Buddhist Epistemology in the Geluk School

The Library of Tibetan Classics is a special series being developed by the Institute of Tibetan Classics aimed at making key classical Tibetan texts part of the global literary and intellectual heritage. Eventually comprising thirty-two large volumes, the collection will contain over two hundred distinct texts by more than a hundred of the best-known authors. These texts have been selected in consultation with the preeminent lineage holders of all the schools and other senior Tibetan scholars to represent the Tibetan literary tradition as a whole. The works included in the series span more than a millennium and cover the vast expanse of classical Tibetan knowledge—from the core teachings of the specific schools to such diverse fields as ethics, philosophy, linguistics, medicine, astronomy and astrology, folklore, and historiography.

Buddhist Epistemology in the Geluk School: Three Key Texts

This volume includes translations of three separate Tibetan works composed by individuals who are now regarded as iconic figures of the Geluk school of Buddhism. The first work is *Banisher of Ignorance: An Ornament of the Seven Treatises on Pramāṇa*, by Khedrup Gelek Palsang (1385–1438), and the second is *On Preclusion and Relationship*, by Gyaltsab Darma Rinchen (1364–1432). The authors—popularly known as Khedrup Jé and Gyaltsab Jé—are represented as the foremost disciples of Tsongkhapa Losang Drakpa (1357–1419), and each succeeded him as the Ganden throneholder. The third text, *Mighty Pramāṇa Sun*, a commentary on parts of Candrakīrti's *Clear Words* (*Prasannapadā*), is by Jamyang Shepa (1648–1721), a later luminary in the Geluk school.

These works concern themselves primarily with the Buddhist theory of knowledge—the means by which we are able to know things and how we can be certain of that knowledge. Encapsulating this theory is the notion of *pramāṇa*, a concept derived from India, the Buddhist understanding of which was shaped most significantly by the masters Dignāga (fifth to sixth century) and Dharmakīrti (seventh century). Based on their explanation, *pramāṇa* is often translated as "valid cognition," a literal reference to the kind of cognition that they proposed could be relied upon to supply indisputable knowledge. In recognition of the crucial role that reasoning is held to play in gaining certain knowledge, the Buddhist Pramāṇa tradition that the treatises of Dignāga and Dharmakīrti gave rise to is described as a logico-epistemological system.

The works in this volume demonstrate how important a component scholastic rigor has been to Tibetan religion. They illustrate how those who follow the tradition have viewed the ordered, systematic approach as necessary not only for textual analysis, for those seeking to unravel the complexities of the Indian Buddhist scriptures and treatises, but also for practitioners aiming to progress along the spiritual path and achieve the higher Buddhist goals.

THE LIBRARY OF TIBETAN CLASSICS • VOLUME 21
Thupten Jinpa, General Editor

Buddhist Epistemology in the Geluk School

Three Key Texts

Khedrup Jé, Gyaltsab Jé,
and Jamyang Shepa

Translated by Jonathan Samuels

Wisdom

Wisdom Publications, Inc.
132 Perry Street
New York, NY 10014 USA
wisdom.org

Library of Congress Cataloging-in-Publication Data
Names: Dge-legs-dpal-bzang-po, Mkhas-grub-rje, 1385–1438. | Dar-ma-rin-chen, Rgyal-tshab-rje, 1364-1432. | 'Jam-dbyangs-bzhad-pa Ngag-dbang-brtson-'grus, 1648–1721. | Samuels, Jonathan, 1963– translator. | Dge-legs-dpal-bzang-po, Mkhas-grub-rje, 1385–1438. Tshad ma sde bdun gyi rgyan Yid kyi mun sel. English.
Title: Buddhist epistemology in the Geluk school: three key texts / Khedrup Jé, Gyaltsab Jé and Jamyang Shepa; translated by Jonathan Samuels.
Description: New York, NY, USA: Wisdom, [2025] | Series: The library of Tibetan classics; volume 21 | Includes bibliographical references and index. | Text in English. Translation from Tibetan.
Identifiers: LCCN 2024046688 (print) | LCCN 2024046689 (ebook) | ISBN 9780861714605 (hardcover) | ISBN 9781614299561 (ebook)
Subjects: LCSH: Buddhism—Tibet Region—Early works to 1800. | Buddhist logic—Early works to 1800. | Knowledge, Theory of (Buddhism) | Tsong-kha-pa Blo-bzang-grags-pa, 1357–1419.
Classification: LCC BQ7549 .D554 2025 (print) | LCC BQ7549 (ebook) | DDC 294.3/923—dc23/eng/20250211
LC record available at https://lccn.loc.gov/2024046688
LC ebook record available at https://lccn.loc.gov/2024046689

ISBN 978-0-86171-460-5 ebook ISBN 978-1-61429-956-1

29 28 27 26 25
5 4 3 2 1

Cover and interior design by Gopa & Ted2, Inc.

Printed on acid-free paper that meets the guidelines for permanence and durability of the Production Guidelines for Book Longevity of the Council on Library Resources.

Printed in Canada.

Message from the Dalai Lama

THE LAST TWO MILLENNIA witnessed a tremendous proliferation of cultural and literary development in Tibet, the "Land of Snows." Moreover, due to the inestimable contributions made by Tibet's early spiritual kings, numerous Tibetan translators, and many great Indian paṇḍitas over a period of so many centuries, the teachings of the Buddha and the scholastic tradition of ancient India's Nālandā monastic university became firmly rooted in Tibet. As evidenced from the historical writings, this flowering of Buddhist tradition in the country brought about the fulfillment of the deep spiritual aspirations of countless sentient beings. In particular, it contributed to the inner peace and tranquility of the peoples of Tibet, Outer Mongolia—a country historically suffused with Tibetan Buddhism and its culture—the Tuva and Kalmuk regions in present-day Russia, the outer regions of mainland China, and the entire trans-Himalayan areas on the southern side, including Bhutan, Sikkim, Ladakh, Kinnaur, and Spiti. Today this tradition of Buddhism has the potential to make significant contributions to the welfare of the entire human family. I have no doubt that, when combined with the methods and insights of modern science, the Tibetan Buddhist cultural heritage and knowledge will help foster a more enlightened and compassionate human society, a humanity that is at peace with itself, with fellow sentient beings, and with the natural world at large.

It is for this reason I am delighted that the Institute of Tibetan Classics in Montreal, Canada, is compiling a thirty-two-volume series containing the works of many great Tibetan teachers, philosophers, scholars, and practitioners representing all major Tibetan schools and traditions. These important writings are being critically edited and annotated and then published in modern book format in a reference collection called *The Library of Tibetan Classics*, with their translations into other major languages to follow later. While expressing my heartfelt commendation for this noble project, I pray and hope that *The Library of Tibetan Classics* will not only make these important Tibetan treatises accessible to scholars of Tibetan studies, but will create a new opportunity for younger Tibetans to study and take interest in their own rich and profound culture. Through translations into other languages, it is my sincere hope that millions of fellow citizens of the wider human family will also be able to share in the joy of engaging with Tibet's classical literary heritage, textual riches that have been such a great source of joy and inspiration to me personally for so long.

The Dalai Lama
The Buddhist monk Tenzin Gyatso

Special Acknowledgments

THE INSTITUTE OF TIBETAN CLASSICS expresses its deep gratitude to the Ing Foundation for its generous support of the entire cost of translating this important volume. The Ing Foundation's long-standing patronage of the Institute of Tibetan Classics has enabled the institute to support the translation of multiple volumes from *The Library of Tibetan Classics* and has also enabled the general editor of the series to oversee the entire translation project over many years.

Publisher's Acknowledgments

THE PUBLISHER WISHES TO extend a heartfelt thanks to the following people who have contributed substantially to the publication of *The Library of Tibetan Classics*:

Pat Gruber and the Patricia and Peter Gruber Foundation
The Hershey Family Foundation
The Ing Foundation

We also extend deep appreciation to our other subscribing benefactors:

Anonymous, dedicated to Buddhas within
Anonymous, in honor of Dzongsar Khyentse Rinpoche
Anonymous, in honor of Geshe Tenzin Dorje
Anonymous, in memory of K. J. Manel De Silva—may she realize the truth
Anonymous, in memory of Gene Smith
Dr. Patrick Bangert
Nilda Venegas Bernal
Serje Samlo Khentul Lhundub Choden and his Dharma friends
Nicholas Cope
Kushok Lobsang Dhamchöe
Diep Thi Thoai
Tenzin Dorjee
Richard Farris
Gaden Samten Ling, Canada
Evgeniy Gavrilov & Tatiana Fotina
Petar Gesovic
Great Vow Zen Monastery
Ginger Gregory
the Grohmann family, Taiwan
Gyaltsen Lobsang Jamyang (WeiJie) and Pema Looi
Rick Meeker Hayman
Steven D. Hearst
Jana & Mahi Hummel
Curt and Alice Jones
Julie LaValle Jones
Heidi Kaiter
Paul, Trisha, Rachel, and Daniel Kane
Land of Medicine Buddha
Dennis Leksander

Diane & Joseph Lucas
Elizabeth Mettling
Russ Miyashiro
Kestrel Montague
the Nalanda Institute, Olympia, WA
Craig T. Neyman
Kristin A. Ohlson
Arnold Possick
Magdalene Camilla Frank Prest
Quek Heng Bee, Ong Siok Ngow, and family
Randall-Gonzales Family Foundation
Erick Rinner
Andrew Rittenour
Dombon Roig Family
Jonathan and Diana Rose
the Sharchitsang family
Nirbhay N. Singh
Wee Kee Tan
Tibetisches Zentrum e.V. Hamburg
Richard Toft
Alissa KieuNgoc Tran
Timothy Trompeter
Tsadra Foundation
the Vahagn Setian Charitable Foundation
Ellyse Adele Vitiello
Jampa (Alicia H.) Vogel
Nicholas C. Weeks II
Richard and Carol Weingarten
Claudia Wellnitz
Bob White
Kevin Michael White, MD
Eve and Jeff Wild

and the other donors who wish to remain anonymous.

Contents

General Editor's Preface xv

Translator's Introduction 1

Technical Note 71

Banisher of Ignorance:
An Ornament of the Seven Treatises on Pramāṇa

KHEDRUP GELEK PALSANG

1. Introduction: The Aim and Subject Matter of Pramāṇa Treatises 75

PART 1. DESCRIPTION OF THE OBJECT: THE THING KNOWN

2. Object: Equivalents and Definition 93
3. Evident and Hidden Things 101
4. Specifically and Generally Characterized Entities 115
5. The Two Truths 161
6. The Four Kinds of Objects: Appearing, Held, Conceived, and Engaged 179

PART 2. DESCRIPTION OF COGNITION: THAT WHICH KNOWS THE OBJECT

7. Awareness That Is Not Valid 189
8. The Definition of Valid Cognition 195
9. Valid Perception 213

10. Sense Perception 219
11. Mental Perception 269
12. Self-Cognizing Perception 285
13. Yogic Perception 297
14. Valid Cognition and Its Results 321
15. Valid Inferential Cognition 345
16. The Proof Statement 349
17. The Logical Reason 367
18. Varieties of Correct Reason 389
19. Incorrect Reasons 441
20. The Thesis of a Proof 465
21. The Consequence 491

PART 3. HOW COGNITION ENGAGES ITS OBJECT
22. Varieties of Object and Ways of Cognizing 503

On Preclusion and Relationship
GYALTSAB DARMA RINCHEN (1364–1432)

1. Preclusion 533
2. Relationship 547

Mighty Pramāṇa Sun, "Banisher of Gloom from the Hearts of the Fortunate," Totally Illuminating the Profound and the Expansive: An Exposition on Valid Cognition in the Thousand Measures of Clear Words
JAMYANG SHEPA NGAWANG TSÖNDRÜ (1648–1721)

1. Introduction 555
2. Defense of Nāgārjuna's *Fundamental Treatise on the Middle Way* 561
3. General Refutation of Others' Assertions about Valid Cognition 571
4. Specific Refutation of Others' Notions about Perception 605

5. Valid Cognition according to the Prāsaṅgika System 639
6. The Objects of Valid Cognition 667

Appendixes
1. Table of Tibetan Translation 679
2. Text Outlines 683

Notes 713
Glossary 811
Bibliography 821
Index 835
About the Translator 871

General Editor's Preface

For far too long, I have had a wish to see an English translation of Tibetan epistemological texts that is not merely accurate but lucid and engaging to the contemporary reader. The translator of our volume, Jonathan Samuels, has today made this wish a reality. It is a great joy to know this volume can now be shared with interested readers in the international audience. Jonathan's translation of Khedrup Jé's *Banisher of Ignorance* in particular, the lengthiest work in the present volume, is a masterpiece of translation. I am convinced that it will be appreciated by generations, for it offers the reader a rare key to unlock the challenging and complex treasure house that is Buddhist epistemology. Khedrup Jé's voice, with its characteristic directness, clarity, and swaggering humor, comes through in a manner that is vivid and lively. So let me, at the outset, express my deep appreciation to Jonathan Samuels and my admiration for his majestic translation of the three important epistemological works featured in this volume.

The works belong to a field of study crucially important in Tibetan Buddhism, especially in the training in the major scholarly monastic institutions. The discipline is known as *pramāṇa* in Sanskrit (*tshad ma* in Tibetan), a word that connotes "validity" or "reliability" but has no direct correlate in English. The term can refer to what in contemporary language one might label "logic and epistemology." It can also refer to epistemic instruments—sources of knowledge, such as perception and inference. When used in the sense of a discipline or a field, it is helpful to keep in mind two distinct but related meanings. For *pramāṇa* as a discipline covers both the analysis of the forms and structures of argument—what makes a form of argument valid—and the inferences such valid arguments generate. For convenience, translators, including myself, render the term as "epistemology" when used in this general sense of a discipline. Hence the Geluk school of epistemology in contrast with the Sakya school of epistemology.

It would be no exaggeration to state that *pramāṇa* is the most challenging among the five subjects in the Geluk monastic curriculum—the other four being Perfection of Wisdom literature, Madhyamaka philosophy, Abhidharma cosmology, and Vinaya discipline—whose mastery culminates in the conferment of the *geshé lharam* degree. Typically, the student will memorize key sections of Dharmakīrti's premier *Commentary on Pramāṇa* (*Pramāṇavārttika*), train in the basics of debate based on "selected topics" (*bsdus grwa*) drawn from this text, and study the types and taxonomy of cognitions (*lo rig*) as well as the forms and structures of argument, a topic referred to as the "science of reasoning" (*rtags rigs*). In addition, in the Geluk monastic centers, a student will spend one month of the year in the winter devoted to the study of *pramāṇa*. A central question motivating the investigation of *pramāṇa* is "If ignorance entraps us in suffering and bondage, and if the knowledge of the nature of reality is what dispels ignorance, by what means can such knowledge of reality arise?" So, the discipline of epistemology (*pramāṇa*)—that is, the means to reliable knowledge—is intimately connected in the Indian philosophical context, including especially Buddhism, to soteriology: the quest for liberation or enlightenment.

As editor of the critical Tibetan editions that are the foundation of *The Library of Tibetan Classics*, I had the opportunity to select the texts featured in this volume. The main text, Khedrup Jé's *Banisher of Ignorance*, surveys the topic of logic and epistemology in the Buddhist tradition. Its subtitle, *An Ornament of the Seven Treatises on Pramāṇa*, with its explicit reference to seven works of Dharmakīrti, indicates the broad overview nature of the work. Anyone who studies this work can justifiably claim to have obtained a comprehensive introduction to Buddhist epistemology. The second text, which is by Gyaltsab Jé, focuses on the singular topic of "relationship"—whether of *invariability*, such as between cause and effect, or of *preclusion* (or incompatibility)—that facilitates the drawing of inference in the context of a reasoning. The final text, by Jamyang Shepa, seeks to establish what the author sees as epistemological views unique to the Prāsaṅgika-Madhyamaka, especially those of Candrakīrti. The text is, in fact, a detailed commentary (based on an outline developed by Khedrup Jé) on the section of Candrakīrti's *Clear Words* (*Prasannapadā*) that critiques epistemology as espoused by what Candrakīrti viewed as realist schools, including a focused critique of the views on perception by the fifth-century founder of Buddhist epistemology, the master Dignāga. Jamyang Shepa, following Tsongkhapa, does not read Candrakīrti as rejecting epistemology wholesale, even when critiquing Dignāga, but as questioning the underlying ontology that assumes unique particulars to have true existence.

Two primary objectives have driven the creation and development of *The Library of Tibetan Classics*. The first aim is to help revitalize the appreciation and the study of the Tibetan classical heritage within Tibetan-speaking communities worldwide. The younger generation in particular struggle with the tension between traditional Tibetan culture and the realities of modern consumerism. To this end, efforts have been made to develop a comprehensive yet manageable body of texts, one that features the works of Tibet's best-known authors and covers the gamut of classical Tibetan knowledge. The second objective of *The Library of Tibetan Classics* is to help make these texts part of the global literary and intellectual heritage. In this regard, we have tried to make the English translation reader-friendly and, as much as possible, keep the body of the text free of unnecessary scholarly apparatus, which can intimidate general readers. For specialists who wish to compare the translation with the Tibetan original, page references of the critical edition of the Tibetan text are provided in brackets.

The texts in this thirty-two-volume series span more than a millennium—from the development of the Tibetan script in the seventh century to the first part of the twentieth century, when Tibetan society and culture first encountered industrial modernity. The volumes are thematically organized and cover many of the categories of classical Tibetan knowledge—from the teachings specific to each Tibetan school to the classical works on philosophy, psychology, and phenomenology. The first category includes teachings of the Kadam, Nyingma, Sakya, Kagyü, Geluk, and Jonang schools, of miscellaneous Buddhist lineages, and of the Bön school. Texts in these volumes have been largely selected by senior lineage holders of the individual schools. Texts in the other categories have been selected primarily in recognition of the historical reality of the individual disciplines. For example, in the field of epistemology, works from the Sakya and Geluk schools have been selected, while the volume on buddha nature features the writings of Butön Rinchen Drup and various Kagyü masters. Where fields are of more common interest, such as the three codes or the bodhisattva ideal, efforts have been made to represent the perspectives of all four major Tibetan Buddhist schools. *The Library of Tibetan Classics* can function as a comprehensive library of the Tibetan literary heritage for libraries, educational and cultural institutions, and interested individuals.

It is a source of profound joy and satisfaction to see this volume in such an excellent and lucid translation. Editing the Tibetan source texts offered me a chance to closely reengage with three texts I had studied carefully when I was a scholar monk at the Shartsé College of Ganden Monastery in South India. I wish first of all to express my deep personal gratitude to H. H. the Dalai Lama for always being such a profound source of inspiration. I would like to thank Jonathan Samuels for producing masterful translations of these Tibetan texts, and that too with such care, diligence, and patience. I owe thanks to our long-time editor at Wisdom, David Kittelstrom, whose incisive editing always helped bring a level of clarity and accessibility to the translations that translators who work with him are grateful for. I thank my wife, Sophie Boyer-Langri, for taking on the numerous administrative chores that are part of a collaborative and multi-year project such as this.

Finally, I would like to express my heartfelt thanks to Nita Ing and the Ing Foundation for their long-standing patronage of the Institute of Tibetan Classics, whose generosity not only made the translation of this volume possible but also enables me to continue to oversee this translation series. It is my hope that this volume will be for many people a source of deep intellectual enrichment—offering an opportunity to sharpen their critical thinking, evaluate the soundness of arguments, and crystalize their thought—and of philosophical and spiritual insight.

Thupten Jinpa
Montreal, 2025

Translator's Introduction[1]

Pramāṇa Epistemology

The Geluk epistemological system is built upon thinking and practices formulated in eleventh-century Tibet, which in turn traced their roots back to Indian authors living between the fifth and seventh centuries. If there is one thing that could be said to characterize the tradition, it is the pursuit of *certainty*. The tradition's basic understanding of our situation is a standard Buddhist one. The principal predicament is that sentient beings are caught within samsara, a state characterized by dissatisfaction and suffering. The Buddha diagnosed this malady, fully exposing its hidden depths and identifying its causes. Then, driven by an incomparable altruism, he gave teachings that in the short term offered solace to those who suffered and could ultimately release them from their plight. Based on this understanding, those in the Indian and Tibetan epistemological tradition acknowledged the Buddha as the unsurpassed physician and the supremely compassionate one, but they also fostered a new image. This emphasized the Buddha as the ultimate and unerring authority, an entirely trustworthy and reliable *source of knowledge*.

The tradition's quest for certainty has manifested in two distinctive ways. The first was its development of a comprehensive theory of knowledge. The epistemological tradition rejects the idea that spiritual practice should be defined by pure faith, especially in revelatory scriptures and ritual performance. Specifically, in terms of the Buddhist path, it also dismisses the view that realization should be approached solely as a mystical process, the only access to which is through experience. The tradition regards spiritual realization as falling within the domain of knowledge. As such, it is something that must be based on identifiable principles, which could serve as the basis of a theory. The epistemological tradition has therefore, perhaps more than any other in Buddhism, been prepared to stand apart from the path of realization, to analyze and discuss the workings of the processes it involves.

The second distinctive way that the tradition's quest for certainty has manifested is its engagement with other traditions and those holding different views. A passage by Bhāviveka cited by one of our authors in this volume points to the issues at stake:

> Being a text handed down in an unbroken tradition,
> it is claimed, is what makes it a "scripture."
> But since the same applies to everyone's texts,
> what is it that gives [what they say any] certainty?[2]

That is, the tradition has been shaped by the awareness that Buddhism did not stand in isolation. Other religious schools had their own understandings of reality, of the main dilemma faced by beings, and of the solution to that dilemma. They also claimed that their scriptures and teachings embodied certainty. Hence, in addition to the deeper questions about how it was possible to be certain that what the Buddha taught was correct—and indeed, how one can be certain of anything at all—there was the issue of how Buddhists distinguished themselves from others, especially when, in medieval India, there were so many commonalities among different religious traditions. Those in the Indian Buddhist epistemological tradition, and then later those in Tibet, have therefore always kept a very keen eye on what might be termed "the opposition," meaning those who express alternative views and who call into question aspects of the Buddhist account. The tradition's authors tend to structure their writings as discourses, and the extent to which they are prepared to represent differing points of view and engage with those holding them is exceptional.

The view that definite knowledge of things is possible was not exclusive to Buddhism, nor did it likely have its origin in Buddhism. Early Indic philosophers had wrestled with the issue of how knowledge was gained, and they developed the idea that it was possible to distinguish particular sources that could yield incontestable knowledge, and they referred to these sources as *pramāṇa*. And as our authors saw it, Indic religio-philosophical schools were in agreement about the possibility of indisputable knowledge and the fact that religious practice should be premised upon it. According to many Tibetan scholars, even deniers of religion like the early materialist thinkers, who claimed only to trust their senses, thereby implicitly accepted at least one form of pramāṇa. But these schools held competing notions of exactly what constituted pramāṇa and diverse understandings of how such notions supported their own tenets and made them superior to those of others. Reflecting how seriously the issue of certain knowledge was treated in some

Buddhist quarters, the composers of the Sanskrit treatises that are the focus of the present volume are now commonly described as having belonged to the Pramāṇa school or tradition and are simply referred to by many as "Pramāṇaists."

The Indian Pramāṇa tradition is especially associated with Dignāga (fifth to sixth century) and Dharmakīrti (seventh century), whose deliberations and writings had a massive intellectual impact in India and neighboring lands, particularly in Tibet.[3] Dignāga and Dharmakīrti are generally seen as the two most significant Buddhist contributors to the Indian discourse on pramāṇa, those who went furthest in the development of a distinctively Buddhist epistemology. Other Indian schools of thought recognized a wide range of things as pramāṇa. Scripture, personal testimony, and even tradition itself were identified as sources of incontestable knowledge. Dignāga, Dharmakīrti, and their followers pursued a more radical line. Disputing the reliability of many of these proposed sources, they advocated a notion of pramāṇa rooted in awareness, arguing that the only actual pramāṇas—epistemic means that could be relied on to provide certain knowledge—were *cognitions* within the individual's own continuum. Of the various kinds of cognition, they said that only two, perception and inference, could be pramāṇas. Accordingly, in the Buddhist context, pramāṇa is frequently translated as "valid cognition," and the defense of the assertion that pramāṇa is limited to these two forms—along with the explication of their workings and the refutation of alternative sources of certain knowledge—serves as the intellectual wellspring for the tradition.[4]

The assertion that these were the only two kinds of pramāṇa especially challenged the idea that revelation and scripture in themselves were reliable sources of knowledge or articulations of truth. While Dignāga famously hailed the Buddha as pramāṇa on the grounds that he was unerring, this was not meant entirely literally. Even the veracity of the Buddha's own words—as recorded in the Buddhist scriptures—could not be accepted unquestioningly. According to an oft-cited passage on assaying gold, the Buddha invited his followers to test what he taught. But given that so much of this related to phenomena outside the experience and immediate perceptual range of ordinary beings, including realizations of ultimate reality, how might they go about this? It was here that the tradition said systematized analysis and logic found their place. It encouraged structured thinking, partly to combat the idea that religion should be left to blind faith, but equally aware that misguided direction or a lack of rigor could result in dubious or even mistaken deductions. For inferential cognitions to be pramāṇa, they must be based on sound, incontrovertible reasoning, grounded in logical principles. Part of the task, as Dignāga and Dharmakīrti saw it, was to set out these principles, identify the rules of correct reasoning, and in the process, root out spurious arguments and erroneous systems of thinking. Not only would individuals with a thorough grasp of correct reasoning have at their disposal the means of generating inferential cognition for themselves, but they would also be in a position to present correct lines of reasoning to others and allow them, in turn, to develop their own inferences.

If liberation from suffering (that is, nirvana) and full enlightenment were realities, it would not be sufficient to simply claim that certain beings had experienced them. Their possibility and existence, together with details of the various stages of the path, must be knowable to those who might aspire to achieve them. Inference was what made knowledge of the path and its goals accessible to such individuals, and as potential objects of inference, this path and its goals were viewed as amenable to methodical examination. Consequently, an analytical approach associated with correct inference was held to provide the means for testing what the Buddha had taught.

Within the writings on pramāṇa, as exemplified by the three works translated in this volume, we therefore see vital intersections among the spheres of textual analysis, logic, and spiritual practice. For our authors, the Buddhist path could be charted out in a detailed, graduated fashion. Both the understanding of that path and the progression along it were governed by coherent, determinable rules. This meant that advancement to its highest levels was in theory open to all, rather than just the extraordinary few whose greatness seemed preordained.

Models of Understanding

Referencing some basic models and frameworks structuring Tibetan Buddhism provides us with a clearer picture of the place of pramāṇa within that tradition. Introductions to Mahayana Buddhism usually discuss the two great schools of thought: Cittamātra ("Mind Only") and Madhyamaka ("Middle Way"). We encounter various characterizations of them outside the Tibetan tradition. Opinions differ on how fitting it is to describe Cittamātra philosophy as a form of idealism; and Madhyamaka, with its emphasis on negation rather than affirmation, has a long history of being represented as a kind of nihilism. Exactly where these two schools have stood in relation to each other, philosophically and historically, is also a source of much discussion, but they are frequently depicted as rival systems. Within the Tibetan tradition, however, the predominant trend has always been to find a means of accommodating both philosophies. Apparent clashes and tensions between their views and any qualms regarding their chronology and historical popularity have been ironed out and explained through the application of joint hermeneutic and doxographic models. The two systems have been represented not simply as plausible or valid interpretations of the Buddha's teachings but exactly what he intended to convey. The differences in them related to their audiences—those individuals and groups to whom the Buddha spoke directly—whose capacities and dispositions he had in mind when delivering the teachings in question. The perspective of a Mahayana instruction was oriented toward either Cittamātra or Madhyamaka, depending on its intended recipients.

The different views espoused by the Buddha were collated and elucidated by some of his foremost followers in later centuries. The treatises and commentaries they composed served as the basis for the formation of different schools of Buddhist philosophy. For those in the Tibetan tradition, the fact that the Buddha was the initiator of this process and approved of the multiplicity of views it gave rise to has not been understood to imply spiritual relativism. The schools had varying presentations of the path and had different versions of what constituted ultimate reality, so not all of them could be *the* truth. Tibetan thinkers, seeking to comprehend and organize the Indian Buddhist legacy, most commonly referred to four distinct Buddhist philosophical schools in India and ordered these hierarchically. In ascending order these were the Vaibhāṣika and Sautrāntika, the two schools belonging to the Śrāvaka or Hinayana system, holding a philosophical view that lent toward realism. Above these were the Cittamātra (or Yogācāra) and Madhyamaka, the two schools of the Mahayana system. Although each individual eventually had to progress to the highest of the four views, the lower ones could partly act as steppingstones, bringing about a gradual refinement of understanding.

Over many centuries, Tibetan scholars engaged in a vast project of gathering, translating, and commenting on Buddhist works originally composed in various languages, principally Sanskrit. There was general agreement that Madhyamaka represented the highest view, and there are no accounts of Tibetans who identified themselves as outright adherents of the Vaibhāṣika or Sautrāntika systems. But this did not mean that Tibetan scholarship ignored the teachings of the lower schools. First, to disparage any of these teachings, or worse, to deny that they actually derived from the Buddha, was portrayed as the most heinous of offenses, one that undermined the Buddha's intention. More importantly, and absolutely key to understanding the culture and mentality of the authors of our works, it was the duty of a true Tibetan scholar to understand each of these schools of thought—mainly through the treatises in which their views were set out—*in their own terms*, rather than beginning from the premise that they were inferior to the Madhyamaka and thus warranted little interest. Apart from the grounding that some of these lower schools' works provided, it was acknowledged that they covered numerous aspects of the path, discipline, and mental trainings in far more depth and detail than in Madhyamaka texts. Thus scholars devoted much time and intellectual energy to studying and explaining aspects of Buddhist systems despite seeing their descriptions of reality as partial and provisional.

In terms of the aforesaid model of the four schools, Tibetan scholars generally viewed Dignāga and Dharmakīrti as representatives of Cittamātra thinking. While this view was evident in the Pramāṇa writings of these two figures, large portions of Dharmakīrti's works also accommodate the Sautrāntika perspective. This feature is reflected in the first two works of this volume, especially the first, where the Cittamātra is projected as the main system but the Sautrāntika is foregrounded on many matters. Only in the last work of the volume do we see parts of these systems brought into question. Having further divided Madhyamaka into two subschools, Svātantrika and Prāsaṅgika, and depicting the latter as superior, its author presents a Prāsaṅgika critique of the Pramāṇa system of Dignāga and Dharmakīrti and considers its implications. However, the inclusive nature of the Tibetan system means that this is far from a total rejection of everything for which the Pramāṇa tradition stood.

Historical Aspects of the Pramāṇa Tradition: Evolution and Authority

Dignāga and his foremost commentator, Dharmakīrti, are currently regarded as the key figures in the formulation, and systematic presentation of what became known as the Buddhist Pramāṇa tradition. Tibetan scholarship agrees with this assessment of their importance and, as the first work in this volume demonstrates, often seeks to plot a direct line between their writings and the teachings of the Buddha. Historically, there were more steps in the evolution of Buddhist Pramāṇa thinking, especially with regards to logic. Earlier writings, such as the *Compendium of Abhidharma* and *Foundation for Yoga Practitioners: The Levels of Spiritual Practice* by Asaṅga (fourth century CE) contain sections on logic. More significant still were writings by Vasubandhu (ca. fourth century CE) that are known to have made a substantial contribution to the systematization of logic. But this was made in three works by him that unfortunately do not survive, although an attempt has been made to reconstruct one of these based on passages cited by Dignāga.[5] These works by Vasubandhu appear never to have reached Tibet, but the tradition of scholarship there has a residual memory of his contribution. Hence in some works, such as the *Blue Annals* by Gö Lotsāwa (1392–1481), there is reference to a Pramāṇa "lineage"[6] in which Vasubandhu is represented as Dignāga and Dharmakīrti's predecessor.

Such lineages do not generally feature in Geluk scholars' descriptions of the Pramāṇa tradition. Among the three works translated in this volume, the Tibetan conception of the Buddhist Pramāṇa system at its most expansive is presented in the first. Its author, Khedrup Jé, rejected the idea that Buddhist Pramāṇa was the product of later intellectualization. Rather than inventing a system, Dignāga and Dharmakīrti were clarifying principles, categories, and indeed an approach that had its origins in the Buddha's own teachings. The opening section of Khedrup Jé's work demonstrates this by identifying various portions of scripture in which the Buddha had revealed his commitment to rationality and rigor. Such is Tibetan scholarship's respect for Dignāga and Dharmakīrti that "lords of reasoning" became one of its most common epithets for them. The perceived accurateness of Dharmakīrti's representation of Dignāga's thought is conveyed in the description of the two as "ārya father and spiritual son." Beyond mere respect, within the Pramāṇa tradition they hold a towering status akin to that of the Buddha. They represent unquestioned authority, and their works assume canonical infallibility. The task of those who followed them, both in a temporal and devotional sense, was to offer further clarification and rectify subsequent misinterpretations of their intention.

The Tibetan tradition frequently refers to a group of works by Dharmakīrti known as the Seven Treatises on Pramāṇa,[7] as illustrated in the title of Khedrup Jé's text translated in this volume. But when Tibetan scholars like Khedrup Jé refer to this group, they usually include implicitly an eighth text, Dignāga's *Compendium of Pramāṇa* (*Pramāṇasamuccaya*), which they projected as the foundation and source of the Buddhist Pramāṇa tradition. The seven treatises composed by Dharmakīrti are viewed as either direct commentaries or further explorations of topics introduced in Dignāga's treatise. The seven are:

1. *Commentary on Pramāṇa* (*Pramāṇavārttika*)
2. *Ascertainment of Pramāṇa* (*Pramāṇaviniścaya*)
3. *Drop of Logic* (*Nyāyabindu*)
4. *Drop of Reasoning* (*Hetubindu*)
5. *Analysis of Relation* (*Sambandhaparīkṣā*)
6. *Verification of Other Minds* (*Sāṃtānāntarasiddhi*)
7. *Science of Disputation* (*Vādanyāya*)

The first among these, the *Commentary on Pramāṇa*, eventually came to dwarf the others in importance. In the Tibetan tradition it is commonly referred to simply as the *Commentary* (*Rnam 'grel*), with the *Pramāṇa* of the title understood to denote Dignāga's *Compendium of Pramāṇa*.

The first two texts in this volume present explanations squarely from the perspective of the Pramāṇa tradition. While they occasionally cite other giants of the Mahayana tradition such as Nāgārjuna and major Cittamātra thinkers such as Vasubandhu and Asaṅga, their focus rests on the legacy of Dignāga and Dharmakīrti. The first text cites Dharmakīrti at almost every turn. It also references Dignāga's writings but tends to cite Indian commentaries on Dharmakīrti's works more frequently and at greater length. Among these commentators, particular prominence is given to Devendrabuddhi (ca. 630–690), Śākyabuddhi (ca. 660–720), and Prajñākaragupta (ca. 750–810)—who each composed works on Dharmakīrti's *Commentary on Pramāṇa*—and Dharmottara (ca. 740–800)—who wrote on the *Ascertainment of Pramāṇa*. It should be noted that however highly these later Indian commentators have been regarded in the Tibetan scholarly tradition, their interpretations are not unquestionable. Khedrup Jé and Gyaltsab Jé, for instance, sometimes appear to have different understandings of Dharmakīrti's thinking and do not totally agree on which of his Indian commentators is most accurate, and they display no qualms about stating their preferences for one interpretation over another. Khedrup Jé's text, for example, contains criticisms of Dharmottara, whereas Gyaltsab Jé seems to express more support for Dharmottara's interpretations. Dharmakīrti's Indian commentators must therefore be recognized as a second tier of authority. When Tibetan scholars composed their own explanations of the correct understanding of

Dharmakīrti's thought, they did not feel obliged to incorporate everything these Indian commentators wrote and, on some points, openly rejected their interpretations. However, the questioning of their authority is limited, as our authors see themselves as belonging to the same Pramāṇa tradition as their Indian forebears. They work within the same parameters and generally make their choices among the available interpretational options rather than offering alternative explanations. In line with others in the Tibetan tradition of scholasticism, the authors in this volume reserve most of their criticisms for their fellow Tibetan commentators.

Pramāṇa thinking, like that of Madhyamaka, was first introduced into Tibet during the so-called earlier diffusion of Buddhism, concurrent with the era of Tibetan empire during the seventh to ninth centuries. A number of mainly shorter works were translated from Sanskrit into Tibetan, and a translation of Dharmakīrti's *Commentary on Pramāṇa* is also reported to have begun,[8] but it did not survive. The impact of these Pramāṇa works during this earlier era appears to have been limited. Śāntarakṣita and Kamalaśīla, two major figures from India, took up residence in Tibet during that period, and their brand of Madhyamaka fully embraced many aspects of Pramāṇa thinking. The texts in this volume occasionally cite their writings as authoritative on matters of Pramāṇa. Some contemporary writings vaguely suggest that the Tibetan Pramāṇa traditions began during the period of the earlier diffusion with Śāntarakṣita and Kamalaśīla and continued through to the "later diffusion." No historical evidence is offered to support this, and it runs counter to the descriptions in the "religious histories" (*chos 'byung*), which state that the tradition began during the later diffusion. The authors in this volume also never acknowledge the existence of a Tibetan tradition of Pramāṇa during that earlier period.

The indigenous Tibetan tradition of Pramāṇa writing and thinking, as recognized by our authors, the religious histories, and modern scholarship, truly established itself during the early decades of the later diffusion. Taking the broadest historical sweep, we must speak of three successive waves of Tibetan Pramāṇa interpretation related to:

1. Sangphu scholarship
2. Sakya scholarship
3. Geluk scholarship

This presentation in no way depreciates the significant intellectual contributions made by individual scholars outside these matrices. But if we view the progression of the Tibetan Pramāṇa tradition in terms of organized groups of scholars working in concert and establishing abiding institutions, it is these three groups that deserve to be singled out. With the first, we see the Tibetan Pramāṇa tradition's true foundation, and with the subsequent two, separate movements that seriously questioned previous scholarship, engendering major new lines of reinterpretation that produced enduring historical effects.

Sangphu Monastery, situated close to Lhasa, was undoubtedly the epicenter of the first wave, although the network of scholars involved spread much wider. The monastery was founded in 1073 by Ngok Lekpai Sherab, an immediate disciple of Dīpaṃkaraśrījñāna (982–1054), the Bengali teacher popularly known as Atiśa. Some of Atiśa's later Tibetan followers promoted a new religious tradition centered around him, which came to be known as the Kadam school. Sangphu's association with some of Atiśa's chief disciples led some to describe it as a Kadam monastery, but its alignment with the tradition was loose. When Ngok Loden Sherab (1059–1109), a nephew of the monastery's founder, acceded to the Sangphu throne as its second abbot, the monastery appears to have taken a new direction. Ngok Loden Sherab is still celebrated primarily as a translator, as indicated by his most common sobriquet, Ngok Lotsāwa, "the Ngok (clan) translator," even though this seriously underplays his intellectual range. In addition to his tremendous industry in the field of translation, he produced numerous summaries of Indian Buddhist treatises and composed the first substantive Tibetan commentarial writings—on Dharmakīrti's *Ascertainment of Pramāṇa* and Dharmottara's *Extensive Commentary on Drop of Logic*.

Some scholars working in the decades immediately prior to Loden Sherab, including Ma Lotsāwa (1044–89?)—who was the first to translate Dharmakīrti's *Commentary on Pramāṇa* into Tibetan—and Khyungpo Draksé (fl. eleventh century), were described in some later texts, such as the *Blue Annals*,[9] as having espoused a system known as the "old Pramāṇa."[10] But their writings on the topic have not survived, and our knowledge of their activities and assertions remains sketchy. Nevertheless, Loden Sherab's work was clearly groundbreaking. Not least because of his position at Sangphu, we can be certain that he was a principal driving force behind the formation of early Tibetan scholasticism in the eleventh and twelfth centuries. The other figure most strongly associated with this Sangphu tradition, cited a number of times in this volume, was the sixth abbot of Sangphu, Chapa Chökyi Sengé (1109–69).

In the early days of Tibetan scholasticism, there was an understandable adherence to the Indian model of scholarly writing. The majority of commentarial works therefore chose as their subject a single scripture or treatise. The Tibetan translators of Indian writings frequently felt they were best qualified to compose commentaries on them, as demonstrated by some of Ngok Loden Sherab's own writings and those of scholars such as Patsab Nyima Drak (1055–?). However, a noteworthy feature of early scholasticism was its independent thinking. Sangphu became known especially for its development of the "summaries" genre. This was pioneered by Ngok Loden Sherab and, as the name suggests, began simply as outlines of the contents of individual works. The new format was not intended to displace that of traditional commentary. As developments in the area went on to show, it was partly inspired by pedagogical considerations. Chapa Chökyi Sengé went even further in adapting the summaries for the native Tibetan audience. Using a structure and sets of classifications that he appears to have devised himself, Chapa composed at least one major work, *Banisher of Ignorance*, that set out to isolate the essential contents of the Indian Buddhist Pramāṇa writings as a whole and deal with them systematically. In breaking completely from the commentarial mode, it created a new format.

The second wave of Tibetan interpretation was initiated by Sakya Paṇḍita (1182–1251) from his base at Sakya Monastery. Sakya Paṇḍita revised the translation of the *Commentary on Pramāṇa* and promoted this work over the *Ascertainment of Pramāṇa*. His magnum opus on Pramāṇa, *Treasure of Pramāṇa Reasoning*—which our authors cite several times—was unique among Tibetan writings on Pramāṇa in that it spawned its own major commentarial tradition. It attempted to convey the information in an even more accessible manner than the Sangphu summaries, through thematic chapters. In this and other works, Sakya Paṇḍita's critical comments about earlier Tibetan interpretations of Pramāṇa were seen as being directed against Sangphu scholarship.

The third wave, of which the first two works in this volume must be considered a part, began in the early fifteenth century. By this time the Buddhist scholastic institutions in India had crumbled, and Tibetan scholasticism had become a mature and autonomous tradition. With no new external interpretations with which to contend and the project of translating Indian Pramāṇa writings essentially completed, the Indian canon of works was largely settled. A Tibetan pantheon of authority had been established, and Sakya Paṇḍita's position within it was fixed. Unlike the second wave, the third one involved no overt or self-declared challenge to the existing order. Nevertheless, from the criticisms that Sakya authors made of the new writings and their contents, it is obvious that a new direction had been taken. With Sangphu Monastery and independent supporters of its intellectual traditions in a state of decline, authors and institutions associated with the Ganden tradition—which later came to be known as Geluk—were now in the ascendent. The system of Pramāṇa interpretation they promoted descended from both predecessors while being a direct continuation of neither. Eventually, backed by Geluk political institutions and the power of their educational centers, it went on to dominate in Tibet.

Alongside Pramāṇa, Madhyamaka developed into one of Tibetan scholasticism's main fields, and we find evidence of their interaction and mutual influence over the centuries. But in the Geluk school, the practice of delineating the two into separate spheres, which was already apparent in the earlier tradition, became further ensconced. As such, the two were studied as distinct disciplines, and the writings on them remained largely discrete. The Geluk doxographic framework allowed them to be treated in both commentarial and educational spheres as coherent, self-sufficient systems. They were generally not subjects of comparison, and there was no major incentive for integrating them. For the Geluk school, *Entering the Middle Way* (*Madhyamakāvatāra*) by Candrakīrti (ca. 570–650) came to be regarded as the definitive Indian interpretation of Nāgārjuna's epoch-making writings on the Middle Way. Its perceived championing of the Prāsaṅgika view as the final one meant that the treatises of scholars such as Śāntarakṣita and Kamalaśīla—which were seen to accord with Svātantrika thinking and had been favored during the earlier diffusion—as well as some of those associated with the earlier Sangphu tradition were now relegated to a lower rank. By the time of Jamyang Shepa, our third author, *Entering the Middle Way* reigned supreme as far as Geluk scholarship was concerned. This meant that interest in *Clear Words* (*Prasannapadā*), Candrakīrti's other major commentary on Nāgārjuna's influential *Fundamental Treatise on the Middle Way* (*Mūlamadhyamakakārikā*), had greatly waned. This was despite the fact that the work's importance was clearly appreciated in the early tradition of scholasticism, as evidenced by writings on it by figures such as Patsab Nyima Drak and Thangsakpa (eleventh century). The extent to which *Clear Words* was studied in the centuries following these earlier writings is unclear, although there were sporadic reports, such as that seen in the *Blue Annals*,[11] that some tradition of teaching both of these works continued at least into the fourteenth century. Insofar as Jamyang Shepa's work is a commentary on key sections within *Clear Words*, it must have gone some way to reviving the earlier tradition in Geluk circles.

Jamyang Shepa framed his work not as a commentary on the whole of *Clear Words* but as one that was interested in Candrakīrti's standpoint on the matter of Pramāṇa. In *Clear Words*, the criticisms of the Pramāṇa tradition are far more vocal than those expressed in *Entering the Middle Way*—to the extent of virtually identifying Dignāga as an opponent—and the topic of valid cognition is addressed more squarely. Previous direct and confrontational questioning of the Pramāṇa tradition seems to have largely been filtered out of Geluk discourse. The standing of Dignāga and Dharmakīrti's Pramāṇa tradition in Tibetan scholasticism also meant that aspects of the Madhyamaka perspective on valid cognition were in general poorly represented in Tibetan scholastic writings, including those of the Geluk school. Explorations of the Prāsaṅgika viewpoint on valid cognition were very rare. Jamyang Shepa addressed what was probably the main potential fault line within Pramāṇa thinking. Candrakīrti, like Nāgārjuna before him, makes specific reference to a *fourfold* division of Pramāṇa, which Jamyang Shepa did not seek to undermine. This fourfold division—comprising, in most accounts, perception, inference, scriptural testimony, and analogy—seems to correspond with that espoused by the non-Buddhist Nyāya tradition. A number of contemporary writers suggest that the Buddhist tradition borrowed from the Nyāya, and even argue that this would be entirely in keeping with Candrakīrti's view that the Buddhist philosopher should not fight worldly conventions but be prepared to accept prevailing ideas. This, however, raises huge questions about what counts as a valid convention, especially when two systems of convention seem to be in conflict. Furthermore, Jamyang Shepa would not have flippantly dismissed the twofold division of the Pramāṇa tradition. In the third work in this volume, he took up the challenge of seeking a compromise between the fourfold and twofold schemes.

Binaries and Realities

Several basic binary divisions—of which the samsara-nirvana distinction can be viewed as the foremost—structure the whole of Buddhist thinking and much of its practice. A number of these divisions represent dichotomies, the two portions of which form an opposition, in that one is characterized as the absence of the other or some main feature of that other. Aside from the samsara-nirvana distinction, perhaps the most basic dichotomy is that of the two truths, according to which everything that can be said to be true must be so in either an ultimate or a conventional sense, and must therefore be classified as either an ultimate truth or a conventional truth. The reliance upon organizational divisions and classifications is fundamental to the understanding and transmission of the Buddha's teachings and represents a foundational concept for all traditions of Abhidharma. Scholastic Buddhism has been an eager consumer and generator of these schemes. The regularity with which the binaries feature in the writings translated in this volume will convince any reader of the special place afforded to them within the Indian Buddhist scholarly tradition and of the fact that Tibetan Buddhist scholasticism subsequently foregrounded them to an even greater extent. It could be said that the application of binary divisions, especially the oppositional dichotomy, has been regarded as the most essential way of categorizing, understanding, and explaining individual phenomena and indeed the whole of reality. The reduction to binaries has an equally prominent role in analysis and the refutation of opposing views. Tibetan scholasticism favors a dialectical approach, based on the idea that truth—both in the sense of what the Buddha really meant and in the sense of how things actually exist—can be reached by analytically whittling away incorrect understanding in its multifarious manifestations as presented by actual and fictional opponents. This oppositional approach also expresses itself in the language and imagery of the tradition's writings. Readers may be struck by the vehemence of the attacks, the abrasive strength of the insults, and the mocking depictions that authors employ in challenging the positions of other scholars. The authorial space within which they functioned gave license to conflating the refutation of others' views with the epic battle against delusions, to the extent that rival scholars might even be depicted as enemies of truth.

The thinking in the Pramāṇa tradition has been molded around a particular set of closely aligned dichotomies, each of which is based on the kind of opposition mentioned above—a more affirmative portion set against a negative one—with the two portions of a dichotomy broadly equivalent to those of the other dichotomies. All of these were inherited from the Indian Pramāṇa tradition, but the Geluk school had its own spin on certain aspects. The first of these dichotomies attracting our attention is that of the two truths. The understanding of the two truths varied among different Buddhist thinkers, and the Tibetan tradition organized these understandings within its doxographic model of tenet systems. For the Pramāṇa tradition, the ultimate is found in activity and efficacy. This stance has a key soteriological dimension, since insights into the sphere of activity had a practical application in the path with respect to actions and their results. The Buddha's authority could be said to rest primarily in his knowledge of action or karma. It was his complete comprehension of the principles of karma that allowed him to see exactly which actions brought about which results and what path of action could eventually lead to release from suffering, and it furnished him with the ability to reveal this path to others in an unmistaken fashion. This authority was the subject of Dignāga's praise to the Buddha at the start of his *Compendium of Pramāṇa*. However, the conscious sphere of actions among the animate—the ability of agents to understand and exercise choice in what actions to pursue or refrain from, in order to steer a course toward desired results—is grounded in features of the phenomenal world. Ontologically, activity and efficacy also applied to *things*: objects such as a pot[12]—a favorite example used in the Pramāṇa tradition—together with its materials and parts. They are produced and give rise to effects. Although enmeshed within a causal nexus and subject entirely to productive forces and conditions, to the extent that their function in that sphere does not rely on the conceptual mind, they exist as independent realities.

A second dichotomy reinforces this. It divides things into entities (Skt. *vastu* or *bhāva*) that are actual and non-actual. Here again, actuality is understood in terms of causality—embodied by that which is derived from causes, produces its own effects, and is functionally active. A third dichotomy views these divisions from another perspective. The same causal phenomena are classified as being impermanent. With grosser objects like pots, transitoriness is obvious in their finiteness. But even for the duration that they apparently survive as solid, coherent, functional entities, they are on a subtler level, like the particles comprising them, subject to constant changes that are largely unperceived. In addition to the physical, this principle of dynamic transitoriness also encompasses consciousness and other phenomena within the empirical world. Hence this third dichotomy distinguishes between the impermanent and the permanent.

The fourth dichotomy, arguably the most important for the Pramāṇa tradition, concerns certain types of characteristics (Skt. *lakṣaṇa*). From the epistemological perspective, what really distinguishes those things among the "ultimate-causal-impermanent" category is their own characteristics. They are individual and occupy identifiably separate spaces and times, which they do not share with others. Most crucially, they are independent and autonomous in the sense of not being reliant on the mind for such an existence. They may be subject to conception, classification, and designation, but that does not make them what they are. Their foremost quality of being active, functioning entities outside the domain of thought is seen by the Pramāṇa tradition as encapsulating their existence and qualifying them as real. Therefore, this last dichotomy separates characteristics that are specific or individual from those that are generalized, with the latter described largely in terms of the converse of the former—that is, lacking independence from mind and so on. The two sides of this latter dichotomy, especially based on the Geluk explanations, are commonly translated as "specifically characterized phenomena" (Tib. *rang mtshan*, Skt. *svalakṣaṇa*) and "generally characterized phenomena" (Tib. *spyi mtshan*, Skt. *sāmānyalakṣaṇa*). Implicit within these terms are two aspects of the Geluk slant. First, these are not just the characteristics themselves but also the things with those characteristics. That is, rather than just individual elemental bits (the particles of matter and portions of consciousness existing in time), these are also the substrata to which they belong. Using the classic example of the pot as illustration, it is a gross entity within which various features, attributes, and materials inhere. This pot, like the more fundamental constituents comprising it, occupies its own space and time, is independent of thought, and is no less real than its constituents. Thus the pot and its parts, constituents, and so on belong to the same category. The translation "specifically characterized phenomena" is intended, therefore, to embrace not just the characteristics but also the things characterized.

Second, an even more important distinguishing feature of the Geluk standpoint is that the things in question are sometimes referred to as "specifically characterized *phenomena.*" This brings our attention to the other side of the dichotomies mentioned above. Interpreters of Dharmakīrti agree that what lies on the other side of the positive portion of the dichotomies are things that do not occupy identifiable spaces and times, are not subject to change, and lack any existence independent of mind. Probably for most scholars—inside and outside Tibet, historical and contemporary, academic and religious—this is unreality, or at best some vague or liminal presence within the confines of thought. This is decidedly not the case for the Geluk. While distinguished from the affirmative side, those that are conventional, non-actual, permanent, and generally characterized *are* things. They are not purely imagined but have the status of phenomena. Their existence is defined—not fabricated—by mind, concept, and name. These are constructs that rely on the intervention of mind, such as those arrived at through a process of negation. The status of these constructs differs from that of things that have simply been imagined. The latter group are described as "nonexistents." When Geluk scholars refer to these, they generally reach for the stock examples supplied by their Indian predecessors. The nonexistence of these things is embodied by their impossibility. The Geluk scholars' favorite example is a hare's horn.

As both their explanation of the Pramāṇa tradition and Madhyamaka critique of it show, Geluk scholars are insistent about the primacy of the dichotomy. A strand of thinking that is particularly well represented in Tibetan philosophical discourse is the notion of the transcendent category. For instance, ultimate truth is argued to be beyond dualistic distinctions and is therefore not containable within a dichotomous division. Geluk scholars reject the idea of such a category (or non-category). The absence or negation of a pot in a certain location exists and is a reality, just like the absence of the self that is negated in selflessness. Selflessness and emptiness—the realization of which forms the very basis of the path—are also classified as permanent, or perhaps more accurately as realities that are *unchanging*. Being objects of cognition, they too are existents.

The single most commonly cited passage by the Tibetan authors in this volume is Dharmakīrti's statement "As there are two objects of comprehension, there are two valid cognitions." This binds the last dichotomy, an ontological one, to the most crucial epistemological one for the Pramāṇa tradition. The two objects of comprehension are the aforesaid specifically and generally characterized phenomena. There are only two sources that can bring knowledge of the phenomena within these categories. These are, as identified above, the two forms of valid cognition: perception and inferential cognition. Phenomena that are specifically characterized belong to the domain of perception, whereas those that are generally characterized fall within the domain of inference. For the Geluk school, this is not quite as straightforward as saying that perception only cognizes the specifically characterized, whereas inferential cognition is limited to knowing the generally characterized. Rather, it means that the sights, sounds, and other objects of the phenomenal world are essentially affirmative, independent things, which present themselves to the cognitions that perceive them. Perception experiences them as they are—that is, in a manner that corresponds to their reality. In experiencing them, perception validates or confirms their existence. Inferential cognition, by contrast, works within the realm of thought and is a type of conceptual consciousness, a category that includes suppositions, memories, and delusions, in addition to random and unstructured thoughts and impressions. The logical deductions that inferential cognitions rely upon involve the manipulation of concepts. Ordering and categorization always feature, and negation frequently plays a part. At least some portion of the phenomena with which inference engages necessarily lies outside the realm of immediate experience.

All of Geluk understanding of epistemology in the Pramāṇa tradition of Dignāga and Dharmakīrti derives from the distinction referred to in the above statement that delineates the two objects—the specifically and generally characterized—and couples them with the two forms of valid cognition. The third text in this volume sets out how the same dichotomy is seen by Candrakīrti to epitomize the thinking of the Pramāṇa tradition and how, as a result, it becomes one of his principal targets. For a Geluk author like Jamyang Shepa, the question is what to make of Candrakīrti's criticisms, since rejecting them is simply not an option.

While the dichotomies identified thus far count among the most significant ones structuring Pramāṇa thinking, there are other binaries that are equally integral to the tradition. Among these are subject and object (i.e., a cognition and what it cognizes), particular and universal, affirmative and negative phenomena, as well as definiendum and definition (i.e., the thing defined and what defines it). The last is especially important in the Tibetan tradition of scholasticism. The exercise of defining something—for example, what it means to be impermanent, generally characterized, or even a pot—itself became a defining feature of scholasticism, and each new section within Khedrup Jé's text begins by delineating the phenomenon in question.

Pramāṇa Epistemology in Practice

A distinctive feature of the Geluk system is its emphasis on the soteriological dimension of Pramāṇa. Another of Khedrup Jé's works, *Guide Through the Path of Pramāṇa*, articulated the vision of an epistemology directed toward enlightenment and contributed to Geluk thinking in this area. Details of this vision are scattered throughout the works in this volume, making it difficult to see where the topics covered stand in relation to the whole. A concise description of how some of these elements fit together in Geluk understanding of the process of realization may therefore be helpful. Never seeking to displace the traditional version of the stages of the path, this model examines what progress along sections of that path might actually entail. Its emphasis on what makes valid cognition and logic necessary to that progression helps us understand why our Tibetan authors felt compelled to analyze and write about them in such detail.

Although the accurate comprehension of qualities such as impermanence, selflessness, and emptiness is regarded as powerful, the truly transformative effects of their realization can only be unlocked with their direct perception during meditation. On the epistemological level, perception also forms part of the goal, since it is the only kind of valid cognition that is manifest at the stage of enlightenment, given a buddha's transcendence of conceptuality. According to the Pramāṇa tradition, there are four types of perception—sense, mental, self-cognizing, and yogic. A practitioner cannot gain the yogic perceptions of buddhahood without first having generated yogic perceptions on the paths of seeing and meditation. However, perception itself offers no direct path here, because none of the other three kinds of perception can be cultivated or developed into those of the yogic variety. Nor can yogic perception arise spontaneously according to this gradualist vision of awakening. Instead, the route to this kind of perception is conceptual. The process, as it is commonly depicted, involves an individual building an understanding of the target object of realization on the conceptual level. Through a procedure usually described as being made up of three stages—learning, deliberation, and meditation—the individual strives for acuity. During the final stage, supported by the concentrative powers and analytical abilities that the individual has patiently developed, this conceptual understanding gives way to perception—that is, direct experience—of the object. In general terms, Geluk scholasticism agrees with this depiction, placing trust in the ultimate efficacy of meditation, but its own version stresses inferential cognition's role in the advancement to that stage.

What then is this role according to the tradition, and how is an inferential cognition produced? One clarification concerns what appear to be two forms of inference after which Dharmakīrti names the first and fourth chapters of his *Commentary on Pramāṇa*. These translate literally as "inference for oneself" (*svārthānumāna*) and "inference for another" (*parārthānumāna*). Since it is only realization experienced within the individual's own continuum that can be of any genuine impact, inferential cognition is necessarily of the first kind—that is, it is always in the personal domain. Inference for another, therefore, does not actually denote a separate variety of inference. Rather, it is an acknowledgment of the fact that generating an inferential cognition is rarely a solitary enterprise; it is likely to involve two parties and include acts of communication.

More specifically, the latter, "inference involving a second party," refers to the *proof statement*. The established paradigm for explaining the production of an inferential cognition involves the interaction occurring between a Buddhist and non-Buddhist in the context of a debate. The process is initiated by the Buddhist interlocutor who, having already realized the object or point for himself, is seen to be in a position to direct the non-Buddhist interlocutor to the same correct understanding. In the debate scenario, as described in the Indian Pramāṇa treatises, the Buddhist is cast as the "proponent"—the one who presents the correct proof. The non-Buddhist is the "opponent," who contests the proof, arguing against it by means of a *discrediting statement*. On one level, such statements were simply attempted refutations, although in public disputations between opposing parties in medieval India, which could be either intra- or cross-tradition in nature, there were clearly rules about how these refutations were to be formulated. However, in Tibetan scholasticism, the discrediting statement became increasingly associated with the "consequence"—a form of argumentation elaborated on below—with many authors, such as Khedrup Jé, regarding the two as equivalent. From this perspective, it could be the Buddhist who employed the discrediting statement. For instance, the correct understanding that the Buddhist wished to induce in the non-Buddhist opponent might directly challenge a strongly held view, such as one that was integral to a system of beliefs to which that individual subscribed. In such a case, directly presenting the opponent with the correct view would likely be met with stubborn resistance. The Buddhist might first therefore employ a discrediting statement aimed at undermining the position that was the source of that resistance.

Another element mentioned in our texts is the *false rejoinder*. This is the attempt of one interlocutor, who is invariably the non-Buddhist, to thwart the challenge to his position through deflection; rather than sticking with the topic at hand, he launches a counterargument. As its name suggests, such a response is necessarily self-defeating, and the sixth chapter of Dignāga's *Compendium* is devoted to identifying the grounds on which such rejoinders fail. The topic is not dealt with at length in Dharmakīrti's *Commentary*, and so Tibetan authors generally treat it as tangential, sometimes only providing examples from debates between followers of different non-Buddhist traditions.

To return to our original scenario, if there is no overt resistance from the non-Buddhist opponent's side, he may well be ready to generate an inferential cognition of the correct view. Every such cognition relies on a correct proof, which the Buddhist has realized earlier but of which the non-Buddhist interlocutor may be unaware. The Buddhist must therefore communicate the proof to the non-Buddhist, and the vehicle for this is the aforementioned proof statement.

Among the three main elements introduced thus far—the discrediting statement or consequence, the proof statement, and the proof—the tradition identifies the first two as "speech," configurations of words verbalized by one interlocutor and directed toward the other. The proof itself, however, is what the proof statement conveys. The subject—that about which a thesis is being established—is an essential component of the proof. So if the subject of the proof in question was "pot," the word *pot* must form part of the proof statement, and the actual subject of that proof must, in some sense, be the pot itself. Great emphasis is placed on the proof statement being formulated in the right manner so that it can produce the intended effect. The words are not designed to elicit an emotional response, such as to inspire, or in the didactic sense, to impart instruction (uses of language that we might be more familiar with in the religious context). Here, the aim is that the words trigger an inferential realization—that is, a *pramāṇa*—and that these words both guide and structure the knowledge the realization brings.

When the non-Buddhist party personally generates the anticipated inferential cognition, the goal of the interaction has been achieved. The tradition's reference to debate situations could create the impression that inference, the process of its production, and the associated learning belong to the domain of argument and disputation. The fact that the subject matter often relates to medieval Indian encounters can further contribute to the sense of its remoteness. Historically, some Tibetan Buddhists therefore judged the process of inference production as irrelevant to their personal development. Geluk authors aimed to counter this by projecting their reimagining of debates between Indian protagonists and their own disputes with their fellow Tibetan scholars as part of a wider mission to rectify specious views and eradicate delusions—a mission that must, finally, be pursued on the personal level.

Geluk scholasticism offers some more specific reasons as to why one cannot choose to sidestep inference. The three stages, involving the development of a conceptual understanding of the intended object and then eventual advancement beyond it, remained the general model for the process of progression. But Geluk scholars were especially interested in the epistemological mechanics, and within this, an emphasis on the ontology of phenomena, according to which everything can be classified as either evident or hidden. This differs from some of the binaries mentioned above, such as the impermanent-permanent dichotomy, in that this division takes account of *perspective*. Eager to demonstrate its soteriological value, our authors impress on their readership that the standpoint it represents cannot be an enlightened one, since everything is evident to a buddha. Rather, it derives from ground-level epistemology taken from the perspective of ordinary beings and is oriented toward showing them the route out of their current predicament. The acknowledgment that, from this ordinary perspective, certain things are hidden means neither that direct experience of them is impossible, nor that their comprehension simply requires greater effort. Perhaps more drastically, it means that initial cognition of them is *necessarily* inferential. Geluk scholasticism is adamant about this point. By implication, no matter how devoted one might be to meditation or an enlightened spiritual guide, if one's practice does not fully embrace inference rooted in correct logic, it cannot prove effective. And without such inference, however *convinced* the practitioner may be about emptiness, selflessness, impermanence, and even the existence of past and future lives, there can be no pramāṇa—no certain knowledge of them. Consequently, spiritual goals like the elimination of delusion and freedom from samsara will remain elusive. It would seem therefore that the application of logic is indispensable. The one possible proviso to this is explored below.

The logic discussed in the Pramāṇa treatises is complex, and the usual examples of hidden phenomena are the likes of emptiness. These reasons could make the prospect of realization through inferential cognition seem distant. However, perspective is all important here. A standard proof cited in the treatises is the one used to infer the presence of fire from smoke. The inference is not directed toward discovering some opaque facet of fire. Nor is there anything about fire's nature that makes it obscure. The fire in question is a completely mundane object, and only the individual's relative position makes it hidden in the sense that his distance from it temporarily prevents him from seeing it. Crucially, not only do certain hidden objects lie well within the grasp of the ordinary person, so do certain inferential valid cognitions that realize hidden objects. A largely unstated but noticeable and perhaps reassuring premise of the tradition is that humans have innate abilities for rationality and rudimentary powers of reasoning. The system of logic set out by Dignāga and Dharmakīrti is not entirely alien to us. It helps us uncover and employ immanent principles and powers. However abstruse the discussions on logic are, their primary aim is simply to identify the correct proof and its constituent elements, which, once successfully isolated, allow the individual to draw conclusions beyond the sphere of the everyday.

The tradition brings to the fore knowledge that is requisite to ensure the success of even a mundane act of inference. For an inference of fire from smoke to be accurate, one must be aware that any instance of smoke is necessarily associated with an instance of fire. That means one must be certain that smoke has an unfaltering relationship with fire. Knowing that the two are related requires, in turn, the understanding that they can be viewed as groups or categories of things. Only with this awareness can knowledge of what is generally true of smoke and fire be transposed to the specific situation at hand. In short, it necessitates not just the possession of individual pieces of information but also the ability to manipulate spheres of knowledge and move between empirical and abstract domains. This model of knowledge raises various questions that the tradition seeks to address. Inference may be a conceptual process, but it involves an interplay between the universal and the particular: drawing information from the domain of perception of individual cases—for instance, of smoke and fire—into the generic domain of categories. Obviously objects within the perceptual and conceptual spheres cannot be equated, but at the same time, without some form of recognizable correspondence between, for instance, the versions of smoke in the chimney and in thought, there could be no interplay between the spheres. Thus the nature of objects, especially in the conceptual domain, and the mode in which a universal is connected with its particulars are areas that greatly absorb Tibetan scholasticism.

Two notions essential to the tradition's model of logic are relation (*sambandha*) and pervasion (*vyāpti*). The tradition recognizes only two kinds of relationship that serve as the basis for logical deductions. One is where two things have a causal relationship, with the effect related to the cause, such as smoke being related to fire. The other relationship is the (same-)nature relationship, where the two things in question are not sequential but exist simultaneously, such as production and impermanence, characteristics that are equally present in all actual things. What links the two types of relationships is the idea that it is impossible to have one component of the relation without the other. It is therefore unfeasible to have smoke unless it has been preceded by fire or to have a pot that is produced but not impermanent. The fact that one component cannot exist without the other—that there is an unfaltering relationship between them—is developed into a theory of entailment that serves as a logical foundation for the system. Once one is certain that two things are related, then even if one of them should lie beyond the range of one's immediate cognition, it would be possible to *deduce* its presence or absence from the presence or absence of the other. The notion of pervasion rests upon this relational foundation. The classic explanation of this notion views *x* and *y* as categories, and saying that *x pervades y* conveys that *x* subsumes or encompasses every instance of *y*.[13] That is—depending on the nature of the elements, categories, and so forth, involved—there can be no instance of *y* that is not also *x*, or no instance of *y* that is not attended by *x*. Hence the category of impermanence pervades that of the produced, since any instance of something produced must also be an instance of something impermanent, and the category of fire pervades that of smoke, since for every instance or occurrence of smoke there is an occurrence of fire.

The essence of thought, as a cognitive process, lies in the conceptual mind's power to abstract, which is attributed to its ability to isolate its object. The Pramāṇa tradition explains this ability by means of its theory of other-exclusion (Skt. *anyāpoha*). This capacity for selectivity derives from the fact that thought, rather than grasping an object affirmatively, engages it by blocking out what is other than that object. This idea is developed even further in Tibetan scholasticism through reference to the idea of "conceptual isolations" (Tib. *ldog pa*). What separates inferential cognition from other forms of thought is its being a source of valid knowledge. It should be apparent even from this short description how much relations and pervasions, as principles, rely upon abstraction. To realize relations and pervasions, we must identify them through isolation by drawing from experience, such as having observed how the likes of fire and smoke act. As a principle, a relation is a construct, but as with other conceptual schemes, it may manifest or be instantiated in the world of real things. Therefore, in explaining the link between constructs and objective reality, Geluk scholasticism does not equate the universal with the purely abstract or the particular with the real but holds that a universal can, in some sense, exist in the real world. When our authors discussed such topics, they were clearly engaged in philosophical inquiry. But their main aim was to provide a credible explanation of how inference works, since they regarded it as fundamental to their models of epistemology and soteriology.

Faith in Logic

In various branches of Tibetan Buddhism one hears reference to relying on a combination of *scripture* and *reasoning*. This rubric was inherited from India. It is mentioned, for instance, by Candrakīrti in his *Entering the Middle Way Autocommentary*[14] and Atiśa in his *Instruction on the Middle Way*.[15] More generally, it is used to express that while faith in what the Buddha said may be vital, the place of rational thinking is also integral. But scholars of the Geluk school are particularly fond of referring to this combination, and identifying the reasoning with their analytical approach and reliance on logic. The logic they mean is not concerned with abstract notions, such as that of possible worlds. Nor does it engage in the analysis of statements in terms of modalities. While it may deal with matters of belief, the tradition says its primary interest lies in *certainty*. If queried on this, our authors would undoubtedly clarify that logic is primarily employed to gain certainty in the epistemological sense—that is, within the realm of knowledge. A proof can only be correct if it is based on unimpeachable logic, and the main purpose of such a proof is to generate a correct inference. However, our authors would add that logic is just as necessary for reliable textual analysis and even structured conversation with others about philosophical matters. The Pramāṇa tradition developed a system of formal logic, and for Geluk scholars, the two most important structures within this system are the *proof* and the *consequence*. There are also more informal ways in which our authors approach argumentation. Before discussing any of these, we return briefly to the relationship between scripture and reasoning.

Those in the Indian Pramāṇa tradition were particularly critical of what they saw as the unquestioning reverence given to the Vedas. It would have been difficult to argue that such reverence should simply be switched from the words of the Vedas to those of the Buddha. Accordingly, Pramāṇa thinkers were known for expressing skepticism about the notion of scripture as divine revelation and for adopting a questioning attitude to the acceptance of tradition. Rather than abandoning scripture to the realm of pure faith, they devised a logical method that could be applied to the Buddha's scriptures for the purpose of analysis and as a way of generating inferences. Dignāga in particular is credited with having shown how conviction could be brought into the domain of inference. Reference has already been made to hidden phenomena and how inference is required to access them. The Indian Pramāṇa tradition divided these hidden phenomena into different spheres and paired each with its own variety of inferential cognition. Those things within the sphere of "extremely hidden phenomena" might seem the most problematic, in that what falls into this category—including the various finer workings of karma—can only be experienced by someone who has achieved full enlightenment. To gain any certainty about the Buddha's pronouncements on such matters, the individual has no choice but to rely on what is literally designated "inference of conviction" or "scriptural inference." Whatever the names might suggest, the method here is not that of generating the inference "*X* is true, because the Buddha said *x* is true." Since extremely hidden phenomena themselves lie outside the sphere of usual analysis, attention turns instead to the words that convey them. Thus, with this kind of inference, one takes a particular pronouncement by the Buddha and examines it to see whether it passes a number of prescribed tests in order to make deductions and yield certain knowledge about its content. As the works in this volume show, some of the key principles shared by Indian Pramāṇa thinkers and the Geluk scholars who followed them are embodied in the way that they tackled the issue of scripture.

The proof and the consequence were briefly introduced in the context of the discussion on how an inference is induced. What remains to be explained is how the two differ in terms of their configuration and usage. Regarding the latter, the focus here is upon usage within Geluk writings. A point never overtly stated by our authors is that, generally speaking, they see proofs as objects of analysis. Consequences, by contrast, are what they employ as the means of analyzing those proofs. In addition, consequences are the formulaic mode of communication relied on by Geluk scholars in their analytical discourse. To help further clarify the distinction between the two, the proof and consequence will now be dealt with separately.

Logical Proofs

Tibetan scholasticism's goal of understanding the Indian Pramāṇa treatises involves very precise identification of the proofs that the Indian masters were advancing. The intellectual and religious motives for this are intertwined. A correct proof is the embodiment of a set of logical rules that, once fathomed, can in theory be extended to develop further proofs and applied to new situations. It is believed that *only* correct proofs give rise to inferences yielding certain knowledge, by means of which genuine spiritual progress is gained. However, Indian Pramāṇa writings—especially those of Dharmakīrti—are extremely elliptical, meaning that identifying and extracting the proofs is not always a straightforward matter. That said, there is a good deal of agreement among Tibetan scholars about the proofs that Dignāga and Dharmakīrti advanced. The differences of opinion are about exactly how they should be formulated, and we encounter multiple minor variants of the same proof, as each scholar tweaks versions proposed by his predecessors, with the apparent aim of arriving at the flawless formulation. Such attention to minor, technical distinctions is illustrative of the Tibetan discourse on Pramāṇa more generally. Not all the proofs within our texts have direct Indian origins. For clarity of expression or to facilitate further analysis, our authors occasionally present the stance of a Tibetan opponent in the form of a proof—irrespective of whether the opponent originally expressed it that way.

It is also the case that during earlier periods of Tibetan scholasticism and among non-Geluk thinkers, reliance on the proof as a logical formulation was more widespread. But when our Geluk authors refer to proofs, they tend to mean the reasoning expressed in the Pramāṇa treatises. They are generally disinclined to use it as a vehicle for their own arguments and to thereby introduce new proofs into the mix. In keeping with Tibetan scholasticism, our authors' conservative attitude to the content of the treatises generally manifests in their reluctance to transpose it to their own situation. As an object of description and analysis, a proof is carried from the treatise together with its original context into the realm of Tibetan scholarly discourse. Accordingly, certain proofs are embedded in debates with non-Buddhist opponents or proponents of Buddhist schools that never existed in Tibet. This is not to say that every proof discussed is buried in the obscurity of sociocultural detail pertaining to the subcontinent. Many proofs come with no such trappings, as illustrated by the proof inferring fire from smoke, whose universality is apparent. Still, it may be useful for the reader to be aware that when proofs are accompanied by references, these will be Indian rather than Tibetan. This applies not just to opponents—from schools such as the Nyāya or Sāṃkhya—but also flora and fauna, and even the occasional figurative appearance (or nonappearance) of a certain grisly spirit. No attempt is made to supply more "culturally appropriate" examples.

As pointed out, a correct proof in Buddhist logic must conform to a precise pattern. Although in Indian Pramāṇa treatises there was some variation in this pattern,[16] in Geluk understanding, there was not. Generally speaking, the logic does not make use of symbols, and in practice, proofs are always conveyed together with content. However, to introduce the different components of the proof, it is helpful to use letters to represent them. The basic proof takes the form: A is B, because of C, just like D. The most familiar proof is "Sound (A) is impermanent (B), because it is produced (C), just like the pot (D)." The content here has genuine philosophical import, but it should be recognized that the frequency with which this particular proof appears in the Buddhist Pramāṇa literature (and indeed even in non-Buddhist works) is also due to it being chosen to represent a standard model for analysis and explanation, since again, there was traditionally no custom of reducing proofs and their components to symbols. Each of the components has a technical name: subject (A), predicate (B), reason (C), and example (D).[17] Hence, in the illustration, "sound" is the subject, that about which something is being established, "impermanent" is the predicate, what one is establishing to be a property of sound, and "produced" is the reason, by means of which one establishes that sound is impermanent. The pot is an ancillary component used to facilitate the process of linking other elements within the proof. In rough terms, just as the pot is something that is both produced and impermanent, this must also be the case for sound. More specifically, pot is a *similar example*, one that clearly belongs to the same categories—being produced and so on—as the elements it helps to link. But one might alternatively use a *dissimilar example*, since it is feasible to make the same point in a negative fashion. Other items of terminology relating to the proof also refer to clearly delineated technical roles. *Thesis*, for instance, corresponds with the familiar usage of the term in that it denotes something that an individual may propose and set out to establish. But in this context, it refers only to "A is B." This equally applies to the designations *reason*, *subject*, and so forth: while having similarities with terms in popular usage, their versions in this sphere of Buddhist logic are very strictly defined.

Compared to logical formulations found in other Indian religio-philosophical schools, the Buddhist proof is concise. This brevity is largely explained by the conviction—evident in Indian Pramāṇa writings, especially in their reports of debates with non-Buddhist opponents, and also in our own texts—that correct identification relies on a process of analytically boiling down the "stuff" of discourse to logical essentials. Correct understanding and formulation are not just about getting rid of conceptual "impurities" but also shedding anything deemed excess to requirement. A proof is supposed to be a lean, concentrated entity, from which all extraneous content has been removed. Precise and concise formulations are viewed as allies of analysis.

Components that are cluttered with content are prone to vagueness. They may introduce unknown elements and unquantifiable or uncertain variables.

The second standard proof-model found in the treatises is that in which smoke is used to infer fire: On the smoky mountain pass (A), there is fire (B), because there is smoke (C), like in the kitchen hearth (D). This proof continued to serve as a standard model partly because of the mundanity of its content, making it easier to analyze and understand the essentials at play. Reiterating the earlier point, even the understanding of everyday cognitive processes serves a spiritual purpose, if it helps to identify the elements vital for correctness, which might then be harnessed and directed toward higher ends. The need for exactitude and conciseness here feeds directly into the way Geluk scholars envision Buddhist meditational practice. Vagueness and ambiguity are viewed as antithetical to effective meditation, which is a sustained activity focused on a precise and well-defined object. Such an object is first cognized through inference based on a correct, clearly formulated proof.

It must be said that the economy of expression to which the correct proof aspires contrasts with the analytical discourse attached to it. A seemingly simple act of inferring fire from smoke can generate a tremendous amount of involved discussion. But as already indicated, there is much more at stake than the individual proof in question. Each inherited proof is used as the basis for posing broader questions about principles, definitions, and classifications.

While a correct proof requires all the components enumerated above, the most important component is the reason. In the most general sense, a reason can be described as a piece of evidence presented in support of a thesis. The Buddhist Pramāṇa tradition sets strict criteria for what counts as a *correct* reason—that is, one that serves as the basis for a correct, inference-inducing proof. Dignāga distinctively defined the correct reason in terms of three characteristics or criteria.[18] These do not distinguish a special class of phenomena as reasons. Instead, these criteria are essentially the relations that the reason is required to have with the proof's other components, and as such, the reason is a literal embodiment of the whole structure of the proof and the manner for determining its logical correctness.

The technical terms for the three criteria are the *property of the subject*, the *forward pervasion*, and the *reverse pervasion*. Explained roughly, with reference to the first of our standard expositional models—Sound (A) is impermanent (B), because it is produced (C), just like the pot (D)—these mean that (1) being produced is a quality of sound, i.e., C is a property of

A, (2) that something produced is necessarily impermanent, i.e., C is always B, and (3) that something not impermanent is never produced, i.e., non-B is never C. An individual who is in the position to take the logical step of establishing the proof's thesis does so only when he is sure that the reason satisfies the three criteria. Dignāga and Dharmakīrti may have formulated the three criteria precisely, but they trigger plenty of discussion. Hence, aside from the role the proof plays in the generation of knowledge, the proof itself becomes one of the principal objects of analysis for Pramāṇa writers as they disassemble individual proofs advanced by the figures of authority and discuss their mechanics and the theory behind their use.

Consequences

Although the importance of the proof for the Pramāṇa tradition is massive, within Geluk dialectical writings, in practical terms, the real tool of formalized argumentation is the consequence. In the present texts, our authors find little reason ever to make direct reference to consequences, but this is because their reliance on them is so pervasive. To better understand the specific function here, it may be helpful to distinguish among a variety of things that "consequence" might denote in the context of Buddhist writings. First, the consequence is often used to refer to Nāgārjuna's distinctive form of refutation, a method that many describe as a kind of *reductio ad absurdum*. Second, it has a central place in Candrakīrti's attack on Bhāviveka. Particularly well known in the Tibetan tradition, it serves as a springboard for distinguishing between the Prāsaṅgika and Svātantrika schools of Madhyamaka thought. Third, within Tibetan scholasticism, the consequence is a subject of analysis, especially among early exponents of the tradition. Both Chapa Chökyi Sengé and Sakya Paṇḍita were interested in classifying consequences according to their type. Fourth, in Tibetan Buddhist debate, the consequence is a verbal formula by means of which a challenger attacks the position of the respondent. The first three iterations of the consequence are embedded within specific discourses—namely, discussing Nāgārjuna's approach, what characterizes Candrakīrti's Prāsaṅgika thinking, together with the potential role of the consequence in inducing inference, and what defines the various subcategories of consequence. The iteration that comes closest to the consequence as used in our texts is the fourth one—the verbal formula used in monastic debate—in that in neither case is the consequence itself held up for scrutiny or discussed on the level of theory but rather belongs to the realm of practice, where it is employed both as a tool for analysis and a vehicle of communication. On the surface, a consequence resembles a proof in that it usually has something akin to the characteristic "A is B, because of C" formula. As with a proof, one can also refer to a consequence's subject, predicate, reason, and pervasion.[19] But unlike a proof, a consequence necessarily includes the words "it follows." Packed into this seemingly minor distinction is a whole world of difference. "It follows" is used when one party is pointing out what he believes to be a logical implication or consequence of something the other party in the discourse has asserted. Theoretically, a correct proof should be capable of inducing a correct inference. This is possible because the various elements from which it is constructed are factual—that is, the proof's content reflects reality. In contrast, the consequence is purely a verbal formula. It must be grounded in one or more positions accepted by the other party, and it is from these that it derives a logical conclusion. But its content has no loyalty to any objective reality. So while the proof may be the vehicle for conveying positive theses and assertions, for critical analysis in Geluk scholasticism, the consequence is the more important tool and is most representative of its style of dialectical discourse. Since the consequence primarily acts as the medium for analysis and argumentation, direct references to it in our texts are only occasional. Nevertheless, indirect reminders of the consequence's *presence* are constant, as the authors explore the range of possible answers that an opponent might give to what is referred to in the translation (in brackets) as the "argument."

The textbook explanation of how the consequence works, in terms of theory, calls upon us to imagine an individual who accepts that sound is permanent. Perhaps because he is strongly committed to the idea, a proof that overtly presents the opposite thesis, such as the standard "Sound is impermanent because it is produced," may make little impact. So he may be presented instead with a consequence, such as "It follows that sound is not produced, because it is permanent." Although the consequence may seem to do little more than reorder the elements in the proof, a crucial bit of information (sometimes missing from these explanations) is that ordinary individuals are said to be able to perceive that sound is produced but not that it is impermanent. That sound is produced is therefore something that the individual implicitly accepts, and denying it would fly in the face of common experience. The consequence is supposed to confront him with the conflict of trying to hold that something he knows to be produced is simultaneously not subject to change. Pointing out to him a logical implication of his incompatible positions is likely to be more successful in breaking down his misconception than presenting him with the standard proof.

The main concern with such examples is with technical correctness and making the relationship between the consequence and the proof associated with it a transparent one. But this explanation relies on a highly artificial situation, and it gives little indication of how a consequence might actually be used either in a live debate or in our texts. To demonstrate the latter, we can do no better than turn to the first occasion that a consequence appears in the translation. Our author, Khedrup Jé, is assessing the view of those who believe that the Pramāṇa treatises have no real place in Buddhism. These individuals feel that learning in Buddhism should be closely aligned with the true aim of spiritual practice—namely, to bring about internal change. Identifying this interior aspect as supreme, one of these individuals talks of a "*piṭaka* (collection) of internal learning." What he is suggesting is not that there is a separate *piṭaka* of the Buddha's teaching beyond the commonly accepted threefold division (i.e., the *tripiṭaka*) but that the affinity of purpose shared by these three can be extended to encompass other treatises with similar intents. He claims that the very subject matter of the literature on Pramāṇa excludes such writings from this category. It is to this opponent that Khedrup Jé directs his argument: "It follows that the Conqueror's own teachings do not belong to the *piṭaka* of internal learning, because they also teach the two types of valid cognition, logical reasoning, and so forth." When markers are inserted to help separate the component parts of this consequence, it reads:

> It follows that the Conqueror's teachings (A)
> do not belong to the *piṭaka* of internal learning (B),
> because they also teach the two types of valid cognition and
> so forth (C).

In the reason, Khedrup Jé makes more explicit the topics that the Pramāṇa treatises teach, such as valid cognition and logical reasoning. That aside, the formula clearly reuses the opponent's own assertion that a Pramāṇa teaching cannot belong to the aforesaid *piṭaka*. This means that the *first essential* for a correct consequence—that it is based on the opponent's own assertion—has been fulfilled. The author also introduces a new element, the teachings that the Buddha himself gave, as the subject. This produces a new conclusion, akin to the thesis of the proof that A is B. This conclusion that the Conqueror's teachings do not belong to the *piṭaka* of internal learning is clearly one that the opponent does not welcome. This fulfills the *second essential* for a correct consequence, that the conclusion it reaches is one that is undesirable for the other party. In technical language, the consequence's pervasion is the opponent's own position. Described in more vernacular terms, the opponent has made a generalization without giving full thought to its implications. It often seems that the aim of the consequence is not so much to address a claim directly but to exploit implications that the opponent had failed to foresee. It should be apparent to the reader that, while the content of the consequences used in the text is often technical, the consequence itself only really aims to satisfy the two essential criteria just identified rather than any complicated technical definition.

In the situation described, the opponent cannot simply reject the consequence out of hand. The commitment of both parties to the rules of the discourse means that they agree not just that usage of the proof is the correct way to formulate an assertion but also that the usage of the consequence is the correct way to formulate a criticism. The opponent's response must therefore be directed at either the conclusion or the grounds upon which it has been reached, (the grounds here being *vaguely* comparable to the argument's premises). The first of these is rarely a viable option for the opponent. It would involve him either accepting or rejecting the conclusion "A is B." He is unlikely to accept it, since by its very design, the consequence is intended to present him with an unwanted conclusion. And he can only reject the conclusion if he can identify the exact fault in the grounds upon which the conclusion is based. This effectively leaves the opponent with only two choices, denying either the reason or the pervasion. The example from the text can again be used to illustrate these choices. First, if the opponent rejects the reason, he is saying that he does not accept it to be true of the subject. In other words, he does not accept that the Conqueror's teachings deal with topics such as the two types of valid cognition—that is, he rejects that C is true of A. Second, he could challenge the pervasion, meaning that he would deny that something teaching topics such as the two types of valid cognition is excluded from the *piṭaka* of internal learning—he rejects that what is C is necessarily B. To deny this would obviously be problematic, since it is exactly the position that is supposed to be his own, and upon which the consequence is based. In the text it is actually the first of these two options that Khedrup Jé is interested in, since he goes on to provide evidence of the Buddha having taught about valid cognition and his commitment to the logical approach. As to how the discussion unfolds, the text will speak for itself.

Such a consequence could quite feasibly be presented in a live monastic debate, but the other party would not be quite as constricted as the description above might suggest. The individual has more scope for avoiding the conclusion, often by challenging the accuracy with which his position has been characterized in the consequence.[20] In the textual sphere, as represented in this volume, the opponents and their positions may be real, but only in very rare cases are the debates a true record of what was said during an actual encounter. While the discourse can be said to be imagined, it reads like a credible interaction between two parties engaged in a dialectical exchange. There may often be questions about the author's representation of an opponent's view. The way an opponent responds to the consequences is also entirely at the author's discretion, but the opponent is frequently granted a "right of reply," in which he may set about trying to refine his position. Although the author's attacks always prevail ultimately, in addition to providing lessons in scholasticism's reductive technique, these imagined debates are an interesting way of further exploring the positions of opponents, many of whom were no longer alive at the time that the texts were composed. A particularly interesting feature of our first author's use of the consequence is a variation he regularly deploys. This involves the evocation of the *three spheres* motif, a point explained by the author and clarified in the accompanying notes. This variation, which appears to be entirely of Tibetan origin, is used to underline that the primary aim of the consequence is not just to criticize the opponent's position but to deprive him of any means of response.

Other Aspects of Argumentation

While the proof and consequence represent the formal instruments of assertion and criticism, they belong to a wider spectrum of practices relating to argumentation. In a general sense, the *reason and scripture* formula serves as an accurate description of the materials used by any scholar to construct an argument. The notion of scripture stretches beyond the words of the Buddha to encompass passages from works by any figure that all parties in the discourse regard as being of complete authority, and in the Pramāṇa context this is usually Dignāga and Dharmakīrti. The hermeneutical approach means that in theory any passage is open to interpretation, usually according to context. While it is true that there is total agreement on certain passages, such that their meaning is no longer questioned, much of the discourse leads back to matters of interpretation. Typically, in support of a position that he proposes, a scholar will cite relevant passages of scripture and advance lines of reasoning. Another scholar who wishes to challenge him is expected to supply scriptural passages and lines of reasoning of his own that undermine or contradict those of the first. How each scholar interprets the passages in question is likely to feature centrally in the discourse.

Scholarly descriptions of the discourse emphasize its logical aspect and generally use the proof as their model. This stems from the preference for representing the tradition of scholasticism as systematic, rigorous, and above all one that has an objective methodology. But our authors, like those in other eras and cultural settings, are in the business of convincing the readership of their case. Notwithstanding the huge status of formalized techniques—which make the approach so distinctive—our authors also rely on various informal methods, including *rhetoric*. Among the most common of those deployed to undermine an opponent's position or even the opponent himself are humor, mocking, and even ridicule. These should be recognized as strategic devices. They are consistent with the assertive persona that the Tibetan monastic debate culture encourages the individual to adopt for the purpose of dialectical discourse. They are accepted ways of strengthening the force of what one says but are clearly not regarded as substitutes for a coherent argument. Tibetan scholars never developed a system of classification for such types of rhetoric, but when used, they rarely aim at subtlety, and no further clarification seems necessary.

It is in fact only for the proof and the consequence that the tradition developed any sort of descriptive analysis and system of classification. The reader is likely to notice many other elements of logic that seem formalized in their language and structure. Most of these have no technical names in Tibetan and have traditionally been learned through practice rather than from any manual or rulebook, since neither appears to have ever been written. An example is the parallel argument, in which the author, usually for the sake of refutation rather than assertion, develops a line of reasoning analogous to the actual one held by an opponent. While not directly countering the opponent's position, it may be seen to reduce it, by demonstrating that a line of reasoning comparable to the one proposed by the opponent could be used to reach an unwelcome conclusion with which he could not agree. The use of this type of argumentation in the writings of Chapa Chökyi Sengé has been examined by Pascale Hugon,[21] but its place in Geluk writings such as those in this volume has yet to be investigated. Our authors do use hypothetical arguments partly intersecting with this type of argumentation, usually prefaced by questions such as "What would you say if someone argued such and such?" The author who employs this kind of argument generally endorses neither it nor its conclusions. The aim is rather to show that in committing to a chosen position, the opponent's ability to support or defend another has been diminished. In addition, we see reliance on a welter of analytical schemes, sometimes with hermeneutical or etymological slants. These were for the most part taken from the earlier tradition, and when combined, they form the stock-in-trade of Tibetan scholasticism, although our authors sometimes employ them in novel ways. Because our authors expected their original audience to be familiar with these, they rarely feel the need to formally introduce them, but notes attached to the translation clarify some of the less obvious ones. On the one hand, these schemes are simply the means of examining and processing the materials in scriptures and treatises. But in argumentation, they are frequently presented as evidence, since the case for a particular position could only be enhanced if it is seen to stand up to the analyses based upon them.

A few more points about the thinking behind arguments can help to orientate readers. Geluk scholasticism relies heavily on its *theory of definitions*, and as mentioned above, a huge amount of its discourse centers on how something should be correctly defined. Apart from being a means of identification, the formulated definition can be used within a proof to allow further deductions. Aspects of the theory are revealed gradually throughout the texts, but it is useful to know beforehand that much of the thought is guided by a kind of dictionary logic. Here, a clear distinction is made between a thing defined, called the *definiendum*, and the characteristic(s) that embody it, called the *definition*. These are not equivalent to a word and its meaning in a lexicographic sense, but there are noticeable commonalities between the principles in the two fields. Thus, just as a lexicographer would try to create a definition or meaning that is easier to comprehend than the word it explains, here there is also a requirement that a definition is easier to realize than its definiendum. Reflecting the observation that a lexicographer who tries to define a word by citing the word itself would be seen as ineffective, here the stipulation is that no part of the definiendum should be explicit in the definition. It is perhaps always the case, however, that these "shared" principles are applied more strictly here than during the compilation of a dictionary. So while a lexicographer might aim for some degree of inclusiveness in addition to clarity and consistency, here the definition must be absolutely watertight. Since it is expected to serve a logical function, it must be exactly equivalent to—which here means coterminous with—what it defines. These are some of the principles that our authors take as given but rarely feel the need to spell out or reiterate.

Arguments can also often seem reductive—a description that generally carries largely negative connotations with regard to discourse. There are indeed strong grounds for suspecting that the positions of certain opponents are being oversimplified. Furthermore, having attacked an opponent's position, an author will often invite the opponent to respond but in a manner that apparently forces him to choose from a very limited number of options. However, it is useful to remember that this partly arises from the areas of agreement between the two parties. In these texts, discourse frequently revolves around some particular epistemological or analytical model, each of which has a set of constituents and associated technical terms. When an author presents an opponent with limited options, it is often these models that are being referenced. An opponent, whether real or imagined, generally does not protest, simply because he agrees that the choices with which he is being presented are the only ones available.

Aspects of Shared Indian Heritage

With their stated aim of determining the true intention of Dignāga and Dharmakīrti, Tibetan writers on Pramāṇa set out to clearly distinguish between the views these two masters held from those they did not. Far less of a priority for them was distinguishing views that were unique to Dignāga and Dharmakīrti from those that they simply held in common with others. The vagueness about provenance can leave readers of Tibetan Pramāṇa works with the sense that *everything* correct or acceptable in some way derives from the two masters, especially as it appears that the only contributions that Indian non-Buddhists bring to the discourse are views that are patently wrong. Works on Indian philosophy and logic that are not purely written from the Buddhist perspective can help give a clearer impression of how much different traditions shared.[22] For the present purposes, it is sufficient to briefly highlight a few areas of commonality with non-Buddhist traditions, not only to create a more balanced picture but also to give the reader a better sense of the thinking behind some of the debates and the issues that lie at their heart.

As is often pointed out, Dignāga and Dharmakīrti's system of Pramāṇa arose from the crucible of religio-philosophical discourse in medieval India. Tibetan writings sometimes name individual proponents of non-Buddhist views, but more commonly they represent the opponents of the Buddhist Pramāṇa system as organized schools of thought. Although Tibetan authors generally agree that these schools must conform to an even-numbered scheme (of usually four, six, or eight), they differed on the identification of core groups and the borders between them. Nevertheless, the six non-Buddhist interlocutors presented in our volume belong to one of the most common enumerations. The six schools in question are the Nyāya, Vaiśeṣika, Mīmāṃsā, Sāṃkhya, Nirgrantha (Jain), and the Cārvāka (or Lokāyata). This classification should not be confused with what are now commonly presented as the six main schools of Hindu philosophy. These are the so-called *āstika* schools, which are contrasted with the *nāstika*. The *āstika-nāstika* classification appears primarily in Indian non-Buddhist sources. The distinction it makes is between the schools that affirm a fundamental entity or principal and those that deny it. Some identify the fundamental entity or principal in question as the deity Īśvara, while others say it is the authority of the Vedas. The *āstika* classification includes the Yoga and Vedānta schools; Tibetan authors disagree on whether to count these as independent traditions. The two schools that take their place in the Tibetan sixfold division are the Nirgrantha and the Cārvāka. In non-Buddhist sources, these two schools together with the Buddhists are the most prominent "deniers" (*nāstika*). We indeed find commonalities between Buddhist and Jain traditions, although Tibetan sources give no hint of this, and our authors in general find it difficult to acknowledge affinities with non-Buddhist traditions. The one issue on which Buddhist authors feel themselves able to express common cause with most non-Buddhist schools (although usually tacitly) is in what they perceive to be their united opposition to the materialists (the Cārvāka or Lokāyata),[23] who are often portrayed not so much as philosophers but as overt hedonists or at least those bent on rationalizing hedonism. It is difficult to imagine our authors being willing to admit sharing a category with the Cārvāka, but these materialist philosophers were, like the Buddhists, "deniers." Our authors make no overt reference to the *āstika-nāstika* classification, but when distinguishing their tradition from others they regularly focus on Buddhism's denial or rejection of particular iconic beliefs associated with the Indian *āstika* schools. The chief among these are the beliefs in a supreme being, the ultimate authority of the Vedas, and the existence of a form of self that is known as the *ātman*—all of which are targeted by our authors. As with their forebears in the Indian Pramāṇa tradition, our authors constantly emphasize the divide between Buddhist and non-Buddhist philosophical thinking, but before engaging with this perspective, it is worth considering just how much is shared across that divide.

The most conspicuous affinity shared by the Buddhist and non-Buddhists schools (excluding the materialists) is their primary religious worldview with its Indic system of belief in samsara, liberation, and karma. For our authors, acceptance of this worldview is a given, so they rarely feel the urge to step outside the adversarial framework to acknowledge any sort of solidarity about it. On a more philosophical level, an area of commonality already identified is implicit in the notion of *pramāṇa* itself. Dharmakīrti may well have been exceptional in his "relentless pursuit for certainty,"[24] but as already mentioned, the concept of pramāṇa may predate Buddhism, as do elements of the discourse pinpointing trusted sources of knowledge. Buddhists and non-Buddhists were drawn into debates about the correct identification of these sources by a good deal of agreement about fundamental principles.

Among the philosophical Hindu schools, the one with which the Pramāṇa tradition shares the closest intellectual affinity is the Nyāya. This school is known for its early systematization of thought, and developments in the fields of logic and epistemology, as expressed in the *Nyāyasūtras* (ca. 150 CE) attributed to Akṣapāda Gautama. Throughout the era that Buddhism thrived in India, those in the Nyāya school were held to be the Hindu specialists on logic, and over the centuries, other Hindu traditions came to accept much of their system. Many of the discourses in Pramāṇa literature parallel those in Nyāya writings, and in a number of cases, there is clear evidence of interaction between adherents of the two traditions. Despite their commonalities, the Buddhist and Nyāya traditions regarded themselves as rivals rather than comrades, and works like Nāgārjuna's *Treatise on Pulverization* and Dharmakīrti's *Science of Disputation* are specific refutations of different aspects within the Nyāya system. In the works translated in this volume, like those of most other Tibetan authors dealing with Indian non-Buddhist philosophical traditions, the Nyāya is portrayed as just one school among many. However, in the third work, by Jamyang Shepa, a fourfold division of pramāṇa has a key place. This division is generally understood to originate with Nyāya thinkers, and it is a perfect example of how aspects of their epistemological and logical traditions came to be accepted as standard.

A key example of a concept that structures Pramāṇa thinking and has Indic rather than specifically Buddhist roots is the notion of *substance* (Skt. *dravya*, Tib. *rdzas*). A substance is commonly viewed as a substratum separated from the properties it possesses, which inhere or subsist within it. Two discussions that feature in our texts concern whether certain mental faculties constitute substance and how substantial existence contrasts with imputed existence. These specific questions are largely internal ones debated among different Buddhist schools. However, the basic notion of substance as the foremost category—a possessor of qualities that is contrasted with a category of less concrete phenomena—is as fundamental to Nyāya, Vaiśeṣika, and Jain thinking as it is to the Buddhist Pramāṇa tradition. Dignāga and Dharmakīrti certainly disagree with their non-Buddhist peers on what counts as a substance, but the ontology itself is one that they, like other Buddhist philosophers, inherit from earlier times and largely accept. It is only at the hands of the Buddhist Prāsaṅgika Madhyamaka that we see aspects of this ontology being challenged.

Some variety of separation between a thing and its properties is fundamental to the Pramāṇa tradition and pervades every facet of its thinking. This is indicated by the proliferation of terms related to the divide. On the one hand there is the *basis* or *subject*, and on the other there is the *property* or *predicate*, the *quality* or *attribute*, and the *characteristic*. This separation is core to the Pramāṇa tradition's model of analysis. The same model structures the logical proof, which asserts that the subject has a certain property. Two parties may find themselves at philosophical odds on a particular issue, and the ensuing debate will be characterized by a series of affirmations and negations. These all rely on the subject property model, and it is the degree of consensus about it that allows Buddhists and non-Buddhists to engage each other in structured debate.

Despite this common conceptual framework, the greatest exemplifier of the divide between the Buddhist and non-Buddhist schools is the former's attitude to a particular variety of realism, which serves as a principal driving force for Buddhist Pramāṇa thinkers and also as an issue behind several recurring arguments. As attested by our texts, in Tibetan Buddhist philosophical literature, there is a pejorative dimension to being labeled a *realist* (Skt. *vastusatpadārthavādin*, Tib. *dngos smra ba*). In our first two texts, the two non-Mahayana Buddhist schools—Vaibhāṣika and Sautrāntika—often find themselves unfavorably classified together with the non-Buddhists as realists, whereas in the third text, it is Dignāga's Pramāṇa tradition itself that seems to be the recipient of this disparaging designation. While anti-realism is strong in Buddhist thinking generally, the particular brand of realism that is subjected to an unremitting onslaught by Pramāṇa thinkers is embodied by the Nyāya and Vaiśeṣika schools, and to some degree the Sāṃkhya too. The above-mentioned common conceptual framework means that they, like the Buddhists, accept such distinctions as those between a thing and its properties, the whole and its parts, the universal and the particular, and the object and its name.

According to a Buddhist critique, these schools are guilty of reifying the elements on both sides of the distinction as well as the distinction itself. It must be stressed that these non-Buddhist schools do not have a uniform set of views; there are variations among their positions. However, the Buddhists believe they are addressing a tendency of thought that all the non-Buddhist schools are liable to exhibit. For these non-Buddhist schools, the mind cognizes things—horses, cows, and so forth—and the differences between them, but it has no direct role in producing either the things or their differences. The mind's ability to cognize these things and differentiate between them is due to the fact that they have individual, affirmative essences, such as horseness or cowness. Substances are portrayed as independent and indivisible. To support the rigid classifications of phenomena that these schools assert, even the qualities or attributes that inhere within these substances are granted some degree of independent reality as qualities or attributes. They maintain that the separation between these various elements is real while simultaneously denying a role for conception; this is a weakness that Buddhist Pramāṇa scholars constantly target. They draw attention, for instance, to the ensuing contradictions when these schools are pressed to explain the relation between the whole and its parts. This approach parallels the lines of argumentation found in the Madhyamaka analysis of self. The bottom line for Buddhist thinkers is the need to take account of the mind, by not seeing it as a passive cognizer that merely confirms the existence of its object but understanding its role in *creating* that existence. Due to the nature of the binary divisions discussed above, for Pramāṇa scholars, the emphasis here is on constructs (non-actual things), and the centrality of conceptuality to their existence. Things on the other side of the divide, such as sounds and pots, as well as their features of production, impermanence, and so forth, also form part of the discussion. They may be actual things, but what determines that they belong to certain categories and are assigned the roles of subject, predicate, or reason in a proof, like the categories and roles themselves, is thought. The Buddhist Pramāṇa thinkers reduce the real, solid distinctions held by the non-Buddhist schools to linguistic and analytical conveniences.

The most regular object of criticism in our texts is the realist theory of language and its understanding of the relationship between an object and its name. For these non-Buddhists, there is a unique, semi-mystical bond between a word and the thing it denotes, whereas for Pramāṇa thinkers, the connection between the two is a matter of arbitrary choice and subsequent convention. In short, these non-Buddhist schools have a realist vision of the world as one populated by real, independent objects endowed with affirmative essences and belonging to actual categories. This is subjected to an incessant assault on every available occasion by our authors who, like other Buddhist Pramāṇa thinkers, seek to dismantle notions of substantive, independent existence and expose the pervasive role of conception.

Pramāṇa Views from the Geluk Perspective

Some describe Geluk understandings of Pramāṇa and interpretations of Dharmakīrti's writings as unorthodox. This says nothing about their popularity. The Indian Pramāṇa system had a historical impact on Buddhist traditions in China, Korea, and Japan, among others, but especially in Tibet, where it served as the foundation of scholasticism. The institutionalized learning of Pramāṇa in the main Geluk monasteries appears to go back to Khedrup Jé's tenure as Ganden throneholder (see below), and these monasteries served as massive centers for the promotion of the Pramāṇa interpretations of Tsongkhapa and his followers. Given the stability and continuity of the major Geluk monastic centers, their model of largescale education, and their successful export of this model within Tibet and beyond, it seems unlikely that there has ever been another system to rival the Geluk one in terms of the number of scholars it has trained in Pramāṇa.

Even though Geluk Pramāṇa interpretations cannot be regarded as marginal in terms of their popularity, on certain points they do not conform with the historical mainstream. This mainstream is determined not by how many people have accepted the points of interpretation but the number of scholars, throughout Asia rather than just in Tibet, who have expressed support for them in their writings. It is important to keep a sense of proportion on what divides Geluk and mainstream understandings. The differences are highlighted by contemporary specialists on Dharmakīrti's writings, who tend to approach them from a philosophical rather than from a religious perspective. To the nonspecialist, the separation between interpretations could well seem relatively minor. Perhaps the main differences in Geluk interpretations surface in relation to the division between specifically characterized and generally characterized things, aspects of which are discussed above in the section "Binaries and Realities." There is agreement that generally characterized things are conceptual constructs. In reinforcing the basic dichotomies already outlined and attacking the realism of non-Buddhists schools, Dharmakīrti is keen to contrast the reality of the causal world with the concept-reliant schematic one. As such, he never explicitly assigns to the constructs anything more than a shadowy, insubstantial status. The prevalent view is that such things have no actual existence. Geluk scholars, however, regard this position as highly problematic, as it makes no clear distinction between these constructs and things that are totally imagined. For them, it is essential to maintain a strict divide between these two: the former shape our understanding of reality, whereas the latter, such as the hare's horn(s), are pure fictions. Just as valid cognition must be able to confirm the nonexistence of the fictional, it must also be able to confirm the existence of these constructs, without ever denying the conceptually bound nature of that existence. An overriding concern is with the likes of selflessness and emptiness. These are unquestionably negations and thus cannot exist separate from mind. But to conclude that they therefore have no existence would mean, for example, that selflessness has no more reality or truth to it than the self that it negates. For Geluk scholars, this would undermine not just the epistemological model but also the soteriological one. Thus they rebut any suggestion that such transformative, ultimate realities are anything less than existent. As illustrated by this example, Geluk thinkers aim for what they see as *logical* consistency throughout the whole system. As Dreyfus rightly observes, it is often the case that they deem philosophical principles as higher than exegetic ones.[25] Their views are frequently arrived at through having pushed certain lines of thinking to their logical conclusions.

The view on constructs just described is nowadays most commonly associated with the Geluk school and is seen as characteristic of their system. The first two works in the present volume belong to the earliest stage of writings that the Geluk tradition would later come to identify as purely its own. In these, the idea that constructs exist is not one that the authors simply entertained or are gradually moving toward; it is presented as a firm, unambiguous position. There is no clear picture of how such unanimity was reached, and our authors never describe such matters in terms of an intellectual evolution. But this does not mean that the view originated with Tsongkhapa or his followers. Questions regarding the category of noncomposed or unconditioned things—including uncaused space, selflessness, and various types of cessation or absence—go back a long way in Indian Buddhism, centuries before Buddhism's arrival in Tibet. In earlier Tibetan scholasticism, there was no uniformity about the status of the category. Some, like many later non-Geluk scholars, simply place them outside the categorical schemes that demand they be classified as either existent or nonexistent. Others reject this, and explore both the existence and nonexistence options as viable, but never express a firm opinion on which is correct. But Tibetan scholars seem increasingly to identify the category of noncomposed things with the category of constructs (i.e., generally characterized things). A couple of generations before Tsongkhapa and his followers, Chomden Rikpai Raldri (1227–1305) expressed a position that has some correspondence with Geluk views on this matter.[26] Chomden Rikpai Raldri became a very prominent teacher at Narthang Monastery, an early Kadam stronghold. He helped develop the Narthang branch of scholarship, an offshoot of the Sangphu tradition, and seems to have been very influential on Tsongkhapa. Thus, in many instances, Tsongkhapa and his followers seem to have brought ideas that earlier scholars had expressed to what they saw as their logical conclusion.

In common with other Tibetan scholars, those of the Geluk tradition were also prepared to augment terminology and develop categories that they saw as implicit in Dharmakīrti's writings. To give one example, the fact that the absence of a thing could be used to make logical deductions is key to Dharmakīrti's thinking, and this absence is the basis of the category of "nonobservation reasons" that he describes at length. But he does not explicitly set out the subdivisions for the category that we see explained in the first work in this volume. The subdivisions seem to have derived from Tibetan scholars who noticed that one of the nonobservation proofs cited by Dharmakīrti did not fit comfortably within the parameters he appeared to set for the category. They took this to mean that he actually acknowledged that the category contained two varieties, and they went on to clarify the differences between them. The original scholars responsible for distinguishing between the two varieties belonged to the earlier tradition of Tibetan scholasticism. But it is in Geluk literature that the distinction is explored with greatest alacrity and to its furthest extent.

There is also a very clear strategic dimension to the way that Geluk scholars deal with Pramāṇa writings. These writings, like the Cittamātra system more generally, are regarded as a preliminary to engaging with Madhyamaka. Signs of this dimension are detectable in Geluk presentation of certain aspects of the Pramāṇa system, especially those pertaining directly to emptiness and processes of imputation. Even if the positions in question are eventually superseded by higher ones, they may still be valued as a means of refining thinking and offering their own insights. Geluk scholars also distinguish between the intent of the author and his work. They agree that Dharmakīrti's Seven Treatises are presented from the Cittamātra perspective. But this did not necessarily mean that Dharmakīrti personally subscribed to the Cittamātra system, since some of the scholars argued that his final view was Madhyamaka. Geluk scholars also agreed that both Sautrāntika and Cittamātra systems were represented in Dharmakīrti's works. The Sautrāntika perspective, with its more realistic standpoint, often seems to serve as a default in Geluk Pramāṇa writings. It is only on issues about which the two systems strongly differ that their respective positions are explicitly spelled out. The existence of externally established objects and the corresponding theories of perception are among the most obvious areas of disagreement. Hence, in the first work, Khedrup Jé devotes separate sections to the two systems' competing explanations of the three conditions that give rise to perception, since this is related to the consideration of whether there is an object *out there* acting as one of the perception's causes. But for the most part, Geluk scholars prefer not to go through the Pramāṇa materials systematically by carving them up into Sautrāntika and Cittamātra sections.[27] Instead they understand the majority of the Pramāṇa writings as expressing a set of principles in the sphere of epistemology and logic that are not just acceptable to both Sautrāntika and Cittamātra but even have extension beyond their systems.

On the other side of the fundamental dichotomy there are some significant differences in the way that Geluk scholars understand specifically characterized things. Rather than preempting the authors' own explanations of these, some of the major differences, along with a number of other distinctive features of Geluk epistemology, are listed below in bullet-point style. Given the technical nature of these features, readers may find such a list helpful as a point of reference as they delve into the texts. Furthermore, this list, which is in no way intended to be comprehensive, can alert readers to the areas where they are likely to encounter discrepancies between Geluk and other interpretations of the Pramāṇa system. Those who wish to learn more about the diverging interpretations of Pramāṇa, especially in the Tibetan context, and to seek more contemporary analysis of the finer distinctions between Geluk scholars and those of other schools, particularly the Sakya, may do well to consult *Recognizing Reality* by Georges Dreyfus.

- Conceptual constructs—those on the generally characterized (*sāmānyalakṣaṇa*) side of the dichotomy mentioned in the earlier section—are realities and are existent.
- Actual things—those on the specifically characterized (*svalakṣaṇa*) side of the dichotomy—have an equal ontological status. The grosser entities that are constituted of individual particles or instants of consciousness are no less real and existent than those constituents.
- Particulars do not equate exactly with specifically characterized things, nor do universals equate exactly with those that are generally characterized.
- There is a "moderate realist" view on particulars, and this contrasts with the "antirealist" view of Sakya Paṇḍita and other Sakya scholars.
- While specifically characterized and generally characterized things are mutually exclusive categories, universals and particulars are not.
- The basic criterion for being a universal is to have particular instantiations. Hence a universal can be either an actual thing (e.g., pot) or a conceptual construct arrived at through negation (e.g., the absence of pot).
- The basic criterion for being a particular is to belong to a type, or in other words, to have a universal. This explains why something like pot can simultaneously be a particular—an instantiation of the universal *existent thing*—and also a universal—that to which individual pots belong.
- Rather than transcending categorization, the ultimate lies within the sphere of valid cognition and has a definite ontological status. It lies within the reach of thought and language, and is accessible through logical reasoning.
- There is adherence to a theory of definitions developed at Sangphu, involving a three-way split among the definition, definiendum, and illustration.
- The standard model of representationalism in perception is refuted, as exemplified by the distinct way that the *object-aspect* is identified.

There are also two basics of Geluk logic that it is essential to be aware of when reading the dialectical exchanges within this volume:

- A double negation equates to an affirmation.
- In argumentation, stating that one does not accept a particular assertion is seen as tantamount to holding the converse of that assertion (i.e., not accepting the claim that *x* is *y* is equivalent to asserting that *x* is not *y*).

Geluk Pramāṇa in the Context of Tibetan Schools

All three works in this volume are now regarded as Geluk writings, but only the third was composed by someone who identified himself as belonging to the Geluk school. At the time the first two works were written, the Geluk school did not yet exist. Tsongkhapa is commonly represented as the school's founder, although it would be more accurate to view him as the central figure around whom the school's identity coalesced. As with other Tibetan religious traditions, most of the work of carving out a distinct identity and presenting it as an independent school was undertaken by disciples and later followers. The origins of the Geluk go back to individuals who were drawn to Tsongkhapa and eventually formed a community. This group gained its first stable base with the founding of Ganden Monastery near Lhasa in 1409, due to which, one of the names they were originally known by was Gandenpas (i.e., those associated with Ganden). The Geluk *identity* as a school was what developed in subsequent decades and centuries. For a variety of reasons, including its relatively late formation and centralized structure, many aspects of the Geluk tradition have greater uniformity than those of other Tibetan schools. This is certainly true of its teachings and philosophy, as set forth in the writings of Tsongkhapa, Khedrup Jé, and Gyaltsab Jé, which soon took on canonical status within the tradition.

The high degree of intellectual homogeneity among Geluk thinkers did not originate in anything resembling an organized church. There has never been a senior council or authority determining policy and prescribing official thought. The same is true for the consistency we see among the writings of Tsongkhapa, Khedrup Jé, and Gyaltsab Jé. The latter two were neither neophytes brought up in Tsongkhapa's tradition nor exactly converts to it. Prior to meeting Tsongkhapa, they were noted scholars in their own right. And given Khedrup Jé's independence of thought (discussed below), it may seem slightly surprising that there was such agreement among them on philosophical matters. In the field of Pramāṇa, Khedrup Jé indeed retained some of his individuality. Gyaltsab Jé's interpretations are held to be closer to those of Tsongkhapa, to the extent that Gyaltsab Jé's *Illuminator of the Path to Liberation*, his explanation of Dharmakīrti's *Commentary on Pramāṇa*, is regarded as expressing Tsongkhapa's own thought, since it is reportedly based on teachings that he gave—Tsongkhapa himself apparently did not compose a full commentary to Dharmakīrti's work. A number of works attributed to Tsongkhapa follow this pattern, with the colophons describing them as Gyaltsab Jé's notes on Tsongkhapa's teaching. Although this might be seen to cloud the boundary between the input of the two individuals, these works are traditionally regarded as faithful recordings of Tsongkhapa's words.

Khedrup Jé's own thinking on Pramāṇa, as expressed most comprehensively in the *Banisher of Ignorance* (contained in this volume) and his own commentary on Dharmakīrti's treatise, differs in some respects from that of Gyaltsab Jé, although this does not result in radically diverging interpretations. But importantly, rather than trying to gloss over these differences, the tradition found ways of absorbing them. Khedrup Jé's "variations" are celebrated as aspects of his own individuality and even held to embody scholasticism's principle that the sphere of commentarial interpretation should encompass multiple voices. Later generations of Geluk writers went on to compose textbooks (*yig cha*) that serve as the main study materials within the various colleges (*grwa tshang*) of the main Geluk monasteries. In the textbooks on Pramāṇa, authors also expressed minor differences of interpretation. Jamyang Shepa, the author of the third text translated in this volume, whose textbooks were adopted by Gomang College, was more favorable to Khedrup Jé's interpretations than other textbook writers. But variations of interpretation at the textbook level have again never been seen to threaten the school's integrity. Indeed, these textbooks together with their variations are generally perceived to be a major strength of the college system functioning within the great Geluk centers.

On the topic of schools, there are two more important points to be made. Geluk scholasticism has been seen as exemplifying an unusually analytical approach to Buddhism, and arising from this, it has regularly drawn a set of criticisms. There are charges that it is overly intellectual and discursive, concerns itself with topics that are too abstruse, and that its beloved Pramāṇa is a field of knowledge that is not "properly" Buddhist, since aspects of its logic are shared with Indian non-Buddhist schools and are (according to some) of non-Buddhist origin. But perhaps the two most enduring criticisms are that the school's analytical approach is not compatible with the contemplative spirit that many have felt should characterize Buddhism, and that there is something unseemly and even *un*-Buddhist about the way that its tradition of scholasticism appears to encourage and perhaps even revel in faultfinding, disagreement, and combative argumentation. In the contemporary setting, positions on the dialectical approach are often seen purely through the prism of schools and sectarian divides. But while those in the Geluk tradition may latterly have been the foremost advocates of dialecticism in Tibet, this mantle was one they inherited, together with the associated discourse and tensions, from earlier Tibetan scholasticism, which first arose in the eleventh century.

Furthermore, in historical terms, what are now described as the Tibetan religious schools were never clearly separated into opposing camps of proponents and detractors of the analytical approach associated with Pramāṇa. David Jackson makes some valuable points pertinent to this.[28] As he observes, the criticisms mentioned above have not always clustered together neatly such that they can be arranged into two clearly identifiable sides—the *pro-* and *anti-*factions. Among what might broadly be termed "Pramāṇa critics," there were actually various strands of thought, and Jackson provides glimpses of their shades. Furthermore, as Jackson observes, in addition to Sakya authors (who were more readily associated with forms of scholasticism), various luminaries among the branches of Kagyü were staunch supporters of Pramāṇa long before the Geluk tradition appeared on the scene. This is true, for instance, of the Drikung Kagyü, since figures such as Jikten Gönpo (1143–1217) cannot be viewed simply as lone voices or historical outliers. If we stick with the traditional picture of Tibetan religious affiliation, the schools cannot, therefore, be arranged to form a neat, oppositional divide. Their engagement with the analytical approach, exemplified by an interest in Pramāṇa, can be seen as spanning a range, akin to the various Buddhist traditions' relations with anti-realism. And if we are prepared to go deeper, taking into account the inclinations of individual religious figures and branches within those schools, as well as considering different stages in history, then even this more realistic picture presents some challenges.

It is, nevertheless, fair to say that the issue of Pramāṇa has tended to act as a lightning rod for criticism, with much of the historical discourse coming down to questions about the worth of Pramāṇa study and its relevance to the Buddhist notion of an escape from suffering. The whole initial section of our first text, by Khedrup Jé, is essentially a defense of Pramāṇa in terms of the path and, more generally, of scholasticism's analytical approach. In setting out to establish Pramāṇa's pivotal role in the Buddhist vision, it reaffirms principles shared with the system's detractors—namely, a belief in the primacy of meditation and a conviction that whatever means are employed to reach the final goal (and in this case, however analytical or argumentative those means might be), these should never be mistaken for ends in themselves: there must always be a clear-sighted recognition that the goal is to overcome suffering by eradicating deluded thoughts. The section of defense in Khedrup Jé's work was by no means original. By his time, the argument was well rehearsed, and defense sections or apologia taking a very similar form and often drawing upon the same set of quotations can be found in works from earlier centuries. Intriguingly, a large portion of the section in Khedrup Jé's text almost matches verbatim the opening passages in Gyaltsab Jé's *Extensive Pramāṇa Memorandum*, the contents of which, the colophon reports, derive from a teaching delivered by Tsongkhapa.

Even if such defenses had become standard prefaces for the more expansive works on Pramāṇa, it still seems reasonable to wonder whether our authors had specific parties in mind when they wrote them and whether some of their remarks were directed at particular individuals. If so, they never reveal the identity of those who seem to have opposed the Pramāṇa tradition, reserving their main criticisms for their fellow scholars, all of whom were steadfast proponents of Pramāṇa. However, at one point in his defense section, Khedrup Jé makes a disparaging comment about those who rely on "personal instructions." This may lead us to wonder whether certain Kagyü traditions, which lay great stress on instructions communicated directly from master to disciple, are the target. Gampopa Sönam Rinchen (1079–1153), who is seen as the founder of the Dakpo Kagyü tradition, was not drawn to the analytical approach and does not seem to have favored the study of Pramāṇa. However, it was among some of his followers that this developed into a pronounced opposition. For instance, in his *Ornament Clarifying the Essence (of Gampopa's Four Dharmas)*, Layakpa Jangchup Ngödrup, one of Gampopa's disciples, cites a passage by Maitreya[29] that also appears early in Khedrup Jé's work. But while Khedrup Jé uses it in defense of the Pramāṇa tradition, Layakpa argues that it supports his conclusion that there is no place for logical reasoning in the Buddhist path.[30] A strain of anti-Pramāṇa sentiment within the Dakpo Kagyü traditions is therefore undeniable, although historically, these cannot be characterized as traditions that were totally hostile to the study of Pramāṇa or that rejected the notion of *pramāṇa* itself. Founders of the Dakpo Kagyü subschools, including Düsum Khyenpa (posthumously designated the First Karmapa, 1110–93), Phakmo Drupa Dorjé Gyalpo (1110–70), and possibly also Shang Tsalpa Tsöndrü Drakpa (1122–93), had all studied Pramāṇa with Chapa Chökyi Sengé. The Seventh Karmapa Chödrak Gyatso's (1454–1506) deep engagement with Pramāṇa also resulted in one of the finest expansive Tibetan commentaries on Dharmakīrti's writings.[31]

There is, however, emerging evidence of discourse among those who would commonly be identified as followers of Atiśa and belonging to the Kadam tradition. Certain individuals involved in this discourse did not reject the notion of pramāṇa outright but disagreed with the strict twofold division of it advanced by Dignāga and Dharmakīrti. These individuals—who were clearly conversant with the language of the Pramāṇa tradition emanating from Sangphu—began using it to develop alternative models, in which the aforesaid "personalized instructions" were recognized as one type of pramāṇa (i.e., a valid source of knowledge).[32] Although some of the discussion about different varieties of pramāṇa has its origins in earlier Indian textual traditions, we clearly see aspects of a Tibetan discourse in which Pramāṇa thinking is informing the development of new epistemological models that some regarded as better suited to the Tibetan situation or the Tibetans' own understanding of Buddhist meditational practice. Hence, if it is apt to talk of an opposition against whom these Geluk authors saw themselves as defending Dignāga's and Dharmakīrti's Pramāṇa tradition, it must be seen to have comprised not just those who denied the validity of the analytical approach but also those who were prepared to be more creative with the Indian inheritance.

One thing we can be sure of, however, is that in his remark on personalized instruction, Khedrup Jé is not denying this as a model of transmission. His own collected works include several writings that owe their roots to the very same type of instruction. It is for this reason that the need to add a proviso was mentioned in the earlier discussion about the Geluk school's insistence on the importance of logic in the path. While for Geluk scholars, individualized instructions have no place in the Pramāṇa tradition and the practices of scholasticism associated with it, in other fields, especially those of meditation and tantra, such means of transmission are viewed as essential. As remarked above, Geluk scholasticism divides subjects into distinct fields and treats many of them very separately. This separation also extends into other spheres, such as the domains in which knowledge is stored and the mediums through which it is transmitted or conveyed.

How then are we to view the remarks of a figure like Khedrup Jé, who seems to attack personalized instructions here but in other works expresses implicit faith in the same medium? Tibetan scholasticism has misgivings about opaque processes *in certain contexts*. When particular scholars challenge personalized meditation instructions, they are very unlikely to be questioning the veracity of the style of transmission in general terms, especially as they regard it with reverence themselves. Instead, they are expressing their suspicions that this institution can sometimes serve as a cloak for ineffectual or misguided direction, especially if the recipient is being instructed to turn away from inquiry and learning. In summary, with respect to Pramāṇa and other fields viewed as falling within the domain of scholasticism, the Gelukpa prefer clinical explanations over empirical ones and public practices of knowledge transmission over private ones. A common thread running through their analytical methods is the belief in accountability: individuals should be prepared to submit their views to scrutiny and, if called upon to do so, defend them.

Aspects of such thinking are apparent in the present works, but it does not mean that they pervade every form of Geluk literature. Little of the clinical logician may be evident in devotional writings or certain tantric works, where we often seem to be presented with a different side of the author altogether. These different *versions* of the author are also very rooted in the Geluk approach. Its scholasticism has found ways of compartmentalizing fields of learning but also ways of prescribing the various outlooks, viewpoints, and sets of locution that should accompany each. The visions of the path associated with each field may also differ, as can the descriptions of the means and criteria for the attainment of knowledge. How these can all be integrated within a single vision is not always immediately apparent, even though the Geluk tradition's hierarchical organization of systems makes it clear that some supersede others. The stance of Geluk writers on the necessity for inference and logical reasoning as the paths to true realization may appear uncompromising. But this begs some obvious questions: How much weight do such assertions carry, if within the Geluk's own model of knowledge, the Pramāṇa system is eventually to be surpassed by those of Madhyamaka and tantra? When one moves outside the Pramāṇa paradigm, do such assertions simply cease to be valid?

Two observations are in order here. First, certain aspects of Pramāṇa are admittedly bound to specific commentarial or didactic contexts. But drawing upon my many years of personal involvement with the tradition, I would say that Pramāṇa as a system has meant far more to Tibetan scholasticism and the Geluk than just one among a number of fields of learning, and this is due chiefly to its inextricable relation with logic. The logic deriving from the Pramāṇa system is most important for what it is seen to stand for—namely, a rational, critical approach to Buddhism, which is opposed to fuzzy and cluttered thinking. Hence, rather than being a perspective that is adopted provisionally, it is a *mentality*, which Geluk scholars feel permeates the whole of their tradition. It expresses itself not only in the order and structure of the texts but also in the Geluk educational system, especially in the practice of debate. Thus, in this sense, Pramāṇa thinking is never completely surpassed. In relation to the third text in this volume, by Jamyang Shepa, readers can judge for themselves how much, in the Geluk interpretation of Candrakīrti, Madhyamaka is actually being allowed to supersede Pramāṇa thinking. More generally, Geluk works on Madhyamaka do not set about totally deconstructing the aspects most strongly associated with Pramāṇa thinking, including its theory of definitions. That the shift in context should have brought some change in the understanding of such things is implied, but is rarely addressed directly.

Second, Geluk scholars, like those of other religious traditions in Tibet, extol the virtues of tantra and regard it as the highest system. We often hear that the tantric system is superior to the sutra one because it offers alternative techniques by means of which the same or homologous goals can be reached more swiftly. Accordingly, Geluk works on tantra deal with a plethora of esoteric techniques, meditational practices, and versions of the path, together with their alternative epistemologies. In such works, Geluk scholars seem to operate in a different space than in their writings on Pramāṇa. We see no concerted attempt to show how Pramāṇa thought can be incorporated into tantra or how a fusion of the systems might be possible. But if certain aspects of the Pramāṇa vision, including the reliance on inference and logic, are barely mentioned in these tantric writings, this does not mean that the authors feel these aspects have effectively been displaced. The Pramāṇa model is never overtly dismantled. A careful reading of tantric writings reveals occasional references, ranging from the terse to the oblique, that suggest that processes of reasoning have necessarily *preceded* the topics under discussion. Hence, even in the most advanced of tantric meditational techniques, while understated or virtually imperceptible, Pramāṇa thinking is nevertheless always present.

The Authors

The composers of the first two texts in this volume, Khedrup Gelek Palsang (1385–1438), popularly known as Khedrup Jé, and Gyaltsab Darma Rinchen (1364–1432), popularly known as Gyaltsab Jé, were direct disciples of Tsongkhapa Losang Drakpa (1357–1419). Khedrup Jé and Gyaltsab Jé are now celebrated as Tsongkhapa's chief disciples, with the three of them forming the "father and spiritual sons" triumvirate of the Geluk school. These three figures were also the first three Ganden throneholders. Despite the iconic status of our authors, the following brief sketches of their lives are not condensed hagiographies. They are instead restricted to corroborated details that are historically informative. These descriptions aim to give some sense of our authors as individuals, identify the key events in their lives, and contribute to the reader's engagement with and appreciation of the works in this volume. Significant religious figures such as these received various names during their lifetimes—birth name, ordination name, and names incorporating titles and epithets. On grounds of expedience, I have mostly referred to them by the same name throughout.

Khedrup Gelek Palsang (Khedrup Jé)

Although our first author composed the most important early biography of Tsongkhapa, *Entrance Point for the Faithful*, contemporary materials on his own life are more limited. He left no autobiography, but writings such as his *Record of Teachings Received* provide valuable details. He later became the subject of much creative narrative and genealogy, the prime example of which is his retrospective recognition as the first Panchen Lama (one that is not universally accepted). Such recognitions reveal something about the political, regional, and religious situation during the times of their conception and are informative about Tibetan hagiographical mechanisms, but they generally tell us very little about the individuals supposedly at their center.

Gelek Palsang, who later acquired the name Khedrup, was born in the Doklung Valley in Tsang, the western region of the Tibetan Central province (Ü-tsang), in 1385. His father was a local official within the Sakya polity in the former myriarchy (an administrative division created by the Mongols) of Latö Jang. Ngamring Monastery and the structures close to it served as the administrative hub for the territory. Having taken novice vows while still a young child, Gelek Palsang entered this monastery, began his studies, and probably stayed throughout his teens. At the beginning of his twenties, it seems that he moved to Sakya Monastery, also in Tsang. According to his own account, in 1403 he took full ordination from Jetsun Rendawa Shönü Lodrö (1349–1412) in the temple of Muzing. With Rendawa, he studied core subjects of scholasticism and received tantric teachings. In preceding years, Rendawa had also taught Tsongkhapa and Gyaltsab Jé, and Tsongkhapa considered Rendawa his most significant spiritual guide. Rendawa was also extremely important to Khedrup Jé, and he is second only to Tsongkhapa in the number of expressions of honor he attracted in Khedrup Jé's writings.

Khedrup Jé's early life was steeped in the Sakya tradition. But in his mid-twenties, he left the environs of the Sakya strongholds of Tsang and journeyed to Ü, the eastern region of the Tibetan Central province. Later Geluk writings say that he traveled with the sole purpose of meeting Tsongkhapa and that he carried with him a letter of introduction from Jetsun Rendawa. The single-minded goal of his journey may well be a narrative simplification: it was a common practice for learned monks of his age to undertake a journey to visit the major centers of scholastic learning within Ü and Tsang. By Khedrup Jé's own account though, once in Ü, he was presented with many auspicious opportunities, such as that of receiving instructions on Atiśa's "three combined rivers of bodhicitta" from Tsongkhapa before the Jowo statue in Lhasa on the fifteenth day of the month of miracles. The prospect of such opportunities would surely have entered into his decision to travel to Ü.[33] What is certain is that Khedrup Jé's journey led to his first encounter with Tsongkhapa and he became part of Tsongkhapa's circle soon after. In addition to repeating the study of core subjects of scholasticism that he had earlier undertaken with Jetsun Rendawa, he took other teachings and empowerments from Tsongkhapa and joined him in meditational retreats. The exact duration of this stage in his life is uncertain, and there are ambiguities about the sequence of events in the years that immediately follow.

However, Khedrup Jé's next step was definitely to return to Tsang. There is no suggestion that this represented any sort of acrimonious break with Tsongkhapa and his circle, but the reports that Khedrup Jé returned with the clear purpose of promoting Tsongkhapa's teachings after having made copious notes from the time he spent with him, and that Tsongkhapa was involved in the creation of such a plan, are quite likely to be later narrative embellishments. For instance, in the work translated in this volume, which was composed after his return to Tsang, Tsongkhapa is mentioned only once, at the end, albeit in a manner that affirms his personal importance to Khedrup Jé. It is sensible to remain open-minded to the possibility that Khedrup Jé was exercising his own prerogative in the return to Tsang rather than executing some proselytizing master plan. It seems Khedrup Jé initially returned to Ngamring, his original monastery, and was eventually invited to take up the role of abbot of Changra Monastery, which had been built in 1413. Changra was to remain Khedrup Jé's main center for many years. At some point he acquired the academic title of *kachupa*, most likely before his stay at Changra. Whatever the case, thereafter Khedrup Jé was most commonly referred to by himself and others as the Changra Kachupa or the Changra Abbot. Within the same period of his residency in Tsang, Khedrup Jé also founded the monastery of Riwo Dangchen in Panam, close to Changra. Later, in Gyantsé, while still in his early thirties, he became involved in the establishment of Palkhor Chödé Monastery. He eventually withdrew from the project following a souring of relations with its patron, Rabten Kunsang Phak (1389–1442), the ruler of Gyantsé, but was resident there for some time and completed at least one of his major compositions there. It seems that he returned to Riwo Dangchen after that. One of his later biographies names other monasteries that he founded, but details are sparse.

Khedrup Jé did not shy away from dispute. At the tender age of sixteen, he crossed swords with the well-known scholar Bodong Choklé Namgyal (1376–1451) in a public debate during the latter's visit to Ngamring. Although a later, much-anticipated public showdown with the major scholar Rongtön Sheja Kunrik (1367–1449) never materialized, the two took up cudgels via the written medium. But he was not unknown for fractious relations even outside the domain of formalized disputation and became involved in various clashes, such as the one with the forementioned Rabten Kunsang Phak, reportedly in relation to Rongtön. Another was with Ngorchen Kunga Sangpo, in relation to Palkhor Chödé's foundation but centered on diverging views on the Hevajra body maṇḍala.[34] Khedrup Jé also had differences with other elements within the Sakya hierarchy. Furthermore, even by the standards of Tibetan scholasticism, which accepts or even encourages boldness and vociferousness in argumentation, Khedrup Jé's outspoken style pushed the limits, as the first work translated in this volume attests, and he is regarded as having few rivals in terms of his swagger and abrasiveness.

After his return to Tsang, it is unclear how much direct contact Khedrup Jé had with Tsongkhapa and the circle of followers who lived together with him over a number of years in Ü. Khedrup Jé made no secret of the fact that some of the events he recounts in Tsongkhapa's biography were reconstructed, based on reports he gathered from others who witnessed them in person. But simultaneous with Khedrup Jé's own efforts developing monastic institutions in Tsang, the mobile, loose-knit group of disciples surrounding Tsongkhapa in Ü transformed into a residential monastic community with Tsongkhapa's founding of Ganden Monastery in 1409. The establishment of other major centers followed swiftly. After Tsongkhapa's passing in 1419, Gyaltsab Jé was appointed the second Ganden throneholder. In 1431, he traveled to Nenying Monastery in Tsang and requested Khedrup Jé to be his successor. It seems they then journeyed back to Ü together, and Khedrup Jé took up the post almost immediately, at the age of forty-five. He remained the throneholder for close to eight years, until his passing. During his tenure, his decision to set up a Sangphu-styled center for dialectical study at Ganden had what appears to be a major impact on the monastery and perhaps the character of the Geluk tradition itself. Another notable act involved the construction of two side-by-side structures housing the remains of Tsongkhapa and Gyaltsab Jé at Ganden. Following his own demise, another structure with his own relics was created so that Tsongkhapa's structure was flanked by his and Gyaltsab Jé's, an arrangement that appears to have inspired the iconographic depiction of the Geluk triumvirate.

Khedrup Jé's literary legacy is contained in the eleven volumes of his collected works (or twelve volumes in some editions). Among his scholastic writings, his works on Pramāṇa are highly respected. Also much admired are the *Thousand Measures: Providing the Fortunate with Sight* on Madhyamaka and the *Appearance of That Difficult to Realize*, his explanation of Haribhadra's commentary on the *Ornament of Realizations* (relating to aspects of Prajñāpāramitā literature.) The larger portion of his works are about tantra, and among these, he is best known for his considerable writings on Kālacakra and Hevajra as well as his exegesis on the classes of Buddhist tantra. His biography of Tsongkhapa also counts as a very significant work. More generally, he is known for his numerous versified eulogies. Apart from its content, Khedrup Jé's writing is celebrated for its aesthetic value. This derives from his love of the *kāvya*-style poetry, and Khedrup Jé's verses are saturated with figures and allusion from that tradition. Despite its complexity, Khedrup Jé's style remains admired for its rich imagery and expressiveness. Some later Geluk writers composed commentaries on it, and his versified works have been treated as a yardstick, with subsequent generations of authors (particularly those belonging to the Geluk tradition) seeking to emulate them. It is unsurprising that Khedrup Jé's compositional skills were also employed to great effect against those he sought to criticize, often cuttingly. It should be noted that even at its most excoriating, Khedrup Jé's writing is still held up and celebrated as the exemplification of a particularly rambunctious style of Tibetan writing.

Finally, certain scholars have portrayed Khedrup Jé as having rejected his Sakya roots and even having rebelled against the Sakya order. Such portrayals usually rely on oversimplifications regarding Sakya homogeneity. Khedrup Jé clearly had disagreements with individual scholars and also with elements of what might be termed a Sakya establishment,[35] but there was never a wholesale rejection of Sakya teachings. The current work is prima facie evidence of the respect that Khedrup Jé held for Sakya Paṇḍita's Pramāṇa interpretation, and this respect was certainly not limited to that field. This notwithstanding, in Khedrup Jé we undoubtedly encounter one of Tibetan religious history's real *characters*, who was clearly no stranger to controversy. His independence and outspokenness have served more to endear him than damage his reputation among many Tibetans, and perhaps make his faith in Tsongkhapa the more touching.

Gyaltsab Darma Rinchen (Gyaltsab Jé)

Since contemporary biographical sources for our second author are even more limited than for our first one, we know very little about his early life. Darma Rinchen was born in 1364, and like Khedrup Jé, he was a native of Tsang. Darma Rinchen gained the reverential epithet of Gyaltsab later in life, probably when he ascended to the throne of Ganden, as Tsongkhapa's "regent." Details of his ordination survive, but we do not know his first monastery or any institution with which he maintained a lasting relationship, and consequently we know little about his early learning and education, save for the fact that he engaged in study at various monasteries in Tsang, which must have included Sakya and also Nenying (he renewed his relationship with Nenying in his later years.) Jetsun Rendawa was among the group who granted him ordination, and having studied with him, Gyaltsab Jé, like Khedrup Jé, considered Rendawa one of his principal teachers. Although little is known about his life before he met Tsongkhapa, in his early decades he gained a considerable reputation as a scholar. One fact that has recently been drawn attention to is what was apparently the instrumental role he played in the development of the new scholastic degree, *kachupa*.[36] It is also clear from reports of his examinations that he spent some time at Sangphu. He first encountered Tsongkhapa immediately after having completed these examinations. Gyaltsab Jé had traveled from Tsang to Ü. It seems almost certain that meeting Tsongkhapa was one of the aims of this journey, but it may also have been motivated by a wish to submit to scholarly examination at Sangphu. Almost immediately it seems, Gyaltsab Jé joined the close circle of companions and disciples surrounding Tsongkhapa. Unlike Khedrup Jé, however, he chose to stay in Ü, accompanying Tsongkhapa rather than returning to Tsang. Although Gyaltsab Jé taught within his own right, he was one of the chief among Tsongkhapa's followers who helped establish Ganden Monastery.

Gyaltsab Jé also engaged in significant public disputations with notable figures of the day. These included Rongtön Sheja Kunrik and Yaktön Sangyé Pal. Reports of these confrontations are largely restricted to the pre-Tsongkhapa period of Gyaltsab Jé's life. It is uncertain whether this reflects the limitations of available historical sources or a change in the nature of his activities following his joining of Tsongkhapa's circle. What can be said with greater certainty than in the case of Khedrup Jé is that Gyaltsab Jé's activities in the fields of teaching and establishing monastic communities in Ü were directly supported by Tsongkhapa. Gyaltsab Jé became one of his most trusted disciples, and just prior to Tsongkhapa's passing in 1419, he handed over two of his few personal belongings (his cloak and staff) to Gyaltsab Jé. Shortly afterward, a delegation of Tsongkhapa's other disciples, apparently headed by Duldzin Drakpa Gyaltsen (1374–1434), requested him to take up Tsongkhapa's mantle. He agreed and became the second Ganden throne-holder, a post he held for eleven years.

Gyaltsab Jé wrote numerous works, most of which are contained in the eight volumes of his collected writings. Some coined a specific label for his oeuvre, referring to them as the Darṭik ("Dar commentaries")—a name that incorporated the first syllable of his name Darma. This highly unusual distinction is a testament to the impact of Gyaltsab Jé's writings. But the name was generally used unflatteringly by those outside the Ganden tradition, particularly those who felt troubled by what they saw as his reinterpretations of aspects of Pramāṇa. Later collators of his writings controversially chose not to include his commentary on Sakya Paṇḍita's *Treasure of Pramāṇa Reasoning* within his Collected Works. Two of his texts came to have massive importance in Geluk scholastic education—his main work on Pramāṇa, *Illuminator of the Path to Liberation*, which is his explanation of Dharmakīrti's

Commentary on Pramāṇa, and *Ornament Essence*, which is his principal writing on the Prajñāpāramitā-related field of study known in Tibetan as Pharchin. According to oral tradition, these works were based on notes made from Tsongkhapa's personal teachings on the subjects, and they are de facto regarded as representing Tsongkhapa's real intention, and in the Geluk mainstream are treated as the school's most definitive works in their respective fields. Outside the main curriculum, various other works by Gyaltsab Jé, including his commentary on Śāntideva's *Entering the Bodhisattva Way*, are also considered very important. Many of his works are commentaries to treatises on which Tsongkhapa left no separate writings. It is fair to say that what became mainstream Geluk thinking is represented most notably in works composed by Tsongkhapa and those that are in Gyaltsab Jé's name but are thought to have been written with Tsongkhapa's approval. Most of Gyaltsab Jé's major works were written late in his career, during his time in Ganden, when he and his companions were consolidating Tsongkhapa's legacy.

It was a year prior to his passing that Gyaltsab Jé requested Khedrup Jé to replace him as the Ganden throneholder. This choice proved controversial, since it was felt in some quarters that Duldzin Drakpa Gyaltsen was his natural successor. Drakpa Gyaltsen had been another of Tsongkhapa's most trusted disciples, and as already noted, he also appears to have been among the foremost of those who had entreated Gyaltsab Jé, just over a decade earlier, to take on the position of the second throneholder. There also seems to have been some disquiet about Khedrup Jé, who had become a more distant and perhaps independent figure, outside Tsongkhapa's close circle. However, Drakpa Gyalsten seemed mainly inclined toward monastic discipline and meditational practice, and the only works he is known to have composed were on Vinaya and tantra. Gyaltsab Jé likely saw Khedrup Jé as better suited to supporting the burgeoning project of monastery establishment that Tsongkhapa's disciples had embarked upon. Furthermore, Gyaltsab Jé and Khedrup Jé clearly shared a vision of the new tradition that placed scholasticism at its heart.

Jamyang Shepa

The biographical materials for Jamyang Shepa,[37] who was originally named Ngawang Tsöndrü, are more comprehensive than those for our first two authors. They include his *Autobiographical Verses*, a self-penned account of his first three decades (until about 1680). He was born in the town of Lhetra Ting in Amdo, Eastern Tibet, in 1648. He recounts that he was a sickly child and at the age of five received a hand blessing from the Fifth Dalai Lama, Ngawang Losang Gyatso (1617–82), who was apparently on his way to Beijing. This encounter forged a "Dharma connection" between them and, he implies, had a restorative physical effect upon him. He began reading texts at the age of seven, but it was not until thirteen that he became a pre-novice. His autobiographical verses detail the many topics he learned and the meditations he engaged in but do not reveal whether he joined a monastery. In 1668, at the age of twenty-one, like our two previous authors, he traveled to Ü—where the Geluk monastic centers, by now well established, were situated—and was admitted to the Gomang College of Drepung Monastery, where he began studying. He also renewed his acquaintance with the Fifth Dalai Lama, who granted him novice ordination in that same year. We can probably infer that his ordination had been deferred until that time so that he could receive it from the Fifth Dalai Lama in person.

Arising from encounters during this period, two individuals that he refers to as his "root" teachers are Phabongkha Jamyang Drakpa and Döndrup Gyatso. His autobiographical verses describe this first period in Gomang but concentrate almost exclusively on the many texts he studied and the empowerments he took. It is said that he received the name Jamyang Shepa ("Mañjuśrī Smiles") as the result of a statue indicating approval of the incredible effort he put into his religious exercises. This apocryphal account presumably refers to this period of his life. Our knowledge of Jamyang Shepa's education relies heavily on his own account, but we can be sure that he was an exceptionally dedicated student who made rapid progress. At the age of twenty-five he underwent examination, primarily at Sangphu Monastery, and emerged, like our previous two authors, with the scholastic title of *kachupa*.

His full ordination was likely to have taken place in 1674. In 1676, he entered Gyümé Tantric College, where he formed a firm bond with Changkya Losang Chöden (1642–1714). Upon the latter's demise, Jamyang Shepa was called upon to officially recognize his reincarnation. Later, when Jamyang Shepa himself passed away, the second Changkya in turn recognized his reincarnation. This reciprocal arrangement between the two lines was to prove key to the development of Geluk institutions in Amdo.

With his formal studies completed, Jamyang Shepa entered a new stage of his life from 1680 (his autobiographical account ends at this time), when he took up residence at Riwo Gephel, the retreat area above Drepung Monastery. There he embarked on a long period of meditation and an extremely productive phase of authorship, during which many of his most important works were composed. He also occasionally gave teachings and received instructions.

The next stage of Jamyang Shepa's life was marked by his transformation into a public figure and saw him being thrust into the center of the turbulent politics of the time. The Fifth Dalai Lama's passing in 1682 had been kept secret until 1697 by his prime minister turned regent, Desi Sangyé Gyatso (1653–1705). The interregnum had given the regent time to discover the individual who was to be recognized as the Sixth Dalai Lama and have him enthroned in Lhasa. Jamyang Shepa, who was now one of the most respected Geluk figures, accepted to serve as a principal guide of the Sixth Dalai Lama, Tsangyang Gyatso (1683–1706). Despite the best efforts of Jamyang Shepa and others, the Sixth Dalai Lama eventually rejected the life of monasticism planned for him and soon spiraled out of the scholastic orbit. In his public role as a member of the Lhasa establishment, Jamyang Shepa had frequent contact with the regent, who was probably instrumental in getting him appointed as the thirty-second abbot of Gomang by the Sixth Dalai Lama, in 1702.

The regent was himself a notable lay scholar, and evidence suggests that he and Jamyang Shepa maintained a healthy respect for each other's learning. However, they had differing understandings of the boundaries and obligations that their official relationship imposed on them. On two occasions the regent is said to have requested that Jamyang Shepa compose certain texts with a particular commentarial slant. As recounted in Gene Smith's short English introduction to Jamyang Shepa's explanation of Dharmakīrti's *Commentary on Pramāṇa*, the regent is said to have asked the author to compose a work that favored Dharmottara's interpretation. The fact that the regent was not in agreement with Khedrup Jé's positions was a factor here. On being shown the first chapter of the resultant work, the regent is said to have exhibited displeasure at Jamyang Shepa's failure to comply with his recommendation. Assuming that the report of this event is accurate, it is difficult to say whether Jamyang Shepa's action represented a stand for scholarly independence or was simply the expression of a preexisting interpretational preference that he saw no reason to conceal.

Central Tibet was plunged into turmoil when Qoshot Mongol forces, under the leadership of Lhasang Khan (d. 1717), challenged the legitimacy of the Sixth Dalai Lama. Lhasang Khan led his forces into Lhasa in 1705, attacked Drepung Monastery, and was complicit in the murder of the regent and probably also the Sixth Dalai Lama. Jamyang Shepa had enjoyed cordial relations with the Qoshot leader prior to this series of events, but his efforts to restrain Lhasang Khan met with limited success. He stepped down from his post at Gomang in 1707 and returned to Amdo in 1709. Following this return, which was against the wishes of Lhasang Khan, he managed to secure the safety of the individual who was to be recognized as the Seventh Dalai Lama, Kalsang Gyatso (1708–57). In one of his most significant deeds, Jamyang Shepa founded Labrang Tashikhyil Monastery, which developed into the region's largest. His native area in the vicinity of Lake Kokonor (Tib. Tso Ngön) was ethnically diverse, and his move proved popular with other Mongolian groups, including the Dzungars, who settled there and went on to depose the Qoshot in Central Tibet in 1717.

Having reestablished himself in Amdo, Jamyang Shepa resumed writing. He was a prolific author, and the most extensive version of his collected writings contains sixteen volumes. In terms of their historical influence, his most important compositions were those jointly adopted as textbooks for Gomang and Labrang. By Jamyang Shepa's time, the Geluk tradition had developed a clear study program in their major monastic centers. Textbooks became the main materials of the scholastic curriculum, serving as the prism through which the principal Indian treatises and even the thought of Tsongkhapa and his chief disciples were to be understood. These are all post-fifteenth-century compositions and vary among the different colleges. Through the figure of Jamyang Shepa and use of his textbooks, Gomang and Labrang developed an abiding affinity with each other. These two centers also gave rise to numerous branches, which were particularly welcoming to those hailing from Amdo and various Mongolian groups. On various measures—such as the geographical spread, quantity, and ethnic diversity of the monastic populations who have relied on them—Jamyang Shepa's textbooks are unrivaled in their diffusion.

Apart from his *Decisive Analysis of the Pramāṇavārttika*, which comments on the first three chapters of the treatise, his *Presentation of Tenets* and *History of the Yamāntaka Tradition* are held in particularly high regard. During his later years, Jamyang Shepa gradually delegated the running of Labrang to others, focusing more on spiritual practice until his death in 1721 or 1722.

Some of Jamyang Shepa's followers have been accused of being overzealous in expressing their commitment to the Geluk tradition, to the point of engaging in sectarianism. The main controversy associated with Jamyang Shepa himself is probably the issue of whether he could have done more to curb the excesses of the Dzungars when they arrived in Central Tibet, especially to deter their persecution of followers of the Nyingma tradition. At present there is little clear evidence on how much personal leverage he had with the Dzungars. As we saw in the case of the Qoshot, good relations with a leader or group, even if of a religious nature, have not always translated into the ability to influence their actions. Sangyé Gyatso's reported dislike for Khedrup Jé's interpretations seemed to be based on the fact that they did not always accord with those of Gyaltsab Jé (and perhaps indirectly, those of Tsongkhapa). Sangyé Gyatso's intervention could well be seen as an attempt to create a Geluk orthodoxy, at least in the sense of commentarial interpretation. Whether or not Jamyang Shepa's resistance to this was partly a matter of principle, his siding with Khedrup Jé's thinking helped to reinforce the idea that the Geluk tradition had a place for differing interpretations. It also had the effect of situating Jamyang Shepa slightly outside the commentarial mainstream, an area of affinity that he continues to share with Khedrup Jé and has filtered through to the many institutions and communities that align themselves with Jamyang Shepa.

The Texts

Text 1

There are four attested works on Pramāṇa composed by Khedrup Jé. Those generally seen as his major contributions are the two longest ones, which are *Banisher of Ignorance*, translated in the present volume, and *Ocean of Reasoning*, his explanation of Dharmakīrti's *Commentary on Pramāṇa*.[38] In setting out to explain a single root text, the latter fits firmly within the traditional commentarial mode. The former belongs to the more select group that attempts to describe the essentials of the Pramāṇa field as a whole. Sakya Paṇḍita's *Treasure of Pramāṇa Reasoning*, composed about 1219, has the same aim, as does the *Ornament of Reasoning* by Gendun Drup, the First Dalai Lama, which was written in 1437, not long after Khedrup Jé's work.

The exact year(s) of composition for this work by Khedrup Jé are unknown. He did not include dates in the colophons of his writings, and other clues are sparse. However, he states that Changra was the place of composition. We can be reasonably sure that this was undertaken during his time as abbot of Changra (the monastery was apparently built in 1413), prior to his involvement with Palkhor Chödé and his eventual return to Riwo Dangchen. By that reckoning, the work would have been produced when he was in his late twenties or early thirties, most likely somewhere between 1412 and 1415.[39]

Leonard van der Kuijp observes that Khedrup Jé cites *Banisher of Ignorance* many times in his *Ocean of Reasoning* and concludes that it must have been completed before that latter work.[40] However, a closer inspection reveals that the *Ocean of Reasoning* is also mentioned several times in *Banisher of Ignorance* (although not by name). The references Khedrup Jé makes to specific sections in the *Ocean of Reasoning* are phrased in a manner that could suggest they were not yet finished, but when speaking of the work as a whole, he gives the impression of a completed task. It seems safe to say that work on the two texts overlapped and that at least a substantial part of the *Ocean of Reasoning* was already in existence when *Banisher of Ignorance* was finalized. The possibility remains that Khedrup Jé wrote sections of the two texts in tandem and that their different formats sometimes allowed him to treat the same material in alternative ways.

The present work is highly structured and unusually systematic, even by the standards of Tibetan scholasticism. Although it had been common for some centuries to organize the discussions using a threefold framework—the refutation of others' assertions, followed by setting out our own position, and then dealing with objections to that position—Khedrup Jé employs these with noteworthy consistency. These he applies most regularly to what counts as the correct definition of the object or feature at hand. The *Banisher of Ignorance* is divided into three major sections, the third of which employs a novel structure with nine subsections exploring some of the major ontologies of scholasticism through a series of mainly binary divisions. Although Khedrup Jé does not seem to be imitating any earlier work, we note that the first two major sections mirror the first two chapters of Sakya Paṇḍita's *Treasure of Pramāṇa Reasoning*, and almost half of the nine subsections in the third portion correspond to independent chapters in that work.

Certain Geluk works that rely on a dialectical format—such as those of the Collected Topics (*bsdus grwa*) genre, which are primarily used for educational purposes—use fictional opponents to voice theoretical arguments and positions. This is not the case with the present work. While a large amount of the dialogue exploring the views and responses of others is necessarily imagined, we can be almost certain that when Khedrup Jé refers to the assertion or claim of "someone," he has in mind real scholars, and the views that he attributes to them are ones that they genuinely expressed, primarily in their writings. Khedrup Jé seems to devote most of his energy to refuting his contemporaries. Thus, even though the figures are generally anonymized, this work is undoubtedly one of the most complete surveys of Tibetan scholarly opinion on Pramāṇa during the late medieval period. According to oral tradition, this work was composed after a public disputation with Bodong Choklé Namgyal. The event was very real, although the work was actually composed at least twelve years later, and Bodong Choklé Namgyal is never named by Khedrup Jé. Nevertheless, various other sources allow us to identify Bodong as one of Khedrup Jé's targets, and therefore this work has the highly unusual feature of having been derived partly from exchanges that occurred in a face-to-face disputation.[41]

As mentioned above, Chapa Chökyi Sengé composed a work entitled *Banisher of Ignorance* in the twelfth century. This text has only recently reemerged, having long been considered lost, and has immense importance for the development of the Pramāṇa tradition in Tibet. It is understood to be the first example of a "Pramāṇa Summary" (*tshad ma bsdus pa*), which despite its unassuming title, represented an entirely fresh Tibetan conception of how to present the material of the Pramāṇa tradition. Khedrup Jé's *Banisher of Ignorance* and Gendun Drup's *Ornament of Reasoning* are later manifestations of this genre. But its heyday was during the early centuries of Sangphu scholasticism. Sakya Paṇḍita's *Treasure of Pramāṇa Reasoning* was intended as an alternative to this genre of writing and clearly sought to challenge it. Although Khedrup Jé's *Banisher of Ignorance* is inspired by the format of the Sangphu "Pramāṇa Summary," he sought to distance himself from aspects of Sangphu scholarship, and on a number of occasions in this work claims allegiance to Sakya Paṇḍita's *Treasure of Pramāṇa Reasoning*. Further research is required to determine the exact relationship between Khedrup Jé's *Banisher of Ignorance* and the one composed by Chapa Chökyi Sengé. However, it seems inconceivable that Khedrup Jé would have been unaware of the existence of that work and of the possibility that his evocative reuse of the name would be interpreted as a reference to it, even though it was obviously not intended as an endorsement of Chapa Chökyi Sengé's system.

Khedrup Jé's *Banisher of Ignorance* achieves the rare feat of dealing with topics of a complex and profound nature in a rigorous, technical manner while providing what can best be described as moments of entertainment. The serious, demanding material is regularly punctured by his bursts of bravado, in which all his wit and craft with language and imagery are on display.

On a personal note, by some quirk of karma, and quite unrelated to my being commissioned to translate this work, *Banisher of Ignorance* was the very first Tibetan text that I ever bought, when I, at the very start of my efforts to learn the language, and with only the crudest understandings of what the text was, stumbled across it in a monastery bookshop when attending a Kālacakra initiation by H. H. the Dalai Lama in Rikon, Switzerland.

Text 2

This text is by Gyaltsab Jé, the second Ganden throneholder, who composed no less than eleven known works on the topic of Pramāṇa.[42] Although undated, it is clearly a mature work. The colophon states that it was composed at Ganden Monastery, so it must have been produced between 1409 and 1432. Taking the contents into consideration, it seems most likely that it was produced in the 1420s. The text is not a commentary on a root text and is relatively brief, as a result of which it has been regarded as a minor writing and somewhat overlooked. It explores one of the topics that Dharmakīrti highlights in his *Analysis of Relation*, which is a "branch" work among the Seven Treatises, according to Tibetan scholasticism. Dharmakīrti's *Analysis of Relation* gave rise to its own commentarial tradition in India and enjoyed an afterlife in Tibet in at least one work, the *Analysis of Relation: Floral Ornament*, by Chomden Rikpai Raldri (1227–1305). In the present text, Gyaltsab Jé does not follow that tradition. Instead he unites explication on the topic of relation with that of preclusion. Sakya Paṇḍita had earlier come close to doing so in his *Treasure of Pramāṇa Reasoning*, in which the sixth and seventh chapters are respectively devoted to those two topics. Gyaltsab Jé's text aligns its content far more closely with the later Tibetan writings arising from that work by Sakya Paṇḍita than with any specific Indian commentarial tradition.

The importance of the two topics that are the focus of Gyaltsab Jé's work was summed up by the later Sakya scholar Shākya Chokden (1428–1507) in his pithy remark, "The main immediate subject matter of the texts on logic is refutation and establishment. The root that these rely upon is preclusion and relationship."[43] By making preclusion and relationship the subject of a separate text, Gyaltsab Jé highlights their importance in Pramāṇa writing and thinking. He wishes to show that not only do the pervasion of a formal proof and hence the proof itself necessarily rely on preclusion and relationship, but *any* form of establishment or negation also implicitly depends on those two. Thus Gyaltsab Jé's work drills down to the principles at the heart of Buddhist logic and reasoning.

While Gyaltsab Jé refers to the positions of Indian commentators, his concerns lie in the reception and interpretation of their writings by earlier Tibetan scholars, particularly those from Sangphu. He also wants to convey that preclusion and relationship have significance well beyond the sphere of Pramāṇa. For him, these are principles with universal application, which the Madhyamaka system does not set about dismantling. He further highlights this point by emphasizing the role of preclusion in the paths that counter delusion. More generally, he argues that without a clear understanding of the principles of preclusion and relationship, higher levels of realization are unfeasible.

Text 3

Jamyang Shepa does not inform us in this work when he composed it, but he mentions his own commentary on Candrakīrti's *Entering the Middle Way*, which he completed in 1695. Although simultaneous composition cannot be entirely ruled out, the present work is probably of a later date. The colophon says it was written at Riwo Gephel, suggesting the work was completed during his long period of relative seclusion there, at some point between 1695 and his appointment as the abbot of Gomang in 1702. But the same colophon mentions a Tri Rinpoché (i.e., "throneholder") as one of his teachers. This would appear to be Döndrup Gyatso (1655–1727), and *if* this is a reference to his time as Ganden throneholder (1702–8), it would make the composition slightly later.[44]

The title gives the impression that the work is a commentary on Candrakīrti's *Clear Words*. But since Jamyang Shepa's main concern here is with the topic of valid cognition in the foundational writings of Madhyamaka, he only concentrates on the first chapter of Candrakīrti's work. Mirroring that chapter's content, Jamyang Shepa carefully sets out Candrakīrti's argument that even epistemological understanding must respect the conventions of everyday language. In addition to *Clear Words*, Jamyang Shepa draws from relevant sections in Candrakīrti's other commentaries on treatises by Nāgārjuna and Āryadeva, as well as Nāgārjuna's own *Dispeller of Dispute*.

Jamyang Shepa's work shares its abbreviated name with one by Khedrup Jé, the *Thousand Measures: Providing the Fortunate with Sight*.[45] The tradition of assigning the name *Thousand Measures* to works relating to *Clear Words* goes as far back as Patsab Nyima Drak, who first translated *Clear Words* into Tibetan in the late eleventh or early twelfth century. It represents a partial play on words, as the Tibetan syllable for "thousand" (*stong*) also means "empty," as in "emptiness." Although the allusion is less certain, the

Tibetan word for "measure" (*thun*) is the same as the one for "session," as in an allotted period for meditation. The name of Khedrup Jé's work might seem to indicate that Jamyang Shepa had been anticipated here, but Khedrup Jé's *Thousand Measures* is not a commentary on *Clear Words*, despite containing much related content. Neither does the manner in which Jamyang Shepa cites Khedrup Jé's *Thousand Measures* suggest that he is directly relying on its commentarial interpretation. However, appended to Khedrup Jé's *Thousand Measures* are a number of sections written by other authors, including Shangshung Chöwang Drakpa (1404–69), a principal disciple of Tsongkhapa. Chöwang Drakpa describes his sections as being derived from notes he took during teachings. In one of them, he clearly identifies Khedrup Jé as the source. Another short section by him is based on parts of *Clear Words* and covers some of the same areas that Jamyang Shepa's work does. Again, it is described as Chöwang Drakpa's "notes," but the source of the teaching is not specified. Jamyang Shepa never mentions the sections bearing Chöwang Drakpa's name, and it is unclear at what stage they were appended to Khedrup Jé's text. Notwithstanding doubts about these matters, it seems clear that Khedrup Jé had some role in inspiring Jamyang Shepa's work.

Acknowledgments

I wish to express my sincere gratitude to the general editor, Thupten Jinpa. The degree of patience he has shown over the very long period it has taken me to complete this work has been prodigious. I also want to thank the editor, David Kittelstrom, who revived the project when it faltered and guided it over the finishing line. My thanks also go to Ben Gleason and others at Wisdom Publications for the valuable contributions they have made.

Technical Note

The three translations in this volume rely on the annotated Tibetan critical edition of the three texts contained in *Dpal dge ldan pa'i tshad ma rig pa'i gzhung gces btus* (*Anthology of Pramāṇa Works of the Glorious Gedenpa*), published in New Delhi in modern book format by the Institute of Tibetan Classics (2006, ISBN 81-89165-19-4) as volume 21 of the *Bod kyi gtsug lag gces btus* series. The three Tibetan works are: *Tshad ma sde bdun gyi rgyan yid kyi mun sel* (*Banisher of Ignorance: An Ornament of the Seven Treatises on Pramāṇa*) by Khedrup Gelek Palsang, *'Gal 'brel gyi rnam gzhag* (*On Preclusion and Relationship*) by Gyaltsab Darma Rinchen, and *Tshig gsal stong thun gyi tshad ma'i rnam bshad* (*An Exposition on Valid Cognition in the Thousand Measures of Clear Words*) by Jamyang Shepa. The Tibetan critical edition was prepared specifically for *The Library of Tibetan Classics* series. Bracketed numbers embedded in the text of the translation refer to page numbers in the critical edition, which can be viewed online at http://purl.bdrc.io/resource/WA3KG150.

The conventions for phonetic transcription of Tibetan words are those developed by the Institute of Tibetan Classics and Wisdom Publications. These reflect approximately the pronunciation of words in modern Central Tibetan dialects. Transliterations of the phoneticized Tibetan terms and names used in the text can be found in the table in the appendix. Sanskrit diacritics are used throughout except for Sanskrit terms that have been naturalized into English, such as samsara, nirvana, sutra, and Mahayana.

Pronunciation of Tibetan phonetics

ph and *th* are aspirated *p* and *t*, as in *pet* and *tip*.

ö is similar to the *eu* in the French *seul*.

ü is similar to the *ü* in the German *füllen*.

ai is similar to the *e* in *bet*.

é is similar to the *e* in *prey*.

Pronunciation of Sanskrit

Palatal *ś* and retroflex *ṣ* are similar to the English unvoiced *sh*.
c is an unaspirated *ch* similar to the *ch* in *chill*.
The vowel *ṛ* is similar to the American *r* in pretty.
ñ is somewhat similar to the nasalized *ny* in *canyon*.
ṅ is similar to the *ng* in *sing* or *anger*.

Abbreviations

Catuḥśatakaṭīkā	Candrakīrti. *Commentary to Four Hundred Stanzas*. Toh 3865.
Pramāṇasamuccaya	Dignāga. *Compendium of Pramāṇa*. Toh 4203.
Pramāṇavārttika	Dharmakīrti. *Commentary on Pramāṇa*. Toh 4210.
Pramāṇaviniścaya	Dharmakīrti. *Ascertainment of Pramāṇa*. Toh 4211.
Pramāṇaviniścayaṭīkā	Dharmottara. *Direct Commentary on the Ascertainment of Pramāṇa*. Toh 4229 (chapters 1 and 2) and Toh 4227 (chapter 3). A.k.a. *The Correct* (*'Thad ldan*).
Prasannapadā	Candrakīrti, *Clear Words*. Toh 3860. All citations are from chapter 1 unless specified otherwise.

Banisher of Ignorance

An Ornament of the Seven Treatises on Pramāṇa

Khedrup Gelek Palsang
(1385–1438)

1. Introduction: The Aim and Subject Matter of Pramāṇa Treatises

In Sanskrit, this work is entitled *Pramaṇaśāstrasenasaptālaṃkāramanata.*[46] In Tibetan, it is called *Tshad ma'i bstan bcos sde bdun gyi rgyan yid kyi mun sel.*

Homage to the Noble Mañjughoṣa!

The blue-throated [Śiva], sporting his lunar diadem and an abundance of streaming locks, rushes to your lotus feet with the enthusiasm of a bee making for a flower.
The splendor of your physical presence outshines even that of the mountain of precious jewels; so immense is its grandeur that the earth, girdled by the oceans, must surely shudder, as it strains to support it.
Your enlightened activity is like the dawn light; as its first shafts appear, the commander of the dark forces discards his arrows and is stunned into inactivity.
Your speech is a great lake, exquisitely rimmed by trees with the sixty branches [of verbal qualities];
through it, Mighty Sage [Śākyamuni], may you relieve the world of all ills!

While Śiva has his lunar diadem, your insignia is the crown jewel of compassion, symbol that you have taken upon yourself the burden of helping limitless beings in samsara.
The devoted offering of just a handful of flowers in celebration of your qualities is all it takes [to invite] a brilliant flash of insight, bursting into my mind like blazing sunlight, banishing the murky gloom of unknowing.
Just as soothing moonlight falls upon every night lily on the lake's waters, the wonderful pervasive power of your omniscient awareness saturates the lotus mind of every living being.

At your lotus feet, Mañjughoṣa, nurturer of the lotus, I invite you, amid a flourish of your dazzling orange petal-like digits, to mature my lotus mind, bringing it to its full glory.

Formed from the moonstone of the two collections,
that sphere of the three trainings, who emanated the cool rays of correct reasoning
and emerged unscathed, despite the attacks of Rāhu-like adversaries.
Reverentially, I raise to my crown the celebrated lunar orb that is Dignāga.

I prostrate myself at the feet of my spiritual tutors, those mighty elephants.
Their faces are caparisoned with the golden gauze decoration of the teachings of the Able One [Śākyamuni].
Their gaits are the four methods of attracting disciples. Their brows are elevated with intelligence.
Their purity of knowledge and tenderness are reflected in the brilliant ivory-like whiteness of their tusk-like teeth.

The great Dharmakīrti perfectly distinguished the flawless thought of the lord of reasoning [Dignāga].
Having gained the insight allowing me a share in this knowledge equal to his own, I will impart it clearly and correctly using the path of reason.

Due to their sightless faculties, other religious guides have been unable to clarify even a scrap [of Dignāga's intention].
They have frittered away their youth in the turgid recital of the texts.
Let them now give it a rest!

From deep within the storm cloud of my intellect,
I summon forth ten million thunderbolts of scripture and reason.
Unleashing them, I obliterate the forest of corrupt assertions.
I demolish the mountain of false accounts.

Inebriated by the noxious beverage of your false accounts
and constrained by your limited knowledge of Buddhist scripture,
some of you have peddled your own fabricated doctrine.
I warn such spiritual guides: Your time has come!

This marvelous work is a scintillating sun.
May its rays sustain the multipetaled flowers of reason
and its dawning be greeted by the melodious bee-like hum
of eager, young intellects setting about their inquiry.

Outlining the content of this work

This work explains the true thought of the Seven Treatises on Pramāṇa and their source [the *Compendium of Pramāṇa*] composed by the father and [spiritual] son, the great masters Dignāga and Dharmakīrti, who are the progeny born from the very heart of the noble Mañjughoṣa. These writings reveal what the Sugata meant in his various pronouncements forming the Abhidharma *piṭaka*, that profound treasury of his precious words. They reveal in their entirety all the essentials relating to the three vehicles, the means by which those who earnestly engage in the quest for freedom may be conveyed to liberation and omniscience. They explain these essentials following the path of Pramāṇa, thereby preventing any danger of misinterpretation. The intention of the Pramāṇa treatises is set out in four sections: [4]

1. The aim of the Pramāṇa treatises
2. How [the achievement of] that aim depends on these treatises
3. A call to value treatises that have such an aim
4. The core subject matter of these treatises

The aim of the Pramāṇa treatises

1. Countering certain misconceptions associated with the aim
2. The actual aim

Countering certain misconceptions associated with the aim

1. Countering the misconception that Pramāṇa treatises are not relevant to those engaged in the quest for liberation
2. Countering the misconception that Pramāṇa treatises are not relevant to the location in question
3. Countering the view of those who, while conceding that the Pramāṇa treatises have an aim, believe it to be an inferior one

Countering the misconception that the Pramāṇa treatises are not relevant to those engaged in the quest for liberation

Someone claims that Pramāṇa treatises are of no use in the quest for liberation. He says that these are treatises concerned with logic and thus fall outside the gamut of the *piṭaka* of internal learning.

[Response:] We point out that "logic" can denote two distinct things. We acknowledge that the type of reasoning advanced by non-Buddhist philosophers such as the sage Lingkyé[47] is the stuff of pure invention. However, the second is the variety referred to in the *Ornament of the Mahayana Sutras*:

> Logical reasoning is held to be dependent and lacking certainty.
> It is not comprehensive, [but] is conventional and inferior.
> It is that on which the juvenile rely.[48]

As this indicates, it is first necessary to determine the real nature of a thing conceptually by holding an *object universal*.[49] At that [initial] stage, when its nature is not manifest, the individual approaches it through conceptual logic. It is in this respect that treatises explaining such matters are described as treatises on logic.

Not even this detractor suggests that Pramāṇa treatises deal with the first variety of [non-Buddhist] material. And no logical argument could establish that these treatises are concerned with that sort of material, since they are all [Buddhist] works derived from following our teacher, the Omniscient One. The type of conceptual logic that these treatises work with must therefore be of the second variety. To suggest that those engaged in the quest for liberation can do so without such logical understanding is to regard the supreme dharma level[50] and everything that precedes it us unneeded, because the only way one can understand reality before that level is necessarily by taking an object universal as one's object.

The claim that the Pramāṇa works are not treatises dedicated to the field of internal learning is also untenable. A treatise belonging to the field of internal learning denotes a work that concentrates on communicating the means that should be employed to eliminate ignorance and cultivate the wisdom that realizes selflessness, the antidote to that ignorance. [6] The Pramāṇa works clearly delineate the selflessness of persons and phenomena in a logical fashion, and they definitely focus on teachings belonging to the higher training in wisdom. If you say that this is insufficient grounds for counting something as belonging to the field of internal learning, then you must identify which works within the canon constitute the *piṭaka* of internal learning!

Quite apart from that, the general notion that something that does not belong to the field of internal learning is by virtue of that fact useless to those engaged in the quest for liberation is totally erroneous. Enlightenment remains beyond the reach of those who fail to master the five fields of learning. The *Ornament of the Mahayana Sutras* states:

> Without application in the area of the five fields of learning,
> even the most supreme of ārya beings cannot gain full omniscience.
> Thus, to prevail over others, [then] guide them, and achieve full
> personal knowledge,
> one must strive in [all of] these fields.[51]

If these treatises belong to the *piṭaka* dealing with the field of internal learning, someone might question whether they can be considered treatises on logic.

[Response:] In addition to belonging to that *piṭaka*, the Pramāṇa works are *also* treatises on reasoning. The science of reasoning[52] is the field of reasoned analysis. These works provide the principal means by which those engaged in the quest for spiritual goals can gain a systematic, reasoned understanding of what they should pursue and reject. Treatises belonging to the field of internal learning and treatises on logic are therefore not mutually exclusive. A treatise such as [Guṇaprabha's] *Vinaya Sutra* belongs exclusively to the field of internal learning. Works such as Dharmakīrti's Seven Treatises on Pramāṇa belong to both categories. The [*Nyāyasūtra*] works by the Brāhmaṇa Akṣapāda [Gautama] teaching the sixteen categories of logic belong purely to the category of logic. Medical texts, on the other hand, fall into neither of these categories. Thus there are four points of demarcation between the two categories.[53]

Some may still argue that the mere fact that a work teaches the two kinds of valid cognition, logical reasoning, proof statements, and discrediting statements means that it falls within the field of logic and that this alone excludes it from the field of the internal learning.

[Response:] If that is so, it would follow that the Conqueror's own teachings do not belong to the *piṭaka* of internal learning, because they also teach the two types of valid cognition, logical reasoning, and so forth. The *Abhidharma Sutra* contains the passages "With a visual awareness one cognizes blue but does not think 'blue'"[54] and [7] "A visual cognition is produced in reliance upon the eye and form."[55] In these, the Buddha delineates what sense perception is and sets out the three conditions for its production. Also, the *Ten Grounds Sutra* says:

> One becomes aware of fire by smoke.
> One becomes aware of water by [certain] waterfowl.
> Similarly, one becomes aware that [someone has] the lineage
> of an intelligent bodhisattva by various telling signs.[56]

This presents an *effect reason* as well as the inferential cognition that arises in dependence on it. The passage "Whatever is subject to production is also subject to cessation"[57] presents a [*same-*]*nature reason*, as well as the proof statement within which it is formulated. The words "I, or another such as myself, can fully assess an individual"[58] feature a *reason involving the nonobservation of something that should be apparent*. "An [ordinary] person cannot fully assess another . . ."[59] uses a *reason involving the nonobservation of something that is not accessible*.[60] In response to Dīrghanakha's remark "I do not tolerate anything," the Blessed One inquired of him, "And is the view that you tolerate nothing tolerable to you?"[61] The Blessed One was using a consequence and a discrediting counter. In declaring "The presence of this [one thing] necessitates the occurrence of that [other thing],"[62] the Buddha was revealing a [logical] relationship. In explaining how, once the antidote is introduced, the undesirable element will be discarded, and also in comparing that process to how light rids a place of darkness, he was teaching about preclusion. That is to say, the majority of those subjects discussed in [Dharmakīrti's] Seven Treatises can be individually matched with relevant passages found within the Conqueror's own teachings. I will not elaborate on this further as it will take up too much space.

To reiterate the point, if one advocates that Pramāṇa literature does not belong to the *piṭaka* of internal learning, one must concede that the same is true of the teachings of the Conqueror. Furthermore, the Blessed One himself stated:

> Bhikṣus and wise ones,
> follow me not through mere respect
> but once you have examined what I say,
> as though you were assaying something:

burning, cutting, and rubbing it
to test if it is [truly] gold.[63]

He thereby encouraged us to investigate the real import of his pronouncements by means of valid cognition. The noble Maitreya also said, "[Having] a mind that logically analyzes the good Dharma, never [being subject to] obstructions from evil spirits . . . ."[64] *Entering the Middle Way* also says: [8]

While ordinary individuals are bound by the conceptual,
yogis without conception have gained freedom.
The wise declare that the arrest of conceptual notions
results from the exercise of one's analytical [powers].[65]

It is therefore the judgment of all āryas that a "faith-based devotee" is someone who disregards the reasoned, logical approach in favor of one that involves simply accepting what the teachings say at face value; he is an individual of inferior intellectual powers. Conversely, someone who adopts a reasoned, logical approach to distinguish what should be adopted from what should be rejected is lauded by the wise as a "practitioner with devotion to the Dharma." So if confronted by someone making the diabolical claim that to embrace reasoned analysis is to take the approach of logic and that this is something those engaged in the quest for liberation should avoid, sensible individuals would be well advised to simply block their ears!

Countering the misconception that the Pramāṇa literature is not relevant to the location in question

Someone proposes that the sole use of the collection of [Dharmakīrti's] Seven Treatises is for attacking the views of those who belong to [Indian philosophical] schools outside the Buddhist tradition and that consequently in locations where members of other schools do not exist, study or reflection on the treatises becomes a pointless exercise.

[Response:] This misconception is extremely grave, and it constitutes the spurning of Dharma. These treatises provide us with a broad range of means to counter extreme positions that involve exaggeration or denial [of what exists]. These positions include the beliefs that being concerned with virtue and vice is pointless because there are no past and future lives, and that straining in pursuit of paths that lead to liberation or enlightenment is pointless because liberation and enlightenment do not exist, and the impressions that one's [physical and mental] aggregates are pure, of a pleasurable nature, a fixed character, and have a self. So does [the aforementioned individual] really think that in those locations where there are no non-Buddhist "outsiders," we do not need to concern ourselves on a personal level with eliminating distorted notions, developing an understanding of the impermanent, suffering, empty, and selfless nature [of the aggregates], and determining with certainty whether there are past and future lives, what the relationship between actions and results is, and whether liberation and enlightenment actually exist?

Unless one can rid oneself of distorted notions of the "learned" variety, there is no way that the path of seeing can eliminate those elements it is supposed to counter. Misconceptions of this learned variety are promulgated by various philosophical schools. The Pramāṇa treatises refute the views held by non-Buddhist philosophers not with the narrow goal of engaging in disputation with these philosophical extremists but to attack the distortions themselves. [9]

Countering the view of those who, while conceding that the Pramāṇa treatises have an aim, believe it to be an inferior one

Some grant that studying the Seven Treatises helps one develop a keen critical eye for judging an argument and agree that this can be helpful when interpreting what is being taught in the writings of various other traditions. In this respect, they liken such study to the salt that is used for flavoring food; it does not in and of itself represent a goal of any particular worth or significance.

[Response:] This notion is also incorrect. All the issues vital to the three vehicles—namely, what things within the framework of the four truths are to be adopted or discarded, together with the method employed in pursuit of this exercise, in addition to the topics of the selflessness of phenomena and so forth—are comprehensively laid out in a systematic, logically argued fashion in these treatises. In that sense, no other works are capable of offering a more worthy focus for one's learning, deliberation, and meditational practices.

The actual aim

Dharmakīrti's Seven Treatises on Pramāṇa and their source text [the *Compendium of Pramāṇa*] set out to prove that Śākyamuni is the sole unerring authority in matters concerning the quest for liberation. They achieve this by demonstrating that both the teacher and his teachings are totally flawless. These teachings exist in two forms: the communicated word and that which has been internalized. Regarding the first of these, [the *Commentary on Pramāṇa*][66] says:

> A statement that is coherent, communicates the method
> corresponding [to the goal] and that [real] human goal
> is one that is [worthy] of thorough analysis.
> Others are not.[67]

Hence the teaching in its communicated form is a type of utterance that is marked by three attributes: (1) it shows the goal for which the person in pursuit of liberation aims, (2) it shows that the sacred means that corresponds to that goal has the power to achieve it, and (3) it presents these in a coherent fashion. The way to establish that this communicated form of the teaching is flawless is by examining its contents—using valid cognition to authenticate the things it says about evident and hidden phenomena, and also verifying those sections that deal with profoundly hidden phenomena by subjecting them to the threefold investigation. As the *Commentary on Pramāṇa* says:

> One should accept a treatise [whose respective statements] about the things that [we] see and those that [we] do not see are not discredited by proven reasoning or its own words. To [determine that those words do not contradict one another we] should analyze [the treatise's statements].[68] [10]

Alternatively, one approaches the teaching by authenticating what the teachings have to say on matters of crucial importance. Once the teachings' veracity on these matters has been confirmed by means of valid cognition, using the fact that the pronouncements on the issues of less importance emanate from the same teacher, one establishes that these pronouncements must also be free from error. That the Buddha is an unerring authority regarding the major issues but unreliable about minor ones is untenable.

What the communicated instruction discusses falls into two main areas: the elevated, comfortable states in cyclic existence and the truly worthy—the latter referring to the states of liberation and enlightenment—together with the means for their achievement. In terms of the sequence in which these goals are personally accomplished, one first gains an elevated state of existence, after which one can achieve the truly worthy. When viewed in terms of relative importance, the elevated states are subordinate to the truly worthy. With regard to the process of confirming their existence with valid cognition, it is the truly worthy and the means to achieve it that must come first, with the confirmation of the more elevated states following after. The process is described in the passage:

> One properly ascertains how things are regarding what is to
> be adopted and what discarded, together with the means
> [to pursue these].
> Thereby [one finds the Buddha to be] unerring with respect to
> the principal matter.
> And thus [one can] infer [the same] with respect to the other
> [matters].[69]

The teachings in their internalized form are the paths of the three vehicles and the results gained through them. These are none other than the states of the truly worthy and the means by which they are achieved. One verifies their existence with valid cognition and thereby establishes the veracity of the teaching in its communicated form, the medium expressing that content. Once one has verified that the communicated form of the instruction is flawless, one can employ this as a reason to establish that its teacher is a person of valid authority and also that the Sangha, those who actually put the teachings into practice in the prescribed manner, are totally trustworthy.

Once someone has established that the Buddha alone is a person of valid authority for those engaged in the quest for liberation, if he is of Mahayana persuasion—someone with the compassion and the exceptional resolve to ensure that the needs of every spiritual type are served—he will gain the ascertainment that no one except a buddha has the power to actually satisfy the needs of beings of all three [spiritual] types. This ascertainment will serve as the cause for him to develop bodhicitta, with its personal determination to gain enlightenment. [This ascertainment] can either [prompt] the initial generation [of bodhicitta] in those who have not previously experienced it or make it irreversibly steadfast in those who have. Even when the individuals involved aspire to nothing more than the achievement of personal liberation, it is this trust that the Buddha alone is the guide in the quest for it that leads to the informed conviction that (1) only the path taught by him can facilitate release from samsara [11] and (2) the instructions of figures like Kapila, who fall outside this tradition, do not offer a means to achieve such release. The faith that such an individual gains in this Dharma and its teacher will be one that is *knowledge based*.

Even for those whose interests and aspirations stretch no further than the achievement of happiness and comfort in future existences within samsara, confirmation that the Buddha is the sole person of valid authority will inspire them to adopt him alone as their *refuge*, the one able to help protect them from pain and sufferings in future existences. They will also develop the conviction that the likes of Śiva and Brahmā, constrained by their own shortcomings, are in no position to provide protection for others.

Once [the individual] has verified that the communicated and internalized forms of the teachings are without fault of any description, he can set about systematically resolving remaining questions about the identity, variety, sequence, and respective capacities of the paths included in the three vehicles. Through this process, the claims of others—such as that the sacrificial offering[70] of cattle can secure comfortable future states of existence, or that by taking Śaivite empowerments or practicing punishing physical austerities one can purify the negativity of one's past deeds and gain liberation—are revealed to be immature nonsense. One will come to see the adoption of such practices as comparable to the action of someone who, in an attempt to escape the oppressive heat of the sun, leaps into a flaming pit. One will reach the conclusion that the communicated teachings of the Conqueror alone should act as the focus of one's learning and deliberation, and that the internalized form of the teachings should serve as the exclusive foundation of one's meditation. And it is by learning, deliberating, and meditating on these communicated and internalized forms of the teachings that those seeking liberation and enlightenment embark on their quest in earnest.

Some, due to the disinformation peddled by schools such as the Cārvāka have had their innate judgment blinded and have wantonly engaged in the taking of life for reasons of immediate gratification. Even they will turn away from such amoral practices when they generate valid ascertainment of the flawlessness of the teachings of the Conqueror. Those seeking favorable conditions in their future existences will be led by this ascertainment to eschew those practices that are incompatible with the achievement of such an aim, and they will instead adopt a wholesome code of conduct. The intelligent therefore recognize that bringing about [these results] is the true aim of the Seven Treatises and the *Compendium of Pramāṇa*. [12]

How the achievement of that aim depends on these treatises

An ordinary, myopic individual[71] cannot hope to gain valid knowledge that the Teacher and his teachings are flawless by direct observation, as if that flawlessness were an obvious visual object that could simply be gazed upon. Instead, certain knowledge of that flawlessness is something gained through a valid inference. The development of such a valid inferential cognition in turn necessarily relies on an incontrovertible logical reason proving that the Teacher together with his Dharma in both its communicated and internalized forms are faultless. Verification that such a logical reason is incontrovertible depends on one's establishing by means of valid cognition that it fulfills the *three criteria*.[72] In the final reckoning, each of the three criteria must be accessible to and resolved by the perceptual experience of a myopic person, since if they had to depend exclusively on further inferences to support them, it would result in an infinite regress.

To sum up, if an individual has developed a desire to achieve either the elevated states within cyclic existence or the truly worthy, this valid ascertainment of the flawlessness of both the Buddha and his teachings will guarantee that he forsakes paths contrary to the achievement of those goals and develops the resolve to train properly in the right paths with such dedication that he will not be distracted from his purpose. This ascertainment is gained by relying on logical reasons and the valid cognitions verifying that the reasons satisfy the three criteria. A comprehensive treatment of these matters—presented in the form of a systematic investigation involving the logical refutation of all positions to the contrary—is an approach that is found in few commentarial treatises attempting to elucidate the intent of the Buddha apart from those of the two lords of reasoning, Dignāga and Dharmakīrti. Therefore it is not difficult to establish that one should rely on them.

A call to value treatises that have such an aim

Any individual endeavoring to secure release from cyclical existence, either for himself or for others, should view the treatises that reveal the proper method for severing the very root of samsara as a valuable asset. We can see for ourselves that even someone who aspires to just keeping his own stomach full will maintain his preoccupation with food and drink to the exclusion of all else. [13] Here, we are concerned with someone who has undertaken to strive for the most supreme of states and, following the example set by those of sharper faculties, has committed himself to engage in careful assessment prior to acting. If such a person fails to appreciate these treatises as the very thing that can provide him with the means to gain valid knowledge of the supreme goal he aspires to attain and the method for achieving that goal, and instead regards them as superficial chaff belonging to a tradition that interests itself only with controversy and disputation, he must be totally unacquainted with the notion of distinguishing between right and wrong paths of action. It hardly seems necessary to comment on whether he is of wise judgment. Self-absorbed in the smugness he derives simply from having spent time in a cave, such a foolish person clings to the idea that a few garbled words he chooses to refer to as "personal instructions of a contemplative" contain vital significance within them. The notion that he is of sharper faculties can be entirely dismissed. Indeed, he is not even worthy of the label "faith-based practitioner," since he places his faith in unworthy objects. Accordingly, his mental state lacks the stability required for sound judgment. We may liken him to someone trying to gain his footing on a bubble.

One who learns, deliberates, and meditates on the present corpus of works should direct his efforts toward the exercises of analytical study, reflection, and so forth with the intention of discovering the process by which both he and others are caught up in samsara and how they might find their way out of it. If instead, he performs these exercises solely for the purpose of engaging in verbal sparring with his companions, not only will doing so demean him personally, it will also cause others to disrespect the treatises. Intelligent individuals should never allow the taint of their own mind to sully the brilliant works of true masters!

The core subject matter of the Pramāṇa treatises[73]

1. Identifying the core subject matter of the treatises
2. Explaining that core subject matter at length

Identifying the core subject matter of the treatises

Entrance to Reasoning states:

> Perception, inference, and pseudo [forms of them
> are] for the sake of personal knowledge.
> Proof [statements], discrediting [statements], and pseudo [forms of them
> are] for the sake of knowledge in others.[74] [14]

That is to say, the subject matter is twofold: (1) those means by which one personally gains valid ascertainment of the fact that the Teacher and what he teaches are flawless and (2) those means one subsequently employs to offer guidance to others.

Perception and *inferential cognition* make up the first of these. Whether one's description of things accurately reflects the way they really are will depend on whether the cognitions responsible for providing the information about them are accurate. Since the correct cognition that allows one to ascertain hidden phenomena is inferential and the correct cognition that allows one to ascertain evident phenomena is valid perception, these treatises teach the valid forms of these two. Other types of cognition tend to mislead one, and so pseudo forms of perception and inferential cognition are also discussed as a subsidiary, in order to rule out [inauthentic forms] of these two.

Having ascertained the facts for oneself, one induces realization in others. The essential elements required for this process are the correct and the pseudo forms that comprise the second set of four. *Discrediting statements* are taught so that they can neutralize the most strident of mistaken convictions, while *proof statements* are imparted to counter indecision that wavers between two views. The pseudo forms of those two are discussed to rule out [inauthentic forms] of them.

Therefore the core of the Pramāṇa treatises is covered in the three chapters on perception, personal inference, and inference for others. Why then does the *Compendium of Pramāṇa* explain these in six chapters?[75] The [subject matter of the] *Compendium's* "Analysis of the Example" and "Analysis of Exclusion" are subsumed into the *Commentary on Pramāṇa*'s [first] chapter, "Personal Inference," whereas [the *Compendium*'s] "Analysis of False [Self-Defeating] Rejoinders"[76] is subsumed within [the *Commentary on Pramāṇa*'s fourth chapter,] "Inference for Others."

So among the Pramāṇa treatises, the *Compendium of Pramāṇa*, *Commentary on Pramāṇa*, *Ascertainment of Pramāṇa*, and *Drop of Logic* are expositions that deal with the entire core subject matter. The four remaining works among the Seven Treatises are offshoots of these and do not cover the whole range of subjects. More specifically, the *Drop of Reasoning* and *Analysis of Relation* are derived from the chapter "Personal Inference," whereas the *Verification of Other Minds* and *Science of Disputation* are derived from the chapter "Inference for Others." Why then does Dharmakīrti's commentary to the *Compendium* have four chapters [rather than three]? The principal topic addressed by the treatise is how one goes about proving that the Teacher and what he taught are flawless, and it was to address this matter specifically that the [second] chapter "Establishing Validity" was taught. [15] The fact that the Teacher and his teachings are flawless must be confirmed by valid cognition. This is gained by relying on a correct logical reason. The chapter "Personal Inference" was set forth to describe such reasons. To serve as a flawless reason, something must fulfill the three criteria, which ultimately need to be substantiated by the direct experience of perception. Thus the [third] chapter, "Perception," was set forth primarily to describe valid perception. The [fourth] chapter, "Inference for Others," was then presented to discuss the means of conveying to others what one has ascertained for oneself. This delineates the core subject matter of the treatises.

The Seven Treatises are the source of the honey-like path to liberation.
The commentary [on Pramāṇa] is the lotus, with its pistil visible.
Other supposed scholars shed no more light on it than its nemesis,
the moon.
Only the solar power of my intellect can truly illuminate it!

PART 1

Description of the Object: The Thing Known

2. Object: Equivalents and Definition

Detailed exposition

Second, the detailed exposition is set out under three major headings:

1. Description of the object: the thing known
2. Description of cognition: that which knows [the object]
3. How cognition engages its object

Description of the object: the thing known

1. Enumeration [of equivalents]
2. Defining characteristics
3. Varieties

Enumeration of equivalents

1. Refutation of others' assertions
2. Setting out our own position
3. Dealing with objections to that position

Refutation of others' assertions

Someone[77] claims that *object* and *known thing* are equivalent. But he says that object and *comprehended thing* are not equivalent. He argues that [if object and comprehended thing were equivalent,] it would follow that the conceptual mind [mistakenly] holding sound to be permanent *comprehends* the object universal of sound being permanent [since that object universal is its object]. He also denies that *known thing* and *comprehended thing* are equivalent, asserting that if they were, all cognitions would be valid cognitions.[78]

[Response:] The opponent who says this is under the impression that if being an object entails being comprehended, then being the object of any given cognition must entail being comprehended by that cognition. [16] By that logic, since anything that is a cause is also necessarily an effect, it would follow that the cause of any given fire must also necessarily be that fire's effect! Furthermore, it would follow that the term *pot* knows what it refers to [because pot is its object].[79] If he denies the pervasion [that something with the term *pot* as its object necessarily knows what that term refers to], it would go against[80] his assertion that object and known thing are equivalent. He has also accepted the point at which the "push" has occurred.[81]

Several [other individuals] deny that object and comprehended thing can be regarded as equivalent, because they say a thing that is comprehended is necessarily specifically characterized. [In support of this,] they cite the passages "Only specifically characterized [things] are comprehended"[82] and "If you say that only [specifically characterized things are comprehended,] I too accept this."[83]

[Response:][84] This is to assert that generally characterized things cannot be comprehended, which essentially endorses the Cārvāka view that inference is not a valid source of knowledge. Furthermore, how would those in question respond if someone were to advance this argument "Inferential valid cognition must therefore be impossible, since it is impossible to comprehend a generally characterized thing"?[85] The response may be to deny this pervasion. But that would be tantamount to asserting that it is possible for certain valid cognitions to comprehend *nothing* whatsoever, or that anything an inferential cognition comprehends is necessarily specifically characterized. Neither of these is tenable. To maintain that there are valid cognitions that do not comprehend anything opens the way to all kinds of [objectionable] consequences, such as that similarly, there can be causes that do not produce effects. Asserting that valid inferential cognition comprehends what is specifically characterized also openly contradicts another position that one of the [aforementioned individuals][86] has proposed—namely, that no conceptual cognition has something specifically characterized as its object. It would also place these individuals outside [the Pramāṇa tradition], the treatises of which state:

> [Such things] are not [according to you] comprehendible, because
> it is certain that they do not exist.
> But [in that case, we say, this nonexistence] must be either something
> of which one cannot be certain
> or something established by a second [form of] valid cognition
> [other than perception].[87]

At this point, the response of these individuals may be to concede the main argument, by admitting that valid inference is impossible.

[Response:] But from this it would follow that no hidden phenomena can be observed by valid cognition! If one were to accept this, it would follow that things such as past and future lives, buddhas, and fires [obscured] on smoky mountain passes do not exist, because they are not observed by valid cognition, whereas if they did exist, they should be apparent to such a cognition. The first portion of the reason [that such things are not observed by valid cognition] is what they themselves have acknowledged. The pervasion [that if something is not apparent to valid cognition it does not exist] also holds. This is because the Seven Treatises contain numerous pronouncements such as "[Something that shows] no presence [though] it should be apparent can only be [something that] is not observable."[88] That is, they frequently reiterate that when the thing in question should be observable if present, its failure to appear must mean that it does not exist [there]. [17] If this was [not enough] to establish its nonexistence, since there are no grounds besides these for negating the presence of a horn on the head of a hare, one would be unable to rule it out! Accepting this would mean that there are no such things as past and future lives or a buddha. The conclusion one would have to draw is that all endeavors to perform virtue, refrain from nonvirtue, and train in the path are exercises in futility. It would also follow that there is no fire on the mountain pass from which smoke emanates and such smoke must therefore occur randomly, independent of any cause.

In an attempt to escape such faults, these individuals might propose that while generally characterized things can be comprehended, this occurs only in a conventional sense.

[Response:] Logicians who count themselves as followers of the lords of reasoning do not hold the view that something that is generally characterized can be comprehended *ultimately*. So what exactly does this finesse achieve in terms of distinguishing their position? What is more, it would follow from what they say that generally characterized things are observed by valid cognitions dealing with conventional [i.e., nominal] realities, because they are comprehended, albeit only in a conventional sense. If these individuals accept this [argument], they would be going against their stance that only *specifically* characterized things can be comprehended. [The argument's] pervasion holds, because what exists in a conventional sense is established by conventional valid cognition, whereas what exists in the ultimate sense is established by valid cognition investigating the ultimate. This is because while the fact that something is established by valid cognition is enough to determine that it exists, determining what exists conventionally is not the task of valid cognition of the ultimate and determining what exists ultimately is not the task of valid cognition of the conventional.

They may claim that to exist conventionally just means that the thing in question is held to exist by a mistaken cognition.

[Response:] If that is the case, it would follow that permanent sounds exist conventionally, since certain mistaken cognitions hold that some sounds are permanent. By the same token, it would follow that all sounds are impermanent in the conventional sense, because they are held to be so by mistaken cognitions! Thus, with the three spheres in place, [his position is seen to be irredeemably flawed.][89]

A certain individual with scholarly pretensions, confused about how to establish the criterion for a thing's existing conventionally, was forced to assert that from the *excluding perspective*,[90] sound can be both permanent and impermanent.

[Response:] If that were the case, one would have to conclude that according to this system, conventionally there is no such thing as a direct preclusion.[91] It would also mean that when determining what exists on a deceptive [conventional] level, we must conclude that the ears and the horns of a hare have equal status; either they both exist or they both do not exist on the hare's head. Similarly, sound must be equally permanent and impermanent. To accept this would be to concede that all correct reasons exist only in the deceptive domain of convention, not ultimately. [18] Accordingly, "being produced" could serve equally well as a reason that establishes sound to be permanent or one that establishes that sound is impermanent. Any sensible person should ask himself what more wretched position there could be than this.

Both of these opponents have also advocated that *existent* and *actual thing*[92] are equivalent, but object and existent are not.

[Response:] It would follow that generally characterized things do not exist, because [existent and actual thing are equivalent]. If [these opponents] were to accept this conclusion, exactly the same faults would apply [to their position] as have been set out [for the ones] above. Thus it would [again] follow that there can be inferential valid cognitions that comprehend nothing whatsoever. Thus you [the opponents] should just exchange the comprehended thing and the existent that you are intoning and run through [the same arguments] again.

It would also follow that selflessness does not exist, because selflessness is not an actual thing. They cannot deny the reason, because they have committed themselves to the stance that all straight negations are not actual things.[93] To claim that such negations are otherwise does not stand up to logical analysis. If they accept that selflessness does not exist, it would follow that there *is* a self.

Furthermore, it would follow that the relationship between the reason and predicate in any correct logical proof does not exist, because it is not an actual thing. The *Commentary on Pramāṇa* says:

> Because it is ascertained that the absence of one would necessarily mean that of the other,
> [whereas] false reasons are other than these [correct ones].[94]

In passages like this and also on numerous other occasions, the treatises state that unless the relationship between the reason and the predicate has been established [by valid cognition], the proof counts as a false one. So to assert that the relationship does not exist places one outside the Pramāṇa tradition. That such relationships are not actual things is also something that you [the opponents] are in no position to challenge, because you have [elsewhere] asserted that they are not. It is, in addition, something that is established by means of logical reasoning. You are also in no position to reject the argument's reason [that existent and actual thing are equivalent].

There are moreover those who assert that actual things are limited to temporally indivisible moments of consciousness and directionally indivisible physical particles. They also propose that only actual things exist.[95]

[Response:] You, the supposed scholars who assert this, pay heed! It follows that in the space before us, it is impossible for a *piśāca* spirit,[96] which is a *remote* entity, to exist, because for a *piśāca* spirit to exist, it must be either temporally indivisible moments of consciousness or directionally indivisible physical particles. The pervasion [that anything that exists must be either of those two] is one that you proposed. The reason is also established, since the *piśāca* is neither. This is because it is a necessarily a living being that is an assemblage of four aggregates. But if you accept the argument, it would follow that [you are stating definitively] that there is no *piśāca*, a remote entity, in the space before us!

Setting out our own position

Object, *known thing*, *comprehended thing*, *existent*, and *established basis* are all equivalent and synonymous. [19]

Dealing with objections

How then are we to understand the passages "What is comprehended is exclusively specifically characterized"[97] and "Only specifically characterized [things] are comprehended"?[98]

[Response:] These remarks occur in the context of investigating what has the efficacy to yield the result that the person desires. What the person needs to *comprehend* therefore is which actions he should engage in so that this efficacy can be gained. [Alternatively, the passages can be understood to refer to the fact that] those things that are by nature affirmative and have an independent existence, and which the person also needs to *comprehend*, will necessarily be specifically characterized. But I will not go further here into the evidence supporting this understanding of these passages.

We also need to account for the words "Just as being an effect and being existent [are each reasons establishing that a thing will] perish,"[99] since these appear to suggest that sound is impermanent on the grounds that it is an existent. We explain this by saying that *existent* here should not [be understood] as the type referred to in passages such as "Being existent is not other than being observed,"[100] in which what exists is equated with what is observed by valid cognition. Instead, *existent*, a term with a wider application, is used here [in the first passage] to denote a particular variety of existence—namely, that of entities that have their own independent existence. The passage in question proposes that this type of existence is a correct reason that can establish that sound is impermanent. Thus we may talk of two types of existent things: one that exists by virtue of having its own affirmative and independent nature, and one that exists only by virtue of the elimination of some negandum.[101] As both are verified by valid cognition, they both count as *authentic* forms of existence, but the passage in question uses the term in its [first] narrower sense, such that it refers only to something that has an affirmative and independent nature. That is, it uses a term with general application to designate one of its specifics. It is this form of being existent that it identifies as the correct reason establishing that sound is impermanent. In line with this, the autocommentary to *Commentary on Pramāṇa* says, "It is because [the quality] that is posited to be present in sound entirely exists within [sound] by way of its own character . . . ."[102]

In his own explanation of the aforesaid passage, someone dismisses the idea that it identifies "being existent" as the correct reason establishing that sound is impermanent. Instead, he contends, the reason it conveys is "[It] exists among actual things."

[Response:] This contradicts the view that the reason identified in the passage belongs to the *plain* subcategory of nature reasons. The reason proposed by the opponent here cannot belong to that subcategory. This is because "[It] exists among actual things" cannot be brought to mind without "exists" appearing as something qualified by "actual things." Unless one explains it like this, then it could equally be argued that "[It] has productive origin" does not count as a nature reason belonging to the *specified dependence* subcategory in the proof that sound is impermanent.[103] [20]

Defining characteristics of object

1. Refutation of others' assertions
2. Setting out our own position
3. Dealing with objections [to our position]

Refutation of others' assertions

Someone claims that an object is defined as "a phenomenon cognized by awareness." He believes that unless one stipulates that an object must be a phenomenon, something such as a double moon, grasped by a mistaken [i.e., dysfunctional] sense consciousness, would qualify as an object. He also states that *object* is equivalent with *known thing*, and that *[knowing] consciousness* is equivalent with *[cognizing] awareness.*[104]

[Response:] It would follow that the double moon grasped by a mistaken sense consciousness is a known thing, because it is something cognized. He cannot accept the conclusion, since it would directly contradict his own position. If he denies the pervasion [that what is cognized is necessarily known], he would be going against his stated view that *[knowing] consciousness* and *[cognizing] awareness* are equivalent. He has also accepted the point at which the "push" has occurred.[105] Equally, he cannot challenge the reason [that the double moon is a cognized thing], since in doing so he would go against [his implicit assertion] that it is cognized by awareness.[106]

Setting out our own position

An object is defined as "that which is cognized by awareness."

Dealing with objections to our position

Others argue against this, saying that if an object is defined as that which is cognized by an awareness, it follows that any subject would necessarily be an awareness. They also allege that our position makes it impossible for any cognition to be a false one.[107] These opponents also advocate that *object* is equivalent to *comprehended thing*.

[Response:] We would point out that based on their position, it must [equally] follow that a subject is necessarily a valid cognition, because to be an object is necessarily to be comprehended. Thus the three spheres [are in place, and their position is shown to be irredeemably flawed.]

Their charge about the impossibility of false cognition is based on the following thinking. If the sense cognition in question were aware of the double moon it grasped, that double moon would constitute its object. And if it had an object, the cognition could not be counted as a false one. This, in turn, depends on their reasoning that since being cognized by awareness is to be an object, then being the thing comprehended by *any* given consciousness is to be an object. This is essentially the same line of reasoning as that advanced [by the first individual] who argued against us in the Enumeration [of equivalents] section.[108] It is exactly the sort of nonsense that can be expected from someone who fails to differentiate between pervasion *as it applies generally* and *as it applies to specifics*.[109] I have refuted this line of thinking above, and I make the following observation:

The general pervasion is the whole expanse of the heavens,
and the specific case what is seen through two apertures [i.e., eyeholes]
  punctured in a wall.
If those who equate them can be counted as intelligent,
who might be judged as a fool?

Those unfortunate individuals languish in a bleak pit of despair, [21]
where more light is gained from the firefly than the sun.
On the ground where only poisonous trees flourish,
what chance is there that this healing medicinal plant may sprout?

3. Evident and Hidden Things

Varieties of object

1. Refutation of others' assertions
2. Setting out our own position

Refutation of others' assertions

Someone claims that the three kinds of object are: actual thing, non-actual thing, and mutual phenomenon. He defines these respectively as "something able to perform a function," "something incapable of any function," and "a phenomenon jointly concomitant with both actual and non-actual things."[110]

[Response:] This is untenable. This division is perhaps intended to be a definitive one, but every known thing can be definitively categorized as either an actual thing or a non-actual thing. So the third category of the "mutual phenomenon" is superfluous. If, on the other hand, the division is supposed to be a typological one, since there is no phenomenon that is neither an actual thing nor a non-actual thing, a third category is again redundant. If, alternatively, this division is set out to categorize the individuations of objects, since there are countless individuated examples of objects beyond the three that he proposes, such a categorization would need to represent each one of them separately. Also, it follows that pot is a phenomenon that is jointly concomitant with both actual and non-actual things, because it is a mutual phenomenon. It must be a mutual phenomenon, since it is a phenomenon that has joint concomitance with the many things that instantiate it.

In fact, there are countless such faults with his position. For example, if being a mutual phenomenon means that something needs to be jointly concomitant with both actual thing and non-actual thing, then it follows that being a phenomenon that is a common locus means that something needs to be a common locus of both actual and non-actual thing. Similarly, it would follow that anything jointly concomitant with pillar and pot is necessarily also concomitant with non-actual thing.

Setting out our own position

Objects can be divided in four ways. The first of these is in terms of how objects are comprehended or appear to the valid cognitions that are their subjects. Looked at in this way, they can be divided into the *evident* and the *hidden*, or into the *specifically* and *generally characterized*. The first to be explained is the division into evident and hidden. [22]

Evident and hidden things

1. Defining characteristics
2. Varieties
3. Analysis of whether evident and hidden things preclude each other

Defining characteristics

1. Refutation of others' assertions
2. Setting out our own position

Refutation of others' assertions

Some say that an evident thing is defined as "that which is realized by means of a perception that has an experiential aspect,"[111] whereas a hidden thing is defined as "that which inferential cognition realizes in a generalized fashion through reference to relationships."[112]

[Response:] I do not believe that these are correct in the present context. It is inappropriate to ascribe to the Sautrāntika school the view that evident phenomena such as the color blue are realized by means of perceptions that have an experiential aspect. As far as the Sautrāntika is concerned, such phenomena are externally established entities, and as such, consciousness is not divided into experienced and experiencer [with regard to them].[113]

Furthermore, having provided these definitions, when identifying the varieties, this individual portrays the likes of a fire on a mountain pass as an *occasional* hidden phenomenon—a thing that sometimes one realizes by depending on a reason and at other times one can realize directly by perception. He also maintains that evident and hidden things preclude each other. These positions are contradictory, since if evident and hidden things preclude each other, it follows that this would also be the case for those things realizable by perception and those realizable by inferential cognition. He cannot dispute the pervasion [that if evident and hidden things preclude each other, that would also be the case for the things realizable by perception and inferential cognition], because that would go against the way he defines the two phenomena. Equally, he cannot deny the reason [that the two phenomena preclude each other], since that would be to blatantly contradict his own thesis. If he accepts [the consequence, agreeing that things realizable by perception and valid inference respectively preclude each other], he would be going against any notion that the fire on the mountain pass is sometimes realized by depending on a reason and at other times realizable by perception.

Others define an evident phenomenon as "that which, by virtue of its own identity, can be realized by perception" and a hidden phenomenon as "that which inferential cognition can realize in a generalized fashion." They too maintain that evident and hidden phenomena preclude one another.

[Response:] It follows that something realizable by valid perception would thereby be precluded from being realizable by inference, because evident and hidden phenomena preclude each other. They have endorsed both the reason and the pervasion [of this argument]. If they agree with the conclusion, it ludicrously follows that the fire on the smoky mountain pass would not be amenable to realization by *any* valid perception! Furthermore, the same criticism can be made of anyone who defines evident and hidden phenomenon in terms of their respective realizability by perception and inferential cognition while also maintaining that evident and hidden phenomena preclude one another.

There are others who also define an evident phenomenon as "that which, by virtue of its own identity, can be realized by perception" and then divide such phenomena into [external] entities and consciousnesses. However, they also contend that when the *perceptions of those entities* cognize them, they do not do so by virtue of those entities having their own identities.[114] [23]

[Response:] This is nothing more than an attempt to hold positions that overtly contradict one another.

[Qualifying their assertion,] they may claim that what they are denying is not that such an entity's own identity can be realized but only that this identity can *appear* to perception.

[Response:] What reason do they have for saying that the identity does not appear? Perhaps they feel that they must deny that the object's identity can appear to perception in order to avoid the charge that since the object is viewed as pleasant by some and unpleasant by others, despite being a single thing, it must have multiple identities. This is perhaps why they assert that when one perceives something, it is actually the [image] aspect of the object that appears and that one interprets this as the object having appeared.[115] But they are still asserting that the identity of the object is realized. So it still follows that a single object would have multiple identities, some pleasant and others unpleasant. Besides that, we could just as well argue that when one perceives something, it is actually the aspects of the object that are *presenting* themselves and that this is what one interprets as the object having appeared. How could they respond to such an argument? It parallels theirs in every respect.[116]

Setting out our own position

An evident phenomenon is defined as "that which is realized overtly by valid perception," whereas a hidden phenomenon is defined as "that which is realized overtly by inferential valid cognition."

Varieties

1. Refutation of others' assertions
2. Setting out our own position

Refutation of others' assertions

One individual advances the position that something such as consciousness is wholly evident, whereas a specifically characterized thing, such as sound and impermanence combined,[117] is only occasionally so. He also asserts that a physical sense power such as the one associated with vision is wholly hidden, whereas again sound and impermanence combined, something that is specifically characterized, is only occasionally so.

[Response:] This is incorrect. What grounds are there for classifying consciousness as "wholly" evident? Is he saying that this is because it is evident to every individual being? Or does he mean that this is because it is evident only to certain beings? Or is it simply because a consciousness is always evident to the person in whose continuum it exists? The first of these alternatives is not credible, since there is no phenomenon that the valid perception of every single being shares, in the sense of overtly comprehending it. If he uses the second alternative as the grounds, then it follows that sound and impermanence combined, something specifically characterized, would be wholly evident, because it is evident to certain beings. He cannot deny the [argument's] pervasion, as that would go against his own assertion. He cannot accept the conclusion, since that would go against his assertion that the aforesaid combination is an occasional hidden phenomenon. Equally, he cannot deny the reason [that the combination is evident to certain beings], since to do that would be to abandon his contention that it is an occasional evident phenomenon. [24]

If the third alternative were correct, it would follow that the thinking of a person other than oneself, who is motivated to verbalize "pot"—[when such a verbalization is] outside of the five situations—is wholly evident, because it is necessarily evident to the person in whose continuum it exists.[118] The reason and the pervasion [of this argument] are the very ones that this individual proposes. He cannot accept its conclusion because doing that would go against his position that the specifically characterized combination of sound and impermanence is an occasional hidden phenomenon.

He is also wrong to assert that the physical sense power associated with vision is a wholly hidden phenomenon. If it was, it would follow that valid perception can never comprehend it. That would preposterously mean that it is impossible for a buddha's omniscient wisdom [to comprehend it].[119] The individual in question may suggest that this is not a charge that can be leveled against his position, since the classification of phenomena into evident or hidden is made purely from the perspective of how they are perceived by myopic individuals.

[Response:] If, as this suggests, the physical sense powers are classified as hidden phenomena since they are not perceived by myopic individuals, it would follow that an ordinary being is not capable of attaining the divine eye, because it is not possible for an ordinary person to comprehend a physical sense power by means of perception. This would absurdly mean that all gods are āryas! That would have to be the case, because the divine eye can see without obstruction every physical form, gross or subtle, distributed throughout three thousand worlds.[120]

Setting out our own position

There are two varieties of evident phenomena: the objects directly engaged by two types of perception—namely, self-cognizing perception and other-cognizing perception.[121] A hidden phenomenon can be any one of three varieties: either something comprehended by inferential cognition dealing with demonstrable facts, by inferential cognition regarding a matter of agreement, or by inferential cognition associated with scripture.

Analysis of whether evident and hidden things preclude each other

Someone argues that evident and hidden things must preclude each other, since what is evident to any one individual is necessarily not hidden from him, and what is hidden from him is necessarily not evident. Thus there is a clear delineation between what is evident and what is hidden as long as the standpoint is that of a single individual who realizes the phenomena in question. The alternative approach, he notes, would be to take into account the perceptions of different individuals, in which case the two could not preclude each other, because what is either evident or hidden for one individual will not necessarily be so for another. But [the problem with that alternative, he proposes,] is that one would be forced to the conclusion that valid and nonvalid cognition do not preclude each other, since a single cognition can be valid with respect to one of its objects but not with respect to another. He contends that similarly, the existence and nonexistence of a pot would not preclude each other, since the pot can be present in one location while being absent in another.

[Response:] Attacks corresponding to those he makes [against the position that multiple observers are the basis for judgment] can be made against his own stance that the basis is a single observer. That is, if we were to count certain phenomena as preclusive because they preclude each other from the perspective of one individual, it would follow that we must equally count certain phenomena as evident because they are evident to a particular individual. Thus the three spheres [are in place, and his position is shown to be irredeemably flawed].

Furthermore, it follows that cause and effect preclude one another, since whatever is a cause of a specific thing cannot be its effect, and whatever is the effect of that thing cannot be its cause. The conclusion is one that his view implicitly sanctions,[122] and hence the three spheres [are in place]. [25]

Something that is overtly comprehended by perception is not thereby precluded from being overtly comprehended by inferential cognition. Since this is the case, being an evident object of comprehension and a hidden object of comprehension *do not* preclude each other. That notwithstanding, what is evident to a particular cognition is necessarily not hidden from that cognition. Hence, from the standpoint of a single awareness, any one phenomenon cannot be both evident and hidden at one time.

Someone may [challenge this with the argument] that since objects of comprehension that are evident and hidden do not preclude each other, it follows that the same must be the case for perception and inferential cognitions. He may say that the pervasion to this argument must hold, otherwise it could not be said that the definitive dichotomy of valid cognitions that classifies them as either perception or inference derives from the definitive dichotomy of comprehended objects that classifies them as either evident or hidden.

[Response:] According to that logic, since the *property of the subject*, *forward pervasion*, and *reverse pervasion*[123] do not preclude one another, it follows that the same must be the case for *unconfirmed*, *contrary*, and *inconclusive* reasons. He must accept that the pervasion [of this argument] holds; otherwise it would follow that the definitive threefold division of incorrect reasons into the unconfirmed and so forth does not derive from the definitive threefold division of the characteristics of the correct reason. He may respond by agreeing that the threefold division of incorrect reasons is not a definitive one. But we would say that the same must then be the case [for the division of the three criteria of the correct reason].[124] He may then challenge us to account for the passage:

> There are no comprehended things apart from the evident and the hidden. Thus, because the things comprehended are twofold, valid cognition is regarded as twofold.[125]

We could equally challenge him to account for the passage:

> [Dignāga] stated that [the fulfilling of each of the] three criteria must also be "ascertained"
> to counter the [idea] that [reasons that were either] unconfirmed, reversed, or mistaken [qualified as correct ones].[126]

To sum up, the fact that evident and hidden objects of comprehension do not preclude each other does not mean that the same is true of perception and inferential cognition. Despite the fact that these two objects of comprehension do not preclude each other in a general sense, this does not mean that something that is evident for a specific valid cognition is not thereby ruled out from being hidden [for the same cognition]. Devendrabuddhi remarks:

> It is in reference to a [specific] individual doing the realizing and a prevailing set of circumstances that the evident and the hidden [are said to] have characteristics that distinguish them.

> Without this [single point of reference], what is evident or hidden will vary depending upon changes of the viewer and the viewpoint, and the boundaries delineating the two become indistinct.[127] [26]

This tells us that the clear delineation between evident and hidden phenomena holds as long as the point of reference for it is one party and one set of circumstances. There is no clear delineation between the phenomena if, instead of using a specific referent, one takes any or all perspectives into consideration, because what is evident for one may be hidden for another, just as what is hidden for one may be evident for another. It is owing to this that the passage describes the boundaries between them as being "indistinct," meaning that the two phenomena do not preclude each other. This is entirely consistent with Śākyabuddhi's comment on the words "They seem to be indistinct because what is obvious may also become hidden, and what is hidden may, in another [set of circumstances], become obvious."[128]

Given this agreement, those who continue to cite Devendrabuddhi's remarks—referring to an individual involved in the realization—as though it establishes that the evident and the hidden preclude each other should stop circulating this corrupt interpretation.[129]

I will now address the following qualm. Under the impression that an object of comprehension that is hidden from the point of a particular subject cannot be overtly realized by that same subject, someone might suggest that we are wrong to define a hidden thing as "that which is realized *overtly* by an inferential valid cognition." This person should pay heed to what I now say on this matter. Different ways of realizing an object preclude each other, and so for someone to realize something in an evident[130] fashion precludes their realizing that same thing in a hidden fashion. There is, nevertheless, no contradiction involved in one thing being both a hidden object and one that is realized overtly. If inferential cognition could not realize the thing it comprehends overtly, it would have to do so implicitly, since there is no third way for valid cognition to realize an object beyond these two. The position that inferential cognition realizes its object of comprehension implicitly is unsustainable, because it would require inferential cognition to realize something that *is* its own object of comprehension by dint of the overt realization of something that is *not* its object of comprehension.

So what do "overt realization" and "implicit realization" mean? First I will deal with them in a general sense and then in terms of perception and inferential cognition individually. [27] An object can be said to have been realized overtly when a particular valid cognition focused on that object arises in the aspect [of that object] and is [alone] able to induce [in the person] ascertainment of that object, without his needing to rely on another, subsequent cognition. Implicit realization of an object *x* occurs when a valid cognition is focused on an object other than it *y*. If, despite this, in the process of overtly understanding its own object of comprehension *y*, that valid cognition still manages to get rid of certain relevant distorted notions regarding the object *x* to the extent that at some later point in time, all [the person] need do is turn his attention toward object *x*, and in doing so he will be able to ascertain it without needing to rely on any other valid cognition; then he can be said to have realized object *x* implicitly.

Valid perception overtly realizes a thing—its object of comprehension—when it arises in the aspect of that thing and eliminates distorted notions about that thing. This occurs, for instance, when the valid perception that apprehends blue overtly arises in the aspect of that blue and eliminates distorted notions about it. Valid perception realizes implicitly when, in the process of overtly arising in the aspect of its own object of comprehension and eliminating distorted notions about that object, it also eliminates distorted notions about another phenomenon, the aspect of which it does not take on. This is what occurs, for instance, when a perception overtly arises in the aspect of and thereby ascertains a specific location [where there happen to be no pots]. Despite the fact that the perception does not overtly arise in the aspect of the *absence of pots*, the individual is nevertheless divested of any distorted notion that there are pots present. So [later,] simply by turning his attention to the fact, he can ascertain that the location was one with no pots in it.

The valid sense perception that apprehends a location—and has the capacity to induce, through its own power, an ascertainment of the fact that there are no pots in that place—cannot directly *perceive* that absence. The location and the absence of pot represent discrete entities, and the perception does not overtly arise in the aspect of the absence. Nor can it be said that this cognition is an inference [of the absence of pots], because the object universal of that absence is not something that appears to it. In spite of this, it is still counted as a valid cognition *of* that absence. This valid perception must be counted as a valid cognition of the absence of pots in that location on the grounds that: (1) this absence is one of its objects, and (2) it is a valid cognition that can independently induce ascertainment of that absence through having eliminated distorted notions running counter to the fact of that absence.

To deny that the absence of pot forms the object of this perception would amount to asserting that only those things of which a cognition is overtly aware can count as its object. This would also mean, absurdly, that a statement of speech can only communicate the things it expresses overtly. [28]

Some might claim that by asserting that the perception in question is a valid cognition of the absence of pots, while denying that it is either a perception or an inference of that absence, we are undermining the position that the division of valid cognition into perception and inference is a definitive one.

[Response:] We would reaffirm what is actually meant when this twofold division of valid cognition is described as a "definitive" one. It denotes that any specific valid cognition must be either a perception or an inference. But while any valid cognition must be either of those two, what does not follow from this is that when some awareness validly cognizes a certain thing, this awareness must be either a perception or an inference of *that* thing. If it did, [one might equally argue that] because any object is necessarily an appearing object, a held object,[131] a conceived object, or an engaged object, it would follow that if something were the object of a particular phenomenon, it must be the appearing, held, conceived, or engaged object of *that* phenomenon. The pervasion and the reason [of this argument] are the ones proposed [by these individuals]. But if they accept its conclusion, it would follow that the *śabdārtha* of pot[132] is the appearing object, or held object, and so on, of the term *pot*, because it is the object of that term.

Inferential cognition overtly realizes a thing—its object of comprehension—when it takes on the object universal of that thing and [in doing so] eliminates distorted notions about that thing. This is what happens, for instance, when an inferential cognition realizing that sound is impermanent overtly takes on the object universal of sound being impermanent, thereby eliminating the distorted notion that sound is not impermanent.

When, [in the process of] an inferential valid cognition taking on the object universal of a thing, that cognition [overtly] comprehends that thing and eliminates distorted notions about it, and also, by dint of that, eliminates distorted notions about some other phenomenon, the object universal of which it does not take on, it is said to have realized that other object *implicitly*. This is what occurs, for instance, with the inferential valid cognition realizing sound to be impermanent. The cognition does not take on the object universal of the absence of permanence in sound, but it still manages to eliminate the distorted notion that any form of permanence is present within sound. Thus [it ensures that at a later point, the individual] will be able to ascertain that sound lacks any permanence simply by his turning attention to that fact, without his needing to rely on any other valid cognition. This inferential cognition can be a valid cognition of sound's lack of permanence *without* needing to be either a perception or an inference of it, a point that can be understood by referring to the reasoning provided above.

[The opponent] may argue that since we are proposing that a perception can validly cognize the absence of pot, it follows that this absence would be something that is its object of comprehension. But if we agree to that, he might say, "It would follow that valid perception comprehends something that is not specifically characterized." For our part, however, both of these are conclusions that we fully welcome! The authoritative pronouncements that things comprehended by valid perception are specifically characterized must be construed to mean that any perception of a myopic individual must always perceive *something* that is specifically characterized, and not that a valid perception can comprehend only those things that are specifically characterized. [29] If it really were the case that valid perception could only comprehend things that are specifically characterized, it would ridiculously follow that a buddha's omniscient awareness would be limited to comprehending things that are specifically characterized. It would also be inconsistent with authoritative statements about logical proofs that use as their reason the nonobservation of something that has the same nature [as what they are actually negating], since such statements declare that the *property of the subject*[133] in such a proof can be confirmed by valid perception. Nor would it be compatible with passages such as "As there are two objects of comprehension, there are two valid cognitions."[134]

This individual may concede that valid perception is able to establish the property of the subject in a proof that uses a reason of nonobservation, but he may still deny that this property is something that the valid perception is able to comprehend. This suggests a situation where valid perception has established a property without having comprehended it. He must therefore be asserting that valid cognition can establish something but that this is no guarantee that it has comprehended that thing. But then it would absurdly follow that something does not have to be comprehended to [qualify as] an established basis.

He may then argue that since the relationship linking cause and effect is something established by valid perception, it must follow that this relationship is comprehended by valid perception. If we agree to that, he may feel that it would force us into the unacceptable conclusion that this relationship cannot be a conceptual construct.

[Response:] We concur with the first conclusion [that the relationship can be comprehended by valid perception]. We maintain, however, that the second one [that this rules out the relationship being a conceptual construct] is not warranted, because although a myopic person cannot *perceive* phenomena that are conceptually constructed, this does not mean that he is unable to *comprehend* them by means of valid perception.

[Our opponent] believes that anything valid perception is able to comprehend must be specifically characterized. [He reasons that] if something is a valid perception and it validly cognizes some phenomenon, it will necessarily be a *valid perception of that same phenomenon*.

This logic, however, leads to the ludicrous conclusion that the inferential valid cognition realizing that sound is impermanent must be a cognition that is mistaken about sound being impermanent. This is because it is a mistaken cognition that is valid and it also validly cognizes that sound is impermanent. He has no adequate response to this argument. With this, the view that to validly cognize some phenomenon [the subject] must either perceive or infer it is dealt a final withering blow. I have many other such gems of reasoning, but I will not relate more of them here, as I fear that would take too much space. [30]

Instead, I want to explore another question: Is it or is it not the case that whatever a valid inferential cognition overtly comprehends must form a *probandum* to be established by means of a correct logical reason? If this is not the case, then how are we to interpret the passage "Inference is of two kinds: [the first, which is] for personal ends, understands an entity by means of a reason [embodying] the three criteria"?[135] On the other hand, if whatever valid inferential cognition overtly comprehends must be the probandum in a logical proof, then one could face the following argument: Generally characterized [thing] must form the probandum [to be established] in dependence on a correct reason, because it is something that valid inferential cognition overtly comprehends.[136] One cannot dispute that what is generally characterized is overtly comprehended by inferential valid cognition, since to do so would contradict lines such as "As there are two objects of comprehension, there are two valid cognitions."[137] But if one accepted that *generally charac-*

terized [thing] forms the probandum, would one not be forced into agreeing that the generally characterized [thing] in question must represent a grouping made up of both a subject and a predicate?[138]

It is legitimate for sensible persons to concern themselves with such issues. I therefore encourage such individuals to pay attention to what I have to say on the matter. What is generally characterized is overtly comprehended by inferential valid cognition. But that does *not* mean that what is generally characterized needs to form the probandum established by means of a correct logical reason. This should not be seen as contradicting the passage "Inference is of two kinds: [the first, which is the] personal [variety], understands something by means of a reason [embodying] the three criteria."[139] What these words describe is how a valid inferential cognition necessarily comprehends [at least] one probandum that is being proved by means of a logical reason. It does not mean that every thing that inferential valid cognition comprehends constitutes such a probandum.

Assuming then that valid inferential cognition comprehends some form of general characterization, the next issue is this: Does the cognition comprehend that general characterization in connection with some basis or not? The cognition comprehends it in connection with a basis, because it is always by depending on a correct reason that valid inferential cognition comes to comprehend its object.[140] Valid inferential cognition comprehends general characterization overtly [when it, for instance,] overtly comprehends that the *śabdārtha* of pot is generally characterized. This must be something that valid inferential cognition overtly comprehends, because there is a correct reason that establishes the probandum "The *śabdārtha* of pot is generally characterized."[141]

However, this does not make it the proof's probandum: *x* may be something that it is necessary to establish by means of a correct reason in connection with a particular basis. But this, by itself, does not mean that *x* necessarily counts as a *probandum* that is established by means of a correct reason. [This contrasts with the situation regarding comprehension, where] if something is comprehended by valid inferential cognition in connection with a particular basis, that is sufficient for it to be counted as an object of comprehension for inferential valid cognition.

[An opponent] might raise an objection by referring to the case of someone who has validly ascertained impermanence and retains a [clear] recollection of it. If at some later point the person has a valid inferential cognition realizing *sound* to be impermanent [the opponent might say] it would follow that impermanence is still what the inferential cognition of this person comprehends, since it is realizing that impermanence [connected with] the basis sound. [The opponent] might then claim that the inference in question must therefore count as a *subsequent cognition* [of impermanence]. And this, he might argue, would make one of the two forms of valid cognition [i.e., inferential cognition] redundant. [31]

[Response:] We are quite willing to accept that the cognition in question comprehends impermanence, but we reject the idea that it therefore counts as a subsequent cognition [of impermanence]. Both the original and later valid cognitions [of that person] comprehend impermanence, and in this respect there are no grounds for distinguishing between them. However, they differ in the ways they comprehend that impermanence. The original cognition does not realize impermanence in connection with sound, whereas the latter does.

If [the opponent] is going to claim that because this cognition comprehends only the [particular] impermanence connected with sound, it should not be counted as a cognition of impermanence, then he would surely also have to assert that the apprehension of the second moment of blue does not constitute the apprehension of blue. In that case, the visual cognition of that second moment of blue would also not count as a visual cognition apprehending blue.

Generally speaking, merely comprehending a thing that an earlier valid cognition has already comprehended is not enough to qualify something as a subsequent cognition. I will elaborate on the reasons for this below. We note that the majority of self-proclaimed scholars have never even entertained doubts on these matters, whereas the few who have tentatively approached them found themselves floundering. Hence I have cause to remark:

My understanding is the moonstone, from which a steady trickle of *pearl-wisdom drops* tumble.
My intellect is the sun, from which brilliant light descends.
Nourished by them, this lotus masterpiece blooms and flourishes.
Of such stunning beauty are these two that the three worldly planes have ne'er seen their like.

4. Specifically and Generally Characterized Entities

The specifically and the generally characterized

1. How the perceptual and inferential dichotomy of valid cognition is determined by the specifically and generally characterized dichotomy of comprehended things
2. Etymological derivation of the terms "specifically characterized" and "generally characterized"
3. Description of specifically and generally characterized entities

How the perceptual and inferential dichotomy of valid cognition is determined by the specifically and generally characterized dichotomy of comprehended things

The passage "As there are two objects of comprehension, there are two valid cognitions"[142] informs us that comprehended things are definitively divided into two—those that are specifically and those that are generally characterized—and also that this division is the reason that there are just two forms of valid cognition, perception and inference. A fuller sense of this [distinction] is conveyed in passages such as "Comprehended things are asserted to be of two types, because there are those that are realized by way of [having] their own [identities,] and those that are realized by way of [having identities shared with] others."[143] It is this that I will now explain. The strict dichotomy classifying comprehendible things into those that are specifically and generally characterized is presented as the reason why perception and inference are the only two forms of valid cognition. The argument advanced here is *not* that anything serving as the actual comprehended object[144] of valid perception must be specifically characterized whereas anything that is the actual comprehended object of valid inferential cognition must be generally characterized. [Such could not be the case] because the valid inferential cognition realizing sound to be impermanent validly cognizes something that is *specifically characterized*—namely, that *sound is impermanent.* [32]

Nor is the argument that [the strict division of comprehended things determines the strict division of what validly cognizes them] on the grounds that anything that valid perception comprehends is necessarily specifically characterized whereas anything that valid inference comprehends is necessarily generally characterized. These cannot be the grounds, because certain generally characterized things, such as the absence of pot in a location where there are no pots, can be comprehended by valid perception, whereas certain specifically characterized things, such as sound being impermanent, can be comprehended by valid inferential cognition.

Instead, [the statement] "As there are two objects of comprehension, there are two valid cognitions"[145] means that valid cognition is strictly divided into perception and inference on the grounds that there are two ways in which the comprehension of an object can occur, with either something specifically characterized or something generally characterized serving as the object *held* by the cognition. This is the point made in the passage "Comprehended things are asserted to be of two types, because there are those that are realized by way of [having] their own [identities], and those that are realized by way of [having identities shared with] others."[146]

In a similar vein, the line "Because there are those capable of functioning and those that are not"[147] should also be understood to mean that there are two forms of comprehension of a thing, depending on whether the object held [by the cognition in question] is a functioning phenomenon or a phenomenon devoid of function.

Etymological derivation

Why then are the two called "specifically" and "generally characterized"? Something is described as "specifically characterized" on the grounds that it has its own characteristic identity—one that can present itself independently without needing to rely on a negandum or any other such thing. Something is described as "generally characterized" due to it having a purely generic nature; one that lacks any independent character.

Description of specifically and generally characterized entities

1. Delineating specific characterization
2. Delineating general characterization

Delineating specific characterization

1. Defining characteristics
2. Identification of the illustration

Explanation of what defines specific characterization

Some contend that what defines a thing as specifically characterized is that it "occupies a determinate location and time and [possesses] its own individual nature." [33] Others have said that its "being able to function" is what defines it. However, these and various other positions turn out to be unsustainable once we take into account how things are explained by the Prāsaṅgika school. According to the Prāsaṅgika standpoint, specific [or *self*][148] characterization represents the principal negandum for the analytical reasoning that gets at what exists ultimately. Therefore [the quality] that for the realist [Buddhist] schools encapsulates what it is to be specifically characterized[149] is the very one that the Prāsaṅgika negates in [order to realize] ultimate reality. What the realists identify as the essence encapsulating self-characterization must therefore be something that the Prāsaṅgika denies has existence, even conventionally. Given this fact, neither having "determinate location, time, and individual nature" nor being "able to function" can be identified as this essence, because the Prāsaṅgika accepts that both of these exist. Hence, while both of these descriptions may help to illustrate what specific characterization is, neither can be counted as what defines it.

In our own system, a specifically characterized [entity] is defined as "an actual thing that is not constructed by thought but exists from its own side, according to its own unique nature."

Identifying the illustration of specific characterization

The illustration of specific characterization is "being something that occupies a determinate location and time and [possesses] its own individual nature."[150]

As to what it means to have a determinate location, time, and individual nature, some propose that (1) determinate location refers to the fact that if something is present in the east, it cannot be found in the west, (2) determinate time means that if something existed yesterday, it cannot remain today, and (3) individual nature denotes that what is [a quality] of the light[-colored] cow cannot be present in the dark-colored cow. One individual who agrees with this understanding of [the expressions] argues that because things such as pot[151] and actual thing need to maintain a concomitance[152] with the various things that instantiate them, they must be generally characterized, not specifically characterized. In addition, he says that the only types of specifically characterized entities are temporally indivisible moments of consciousness and directionally indivisible physical particles. He also asserts that a thing's being able to perform a function is no guarantee that it is specifically characterized, whereas its being able to perform that function "ultimately" is such a guarantee.

Another individual, conceited with the idea of himself as some sort of authority, says that actual things are necessarily specifically characterized.[153] In his opinion, it is impossible for something that is specifically characterized to be concomitant with various instances. Thus, for him, the only *actual* things are those that are indivisible. Based on these grounds, he says that the likes of actual thing and pot do not constitute substances, since the assertion that they do would entail various logical faults. He outlines these faults in the following manner. Do actual thing and pot constitute a single, identical substance or discrete ones? If they were discrete substances, pot could not count as an actual thing. Whereas if they constituted an identical substance, it would follow that the perception of pot would also be a perception of actual thing. He says that the pervasion of this line of reasoning [that if the two of them were a single substance, the perception of one would also require that of the other] cannot be disputed, as this would lead to the unacceptable conclusion that perception is not a comprehensive engager [of its object].[154] [34]

He also argues that if actual thing and pot did constitute an identical substance, then their production and destruction would need to be simultaneous. By the same token, the production and destruction of pillar and actual thing would also need to be simultaneous, because they would also have to represent an identical substance. But from that it would follow that pillar and pot would be produced and cease simultaneously.

He argues that because pot is the same substance as actual thing, and pillar is also the same substance as actual thing, it follows that pillar and pot themselves must constitute a single substance. He asserts that each of the conclusions about the faults of the two being the same substance would follow, because if one thing is the same substance as another, it must be *identical* to it. That in turn follows, because specifically characterized phenomena that constitute the same substance, such as sound and its impermanence, must be indistinguishable from one another. Sound and its impermanence are indistinguishable, he says, in that the perception apprehending them sees them as the same thing.

In addition, he thinks that there is a problem with asserting that the perception of pot can *see* actual thing. As far as he is concerned, this would necessarily require it to apprehend a *purely abstracted thing*,[155] and that would mean that it cognizes a universal. There must, he says, be a pervasion between these two, otherwise it would go against the notion that this purely abstracted thing is a universal. But if one accepted that perception cognizes a universal, he says, it would absurdly mean that perception is conceptual.

[Arguing against] pot being an actual thing, he questions whether pot is supposed to constitute a substance identical to the visual form, smell, taste, tactility, and the elements of earth, water, fire and air that belong to it, or whether it stands as a substance that is separate from them. He says that if pot forms a substance identical with that of the eight, it would follow that those eight substances constitute just one single substance. [But equally,] he says, the idea that the pot and those eight could be discrete substances is unmaintainable, because no pot substance can be found separate from the substance of the eight constituents belonging to that "pot." There is, he says, no visual form, smell, taste, tactility, earth, water, fire, air, or even sound that can be said to be the substance of pot while being a substance separate from those eight [constituents]. Still, pot is external gross matter, and as such, it must be identified as either [one of the four primary] elements or [one of the four] element derivatives.

He challenges the view that a purely abstracted pot can be a substance, questioning whether the substance that is supposed to constitute that pot is the same one that constitutes golden pot or not. He says that if the substance that the pot is constituted from is that of golden pot, it could not also be concomitant with that of silver pot. Conversely, if such a substance did not constitute pot, how could the substance of pot be identical with that of golden pot?

He also wonders whether this purely abstracted pot is a substance that belongs to the past or the future, or a substance that belongs to the present. If it belonged to the past or the future, it could not be concomitant with the present instances of pot, whereas if it belonged to the present, it could not be concomitant with the instances of past and future pot. He proposes that the alternative, that pot is none of them, would entail that it is not made up of any substance.

He next considers whether this pot can ever cease. If not, it cannot be an actual thing. [35] But if it can, something such as a golden pot that is manufactured only after that pot has come to an end would be left in want of a universal.

Seeing how this same line of reasoning can be used against names and word combinations, he also denies that they constitute substances. He is even prepared to claim the same is true of letters. He reaches such a conclusion by the following reasoning. The fundamental [Sanskrit] letter, *a*, comprises sixty-five temporal portions. If the letter itself constituted a substance, he says, that substance would need to be either identical to or distinct from those temporal portions. That being the case, he questions whether at the juncture when its first temporal portion has ceased, this letter has also come to an end, or not? If it has come to an end, the question of whether the substance it forms is identical to or distinct from that of its later temporal portions does not arise, since at the point when those later temporal portions come into existence, the letter does not constitute any sort of substance at all. Conversely, if the letter does not come to an end at that juncture, we must conclude that it never will, because if it were going to, it surely would have done so already. However, he says, to accept the [conclusion that the letter does not form a substance that is either identical to or distinct from those later temporal portions] is to abandon any notion that it is an actual thing. He engages in a great deal of this type of discussion.

He even goes on to conclude that coarse entities and continua do not constitute substances. Does something such as a pot, he asks, which is supposed to be both a coarse entity and one that constitutes a substance, constitute a substance identical with or distinct from its essential component parts? If it constituted a substance that was identical with that of those components, all those components would have to constitute a single, unitary substance. On the other hand, if the pot constituted a substance discrete from that of its component parts, it would have to represent the *whole* that encompassed those parts: a substance that stood outside its essential component parts. To agree to that, he says, would leave one without any grounds for refuting the position espoused by the [non-Buddhist] Vaiśeṣika.

He proposes that the same type of analysis—inquiring whether the thing in question is the same substance with or a different substance from the earlier and later temporal portions that constitute it—can be used to refute the idea that any continuum can constitute a substance. In addition to this, he maintains that something can only count as an actual thing if it belongs to the present. He denies that the likes of pot and established basis can be actual things. He also rejects the idea that such things as the visual form of pot can count as substances.

Someone else adds to this discussion by claiming that when called on to identify the illustrations of actual thing, one should point to temporally indivisible moments of consciousness and indivisible physical particles. Another individual with scholarly pretensions is not even willing to go this far. For him, the illustration can only be phrased in hypothetical terms, and so one should state, "*If* something were to be a temporally indivisible portion of the visual form of a pot, then it would count as an actual thing." The latter two individuals are also both of the opinion that the likes of actual thing and pot are generally characterized.

Finding himself the victim of a severe punishment, with his body pinned down by staves and deprived of control over what he says by the noose that constricts his throat, a cowardly wretch is reduced to emitting a stream of disjointed inanities. In a similar fashion [these individuals] desperately flail around attempting to elicit some semblance of real meaning from a froth of words they use to surround what is essentially a contradiction. [36]

I will deliver a refutation of their position in two sections:

1. Countering the view that an actual thing need not be specifically characterized
2. Countering the position that the likes of actual thing do not constitute substances

Countering the view that an actual thing need not be specifically characterized

[Response:] Based on the assertions of these individuals, it follows that it would be possible to have a valid perception that comprehends a generally characterized thing as its held object. This conclusion is inescapable, because according to them the valid perception of pot has a held object that is generally characterized. They find themselves unable to dispute that the held object of this perception is generally characterized, since if they did, they would be going against their stance on pot being generally characterized. But accepting the [argument's] conclusion would leave them with a number of faults. Namely, it would follow that there is (1) a valid perception, the held object of which is a *śabdārtha*, (2) a perception that is conceptual, and (3) an inferential valid cognition that takes something specifically characterized as its held object.

Their assertion that there are some things that perform functions but are not specifically characterized cannot be correct. If it were, *Commentary on Pramāṇa* would not have presented "because there are those capable of functioning and those that are not"[156] as the reason that supports the strict division between comprehended things that are specifically and generally characterized.

They may claim that it is only those things that are *ultimately* able to perform a function that qualify as specifically characterized. But this claim cannot be reconciled with their denial that things such as blue are specifically characterized. According to their reckoning, it follows that blue would be something that qualifies as specifically characterized, on account of the fact that it is ultimately able to perform a function. They have obviously already endorsed the pervasion [between ultimate functionality and specific characterization]. The reason [that blue performs its function ultimately] is also one that they cannot contest, because the valid cognition verifying that it performs a function [must be classified as] a cognition that analyzes the ultimate. Why? Because it is a valid perception. The pervasion between perception and cognizance of the ultimate is something that I will expand on later.

They believe that temporally indivisible portions of consciousness and indivisible physical particles are specifically characterized. But this is inconsistent with their assertion that something such as a pot is *not* specifically characterized. Are there or are there not numerous things that instantiate the temporally indivisible portions of consciousness? If not, it would follow ludicrously that there is only one single temporally indivisible moment of consciousness in the whole universe. But if there are many things that instantiate these moments, it would follow that the temporally indivisible portion of consciousness is generally characterized, because it must be concomitant with all these various instantiations. The pervasion is the one that [these individuals] themselves proposed, since they said that anything maintaining a concomitance with many instances is necessarily generally characterized. They must also accept the reason [that the temporally indivisible portion of consciousness is concomitant with the various things that instantiate it], otherwise it would go against the position that there are various things that can actually *be* these portions. They might resort to claiming that while there are various things that instantiate the temporally indivisible portion of consciousness, this still does not mean that this indivisible portion is concomitant with these individuations. But then we would urge them to consider why it is that pot must be concomitant with its various instances. [37]

They may say that the temporally indivisible portion of consciousness itself is not specifically characterized; it is only *if* there were something that happened to instantiate it that such a thing would need to be specifically characterized. According to this position, the apprehension of the illustration for what is specifically characterized can only be approached in a hypothetical fashion. This essentially mirrors the one proposed above for identifying the illustration of actual thing, and I intend to refute these below.

Countering the position that the likes of actual thing do not constitute substances

The perception that apprehends pot must be an actual thing, since it directly sees pot. [Our opponent] cannot challenge the fact that this perception actually sees pot, because if he did so, he would be going against his [earlier] assertion that if pot and actual thing constitute a single substance, then any perception of pot would also necessarily perceive actual thing. Neither can he call into question the [argument's] pervasion, because that would violate the basic tenet that perception is always an actual thing, which he also accepts.

The question then is whether the perception of pot is a substance identical to or distinct from the substance of its own first temporal portion? If the substance of the perception apprehending pot was identical to that of its own first portion, the production and cessation of that perception would need to be simultaneous with that of its own first temporal portion. Thus, with the three spheres [in place, the opponent] would be left without any possible response.

The alternative is the position that the perception of pot forms a substance distinct from that of its own first temporal portion. But if that were the case, it would follow that the first instant of that perception could not *be* a perception apprehending pot, in that it would be a substance entirely distinct from that perception. Thus, with the three spheres [in place, the opponent] would be left without any possible response.

[The individual may argue that] actual thing and pot cannot constitute a single substance, since if they did, the substance of actual thing and the substance of pot would have to be identical, because if the two constituted a single substance, the production and cessation of each one would need to be simultaneous with the production and cessation of the other. All those committed to the aforesaid viewpoint could be expected to approve of this line of reasoning. They should pay particular heed to what follows.

[Response:] Based on his reckoning, it must be logical to assert that, because light cows and dark cows belong to the same type of thing, the type that the light cow belongs to must be identical with the one to which the dark cow belongs. However, such a conclusion is unacceptable. The light-cow type is an *exclusion*, formed by the elimination of *non*-light cow, whereas the dark-cow type is not that.[157] Just show me the scholar who is able to counter this argument. If there is such a person, he would certainly receive my support! [38]

Also, since "actual thing derived from effort" and "actual thing not derived from effort" are individually related to impermanence in that they each share the same nature as it, then it must follow that they are also related to each other and share each other's nature.[158] [Our opponent] cannot dispute the pervasion that this conclusion is based on, as that would go against his earlier argument that if pot and pillar individually share the same substance as actual thing, then they must also share the same substance as each other. On the other hand, if he accepts the argument's conclusion, it would go against his original position that pot and pillar do not form a single substance. [His only option] would be to reject the argument's reason.[159] But rejecting that would contradict his assertion that "The sound of a conch is impermanent because it is derived from effort" can be classified as a proof in which the reason "derived from effort" is related to the predicate "impermanent" in the sense of their sharing the same nature.[160]

Another conclusion to be drawn from what he says is that because the perception of pot is an awareness that sees pot, it follows that it must be one that cognizes a universal. If he were to accept this conclusion, it would directly go against one of his own basic theses. If, on the other hand, he disputed that there is pervasion between an awareness that cognizes a pot and one that cognizes a universal, it would go against his assertion that pot is a universal. Similarly, he cannot challenge the reason [that the cognition in question sees pot, since] that would go against his position that it is a comprehensive engager.

He might propose that while pot *is* a universal, the fact that a perception sees it does not mean that this perception counts as one that cognizes a universal. But this would go against his [earlier] argument that because actual thing is a universal, if the perception of pot were to see it, that perception would have to count as one that was seeing a universal.

The belief that any two phenomena that share a single substance must be the same thing ultimately rests on only two lines of thinking: the notion that (1) things that share a single substance, such as sound and its impermanence, appear the same to the perception that apprehends them and (2) that if two things appear to be the same to a cognition of the unmistaken variety, then that is indeed the way that they must be. However, this fails to differentiate between two forms of unmistaken awareness—namely (1) an unmistaken awareness that *observes* that two or more things are the same and (2) an unmistaken awareness that does *not observe* that they are distinct. It may be the case, for instance, that someone's auditory cognition of a sound is not aware of the fact that the sound and its impermanence are distinct, but this in no way means that it actually *observes* that they are the same. If this perception's failure to detect that sound and its impermanence are distinct amounted to its actually observing that they are the same, we would also have to conclude that the failure of this perception to cognize that sound has no self-existence [i.e., sound is selfless] must mean that it sees sound as self-existent!

Someone might offer a response to this by saying that *if* the selflessness of the sound actually constituted [part of] the substance of sound, the auditory cognition that sensed sound would also have to perceive that selflessness. But in fact, the cognition in question is not aware of the selflessness since that selflessness does not constitute [part of] that substance. Therefore, although the auditory cognition does not observe selflessness, this does not mean that it perceives sound to be self-existent.

[Response:] The same must apply here. *If* the feature of sound and its impermanence being distinct from each other[161] constituted a substance, [the auditory cognition should indeed be able to perceive it]. Thus if the cognition did not see the two [sound and its impermanence] as separate, this would be tantamount to its affirming that they were the same thing. However, the feature of them being distinct does *not* constitute [part of the] substance [of sound] and is therefore not something observed by auditory cognition. [39] This feature of the distinctness of sound and its impermanence does not form a substance. If it did, this distinctness would have to be embodied in reality, and thus [sound and its impermanence would need to be discrete from one another in a true sense.

[Our opponents] may allege that our position is inconsistent. If we acknowledge that (1) sound and impermanence individually constitute substances and (2) that sound and impermanence are also different from one another, then we should, they may say, accept that the feature of their distinctness also constitutes a substance.

[Response:] According to this, it would follow that anything that is the selflessness of temporally indivisible portions of sound and temporally indivisible portions of impermanence must itself be a substance, because such a thing is necessarily a substance and selfless. They would have no response to this argument.[162] Thus, while both sound and impermanence are made up of substance and are also different from each other, the feature of them being distinct from each other does not constitute [part of] that substance. For this reason, perception cannot be expected to observe them *as* discrete.

The objection to this may be that, if the feature of them being distinct was not established in substance, any separation between them would amount to just a fictive one. Hence them being distinct could have no credence. But based on that, it would follow that no conventional thing is an established basis, because every one of them is a construct of thought and [according to the opponent, that makes them] liable to being undermined by valid cognition. He cannot challenge this [argument's] reason, since that would go against his assertion that being discrete could have no credibility if it were only a construct of thought.

Our opponent argues that pot and actual thing do not form a single substance, saying that if they did, the perception that apprehends pot would also have to see actual thing, because that perception is a comprehensive engager of pot. This is exactly the type of drivel that can be expected from those who lack the wit to penetrate the meaning of the passage "Thus, in seeing [i.e., perceiving] the actual thing, one sees all of its qualities [without exception]"[163] and instead content themselves with the most superficial reading of the words.

To these persons, we pose the following question about *forms with physical resistance*.[164] Is it possible for something to actually instantiate a single temporally indivisible portion of this variety of form or not? If they deny that such [an instantiation] is possible, it would go against their assertion that it is possible for the pot's visual form. If, on the other hand, there is something that can instantiate the temporally indivisible portions of [these obstructed] physical forms, does such an [instantiated] portion and the tactility belonging to it constitute a single substance or distinct ones? If they say that the two are distinct substances, it would go against their position that it is impossible to have a substance that stands separate from the essential component parts belonging to it. Conversely, if they agreed that these two constitute a single substance, it would follow that the visual cognition that apprehends such an obstructed physical form must also "see" its tactility, because (1) the cognition in question is a comprehensive engager of that portion and (2) that portion and its tactility constitute a single substance. Thus the three spheres [have been embraced]. [40]

Their line of reasoning would give rise to further faults if it were applied to the Vijñaptika view of things.[165] It would follow, for instance, that when one has a visual consciousness apprehending blue, the subject-aspect element[166] of that consciousness would also have to overtly take blue [as its object]. That is because (1) this self-cognitive element is a direct comprehensive engager of the visual consciousness apprehending blue and (2) the visual consciousness of blue and the blue that it apprehends constitute a single substance. But if [our opponents] agreed with this conclusion, they would lose the distinction drawn between the visual consciousness that apprehends the blue and the subject-aspect of that consciousness, according to which the two are classified respectively as the other-cognition and self-cognition.

The only feasible way for that subject-aspect to overtly realize the blue would be for it to take on the aspect of that blue. But if that were the case, would the aspect of blue that the visual consciousness takes on be the same as the one taken on by the subject-aspect, or would they be separate from each other? If they were the same, it would absurdly follow that the visual consciousness apprehending blue and the subject-aspect [aware of that consciousness] would be the same thing. The conclusion that the two are separate things is equally unacceptable, since it would mean that, when a person views blue by means of his visual consciousness, there would need to be two aspects of blue occurring simultaneously.[167]

Regardless of whether the perspective is Sautrāntika or Cittamātra, the position—that two or more things that are a single substance must be identical—can be attacked in the following way. Since the subject-aspect of the visual consciousness of blue forms a single substance with the object-aspect of that consciousness, it would follow that the two aspects are identical. This would lead to the ridiculous situation of the self-cognition and other-cognition being the same thing. The fact that the [subject-aspect and object-aspect] form a single substance cannot be disputed, otherwise how could one say that the subject-aspect is a self-cognizing perception of that visual consciousness?

What the passages "[If those things that] form a single entity..."[168] and "Thus, in seeing [i.e., perceiving] the actual thing, one sees all of its qualities [without exception]"[169] refer to is those things [i.e., features] that belong to the same *simultaneous substantial entity*[170] as the phenomenon. Any such [feature] is indistinguishable from the phenomenon in the sense that a perception that sees that phenomenon must also necessarily see that [feature]. Thus it is also stated that "[Even though] a particular [thing in its entirety] without parts is [what] perception grasps . . ."[171] In addition, in support of the passage "Thus in seeing the actual thing, one sees all of its qualities [without exception]," the reason that the autocommentary gives is: "because seeing [the whole] facet of [an actual thing] and not the parts would be unfeasible."[172]

Another thing that would follow [from the opponents' position]—that anything which constitutes a single substance with another phenomenon must be identical with that phenomenon—is that such a thing would need to form a single unit with that phenomenon, being identical with it in *every respect*. The pervasion [between being identical and being identical in every respect] holds, as this other thing could hardly be counted as identical to that phenomenon if it differed from it in certain respects. Viewed again from the Vijñaptika perspective, this would force one to conclude that the visual consciousness perceiving blue and that blue must also form a single unit, indistinguishable in any respect. [41] But the blue appears to that consciousness to be something *out there*. So we would have to conclude that the visual consciousness itself similarly appears to be *out there*.

Also, for both the Sautrāntika and Cittamātra schools, a conceptual cognition and the self-cognition experiencing it constitute a single substance. Following the reasoning [of our opponents], this must mean that they are fused together into a single, inseparable unit. If that were the case, it would absurdly follow that the *śabdārtha*—which overtly appears to the conceptual cognition—also overtly appears to the self-cognizing perception. If that were the case, it would follow that the self-cognition was not a perception.[173]

Furthermore, it would follow that the visual form of pot constitutes a substance. This is because the analysis that they put forward—when attempting to refute that pot constitutes a substance—asserts that the pot cannot be a substance since it is neither the same substance as nor a separate substance from that of its visual form. The predicate and reason [of this argument] are the ones that they proposed.

They have also argued that if the pot and the eight atomic substances belonging to it, such as its visual form, were to constitute a single substance, those eight atomic substances would also count as just one single substance. In this they effectively admit that the visual form and so forth *do* form the substance of that pot. However, this position directly contradicts them [elsewhere] denying that pot's visual form actually constitutes a substance.

They maintain that the pot is gross matter of the external variety, but they also claim that it is a non-actual thing. Thus they toil beneath a massive burden of self-contradiction.

They have also said that unless pot is made up of the substance of golden pot, it cannot be the same substance as golden pot. This can be countered by a parallel argument. Because clay pot and golden pot belong to a single type of thing, it follows that the type that clay pot belongs to must be the golden pot type. I have already explained the reasons why if [two things] share the same substance it does not follow that one of them has to constitute the substance of that other.

They have also used the argument that if the pot was a substance belonging to the present it could not be concomitant with past or future instantiations of pot. However, this is not a fault in our position. If, by "past pot" and "future pot," they mean something that *is* a pot but belongs to the past and something that *is* a pot but belongs to the future, then we would say such things are not established in any sense. Whereas if they were to suggest that, for instance, yesterday was to be taken as an example of a past time, and the "past pot" is one that existed at that time, we would say that such a pot *did* actually belong to the present. So in that sense, there is no inconsistency in our asserting that the pot is concomitant with those various instances while also maintaining that it constitutes a substance that belongs to the present.

Their contention that if pot ever comes to an end, the golden pot that is manufactured only after that will be left in want of a universal also fails. [42] The golden pot that is manufactured only after pot has come to an end will not be left in want of a universal, because even though *pot* may have come to an end, the *pot that is manufactured subsequent to that* will [then exist, and that pot will] be concomitant with the golden pot in question. They might claim that this is an impossibility since once pot ceases, no [further] pot can arise. But if that were the case, it would be impossible, once the current actual thing comes to an end, for there ever to be a current actual thing again.

The refutation directed against the view that letters constitute substances is also flawed. Does the thing that instantiates a particular day of the month constitute a substance, or not? If it does, this day must form a substance that is either identical with or distinct from the substance of its own earlier, middle, and later portions. That being so, once its earlier, or morning portion is over, has that day ended or not? If it has, the question of whether it forms a single substance that is identical with or distinct from the later portion does not arise, because at the latter stage of the day, it would no longer form any sort of substance at all. So it would be logically inconsistent for [our opponents] to hold that the day ends [when the morning does]. Conversely, if they propose that the day in question has not already ended [at that latter stage], we could attack them [with the reasoning they earlier used themselves,] concluding that it must therefore be something that will never come to an end, since if it were going to come to an end, it would have done so already. So once again the three spheres are in place.

This argument of theirs that "[It is something that] never [ends], since if it were going to come to an end, it would have done so already" is a [line of reasoning] we might also turn against [the opponents'] own assertion that any instantiation of a temporally indivisible portion of the visual form of the pot is necessarily an actual thing. Based on their logic, it follows that the thing that instantiates such a temporal portion must be one that never comes to an end, since if it were going to come to an end, it would have done so already. The pervasion is the one they proposed themselves, but the conclusion is hardly one that they can accept, because it would go against the idea that this temporal portion is an actual thing. So once more, the three spheres [are in place]. They may therefore say that the temporal portions in question have already ceased, but from this it would again follow that the temporal portions are not actual things, in that they are things that belong to the past. With the three spheres [in place, these individuals are left] without any form of response.

The alternative to this is to assume that a thing instantiating a particular day in the month does not constitute a substance at all. But then the same would have to be true for the likes of month, year, and eon. Then it would ludicrously follow that gaining enlightenment after having accumulated merit for the period of three countless eons is a total impossibility![174] There are copious other ways to attack their thesis that letters do not constitute substances. I will deal with these below.

The view that coarse entities do not constitute substances is also unsustainable. One would have to conclude, for instance, that because blue is a coarse entity, it cannot form a substance. But this conclusion goes against [another of] the opponents' own assertions, since they have said that no temporally indivisible portion of a visual consciousness of blue can be produced unless blue serves as its observed [object] condition.[175] They might refuse to accept that blue is a coarse entity. However, it must be a coarse entity, because apart from infinitesimally small particles, all externally established entities are necessarily coarse ones. Blue cannot be this sort of tiny particle, since it is a collection comprising many constituent parts, each of which share the same essential nature as it, but none of which is individually that collection. What is more, if one were to assume that blue did not constitute a substance, it would follow that it is nothing more than a construct of thought, something that is true for any object of comprehension that does not constitute a substance. [43] But if blue is nothing more than a construct of thought, then how could there be an unmistaken cognition of such an external entity that overtly takes on the aspect of blue? And if there were no unmistaken cognition that was able to overtly take on such an aspect, nothing would ever actually *be* a visual consciousness of blue.

The [opponents' arguments] lead to the conclusion that the perceptions of myopic individuals [directed at the] external world can never overtly comprehend substances. This follows, because [they assert] that (1) the coarse entities [comprehended by myopic individuals] do not constitute substances and that (2) indivisible physical particles cannot be overtly comprehended by the perception of those individuals. As the opponents have obviously argued that coarse entities do not constitute substances, they might try to deny [the second position] that it is impossible for myopic individuals to directly perceive indivisibly tiny physical particles. If they did that, they would be accepting that it is possible for an ordinary being to directly realize the *minutest units of time*. If they were to accept that, it would follow that such an ordinary being would be someone capable of obliterating the seed-potentials that give rise to distorted notions holding [impermanent things] to be permanent. But accepting that would lead to the ridiculous conclusion that such an individual would simultaneously be both an ordinary being and an ārya!

Furthermore, [to pursue another line], the Madhyamaka school, as is expressed in passages such as "because all phenomena are akin to dreams,"[176] maintains that all phenomena are analogous to those in a dream, in the sense that they lack any truly existent nature. The Buddhist realist schools attack this position, arguing that if it were the case, the absurd conclusion would be that even the virtuous and nonvirtuous karma accumulated by actions performed through strong attachment *during waking hours* could not yield pleasure or suffering as their results, because they lack any sort of truly existent nature. Now if [our opponents' understanding of the realist's standpoint] is correct, then the Mādhyamika could legitimately rebut the realists' attack by hurling the argument right back at them, since the three spheres are directly in place. This is because (1) the consequence's predicate [that the actions do not yield those results] is something that is ruled out by valid cognition,

(2) the consequence's pervasion [that if things are not truly existent, such actions cannot yield those results] is something that the realist themselves openly declare to be the case, and (3) according to you [opponents], the reason of the argument—namely, that these actions have no truly existent nature—represents one of the most fundamental tenets of the Buddhist realist schools. We would request you "far-sighted" individuals to show us where exactly these Buddhist realists, capable of employing such an attack without entirely undermining their own fundamental tenets, are supposed to be. In actual fact, it is precisely *because* the realist schools hold as one of their most basic tenets that coarse entities and the karma deposited upon the mental continua are things that exist in the ultimate sense that they direct the aforementioned attack at the Mādhyamika, who denies their true existence. [44]

In reply, [our opponents] may suggest that this would be inconsistent with the portrayal of the views of the Buddhist realist schools found in [Haribhadra's] *Clear Meaning: Commentary* on the *Ornament of Realizations*. There, the view attributed to them is that ultimately, the slain and the slayer do not exist.

[Response:] The concept of "ultimate" in the section mentioned is based on the etymology of the [Sanskrit] term *paramārtha*, and it glosses the unmistaken valid cognition that scrutinizes what ultimately exists as "ultimate." According to the realist schools, such cognitions do not apprehend the isolated identities of coarse entities, continua, and the various components of an action. This is because, they claim, these identities must be posited as "wholes." As wholes, [actions comprising] the slain and the slayer, the produced and the producer, as well as coarse entities, continua, and so forth each possess a [series of] earlier and later temporal portions, a variety of stages, and numerous component parts. The realists say that it is untenable for this kind of *part-possessing whole* to overtly appear to an unmistaken awareness.

[Our opponents] may then allege that this represents a contradiction, arguing that [the realist schools] cannot maintain that blue is (1) a coarse entity, in addition to being (2) something that overtly appears to the visual perception apprehending it, if they also hold that it is (3) impossible for a whole, in possession of various parts, to overtly appear to an unmistaken awareness.

[Response:] There is no such inconsistency [on the part of the realist schools]. Blue is a coarse entity, and it does overtly appear to the visual consciousness that apprehends it. Despite this, the fact that it *is* a coarse entity does not appear to that consciousness. The reason for this is as follows. If blue were to appear to the visual consciousness apprehending it *as* a whole possessing various parts, then the blue and those constituent parts would need to appear to that consciousness as though distinct from each other, and this would have to mean that the blue and its constituent parts actually form separate substances.

Even among those who [correctly] acknowledge that coarse entities constitute substances, there are those who invite this same attack upon themselves, due to the fact that they advocate things can appear to sense consciousness as having a coarse aspect. [What we say is] that while blue is a coarse entity and overtly appears to the visual consciousness apprehending it, when this blue *presents*[177] itself to that consciousness, it does so neither in the aspect of a coarse entity nor in the aspect of something [made up] of particles. The aspect that it overtly presents is simply that of blue, qualified by neither of these two [features]. This is why sense consciousnesses are described as subjects that cognize the characteristics of "sense bases,"[178] not those that cognize the characteristics of substances. The feature of *being blue* is considered to be a characteristic specific to a sense basis, because it is by virtue of being blue that a blue is counted as a visual-form sense basis.

One individual claims that a coarse entity cannot form a substance and that particles can never overtly appear to the perceptions of myopic persons. But he also accepts that a sense consciousness needs to have a thing that is external and specifically characterized as its overt object. [45]

[Response:] He blatantly fails to recognize how these positions conflict with each other. Based on what he says, it would follow that external entities that are neither coarse entities nor particles are substances. But if he accepts this, it would go against his claim that it is impossible for coarse entities or continua to constitute substances.[179]

Elsewhere, someone asserts that while the entity that a sense consciousness deals with may be [composed of] particles, this entity appears to the sense consciousness in the aspect of a coarse entity.

[Response:] This is incorrect. It would follow that the sense perception was mistaken about the object that appears to it, because the entity it deals with would appear to it as a coarse entity, in spite of the fact that it is not so. That would lead to the unacceptable conclusion that the entities in question do not present an accurate resemblance of themselves[180] to the consciousnesses that apprehend them.

In an attempt to counter this, the individual may allege that it is in fact *our* position that leads to the unwelcome conclusion that blue does not present itself accurately to visual consciousness, because we are the ones who propose that even though blue is coarse, it does not present itself *as* coarse to that consciousness.

[Response:] The phrase "presenting an accurate resemblance of itself" needs to be understood purely in terms of its identity as blue. What it overtly presents itself as is blue, and that is exactly what it is [in reality]. If instead, [as he claims, the only way] a whole, in possession of various parts, could be said to present an accurate resemblance of itself would be if it presented itself *as* such a whole, then it would also follow that the only way that the blue lotus (*utpala*) could present an accurate resemblance of itself to an unmistaken visual consciousness would be if it presented itself as something *with* a smell and taste. This would have to be the case, because the blue lotus is supposed to be something that presents itself accurately to that perception and is also something that has a smell and a taste.

Now if, as we say, [an object] does not appear to sense consciousness *as* a coarse entity, a question may arise as to how to interpret the passage "How is it then that these particles could make something in [their] likeness, if what appears is [something that is] coarse?"[181] This passage represents part of an argument directed by the Cittamātra against the Sautrāntika. The question posed by the Cittamātra is this: If [as the Sautrāntika proposes] the object generates the consciousness in a form that resembles itself, is that consciousness one that resembles that object in every respect, or only in some? The aforesaid passage considers the first of these options, which it rules out on the grounds that it would entail the sense consciousness also being generated as something with the aspect of a coarse entity. The passage does *not* refute that the Sautrāntika himself asserts that things appear to sense perception in the aspect of coarse entities.

I have already covered some of the arguments that damage the view that continua cannot constitute substances. Here is another: Because sound constitutes a continuum, it would follow, based on the aforesaid view, that it cannot form a substance. [46] Sound [obviously] constitutes a continuum, in that it is an actual thing made up of the various temporal portions that form its component parts. This point can hardly be disputed, since that would oblige one to accept that there is nothing to sound other than a single instant. It must be granted that [on occasions] sound is described as something that does not have a continuum.[182] However, these [statements only] refer to sound's not having a continuum [composed] of like moments.[183]

Otherwise, [such statements would be denying that] sound is a continuum made up of various constituent temporal portions. This would make it a composite [phenomenon] that did not form any sort of continuum at all, and thus it would necessarily be something of the absolute shortest possible duration. It would absurdly follow that sound is something that myopic persons could not possibly realize through perception. In summary, a "continuum" is a time duration composed of various temporal portions as its constituent parts, whereas a "coarse [entity]" is a physical mass composed of various particle substances that are its constituent parts.

Attempting to counter our position, some may argue that since two indivisible physical particles [just as much as one] are indivisible particles, they must also be counted as one of the absolute smallest possible units of form.[184] They might say that the pervasion between being this type of particle and the smallest unit(s) of form is one that we have already acknowledged. But if we were to agree that the two particles constitute one of these smallest units, [these opponents] would argue that the two must therefore be incapable of extending beyond the area covered by a single particle.

[Response:] Based on that logic, it would follow that even a hundred of the shortest possible units of time can last no longer than the duration of a single one of such units, because they [just as much as one] are units of the *shortest possible* duration. The pervasion and predicate [of this argument] are exactly the ones that these individuals themselves have proposed. If they were to dispute the reason [that a hundred of these are units of the shortest possible duration], they would be compelled to agree that [the very notion of] having a number of these shortest possible units of time becomes an impossibility, and in that case there could only ever be one of them!

[What one must say, therefore, is that] while a hundred of these shortest possible units *strung together* in a sequence do constitute a continuum, any number of them [individually, outside that sequence,] still represent only the shortest possible unit of time. These individuals may say that this would oblige us to accept that [the duration] of a hundred such shortest units is equal to that of a single one. But this is something with which we wholeheartedly agree. The fact that the duration of the hundred [individual] units is no more than that of one might lead these opponents to argue that even if a hundred of them were strung together, they could still not form a continuum. We deny any such flaw. The two may match one another in that they are both the same [form of] duration, but they differ in terms of the duration they could be said to *have*. However, these matters can only be appreciated by individuals such as ourselves, who enjoy an extraordinary degree of penetrative insight. As for you, my pretty ones, you must content yourself with dreams of how wonderful it would be if you could comprehend points of such profundity!

According to [one opponent's analysis], continua cannot be substances, because if a continuum were a substance, it would need to form either the same substance as the earlier and later temporal portions that it possesses or a substance that was distinct from them. He then questioned whether or not that continuum ceases at the time of the earlier temporal portions. [47] He said that if the continuum ended at that earlier time, then it could form neither a substance that was the same as the later temporal portions nor a substance that was distinct from them, since it would not exist [at all] during their time. He proposed that if, on the other hand, the continuum had not ended at that later point, then neither could it be expected to do so at any time subsequent to that, and we would have to conclude that it is permanent.

[Response:] This logic is erroneous. It would follow that indivisible particles in the west and indivisible particles in the east cannot be distinct substances, because in the eastern particles' location none of the western particles are present, and in the western particles' location none of the eastern particles are present.[185] He has no response to this.

It is due to having placed his confidence in this insubstantial analysis that he is obliged to maintain that cause and effect do not constitute substances. But from this it would ludicrously follow that there are no actual things that are produced from causes. Furthermore, it would follow that once smoke has been produced, its cause, fire, can no longer be judged to be a cause, because when smoke has been produced, its cause, fire, must already have ceased. He might deny the pervasion between these two. But this would go against the line of reasoning that if the production of the effect requires the cessation of the cause, cause and effect can form neither the same substance nor separate ones. If, on the other hand, he accepts the conclusion [that once smoke is produced, fire no longer counts as its cause], then it would follow that smoke's being an effect disqualifies fire from being a cause. Agreeing with this would force him to accept that if there *is* smoke, then there is necessarily *no* fire. In that case, the argument "There is no fire, because there is smoke" becomes a correct one! Thus the three spheres [are in place]. In response, he may argue that if the cause, fire, still constitutes a substance even after its effect, smoke, has been produced, it must mean that the fire has not ceased. He might claim that cause and effect would therefore need to exist simultaneously.

[Response:] By this reckoning, being a produced effect would necessarily mean being something without a cause, and thus [as they would be causeless phenomena] all such effects would be permanent.

We also wonder whether he considers fire and smoke to be cause and effect [of one another] at the smoke stage, at the fire stage, or whether he denies that they are cause and effect at all. If it were the first of these, it would follow that fire is present at the smoke stage, because it is at this time that it is the cause of smoke. Thus the three spheres [would be in place]. Conversely, if it were the second option, it would follow that smoke is present at the fire stage, because it is at this time that smoke is the effect of fire. Again, the three spheres [would be in place]. The absurd consequence of the two not being cause and effect at all is that it would be impossible for smoke to act as a correct effect reason proving the presence of fire on a smoky pass [when the fire is obscured from sight].

He may suggest that our own position is susceptible to the exact same criticisms that we have made of his. But our assertion that fire and smoke are cause and effect is based on a [different] understanding of the time [frame] being referenced. For us, the "time" here is something made up of *both* the fire stage and the smoke stage. But for him this is not an option, since it would invalidate his position that a continuum can never constitute a substance. [48]

Next, we turn to those who, when called upon to provide an illustration of an actual thing, phrase their response in hypothetical terms by stating that only "*if* something were to be a single temporal portion of the pot's visual form would it count as an actual thing." Let us look then at this single temporal portion of the pot's visual form. Are these individuals of the opinion that there is something that actually instantiates this temporal portion or not? If there is no such thing, then [how are we to see] the response they gave when called upon to provide an illustration of actual thing? It is very much like someone declaring that "*If* something were the horn on the head of a hare, it would be an actual thing." Thus, with a single utterance, the full extent of their flawed understanding is exposed.

The alternative would be for them to assert that there is something that instantiates that temporal portion. But then how could they respond to the following argument? Any single temporal portion of the pot's visual form is an impossibility, because the pot's visual form is not subject to any momentary disintegration. [The opponents] would obviously not be inclined to accept this conclusion, since it would be directly at odds with what they have just asserted [about an instantiation of pot existing]. Neither could they deny the pervasion it is based on, because this would run counter to their view that something with temporal portions necessarily disintegrates. Equally, they cannot challenge the reason—namely, that the pot's visual form is not subject to disintegration—because to do that would be to admit that the form disintegrates, which would go against their view that it is a not an actual thing.

But if there is something that instantiates a single temporal portion of pot's visual form, it would follow that it must be either the same substance as or a distinct substance from the earlier and later temporal portions of the pot's visual form, since such a thing would necessarily constitute a substance. The reason and the pervasion of this argument are exactly the ones that [the opponents] proposed. Assuming then that they accept the conclusion, there is then the question of whether this indivisible temporal portion of pot's visual form perishes along with the disintegration of the earlier temporal portions. If it does, it would mean that no later temporal portions of pot's visual form could count as indivisible ones. On the other hand, if it failed to disintegrate together with those earlier temporal portions, then neither could it [be expected to] disintegrate subsequently, meaning that it would have to be permanent. That is to say, every one of the attacks that he tried to use to undermine [the views of others] can be turned against his own system to equally good effect.

It was due to their reluctance to make the assertion that there is no illustration for actual thing that they were obliged to peddle this fiction of theirs. It would have been far better if, right from the outset, they had cut short any discussion by admitting that they had nothing to offer on the matter, and thus all this bother could have been avoided.

Their refusal to accept that sound is an actual thing has forced them to contend that it must be a non-actual thing. And because of this, they have to concede that it must be permanent. The problem with maintaining this position is that it would make the valid inferential cognition that realizes sound to be impermanent, using the reason that it is produced, into a false cognition—one that is mistaken about the object it engages. Thus I declare:

In the assemblies of the learned, those with scholarly pretensions parade as
 though they are trophies.
Deporting themselves publicly in this manner, acting for all the world like
 they are Vasubandhu, is just their nature.

How telling, though, that in seeking to describe the true state of things,
they instead end up revealing their own internal state, [49]
and with the very words that they use to criticize others,
it is upon themselves that they inflict defeat.

Next, I will explain our own position on the aforesaid issue. To say that a thing has its own "determinate location, time, and individual nature" basically means that it exists in the exact opposite way to how things exist according to thought, where [aspects of a thing's location, time, and nature] seem to be *merged*.[186] Our own experience tells us that [to merge the times of a thing] is not to labor under the impression that, [for instance,] something that exists in the earlier portion of the day must also exist in the later part. [Similarly, to merge the nature of a things] is not to assume that something present in a mottled cow must also be present in the pale yellow cow.[187] Nor [when merging locations] are we imagining that something that is in the east must also be in the west. Also, when a single specifically characterized thing is described as *having* its own determinate location, time, and individual nature, it does not mean that if something exists in the earlier portion of the day it cannot also exist in the latter, that if it is present in the east it must be absent from the west, or that if it is something found in the mottled cow, it must necessarily be missing from the pale yellow one.

Instead, the type of assumptions we make about a thing when [aspects of] its location, time, and nature are seen to merge are as follows. For example, we have the sense that the very same pillar that exists in the earlier part of the day is the one that [continues to] exist in the later part of the day. We feel that when that pillar is in physical contact with various other material substances located to its east and west that the thing touching the substance situated to its east is the same one that is touching the substance situated to its west. And as far as "cow" maintaining a concomitance with all particular cows goes, [we have the sense that] the thing that is concomitant with the mottled cow is the exact same thing as the one that is concomitant with the pale, yellow cow. [In line with this,] for a thing to have a determinate identity means the following. Saying that a pillar, for instance, has a *determinate time* is not to suggest that because it exists in the earlier part of the day it cannot exist in the later part. Instead, it means that the pillar of the earlier period is not the same one that exists at the later time. To say that a thing occupies a *determinate location* does not suggest, for example, that a material substance can have no physical contact with another thing to its west because it has contact with something situated to its east. Instead, it means that the [part of the] material substance that is in physical contact with something situated to its east is not the same as that [part] in contact with another thing situated to its west. To say that an object has a *determinate nature* does not imply that the mottled cow and a pale yellow cow, for instance, cannot share a nature. Instead, it means that the nature that belongs to the mottled cow is not the same one that belongs to the pale yellow cow.

Pot, actual thing, and so forth are therefore concomitant with each of their individual instances, but this fact [should not be seen] as incompatible with them having their own determinate locations, times, and natures. Actual thing is specifically characterized, but this specifically characterized [identity] is completely consistent with its being a universal, maintaining a concomitance with each individual actual thing.

Numerous lines of reasoning and passages in authoritative texts disprove that universal [itself] is an actual thing. [50] But none of the treatises by the father and spiritual son [Dignāga and Dharmakīrti] present logical proofs or authoritative statements in support of the claim that something that *is* a universal is thereby precluded from being an actual thing. Neither is there a single line in the principal commentaries to the Seven Treatises stating that [something that is] a universal cannot be an actual thing.[188]

How then do we account for passages like "Those objects that are within consciousness"?[189] What passages such as this are discussing is the *śabdārtha*. This is a [purely] conceptual object; it is what serves as the point of reference and the foundation for our applying conventions to things, [allowing us to] deal with them in general terms and as things that form common groups.[190] Such passages do not indicate that a universal cannot be specifically characterized. Actual thing is a universal and is also concomitant with each specific actual thing. It must be able to maintain this concomitance, otherwise we would end up with the ridiculous situation in which it would be impossible to have many different objects that were [all] actual things.

A universal does not have to be generally characterized. If it did, it would necessarily be a conceptual construct. That would mean that anything that had a number of instances of itself would need to be a conceptual construct, and anything that was a substance could never have more than a single instance of itself in the whole of existence. What the term *universal* actually refers to is "commonality," so all that is required for something to qualify as a universal is for it to share an association [of identity] with [at least] two things.[191] This in no way precludes the thing in question from being a specifically characterized one. The passage "Because there are those capable of a function and those that are not" tells us, for instance, that anything able to perform a function is necessarily specifically characterized, while the Seven Treatises frequently reiterate the point that in the logical proof establishing that sound is impermanent [by reason of its being produced], "produced" must be concomitant both with pot, the similar example of the proof, and with [the subject] sound itself.

Effect is also specifically characterized, as explained in the words "It is stated that it is a cause and an effect [and is] asserted to be specifically characterized."[192] Effect is also a universal, as declared in the passage "It is due to its concomitance with the thesis [being proved] that the effect, a universal, is able to establish [that thesis]."[193]

We are informed that *general characterization* [on the other hand] denotes "something that cannot be realized by way of its own identity and whose character can only be understood in generic terms."[194] This indicates that a generally characterized thing must be conceptually constructed, and thus it is precluded from being an actual thing. The passage "because there are those capable of a function, and those that are not"[195] also affirms the point that a generally characterized thing is incapable of functioning. This is also [supported] by the section that includes the words "The others exist conventionally."[196] This tells us that a thing that serves as the illustration for specific characterization is one that exists in an ultimate sense, whereas the illustration for general characterization is one that exists in a conventional sense. [51] Thus, while universal, coarse entity, and continuum [themselves] are conceptual constructs and do not constitute substances, this fact does not rule out any of the things that *are* universals, coarse entities, or continua from being substantially existent and specifically characterized. Such things are not necessarily generally characterized. Pot, for instance, is one such thing that should be understood to be a universal, a coarse entity, a continuum, and specifically characterized but not generally characterized.

What reasons are there then for rejecting the belief of the non-Buddhist philosophies that the universal is an actual thing? As far as the Sāṃkhya are concerned, the very same primordial principle[197] that forms the nature of the blue is the one that forms the nature of yellow. They hold this primordial principle to be an eternal substance, and because of this, they find it necessary to maintain that the nature of the blue and of the yellow form an indivisible, unitary whole. This stance leaves them open to the same attacks that have been set out above—namely, that the production and the cessation of the blue and the yellow would therefore have to be simultaneous, and that there should be no distinction in the way blue and yellow appear to a correct, unmistaken cognition. These are the criticisms made in passages such as "[They must either be] distinct or their production and cessation must be simultaneous."[198] [Since they specifically target that incorrect position,] it would be quite wrong to interpret these lines as arguing that any universal and particular that are of the same substance would need to have simultaneous production and cessation.

The Vaiśeṣika espouse that the universal and its particulars are distinct substances. They claim that the universal that is concomitant with the mottled cow is the same one that is concomitant with the pale cow, but that this universal is still an indivisible, partless unit. If that were the case, then the universal pot and the first temporal portion of a pot must form a single, indivisible unit. It is against this position that [Dharmakīrti] launched the attack outlined above, saying that if this were correct, the pot that is produced only after that first temporal portion has ceased would be left without a universal. Those who do not interpret this as a consequence [based on the Vaiśeṣika's own view] need to consider just how they are going to account for the line "[Given that it also] exists later on and is something that has no parts,"[199] [which appears in the same section].

Similarly, "There is no effect that arises from this concomitance"[200] tells us that because universal—a thing that maintains a concomitant association with its various instances—is a conceptual construct, it does not give rise to any results. The passage does *not* indicate that simply being a universal is enough to disqualify something from giving rise to an effect.

Even when we do find certain non-Buddhist philosophers who are prepared to admit that coarse entities can constitute substances, the kind of substance that they have in mind is the whole—a coarse entity that possesses its component parts but is still a partless, indivisible unit. But they believe this whole is a substance that is identical with that of its components, which should mean that those components also form a single, indivisible unit. It is this position that [Dharmakīrti] attacks, arguing, for example, that any movement in one of the components would therefore have to involve movement in all of them. If these [non-Buddhist philosophers] were to accept [the alternative] that the whole possessing its components is a substance different from that of its components, then they would be attacked on the grounds that this would require a whole that stands aloof and separated from those components. [52] There are absolutely none of these non-Buddhist philosophers who advocate that the whole is the same substance as its components and that it is also something that has various parts.

According to our system, however, something such as the pot is a coarse entity as well as one that has parts. It is also a substance that is the same as that of the components constituting its parts. The aforesaid criticisms cannot be made of this position. A single day, for instance, is a continuum that constitutes a substance. As such, (1) the analysis as to whether when its earlier portion, the morning, finishes, [the day] itself must also come to an end, and (2) the argument that there is no way that such a thing could be momentary, are irrelevant. The day itself commences with its own early portion, and so the day exists [at that time] and is not yet at an end. The first day reaches its conclusion immediately prior to the start of the early portion of the second day. In the very next moment after this point, the first day will have passed. The fact that something does not last into a second stage beyond the time of its coming into existence is the very quintessence of what it is to be *momentary*. The example [of the day] provided here should serve to illustrate this principle for all those actual things that are continua.

Delineating general characterization

1. What defines general characterization
2. Identification of the illustration

What defines general characterization

[A generally characterized thing is] "a phenomenon that has no identity existing in any objective sense from its own side but is one constructed purely by thought."

Identification of the illustration

The illustration of [a generally characterized thing] is that object held by a conceptual cognition that merges location, time, and nature. To appreciate just what this means, it is necessary to understand (1) the manner in which an object appears to conceptual cognition and (2) just how conceptual cognition engages that object. Therefore, employing an example, I will elaborate on these.

Let us take the thought that judges the golden pot to be a pot. [53] Both the golden pot itself and the object overtly held by this conceptual cognition appear to it as pot. Thus [this conceptual cognition] does not differentiate between [two] appearances, that of (1) the golden pot appearing to be pot and (2) [the cognition's] overt, held object appearing to be pot. They seem to it to be fused together. It is precisely because the [first] appearance[201] and the construct[202] seem indistinguishable [to the cognition] that they are described as being "merged into one." The appearance [of the object] is the actual specifically characterized pot, whereas the construct is the *śabdārtha* of pot.[203]

To what exactly does the *śabdārtha* of pot refer? The golden pot appearing as a pot [to that conceptual cognition] counts as the *śabdārtha* in this case, as does what appears to [that cognition] seeming to be the complete reverse of a non-pot. To this conceptual cognition, the golden pot seems to be a pot as well as the opposite of a non-pot, but so does the thing that the conceptual cognition overtly holds [i.e., the thought construct]. These two appear to the conceptual cognition to be merged into one. But while undifferentiated in the way that the two present themselves to the conceptual cognition in question, this *does not* mean that the cognition actively conceives of them as being identical. [True,] this conceptual cognition can be described as "mistaken" with regard to what appears to it, in the sense that these two [together] seem to it to be real external entities and the complete reverse of non-pot when in fact they are not. [It is also true that] in engaging its object, this conceptual cognition latches on to[204] the appearance of the golden pot to be a pot as though it were an external entity when in reality it is not. Despite this, in terms of what it *conceives to be the case*, it judges golden pot to be a pot and does not think "The *śabdārtha* is a pot," or "The appearance of the golden pot is a pot." To that extent we can say that it is not in error with respect to its conceived object.

The essential point to be appreciated is that there are two dimensions to thought: the way that things *appear* to it and the way that it *conceives* them to be. Both the appearance that the golden pot is a pot and the [object] that the conceptual consciousness overtly holds present themselves [to that consciousness] as though they were external entities, whereas in point of fact, they are not. They also present themselves as if they were the complete reverse of non-pot when [again] they are not. It is in view of this that conceptual consciousness is said to be "mistaken" [i.e., in error] with respect to the object that appears to it. [Contrasting with this is] the way that it *conceives* things to be. It is the golden pot that the conceptual cognition judges to be a pot, and it is indeed the case that golden pot is a pot. And even though the appearance, which is not an external entity, presents itself as such to that cognition, the cognition does not think "The appearance is a pot" or "The appearance is the complete reverse of non-pot." Therefore it is not said to be "mistaken" with respect to its conceived object.

Some have asserted that the object-aspect of conceptual cognition appears to that cognition as though it were an external entity. [54]

[Response:] This is not tenable. It has been stated that the object-aspect of a conceptual cognition refers to the cognition itself. And it would be quite impossible for the conceptual cognition to appear to itself as though it were external. As this object-aspect is a conceptual cognition, this would also create an infinite regress, since each object-aspect would require another conceptual cognition to which it appeared as external, ad infinitum. The issue of why the object-aspect of a conceptual cognition should not be regarded as different from the conceptual cognition itself is one that I will deal with below. Equally implausible is someone else's suggestion that this object-aspect is the *śabdārtha*. The object-aspect constitutes a substance of the conscious variety, whereas the *śabdārtha* is necessarily a conceptual construct.

Another individual identifies the *śabdārtha* of pot as "the [quality of] being an external pot that we superimpose upon the reflected image[205] of the pot that appears to thought."

[Response:] This is also incorrect. If this so-called reflected image is supposed to mean the object-aspect, [the assertion must be wrong,] because [again] it is impossible for this object-aspect to appear as though it is something external. If, on the other hand, it is supposed to denote what appears as a pot to that conceptual cognition, then in what sense can it be said that we "superimpose an external pot" upon that? If what he intends by this phrase is that the cognition in question conceives [the appearance to be] an external pot, we reject the suggestion that the cognition superimposes in that manner. The conceptual cognition of pot does not judge what appears to it to be an external pot. If it did, it would be a false cognition, mistaken about the thing it conceived. To engage the external pot, it is necessary for conceptual cognition to latch on to what appears to it to be a pot, but it need not conceive of that appearance *as* an external pot.

If, alternatively, this individual used "superimpose" to refer to the way that the appearance is not [out there] in the external pot but presents itself as though it were, then what he would actually be asserting is that the conceptual cognition of pot superimposes *external pot* upon what appears to it. But this would lead to the absurd conclusion that every conceptual cognition mistaken about the object that appears to it must be considered a superimposing distortion.

What presents itself to conceptual cognition when the golden pot appears as a pot is the *śabdārtha*. In spite of this, not everything that presents itself to thought as if it is a pot has to be a *śabdārtha*. For instance, the golden pot is not a *śabdārtha*, but it *does* appear to conceptual cognition as a pot. The *śabdārtha* of pot cannot be counted as a universal of the various instances of pot, nor can those individual instances of pots be considered its particulars. This is because something being a pot precludes it from being a *śabdārtha*. But this does not disqualify something that *instantiates* the *śabdārtha* of pot from being the universal of the various individual pots, nor does it prevent those individuations from being the particulars of that instantiation. *That which presents itself to conceptual cognition as if it were a pot* is, for example, something that instantiates the *śabdārtha* of pot in addition to counting as a universal of pot's various individuations. It counts as the universal of those individuations on the grounds that it has a concomitant association with every one of them, and those individuations are also its particulars. [55] We may therefore say that there are two types of universals that have a concomitant association with the various individuations of pot: the actual, objectified variety and the nonmaterial, nonobjective variety. Pot is an actual, objectified universal that has a concomitant association with each individual pot. That which presents itself to conceptual cognition as if it were a pot, on the other hand, is a nonmaterial, nonobjective universal that has a concomitant association with each individual pot.[206]

Hence, as described above, the *held objects* of conceptual cognition are generally characterized. And being generally characterized does not preclude something from being a universal. So what presents itself to conceptual cognition when the golden pot appears to it to be a pot is the *śabdārtha* [of pot]. It is also necessary for conceptual cognition to latch on to this appearance in order for it to determine that the golden pot is a pot. However, the judgment [derived from this] that a specific golden pot is a pot is one rooted in objective reality. Conceptual cognition can therefore accurately reflect the way that things are. Despite this, not everything that presents itself to conceptual cognition is specifically characterized. These facts apply to every conceptual cognition that is not mistaken about its conceived object.

How is it then that a conceptual cognition can still help us to secure something that *is* specifically characterized? The perception of something that is specifically characterized is what acts as the cause, forming a propensity to conceive of the thing in question. Then, in dependence on this sort of propensity, one gets a conception of that thing. That conceptual cognition allows us to engage the specifically characterized thing and [eventually] secure it. This is the process that is revealed in passages such as "The various different things that [share the same] designation and meaning are the seed [for the concept of them]."[207]

Making a lengthy case, including the exploration of a number of related issues, someone argues that no specifically characterized thing can ever serve as an object of thought. He asks whether sound and its production, its impermanence, and so forth are supposed to form a single substance or separate ones. He rejects the first of these alternatives, saying that it would force one to the conclusion that when a conceptual cognition ascertains a specifically characterized sound, it must also ascertain its production and impermanence. He says that this would follow, because (1) [it is generally agreed that there is such] a conceptual cognition that ascertains specifically characterized sound and because (2) sound, together with its production and impermanence, form a single substance. He believes that this is the argument advanced in the passage "If inferential cognition also apprehended an actual thing, then when it ascertained one [of that thing's] features, it would have to apprehend every one of them."[208] He also dismisses the second alternative [that sound, its production, and so forth each constitute separate substances] on the grounds that there is no unmistaken cognition to verify [that they exist in this way]. Returning again to the first alternative [of them comprising a single substance], he says that it would also lead to the ridiculous conclusions that when a conceptual cognition analyzing sound verified one of its features, it would have to verify every one of them, and that if it negated one of its features, it would be negating all of them. [56] This again would follow, he says, because as stated before (1) [it is generally agreed that there is such] a conceptual cognition that ascertains specifically characterized sound and because (2) sound, together with its production and impermanence, form a single substance. He suggests that this is the point made in the passage "If that were not so, the [features] of the entities . . . ."[209] This is the reasoning that leads him to conclude that no specifically characterized thing can ever serve as the overt basis for any sort of negation or affirmation.

Someone else raises an objection to his position [that specifically characterized things cannot act as objects of thought]. He cites the passage "How can something be cognition if it provides no knowledge of a specifically characterized thing?"[210] and claims that it stipulates that a valid cognition must realize something that is specifically characterized. However, the [first individual] denies that the point made by the passage is that every cognition has to realize something that is specifically characterized itself and asserts that it only says that it must *give rise to* knowledge of that type of phenomenon.

[Response:] The [first individual's] analysis is laden with arguments that are unsustainable, illogical, and [in some cases] self-defeating. Let me explain. [Based on his logic,] it follows that a valid [perception] comprehending a specifically characterized sound would also realize the production and impermanence of that sound. Why? Because (1) [it is generally agreed that there is] a valid cognition that comprehends that sound and because (2) that sound, together with its production and impermanence, comprise a single substance. So how might this individual respond to such a line of reasoning? He could accept the argument. But if he does that, why would he not also accept that a conceptual cognition ascertaining sound also ascertains its production and impermanence? He may object to this position, saying that it leads to the unwanted conclusion that [once sound has been ascertained], there could be no role left for subsequent cognitions ascertaining that sound is a product, sound is impermanent, and so forth, rendering such cognitions redundant. We would point out that by the same token, one must conclude that [once sound has been perceived], there could be no role left for subsequent valid cognitions comprehending that sound is a product, sound is impermanent, and so forth, and they would also therefore become redundant.

In any case, the pervasion [underlying his response] is wrong. If it was correct, the conclusion to be drawn, paralleling his own, would be that because the first temporal portion of the conceptual cognition of sound ascertains that sound, all later temporal portions of that conceptual cognition must be considered redundant. This individual might reject the suggestion that there is any parallel between the two [situations]. He may acknowledge that when the valid [perception] in question realizes sound, that sound [and its features of] production, impermanence, and so forth [all] comprise a single substance, but despite this, he may say, one realizes only those [features of sound] for which the prerequisite conditions for realization—such as familiarity and clarity—are in place, not those for which they are absent. We would point out that the situation is similar with conceptual cognition, in that when a conceptual cognition ascertains sound, it can only ascertain those of sound's features of production, impermanence, and the like for which the conditions of ascertainment are in place, not those for which such conditions are absent. Addressing next the later consequences [he presented], we can again set forth an argument that parallels his own. Namely, it would follow, based upon his logic, that any valid [perception] that comprehends sound, in verifying any one of its features, must verify all of them, because (1) [it is generally agreed that] there is a valid [perception] comprehending that sound exists and because (2) sound, together with its features such as production, constitute a single substance. [57] Likewise, according to his logic, he must also agree that the inferential valid cognition that gives rise to knowledge of that specifically characterized sound also gives rise to knowledge of its production, impermanence, and so forth because (1) there is an inferential valid cognition that gives rise to knowledge of sound and because (2) sound, together with its production and impermanence, constitute a single substance. The three spheres [are in place].

Furthermore, he has already asserted that perception can only comprehend specifically characterized things, but now he is trying to claim that every one of these valid perceptions needs to induce [a conceptual] ascertainment of the thing it comprehends. At the same time, he is saying that it is impossible for conceptual cognition to ascertain a thing if it is specifically characterized. This is just a mass of contradictions!

His thesis that a specifically characterized thing cannot serve as the basis for any sort of negation or affirmation is also [undermined by his own argument], because the very basis that he has used to argue against such negation and affirmation is a *specifically characterized thing*. This is a line of reasoning—to which he has no response. [What is more,] this is [exactly] the line of reasoning that is presented in the passage "As to your rejection of it, how can you derive a rejection from something that does not exist?"[211] This rebuts the notion that a specifically characterized thing cannot be used as the basis for affirmation and negation. But [even the more particular position—that there can be no affirmation or negation when a specifically characterized thing is serving as the *overt* basis—is also untenable, because if one can neither overtly affirm nor negate anything about a specifically characterized thing, then neither can valid cognition have any overt knowledge of such a thing. This must follow, because the way a valid cognition operates is by affirming the thing it comprehends while negating its inverse. If it did not operate in this way, it would mean that valid perception and inference [could not be relied on] to rule out [mistaken notions] such as that sound is not a thing heard, or that a pot is permanent.

Furthermore, if [as he proposes] conceptual cognition is incapable of realizing an actual thing, it would follow either that [what purports to be] the valid inference realizing sound to be impermanent does not in fact realize that sound is impermanent [at all], or that the sound and the impermanence [that it realizes] are not actual things. But if the valid inferential cognition that realizes that sound is impermanent does not actually realize it, then what does it comprehend? It certainly could not comprehend the *śabdārtha* of sound being impermanent, since it is a false cognition with respect to that.[212] And as there is no other [reasonable] choice [for this inferential cognition's object] apart from those two [i.e., sound being impermanent and the *śabdārtha* of sound being impermanent], it would ridiculously follow that this inferential cognition is not a valid cognition!

The [other option] would be to suggest that sound and impermanence are not actual things. But from that it would follow that they are non-actual things, and sound and its impermanence must therefore be permanent. If he concedes this, it would mean that when one uses the reason that sound is produced to prove that it is impermanent, the reasoning [is flawed], because the property of the subject is one that cannot be established and the pervasion is completely contrary to what is actually required. A great deal more could be said on this, but to keep my treatment of the topic concise, I will elaborate no further here. [58]

This still leaves the question of how to understand the words "If inferential cognition also apprehended an actual thing. . . ."[213] The point that this passage makes is that *if* inferential cognition were a comprehensive engager, then the inferential cognition that ascertained sound would also need to ascertain all of the features of that sound. The passage is definitely *not* saying that an inferential cognition cannot have an affirmative thing as its object, on the grounds that if it did, it would have to be a comprehensive engager. A cognition does not become a comprehensive engager simply by virtue of having an affirmative thing as an object. If it did, we would similarly have to conclude that a cognition that has something negative as an object would necessarily be an excluding engager. This is obviously unacceptable, as it would mean that the perception that apprehended a spot where pot is absent must also be an excluding engager, since it has an object that is an exclusion. That is obviously the case for the perception in question, as the *absence* of pots in that spot is [one of] its objects.

[This individual's interpretation of] passages such as "If that were not so, the [features] of the entities . . ."[214] [is also incorrect]. These words do not refute the idea that something specifically characterized can serve as the basis for any negation or affirmation. They only refute that the thing's identity *as* such a basis is established in any ultimate sense. Sound, for instance, can be used as the basis for negation and affirmation. But if sound's identity as this basis was established in an ultimate sense, then all of the negation and affirmation undertaken in relation to sound, [despite the fact that it only occurs] in the domain of thought, would also have to be established in an ultimate sense, and as such, the conceptual cognition [engaged in this negation and affirmation] would have to be an unmistaken one. And if the cognition was an unmistaken one, it would necessarily be a comprehensive engager. If conceptual cognition were a comprehensive engager, it would mean that when it confirmed any one of sound's features, it would necessarily confirm them all. That [is what the passage in question] says.

Furthermore, when the subject and its property, the thesis and reason, and so forth are described as being "conceptual constructs," it is negating them being established ultimately. This is not to deny that "sound," for instance, is the proof's subject of interest, that "impermanence" is the property of the probandum, and that "produced" is the reason but only that they are established as such in an ultimate sense. The logic behind this is as follows. If sound were the subject—and so on for the others—in an ultimate sense, then the [order in which someone proceeds when establishing the proof]—first establishing sound, after that establishing that the sound is produced, and after that establishing that sound is impermanent—would need to be established ultimately. Since [this order would therefore need to reflect something existing in reality, it must actually be the case that] first the subject of interest was established [i.e., existed], after which the property of the subject would be established, only after which the property of the probandum would be established in the subject of interest. If one accepted that, it would follow that the cause of sound did not generate [sound's qualities of being] produced and impermanent. [59] What one must therefore assert is that sound, impermanence, and production are *themselves* ultimately established. And while they count, respectively, as the subject of interest, the property of the probandum, and the reason, it is only in a conventional sense that they have the identities of the subject of interest and so forth, and not in an ultimate sense. It is with this point in mind that [Dharmakīrti] says:

> Classifications [such as that] of property and subject, or different and non-different, have no regard for how things are ultimately. Just like such matters are accepted in the world, all the

classificatory schemes of the *probandum* and *probans* have been created by the wise solely to provide access to the ultimate.[215]

Broadly speaking, everything mentioned in the teachings of the Conqueror is said to be either one or the other of the two truths. Those that are true in a conventional sense were taught solely to help us gain realization of what is ultimately true. More precisely, the schemes according to which things are classified as either the subject or property [of that subject], or as the probandum and probans are [truths] of the conventional variety. It is these that serve as the foundation for determining the actual state of things, the means by which one can realize the ultimate, and it is these that the words "solely to provide access to the ultimate"[216] refer to in the above passage.

Sound is the subject [of the logical proof], but this does not mean that sound is a conventional existent. On the other hand, the [identity of the] subject that is assigned [to sound] *is* that sort of [conventional] construct. A good deal of skill is therefore required when negotiating the distinctions between the identity itself and the thing that has that identity. Those who believe that reality is not something that can be arrived at through thought and conceptual schemes involving negation and affirmation may never have engaged in personal dialogue with the Chinese teacher Heshang, but they are still in alliance with him and his view that entertaining any type of thought at all is a nonvirtuous activity. As such, they are butchers, slaughtering the very life of the path to liberation.

Having understood why true establishment is rejected for such things as the subject and its property, one can extend this knowledge to the universal and common locus. Again, what this means is that the universal and the common locus *themselves* are not established in any true sense. It does not mean that those things [bound together] by them lack true establishment, because, just as I have explained above, actual thing is a universal, and the *utpala* can be the common locus of [*utpala* and] a thing that is blue. [60]

The refutation of true establishment with respect to the universal takes two forms. Non-Buddhist philosophies imagine the universal to be some sort of primordial nature. We deny that this type of universal is true either in the ultimate sense or on the conventional level. The kind of universal of our own system, on the other hand, is something for which we refute true establishment but do not deny the existence of on the conventional level. The reasoning refuting true existence of the universal runs as follows. If the universal existed in any true sense, the conceptual cognition [responsible for] apprehending it would need to be *unmistaken*. Things would therefore have to exist in exactly the way that it holds them to exist. But this consciousness is one that merges various things together [as though they had a single] nature. This should mean that the various instances of a thing are [also in reality] merged together as part of a single nature, such that every one of them was concomitant with all of the others. But this is simply not credible. That is why it is said that the universal does not, in any true sense, exist in the way that a conceptual consciousness thinks it does. This is the point made in the passage:

> The way that it envisions them
> is not the way that they ultimately are:
> The individual instances are not concomitant.[217]

Others have come up with alternative ways of interpreting this passage. Some [use it to argue against the view that] the universal and its individual instances constitute a single substance, claiming that what the passage states is that if they did, each individual instance would have to constitute the substance of every other. Someone else interprets it as a refutation of the non-Buddhist notion of an indivisible, unitary universal. In this they are both so far away from the master [Dharmakīrti's] actual intention that it is as if they were separated from it by a great ocean. What is more, those belonging to the latter group would have to interpret "it" in the line "the way that it envisions them" as referring to "the [non-Buddhist]." Such a reading would oblige them to understand the [immediately preceding] line "due to thinking about them"[218] as meaning "It is due to the non-Buddhist thinking about them." This just goes to show what a ridiculously ill-considered interpretation this is.

The common locus is judged not to be established in an ultimate sense on the following grounds. There is a common locus of an *utpala* and something blue. But if their common identity had any ultimate reality, then similarly, their identity as distinct things would also have to be something that was established in true fact, since it makes no sense to talk of commonality when there is only one thing. However, if the distinctness of the *utpala* and the blue thing was a true fact, the two would have to constitute substances that are totally separate from each other—things that could not be embodied in a single locus. The vital point to be appreciated is our affirmation that there is a common locus instantiating an *utpala* and a blue thing, and also that *utpala* and blue are substances. But being the common locus of the two does not constitute any sort of real substance—it is merely something assigned to them by a consciousness dealing in conventional ideas. This is what is referred to in lines such as "At that point it is from the side of the mind that the commonality [of the objects] exists."[219] [61]

There are those who refuse to accept that any such conceptual construct can be substantiated by valid cognition. In this, however, they are denying the establishment of anything that is true in the conventional sense. As such, they clearly stray toward the philosophy of the nihilists.

Someone rejects the view that something specifically characterized can act as the *referent for labeling*.[220] He says that this is what is meant by the passage:

> Through verbalization, a name is assigned to a thing,
> such that it [becomes a] convention.
> [But] by that [latter] stage, that specifically characterized [thing]
> no longer exists.
> So the name is not its own.[221]

In his judgment, there would be no point having something specifically characterized as the *referent for labeling*, because the thing that is present when the name is initially given cannot maintain a concomitant association with the specifically characterized things to which the term will apply once it has gained acceptance, whereas the whole purpose of assigning a name should obviously be so that it can facilitate [this later] accepted usage.[222] He [backs this assertion] by drawing attention to the fact that the individual instances of specifically characterized things are countless, which makes the idea of assigning a name to each of them impractical. He says that this is what is meant by the lines "because assigning each of them individually would be a troublesome, unachievable, and futile endeavor."[223] He concludes therefore that according to our own [Buddhist] system, the thing to which the name is initially assigned is the *śabdārtha*.

[Response:] According to that, it must follow that assigning a name to the *śabdārtha* would be an equally pointless exercise, because the *śabdārtha* involved in the initial process of labeling is one that would have no concomitant association *either* with the referent for labeling at the [later] stage when the term has passed into use or with any of the specifically characterized things [it is supposed to denote]. The reasoning we use here parallels exactly that of his own argument. Furthermore, based on his own reasoning, it follows that the initial act of labeling cannot be directed toward the *śabdārtha*, because their number is countless, since they must be exactly equal in amount to that of the individual instances of a thing. This argument is one for which he has no response.

Let us look at what one labels[224] during the initial naming process. When the name "cow" is initially given, one uses a particular specifically characterized thing, such as a light[-colored] cow, as the basis for the application.[225] It is thanks to this initial labeling that during the stage when the term has passed into accepted usage, one understands that the dark cow and others are also cows. This [subsequent recognition] can only occur because when one initially applied the cow label to the light cow, it was on the grounds that it had the [characteristic] hump and other [distinctive features], and because these are the same [type of features that one later sees] in the dark cow and others. The light cow is said to have served as the basis for the initial application of the name because the labeling process must be something that helps one to understand, both during the process itself and later, when the term has passed into accepted usage, that any creature possessing the hump and other requisite features is a cow. By the same token, what serves as the basis for the labeling is *not* some sort of composite of the "light[-colored] creature" and "cow." The process is not one [aimed] to help one, at the later stage of accepted usage, to be able to identify a dark cow or any other one as a composite of the light-colored creature and cow. [62]

Thus, when one engages in the initial process of labeling "cow," using the light cow as one's basis, the principal referent for labeling is both cow and the other-exclusion that is the complete reverse of non-cow.[226] The *śabdārtha*, which is the light cow's appearing [to the conceptual cognition] to be the complete reverse of a non-cow, also counts, in a minimal sense, as a referent for labeling. Since a [real] cow serves as a referent for labeling here, the assertion that this referent cannot be an actual thing is obviously not tenable. Despite the fact that the cow is the referent for labeling, this is not an identity that it has in any ultimate sense. So what the passage "Through verbalization a name is assigned to a thing . . ."[227] negates is that a specifically characterized thing can be the referent for labeling in an ultimate sense. The reason that the term "cow" is not one that can be assigned to the light cow in any ultimate sense is that the light cow is not the thing that has a concomitant association with the dark cow and others at the later stage, when the term has passed into accepted usage. This must be the case, because if the light cow's identity as the referent for labeling was one that it had in an ultimate sense, then the conceptual consciousness assigning the term "cow" to the light cow [would need to be correct, and] things would have to exist in exactly the way that it holds them to exist. But as the conceptual consciousness in question fails to differentiate between cow and the light-colored cow, this would logically entail the two of them being identical. And if cow really were identical with the light-colored cow, then it would be necessary to accept either that it was not concomitant with the dark cow or that the light-colored cow was concomitant with the dark one.

The point that [again] needs to be understood is that subject, subject property, universal, common locus, probandum, probans, referent for labeling, and so on, as individual isolates,[228] are *all themselves* conceptual constructs, and as such, they must be generally characterized. But when it comes to the instantiation isolates [i.e., the things that instantiate those identities], they neither have to be conceptual constructs nor have to be generally characterized. This concludes the detailed explanation of what defines general characterization.

Next, we turn to several ancillary topics that have special significance with regard to the discussion on specific and general characterization. First, we have the passage:

> Because every actual thing maintains an identity by way of possessing its own individual character
> each one of them is thereby differentiated,
> [both] from those things that are similar to it, and others [that are not].[229]

This describes how each specifically characterized thing retains its own determinate identity, which is not merged with that of any other phenomenon—whether that phenomenon is a similar type of thing to it, or a type that is dissimilar to it. [This also applies to] conceptually constructed phenomena, some of which can be classified as either the same type or different type of thing. [63]

What then does it mean [to say that two things] are either the same type or different ones, or that they are similar types or dissimilar ones? Things may be described as "types that are alike or not alike," "types that are similar or dissimilar," and "types that are the same or different."[230] The three notions of *likeness*, *sameness*, and *similarity* of types can be described from two [perspectives: those of] substance types and those of isolated type identities. Things that are a *similar substance type* and so forth are classified as such because they were produced from the same "substantial cause."[231] So if there are various different actual things that have all arisen from a *single* substantial cause, they are said to be "similar," the "same," or "alike" in their type. Several separate seeds of barley grown on the same stalk produced by a single barley grain, for instance, are described as [things] that are a "similar substantial type."[232] This is because they are (1) all derived from the same substantial cause and (2) are separate things.

Conversely, the light-colored cow and dark cow, while both equally cows, are derived from different substantial causes and are thus described as [things that are a] "dissimilar substance type." Śākyabuddhi offers a particularly clear articulation of this point:

> Thus [the distinction according to which] all external and internal things are classified as those that are distinct or nondistinct [from one another] is determined by their substantial causes. Without these substantial causes, the production of things would never even occur.[233]

And:

> So the classification of different continua [as being either] similar or dissimilar types is determined by [their] substantial causes.[234]

Once this point has been understood, one will be in a position to correctly judge what was intended by the words "[Their] diversity is derived from the diversity of their causes."[235]

On the other hand, to say that things are the same isolated *type*[236] means the following. In the philosophies of those outside [the Buddhist tradition] such as the Sāṃkhya, things like sandalwood, *śiṃśapā*,[237] and cow are each counted as separate substances. These [philosophies] say that thought and language deal with sandalwood and *śiṃśapā* as the same type of thing but sandalwood and cow as different ones. This is because, they say, the sandalwood and *śiṃśapā* share a primordial universal *tree-ness*, but the sandalwood and cow do not. The master [Dharmakīrti] rejects this position, instead asserting that the association that exists between sandalwood and *agaru*—from which cow is excluded—is that they are of a similar type, derived from the exclusion of things other than tree. It was with this point in mind that he declared: [64]

> Separate [things] that are alike are the [same] type.
> It is due to their close [resemblance] that [a consciousness] engages them while not [engaging] others.
> And this [closeness] is the grounds for language and thoughts [judging them to be the same type].[238]

The light-colored cow and the dark cow are classed as the same type of thing. Why this is the case essentially stems from the fact that there is a cow-universal that maintains a concomitant association with both of them equally. Still, one cannot give "because there is a universal for cow that maintains a concomitant association with both of them" as the reason for asserting that they are the same type. By that logic, it could equally be argued that permanence and impermanence must be the same type of thing, because there is a universal that maintains a concomitant association with both of them—namely, known thing. What is more, since known thing is a universal that has a concomitant association with every phenomenon, one would be forced to the conclusion that all things are the same type—which would undermine any possibility of different types of things existing.

Moreover, to establish that the light-colored cow and the golden pot are not the same type of thing, one cannot use [the reason] "because the light-colored cow is a cow, whereas the golden pot is not." Someone [could simply counter this, making a] similar case for the light-colored cow and the dark cow not being the same type of thing, because the second cow is dark whereas the first is not. Thus, based on that logic, one would eventually be obliged to agree with the conclusion that just about every known thing must be a different type of thing from almost every other.

One should also be aware of the fact that there are two ways in which things can be the same type. There is the way that various affirmative, objectively real things, such as pots, can be the same type of thing and the way that negative phenomena, such as absences of pots, can be the same type. With the first of these, [the judgment that] two phenomena are the same type of thing [is based on] their sharing a resemblance. If a simple glance at the two gives rise to a spontaneous sense that the two are *alike* in anyone paying sufficient attention—irrespective of whether that person has acquired language—they are said to be the same type of thing. Things that are the opposite of this are said not to be the same type. Anyone paying sufficient attention, who catches sight of a light cow and a dark cow, for instance—without any sort of deliberation and irrespective of whether that individual has acquired language—will have the sense that they resemble each other, but they will not have the same sense when encountering a light[-colored] cow and a pot. Hence the light cow and dark cow are described as the same type of thing, whereas the light cow and the pot are different types of thing.

There are two separate conditions that make things appear to us as either alike or unalike. On the *internal* level, the habit of considering the light and dark cows as the same type of thing is something that we have always had, since time without beginning, and stems from the *predisposition for linguistic formulation*.[239] No such habit exists, however, when it comes to the light cow and the pot. On the *external* level, the correspondence between the light cow and the dark cow is found in the fact that they share the various characteristic features, such as the [cow] hump—features that the light-colored cow and the pot do not share. [65]

The criticism that since [diverse objects] are alike in being actual things, they must all be of the same type cannot be leveled at the position [I have just laid out]. A light cow and a human may well both be actual things, but our experience tells us that we do not get the sense that they are the same type of thing. The light cow and the dark cow, on the other hand, which share various characteristic features such as the [cow] hump, do evoke a sense that they are the same type of thing, spontaneously and without any deliberation, in everyone from a child to a scholar.

As far as non-actual, negative phenomena are concerned, their type is determined on the basis of whether or not their neganda are the same type. The only way to distinguish negative phenomena is by way of these negated elements, as they do not have their own individual identities by means of which they can be differentiated.

Once one has understood these matters, nothing about the categorizations of alike or unalike will prove perplexing. In this snowy mountain land [Tibet], only I, the world's glory,[240] can claim to have elucidated them. This concludes the detailed discussion on specific and general characterization.

5. The Two Truths

Division of objects by way of their identities

Next is the description of how objects are classified as being those that are true in either the conventional or the ultimate sense.

1. Etymological description of the two truths
2. Defining characteristics
3. Identification of their respective illustrations

Etymological description of the two truths

[Regarding the first, Dharmakīrti states]:

> It conceals the nature of other [things], in that even though those [things] have different natures, the concealer of that [fact] . . . .[241]

In the earlier translation,[242] "concealer" was rendered "misleader."[243] The vast majority of those following the various Buddhist philosophical schools agree that *concealer* refers to the concealment of things, [such that one is prevented from] seeing them as they actually are. The term's etymology is built on the notion that it is the conceptual consciousness dealing with universals that misleads. It does this by standing in the way of our directly engaging with the specific characteristics that are the real nature of actual things. Therefore the conceptual consciousness dealing with universals is the basis for the designation *conventional*. And since the things that are "true" for that consciousness—the etymology's basis—are generally characterized ones, they are denoted "conventionally true." [66] While conceptual consciousness may serve as the basis for the designation, since it is said to mislead, it does not itself genuinely count as one of these "misleading things." This is because it is a consciousness, and as such, it must be something established in an ultimate sense. *Conventional truth* is not supposed to convey a thing that is both misleading and true. If it did, one would have to advocate that there are things that are false but true, and this is a contradictory position.

Regarding the etymological description of the term *ultimately true*, at least some of those from the śrāvaka-based Buddhist tenet systems hold that the term refers to something "true" in the sense that it can withstand logical analysis. Those Sautrāntikas who are followers of the logic presented in [Dharmakīrti's] Seven Treatises concur with the Cittamātra school on this matter. For them, the "ultimate" referred to in the term, and the one that the term is built on, is *unmistaken* cognition. Entities that are true from the perspective of that consciousness are said to be "ultimately true." And since such entities are the *held objects* of such a consciousness, they are also said to be "established ultimately." But while the Sautrāntika and Cittamātra agree that a cognition with an ultimate entity as its overt object is an unmistaken consciousness, they differ on what counts as an illustration of unmistaken cognition. For the Cittamātra, *all* perceptions that are other-cognitions are mistaken cognitions, whereas for the Sautrāntika, these are unmistaken.

Defining characteristics

Something ultimately true is defined as "a phenomenon that is not merely constructed by thought but is established from its own side." Something that is conventionally true is defined as "a phenomenon that is constructed entirely by thought."

Someone claims that the passage including the words "Whatever is capable of performing a function ultimately: that here is what exists ultimately"[244] sets out the characteristics defining what it is to be ultimately true and also the characteristics defining what it is to be specifically characterized.

[Response:] This individual has obviously not even bothered to look properly at the text in question. The stanza [ends with the words] "Those two are called the specifically and the generally characterized," not "Those are said to be the defining characteristics of the specifically and generally characterized." In any case, the choice of the words such as "whatever" and "that" in the passage, in addition to the context in which they appear, tell us that what the above lines are really meant to communicate is the pervasion between (1) things that are able to perform a function from the ultimate perspective and (2) those that exist ultimately. So what is the context for this passage? It appears in the section verifying that the reason "as there are two objects of comprehension" [is a correct one for establishing that there are two types of valid cognition]. [67] And it is in this regard that it is also necessary to establish the pervasion [underlying the statement] "because there are those capable of performing a function and those that are not."[245]

The meaning of the stanza "Whatever is capable of performing a function ultimately . . ."[246] can be summed up as follows. The definitive twofold division of objects of comprehension into those that can and cannot perform functions corresponds exactly to the twofold division of objects of comprehension into those that are specifically characterized and those that are generally characterized. This is because those that are able to perform a function in the ultimate sense are necessarily ultimately existent; such ultimate existents are described as "specifically characterized." Those that, from the same perspective, have no capacity to function are necessarily existent in a conventional sense; such things are described as "generally characterized."

This matter is one that Devendrabuddhi and Śākyabuddhi agree about. In his explanation of the context and place of this passage, Yamāri states, "In a marginal sense, this [passage can also be said] to reveal the two types of truth according to the inferior vehicle." The Sautrāntika school belongs to the Hinayana, which in comparison to the Mahayana is "inferior." Thus he apparently believes that the version of the two truths described in the passage is that of the Sautrāntika. But this is not tenable. If the notion of the two truths to which he refers is one that the Sautrāntika school shares with the Cittamātra, it would hardly be right to describe it as belonging to "the inferior vehicle." The alternative would be to understand the version of the two truths presented in the passage as that of the Sautrāntika alone. However, it would mean that there must be those of the Cittamātra school who do not believe that what ultimately performs a function is necessarily ultimately existent. But the idea that any follower of the Vijñaptika system in the land of āryas [India] espoused such a view is unheard of! Therefore this passage must be read as one that both followers of the Sautrāntika and the Cittamātra accept, although they still disagree about what counts as the illustration of those that function ultimately.

Identification of their respective illustrations

1. Refuting others' assertions
2. Setting out our own position

Refuting others' assertions

According to one individual, the above statement—affirming that things that are able to perform functions are ultimate truths—is not made from the perspective of "ultimate indivisibles."[247] Rather, he says, it speaks from the point of view that "correct conventional phenomena"[248] constitute the ultimate truths. However, in actuality, he says, temporally indivisible units of consciousness and directionally indivisible physical particles are the only things that are true in an ultimate sense. He argues that if being able to perform a function were alone enough to qualify something as an ultimate reality, it would follow that such things as pot must be considered ultimately true. He proposes that the version of the two truths presented in the passage is not the correct one but is that of the Sautrāntika school, and their understanding corresponds with the *Treasury of the Abhidharma* where it states: [68]

> A conventionally existent thing is one that the mind can no longer engage
> once that [thing] has been physically destroyed or mentally dismantled.
> [These are things] such as pots and water.
> Those that exist in the other way are ultimately existent.[249]

According to this explanation, the likes of pot and water are known to be "misleading" in that they are things that, upon disassembly, lose their recognizable identity.

[Response:] This position is not viable. For one thing, it would absurdly follow that a thing does not need to be specifically characterized to qualify as ultimately existent. This is because there are certain phenomena that retain their recognizable identity despite disassembly but are not specifically characterized. If the individual were to accept this conclusion, it would directly contradict both the passage and his own stated position. Nor can he challenge the reason [that there are such phenomena], since even after disassembly, a permanent thing still manages to retain a recognizable identity. He could try to deny this by claiming that if we mentally dismantle a permanent thing, we destroy its recognizable identity. But we reject this. It makes no sense for him to differentiate between permanent phenomena and indivisible physical particles, saying that the recognizable identity of one can survive disassembly while the other cannot. [They are equal in that] (1) neither has component parts constituting any sort of substance [that might be dismantled], and (2) any parts that they have are simply [conceptually] isolable portions[250] of their identity. Both [permanent phenomena and indivisible physical particles] must have various such isolable portions, because for as many things that [such phenomena and particles] are not, there exist an equal number of isolable portions that are the reverse of these, that [such phenomena and particles] are.[251] Furthermore, although the passage cited from the *Treasury of the Abhidharma* and the one [from the *Commentary on Pramāṇa*] under discussion both present accounts of the two truths that are [accepted by those following] the Sautrāntika system, in the final analysis, they do not represent the same position. The view set out in the *Treasury of the Abhidharma* is that of Sautrāntikas who maintain that the only things constituting substances are indivisible ones. For them, colors can be substances, because they believe that there is such a thing as "color-substance"[252] even on the level of particles. Shape, on the other hand, does not constitute a substance, as there is no such thing as a shape-substance to be found on the level of particles. In line with this view, [the *Treasury of the Abhidharma*] says, "[Shape] would be apprehended both [by visual and physical consciousness, and thus, it] does not exist as particles."[253]

Conversely, here [in the Pramāṇa system], it would be wrong to suggest that shape does not constitute a substance, since we find various passages such as the one including the words "How is it then that shape and so forth [constitute things that] are really established?"[254] This tells us that shapes are effects, and thus they necessarily constitute substances, as even you [the opponent] would acknowledge. As "those" Sautrāntika [following the *Treasury of the Abhidharma*] and "these" Sautrāntika [following the *Commentary on Pramāṇa*] have systems that differ, one should take care not to conflate them. [69]

Someone may then argue that since "these" Sautrāntika and "those" Sautrāntika have differing notions of what is ultimate, there must also be a difference between the ways of delineating what it means to be ultimately true as asserted by the brothers [Asaṅga and Vasubandhu] and [the *Commentary on Pramāṇa*].[255]

[Response:] The two Sautrāntika systems differ on the issue of whether certain [gross] physical material things constitute substances, in that they disagree on whether a shape constitutes a substance. [Based on our opponent's logic,] it would therefore follow that the two Cittamātra systems must also disagree on whether certain cognitions constitute substances.

What is more, it must follow that the visual form of a pot is *false*, since it is conventional. He cannot challenge this reason as that would go against his claim that the visual form of pot is a correct conventional [phenomenon].

But if he were to accept the argument's conclusion, it would follow that the visual form of the pot is a conceptual construct. And that would mean that it is impossible for it to be an object apprehended by perception.

We also note that the term "ultimate indivisibles" [that our opponent uses] is one not found in any scriptural or commentarial tradition. Nor is it accepted by any of the erstwhile scholars. It seems instead to have only ever been employed by the ignorant as a way of advertising their own foolishness.

Someone else advocates that the classification of phenomena—according to which those that are able to perform functions are ultimate and those that lack the capacity to function are conventional—is made purely from the perspective of valid cognitions operating solely within the conventional sphere.[256] As such, he says, the classification [concerns itself only with] categorizing correct conventional and impaired conventional [phenomena][257] respectively as the "two truths." He suggests that from the standpoint of valid cognition dealing with the *final* [state of things], the only entities that prove to be true in an ultimate sense are temporally indivisible portions. He says that all phenomena other than these are only true in a misleading sense. He holds that since all [of the elements] within an action, such as the object and the actor,[258] are explained as being conceptual constructs, and since all elements, such as the produced and the producer, are subsumed within that scheme, produced, producer, cause, effect, and every other such thing do not exist ultimately.

[Response:] According to his reckoning, it follows that selflessness is an impaired conventional phenomenon, because it lacks any capacity to function. The pervasion that this argument is based on is exactly the one he proposes. The reason [that selflessness does not function] is confirmed by valid cognition. He is therefore obliged to accept the conclusion. But if selflessness is an impaired conventional phenomenon, it follows that any cognition with selflessness as its apprehended object would be a false cognition. It therefore absurdly follows that *any* awareness cognizing selflessness is necessarily false. This argument entirely destroys the positions of both the present and the previous opponents.

It would also follow that the straightforward exclusion[259] of the subject and object truly existing as two separate realities is an impaired conventional thing, because it is a phenomenon that has no capacity to function. [70] But if he accepts this, he would have no response to the argument that this exclusion therefore cannot count as a perfect, immutable nature.[260]

What is more, based on his stance, it would follow that ultimately, there is no such thing as comprehended and comprehender, because ultimately, none of the elements in an action exist. The argument's pervasion and reason are the ones that he himself proposed. But if he accepts [its conclusion], using the same line of reasoning, it would also follow that ultimately, there is no such thing as valid cognition. This would be entirely at odds with his own asserted position. Was it not he [the opponent], after all, who was so vociferous in declaring that a valid cognition is defined as "a cognition that is fresh and entirely nondeceptive with regard to what it comprehends"?

If he is prepared to grant that [ultimately] there is no such thing as valid cognition, it would follow that ultimately, neither can his temporally indivisible portions of things exist, because if they did so in any ultimate sense, valid cognition should be able to observe them, whereas [according to his reckoning] it does not. If he accepts this [conclusion that these temporally indivisible portions cannot be cognized ultimately], it would go against his assertion that they are ultimately true. On the other hand, if he denies the pervasion [that if they existed in the ultimate sense, valid cognition should be able to observe them, and its failure to do so must mean that they do not exist], he would be calling into question [the foundation of the] category of logical reasons known as "nonobservation of what should be apparent." Of the two parts of the reason itself, he cannot deny the first, since that would undermine his view that there is such a thing as valid cognition that has access to the final [state of things]. Nor can he deny the second part [that indivisible things are not observed ultimately], as that would go against his position that valid cognition itself cannot verify temporally indivisible portions in the ultimate sense.

Aside from this, if he is proposing that things established ultimately are not causes, then it would also follow that they lack any capacity to function. But this would overtly clash with his assertion that lacking the capacity to function is the very characteristic that defines something as a non-actual thing. How, in any case, can he escape the charge that what he is trying to claim about these ultimately established objects is that they are permanent? He might reject the suggestion that they could be permanent, citing the fact that it would [lead to the unacceptable conclusion] that they are not subject to disintegration. But since he is proposing that these indivisible entities are not effects, it would mean that they were not produced. He might agree to this, but in accepting that these entities are not produced, he is thereby [again] effectively admitting that they are not subject to any sort of disintegration. He may argue that because the possibility of the purely abstracted actual thing not disintegrating has been ruled out, it must also have been ruled out for these "true things" that are its particulars.[261] Since I am fully conversant with reasoning, I could oppose him in kind for eons. Thus I say that because he has ruled out the possibility that actual thing in its purely abstracted form is something not produced, he must also have ruled this out for the "true things" that [he says] are its particulars.

[The claims that he makes regarding] these "true things" also mean that there is no way of formulating a logical proof to establish that they are impermanent. He cannot use "they are produced" as the reason that establishes their impermanence because [according to him] that is not a property of the subject. Similarly, if he presented something such as "[because] they are known things," it would count as an inconclusive reason, whereas "[because] they are non-actual things" would be a *contrary reason*. [Finally], he cannot establish [that true things are impermanent] by using "[because] they are actual things" as the reason, since then the probans would essentially be no different from the probandum he wants to establish. And if such an approach were permissible, it would follow that one could use the reason "[because] it is sound" to establish the thesis "The sound of a conch is impermanent." [71]

In addition, we also observe that he tries to maintain a whole mass of other positions that directly contradict one another. He advocates that an actual thing must belong to the present but that none of his "true things" are produced. At the same time, he accepts that what defines something as belonging to the present is the fact that it has been "produced but not yet ceased." This suggests that something that was never produced could have ceased. [But if he holds that position,] how would he counter the proposition that in the ceasing of a thing that was not produced, a nonthing has ceased?[262]

Let us assume, furthermore, as the opponent claims, that these "true things" are not produced. Why then would the Mādhyamika bother to prove to the Buddhist realist schools that because things are not produced in any of the four alternatives ways, they are not produced ultimately? [If our opponent was right,] it would follow that there is no need to prove that to them, because those in the realist schools would already have established that things lack any sort of production ultimately. If [our opponent] accepts this, given that the Mādhyamika do not need to rely on the reasoning to establish to themselves that things lack such production, it would follow that the whole proof is redundant.

[Our opponent's] position is a tangle of irreconcilable assertions. Through it, one is compelled to either agree that those of the realist camp have internalized the Middle Way view or throw in one's lot with the Cārvāka, adopting their stance that true things arise causelessly! The baseness of his position is therefore quite unprecedented, although the standard of views in this age we live in has sunk to such a wretched level that there is no guarantee that such positions will not prevail.

[In line with] his position that actual things are necessarily established in an ultimate sense whereas coarse entities are not, someone else proposes that things such as pots are [not coarse objects] but are in fact particles. He reasons that just as a heap made up of numerous jewels is still "jewels," an aggregation composed of various particles must still amount to particles.

[Response:] By this reckoning, since anything composed of many particles must itself be particles, it follows that any collection composed of various essential parts must itself *be* those essential parts. He must accept [this argument's] reason and pervasion, as he himself proposed them. But if he agrees with its conclusion, he would be obliged to accept that a collection composed of arms, legs, and so forth must actually be those limbs. Thus he must also agree that a male can be reduced to the [constituent that is] the masculine essence and that a female can be reduced to the feminine essence.[263] This is just an illustration of the kind of arguments that can be made against his assertion. The notion that actual things cannot be coarse entities is the one I have refuted above.

I have already remarked on the attempts of some to explain away the [unacceptable position] that one can have actual things that are not produced from causes by blaming the realist schools themselves and saying that it represents an internal contradiction within their system.[264] But if someone is going to [resort to this defense], he could just as well claim that when he was forced to concede that an actual thing must be both permanent and impermanent, he was simply reporting on an internal contradiction that existed in the realist schools, and this fault is not one for which he can personally be held responsible. Thus he could portray all of his own faults as those for which the great masters—whose knowledge of reasoning was complete—can be blamed, while he coolly [sits] plucking hairs from his chin, unmoved by any of the criticisms directed against him.[265] [72]

To sum up, even though coarseness is a conventional [reality], this does not mean that every coarse entity is conventional, just as despite the fact that the [identities of] the elements of an action—such as the object and the actor—are conceptual constructs, it does not follow that everything with those [identities] must be a conceptual construct. Again, this is a matter where one must be able to distinguish between the identity itself and the thing that has that identity.[266]

If, as we maintain, [it is permissible] for something to be both a coarse entity and ultimately true, someone might raise the following objection. The Vaiśeṣika asserts that "the whole exists as a substance distinct from its parts." The Buddhist criticism is that the claim's reference to a "[part-possessing] whole"[267] necessarily implies it is a conventional reality—one that is nothing more than a collection of the component parts. [Our opponent] might say that the position we propose makes it possible to have a whole that is not a conventional entity. [He might then argue that] the Vaiśeṣika could therefore [equally] talk of a "whole" *without* this implying that it was a conventional entity. But if this were the case, [the opponent] might ask, what grounds would remain for the Buddhist to allege that the Vaiśeṣika statement "The whole exists as a substance distinct from its parts" is one in which the overt and implied assertions contradict one another?

[Response:] We deny that this is a flaw in our position. Stating that a phenomenon is a "[part-possessing] whole" necessarily implies that the component parts *do not* constitute a substance separate from that whole. This is because in order for something to be a whole with integral parts, those parts must be the components comprising the entity. This overtly runs against the thesis that the whole represents a substance that is separate from those parts, and we are therefore justified in throwing [the Vaiśeṣika] assertion back at him, declaring that it is self-contradicting.

If having integral parts that are not of a thing's own nature makes that thing a [part-possessing] whole, it means that indivisible physical particles must also [be counted] as this kind of whole. This is because they can be said to have parts—in that they have western and eastern points—but these do not actually comprise the particles. [They must have] these eastern and western points, as without them, there would be no way that these particles could be located in any of the ten directions or at any focal point in space, and as such, they could not be counted as physical objects.

Again, there are some who try just to dismiss the Sautrāntika claim that while these particles are directionally indivisible, they can still be spoken of in terms of physical dimensions of east and west as another one of that system's "internal contradictions."

[Response:] Once more, this is not in fact the case. [The Sautrāntika speaks about] parts such as the eastern directional-part and the western directional-part[268] that are different substances [from each other]. These may comprise a thing, without [individually] being identified as that thing. What [the Sautrāntika] means by "indivisible" is something without such [directional] parts. But [for him] "indivisible" does not generally mean that it has no eastern or western [dimensions]. From the west of one of these minutest particles is another minute particle, which is a substance separate to it and does not form one of its integral parts. So [the Sautrāntika would say] one can talk about the east of an indivisible particle without this entailing that the particle itself has directional parts.[269]

Similarly, when the minutest units of time are described as "temporally indivisible," what this is supposed to convey is that they are not constituted of infinitesimally small earlier and later integral [portions]. Just because one can plot points in time that precede or follow one of these units does not make it something that is temporally *divisible*. Indeed, unless these minutest units of time had [moments preceding and following them], they would be quite incapable of performing functions and could have no causes. [73]

Setting out our own position

The father and spiritual son [Dignāga and Dharmakīrti] maintained the following. The Blessed One turned the wheel of Dharma in three stages. During the First Discourses, he taught the selflessness of phenomena. But since [the teaching] was [also] intended to cater to those of the śrāvaka persuasion, who were not yet fit receptacles for explicit instruction about [that] selflessness, he delivered discourses that gave prominence to the notion that external entities exist and revealed only the selflessness of persons. In the Middle and Final Discourses, catering to those of the Mahayana persuasion, he taught the selflessness of phenomena. In the Middle Discourses, however, he declared that all phenomena were "characterless." What the Blessed One really intended by such statements can only be explained with the aid of the Final Discourses. The statements of the Middle Discourses cannot therefore be taken at face value, and the teaching is hence classified as one that *requires interpretation*. The Final Discourses, on the other hand, are teachings for which no "other" intent need be sought; they can be taken literally. Hence they are described as *definitive*.

Correspondingly, in these [Seven Treatises] there are also two approaches. In the first, the aim is to embrace those of the śrāvaka persuasion. [Consequently,] the focus is on the selflessness of persons, and in accordance with the teaching of the First Discourses, the stance adopted does not question the belief in the reality of external entities. In the second approach, where the aim is to teach our own Mahayana system, the focus is on presenting the selflessness of phenomena. In keeping with the Final Discourses, the existence of external entities is rejected. Suchness is explained in terms of the nondualistic consciousness, and the Middle Discourses are accordingly described as teachings that require interpretation.

Of these two approaches, the one that does not question the reality of external entities is consistent with that of the Sautrāntika system. [Śāntarakṣita's] *Ornament to the Middle Way* distinguishes three kinds of Sautrāntika: (1) Opponents of Parity,[270] who believe that [when a perception occurs] there is a single cognition to which the multiple aspects [of the object] appear, (2) Proponents of Equal Measure,[271] who assert that there is a single cognition to which [the object] appears in a single aspect, and (3) Proponents of Parity,[272] who hold that there are multiple cognitions to which the multiple aspects [of the object] appear. Here [in the Pramāṇa treatises], wherever the Sautrāntika standpoint is taken, the position reflected is that of the Opponents of Parity. [74]

Within the Cittamātra system, we find the True Aspectarians and the False Aspectarians.[273] The first group contends that the object-aspect of a cognition constitutes a substance, whereas the second say that it is a conceptual construct. There are three branches of True Aspectarians corresponding to the above-mentioned Opponents of Parity and so forth. The False Aspectarians are divided into the Opponents of [the notion of] Taint and Proponents of [Intrinsic] Taint.[274] The first argues that every conventional appearance has its origins in the imprint [left on the mind by] ignorance and that these appearances will halt once one disposes of this imprint. Through this reasoning they reach the conclusion that a Buddha is not subject to any conventional appearances. The second contends that the appearance of conventional entities has absolutely no link with ignorance and that ridding oneself of that ignorance will do nothing to prevent it. Even a Buddha, they assert, [experiences] the appearance of conventional entities.

Devendrabuddhi and Śākyabuddhi both portray the master [Dharmakīrti] as a True Aspectarian. The author of the *Ornament* [Prajñākaragupta][275] says that he was a False Aspectarian and an Opponent of Taint, whereas Dharmottara classifies him as a Proponent of Taint. My own lamas judge the philosophical horizons of the True Aspectarians to be broader than those of the False Aspectarians and that Dharmakīrti's own view was that of the former. Numerous passages found in the treatises, as well as various lines of reasoning, convince me that the final intention of [Dharmakīrti's] Seven Treatises is that of those True Aspectarians who are Opponents of Parity. I will now justify this conclusion in a brief account of the topic.

Direction on how to interpret the intent behind the declaration in the Middle Discourses that all phenomena are "characterless" is provided in the following lines:

> The divisions that exist between things
> derive from the divisions there are in it [i.e., thought].
> And since it is infected,
> all the divisions between those [things] must also be infected.
> Apart from the aspects of object and subject,
> there are no other characteristics.
> And it is because they lack these characteristics
> that [the Buddha] declared that they have "no nature."
> Classifications such as the aggregates and so forth,
> which distinguish by way of such characteristics,
> are [similarly] therefore not there in reality.
> In that sense also, those things are devoid of characteristics.[276]

The first two stanzas explain that thought is responsible for separating things into various dichotomies,[277] such as cause and effect, defined and defining, produced and producer. This is the same thought to which object and subject appear to be two separate substances. Since logic, however, disproves that object and subject can be separate substances, it confirms that thought is mistaken. Every classification assigning things to dichotomies—designating them, for instance, as either the thing defined or the characteristic that defines it—is therefore no more than a conventional reality that is constructed by an erroneous consciousness. [75] These divisions are not established in any ultimate sense. It is with this point in mind that [the Buddha] declared all phenomena to be "characterless" and "without nature."

The last stanza informs us that characteristics are what distinguish things. Being *fit to be [regarded as] form*, for instance, distinguishes an aggregate of form. Because of this, that fitness is classified as the "defining" characteristic. Form is the thing that is distinguished by that characteristic and is thus classified as the "defined." If definer and defined were established in any true sense, form and that fitness would have to be *truly* different, such that form—as the thing defined—and being fit to be [regarded as] form—as the thing that defines it—would need to constitute separate substances. All phenomena are included within the scheme of definer and defined, and definer and defined are classified as actor and object. And since their identities *as* either the object or that which acts on the object are not established in any ultimate sense, all phenomena are described as "characterless" and "without nature."

Someone reads the last stanza as describing the Sautrāntika view of things. This is not credible. The majority of those belonging to the śrāvaka-based schools, such as the Sautrāntika, do not acknowledge the Mahayana teachings as the authentic word of the Buddha. Consequently, it is not incumbent on them to try to account for the real intention behind [statements in] the Middle Discourses. Furthermore, the word "also"—in the phrase "in that sense also" of the last sentence—indicates that its content is a continuation of what appeared in the preceding lines. Thus both the earlier and later parts of the passage represent the Vijñaptika system's own explanation of the way things are.

[Dharmakīrti's] Seven Treatises presents things in two ways: one version also takes the Sautrāntika tenets into consideration and is able to accommodate them, whereas the other one outlines [Dharmakīrti's] own Vijñaptika system. But they are united in their assertion that a specifically characterized phenomenon is necessarily true in an ultimate sense and that an actual thing must be specifically characterized. Correspondingly, they also agree on the characteristics that define something as true in an ultimate sense. Where the systems diverge is on the issue of what count as the illustrations of the two truths. So while they both advocate that a specifically characterized thing is ultimate and that a generally characterized thing is conventional, the Sautrāntika believes that externally established entities are specifically characterized, ultimate existents, whereas the Cittāmatra holds that there are no externally established entities.

As the systems agree that an actual thing is ultimately true and that a nonactual thing necessarily only exists in a conventional sense, one can work out the illustration for each of the two forms of truth. [76] A thing that is able to perform a function necessarily does so ultimately, because something that functions cannot be merely constructed by thought; it must be a substantial entity. Both Devendrabuddhi and Śākyabuddhi frequently remark that a phenomenon totally devoid of any capacity to function is a conventional one, whereas something that displays even the slightest capacity to function is specifically characterized and ultimately existent.

An objection to our position might be that if only actual things count as ultimate ones, it would follow that selflessness is a purely conceptual construct. And as such a thing could never be overtly comprehended by perception, one would have to conclude that an ārya could never realize selflessness directly.

[Response:] The conclusion that selflessness is a conceptual construct is one that we welcome! But the kind of "conceptual construct" referred to here is not one that is a complete distortion, creating an identity for something when the facts say otherwise. Instead, it is a conceptual construct in the sense that it has only a *designated existence*.[278] The reason it is classified as a designated existent is that it has no independent identity; it can only appear to the mind when something else is negated. A substantial existent, on the other hand, has a [real] identity, created by causes. And as such, it is able to present itself to the mind in its own right, not by virtue of excluding something else.

What a learner ārya's transcendent meditative equipoise directly perceives is that actual things are just fleeting, momentary entities, none of which have any self. The *straight negation* of this self is a fact that is comprehended implicitly [through this perception], not one realized overtly. Myopic beings cannot overtly perceive any objects of the non-actual variety, because this kind of thing is incapable of presenting an aspect of itself to the perception of such a being. If it were capable, one would have no way of fending off the contention that a non-actual thing can [produce] a perception in a myopic being by acting as its observed [object] condition.

How then does the transcendent awareness of a complete buddha gain knowledge of these non-actual things? Does it realize them overtly or implicitly? The transcendent consciousness of a complete buddha gains knowledge of all phenomena by dint of having eliminated—in such a manner that there is no possibility of their ever returning—the obscurations to knowledge, together with the imprints of those obscurations, which had formerly prevented the full knowledge of things through having concealed them. [77] [The way this transcendent awareness] realizes a non-actual thing is not then [the usual one], where through the overt realization of an actual thing, knowledge of [a non-actual one] is gained only implicitly, through a mental act of excluding something. Instead, the transcendent awareness realizes such things in an explicit manner, [an ability] derived from [the individual in question] having eliminated the obscurations to knowledge.

A possible objection to this might be that it would still surely involve the aspects of these non-actual things appearing [to the awareness]. And since these aspects could not [for a buddha] be said to originate in predispositions within the awareness, as is the case with those aspects that appear to thought, one must conclude that these non-actual things indeed have the capacity to present aspects of themselves to the awareness that apprehends them.

[Response:] What we assert is that when the aspect of a non-actual thing appears to the transcendent awareness of a buddha, it is neither that the object presents an aspect of itself, nor that the aspect derives from imprints [in the mind]. Instead, the aspect appears by virtue of the obscurations having been eliminated.

Someone might also point out that a buddha's transcendent awareness would necessarily have to [experience] the aspect of a non-actual thing in a clear, distinct fashion. The aspect could not appear to it in a vague fashion, he might say, because that would mean that the awareness was a conceptual one. So this awareness must be a valid cognition that realizes a thing that is non-actual by means of the aspect of that thing appearing to it distinctly. From this it would then follow, he might say, that the awareness is a valid perception of something non-actual. This, he might suggest, would force one to conclude that a non-actual thing *manifests* itself to the transcendent awareness of a buddha. But in that case, he might argue, this non-actual thing must count as an evident phenomenon, since it would be something comprehended in a manifest fashion by the transcendent awareness of a buddha.

[Response:] We agree that this non-actual thing is manifest to the transcendent awareness of a buddha. But we deny that if the phenomenon appears to a buddha in a manifest fashion, it must be counted as something that is evident. If this were [a correct criterion], we would also have to conclude that certain unpleasant tasting things must be considered the most exquisitely flavored fare, because that is how they are experienced by a buddha. This is the point made in the *Ornament of Realizations* where it says, "[To him,] unpleasant tastes seem exquisite."[279]

[The opponent may] claim that this does not indicate that [a buddha] experiences something to be delicious when in fact it tastes unpleasant but that, even when the foodstuff in question is one *generally* considered to have an unpleasant taste, once it is set before a buddha for him to eat, it will be transformed into a gloriously flavored victual, and this is what he will experience as delicious.

[Response:] Using a corresponding line of reasoning, we would point out that here also, we are not arguing that a buddha] experiences some object of comprehension as evident when in fact it is not, but that even though the object in question is one generally considered to be a hidden phenomenon, from the perspective of the transcendent awareness of a buddha, it is manifest and also appears as manifest to that awareness.

[The opponent might argue that] it would follow that the transcendent awareness of a buddha is a mistaken one, because something such as a non-actual thing, which is not generally evident, appears to it to be so. [78]

[Response:] According to that logic, it would follow that a buddha's perception of taste is mistaken, in that although some kinds of food are generally not flavorful, they are experienced as such by the taste consciousness of a buddha.

[The opponent might answer by] saying that while a buddha experiences the taste that way, this does not represent a mistaken [perception], since [such an experience] is due not to an error but rather to the way that a buddha perceives things thanks to his having completed his accumulation of merit.

[Response:] Once more, we could present the corresponding argument that in our case also, even though the phenomenon is not, in the general sense, an evident one, and while it indeed appears in a manifest fashion to the transcendent awareness, this does not represent a mistaken [perception], since [this experience] is not due to an error but is rather the way that a buddha perceives things thanks to his having completed his accumulation of transcendent understanding.

Even though the transcendent awareness of a buddha experiences a non-actual thing in a manifest way, it does not consider it to *be* an evident phenomenon. The criticism he makes against our position—that it leads to the conclusion that a non-actual thing must be an evident one, because there is a valid cognition that understands it as such—cannot therefore be leveled against it. So are we saying that something can appear to valid cognition in a manifest fashion but not be seen by that valid cognition *as* manifest [i.e., evident]? Yes! For instance, the impermanence of a sound appears in a manifest fashion to the auditory cognition of sound, but that cognition does not view it as something manifest.

There are a great many issues arising from this topic, but I must forgo further discussion of them for the time being and draw this account of the two truths to a close.

6. The Four Kinds of Objects: Appearing, Held, Conceived, and Engaged

Categorizing objects in terms of how their subjects apprehend them, [conceive them,] and so forth

Now we have the fourth way of categorizing objects. It is necessary here to explain the appearing object, held object, conceived object, and engaged object of consciousness:[280]

1. Refutation of others' assertions
2. Setting out our own position

Refutation of others' assertions

Someone claims that a conceptual cognition has no appearing object. He argues that if it did, it would have to be regarded as a cognition that engaged its object *by virtue of* that object appearing to it. But if that were the case, he says, it would follow that the cognition was not an excluding engager. He thus concludes that while an object universal counts as the actual, overt object of a conceptual cognition, it cannot be its appearing object.

[Response:] It would follow that a conceptual cognition engages its object *by virtue of* an actual thing, because such a cognition has an overt object [appearing to it].[281] This argument shows that the three spheres [are in place] and is one for which he can offer no response.

Furthermore, his suggestion that conceptual cognition has no object appearing to it clashes with the *Ascertainment of Valid Cognition* where it says, "The thing that appears to thought is precisely the one that it treats as its own object."[282] [79] What he proposes also goes against the numerous other statements about the *śabdārtha*, which identify it as an *exclusion of other* that appears to conceptual cognition.

Someone else equates appearing object with *overt [actual] object*. For him, both appearing object and overt object denote an object that a cognition has direct contact with, where there is no aspect standing between the object and the cognition. Therefore he says that there are only two things that can qualify as appearing objects: an object universal and consciousness—the first, because it serves as the appearing object of a conceptual cognition, and the second, because it serves as the appearing object of a self-cognition. According to him, because an aspect necessarily stands between a sense cognition and its object, such a cognition does not realize external entities in any actual, overt sense. [To support this,] he points to the situation where there are two people, an adversary and a friend of a specific individual.[283] If there were no [image] aspect mediating between the perception and the object it realizes, he says, it would follow that when both of those people see the physical form of this individual, that form must have multiple identities, because it appears as pleasant and unpleasant to the perceptions of the respective observers, and they realize that form without the mediation of any aspect.

[Response:] Well then, it would follow that the overt object of a conceptual cognition is an externally existent entity. Why? Because the overt object of a conceptual cognition appears as if it is something "out there," and [according to this opponent,] there is no aspect standing between the conceptual cognition and that overt object.

It would also follow that blue is not evident to the valid perception of blue, because there is an aspect mediating between the blue and that perception. Both the reason and the pervasion [of this argument] are ones he advanced. But if he agrees with its conclusion, he will also be obliged to accept that whenever an other-cognizing valid perception has an awareness as its object of comprehension, for that valid perception, the awareness must be something hidden. So we [like Dharmakīrti] would have occasion to lament, "Oh, how miserable this is!"[284]

Also, we can refer back to [the scenario] where two people—one an adversary and the other a friend of a particular individual—observe that individual's physical form. Based on [our opponent's] view, it would follow that the aspect of that individual's form *is* both pleasant and unpleasant, because it appears as pleasant and unpleasant to the subject-aspects [i.e., self-cognitions] of the respective observers, and they realize that form's aspect without the mediation of any aspect. Again, the three spheres [are in place], and he has no response to the argument. The contention that a self-cognizing awareness can operate without an aspect is one that I will refute below.

Someone says that the conceived object of a conceptual cognition can never be specifically characterized. This is because, he says, a conceptual cognition can never realize a specifically characterized thing. He proposes that the object universal serves as the conceived object, since this is what the conceptual cognition thinks of as external. [80] He concludes that every conceptual cognition therefore requires a conceived object.

[Response:] This also is untenable. We have already refuted theses such as these, which assert that it is impossible for a conceptual cognition to have a specifically characterized thing as its object and that a conceptual cognition thinks of its overt object as something external. His claim is that every conceptual cognition requires a conceptual object and that this object can never be specifically characterized. But this fails to distinguish between conceptual cognitions that are *factually correct* and those that are *factually incorrect*.

Someone else proposes that an awareness only has two kinds of object: the held object and the conceived object. He says that the objects held by a valid perception are individual temporal portions but that these portions cannot serve as the *objects of engagement* for such cognitions, since they are not things that a person could [set out to] obtain. He also notes that the held object for an inferential cognition is necessarily a non-actual, conceptually constructed thing. He therefore concludes that neither can this [held object] be the object of engagement for such cognitions. Drawing attention to the passage "Both valid cognitions have objects that are actual things"[285] in the *Ascertainment of Valid Cognition*, he says that it confirms that the object of engagement for any valid cognition has to be an actual thing, which a conceptual construct can never be.

He also maintains that a coarse continuum cannot be a conceptual construct. But [elsewhere] he claims that the objects of engagement for valid cognitions are just a series of temporal portions strung together, which we designate "continuum," or just a collection of different particles, which we designate "coarse." He attributes responsibility for this labeling to an *ascertaining awareness*, something that is induced by valid cognition.[286] In cases where a valid perception induces an ascertaining awareness, he suggests that the conceived object for that awareness can also be counted as the conceived object for the valid perception, since it is only owing to the fact that the object has been perceived that it can become something conceived. He proposes that the situation is comparable to the way that it is permissible, for instance, to say that "The king has executed someone" when it is in fact the executioner who has performed the act under the king's orders.

[Response:] None of these assertions are tenable. Is he proposing that the collections of various temporal portions labeled "continua" and the clusters of various particles labeled "coarse" constitute actual things or not? Assuming that he considers them to be actual things, is he suggesting that each individual temporal portion is an actual thing, or is it only the coarse continuum that constitutes the actual thing? If he were to say the first, it would follow that they cannot be objects engaged by valid cognition, since they are [only] individual temporal portions. The three spheres derive directly [from his assertions]. The alternative, that coarse continua are actual things, must also be ruled out, because [for him] a continuum is disqualified from being an actual thing. [81] So again, the three spheres derive directly [from his assertions]. On the other hand, if he says that they are not actual things, it must follow that they cannot be the [kind of] objects that valid cognition can engage. So once more, the three spheres derive directly [from his assertions].

He may attempt to dismiss our criticisms, insisting that although the individual temporal portions cannot be [actual objects], they can form composites and that while the objects may not, properly speaking, be coarse continua, they are still labeled as such.

[Response:] We would question whether these designations are factually correct. If they are correct, then it follows that these objects must indeed be coarse continua, because it is factually correct to assign the labels "coarse" and "continua" to them. Conversely, if the designations are not factually correct, then it follows that the thought labeling them "coarse" and "continua" must be factually incorrect, because its designation of these labels does not correspond with the facts. But if he accepted that the thought is factually incorrect, it would go against his thesis that the thought in question can be an ascertaining awareness that has been induced by a valid cognition.

The view that a coarse continuum is necessarily a conceptual construct is one that I have already refuted. Further, we would ask the opponent whether he believes that a valid perception is precluded from being an ascertaining awareness. If he says that it is not precluded, this contradicts lines such as "Perception is not responsible for the ascertainment of anything."[287] It would also mean that perception could be conceptual. The alternative is to deny that a valid perception can be an ascertaining awareness. But it must follow [based on his reasoning] that the valid perception of blue ascertains its object, since the object ascertained by the conceptual cognition induced by that perception is the same object [the perception itself] ascertains. That must be the case, because it is only due to the object having been perceived that the [subsequent] conceptual cognition is able to ascertain it. Again, the three spheres are in place, and he is left without any reasonable response.

Someone else claims that every object a conceptual cognition has—apart from itself—is necessarily its conceived object.

[Response:] This is also wrong. We have already explained that while the appearing object of a conceptual cognition might present itself as though it is external, the cognition neither actually conceives of it as such nor thinks, "It is out there." Such appearing objects cannot therefore count as the objects *conceived* by such cognitions.[288]

Some propose that it is impossible to have a conceptual cognition that has no conceptual object. But [elsewhere] they divide communicative sounds into those that have and do not have objects to which they conceptually adhere.[289]

[Response:] This is an internal contradiction in their position. In any case, it is inappropriate to describe a communicative sound as something that conceptually adheres to [what it conveys]. Is this description supposed to indicate that there is something to which the *sound itself* adheres? Or is it supposed to mean that the object communicated by that sound is the same one conceived by the thought that triggered the verbalization of that sound? The first of these alternatives is not acceptable because sounds are physical matter. The second alternative must similarly be rejected, as it would force one [for consistency] to concede that the sound also has an appearing object.

Someone reasons that a conceptual cognition must have a held object, since there is something that it holds and that is also its object. [82] But he has then gone on to deny that a factually incorrect conceptual cognition has a conceived object.

[Response:] Again, he is contradicting himself. It would follow that a factually incorrect conceptual cognition has a conceived object, since there is something of which it conceives and that is also its object. The three spheres [are in place].

In support of their claim that conceptual cognition has no held object, some cite [the *Commentary on Pramāṇa*] where it says, "Except for a causal thing, there is nothing that is 'held.'"[290] They also quote Devendrabuddhi's subsequent explanation of this line, in which he states, "The cause that establishes [i.e., sets down] the aspect is the object itself."[291]

[Response:] This interpretation of the passages is flawed. They should be understood to be speaking purely from the perspective of other-cognitions. Unless one reads them that way, one would be forced to accept [they assert] that only phenomena that are causes can be objects.

Someone else argues that a coarse [entity] cannot be an object of sense perception. We have already dispensed with this view.

Setting out our own position

The *appearing object* and the *held object* [of any cognition] are equivalent. In the case of a nonconceptual cognition, the phenomenon that overtly presents a clear aspect of itself through the cognition and in doing so becomes the object of that cognition is its appearing object and held object. So external entities and awarenesses are the held objects and appearing objects of nonconceptual cognitions. And the "subjects" that have these two as their objects are [respectively] the majority of nonconceptual other-cognizing awarenesses and self-cognizing awareness.

What then of a mistaken sense consciousness? Does it actually have a held object? Mistaken sense consciousness comes in two varieties. [First,] there are those where [apart from] the *immediate condition* that has just preceded it, the only thing making the aspect of the object appear is a defect in the sense power that serves as the *governing condition*. A consciousness of this variety does not depend [for its production] upon some external object that is in close proximity [to the observer]. An example is that of [someone with the condition of] "floating hairs."[292] The second variety of this mistaken cognition occurs due to [the combination of] a defect in the sense power serving as the governing condition and the close proximity of some external object. An example is a visual awareness to which a single moon appears as if double.

The first kind of cognition does not have a held object. The aspect of something presents itself in the consciousness but does so independent of any object. The only thing occasioning it is a defect in the sense power that is its governing condition. So the sense cognitions that seem to see hairs floating and suchlike will occur as long as the other conditions come together, in spite of the fact that there is no [external] object. The second kind of cognition, on the other hand, has a held object. We know from experience that if we apply pressure to our eye, we would not see the moon as double unless the moon was in our [visual] range; but when the moon is in our visual range and the other causes and conditions come together, we will see the double moon. [83] So the appearance of the moon as double depends on the presence of a single moon. Therefore, when one sees the single moon as double, the aspect of a single moon must have appeared. The impairment of the sense power is responsible for the failure of that aspect of the moon to appear accurately. Since sense cognitions such as those that see floating hairs do not depend on an object, they cannot be said to have a *held entity*.[293] This is the point behind the statement "The [cognition] to which hairs appear is one that has no object."[294] [The second variety of] mistaken sense cognitions—such as those that see the tip of a lamp's flame as a corona of light or a single moon as double—depend on an object within close range presenting an aspect of itself, and thus have an entity that they hold. This is the point being made in the line "It is purely due to the lamp that it exists."[295] Not all of the held objects of nonconceptual cognition count as *held entities*. There are many passages in the treatises and their commentaries explaining that the held entity presupposes an externally established object, such as "Because it is produced due to an entity."[296]

The held object of a conceptual cognition is the object that appears to thought as though it is right there before oneself—as if there is no mediating object universal. Thus, in terms of conceptual cognition, the appearing object and held object can only be the *śabdārtha*.

[Despite the opponent's assertion,] the fact that a cognition holds an object does not necessarily mean that the object qualifies as that cognition's *held object*. If it did, it would follow that *sound is impermanent* must count as the entity held by the valid inferential cognition realizing that sound is impermanent, because it is an entity that is held by that inferential cognition. [That opponent] cannot agree with this [argument's] conclusion, since it directly contradicts his assertion that *sound is impermanent* does not count as a held entity. There are also various authoritative passages and logical reasons that disprove such a position.

Some have distinguished between what they refer to as "overt" and "mediated" varieties of the held entity. This [distinction] is surely a source of great mirth among the gods.

The *conceived object* is the object to which a conceptual cognition adheres. In the case of the conceptual cognition of pot, for example, this is the pot itself. Those [cognitions] that conceive of their objects in a factually correct manner, such as the conceptual cognition that sound is impermanent, have conceived objects. Those that do not conceive of their object in a factually correct manner, such as one that considers sound is permanent, have no [actual] conceived object. [84]

The *object of engagement* is a phenomenon, the mode of existence of which matches exactly the one valid cognition explicitly determines it to have. The subjects that have objects of engagement are the two varieties of valid cognition and persons who have these cognitions. The issue of whether the object that a valid cognition engages has to be specifically characterized is one that I will discuss below.

Someone argues that rather than saying that the valid cognition has the object of engagement, it would be more accurate to say that valid cognition *informs* [the person] of that object. He obviously reaches this conclusion by reasoning that the object in question is one with which the valid cognition can never itself engage, in that by the time that [the person] is informed about the object, the valid cognition of [that object] has already ceased to be, and by the time that [the valid cognition] has engaged with the original object, [that object has similarly] ceased to be.

[Response:] This [line of reasoning is undermined, since it can] equally well be directed at the person [doing the cognizing]. A great deal could be said on such matters, but I will not write more on them here as it will take up too much space. I will, however, return to some of the points later.

It is as though an individual of unparalleled intelligence and high-minded intent
has taken up the fine artist's brush of Mañjughoṣa,
and working with a brilliant palette of reasoning,
has created a masterpiece in which all things are made clearly visible.

My intellect has the splendor of garuḍa, the king of birds,
a fact that the horde of vain philosophers find unbearable.
With the beating of my wings, I unleash a gale
that smashes the rocky edifice of our adversaries' pride.

This concludes the description of the object: the thing known.

Part 2

Description of Cognition: That Which Knows the Object

7. Awareness That Is Not Valid

Awareness, *consciousness*, *mind*, and *cognition* are all equivalent. Awareness is defined as "that which is produced to [consciously] experience." There are two different ways of dividing awareness. The first is by way of its functions:[297]

1. Awareness that is not valid
2. Awareness that is valid

Awareness that is not valid

1. Conceptual cognition
2. Nonconceptual false cognition

Conceptual cognition

1. Defining characteristics
2. Varieties [85]

Defining characteristics

Someone asserts that a conceptual cognition can be defined as "an awareness that merges the name [of the thing] with the thing [itself]."[298] Someone else judges it necessary to add that a conceptual cognition is one that either merges [the name and the thing] or sees them as being "mergeable."[299] [He believes that] if the definition included only the first of these, it would not cover the conceptual cognitions of those who have not acquired language. Similarly, he says, if the definition included only the second, "mergeable," it would not cover the conceptual cognitions of those who have acquired language. For this individual, "merges" refers to the way that the name and the thing seem to be as one to a conceptual cognition. Both [individuals] also interpret "name" and "thing" in the phrase "merges the name and the thing" as referring separately to the sound universal[300] and object universal respectively. It is also the case that there are many who suggest that conceptual cognitions can be divided into those that hold only a sound universal and those that hold only an object universal.

[Response:] These individuals are contradicting themselves. They have defined a conceptual cognition by saying that it must be either (1) something that merges the sound universal and the object universal, or (2) something that sees those two as "mergeable." But this goes against their assertion that there are conceptual cognitions that only hold a sound universal. They also asserted that the term "mergeable" does not cover the conceptual cognitions of those who have acquired the use of language. But this is contradicted by their explanation of "merge," which they say refers to the way that the name and the thing seem to be as one to a conceptual cognition. According to that, the term "mergeable" must mean "the name and thing seem as though they can [potentially] be merged." This creates an internal contradiction since, to the conceptual cognition of someone who has gained the use of language, the name and the thing must seem to be as one, but *not* seem mergeable.[301]

They are also wrong to interpret [Dharmakīrti's use of the term *śabdārtha* as one in which] "sound" and "object" separately denote "sound universal" and "object universal," respectively. This is because it obliges them to read the "name" and "thing" in the passage "Any consciousness that holds the *śabdārtha* [relating to a certain thing] is a conceptual cognition [of that thing]"[302] in exactly the same manner. This would in turn compel them to read [the next line], "The nature [of that awareness] is not that of a *śabdārtha*,"[303] [as similarly referring to the same dual elements. Thus it would be] saying, "The nature [of the thing in question] is *neither* that of a sound universal *nor* that of an object universal." In this way they end up with a totally inelegant reading.

Thus, according to our system, conceptual cognition should be defined as "an awareness that holds a *śabdārtha*." The [key expression, *śabdārtha*,] should not be split into its [literal] constituents, "sound" and "object," and then read as two separate things, "sound universal" and "object universal." Instead, it should be understood to denote the appearing object of a conceptual cognition—namely, the *śabdārtha*. That is, this is the same thing referred to in the words "The features of the *śabdārtha* are threefold."[304]

How then are we to account for the passage in the *Ascertainment of Valid Cognition* that says "Conceptual cognition is a consciousness to which what appears [to it seems] mergeable with words"?[305] The meaning of this is as follows. What appears to a conceptual cognition is the *śabdārtha*. Since the *śabdārtha* [has direct involvement with] the assigning of the name [to the object], the description used is "mergeable with words." [86] Due to this, the conceptual cognition is said to be "that to which what appears [to it seems] mergeable with words." It is not saying that a sound universal and an object universal seem to be mergeable [with each other].

Varieties of conceptual cognition

In functional terms, conceptual cognition can be divided into two [varieties], those that attach names and those that attach object-meanings. The first is defined as "a consciousness that apprehends [a thing] having made a connection between the name and the object-meaning [encountered at] the respective stages of labeling and usage." This occurs, for example, when someone encountering a certain white creature thinks, "This animal is 'a cow.'" The second is defined as "a conceptual cognition that apprehends [something] having made a connection between the basis of the property and the property, through their respective object-meanings." This occurs, for instance, when one encounters a certain individual and thinks, "This person is one with a [wooden] staff." These two varieties of conceptual cognition do not preclude each other, since the inferential cognition realizing that sound is impermanent is an example of both.[306]

Typologically, conceptual cognition is divided into that which does not realize [an object] and that which is an ascertaining cognition. The first of these is defined as "an awareness that conceives of something that can be overtly overruled by valid cognition." It has two varieties: false conception and doubt. The first of these is equivalent to *conceptual false cognition* and is defined as "a conceptual consciousness whose conceived object does not exist even conventionally." This is equivalent to [*mental*] *distortion*. An example of this is a conceptual consciousness that holds sound to be permanent. Some have proposed that a false conception necessarily takes the form of an unequivocal conviction.

[Response:] This is not tenable, since it excludes the notion "Sound is more than likely permanent" from the category of false conception. Given that this conception is a mental distortion, such a position is unacceptable. False conception and doubt do not therefore preclude one another.

Doubt is defined as "an awareness that has the aspect of wavering between two alternatives with regard to its apprehended object." This has two varieties. The first has indecision in equal measure with respect to both alternatives, such as in the thought, "I wonder whether sound is impermanent or permanent." The [second variety] is doubt where the qualms are stronger with respect to one of the alternatives, such as that which tends toward what is correct, as in the thought "Sound is more than likely impermanent," or that which tends toward what is incorrect, as in the thought "Sound is more than likely permanent."

Someone describes a thought "Surely there must be some water in the old well" as a form of "latent doubt."[307]

[Response:] This is incorrect. [87] Is such a thought designated "latent doubt" because it is both latent and doubt? Or does the expression refer to that which does not presently manifest in the aspect of doubt but will transform into such when the individual encounters evidence that is either contrary to or supports the exact opposite of what he currently holds to be the case? The first of these options is untenable. To be "latent" is to be in the nature of something that is merely a potential, capable of producing effects only if certain dormant conditions come together. Such a thing could not have a cognitive aspect or observed object.[308] Nor is the second option acceptable, otherwise it would follow that every factually incorrect conceptual consciousness counts as latent doubt. The term *latency for doubt* should therefore be understood as referring to something that has neither a cognitive aspect nor an observed object but has the nature of a seed [potential], which will generate doubt if it meets certain conditions. Thus it may be a cause for doubt but cannot itself be doubt.[309]

The second type [of conceptual cognition], ascertaining cognition, is defined as "an awareness that is either itself a valid cognition or one brought about through the power of a valid cognition, and that ascertains the object it apprehends." It is divided into valid inferential cognition and subsequent cognition. The former will be explained later.

Subsequent cognition is explained under the two headings:[310]

1. Refutation of others' assertions
2. Setting forth our own position

Refutation of others' assertions

Someone says that while the first temporal portion of an inferential cognition is valid, each of the following temporal portions, from the second onward, is a subsequent cognition. [He argues that] those later portions of awareness could not be valid cognitions because they just maintain recollection of an object that has already been apprehended by valid cognition.

[Response:] This is not correct. [His example of a subsequent cognition is] an awareness realizing sound to be impermanent that is generated only after [the initial] valid inferential cognition has realized sound is impermanent, using the reason "[because] it is produced." But [we say this later temporal portion of awareness] is not an inferential cognition. This is because such an awareness does not result *directly* from recalling the ascertainment by valid cognition that the reason satisfies the three criteria. Instead, it is only an ascertainment induced through the power of the inferential valid cognition. If it were otherwise, so that even an awareness that came about as an indirect result of recalling the three criteria could count as an inferential cognition, it would absurdly follow that an ārya's transcendent wisdom of meditative equipoise realizing the selflessness of the aggregates would also count as an inferential cognition. Thus since the awareness realizing sound to be impermanent that arises after that valid inference does not itself count as an inference, it is impossible to have an inference that is a subsequent cognition.

Someone else claims that the inferential valid cognition realizing sound is impermanent is a subsequent cognition with respect to impermanence.

[Response:] This also is erroneous. It is not the case that this cognition ascertains impermanence by recalling the same impermanence that has already been ascertained. Rather, it represents the fresh ascertainment of an impermanence that was not formerly ascertained—namely, the one connected with sound. [88]

The assertion that all later temporal portions of perception are subsequent cognitions is a careless one. Subsequent cognition is after all an awareness that recalls an object that has formerly been ascertained, and a consciousness that recollects is necessarily conceptual. If this were not the case, and an awareness could qualify as a subsequent cognition [simply] on the grounds that it apprehended something that has already been apprehended by valid cognition, then it would absurdly follow that the all-knowing wisdom is a subsequent cognition from its second temporal portion onward. It would also make the valid perception of selflessness a complete impossibility. There are a huge number of arguments that can be used to counter the assertion but these I will discuss later.

Setting forth our own position

Regarding the line "Because it apprehends [something] that has already been apprehended, the conventional [is not asserted to be valid cognition],"[311] Devendrabuddhi, Śākyabuddhi, and the author of the *Ornament* [Prajñākaragupta] all agree that it describes subsequent cognition as a form of recollection. The Dharma lord [Sakya Paṇḍita] also makes statements such as "Subsequent cognition is the recollection of what has passed."[312] The majority of those who properly understand logical reasoning the way we do are therefore of one thought and one voice on this matter, identifying subsequent cognition as a kind of recollection. Subsequent cognition can thus be defined as "an awareness that ascertains by recalling the object already ascertained by the valid cognition that induced it."[313]

Nonconceptual false cognition

Nonconceptual false cognition is defined as "an [outwardly directed] other-consciousness to which the aspect of something clearly appears but does so due to some impairment in the sense power that is its governing condition."

Someone defines it as "a consciousness that is concomitant with its governing condition, a sense power, which is impaired."

[Response:] This is incorrect. It would follow that in the case of a sense consciousness to which two moons appear, the valid self-cognizing perception experiencing that consciousness must count as a nonconceptual false cognition.[314]

There are different varieties of nonconceptual false cognition, those that are mistaken with regard to (1) *shape*, such as the visual consciousness to which a swiftly rotating firebrand appears to form a circle, (2) *color*, such as the visual consciousness to which the white conch appears as yellow, (3) *activity*, such as the visual consciousness of someone traveling in a boat, to which the trees [on the bank] appear to be moving, [89] and (4) *number*, such as the visual consciousness that mistakes one moon for two, (5) something's *nature*, such as the visual consciousness [of someone with myodesopsia] to which bits of hair appear to fall before the eyes, (6) *time*, such as the dreaming consciousness to which the sun appears to be shining in the middle of the night, and (7) *scale*, such as the visual consciousness to which a small physical mass on a barren plain appears as large when viewed from a distance. Of these, the dreaming consciousness is a mental one, while the remainder are sense consciousnesses.

As an example of a mistaken consciousness, someone provides "that [sense consciousness] to which the setting sun appears to be resting on top of the mountains in the west."

[Response:] What actually happens when the sun is about to disappear behind the mountains is that the sense consciousness to which the orb of the sun appears simply does not see any space between the orb and the mountains. It is not that it perceives the sun to be resting on top of the mountains. There are many further points that could be made here, but I find it necessary to curtail the discussion for now.

8. The Definition of Valid Cognition

Description of valid cognition

1. Defining characteristics
2. Varieties

Defining characteristics

1. Refutation of others' assertions
2. Setting forth our own position

Refutation of others' assertions

The *Commentary on Pramāṇa* provides two passages: "Valid cognition is a consciousness that is nondeceptive"[315] and "Also, [it] illuminates something that had not been known."[316] These two passages reveal the defining characteristics of valid cognition.[317] Both Devendrabuddhi and Śākyabuddhi advocated that each of these lines individually supply the full set of defining characteristics. They evidently maintained that the former reflected the way of defining valid cognition according to popular, worldly understanding, whereas the latter reflected the way it is defined according to scholarly understanding, as represented in the treatises. Devendrabuddhi says:

> Thus it states that "nondeceptive" is one defining characteristic
> of valid cognition.
> "Also, [it] illuminates something that had not been known"
> is another, second characteristic.[318]

In his *Explanation*, Śākyabuddhi comments, "What 'another, second characteristic' denotes is that the [earlier characteristic] is the one affirmed by the world, whereas this is another, second one."[319]

[Response:] I do not feel that this interpretation is the right one. If the earlier line does indeed reveal that being "a fresh and nondeceptive consciousness"[320] is what defines valid cognition, there should be no grounds for distinguishing between what the earlier and later lines convey, by suggesting that they respectively refer to such things as a "scholarly understanding" and a "popular understanding," or that the two [versions of the definition] differ in terms of whether or not they dispel particular misconceptions [regarding the characteristics]. [90] It is also the case that if [the first passage] was saying that being a "nondeceptive consciousness" alone defines valid cognition, subsequent cognition would also qualify as valid. Thus the definition would be unsound. In response to Devendrabuddhi's contention, the *Treasure of Pramāṇa Reasoning* says:

> If it were demarcated in two definitions,
> there must also be two definienda.[321]

Later followers of this treatise explained that this passage means "If there were two sets of defining characteristics, there must correspondingly be two definienda—that is, two valid cognitions."[322] But since they [have elsewhere] agreed that there are two sets of defining characteristics for the *probandum* [of a proof], a similar argument could justifiably be thrown back at them, saying that there must also therefore be two definienda for the probandum. The three spheres are in place, and they have no reasonable response.

My own view on what the Dharma lord [Sakya Paṇḍita] intends is as follows. Devendrabuddhi reasons that the two passages could only provide two different [sets of] defining characteristics if they served two separate purposes, each of which required a different set. Because there are no such purposes, we must conclude that the defining characteristics presented in the two passages are synonymous and interchangeable. However, if that were the case [Sakya Paṇḍita says] both sets of characteristics would serve as definers. And as two identifiably separate *isolated encapsulations* are required here to set out what is defined, there must correspondingly be two individual isolates for valid cognition.[323]

Although the author of the *Ornament* [Prajñākaragupta][324] asserts that the earlier [feature of being a nondeceptive consciousness] represents the defining characteristic of conventional valid cognition and the latter [feature of illuminating something that had not been known] is the defining characteristic of ultimate valid cognition, this position is not sustainable. Taking ultimate valid cognition [as our subject], if it is nondeceptive with respect to what it comprehends, it follows that it must be a conventional valid cognition, because it [fulfills the criteria of being] a valid cognition that is nondeceptive with respect to what it comprehends. Conversely, if it is *not* a nondeceptive valid cognition with regard to what it comprehends, it follows that it would not be valid cognition at all, because it is deceptive with regard to the thing it [supposedly] comprehends.

In defense of the position, some may propose a third alternative, [somewhere] between deceptive and nondeceptive. But if such an alternative were really possible for valid cognition and it could occupy a domain outside [the boundaries] of deceptiveness and nondeceptiveness with respect to what it comprehended, then [correspondingly] it would have to be possible for the object to occupy a state outside [the boundaries] of either being or not being the way valid cognition comprehends it to be.

The earlier generation of [Tibetan] scholars claimed that the great brahmin [Śaṃkarānanda] was of the opinion that valid cognition is defined as "that which has the three qualities of realizing a true entity."[325] According to them, the three were (1) the quality of its object, in that the object is something not previously realized, (2) the quality of its mode of apprehension, in that it is an unmistaken cognition, and (3) the quality of its function, in that it is a cognition that eliminates distortions.

[Response:] But this strikes us as little more than some form of inane incantation that has unthinkingly been handed down. In none of the great brahmin's works translated into Tibetan do we find even an oblique reference to such a view, and apart from those, we have no other source for the attribution of such a view to him. [91]

It was also widely accepted among this earlier generation that Dharmottara defined valid cognition as "that which has the three qualities of nondeceptiveness" and that these three were (1) the quality of its nature, in that the cognition has the capacity to achieve its purpose, (2) the quality of its object, in that the cognition secures an engaged object that it has accurately discerned,[326] and (3) the quality of its function, in that the cognition possesses the intrinsic ability to discern an object accurately. They also said that Dharmottara deemed it necessary to add "an extra part to the definition to ensure that it encompassed everything that it was supposed to."

[Response:] In offering such a reading, what they succeed in doing is demonstrating they lack the competence to interpret the real intention of the [master] commentator. Dharmottara does not assert that valid cognition itself secures its object of engagement. [His understanding is reflected] in the passage "By engaging their objects precisely, they are nondeceptive with regard to the task they perform," which asserts that it is by virtue of the valid cognition accurately discerning the object it engages that an individual gains insight into the nature of that object.

In *The Correct*, Dharmottara says, "It is taught that accurate discernment is engagement"[327] and "Engagement is nothing other than the gaining of insight. So every valid cognition has the function of [realizing something] that has not been realized."[328] As for attributing to Dharmottara the assertion that [it is necessary to add] "an extra part to the definition to ensure that it encompassed everything that it was supposed to," we find absolutely no trace of this in any of his works, and so it turns out to be something that was passed on unthinkingly by the former generation.

Another Tibetan defines valid cognition as "that which [realizes] something that is true and had not formerly been realized, and thereby precludes a distortion that is the opposite of that truth."[329]

[Response:] If valid cognition [realized only truths], it would be impossible for it to comprehend what was deceptive. But that would be to deny [the existence] of anything that is a conventional truth.

Elsewhere, someone says that the passage "Valid cognition is a consciousness that is nondeceptive"[330] reveals that valid cognition is defined as "A consciousness that is fresh and nondeceptive with respect to its comprehended object." According to him, the [second] passage, "Also [it] illuminates something that had not been known,"[331] does not convey a second definition. Instead, he says, it [is intended to] counter any criticism that the definition is too broad. This is because based only on the first definition, someone could argue that "conventional" [subsequent] cognition also qualifies as valid cognition. [92] So he suggests that "also" [in the second passage should be understood negatively, as conveying that][332] the definition of the first passage can be faulted "neither" on the grounds that it is too narrow, such that it excludes valid consciousness that derives from some form of communication,[333] "nor" on the grounds that it is too broad, such that it includes conventional [subsequent] cognition.

[Response:] This is not correct. With the passage "because it apprehends [something] that has already been apprehended, the conventional is not asserted [to be valid cognition],"[334] [Dharmakīrti] has already averted any risk that the [definition of] valid cognition might be [interpreted] too broadly, as one that encompasses subsequent cognition. And if [these words] are not equal to the task of averting that risk, then neither can the passage "because the [cognition] that derives from communication can also guide one to what one actually desires"[335] avert the risk [that the category is understood] too narrowly and that valid consciousnesses that derive from communication are excluded from it.

Someone else proposes that the line "Valid cognition is a consciousness that is nondeceptive"[336] presents the defining characteristics in an abbreviated form, whereas the passage "They exist as things with the capacity to perform functions . . ."[337] provides a full description, and the line "Also [it] illuminates something that had not been known"[338] offers a closing summary of the section. He says that "also" indicates that not only does what is conveyed in the first passage counter any criticism that the defining characteristics suffer from any of the three flaws—being (1) too narrow, (2) too broad, or (3) impossible [i.e., having no examples of instantiation]—but that the second passage, "Also [it] illuminates something that had not been known," is *also* able to counter any such criticisms. He concludes that the defining characteristics presented in the former and later passages are one and the same.

[Response:] We would pose the following question. Is he suggesting that not only the earlier but also the latter *passage* is able to counter criticism that there are the flaws of [the definition] being too narrow, too broad, or impossible? Or is he saying that not only does the *definition* revealed in the earlier passage not have these flaws, but neither does [the definition] revealed in the later passage have them? If it is the first of these alternatives, then the [first] passage, "Valid cognition is a consciousness that is nondeceptive,"[339] would reveal that valid cognition is defined as "a consciousness that is fresh and nondeceptive with respect to its comprehended object," and in so doing, it must already have countered any possibility of criticism on the grounds of [the definition] being too narrow, too broad, or impossible. But if [these potential criticisms have already been dealt with], it would make the later passage, "because the [cognition] that derives from communication . . . ," redundant.

If it is the second alternative, since the definitions indicated by both the earlier and later passages are held to be the same, then one would be forced to read [the passages, in combination, to be saying], "Not only does 'a consciousness that is fresh and nondeceptive with respect to its comprehended object' counter the three criticisms, 'a consciousness that is fresh and nondeceptive with respect to its comprehended object' also counters the three criticisms." This would plainly be ridiculous.

Having thus dispensed with misconceptions pertaining to the distinction between the earlier and later passages, I will now address those related to the import of the word "something" in the line "Also [it] illuminates something that had not been known." [93] In reference to this, someone argues that because "something" here denotes a specifically characterized phenomenon, valid cognition should be defined as "an awareness that realizes a specifically characterized object that had not previously been known." Thus he claims that valid cognition must have an engaged object that is specifically characterized. He asserts that in the case of an inferential cognition comprehending a non-actual thing such as noncomposite space, the engaged object must be something that is specifically characterized and can serve as the basis for negating the presence of the *grouping* of noncomposite space and non-actual thing. [He says that even] in the case of the inferential cognition that comprehends [the thesis] "permanence is devoid of production" using the reason "[because it is] devoid of functional activity," there must also be an engaged object that is specifically characterized. He identifies this object as "that specifically characterized product, whose nature is produced, which is the reverse of something permanent, whose nature is devoid of production." He also claims that although the aforesaid specifically characterized *basis of negation* together with "product, which is the reverse of something permanent,"[340] are the engaged objects of the valid cognition in question, they are not the objects comprehended [by that cognition].

[Response:] Does the object that a valid cognition engages need to be one that it comprehends? If it does, then [contrary to his assertion] it would follow that "product, which is the reverse of something permanent," is the object engaged by the inferential cognition of [the thesis] "permanence is devoid of production" because it is indeed the object that this valid cognition comprehends. Hence the three spheres [are in place, and his position is shown to be irredeemably flawed]. Conversely, if the object that a valid cognition engages does not need to be one that it comprehends, then it follows that the object engaged by a valid cognition does not need to be one that is an established basis, since such an object does not need to be the comprehended object of valid cognition. The reason [derives] directly [from his assertion]. But if he accepts the [argument's conclusion,] it would go against his claim that such an object must be specifically characterized. On the other hand, he can hardly deny the pervasion, because that would go against the position that *established basis* and *comprehended object* are equivalent.

It would also follow that *every* negation depends on a basis of negation that is specifically characterized, because [according to him,] an inferential cognition that relies on a negative reason necessarily takes as its object a basis of negation that is specifically characterized. This [argument's] reason is one that he has proposed. But if he were to accept [its conclusion], it would absurdly mean that if one is seeking to negate that [the subject] permanent is specifically characterized, the *basis* for the negation must be specific characterization.

The opponent may attempt to counter this by saying that such a process [of negation] involves taking a specifically characterized phenomenon as one's basis and then negating that the combination of permanence and specific characterization is present within it. [94]

[Response:] What he is proposing therefore is that the way to go about negating that permanent is specifically characterized is to take some basis *other* [than permanent] and then use it to negate the presence of a combination of permanence and specific characterization. But then it would follow that the way to establish that sound is impermanent should [correspondingly] be to take some other thing and then use it as the basis for affirming the combination of sound and impermanence, because the way to negate permanent being specifically characterized is to take some other thing and then use it as the basis for demonstrating the absence of the combination of permanence and specific characterization.

Furthermore, [in the earlier example of] a valid inferential cognition comprehending that permanent is devoid of production, he asserted that the object the cognition engages is "specifically characterized product, which is the reverse of something permanent." But if that is the case, it follows that the very thing engaged by the valid cognition comprehending the proof's thesis is that which is supposed to be the property that the proof negates![341] He has no response to this argument. The various other attacks that could be made on his position are simply too numerous to record here.

Someone else asserts that the engaged objects of the valid cognitions mentioned above are their respective object-aspects.

[Response:] This is not tenable. As [I have already stated], the object-aspect of any given consciousness is none other than the consciousness itself.[342] So, based on his view, it would follow that every consciousness is its own engaged object. This pernicious notion—that the object-aspect of a consciousness can be its own object—is one that I will refute below.

Someone else claims that when [valid cognition] is said to "secure the engaged object," what this refers to is the way that [the valid cognition] brings with it the precise ascertainment of the nature of the object that the person [who has the cognition] seeks to gain.

[Response:] This also is incorrect. If it were true, it would mean that whenever a person properly ascertains the nature of an engaged object, he could be said to have secured that object. From this it must follow that someone who seeks to gain fire would secure it merely by ascertaining that it is something with the capacity to cook and burn. Also, someone who wishes for sustenance could be said to have secured it simply by ascertaining the nature of food and drink. What is more, if [this individual] is saying that a person having a "proper ascertainment of the nature of the object" is *not* sufficient grounds for asserting that the object has been secured, then neither can he claim it is sufficient grounds for someone to have secured an *engaged* object. Conversely, if he says that this *is* sufficient grounds for asserting that a person has secured a thing, then it leads to the ridiculous conclusion that a complete buddha has secured for himself the sufferings of the lower realms! There are endless such absurd consequences to be derived from this position, such as that once someone seeking to gain enlightenment properly ascertains the nature of buddhahood, he would have attained buddhahood. This standpoint does little more than expose the inadequacies of its proponents' understanding.

Someone else [also] claims that valid cognition requires, by necessity, an engaged object that is specifically characterized. In the case of the inferential cognition comprehending that noncomposite space is not an actual thing, he identifies this [specifically characterized] engaged object as "the ascertainment that realizes noncomposite space is a non-actual thing." [95]

[Response:] This position is flawed in a similar fashion [to the previous one.] The initial ascertainment—generated in an individual's continuum—realizing that [noncomposite] space is a non-actual thing is an inferential cognition. Thus it would follow that this inferential cognition serves as its own engaged object.

[Attempting to defend his position, this opponent] may concede that the inferential cognition is a form of ascertainment but claim that it does not [qualify as] the engaged object here, and that the ascertaining cognitions that arise after the inferential cognition should instead [be identified as] the engaged objects.

[Response:] In the case of an inferential cognition that comprehends space to be a non-actual thing, the ascertainment induced by that cognition cannot serve as its object, because that ascertainment is the *effect* of that inferential cognition.

The misconceptions of the dull-witted are like firewood,
but however plentiful their supply,
they are destined to serve as kindling
to fuel the flames of my intellect.

However, the potential for comment is limitless,
so here I should let the issue rest.

Let us next address misconceptions surrounding the phrase "that had not been known" [in the *Commentary on Pramāṇa*'s second passage]. Some assert that it was necessary to include this phrase when defining valid cognition in order to exclude those cognitions that realize objects that [a person] has already realized. Thus, a valid cognition could not be one that comprehends an object that an earlier valid cognition has realized and of which a memory is retained.

[Response:] This is totally erroneous. What about those things that are comprehended by the first temporal portion of an omniscient consciousness? Are they realized by the second temporal portion or not? If not, it must follow that the consciousness is not an omniscient one. But if they are, then it follows that from the second temporal portion onward, all the instances of the omniscient consciousness would be rendered nonvalid cognitions.

The defense to this may be to say that the defining characteristics are given from the point of view of the valid cognitions of myopic beings.

[Response:] As the passage "[Because his consciousness] possesses [those qualities] the Blessed One is himself valid"[343] informs us, the valid cognition of the buddha also shares these defining characteristics. This is just an illustration of how lightweight [the individuals in question] are intellectually. In addition to the above criticism, it also follows [based on their view] that a valid perception realizing a specifically characterized entity to be selfless would be an impossibility. Why? Because the only way that [such a] cognition realizing selflessness directly can come about is if [earlier, on the] path of preparation, the [individual in question] has gained familiarity with the selflessness that has been determined by valid *inferential* cognition. [96] So by subscribing to their view, one would be forced to concede that there could be no āryas who have in their continua valid cognitions that comprehend the way things actually are.[344]

Furthermore, it would also follow that it is impossible for anyone who has acquired language and is not deaf to have an auditory perception of sound that is a valid cognition. Why? Because such an individual retains a recollection of sound derived from the valid auditory cognitions they had before they acquired language.

These [opponents] may deny that there is any such flaw in their standpoint. They may claim that the sound realized at that earlier stage has ceased, whereas the sound realized now that the individual has acquired language did not exist at that earlier stage.

[Response:] Does the auditory valid perception of the individual who has not yet acquired language realize sound or not? If it does not, the idea that it is a valid perception of sound must be dismissed. If that [earlier] perception realizes sound, then does the auditory perception of the individual once he has acquired language [also] realize sound? Again, if it does not, it would follow that it cannot be counted as a perception of sound. But if it does, the criticism would still remain, in that it must follow that such a perception does not qualify as a valid cognition, since it would be an awareness that realizes an object that has already been realized by an earlier valid cognition. This argument also undermines the reasoning of those who assert that the later temporal portions of the perception of blue are not valid cognitions because they apprehend what earlier valid cognition has already apprehended.

[The opponents also propose that] since the later temporal portions of a perception of blue are cognitions of blue that realize what earlier valid cognition has realized, they must be counted as subsequent cognitions.

[Response] Let us assume that Devadatta[345] has, at an earlier stage, validly ascertained sound and impermanence independently of each other, and retains recollection of both. If he later has a valid inferential cognition that realizes sound is impermanent, it follows that it is a subsequent cognition, because it is an awareness that realizes the impermanence that has already been realized by the earlier valid cognition. The three spheres [are in place].

They may try to deny that this scenario corresponds to [that of the perception of blue], by arguing that this inferential cognition *newly* realizes something—namely, that sound is impermanent.

[Response:] But then similarly, even if someone has previously realized just blue, he can still *newly* realize later temporal portions of blue.

Someone else proposes that valid cognition always induces an ascertainment of the thing it comprehends in the continuum of an individual.[346]

[Response:] If he were correct and that was a requirement of valid cognition, it would follow that a valid cognition in the continuum of a complete buddha is impossible, because an ascertaining cognition cannot feasibly exist in the continuum of such a being. He cannot deny that such a cognition in the continuum of a buddha is unfeasible because that would contradict his own position that ascertaining cognitions are necessarily conceptual. Various logical arguments also fatally undermine [such a view]. [97]

Someone else advocates that valid mental perception is extremely hidden and also that valid cognition always induces ascertainment with regard to its object.

[Response:] These two positions are incompatible.[347] The same type of reasoning can also be used to refute the view that a valid cognition is necessarily the eliminator of distortions in the continuum of the individual.[348]

Setting forth our own position

1. The actual defining characteristics of valid cognition
2. The valid cognition that ascertains those defining characteristics

The actual defining characteristics of valid cognition

Valid cognition is defined as "a consciousness that is nondeceptive with respect to its comprehended object and accurately discerns [that object] through its own power." This is revealed in the *Ascertainment of Valid Cognition* where it says, "By engaging its object precisely, it is nondeceptive with regard to the task it performs."[349] This is also what is indicated by the words "Valid cognition is a consciousness that is nondeceptive."[350] The passage "Because it apprehends [something] that has already been apprehended, the conventional is not asserted [to be valid cognition] . . ."[351] excludes subsequent cognition—which is induced by a valid cognition and recalls the object already comprehended by it—from being valid cognition. It is not saying that a cognition apprehending something that an earlier valid cognition had already apprehended is thereby precluded from being valid cognition.

The words "Also [it] illuminates something that had not been known"[352] express how valid cognition makes known an object that is not already known. But it should be understood that this refers merely to valid cognition having the *capacity* to make known what has not previously been known. If, in its making known something that is not already known, this awareness were instead required either to (1) know something by countering some unknowing that is present in an individual's continuum or (2) make known something of which [the individual] previously had no knowledge, then when light expels darkness, [one must similarly say] that the light must be either expelling some darkness that is already present or expelling some darkness that had not previously been there. And when light appears in a particular location, it would mean that even though [the first temporal portion] of light dispels darkness, the subsequent temporal portions of it do not [act in that way]. Therefore what "Also [it] illuminates something that had not been known" conveys is that any valid cognition necessarily has the *capacity* to know some object of comprehension that is not already known. That said, this passage does not reveal a defining characteristic of valid cognition.

One can talk of an "engaged object for valid cognition" in two different senses. A person may engage with an object because he earnestly wishes to secure the results that it can yield. [98] As the valid cognition in the continuum of that person accurately discerns the object he wishes to engage, that object may be described as the "engaged object of valid cognition." [In the second sense,] there is no reference to the person engaging with an object to gain the results that it can yield. The description "engaged object of valid cognition" refers [only] to valid cognition's engaging with the object through performing its function of accurately discerning it. The engaged object in the first sense is necessarily specifically characterized, since no rational person would engage with a phenomenon to gain the results it could yield if that phenomenon were incapable of productive activity. The following passages were delivered with this point in mind:

> Only specifically characterized [things] are comprehended,
> because it is from them that [valid cognition], investigating what does and does not exist,
> can establish whether they perform [the actions that are attributed to them].[353]

And:

> Aspiring for something with a specific nature,
> the person engages with that specific thing
> [to investigate] whether there is proof [that it can yield] the desired result.[354]

And also:

> What would be the point of aspirants investigating something that is devoid of function?[355]

With respect to the engaged object of the second sense, however, there is no requirement that it be specifically characterized, because valid cognition engages *every* comprehendible [object] through performing the action of accurately discerning it. So, for instance, the engaged object of the inferential cognition comprehending that space is not an actual thing is the combination of space and non-actual thing. All inferential cognitions that depend on negative reasons should be understood to work in this fashion.

There are two ways that the "nondeceptive" of the passage "Valid cognition is a consciousness that is nondeceptive" can be understood. This is because, as has just been outlined, there are two ways to gloss the engaged object and hence two different things regarding which valid cognition can be said to be "nondeceptive."

Regarding the first of the engaged objects mentioned, valid cognition is nondeceptive in that it comprehends the object's function, and the object functions in exactly that way. This is what is referred to in the line "[Valid cognition is] nondeceptive [since the object] is able to perform the function [that it cognizes]."[356]

In terms of the second sense of engaged object, valid cognition is described as "nondeceptive" in that it has the capacity to understand the nature of an object that one had not previously understood. This is the point made by the words "Also [it] illuminates something that had not been known." "Also" here should therefore be understood to mean "Valid cognition is nondeceptive not only because it comprehends the function of its object but *also* because it illuminates something that one had not known." [99]

How then are we to understand the passage "because [Dignāga's] intended meaning was that [valid cognition] knows the specific characteristics of something that was not known . . ."?[357] Let me, as the only person with the privilege of understanding this, explain. This passage contains [Dharmakīrti's] response to an opponent who argues the following: "[Given what you have asserted,] when a visual perception has realized an actual blue, and is then followed by a conceptual consciousness, which understands blue in the general sense [of a universal], that second consciousness must also count as a form of valid cognition, because it is an awareness that understands blue in a general sense, something that had not previously been known." In his response, "because [Dignāga's] intended meaning . . .," [Dharmakīrti] is saying, "It does not follow that the conceptual consciousness is a form of valid cognition. That is because what [Dignāga] intended was that of the two consciousnesses referred to, only perception—the one with the capacity to know the specific characteristics of blue, which had not been known before—is a valid cognition. The conceptual consciousness that arises after it and apprehends blue in a general sense is nothing more than a recollection of the specific characteristics of blue already discerned by perception."

What this passage affirms therefore is that of these two—the perception of blue and the subsequent cognition, generated after it, which apprehends the generality of blue—only the *perception* is a valid cognition. It does *not* say that only those cognitions that are valid with respect to specifically characterized phenomena qualify as valid ones. Such a position, if adhered to, would mean that nothing generally characterized could be comprehended by valid cognition, and so unless something was an actual thing, it could not be an established basis.

There is also the question of how the line "Both valid cognitions have actual things as their objects" should be construed. This should be understood as Dharmottara explains, "Thus there is no distinction between the two of them in terms of their [ability to] gain the things that are their objects of engagement. As it is stated, 'Both valid cognitions have actual things as their objects.'"[358] Such passages are *not* asserting that the engaged object of a valid cognition is necessarily an actual thing. Instead, they are intended to address a particular qualm. That is, there may be those who have no doubt that because a valid perception is a cognition with a specifically characterized object, it must have the capacity to secure the actual thing that is its engaged object, but they doubt whether inferential valid consciousness also has such a capacity, since it is a cognition that has a generally characterized thing as its object. Such passages explain that even if one relies upon an inferential valid cognition, it is still possible to secure an engaged object that is an actual thing.

There is another statement by Dharmottara:

> Therefore, since the temporal portions of an initial perception and an inference are able to ascertain the continuum of an actual thing that performs a function, they take [these] as their engaged objects. Later [temporal portions] that are indistinguishably part of the same continua [of consciousness] have relinquished their validity.[359] [100]

Some have interpreted this as an assertion that because the later temporal portions of a perception, such as one that apprehends blue, are only discerning an engaged object that has already been discerned by the earlier [i.e., initial instant of that] valid perception, they do not qualify as valid cognitions.

[Response:] The question of whether this is what the master Dharmottara actually believed should be looked into. But *if* Dharmottara did assert this, it would mean that there was a major inconsistency in his position, because [elsewhere he declared] that a mental perception that is a valid cognition necessarily comprehends the last instant in the continuum of the thing comprehended by the sense perception that acted as its immediate condition.[360]

Description of the defining characteristics relating to valid cognition: The valid cognition that ascertains those defining characteristics

1. Setting forth our own position
2. Refutation of others' assertions

Setting forth our own position

What verifies a valid cognition's identity, establishing that it is something nondeceptive with regard to the object it comprehends, is a self-cognition. This is conveyed in the line "Thus its identity is realized through itself."[361] The realization that an awareness that is nondeceptive with respect to the comprehended [object] it discerns accurately is a valid cognition depends on [the individual] correctly ascertaining [i.e., distinguishing] which bases can appropriately be assigned the designations *valid* and *nonvalid*. That is what is meant by the line "Validity is [approached] through terminology."[362] Not every individual can independently distinguish which bases are appropriate to designate *valid* and *nonvalid*. Otherwise, there would obviously be no grounds for confusion regarding the classifications of the two. The treatises teaching the definition of valid cognition were therefore composed to provide a means [for such individuals] to accurately identify how to correctly apply the terms *valid* and *nonvalid*. This is what is intended by the words "The treatises aim to counter confusion."[363] My ability to present such an accurate account of these passages stems from my personal insight into them,[364] allowing me to see what others have previously not.

Refutation of others' assertions

Someone claims that a perception of the color of fire in the distance that directly induces doubt as to whether what has been seen is fire or not is an example of what is referred to as a "valid cognition that ascertains dependently."[365] [101]

[Response:] This is incorrect, as the perception in question is quite capable of *independently* inducing ascertainment that the intense glow it sees is an intense glow. This is despite the fact that it fails to validly cognize that this intense glow is the color of fire.

[He may] argue that the perception is a valid cognition with respect to the intense glow being the color of fire, because it prompts [a person] to investigate whether [the entity in the distance] is fire. This investigation will in turn give rise to either (1) a perception that sees [the entity] is that which performs the functions of cooking, burning, and so forth or (2) an inferential cognition that realizes it is fire [in dependence on the reason] smoke. Thus, he might say, the perception is capable of inducing an ascertainment of fire.

[Response:] Many ludicrous conclusions could be drawn from such a position. For instance, it follows that the doubt induced by that perception would also count as a valid cognition with regard to the intense glow being fire. It would also follow that the visual perception that sees the sparkle of the jewel through the crack in the door must also be a valid cognition with regard to the jewel.[366] By extension, we can also dismiss the assertions of some others who posit the "[perceptions of] beginners and the inattentive"[367] as examples of valid cognition that ascertain dependently. Others have certainly had a lot to say on these matters. But the majority of these seem to be floating in space[368] and do not warrant any further attention here.

There is a widely held belief that Devendrabuddhi, Śākyabuddhi, the author of the *Ornament* [Prajñākaragupta], and others regard the consciousness that considers the sparkle of the jewel to be the jewel as an example of valid cognition.

[Response:] Since that consciousness is conceptual, it cannot be perception, and since it is a *false cognition* that does not depend on a reason, neither can it be a form of valid inferential cognition. It is therefore impossible that anyone thinking in a logical manner would of his own accord make such an assertion. So let me now explain the actual intention of these commentators. When Devendrabuddhi and Śākyabuddhi talk of valid inferential cognition [in relation to such a consciousness], they are certainly not proposing that the thought that considers the sparkle to be the jewel can count as a valid inferential cognition. Rather, they are affirming that the conceptual consciousness derived from the perception of the jewel's sparkle and ascertaining that there is a jewel in that place is a valid inferential cognition. They advocate that the situation should be viewed as on a par with that of when someone perceives smoke [emanating from] somewhere and [on the basis of this] has an inferential valid cognition realizing that there is fire in that place. Unless one views the two cases as on a par with each other, the assertion that an inferential valid cognition realizes fire in dependence on smoke would amount to claiming that there is a valid cognition that holds smoke to *be* fire!

The author of the *Ornament* states the following:

> Thus the awareness that apprehends "jewel"
> and is [derived] from the sparkle of the jewel
> must, with respect to that,
> be either a perception or an inference.[369] [102]

What this means is that the visual consciousness that sees the sparkle of the jewel and induces a [later] awareness apprehending the jewel is a perception, whereas the cognition that realizes the *presence* of the jewel based on the jewel's sparkle is an inferential one. Hence he identifies the perception of the jewel as the valid cognition that helps establish the *property of the subject* and the apprehension of the jewel as an inferential cognition.

Were it possible to weigh upon the scales
my own intellect against that of others,
would it not be like comparing
the mighty Mount Meru to a grain of sesame?

The varieties of valid cognition

Now second, I will describe the varieties of valid cognition. Taking simply valid cognition as the thing being divided, it has two varieties: valid perception and valid inferential cognition. There are two [alternative] grounds for regarding this twofold division as definitive. The twofold division of valid cognition into perception and inference is definitive because (1) the ways that an object can be comprehended are limited to two in that: either a generally characterized phenomenon will serve as the held object [of a cognition] or a specifically characterized phenomenon will serve as the held object observed [by a cognition]. Or (2) the ways that an object can be comprehended are limited to two in that: the object of [the cognition] is comprehended either in a manifest or an obscure fashion.

Generally speaking, definitive categorizations themselves are of various [kinds]. (1) The division of objects of knowledge into those that are permanent and those that are impermanent is a definitive categorization of the *excluded third* variety, with the two directly preclusive elements of the division being jointly exhaustive.[370] (2) A division such as that of inferential cognitions into those for personal ends and others' ends is a definitive categorization of the *purposive* variety. In reality, all inferential cognitions are for personal ends, but there is some objective behind presenting the twofold division. (3) There are also definitive categorizations of the *typological* variety. The division of the perfections into six, for example, is said to represent a definitive categorization of all paths of a buddha. It is not the case that every single instance of a path falls into one of the six divisions, but when organized according to types, paths can be said to fit into the sixfold divisional scheme. [103] Furthermore, there may be those who, having identified valid cognition as the thing divided, contend that it is necessary to add another category of valid cognition that is neither perception nor inference. There are others who reject the idea of the twofold division [into perception and inference] itself. The twofold division of valid cognition was made to counter such misconceptions. (4) Thus there are definitive categorizations of the *misconception-countering* variety.

From among these [four], only a definitive categorization of the [first variety], with its directly *preclusive, jointly exhaustive* elements, [categorically] rules out the possibility of something that does not belong to either one of the twofold divisions of the phenomenon in question.[371]

9. Valid Perception

1. Defining characteristics
2. Varieties
3. Valid cognition and its results

Defining characteristics

Valid perception is defined as "a consciousness that is free from conception and is not mistaken due to some adventitious source of error." The "conception" from which such a consciousness is said to be free is the conceptual cognition that holds a *śabdārtha*. As [Dignāga] stated, "Perception [is a cognition] that is free from conception, [the latter being what deals with] conjoining names, types, and so forth."[372]

Anything that is not mistaken is necessarily free from conception, but it is still necessary to mention both characteristics. This is because ["free from conception"] counters the misconception of some non-Buddhist philosophers who claim that there are conceptual sense perceptions. And if one failed to stipulate that [perception] must not be mistaken, it would follow that nonconceptual false cognitions would count as perceptions.

One should not interpret "conception" in the phrase "free from conception" as referring to conceptual cognition in the sense of a substance. If one did, it would exclude self-cognizing perceptions that experience conceptual cognitions from [the category of] perception.[373] Neither should one interpret it as referring to conception in the sense of an individual isolate, because by that criterion, even inferential cognition would not count as conception.[374] It should therefore be understood to mean that [a perception] is something that is not produced in the nature of a conceptual cognition.

The [perception's characteristic of] being unmistaken must be understood in terms of *not being mistaken due to some adventitious source of error*, as is spelled out in the *Ascertainment of Valid Cognition*: "It is something that is not [made] mistaken due to such things as blurredness, swift rotation, traveling in a boat, or [physical] imbalance."[375] This being the case, these defining characteristics encompass both the Sautrāntika and Cittamātra systems. In the Cittamātra system, sense perceptions are mistaken consciousnesses in that they are influenced by the propensity for seeing duality. [104] This propensity is said to have always been within us, and due to it, the objects we observe seem to be external to us even though they are not. Despite this, the Cittamātra still hold that no perception is mistaken due to the adventitious sources of error such as blurredness of vision.

Some have chosen to define perception simply in terms of being "that which is free from conception and unmistaken." They have also claimed that such a definition is acceptable in the Vijñaptika system, because it [like the Sautrāntika] stipulates that a perception must be consciousness that is not affected by any of the adventitious sources of error.

[Response:] These individuals are guilty of implying that in the Cittamātra system, simply being unaffected by the four sources of error is enough [to qualify] something as being unmistaken.

Others have suggested that while being "free from conception and unmistaken" may be sufficient to define perception, it is insufficient when it comes to defining *valid* perception, because a valid cognition necessarily induces ascertainment [of an object]. Based upon this, they maintain that if a visual perception sees the color of a mirage and gives rise to the mental distortion that holds the mirage to be water, or if an auditory perception of sound occurs when the attention of a person is engrossed in a beautiful [visual] form, these are cases of perception but not valid cognition.

[Response:] This is incorrect. The idea that valid cognition necessarily induces ascertainment has already been dealt with. Anyway, the perception that sees the color of a mirage *is* valid with regard to that bluish shimmer. It also induces ascertainment of that, because if one failed to ascertain even the bluish shimmer, how could one project "water" upon it? And if when someone's attention was engrossed in an attractive physical form, he did not ascertain that he had an auditory perception, how could one establish that such a [cognition] was a perception? But if the person did ascertain [with certainty] that the [auditory] perception had occurred, how is it possible that he could have ascertained that he had heard sound but did not ascertain sound itself?

Thus what the passage "Because of being attached to something else, the consciousness is rendered incapable of grasping another object"[376] reveals is that even if someone is in close proximity to a particular sound, when his mind is thoroughly engrossed in a highly attractive visual form, it will prevent the auditory perception being produced [at all]. It does not mean that the individual has an auditory perception but that it fails to ascertain sound.[377]

So is an auditory consciousness necessarily a perception with respect to the impermanence of sound, or not? If not, it would mean that to perceive sound is not necessarily to perceive the impermanence of sound. If, on the other hand, the auditory consciousness *is* a perception with respect to that impermanence, it should mean that an auditory consciousness is necessarily a valid cognition with respect to the impermanence of sound. [105] But if that were the case, there would be the incongruity of an individual who, at the very time that he is misconceiving that sound is permanent, has a valid cognition in his continuum realizing that it is impermanent!

It is certainly possible to have this qualm. What should be understood is that while a perception is necessarily a valid perception, something can be a perception with respect to a thing without being a *valid* perception of that [thing]. By analogy, while a valid inferential cognition is necessarily a mistaken consciousness, it can be a valid inferential cognition with respect to a thing without being a mistaken consciousness of [i.e., a consciousness mistaken about] that thing. Thus an unmistaken auditory consciousness can be a perception with respect to sound's impermanence without having to be a *valid* perception of that impermanence. Despite this, generally speaking, an unmistaken auditory consciousness is necessarily a valid perception.

Furthermore, if perceiving a thing were enough to make [an awareness] a perception of that thing, it would follow that the sense perception to which a single moon appears as two is the perception of a single moon, because it sees that single moon. An opponent may deny that it sees the single moon.

[Response:] If that were correct, it would follow that a single moon does not appear to it. It would also follow that the sense consciousness to which the tip of the flame on a butter lamp appears as a halo of light does not see the tip of the flame, but we know from our own experience that we actually see these things directly.[378]

If [this opponent] grants that we do indeed see these things, we would press him further. Does he want to assert that the first is a perception of the single moon but is not a perception? Or is he saying that it is a perception? If he denies that it is a perception, then he should consider how he would counter someone claiming that a cognition can be valid with respect to something but not itself be a valid cognition. If conversely, he asserts that it is a perception, it would contradict [the treatises], which identify the cognition of the two moons as a form of pseudo perception.

Based on his position, it would also follow that the conceptual cognition of pot is an inferential cognition of pot, because it realizes pot in an obscure fashion. The pervasion of this argument [that what realizes an object in an obscure fashion is necessarily an inferential cognition of that object] is something he has already accepted. He may respond by denying that there is any parallel between the two situations, saying that while that conceptual cognition realizes pot in an obscure fashion, it cannot be counted as an inferential cognition of pot, because it does not realize it in dependence on a reason.

[Response:] We could argue along similar lines, saying that [while the cognition] perceives the single moon, it cannot be counted as a perception of the single moon, because it does not accurately discern [the single moon] through the force of its own experience.

He might object to [our introduction of "accurately discern" into the discussion], saying that this is the meaning of *valid* perception, not of perception.

[Response:] Equally, can it not be said that the "dependence on the reason" refers to *valid* inference, not [simply] inference?

[He may attempt to justify his introduction of the phrase "dependence on a reason" on the grounds that] (1) something that does not depend on a reason would fail to satisfy the literal etymology of the term *inferential cognition* and (2) nowhere do the treatises indicate that an awareness that does not depend on a reason can qualify as an inferential cognition. [106]

[Response:] Again, [our reference to "accurately discern" can similarly be justified,] because (1) something that does not accurately discern its object through the force of experience would fail to function as a perception and (2) nowhere in the Seven Treatises on Pramāṇa or the *Compendium of Pramāṇa* is there differentiation between perception and valid perception.

He might deny that a perception necessarily performs such a function.

[Response:] Similarly, an inferential cognition does not have to satisfy the literal etymology of the term. If everything was required to satisfy its literal description, it would follow that every perception depends on a sense power, because "dependence on the respective sense power(s)" is part of the literal description of perception. Many such points could be brought up here, but I will not pursue them for the time being.

At no point do the master [Dignāga] and his [spiritual] son [Dharmakīrti] make any major differentiation between perception and valid perception. In line with this, the Dharma lord [Sakya Paṇḍita] also states, "Simply through being free from conception and unmistaken, perception establishes itself as valid cognition."[379]

There are four categories of valid perception: (1) sense valid perception, (2) mental valid perception, (3) self-cognizing valid perception, and (4) yogic valid perception. This division works for both the Cittamātra and Sautrāntika systems. The claim that there is no place for sense and mental perception in the Cittamātra system is flawed, since that system asserts such things as visual and auditory perception and also that these are produced by the sense powers that serve as their governing conditions. Furthermore, if the claim [that the system does not accept such perceptions] was correct, it would follow that [Dignāga's] *Analysis of the Objects of Cognition* does not provide an explanation of three conditions for sense consciousness according to the Vijñaptika system.

It would also absurdly follow that a sense perception is defined not on the basis of being derived from the [physical] sense power that [serves as] its governing condition but on the basis of being derived from an external object that is its observed condition.

Some may grant that the cognitions under discussion [in such passages] are sense perceptions, but they may still be unwilling to accept that they are valid cognitions.

[Response:] Such a position is not sustainable. The *Ascertainment of Valid Cognition* has statements such as:

> Due to stable imprints they will be associated, inseparable until the end of samsara.
> Since in the conventional sense they are nondeceptive, here they are valid cognitions.[380]

Such statements indicate that while a sense consciousness such as that which sees two moons and a visual perception of blue are both mistaken, it is still legitimate to distinguish them based on whether they arise from stable or unstable imprints. [107] Thus, in conventional terms, these [consciousnesses] can be divided based on whether they are deceptive or nondeceptive, and as such, whether they are valid cognitions or nonvalid cognitions. If the distinction between nondeceptive and deceptive did not apply to the visual perception of blue and the [consciousness] to which the two moons appear, it would follow that the blue and the two moons are equally substances. But if that were the case, it would undermine the whole discussion to establish that blue is the same substance as the consciousness [apprehending it] using the line of reasoning known as *simultaneous observation.*[381]

When explaining the passage of the *Treasure of Pramāṇa Reasoning* that states "The system of four perceptions is [that of] the Sautrāntika. The Vaibhāṣika has three, the Vijñaptika, two,"[382] the commentary says, "The thought of the glorious Dharmakīrti is that in the Vijñaptika system, no other forms of valid cognition than self-cognition and yogic perception are possible."[383] This effectively rejects the idea that the likes of a sense perception to which a single moon appears can be a valid cognition. However, this directly contradicts the commentary's remarks on the *Treasure of Pramāṇa Reasoning* passage "What is true and what is false is determined by whether the imprints are stable or unstable,"[384] where it explains that the Cittamātra system also distinguishes between [consciousnesses] to which a single moon and a double moon appear with respect to whether or not they are valid. I therefore suspect that this [earlier comment] does not reflect the actual thought of the root text's composer.[385] The issue of what he actually intended is something that I will discuss elsewhere.

10. Sense Perception

Valid sense perception

Of the four types of perception, I will first deal with sense perception.

1. Literal meaning of *sense perception*
2. Defining characteristics
3. Varieties
4. Explanation of the three conditions

Literal meaning of "sense perception"

The designation *sense perception* derives from the fact that these are perceptions produced in dependence on sense powers serving as their governing conditions. Visual perceptions of form as well as the remaining [sense] perceptions share the [characteristic] that they arise from three conditions, and all are known as "sense consciousnesses." Their individual designations, *visual consciousness* and so forth, derive from their respective governing conditions, not their observed [object] conditions. The reason for this is that sense and mental consciousnesses share certain objects, so any designation made on the basis of their objects would fail to convey that they are distinct [from one another]. [108] Their respective governing conditions, on the other hand, are unique to each of them, and so a designation based on these is capable of communicating their distinctness. Hence their labels are assigned to them based [on these governing conditions] rather than their objects. This is the point [made by Dignāga] in the passage "Because they are causes that are unique [to each], the designations are made in terms of the sense powers."[386]

Defining characteristics

Sense perception is defined as "an other-knowing consciousness that is free from conception, unmistaken, and directly produced by its governing condition that among the two, a [physical] sense power and a mental sense power, is only a physical sense power."

Others define sense perception as "an other-knowing consciousness that is free from conception, unmistaken, and directly produced by its governing condition, a sense power that is physical form." In their explanation of these characteristics, they fail to indicate any distinction between the Sautrāntika and Cittamātra positions. But later, in presenting the Cittamātra system, they explain that for a sense perception, both an earlier consciousness of the same kind as that sense perception and a capacity present in that earlier consciousness play the roles of governing conditions. This is inconsistent.

Varieties

There are five varieties of sense perception, ranging from sense perception that apprehends visual form to sense perception that apprehends objects of touch. The first is defined as "an other-knowing consciousness that is free from conception, unmistaken, and directly produced by a visual sense power that is its governing condition." The defining characteristics of the remaining four follow a similar pattern.

Explanation of the three conditions

1. An analysis of whether the group of causes for a sense consciousness is limited to the three conditions
2. Setting out the nature of each of the three conditions

An analysis of whether the group of causes for a sense consciousness is limited to the three conditions

1. Refutation of others' assertions
2. Setting forth our own position

Refutation of others' assertions

Someone asserts that the division of the three conditions is a definitive categorization that encompasses each and every one among the group of causes of a sense consciousness.

Response: This stance is unsustainable, since there are numerous indirect causes of a sense consciousness that are not classified as any one of these three conditions. If each of the indirect causes of a sense consciousness also had to be classified as one of the three conditions, it would follow that the gustatory sense power is one of the three conditions that produces an auditory consciousness hearing communicative sounds, because it is an *indirect* cause of that auditory consciousness. And this is because that sense power is a cause of communicative sound. If he were to accept this, it must follow that the gustatory sense power is the governing condition of that auditory consciousness, since it is definitely neither [that consciousness's] object condition nor its immediate condition. It cannot be its observed [object] condition, because it is not its object, and it cannot be its immediate condition, because it is not a consciousness. [109] If he agreed with this conclusion, he would be forced to maintain the pitiful position according to which auditory consciousnesses can be derived from governing conditions that are gustatory sense powers. The stance would also force him to accept other unwanted conclusions. It would also follow, for instance, that the visual form of [a lump of] molasses at an earlier point was one of the three conditions that [produced] the gustatory consciousness experiencing the taste of [a lump of] molasses at the present time.

There is a widespread notion that an indirect cause does not constitute a cause.

Response: But if it does not, it must follow that [when Dharmakīrti declared] "Due to that, [the Buddha] taught that ignorance is the cause of all faults,"[387] he was *not* in fact saying that ignorance is the cause of all faults, since ignorance does not produce all faults *directly*. The aforesaid notion actually leads to a whole host of other ridiculous conclusions. For instance, it would follow that delusions, those things responsible for the karma that propels one into samsara, are not causes of samsara. It would also follow that ignorance is not the cause of aging and death. Furthermore, it would follow that none of the Mahayana paths—from the paths of accumulation and preparation up through the ten grounds, including every stage preceding the final continuum—constitute the causes of buddhahood! It would also follow that something that was indirectly related to another thing could not in fact be related to it. And if that were the case, then neither could something that indirectly precluded another thing preclude that thing. Thus it would follow that product and permanent do not preclude each other. Basically, to hold the aforesaid notion is to reject the whole idea of samsara and nirvana.

While someone claims that the direct causes of a sense consciousness are limited to the three conditions, another individual objects to this. Referring to the light allowing one to see a visual form, he questions which of the three conditions of a visual consciousness it is supposed to be. The first individual's response to this is to propose that the light is *both* the observed [object] condition and governing condition. In support of this, he cites the passage:

It is not that something can only govern [the production of one sort of result],
since it is possible for one thing [to give rise] to discordant forms of seeing.
Light, for instance, simultaneously serves
as [the factor] that [can] both impede and facilitate the eye seeing form
for the nocturnal venturer and those with other [kinds of] sense power.[388]

He says that this passage states that light is a governing condition of visual consciousness, and that the line "There is no light/appearance that is not apprehended"[389] affirms that light is also the observed [object] condition.

[Response:] The first individual's position that [light] is a common locus of the observed [object] condition and governing condition is not plausible. If light were the governing condition of visual consciousness, it would absurdly follow that unless there is light, there can be no visual consciousness apprehending form, but our experience tells us that we have visual consciousness that sees darkness. [110] It is also frequently stated in the Abhidharma that darkness is a color. The reason he provides to establish his thesis is also erroneous. The actual meaning of the section "Light, for instance . . ." is as follows. Light, such as that of the rays of the sun, is a *governing cause* that is not conducive to the production of a clear visual consciousness of form for beings who have visual sense powers like those of the owl, the "nocturnal venturer." On the other hand, it is a governing cause that is conducive to the production of a clear visual consciousness of form for beings with visual sense powers like those of humans. The passage informs us, therefore, that light is a governing cause that brings the sense powers of humans and owls to a state in which they are [respectively] either able or unable to produce visual consciousnesses as effects. As such, rather than describing light as the governing cause of visual consciousness, it says that it is the governing cause that enables *certain* sense powers to produce visual consciousnesses as effects. This interpretation is also favored by the master Devendrabuddhi, who states in his commentary:

> [The passage] "Light, for instance, simultaneously serves as [the factor] that [can] both impede and facilitate the eye seeing form for the nocturnal venturer and those with other [kinds of]

> sense power"—[in other words,] the nocturnal venturer and the human—means that it [light] facilitates the human eye seeing form but impedes the eye of nocturnal creatures seeing form.[390]

Thus he explains the passage in terms of the [physical] eye, not visual consciousness.

As regards "There is no light/appearance that is not apprehended," [the second passage he cites,] there are two different [versions and] explanations of it. According to the first, [it forms the third line] of the following passage:

> [We say,] "The apprehended [object] is not separate from [the earlier consciousness] that produces [the later consciousness]."
> [He responds,] "[The earlier consciousness] that produces [the later consciousness] is not the genuine apprehended [object of that later consciousness],
> [because what] appears to [the earlier consciousness] is not the apprehended [object of the later one]."[391]

This is interpreted as expressing the views of another system. In the [second version, it forms the second line] of the following passage:

> The producer has the characteristic [required] of the apprehended [object].
> There is no [form and so on] appearance that is not [such an] apprehended [object].[392]

This [second passage] is interpreted as expressing the views of our own system. According to the first [version], it could make sense to understand "appearance" as referring to the light that provides illumination [for seeing] forms. But to interpret it as light in the second [would make it] irrelevant to what the passage is discussing. So it should instead be understood as referring to the visual forms and suchlike that "appear" to sense consciousness. And what [Dharmakīrti's original passage] means is: What defines an apprehended [object] is that it produces the consciousness that apprehends it. This is because none of the forms and suchlike that appear to consciousness—[and are thereby the objects] it apprehends—do not produce that consciousness.

There is plenty to say about the meaning of this passage, but it is too much to write here. However, the pronouncements of others on the matter are not to be trusted.[393] [111]

Setting forth our own position

Every one of the numerous things [constituting] the group of direct causes of a sense consciousness fits into the definitive threefold classification of conditions. This is confirmed by the passage:

> So, apart from the sense power, the entity, and the awareness,
> or the earlier mental attention
> that [constitute] the causal group,
> nothing else is related [to the perception's production].[394]

Despite this, a cause of a sense consciousness will not necessarily be one of the three conditions. And in the production of any individual resultant sense consciousness, the three conditions are mutually exclusive.

Setting out the nature of each of the three conditions [that produce a] sense consciousness

[This is explained according to the] Sautrāntika and Cittamātra systems.

The three conditions according to the Sautrāntika system

1. The governing condition
2. The observed [object] condition
3. The immediately preceding condition

The governing condition

Someone defines the governing condition as "that which independently produces its governed result."

[Response:] This cannot work, as it is a *circular definition*. [Anyone who] ascertains that a phenomenon *x* is the governed result of a thing *y* must already have ascertained that *y* is *x*'s governed condition. But [according to this definition, someone who] ascertains that *y* is *x*'s governed condition must already have ascertained that *x* is *y*'s governed result.

The thing specifically being defined here is the governing condition of a *sense consciousness*. This is "the sense power that plays the dominant role in ensuring that its result, a sense consciousness, has the unique character that it does." We note that a sense consciousness, such as that of the visual variety, has three separate qualities: (1) its nature is that of conscious experience, something that is clear and aware, (2) it has taken on the aspect of the visual form [it perceives], and (3) it is limited to the apprehension of visual forms and is incapable of apprehending other things, such as sounds.

The condition chiefly responsible for ensuring that the visual consciousness has the first of these qualities is its *immediately preceding condition*. However, this quality is not unique to visual consciousness, since every consciousness has this same nature of being a clear and aware conscious experience. The *observed [object] condition* is chiefly responsible for ensuring that this consciousness has the second quality. But again, this quality is not exclusive to visual consciousness, as some mental consciousnesses also take on the aspect of the visual forms [they perceive]. So only the third of the qualities can be said to be unique to visual consciousness, distinguishing it [from other consciousnesses]. [112] And it is the *governing condition* that is chiefly responsible for this quality. In the case of visual consciousness, the governing condition is the visual sense power. And because this sense power is the thing principally responsible for supplying the visual consciousness with its own unique character, it is said to "play the dominant role" [in its production]. The auditory and other sense powers should be understood in a similar way.

Let us next turn to the nature of this visual sense power. The existence of a cause [of visual consciousness] apart from its immediately preceding condition and observed [object] condition can be inferred from the fact that the presence of those two alone will not lead to the production of a visual consciousness even on the odd occasion. Such a cause must also be what ensures that the visual consciousness apprehends only visual forms. This is because it is only logical to conclude that one of visual consciousness's principal causes must be responsible for this, but neither the immediately preceding condition nor the observed condition can plausibly be asserted to be that cause. This [other] cause of the visual consciousness—distinct from its immediately preceding condition and observed [object] condition, and chiefly responsible for ensuring that it apprehends only visual forms—is known as the "visual sense power." It is designated "sense *power*" in that it plays the predominant role in shaping the [nature] of its resultant visual consciousness by supplying it with its distinctive character.

This sense power is asserted to be physical material. If instead, it were posited to be consciousness, since no one could seriously maintain that it is conceptual, one would have to assert that it is a nonconceptual consciousness.

Since it would be unreasonable to suggest that it could be a nonconceptual false cognition, it would have to be a valid perception. But the treatises inform us that the view that sense powers can be valid is exclusive to the Vaibhāṣika system. If the Sautrāntika system also had this view, it would follow that it would have a presentation of *valid cognition and its results*[395] that is based on the idea that the sense powers are valid.

We are told that some Abhidharma followers ascribed a shape and a color [to these sense powers], saying that certain of them are, for instance, like those of the flax plant. Whether such views were held by members of this [Sautrāntika] school is difficult to determine. The nature of other sense powers, the auditory and so forth, can be understood by extrapolating from what has been said about the visual consciousness.

The observed [object] condition

The observed [object] condition is that thing directly responsible for making the consciousness apprehending it into something that bears its *aspect*. The observed [object] condition of a sense consciousness and the entity held by that consciousness are equivalent. How the aspect of the object presents itself to sense consciousness and what kind of things serve as the illustrations of the observed [object] condition and the entity held are matters that I have dealt with already, in the section explaining the object. [113] The conclusion was that even though the held entity of a sense consciousness can be a coarse object, this does not mean that the aspect of a coarse object *presents* itself to that consciousness.

The entity held by the sense consciousness, which is responsible for making that consciousness into something that bears its aspect, can never exist simultaneously with that sense consciousness. If the two existed simultaneously, then at such a time, they would already have been fully produced. And since [the idea that] fully produced, fully existent things require any sort of *re*-production is not credible, it would mean they could not be cause and effect.

By the same token, since [that entity] is a cause of the sense consciousness, it would be unfeasible for it to come about later than the [consciousness] that apprehends it. Thus the held entity of a sense consciousness necessarily precedes that consciousness.

However, the fact that the held entity must precede the consciousness does not prevent that consciousness from having it as an object. In being produced, that consciousness takes on the aspect of the object that it holds, and indeed for [a consciousness] to *arise* in the aspect of some phenomenon is exactly what the phenomenon being the object of that consciousness means.

Someone might then ask whether at the time that the sense consciousness [exists], the object it holds has ceased or not. If it has ceased at that time, he might say, then that consciousness could not apprehend it. Conversely, if the object has not ceased, it could not be counted as the cause of that consciousness.

[Response:] By the time that the consciousness [exists], the object that it holds has ceased, but this does not mean that the object cannot be apprehended. The way in which the sense consciousnesses and their respective held entities are posited as subjects and objects with respect to each other is similar to how things are regarded as cause and effect, as I explained earlier. Hence the "time" that the consciousness and the held entity count as subject and object is [a duration] comprising the respective stages during which the two exist and that are its portions.

Someone proposes that those of the Sautrāntika school are also of the opinion that once cognitions are subjected to logical analysis, they are found not to apprehend external entities.

[Response:] Personally, I do not believe that this is what the Sautrāntika system says on the matter. It would follow that [for the Sautrāntika], when subjected to logical analysis, external entities are not established, because once subjected to such analysis, valid cognition no longer verifies them. The reason and predicate [of this argument] are the ones he proposed. The pervasion is also one that he has implicitly acknowledged. The three spheres [are in place].

Generally speaking, there are four distinct ways for an object's aspect to appear in consciousness.[396] It can appear due to (1) *the object*, such as when the aspect of the held entity appears for the perception of a myopic individual, (2) *mental imprints*, such as when the aspect [of something] appears for conceptual cognition, (3) *concentration*, such as when the aspect of the whole range of physical forms, whether gross or subtle, appear for the clairvoyance of divine eye, and (4) *completing the two collections*, such as when the aspect of every single phenomenon appears for an omniscient consciousness. [114]

Entities such as sounds, pots, and the like have two natures: one exclusive to each of them individually and one that they share with others. To the perceptions holding their respective [objects], the aspect of the individual nature appears, whereas the shared one cannot. And to the conceptual cognitions holding their respective [objects], the shared nature appears, whereas the individual one cannot. So an aspect of pot appears both to the perception and the conceptual cognition of pot. But the aspect that appears to the conceptual cognition is referred to as "pot's universal aspect,"[397] whereas the aspect of pot that appears to perception is not called a "universal aspect."

But would this not mean that the inferential cognition realizing that sound is impermanent does not [actually] take a nature that is exclusive to an individual sound and its [quality of] impermanence as its object? And if that were the case, would this not contradict the assertion that this inferential valid cognition takes a *specifically characterized* sound and impermanence as its object(s)?

[Response:] We affirm that this inferential cognition takes a nature that is individual to sound and [its] impermanence as its object. But while this nature is individual to sound and its impermanence, this is not how it appears. [To that inferential cognition] it seems to be a shared nature. We are able to maintain this position without any contradiction due to the distinction we make with respect to conceptual cognition, our assertion being that it is mistaken not about its conceived object but its appearing object.

Someone contends that unless that nature appears [to inferential valid cognition] the idea that [sound and its impermanence] have that nature is undermined.

[Response:] Based on that logic, it would follow that sound and its impermanence do not *appear* to inferential valid cognition in an unclear fashion, because they do not *exist* in an unclear fashion. He cannot challenge this argument's reason, since sound and its impermanence exist in a clear fashion, because that is how they appear to valid perception.[398] So the three spheres [are in place, and his position is therefore irredeemably flawed].

A consciousness such as the visual consciousness apprehending form can be said to have two different facets—the aspect of an external form that it presents in[399] and its identity as a clear and aware conscious experience. The first of these is referred to as the "object-aspect" of the visual consciousness. There is no distinction between this [object-aspect of the visual consciousness], the visual consciousness that apprehends form, and the aspect of form that presents as the visual consciousness apprehending form. The object-aspect of the visual consciousness is therefore the consciousness itself. Thus, when it is said that the aspect "presents" as this consciousness,[400] this should not be interpreted to mean that there is some aspect *separate from* the consciousness, presenting itself to [that consciousness]. Instead, it means that the consciousness itself, by virtue of the particular causes that create it, takes on the aspect of the object. The second facet of the visual consciousness, its identity as a clear and aware conscious experience, is referred to as its "subject-aspect." [115] There is no distinction between this and the self-cognizing perception that experiences the visual consciousness [of form].

What justification do we have for identifying the object-aspect of the visual consciousness as the visual consciousness itself? Let me explain. If one did not identify the object-aspect of a visual consciousness as the visual consciousness itself, the absence of any other suitable candidate would oblige one to identify it as the *object* of that consciousness. But this [option] is not tenable, since from this it would follow that the visual consciousness is a self-cognizing perception, because it would be a perception with *its own nature* as the object it cognized. It would also follow that the visual consciousness is a self-cognizing perception of the object-aspect, because it is a perception of that [object-aspect] but not an "other-cognizing" perception of it.

Someone might disagree [with the latter], claiming that the visual consciousness *is* an other-cognizing perception [of its object-aspect].

[Response:] It would follow that what presents to the visual consciousness is the aspect of its own object-aspect, because it is an other-cognizing perception with respect to its own object-aspect. But if one accepted that, it would follow that the aspect of that object-aspect also requires an aspect [to appear to the visual consciousness] and so forth, creating an infinite regress.

Someone else says that a visual consciousness does not realize external objects in a direct fashion, since there is the mediation of an aspect. He says that what we refer to as the sense consciousness "directly" realizing an external object is actually the visual consciousness directly realizing the aspect of that object.

[Response:] It would follow that nor is the aspect itself directly realized, since there must be an aspect mediating in the process. So the three spheres [are in place].

In terms of the Sautrāntika system, the claim that a visual consciousness is an other-cognizing perception of its own object-aspect has a critical flaw. It would follow that the object-aspect of the visual consciousness must really be an entity that is separate from that consciousness, because that consciousness cognizes it to be something other than itself. But if that were the case, the object-aspect of the visual consciousness would appear to that consciousness to be situated some distance away from it. From this it would follow that the visual consciousness is a *mistaken* one, since the object-aspect seems to it to be situated some distance away, when in fact it is not. This argument is one to which [those who propose the position] have no response.

Anyway, irrespective of whether the position proposed by the aforesaid individual is supposed to represent the Sautrāntika or Cittamātra system, it still follows that a visual consciousness directly realizing blue would [in fact] be a consciousness directly realizing the *aspect* of blue, since [according to him] it is only by virtue of the aspect of blue directly presenting itself to the consciousness that the visual consciousness can be said to realize blue. [116] And for the aspect of blue to directly present to visual consciousness simply means that the aspect of blue directly *appears* to that consciousness. But if he accepts this argument, it would absurdly follow that the blue can only be realized *implicitly* [i.e., indirectly] by this visual consciousness.

Someone else similarly claims that due to the mediation of the aspect, a sense consciousness can never be directly aware of an external entity. He believes that a sense consciousness has no appearing object, since "appearing object" refers to an object that a cognition is able to get at *without* the mediation of an aspect. Thus, according to him, the only kinds of cognitions that have appearing objects are self-cognition and conceptual cognition, the appearing objects of which are respectively an object universal and a consciousness.

[Response:] His assertion about the meaning of appearing object contradicts his claim that a sense consciousness directly apprehends its own object-aspect. It would follow that the object-aspect of a sense consciousness is an object that [the sense consciousness] is able to get at *without* the mediation of an aspect, because it apprehends it directly. The reason and pervasion [of this argument] are the ones that he himself endorsed. But if he now accepts its conclusion, it would follow that the object-aspect of that sense consciousness qualifies as the appearing object. Thus the three spheres are in place, and he is left without any reasonable response.

He also declares that the Sautrāntika system does not differentiate between the appearing object and the held object of a sense consciousness. In another statement, he says that the object held by a sense consciousness is necessarily a cause of that consciousness. But now he must also admit that the object-aspect counts as the appearing object of the sense consciousness. So [we can argue] it would follow that the object-aspect of the sense consciousness is the cause of that consciousness, because it is the object held by that consciousness. The reason and pervasion are ones he himself endorsed. But if he accepts that the object-aspect of the sense consciousness is its cause, it creates various problems for him. For instance, it contradicts a claim [he made elsewhere] that an aspect of whatever variety must be the same entity as the cognition that apprehends it. Thus it would follow that cause and effect can form the same substance, and that a cause and its effect can exist simultaneously. However, in the passage "Except for a causal thing there is nothing that is 'held' [by a cognition],"[401] [Dharmakīrti] stipulated that anything that is the held object of a consciousness must be a cause of that consciousness. Thus his claim that the object-aspect of a sense consciousness can be its cause is one that has absolutely no viability.

According to [this individual], what the "object-aspect of a sense consciousness" properly denotes is the aspect of the object held by that sense consciousness. If he now [claims that] this aspect is the sense consciousness's held object, it must follow that the aspect of blue appearing to the sense consciousness is the blue that appears to that sense consciousness, since the aspect of the sense consciousness's held object is that consciousness's held object. [117]

To sum up, if one rejects the position that the object-aspect of a sense consciousness is the sense consciousness itself, one is obliged to identify it as the object held by that consciousness. That view is susceptible to the various criticisms I have already set out, as well as others that will follow. Similar arguments can be directed against those who do not identify the object-aspect of a conceptual cognition as the conceptual cognition itself.

Someone claims that in the case of self-cognition, an aspect of the object does not present itself.

[Response:] This is untenable. If he claims that there is no aspect of the object in the case of a self-cognition, then if someone were to propose that [similarly] in the case of a visual consciousness, no aspect of [the object] form presents itself, how would he counter it?

He might say that in the case of a visual consciousness, there is little choice but to accept that an aspect of the object is involved. [Turning to the scenario of two people,] a friend and an adversary of an individual, [he might say,] if no aspect were involved, it would follow that when the two people see the physical form of this individual, it must have multiple identities, *both pleasant and unpleasant*. This is because it appears as pleasant and unpleasant to the visual consciousnesses of the respective observers, and their consciousnesses perceive that form in its raw state, without [the mediation] of any sort of aspect. [This individual] might say that this is the argument made in the passage "These cannot be [in the entity's] own nature, since there would be the fault of it having multiple identities."[402]

[Response:] [This is not correct,] since as I outlined in the section on the appearing object, the exact same argument can be made in the case of self-cognition. Quite aside from that, [he is wrong to suggest that] the passage "These cannot be [in the entity's] own nature, since there would be the fault of it having multiple identities" represents a Sautrāntika attack on the Vaibhāṣika view that objects are cognized without the involvement of aspects. This is because the Sautrāntika cannot use this argument to criticize the Vaibhāṣika without corresponding criticisms applying to their own system. This can be explained in the following manner. In the Sautrāntika system, are the visual consciousnesses of the two persons counted as correct? If not, [then their position corresponds to the Vaibhāṣika], because neither would be asserting that this is a case of mistaken cognitions that are able to apprehend the actual entities in a raw state, without the involvement of aspects. If, on the other hand, the Sautrāntika believes that these consciousnesses are correct ones, they would be obliged to maintain that the form of the individual presents an accurate aspect of itself to those two consciousnesses. But in that case, the form of that single individual would be presenting a pleasant aspect to one visual consciousness and an unpleasant aspect to the other. And since those aspects are accurate reflections, one would be forced to conclude that the form must indeed have both pleasant and unpleasant identities. So the Sautrāntika position would be equally vulnerable to the criticisms that apply to the Vaibhāṣika one.

How then is the passage in question to be understood? I explain it like this. The Sautrāntika stance is that the aspect that presents within sense consciousness is provided by the actual entity. Followers of the Cittamātra say that if such were the case, there must be a real [external entity] matching what the aspect reflects. [118] They then attack the notion [that such an object exists,] arguing that it leads to the ridiculous conclusion that the single individual's physical form must have a multiplicity of identities, some pleasant and others unpleasant. According to the Cittamātra system, the aspect is not something supplied by the entity itself but one that arises due to imprints [in the mind]. This still leaves a question about how to account for the line [in the same stanza] that says, "Even if there was an external entity. . . ."[403] This is something that I will discuss later, when explaining the third *conceptual analyses of valid cognition and its result*.

I have already provided some arguments refuting the view that an object can be apprehended without the [involvement of] an aspect, and there are more to follow. Finally, however, they come down to this: If an aspect of a [visual] form, for instance, does not present itself within visual consciousness, then the same must be the case with all other aspects. One thereby loses the grounds for being able to distinguish visual consciousness as that which apprehends visual form but not, for instance, sound. If one asserts that visual consciousness apprehends form without relying on an aspect, this invites the unwanted conclusion that it must equally apprehend everything, sound and all.

The situation is similar with self-cognition. If the subject-aspect of the visual consciousness were to apprehend the object-aspect of that consciousness without reference to an aspect, everything would be similar in not presenting an aspect. And there would be no basis for differentiating between what the self-cognition does and does not apprehend. Thus, if the self-cognition apprehended the object-aspect of the visual consciousness, it would also apprehend that of the auditory one. [What actually happens] therefore is that an aspect of the object-aspect presents itself to the subject-aspect. And as previously stated, what it means for an aspect to "present itself" is that the consciousness, by virtue of the particular causes that create it, itself takes on the aspect of the object.

Someone may argue that if [as we propose] the consciousness apprehending blue is what "presents" in the aspect of blue, it would follow that the [perception of blue] also requires another aspect of blue presenting to [and occasioning] that consciousness. But that in turn, he might say, would require a further aspect and so on, creating an infinite regress.

[Response:] Our position incurs no such fault. Since "present" here simply denotes that the aspect of blue is produced, the [opponent's] argument amounts to no more than him saying, "The production of the aspect of blue requires the production of the aspect of blue." And this is something with which we would agree. There are no more grounds for asserting that this leads to an infinite regress than does the statement "The production of smoke requires the production of smoke."

This explanation regarding what it means to "present an aspect" is one on which both Sautrāntika and Cittamātra would concur. Where they differ is in their identification of the causes responsible for visual consciousness taking on the aspect of form. For the Sautrāntika, it is an external form that causes this, whereas for the Vijñaptika, it is an imprint [in the mind]. It should be noted, however, that of the Vijñaptika system who assert this are those of the True Aspectarian persuasion. [119]

So, when a visual consciousness apprehends an assortment of colors, do the aspects of blue, yellow, and so forth that present themselves [each] count as the visual consciousness apprehending that assortment?

[Response:] The aspect, as a whole, which is composed of and possesses those portions, is the visual consciousness apprehending the assortment of colors. It should be understood that the whole and the portions form a single substance. But the portions are still separate substances from each other. This explanation finds favor with the Opponents of Parity in both the Sautrāntika and the Cittamātra schools.

Someone might question whether or not there are self-cognitions directly experiencing each of the aspects of blue, yellow, and so forth present in the visual consciousness apprehending the assortment of colors. He might say that if not, it would surely disqualify these [aspects] from being object-aspects. Conversely, if self-cognition does experience them, wouldn't the fact that each of the aspects forms a substance distinct from the others mean that there would need to be separate self-cognitions, one for each of them? In that case, he might say, the visual consciousness apprehending the assortment of colors would have numerous subject-aspects, each of them a separate substance. So it must follow that the self-cognizing "experiencer" of that visual consciousness would also need to have many separate substances.

Once again, however, there is no such fault [with our position]. We grant that the subject-aspects experiencing the aspects of blue, yellow, and so forth are separate substances from one another. But the "experiencer" of the visual consciousness apprehending the assortment of colors is not these individual [portions of self-cognition]. Instead, it is the subject-aspect that forms the whole, *made up* of these portions.

The immediate condition

The immediate condition is "that consciousness which, without the interruption of any other cognition, occurs immediately prior to the consciousness in question and is responsible for making it into something that has the identity of a conscious experience." It is "immediate" in the sense that there is no other intervening consciousness. It is a "condition" in that it is a cause. And it "corresponds" in that it shares an identity of consciousness [with the consciousness in question]. This is how the term *corresponding immediate condition* should be understood.[404] A corresponding immediate condition [of another consciousness] does not need to be similar to it in every single respect. There are, for instance, cases of some nonconceptual consciousnesses acting as substantial causes for the conceptual consciousnesses that are their results.

Here, someone might raise the following question. An individual who has remained in meditative equipoise on an uncontaminated transcendent path will arise from that state straight into a state in which his mind is a contaminated one. So what can be posited as the substantial cause for the first temporal portion of the contaminated mind that arises immediately after [the uncontaminated one]? It must surely be the last temporal portion of consciousness of the uncontaminated meditative equipoise. But then it would follow that the last temporal moment of the equipoise is contaminated, because it supports [the production of] a contaminated effect. [120]

[Response:] Something may be contaminated by virtue of being the effect of a "contaminant." But just because something supports [the production of] a contaminated effect in no way means that it must itself be contaminated. Otherwise, any authoritative statement indicating that an [effect] is in some way connected with a cause that is contaminated [must be interpreted to mean that] the effect itself is contaminated. But since a path of seeing necessarily arises as the result of the supreme dharma level of the path of preparation in the continuum of an ordinary being, it would then follow that all paths of seeing are contaminated!

Someone may then ask us to identify the substantial cause of the first temporal portion of consciousness in an individual who has just arisen from the state of suspension absorption.[405]

[Response:] My own position on this matter is as follows. However attenuated the subtle operations of mental consciousness may have become during the state of suspension absorption, it is undeniably the case that they continue in a dim form within the individual's continuum. This is a stance that we are obligated to maintain, given that the [particular philosophical system] we are exploring here denies the existence of the "foundational consciousness."[406] In the absence of the foundational consciousness, any notion of a "deluded awareness,"[407] which is supposed to fixedly observe that consciousness, also becomes untenable. But even those who posit the existence of the foundational consciousness do not believe that the deluded awareness is present during the suspension absorption. They assert that the five "portal" sense consciousnesses,[408] in addition to the coarser level of mental consciousness together with their attendant functions have all been halted. Despite [all of these having been suspended], it would be unacceptable to advocate that consciousness is totally absent from that state.

But why is the absence of consciousness during that state deemed so unacceptable? It is unacceptable because it would be at odds with the sutra passage that states, "The consciousness in the suspension absorption does not [become] disconnected from the body."[409]

[Response:] [If consciousness became decoupled from the body,] it would lead to various ridiculous consequences, such as (1) the [entity it belonged to] would no longer be a sentient entity, (2) the body of someone engaged in the suspension absorption would be comparable to a corpse, and (3) the body of someone engaged in the absorption would need to remain for a prolonged period without being sustained by consciousness, and it would consequently undergo decomposition. [Such an absence of consciousness] would also contravene one of our most basic philosophical tenets—namely, that a living being is a composite of four or five aggregates.

[Considering the] nature of the suspension absorption itself [at that time], if it were some form of consciousness, it could only be a mental consciousness. It could not be the body because that would absurdly mean that it is physical matter. And even if one asserted that the absorption is a composite of the body and mind, as with a person, that would in fact confirm the presence of consciousness. If one denies all three of these alternatives, one would have no choice but to align oneself with those who claim that [the absorption] is simply an imputation, the existence of which is attributed to the body during the spell where the coarser levels of sensation and discrimination have been halted. But given the context within which we are presently working, one would thereby be required to concede that the absorption is not an actual thing, because in this system, an actual thing cannot be an imputed existent.[410] [121] And if the absorption were not an actual thing, one would have to admit that it could not have the capacity to bring about a state of sustained pleasurable comfort in the here and now.

Someone might object to the idea that mental consciousness is present during the state of absorption, on the grounds that mental consciousness is always accompanied by sensations and discrimination. Thus, if consciousness were present, he might say, it would contradict the position that these two are supposed to be halted during the absorption.

[Response:] The sensation and discrimination that are said to be halted within the absorption are those of the *coarser* variety, and I myself would oppose any suggestion that these are present. If those who object to our assertion that consciousness is present are trying to claim that even the dim level of sensation and discrimination are absent during the absorption, they are also setting themselves against those who believe that the foundational consciousness is present, because [advocates of that consciousness] frequently reiterate that the five omnipresent mental functions including that of sensation necessarily accompany the foundational consciousness.

Some may suggest that our [depiction of] the suspension absorption makes it indistinguishable from the "absorption of nondiscrimination."[411] We accept that both of them are aimed at halting the five portal [sense] awarenesses, in addition to the coarser level of mental consciousness and all its associated functions. But there is still a world of difference between the two absorptions in terms, for instance, of whether the paths they employ are mundane or transcendent and whether the mental perspective adopted during the absorption is factually correct or not.

Let us look now at the reasons for this system rejecting the foundational consciousness. If a foundational consciousness were to exist, we could first rule out any idea that it might be a conceptual consciousness. This is because proponents of the foundational consciousness state that it operates uninterruptedly up until the attainment of buddhahood. So it would obviously need to be present in the continuum of someone at the time that he had a conceptual mental consciousness. But [the foundational consciousness] could not exist concurrently with that conceptual mental consciousness, as that would contradict the fundamental tenet [stated by Dharmakīrti] that "No two conceptual consciousnesses can operate simultaneously."[412]

One would therefore have to assert that it must be nonconceptual. But it could not be a nonconceptual false consciousness, because from that it would absurdly follow that we have a false consciousness present in us uninterruptedly, right up to the point of enlightenment. As this is unfeasible, it would be necessary to posit that the foundational consciousness is a perception. But this would contradict our basic philosophical tenets, according to which the perceptions of myopic beings *are* able to distinguish the things they observe and operate with a very high degree of lucidity. This is because those who advocate the existence of a foundational consciousness find it necessary to claim that it is *not* able to properly distinguish [objects], and that while it sees "the world"—comprising the various domains and inhabitants—that the individual shares with other sentient beings in any particular existence, it does so without any real lucidity, to the extent that it has even less clarity than conceptual mental consciousness. [122]

Also, perception is divided into sense, mental, self-cognizing, and yogic varieties. Thus if the foundational consciousness was a form of perception, one would be forced to assert the existence of another kind of perception that does not fit into the fourfold scheme.

Those who accept the existence of a foundational consciousness also find it necessary to posit the "deluded awareness," which [they say] observes the foundational consciousness. They are also obliged to maintain that this deluded awareness is always accompanied by the "view of self," "attachment to self," "confusion regarding the self," and "pride in self"—a series of four [mental notions] that are exclusive to it. That would mean that the view of self and the attachment to self exist concurrently. But *Commentary on Pramāṇa* informs us that the view of self is the cause of attachment to self, indicating that what [Dharmakīrti] holds is that the two occur sequentially.

Those who believe in the existence of the deluded awareness say that it has the aspect of a conceit in the self. This should mean that it is a conceptual consciousness that holds a *śabdārtha*. But those who believe in this deluded awareness all claim that, with a few exceptions—namely, when an individual remains in the meditative equipoise of a transcendent path, is engaged in the suspension absorption, attains the state of arhatship in the Hinayana, or attains the eighth ground in the Mahayana—its presence is constant throughout every stage of cyclic existence. So they are compelled to admit the possibility that someone can simultaneously have two conceptual consciousnesses. But this would contravene the philosophical principle [that Dharmakīrti] conveys in the line "No two conceptual consciousnesses are seen simultaneously."[413]

Those who believe that there is a deluded awareness also treat the view of self and confusion regarding self as though they were two separate things. But this position does not correspond with that of the present system. [Dharmakīrti] considers these two as equivalent, since according to him, the *view [associated with the] transitory composite*[414] and *deluded ignorance*[415] are equivalent.

As it has now been demonstrated that the deluded awareness is not accepted [in this system], it is also logical to conclude that neither is the foundational consciousness. Belief in the foundational consciousness is inextricably linked with belief in the deluded awareness. Those who posit the foundational consciousness contend that it serves as the referent object for the notion of self. It is the awareness that refers to the foundational consciousness and then develops a conceit in the self that they label the "deluded awareness."

Those who assert that there is such a thing as the foundational consciousness also claim that every individual foundational consciousness in the continua of beings belonging to either of the two lower realms [i.e., the desire realm and form realm] directly sees such things as the visual sense powers of both themselves and other beings. [123]

If this were accepted [in the present system], it would need to assert that any ordinary being belonging to the desire or form realm necessarily has in his continuum a consciousness whose overt objects are the visual and other sense powers. But [the present system] disagrees with this.

To sum up then, belief in the foundational consciousness is incompatible with a great number of basic tenets set forth in the Seven Treatises. Hence there is no place for the foundational consciousness here, and those who assert it within the context of the Seven Treatises can be likened to sightless individuals attempting to examine an elephant. However much of their [uneducated] cowherd's version of reasoning they repeat, nothing in it will be to the liking of real scholars.

Although the foundational consciousness is not accepted here, the position that there is no consciousness during the suspension absorption is unsustainable. The various arguments refuting the presence of other types of consciousness than the mental one during the absorption essentially establish the case that the consciousness that is present must be mental consciousness. The very last temporal portion of that consciousness, which occurs just prior to the person leaving that state of absorption, should therefore be identified as both the substantial cause and the immediate condition for the first temporal portion of consciousness that arises outside that state [of absorption], and there is no need to search for any immediate condition beyond this.

Someone else suggests that the last temporal portion of an individual's consciousness as he is about to enter the absorption should be identified as the immediate condition for the first temporal portion of his consciousness that occurs as soon as he leaves that state. Elsewhere, [this individual] claims that the physical body cannot act as the substantial cause for consciousness. He also explains that the term "immediate" refers to the fact that no other consciousness interrupts [that condition and the consciousness it produces].

[Response:] What about the first temporal portion of consciousness [of the person] who has just left such a state of absorption? Does it have a direct substantial cause, or not? If it does not, it would follow that it was disqualified from being an actual thing. So if that [cause] exists, what is it? Does the consciousness of the person at the point he is just about to leave the absorption serve as the direct substantial cause for the first temporal portion of his consciousness outside the absorption? If that is accepted, it would follow that the consciousness of the person who is on the verge of entering the absorption is not the immediate condition of his consciousness as he is about to leave it, because those two consciousnesses would be interrupted by the direct substantial cause [of the latter]. Thus the three spheres [would be in place]. The [individual] might identify the last [temporal portion] of the person's physical body just as he is about to leave the absorption as the direct substantial cause here. But that is not eligible to be the direct substantial cause of consciousness, since it is a physical body. Thus again, the three spheres [would be in place].

He may say that the last temporal portion of consciousness of the person entering the absorption acts as the substantial cause here. But is he proposing that the absorption is the result of that consciousness or not? If it is not, in the absence of any other suitable candidate as its cause, we would have to conclude that the absorption occurs [randomly,] without causes. [124] But if he agrees that the absorption *is* the result of that consciousness, it would follow that the final temporal portion of the person's consciousness as he is about to enter absorption cannot be the *direct* substantial cause of the first temporal portion of his consciousness as he leaves it, because another result of that final temporal portion [namely, the absorption] interrupts the two consciousnesses. So once more, with the three spheres [in place, this individual's position is shown to be irredeemably flawed].

Now if he can come up with something other than the three things mentioned that could serve as the direct substantial cause, it would certainly be permissible to posit that it is also the immediate condition. And there would be no need for him to argue that the consciousness of the person as he is about to enter the absorption is the immediate condition. But if he cannot come up with a direct substantial cause apart from those three, the conclusion must be that such a thing does not exist—a position that seems highly unsatisfactory.

Someone else identifies the final temporal portion of the physical body of a person about to rise from the absorption as [both] the substantial cause and the immediate condition for the initial temporal portion of his mind after he has just arisen. He also claims that when a being in the formless realm is on the verge of death, it is the final temporal portion of his consciousness that serves as the substantial cause for the first temporal portion of the physical body he is about to adopt as he passes into the intermediate existence of one destined for rebirth in the form or desire realm.

[Response:] This view—that consciousness can act as the substantial cause of the physical body and the physical body can act as the substantial cause of consciousness—belongs to the non-Buddhist schools. None of those who espoused Buddhist philosophical tenets in the land of āryas ever maintained such a thing. It is [a view] that [the Pramāṇa] treatises counter. They refute it, for example, through an analysis that questions whether the physical body that [the non-Buddhist philosophers propose] is acting as the substantial cause of consciousness has sense powers or not. They also refute it with various consequences, such as it meaning that a person's continuum would simultaneously have multiple mental consciousnesses.

It would also follow that both the body and mind of the person who has just arisen from the absorption must be the same kind of substance, because they derive from a single substantial cause. Moreover, if the physical body were able to act as the substantial cause for the mind, it would essentially be impossible to prove the existence of past lives. The problems with his view are very serious and abundant. Still, the fallacies arising from what is an antithetical position [for Buddhists] are not worthy objects of scholarly analysis. [125]

[Supposing, however, as he asserts, that] the final temporal portion of consciousness for a being in the formless realm who is on the verge of death serves as the substantial cause for the first temporal portion of the physical body he is about to adopt as he passes into the intermediate existence of one destined to be reborn in the desire realm. It would follow that the visual and other sense powers belonging to that new body in the intermediate existence must all be the same kind of substance, because they all derive from a single substantial cause. It would also mean that the first temporal portion of all five visual and other sense powers arose with a mental consciousness [acting as] their substantial cause. But if this was the case for those first temporal portions, it must also be the case for subsequent ones. It would absurdly follow that every individual physical body necessarily has its origin in a mental consciousness [that acted as] its substantial cause. Both of these theses deviate from the parameters laid down in passages such as "Any consciousness has ignorance as its substantial cause"[416] and "It is also established that a thing that is not a consciousness cannot be the substantial cause of one that is consciousness."[417]

Someone attempts to deal with these criticisms by saying that if the second chapter of the *Commentary on Pramāṇa* was basically a Sautrāntika text, [the view that physical form can have consciousness as its substantial cause] would indeed be contradicted [by what the two passages say]. But he proposes that there is no such problem, since "The [second chapter is a] text shared by [both] vehicles."[418]

[Response:] O you, whose intellectual [abilities] must arouse mirth among the gods! Let us examine this idea of yours that a text can be shared by both vehicles. If by "shared" you mean that both the Sautrāntika and the Cittamātra systems agree with what the text asserts, then your argument effectively says, "The Sautrāntika school espouses a position that is contradicted by the content of the text's passages, but this is not a problem, because *both* the Sautrāntika and the Cittamātra schools agree with the content of these passages." And with a single comment [I have] laid bare the full extent of your intellectual powers! If the text were exclusive to either the Sautrāntika or the Cittamātra system, it could not be counted as one that is "shared" by both vehicles. Otherwise, a text being exclusive to any one vehicle would be an impossibility. But when you state, "The text is shared by [both] vehicles," you have no choice but to explain [the vehicles] as referring to the Sautrāntika and the Cittamātra, because even you would not claim that this text is shared by the likes of the Vaibhāṣika or the Madhyamaka, who clearly have no place in the present discussion. Again, there are a great many things that might be said on this matter, but I will refrain from doing so, as it will take up too much space.

So what then do I identify as the actual substantial cause for the first temporal portion of the physical body of someone who has just passed from the formless realm into the intermediate existence of one destined for rebirth in the desire realm? I say that the substantial cause is an imprint [stored] in the mental consciousness of the individual who is passing from the formless realm. This imprint was laid down by some action previously performed by that individual, and it now propels him into a rebirth in the desire realm. This position is in keeping with the majority of treatises by the great pioneers and is also the point made in the *Commentary on Pramāṇa* where it says: [126]

> [So] they depend upon mind.
> And as [mind] is the cause of the sense powers,
> the sense powers are [said to be] derived from mind.[419]

Similarly, this is what [Prajñākaragupta's] *Ornament* refers to where he says, "Also, when it comes to the production of a [new] body for those who, upon death, pass from the formless realm, this is the cause that forms things."[420] Here [that which] "forms" is another way of referring to karma [action]. Furthermore, Ravigupta remarked, "Also, when it comes to the production of a [new] body for those beings who, upon death, pass from the formless realm, the cause is the imprint that forms a body composed of the five sense bases."[421]

Some might challenge our identification of an imprint as the substantial cause, saying that this contradicts our position that consciousness cannot be the substantial cause [of physical bodies], because, [they might assert,] imprints are [in the nature of] consciousness.

[Response:] The claim that imprints are conscious [phenomena] represents the senseless prattle of those who lack any acquaintance with the great treatises. Supposing [for a moment] that an imprint is something conscious, is it to be equated with the consciousness to which it belongs, or is it separate from that consciousness? If it is the former, it would follow that all imprints in a mental consciousness that is virtuous would themselves also need to be virtuous. But if that were accepted, it would absurdly follow that simply due to being [present] in a mental consciousness that was in a virtuous [state], even those imprints that are obscurations would also be virtuous!

What is more, it would follow that the imprints for such things as desirous attachment, hatred, and so forth that are present in the mental consciousness are themselves mental consciousness. But if that were accepted, it would follow that one person has multiple primary mental consciousnesses, which are separate substances from one another, present in his continuum at any one time.

Some might deny that such imprints are separate substances from one another.

[Response:] It would follow that these imprints do not derive individually from separate substantial causes. And if he accepts that, it would follow that desirous attachment and hatred are not separate substances.

The alternative position, [that an imprint] is a sort of consciousness but one that is separate from the consciousness that it belongs to, is also untenable. If one divides consciousness, there is no third alternative beyond conceptual and nonconceptual varieties. So which of these two is the imprint? If it is a conceptual consciousness, then since it is permissible for a person to have many imprints at the same time, it follows that multiple conceptual consciousnesses that are different substances can exist simultaneously in one person's continuum. Alternatively, if the imprints are nonconceptual, since they obviously could not be nonconceptual sense perceptions, they could only be mental consciousnesses. [127] But then the criticism that this would allow multiple mental consciousnesses that are different substances to be present simultaneously in a person's continuum would remain.

Someone might say that the imprint of a visual perception is a visual perception, the imprint of an auditory perception is an auditory perception, and so on, and that this is the way to understand the assertion that imprints are consciousness.

[Response:] It would follow that the five portal [sense] consciousnesses are present in the continuum of someone in the formless realm, because he has the imprints of those consciousnesses.

Thus the view that imprints are consciousness is not one found among the very learned and is just the vulgar creation of those who do not understand the application of logical reasoning.

Someone may dispute [our position], claiming that if one asserts imprints can be substantial causes, one must also accept that the actions responsible for laying down those imprints can be substantial causes. But since actions are consciousness, he might say, this would confirm that there are cases of consciousness acting as the substantial cause for the physical body.

[Response:] We reject this criticism. The kind of imprints laid down by actions [i.e., karma] are substantial causes. As for the karmas themselves, they are not substantial causes but the governing conditions of *maturing effects*.[422] Indeed, in response to [the opponent's proposition that "No criticism [can be made of our position: beings have varying degrees of delusion], just as they have varying degrees of physical attractiveness," this is the very point [Dharmakīrti] has in mind when he says, "The same argument applies to your position: If [it was the elements that] governed [the attractiveness of beings], not their karmas, [they should all be equally attractive]."[423] He thereby affirms that karmas [i.e., actions] serve as the governing conditions of such things as the physical forms of living beings.

This concludes the presentation of the three conditions according to the Sautrāntika system and the discussion of various ancillary issues.

The three conditions according to the Cittamātra system

1. Identification of the object condition of sense perception
2. Identification of the governing condition of sense perception
3. Identification of the immediate condition of sense perception

Identification of the object condition of sense perception according to the Cittamātra system

1. An account of the object condition
2. Subsidiary topic: a discussion about the reasoning [establishing] the *simultaneity of object and perception*

An account of the object condition

Someone advocates that [in the Cittamātra system] a number of things can permissibly be identified as the object condition in the case of a visual consciousness, such as that of blue. These are (1) the aspect of blue that presents itself to the visual consciousness of blue, (2) [the thing that] appears as blue, (3) blue, (4) the earlier consciousness that served as the immediate condition for the visual consciousness of blue, and (5) the capacity present in that earlier consciousness to produce a visual consciousness that has the aspect of its object. [128]

[Response:] Of these, he is wrong to assert that (3) blue, (2) [the thing that] appears as blue, or (1) the aspect of blue that presents itself to the visual consciousness of blue can serve as the object condition. Only something that is the cause of another thing can serve is its object condition. But those three that he proposes form part of the visual consciousness's own *nature* and hence cannot be its cause. If some phenomenon is part of a thing's nature, it is precluded from being that thing's cause. Otherwise, it leads to the absurd position of self-production.

Some may dispute this, saying that what self-production [refers to] is a thing that produces *itself*, and that something produced by a phenomenon that forms part of its own nature does not count as self-production.

[Response:] By that reckoning, the Sāṃkhya's view that a pot is produced from the raw clay that is part of its own nature would not amount to an assertion of self-production. This would invalidate the whole line of reasoning pursued by the great pioneers such as Ārya Nāgārjuna and his spiritual son [Āryadeva], who argue against the notion that a pot is produced from the raw clay that is part of its own nature, on the grounds that this *does* constitute an assertion of self-production. And [if the Sāṃkhya's view did not count as self-production,] since there is no one who supports the idea that pot actually arises from itself, this would mean that absolutely no one promoted the philosophical extreme known as "self-production." Therefore the [individuals in question] give every indication that they have fundamentally failed to understand the real import of self-production.

In addition to that, the aforementioned three things cannot be the object conditions of the visual consciousness of blue [in the Cittamātra system], because they each exist simultaneously with that consciousness and constitute the same substance as it. If this did not exclude them from being object conditions, it would follow that cause and effect can exist simultaneously and constitute the same substance. None of those three can qualify as the object condition of the visual consciousness of blue, because each of them exists simultaneously with it, and the object condition of that perception must be something that is not simultaneous with it.

Someone might challenge this last point and assert that the object condition can be simultaneous with the consciousness. But then it would follow that the immediate condition of the perception is also simultaneous with it. Why? Because the object condition is simultaneous with it, and if it is the case that the object condition is the consciousness's direct cause, the immediate condition must also be its direct cause. Basically, anyone who claims that the aforementioned blue and so forth are the object conditions of the visual consciousness of blue is forced into [one of two positions]. Either he must grant that the three are *not* simultaneous with that consciousness and are of a substance that is separate from that of the consciousness, or he must concede that the immediate condition is *also* [like the object condition] simultaneous with that consciousness and is the same substance as that consciousness. [129] Thus reconciling the schemes in a coherent manner becomes difficult.[424]

Someone maintains that there is a way to posit blue as the object condition of the visual consciousness without it entailing that cause and effect constitute the same substance. He suggests that it is only upon logical analysis that the [object condition and the visual consciousness] reveal themselves to be of the same substance and thus cannot [viably] be cause and effect. He suggests that when they are not subjected to such analysis, they are cause and effect, without being a single substance. He furthermore proposes that the type of analysis he refers to here is one that seeks to determine whether or not the things in question are substances, and that this is not the variety that looks into their ultimate status.

[Response:] In the context where the two are counted as cause and effect, is it or is it not appropriate to analyze whether the two are substance(s)? To say that it is inappropriate would amount to asserting that it is possible to have cases of cause and effect where the two things involved neither are nor are not substance(s). Thus assuming that this form of analysis is appropriate, the issue then is whether or not the two are substance(s). If they are not, it follows that cause and effect in which neither thing concerned is actually a substance would be viable. If, on the other hand, the two things are substances, then they must, in the context in question, constitute either the same substance or separate substances. Once he concedes this, he would have to agree that they should, in this context, be separate substances, because he has freely admitted that they must be either the same substance or separate substances but that there is no need for them to be a single substance. He has accepted both parts of this reason, so [presumably] would agree with the conclusion. But if he does, it would follow that the two are separate substances, because they are cause and effect. So, with the three spheres [in place, his position is shown to be irredeemably flawed]. What is more, [this individual] has ventured that a logical analysis into whether certain entities count as substances is not one that looks at their ultimate status. But this is totally incompatible with the assertion [he makes elsewhere] that to be a substance is to [exist in the] ultimate sense.

Also, if, as he asserts, when [blue and the perception of blue] are subject to analysis, they are [seen] not to be cause and effect, it would follow that in the same context, [the blue] does not count as the object condition of the [visual perception]. But there is nothing else that could [be posited] as the object condition in that context. It would follow, therefore, that it is possible to have a sense perception that is not derived from any of the three conditions, because even when subjected to analysis, there is still a sense perception [remaining], but it is one not produced by the three conditions. But he cannot agree to this without contravening his own basic tenet that such a thing is impossible.

It might be suggested that the consciousness that is the immediately preceding condition [of the visual perception] could also be its object condition.

[Response:] This is untenable. One would have to accept that this same earlier consciousness also serves as the governing condition. [130] So apart from the consciousness that is the immediately preceding condition, the sense perception would have no other direct cause. But such a position is fatally undermined by the logical arguments explained [in authoritative works] establishing that it is impossible to have an effect that is derived from a single direct cause. [His position also implies that] a substantial cause can produce a result without having to rely on contributory conditions.

Someone else refers to the capacity within the earlier sense consciousness to make the sense consciousness following it into one that has the aspect of that later consciousness's object. According to him, it is this capacity that is the object condition of the later consciousness. He [similarly] identifies the governing condition as a capacity existing in the earlier sense consciousness to make the later consciousness into one that ascertains different objects. Likewise, [he says,] the immediate condition is the capacity [in the earlier consciousness] responsible for making the following consciousness into something that has the nature of a conscious experience. He believes that none of these capacities exist separately from the thing that possesses them, and that while we may talk of *three* conditions [producing] a later sense consciousness, these are all in fact nominal distinctions of identity made within a single entity.[425]

[Response:] Effectively, he says that what establishes that the three conditions must be the same entity are that (1) they are capacities within a single consciousness and that (2) the capacities do not exist separately from the thing that possesses them. But we say that this is not a conclusive reason. If it was, then by extension, when a visual consciousness sees a variety of colors, such as blue, yellow, white, and red, it must follow that those colors all count as a single entity, because (1) they are all the overt object of a single sense consciousness and (2) the overt object of a sense consciousness does not exist separately from that consciousness. This argument's reason and the pervasion are the ones that he advanced. But he cannot agree with its conclusion, since it contradicts the passage "a blue and yellow, which are different from one another . . . ,"[426] where [Dharmakīrti] affirms that even in the Cittamātra system, blue and yellow are separate substances.

Someone proposes that the object condition derives its name from the fact that it is both the thing observed [by the consciousness] and the condition [that helps produce it]. But in other pronouncements on the topic, we find him asserting that (1) the object condition of any given consciousness is the consciousness that occurred just prior to it or some capacity present in that earlier consciousness, (2) the object condition of any sense consciousness needs to be one that has *simultaneity* with it,[427] and (3) things that have such simultaneity must exist concurrently.

[Response:] These positions are basically at odds with one another, because it would absurdly follow that the earlier and later sense consciousnesses occur simultaneously.

It also implies that the [object condition] is an entity confined to the internal cognitive domain of the later consciousness that holds it. But if that were the case, a later sense consciousness could never shift to an object that was different to that of the earlier consciousness. [131]

What then is the correct stance on the object condition? In his *Analysis of Objects of Cognition*, Dignāga provides us with two descriptions of the object condition. In one of them he states:

> The thing one knows is internal, [despite] appearing as external.
> This thing is the [object condition]

> because it is in the nature of [that] consciousness
> and because it is also the condition.[428]

In the other, he says:

> Alternatively, it is [the object condition] because it provides the capacity, in successive stages.[429]

The meaning of the first passage is as follows. Things such as blue, which appear to the sense consciousnesses as if they were external entities, are the objects of those consciousnesses. They are the objects observed by those consciousnesses, as well as the conditions that produce them, and are hence known as "object conditions." Then "It is in the nature of [that] consciousness" informs us why that [blue] is counted as the thing observed—namely, because it is the object that is in the nature of the consciousness observing it. As to why it is considered to be a condition, the same treatise states, "Even though it is one portion [of the consciousness], it is [still] the condition, since it is unfailing."[430] The blue that appears to a sense consciousness is a cause. It makes up one portion of that particular sense consciousness's entity and must therefore be simultaneous with that consciousness. In spite of this, it can still legitimately be regarded as the condition. This is because, as the treatise states, its concomitance with that consciousness is unfailing; as long as it has this [blue] as its object, the consciousness will arise, but without this, it will not.

Proposing a different interpretation, some have [linked] the line "It is in the nature of [that] consciousness"[431] with "appearing as external" and added the qualifications "conventional" and "ultimate." They say what [Dignāga] asserts here is that "It is in the conventional sense that it is seen as the external object, because in the ultimate sense, it is in the nature of consciousness."

[Response:] If that were the case, "It is in the nature of [that] consciousness" would represent a repetition of what has already been stated in the line "The thing one knows is internal."[432] Also [this explanation cannot be correct] because in the present [Cittamātra] context, the belief is that the existence of external objects is refuted by logic even in a conventional sense. Furthermore, if what the passage asserts is that "in the ultimate sense [the object] is in the nature of consciousness," it would make [Dignāga's] reason "being the object observed and being the condition" into one that was irrelevant, established nothing, and thus unfitting for the occasion. For these three reasons, this interpretation is in fact so far from what the passage intends to convey that it is obviously [derived from someone] who is only familiar with the treatises in the sense of having trained his ears.[433]

The description of the object condition in the [first] passage [by Dignāga] is actually based on a version of things presented by earlier masters such as Vasubandhu, following the Abhidharma system. As such, it entertains the possibility that a cause and an effect can exist simultaneously and may not be separate substances. While the lord of reasoning [Dignāga] outlines this position here, he does not personally endorse it. For his own view regarding the object condition, we must turn to the [second] passage, "Alternatively, it is [the object condition] because it provides the capacity, in successive stages." [132] In this line, the term "alternatively" is meant as a paratextual remark within [Dignāga's] commentary, which creates a contextual bridge [between the two passages]. Effectively, what he says is "Earlier masters certainly explained the object condition in the way [that I have just described]. *Alternatively*, there is the way that I, [Dignāga,] explain it." The words "it is [the object condition] because it provides the capacity, in successive stages" convey that "The capacity present in each preceding consciousness to produce its result, a succeeding consciousness, which has the aspect of its object [A] is the object condition of each successive consciousness [B], because it is the condition responsible for providing its result, the consciousness that succeeds it, with the aspect of the object [C]."[434] [Thus Dignāga describes] a logical proof, the subject of which is conveyed by "capacity" and the probans [i.e., reason] by "provides." He does not intend that these two should be fused together to produce a single reason, "[because] it provides the capacity." Such a reason would be unconnected [to the context.]

[The proof Dignāga intended his reason to be used in could not have been:] (1) "Something [A] is the object condition for the later consciousness [B] because it provides that *later consciousness* with the capacity [C]." Why? Because the pervasion would be unconnected. [Nor could it have been:] (2) "Something [A] is the object condition for the later [consciousness] [B] because it provides the *earlier consciousness* with the capacity [C]." Why? Because then it would follow that the object condition of a sense consciousness was the *indirect* cause of that sense consciousness.[435]

When [Dignāga] says that the capacity present in the earlier consciousness is the object condition for the later consciousness, this does not amount to an assertion that the capacity qualifies as such because it is both the object observed by that later consciousness and a condition [that produces] it. Instead, he is saying that the capacity is referred to as the "object condition" due to the fact that it is the principal condition responsible for making the later consciousness into something that has the aspect of the object [it observes]. In the Cittamātra system, the aspect is not presented to the sense consciousness by an [external] object; it arises from an imprint. It is an imprint present in the earlier sense consciousness that is responsible for giving rise to the later consciousness and making it into something that has the aspect of the object. This imprint, taking the form of an *imprint for a continuity of kind*,[436] is the aforesaid capacity. As this is the condition chiefly responsible for making its result—that later consciousness—into something that has the aspect of the object, it is described as the "object condition" of the later consciousness. This is an extremely sophisticated position that has its origins in a commitment to certain philosophical tenets.

Given all this, how are we to interpret [Dignāga's] statement—in his autocommentary to the *Analysis of Objects of Cognition*—where he says that the object condition is something with two characteristics?[437] [133] Those who hold that the object condition of a sense consciousness is an [external object] such as the blue that appears to that sense consciousness [can interpret the statement as referring to the fact that] this blue qualifies as the object condition because it has two characteristics: it is (1) the thing that the consciousness in question observes and (2) the condition [that produces] the consciousness. Whereas for those such as Dignāga himself, who hold that the object condition is a capacity, this statement should be taken to refer to the fact that this [capacity] qualifies as the object condition because it has two characteristics: it is (1) the thing responsible for supplying the aspect that the sense consciousness observes and (2) the condition [that produces] the consciousness.[438]

It is in the same context that the following passage from the autocommentary to the *Analysis of the Objects of Cognition* occurs: "[One may] on certain occasions [speak of] the consciousness arising in the aspect of the object from the maturing of a capacity and, on other [occasions,] of the capacity arising from the aspect of that [consciousness]. One may choose to describe those two as being either distinct or nondistinct from consciousness. Thus it is the internal object with the two features that can correctly [be described as] the object condition."[439]

To conclude, according to our system, something qualifies as the object condition of a sense consciousness by virtue of being the thing responsible for making that consciousness into something that has the aspect of [the object] it observes. However, this does not necessarily entail that this thing is *observed* by that consciousness.[440]

With my own intellect as the observer
and all knowable things as the observed,
I have explained the object condition of sense consciousness with
unfailing accuracy,
just as taught in the *Analysis of Objects of Cognition*.

A discussion about the reasoning [establishing] the "simultaneity of object and subject"

1. Discussion on the aim of this proof
2. Formulating the proof and identifying its three components
3. Establishing [the reason's fulfillment of] each of the [three] criteria

Discussion on the aim of this proof

This proof is presented by someone of the Cittamātra school, taking the role of the proponent, to a member of a [Buddhist] realist school, taking the role of the respondent. It aims to prove that the blue and so forth that appear to sense consciousness to be "outside" are not in fact external entities. By means of the proof of simultaneity,[441] the follower of the Cittamātra seeks to establish that the object and subject are not separate substances. [The Cittamātra belief is that] unless the object is the same substance as the consciousness apprehending it, one must accept that it is external to that consciousness. [134] Similarly, [the Cittamātra maintains that] unless the visual forms, sounds, and the like are the same substance as the sense consciousnesses of the myopic beings who apprehend them, one must accept that they exist in exactly the way they appear to those consciousnesses—namely, located at a distance from them [in space]. This would oblige one to accept that they are entities external to consciousness. What the proof of simultaneity sets out to establish, therefore, is that those objects are *not* substances separate from the sense consciousnesses of the myopic beings who apprehend them.

This proof is not [designed] to establish that Devadatta's mind, for instance, is not a separate substance from the superknowledge that knows others' minds.[442] And it would not follow, from its inability to establish such a thing that Devadatta's mind was an external entity. Such [superknowledges] are not the type of consciousnesses referred to when the proof of simultaneity is used to establish that certain objects and subjects are not substances separate from each other. The proof of simultaneity is used to establish that [sense] objects, such as blue, are the same substance as the consciousnesses, such as visual and other consciousnesses that apprehend them—but [only] in those cases where one would otherwise be obliged to accept that the objects must be external entities. The proof's aim is not [furthermore] to establish that every consciousness with an object such as blue must be the same substance as that object. Otherwise, it would follow that objects such as blue are the same substance as omniscient wisdom. If, on the other hand, one follows the opinion of our Tibetan "logicians," the majority of whom say that for the Cittamātra, *no* subject and object can be distinct substances, one can only end up with the conclusion that the omniscient wisdom directly perceiving selflessness is the same substance as self-grasping! And thus the very notion of separate substances in the Cittamātra system becomes unviable.

Formulating the Proof and Identifying Its Three Components

The proof is formulated in the following manner: "Whatever is ascertained to have observational simultaneity with another thing is of a substance that is not separate from that thing, just as is the case, for example, with a sound and a *heard thing*. The blue that appears to a visual perception apprehending it and that visual perception of blue are ascertained to have observational simultaneity."

Regarding the three components of the proof—the reason, the predicate, and the subject—someone identifies the aspect of blue as the subject.[443]

[Response:] This is incorrect. Among the respondents to whom the proof [might be] presented, the Sautrāntika has already established that, with respect to the visual perception apprehending blue, what presents as the aspect of blue is not a separate substance from that perception.[444] And the Vaibhāṣika, for his part, does not believe in the existence of an aspect, and so an [aspect could not serve as] an agreed subject for the [proponent and respondent].

Someone else posits that "the appearance as blue" is the subject of this proof.

[Response:] This is also wrong. The [appearance as blue] cannot serve as the subject, since there is no way to establish that it has simultaneity with the visual consciousness of blue. Why? Because it is something that is present in that visual consciousness.[445] Also, the appearance as blue to the visual consciousness that apprehends blue cannot be the subject here, because for the Vaibhāṣika, there is no such subject. [135] As far as [the Vaibhāṣika] is concerned, it is the sense power, not the visual consciousness, that apprehends the object. That being the case, he does not accept the existence of the "appearance as blue."

But what evidence is there for asserting that the Vaibhāṣika does not believe that a visual consciousness apprehends its object? The Vaibhāṣika's line of thinking is that visual consciousness, [being consciousness,] cannot be impeded by physical entities, and so if it were able to apprehend objects, vision would not be blocked [even] by such things as mountains. The Vaibhāṣika therefore concludes that what apprehends physical form is the visual sense power, not the visual consciousness that depends on that sense power. This is the position described in the *Treasury of the Abhidharma* when outlining the Vaibhāṣika's views:

> It is supposedly the eye that is the basis for seeing forms,
> not the consciousness that depends on that [eye].
> Why? Because [we] do not see those forms
> that are blocked [from our sight].[446]

According to our system, the [subjects] that Buddhist realists and idealists share and that serve as the basis for their dispute over whether or not they exist external to the sense consciousnesses of the myopic beings that apprehend them, are *the five objects, such as form and sound*. It is those five objects that the two Buddhist realist schools attempt to establish are external entities, whereas the idealists—using their proof of simultaneity—wish to demonstrate that these are the same substance as the sense consciousnesses that apprehend them. Thus it is the five objects, form and so forth, that are the *subject* in the proof of simultaneity, the reasoning establishing that they are the same substance as the respective sense consciousnesses that apprehend them. So, [more specifically,] where the proof of simultaneity is [employed] to establish that [the object] apprehended by the visual consciousness of blue is not a separate substance from that consciousness, *blue* is the subject.

Let us now briefly deal with some of the incorrect views regarding this point. [136] Someone proposes that blue and the like cannot be the subjects [of the proof] for the Cittamātra, because as far as the Cittamātra is concerned, blue and the like are not established bases. He reasons that if things such as blue were established bases, it would mean that physical material is also established, and this would in turn entail the existence of [genuine] external entities. Thus he says that in the Cittamātra system, form and so forth cannot be established bases.

[Response:] Based on this logic, it follows that there could be no account of the five aggregates in the Cittamātra system, because the form aggregate would not be an established basis according to that system. And if he accepted that, he would also have to concede that neither could there be accounts of the eighteen elements or the twelve sense bases in the Cittamātra system. If he accepted that, he would either be accusing the Cittamātra of disparaging the majority of the scriptural corpus by denying that they contain such accounts, or he would be declaring his intention to brazenly disregard the presence of the numerous accounts of the aggregates and so forth that appear in the majority of Cittamātra works.

What is more, if he is correct [to claim that] the likes of blue and yellow are not established bases in the system that advances the proof of simultaneity, it follows that [adherents of that system] would not offer [the likes of blue and yellow] as instances of things that are distinct substances when they present a *dissimilar example* [in support] of that proof. But this is hardly something that he can concede, as it would amount to rejecting all passages relevant to this in the *Commentary on Pramāṇa* and the *Ascertainment of Pramāṇa*, such as "[Just like] there is no guarantee that a blue and yellow, which are different from each other, will be experienced [together]."[447]

In fact, subscribing to the position [of this individual] makes it impossible to endorse any accounts of [what exists in] samsara and nirvana, including descriptions of the three realms and the three bodies [of a buddha]. This is a position that we can see leading only to untold grief.

Elsewhere, someone asserts that while blue, yellow, and so forth may be established bases, blue is not [actually] blue but is consciousness. Likewise, he says that in the Cittamātra system, all things such as blue and yellow are necessarily the consciousnesses that apprehend them. Stated succinctly, he proposes that the likes of blue must be judged to be the visual perceptions that apprehend them, because the alternative would be that blue and yellow are physical material, meaning that they must be externally established entities.

[Response:] This position also is untenable. If blue is necessarily the consciousness that apprehends it, it follows that every individual blue would in fact be an instance of omniscient consciousness. By this reckoning, one would eventually be forced to accept that every single established basis is in reality an example of omniscient consciousness. [137] And as he basically asserts that a thing is the perception that apprehends it, then it would also follow that blue is [actually] a self-cognizing perception. But if that were the case, it would go against [his own] assertion that [blue] is a visual perception. So if one uses his logic, one is unwittingly forced into maintaining that every established basis is a self-cognizing perception!

Added to this, it follows that wherever there is a living being with corporeal form, there must also be a visual perception, because [according to him] any form is necessarily a visual perception. But if that were the case, it would be impossible to have someone who was blind! And since one would also have to maintain that a sound is in fact an auditory perception, it would similarly make a deaf person an impossibility. Also, since something that has a visual form, sound, smell, taste, and tactility—such as a pot—is [experienced by] all five portal sense perceptions, one would eventually be obliged to concede that every such thing—pillars, pots, and the like—must in fact be living beings. Thus this view would obviously be that of the Cārvāka and the Nirgrantha, who deem elements such as the earth element to be living creatures and [vegetation] such as trees to be sentient.

Also, it would follow that every individual blue is a conceptual consciousness of blue, since [according to him] any blue is necessarily the consciousness that apprehends it. The reason is the one that he has proposed. But if he were to accept [the argument's conclusion], we would ask him whether or not something that is a perception apprehending blue is thereby disqualified from being a conceptual consciousness. If not, it would make conceptual perception a possibility! But if he agrees that to be a perception is to be disqualified from being a conceptual consciousness, it would follow that blue *cannot* be a conceptual consciousness, because it is a perception apprehending blue. The three spheres [are in place, and his position is therefore shown to be irredeemably flawed].

What is more, it would follow that when an adversary and a friend of a person gaze at his physical form, their visual perceptions do not preclude each other, because their visual perceptions are [in actuality] the form of that person. This illustrates how [the above view] eventually forces one into the position that visual consciousnesses can *never* contradict each other. [Similarly,] since the form, smell, and taste that are physical [features of] Devadatta's body are, according to this view, the tactual, visual, and other consciousnesses [that cognize them], it would mean that even when resting in suspension absorption, Devadatta would still have these consciousnesses. And it would follow, from this, that even during the meditative state of absorption in which [gross consciousnesses] are suspended, the five portal sense perceptions would still be present!

Furthermore, one would also have to accept that when disciples who are ordinary beings behold the major and minor marks [adorning] the emanation body of a complete buddha, those marks are the visual perceptions of those disciples. Thus it would absurdly follow that the major and minor marks of a buddha are the visual perceptions of ordinary individuals! [138] The criticisms that could be made of this position are very grave and abundant, so much so that one cannot hope to enumerate them all. I leave to the intellectually gifted the task of extrapolating them from what I have set out here.

The analysis that we would press on all those who advocate that in the Cittamātra system things are consciousness and those with very shallow intellects who propose that any object of knowledge is necessarily a mind would be one that forces them to identify what type of consciousness they mean in each case. Basically they have no choice but to answer by pointing to the consciousnesses apprehending the respective objects, and in doing so, they bring upon themselves the oppressive burden of flaws such as those mentioned above.

Someone else asserts that blue and so forth are, conventionally speaking, external entities, but in the final, ultimate sense,[448] they are consciousness.

[Response:] We find a great number of failings with both parts of this assertion. To accept that being an external entity in a conventional sense is enough to count as an external entity is to acknowledge [the existence] of external entities. But the whole notion of such entities has been rejected by the reasoning set forth [by Vasubandhu] in passages such as "[If an aggregate is supposed to be formed of] a partless particle surrounded [by others on its] six [sides], then it follows that the partless particle has six portions."[449] [So anyone who holds that external entities exist conventionally] does not have even the slightest hint of the Vijñaptika about him. If, conversely, being an external entity in a conventional sense is not enough for something to count [as an external entity], a similar state of affairs must also apply to the status of other things. Existing in the conventional sense would not, for instance, be enough for something to count as existent. Thus one would be guilty of the same error made by nihilists, who totally deny that things can be conventionally true.

Someone may acknowledge that being an external entity conventionally is only ever enough for something to count as an external entity conventionally, not ultimately. He may also propose that since there is no third alternative for external entities beyond conventional and ultimate [existence], it would be incorrect to analyze whether something counts as an external entity without first stipulating if this is in a conventional or ultimate sense.

[Response:] We agree that there is no third alternative outside these two senses of being true, but we reject his suggestion that it is necessary to explicitly add the qualification of either of the two truths at the very outset of the analysis. [If that were correct,] it would follow that because the simple inquiry as to whether Devadatta is going somewhere has neglected to add the qualification "in the conventional sense," [it implies the existence of] some Devadatta who was true neither in an ultimate sense nor a conventional one. Similarly, it follows that if someone were to give the reason "[because] there is smoke," without specifying whether the smoke in question is physical material or consciousness, it would amount to the assertion that a variety of smoke that is neither physical matter nor consciousness existed. [139] When we asked [the individual here] whether to exist conventionally constitutes existing, he responded by insisting that we stipulate whether the question is about existence in the conventional, ultimate, or some sense other than these two. This response is a *self-defeating rejoinder* of the *similar effect* variety.[450]

If he denies that it is such a response, then it would similarly be the case that—when a person who has been presented with the proof "Sound is impermanent because it is produced" [seeks to thwart it] by questioning whether the production [referred to in the proof is a quality] of sound, pot, or another produced thing—he has *not* used a self-defeating rejoinder similar to [what it is supposed to refute] with respect to being an effect. All we are actually dealing with here are the antics of an individual who, having realized his inability to respond, tries to stymie proceedings by introducing a particularly slippery subject that is hard to pin down in the discussion. The [other] part of his position, where he claims that [blue and so forth] are in the ultimate sense, consciousness, is open to exactly the same criticisms that have already been directed at the contention that form is [in actuality] consciousness.

Someone else proposes that the object-aspect of the visual perception apprehending blue must, in a conventional sense, be both an externally real entity and blue. He argues that this must be the case, because it is this object-aspect that the thought following [the perception] conceives to be blue and an externally real entity.

[Response:] This position is also one that does not hold.[451] It would follow that the subject-aspect of that visual perception is, in a conventional sense, a cognition with overt awareness of an object that is an externally real entity.

Why? Because the object-aspect of the visual perception apprehending blue is conventionally an external entity. But if this were accepted, it would follow that conventionally, this subject-aspect is an other-cognition. And this would mean that on the conventional level, any form of self-perception would be an impossibility![452]

Based on what he asserts, it would also follow that the Cittamātra model of valid cognition, its result, and comprehended object[453]—according to which, (1) the object-aspect is the thing comprehended, (2) the subject-aspect is the valid cognition, and (3) the self-cognition is the result—is a description [of the three] on the ultimate level. This is something that he is forced to concede, because for him, in the Cittamātra system, the object-aspect is conventionally an external entity. But if he accepts this, he would be agreeing that on the ultimate level, the object, subject, and self-cognition remain distinct from one another. So [once more] he does not have even the slightest hint of the Cittamātra about him.

Moreover, it is conventional valid cognitions, not mistaken awarenesses such as later thoughts, that determine conventions. Otherwise, as I have already explained, it would become necessary to accept that in the context of determining conventions, whatever inconsistencies there might be reflect reality itself.[454] [140] What others have said on this matter, therefore, amounts to little more than a shallow play of words.

Our own system must also address the question of whether things such as blue are consciousness or physical material. If they were physical material, this would require them to be constituted of particles, which would mean that they are externally real entities. Conversely, if they were consciousness, all the charges outlined above could be made. Therefore neither of these two options is acceptable. Despite appearing to occupy a physical space at some distance from the sense perceptions of the myopic beings that apprehend them, blue and so forth are [in fact] the same substance as those perceptions. For this reason, they are asserted to be part of the nature of those respective sense perceptions, and they are neither matter nor consciousness.

But does this not also entail them being part of the nature of omniscient wisdom? What we maintain is that the situation is not comparable. The proof of simultaneity establishes that the blue and so forth appearing to the sense perceptions of myopic beings are the same substance as those perceptions. However, in the case of omniscient wisdom and things such as blue, there is no way to establish that they are the same nature. One could not, for instance, employ the proof of simultaneity, because [those to whom the proof might be presented] could not have confirmed the property of the subject,[455] and there are no alternative proofs that can be employed [to establish that they are the same nature]. In any case, the view that actual things other than physical material and consciousness are impossible derives from a lack of proper analysis. For the Vaibhāṣika, there is space and the like, for the Sautrāntika, there is the person and so forth, and for the Cittamātra, there is suspension absorption and so on. Thus the majority of Buddhist philosophical schools individually assert [the existence of] things that are neither physical material nor consciousness. In addition to this, there are many entities, such as *imprints*, that they all agree are neither physical material nor consciousness. So even if one has, since childhood, become accustomed to intoning "If one divides actual things, there are the two, physical material and consciousness," this is no excuse for internalizing it [unquestioningly].[456] Here we conclude discussion of the subject [of the proof of simultaneity] and various related issues.

Next, we turn to the predicate of the proof [of simultaneity]. Others have proposed that as far as the True Aspectarian is concerned, what the proof seeks to establish is that [the perception and its object are] the same substance, whereas for the False Aspectarian, it is only to establish that the two are not separate substances.

[Response:] Now, if what served as the subject of the proof was the aspect, this proposition would be correct, but this has already been rejected. [141] We find that True Aspectarians and False Aspectarians agree that blue and so forth are the same substance as the visual and other perceptions apprehending them. And as elaborated above, they also agree that things such as blue should be identified as the subjects being debated. Hence neither of them would have the slightest objection whether we say that the proof is intended to establish that [the perception and the blue] are the same substance or we say that they are not separate substances. Either of these can be said to satisfy their objective, since they both wish to negate the existence of external entities.

Regarding what the "simultaneity" within the proof actually denotes, someone claims that it refers to the fact that the self-cognizing perception observes [that the object and subject, such as blue and the perception of blue,] exist concurrently with itself.

[Response:] This cannot be correct, because if the self-cognizing perception experiencing the visual consciousness of blue were to overtly see blue, it would have to count as an other-cognition. It would also require that the self-cognizing perception experiencing the visual consciousness of blue overtly take on the aspect of blue. If, in response, he tries to assert that it does indeed take on that aspect, it would follow that just like the visual perception, the [self-cognizing] subject-aspect must itself have both an object-aspect and a subject-aspect.

Someone else formulates the reason [in the proof of simultaneity] as "[because] there is [observational] simultaneity [of subject and object] with respect to the cognitions of all sentient beings."

[Response:] This is not tenable, because nothing can be observationally simultaneous with the cognitions of all sentient beings, since that would mean that every successive instant of all sentient beings' cognition must be alike.

Someone else tries [to justify the reference to] "the cognitions of all sentient beings" by saying that when blue is observed by the cognition of one sentient being, the cognition of the same sentient being also necessarily observes the visual consciousness of [blue], and that this [is extendable] to *any* sentient being.

[Response:] If that really [justifies] this formulation, it would follow that [the same applies to] the wisdom directly realizing selflessness and the self-grasping attitude that it counteracts. They must be the antidote and the element eradicated with respect to the cognitions of *all* sentient beings, because the production of the wisdom directly realizing emptiness in the continuum of one sentient being spells the eradication of the specific self-grasping that it counteracts [for that sentient being], and this is [extendable to] the continuum of *any* sentient being. But if he accepts that, it would follow that the wisdom directly realizing emptiness is the antidote with respect to the mental continua of all sentient beings. [142] But from this it would absurdly follow that a sentient being who does not have the antidotal wisdom realizing emptiness in his continuum is an impossibility.

One [individual] says that the reason should not simply be formulated as "[because] they are observed simultaneously," since this would [also encompass] such things as *apparent forms*,[457] which are [only] observed to be simultaneous with the cognitions of *some* sentient beings. So it would follow that these [apparent forms] also are not separate substances [from the cognitions observing them].

[Response:] Here is someone who is clueless about how to identify a fault. It follows from what he says that if something is simultaneously observed with respect to the cognitions of only some sentient beings, it would be simultaneously observed. This must be the case, because [he proposes that] one could not use the reason "[because] they are observed simultaneously" to establish that [object and subject] are not separate substances, since [that reason also encompasses] certain apparent forms, which are only simultaneously observed with respect to the cognitions of *some* sentient beings. But if that conclusion is accepted, it absurdly follows that a pot and its location have [observational] simultaneity. And that would mean that the presence of one necessarily required that of the other. In [seeking to] undermine the master [Dharmakīrti's] formulation of the reason "[because] they are observed simultaneously,"[458] this individual has only succeeded in revealing his own deficiencies.

Many are of the opinion that what simultaneous observation denotes is that the cognition overtly observing blue must also overtly observe the visual consciousness of blue, and the cognition that overtly observes the visual consciousness of blue must also overtly observe blue.

[Response:] This view is not viable. It would follow that the visual consciousness of blue overtly observes itself, because it overtly observes blue. But this [conclusion] cannot be accepted: as will be explained in the section dealing with self-perception, there are various logical arguments that discredit it. Furthermore, it would follow that the self-cognizing perception experiencing the visual consciousness of blue must also overtly observe blue, because it overtly observes that consciousness of blue. But [this conclusion] also cannot be accepted, since the arguments outlined above, such as that it would mean [that the self-cognition] is an other-cognition, have already disproved it. [Similarly,] it would also follow that the valid mental perception of blue overtly observes the visual consciousness of blue, because it overtly observes blue. [143] [These individuals] have no response to this.

[In defense of the position,] some might argue that it was not meant to apply to any blue and [cognition of it] but specifically to the visual consciousness of blue and the blue that appears to that consciousness, and that what it proposes is that if a cognition *overtly* observes one of them it must also overtly observe the other.

[Response:] We would point to a situation where there is a single blue, which is the common object overtly observed by the visual consciousnesses of both Devadatta and Yajñadatta. It would follow that the visual consciousness of Devadatta overtly observes the visual consciousness of Yajñadatta, because it overtly observes the blue that appears to the visual consciousness of Yajñadatta. They have no response [to this argument].

There may be those who wonder whether simultaneous observation implies that the presence of either one of the things necessarily entails that of the other, in the same location and for the same duration.

[Response:] This [alone] cannot be what is meant by simultaneous observation, because if it did, the taste and visual form of [a piece of] molasses at a particular time would count as things that are simultaneously observed and therefore as substances that are not distinct from each other.

The actual meaning of [two] things having simultaneity is as follows. "Simultaneous," in this context, refers to things having the same location and duration. "Observation" denotes that they are observed by valid cognition, whereas "necessary" signifies that there is a necessary concomitance between the things in question. Essentially then, the terms should be understood to mean that [two things are linked in such a way that] the observation of the first by valid cognition will necessarily also be accompanied, at the same time, by observation of the second, and vice versa. So, for instance, at the exact same time that blue is observed by valid perception, that perception will necessarily be observed, simultaneously, by the valid self-cognizing perception that experiences it. And at the same time that the valid perception of blue is being observed by the valid self-cognizing perception, blue will also necessarily be simultaneously observed by the valid perception that apprehends it.

Some may wonder whether this might equally be said to apply to the taste and visual form of molasses at a specific point in time. But the situation with those two is not a corresponding one. If it was, it would mean that whenever one saw the form of molasses one would have to experience its taste! This concludes the section on the reason of the proof of simultaneity.

There are those who accept that "observation" in the context of the proof of simultaneity refers to [an action performed by] valid cognition, but they go on to claim that "just like the error of the sense consciousness to which the moon appears double" serves as the *similar example* for the proof.

[Response:] These individuals obviously cannot be in their right minds, because it would ludicrously follow that a double moon is something observed by valid cognition![459] [144]

There are also those who identify the similar example as "just like the aspect of a double moon and the sense consciousness to which it appears."

[Response:] If that were correct, there would be the flaw of the similar example remaining unestablished for the likes of the Vaibhāṣika and various others to whom the proof [of simultaneity] is presented. This is because they are opponents who claim that cognition occurs without the [mediation] of an aspect.

What then did [Dharmakīrti] intend by the passage "It is just like [when], due to an error in the consciousness, two moons, which do not exist, are seen as separate"?[460] This passage follows on from the section [in which Dharmakīrti asks his opponent], "By what means can it be proved that the object that can necessarily only be experienced simultaneously with the cognition is separate from that [cognition]?"[461]

[In response, the opponent inquires] how it is that blue and the like seem to occupy a space at some distance from the sense consciousnesses to which they appear if they are [in fact] not separate from those consciousnesses. The passage "It is just like [when], due to an error in the consciousness, two moons, which do not exist, are seen as separate"[462] is [Dharmakīrti's] answer to this question, where he says that the [situation] comes about due to a mistake [in cognition]. Essentially then, what this passage does is to provide an *analogy* helping to illustrate how it is that despite them not being separate from the [various] sense consciousnesses, blue and so forth can still appear to be so. It does *not* present the *similar example* [used in the proof of simultaneity], establishing that [the subject and object] are not separate from each other.

Establishing [the reason's fulfillment of] each of the [three] criteria

The cognition responsible for confirming the *property of the subject* in the proof of simultaneity is the self-cognizing perception.

The *forward pervasion* is established in the following manner. [Things] that have [observational] simultaneity cannot be separate substances. For a start, a relationship between [two things] is confirmed to exist if they are different from each other, but observation of one of them necessarily requires that of the other. As the things in question are necessarily observed simultaneously—that is, at one and the same time—the possibility that the relationship between them is one of cause and effect is excluded. Simultaneity therefore demands that the relationship that the things in question share is that of being *part of the same entity*,[463] and it is this fact that rules out any possibility of them being separate substances.

The *reverse pervasion* is conveyed by the words "[Just like] there is no guarantee that a blue and yellow, which are different from one another, will be experienced [together]."[464] The logic used is that things of separate substances are precluded from having simultaneity, because if entities that were separate substances but had simultaneity actually existed, they should be observable, but no such things are observed. This logical reason [belongs, therefore, to the category] of those involving the *nonobservation of what should be apparent*. Thus one establishes [the pervasion] by ruling out [the possibility] that entities with separate substances can have simultaneity. [145] The reason that if such things did exist, they would be observable [means, in the present case,] that entities with [observational] simultaneity are necessarily apparent to valid cognition.

With reference to this, someone claims that a basic awareness and the cognitive functions associated with it[465] must therefore also have simultaneity, because when one of them is observed by valid perception, the same is necessarily also the case for the other. This, he argues, must be the case, because at the same time that the self-cognizing perception experiences the basic awareness, it also experiences the cognitive functions associated with that awareness. But, he points out, accepting that they have simultaneity would force one to accept that they are the same substance.

[Response:] We agree that a basic awareness and the cognitive functions associated with it are indeed counted as the same substance. If they were separate substances, they would be debarred from having any sort of relationship by way of being part of the same entity. And since existing at the same time also disqualifies them from having a cause-and-effect relationship, it would follow that they must be distinct, unconnected things. This would absurdly mean that they do not depend on each other in any way. But to grant this would amount to admitting that the whole model for explaining a basic awareness and its associated cognitive functions is the stuff of imagination. It would also follow that it must be *possible* for [a single individual] to have numerous conceptual consciousnesses of the same variety but separate substances in his mental continuum at the same time, because a basic conceptual mental awareness and the conceptual cognitive functions associated with it are separate substances [simultaneously present in that individual's continuum].

How then, someone asks, can we explain what the master Asaṅga says in statements such as "since five are not tenable,"[466] where he [apparently] issues a series of refutations of the view that a basic awareness and its cognitive functions are the same substance? He also [seems to] use arguments against the view that main mind and mental functions are the same substance, such as when he says it would follow that the definitive enumeration of aggregates into five is untenable, "because the aggregates of consciousness, feeling, and so forth are all just a single substance."[467]

[Response:] [The master Asaṅga] cannot have intended [in these statements] to refute the view that the two are the same substance. That is because the very same arguments that he seems to use here could equally be turned against his own position. With an analysis corresponding to his own, one could question, for example, whether the form [aggregate] and so forth are of a substance that is the same as that of consciousness, or one that is distinct from it. If they were distinct substances, it would follow that there are real, external entities. If, on the other hand, they were the same substance, it would follow that enumerating the aggregates definitively as five is untenable, since the aggregate of form and the aggregate of consciousness would actually be just a single substance. Hence with the three spheres [in place, anyone holding such a view] would be left without any reasonable response. The majority view, including that of both the ārya Asaṅga and his brother [Vasubandhu], as well as the two lords of reasoning [Dignāga and Dharmakīrti], is that a basic awareness and its cognitive functions are the same substance.[468] [146] There are many related issues that still need to be discussed, but I must put them aside for the time being.

This concludes the description of the establishment of the proof's three criteria together with certain related matters. This proof of simultaneity is a source of considerable scrutiny and discussion among the scholarly and is of extreme importance in the Vijñaptika system of tenets, but no confidence can be placed in the present-day "logicians." For this reason, I have dealt with the topic at some length here, and the illumination of my well-expressed pronouncements on it will bring clarity to the world.

Vying with one another to discover their furthest bounds, the heavens and
  my own intellect will surely grow weary,
and the great lake, anxious lest in an instant my mind should fathom its
  depths, disappears behind the mountains.

Having cleared their throats, the gods of virtue send forth their words
  to the realms of Brahmā as messengers
to announce that the brilliance of my pronouncements has brought
  a smile of approval to the lotus-visage of the Buddha.

Such is the expression of wonderment! In this way I conclude this lengthy account of the object condition of sense perception according to the Vijñaptika system together with certain topics arising from it.

Next, I will deal with the governing and immediate conditions. The [Cittamātra system] defines the immediate condition in exactly the same manner as the Sautrāntika. This has already been explained, so there is no need to repeat it here. But the Sautrāntika and Cittamātra views on the governing condition differ. Both agree about the character of the visual sense power, which is the governing condition of the visual consciousness: it is distinct from the other two conditions and has the unique feature of being the cause that is chiefly responsible for making visual consciousness apprehend, among the five sense objects, only visual form and not the others, such as sounds. But their positions differ in that the Sautrāntika system identifies this [sense power] as physical material, whereas the Cittamātra posits that it exists in the form of a potential, present in the awareness acting as the immediate condition [for the cognition in question]. It is with this point in mind that Dignāga stated:

> The cooperating [condition] is the sense power,
> the nature of which is a capacity and [which is] also a sense power.
> For the Vijñaptika, there is no contradiction [in this].[469] [147]

This concludes the section explaining the three conditions of sense perception according to the Vijñaptika system.

11. Mental Perception

Valid mental perception

1. Refutation of others' assertions
2. Setting forth our own position
3. Dealing with objections [to our position]

Refutation of others' assertions

One individual, employing various arguments to back his assertions, attempts to characterize the position of the author of the *Ornament* [Prajñākaragupta]. According to him, [Prajñākaragupta] defined mental perception as "a consciousness that makes an object manifest by dint of familiarity [with it and is also one that itself] depends upon the mental [faculty]." He says that [for Prajñākaragupta,] mental perception is differentiated from sense perception in terms of its function. Thus, while a sense perception is only able to register the appearance of an object, mental perception is able to ascertain it. However, this ability to ascertain things does not mean that mental perception should be counted as a conceptual cognition. For the way that a conceptual cognition apprehends its object involves that object being concealed from it, whereas a mental perception ascertains an object in a manifest fashion. But would this not contradict passages such as "Perception is not responsible for the ascertainment of anything?"[470] This individual denies that this presents any problem, arguing that when such passages talk of perception, they are referring solely to *sense* perception. [Justifying this claim,] he has pointed out that the term *akṣara*[471] refers to something that depends on a sense power.

[Response:] The individual in question has [obviously] written this characterization without any reference whatsoever to the *Ornament* or its commentary [by Yamāri], and he has correctly represented neither [Prajñākaragupta's] intent nor the way that he expressed himself. According to the description of a mode of production for mental perception that is *attributed* to [Prajñākaragupta], the first thing produced is a temporal portion of sense perception. This is followed by a single [temporal portion of] mental perception. Then once again, there is one of sense perception. That is, the process of perception is initiated by sense perception and then completed by mental perception. So throughout their production, sense and mental perception are completely bound together, arising alternately.

Now while this interpretation may be one bandied around in scholarly circles, it is not found in any of the treatises by this author or his followers appearing in Tibetan translation. It is also incorrect since if mental perception were an ascertaining awareness, it would follow that when it holds its object, it ascertains all those features that are inseparable from the substance of that object. [148] That is because a mental perception is necessarily a comprehensive engager and is also [according to these individuals] necessarily an ascertaining awareness. If that [argument] is accepted, it would follow that every time mental perception held something such as a visual form or a sound, it would necessarily ascertain that the form or sound in question shares its nature with consciousness. But that would be ridiculous, as it would make it impossible for any person to have a mental perception in his continuum *unless* he had gained ascertainment of the philosophical tenets of the Cittamātra!

Also [this characterization] gives mental perception far greater palpability than sense perception. This is because it ascribes to mental perception the certainty of ascertaining its object, making it seem more robust. Sense perception, on the other hand, only registers the appearance of an object, suggesting that it is more insubstantial. But if that were really the case, the grounds for developing distorted notions and denying the existence of mental perception should be much weaker than those for developing comparable notions about sense perception, making the situation analogous to that of conceptual cognition and perception.

Their assertion that mental perception follows a pattern of "alternate production"[472] is also not credible. Based on that, it would follow that all sense perceptions from the second moment onward lack direct substantial causes. That is because there would always be a mental perception standing between earlier and later sense perceptions of the same kind, interrupting [production].

Dharmottara says that although there are references in authoritative works to mental perception, the valid cognition of a myopic being, dealing only in demonstrable facts and realities, cannot ascertain such perception. [Dignāga, for instance,] asserts the existence of mental perception in the source treatise [*Compendium of Pramāṇa*]. But this was attacked by those who maintained that this assertion would force him to accept that subsequent cognitions can be valid cognitions and that it must be possible for a blind person to see visual forms. Dharmottara states that it was to rebut this attack that Dharmakīrti proposed (1) that a mental perception can be produced from a sense perception serving as its immediately preceding condition and (2) that there is no inconsistency involved in maintaining that the mental perception apprehends the second temporal portion [of the object apprehended by the sense perception]. For Dharmottara, all Dharmakīrti intended in that section was to point out that there were no logical arguments that [Dignāga's detractors] could offer against the idea that a mental perception is produced from such a causal condition.[473] In Dharmottara's interpretation, mental perception is an extremely hidden phenomenon, and it can thus only be verified by means of scripture, not by valid cognition dealing with demonstrable facts and realities. And while neither scripture nor reasoning can be used to establish exactly what causal condition gives rise to a mental perception, he asserts that neither are there any logical arguments able to *disprove* that the aforesaid causal condition is the one that produces the mental perception. [149] Someone accuses Dharmottara of having contradicted himself in claiming that perception is an extremely hidden phenomenon while simultaneously suggesting that its causal conditions, its manner of production, and other details about it can be substantiated by valid cognition dealing in demonstrable facts and realities. But he has failed to comprehend Dharmottara's position, and consequently his refutation falls completely wide of the mark.

As to [Dharmottara's actual] view on the way that mental perception is produced: for him, it is illogical to suggest that during a time that the sight [of a person] is operating, the awareness to which visual form appears clearly is any other than his visual awareness. So he explains that when the person's sight is in operation, the mental perception has yet to be produced, but the sense consciousness [in operation] will act as the immediate condition for its production. Thus the mental perception of visual form will only be produced once the sequence [of instants comprising] the sense perception of form has come to an end. He says that there is just a single instant of this mental perception. If there were anything more to it than that, such that the mental perception occurred in a longer sequence, it would mean that one could ascertain it through direct experience, so there would be no danger of developing the distorted idea that it does not exist.

What I have recounted here is the true thought of the master Dharmottara. Many Tibetans—who consider themselves learned when in fact they are ignorant—have judged Dharmottara's view on [the production of mental perception] to be the correct one. I personally do not share in this opinion.[474] For one thing, it would follow that the myopic being would have no self-cognizing perception experiencing that mental perception, because the mental perception remains extremely hidden to his mind. But if one were to accept this, it would mean that the mental perception's status as a consciousness would be undermined.[475] Given the frequency with which the master [Dharmakīrti] expressed his categorical opposition to the notion that [any portion of a person's] own awareness might be hidden from him, the idea that [part of that awareness] might be *extremely* hidden from him strikes me as deplorable.

Someone may question why, when an individual's own conscious experience is not hidden from him, it is still necessary to prove to followers of the Vaiśeṣika school that things such as pleasure are actually [forms of] consciousness.

[Response:] Although pleasure and the like in the continuum of a Vaiśeṣika are not hidden from him, he is unaware that such things should be categorized as consciousness. So what is hidden for him is the fact that these things *are* consciousness. The situation is analogous, for instance, to [when one is proving to someone that sound is impermanent: in that scenario,] what needs to be established is not sound itself but the fact that it is impermanent.

We would also question what justification [Dharmottara] has for claiming that mental perception is extremely hidden. He may say that it must be extremely hidden because it cannot be ascertained by the valid cognition of a myopic being and its [existence is only substantiated] by the fact that it has been mentioned in scripture. [150] But why exactly does he maintain that the valid cognition of a myopic being cannot ascertain it? If it is simply on the grounds that it lasts for just an instant, then we wonder what the instant he refers to means. Is this an instant in the sense of things not enduring from one moment to the next, or in the sense of the *minutest unit of time*? If he means the first of these, it follows that *no* actual things can ever be ascertained by the valid cognition of a myopic being. But if he is referring to the second option, what reason does he have for believing that [the mental perception] must be just one of those *minutest units of time*? He may well respond by saying that mental perception must be one of these units;

otherwise it would necessarily constitute a continuum. And if it were a continuum, ascertaining it would become a very straightforward matter, and there would be no reason for developing the misconception that it did not exist. Why then would anyone develop the notion that past and future lives do not exist? They must, after all, constitute a continuum. [Dharmottara] would probably deny that this example is comparable to the one at hand, saying that while past and future lives represent continua, this is not the type of continua that is confirmed empirically. By contrast, mental perception, he may say, is the type of thing that, if it were a continuum, would need to be accessible to the empirical experience of those who have it. However, it is not impossible for an individual to deny what he has established empirically. Otherwise, it would follow that because a Cārvāka empirically establishes the individual who is his father, he could never develop the erroneous idea that he has no father.

Furthermore, if [Dharmottara] really were asserting that the valid cognition of a myopic being can never ascertain a thing that [lasts only] the minutest portion of time, then one would have to accept that any actual thing that does not have parts would necessarily count as extremely hidden.

Thus we find no evidence to support the thesis that mental perception is an extremely hidden phenomenon or that it is only produced for a single instant. Nor are the reasons that were given to establish that mental perception only occurs once when the sequence of sense perception has ended sound ones. The argument says that it is illogical to believe that during a time that the sight [of a person] is operating, the awareness to which visual form appears clearly would be any other than his visual awareness. However, this is not correct, since there are numerous examples where form clearly appears to the concentration of an individual, whether an ordinary being or an ārya, despite the fact that the sight of that individual is still operating.

Certain others have criticized Dharmottara's stance on the way mental perception is produced by directing a consequence against it, saying that the mental perception would be produced after a sense perception of color has apprehended the last instant of that color's continuum. But this does not damage Dharmottara's position. He claims that if a mental perception is produced, it can only occur once the sequence of the sense perception has come to an end. He does not say that *every* continuum of sense perception necessarily culminates in the production of a mental perception.

Someone else attacks Dharmottara, arguing that if the mental perception can be produced at the end of the sense perception sequence, it can just as well be produced before that [endpoint] is reached, because there is nothing to set apart the causes that can produce the mental perception at the endpoint of the sequence from [those that are present] prior to that endpoint. [151]

[Response:] Again, this does not damage Dharmottara's position. Dharmottara could justifiably respond to this attack as follows. While acknowledging that the two occasions cannot be distinguished in terms of the particular *set of causes* [capable of producing the mental perception]—since those causes are equally present in their entirety before the sense perception sequence has come to an end as they are once it has ceased—he could say that it is still necessary to differentiate between [the two occasions], since the *conditions detrimental*[476] to [the production of the mental perception] are not present on both [occasions]. This is because, up until the end of the sequence, sense perceptions occur in an uninterrupted stream, thus leaving no opportunity for a mental perception to be produced. We see many such cases where earlier [Tibetans] attempted to refute certain masters from the land of āryas without properly understanding what they said, or where, with only the briefest exposure to the works of these masters, [these Tibetans] cited a small portion of what they said and then hurled some quite unwarranted criticism at them.

Another Tibetan proposes that when there is a perception of a sense object, only the first instant is [actual] sense perception, whereas all those that follow from the second moment onward are mental perceptions. [These subsequent instants] must, he argues, be [mental perceptions], since they are nonconceptual, unmistaken mental cognitions for which the sense perception—existing concurrently with the [sense] object from its second instant onward—has acted as the immediate condition. He reasons that these perceptions must be mental cognitions, because the governing conditions that give rise to them are *mental sense powers*. And he says that "The governing conditions that give rise to them must be mental sense powers, because they are perceptions that can only arise once the earlier awareness of a kind similar to themselves has come to an end." He states that if a cognition that arose from a governing condition that was a mental sense power were not [thereby counted as] a mental cognition, then neither would one arising from a physical sense power be a sense cognition. According to this opponent, sense perception is defined as "a consciousness that is nonconceptual and unmistaken, and is derived from its governing condition, a physical sense power."

[Response:] His position is not tenable. Based on what he says, it follows that in the case of the first instant of a sense perception also, the governing condition that gave rise to it would be a mental sense power, because it is a perception that can only arise once the earlier awareness that is its substantial cause has come to an end.[477] The pervasion [of this argument] is the one he himself proposed. Furthermore, the reason [that it is produced from such a substantial cause] must be correct, because the sense perception is also produced from an immediate condition that is *mental*—in this case, the [instant of] *mental attention* that preceded it. But if he accepts the argument, then it would follow that [the first instant of sense perception] must be a *mental* perception, because it is a nonconceptual and unmistaken cognition, derived from its governing condition, a mental sense power. The [argument's] reason and predicate are clearly those that he himself advanced. But if he challenged its pervasion, it would go against his own original assertion that any nonconceptual, unmistaken cognition with a physical sense power as its governing condition is necessarily a sense perception. Also, if he denied the pervasion, it would go against his drawing of a parallel [between sense and mental consciousnesses], in which he said that just as a cognition derived from a governing condition that is a physical sense power must be a sense perception, one derived from a governing condition that is a mental sense power must be a mental cognition. [152]

What is more, it would follow that if some phenomenon is a mental sense power and it produces a thing, it necessarily does so by acting as the thing's governing condition. This is because, as he proposes, "The governing conditions that give rise to [the thing in question] must be mental sense powers, because [that thing is a] perception that can only arise once the earlier awareness of a kind similar to itself has come to an end." But if he accepts that [argument], it would follow that all the effects of any main awareness must be [classified as] its governed effects. Let us not then treat the accounts of this individual with too much awe. He is, after all, someone whose intellect is not refined enough to be able to properly distinguish between the immediate condition and the governing condition. There are many other points that could be made pertaining to this topic but they are of no great import, and so I will leave them for the time being.

Another Tibetan, who misguidedly views himself as a genuine scholar, together with certain commentators on [Sakya Paṇḍita's] *Treasure of Pramāṇa Reasoning* talk of the physical sense powers existing in uninterrupted streams, with each successive instant arising from a preceding one of a kind similar to itself. On the other hand, they identify a mental power as a sense consciousness that has just ceased. Hence [they claim] there is no continuous process involving one mental sense power arising from another, and consequently one cannot talk of a continuous stream of mental sense powers. They claim that since the physical sense powers that act as the governing condition for the sense consciousnesses form a sequence, the sense consciousnesses derived from them also constitute continua, whereas since the mental sense power that serves as the governing condition for the mental perception does not constitute a continuous sequence, the same must be true for the mental perception derived from it. It is for this reason, they assert, that mental perception is more difficult to ascertain than sense perception.[478]

[Response:] This is totally wrong. First of all, if what they are trying to establish is that the mental sense power is not involved in a continuous process of production, why do they state that this mental sense power is "a sense consciousness that has just ceased"? What possible relevance has this to their argument? They might respond that what they meant was that the sense power had just ceased and, thus, could no longer be counted as an actual thing capable of producing an effect. But if that is the case, it follows that the mental sense power is not an actual thing because it is nothing more than "a sense consciousness that has just ceased." The reason and pervasion [of this argument] are the ones they proposed. But they cannot accept its conclusion [that the mental sense power is not an actual thing], as it goes against their assertion that this sense power is the governing condition for the mental perception. They could not reject the pervasion, as this would go against their assertion that a non-actual thing is incapable of producing effects.

What is more, identifying the mental sense power as a consciousness that has just ceased is to deny it any substantial existence. Maintaining that it is the governing condition of the mental perception, on the other hand, is to affirm its substantial existence. Thus they have managed to pile up a whole mountain of self-contradiction for themselves! [153]

The claims of this group of opponents are also incompatible with their stated position that the number of mental perceptions [produced] is equal to that of the sense perceptions. If the two were produced in equal number, it would contradict their thesis that one of them exists in a continuous sequence whereas the other does not. They may defend this thesis, arguing that it is the position advocated in the *Treasure of Pramāṇa Reasoning*:

> One physical sense power is produced from another.
> Thus sense cognition [occurs as] a continuous sequence.

One mental sense power does not [derive] from another.
Thus it has no continuous sequence.[479]

But is it really likely that this lord of the Dharma would make such a patent error? I will explain later how distorted views such as this are misrepresentations of the *Treasure of Pramāṇa Reasoning*'s true intent.

Someone else defines mental perception as "a mental consciousness that is a nonconceptual and unmistaken other-cognition, and is derived from its immediate condition, a physical sense consciousness." However, the fool has gone on to acknowledge that the thing referred to as mental perception is not a [real] established basis!

Granting it no more existence than a set of hare's horns,
he yet claims for it production from an immediate condition
and the status of an other-cognizer.
I am far from finished with this position.

Thus, enveloped in a foul gloom,
they follow witlessly in the trails of fools
while reciting the fine words of real scholars.
But what point is there in reasoning with those
who remain oblivious even to glaring contradictions?
Explanation is of little use with a cow;
it is the stick that guides it onto the path.

Setting out our own position

1. Defining characteristics
2. Varieties
3. Manner of production
4. Subsidiary topic: identifying the mental sense power

Defining characteristics

Mental perception is defined as "a mental consciousness that is an unmistaken other-cognition and is directly derived from its governing condition, a mental sense power."

Varieties

There are five varieties, one for each [of the sense objects]: those that apprehend visual forms, [sounds,] and so forth.

Manner of production

First, a single instant of sense perception occurs, following which there is a second instant. This second instant of sense perception is produced with (1) the first instant acting as its immediate condition, (2) the physical sense power present at the same time as that first instant acting as its governing condition, and (3) the second instant of the entity it apprehends serving as its object condition. Simultaneous with this second instant of sense perception, the first instant of mental perception occurs. [154] This mental perception shares the same immediate and observed [object] conditions as that second instant of sense cognition. What differentiates the two perceptions are their governing conditions. The mental perception is produced not from a physical sense power but from the mental one that was present at the same time as the first instant of sense perception. The second instant of the mental sense power and the second instant of the sense perception occur simultaneously. Following that, the process continues in the same fashion, with an instant of mental sense power and an instant of sense perception being produced in tandem, until eventually it reaches its conclusion, with the sense power and perception ceasing simultaneously.

This view of the way mental perception is produced has long been ascribed to the great brahmin [Śaṃkarānanda], but there is nothing in any of his treatises appearing in Tibetan translation that might serve as its source. It is clearly the view favored in the *Treasure of Pramāṇa Reasoning*, and it is this work that assigns the name "perception in three ways"[480] to this manner of production. The three referred to are (1) the sense perception and (2) the mental perception that are generated simultaneously—both of which are other-cognitions—and (3) the inwardly directed self-cognition. There may be those who [accept this but] see no point in representing the process in terms of exactly how many perceptions are in operation. If that is the case, they should not feel obliged to analyze [the process] in this manner. If, however, one chooses to describe the production using such a scheme, this version of the threefold scheme provided by this Dharma lord [Sakya Paṇḍita] must be regarded as the correct one.

Another individual has come up with a whole array of schemes here, claiming that the [perceptions] can be approached in various "ways,"[481] such as "the way of reckoning them through their respective governing conditions," "the way of reckoning them through their respective objects," and so forth. His creation of all these schemes simply reflects his failure to comprehend the [perception in three] ways and his delight in verbiage. The point of counting perceptions in terms of these "ways" is to work out how many different *types* of them are operating during the process of perceiving an entity. It is not meant to serve as an analysis of how many objects, governing conditions, or substances there might be at the time.

Identifying the mental sense power

The claim of certain others—that the mental sense power is any one of the six kinds of consciousness that has just ceased—has been refuted in the foregoing discussion. So let me now explain our own position. The *Treasury of the Abhidharma* states:

> Any of the immediately preceding six
> consciousnesses [can be] the mental [element].
> It was to establish that the basis for the sixth [consciousness is mental]
> that the constituents were asserted to [number] eighteen.[482]

This tells us that in the Abhidharma system [of the Vaibhāṣika], the mental sense power serves as the basis for the sixth consciousness, the mental consciousness, alone, and [due to this,] the mental sense power in question is not posited as something that provides the opportunity for any of the other five consciousnesses to arise. [155] And since [adherents of that system] held that a number of consciousnesses of different types cannot be present in the continuum of a single individual at any one time, the passage says that it is only once the group of all six previous consciousnesses has ceased that this later mental one can be produced. Thus it is the passing of the group of six *previous* consciousnesses that present the opportunity for the later mental consciousness to arise. And they identify the capacity for the presenting of that opportunity as the mental sense power. For this reason, [the other translation of the passage says,] "The six [consciousnesses] that have immediately ceased . . . ."[483] This indicates that it is only with the cessation of all six of the consciousnesses, not just any one of them, [that the mental consciousness can be produced].[484] Those [following this Abhidharma] system certainly do not accept that a thing just ceased is the mental sense power. Although even if they made such a claim, it would not be incompatible with their own fundamental tenets, since they argue that [even] things belonging to the past still constitute substances. However, the same cannot be said for the present [Pramāṇa] system, where any such claim would represent an abandonment of its philosophical principles.[485]

Those who are of the view that a number of basic consciousnesses of different types *can* be present [in a single individual's continuum] at any one time are following the lead set by the ārya Asaṅga. With respect to the mental sense power, he refers to "the thing that will immediately become a mental consciousness."[486] This characterizes the mental sense power as an [abstract] quality, that of creating the opportunity for the consciousness that immediately follows it to arise. That opportunity may be created by any one of the six consciousnesses that is about to end. It does not depend on *all six* of them having ceased. This is also the stance taken in the *Treasure of Pramāṇa Reasoning*. Therefore the mental sense power is the [abstract] quality that is *the opportunity, created by an earlier consciousness that is about to end, for a subsequent consciousness to be produced.*

I personally see nothing to substantiate the view [mentioned above] that because there is no [continuous] sequence of mental sense powers with each one successively producing the next, they can have no continuum. Such a notion is also at odds with what we find in the great treatises, where *mental sense power* is frequently described as synonymous with *main awareness*. [Those who deny mental sense power has a continuum] must either assert that what determines whether an effect forms a continuum is whether its cause formed a continuum, or that the one has no bearing on the other. If they hold the latter to be the case, then the fact that the mental sense power does not exist in the form of a continuous sequence would not mean the same is true for [its effect,] the mental perception. If, on the other hand, they hold that the cause does determine whether the effect forms a continuum, we would point out that the object condition and the immediate conditions of the mental perception *do* arise as continuous sequences. Hence [these individuals] would be forced to agree that the mental perception itself must form a continuum. However, this would completely wreck their position—in which the sense perception is the cause of the mental one, and although this sense perception forms a continuum, the mental one does not. The efforts of so many with scholarly pretensions to explain the mental sense power can be compared to the attempts of the blind to gaze upon a visual object. [156]

Dealing with objections [*to our position*]

What leads us then to the conclusion that the mental perception occurs *together* with the later moment of sense perception? We are brought to it logically, through all other possibilities having been rejected. We are told that a mental perception must derive from its immediate condition and that this is a sense perception. Thus it can only occur after the first moment of sense perception. The only options, therefore, are that the mental perception occurs when all the later moments of sense perception have come to an end or at some point before they end. Likewise, there are two options for the mental perception occurring before the other sense perceptions have ended. It must either alternate with the sense perception, or not. If it is the latter, it would operate concurrently with the sense perception. In the foregoing analysis, production at the end of the sequence [of sense perceptions] and alternating production have both been ruled out. Conversely, no evidence to challenge the notion that [the two perceptions] exist concurrently has been encountered.

Someone might object here, arguing that according to this view of production, the first moment of mental perception and the second moment of sense perception derive from a single substantial cause, which should logically mean that they are the same *type* of thing. He might say that granting this would endorse the idea that two consciousnesses of the same type but different substances can occur simultaneously in the continuum of a single individual. And that, he could contend, leads to the absurdity of a single individual with two separate continua of consciousness!

[Response:] This is an issue worthy of scholarly attention and one that I should therefore address. As has already been explained, if two things originate from a single substantial cause, they will necessarily be of the similar substantial type.[487] However, this is no guarantee that they share the same *isolated type*.[488] If the two consciousnesses present in that individual's continuum at the same time were of the same isolated type, it would entail the absurdity of that individual having multiple conscious continua, but there is no such consequence if the two are only of the same type of substance. But if [someone did make that argument, we could respond]: It follows that when Devadatta [cognizes blue], the two cognitions that arise simultaneously in his continuum—(1) the initial instant of a conceptual ascertainment of blue, directly induced by the first instant of visual consciousness apprehending that blue, and (2) a second instant of visual consciousness that succeeds the [first instant of visual consciousness]—must be the same type of thing, because they both derive from the same substantial cause [the initial instant of sense perception]. So how would he answer this? This [argument's] reason and pervasion are the ones that he himself proposed. But if he accepts the conclusion, it would follow that there are two consciousnesses—with different substances but the same type of thing—present at one time in the continuum of a single individual. The three spheres [would be in place]. He may try to deny that it is possible for someone to have a conceptual apprehension of blue derived from the first instant of the visual consciousness of that blue at the same time that he has a second instant of visual consciousness of blue. [157] But from this it would follow that a visual consciousness that can directly induce a [conceptual] ascertainment of blue would necessarily be one that was incapable of generating later instants of a kind similar to itself.

In conclusion, we can say that if two consciousnesses that are separate substances but share the same isolated type—such as two visual perceptions—were present in a single continuum at any one time, it would entail the person having multiple continua of consciousness. However, even if the two consciousnesses in question are the same type of substance, as long as they have different isolated types—such as sense and mental perceptions—their simultaneous presence in the continuum creates no such problem.

Another objection that might be raised against *production in three ways* is that if the sense perception and mental perception are considered separate substances, then this should also be the case for the self-cognitions that experience each of them. And the process should therefore be more properly described as production in "four ways." Equally, however, taken from the perspective of "kinds" of thing, if the two *experiencers* are to be counted as one on the grounds that they are both self-cognitions, then the two that are *experienced* should also be counted as one, because they are both cognitions of [other] entities. Thus, [the objector might conclude,] one would end up with just "production in two ways."

[Response:] This is not a legitimate criticism. The scheme of "ways" provides a means of counting how many *different types* of perception are in operation at a given time. So while the two experiencers are separate substances, in terms of their identity they are both essentially just self-cognitions, and do not represent different *types* of thing.[489] This is to be contrasted with the things that they experience. While these two are both cognitions of [other] entities, they are distinguished by the fact that one of them is a sense perception whereas the other is a mental one. We thus see a major difference between them on the level of their isolated *type*. Furthermore, in terms of their classification as valid cognitions, these experiencers again both fall into a single category, whereas the two that are experienced belong to different categories from one another. Unless one accepts this, it would equally follow that the typological scheme distinguishing four varieties of valid perception is untenable, because in the same way that sense perception and mental perception are two separate substances, so are the [self-cognitions] that experience them. Hence a fivefold categorization would be required. Or, just as the two experiencers are counted as one because they are both self-cognitions, so the sense and mental perceptions should be counted as one in that they are both cognitions of [other] entities. Thus a threefold categorization would be necessary. The three spheres [would therefore be in place with respect to the objector's position]. This concludes the section on mental perception.

12. Self-Cognizing Perception

Self-cognizing valid perception

1. Refutation of others' assertions
2. Setting forth our own position
3. Dealing with objections [to our position] [158]

Refutation of other's assertions

1. Refuting the idea that every awareness is essentially a self-cognition
2. Refuting the view that a self-cognizing perception has no object

Refuting the idea that every awareness is essentially a self-cognition[490]

Someone proposes that every awareness must be a self-cognizing perception of its own nature, since awareness of [other] objects can only proceed from awareness of oneself. In support of this vacuous claim, he cites the passage that says, "If that [consciousness] does not know its own [nature], how can it know another's nature?"[491]

[Response:] This is untenable. We may consider, for instance, the nature of the valid inferential cognition that realizes sound is impermanent. It would follow that this nature is an overt object of comprehension for this valid cognition, because it is a valid cognition that overtly comprehends its own nature. He cannot deny the reason, as that would go against [his assertion] that an awareness must be a self-cognizing perception of its own nature. But if he agrees [with the argument's conclusion], then it would follow that the nature of that inferential cognition is a hidden [phenomenon] for the mind of the individual in question, because it is the *overt object of comprehension for the inferential valid cognition* in the continuum of the person who has that cognition. This reason is one that [the opponent] has already accepted. But if he agrees [with this conclusion], this would mean that [contrary to his original assertion] it is possible for someone's own mind to remain hidden from him!

It also follows that the valid inferential cognition in question would be a consciousness to which its held object—a specifically characterized phenomenon—vividly appears. But that would mean that this valid inferential cognition is nonconceptual. He cannot deny the reason [that a specifically characterized object vividly appears to it,] since this would go against his assertion that it is an awareness to which its own specifically characterized nature directly appears.

Moreover, it follows that he is proposing a model of valid cognition and its results according to which (1) the thing comprehended is the nature of awareness, (2) the thing validly cognizing it is itself, and (3) the result is self-cognition. This must be the case, since this is the model yielded by his assertion that every awareness is necessarily a self-cognizing perception of its own nature. If he denies the pervasion [that his assertion yields such a model], we would call on him to consider how one can substantiate the model of valid cognition and its results according to which (a) the thing comprehended is the object-aspect, (b) the valid cognition is the subject-aspect, and (c) the result is self-cognition.[492] If he accepts [the viability of the first model], then it would follow that the model of valid cognition and its results that he has agreed to it is that (1) the thing comprehended is the subject-aspect, (2) the valid cognition is the object-aspect, and (3) the result is self-cognition. This must be the case, because what *own nature* primarily refers to with respect to awareness is the *subject-aspect*—namely, the [self-]experiencing dimension of something that is clear and aware—whereas the *object-aspect* of an awareness, as has been established above, refers to that awareness itself.[493] [159]

What is more, by his reckoning, it would follow that the false cognition that sound is permanent perceives its own nature and is [therefore] aware of the fact that it is a false cognition. This must be the case, because it perceives its own nature, and being a false cognition is inseparable from that nature, with the two of them forming part of a single substance. But if he were to accept this [conclusion], then it would also follow that the consciousness holding sound to be permanent cannot be a false cognition, because it is an awareness that apprehends the cognition holding sound to be permanent is a false cognition.

[Returning to] the valid inferential cognition that realizes sound is impermanent, it follows that the cognition's own nature *cannot* be its object, because although it is an ascertaining cognition, the thing that it ascertains is not its own nature. He cannot dispute this [argument's] pervasion, since that would contradict the [*Commentary on Pramāṇa*] passage "How can something that those ascertaining cognitions do not ascertain be their object?"[494] But [equally], if he accepts [the argument's conclusion], he would directly [go against his original position]. So he must challenge [its reason] and thus deny that what the cognition ascertains is not its own nature. But then it would follow that the inferential cognition is an ascertaining awareness of its own nature, because it is a conceptual cognition that ascertains that nature. And if he accepts this, it goes against his assertion that this cognition is a *perception* of its nature.

If every awareness had its own nature as its object, it would also invalidate one of the attacks on the Nyāya. The Nyāya school claims that pleasure is comprehended by sense perception. The [Buddhist] response to this, contained in the line "Because a sense consciousness definitely [has only a physical object],"[495] is that sense perception cannot have pleasure as its object, because it is definitely only a subject of external things.[496] What [our opponent] says is therefore without doubt little more than drivel, against which any number of criticisms can be made. But since cataloguing them all would take up too much space, I will stop here.

Someone else agrees that awareness of one's own [nature] is a necessary prerequisite for awareness of another's [nature], and that every consciousness must therefore be a self-cognition of its own nature. But he does not believe that every awareness must be a self-cognizing *perception*.

[Response:] This is an even more flagrant piece of nonsense. Does he suppose then that an awareness realizes its own nature while that nature remains hidden from it? Or if he says that [conversely] it realizes the nature in a manifest fashion, is the nature something that it realizes overtly or only by implication? Some may be ready to maintain that the awareness in question can realize itself even though its nature remains hidden from it, or that it can realize that nature implicitly. We do not deem it necessary to refute such persons; their own claims are quite enough to discredit them. The only remaining option, therefore, would be that the awareness overtly realizes its own nature in a manifest fashion. But this goes against his assertion that an awareness is not a perception [of its own nature].

Someone else claims that even though every consciousness is a self-cognizing perception of itself, this does not mean that every one of them is a self-cognizing perception.

[Response:] Once again, this is someone who has barely given the matter any thought. He subscribes to the view that what it means to be a "self-cognizing perception" is to be a consciousness that knows its own nature. So, if he now goes on to claim that [knowing its own nature] is not enough for a consciousness to qualify as a self-cognizing perception, is this not tantamount to asserting that something both is and is not a self-cognizing perception, simultaneously? He needs to think the matter through properly. [160]

Also, it would follow that being the inferential cognition of an object is not sufficient for something to qualify as an inferential cognition, because being the perception of an object is not sufficient for something to qualify as a perception. He has accepted [the argument's] reason. But if he agrees with [its conclusion], it would leave him incapable of proving even that the inferential cognition realizing sound is impermanent is an inferential cognition.

If it is necessary for something to be aware of itself in order to be aware of another, it would also follow that something must comprehend itself in order to comprehend another. But that would absurdly mean that every valid cognition validly cognizes itself. Therefore the passage "If that [consciousness] does not know its own [nature], how can it know another's nature?"[497] cannot be interpreted to mean that nothing can be aware of another unless it is aware of itself. Instead, it indicates that there could be no awareness of another thing unless [a consciousness] had a subject-aspect [to it] that is aware of [the consciousness] itself.

Refuting the view that self-cognizing perception has no object

An individual who prides himself on being a scholar says that in discussion of self-cognizing perception, there can be no distinguishing between "knower" and "known," and that self-cognition should be described as "that which is simply produced as awareness, the opposite of physical material."[498] [In support] he cites the *Treasure of Pramāṇa Reasoning* where it says, "Self-cognition is just the opposite of physical matter."[499] This leads him to say that self-cognizing perceptions do not have objects. In very strident tones, [he dismisses the idea] that self-cognition is aware of itself. It would follow, he argues, that the lamp, in addition to being a lamp, is both illuminator and illuminated, because [it is permissible for] a self-cognition, in addition to being a self-cognition, to be both knower and known. Here he cites the passage:

> Because [he has accepted that] it is in the nature of the thing,
> when the illuminator properly illuminates,
> he must concede that it is illuminating itself.[500]

[Response:] What he generously supplies us with here is a target of very ample proportions, upon which a torrent of criticisms—such as that he contradicts his own assertions and is guilty of the same errors he claims to find in others—can rain down. Let me mention just a small sample of these. The *Treasure of Pramāṇa Reasoning* says, "It [valid cognition] has [the two features] of being nondeceptive and illuminating something that was not already known. It realizes a specifically characterized thing and is in accordance with the way things are."[501] You[502] have explained it by saying "Put concisely, being a fresh and nondeceptive cognition of the specifically characterized thing of which it is aware is the characteristic that defines valid cognition."[503] However, you go on to state that a self-cognizing valid perception does *not* comprehend an object. How can this be counted as anything other than the most blatant self-contradiction? [161] A valid cognition necessarily comprehends a thing. Thus to claim that a self-cognizing valid perception has no object is to place oneself outside the tradition to which passages such as "Valid cognition is consciousness that is nondeceptive" belong. It would also follow that the lamp has nothing to illuminate, because self-cognition has no object [to comprehend]. The three spheres [are in place], and you have no response. [Your position] also makes the [standard] model for valid cognition and its results unsustainable. This is because in that model, (1) the thing comprehended is the *object-aspect*, (2) the valid cognition is the *subject-aspect*, and (3) the result is the *self-cognition*. But according to you, a self-cognition does not comprehend anything.

You answer these criticisms by saying that while the aforesaid model treats the object-aspect like the object of the subject-aspect, to accept that it [really] is the object would be to hold that the *excluding perspective* reflects the way things actually are. However, you say, it does not, since [contrary to the way they appear to it,] the object-aspect, the subject-aspect, and the self-cognition are not distinct from one another in any real sense. And for this reason, the whole model of valid cognition and its results that treats them as though they were distinct is not, properly speaking, correct. Instead, you say, the model is designed to reflect the way that these things appear to a mistaken [conceptual] consciousness—namely, as distinct from each other. You argue that [opponents who say otherwise] must accept that the illusory horses, oxen, and other things that appear to the eyes of those under the spell of the illusionist's mantras and substances are actual horses, cows and so on, because [these opponents assent to the idea that] the object-aspect, subject-aspect, and self-cognition of a specific consciousness are [actually] distinct from one another. Some respond to this by rejecting the idea that [the fiction of the conjured animals is a fitting] analogy for the actuality [of cognition]. You insist, however, that this linkage is exactly the one made in passages such as "These distinctions are not present in their nature, but only because of the mind."[504]

[Response:] Is the linkage [you make between] the analogy to the actuality [derived from] the excluding perspective on things or the *appearing perspective*? If you say that it is the latter, it would go against [your assertion] that the model of valid cognition and its result originates in the excluding perspective. So you must say that [the linkage of the analogy to the actuality is similarly derived from] the excluding perspective. But then it would follow that what is the case from the excluding perspective must be [true], because it is on the basis of the linkage of analogy and the actuality being correct that [you judge] the object-aspect, the subject-aspect, and the self-cognition not to be distinct [from each other]. The three spheres [are in place, and] you have no response.

You assert that the distinction between the subject-aspect and the object-aspect is constructed by a mistaken consciousness, and then you seek to use this to justify the conclusion that the subject-aspect has no object. This amounts to a nihilistic attack on the whole notion of an awareness having an object. [162] It would follow, for example, that a conceptual consciousness can never have an object, because things appear to such a consciousness as though they existed externally, but this appearance is simply constructed by mistaken consciousness.

Similarly, from the Cittamātra view of things, it would follow that the visual perception of blue has no object, because the apparent separation between that visual perception and the blue it apprehends are simply constructed by mistaken consciousness. If you grant this for sense perception, it must equally apply to all other-cognitions. This would mean that according to the Cittamātra system, no awareness has an object. And if there are no objects that valid cognition comprehends, then neither are there any that it establishes. Thus you would be compelled to avow, as a fundamental tenet, that no object can exist!

You assert that self-cognition is a substance and that it should not be considered separate from the object-aspect. You also vigorously maintain that it is the thought of the *Treasure of Pramāṇa Reasoning* that the actual perspective of the Seven Treatises is that of the False Aspectarian. This represents a massive internal contradiction. The False Aspectarian says that aspects are constructs. This means that the object-aspect of any given awareness is true only in a conventional sense. But as you also claim that self-cognition constitutes a substance, it must be true in an ultimate sense. And if one of them is conventional whereas the other is ultimate, they are obviously separate things!

In your discussion on valid cognition and its results, having declared the final thought of the Seven Treatises to be that of the False Aspectarian, you identify the False Aspectarian's version of the model as that in which (1) the thing comprehended is a conceptually constructed object-aspect, (2) the valid cognition is that which apprehends that aspect, and (3) the result is a putative self-cognition, which apprehends that valid cognition. This [formulation] effectively denies any place for [genuine] valid self-cognition in the Seven Treatises' own system. But in your account of self-cognizing perception, you say that the system accepts something that is "awareness, the opposite of physical matter" as genuine self-cognition. How can this be judged as anything other than you directly contradicting your own position?

What is more, based on your view, it follows that there can be recollection that has no object, because there is self-cognition without any object. If you reject the [argument's] pervasion, you would be saying that recollection is *not* the [decisive] reason establishing the existence of self-cognition, in that subsequent recollection [can only] recall the object that the [earlier] self-cognition experienced. So if you deny that, we invite you, "expert logician," to explain what relevance recollection has in establishing the existence of self-cognition![505] [163]

You reject the idea of distinguishing between object-aspect, subject-aspect, and self-cognition on the grounds that this form of distinction is derived from assenting to the excluding perspective on things. This is essentially to claim that nothing derived from that perspective should be regarded as correct. But this is basically saying that nothing that is true in the conventional sense has any existence. The Conqueror and those who have successively upheld his tradition have all agreed that it is necessary to rely on what is true conventionally in order to realize what is true ultimately. Whereas you now inform us that anything that is true in a conventional sense has no existence at all. This means you are asserting that there is no way to realize what is ultimately true. Your stance thus regards all phenomena in samsara and nirvana, together with those of the afflicted and purified categories, nihilistically. So while you may try to disguise it as Buddhist Dharma, what you espouse is actually the system of the Cārvāka!

Setting forth our own position

Every consciousness has two portions: one that is clear, aware, and experiences its own nature and one that presents in the aspect of its object. The first is referred to as the "subject-aspect" and is regarded in both the Sautrāntika and Cittamātra systems as the illustration [that embodies] self-cognizing perception. The second is referred to as the "object-aspect" and is that which the self-cognizing perception is said to experience. Thus the clear, aware, and experiencing portion of consciousness is the basis for designating the subject-aspect a *self-cognition*. And it is this [feature] that the *Treasure of Pramāṇa Reasoning* refers to when it declares that "Self-cognition is just the opposite of physical matter."[506] The statement should not be construed as the author defining self-cognition as "awareness [that] is the opposite of physical matter," and thus it does not convey that self-cognition has no object. If it did, simply "being an awareness" would be all the evidence required to prove that an awareness had no object, and any given awareness would necessarily *not* be aware of an object. However, this would lead to the dire position of having to champion the totally perverse view that an object is necessarily a thing that is *not* known by an awareness!

The Vaibhāṣika accept that consciousness has a clear, aware, and experiencing part, but they do not recognize this as self-cognition. [164] The reason for this is that they lack any notion of consciousness as a thing with aspects, and thus have no conception of anything such as an "object-aspect." Without this, they cannot assert that the clear, aware, and experiencing part of an awareness is a self-cognition. For them there seems to be no sense in speaking of a self-cognition when there is nothing to "cognize," nor in speaking of an experiencer when there is nothing to "experience." Only those who assert that consciousness has [various] aspects to it can posit object-aspects. Once they establish that this object-aspect need not be an entity that is separate from the clear, aware, and experiencing side of awareness, it is easy for them to establish that there is such a thing as self-cognition. This is what is meant by the statement "Thus, by means of the two sides [to consciousness] also, self-cognition is established."[507]

If that were not the case, and the clear and aware side of consciousness could be a self-cognition without any requirement that it be aware of an object, there would be no inconsistency in maintaining that self-cognition exists but that the object-aspect does not. But sensible individuals are well-advised to reflect on why it is said to be necessary to establish the object-aspect in order to confirm self-cognition. The clear, aware, and experiencing part of consciousness is the *experiencer* whereas the object-aspect of that same consciousness is the *experienced*, and those with an intellectual grasp of this point declare that self-cognition exists.

As far as the Sautrāntika is concerned, this perception is *self*-cognizing in that the object it perceives is its own nature. For the Cittamātra school, on the other hand, the perception is *self*-cognizing due to having no sense that the object it is aware of is separate from itself; he does not cite the fact that the perception is aware of its own nature as the grounds for designating it self-cognition. For him, when there is a perception of blue, the blue that is apprehended is also part of the nature of the visual perception, despite which, the perception must still be counted as an *other*-cognition. In the Sautrāntika system, one distinguishes a self-cognition from an other-cognition in terms of whether the object is a separate entity from [the cognition]. In the Cittamātra system, the basis for the judgment is whether, within the apprehension of the object, there is any sense of [subject-object] duality. Reflecting this [difference in stance], the Sautrāntika and the Cittamātra systems define self-cognizing perception in different ways. According to the Sautrāntika, it is "a consciousness that is nonconceptual and unmistaken, and is overtly aware of an object that is in its own nature." For the Cittamātra school, it is "a consciousness that is nonconceptual and unmistaken, and overtly realizes the object it holds without any sense of dualistic separation." [165] To say that "self-cognition is the nature of the consciousness" and that "consciousness has self-cognition" would therefore be legitimate assertions. But one should not say that "a consciousness is, *in its nature*, a self-cognition" or that "a consciousness *is* a self-cognition."

The thing that self-cognition holds—what is termed the "object-aspect" of the consciousness—is the consciousness itself. The phrase "the aspect presents" simply means that the [consciousness] is produced with the aspect. As I have established in the lines of reasoning set out above, it should not be interpreted as indicating the presence of a [separate] aspect standing between the object and the awareness like some sort of partition.[508] This [position] represents a philosophical tenet for both the Sautrāntika and the Cittamātra. Thus, when describing the view of those [Buddhist] realists who assert that consciousness is aspected, "Entrance into the Yogācāra Thatness," [the fifth chapter of] the *Blaze of Reasoning*, says:

> When a consciousness with an object and a subject operates, the aspects of various objects, such as visual forms, vigorously appear.

> What is it that makes the aspects of these various [objects] appear so vigorously? It could only be [either] that the consciousness has completely become the aspect of the object or . . . .[509]

Dealing with objections [to our position]

Someone claims that unless we accept that every consciousness is a perception of its own nature, we go against the *Commentary on Pramāṇa* where it states:

> The nature [of that awareness] is not that of a *śabdārtha*,
> thus all [cognitions of it] are perceptions of it.[510]

[Response:][511] What these words actually indicate is that the nature of consciousness is not that of a *śabdārtha* but that of a specifically characterized entity. For this reason, all those valid cognitions that engage [that consciousness] through *experiencing* it are perceptions of it. [Dharmakīrti] is *not* saying that every consciousness perceives its own nature.

Elsewhere, someone argues in the following way. Conceptual cognition must be either awareness or physical material [with respect] to itself. If it is neither of these two, then conceptual cognition cannot be an [actual] entity [with respect] to itself. [Likewise,] a consciousness must be either a self-cognition or an other-cognition [of itself]. And as it cannot be an other-cognition [of itself], one must assert that consciousness is a self-cognition [of itself].

[Response:] This analysis is by a person with a very crude intellect. For one thing, as I have already demonstrated, an actual thing can be something that is neither awareness nor physical material. [166] And while we readily agree that a consciousness is [classifiable] as either a self-cognition or an other-cognition, as should be apparent from the numerous times I have already addressed this point, the fact that something is an awareness with respect to another thing in no way entails it being either a self-cognition or an other-cognition with respect to that thing.

The unscholarly produce a never-ending sequence of errors, and using logic to disprove them all would serve no great purpose. Therefore I will devote no more space to this except to declare:

Until the keen-sighted person steps up,
the elephant is left in the hands of the blind throng,

whose inspection of it results only in the cacophony
of a hundred conflicting descriptions, all of them wrong.

Similarly, until I stepped up with my keen intellect,
this matter was left to the crowd of supposed scholars,
whose best efforts at investigation
led to nothing but false descriptions.

This concludes the section on self-cognizing perception.

13. Yogic Perception

1. Defining characteristics
2. Varieties
3. Description

Defining characteristics

A yogic perception is defined as "a transcendent awareness that depends on its governing condition, a concentration, and realizes its object, one of the aspects of the [four] truths,[512] by perceiving it."

Varieties

There are the śrāvaka's yogic perceivers, pratyekabuddha's yogic perceivers, and Mahayana yogic perceivers. There are also those that are included within the paths of seeing, meditation, and no-more learning. Elsewhere, I have established by means of scriptures and logical reasoning that the path of preparation is not a yogic perception.[513]

Description of the four truths

1. General discussion on the four truths
2. Specific discussion about the aspect of selflessness

General discussion on the four truths

1. The identity of each of the four truths
2. Their definitive enumeration
3. Their definitive order

The identity of each of the four truths

True sufferings

A thorough description of the topic would provide a whole range of illustrations, showing how true sufferings manifest in [both] the domains and the inhabitants that constitute the impure worlds. [167] Here [in the Seven Treatises], however, the only things overtly presented as illustrations of true sufferings are the contaminated aggregates [that a person has] appropriated. The reason for this focus is that unless one recognizes that these very aggregates have a dissatisfactory, suffering nature, there will be no opportunity to develop the genuinely renounced attitude that spurns samsara or to [generate] the sincere aspiration to reach nirvana. Whereas once one has recognized their dissatisfactory, suffering nature, the wish to spurn samsara will develop naturally. [Dharmakīrti] therefore illustrates true sufferings by stating, "Suffering is having samsaric aggregates."[514] In doing so, he primarily aims to present true sufferings as a subject for yogic [meditational] practice.

The four aspects of true suffering are meditative antidotes to the distorted notions that these appropriated aggregates are pure, pleasurable, permanent, and have a self. The four aspects of true suffering are as follows. The aggregates are (1) *impermanent*, because they are undergoing disintegration moment by moment. They are (2) *suffering*, both because they are under the control of karma and delusion and because they are in [a state] that is not congruent with that of āryas. They are (3) *empty*, in that they have no self that is separate from them. And they are (4) *selfless*, because they do not have a self that is [part] of their nature. Unless one realizes by means of valid cognition these four aspects of suffering in their entirety, one cannot fully develop the genuine thought of renunciation. How is this the case? Realization that the [aggregates] have a dissatisfactory, suffering nature will trigger the desire to be separated from samsara. But without also realizing their impermanence, one will fail to appreciate that eventual separation from these aggregates is inevitable, and thus the craving attachment[515] one has for them will continue unabated. And unless one realizes their selflessness, there will naturally be a craving attachment for the senses and the like as "mine."

While the realization that one's own aggregates are impermanent and have a dissatisfactory, suffering nature will give rise to some sort of desire to be rid of them, an [underlying] self-grasping will ensure that thoughts then turn to other [kinds of aggregate], believing that it is through [obtaining] them that "my happiness" can be secured, in spite of the fact that they are also contaminated. Thus, while realization that the aggregates are impermanent informs one that separation from them is inevitable, and recognition of their dissatisfactory, suffering nature arouses in one the wish to be rid of them, the *genuine* yearning for liberation, in which there is a total disaffection with contaminated phenomena in all of their forms, only comes about once one understands the aspect of true suffering that is the absence of any [actual] self within oneself and others. [168]

True origins

Self-grasping—the root of samsara—the desirous attachment and other [delusions] arising from self-grasping, and the karma one accrues under the influence of delusions are all referred to as "true origins." This is because they are the causes responsible for [bringing about] their result, suffering, in the form of the various contaminated entities. On this topic, [the *Commentary on Pramāṇa*] says:

> Even though ignorance is the cause of existence,
> [here] craving attachment and not it [i.e., ignorance] is described as such,
> because craving attachment perpetuates the process and is its immediate [condition].
> Karma [like ignorance] is [also] not [so described].[516]

This tells us that while ignorance is the [real] cause of samsara, in his discussion on [true origins'] aspects of "irresistible production" and "condition," [Dharmakīrti] chose not to overtly present it as such, focusing instead upon craving attachment as the cause. Karma [i.e., action] is also one of the causes of suffering, but again there is no explicit acknowledgment of this fact in the section. Why then did [Dharmakīrti] choose to represent only craving attachment [as the cause of samsara]? He communicates his reason for this in the words "Craving attachment perpetuates the process and is its immediate [condition]." This is not to deny that ignorance and karma are properly classified as true origins. In numerous other sections of the treatise, such as "Once there is [sense of] self, there is consciousness of other . . ."[517] and "Thus the wish for release attacks the root . . . the view of the transitory composite . . . ,"[518] [Dharmakīrti] affirms that delusion and the karma associated with it do indeed act as causes of samsara.

Failing to notice that [Dharmakīrti] acknowledges this fact, some claim that the *Commentary on Pramāṇa* teaches that true origins are limited to three kinds of craving attachment—directed at the desire [realm], the disintegrating [aggregates], and existence. This [misinterpretation] disregards the vast majority of causes for suffering and in so doing denies their existence.

There are four aspects of true origins, which [the treatise] sets forth to counter four distorted notions related to true origins. The notions are that (1) suffering is causeless, (2) a single cause is responsible for all suffering, (3) suffering is created by manifestations of *śabdabrahman*,[519] and (4) suffering is part of some [grand] design by Śiva or another ["divine"] agent. The four aspects [countering these] are as follows. A true origin is (1) *cause*, in that it is what creates suffering itself. It is (2) *origin*, in the sense of being the source of every single type of substance that gives rise to suffering. A true origin is also (3) *powerful producer*, in that it generates suffering in an overwhelmingly forceful manner. And it is (4) *condition*, since it incessantly sustains the sequence of suffering.

True cessations

A true cessation is brought about by a true path and is a *separation* from any seed [of delusion] that is to be eliminated by a true path. For true cessations there are again four aspects, set forth to counter four distorted notions. These notions are that (1) there is no liberation whatsoever, (2) certain contaminated phenomena [that can be gained] without having rid oneself of delusion constitute liberation, (3) there is a form of liberation that is superior to the cessation of suffering, [169] and (4) while temporary respite [from suffering] may be possible, no enduring state of liberation from it exists. The four aspects that stand in opposition to these notions are as follows. A true cessation is (1) a *cessation*, in that it marks the elimination of suffering. It is (2) *peace*, since it represents the elimination of delusion. A true cessation is (3) *most excellent*, in that nothing is greater than it. And it represents (4) *release*, as there is no regression from it once attained.

True paths

A true path is an ārya's transcendent awareness, encompassing an *uninterrupted path*—the antidote that directly eliminates that portion of the seeds of defilement that are allotted to it for eradication—and a *released path*—one that has prevailed in that [process of] elimination. One meditates on the four aspects of true paths to counter the four distorted notions, that (1) there is no path to liberation whatsoever, (2) the wisdom realizing selflessness is not the path to liberation, (3) this wisdom misapprehends the way that things exist, and (4) this wisdom is incapable of bringing about a total eradication of suffering. The four aspects of a true path are as follows. It is (1) a [genuine] *path*, in the sense that it takes one [to the destination]. It is

(2) *appropriate*, in that it is what acts as the antidote to delusions. It is (3) *productive*, as it makes the mind correct. And a true path is something that is (4) *assured extrication*, in the sense that it is certain to deliver one to the enduring state. Here "enduring state" denotes the state from which there is no regression.

The path of no-more learning is the result of a true path but does not count as a true path itself. This is because a true path should be a genuine path and must lead somewhere. And if the path of no-more learning were that, it would absurdly follow that there is some higher state that one can progress to beyond that of buddhahood. The paths of accumulation and preparation also do not count as true paths, because it is impossible to have a path of accumulation or preparation that is an uninterrupted path serving as a direct antidote to any of the seeds that should be eliminated. Therefore only the paths of seeing and meditation can be classed as genuine true paths.

Someone defines *analytical cessation*[520] as "a cessation that is the abstracted absence of some element that a mind cognizing suchness has eradicated." We note that he also goes on to declare that true cessations are necessarily composite phenomena.

[Response:] It would follow that an abstracted absence of the seeds to be eradicated by the path of seeing counts as an analytical cessation, because it is a cessation and it is the abstracted absence of an element eradicated by a mind cognizing suchness. [170] But if he were to accept this, then it would follow that the cessation in question is a composite phenomenon, because that is what he has asserted [for all true cessations]. He has accepted both the reason and pervasion [of this argument]. But if it is composite, it would follow that it is not a *straight negation*. In point of fact, an analytical cessation is *necessarily* a straight negation. By claiming that such a cessation is a composite thing, he has simply revealed himself not to be a person of learning.

Among the various Buddhist philosophical schools in the land of āryas, there were admittedly those—namely, the Vaibhāṣika—who believed that true cessations constituted substances. But as far as they were concerned, these were permanent substances rather than impermanent ones. The Sautrāntika, on the other hand, ruled out such an idea, saying that something such as noncomposite space could no more constitute a substance than could the son of a barren woman. And because both analytical and nonanalytical cessations[521] also belong to the category of noncomposite phenomena, neither of them could be a substance for the Sautrāntika. Expressing this is the passage:

> Space is comparable to a barren woman's son,
> and cessations correspond to space.
> There is nothing composite or material about them.
> They are not divided according to the three times
> and have no form with physical resistance.
> These are the facts, we are told, according to the Sautrāntika.[522]

You[523] also interpret the passage literally, something that squarely contradicts your position [on cessations].

A true cessation is said to be the "result" of a [true] path. This is intended to convey that a true cessation can only be actualized in dependence on a [true] path. There is no suggestion here that the path and the cessation are [actual] cause and effect, like fire and smoke, since that would necessarily entail [the cessation] was something newly produced, having hitherto not existed. The treatise explains that there is no such thing as a permanent, self-arisen valid cognition. But since nobody claims that a true cessation is a valid cognition, there is no fault here. There are many other issues that I could address on this topic, but I set them aside for the time being.

The definitiveness of the [fourfold] enumeration

Why then is this fourfold division of the truths said to be the definitive way of enumerating them? There are two [classes of phenomena]: (1) the afflicted class,[524] made up of those things one needs to eradicate, and (2) the pure class,[525] those one should embrace. These two classes comprise everything that one needs to strive for and rid oneself of, and they are therefore regarded as definitive. The constituents in each class are also divided definitively into those that are causes and those that are effects.

The definitiveness of the order [of the four truths]

The textual tradition presents the four truths in a number of different sequences. Thus the four may be arranged into sets of cause and effect, [or they may be organized according to] how difficult they are to ascertain, the sequence in which they are described and explained, the order in which they are actually realized, or ranked in terms of their relative superiority and inferiority—in either ascending or descending order—or the chronological sequence in which they occur. [171] Here [in the *Commentary on Pramāṇa*], they are presented in the sequence that the subject realizes them. This can be explained as follows. To develop a genuine desire for liberation, a person must first recognize how samsara, in its very nature, is fundamentally dissatisfying. Only this recognition can engender the wish to be free from samsara. The next thought that will occur to any rational person who has recognized this nature is that there can be no hope of getting rid of the effect without tackling its causes. The individual will therefore start to investigate whether suffering actually has a cause, and using the reason that suffering only arises on certain occasions, he will establish that suffering does indeed depend upon causes. Having determined that these causes must be either permanent or impermanent, the person will then be guided by the logic communicated in passages such as:

> Because [āryas] observe that as long as the cause is present, there can be no reversal of its effect.[526]

Seeing that the necessary association [between effect and cause] could not be possible if these causes were permanent, the individual will conclude that they must be impermanent and then endeavor to identify these impermanent causes of suffering. Grasping at the notion of self directly spawns a craving that is attached to the self. This in turn creates a craving attachment for *my happiness*. Feeling that the self is independently unable to achieve this happiness, a craving attachment for *my senses* and the like develops, under the impression that they can facilitate the achievement of personal happiness. In pursuit of that goal, while exploiting the senses and so forth like slaves, one performs physical, verbal, and mental actions. Striving for pleasure in this life, some individuals are driven to perform all sorts of nonmeritorious actions, such as killing, and through these actions they form for themselves [new] sets of aggregates belonging to the lower realms of existence. Others, attached to the [idea of] experiencing sensual pleasure in future existences, will engage in various meritorious actions, and in so doing, forge for themselves [new sets of] aggregates of either the human or celestial variety belonging to the more pleasurable existences in the desire realm. Still others, attached to the pleasure associated with minds of concentration, will perform actions of the "unwavering" variety, and thereby fashion for themselves the aggregates belonging to one of the two higher realms. Thus, guided by the logical reasoning expressed in lines such as "One who sees a self [always clings to 'I'] . . . ,"[527] a person engaged in the investigation will realize that the causes of the suffering aggregates he has appropriated are their origins, taking the form of karma and delusions. [Reflecting this order, the treatise] teaches first about suffering and then later about its origin.

Someone who has developed the wish to eradicate these origins will start to investigate whether self-grasping—the root of all such karma and delusion—can actually be eliminated. [172] In the course of this investigation, seeing how this self is fatally undermined by various lines of logical reasoning—such as those establishing that it can be neither the same nature as the aggregates nor a nature that is distinct from them—he will come to realize that self-grasping can indeed be eliminated. Realizing the possibility of eradicating [the cause] self-grasping, the person next becomes aware that separation from the effect, suffering, must also therefore be possible. At this point, he realizes that a cessation in which suffering has been eliminated must be achievable. Hence the treatise teaches true cessation third in the order.

Next, it occurs to the person that unless he is prepared to work at the cause—the path—[such a cessation] can never be brought about. It is at this point that he develops the desire to train in the path. It is [only] last in the order therefore that the treatise teaches the true path.

Specific discussion about the aspect of selflessness

1. Identifying the two selves that are to be negated
2. Explaining the logical proofs that refute them
3. How one meditates on selflessness
4. How one eradicates self-grasping by means of that meditation

Identifying the two selves that are to be negated

We can distinguish between two forms of "self" that are to be negated, the self of persons and the self of phenomena. Negations of the self are accordingly also twofold—namely, the selflessness of persons and the selflessness of phenomena.

What then is the person? And what is the "self" of the person? There is a notion that has always been present in sentient beings from time without beginning, whose referent is the [actual] person [or] "I." But instead of [seeing this] for what it is—that is to say, no more than a designation that is given to either the collection of the [individual's] aggregates or the continuum of the aggregates over time—this notion misapprehends the person to exist as a self-supporting substance, the nature of which sets it apart from the aggregates. Because this notion has the person as its referent and grasps at it as a self it is known as "self-grasping."

The person is an identity assigned to a set of aggregates that are a composite in a state of flux and disintegration. Due to viewing the person as having a nature that sets it apart from this transitory, composite character, [self-grasping] is called the "view [associated with] the transitory composite."[528] As this has always been present in the person's continuum from time without beginning, it is described as "innate."

What acts as the referent object for self-grasping is just "I."[529] It is to this that terms such as "person" and "living being" are affixed. It is also what acts as the basis for the [workings of] cause and effect. If the "person," "living being," or "sentient being" did not exist, there could be no cause and effect, since there would be neither the performer of the actions, who thereby accumulates karma, nor the experiencer of the maturing and other effects [of those actions]. [173] But self-grasping holds the person to be a "self-supporting substance, the nature of which sets it apart from the aggregates."[530] This constitutes a self of persons and as such, is ruled out by valid cognition. This sort of self lacks any kind of existence, even in a conventional sense. The abstraction that is the simple absence of this type of self is called the "selflessness of the person."

The referent object for the innate view [associated with] the transitory composite is therefore the person and *not* a self of persons. Conversely, what it holds is a self of persons, not the actual person. If there were no distinction between the person and the self of the person, it would entail that the person does not exist even in a conventional sense, meaning that the accumulator of actions and the experiencer of their results, the very basis of karmic effects, would be completely lost. Alternatively, it would entail that a self of persons really exists.

Some may challenge the assertion that a self of persons does not exist conventionally. They might say that when refuting a self of persons, what one rules out is that such a thing exists in any ultimate sense, which is not to say that it cannot exist conventionally. They may claim that while one must obviously reject the existence of a permanent, unitary, and independent self of persons[531] even in the conventional sense, there is nothing wrong with acknowledging that a mere self of persons exists.

[Response:] What objection would they have if someone were to assert that similarly, on the conventional level, there is a self of phenomena? It could be claimed that such a self is the separation between the object, the subject, and the self-cognition with respect to a single awareness. On the ultimate level, this separation is negated. So [one could maintain that] a "mere self" of phenomena is an established basis, whereas the self of phenomena that is to be negated even on the conventional level is the aforesaid object, subject and self-cognition being separate *substances*.

These individuals may be prepared to accept this and agree that the [first] self of phenomena could exist. But what we say is that anyone ready to maintain that both the self of person and self of phenomena have a place in our own system, as things to which we ascribe definite existence, lacks not just the faintest whiff of the Buddhist about them but also any hint of the taste. [The existence of such a self] has all sorts of absurd consequences. It would follow, for instance, that the self is something that no logical proof could refute. It would also follow that the awareness that realizes selflessness is erroneous. And it would follow that there is no antidote that can eradicate self-grasping.

If [upon consideration, these opponents] accept that a self of phenomena does not exist, they might still deny that this corresponds to the situation with the self of persons. They could maintain that whereas the aforesaid object, subject, and self-cognition being separate substances would constitute a self of phenomena, the three merely being different does not. [174]

[Response:] We would point out that this situation corresponds exactly to that of the person, because whereas being a person that is a self-supporting substance—the nature of which sets it apart from the aggregates—would constitute a self of persons, merely being a person does not. Moreover, if there is no distinction between person and a self of the person, it must equally be the case that there is no distinction between phenomena and a self of phenomena. So it would follow that to be an established basis is to have a self!

The wisdom realizing selflessness is the antidote to self-grasping, the thing to be eradicated. This can only be the case if those two have the same referent object but diametrically opposed ways of apprehending it. But if there really was no distinction between person and a self of the person, it would absurdly follow that just like the [mind] grasping at a self of persons, the wisdom realizing the selflessness of persons also observes the self of persons. Although the referent object of both the antidotal [wisdom] and the [self-grasping] that it is supposed to eradicate is the mere person, the two differ in their aspect, with [self-grasping] viewing this as a self and the antidote seeing that it is self-*less*. It is therefore necessary to differentiate between person and a self of person in exactly the same way that we differentiate between phenomenon and a self of phenomenon.

The various [Buddhist] tenet systems have divergent views on what constitutes a self of phenomena. The present [treatise], as mentioned above, sets out the paths for the [spiritual] trainees of all three persuasions. Thus one version [of the path] it presents is given from the perspective of the śrāvakas, those who follow the First Discourses [of the Buddha]. This is the version that, in accordance with the Sautrāntika system, accepts the reality of external entities. [The other] version [of the path] presented in the treatise is that of the Mahayana. It follows the pronouncements of the Final Discourses and thus treats the Middle Discourses as interpretive. This version accords with the Vijñaptika school of tenets and rejects the idea of external entities.

The first of these [two versions] only countenances the selflessness of persons, not the selflessness of phenomena. That being the case, there was obligation to say what would constitute a self of phenomena. The Vijñaptika system [on the other hand] does talk of a self of phenomena, which it identifies as the [fiction] that *the object, subject, and self-cognition within a single cognitive act are separate substances*. The negation of this is the selflessness of phenomena.

These are major subjects of scholarly examination and principal topics taught by the treatises. Unless they are properly comprehended, liberation and enlightenment remain unachievable goals. But once understood, they serve as the main focus of meditation. Although these are matters of vital importance, since a full treatment of them would demand that I write a huge amount more, I will deal with them no further here. [175]

Explaining the logical proofs that refute the two selves

What refutes the self of phenomena is the logical reasoning that negates the object and subject being separate substances. The chief reasoning is the proof of simultaneity, which has already been explained at length. So next we turn to the logical reasoning that refutes the self of persons.

1. Formulating the [proof's] reason
2. Establishing the reason's [fulfillment of the] three criteria

Formulating the [proof's] reason

The proof is formulated in the following manner: (a) Whatever is neither the same nature as nor a different nature from its own aggregates necessarily has no nature at all. (b) Such a thing is analogous, for example, to the horns on the head of a hare. (c) A person that is a self-supporting substantial thing with a character that sets it apart from the aggregates—rather than simply an identity assigned to the composite or the continuum of the aggregates—is neither the same nature as nor a different nature from the aggregates. This proof's reason is classified as one that involves the nonobservation of a nature.

Establishing the reason's [fulfillment of the] three criteria

1. Establishing the pervasion
2. Establishing the property of the subject

Establishing the pervasion

This requires two cognitions: a valid cognition that ascertains that being the same nature and different natures overtly preclude each other and a valid cognition that ascertains the property of the subject. It is the combination [of the information] provided by these two that allows one to establish: (1) the reverse pervasion—the certainty that [what serves as] the reason is totally absent from the class of dissimilar instances—and (2) the forward pervasion—the certainty that [what serves as] the reason is always present within the class of similar instances.

Establishing the property of the subject

That the aggregates and a self-supporting person do not constitute two different natures [and thereby, separate entities] is something that those with sharper mental faculties are capable of perceiving for themselves. For those with duller faculties, on the other hand, it is something that must be confirmed by inferential cognition.

The reasoning that confirms that the two are not the same nature is as follows. The aggregates in someone's continuum (A), cannot be the same nature as that of a self-supporting person (B), because these aggregates are impermanent and dependent on other [causal forces] (C). The pervasion [that whatever is impermanent and dependent on others cannot be the same nature as a self-supporting person] is established, since if the person was something self-supporting, with a character that set it apart from that of the aggregates, it would need to be *permanent* and *independent*. The [second part of the proof's] reason is also confirmed, in that the [aggregates] are dependent on other forces, because they are formed by karma and delusion. That the aggregates are formed in such a way is, in turn, verified by the reasoning conveyed in the passage "One who sees a self [always clings to

'I'] . . . ,"[532] which was cited above. The [first part of the] reason is also confirmed, in that the aggregates are impermanent because they are produced. The way that each of the components of this proof are confirmed will be discussed below. [176]

Thus the basic proof used to establish that the aggregates lack a self uses a reason [that belongs to the] *nonobservation of a nature* [category]. The reason employed to confirm the proof's pervasion [belongs to the category known as the] *observation of something that is preclusive* [with what is being negated].[533] The reason used to confirm the first part of the property of the subject is of the *nature* variety, while that confirming the reason's second part is of the *effect* variety.

To eliminate self-grasping, one must ascertain that the aggregates are selfless. A myopic being cannot do this through perception but must rely on a logical reason. As has just been explained, that logical reason can itself only be ascertained by depending on further logical reasons, using evidence [related to] effects, natures, and nonobservation. So those who direct no attention to the logical approach may devote much effort to meditating on selflessness, but this effort will ultimately prove futile.

"Being an aggregate ruled by karma and delusion" encapsulates what it means[534] to be an "aggregate of compositional factors." Until one has ascertained that the aggregates both have such an identity and are also impermanent, it is impossible to be certain that their nature is not the same as that of a self of persons. For this reason, realizations that the aggregates are impermanent and are in the nature of suffering represent the sacred means by which their selflessness can be realized. In order to convey this point, [the treatise] says:

> Due to this, [the Buddha] taught that from impermanence
> [there is] suffering,
> and from suffering [there is] selflessness.[535]

Realizing the selflessness of persons, then, means realizing that the aggregates are empty of a self-supporting person. Realizing that the aggregates are impermanent and ruled by karma and delusion does not itself constitute a realization of selflessness. If it did, just meditating on the impermanence and suffering nature of the aggregates would also count as meditation on selflessness, and just by reflecting on the faults of samsara, one would be performing a special insight meditation! So although it is true that knowledge of the sixteen aspects [of the four truths], including that of impermanence, is necessary to realize the selflessness of persons, those who say that what realizing the selflessness of persons means is realizing the sixteen aspects are entirely mistaken.

How one meditates on selflessness

There is a definitive division of paths according to which, in general terms, every path can be classified as either a *path that matures* or a *path that releases*.[536] [177] A path that matures is one that makes the [mental] continuum into a receptacle fit for an uncontaminated transcendent awareness. A path that releases, on the other hand, is an uncontaminated transcendent awareness that is an antidote—one that frees the [mental] continuum from the seeds of any of the elements to be eradicated. One cannot generate a path that releases in the continuum without having first [cultivated] meditation on a path of maturation. It would be like lancing an abscess prematurely without having allowed it to ripen, which can result in sickness. Thus one must first engage in [the cultivation] of meditation on a path of maturation.

The stages of practice for such a path are as follows. Unless one develops the genuine yearning to escape samsara based on a total rejection of it, there can be no desire to achieve liberation and thus no training in the path to that liberation. Therefore one should initially work to engender a sincere desire to completely reject samsara. This requires real knowledge and conviction that samsara is [in the nature of] suffering. Merely making statements about the pointlessness of samsara does not amount to a true rejection; disenchantment with it must be total, something that can only come about through recognition of its flaws. Suffering in samsara takes three forms. The torments of hell or the pangs of hunger and thirst are things that all samsaric beings naturally recognize as suffering as soon as they occur. These are "self-evident sufferings."[537] In contrast, contaminated pleasure may not immediately be recognized as suffering. It becomes recognizable to everyone as such at the point it degenerates [into discomfort]. This represents the "suffering of changeability." Finally, there is a form of suffering that is present in all samsaric beings. This is the "suffering of compositionality," which stems from the fact that everyone is equally impermanent and bereft of independence. An individual cannot genuinely reject samsara in its entirety without having gained insight into this compositional suffering. Most beings do not need the aid of meditation to understand the unsatisfactory nature of the other two [forms of suffering]: they know it from experience. Such recognition alone does not therefore directly spur someone to reject samsara in its entirety. If it did, then everyone, including even denizens of hell, would quite effortlessly have rejected samsara by now. Recognizing things such as self-evident sufferings does not directly engender a total rejection of samsara, because as already remarked, despite this recognition, an individual can still harbor a craving attachment for certain situations within the higher realms of samsara, such as the states of Brahmā, where there is no self-evident suffering. [178] A total rejection of samsara, from the very core of one's being, can only occur when one has properly realized the real character of compositional suffering. Meditation must therefore focus on how these appropriated aggregates are by their very nature dissatisfactory. This point is conveyed in the passage:

> It was with the suffering of compositionality in mind
> that [the Buddha] instructed us to meditate on suffering.[538]

Once the dissatisfactory nature of the contaminated aggregates that a person has appropriated fully dawns on him, he will wish to be rid of them. Liberation promises freedom from the aggregates, and once the person has the desire to achieve it, he will investigate whether the eradication of this suffering is actually feasible. This will lead to the realization that the only way to ensure that he can be rid of suffering so that it can never return is to eliminate what causes it. His thoughts will then turn to discovering the cause. It is reflection on this that brings about the recognition, in the manner already outlined, that self-grasping lies at the root of suffering. At that juncture, the person who wishes to gain freedom from the sufferings of samsara will be motivated to examine whether he can eliminate this self-grasping, the root of samsara. What determines whether the seeds of [self-grasping] can be eradicated is whether or not self-grasping's notion of things has some foundation in reality. If the way that self-grasping holds things to be corresponds with how they actually are, self-grasping must form part of the very nature of the mind, and hence its seeds could never be removed. Conversely, if they do not correspond, then the way that self-grasping understands things can be challenged and discredited so that, with the deployment of an antidote, self-grasping itself can eventually be halted altogether.

To sum up, the way to investigate whether self-grasping can be eradicated is to determine whether its understanding of things is founded in reality. The question then is essentially this: Does the self to which it holds really exist?

This is the point that should be examined using the lines of reasoning such as those set out above that prove there can be no such self. Through this, one is brought to an ascertainment of selflessness and with it, the knowledge that self-grasping itself can be eliminated. One understands that if this is the case with self-grasping, it must also be possible to rid oneself of its effects, samsaric sufferings. The same reasoning [establishing that self-grasping can be eliminated] also brings one to the conviction that there is a state in which all forms of samsaric suffering have been eradicated—namely, nirvana. [179] How does it do this? If the causes giving rise to a thing have some irresistible force that can counter them, then [continued exposure] to that antidotal force over time will dissipate that thing. We observe, for example, that goosebumps resulting from the cold diminish and finally disappear as one comes close to a huge fire. Similarly, we observe that there is an irresistible force that can counter the causes giving rise to the appropriated aggregates. Anything that is seen to have an irresistible counter force will necessarily dissipate through [continued exposure] to the power of that antidotal force. This is just as, for example, the sensation of cold is seen to diminish and disappear when one moves into close proximity with the fire.[539] Likewise, there is seen to be an irresistible force that can counter the conception grasping at the idea that the object, subject, and the self-cognition within a single cognitive act are truly distinct from each other. Using the fact that such an irresistible force is observed [by valid cognition] as the reason, one logically establishes the existence of a state in which all grasping at a self of phenomena has been extinguished. Having confirmed this, one employs *reasoning dealing with demonstrable facts* to verify that it must also therefore be possible to completely imbue the [mental] continuum with understanding of the four truths. Thus the existence of omniscient awareness is also something that can be established by the reasoning of demonstrable facts, because "omniscient awareness" denotes the transcendent awareness whose comprehension of the four truths has been optimized by the total elimination of any grasping at a self of phenomena.

Some, at this point, might have a misconception, acting upon them like an impediment. They might wonder whether the wisdom realizing selflessness is really capable of totally eradicating self-grasping. They might think that this would essentially require an infinite progression of the wisdom realizing selflessness, as it becomes familiar with its object over many lifetimes. But they might rationalize that [such things have limits]. For example, exposing water to [a source of] heat can increase its warmth to a limited extent, but this can never transform it into anything like fire itself. Likewise, [when training to] jump, accustoming oneself with the action can be expected to bring modest improvement, but the extent of this is limited. One will never be able to jump, for instance, further than the distance of a league. Similarly, they might conclude that while some modest development in the wisdom that realizes selflessness may be possible, the potential for progress is finite.

The logical reasoning used to dispel this misconception is that which establishes that the lucidity the wisdom realizing selflessness has with respect to the object with which it has gained familiarity can be developed beyond any bounds. The reasoning is as follows. As long as the wisdom realizing selflessness is engaged in a process of familiarization with its object, in which it remains conjoined with those factors that support [continued] familiarization, the lucid experience it can develop of that object has no bounds. [180] This is because (1) the support [for the awareness] is stable, and (2) not repeatedly needing to exert effort with regard to something once familiarity with it has been gained is a natural feature of the conscious continuum. Desirous attachment, for instance, is [an obvious] case of this. The reason used in this proof is of the nature variety.

Here, the "support" referred to is simply the clear and aware [entity] of consciousness. But how can the stability of this support be demonstrated? Through establishing that a basic awareness has neither a starting nor an end point. Let us consider the awareness of someone who has just been born. Any idea that it could have arisen without a cause is ruled out by the fact that the occurrence [of such a thing] is only occasional. So is whatever causes it permanent or impermanent? If it were a permanent thing, there would necessarily be no location or time in which it could be said not to be present. Consequently, there would be no way that it could maintain a concomitant [relationship] with any specific effect.

We must assume then that the cause [of this initial awareness] is impermanent. Since the thing(s) from which it arose are limited to physical material or consciousness, it must have been produced by either of these. If the substantial cause [that gave rise to the awareness] were a physical material, it would need to be either something linked with the [internal] physical sense powers or be some sort of external material. If it were the former, would the whole group of sense powers need to be involved [in the production of that awareness], or would just a single one of them suffice? If all the sense powers were required, it would mean that in the absence of even one of them, [such as] the visual sense power, the mental awareness [of a person] could never have arisen. Whereas, if just a single sense power [such as the visual one] had served as the cause, the person's conceptual consciousness would be able to apprehend visual form in the same vivid manner that visual perception does.

The alternative is that the substantial cause [for the initial awareness] was some sort of external material. But would the material [that caused the awareness] be a substance that was a whole, in possession of its various components, or the individual particles themselves? If it were a substance as a whole, would this be something that could be divided [into further parts] or something indivisible? If it were the part-possessing whole that served as the substantial cause, then again, the question is whether it would be necessary for the entire collection of these separate parts to come together for [that substance to act as the cause] or whether just a single one of them would suffice? But both possibilities are ruled out by the same logic as above. What acted as the substantial cause must therefore have been an indivisible whole that possesses its portions but is of a substance distinct from them. However, the idea that such a thing could act as the cause leads to various absurdities. It means that, for instance, if the face is veiled, then all portions [of the whole] must be veiled. If not, then it would have to be possible to distinguish between veiled and unveiled portions [of the whole]. The response [from those who believe in the indivisible whole may be that] the division into veiled and unveiled portions is one that is found among the portions themselves but not in the whole that possesses them. But if that were true, it would follow that even when the face is veiled, the "whole" face that possesses it would remain clearly visible! [In the *Commentary on Pramāṇa*, Dharmakīrti] similarly evokes the examples of movement and the dyeing of cloth to discredit the position [of the indivisible whole].

Let us return to the notion that particles could act as the substantial cause [for the initial awareness]. If individual particles were capable of acting independently, it would mean that each of them could produce separate mental conceptual consciousnesses, and therefore numerous such consciousnesses would be produced simultaneously. If, on the other hand, the process [of production] required the entire collection [of particles] coming together, then there could be no production if even a single particle were not in place.

Reasoning in such a manner, through a process of elimination, one eventually establishes that the substantial cause [of the initial moment of awareness] must [have been another awareness]. [181] That consciousness could [potentially] have been one that belonged to either the individual's own continuum or another's continuum. If the awareness that acted as the direct substantial cause [for the initial moment of awareness in the present life] was included in the continua of others, such as the individual's parents, it would absurdly follow that whether the son became, for instance, a skilled craftsman or a total idiot would be something that depended solely on his father. It is only logical to conclude therefore that the awareness that acted as the substantial cause for the initial [moment of] an individual's awareness in one life must have been an earlier awareness that was his own. And these are the grounds for asserting that awareness has neither beginning nor end, thus confirming the existence of past and future lives.

Something such as heat cannot act as a stable support for water. We know from experience that if the water is boiled excessively, it will completely evaporate. And with [an activity] like jumping, there is no consecutive sequence through which momentum can be built up and carried forward. Each occasion that one jumps requires its own effort. In contrast, love, wisdom, and so forth [are qualities] that develop by the force of momentum carried through from previous moments [of themselves]. And familiarity with them, once bred, ensures that fresh effort is not required [every time]. This fact, which serves as the reason [in the aforesaid proof establishing that wisdom and so forth have no bounds to their development], is one that can be confirmed by our own self-cognizing perception.

It is then, by a thorough process of reflection, during which a wide range of lines of reasoning are employed, that one is brought to the recognition that samsara is fundamentally dissatisfactory. Next, one discovers that the cause of samsara is self-grasping and that it should and can be eliminated. Liberation therefore definitely exists. And once one has knowledge and conviction of this and has generated an ardent desire from the depths of one's being to achieve that liberation, one can be said to have developed, in the complete and authentic sense, the mind that seeks nirvana. Until one is driven by this mind of yearning, whatever worthy practices one might perform will all count as "[virtues] associated with merit[-making]."[540] As such, the results they produce while pleasurable, can still only manifest within samsara. In contrast, once driven by the yearning for liberation, even the most rudimentary of worthy practices, such as providing someone with a single mouthful of food, will act as a cause [for the achievement] of liberation and of finally turning one's back on samsara. As such, these activities will count as "virtues associated with liberation."[541]

This resolve to attain liberation must be firmly anchored in a conviction arrived at through a process of logical analysis. If instead, the resolve is based solely on the reports of others, while it may seem very fervent in the individual involved, when he is beset by the most harrowing forms of suffering, it can still be shaken by spurious arguments or affected by things that others might say. And as soon as the individual experiences a slight respite from the extreme suffering that he had been assailed by, he may once again be lured by certain pleasures of the present existence. [182] With his resolve lost, he may once more find himself back at the stage he was at before he "rejected" samsara. This is the situation reflected in the words "Once that is lost, one reverts to one's original state."[542]

How one eradicates self-grasping by means of that meditation [on selflessness]

Someone who has generated within his continuum the complete and authentic wish to gain liberation will see that it cannot be achieved unless he is prepared to work at the causes that can bring it about. This is what leads him to train in the path. Looked at in this way, there are three kinds of individual who train in the path. The principal concern of someone whose faculties are, by nature, of a duller order is that of freeing himself from the sufferings of samsara. Such an individual will actualize the path of the śrāvaka in his continuum and eventually attain the state of the arhat. Someone whose faculties are of a medium order will [also] principally be concerned with freeing solely himself from samsara. Having actualized the path of a pratyekabuddha in his continuum, he will eventually attain the goal [of that path]. Finally, there are those whose faculties are of a sharper order. A person of this type will discern that just like himself, all samsaric beings are tormented by the sufferings of samsara. He will also become aware that because the [cyclical] process [of existence] has no beginning, each and every sentient being must at some point or other have acted as mother to him and, as such, has been incredibly kind. Finding the present situation unbearable, great compassion will manifest within him with the thought "How wonderful it would be if sentient beings could be free from suffering!" This great compassion will help engender in him the desire to personally [work to] free all sentient beings from suffering. However, the individual will realize that in his current state he is in no position to remove all others from suffering. A thorough investigation of the matter will eventually convince him that the capacity to free all beings from suffering is one that only a buddha possesses. At that point, the individual will develop the Mahayana mind generation (*bodhicitta*) that is determined to personally attain the state of buddhahood in order to free all sentient beings from suffering. He will then train in the Mahayana path and finally actualize that state of buddhahood. [183]

There are [correspondingly] three different ways of engaging in the path. The only selflessness that those who propound the śrāvaka tenets believe in is the selflessness of persons. Because they only assert one sort of selflessness, for them, it is not meditation on [different types of] selflessness that distinguishes the structure of these three paths from one another. [Instead] those of the śrāvaka persuasion familiarize themselves with [selflessness] over a very short duration, such as three lives. Together with this, they undertake a very modest [practice] building up a collection [of merit] and then eventually reach the state of a śrāvaka arhat. Those of the pratyekabuddha persuasion combine a [practice] building up a collection [of merit] for up to a hundred eons with meditation on the selflessness of persons. Then finally, they attain the state of a pratyekabuddha arhat. Those of the Mahayana persuasion perform a [practice] building up collections over periods such as three "countless" eons. This they combine with a meditation on the selflessness of persons, in which a whole host of techniques to realize that selflessness are used. It is through this practice that they eventually attain complete buddhahood, a state in which they are said to have rid themselves of nonafflicted ignorance, every knowable thing has become clear to their mind, and every possible source of failing, frailty, and limitation has been removed.

The scheme for the attainment of liberation and omniscience that [Dharmakīrti] explains in the second chapter [of the *Commentary on Pramāṇa*] is one that can accommodate the views of these things in the śrāvaka's tenet system. Because he wants to present the topic in a way that both the [Hinayana and Mahayana] tenet systems can agree with, he chooses only to refer to the selflessness of persons. Likewise, when he discusses what distinguishes the paths of the greater and lesser vehicles from one another, he points only to the range of techniques that each of them uses and the duration of their practices of accumulation. [Dharmakīrti] explores these topics at some length in passages such as:

> [He relied on] multiple techniques with numerous aspects
> and gained familiarity [with objects] over a great length of time,
> due to which [his mind achieved] total clarity
> with respect to the faults and qualities [of those objects].
>
> And because [his] mind is illuminated,
> [he achieved] eradication of the causal imprints.

> [This] great Able One has worked [altruistically] for the sake of others,
> and [his path is thereby] distinguished from those of the rhinoceros-like [pratyekabuddha] and so forth.[543]

The [other] version of how to train in the path to attain liberation and omniscience [presented by Dharmakīrti] is one exclusive to the Mahayana [tenet system]; it is the Vijñaptika's own account. This says that those of the śrāvaka persuasion familiarize themselves only with the selflessness of persons, and in doing so rid themselves of the obscuration formed by delusions[544] and reach the śrāvaka goal. [184] Those of the pratyekabuddha persuasion, working to achieve their own ends, familiarize themselves with selflessness over periods of a hundred eons or so. This selflessness includes not just that of persons but also a form of the selflessness of phenomena that is restricted to the object. In this way, they eliminate [both] the obscuration formed by delusion and just that portion of the obscuration to knowledge [made up of] concepts related to the object. They thereby eventually reach the pratyekabuddha goal. Those of the Mahayana persuasion combine the method [side of the path], great compassion, with the process of logical reasoning that leads them to an understanding of all forms of selflessness relating to both the person and phenomena. They first ascertain these forms of selflessness by valid inferential cognition. Following that, using the single-pointed [concentration of] calm abiding, they gradually gain familiarity with them.

Once the cascade of discursive thought has subsided, the transcendent awareness of the path of seeing will emerge [in the practitioner], bringing with it the [first] perception of truth, in terms of the two varieties of selflessness. It is in this way that he rids himself of the portions of the two obscurations—those formed by delusions and those preventing omniscience—that are countered by the path of seeing. The process of familiarization continues over an extremely long period of time, until finally [the practitioner] eradicates all forms of obscuration that are to be countered by the path of meditation and thereby actualizes the wisdom of the omniscient consciousness.

Hence, when the third chapter [of the *Commentary on Pramāṇa*] describes in considerable detail the selflessness of phenomena, [Dharmakīrti] is giving a presentation [of the path] that is exclusive to the Mahayana [tenet system]. Elsewhere, I have dealt at some length with issues such as how exactly the two varieties of obscuration are eliminated by their antidote, the path realizing selflessness.[545] I refer [readers] to that section of my writings. There is also a huge amount that could be said about the way that one progresses along the various paths, but fearing that the explanation might become too lengthy, I refrain from expanding it further here.

This marks the end of the concise description of yogic perception and some of the issues related to it.

14. Valid Cognition and Its Results

An account of valid cognition and its results

The "results of valid cognition" can be divided into two: results that are mediated and those that are unmediated.[546] With the first, various [other] things occur [before the results manifest]. What type of results are principally referred to here? [On the one hand,] there are those results that are encompassed by the term "[real] human goal"—namely, [achievement of] the more elevated [comfortable] states of [cyclic] existence and the truly worthy. [On the other,] there are the practices [of someone who], with an understanding of what is to be adopted and discarded in relation to the four truths, and what methods should be employed to do that, works accordingly. This is communicated in passages such as:

> Because that [valid cognition] is the main thing for engaging,
> in [a practice] that adopts [the positive] and discards [the negative].[547]

It is only by means of valid cognition that such results come about, for which reason they are known as "results produced by valid cognition."[548] [185]

Then [secondly] there are the results of valid cognition that are unmediated by the occurrence of other things. These can also be divided into two varieties: those that are not part of the nature of the valid cognition itself and those that are. An example of the first is an ascertaining consciousness that has been directly induced by a valid cognition. Since this is a result that the valid cognition produces directly, it is referred to as an "unmediated result of valid cognition." An example of the second is the facet a valid cognition has for realizing its own object. As to why this is referred to as an "unmediated result of valid cognition," this facet is part of the valid cognition's own nature, and as such no other activity could intervene between [the valid cognition and it]. Added to which, it is through this facet that the valid cognition that has taken on the aspect of its object establishes its identity. However, this facet cannot [literally] be counted as a "result *produced* by valid cognition" for exactly the reason that it is part of the valid cognition's own nature. Describing it as a "result" here should be understood as a reference to the fact that in the sequence of the establisher-established, it is the "result" [i.e., the second in the order].[549] Valid cognition takes on the exact aspect of its object. And only by virtue of that fact can the realization of its object be the identity assigned to this cognition. This is the point made in the passage:

> It is because it has the aspect of different objects
> that the mind realizes different [things].
> Because of that there is this.[550]

The point to be understood is that valid cognition's facet for realizing its object of comprehension—that facet of taking on the aspect of its object—is a genuine result of valid cognition in the sense of being the one established [in terms of the establisher-established sequence]. But this does not mean that it is an [actual] result of that cognition. [Here there are three elements]:

1. That [facet] by virtue of which something is posited to be a "valid cognition" realizing its object of comprehension
2. What is posited, "the result"—namely, the valid cognition realizing its object of comprehension
3. That toward which valid cognition's action of realizing is directed—namely, its "object of comprehension"[551]

Anyone who fails to grasp what each of these three are within the scheme will remain ignorant about the way that valid cognition comprehends its object. As such, he will be unable to use valid cognition to guide his choice of actions when striving to achieve what he desires. Conscious of this fact, the great masters, the father and [spiritual] son [Dignāga and Dharmakīrti] explained at length the scheme of valid cognition, its result, and its comprehended object. Drawing from their explanation, we first concentrate on how this applies to valid perception.

Valid perception and its result[552]

1. Refutation of others' assertions
2. Setting forth our own position [186]

Refutation of other's assertions

The vast majority of individuals proudly proclaiming themselves to be logicians at the present time maintain that the treatises organize [the elements] of the scheme into a series of *three sets*.[553] They refer to these as the first, second, and third "conceptual analyses of valid cognition and its result."[554] They disagree on how the third model should be formulated and also the tenet systems to which it belongs. However, aside from this, these individuals broadly concur that the first conceptual analysis represents a model of valid cognition and its result found only in the Sautrāntika school, whereas the second is exclusive to the Cittamātra system.

Regarding the first conceptual analysis, one of [these individuals] identifies the three [elements] as follows:

1. Comprehended object—an external entity, such as a form
2. Result—the awareness that freshly realizes [such an object]
3. Valid cognition—the consciousness to which the [object's] aspect appears and that cognizes [the object] in a nondeceptive fashion

According to someone else, they are:

1. Comprehended object—an external entity
2. Result—the realization of that external entity
3. Valid cognition—that which derives from that external entity, bears its likeness, and is capable of inducing ascertainment of it

Yet another suggests that the three are:

1. Comprehended object—a hidden entity[555]
2. Result—the realization of that entity
3. Valid cognition—the awareness to which the aspect of that entity appears

As far as the *second conceptual analysis* is concerned, the predominant view is that the three are:

1. Comprehended object—the object-aspect
2. Valid cognition—the subject-aspect
3. Result—self-cognition

However, someone with scholarly pretensions declares that such a model would only be acceptable in the True Aspectarian system. He proposes a different model for the False Aspectarian:

1. Comprehended object—a superimposed [i.e., fictive] object-aspect
2. Valid cognition—that with the aspect of the subject apprehending that [object]
3. The Supposed Result—the self-cognition aware of that [valid cognition]

The same person says that the *Commentary on Pramāṇa* itself follows the system of the False Aspectarian.

Someone else claims that the Cittamātra system [presents two levels of] the scheme. He identifies the [elements of the] one that accords with conventional understanding as:

1. Comprehended object—an external entity
2. Valid cognition—the awareness to which the aspect of that entity appears
3. Result—the realization of that entity

And that of the ultimate[556] as:

1. Comprehended object—the object-aspect
2. Valid cognition—the subject-aspect
3. Result—the self-cognition

[Response:] Let us now turn to the refutation of these positions. The [first] model is supposed to represent the Sautrāntika explanation of other-cognizing perceptions. As such, it is incorrect to identify "an external entity, such as a form" or "an external entity" as the comprehended object of perception. [187] If the [comprehended object is identified in that way], it would follow that in the Sautrāntika system, to be an other-cognizing valid perception is necessarily to be a valid cognition of an external entity, because that system identifies external entities such as form as the comprehended objects in their model of valid perception and its result. If [our opponents] accept this [argument], then it would follow that when someone of the Sautrāntika school sets out his own model, he does not feel the need to use reasoning to establish that form and suchlike *are* external entities, since [according to him] any other-cognizing valid perception is *necessarily* a valid cognition that [realizes] its object is an external entity. But if [our opponents] accept this, it would follow that the numerous lines of reasoning that the Sautrāntika employs when he sets out his own system to establish that blue and so forth are external entities and that external entities exist serve no purpose.

Also, if the Sautrāntika really believed that myopic beings can perceive for themselves that forms and so forth are [real] external entities, then when the adherents of the Vijñaptika deny the existence of such entities, the Sautrāntika should make an appeal to direct experience. But we find no evidence of the Sautrāntika reasoning in this fashion. The alternative to this is that the Sautrāntika *does not* assert that myopic beings can confirm [the existence of] external entities by perceiving them.

In summary, when the Sautrāntika sets out his version of the result according to myopic beings' other-cognizing valid perceptions, he identifies neither "an external entity" nor "an external object, such as a form" as the comprehended object. To claim that he does is to give a clear indication of some inadequacy in one's powers of reasoning.

The assertion [of the third individual] that for the Sautrāntika the comprehended object is a hidden entity is also entirely fallacious and is one that is rebutted by many arguments that I have already set out. Furthermore, if one claims that realization of that entity is the result, it is quite wrong to identify the [awareness to which the] aspect of that object appears as the valid cognition. It would follow that whenever the aspect of an object appears to an awareness, the awareness in question necessarily realizes that object, because the object's aspect appearing [to] an awareness is what determines that it realizes the object. But from this it would follow that the sense awareness to which the single moon appears double *realizes* two moons, because the aspect of two moons appears to it. And if that is the case, the double moon must constitute an [actual] object, because it is something cognized by awareness!

The [last individual's claim]—that the model in which the object-aspect is the comprehended object, the subject-aspect the valid cognition, and the self-cognition the result—is exclusive to the Vijñaptika is also not tenable. The Sautrāntika acknowledges the same model. [188] This must be the case because the Sautrāntika asserts that the subject-aspect of any given awareness is a self-cognizing perception of that awareness's object-aspect. [Our opponents] have already agreed that the Sautrāntika advocates consciousness has aspects, that those aspects are substance and also part of the nature of consciousness, and that self-cognition exists. So if they were to deny that the model just mentioned is accepted by the Sautrāntika, it would mean that their position was a mass of irreconcilable views. One could but marvel at the extent of confusion that they would have created for themselves with their ill-considered pronouncements.

[The model assigned to] the False Aspectarian is also mistaken. It suggests that the False Aspectarian believes myopic beings can perceive that the object-aspect is fictive. But if [the False Aspectarian believed that to be the case], why would he find it necessary to resort to logical reasoning in order to establish that [the object-aspect is fictive] to the True Aspectarian? If it was still necessary to prove by reasoning what a myopic being has already established by valid perception, it would lead to absurd consequences. It would follow that in cases where the property of the subject has been established by perception—such as when smoke is used as the reason to establish the presence of fire on a mountain pass—it would still be necessary to prove [smoke's presence] again by means of logic!

[This individual] says that the first and third conceptual analyses represent the position of the Sautrāntika and the second that of the True Aspectarian. He also says that this threefold division is definitive and exhaustive. However, according to him, the system followed in the Seven Treatises is that of the False Aspectarian. That is to assert that even though the father and spiritual son devoted such a huge portion of their works to discussion of valid cognition and its result, they never managed to set out what their own model was. This is a brazen slander against the lords of reasoning!

He also proposes that the Cittamātra accepts a model of valid cognition and its result in which the thing comprehended, on the conventional level, is a [real] external entity. This is a position that I have already discredited, since I have refuted at some length the idea that the Cittamātra system acknowledges any form of conventional existence for external entities, although I still have more to say on this.

Turning next specifically to the third conceptual analysis, someone has supplied us with two models: an overtly stated version and an implicit version. He claims that the first represents the uncritical understanding of things:

1. Object comprehended—an external entity
2. Valid cognition—[that which has the] aspect of the object
3. Result—an "imagined" cognition of that entity that only exists from the mistaken perspective on things, in which an aspect is interpreted to be an external entity [189]

The second version, he contends, is arrived at through [critical] examination:

1. Object comprehended—the nature of consciousness
2. Valid cognition—[that which has the] subject-aspect
3. Result—the designation "self-cognition"[557]

He insists that the third conceptual analysis is not one that can be attributed to either the Sautrāntika or the Cittamātra in any exclusive sense. He argues that the [model is presented] to encourage those of the Sautrāntika system to adopt the Cittamātra view. So, rather than representing a position that is either Sautrāntika or Cittamātra, the model depends on both.

[Response:] None of this is tenable. [His first model] involves the aspect being interpreted as an object from the mistaken perspective. [It also has] the external entity as the thing comprehended and the valid cognition as the object-aspect. This cannot be right. Why? Because it has the object-aspect [being seen as] an external entity from that mistaken perspective.[558]

Furthermore, he proposes that the model represents an uncritical understanding of things, in which an external entity is the object comprehended, the "imagined" cognition of that entity is the result, and the object-aspect is the valid cognition. But such a model could not be dependent on both the Sautrāntika and Cittamātra systems, since it is at variance with both of them. [Firstly,] for the Sautrāntika, the valid cognition cannot be the object-aspect [of an "imagined" cognition of an external entity], because in that system it is a *genuine* cognition of such an entity. Unless it counted as such, there could be no genuine cognition of an external entity for the Sautrāntika. For the Cittamātra, external entities do not exist at all even in the conventional sense. So even when talking about how things are viewed from the uncritical perspective, they would not assert that an external entity could be the object comprehended. And even if [the Cittamātra] were to assert that talk of the existence of genuine external entities was legitimate from an uncritical perspective, then equally the same uncritical perspective must be adopted for the object-aspect, [meaning that it could legitimately be described] as a *genuine* cognition of an [external] entity. But in that case, to assert that this result—the cognition of an external entity—is just "imagined" would be irrational. What is more, to say that his version of the "critical model"—in which the object-aspect is the object comprehended, the subject-aspect is the valid cognition, and the self-cognition is the result—is dependent on both the Sautrāntika and Cittamātra systems is also untenable. It in fact agrees with neither. In neither system do we find a critical understanding of things according to which the object, the subject, and the self-cognition within a particular cognitive [event] are distinct things. If we did, then either system would have to say that upon analysis, the three are found to be truly distinct from one another. And if either of them was to say that, it would be tantamount to them asserting that the three constitute separate substances. [190]

In response, [this individual] might deny that his phrase "critical understanding" was intended to denote the analysis of the ultimate by valid cognition, saying that it was simply meant to refer to an understanding of things [deriving from] an examination by means of valid cognition. But if that were the case, his "uncritical understanding" of things must denote one that does not involve any sort of examination by means of valid cognition at all. Then it would follow that his assertion "From the uncritical understanding, an external entity is the object comprehended" amounts to the claim that "When it is not comprehended by valid cognition, an external entity is the object comprehended by valid cognition." This [line of reasoning] also serves to definitively refute those who assert that in the Cittamātra model of valid cognition and its result, an external entity is the object comprehended on the level of convention, whereas the object-aspect is the object comprehended on the ultimate level.

Another [individual also] identifies the model of the third conceptual analysis as:

1. Object comprehended—an external entity
2. Valid cognition—the object-aspect
3. Result—the self-cognition

According to him, there are no Buddhists who genuinely subscribe to such a model. It was set forth to help draw those of the Vaibhāṣika and Sautrāntika systems [into the correct view], although this does not mean that the followers of either system actually accept the model. He points to the example of the Blessed One, who, in order to help draw those with excessive craving for physical form [toward a correct view] was prepared to declare to them that there is "no form." [This individual claims that, similarly,] the model in the third conceptual analysis was taught to help those who cling excessively to [the notion of] the object and subject. And by overcoming this clinging, they could be led to a perception of the reality in which no dualistic separation between subject and object exists.

[Response:] This is just senseless prattle by means of which this individual manages to broadcast his own deficiencies. At the point that this object-aspect acts as a valid cognition of the external entity—the object comprehended—is the self-cognition established as the result or not? If it is, it would mean that its identity as a self-cognition is established through the object-aspect depending on an external entity. And from this it would absurdly follow that external entities being in the nature of consciousness is something observed by valid cognition.[559] If on the other hand, the [self-cognition] was not established as such, it would follow that what [this model] communicates—namely, that at the point the object-aspect acts as a valid cognition of an external entity, the self-cognition is the result—cannot lead [those following the Vaibhāṣika and Sautrāntika systems] to a realization of reality in which there is no dualistic separation between subject and object. Why? Because at that point, the self-cognition cannot be the result in that it does not exist. And a treatise system that presents what [has no more existence than] the horns on the head of a hare as something that can lead to realization of ultimate truth would be without precedent! [191]

Moreover, he says that there are no Buddhists who subscribe to the model he proposes for the third conceptual analysis. Does that mean that it represents the assertions of those who follow tenets systems outside the Buddhist one? Or is it the understanding of someone who has been untouched by the influence of any philosophical tenets? Or could it be the case that this is a model that no one actually accepts? It cannot be one asserted by those following non-Buddhist tenets, otherwise it would mean that the whole section "Even if there was an external entity . . . that is true, and in that case even I would not know how [to respond]"[560] must be regarded either as a work that those non-Buddhists could claim as their own or as a report of the views of non-Buddhist opponents. So he might suggest that this model can be attributed to those who have been untouched by the influence of any philosophical tenets. But those whose minds [he proposes] have not been influenced by Buddhist philosophical ideas must in fact have been influenced by those ideas, because they are individuals who advance a model that involves a valid cognition, its result, and the object it comprehends.

The option remaining [for this individual] is to say that this is a model that no one actually accepts. But from this it would follow that the aforesaid passage [of the *Commentary on Pramāṇa*] is one that no one endorses, because the main thing that it teaches is something that no one accepts. The [argument's] reason is the one that he himself proposed. But he cannot agree [to its conclusion], since there are obviously those who accept [the model taught in the passage]. So he might try to deny the pervasion [between the acceptance and endorsement of what the passage teaches]. But from this it would follow that even if no one actually accepted that sound is impermanent, there could still be some party who endorsed the thesis saying that it is, because [the fact that] no one actually accepts the model of the third conceptual analysis does not necessarily mean that no one endorses what is said by the passage teaching that analysis.

It would also follow [that if the intention was to gradually] draw those who cling excessively to physical form [toward the correct view], what should have been taught is that form exists. Why? Because [when the intention was to gradually] draw those who cling excessively to [the separateness of] subject and object [toward the correct view], what was taught is that things comprehended are real, external entities. [This individual] cannot deny the [argument's] reason, since that would go against the idea that it was necessary for there to be a third conceptual analysis teaching that the thing comprehended is an external entity. He also accepted the pervasion. But if he agrees [with the argument's conclusion], it would absurdly follow that the Blessed One was at fault, because to draw in those who cling excessively to physical form, he should have taught that it *exists*, whereas he in fact taught that it does not. [This individual] accepts both parts of this reason.

He also claims that to help draw those following the Sautrāntika system [into that of the Vijñaptika] it was necessary to identify external entities as the things comprehended, the object-aspect as the valid cognition, and the self-cognition as the result. He is also wrong in this regard. [192] One cannot draw a Sautrāntika into the Vijñaptika system by teaching him that what he comprehends are external entities, because the very belief that what he comprehends are real, external entities is the one preventing him from understanding the Vijñaptika tenets!

[Similarly,] identifying the self-cognition as the result cannot help to draw a Sautrāntika into the Vijñaptika system, because the Sautrāntika already accepts the idea of self-cognition, something that elevates him above the Vaibhāṣika. Nor is it helpful to identify the object-aspect as the valid cognition, since the Sautrāntika already espouses the object-aspect as part of his own system. Neither can the Sautrāntika be drawn in by the teaching that this object-aspect is a valid cognition of a real external entity—the thing comprehended—since this notion is exactly what he must bring a halt to, if he is ever going to understand the philosophical tenets of the Vijñaptika. Nor would teaching the Sautrāntika that it is by virtue of the object-aspect becoming a valid cognition of an external entity that the self-cognition is the result help to draw him into the Vijñaptika system. Why? Because the Sautrāntika is aware that valid cognition undermines the idea that it is through reference to an external entity that the self-cognition is established as a self-cognition. This is because the Sautrāntika has already employed various lines of reason to rule out, [to his own satisfaction, the idea] that external entities could be in the nature of consciousness.

It would also be wrong to suggest that the model under discussion could have been presented to help draw the Vaibhāṣika into the tenet system of the

Vijñaptika. For one thing, the idea that the object-aspect is a valid cognition of an external entity—the thing it comprehends—is something that the Vijñaptika tenet system directly seeks to counter. Added to this, the Vaibhāṣika also has his own reasoned arguments that [according to him] rule out self-cognition being the result of an external object of comprehension. And what sensible person is going to adopt an alternative system of philosophical tenets on the basis of a presentation that he can see is ruled out by valid cognition? Even getting the Vaibhāṣika to enter into the Sautrāntika system would require proving to him the existence of self-cognition. So just telling him that self-cognition is the result is hardly going to be sufficient to get him to embrace the Vijñaptika viewpoint. We see therefore that [this individual] has advocated a position without having given it any real consideration. The arguments I have used against him here also serve to refute anyone who might claim that [the model in which the] self-cognition is identified as the result with respect to the thing comprehended—an external entity—was set forth for the sake of drawing those of the Sautrāntika school into the Vijñaptika tenets.

Someone else proposes a [different] model of the third conceptual analysis. In it, an external entity is the thing comprehended and that with the object-aspect is the valid cognition. He explains the result as that which is [found], when subjected to critical analysis, to be a cognition of its own nature but, when viewed uncritically, is [regarded as] a cognition of an external entity. This, he maintains, is the model for valid cognition and its result according to the Sautrāntika system. [193] Someone else challenges this, suggesting that such a model is just a repetition of the one presented in the first conceptual analysis. Another [individual] seeks to defend the model against this charge. He states that the first conceptual analysis represents the Sautrāntika model of valid cognition and its result given from an "uncritical" point of view, whereas the third one is the Sautrāntika version given from the "critical" vantage. Others also defend the model presented by the first individual but on different grounds. They say that the third cannot be considered an unwarranted repetition of the first, because the aims behind the two models are quite distinct. For them, the first conceptual analysis is chiefly intended to refute the view of those such as the Mīmāṃsā. The [Mīmāṃsā] deny that a valid cognition can resemble its object, and so the model is intended to demonstrate to them that it is only by virtue of [the valid cognition] resembling its object that realization of that object can be posited. They say that the model in the third conceptual analysis, on the other hand, is set out to refute the claims of those such as the Vaibhāṣika, for whom awareness has no self-cognizing [facet]. It is meant to demonstrate to the Vaibhāṣika that even when the thing comprehended [seems to] be an external entity, the object that awareness overtly cognizes is not external but in the nature of the awareness itself, and that the awareness, properly speaking, is therefore something that "cognizes itself."

[Response:] None of these stances are credible. It would follow that even according to the Sautrāntika, analysis [necessarily reveals] that an external entity is in the nature of consciousness, because even for them, a cognition that "realizes" an external entity is discovered, upon analysis, to be one that "cognizes itself."

[In an attempt to defend his position,] one of these [individuals] could seek to qualify his original assertion. He might say that the thing counted as the result is [consciousness]. When we talk of it in relation to its own nature, it is that which is "aware" or "cognizant of itself," whereas in relation to an external entity, it is that which is "aware of an external entity." And one can justifiably talk about consciousness as something that is "cognizant of itself," in that every consciousness is aware of its own nature. This, he might say, is what he intended when he asserted that when subjected to critical analysis, [consciousness] is found to be aware of itself, whereas without such analysis, it is just the awareness of another external object, the result. Thus he might deny that he had any intention of suggesting that critical analysis would reveal that [consciousness] being aware of itself was derived from an external entity.

[Response:] It would follow that [equally] the consciousness identified as the result in the context of the first conceptual analysis—namely, the [cognition] that "realizes" an external entity—must be counted as a self-awareness in relation to its own nature, because it is a consciousness. But then it would again follow that the first and third conceptual analyses are essentially the same. They are the same because, on the one hand, a real external entity is identified as the thing comprehended and the object-aspect is the valid cognition. And on the other hand, they are the same in that for both, the result is consciousness—a consciousness that is a self-awareness in relation to its own nature and is an other-awareness in relation to an external entity. The [argument's] reason is one that the individual himself endorsed, whereas its pervasion is obvious. But if he accepts [the conclusion], it would completely contradict his whole argument that what distinguishes the first and third models [from each other] is whether or not they are critical perspectives and [the fact] that they each aim to combat different [misconceptions]. [194]

In any case, [all these individuals assert] that the general model of valid perception and its result that the Sautrāntika advances for a myopic being treats every consciousness as a self-cognition that is aware of its own nature and identifies an external entity as the thing comprehended. But this has already been comprehensively disproved. So why bother attacking something that is already dead? Trying to kill a corpse is, after all, a pointless exercise.

Quite apart from that, the third conceptual analysis cannot be attributed to the Sautrāntika. This is because when setting out this analysis, the *Ascertainment of Valid Cognition* states:

> There is not an entity that presents an accurate aspect of itself [to
> consciousness];
> [otherwise] it would follow that every consciousness has the same
> aspect.[561]

This is a categorical rejection of the idea that there could be an external entity responsible for supplying the sense awareness with the aspect [of the object]. Thus we see that the vast bulk of the analyses that others have provided on this topic amount to little more than empty verbiage.

Now I will set forth our own position.

1. The first conceptual analysis of valid cognition and its result: that involving other-cognition
2. The second conceptual analysis of valid cognition and its result: that involving self-cognition
3. The establishment of those models

The first conceptual analysis of valid cognition and its result: that involving other-cognition

The first is:

1. Object comprehended—blue and so forth
2. Valid cognition—the awareness with the aspect of blue and so forth, which is nondeceptive with respect to blue and so forth
3. Result—the realization of blue and so forth

For reasons already explained, both the Sautrāntika and the Cittamātra systems accept that the valid perception apprehending blue realizes it through taking on its aspect. Their agreement on this fact means that this model for valid cognition and its result is accepted by both schools.

The passage that explains the topic of valid cognition and its result in the source treatise [*Compendium of Pramāṇa*] is:

> Because it has the function of realizing [the object],
> it is regarded as the result of valid cognition.
> [What has this function] is designated "valid cognition,"
> [and what] is without this function is not.[562]

The *Commentary on Pramāṇa* expands on this in the section beginning "That which is said to bring about the function . . ." and ending "This is because we superimpose such distinctions upon things that are different to engage [with them]."[563]

The second conceptual analysis of valid cognition and its result: that involving self-cognition

The second is: [195]

1. Object comprehended—that with the aspect of the object
2. Valid cognition—that which is nondeceptive with respect to that [object] and has the aspect of the subject
3. Result—the cognition of "itself"

Both the Sautrāntika and the Cittamātra believe that it is in reference to the object-aspect of any given awareness that the subject-aspect is asserted to be a self-cognizing perception. Hence they both advocate this same model of valid cognition and its result for self-cognition. The source treatise presents this model in the following passage:

> Or the self-cognition [can be counted as] the result.
> It is [only because the self-cognition knows] the nature of [the feelings associated with the experience of an object] that [we are able to] ascertain it [as something desirable or undesirable].[564]

The *Commentary on Pramāṇa* discusses this at length, in the section beginning:

> [According to the Sautrāntika,] cognitions that know [external] entities are those that know various [things such as blue] . . .

And ending:

> . . . whether we [are talking of] those who accept [that the cognition is of an external entity] or those who do not,
> it is still counted as one that cognizes an entity.[565]

THE ESTABLISHMENT OF THOSE MODELS

In the source treatise, this is taught in passages such as:

> When [an object is comprehended],
> the [thing with] the appearance [of the object] is itself comprehended.
> [This is] the self-cognition and the result.[566]

This is explained at length in the *Commentary on Pramāṇa* in the section "Even if there was an external entity . . . that is true, and in that case even I would not know how [to respond]."[567] Let me explain this. There are those who understand that consciousness has aspects and also [the facet of] self-cognition but still do not fully appreciate the model of the second conceptual analysis, which describes valid cognition and its result in terms of self-cognition. For such people, there are two principal impediments that prevent them from gaining a proper understanding of this model. The first impediment is their belief that the object-aspect, the thing comprehended, [derives from] an external entity presenting itself. The second is their notion that because one can distinguish between an object, subject, and self-cognition within a given cognitive event and describe them respectively as the thing comprehended, the valid cognition, and the result, it must mean that the three are distinct [entities] in a very real sense. The first of these is countered [by the *Commentary on Pramāṇa*] in the section:

> [According to the Sautrāntika,] cognitions that know [external] entities are those that know various [things such as blue] . . .[568]

The *Commentary on Pramāṇa* refutes the second in the passage beginning:

> These distinctions are not present in their nature but only because of the mind . . ."[569]

These passages distinguish between the object, the subject, and the self-cognition within a given cognitive event. But they affirm that the separation between them does not exist in any ultimate sense and that they only appear differently to [the mind that deals in] conventions.[570] It is on the basis of these nominally distinct isolated identities that the representation of them as valid cognition, its result, and the thing comprehended is built, and as such, the model is a conventional one. The [*Commentary on Pramāṇa*] teaches therefore that despite not existing ultimately, the distinctions between them *do* exist conventionally. It does not assert that any apparent distinction between them is something purely imagined, on the basis of the three seeming to be different to a mistaken consciousness. If the latter were the case, since the object, subject, and self-cognition within the cognitive event would not be different from one another, it would follow that they could not be counted as the thing comprehended, the valid cognition, and the result. [196] Thus a model for valid cognition and its result that deals with valid self-perception would be rendered an impossibility. So those with scholarly pretensions who interpret the [*Commentary on Pramāṇa*] in that way are basically undermining the whole notion of valid self-cognition.

There are three impediments standing in the way of a proper understanding of the model for the first conceptual analysis that deals with other-cognitions. These take the form of certain misconceptions pertaining to (1) the thing comprehended, the object that is realized, (2) the valid cognition, that which realizes the object, and (3) the way that the valid cognition realizes that object. The first is the misconception that the thing comprehended, an object such as blue, is an external entity [composed] of a substance distinct from that of consciousness. The second [includes] misconceptions, such as that what realizes and establishes [an object such as] blue can be something other than consciousness, such as the [physical] sense powers, and that the valid cognition and its result constitute separate substances. The third is the misconception that valid cognition comprehends things such as blue in their raw state, unmediated by any sort of aspect.

Of these, the misconceptions that sense powers and the like could be responsible for realizing and establishing things and that valid cognition and its result constitute separate substances are comprehensively refuted by the [*Commentary on Pramāṇa*] in the section discussing the first conceptual analysis. The passages are respectively those that begin "If something else was responsible for verifying that [object] . . ."[571] and "Thus the observation, and that associated with the senses . . . ."[572]

The misconception [related to] the third conceptual analysis,[573] that valid cognition comprehends things such as blue in their raw state, unmediated by any sort of aspect, is one that the [*Commentary on Pramāṇa*] has already dispensed with in the context of the first conceptual analysis. There, it establishes that it is only by virtue of valid cognition taking on the aspect [of its object] that its realization of that object can be asserted. The section where it discusses this says:

> Even though various aspects [related to the senses]
> bring about some diversity in the character of [individual]
> consciousnesses,
> this [realization] is brought about by [valid cognition] combining
> with the [object]
> and it not being a separate entity from that object . . . .[574]

The misconception that the thing comprehended, an object such as blue, is an external entity [composed] of a substance quite distinct from that of consciousness is countered in the [*Commentary on Pramāṇa*] passage "Even if there was an external entity . . . that is true, and in that case even I would not know how [to respond]."[575] Thus the major portion of the section dealing with what is referred to as the "third conceptual analysis of valid cognition and its result" is dedicated to demonstrating how objects, such as blue, which in the first conceptual analysis were identified as the things comprehended, have the same nature as the valid cognitions that comprehend them. It describes how, for instance, when there is a valid perception of blue, the blue that the perception is aware of is [part] of its own nature and not a separate substance external to it. [197] These sections [of the *Commentary on Pramāṇa*] *do not* therefore reveal a "third set" in which the model for valid cognition, result, and comprehended object are distinct from those found in the first [and second] conceptual analyses.[576]

If that is the case, some may question how we can account for a passage such as "Even if there was an external entity . . . ." Some have read this passage as one that presents an argument used by the Sautrāntika, who seek to disprove the Vaibhāṣika claim that there can be awareness of an object without depending on an aspect. These [individuals] have said that the

Sautrāntika argues against the position by pointing to the situation of a person's friend and adversary viewing him [simultaneously]. They say it must follow that his form has multiple characters, because it appears as pleasant to the [awareness] of the first one and as unpleasant to that of the second, and [according to the Vaibhāṣika,] that person's form reaches the cognitions of the two observers in its raw state without the mediation of an aspect.

However, this [is not a correct reading, since] the same type of criticism that these [individuals] have claimed the Sautrāntika makes of the Vaibhāṣika here could just as well be leveled at the Sautrāntika himself, with his belief that an aspect of the object is required for cognition to occur. The reason for this is as follows. If the Sautrāntika and Vaibhāṣika were both denying that the visual consciousnesses of the friend and adversary viewing the person are nonmistaken, the situation would not be one where the Vaibhāṣika asserts there is *cognition* of an object in its raw state without the mediation of an aspect. So the example could not be cited as one that damages his position. If, on the other hand, they both agreed that the visual consciousnesses of the two observers are nonmistaken, then the Sautrāntika must assert that both consciousnesses have an aspect of that person's form. [The Sautrāntika] is obliged to maintain that the aspect accurately represents the object, because if an aspect does not represent the object exactly as it is, it would follow that it is misleading. So the argument that can be made against the Sautrāntika position is, "It follows that the visual form of that person has multiple characters, because the aspect of the person's form that appears to the visual consciousness of his friend is pleasant whereas the aspect that appears to the visual consciousness of his adversary is unpleasant, and because these aspects represent the object accurately." The three spheres are in place for this argument, and it is one to which the Sautrāntika would have no response. In any case, I have already explained that such a reading of this section is completely wrong. I have also on more than one occasion rejected the idea that external entities are identified as the things comprehended in the Sautrāntika's own model for valid cognition and its result.

The actual meaning of the passage is this. The section "Even if there was an external entity . . ." refutes the Sautrāntika contention that when there is a visual consciousness of something such as blue, the aspect of the blue that appears is one that an object has *provided* for the consciousness. [198] It is saying, "Even if the type of real, external blue and so forth that you, the Sautrāntika, believe in actually existed, the aspect of blue comes about due to [mental] imprints projecting it as something *out there*. It does not come to us *from* an object. If it did, then you, the Sautrāntika, would have to accept that when the friend and the adversary of a particular person look at him, the attractive and unattractive aspects of the person's form that they see are presented from the side of the object. Thus it would absurdly follow that this single form has multiple characters."

The section "If one were to accept that [Devadatta had both types of character] . . . We witness [cases where one thing is viewed as attractive and then unattractive by the same individual] within a single lifetime"[577] reveals the problem with accepting that one person's form could have both attractive and unattractive characters. The [next] lines say:

> Hence, even in a [system that believes] the thing comprehended
> is an external one,
> it is right [to assert] that the awareness's experience of itself is the
> result.[578]

This means "When there is a visual perception of something such as blue, if the aspect of the blue that appears was something presented from the side of the object, then the apparent spatial separation—the sense that such an object is located some distance away from one—would have to be the way it actually is. Hence the blue and so forth would indeed be external entities. However, those aspects do not [derive from] the object presenting itself [to the individual's consciousness]. Therefore, even if you believe that the blue and so forth that are the things comprehended exist as external entities, it would be more correct to understand the result as the *experience of blue* that is in the nature of consciousness." The passage thus denies the tenability of the [Sautrāntika] understanding of the result, which identifies it as the realization of the blue and so forth that are external to the individual.[579]

To sum up then, the whole section "Even if there was an external entity . . . It is right [to assert] that the awareness's experience of itself is the *result.* That is how entities are ascertained,"[580] argues that if the aspect of an object such as blue [originates in] some sort of [external] object presenting itself, then it would follow that the physical form of a single individual has multiple [characters, both] pleasing and displeasing. This consequence negates things like blue having such [conflicting] characters and thereby it refutes the idea that such things could be genuine external entities of a substance different from that of consciousness. And it demonstrates that [in the model that has] an object such as blue as the thing comprehended, the result [should be identified as] an awareness of blue that is in the nature of consciousness. In saying this, the passage is only stating that [in the model] that has blue and so forth as the things comprehended and the realization of such things as the result, the things realized are the same nature [as the consciousness], not of some substance separate from it. It does not assert that when setting out the model of valid cognition and its result that one must identify "the realization of blue that is in the nature of consciousness" as the result. [199]

Then, the passage that begins with "In that context, this one to which the objects appear . . ."[581] addresses qualms about [Dharmakīrti's] assertion that when the thing comprehended is something such as blue, the nature of the blue is the same as that of consciousness. There are two such qualms. First, some may feel that because [Dharmakīrti] says that the things comprehended, such as blue, have the same nature as the valid cognitions that comprehend them, these valid cognitions must actually be subject-aspects. The second qualm is as follows. "[Dharmakīrti] asserts that the things comprehended, such as blue, are the same nature as consciousness. If, [in this context, he also asserts that] the object-aspect is the valid cognition, it must mean that the valid cognition and its result have different objects and are of entirely different substances. This must be the case, since if one asks the question 'What is it that the valid cognition, the object-aspect, comprehends?' the answer is 'blue,' whereas if one asks the question 'What realization arises as the result of this comprehension?' the answer is 'realization of its own nature.' What this therefore amounts to is [Dharmakīrti] asserting that the result of valid cognition comprehending blue is [the same valid cognition's] realization of its own nature. But this is comparable to saying that the result of swinging an axe to chop wood is the axe cutting itself!" The thinking here is that if the things comprehended really are the same nature as the consciousness, then because the [valid cognition] comprehends the blue and so forth that are in its own nature, it must be correct to say here that awareness of its own nature is the result.

The first qualm is addressed in the section "In that context, this one to which the objects appear . . . that properly clarifies what is there [in the mind]."[582] It explains that even though blue and the like are the same nature as consciousness, in the model that has them as the things comprehended, there are both reasons why the valid cognition cannot be [identified as] an awareness with the subject-aspect and why that valid cognition must be one with the object-aspect. The [first reason is given in the first] stanza [of this section]:

> In that context, this one to which the objects appear [as external] is
> the valid cognition.
> Despite the fact that there is also [a subject-aspect],
> it is not the one [to which they appear] as separate entities.
> Therefore this [awareness with] subject[-aspect] is not the [correct
> point of] reference with respect to external objects.[583]

What this means is that despite the fact that blue and suchlike are the same nature as consciousness, when [they are counted as] the things comprehended, the [awareness] to which the [blue and the like] appear to have an [external] existence when in fact they do not is the valid cognition. And while an [awareness with] the subject-aspect is present at that time, it is not that to which the blue and the like appear as though they are [external] entities separate from it. Hence, [in the context of talking about] things such as blue appearing to sense consciousness as though they were external to it, an [awareness] with the subject-aspect is not the proper point of reference, and such an [awareness with] the subject-aspect is not the one regarded as the *valid cognition*. [200] This is simply saying that while blue and so forth are the same nature as the consciousnesses, [in the model that treats] them as the things comprehended, one cannot count the self-cognition as the valid cognition, since it is not from it that the dualistic sense—that the blue and so forth are separate [from the awareness that cognizes them]—derives.

The section then gives the reason why the awareness with the object-aspect *should* [in this context] be regarded as the valid cognition, in the [passage] "Because the character of the entity, just as it is . . . that accurately reflects the way they are."[584] [Dharmakīrti] reasons that it is correct to consider the object-aspect to be the valid cognition here, because it is this variety of awareness, the sense consciousness, that can take on the aspect of blue, yellow, attractive, unattractive, and so forth and, in so doing, provide a crisp experience of them in which they are clearly delineated from one another. And it is this experience—one that valid cognition finds entirely consistent with the way that these entities actually are—that allows us to posit and distinguish blue, yellow, and so forth.

The second qualm is dealt with in the passage

> Because the object is the nature of the [sense consciousness] that
> establishes it,

> [that consciousness] is aware of itself but is still regarded as an
> awareness of the object.
> Thus [it is] not that the object [for the two] differs.[585]

The first part of this affirms that in reference to the blue and suchlike that appear to it, the sense consciousness of blue and suchlike is aware of things that are in its own nature. There is, however, no contradiction between this and the assertion that such a consciousness counts as the *result* of the blue and suchlike. This is because the sense consciousness is what induces a subsequent cognition thinking "[I am] aware of blue," due to which the awareness of blue can be posited, and the blue [in question] is the [one that is in the sense consciousness's] own nature.[586] The stanza says that the sense consciousness can still be "regarded as an awareness of the object." The object here is basically the same as the one referred to in the line "The thing one knows is internal."[587] Thus it simply denotes the object that the individual knows. It should not be taken to mean an external entity.

"Establishes" means that the sense consciousness of blue can be posited to be an awareness of blue since the subsequent cognition induced by that consciousness establishes it as such. It does not mean that the *aspect* of the sense consciousness of blue is established as the object of the subsequent cognition. So [those of you saying that it does] should stop promoting such an erroneous interpretation!

What the [final line] "Thus [it is] not that the object [for the two] differs"[588] conveys is that even if the awareness of blue is the result and the blue is in [the valid cognition's] own nature, it does not mean that the valid cognition and the result have different objects. This is because the valid cognition comprehends the blue that is in its own nature.

The [next section] says:

> It is in the examination of the [consciousness's] own nature
> that the self-cognition is described as the result,
> because it is aware of an object that is in its own nature.[589] [201]

This is explaining the line "[That consciousness] is aware of itself but is still regarded as an awareness of the object."[590] This in turn is a commentary on [Dignāga's statement that] in knowing things such as blue, a sense consciousness is "aware of its own nature."[591]

[To say that] blue and so forth are the nature of consciousness is to take it from the standpoint of ultimate analysis. Valid cognitions that deal with conventions are incapable of realizing that blue and the like are the same nature as consciousness. Thus valid cognitions that deal with conventions realize things such as blue, and it is in this sense that an awareness of objects such as blue is described as the result. The type of valid cognition that examines the ultimate and establishes that blue and so forth are the same nature as consciousness is discussed [by Dharmakīrti] in the section "[It] must be simultaneous with the awareness . . . ."[592] This is something that I have explained above.[593]

The passage "Whether it is similar to that, or similar to something else . . . In that case even I would not know how [to respond]"[594] is a synopsis of the preceding account. It teaches the untenability of the position that things such as blue are external entities.

With this I complete my explanation of the passages associated with what has become known as the "third conceptual analysis of the result" and thereby bring to a close my lengthy treatment of valid cognition and its result. The scheme of valid cognition and its result has incredible import. It is essential and wide-ranging in its application. Most Indians and Tibetans who have proclaimed themselves to be "logicians," but are ignorant of real scholarship, have devoted whatever intellectual powers were at their disposal to tackle the topic. But the philosophical tenets involved are of great profundity and the corpus of textual materials difficult to fathom. What is more, the section on what is known as the *third conceptual analysis of the result* is especially prone to misinterpretation, with the words describing it being particularly laden with significance. Consequently, those who have grasped even a portion of them are extremely rare. Much misleading jargon extraneous to the subject in hand has been popularized. Noting how the efforts [to understand the topic] have strained the intellects of the individuals involved, I started to think how wonderful it would be if some cool, sheltered spot of correctness could be created to afford their minds some respite from the fatigue of corrupt views and offer them inspiration. So, from the firm and immense ground of my intellect, which is uniquely able to support a whole array of perfect logical arguments, I brought forth this tree of splendid description.

This marks the end of the exegesis on valid perception. [202]

This flower of fine elucidation, a lotus emanated by Mañjughoṣa,
will surely prove vexing to sensible individuals, as they struggle to determine
whether it is a fresh bloom best suited to sustaining youthful enthusiasm
or a captivating piece of finery for decorating the throats of the mature wise.

15. Valid Inferential Cognition

The second kind of valid cognition, inferential valid cognition, is explained through:

1. Literal meaning
2. Varieties

Literal meaning of inferential cognition

Why then is it called *inferential cognition*? It is literally "a deduction that follows after," in that it logically deduces a thesis—the conclusion—after the reason [used to reach that conclusion] has been understood and the logical relationship [that underpins it] recalled.

The varieties of inferential cognition

It is divided into two, (1) inferential cognition in the personal domain and (2) inferential cognition involving a second party. This is something that is set forth in the source treatise on Pramāṇa [the *Compendium of Pramāṇa*] in the passage:

> Inference is of two kinds: [the first, which is the] personal [variety], understands something by means of a reason [embodying] the three criteria.[595]

Why does [Dignāga] choose to introduce the divisions of inferential cognition before introducing the characteristics that define such cognition? While personal inferential cognition is genuine inference, the kind that involves a second party is something to which the name is only assigned [figuratively]. Hence there can be no single set of defining characteristics that encompass the two types, since anything with the characteristics defining it as an inferential cognition necessarily cannot be something to which the name "inferential cognition" is merely assigned [figuratively]. Every genuine case of inferential cognition is therefore by definition that of the personal variety. So there is no need to provide any set of characteristics of a more general nature other than the one that specifically defines this variety. Thus setting forth the division first is exactly what the treatise really intends.

Someone who prides himself as a scholar attempts to account for [this order of presentation] in another way, citing the following words of Dharmottara to support what he says:

> Because [one] has the nature of consciousness, and the [other] that
> of speech, they are totally different [from one another],
> and as there are no defining characteristics that they share . . . .[596]

Through his very literal reading of this passage, this [individual] has misinterpreted [what Dharmottara says here] about [Dignāga's] choice of referring to the divisions before the defining characteristics. As understood [by this individual, the argument] is that it is impossible to have a set of defining characteristics that is concomitant with both personal inferential cognition and inferential cognition involving another party, because the former is a form of consciousness whereas the latter is a form of sound, meaning that they must be entirely different from one another. [203]

[Response:] According to that logic, it would follow that there can be no defining characteristics that are concomitant with both a conceptual cognition and a communicative sound, because the former is a form of consciousness whereas the latter is a form of sound, meaning that they are entirely different from one another. The reason and pervasion are the ones that [this individual himself] proposed. But if he were to accept [the argument's conclusion], it would ridiculously follow that being "observed by valid cognition," the definition of an existent, is not concomitant with each of those two individually. And if he accepted that, it would follow that one or the other of them must be totally nonexistent!

The reason someone else gives as to why [Dignāga] refers to the divisions [of inferential cognition] before the defining characteristics is "because personal inferential cognition is a form of consciousness, whereas that involving another party is a variety of speech, which means there can be no set of defining characteristics that unite the two." But by that reckoning, it must follow that [equally, Dignāga is] wrong to give the defining characteristics of valid cognition before discussing its divisions, because valid perception is nonconceptual, whereas valid inferential cognition is conceptual, which means that "there can be no set of defining characteristics that unite the two." The three spheres are therefore in place and there is no possible response.

Next, I will explain personal inferential cognition and inferential cognition involving another party.

Personal inferential valid cognition

The literal meaning of the phrase "personal inferential cognition" is as follows. It is referred to as "personal" in that it rids the individual who has it of a distorted conception [and thus achieves something] for him personally. It is known as an "inferential cognition," [literally,] "a deduction that follows after," in that it is an awareness that logically deduces a thesis—the conclusion—after the reason [used to reach that conclusion] has been understood and the logical relationship [that underpins it] recalled.

Personal inferential cognition is defined as "an awareness that accurately discerns its comprehended object and is brought about immediately when the [individual] calls to mind the three criteria [fulfilled by] the reason that serves as the basis [of that inference]."

It has three varieties: valid inferential cognitions that deal with (1) demonstrable facts, (2) the issue of common agreement [about names], and (3) a matter of conviction.

The first is defined as "an awareness that accurately discerns its comprehended object(s)—certain hidden phenomena—and is brought about immediately when the [individual] calls to mind the three criteria [fulfilled by] the reason dealing with demonstrable facts that serves as its basis." [204]

The second variety of inferential valid cognition is defined as "an awareness that accurately discerns its comprehended object—some particular thing that is only the case due to choice—and is brought about immediately when the [individual] calls to mind the three criteria [fulfilled by] the reason dealing with the issue of common agreement [about names] that serves as its basis."

The third variety of inferential valid cognition is defined as "an awareness that accurately discerns its comprehended object—an extremely hidden phenomenon—and is brought about immediately when the [individual] calls to mind the three criteria [fulfilled by] the reason dealing with a matter of conviction that serves as its basis."

The model of valid cognition and its result for valid inferential cognition is:

1. Thing comprehended—a logical conclusion that is deduced about a particular subject and is [arrived at by] using a specific reason
2. Valid cognition—an awareness that, by virtue of taking on the aspect of such a logical conclusion, is nondeceptive with respect to it and comes about due to the overt appearance of the object universal of that conclusion
3. Result—the realization of that [logical conclusion] in the manner [apt for] a thing that is hidden to the one who realizes it

Some [treatise] statements about the scheme for valid inferential cognition and its result say that it corresponds to the one for perception. What they mean is that the two models correspond to each other in their general pattern, not that they are similar in every respect. If they corresponded with each other in every detail, then the way that valid perception and inferential cognition engaged the objects they respectively comprehend would also have to parallel each other in every respect. From that it would follow that the way an overt object is engaged—as something that is *manifest* to the awareness—is exactly the same way as that of object that is *hidden* with respect to the awareness. For *any* model of valid cognition and its result, whether in terms of perception or valid inferential cognition, the thing comprehended is always one that is comprehended *overtly*, never by implication. As I have already had cause to remark, [the process of] implicit realization does not necessarily involve an aspect of that implicit object or the appearance of an object universal. There is in fact no separate model dedicated to valid cognition and its result that is based on things that are realized implicitly, because what is realized implicitly will always be dictated by what one realizes overtly.

16. The Proof Statement

Inferential cognition involving another party

1. The actual account of inferential cognition involving another party
2. What this account conveys overtly: the description of logical reasons [205]
3. What this account conveys implicitly: the description of the probandum that is to be logically established
4. The description of that which prepares the way for the proof statement

The actual account of inferential cognition involving another party

1. List of synonymous terms
2. Literal meaning of the term
3. Defining characteristics
4. Identifying illustrations

List of synonymous terms

"Inference involving another party," "correct verbal formulation of the [proof's] reason," and "correct proof statement" are all equivalent.

Literal meaning of the term "inferential cognition involving another party"

This is referred to as something that involves "another party" in that it is a statement that helps some person *other* than the one who articulates it to realize the thesis to be proven. The term "inferential cognition" is assigned to it in a figurative sense. [There is, however,] a *rationale* and a purpose behind this designation. The rationale [for using this] name is that inferential cognition involving another party is a cause of the resultant [genuine] inferential cognition. It is therefore a case where the name of the result is assigned to the cause. The *purpose* of the designation is that it notifies us of the fact that a statement conveying [a reason fulfilling] the three criteria can induce an inference. The *evidence against* the idea that the designation should be taken literally is the fact that an inference involving another party is a verbal statement and thus necessarily has the nature of physical material.[597]

Someone else proposes a different rationale behind this designation, claiming that it is intended to counter the idea that a "verbal formulation of the theses" is one of the essential components of the proof statement.[598]

[Response:] This assertion is not tenable. [In the *Compendium of Pramāṇa*, Dignāga] includes the term "informs"[599] in his definition of inference involving another party. This has already achieved the purpose [identified by this individual], so it would make [Dignāga] guilty of an unwarranted repetition.[600] This is because by including "informs" in the definition, he has already conveyed that a proof statement that overtly stated something such as the proof's thesis would have the fault of being excessive, and he has thereby ruled out that such things are correct proof statements.[601]

He may [counter this] by saying that our explanation similarly suggests a needless repetition, in that the purpose [behind the designation would already have been achieved]. He says that when someone, in dependence on the designation "inferential cognition," understands that the proof statement conveying the three criteria is capable of giving rise to such an inferential cognition, he would necessarily already have realized that a verbalization of the thesis is not one of the essential components, since an overt expression of the proof's thesis is not able to engender an inferential cognition.

[Response:] There is no such fault [in our position]. [206] A statement that communicates the three criteria is capable of engendering an inference, but that does not mean that each of that statement's components can engender an inference. This is similar to the way that a reason embodying all three criteria has the ability to establish a thesis but that does not mean that each of these criteria individually has such a capacity.[602]

But, [he might say,] isn't the reason one uses to establish that a verbalization of the thesis is not an essential component of the correct proof statement "because the thesis is not the probans"?

[Response:] The reason one should use is "because the thesis is not an essential component of the probans." If, [as he suggests,] one uses "because the thesis is not the probans," there is a problem. Someone could argue that when establishing that sound is impermanent due to being produced, it would follow that expressing the forward pervasion does not count as an essential part of the proof statement[603] "because the forward pervasion is not the probans." If one were to deny [the reason], one would be asserting that the forward pervasion in that proof *is* the probans. This would mean accepting that the forward pervasion has the three criteria [of a correct reason].[604]

[Returning to the literal meanings of the term,] it is called a *correct proof statement* because it is speech that articulates the correct reason of the proof, and it is referred to as a *correct verbalization of the sign* because it is a set of words that articulates a logical reason that fulfills the three criteria.

Defining characteristics

The *Compendium of Pramāṇa* defines inference involving another party with the words "[It] properly informs of something factual that one has realized personally."[605] Each of the three terms—"personally," "something factual," and "informs"—is included to rule out three [potential] flaws [in a proof statement], associated respectively with (1) presumptions, (2) the factuality [of the statement], and (3) the way that [the statement] is formulated.

With respect to the first of these, that things are produced and perish is a fact. The Sāṃkhya have not properly verified the reality of this for themselves. Instead, they content themselves with what their scriptures say on the matter and cite the fact that the mind and pleasure are "produced and perish" as a reason to infer that they are inanimate phenomena. Accordingly, the Sāṃkhya make the mistake of thinking that the proof statement conveying that line of reasoning is correct. Dignāga stipulates that the [content of the] statement [must have been verified by the one who communicates it] "personally" in order to rule out the notion that statements articulating arguments such as this one of the Sāṃkhya can be correct.

"Something factual" is included to counter notions about certain reasons that have no basis in fact. These reasons may simply reflect what people *want* to be the case, or things that are "said" to be so. These cannot serve as correct reasons, and thus neither can the statements that articulate them be correct proof statements. To rule out the idea that they could be, Dignāga stipulates that an inference involving another party must be one that articulates something factual.

We find examples among previous generations of logicians, both from within and outside our own tradition, who [cited correct reasons] that fulfilled all three of the criteria and reflected things that exist in reality, which they had verified for themselves. But with regard to communicating them to others, the formulations of their proof statements were flawed, because they said either too much or too little. This is true, for instance, of the following proof statement:

(a) Sound is impermanent ["thesis"]
(b) because it is produced ["reason"],
(c) just as is the case, for example, with a pot ["example"].
(d) In the same way that pot is produced, so too is sound ["formal linking"].
(e) Sound is therefore impermanent ["summary"].

To counter the idea that a proof statement such as this one, guilty of either a surplus or a deficit of elements, could count as a correct one, Dignāga said that [a correct proof statement] "informs" [the other party that the reason fulfills the three criteria]. How exactly does a "proof statement formulated in five steps"[606] [such as the above] fail in this regard? [207] It fails on the grounds that it includes an overt expression of the proof's thesis, something that is deemed to be excess to requirements. How so? For the proper second party, who is in the process of having the proof established to him, the *thesis* is necessarily unconfirmed and something that he is not yet ready to realize even if it were presented to him.

In addition, there is no point in mentioning the *example* to him. This example does not get across the relation existing between the reason and the predicate and therefore cannot adequately convey the pervasion [to him]. The *formal linking* [of the property to the subject] essentially repeats what happens when one articulates the subject, whereas the *summary* is a repetition of the thesis. Thus a statement of proof that is formulated in five steps with its "five essential components" is flawed.

However, the individual [who presents such a proof statement] is using a reason that [fulfills] the three criteria. [The statement's content] also reflects something that exists in reality, which he has personally verified by means of valid cognition. So why do we still find grounds for criticizing his formulation of the reason [in that statement]?

When presenting the reason to the other party correctly in order to prompt a realization in him, a formulation that either omits some essential component or includes something that is superfluous must be counted as flawed. On this matter, the *Ascertainment of Pramāṇa* says: "The main consideration with the inference involving another party is not so much the facts [one seeks to establish] as the quality of the wording. If it is not phrased in the right fashion, it will only invite disagreement."[607] In his remarks on the phrase "that one has realized personally," the author of the *Ornament* [Prajñākaragupta] says, "It refers both to the one [who directs the process] and the party to whom it is directed. If the communication [of the reason] is correct, there is realization. Thus it [encompasses] both of the [parties]."[608] My impression is that other commentators have, however, interpreted the phrase "realized personally" as referring solely to the person who initiates the process and his [needing to] realize the reason for himself. Here "realized" obviously means that the thing must have been verified by valid cognition.

The term "something factual" denotes the reason that [fulfills] the three criteria. Some might question this, pointing out that the thesis is also "realized" by the initiator of the process. Why then, they might ask, should "something factual" refer only to the reason [fulfilling] the three criteria?

[Response:] It is true that in a more general sense, "something factual that is realized personally" by the one who initiates the process could be understood as referring to both the [proof's] thesis and reason. But in the present context, the phrase must be understood as linked to the term "informs"—that is, something that imparts the information [to the other party]. Hence it can only convey the reason [that fulfills] the three criteria, not the thesis. [208] It is by means of this reason [fulfilling] the three criteria that the other party can be prompted to realize the thesis [of the proof], and in this discussion about inference involving a second party, it is this reason that is said to "inform." The thesis, by contrast, is the thing about which the other party is informed.

Inference involving another party is therefore defined as "a verbal statement through which one party informs another relevant party of a [reason with] the three criteria—which [the former] has personally realized—and does so without [expressing] any more or less than is required."

Identifying the illustrations of proof statements

1. Description of the varieties
2. Examination of whether there can be a proof statement comprising only a single element

Description of the varieties: proof statements that connect similar phenomena and those that connect dissimilar phenomena

Inference involving another party has two varieties: correct proof statements that *connect similar phenomena* and correct proof statements that *connect dissimilar phenomena*. The first is defined as "a correct statement consisting of two component parts that overtly conveys the fact that the [thing serving as the] proof's reason is wholly present among the class of similar instances for that particular proof." An illustration of this is the statement "Anything that is produced is impermanent, just as is the case, for example, with a pot. Sound also is produced."

The second variety is defined as "a correct statement consisting of two component parts that overtly conveys the fact that the [thing serving as] the proof's reason is completely absent from the class of dissimilar instances for that particular proof." An illustration of this is the statement "Anything that is permanent is not produced, just as is the case, for example, with noncomposite space. Sound, however, is produced."

In the present day and age, the "logicians" in this snowy mountain land are all of the same opinion in saying that a correct proof statement connecting similar phenomena must overtly show that the proof's subject and similar example accord with its reason and predicate. Similarly, they say that a correct proof statement that connects dissimilar phenomena must overtly connect and show that the proof's subject and dissimilar example do not accord with its reason and predicate. They believe that what it means for phenomena to "accord" here [depends on whether] the form of assertion in the proof is of the identity or the existence variety. If it is the former, which establishes something about identity, the [elements] accord with one another in terms of an identity-correspondence, whereas if it is the latter, which establishes something about existence, the [elements] accord with one another in terms of an existence-correspondence. [209]

[Response:] This is what I have to say about their position. It follows that in a proof with an assertion of the identity variety, the correct proof statement must overtly show that the subject in the proof is an *instance* of its predicate, because such a proof statement must overtly show that the proof's subject and similar example have an identity that corresponds with its predicate. But if that were the case, it would follow that any correct proof statement connecting similar phenomena would need to overtly verbalize the thesis of the proof. This, however, would fly in the face of all those treatises that insist that articulation of the thesis *cannot* be counted as an essential component of a proof statement. It would also conflict with what [these "logicians"] say on the matter [elsewhere], when they assert that a proof statement that overtly articulates the thesis should be counted as flawed. As it says in the *Entrance to Reasoning*:

> The [proof statement expressing that] the phenomenon are similar shows that what serves as the reason is present in that class of similar instances. For instance, "What is produced is impermanent, just as is the case, for example, with a pot."[609]

And:

> The [proof statement expressing that] the phenomena are dissimilar shows that [in the class] from which the thing one is trying to prove is absent, the reason is also absent. So, [for instance,] "What is permanent is not produced, just as is the case, for example, with [noncomposite] space."[610]

This tells us what connecting similar phenomena and connecting dissimilar phenomena mean. To connect similar phenomena is to overtly show, in conjunction with a similar example, that the reason is wholly present in the class of similar instances for the proof in question. To connect dissimilar phenomena is to overtly show, in conjunction with a dissimilar example, that the reason is completely absent from the class of dissimilar instances for that proof. If, however, [as these "logicians" suggest, the first] overtly connects the proof's subject and similar example with its reason and the predicate, [showing the way that their identities] correspond, while the [second], overtly connects the subject and the dissimilar example with the predicate, [showing the way that their identities] do not correspond, one would be forced to assert that every correct proof statement overtly articulates the proof's thesis.

The pervasion that the proof statement connecting similar phenomena overtly expresses is the forward pervasion, while the reverse pervasion is something that it only conveys by implication. The proof statement connecting dissimilar phenomena [on the other hand] overtly expresses the proof's reverse pervasion while conveying the forward pervasion only by implication. But both kinds of statement express the subject overtly. [210]

Is it therefore strictly necessary to present *both* proof statements—the one connecting similar phenomena and the one connecting dissimilar phenomena—to the other party? Wouldn't just one of them do? It is in fact enough to present either one of them. No rational opponent is going to require both. As long as this other party is a rational person whose thoughts are turned toward logical reasoning and has arrived at the point where the correct proof statement is just what he needs, then once he ascertains that the reason is wholly present in the class of similar instances for the proof, he will understand, by implication, that it must be totally absent from the class of dissimilar instances. Whereas, once he ascertains that the reason is totally absent from the class of dissimilar instances, he will understand, by implication, that it must be wholly present in the class of similar instances. Reflecting this state of affairs, [Dharmakīrti] says:

> Thus, once [he] understands the relationship [between reason and predicate],
> [one can] state either of [the pervasions to him],
> [and] by implication he will understand the other
> [and be able to] correctly bring it to mind.[611]

Some claim that this refers only to an opponent of sharper faculties. They say that it is not necessary to present both proof statements to such an individual; *either* the proof statement overtly conveying the forward pervasion or the one overtly conveying the reverse pervasion will be enough. He would understand the other pervasion for himself by implication. But they say an opponent of weaker faculties would not be able to realize the other pervasion if it were only implied, and so it is necessary to [formally] present both proof statements.

[Response:] This claim blatantly contradicts what these same [individuals] say about the correct proof statement—namely, that it can never have more than two essential components. That is, it would follow that it is possible to have a correct proof statement that overtly expresses both pervasions, because it is possible to have another party for whom it is necessary to overtly present both the forward and reverse pervasions by means of a correct proof statement. But if they conceded this, they would have to acknowledge the possibility of a correct proof statement with *three* component parts. So it would directly go against their original position.

They might deny that their position forces them to accept a proof statement with three component parts by arguing that overt expression of *both* the forward and reverse pervasions should just be counted as a single component, covered by the phrase "expression of the pervasion(s)." They [might liken this to] the way that one [presents the example] but does not refer to this as the "expression of the example" and count it as a component separate from the expression of the pervasion.

[Response:] Well then, based on that logic, it would follow that the expression of the forward and reverse pervasions should [equally] just count as a single component of the proof statement. They must also accept that in terms of the criteria in a correct reason, the forward and reverse pervasions should only be counted as a single criterion. And we too [can liken this] to the way that the example of the reason is not counted as a criterion separate from the criterion of the pervasion. [211] This is an argument that even an omniscient one could not fend off!

They also say that when presented with a proof statement overtly expressing that the reason is wholly present in the class of similar instances, the opponent of weaker faculties will not be capable of understanding, by implication, that the reason must also be totally absent from the class of dissimilar instances. But if that were the case, then neither would such a person be capable of comprehending the fact that sound is impermanent, when presented with the statement "Sound is produced, and whatever is produced is impermanent," as this is also something that the statement only *implies*, and this implicative meaning is no easier to grasp than the other. If they agree that such an opponent is incapable of understanding the implication of the statement, then it must follow that when [Dharmakīrti] states:

> Even [without a proof statement, just being] told that "Sound is produced,
> and all such things are impermanent,"
> [he] will, by implication, know that [sound] perishes.[612]

[he is referring] only to those of sharper faculties. And it would also follow that when presenting a proof statement to someone of weaker faculties, for the proof to [create the desired] impact and bring about realization, it must be necessary to overtly spell out the thesis!

What is more, it would follow that when the opponent to whom one presents the proof establishing that sound is impermanent is someone of weaker faculties, he is able to realize that sound is impermanent but cannot realize that sound is not permanent! That must be the case, because these ["logicians"] assert that when the opponent to whom one presents the proof statement is of weaker faculties, even though he will ascertain that something produced is wholly present in the class of impermanent things, he is still incapable of ascertaining [by implication] that it must be totally absent from the class of permanent [things]. To this these ["logicians"] have no response.

Examination of whether there can be a proof statement comprising only a single element

1. Refutation of others' assertions
2. Setting forth our own position

Refutation of others' assertions

One [group of individuals] claims that when someone is establishing that sound is impermanent by reason of its being produced, there is a situation in which a statement such as "Sound is produced" [alone] can act as a correct proof statement. They say that the other party [in this situation] would be someone who has understood and can recall the relationship [underpinning] the proof's pervasion, and although he may not yet have understood the property of the subject, he has reached the point where he is *ready* to do so. In such a situation, they say that the statement "Sound is produced" can act as the proof statement, because it communicates [one] criterion of the reason in that proof, and by means of this statement alone, the other party will be able to realize the proof's thesis. According to them, this is the point [Dharmakīrti] makes when he says, "To the knowledgeable, all one needs to do is express the reason."[613] [212] And [these individuals] have concluded, therefore, that it is possible to have a proof statement with only a single element.

This position has been attacked in some quarters by those who allege that because the statement in question contains no *expression of the pervasion*, it is incomplete and does not therefore qualify as a correct proof statement. They back their criticism with the passage "[One that] fails to indicate any of the three criteria is said to be 'incomplete.'"[614] Thus they have concluded that the proof statement [proposed by the first group] is a flawed one. They have then given their own explanation of the correct proof statement [to be used] when one is attempting to establish "Sound is impermanent because it is produced." They claim that such a proof statement must be directed toward some other party who has not yet understood the three criteria of the reason but is ready to do so. It must be a verbal formulation that communicates the three criteria of the reason to him, overtly and by implication, in two steps and with two component parts that convey all that is required but employ an economy of expression. They have argued that those who say that it is possible to have a correct proof statement with only one element are obliged to accept that it would also be possible to have a correct reason that [fulfills] only a single criterion.

[Response:] For my part, I see the futility of the effort that has been put into this debate. Like those who believe that a mirage they experience is real water, the two sides then enter into a dispute over whether it possesses all eight qualities that would mark it as water of the finest variety. Both sides are so immersed in their own inane argument that they have no idea what a correct proof statement actually looks like.

So let me explain. First, I will counter the assertion [of the first group] that the statement "Sound is produced" [alone] can serve as a correct proof statement when it is directed at some other party who has not yet understood that sound is produced but is ready to do so. It follows that a verbal formulation of the *thesis*—the thing that is to be proved—can work as a correct proof statement for that opponent, because the statement "Sound is produced" can serve as a correct proof statement for him. The pervasion holds, since the statement "Sound is produced" is one that articulates the thesis to him. That must be so, because for that opponent, the fact that sound is produced is the probandum. But if that is the case, then for this opponent, who has not realized that sound is produced, the statement "Sound is produced" would serve as a correct proof statement. But from this it would follow that for that opponent, the [thing conveyed by] the statement "Sound is produced" is being used as the reason to prove itself. Thus it must also follow that [in an alternative situation] where the other party was someone who did not know that sound is impermanent, the statement "Sound is impermanent" could serve as a correct proof statement for him! Thus anyone who maintains [this group's] position will be forced to accept that the verbal formulation of any thesis must be counted as a correct proof statement. [213] The words "This is something constructed by ignorance"[615] tell the whole story here.

Quite apart from that, there is a view that when, for instance, one is establishing that sound is impermanent by reason of its being produced to a second party who does not yet know that sound is produced, the statement "Sound is produced" conveys to that second party the criteria that the reason [fulfills].

[Response:] This view, which everyone seems to subscribe to, is simply an example of shoddy scholarship. The statement in question does not convey to that second party any of the [three] criteria that the reason [fulfills], because it cannot convey to him either the property of the subject [the first criterion] or the forward and reverse pervasions [the second and third criteria]. It follows that it does not convey the property of the subject to him, because he is someone who is not yet aware that sound is produced, and thus for him, "produced" cannot be considered the property of the subject in that proof. For "produced" to count as the property of the subject, this opponent would need to have ascertained through valid cognition that [the quality of] production is present in sound, in accordance with the form of the proof.[616] But in fact he does not know that sound is produced. These [individuals] have no response to this.

Furthermore, they have [elsewhere] defined the property of the subject as "the thing that is ascertained always to be present, in accordance with the form of the proof, in the subject of interest." So, if they now also assert that the statement "Sound is produced" conveys the property of the subject to the other party in the proof mentioned, they are stacking up a heap of contradictions for themselves. Having agreed among themselves that the aforesaid statement is [sufficient] to convey the property of the subject, they then go on to dispute whether it is a correct proof statement. This is a matter of great wonder![617]

[They cannot claim that] the statement "Sound is produced" is a flawed proof statement for a second party who does not yet know that sound is produced, because if it was, it would follow that the statement "Sound is impermanent" would also have to count as a flawed proof statement for a second party who does not yet know that sound is impermanent. But if they accept that [it is not a flawed proof statement], it would follow that any verbal articulation of the thesis is a flawed statement, because any verbal articulation of the thesis is a flawed proof statement.[618] However, if they accepted that, the conclusion must be that a correct thesis is an impossibility. For this reason, for a second party who has not yet understood that sound is produced but is ready to do so, the statement "Sound is produced" can represent no more than words that *voice* the thesis; trying to determine whether it constitutes a correct or incorrect proof statement makes no sense. [214]

The second group holds that when one is establishing that "Sound is impermanent because it is produced" for a second party who has not yet understood the three criteria of the reason in the proof but is ready to do so, a verbal formulation that communicates to him the property of the subject and the pervasions in two steps and that has two component parts—conveying all that is required but employing an economy of expression—is a correct proof statement.

[Response:] This is incorrect, because for the other party who has not understood the property of the subject or the forward and reverse pervasions in the proof that sound is impermanent due to its being produced, the statements, "Sound is produced," "A produced thing is always present in [the class of] impermanent ones," and "A produced thing is totally absent [from the class of] permanent ones" are all statements that communicate the thesis.[619]

It would also follow, according to their position, that for the aforesaid second party, "produced" is the correct reason in that proof. This must be the case because, for him, a statement that articulates the property of the subject and the pervasion [of the proof] is a correct verbalization of its reason. But if "produced" was the correct reason for him in the proof, it would mean that he must have *ascertained* both the property of the subject and the pervasion.[620] This is why [Dignāga] included "ascertained" among the characteristics that define each of the criteria of a correct reason and stated that ascertainment was necessary for both the one who directs the debate and the opponent. Thus [Dharmakīrti states]:

> The property of the subject is maintained to be something that is
> ascertained by both the proponent and the opponent.
> Likewise, ["ascertainment"] is also expressed for both the presence in
> and the absence from the class of similar instances.[621]

What such passages affirm is that we cannot talk of something as being a correct reason for the other party unless he has ascertained the three criteria. Thus, if the second party is someone who is not aware of those three criteria, statements that express the property of the subject or the pervasions cannot be correct proof statements.

Setting forth our own position

At exactly what point should the correct proof statement be used? What is it intended to achieve? And how should it be presented? Let me illustrate these in terms of a single formal proof, which sets out to establish that because sound is produced, it must be impermanent. There are two kinds of opponent to whom it is necessary to prove that sound is impermanent. The first does not have a strong distorted notion that sound is permanent but doubts on the matter are to the fore in his mind. In the second, it is the distorted notion that predominates. [215]

The first of these persons has not yet given any special thought to the issue of whether sound is permanent or impermanent, or if he paid attention to it at some earlier point, he saw no evidence that could convince him one way or the other. However, he is now preoccupied by the question of whether sound is permanent or impermanent and really wishes to come to a definitive conclusion on the matter. Among those who are like this first type of opponent, some may wonder whether there could be a *third alternative*[622] [of sound being both permanent and impermanent]. Others among them will entertain no such thoughts. If the opponent is someone who is wondering about the [possibility of the third alternative], one should first provide him with a [preparative] countering proof[623] that fatally undermines the idea that sound could be permanent. Only after that should one present the proof statement establishing that sound is impermanent.

When the opponent is someone who seeks to finally resolve the question of whether sound is permanent or impermanent but entertains no notion that it might be both, it is appropriate to respond to his question about which of these two sound is by presenting him with a correct proof statement, establishing that it is impermanent. It is not necessary to go through the step with the [preparative] countering proof that rules out the notion that sound could be permanent.

The second opponent is the one in whom the distorted notion that sound is permanent is more to the fore [than just doubts]. Either he is totally convinced that sound is permanent and clings absolutely to the truth of this notion or he feels that *in all likelihood* sound is permanent. Among those who are like the second person, some will have ascertained that permanent and impermanent form a directly preclusive dichotomy, which rules out the possibility of any third alternative. Others among these opponents will not yet have ascertained this fact. For those who have ascertained it, only one side of the proof—either that which undermines the idea that sound is permanent or that which establishes it is impermanent—is required. Such opponents do not need to be presented with both sides. As soon as they become aware that sound is not permanent, they will ascertain that it must be impermanent. Or as soon as they become aware that it is impermanent, they will ascertain that it cannot be permanent.

For someone who has not yet ascertained that permanent and impermanent form a directly preclusive dichotomy—which rules out any possibility of a third alternative—it will first be necessary to present arguments that undermine the notion that sound is permanent. One might point out, for example, that if it were permanent, it would either have to be always heard or never heard even for a single instant. After this, one would present a proof statement establishing that sound is impermanent.

Next, regarding how the proof statement should be formulated, the second party is someone who is ready to be presented with evidence that will establish that sound is impermanent. A proper first party, who has accepted the role of the one who will present the evidence to establish that, should address this second party, saying something such as, "Whatever is produced is impermanent, such as, for example, a pot. Sound also is produced," or, "Whatever is permanent is not produced, such as, for example, noncomposite space. Sound, however, is produced."

A reason that can establish sound is impermanent [must fulfill the] three criteria. [216] The second party to whom the proof statement should be presented will necessarily be someone who has not yet recognized that "produced" [fulfills] all three criteria. So, while "produced" is *presented* to him as the correct reason in that proof, it has not yet *become* that for him. Correspondingly, the verbal formulation [of the proof] is presented to him as a correct proof statement, but it has not yet become that for him.

Once the proof statement is presented to the second party, it will immediately convey and facilitate realization of the property of the subject and then the two pervasions in succession. If the second party is of sharper faculties, it will not be necessary to repeat the proof statement to him at this point. While he originally understood each of the criteria individually, by recalling the proof statement he has just heard, he will be able to bring together his understanding of all three criteria into a single thought. This is the point at which the proof statement that was presented to him earlier can properly be said to have become a *correct* proof statement, and "produced" that was presented to him earlier as the reason can properly be said to have become a *correct* reason.

A second party who is of weaker faculties will also [initially] gain an understanding of each of the three criteria separately. But even after he has understood them, it will still be necessary to repeat the proof statement to him before he can integrate his understanding of the three within a single thought. This second party has retained an understanding of the criteria individually. The proof statement encompasses all three in the space of *a single utterance*, and so its articulation helps him gather together his separate understanding of each of the three into a single thought. Hence, as soon as the proof statement is presented to him a second time, it can immediately be said to have become a [correct] proof statement.

To sum up, the task of the proof statement is to facilitate re-*collection* of the three criteria that have already been understood. It is not to newly inform someone of those criteria. This is the point that is made in the passage:

The capacity [to establish the thesis] is an element
that is actually innate within the three criteria.
[And only] the words [expressing] the [three criteria]
[can] generate the [necessary] recollection of that.[624]

If the reverse were true, and the proof statement really was able to trigger within someone the initial realization of the three criteria, it would follow that the person would ascertain the three criteria simply [through hearing] the words that express them! And if that were the case, there would have to be a corresponding situation with the [proof's] thesis. That is, mere mention of it would be enough to induce ascertainment of it in someone. But what place would there then be for inference? Would one seriously want to suggest that it is of no use? What actually happens is that [a person first] ascertains the three criteria by means of different valid cognitions. As long as he has not forgotten the three criteria altogether, what the proof statement allows him to do is to recollect his ascertainment of them. And it is this recollection of the three criteria that triggers the inferential cognition that actually realizes the [proof's] thesis.

A proof statement that conveyed just one of the criteria would only be able to prompt a recollection of that criterion. It would not allow someone to recall all three of them simultaneously. Hence a correct proof statement that conveys only one of the criteria is an impossibility. [217]

How then are we supposed to understand the passage "To the knowledgeable, all one needs to do is express the reason"?[625] This appears in the section:

An example is presented to one who does not know
that the [reason] is the same nature or the cause of that [predicate].
To the knowledgeable [on the other hand],
all one needs to do is express the reason.

Thus, once [he] understands the relationship [between reason and predicate],
[one can] express either of [the pervasions to him],
[and] by implication, he will understand the other
and be able to correctly bring it to mind.[626]

What the first stanza explains is that the second party may be someone who does not yet know the relationship upon which the pervasion rests—namely, the relationship that exists between the reason and the predicate. If so, he is presented with an example, which serves as the basis for him to realize that relationship by means of a valid cognition. It says that there are also, however, certain other more astute individuals who *have* already understood the aforesaid relationship but do not yet know the property of the subject. All that they need is that the means for ascertaining the *reason* be expressed to them or that the valid cognition for ascertaining the reason be indicated to them. There is no need to indicate the valid cognitions that ascertain the relationship to such persons. What the first stanza explains therefore are the variations in the ways that those who have not yet understood the three criteria are helped to gain valid understanding of them. The second stanza then describes the way that the proof statement should be presented to a person who has already understood the relationship underpinning the pervasion to help him recall [that of which he is already aware].

Prior to this present explanation of mine, no one in this snowy mountain land has ever given a full and satisfactory account of these passages. Commentators in the land of āryas predominantly interpreted the earlier stanza to be one talking about the valid cognitions responsible for ascertaining the three criteria. This is extremely clear in the autocommentary as well as in the commentaries by Śākyabuddhi and the great brahmin. Any intelligent person can verify this for himself by consulting those works. The [relevant] sections in these commentaries are lengthy, so I have not gone to the trouble of reproducing them here. Yamāri[627] reads, "All one needs to do is express the reason"[628] as referring to inference involving another party.[629] This is either a case of his not having examined the matter sufficiently or a genuine misinterpretation stemming from his own confusion. I have already given reasons why this understanding of the line is incorrect.

There are many points relating to the proof statement that could be discussed, but since I do not want this section to become too long, I have chosen not to explore them further here.

Beside the sun of the Able One, all ordinary suns are pale;
they leave the vast grove of *udumbara*—the most supreme of trees—in darkness.
My mind is like that sun of the Able One,
shining on a lotus arisen from waters, the depths of which are hard to fathom. [218]

17. The Logical Reason

What the account of inference involving another party conveys overtly: the description of logical reasons

1. Description of the correct logical reason
2. Description of its opposite, the fallacious logical reason

Description of the correct logical reason

1. Defining characteristics
2. Examination of the scheme
3. Varieties

Defining characteristics of a correct logical reason

1. Refutation of others' assertions
2. Setting forth our own position

Refutation of others' assertions

Someone claims that a correct logical reason cannot [simply be defined as] something that "fulfills the three criteria." [He believes that] this only establishes that the reason [itself] fulfills the criteria of the property of the subject and the pervasions but says nothing about whether the two parties involved have *ascertained* that it fulfills them. He suggests that there is no such problem, however, if one defines a correct reason as "that which is ascertained [to fulfill] the three criteria."

[Response:] What you say here clashes with your account of the property of the subject. You define it as "that which is ascertained always to be present, in accordance with the form of the proof, in the subject of interest." Hence the property of the subject is *necessarily* something that is *ascertained*, since this is one of the characteristics that define it in your own account.

We could also draw attention to [Dharmakīrti's] pronouncement:

> [Dignāga] stated that [the fulfilling of each of the] three criteria
> must also be "ascertained"
> to counter the [idea] that [reasons that are] unconfirmed, reversed,
> or mistaken [qualify as correct ones].[630]

This stanza does not say that "ascertained" should be given as one of the characteristics that define the correct reason. Rather, it specifically refers to [Dignāga's] stipulation that being ascertained should be included among the characteristics that define the three criteria. This is indeed a point that is made regularly throughout the Seven Treatises, where the term *ascertained* is explicitly taught to be part of the defining characteristics of each of the three. Thus if the three criteria are fulfilled, the property of the subject and the pervasions will necessarily have been ascertained. To hold that the three criteria could be satisfied without those three having been ascertained is simply poor scholarship. In any case, *ascertained* means to have been ascertained by the mind of the second party. Therefore, if the reason has been "established," the second party must have confirmed it by valid cognition. Hence your logic is erroneous.

According to our own system, a correct reason is defined as "that which fulfills the three criteria." [219]

Examination of the scheme of the correct logical reason

1. Identifying each of the three criteria and investigating whether they are mutually exclusive
2. Identifying the foundation for each of the three and investigating whether there can be a correct reason [that establishes something about] a subject that is a nonexistent
3. Examining for whom the reason [must count as] correct
4. Identifying each of the [elements] within the correct proof: the reason, the subject, and the predicate

Identifying each of the three criteria and investigating whether they are mutually exclusive

1. Refutation of others' assertions
2. Setting forth our own position

Refutation of others' assertions

Someone proposes that the property of the subject is "the reason that is ascertained always to be present, in accordance with the form of the proof, in the subject of interest." [He explains] the phrase "in accordance with the form of the proof" as indicating that if the form of the assertion is of the identity variety, the subject *is* [a case of] the reason, whereas if it is of the existence variety, the reason exists wherever the subject is present. He says that the forward pervasion is "that among the reason's three criteria that is the predicate's complete pervasion of the reason."[631] And the reverse pervasion is "that among the three criteria that is the inverse of the reason pervading the inverse of the predicate." In his view, the forward and reverse pervasions are mutually exclusive. This must be the case, he believes, because with the proof "Sound is impermanent because it is produced," at the point that "produced" actually serves as the correct reason establishing the proof, the two pervasions necessarily have to preclude one another. This is because [one pervasion is that] something produced is necessarily impermanent, [whereas the other pervasion is that] something permanent is necessarily not produced. These must be mutually exclusive, because the only thing that can embody the first pervasion is something impermanent, whereas the only kind that can embody the second is something permanent.

Someone else claims that the forward and reverse pervasions are not mutually exclusive, because [in the aforesaid proof, the fact that] if something is produced it is necessarily impermanent does not preclude [the fact that] if something is permanent it is necessarily not produced. That must be the case, he reasons, because if something is an established basis, these two facts are always that.[632] For him, if one did not identify these two [facts] as the forward and reverse pervasions, it would follow that "Whatever is produced is impermanent, such as, for example, a pot. Sound also is produced" is not the proof statement connecting similar phenomena, and that "Whatever is permanent is not produced, such as, for example, noncomposite space. Sound, however, is produced" is not the proof statement connecting dissimilar phenomena. [220] This second individual agrees with the previous one about the characteristics that define each of the three criteria.

[A third individual] concurs with the first two about what defines the property of the subject, but he defines the forward pervasion as "the reason that, due to its relationship with the predicate, is ascertained to exist only in the class of similar instances," and the reverse pervasion as "the reason that, due to its relationship with the predicate, is ascertained to be totally absent from the class of dissimilar instances." He claims that in the case of the proof "Sound is impermanent because it is produced," the [fact that] something produced is necessarily impermanent is the forward pervasion, and [the fact that] something permanent is necessarily not produced is the reverse pervasion. Believing that the only things that can embody the two are, respectively, impermanent and permanent, he concludes that the two pervasions must be mutually exclusive.

[A fourth individual] has offered the same sets of defining characteristics for the forward and reverse pervasions but says that [the two facts]—that if something is produced it is necessarily impermanent and that if something is permanent it is necessarily not produced—do not preclude each other. He thus concludes that the two pervasions themselves are not mutually exclusive.

All these [individuals] agree on what constitutes the *similar instance* and dissimilar instance for the proof "Sound is impermanent because it is produced," saying that an impermanent [thing] is the first, whereas a permanent one is the second.

[Response:] None of the positions held by these individuals are viable. The fault with the first two is this: [the fact that] something permanent is necessarily not produced *cannot* be the reverse pervasion. This follows, because it does not [fulfill] any of the three criteria. This is because it is not one of the essential components of the probans that establishes the thesis.[633] If they were to challenge [this argument's] reason, it would go against [the claim that they make elsewhere] that the components of the probans for this proof are permanent.[634] The same line of reasoning can also be used against [those who identify the reverse pervasion as] "If something is permanent, it is necessarily not produced."

Furthermore, [the fact that] something produced is necessarily impermanent cannot be the forward pervasion. This follows, because [based on their logic, it can instead] be established to be a member of the class of *dissimilar* instances, in that it is a phenomenon that is a non-actual thing.[635] And this is the case "because if something is an established basis, these two facts are always that."[636]

The positions of the next two individuals lead them to embrace open contradictions. It would follow that [the fact of] something permanent necessarily not being produced is ascertained to be totally *absent* from the class of dissimilar instances, since it is the reverse pervasion of the proof in question. They cannot deny this [argument's] pervasion, as that would go against the way they have defined the reverse pervasion. [221] The reason is also something that they obviously themselves asserted. But if they accept [the argument's conclusion], it would go against their claim that the reverse pervasion is permanent.[637] He has also accepted the point at which the "push" has occurred.[638] It similarly follows that [the fact of] something permanent necessarily not being produced is *not* a dissimilar instance within the proof in question, since it is the reverse pervasion. They have accepted both the pervasion and reason [of this argument]. But if they accept [the argument's conclusion], then it would follow that [the fact of] something permanent necessarily not being produced must be a dissimilar instance in that proof, because it is permanent. The three spheres therefore derive directly [from their position, which is therefore shown to be irredeemably flawed].

All of [these individuals] have described the two pervasions in a similar way, saying that in terms of any given formal proof, the forward pervasion is the predicate's complete pervasion of the reason, and the reverse pervasion is [the opposite of that], with the inverse of the reason pervading the inverse of the predicate. This position is one that cannot be sustained. It suggests that in any given proof where the predicate pervades the reason, the inverse of the reason will necessarily pervade the inverse of the predicate. And likewise, if the inverse of the reason pervades the inverse of the predicate, then the predicate will necessarily pervade the reason. This follows a general principle agreed on by logicians about the forward and reverse pervasions—namely, that if either of them holds, then the other one must also hold—a principle that you strive to maintain.[639] But let us apply [your formulation of the principle] to the proof "noncomposite space [A] is a comprehended thing [B], because it is permanent [C]." It follows that impermanent [the inverse of the reason] pervades not being a comprehended thing [the inverse of the predicate] because permanent [the reason] is pervaded by being a comprehended thing [the predicate]. If any of you are capable of a response to this, I will personally grant you a rich reward![640]

They may try to claim that impermanent is the inverse of the reason.

[Response:] It would ludicrously follow that impermanent and permanent do not form a directly preclusive dichotomy!

So they may then question whether something permanent is necessarily a comprehended thing.

[Response:] It would follow that the proof "Sound is permanent because it is a comprehended thing" does *not* fail on the grounds that comprehended thing pervades *both* the class of similar instances [permanent] and the class of dissimilar instances [the inverse of permanent].[641]

It would also follow that in the case of the proof "The person [A] definitely exists [B] because of having a self [C]," "definitely exists" [the predicate] must pervade having a self [the reason], since not having a self [the inverse of the reason] pervades not definitely existing [the inverse of the predicate]. But if one accepted that, it would follow that having a self is not a definite nonexistent because it is pervaded by definite existence! Those with any sense would be well advised to avoid reducing themselves to such a level of idiocy.

Furthermore, [in the case of the pervasion] "A visual consciousness is necessarily a valid cognition because a visual form is necessarily a comprehended thing," it must follow that [if] a visual form is necessarily a comprehended thing, a visual consciousness is necessarily a valid cognition, [because if] something that is not a visual consciousness is necessarily a valid cognition, a visual form is necessarily not a comprehended thing. [222] The pervasion is one that [they] accept. But if they were to agree [with the argument's conclusion], it would follow that all visual consciousnesses are valid cognitions. But that would be ridiculous, because a visual consciousness to which strands of hair floating in the air appear [due to a visual impairment] would thereby be rendered an impossibility. They might then deny that the inverse of the reason pervades the inverse of the predicate in the original proof. But that would mean that a visual consciousness would necessarily *not* be a valid cognition. And in that case, there would be no such thing as a valid cognition that apprehended visual form!

Their assertion that the property of the subject is defined as "that which is ascertained always to be present, in accordance with the form of the proof, in the subject of interest" is also wrong. We might consider, for instance, the proof "Sound is impermanent because it is sound." Sound *is* always sound, and so in that case, it would qualify as the property of the subject!

This way of defining the property of the subject represents a particular inconsistency when the same individuals classify "Sound is impermanent because it is sound" as a proof that is unconfirmed on the grounds that its subject and reason are identical.

Setting forth our own position

The property of the subject is defined as "a logical reason that is ascertained to be wholly present, in accordance with the form of the proof, in the subject of interest of the proof in question, as a property of that subject." An example of this is "produced" when it serves as the correct reason to establish "Sound is impermanent."

The forward pervasion is defined as "a logical reason that is ascertained by valid cognition to be present only in the class of similar instances for the proof in question." The reverse pervasion is defined as "a logical reason that is ascertained by valid cognition to be totally absent from the class of dissimilar instances of the proof in question." In the proof "Sound is impermanent because it is produced," for instance, the "produced" that serves as the correct reason is both of them. This is a point that is made very clearly in the master [Dharmakīrti's] treatises. In the *Ascertainment of Valid Cognition* he says:

> The [fulfillment of] those three criteria [are their] presence in [both] the thing that the inference [is about] and what corresponds with it, and their absence from what is without [that correspondence]. These are ascertained.
>
> Here, "[the thing] that the inference [is about]" is the subject about which there is a wish to learn something and that has various particulars. That [first criterion] is observed either by perception or inferential cognition. Likewise, it is present only among those things that are similar [to it] . . . .[642]
>
> The third criterion is that the logical reason that is present in [the class of things] similar with those about which something is being proved is totally absent [from the class of those that are dissimilar]. That also is ascertained. The "ascertained" at the end of the statement refers to all three criteria.[643]

Also, in *Drop of Logic* he says:

> The logical reason [fulfilling] the three criteria is the one that should be ascertained to be wholly present in the thing that one is inferring [something about], existent only in the class of similar instances and entirely absent from the class of dissimilar instances.[644]

The other treatises, such as *Drop of Reasoning*, also support this.[645] [223]

[Generally,] there are four types of pervasion: forward, reverse, overt, and converse.[646] The first two of these have already been explained. In the context of a specific formal proof, the *overt pervasion* is the predicate encompassing [all cases] of the reason. The *converse pervasion* is the inverse of the reason encompassing [all cases of] the inverse of the predicate. If either the forward pervasion or reverse pervasion within a formal proof holds, the other one will necessarily also hold. But the same is not true for the overt and converse pervasions. When the reason is correct, both the forward and reverse pervasions must hold, otherwise it would not qualify as a correct reason. However, the overt and converse pervasions [of a proof] may hold, and the property of the subject may also be established, but these alone are no guarantee that the reason is a correct one. A case in point is "thing heard" in the proof "Sound is impermanent because it is a thing heard."[647]

Thus, when there is a reason that is to be presented to the other party to help him realize a certain thesis, to work out whether the pervasions hold, it is the forward and reverse ones that must be considered, *not* the converse one. Establishing the [converse] pervasion is not necessarily a requirement; even if it does not hold, this does not necessarily count as a flaw.

[By contrast,] for a correct consequence, the main pervasion that needs to be confirmed is the *overt* one. Thus, when we say that valid cognition has established that the pervasion in a particular consequence holds, the pervasion in question will necessarily be the overt one. There is indeed no guarantee that the forward pervasion will hold. For instance, when faced with an opponent who claims that a sprout is produced independent of causes, one can present him with the consequence "It follows that a sprout [A] can never be produced [B], because it is something produced independent of causes [C]." We can say that the pervasion in this consequence is established by valid cognition, but the pervasion in question is the overt one, not the forward one. If it was the forward pervasion that was established, one would need to be able to ascertain with valid cognition that "something produced independent of causes" is present only in [the class of things] "that can never be produced." But from this it would follow that something produced independent of causes exists!

To sum up, for "something produced independent of causes" to be *present* in the [class] of "things that can never be produced," it would have to exist, but for it to be pervaded [i.e., encompassed] by that does not mean that "something produced independent of causes" needs to exist. It is just the same as with things that are not established bases. Their existence is not a prerequisite for them being pervaded by selflessness. This is just one of many examples. Anyone with intelligence who investigates this matter will be able to grasp it. [224]

There is one type of consequence, the "consequence that projects the probans [of a proof],"[648] where the overt pervasion in its inverted form actually represents [the pervasion in a correct proof]. However, the fact that the overt pervasion in a specific consequence holds is no guarantee that the inverted one also will.

When we talk of the forward and reverse pervasions, we are basically concerned with whether the reason is *concomitant* with the class of similar instances and is [also] the reverse of this—that is, *not concomitant* with [the things that form] the class of dissimilar instances. That the predicate encompasses the reason and the inverse of the reason encompasses the inverse of the predicate, on the other hand, represents only the overt pervasion contained in the words and the converse of that overt pervasion.[649] One should therefore avoid making the serious error of confusing the "reverse" in the sense of *absence* from the class of dissimilar instances with the "converse" [pervasion].

Also, regarding what is meant when it is said that the proof statement connecting similar phenomena overtly conveys the forward pervasion, such a statement is one from which an individual is able to gain the overt realization that the reason is present only in the class of similar instances and, from that, is also able to realize by implication that the reason is totally absent from the class of dissimilar instances. Thus one says that such a statement "overtly conveys" the forward pervasion and "implies" the reverse one. There is no suggestion that the proof statement earns the description of something that "overtly conveys the forward pervasion" on the basis of its communicating that "the predicate encompasses the reason."[650]

This concludes the explanation of the three criteria.

Identifying the Foundation for Each of the Three and Investigating Whether There Can Be a Correct Reason [That Establishes Something About] a Subject That Is a Nonexistent

1. Identifying the foundation for each of the three[651]
2. Investigating whether there can be a correct reason [that establishes something about] a subject that is a nonexistent

Identifying the Foundation for Each of the Three

1. Refutation of others' assertions
2. Setting forth our own position

Refutation of others' assertions

Someone defines the class of similar instances as "that domain of congruity of the subject and predicate, delineated by the universal," and the class of dissimilar instances as "that domain of non-congruity of the subject and predicate, delineated by the universal." What he means by this is that [in the case of the former], the subject and predicate must correspond with one another, whereas [in the latter] there is no correspondence.

[Response:] This position is untenable. Let us consider the proof "Sound is permanent because it is a comprehended thing." It would follow that this is a proof for which there is no class of similar instances, because there is no congruity between [the subject] and [the predicate] in that nothing can be both sound and permanent. He has no response to this.

Quite apart from this, defining the classes of similar and dissimilar instances in this way contradicts what he says on the forward pervasion, which he defines as "[something] ascertained to be present only in the class of similar instances." [225] This can be illustrated with the proof "Sound is impermanent because it is produced." To ascertain the forward pervasion of that proof, it would be necessary to ascertain that something produced is present only in the class of similar instances. This can only be done if one has ascertained that class of similar instances. But as far as he is concerned, the way to ascertain that class is to realize that a particular thing is both a sound and is impermanent. So it must follow that one cannot ascertain the forward pervasion of the proof unless one has already realized the thesis that it is intended to prove!

Someone else claims that the class of similar instances should be defined as "that domain of congruity of the reason and predicate, delineated by the universal." This is just careless. Let us [again] consider the proof "The sound of a conch [A] is impermanent [B] because it is something derived from effort [C]." Based on what he says, it follows that for there to be a class of similar instances for this proof, there must be [complete] congruity between "derived from effort" and "impermanent." But if they are congruous, that would mean there can be no example of a class of similar instances that pervades [the reason] in a divided way.[652]

This individual may say that he was not suggesting that there needs to be complete congruity between the reason and the predicate but only that they need to correspond with one another. The form of correspondence, he might say, is determined by the form of assertion in the proof. If it is of the *identity* variety, the correspondence must be in terms of what the reason and predicate *are*, whereas if it is of the *existence* variety, it must be in terms of [loci] where the reason and predicate are present.

[Response:] We would point to proofs such as "The sound of a conch is derived from effort because it is impermanent" and "Sound is impermanent because it is a comprehended thing." "Derived from effort" and "impermanent" do not correspond with one another in terms of identity, and neither do "impermanent" and "comprehended thing." So it again follows that a class of similar instances for such proofs would be impossible.[653]

Elsewhere, someone claims that at the point that "produced" serves as the correct reason establishing the proof "Sound is impermanent because it is produced," sound does not [count as one of the] class of similar instances. He says that there would be two logical faults if it did. First, he proposes that "similar" must denote some correspondence between sound and impermanent [and that due to this, sound is ruled out], since a thing cannot correspond with itself. Second, he says that if one were to accept that the subject belongs to the class of similar instances in a given proof, it would mean that [in the case of the proof] "Sound is impermanent because it is a thing heard," [the other party involved] knows that thing heard is a member of the class of similar instances, because he has identified a thing heard as a sound. This, he says, would mean that "Sound is impermanent because it is a thing heard" is not an example of an inconclusive proof of the "not shared" variety.[654]

[Response:] Well, according to your first line of reasoning, it follows that even "impermanent" itself cannot count as a similar instance when establishing "Sound is impermanent." Why? Because "similar" here must denote something that corresponds with "impermanent" in the sense of being impermanent, but impermanent cannot correspond with itself. But you have already declared that impermanent *does* count as a similar instance [for this proof]. So the three spheres are in place, [and your position is shown to be irredeemably flawed].

Based on your second line of reasoning, [in the case of the proof] "Sound is impermanent [because it is produced]," it would follow that [the other party involved] knows that "produced" belongs to the class of dissimilar instances, because he has identified produced as a known thing. [226] Since you concede that known thing itself is not impermanent, and that all phenomena that are not impermanent belong to the class of dissimilar instances here, you have agreed to everything in [this argument—its] pervasion, predicate, and reason.

[Based on the earlier definition,] it furthermore follows that the "sound of a conch" must count as a similar instance for the proof "Sound is impermanent." This is because it is a "domain of congruity of the subject and predicate, delineated by the universal." Regarding the reason and predicate [of this argument], we should apprise you of the fact that you are the one who defined the class of similar instances as the "domain of congruity of the subject and predicate, delineated by the universal" and explained that what it denotes is a correspondence between the subject and the predicate. But if you accept [the conclusion] that the sound of the conch is a similar instance in that proof, it would follow that [the other party] must also know that "thing heard" is in the class of similar instances, because he has already identified that the sound of a conch is a thing heard. The three spheres are in place. And if you accept [the argument], it would also follow that "Sound is impermanent because it is a thing heard" could not be counted as the example of an inconclusive proof of the "not shared" variety, because [the other party] knows that thing heard belongs to the class of similar instances. So the three spheres are overtly in place.

Another reason given as to why sound cannot be a similar instance in the proof "Sound is impermanent because it is produced" is that it would mean that it formed two separate foundations for the proof. And if it was two separate foundations, it would accordingly need to constitute two separate criteria of the reason in that proof.

[Response:] That is not necessarily the case. If it was, then it would follow that if something is the reverse pervasion of the correct reason in the proof, it does not need to be an established basis, because if something is the dissimilar example in the proof, it does not need to be an established basis.[655] In any case, whether one holds that "similar instance" refers to "that which has the predicate of the proof in question," "that which has the predicate of the proof in question, in accordance with the form of the proof," or "a domain of congruity delineated by the universal of the predicate," they all lead to the same [problematic] conclusion: that for something to be the similar instance in a proof establishing "Sound is impermanent," it needs to be the predicate of that proof. And that must mean that for something to be the similar instance in that proof, it must be identical with impermanent.

Setting forth our own position

1. Literal meaning of the term
2. Defining characteristics
3. Varieties

Literal meaning of the term

Something is known as the "class of similar instances for establishing that sound is impermanent" due to the fact that it is the class within which sound and impermanent share similarity. Something is known as the "dissimilar class [for establishing that sound is impermanent"] due to the fact that it is the class within which sound and it do not share a similarity. [This explanation in terms of the proof "Sound is impermanent"] can be extended equally well to understand [the class of similar instances and the class of dissimilar instances for] any formal proof. [227]

Defining Characteristics

The class of similar instances is defined as "that which, in terms of the predicate of the proof in question and in accordance with the form of the proof, has the predicate of that proof." The class of dissimilar instances is defined as "that which, in terms of the predicate of the proof in question and in accordance with the form of the proof, is not something that has the predicate of that proof."

Varieties

The similar instance[656] is of two varieties: that which is fully encompassed by the thing presented as the reason and that which is not fully encompassed by the reason.

The dissimilar instance is of three varieties. Something can be a dissimilar instance either in the sense of being (1) other [than a similar instance], (2) precluding [the similar instance], or (3) not existing. For example, with the proof "Sound is impermanent," known thing counts as the first, permanent as the second, and the horns on the head of a hare as the third.

Something that satisfies both the literal meaning and the definition of a *similar instance* in terms of the proof "Sound is impermanent" is the sound from a conch. Something that satisfies the definition but not the literal meaning of *similar instance* in terms of the proof "Sound is permanent" is noncomposite space. It is impossible for something to satisfy the literal meaning but not the definition. Something that satisfies neither the literal meaning nor the definition is noncomposite space in terms of the proof "Sound is impermanent." From these [examples], one can also understand how it works with regards to the dissimilar instance.

Next, we should examine what it means, with respect to a specific formal proof, to say that something is "present," "observed," or "ascertained" in either the class of similar instances or the class of dissimilar instances. Purely in terms of [establishment] by valid cognition, [something being] *present*, *observed*, and *ascertained* are all coterminous. Hence, when the relevant party discovers through a valid cognition that a thing is present in either of the two classes in a particular proof, he will also necessarily ascertain and observe it to be in that class. More generally, although something being present [i.e., existing] for a specific party also means that for him it is also observed and ascertained, this in no way guarantees that this party has really observed or ascertained that thing. Just because an individual is under the impression that something is present or that he has observed or ascertained it does not mean that this is really the case.

Hence the proof establishing "Sound is impermanent" can be used to illustrate what it means for the relevant party to observe that something is in the class of similar instances. "Impermanent" is the predicate in this proof, and what it means for the relevant party to observe that a thing is in the class of similar instances is for him to confirm with a valid cognition that the thing in question *is* impermanent. For him to observe the thing in that class of similar instances means that he has ascertained its basic presence there. [228] However, this does not necessarily mean that he has ascertained that it is present *only* in that class. Why? Even though he has confirmed by valid cognition that the thing in question is in [that class and is therefore impermanent], he may not yet have ascertained with a valid cognition that *any case of the thing in question is necessarily* [impermanent]. Statements [in the treatises] seeming to refer to cases where the forward pervasion is not confirmed because although a thing has been observed in the class of similar instances it has not been *ascertained* there should be understood in this light. They refer to this specific form of ascertainment—that is, ascertainment that the thing is present *only* in the class of similar instances. Once this point has been grasped, one can fully appreciate why the term *ascertained* must be used in conjunction with the word *only* when defining the forward and reverse pervasions. Without this appreciation, one is liable to simply repeat these words like an empty incantation.

This explanation of the way a thing is observed and ascertained in the class of similar instances should be extended to the class of dissimilar instances. [By understanding this,] one can rest comfortably, safe from all sorts of critical attack—such as that of someone arguing that if something is observed to be a known thing, it must follow that it is a member of the class of dissimilar instances with respect to the proof "Sound is impermanent."[657]

Present-day Tibetan "logicians" struggle to give a [coherent] account of the class of similar and dissimilar instances in the same way that the sightless struggle to make out the form of an elephant.

Investigating whether there can be a correct reason [that establishes something about] a subject that is a nonexistent

Some have asserted that the subject of interest in a correct proof must be an established basis. If the subject were not an established basis, they say, how would it be possible for a valid cognition to ascertain that the reason is present within it? And if the presence of the reason could not be ascertained in it, then the whole proof would be flawed, because there would be no way of confirming the property of the subject. They also say if the subject that is supposed to serve as the basis [of the property] is ruled out,[658] the grouping that it forms with the predicate is also ruled out. So there would also be the flaw that the proof's thesis is something actually *disproved*[659] by valid cognition.

[Response:] The [assertion that the subject must be an existent] is incorrect. In the proof establishing that "A self that is a self-supporting substance, the nature of which sets it apart from the aggregates [A], does not exist [B]," the subject is not an established basis.

In an attempt to answer this criticism, someone claims that the proof in question actually uses simply "the person" as its subject and then refutes that it has a self that is a self-supporting substance, the nature of which sets it apart from the aggregates.

[Response:] This is untenable. His formulation of the proof only negates that the person has such a self. It does not rule out the existence of such a self as an individual isolate.[660]

According to one fool, the *śabdārtha* of such a self serves as the subject in the above proof. [229]

[Response:] By making such an assertion, all that he manages to do is advertise his own deficiencies. What he says is tantamount to conceding that this *śabdārtha* itself does not exist!

Others have formulated the proof in [another] way: "Such a self of persons [A] does not exist [B], because it is not observed by valid cognition to be either identical with or distinct from the aggregates [C]." They say that [in the mind of] the other party, the independent person is merged with the *śabdārtha* of such a person, and that when this party engages the subject of interest, he actually engages the two of them together. Thus it is with the *śabdārtha* serving as the basis that valid cognition establishes the reason [in relation to this subject]. [They feel] that it is necessary to have "independent person" as the subject of the proof, because it is only in this way that the proof can rule out the whole notion of such a self. They also believe that they can justifiably identify the *śabdārtha* of such as self as the subject, because [in the mind of] the other party, there is no distinction between the self of persons and the *śabdārtha* of that self of persons. To sum up, these individuals contend that *both* the independent person and the *śabdārtha* of the independent person count as the subject(s) in the proof.

[Response:] Their reasons for asserting that the *śabdārtha* also constitutes the subject of interest in the proof are that (1) when the other party engages the subject of the proof, for him the self will be merged with a *śabdārtha* of the self, (2) even after that point, he will engage the self with the firm impression that it is the same thing as the *śabdārtha* that presents itself as though it were a self of persons, and (3) this *śabdārtha* is what serves as the basis [allowing] valid cognition to confirm the presence of the reason [in the subject]. This they contrast with the situation of a proof such as that establishing "Sound is impermanent because it is produced." Here, although "produced" must also be confirmed, the *śabdārtha* [cannot serve as the basis], because produced is not present in the *śabdārtha* of sound. They conclude by saying that a correct proof must always have a subject that is an established basis, but not everything that counts as a subject for such a proof is an established basis.[661]

Our analysis of this is as follows. Would they formulate the predicate and reason of such a proof as "There is no such self [B], because nowhere is such a self found to be either the same nature as or distinct from the aggregates [C]"? Or would [the proof] simply be "*X* [A] does not exist [B], because nowhere is *x* found to be either the same nature as or distinct from the aggregates [C]"? If it was the first formulation, it would follow that the proof's whole thesis forms its predicate! But if it was the second formulation, it would follow that [the proof is] "The *śabdārtha* of such a self [A] does not exist [B], because nowhere is it found to be either the same nature as or distinct from the aggregates [C]." The three spheres [for this argument are in place].

We could also consider the proof "In that specific location engulfed in a bluish haze [A], there is no smoke [B], because no fire is observed there [C]." [230] [Based on their position] it would follow that, corresponding with the previous proof, the *śabdārtha* of such a location forms the proof's subject.

But that would directly contradict [the Seven Treatises], which say that the subject of this proof is overtly established by valid perception.[662] In my judgment, it will be extremely difficult for them to explain how [their assertion that the *śabdārtha* counts as the subject in one proof] does not also extend to proofs such as "Sound is impermanent because it is produced."

As far as we are concerned, the sort of self already referred to is the *only* subject of interest in the proof in question. Despite this, the proof is not flawed on the grounds that its subject is something not established. The probandum of such a proof is formed through a grouping of the subject and [the predicate] "totally without existence." The very fact that the subject is *not* an established basis is the thesis, and valid cognition's nonverification of that subject is the probans. If the subject were an established basis, the thesis would be one that valid cognition disproved. Thus it can be declared that as long as the subject is not an established basis, the grouping it forms when combined with [the predicate] "totally without existence" will necessarily exist. This is similar to the way that with respect to any established basis, a hare's horn is necessarily totally without existence.

Also, the proof [with a subject that is not an existent] is not flawed on the grounds that there is no way to confirm the reason as a property of the subject. This is because even though the sort of self already referred to is not verified by valid cognition, the fact that nowhere is such a self observed to be either the same nature as or distinct from the aggregates *is* verified by valid cognition. And all known things are [confirmation] of that.[663]

The "subject" literally refers to something that serves as a "basis," with respect to which, through a process of reasoning, various properties—either negative or positive—can, *in the realm of conception*, be ruled out or affirmed. This does not suggest that the basis and its property are two separate things *in objective terms*, or [even necessarily] that the basis actually exists. Consequently, there is no inconsistency [in asserting] that someone might be interested to learn whether something is [a property of] another thing even though that other thing does not actually exist, just as there is no inconsistency in asserting that what is cited as the similar example to help someone ascertain the [proof's] pervasion might not actually be an existent.

This is how we respond to the charge that if the subject is not an established basis, the thesis of the proof would be undermined and there would be no way to confirm the property of the subject. And having now given this response, there is no need to belabor the issue any further.

This is plainly how Kamalaśīla explained the point.[664] There are also passages such as [in Dignāga's *Compendium*], where it says, "[That determined by] perception, inferential cognition, [inferences of] conviction, and of agreement: [each of these has its] own foundation."[665] In this, there is no suggestion that having a subject whose existence is negated necessarily invalidates the proof, only that it requires some subject that is established to serve as a basis, and that without this, the proof would be flawed. This is why he uses the phrase "its own foundation." [231]

Examining for whom the reason [must count as] a correct one

Regarding the point at which something actually serves as the correct reason, it is said that the second party is someone who is curious about the thesis. The [other person] is a proper first party, who has presented the proof's reason to [that second party], having ensured that [he, the first party,] has also already supplied [the second party] with as much verification that the reason [fulfills each of the three] individual criteria of that reason as [the second party] may have required. When the second party has ascertained the [fulfillment of the] three criteria and is on the verge of ascertaining the thesis, it is the [exact] point that the reason becomes a correct one, when it can be said that it actually is the correct reason that will give rise to a valid inferential cognition of the thesis.

There is also the question of whether it counts as a correct reason for the first party. Someone claims that it does not count as a correct reason for that first party on the grounds that it does not fulfill the criteria of the property of the subject for him. Why not? Because the first party does not have the requisite curiosity regarding the establishment of that thesis. To support his assertion [that such curiosity is a definite requirement], this individual refers to the passage "because the reason is stated [to someone who entertains a] doubt."[666]

[Response:] We reject what he says and instead assert that when a proper first party presents "produced" [as the reason] to prove the thesis "Sound is impermanent," produced *does* count as a correct reason for him, because it fulfills the three criteria of such a reason. To deny this is to contradict the pronouncement

> Having ascertained [it] for himself, he wishes to induce ascertainment in another. He need communicate nothing apart from the property of the subject, the relationship, and the thesis.[667]

The words "because the reason is stated [to someone who entertains a] doubt" definitely say that curiosity is a prerequisite for the second party, who is ready to have a correct reason presented to him. What they do not say is that only [in the context of] being presented to such an individual can something qualify as a correct reason.

Some may object to this, saying that if "produced" counts as a correct reason for the first party in the context of that particular proof, then similarly "Sound is impermanent" must count as a thesis that has yet to be established for him.

[Response:] The two cases do not correspond. The fact that the first party has already realized that sound is impermanent can itself be used as the probans establishing that "Sound is impermanent" does *not* count as a probandum for him. [By contrast,] the fact that the [same] first party has ascertained the [fulfillment of the] three criteria by valid cognition can be used as the probans establishing that produced *does* count as a correct reason for him.[668]

One can but marvel at the [antics] of the foolish logicians of the present day. On the one hand, they proclaim that if the first party had not established the property of the subject, the reason would count as one of the unconfirmed variety. But on the other, they now say that something can only qualify as a correct reason if the property of the subject is *not* established for the first party. [232] And how undaunted they show themselves to be as they move around shouldering this enormous burden of contradictions. Such slaves to ignorance!

I could say a great deal more on this topic, but I see no compelling reason to do so. It would only add to the volume of this work, and so I have not bothered.

Identifying each of the [elements] within the correct proof: the reason, the subject, and the predicate[669]

1. Refutation of others' assertions
2. Setting forth our own position

Refutation of others' assertions

Using the proof "Sound is impermanent because it is produced" to illustrate his point, someone proposes that [one can speak of] two sets of these [components]. One set is made up of things that, according to a *misguided impression*,[670] are the subject, the predicate, and the reason, whereas the other set is the things that *actually serve*[671] as those three. The one who presents the proof has the misguided impression that sound (the subject), impermanence (the predicate), and produced (the reason) are *specifically characterized*. But in fact the things that actually serve as the subject, predicate, and the reason are the object universals of, respectively, sound, impermanent, and produced. Specifically characterized versions of produced, impermanent, and so forth cannot really serve as the three [components], because if they were specifically characterized, he claims, there would be no way that the thing serving as the reason could have concomitance with that which serves as the example.

[Response:] This is not tenable. It would follow that when the individual presents "produced" as the correct reason to establish the proof "Sound is impermanent," even though he is under the impression that the produced in question is something specifically characterized, in actuality it is [only in terms of] establishing something about the object universals of produced, sound, and impermanent that it becomes a correct reason. This is because the form of the proof and the way it is presented mean that it is of the identity variety establishing that "Sound *is* impermanent," and even though there is the impression that the sound, impermanent, and produced that act as the subject, predicate, and reason are specifically characterized, only their object universals serve as the three in actuality. If he accepts this, it would follow that the proof in question uses the object universal of produced to establish that the object universal of sound is the object universal of impermanent, and thus the reason of the proof should be classified as *unconfirmed*, whereas its pervasion should be classified as *contrary*. Why? Because the object universal of sound is *not* the object universal of produced, and the object universal of produced is necessarily precluded from being the object universal of impermanent. If the object universal of one thing did not preclude that of another, then it would mean that the [conceptually] isolated identities of produced and impermanent do not preclude each other. [233]

Furthermore, it would follow that whatever instantiates that predicate is permanent, because whatever instantiates it is a non-actual thing. The reason is what you yourself asserted. But if you were to accept [this argument's conclusion], it would blatantly contradict your earlier assertion that only something that is impermanent can count as a similar instance for this proof. And it would also mean, correspondingly, that what instantiates the object of comprehension for the valid inferential cognition realizing that sound is impermanent is permanent.

Similarly, it would follow that permanent is not the anti-predicate[672] for the proof "Sound is impermanent because it is produced," since whatever is the predicate in that proof is pervaded by being permanent. The reason is one that you have accepted. The pervasion also holds. This is because a proof establishes whatever instantiates the predicate, and it negates whatever instantiates the anti-predicate. And *to rule out a pervading [category] is to rule out the members pervaded by that [category].*

Also, you say that it is only according to a misguided impression that sound and impermanent as a group constitute the proof's thesis, whereas the actual thesis is made up of the object universals of sound and impermanent. But from this it would follow that these object universals cannot constitute the thesis of the proof establishing that sound is impermanent, because they are not what the first party believes constitute the thesis. If you deny this reason, it would go against your assertion that the first party is under the impression that sound and impermanent are the thesis.

There are many other ways in which [your position] can be attacked, but as cataloguing them all would require too much space, I refrain from writing any more here. Anyway, extrapolating from what I have set out here, one should reject any assertion that what instantiates the subject, predicate, and reason in the proof establishing "Sound is impermanent" are not actual things. Anyone who denies that a specifically characterized thing can be concomitant with the example [used in the proof] is basically declaring that something specifically characterized can never have a concomitant association with numerous other things with which it shares common features. This is a notion that I have refuted at some length above.

Setting forth our own system

When one is establishing "Sound is impermanent because it is produced," the subject of interest is "sound," the predicate is "impermanent," and the reason is "produced." In themselves, the subject of interest, the predicate, and the reason of the logical proof are conceptual constructs. However, the things that instantiate the subject, the predicate, and the reason in this case are respectively, sound, impermanent, and produced, things that are the very opposite of constructs. [234] Sound, impermanent, and produced are not constructs, but they constitute the subject of interest and so forth in the proof in question. The classification of sound *as* the subject of interest, of impermanent *as* the predicate, and of produced *as* the reason are constructs. The reasoning behind this has already been set out in detail.

18. Varieties of Correct Reason

Varieties of correct logical reason

1. Logical reasons divided in terms of the type of evidence that they use
2. Logical reasons divided in terms of what type of thing they set out to prove
3. Logical reasons divided in terms of the domain with which they deal

Logical reasons divided in terms of the type of evidence that they use

1. Effect as a correct reason
2. Nature as a correct reason
3. Nonobservation as a correct reason

Effect as a correct reason

1. Literal meaning
2. Defining characteristics
3. Varieties
4. Analysis of the scheme

Literal meaning of "effect reason"

The name *effect reason* derives from the fact that with this kind of proof, the thing overtly presented as the reason is an effect, and it is used to learn something about that thing that is overtly presented as the predicate of the proof, a cause of that effect.

Defining characteristics

The correct effect reason is defined as "a reason that fulfills the three criteria and establishes the presence of the cause—that thing overtly stated as the predicate—of its effect—that thing overtly presented as the reason—within the subject of interest for that particular proof."

VARIETIES

1. In the proof "On the pass where there is billowing smoke [A], there is fire [B] because there is billowing smoke [C]," [C] is a correct effect reason of the variety that *overtly proves a cause.*
2. In the proof "The [auditory] cognition hearing the sound of the Vedas [A] must have been preceded by its cause, an impermanent sound [B], because it is an auditory cognition arising from effort [C]," [C] is a correct effect reason of the variety that *proves there was a preceding cause.*
3. In the proof "The sense consciousness of a visual form [A] must have some other cause, in addition to a sense power and a mental consciousness [B], because it does not arise when only a sense power and a mental consciousness are produced [C]," [C] is a correct effect reason of the variety that *establishes the detail of a specific cause.* [235]
4. In the proof "True suffering [A] must have its own cause(s) [B] because it is an actual thing that only arises on certain occasions [C]," [C] is a correct effect reason of the variety that *establishes a cause in terms of an individual isolated identity.*[673]
5. In the proof "The present taste of molasses from the lump of molasses in one's mouth [A] is something that must have been preceded by its cause, the taste of the molasses at an earlier point, which must, [in turn, also] have had the potential to act as the supporting condition [producing] the visible form of the present molasses [B] because it is the present taste of molasses [C]," [C] is a correct effect reason for *deducing a feature of a cause.*

This list does not represent a comprehensive typology of effect reasons. The name assigned to a reason is nothing more than a reflection of what the second party wishes to know and what the first party wants him to infer by means of the proof. As these two factors determine the way a proof might be formulated, the potential for different varieties is essentially limitless. All sorts of others are possible, such as, "A sprout [A] is something that can only be produced from a whole array of causes and conditions assembled together [B] because it is an actual thing that is not produced unless the full range of its substantial cause(s) and various supporting conditions are in place [C]." Thus, while different varieties of effect reasons have been listed here, the distinctions among them are only conventions and do not inhere in the objects themselves. One could equally well classify the [first proof, about] "fire on the pass," as one that belongs to the [third category] that establishes the detail of a specific cause.

Analysis of the scheme

1. Identifying the reason, the subject, and the predicate
2. Explaining which valid cognitions are responsible for ascertaining that each of the three criteria [are fulfilled]
3. Addressing the qualm that this type of reasoning is flawed

Identifying the reason, subject, and predicate

1. Refutation of others' assertions
2. Setting forth our own position

Refutation of others' assertions

Someone claims that in the proof "On the smoky mountain pass [A], fire exists [B] because smoke exists [C]," the predicate is just "fire," as opposed to "fire exists," and that the reason is just "smoke," as opposed to "smoke exists."

[Response:] The same view is particularly widespread among the current generation of "logicians." We, however, know that a huge number of damaging attacks can be made against it. [For instance,] it would follow that the anti-predicate for the proof is "non-fire" because the predicate in the proof is fire. But if one accepts that, it would follow that the proof negates smoke on the smoky mountain pass, because it rules out non-fire in that place. The pervasion holds, because [smoke is in the category of non-fire, and] to rule out a pervading [category] is to rule out the members pervaded by that [category]. [236]

Also, it would follow that at the point that kitchen stove serves as a similar example [for this proof], the congruity that the kitchen stove and the smoky mountain pass would need to share with the proof's reason and predicate would require them to be congruous with those two—smoke and fire—[in the sense of being them]. But how can this be accepted? For the stove to have this kind of congruity with smoke is impossible![674]

Also, if non-fire is what the proof negates, it would follow that anything that instantiates [non-fire belongs to the class of] dissimilar instances. But then it would absurdly follow that the subject "mountain pass," the reason "smoke," and the similar example "kitchen stove" are all dissimilar instances for this proof.

He may respond by denying that non-fire is the anti-predicate for the proof, identifying instead the "nonexistence of fire" as that.

[Response:] If that were the case, it would mean that the predicate affirmed by the proof is not "fire" but the "existence of fire." Why? Because the anti-predicate for a proof must always be identified as the *diametrical opposite of* its *predicate*. Also, [we may consider the proof] "The sense consciousness of a visual form [A] must have a cause other than [just] a sense power and a mental consciousness [B] because it does not arise when only a sense power and a mental consciousness are produced [C]." It follows that "a cause other than [just] a sense power and a mental consciousness" is the predicate.[675] If he accepts that, it would follow that the negation of that is the anti-predicate. But from this it would follow that [what the proof] rules out is that "the sense consciousness of visual form" *is* not "a cause other than [just] a sense and mental consciousness." But that would be ludicrous, since it would be ruling out that the sense power and mental consciousness are causes for that [sense consciousness].[676] Thus such a position can only bring one to grief.

Setting forth our own position

Our position is that in the aforesaid proof, "fire exists" is the predicate, and "smoke exists" is the reason. This may prompt some to ask: If [the proof uses the *presence* or *existence* of smoke as its reason], why is it still described as one that uses an effect as its reason?

[Response:] We could equally well ask them to justify why they are prepared to describe the proof that negates the presence of cold [in a certain place] as one of "nonobservation," even though the thing that is cited as its reason is in fact a valid *observation* of fire.

They may concede that what is overtly presented as the reason in that proof is an observation but argue that, when one gets down to the root of the proof, it is one that deals with nonobservation.

[Response:] In line with this, we can equally well claim that the ["smoke"] proof deserves to be described as one that uses an effect as its reason, because the proof has a cause and an effect at its heart, and when one uses the presence of smoke to infer the presence of fire, what one is relying on is the fact that fire and smoke are cause and effect.

Explaining which valid cognitions are responsible for ascertaining that each of the three criteria [are fulfilled]

In the majority of cases, the cognition that confirms the reason in an [effect] proof will be valid *perception*. And in most situations, the pervasion of the proof is something that [the person] is able to confirm due to having [already] validly ascertained that the things involved are cause and effect. So are the valid cognitions that ascertain cause and effect those [that occur] when the "sets" of valid cognition ascertain fire and smoke to be cause and effect?[677] [237] When the party involved is someone of sharper mental faculties, he will be able to ascertain that smoke is the effect of fire with just "perception in a single set," which observes smoke arising from fire. When someone is of mediocre faculties, he will first require a perception of some location where there is neither fire nor smoke. Next, he requires a perception of fire, and then another of smoke arising in that location due to the presence of the fire. Hence he will be able to ascertain that smoke is the effect of fire with the help of "perceptions in three sets," which allow him to ascertain the affirmative side of the concomitance, according to which smoke will necessarily have arisen due to the presence of fire.

Alternatively, [a person of mediocre faculties] may first have a perception of both fire and smoke, then one that witnesses the expiration of the fire in that same location, and then another, observing that the halting of the fire brings in its wake the expiration of the smoke in the location. Here the "sets" of valid cognitions that help the person to ascertain that smoke is the effect of fire are those concerned with the reversal [of the production process].

[Finally,] when the person is of weaker faculties, he must first have a perception of a location where there is neither fire nor smoke. Next, he must perceive a fire in that location. And this must be followed by another perception, witnessing that the presence of fire brings in its wake the production of smoke in that location. After that, he must have a perception that observes the expiration of fire in that location, followed by another one, observing that the expiration of fire brings in its wake the cessation of the smoke. That is to say, it is with the help of "perceptions in five sets," concerned with ascertainment of both the affirmative and negative sides of the concomitance that he will be able to ascertain that smoke is the effect of fire. This is also the way that it works with other causes and effects.

It is therefore with the help of these valid cognitions that one comes to the ascertainment that fire and smoke are cause and effect, and with it the ability to ascertain that *smoke is produced due to the presence of fire and that the absence of fire guarantees that smoke will also be absent.* Thus it is these perceptions that are said to be responsible for establishing the [cause and effect] *relationship* underpinning the pervasion[678] in the proof that uses the existence of smoke to establish the existence of fire. However, these perceptions can never encounter the relationship between fire and smoke or the relationship that underpins the pervasion in any direct sense, as these [relationships] are conceptual constructs.

It is still true, however, that despite seeing for themselves that smoke is produced due to the presence of fire and is absent when fire is absent, certain ignorant opponents remain unaware that the conventional way to describe this is to say that fire and smoke are "cause and effect." Unless there were such individuals, how could the Cārvāka have dreamed up the idea that there can be such a thing as smoke that is [produced] from no cause at all? Such an individual can only ascertain that fire and smoke are cause and effect if [the fact is presented] to him in the form of a logical proof. The proof is "Smoke [A] is the effect of fire [B] because its appearance or disappearance depends upon whether or not fire has been there to facilitate [its production] [C]." And this is why it was necessary [for Dharmakīrti] to describe that reasoning in the passage "The effect of fire is smoke, because it accords with the features of an effect."[679] [238]

Addressing the qualm that this type of reasoning is flawed

The following qualm has been raised. With this form of reasoning, the presence of smoke on a mountain pass is used to establish the presence of fire there. If fire and smoke were not cause and effect, the proof would not count as one that uses an effect as its reason. But if they are cause and effect, the cause cannot be present when the effect is, and neither can the effect be present when the cause is. This must mean that when the smoke is present on the pass, the fire that had been its cause would no longer be there. So, at the point that it is possible to confirm the property of the subject in the proof, its thesis is countered by valid cognition, and at the point that its thesis can be confirmed, the property of the subject cannot be established, because when there is fire on the pass, its effect, smoke, has not yet arisen.

[Response:] There is no such flaw. The existence of smoke on the pass is not meant to establish that fire exists there *at the time of the smoke.* Rather, it proves the existence of the fire, the cause of that smoke, without making any specification regarding time. The presence of smoke on the pass does not mean that the fire that was its cause is also present [there] at the same time; it just means that it *must have been* there. The afternoon of a certain day, for example, cannot exist without its cause, the morning. But the morning need not exist *when* the afternoon does. Hence we can talk about a specific day and say that the afternoon exists *because* the morning exists. In this, we find no grounds for criticizing the logic, just as the establishment of the property of the subject does not disprove the thesis.

The point to appreciate is that the proof establishing the existence of fire through the existence of smoke makes no specific reference to time. The "mountain pass"—that it uses as its subject and in which it locates the fire and smoke—is a whole comprising two temporal portions, one being the stage in which fire exists and the other being that in which its effect smoke exists.

This concludes the explanation of correct effect reasons.

Nature as a correct reason

1. Defining characteristics
2. Varieties
3. Explaining which valid cognitions are responsible for ascertaining that each of the three criteria [are fulfilled] [239]

Defining characteristics

The nature reason is defined as "a reason—fulfilling the three criteria—that establishes something affirmative regarding a predicate with which it shares the same nature and does so without relying on the two phenomena that are overtly presented as the reason and the predicate being cause and effect."

Varieties

There are two. The first of these, the correct nature reason of the "plain" variety, is defined as "a correct nature reason that is conveyed by words that indicate nothing about the process and causes upon which its production depends."

An example of this is "actual thing" when it is presented as the reason in the proof "Sound is impermanent because it is an actual thing." As noted above, some cite "[it] exists among actual things" as the reason used in this proof, but I have already refuted this.

The second correct nature reason, that of the "specified dependence" variety, is defined as "a correct nature reason that is conveyed by words that indicate the process and causes upon which its production depends."

This can further be divided into those in which the process and causes of production are not [presented as] separate from the thing in question and those in which they are [presented as] separate from that thing. In the proof "Sound is impermanent because it has production," "has production" is an example of the first. The second is further divided into those in which the processes and causes of production are conveyed explicitly and those in which they are conveyed by implication. "Produced from causes and conditions" is an example of the first of these in the proof "Sound is impermanent because it is produced from causes and conditions," whereas "produced" would be a case of the second, in the proof "Sound is impermanent because it is produced."

Explaining which valid cognitions are responsible for ascertaining that each of the three criteria [are fulfilled]

In the case of the formal proof "Sound is impermanent because it is produced," which are the valid cognitions that bring about ascertainment that the three criteria [are fulfilled]? [Considering first] the property of the subject, if the person in question is someone of sharper mental faculties, he will be able to ascertain the property of the subject with the help of a perception of sound arising from its causes and conditions. Certain of those with weaker faculties, on the other hand, will only be able to ascertain it with the help of a valid inferential cognition of the kind that deals with names and expressions.[680]

The pervasions are ascertained with the help of [two] inferential valid cognitions, each of which is founded upon a [correct] reason. In the case of the inferential cognition that ascertains the forward pervasion, the reason used is of the "[preparative] nonreliance" variety,[681] and in the case of the reverse pervasion, it is of the "[preparative] countering" variety.[682]

With the first of these, the proof is formulated thus: "Something produced [A] is, from the very moment of its formation, destined for destruction [B], because its destruction is built into it by its causes and is not something dependent upon the intervention of external agencies [C], just as is the case, for example, with a flash of lightning." The perception of the [lightning] used as the [illustrative] example here is what helps one ascertain the pervasion of this proof. The property of the subject is ascertained by means of a valid cognition that relies on the use of a [preparative] countering proof. [240] One reasons, for instance, [if external agencies were required to cause the destruction of the produced thing,] would the thing's destruction form part of its nature, or would it stand aloof from it as a separate entity? The first of these alternatives can be dismissed, because any feature that forms part of the substance of the produced thing must have been created by the same causes as [the produced thing itself] and therefore could not constitute separate external agents that arose only after the produced thing appeared. However, the second alternative is [equally untenable], because then the destruction for which the external agents are responsible would not be the destruction of the produced thing at all but a destruction that was quite separate and aloof from it.

Second, the [preparative] countering logic that establishes the reverse pervasion [of the main proof is]: "A permanent thing [A] is devoid of [any sort of] production [B] because it is devoid of any functional activity, either gradual or sudden [C], just as is the case, for example, with noncomposite space." The pervasion of this proof is established by discounting the possibility of any third alternative for activity besides those of the gradual and sudden varieties. Regarding the property of the subject, the [possibility] that something permanent could give rise to all effects suddenly [and simultaneously] is countered by perception, which informs one that effects are produced gradually over a period of time. And as these effects are produced gradually, over time, one must accept that the cause(s) themselves have many temporal stages, due to which the results that they yield arise sequentially. Those causes must therefore be impermanent, and any idea that they could be permanent is dismissed.

The master [Dharmakīrti] stated that "One cannot ascertain the pervasion unless there is a relationship."[683] That is, it is necessary to confirm the relationship between [two things] in order to establish the forward and reverse pervasions [in which they are involved]. This can be explained as follows: (1) Production is different from impermanence, and (2) the absence of impermanence guarantees the absence of production. This [formula] encapsulates what it is for production to be related to impermanence. Production's relationship with impermanence[684]—in terms of which "the absence of impermanence also guarantees the absence of production"—is established by the [aforesaid preparative] countering logic. How so? Because through this [preparative] countering proof, it is established that any basis for which impermanence is ruled out is necessarily also one for which production must be ruled out. To sum up, it is through this [preparative] countering proof that one ascertains the [eliminative side of the] formula encapsulating what it is for production to be related to impermanence—namely, any basis for which impermanence is ruled out is necessarily also one for which production is ruled out. It is in dependence upon ascertainment of this, together with a valid cognition of the produced [thing] that serves as the reason [in the main proof], that one comes to ascertain the forward and reverse concomitance [contained] in the proof.

At this point, the following matter should be considered. [241] One uses the fact that what is permanent is not involved in any sort of activity to gain a valid cognition that permanence is devoid of production. But does the valid cognition ascertain that production is impossible for *every* ostensive instantiation of permanence[685] or not? If it does not ascertain that, would this mean that the other party could still harbor doubts about whether some permanent things might be produced? If such doubts still lingered [in his mind] with regard to some things, it would mean that in spite of having generated the inferential cognition that arises from the above-stated [preparative] countering logic, the individual would still not be convinced that the reason [i.e., "produced"] is totally absent from the class of dissimilar instances [i.e., "permanent"]. So in what sense could that valid cognition be the one responsible for ascertaining the reverse pervasion? Conversely, if the individual no longer harbored such doubts but the [preparative] countering valid cognition was not the one responsible for their removal [with respect to every thing], it would be necessary to point to another valid cognition that had performed that task. However, we find no other candidate. In any case, even assuming that it were possible to identify the valid cognition(s) that could perform the task, there would surely need to be an endless number of them, as the ostensive instantiations of permanence are limitless, and each of them would seem to need a separate valid cognition devoted to countering the doubt that it might have been produced.

Someone could therefore argue that if, when the [aforementioned] valid cognition comprehends that to be permanent is to be devoid of any sort of production, it [thereby] ascertains the impossibility of production for *every one* of the ostensive instantiations, then the valid cognition comprehending that to be produced is to be impermanent must similarly [thereby] ascertain that fact with respect to every single ostensive instantiation of production. But if it did so, that valid cognition would also need to ascertain it with respect to sound. However, if that were true, when the opponent ascertains the pervasion of the proof, he would already have realized its thesis [i.e., that sound is impermanent].

[Response:] We deny that there are grounds for such a criticism. The [preparative] countering valid cognition does not itself ascertain that *each one* of the ostensive instantiations of permanence is not produced. However, it still manages to eliminate any occurrence of the distorted notion that there *are* such things. At any later point, whenever the person involved turns his attention to a specific permanent thing, he will be able to ascertain that it is devoid of any sort of production without needing to rely upon any other valid cognition.

However, someone could argue, the distorted notion that to be an instantiation of production does not necessarily entail being impermanent is a notion that the valid cognition ascertaining the forward pervasion should itself therefore be capable of eliminating. But from this, he might say, it would absurdly follow that someone who has ascertained the forward pervasion would thereby also necessarily be rid of distorted notions regarding the thesis.

[Response:] There is no correspondence between these two. If something is encompassed by the universal, it is not necessarily encompassed by [every] particular of that universal, whereas if a universal is ruled out, then all the particulars of that universal are also necessarily ruled out.

This concludes the brief explanation of correct nature reasons.

Nonobservation as a correct reason

1. Defining characteristics
2. Varieties [242]

Defining characteristics

Some define a correct nonobservation reason as "that in which (1) the nonobservation of some phenomenon—one that either should or should not be apparent with regard to the subject for the proof in question—is presented as the reason, and (2) [that thing presented as the reason] is confirmed by valid cognition to have [fulfilled] the three criteria [qualifying it as one that] negates its negandum."

[Response:] This is a wild claim that completely fails to take account [of the whole category of nonobservation reason known as] "reasons [that involve] the observation of something that is preclusive [with what is being negated]."[686]

Others have defined a correct nonobservation reason as "a correct reason used in a proof, the predicate of which is a negative phenomenon."

[Response:] Based on that criterion, it would follow that *every* correct reason is of the nonobservation kind. Why? Because the "predicate" of a proof is a negative phenomenon. This is because the predicate [component] of any proof is a non-actual thing, in that it is constructed by thought. This does not mean, of course, that whatever instantiates the predicate in a correct proof is necessarily a non-actual thing and negative. It just means that the predicate itself is a non-actual thing and negative. One therefore needs to exercise discernment to distinguish between the [constructed] identity itself and the thing to which that identity [is assigned].[687]

In our own system, a correct reason of nonobservation is defined like this: "(1) It is something that fulfills the three criteria of the reason for the proof in question, and (2) whatever is the predicate of that proof is necessarily a straight negation."

[In establishing a thing,] a correct reason must always confirm something that is a negative phenomenon. The proof that sound is impermanent, for instance, confirms by implication that [sound is] not permanent. Consequently, when one has a valid inferential cognition that overtly realizes sound is impermanent, it will also realize by implication that sound is *not permanent*.

However, in cases where the reason is of the effect or nature varieties, the predicate in a proof will be something positive. The proof overtly establishes that this predicate is [present] in the subject and also confirms by implication some negative [fact] about the subject. So it establishes an implicative negation. When the reason is of the nonobservation variety, however, the thing overtly established by the predicate of the proof must be a straight negation. Thus affirmative and negative reasons remain distinguishable from each other. This is why [Dharmakīrti] says:

> because [reasons of this kind] make no assertion with respect to a thing but simply negate.
> That is not the case with the other [kind of] proof; they assert something.[688]

Varieties

There are two types of nonobservation reason: those involving the nonobservation of something that is not accessible and those involving the nonobservation of something that should be apparent. [243]

Proofs using the nonobservation of a thing that is not accessible as their reason

The first is defined as "something that (1) fulfills the three criteria of the reason in a proof negating that a phenomenon definitely exists for a person when (2) that phenomenon exists, despite the fact that it is not accessible to the person in question and (3) his failure to validly cognize it is presented as the proof's reason."

An example of this is the reason as presented in the following proof: "With regard to the space before him [A], the individual for whom a *piśāci* spirit is a remote entity is in no position to express, as certain fact, that the *piśāci* spirit is present [B], because the valid cognition of an individual for whom a *piśāci* spirit is a remote entity does not observe a *piśāci* spirit [C]."

The person to whom one presents such a proof need not himself be someone for whom the *piśāci* counts as a remote entity. It is quite possible that one presents it to some other party with whom one is debating the matter, analyzing whether the individual [referred to in the proof] is actually in a position to make categorical judgments regarding the presence of such a spirit.

Others have formulated the proof in a different way. According to them it should be "With regard to the space before us [A], the presence of a *piśāci* is not something that can be expressed as certain fact [B], because the remote entity, a *piśāci*, is not observed by valid cognition [C]." They say that what this proof refutes is that the presence of the *piśāci* is certain fact. But they deny that it can prove, as certain fact, that the *piśāci* is *not* present. And because of this, [they conclude] that in the location in question, the *piśāci* is *neither* definitely present *nor* absent.

[Response:] Based on that formulation, it would follow that in the location before us, no omniscient awareness observes such a remote *piśāci*, because *no* valid cognition observes a *piśāci* in that space. The [argument's] reason is the one they have asserted. But if they accept [its conclusion], it would go against their own denial that the *piśāci* is definitely absent in that space. Thus, according to their position, by confirming the property of the subject in that proof [i.e., that there is no valid cognition of a *piśāci* spirit in that location], the person would also gain the certain knowledge that there was no *piśāci* there. But this would fly in the face of numerous treatise pronouncements on the matter and would also contradict what these individuals themselves have stated on the topic. Added to that, if the person in question really could know with certainty that there was no *piśāci* in that location, how could it be said that it is a remote entity for him?

Next, we turn to the issue of whether "nonobservation of a thing that is not accessible" should be regarded as a literal or figurative [description]. Why exactly is something referred to by this [designation]?

1. Refutation of others' assertions
2. Setting forth our own position

Refutation of others' assertions

Someone claims that the aforesaid reason [should be classified as] one that involves the nonobservation of a *cause.* [244] Why? Because the anti-predicate of the proof is, he says, "the expression, as certain fact, that a *piśāci* is definitely present," and the cause for such an expression is a valid cognition verifying [the presence] of a *piśāci*. In support of this claim, he cites *Commentary on Pramāṇa* where it says, "because engagement is preceded by cognition."[689] Thus, he argues, since the proof is one that uses the nonobservation of the cause to negate an effect, it must be classified as one that uses the nonobservation of a cause as its reason.

Although [other] ignorant individuals concur with him on this point, one among them says that *because* the proof in question involves the nonobservation of something that "should be apparent" it cannot be [classified as] the nonobservation of something "not accessible." But another among them declares it to be a common locus of both varieties. Someone else holds that this *is* an authentic nonobservation reason of the "not accessible" [variety], although [he adds that] even if a proof involves the nonobservation of a cause, it is no guarantee that it is of the "should be apparent" [variety]. Those who say that the proof is of the "not accessible" variety give as their reason "because even though the referent for the anti-predicate[690] actually exists, it is something that cannot be observed." Whereas those who think it is of the "should be apparent" [variety] say that it must be classified as such "because if the referent for the negated anti-predicate existed, it would be something that could be observed."

[Response:] Those of limited intellect can be expected to come up with an endless supply of such notions, so why bother rebutting them at great length? Allowing ourselves to get caught up in assertions made by those with little wit and too much to say for themselves only robs us of the opportunity of analyzing matters of true significance in real depth. I will therefore address only one of these claims just by way of illustration.

[Based on what you, the first individual, claims,] it would follow that the valid cognition observing the [presence of] a *piśāci* in the location before us must *exist*, because [the cognition] is the cause [that gives rise] to the expression, as certain fact, that a *piśāci* is definitely present. The reason and predicate [of this argument] are exactly the ones that you proposed. Quite apart from that, more generally, we can say, "The valid cognition of a phenomenon is *not* the cause of the factually correct expression of the definite existence of that phenomenon, because [the cognition itself] *is* a factually correct expression of the definite existence of that phenomenon." That is the case, because such a valid cognition is a *cognitive expression*[691] of that fact. We agree that the passage "because engagement is preceded by cognition" conveys that one can only express the presence of a phenomenon as certain fact if that presence has been observed by a valid cognition. However, the passage mentions nothing about the valid cognition being the *cause* of that expression. [245]

Furthermore, the master [Dharmakīrti's *Commentary on Pramāṇa*] treatise, his autocommentary to it, and the commentators on his work have made it abundantly clear on numerous occasions that *all* nonobservation proofs negate that the presence [of some element] in the subject can be stated as a certain fact. The difference between the two varieties of proof is that while those of the "not accessible" [variety] are capable of doing this, they cannot prove, as certain fact, that the [element in question] is not actually present [in the subject]. Conversely, those of the "should be apparent" [variety] are able to negate that the presence [of that element] can be stated as certain fact and also negate the presence of that [element] itself. What this means is that the thought [of the aforesaid authorities] is that whenever the proof is of the "should be apparent" [variety], it overtly establishes that the anti-predicate is not present, and that in proving that is not present, the proof also undermines any notion that one could express the presence of that anti-predicate as certain fact.

[Elsewhere,] you have stated that when, for instance, the nonobservation of pot is used as the reason to establish that the pot is not present, the proof establishes only the *expression*[692] "pot is not present." Therefore you must acknowledge that such a proof negates another expression—namely, "pot is present." Proofs such as this, which cite the nonobservation of pot to establish that pot is not present in a specific location, are recognized as being ones that use reasons involving the nonobservation of a "nature." But [based on your claims] it would follow that even these proofs use the nonobservation of a *cause*. Why? Because such a proof negates an expression, such as "pot is definitely present," and such an expression [according to you] must have been preceded by a valid cognition of the pot's presence, so the proof is one that uses the absence of the cause [the valid cognition of a pot] as a reason to negate the effect [the expression about the presence of the pot]. So the three spheres are in place [and your position is shown to be irredeemably flawed]. And eventually you would be forced to concede that *all* correct proofs of nonobservation are actually those that use the nonobservation of a cause as their reason.

What distinguishes nonobservation proofs of the "should be apparent" and "not accessible" [varieties] from each other is not, then, to be found either in the anti-predicates [they negate] or in the referents of those anti-predicates. Rather, it is this. When the reason that the proof uses is the nonobservation of an element that may exist but is one that the person [in question] would not be able to detect, *even if it were present*, it is of the "not accessible" variety. And when the element is one that should, if it were present, be apparent, and the proof uses the nonobservation by valid cognition—or something that comes down to the same thing—of that element as its reason, then it is known as one of the "should be apparent" [variety]. To sum up then, the "non-observed" thing will either be one that would, if it were present, be apparent or one that would not be apparent, even if it were present. And it is this distinction that forms the basis of the two varieties of nonobservation proof.

Someone asserts that what serves as the reason in a proof of the not accessible variety is something that is not an established basis. But he also seeks to define a reason of this kind as "a correct nonobservation reason for which the referent of the anti-predicate would not be apparent, even were it to exist."

[Response:] He thereby tries to maintain that there is a common locus of something that is *not* an established basis and *is* a correct nonobservation reason. [246] What, once more, does this tell us about his character? His assertion is undercut by a single utterance, and the source of that utterance is himself!

Setting forth our own position

The reason in the proof [about the *piśāci*] is a correct nonobservation, one of the "not accessible" variety. It does *not*, however, use the nonobservation of a cause as its reason. It also goes without saying that it is not a nonobservation proof of the "should be apparent" variety. But while the reason used in the proof is a correct one, what are we to make of the passage "This does not result in certainty as to whether [something] is present or absent. Hence it does not [bring about] valid cognition"?[693]

This remark refers to the person for whom the *piśāci* is a remote entity.

The fact that the *piśāci* represents a remote entity for him means that he is in no position to determine whether or not one is present [in a certain location]. What the passage conveys is that the person's failure to observe, with a valid cognition, a *piśāci* [in the location] cannot be used as a reason to prove to him that a *piśāci* is definitely not present there. It is *not* denying that the person's failure to observe the *piśāci* can be used as a reason to negate that he is in a position to express, as certain fact, that a *piśāci* is present.

Proofs that use the nonobservation of a thing that should be apparent as their reason

The characteristics that define a reason of the second variety of nonobservation proof are as follows: it is "something that (1) fulfills the three criteria of the reason in a proof in which the other party is someone to whom a certain element should, if it were present, be apparent, (2) it is his failure to observe that element that is either used explicitly as the reason or is at the heart of that reason [in the proof], and (3) the predicate of the proof is a straight negation."

This has two varieties: those that involve the nonobservation of something related to [the element negated] being used as the correct reason and those that involve the observation of something that precludes [the element negated] being used as the correct reason.

The definition of the first type is as follows: it is "something that fulfills the three criteria of the reason in a proof that sets out to negate a certain element, and [the proof is one that] uses the absence of something related to that element as its reason."

This first variety is divided into four types, those that involve the nonobservation of (1) a cause of [the element negated], (2) something that encompasses [the element negated], (3) something that is the same nature as [the element negated], and (4) something that is a direct effect of [the element negated].

The first of these is defined as "something that fulfills the three criteria of the reason in a proof that sets out to negate a certain element, when [the proof is one that] uses the absence of a cause of that element as its reason." An example of this is the reason used in the proof "On the nighttime ocean over which a wispy substance hangs [A], there is no smoke [B] because there is no fire [C]."

Someone dismisses the idea that "ocean" could plausibly serve as the subject in this proof. He believes that there can be no one who has identified that something is an ocean but still wonders whether the thing above it might be smoke. [247]

[Response:] This is untenable, as it would follow that [equally] there could never be anyone who wondered whether what [he sees emanating] from the termite mound was smoke.[694]

[Second,] the proof that involves the nonobservation of something that encompasses what is being negated is defined as "something that fulfills the three criteria of the reason in a proof that sets out to explicitly negate a certain element, when [the proof is one that] uses, as its reason, the absence of a thing that encompasses and also shares the same nature as what is being negated." An example of this is the reason in the proof "On the rocky, treeless outcrop [A], there is no *śiṃśapā* [B] because no trees are observed [C]."

Again, someone objects to this, saying that anyone who recognizes the spot as "a rocky, treeless outcrop" would already have ascertained that there is no *śiṃśapā* present, and that this could not therefore serve as the subject.

[Response:] This is incorrect, as it discounts the possibility of a person who has not yet identified that an *śiṃśapā* is a tree.

Someone has stated the opinion that reasons involving the nonobservation of a cause or encompasser of the element that is being negated are employed when that element is such that even if it were present in the *location in question*, it would not be apparent to the valid cognition of the other party. And it is due to the [fact that it would not be apparent] that one must resort to the nonobservation of the cause or encompasser of the element to rule out [that element]. Otherwise, he says, one would use the nonobservation of [something that was] the same nature as that element [to rule it out].

[Response:] Well then, it would follow that a valid cognition capable of ascertaining whether or not smoke is present on the ocean with a wispy substance hanging over it cannot be generated in the continuum of the other party.[695] And thus it would follow that in such a location, smoke is a *remote entity* for that person! Furthermore, [we may cite the proof] "In a location that is totally enveloped by thick smoke [A], no large amount of snow can remain for very long [B], because it is [a place] enshrouded in a great amount of thick smoke [C]." Here also, it would follow that even if the element that is being negated were present [in the location], it would not be apparent to the other party, because if it were, then the proof employed to negate it would have been one involving the nonobservation of something that was the same nature as the element that is being negated, whereas it is in fact one that involves the observation of something [else] preclusive of that predicate.

The reason and the pervasion [of this argument] are the ones he himself proposed. But if he accepts [its conclusion], he would be saying that in that spot, the other party would be incapable of detecting a large amount of snow if it were there but he is capable of detecting a large amount of smoke. This is a scornful denial of common experience. It is also inconsistent for him to maintain that [the other party] would not be able to detect smoke even if it were present above the ocean, but that he *does* perceive the wispy substance of water vapor that hangs there.

How then should we interpret the passage in the autocommentary [to *Commentary on Pramāṇa*] where it says, "If the effect would not be apparent, even if it were present, this [kind of] proof should be employed. If it [would be] apparent, [a proof involving] the nonobservation of the apparent will bring understanding"?[696] [248] The meaning of the passage is this: What the person sees in that location is a bank of water vapor. But mistaking it, he wonders whether there might be smoke there. The reason "because no smoke is observed [there]" could not [help] such an individual to ascertain smoke's absence. Hence, in this situation, one employs the reason "because no fire is observed [there]." In his commentary on the passage, Śākyabuddhi says:

> [When] the resemblance to smoke of something such as rolling water vapor on a great body of water fools [someone], then it is [by means of] the absence of fire, the nonobservation of a nature, that he gains ascertainment.[697] It is not the absence of smoke. In just [such a situation] one employs [the reason involving] the nonobservation of a cause.[698]

[Third,] the proof that uses as its reason the nonobservation of something that is the same nature [as the element that is being negated] is dealt with in two sections:

1. Defining characteristics
2. Identifying the illustration

Defining characteristics

The nonobservation of something that is the same nature as the element that is being negated is defined as "that which fulfills the three criteria of the reason in a proof that sets out to explicitly establish just the absence of a certain element and uses the absence of the valid cognition that observes that element as its reason."

Identifying the illustration

1. Refutation of others' assertions
2. Setting forth our own position

Refutation of others' assertions

Someone asserts that [the formulation] "In the potless place before us [A], there are no pots [B], because there are no pots observed by valid cognition [C]"[699] represents only a rough outline of a proof that involves the nonobservation of something that is the same nature [as the element that is being negated]. As regards the *actual* proof, he says, there are two versions: one that is presented from the perspective of the agent of the action and one that is presented from the perspective of the object of the action. He says that the first of these is "The sense perception apprehending the potless area [A] can give rise to cognitive and verbal expressions of the absence of pots in the spot before us [B], because if a pot were present in this spot, that perception should observe it, but it is a sense perception that observes no pot there [C]." He says that the second version is "The potless area [A] [is one to which] expressions of the absence of pot apply [B], because if there was a pot there, the perception apprehending [the area] should observe it, but it is an area in which the perception apprehending [that area] observes no pot, which should [if it was there,] be apparent [C]."

[Response:] When someone states such a thing, why bother with an elaborate refutation? [Based on his formulation from the agent's perspective,] it would follow that if a pot was present in the spot, it would have to be absent there, because if the pot was present there, it would have to be observed by the sense perception apprehending that the area is potless! This [attack] can be extended to his formulation from the perspective of the object. [249] Now if he wants to go on spouting such self-contradicting positions, then let him! But what I find so astounding is how those with some learning forsake the illustrations provided for them in the tradition's great works in favor of those of their own creation, seemingly determined, thereby, to reveal their own characters.

One view held by certain earlier scholars and one group of "logicians" in the present day is that nonobservation proofs of the nature variety are concerned with names and expressions. So, while [these proofs] may use reasons such as "If pot were present, it should be apparent, but valid cognition observes no pot," what they really concern themselves with is establishing the *legitimacy* of using certain expressions, [such as, in this case,] "pot is absent." This notion leads these individuals to claim that the predicate that any of these proofs aims to establish will necessarily be something affirmative. And on these grounds, they conclude that while proofs of this variety may properly belong to the nature category, they are not "nonobservation" proofs at all.

[Response:] This position is not tenable, since proofs that use as their reason the nonobservation of a cause or encompasser [of the element that is being negated] are also ones that concern themselves with names and expressions. This is a point made [in the *Commentary on Pramāṇa*], where it states, "Thus some, by way of the absence of causes and encompassers, also affirm."[700] And in [Śākyabuddhi's] commentary to this passage, it says, "'Also' refers to [the fact that] in addition to negating, they are reasons [establishing] the expression of the negation."[701] If what [these groups] claim is correct, it would mean that "the description is a legitimate one"[702] would need to form the explicit predicate of such proofs. But if that were the case, then [within the basic threefold division of reasons], they would belong to the category of nature reasons, meaning that the category of proofs using nonobservation as their reasons would have nothing left in it.

Furthermore, do they propose that the party to whom this proof should be presented is someone who has ascertained that there is no pot and is now just wondering whether the "absence of pot" can be expressed? Or should it be presented to someone who has not yet ascertained the absence of pot, to help him to do so? These represent the only two possibilities.

If they propose the first option, [we would say] that an "expression of pot's absence"[703] can denote [one of three things]: (1) a cognition of a pot's absence, (2) the words that convey that absence, or (3) a physical articulation, which is the actions one takes that are informed by that absence. [As for the first,] are we really supposed to believe that there could be someone who has ascertained that there are no pots but is still wondering whether or not there is a cognition that ascertains that there are no pots? [As for the others,] someone who has ascertained that there are no pots may have reservations about expressing that fact. But any concerns he has could be allayed simply by assuring him that expressing that fact will not, for instance, result in him being punished by the ruling authority. What role have logical proofs to play in such matters?

If they propose the second option, [it is also incorrect]. It would follow that even if the proof established [to the party in question] that the expression "There are no pots" can legitimately be used in the location, he would still not be ascertaining the absence of pots there. Why? [250] Because the [verbal] expression "There are no pots" is one that *can* legitimately be used anywhere and with regard to anything at all, simply by virtue of the fact that [such an absence] is one that can be entertained by thought.[704]

These individuals may say that these are not criticisms that can be made of their position, since it is in the *veracity* of what the expression conveys that its legitimacy is established.

[Response:] But then in the context of establishing that sound is impermanent, should we then not also state [to the other party], "One can legitimately use the factually correct term *impermanent* [with respect to sound]"?

They might reply that just by realizing that sound is impermanent, [the other party] will eliminate any distorted notions that sound is permanent. And due to his having ascertained that sound is impermanent, it will not be necessary to expressly prove to him [separately] that the cognitive and verbal expressions of that are legitimate.

Someone else argues that this parallels [the situation with the pots]. So, just by ascertaining that there are no pots in the location, an individual will eliminate any distorted notions that pots are present there, and it will not be necessary to expressly prove to him that the cognitive and verbal expressions of that [absence] are legitimate. This individual also claims that it is impossible for someone who has ascertained that pots are not observed by valid cognition in a particular location not to have ascertained "the absence of pots."

[Response:] Here we have a case of someone who lacks knowledge of even the basic conventions of logical reasoning. If [as he asserts] it is impossible for there to be a situation in which someone has ascertained the characteristics defining a thing but has not yet attached to them the definiendum through which they are expressed, there would be no such thing as a proof that uses a definition as the reason and has the definiendum as its predicate. It would therefore follow that to prove sound is a product, one could never use the reason "[because it] arises from causes and conditions."

Moreover, what "proof establishing an expression" denotes is that between the two, expressions and objects, the proof in question is one that establishes [something about] a phenomenon of the former [category]. In no way does it indicate that such a proof must state as its explicit predicate "It is legitimate to use such and such a term." If it did, it would follow that for a proof to be classified as one "establishing an object," its explicit predicate would need to be "it is an object."

Setting forth our own system

A proof that uses as its reason the nonobservation of a thing that is the same nature as the element it negates can be formulated as in the following example: The lump of clay that in appearance is devoid of any aspect of a "bulbous vessel" [A] has within it no pot [B], because if pot were present, it should be apparent, but the presence of pot within it is not observed by valid cognition. The formulation of such proofs is discussed on numerous occasions in the *Commentary on Pramāṇa* and *Ascertainment of Pramāṇa*, such as in the passage "These [proofs] express the absence of the valid cognition of the [thing] as the reason [establishing] its nonexistence."[705] Although there are many issues relating to this that should be discussed, I will explore them elsewhere. [251]

But if the formulation of such proofs does not explicitly incorporate "It is legitimate to use the term *x*," how are we to explain the following passage [in the *Commentary on Pramāṇa*]?

> The absence of something that should be observable
> is not other than a nonobservation.
> Thus it is from the existence of [something]
> that one establishes a reasonable term and [conceptual]
> understanding.[706]

What this says is that the nonobservation of a phenomenon and the nonexistence of that phenomenon amount to the same thing. And since nonobservation encapsulates what it means [for a thing] not to exist, establishing that something is not observed effectively proves that it does not exist. *However*, there are still certain extremely dimwitted individuals who have not grasped that "nonexistent" is the designation assigned to something that is not observed, and for whom it is necessary to use the reason that [a thing is] not observed to establish that it is nonexistent. The passage is *not* saying that the nonobservation of a thing establishes that it is legitimate to use the term *nonexistence*. So fallacious accounts regarding the purpose of reasons using the nonobservation of a nature and the way that such reasons should be formulated [that say the contrary] can only offend scholarly sensibilities.

But if these reasons [involving] the nonobservation of a nature do not belong to the category of nature reasons, how are we to explain the passage "because it establishes an effect from a cause, this [reason] is subsumed within those of nature"?[707] What this conveys is that such reasons use the *establisher* "cause" to prove the *established* "effect."[708] In such cases, the reason and the predicate are related to each other in the sense of sharing a single nature. And it is because of this that the pervasion and the relation [underpinning the proof] can be established. The way that the pervasion and relation [in proofs using this kind of nonobservation reason] are established therefore resembles those [applied] in the nature category. It is due to the resemblance that the [same nature] category is described as subsuming them. But to be subsumed by something in no way requires being that thing. The textual tradition is as expansive as the ocean. And if those who lack knowledge of even the basic conventions relating to this tradition could refrain from spouting the nonsense [of these fallacious accounts], it would really be far more becoming of them.

A correct reason in a proof [involving] the nonobservation of a direct cause is defined as "that which fulfills the three criteria of the reason in a proof that sets out to explicitly establish the straight absence of the inexorable power of the direct cause of a certain element [to produce that element] and uses the absence of the valid cognition that observes that element as its reason." An example of this is "no smoke is observed" in the proof "Within an enclosed area free from any smoke [A], there is no inexorable power of the direct cause of smoke to produce [B], because no smoke is observed [C]."

Second are reasons that involve the observation of something that precludes [the element that is being negated].[709] This [type of reason] is defined as "that which fulfills the three criteria of the reason in a proof that sets out to explicitly establish the straight absence of some particular element within the subject of interest, and explicitly uses as its reason the observation of a phenomenon that is counter to that element." [252]

There are two varieties of these: (1) reasons that depend on an antagonistic preclusion and (2) reasons that depend on a preclusion of mutual opposition.[710]

The first is defined as "that which fulfills the three criteria of the reason in a proof that sets out to explicitly establish the straight absence of some particular element within the subject of interest, and explicitly uses as its reason the observation of something that is antagonistic to that element."

This type of reason has a number of varieties: (1) the four that involve the observation of a *nature* that precludes [the element that is being negated], (2) the four that involve the observation of an *effect* that precludes [the element that is being negated], and (3) the four that involve the observation of something *encompassed* that precludes [the element that is being negated].

The first four are those involving (1a) the observation of a nature that precludes a nature, (1b) the observation of a nature that precludes a cause, (1c) the observation of a nature that precludes an effect, and (1d) the observation of a nature that precludes an encompasser. The example of these is "[because it is] engulfed in blazing fire" when used [as the reason in proofs] that respectively establish that the absence, in a spot engulfed in fire, of (1a) the tactile sensation of coldness, (1b) goosebumps that are the effects of such coldness, (1c) the inexorable productive power of the cause of such coldness, and (1d) the tactile sensation of frost.

The second four are those involving (2a) the observation of an effect that precludes a nature, (2b) the observation of an effect that precludes a cause, (2c) the observation of an effect that precludes an effect, and (2d) the observation of an effect that precludes an encompasser. The example of these is the observation of "[it being] enshrouded in a large amount of thick smoke" when used [as the reason in proofs] that respectively establish the absence, in a spot enshrouded in a large amount of smoke, of the aforementioned four, the tactile sensation of coldness and so on.

The third set of four are those involving (3a) the observation of something encompassed that precludes a nature, (3b) the observation of something encompassed that precludes a cause, (3c) the observation of something encompassed that precludes an effect, and (3d) the observation of something encompassed that precludes an encompasser. The example of these is the observation of "[it being] engulfed in a blazing sandalwood fire" when used [as the reason in proofs] that respectively establish the absence, in a spot engulfed by such a fire, of the aforementioned four, the tactile sensation of coldness and so on. [253]

The second [variety] of correct reason involving the observation of something that precludes [the element that is being negated] is that which depends on a preclusion of mutual opposition. It is defined as "that which fulfills the three criteria of the reason in a proof that sets out to explicitly establish the straight absence of some particular element within the subject of interest, and explicitly uses as its reason the presence of something that is diametrically opposed to that element." An example of this is [the reason in the proof] "The sprout [A] requires no further production [B] because its nature has already been produced [C]." I see no point in presenting the various divisions of this. This concludes the discussion on nonobservation reasons.

Logical reasons divided in terms of what type of thing they set out to prove

Divided by way of what they set out to prove, correct reasons are of three varieties:

1. Correct reasons [dealing with] demonstrable facts and realities
2. Correct reasons [relating to matters of] conviction
3. Correct reasons [dealing with] the issue of common agreement [about names]

Correct reasons [dealing with] demonstrable facts and realities

The first is defined as "that which fulfills the three criteria of the reason within a [certain] proof, when whatever forms the probandum of the proof in question is necessarily something established by valid cognition(s) dealing with demonstrable facts and realities for myopic beings."

An example is the reason in the proof "Sound is impermanent because it is produced."

Correct reasons [relating to matters of] conviction

1. Refutation of others' assertions
2. Setting out our own position
3. Dealing with objections [to our position]

Refutation of others' assertions

1. Refuting those who reject the feasibility of [using] correct logical proofs in matters relating to conviction
2. Refuting those who accept their feasibility but propose a different model for them

Refuting those who reject the feasibility of [using] correct logical proofs in matters relating to conviction

Someone rejects the whole notion of correct logical proofs relating to matters of conviction. He claims that for such proofs to be possible, there would need to be a [logical] relationship between a scriptural passage and the content it conveys, and that would require that an unfailing relationship could be established between a word and its object.

[Response:] The idea that correct logical proofs cannot deal with matters of conviction is totally spurious. [254] It goes without saying that those who reject such logical proofs are in no position to assert the existence of valid inferences that cognize matters relating to conviction; they must accept that there are no such valid cognitions. And due to this, they are saddled with a series of major faults. [First,] it would follow that there are no valid cognitions comprehending objects that are extremely hidden, since valid inferential cognitions dealing with matters of conviction are impossible. The pervasion holds, because none of the other forms of valid cognition is able to engage an object for which the only verification is its mention in a scriptural passage. But if he accepts the [argument's conclusion], he will be guilty of that grievous denigration that denies the very existence of links between most causes and their effects. He would be refusing to accept, for instance, that engaging in the Dharma action of generosity will mature into a pleasurable effect at some time in the future. Such a view, which is a denial of the existence of karmic cause and effect, is the most repugnant of all wrong views, one that severs the very roots of virtue. It is the position that the Cārvāka holds as his own, and if one with vows should adopt such a view, he would in so doing have embraced the cause for relinquishing every one of his vows. This is the point made in the words "[When] the roots [of virtue] are cut or the [duration] of a night passes, [vows of] the *pratimokṣa* discipline are ended."[711] In certain passages of scripture, the Blessed One identifies a specific action, stipulating exactly what effect it will produce and when. What such a passage conveys—its object—is something that is extremely hidden. And since [this individual asserts that] valid inferential cognitions on matters of conviction are impossible, it would [secondly] follow that no valid cognition is up to the task of counteracting the distorted notions that might develop about the content of such passages, those extremely hidden phenomena. But if he accepts this conclusion, it would follow that there is no way to rid oneself of such distorted notions. Furthermore, it would absurdly follow that defilement is innate to the mind itself, because if there are no valid cognitions to counteract the way that such distorted notions hold things to be, that must indeed be the way that they are!

This still leaves us with the question of how it is possible to have logical proofs dealing with matters of conviction without this requiring some sort of unfailing relationship between a word and its object. The way that this should be explained will be dealt with below. But some analyze the question in the following manner. Is the scriptural passage, they ask, accepted as the proof of the extremely hidden thing [for a person who] has already established that thing with valid cognition, or is it accepted as such without him having established that thing? They rule out the first of these options, arguing that if the person has already established the thing in question, it would be pointless for him to accept the passage as evidence that proves it to him. But they also rule out the second option, saying that it would bring no certainty [to the individual], since he would be accepting that the scriptural passage proves the thing without him having established that thing by means of valid cognition. Thus they conclude that since a scriptural passage cannot itself serve as proof, logical proofs relating to matters of conviction are unfeasible. [255]

[Response:] Well then, is "produced" accepted to be the probans that proves "Sound is impermanent" to an individual who has already established with valid cognition [the thesis] that sound is impermanent, or prior to him having established that? If it is the first option, it would follow that it is pointless to accept that produced is the probans that proves [the thesis to the individual], since he is someone who has already established [that thesis] with valid cognition. The three spheres [for this argument are in place, and thus their analysis of the first option is shown to be irredeemably flawed]. But if it were the second option, [the thesis] would bring no certainty, because one would need to accept that produced is the probans proving [that sound is impermanent for an individual] who has yet to establish by means of valid cognition [that sound is impermanent]. The three spheres [for this argument are again in place].

Furthermore, based on what they propose, it would follow that if one accepts the existence of correct reasons dealing with demonstrable facts, one is thereby obliged to accept that the words articulating a thesis [such as] "Sound is impermanent" can serve as the probans that establish sound is impermanent. If they deny that [accepting the former obliges one to accept the latter], it would go against [their own logic, according to which,] if one accepts the existence of reasons [relating to] matters of conviction, one is thereby obliged to accept that the *words* of the scriptural passage "Practicing generosity gives rise to material resources" serves as the correct probans proving that practicing generosity leads to material resources.[712] Since the reason and the predicate [of this argument] are ones that they have, again, committed themselves to, the three spheres [are in place].

We also note that some other idiots advocate that a buddha is an extremely hidden phenomenon, while they also deny the existence of inferential valid cognition relating to conviction.

[Response:] So they would be forced to admit that there is no buddha, because if one existed, valid cognition would have to observe that.

Faced with this [difficulty], there are those whose reasoning leads them to shamelessly declare that although buddhas exist, they are not apparent to us and thus constitute remote objects.

[Response:] If buddhas are remote objects for you, then why not just openly confess to harboring doubts about their existence? And while you are at it, why not also confess to similar doubts about the existence of the Dharma and Sangha? And in accordance with that, when you go for refuge in the Three Jewels, what you should be saying is, "I go for refuge in the Three Jewels . . . assuming, that is, that they exist"!

Hence those who claim that a buddha is an extremely hidden phenomenon and who also deny the existence of valid cognition relating to conviction will eventually be compelled to concede that all the meditation undertaken on the path over three "countless" eons for the sake of attaining buddhahood is akin to the energy that someone might expend in trying to prove that there are horns growing on the head of a hare. Their adherence to the notion that buddhas are extremely hidden also makes every one of the three types of vow, the twelve categories of [the Buddha's] teaching, and the grounds and paths into things in which no confidence can be placed. And all meditation on the path becomes comparable, they must accept, to trying to prove that there is a *piśāci* spirit in front of us. That a buddha is *not* an extremely hidden phenomenon, the way that one goes about establishing the fulfillment of the criteria in a proof dealing with demonstrable facts, and other such matters have been described at length above. [256]

Refuting those who accept the feasibility [of proofs relating to matters of conviction] but propose a different model for them

Someone formulates a correct proof related to conviction as follows: "Practice of virtuous dharma(s) such as generosity [A] will yield pleasurable maturing effects at some future point [B], because the Blessed One has declared it to be so in a pure scriptural passage [C]." The same individual also identifies "From generosity, material resources; from discipline, pleasure,"[713] as the passage that serves as the reason establishing that material resources are the maturing effects of virtuous practices such as generosity.

[Response:] This is incorrect, since anyone who has ascertained the proof's subject would also already have ascertained its thesis. Why? Because to ascertain that practices such as generosity are *virtuous dharma(s)*, one must already have ascertained that they yield maturing effects that are pleasurable.

He may therefore propose that the subject should be "practices such as generosity" alone and not "virtuous dharma(s)."

[Response:] Even this will not allow him to escape from the criticism, since it would follow that the verbal formulation of the proof's thesis [alone] can serve as the proof statement, because the words of the passage "From generosity, material resources" [alone] can serve as the correct reason proving that generosity yields material resources. That is, if the mere [existence] of the words in a scriptural passage proves [the veracity] of its content, it must be the case that the words "From generosity, material resources" alone establish that generosity yields material resources. But then it would also follow that the words "Sound is impermanent" [themselves] establish that sound is impermanent. To sum up then, [based on his view,] the passage "From generosity, material resources" is simply the verbal formulation of the thesis, and one that itself proves that generosity yields material resources. Thus his assertion that the passage is proof that generosity yields material resources will force him, even though on his part, he has no such wish, to accept that the verbal formulation of a thesis is itself proof [of that thesis].

Furthermore, has [the other party] established the scriptural passage teaching that generosity yields material resources [with regard to] the subject of interest in the proof? If not, he would not have established the property of the subject, so any idea that the proof is correct would collapse. But if [the other party] has established it and thereby the reason's presence in the subject, there are only two ways in which it could be present. According to the [first] form, the presence would be in terms of *identity*, while according to the [second], it would be in terms of *existence*.[714] But neither of these is tenable. For the first to work, generosity would need to *be* the passage of scripture. In order for the second to work, it would be necessary to accept that generosity *has* the passage. But then the same reasoning would have to apply equally elsewhere. So it would follow that everything referred to in a scriptural passage of the Blessed One would need to *have* that passage present within it! [257] And if one accepts that, the same would be the case for the Buddha's enlightened awareness. So it would follow that everything that is an object of that awareness would need to *have* that awareness itself! But if one accepted that, it would ridiculously follow that every established basis has the Buddha's enlightened awareness. To sum up then, the property of the subject [in the proof formulated by this individual] is not established, which means that the proof is not a correct one.

Those who agree with the aforesaid formulation also of course claim that the reason used in a proof relating to a matter of conviction is necessarily of the *effect* variety. Added to this, they maintain that any pure scriptural passage that speaks about an extremely hidden phenomenon can always be cited as the reason within a *conviction proof* to establish the thing about which it speaks. Another fault of their position [becomes apparent when] we consider the proof "Generosity [A] does not yield suffering as its matured effect [B] because certain pure scriptural passages of the Blessed One declare that it does not [C]." It would follow that when the passage in question is presented as the reason in this proof, it must be an effect reason, because it is [the reason] within a conviction proof. The reason and the pervasion [of this argument] are ones that they themselves asserted. But if they accept this [argument's conclusion], it would mean that there can be an effect proof in which the predicate is a *negation*. So they must be asserting that this is something classifiable as both an affirming proof and negating proof!

Someone else rejects [the previous group's version of] the proof relating to conviction. He claims that there are three varieties of conviction proof [conforming with the three types of reason], and that all three proofs are correct ones. As a conviction proof of the effect variety, he gives the example "Śākyamuni Buddha, the Blessed One [A], is someone who must have been preceded by love and great compassion, the things that caused him [B], because he is an individual who has achieved the two end purposes [C]." His example of a conviction proof of the nature variety is "Śākyamuni Buddha, the Blessed One [A] is the ultimate form of valid authority [B], because he is an individual who has achieved the two end purposes [C]." And his example of a conviction proof of the nonobservation variety is "Śākyamuni Buddha, the Blessed One [A], has no flaws such as attachment [B], because he has rid himself of the two forms of obscuration together with their imprints [C]."

[Response:] They also are incorrect. No one who has ascertained that [a buddha] has rid himself of the two forms of obscuration together with their imprints could still be left wondering whether [that buddha] has rid himself of flaws such as attachment. This means that anyone who has established the property of the subject for that proof would also have realized its thesis.

Also, a proof cannot count as correct unless [the other party] has ascertained its subject. But [the other party] who has ascertained the subject in the proof [as formulated by this individual] would already have ascertained that the subject is a buddha. So he could not possibly still be wondering whether the subject has flaws. This means that once [the other party] has established the subject of that proof, he would already have realized its thesis.

Also, if the [proofs presented by this individual] are those that employ correct reasons relating to matters of conviction, it would follow that the predicates that they establish are exclusively extremely hidden things. [258] But if [this individual] agrees with this, he will be forced into the sorry position of having to accept that all the Buddha's [qualities of] abandonment and realization are extremely hidden phenomena. However, as I have already explained, the buddha's [qualities of] abandonment and realization [belong to the domain of] things that can be established by proofs dealing with demonstrable facts and realities.

Setting out our own position

If there is such a thing as a correct logical proof relating to a matter of conviction, what form does it take? The reason in such a proof is defined as "that which fulfills the three criteria of the reason for a proof within which whatever constitutes the probandum is necessarily an extremely hidden thing."

Those of a reflective disposition come to hear about extremely hidden phenomena, together with the rich rewards and serious risks they can bring, depending on whether one engages with or spurns them. Feeling that to neglect them would probably be to squander a major opportunity, they start to wonder about what means there might be of engaging with such phenomena. Following some deliberation on the matter, they become aware that there is no way to approach these entities using other forms of valid cognition, and that it will be necessary to rely on the scriptures [in which they are taught]. But they wonder how to determine whether what those passages of scripture say about [such phenomena] is trustworthy, and so they set about analyzing those [scriptural passages]. Their investigations lead them to the conclusion that they can verify what a particular passage says by subjecting it to the "threefold analysis." That is, they must see whether what the scripture teaches is undermined in the sense of it (1) [contradicting] direct experience, (2) [contradicting] those valid cognitions that deal with demonstrable facts, or (3) containing—within that section specifically teaching about the extremely hidden thing in question—internal contradictions, such as inconsistencies in [the passage's] different parts or between what is overtly expressed and what is implied. Once these individuals verify a particular passage, seeing that it is not undermined on any of these three levels, they ascertain that it is nondeceptive [i.e., trustworthy] regarding the matter in question. At this point, they can act in accord with what the passage teaches, informed by what it says regarding what should be pursued and what should be shunned. This is how one goes about developing the certainty of ascertainment in what a particular passage of scripture teaches. This is something explained in clear and unambiguous terms in numerous sections of the authoritative treatises. But how can those who resemble a lump of clay placed before a tome of scripture be expected to comprehend such things?

As to how a conviction proof is constructed, for the individual inquiring about the contents of a particular passage of scripture, the passage is not the *means* of analysis but its *subject*. This the individual investigates by means of the threefold analysis to determine whether the passage in question passes the test and whether what it says can be regarded as trustworthy. Thus the flawless [formulation] is "The passage 'From generosity, material resources; from discipline, pleasure' [A] is trustworthy with regard to what it teaches [B], because it is a passage that has been verified by means of the threefold analysis [C]." [259]

Which [sections] of the treatise communicate this formulation? [First,] the subject [of the proof] is identified in the passage "A statement that is coherent communicates the method corresponding [to the goal], and that [real] human goal."[715] What this indicates is that a reflective party will not bother investigating just any statement. Rather, he will take a passage with the three features [conveyed in these words] as his basis to investigate whether it is trustworthy regarding what it expresses. Next, the predicate of the proof is given in the line "This [passage] is nondeceptive."[716] [Lastly,] the reason of the proof is provided in the section "Regarding the seen and unseen things [about which it speaks] . . ."[717] Even more succinctly, the line "[These] words of conviction are nondeceptive"[718] presents the thesis. And "One deduces from the universal"[719] shows that the cognition that realizes the [thesis] is an inferential one. What then are these words in which we can have conviction and that will not deceive us? [The *Commentary on Pramāṇa*] identifies these:

> A statement that is coherent communicates the method
> corresponding [to the goal], and that [real] human goal
> is one that is [worthy] of thorough analysis.
> Others are not.[720]

Then it says:

> Regarding the seen and unseen things [about which it speaks],
> [because] there is no [evidence] to counter them
> from either perception or inference,
> this [passage] is nondeceptive.[721]

This sets out what it is that establishes that such passages are trustworthy. It also provides a clear formulation of the reason used in a logical proof dealing with a matter of conviction.

Anyway, to sum up, those who claim that when formulating a logical proof related to a matter of conviction, one uses the passage from scripture itself as the reason [are asserting that] the sort of passage with the features mentioned in the stanza "A statement that is coherent . . ." is not the subject of the comprehensive analysis but the means by which the analysis is conducted. And they are like those who view the treatises' meanings like an expansive ocean far off in the distance.

Regarding the way that a passage of scripture is verified by means of the threefold analysis, someone proposes that (1) the portion of the passage dealing with the "seen"—that is, evident [i.e., manifest] objects—is the one that valid perception establishes, (2) the portion of it dealing with the "unseen"—meaning hidden phenomena—is the one that valid inferential cognition dealing with demonstrable facts establishes, and (3) the [third] portion dealing with the [other] "unseen"—in the sense of extremely hidden phenomena—is the one that [the individual must establish] is not undermined by internal contradictions and so forth within the passage itself.

[Response:] This is not tenable. If it were, then only a passage dealing with *all three*—evident, [slightly] hidden, and extremely hidden phenomena—could be verified by the threefold analysis. [260] This would mean that passages dealing exclusively with extremely hidden phenomena could not be verified by the threefold analysis. So it would ridiculously follow that the passage "From generosity, material resources; from discipline, pleasure" is one that could not be verified by the threefold analysis.

What it actually means to say that [a passage] has been "verified by the threefold analysis" is that the passage in question is not undermined by direct experience, inferential cognition, or inconsistencies and the like in what it asserts. It is this that [the *Commentary on Pramāṇa*] refers to when it says, "[because] there is . . . this [passage] is nondeceptive."[722] Given this fact, the stanza "Regarding the seen and unseen things [about which it speaks] . . ."[723] should not be read as referring to "the portion of the passage dealing with the 'seen'—that is, evident objects . . ." and so forth. Instead, it indicates that there is nothing in the valid perception of evident objects to undermine anything the passage might say about the "seen," nothing in valid inference about hidden phenomena to undermine what it might say about the "unseen," and nothing in the way of inconsistencies, internal contradictions, and so on to undermine what it is saying.[724]

I find myself the first-ever commentator in this snowy mountain land to give a full account of these sections of the [*Commentary on Pramāṇa*] treatise. How astonishing that other commentators could not summon the energy to wield their writing implements to such effect!

The probandum of a [conviction] proof is necessarily an extremely hidden phenomenon, whereas the [reason's fulfillment of the] three criteria are all things established by valid cognitions dealing with demonstrable facts. Some may query this, suggesting that there is a contradiction in our asserting that while the valid cognitions that establish that the proof's reason [fulfills the] three criteria are those that deal with demonstrable facts, what the proof itself establishes is something extremely hidden.

[Response:] This is not the case. The threefold classification—dividing proofs into those that deal either with demonstrable fact(s), the issue of common agreement [about names], or a matter of conviction—does not distinguish them on the basis of whether the fulfillment of the three criteria of their respective reasons are themselves things that one can establish in terms of demonstrable fact(s), the issue of common agreement [about names], or scriptural passages of conviction. Rather, this classification is one that divides logical proofs on the basis of their respective *probanda*. That is to say, is the thesis something that can be established by a valid cognition dealing with demonstrable facts, something that is establishing just a matter of agreement, *or* something that is an extremely hidden phenomenon and [as such] can only be established by means of a passage of scripture?

Furthermore, those advocating that because the probandum the proof establishes is an extremely hidden phenomenon, the three criteria [making up the proof's reason] must likewise be extremely hidden *also* formulate the example of such a proof as "Generosity [A] will, at some future point, yield pleasurable maturing effects [B], because an [authoritative] passage of scripture declares it is so [C]." Thus through their inadequate analysis, they are obviously guilty of a spectacular self-contradiction. [261] Why? Because their formulation of the proof involves citing the passage of scripture itself, or something else that is [in effect] that passage, as the reason, and this is something that, in either case, is established by valid perception.[725] This totally ruins the assertion that a reason [in the domain of] demonstrable fact cannot prove an extremely hidden phenomenon. Thus, to advance that formulation while claiming that the property of the subject in that proof is an extremely hidden phenomenon is an object of scholarly derision.

What is more, since they are [basically] arguing that if the [fulfillment of the] three criteria is established by valid cognition dealing with demonstrable facts, the proof's probandum is necessarily *not* extremely hidden, the same must apply to another of their assertions—namely, that when smoke is used to infer the presence of fire on the smoky mountain pass, what establishes the [fulfillment of the] three criteria is perception. It would follow that the proof's probandum is precluded from being a hidden phenomenon because the reason's [fulfillment of the] three criteria is established by perception. The three spheres are in place, [and their position is seen to be irredeemably flawed].

Which valid cognitions, then, are responsible for establishing [the reason's fulfillment of] each of the three criteria in such proofs? The fact that the passage in question is one verified by the three parts of the analysis can be established by valid perception. The proof's pervasion—that a passage verified by the threefold analysis is necessarily one that is not deceptive with regard to what it says—is established by means of a logical reason. One could realize it, for example, by using the following reasoning: "A passage that deceives is one that represents things to be one way when they are another. The way that such a passage represents things—that is, what it says—is necessarily undermined by [evidence from various] valid cognitions, [whereas] a passage that has been verified by the threefold analysis is one that no valid cognitions undermine."

Also, if the threefold classification of logical proofs [those that deal with demonstrable facts and so on] divided them not in terms of the probandum that each of them sets out to prove but on the basis of the probans each of them uses to establish that probandum, then it would follow that, similarly, the distinction between affirmative and negative proofs is made on the basis of the probans that each of them employs. And if one granted that, it would follow that all sorts of proof, such as [the category of nonobservation proof that] involves the observation of something that precludes the element that is being negated, would count as a proof of the affirmative variety!

Furthermore, based on what you assert, no credence could be given to the fourfold division of valid cognitions made by way of what they *counter*[726]—one of the purposes behind which is to distinguish among the different kinds of things that are countered by valid cognitions relating to conviction and dealing with the issue of common agreement [about names] and so on. According to what you are now saying, what separates them is not what they counter but the basis for each of these valid cognitions, and whether the reasons [they rely on] are those dealing with demonstrable fact, related only to scripture, and so on. You obviously need to give some thought to the passage: [262]

> Therefore, as an acceptance [relating to scripture can also] counter,
> it does not belong outside [the category of] inference.
> [Nevertheless] it has been treated separately
> to indicate a distinction in the object [with which it deals].[727]

Those currently professing to be advocates of logic say that the passage stating that generosity yields material resources [can serve] as the proof's reason. Thus, at the same time that they hear and vocalize the passage themselves, they say that it must be an extremely hidden reason. So, if this is supposed to constitute a position that is logical, who exactly are we to accuse of promoting what is illogical?

Dealing with objections [to our position]

Someone has then said that according to what we assert, if an individual was seeking to establish that sound is impermanent, there would be nothing wrong with presenting the proof "The scriptural passage that asserts sound is impermanent [A] is trustworthy with respect to what it teaches [B], because it is a passage that has been verified by the threefold analysis."

[Response:] The fault here is that such a proof would be pointless. For a party to have established [the reason—namely,] that the passage in question is verified by the threefold analysis—he must already have established, by means of valid cognition, that sound is impermanent, which in turn would necessarily have required someone presenting him with a reason to prove it.

I see the vital importance of reasons [relating to] conviction but judge what others have said about them to be totally unreliable. I have, therefore, explained them at some length in accordance with the true intention of the holy ones.

Correct reasons [dealing with] the issue of common agreement [about names][728]

1. Refutation of others' assertions
2. Setting out our own position

Refutation of others' assertions

Someone denies that the reason "[because it] exists" can serve as a correct one to establish the thesis "The sphere [marked] with the hare [A] can legitimately be denoted by the name 'moon' [B]."[729] It cannot be the reason, he claims, because for such to be the case, there would need to be a demonstrable logical relationship between a word and the thing that it denotes.

Another individual denies that "[because it] exists among objects of thought" can serve as the reason to establish the same thesis. It cannot be that reason, he claims, because the relationship it has with the predicate of the proof is not of a [real] nature, since the relationship between the reason and predicate here is one that we have simply chosen to assign to them. That is the case, he says, because words are just symbols[730] and only able to denote things due to our choosing to agree that they do. And since choices about what [individual] words denote are arbitrary, anything that exists can legitimately be referred to by the term for moon. He concludes that reasons relating to matters of common agreement [about names] are therefore not [logically] correct ones. [263]

[Response:] Neither of these positions are tenable. The former confuses the name and the legitimacy of the name's usage. It would follow that if [the reason] "exists" has a natural relationship with [the predicate] "the legitimacy of being denoted by the name *x*," it must also have a natural relationship with the name *x* itself. This is because if "exists" has the required logical relationship [with the predicate for it] to serve as the reason establishing that it is legitimate to use the name *moon* for *x*, there must also be a natural relationship between the word and what it denotes. If he grants this, it would follow that anything [related to] the name's legitimacy through sharing the same nature as it must also share the nature of the name itself. But if he were to accept this, then it would absurdly follow that all phenomena are in the nature of sound.

The latter [individual] simply fails to make [a crucial] distinction. The fact that the name "moon" is given to particular phenomenon may purely be a matter of arbitrary choice, but the fact that any name *could* be used to denote a phenomenon is not. Anyway, those who use such reasoning to deny that proofs [in this category] are [logically] correct ones are basically arguing that if the pervasion and relationship [that underpin a proof] are governed by choice, they cannot be verified by valid cognition. But to assert that is to embrace the philosophical tenets of those who advocate that to be constructed by thought is to be without any real establishment at all. This is simply to deny that anything can be true in a conventional sense.

There are other [individuals] who accept that "[because it] exists" is a reason establishing that "The sphere [marked] with the hare can legitimately be denoted by the name 'moon'" but classify the proof as one that deals with demonstrable facts. They of course cite the fact that the reason itself is one that deals with demonstrable facts [to reach their conclusion that the same must be true of the proof]. This "logic" is something that I have already refuted.

Another [individual] also classifies the proof in question as one that deals with demonstrable fact. But instead of citing "[because it] exists" as the reason, he formulates the proof, "The sphere [marked] with the hare [A] can legitimately be denoted by the name 'moon' [B] because this is a matter of common agreement in the world." He says that while this is referred to as a "correct proof relating to the issue of common agreement [about names]," the description should not be taken literally. [In explanation] he says that the *rationale* [behind this designation] is that such things are taught to be the means through which a realization of the actual state of things can be gained. [To support this,] he cites the passage "Without reliance on convention, there is no way to realize the sacred [ultimate]."[731] He says that the *purpose* of the designation is to encourage engagement with the conventions of the world. And he claims that the *evidence against* it being a literal description is that the reason is also found to be present in the class of dissimilar instances for the proof.[732]

[Response:] The class of dissimilar instances for this proof—that is, "[that which] cannot be legitimately denoted by the name 'moon'"— is something that does not exist, so his claim that the reason is present in it is not established. [Secondly,] the only conventions referred to in the passage "Without relying on conventions . . ." are conventional truths, which have absolutely nothing to do with the kind of common agreement [about names] dealt with by the proofs under discussion here. [264] Added to this, his formulation of the proof is foreign to the great treatises and their commentaries. Indeed, it is little more than him blathering nonsense, unabashedly. But the range of ideas that the foolish can come up with is so great, how can one ever hope to write enough to counter them all?

Setting out our own position

The reason in a proof dealing with a matter of common agreement [about names] is defined as "that which fulfills the three criteria of the reason within a proof when whatever constitutes the probandum of the proof in question is necessarily a phenomenon that is determined purely by choice."

The example of this is the reason in the proof "The sphere [marked] with the hare [A] can legitimately be denoted by the name 'moon' [B] because it exists among objects of thought [C], just as is the case, for example, with camphor [D]."

Generally speaking, the things that we can comprehend fall into two categories: those realizable through personal experience and those that must be realized by some means other than personal experience. The first are things that valid perception comprehends overtly. The second are of two varieties: phenomena that can only be realized by depending on a passage from scripture and those that can be realized without that. The first are things that form the probanda of conviction proofs and are comprehended by conviction inferences. [The second type,] those realized without depending on scripture, are also divided into two: those things that are not determined purely by choice and those that are. The first are what form the probanda of logical proofs dealing with demonstrable facts and are comprehended by the corresponding inferential cognitions. [The second,] those things determined purely by choice, are those that form the probanda of logical proofs [dealing with the issue of] common agreement [about names] and are comprehended by the corresponding inferential cognitions.

But if nothing more than choice determines these things, how are they comprehended by valid cognition? These two are not incompatible with one another, as I will now explain. Things that are constructed by thought come in two varieties. One variety cannot be substantiated by valid cognition. These are things such as the snake that a striped rope is imagined [to be]. The other variety, those that can be substantiated by valid cognition, also has two kinds. One is those things that cannot be determined *solely* by choice, such as the fact that produced and impermanent are different. The other, such as "moon" denoting the sphere [marked] with the hare, is things that are purely a matter of choice. "Difference" is something that thought assigns to product and impermanent, but this is not something governed only by choice. That is, it is not simply a matter of our choosing to call them "different" but something determined by [the fact that] produced and impermanent have their own attributes. Using the name "moon" to denote the sphere [marked] with the hare, on the other hand, falls purely into the domain of choice. The sound "moon" is used as a symbol to denote something. *What* it denotes is simply a matter of choice. And choice [is without constraint]; it goes where it pleases. [265]

To summarize, it is choice that decides what the sound "moon," as a symbol, should represent. So the fact that it was assigned to the sphere [marked] with the hare must also have been just a matter of [arbitrary] choice. Choice alone, then, decided that the sphere [marked] with the hare was the thing to be denoted by the name "moon," and there was nothing from the side of the object, the sphere [marked] with the hare, that determined it. What valid cognition can establish, therefore, is that the name "moon" can legitimately denote the sphere [marked] with the hare. But this is not something that [falls within the domain of] valid cognition dealing with demonstrable facts. A thing that can be established by that kind of valid cognition is precluded from being one that is decided by choice, since it is determined by the facts themselves.

Now, because choice structures all conventions, the term *agreement* can sometimes refer to choice itself, as the arbiter determining agreement [regarding conventions]. But here "agreement" relates to the fact that a term *can*, legitimately, be used to denote a thing. And something is a "reason of common agreement [about names]" because it is used [in the proof] to establish that fact. The inferential cognition that comes about in dependence on that reason is a valid cognition. Otherwise, it would follow that no valid cognition at all could establish the fact that the name "moon" can be used to denote the sphere [marked] with the hare, since the foregoing discussion ruled out that this is something that can be comprehended by a valid cognition dealing with demonstrable fact. Nor can a passage of scripture alone be used to establish it. If no valid cognition could establish that the name "moon" can be used to denote the sphere [marked] with the hare, then neither could it be established that the name "moon" actually *does* denote the sphere [marked] with the hare. That would mean that "moon" does not convey to us the sphere [marked] with the hare, but that contradicts our direct experience.

Thus, without any real effort, we have been able to establish that proofs [in the category] of common agreement are [logically] correct ones and have also decisively refuted those who claim that the fact that "moon" can denote the sphere [marked] with the hare is a demonstrable one.

Which valid cognitions are responsible then for establishing that the reason [fulfills] the three respective criteria in this type of proof? The property of the subject [i.e., that the sphere marked with the hare exists among objects of thought] is something confirmed implicitly by means of self-cognition. The self-cognition in question is the one that has direct perceptual experience of the conceptual cognition realizing the sphere [marked] with the hare. What the self-cognition overtly experiences is the [thought] that has the aspect of the sphere [marked] with the hare. Implicit in this experience is the understanding that the sphere [marked] with the hare—the object of the cognition—exists among those of which thought can conceive. The proof's pervasion is established by means of logic—namely, "Something that is governed solely by choice can legitimately embrace absolutely anything, just as is the case, for example, with the unbridled imagination. Usage of the name 'moon" is also governed solely by choice." The property of the subject for this proof is also something confirmed implicitly by means of a self-cognition.

At this point, an objection about what we have asserted might be raised. [266] Some may argue, "It follows that the name 'moon' is not an excluding engager [of its object]. Why? Because it does not [engage it] by ruling out things other than the sphere [marked] with the hare. And that must be the case, because 'moon' could be used to refer to absolutely any known object." The pervasion holds, they may say, since [the *Commentary on Pramāṇa*] states:

> If [you acknowledge that] there is an elimination of [what the thing is not],
> then isn't the point [of using names to communicate a thing]
> one that names alone can fulfill?
> So what role is there for some separate universal [such as you propose]?[733]

[Response:] There is no flaw in our position. For the name "moon" to communicate the sphere [marked] with the hare, it need only exclude that the sphere [marked] with the hare is not a moon, which is not to say that it excludes every particular thing that is not a moon, individually. The elimination of non-moon need not eliminate each and every thing that is not a moon.

This concludes the discussion on correct logical proofs [dealing with the issue] of common agreement [about names].

Logical reasons divided in terms of the domain with which they deal[734]

1. Correct logical reasons that establish the thing [meant]
2. Correct logical reasons that establish name and expression[735]

Correct logical reasons that establish the thing [*meant*]

The first is defined as "that which fulfills the three criteria of the reason within a proof, when whatever constitutes the explicit predicate of the proof in question is necessarily a definition."

Examples of this are "produced" when presented in the proof "Sound is momentary because it is produced" and "a brand-new thing that has never occurred before" when presented in the proof "A sound is created by causes and conditions, because it is a brand-new thing that has never occurred before."

Correct logical reasons that establish names and expressions

The second is defined as "that which fulfills the three criteria of the reason within a proof, when whatever constitutes the explicit predicate of the proof in question is necessarily a definiendum. An example of this is "produced" when presented [as the reason] in the proof "Sound is impermanent because it is produced." [267]

Hence, in this context, the "thing" [meant] is a set of defining characteristics, whereas the "name and expression" is a definiendum, the thing defined. "Name and expression" and "thing" here do not [therefore] respectively denote verbal, cognitive, or physical expressions and their objects. They cannot be [referring to them], since *everything* counts as an object either of a verbal, cognitive, or physical expression. So, if the expression denoted here was of that kind, it would make it impossible to have a reason that could establish *only* a name and expression. What is more, if the "name and expression" here was referring to those three forms of expression, then the type of proof under discussion would be one that explicitly set out to establish the legitimacy of such cognitive or verbal expressions. But the assertion that "The expression *x* can legitimately be used to denote *y*" is an *affirmative* one. Hence all proofs in this "name and expression" category would be affirmative. But that would contradict the various accounts saying that reasons establishing name and expression are found in all three categories [of negative reason]—those involving the nonobservation of a cause, an encompasser, and a nature. Furthermore, if one asserted that the proofs here are all about establishing that it is legitimate to use cognitive and verbal expressions, it would follow that *all* correct logical reasons must be counted as "reasons that establish names and expressions." Why? Because all logical reasons legitimate the use of [certain] cognitive and verbal expressions, in that every one of them is presented to produce an inferential cognition realizing a thesis. The [mistaken] reading of "thing" and "name and expression" in the context [I have identified here] represents the predominant understanding in the present day, but it has drifted entirely [from what is correct].

There may be cases of a second party who has ascertained that "momentariness" encapsulates what it means to be impermanent but who has not yet ascertained both impermanent and momentariness in relation to sound. Once such an individual establishes the "thing [meant]" [i.e., the momentariness of sound], he will also establish the "name and expression" [i.e., that sound is impermanent], and vice versa. Hence such an individual only needs to be presented with *one* of the proofs [establishing sound's impermanence or its momentariness].

Some [other] second parties will neither have ascertained that momentariness encapsulates what it means to be impermanent nor established impermanence or momentariness in relation to sound. Such an individual should first be presented with a logical proof that establishes the "thing [meant]" [i.e., that sound is momentary]. If he is someone of sharper faculties, it will not be necessary to then present him with a separate proof establishing the "name and expression." But for someone of duller faculties, that [separate proof] will also be required.

For someone, such as a follower of the Vaiśeṣika system, who will not have established that sound is momentary but who has established that "impermanent," as a label, is used for sound, the proof establishing the "thing [meant]" will alone suffice. Other parties may have realized the "thing [meant]" in relation to sound [i.e., that it is momentary] but have not yet established the "name and expression" *impermanent* in relation to that. If such an individual is of duller faculties and ignorant of the link between the name and the thing [it denotes], he should be presented with a proof that employs the characteristics defining the thing to establish *what* it is that they define [i.e., the definiendum]—for example, "*X* is impermanent because it is momentary." This is classified as a proof that establishes *only* a [name and] expression. Although it [clearly] does not do so by overtly setting out to establish that

"It is legitimate to use the expression *x*." If one presents the [above] formulation to [the aforesaid second party] in the process of establishing the relation and pervasion underpinning the proof, he will become aware of the connection between the defining characteristics and the thing that they define. He will thereby gain the knowledge that the expression *impermanent* can legitimately be used for anything that is momentary. [268] This range of scenarios can also be applied to the formulation of other proofs, to understand how deployment works in those cases.

We see plenty of misrepresentations of the proofs that establish the "thing" and proofs that establish the "name and expression." Here I have tackled what lies at the root of these. I have not detailed all the false notions dreamed up by those who apply scholarly analysis to matters that do not warrant such attention.

This completes the explanation of proofs that establish the thing and those that establish the name and expression.

Next, I will examine another crucial issue related to correct proofs. The master [Dharmakīrti] has declared that the inferential cognition—that which "has the reason"—arises from "the cognition that *grasps* the reason" of the correct proof in question.[736] So now we must identify this cognition.

The cognition that grasps the reason

1. Refutation of others' assertions
2. Setting out our own position
3. Dealing with objections [to our position]

Refutation of others' assertions

The author of the *Ornament* [Prajñākaragupta] proposes that when the proof in question is that of the nature variety, the cognition grasping the reason is identical to the inferential cognition that has the reason, because the reason and what has that reason are not different from one another in the ultimate sense. [Conversely,] he says, when the proof is of the effect variety, the reason is separate from what has the reason, ultimately. Hence the cognitions of those must also be separate. He believes that [in the case of inferring fire from smoke], if the person concerned is very familiar [with the association between smoke and fire], the cognition grasping the reason is the one that perceives smoke. But if the person is unfamiliar [with the association], he must be presented with another proof, convincing him that the thing that he perceives [i.e., the smoke] is the same type of thing [found in] the kitchen hearth. The inferential cognition derived from this [preparatory proof] ascertains smoke, and this cognition is the one grasping the reason [for the first proof].[737]

The master Dharmottara says that the [proof's] reason does not, by its mere presence, bring illumination and make things apparent in the manner of a sense power or the flame of a light. He similarly rejects the idea that [the reason], simply by virtue of appearing to a consciousness observing it, [can induce realization]. If it did, [he argues], it would follow that just by becoming aware of its relationship to the proof's probandum, the person would realize [the probandum itself]. Using this logic, he identifies the cognition that apprehends the relationship between the reason and the predicate as one that *grasps* the reason. Based on this, he proposes that there must be two [separate] cognitions involved in grasping the reason, both of which apprehend the relationship between the reason and the predicate. The first apprehends the relationship in terms of the *example* [used as part of the proof], whereas the second apprehends it in terms of the *subject*. He asserts that although the first one may be described as something that grasps the reason, it is the second one that is "the [actual] cognition grasping the reason."[738] [269]

According to Śākyabuddhi, "The [cognition] that has the reason as its object is the one that arises after the perception. It is referred to as a *valid cognition* since it is the cause of valid cognition."[739] In this passage and others, [Śākyabuddhi] sets forth his case. He says that someone [first] has a valid cognition of the property of the subject. This induces another valid cognition, which is a recollection of that property of the subject, and this recollection, he asserts, is the "cognition grasping the reason."

Little credence can be given to what Tibetans have said on the matter, although we note that one of them has agreed with Śākyabuddhi. Another is of the view that any one of the valid cognitions comprehending *either* the [reason's fulfillment of the] three criteria or the reason itself can count as the cognition grasping the reason. Yet another [takes account of variations in the sequence that things are understood prior to grasping the reason]. He claims that in cases where [the other party] understands the property of the subject before [the pervasion], the [later] recollection of the property of the subject counts as the cognition grasping the reason, even though the recollection of the pervasion interposes between [it and the generation of the inferential cognition]. And in cases where [the other party] understands the pervasion before [the property of the subject], the [later] recollection of that pervasion counts as the cognition grasping the reason, whereas the recollection of the property of the subject is both the cognition grasping the reason and the recollection that interposes [between recollection of the pervasion and] the inferential cognition.

[Response:] These positions are all completely untenable, inconsistent, and either have evidence contradicting them or none to support them. Let me elaborate. [With respect to Prajñākaragupta's claims] regarding proofs of the nature variety, it must follow that the [inferential cognition] with the reason is the proof's probandum, because in the ultimate sense, the reason and what has the reason are not different from one another. Thus the three spheres are in place with regard to the position of the *Ornament*.

I will not bother refuting Dharmottara's view that the cognition ascertaining the relationship [between the reason and the predicate] should be identified as the cognition grasping the reason. The author of the *Ornament* [Prajñākaragupta] has provided a lengthy refutation of this, and there is no point in trying to slay what is already a corpse.

I should, nevertheless, address those Indians and Tibetans who classify the cognition grasping the reason as a valid one. They contend that the cognition grasping the reason can be either a perception or an inference. In the case of proofs of the effect variety, they identify it as the valid cognition that establishes the property of the subject, such as the one that perceives smoke [on the mountain pass]. And with a proof [of the nature variety], such as "Sound is impermanent because it is produced," they identify it as a valid inferential cognition, such as one that comprehends the property of the subject and the pervasion.

[Response:] If you want to assert that, you must first physically erase all the [relevant] remarks in the treatises of the master and his spiritual son! These treatises state, for instance, that the cognition grasping the reason is always *conceptual* and is a form of *pseudo* perception. The treatises also explain that while "inferential cognition" in the passage "inferential cognition and [the thing] derived from inferential cognition"[740] may refer to the cognition grasping the reason, the designation is not to be understood as a literal one, and that, in fact, only the thing it describes as being "derived" from inferential cognition is genuinely inferential cognition. [270]

Furthermore, if it was actually the case that the cognition grasping the reason has two distinct varieties—those that are perceptions and those that are inferential cognitions—then surely [Dignāga] should have specified that a portion of the category [i.e., the first variety] are not *pseudo* perceptions whereas the other portion [i.e., inferential cognitions] are. There would be no point in his creating a single category for all cognitions that grasp the reason and describing it as a category of pseudo perceptions.

As for those Indians and Tibetans who identify the cognition grasping the reason as the one that recalls the property of the subject, their position is flawed. They say that the recollection of the property of the subject—a recollection that has been induced by the valid cognition that comprehended the property of the subject—is *necessarily* (1) the cognition that grasps the reason and (2) the cause that will give rise to the [main] inferential cognition. But this cannot be correct, because such a recollection will not necessarily [produce an inferential cognition], since it also sometimes occurs when the reason is an incorrect one. This is because there are cases where valid cognition has verified the property of the subject, despite the reason itself not being correct. Thus those who claim that one cognition recalls only the property of the subject and another only the pervasion, and that either of these can be the cognition grasping the reason in a specific proof will be forced to concede that even an incorrect proof can have a cognition grasping the reason and that [such a cognition] can be the cause that will give rise to an inferential cognition.

Some may say that it is indeed possible to have a cognition grasping a reason that is *not* the cause of an inferential cognition.

[Response:] How would they counter someone who argued that it must [correspondingly] be possible to have a correct reason that is not capable of establishing a proof?

[While acknowledging the impossibility of this,] they may still maintain that there can be a cognition grasping the reason that is not the cognition of a *correct* reason.

[Response:] But then how would they counter someone who argued that [correspondingly] it should be possible for something to fulfill the three criteria of a reason without fulfilling the three criteria of a *correct* reason, such that one could have an incorrect reason that still fulfills the three criteria?

They might say that the existence of such a thing would contradict [the treatises, which] define a correct reason as "the thing that fulfills the three criteria."

[Response:] We would say that their contention [that something can be a cognition grasping a reason but *not* be the cause of an inferential cognition] equally contradicts [the treatises, which] refer to the cognition grasping the reason as "inferential cognition" but explain that this is not a literal [description] and that the rationale behind it is that the cognition grasping the reason is the *cause* of the inferential cognition—that is, a case where the name of the effect is assigned to its cause. And since [these individuals] also accept this, they are contradicting themselves in what they now say.

[These individuals] may claim that some but not all cognitions grasping the reason are causes of inferential cognition. So, though they may accept that the cognition grasping the reason *is* the cause of inferential cognition, and that on this basis, the [treatises] assign it the name ["inferential cognition"], they might still maintain that the [treatises] do not say that every one of these cognitions is such a cause.

[Response:] But then it would follow that [correspondingly] the [category of actual] things can be referred to by the name "pillar," and that this would be a case of the effect's name being assigned to its cause, because *some* things [in the category of actual] things are causes of pillars. The [argument's] reason and pervasion are the ones that they have proposed.

There are many more things that could be said on this topic, but I will pursue it no further right now. [271]

Setting out our own position

"Fulfilling the three criteria" encapsulates what it means to be the correct reason in a proof.[741] Consequently, the cognition grasping the reason must be an awareness that in relation to what is about to serve as the correct reason in the proof, can recall, within a single cognitive act, that it satisfies *all three* of those criteria. It must also be an awareness that has itself been brought about through valid cognition.

Therefore, explained in literal terms of the phrase's derivation, it is a "cognition grasping the reason" in that it is a cognition that, by means of recollection,[742] grasps that which fulfills the three criteria—the encapsulation of what it means to be a correct reason.

The cognition that grasps the reason is thus defined as "a cognition that has been induced by [earlier] valid cognitions comprehending [that *x* fulfills] the three criteria for the proof in question [individually] and can recall, simultaneously, [that *x* fulfills] all three."

In summation, to bring about awareness that the three criteria [are fulfilled] where there had previously been none, it is necessary for the valid cognitions comprehending [each of] those three to operate. But once that awareness has been gained, it is necessary [for the other party] to generate a cognition that grasps all three by recollecting them together, and this is something achieved by deployment of the *proof statement*. And it is from this cognition that the inferential cognition that "has the reason" is produced.

Dealing with objections [to our position]

Pointing to the passage in the *Compendium of Pramāṇa* that says "Cognition of the reason is not the direct cause of the inferential cognition, because recollection interposes between [the two],"[743] someone may ask, "Doesn't this state that what has the reason [i.e., the inferential cognition] is *not* directly produced from the cognition grasping that reason?"

[Response:] This is not the case. The phrase "cognition of the reason" may [generally speaking] refer either to the valid cognitions that [initially] comprehend the [fulfillment of] the reason's three criteria [individually] or to the [subsequent] recollection of those three [all together]. In this particular passage, it indicates the [first of these] valid cognitions. It is a response to the question "Is the valid cognition that realizes the probandum produced directly from the valid cognitions that [initially] comprehend the [fulfillment of the] three criteria?" [Dignāga] replies, "No, that is not [the immediate] cause, because [the awareness] that recalls [the fulfillment of] all three criteria together interposes between the two." In light of this, the [whole] discussion [introduced by others]—about the inferential cognition not being directly produced from recollection of the property of the subject because recollection of the pervasion interposes between the two—has no place here whatsoever. One can have no confidence in such interpretations. They are comparable to the echoes that prompted the startled reports of the proverbial hare.[744]

But what then [do the treatises] mean when they describe reasons as the causes of the cognitions that grasp the reason?[745]

[Response:] To understand this point, it is necessary to penetrate the meaning of the passage "Whatever a thing is . . ."[746] For this, my own commentary on the treatise should be consulted.

Here I have explained with total accuracy the cognition grasping the reason, and with this, I end the description of the correct logical reason. [272]

As the heads of individuals who had dared to view themselves as scholars bow before me, like those of a thousand once-proud elephants, I, a fearless lion of discourse, sporting the abundant mane of learned tradition and roaring my message of logic, stride out triumphantly.

With hands bathed in the beautifying lamplight of scripture and reasoning,
and with vision made luminous by an incomparable intellect, I purvey
the whole gamut of knowable objects, as I elucidate omniscience and the
true excellence.[747]

19. Incorrect Reasons

The inverse [of the correct reason], the false logical reason

1. Defining characteristics
2. Varieties

The false logical reason is defined as "a reason that does not fulfill the three criteria."

There are three varieties: reasons that are not confirmed, reasons that are contrary, and reasons that are inconclusive.

Reasons that are not confirmed

A reason that is not confirmed is defined as "something presented as a logical reason, but with respect to which, the property of the subject has not been confirmed." There are three varieties of these: reasons that are unconfirmed on factual grounds, reasons that are unconfirmed due to [inadequate] knowledge, and reasons that are unconfirmed due to the protagonists [in the debate].

Reasons that are unconfirmed on factual grounds

Those that fail on factual grounds are divided into five: reasons that are not confirmed because (1) the thing [cited as the] reason is an impossible one, (2) the thing [cited as the] subject is an impossible one, (3) there is no [logical] relationship between the basis [i.e., the subject] and the reason, (4) some portion of the reason cannot be found in the subject, and (5) some portion of the subject cannot be found in the reason.

An example of the first is the reason in the proof "The individual [A] has a self [B] because it possesses the qualities of a self [C]." An example of the second is the reason in the proof "Self [A] pervades everything [B] because its properties, pleasure and so forth, are observed in everything [C]." [273]

The things forming the reasons in these two proofs are *not confirmed* [in that] they do not exist and the predicate each proof is supposed to establish is affirmative in character. The fact that the thing forming the reason does not exist would not, however, necessarily count as a flaw [in the context of another proof], such as when the predicate is a negative one, and what the proof is intended to establish is a straight negation. By the same token, a reason of the affirming variety counts as one that is *not confirmed* if used in a proof attempting to establish something about a subject that does not exist. The fact that the thing forming the subject does not exist would not necessarily count as a flaw if the proof in question seeks only to *negate* something [about that subject].

An example of the third is the reason in the proof "Sound [A] is impermanent [B] because it is something apprehended visually [C]." An example of the fourth is the reason in the proof "The sense consciousness to which two moons appear [A] is a perception [B] because it is a cognition that is nonconceptual and unmistaken [C]." An example of the fifth is the reason in the proof "The three conditions of sense consciousness [A] are causes of the later sense consciousness that is their result [B] because of being things experienced [by self-cognition]."

Reasons that are unconfirmed due to [inadequate] knowledge

These have two varieties: those that fail due to doubts and those that fail because of the subject of interest.

Those that fail due to doubts

The first of these has three varieties: (1) those that fail due to doubts regarding the subject, (2) those that fail due to doubts regarding the reason, and (3) those that fail because of doubts surrounding the [logical] relationship between the subject and the reason.

The respective examples of these are: (1) the reason in the proof "The pot belonging to the *piśāci* in the space before us [A] is impermanent [B] because it is produced [C]" when presented to a person for whom a *piśāci* is a remote object, (2) the reason "[because there is] smoke" used to establish the presence of fire in a certain spot when the other party has not yet ascertained whether the substance above that spot is smoke or water vapor, and (3) the reason in the proof "In the middle dell of three [A] there is a peacock [B] because there is the cry of a peacock [C]" when the other party is someone who has not yet ascertained from which of the three dells that cry emanates.

Those that fail because of the subject of interest

These unconfirmed reasons have three varieties: (1) those that fail because the basis of discussion [i.e., the subject] and the reason are identical, (2) those that fail because the basis and the predicate are identical, and (3) those that fail because the predicate and the reason are identical.

An example of the first is the reason in the proof "Sound [A] is impermanent [B], because it is sound [C]." Why is this reason classified as one that is unconfirmed? [274] Because [to confirm something as] the property of the subject, one must first ascertain the subject of interest and, having done that, ascertain that the thing that serves as the reason is present in that subject. That is, one must be able to think of the subject as the *basis* to which the property belongs, and the reason as the *property* [belonging to that basis].[748] But when sound represents both elements involved, this cannot work. This is not in actuality a case of a reason that is unconfirmed due to the absence of a subject of interest. But I have just included it in the category because the classification I present here is an abridged one. Since there can be no suggestion that the proof fails because "sound is not present in sound," I don't feel that it can be classified as one that fails on factual grounds.

An example of the second is the reason in the proof "Sound [A] is sound [B] because it is produced [C]." Here sound cannot serve as the subject of interest—the thing that the other party wishes to know something about—since he will obviously not think, "I wonder whether sound is sound?" So sound cannot [constitute] the subject of interest [for him]. Thus he cannot ascertain that "[being] produced" is a property of the subject of interest. This is why I have classified this as a proof that fails because the property of the subject is unconfirmed. There can be no suggestion that the proof fails because sound is something that is not produced. So, once again, I don't feel as though it can be classified as one that fails on factual grounds.

An example of the third is the reason in the proof "Sound [A] is impermanent [B] because it is impermanent [C]." The reason is supposed to be presented to the other party to apprise him of the fact that sound is impermanent; something that he had not previously known. But as "impermanent" is both the predicate and the reason, there can be no distinction between them in terms of how difficult they are to ascertain.[749] And because [for the other party] it has yet to be established that sound is impermanent, "impermanent" cannot be used as the probans to prove that fact [to him]. It is on these grounds that [the reason] fails, and it is why I have classified it as one that is unconfirmed. Since this has nothing to do with the facts of the matter, such as sound not being impermanent, again I don't feel it can be classified as one that fails on factual grounds.

Reasons that are unconfirmed due to the protagonists [in the debate]

There are three varieties: (1) those that fail because of the first party, (2) those that fail because of the second party, and (3) those that fail because of both parties.

An example of the first is the reason in the proof "Mind and pleasure [A] are inanimate [qualities] [B], because they are subject to production and destruction [C]." This proof is directed at the Buddhist by the Sāṃkhya. For the Sāṃkhya, describing the mind and pleasure as "produced" means that they *materialize*, [since he believes] that they already existed [prior to becoming manifest]. Likewise, for him, "destruction" is to return to that original, nonmaterialized state. What production and destruction *actually* mean—namely, the production of a brand-new thing and for a thing that had been in existence to totally cease—are [qualities that] the Sāṃkhya denies with regard to mind and pleasure. In this sense, the first party has failed to ascertain through valid cognition the presence of the reason in the subject. [275]

An example of the second is the reason in the proof "Trees [A] are sentient [B] because they die when their bark is peeled [C]." This proof is presented by the Nirgrantha to the Buddhist. The second party here, the Buddhist, has already ascertained by means of valid cognition that "death" means the extinction of life. Hence he has already ruled out, by means of valid cognition, that the reason is a property of the subject [i.e., that death is a property of trees]. Why then is this proof not classified as one that fails due to the first party? Others try to explain this by saying that the first party believes that death for a tree is its drying up when its bark is peeled. Therefore, they say, according to the notion of [death in the Nirgrantha's] own system, the first party has *confirmed* that the tree "dies."

[Response:] It would follow that when the Sāṃkhya presents "production and destruction" as the reason to establish that mind and pleasure are inanimate, it is also a case of a reason that fails due to it being unconfirmed for the first party. This is because [the Sāṃkhya] believes that "production" means that a thing that already exists materializes and that "destruction" means that it returns to its unmanifest state, and he has, according to the understanding of his own system, confirmed these in relation to mind and pleasure. The three spheres are in place [for this argument, and the position advanced by those in question is shown to be irredeemably flawed]. Their reasoning is erroneous. To advocate that the drying up of the tree when its bark is peeled constitutes its death is every bit as unacceptable as advocating that an existent thing [shifting from] states of being manifest and unmanifest constitute its production and destruction.

Admittedly, it is extremely difficult to distinguish between the two aforesaid proofs, asserting that the property of the subject is confirmed for the first party in one case but not the other. But here is what I have to say on the matter. It is not established that the tree "dies" when its bark is peeled. Neither is it established that the tree drying up when its bark is peeled constitutes its "death." Nonetheless, what this first party [the Nirgrantha] holds to be the tree's death—namely, its drying up when its bark is peeled—is something he has confirmed by means of valid cognition in relation to the subject [tree]. [By contrast,] what the Sāṃkhya holds to be the meaning of [a thing's] production and destruction—namely, that it becomes manifest and unmanifest—is nothing more than an assertion. He cannot confirm these in relation to mind and pleasure by means of valid cognition, because they are total impossibilities. It is with this specific point in mind that [Dignāga and Dharmakīrti] distinguish between the two proofs, saying that one of them is confirmed for the first party and the other one not. But they were not saying that there are any such grounds for differentiating between the two proofs in real terms, since in the case of the former proof also [just like the latter], the reason does not count as the property of the subject for the first party. Why? Because that other party, the Buddhist, has already ruled out by means of valid cognition the thesis [that the Sāṃkhya] is attempting to prove. And since the Buddhist has already ascertained that mind and pleasure *are* animate [qualities], he has no interest in them as the subjects in a proof intended to establish a predicate [opposite to this]. [276] So, while it is correct to say that something can only count as the property of the subject when the second party is interested in the proof's thesis, there is no guarantee that a party who has confirmed the property of the subject will maintain an interest. It is necessary to make this distinction.

The latter proof also is one in which the reason does not qualify as the property of the subject for the first party in the debate. If it did, the person in question would need to have ascertained with valid cognition the presence of the reason in the subject. But there is simply no such thing as a valid cognition of the tree's death!

An example of the third, a proof that fails due to not being confirmed for either party, would [occur in the situation] that neither the first party nor the second party had ascertained that sound is produced. In an attempt to establish "Sound is impermanent," whether the first party used "[because] it is produced" or "[because] it is not produced" as his reason, they would be [equally unconfirmed].

Reasons that are contrary [to the thesis proposed]

1. Defining characteristics
2. Varieties

A contrary reason is defined as "that which is confirmed to be the property of the subject in a proof, the pervasion of which is ascertained by valid cognition to be the converse [of the one required to establish the thesis]."

There are four varieties of contrary reasons, those in proofs that derive from the refutation of (1) the nature of the predicate, (2) the nature of the subject, (3) a quality of the predicate, and (4) a quality of the subject. The example and identification of each are as follows. The example of the first is the reason in the proof "Sound [A] is permanent [B because it is produced [C]." The way that the proof should be formulated for the second is dealt with in two sections:

1. Refutation of others' assertions
2. Setting out our own position

Refutation of others' assertions

As the example of a contrary reason [in a proof where] the nature of the subject is refuted, someone gives "The real entity, space[750] [A] is permanent [B] because it is devoid of any functional activity [C]." Despite identifying this as the example, he denies that it can be regarded as a genuine contrary reason of this [second] variety. This is because, he says, it is impossible to have a proof of the "thesis-subject" [type][751] if the thing forming the subject does not exist. This is why he claims that this proof *as stated* cannot constitute one with a contrary reason, whereas the proof *as intended* can.[752] He formulates the intended proof as "Space and the like [A] are permanent, real entities, with a distinct substance [B], because they are devoid of any functional activity [C]." [277] [This individual] says that this is the Vaiśeṣika's [intended proof], because when he states the proof in the way he does, what he [the Vaiśeṣika] really *wants* to establish is that space and suchlike are [all] permanent, real entities, with a distinct substance. And that, [this individual] says, is what is referred to in the passage beginning "the subject of space . . ."[753]

Others disagree, proposing that the reason for the proof in question is an authentic contrary one. They deny that it is flawed on the grounds that the property of the subject is not established. While admitting that [the property of the subject] cannot be established with respect to the *nature* of what is taken as the subject—in that it does not apply to "the real entity"—they say that it does apply to the *quality* of that subject—namely, "space."

[Response:] These and various other assertions [made on this matter] have no real essence to them, as I will now explain. I have already clearly demonstrated that any logical proof of the thesis-subject variety necessarily requires a subject. There is, however, no evidence to support the [first individual] in his contention that one can differentiate between the proof that the person states and the one that he actually intends. So, in this case, it must be [regarded as this individual's] own invention. What is more, according to [this individual, when the Vaiśeṣika] states the proof, what he wishes to establish is that [the subject] is a permanent, real entity, with a distinct substance. It is by virtue of this being what [the Vaiśeṣika] wants to establish that [the individual] comes up with his version of the "intended proof." But let us consider the case of someone who wants to establish "Sound is impermanent because it is produced." [He cannot do so without first] establishing [to the second party that "produced" fulfills the criterion of the reverse pervasion], something that requires the presentation of another proof. So, according to [this individual's logic], when this person presents this other [preparative] proof—namely, "A permanent thing [A] is devoid of production [B] because it is devoid of functional activity" [C]—it would follow that the proof that must be identified as the intended one is "Sound is impermanent because it is devoid of functional activity." Why? Because what he *wants* to establish, when he presents [the reason of this earlier proof, is the thesis of the subsequent one,] that sound is impermanent. This is a criticism [of this individual's position] to which he has no response.

The [second group of individuals] assert that even though the [nature of the] reason is not a property of the [whole] subject, it still counts as the property of the subject, in that it is a quality of that subject. But based on that logic, it would follow that as long as someone used "sound that is selfless" as the subject of his proof, then no matter what he cited as the reason, it could never fail to qualify as a property of that subject. What is more, if what they asserted was correct, then the [treatises'] whole account of proofs that fail because either part of the reason or part of the subject is not confirmed would collapse.

Also, they claim that the reason in the proof "The real entity, space, is permanent because it is devoid of any functional activity" counts as an authentic contrary one. It would follow therefore that the [proof's] pervasion, "Anything that is devoid of functional activity is necessarily permanent," must be the converse [of what is required]. But from this it would follow that "[being] devoid of functional activity" [establishes the converse of the proof's thesis] and, as such, is a *correct reason* establishing that the real entity, space, is *impermanent*! Where in the world could we find stupidity to rival that of the person who is prepared to hold such a view?

All these [individuals] are just floating about in space.[754] Failing to get to the root of the matter, they instead concern themselves deludedly with the offshoots emanating from it. What then is the correct position? [278]

Setting out our own position

The [aforesaid] formulations of contrary reasons—where [distinctions are made between] those in which the nature of the subject is refuted, a quality of the subject is refuted, and so forth—are not separate types, distinguished by way of what serves as the reason and the different things that can be negated within them. In all cases, the thing that is negated and to which the reason is *contrary* is the proof's thesis. That is, what serves as the contrary reason is something that [actually] rules out the *nature* of the predicate being a property of the proof's subject. In this sense, there is nothing to distinguish them from each other. Any distinctions that are made relate to the refutation of views held by various other [non-Buddhist schools] and are based solely on the proofs *deriving* from these debates.[755] This is why [the *Commentary on Pramāṇa*] says, "[Only] in reference to this is it said that some things are the property and [others are] the quality of the subject."[756] It is also what the *Ascertainment of Pramāṇa* means when it says, "They are different only in terms of their presentation, and not in any actual sense."[757]

As regards the contrary reason where the nature of the subject is refuted, what is the context in which this occurs and what is the proof derived from it? The example can be explained as follows. The Vaiśeṣika contends that space forms an actual, substantial entity. But the Buddhist asserts that it is nothing more than a straight negation, the absence of any sort of form with physical resistance. Therefore the two parties do not share a common understanding regarding the nature of space and are not debating whether being a "real entity" is a property of such a space. Instead, their dispute is about space *as the basis* of [any proposed] property, and whether it is a straight negation of physical resistance or something constituting a substance. In the course of the debate, the Buddhist questions the Vaiśeṣika, "Assuming that the nature of space is something 'real,' is it permanent or impermanent?" The Vaiśeṣika responds that it is permanent. The Buddhist then goes on to query what evidence the Vaiśeṣika has to support this claim. His answer is "because it is devoid of any functional activity." In this, he is asserting that "[being] devoid of any functional activity" is a reason establishing his claim "The real entity, space, is permanent." It is this formulation that the master Dignāga attacks in the passage "This is contrary in that it establishes that the nature of the subject is the exact opposite [of the one being ascribed to it]."[758] "Subject" here refers to space and "nature," a real [entity]. The [two parties] have no shared understanding regarding space's nature. So there is no foundation for a debate about whether such a space has the property of being a real entity. [279] In that respect, the debate is unlike [the pattern of others], where both parties have established the nature of a subject, such as, for instance, sound, [which they realize] is something audible, and with that sound as the basis, can then proceed to debate whether or not it has the property of impermanence. Here, [the protagonists have] no shared notion of the nature of the basis, space, with one side [asserting that] it is just a straight negation of physical resistance and the other that it is a real [substantial] entity. It is at this juncture that [the Vaiśeṣika], who believes that it has the nature of a real entity, proposes that "The real entity, space [A], is permanent [B] because it is devoid of any functional activity [C]." This prompts [the Buddhist] refutation: "Being devoid of any functional activity [A] is not a correct probans establishing that the real entity, space, is permanent [B], because that [lack of activity] is the reason that refutes the subject [space] having such a nature [C]. This follows, because the fact that it is devoid of any functional activity is a correct probans establishing that the nature of space is the very opposite of a real entity. Hence it is exactly *contrary* to a reason that is able to prove that the nature of the subject, space, is that of a real entity."

To sum up, when the master said, "This is contrary in that it establishes that the nature of the subject is the exact opposite [of the one being ascribed to it],"[759] he was refuting the idea that the Vaiśeṣika could use "being devoid of any functional activity" as a correct reason to establish that their "real entity, space" is permanent. The [actual] proof with a *contrary reason* [he refers to], therefore, is the one that can either be said to be *derived* from his refutation of the Vaiśeṣika's argument or the one that is *suggested* [in the process] of that refutation. It is this: "Space [A] has the nature of a real entity [B] because it is devoid of any functional activity [C]." That *this* is a proof with an authentic contrary reason is a matter beyond dispute. What [Dignāga] tells us is that if this reason "[being] devoid of any functional activity" were used to refute what the Vaiśeṣika asserts about the [real] nature of the subject, it would count as a correct one. However, if it is presented as one that establishes what the Vaiśeṣika asserts, it counts as a contrary reason. *Nowhere* does he identify "The real entity, space," as the subject, such that the [proof's] subject consists of both the subject [space] and its nature. The proof with the contrary reason that he is discussing is *not*, therefore, "The real entity, space [A], is permanent [B] because it is devoid of any functional activity [C]." This proof may be one that [the Vaiśeṣika] presents to establish the permanence of the subject [space], which he *assumes* has a certain [real] nature, but it is not one that he presents to establish that the subject has such a nature. Therefore the question of whether this is a proof that has a reason contrary to the nature of the subject simply does not arise. [280]

To summarize [my point], the proof "Space [A] has the nature of a real entity [B] because it is devoid of any functional activity [C]" is one in which the reason is contrary to the nature of the predicate. And it is also what negates the nature that the Vaiśeṣika [ascribes to] the subject in the proof that he uses. Through this, I have shown how, from the various contexts of refuting others' positions, one can derive proofs with contrary reasons that are "different" [from one another], while still affirming that all of them are essentially the same, in that what is always negated is that the "contrary reason" is the nature of the *predicate*. In this snowy mountain land, I alone have been able to provide a clear account of this.

Returning to the examples of the contrary reasons, we have those for the third and fourth varieties, in which what is refuted is a quality of the predicate and a quality of the subject.

1. Setting out the correct position
2. Refuting incorrect positions

Setting out the correct position

First, the Sāṃkhya opponent advocates that every object of knowledge is included in their definitive enumeration of twenty-five categories. Among these, they say that the conscious entity that is the person constitutes the "self." All remaining categories are made up of things that are either for the enjoyment or control of such a self. As they are all there to serve the ends of this "self," they belong to it in the sense of being at its personal disposal.

No self-respecting logician is going to advance a thesis without supplying a probans to substantiate it. Accordingly, the Sāṃkhya pursues two lines of reasoning to support what he asserts. One of these seeks to establish that the conscious entity, the person, must be identified as the "self." The other is to establish that things such as the various senses are at the disposal of this "self." The first uses proofs such as "The person [A] is the self [B] because it is the basis for an individual being trapped in or free [from samsara] [C]." I have given a fuller account of these proofs as well as the way they are refuted elsewhere.

With respect to the second line of reasoning, through which the Sāṃkhya wishes to establish that the various senses are at the disposal of that self, we should differentiate the proof as stated by the Sāṃkhya from the one that he actually intends.[760] The proof as he states it is "Sight and so forth [A] serve the purposes of some other [party] [B], because they are composites and collections [C], just as is the case, for example, with things like bedding and seating." However, what he really intends to establish is "Sight and so on [A] serve the purposes of the self [B], because they are composites and collections [C]." [281] Why is it then that the Sāṃkhya does not from the outset just say, "They serve the purposes of the self"? He is concerned that unless he formulates the proof as he does, the Buddhist will deny that this predicate is true of the example [i.e., "bedding and seating"] and will therefore dismiss the proof on the grounds that it lacks a valid example embodying both the reason and the predicate. Consequently, the Sāṃkhya comes up with this disingenuous formulation, which, as it is overtly stated, *seems* to choose an example that both parties know to be concomitant with the predicate but, in terms of what he actually *means*, is intended to establish that things such as the senses are at the personal disposal of the "self."

Thus the Sāṃkhya's basic proof is "Sight and so forth [A] serve the purposes of some other [party] [B], because they are composites and collections [C]." There are two versions of this, depending on how he chooses to formulate it. One is "Sight and so forth, those things [that belong to the] noncomposite one [A], serve the purposes of some other [party] [B], because they are composites and collections [C]." The other is "Sight and so forth [A] serve the purposes of the other, the noncomposite [cognitive] subject [B], because they are composites and collections [C]."

Despite the fact that the Sāṃkhya only cites "sight and so forth" [as the subject], he must, of course, establish that all of his twenty-four remaining objects of knowledge are there to serve the purposes of the self. He knows, however, that if he succeeds in proving that the senses such as sight and objects such as visual forms are at the self's disposal, there will be no difficulty in establishing that this is also the case for the other things. He is also aware that his [Buddhist] opponent does not share his conception of the twenty-four things, so if all twenty-four were cited, the proof would not have a subject accepted by both parties. Thus he chooses [just] the senses such as sight and objects such as visual forms—things that are accepted by both parties—as the subject. And when he says, "sight and so forth," it is [all twenty-four] that he has in mind and sets about trying to prove are at the disposal of the "self." This is how one should understand the subject of the proof.

The Sāṃkhya believes that the conscious entity, the person, is not a material one, whereas all other things are. This is why he describes all those other things as "composites and collections," and reserves the title "noncomposite" for the person. For the Sāṃkhya, "composite" denotes something that is made up of particles that, either gradually or abruptly, come together to compose an assemblage. When he talks of something that is "noncomposite," he means the exact opposite of this. As far as he sees it, coming together to form a composite is the very essence of what it means to be matter. The only [cognitive] subject able to perceive all twenty-four objects is the conscious entity, the person. Thus these twenty-four are said to be the person's objects.

What the Sāṃkhya means, therefore, when he refers to the sight and so forth as "those things [that belong to the] noncomposite one" is that they are the objects of this "self." [282] Thus his subject "sight and so forth, those things [that belong to the] noncomposite one" actually refers to "sight and so forth, the objects of the self." And since he asserts that this self is not a composite but is the subject [that perceives] all twenty-four objects, he designates it "the noncomposite subject." The [particle connecting] "noncomposite" [with "subject" indicates that the two] form a single unit. It is not a [separative] sixth-case, genitive particle.[761] So, when the Sāṃkhya refers to those that "serve the purposes of the other, the noncomposite subject," what he means is that they are there for the sake of something other than themselves, the entity that is not material but is a subject—namely, the "self." And when the Sāṃkhya says that these things "serve a purpose," he does not simply mean it in the productive sense of them being causes that bring about effects. Instead, what he has in mind is that they satisfy an end, just as, for instance, bedding is useful to the individual in that it helps with such things as warding off the cold. Similarly, the senses and so forth satisfy the ends of the "self," because it is by means of the five senses that the self can experience the five [sense] objects. This is what the Sāṃkhya really means when he talks of things being there to "serve the purposes of the self." To be there to "serve the purposes" of the self is to help satisfy its needs and achieve its ends. And as far as the Sāṃkhya is concerned, this "satisfying the needs and achieving the ends of the self" captures the essence of what it is to be at the disposal of that "self." This is why he believes that once he has established that the senses and so forth satisfy those needs and achieve those ends, he will have proved that they are at the disposal of that "self."

So much then for what the phrases in the Sāṃkhya proof mean and what the Sāṃkhya wants to achieve with that proof. When the Sāṃkhya presents his proof, hoping to establish that the senses and so forth are at the disposal of the self, the master [Dignāga] attacks it by asking about the "other" in the phrase "serves the purposes of some other" within the Sāṃkhya's proof. He questions whether what the Sāṃkhya intends by this "other" is the self or simply some "other." [Dignāga] says that if it is only the latter, the Sāṃkhya proof is unsuccessful, since what it aims to establish is something that he [the Buddhist] already knows. If, on the other hand, it means that the senses and so forth are there to serve the purposes of the "self," [Dignāga] says that the reason the Sāṃkhya uses is not a correct one. [Dignāga] asserts that the fact that sight and so forth are "composites" in no way proves that they are there to satisfy the needs and achieve the ends of some "noncomposite" self. Indeed, he says, in relation to the quality of the subject in the proof, the fact that they are composites actually establishes the opposite of what the Sāṃkhya [intends]. Hence the reason must be [classified as] one that is contrary to the quality of the subject. That [reason actually] negates sight and so forth, the *subject* in the proof, being there to serve the purposes of the "noncomposite one," the *quality* that the Sāṃkhya [tries to attribute to them]. [283] The way that the master Dignāga puts this is, "This is contrary in that it establishes that the quality of the subject is the exact opposite [of the one being ascribed to it]."[762]

In summary then, what [Dignāga] tells us as he refutes the Sāṃkhya's proof is that the very fact that the [proof's] subjects are composites rules out the quality that the [Sāṃkhya wants to ascribe to] them. He also identifies "composites" as a reason that is *contrary* to the quality of the subject that the proof seeks to establish.

[Dignāga] is definitely *not* suggesting here that the subject of the proof is "sight and so forth, the objects of the noncomposite one." That is, he is not saying that the [proof's] subject is constituted of the subject that is [supposed to] possess the quality, together with that quality itself, and that this [combined] subject is the one that the proof aims to establish are "there to serve the purposes of self." Such a contrary reason is in fact not possible. Why? Because "composites" could not possibly serve as a correct reason to establish that "Sight and so forth, the objects of the self, are there to serve the purposes of the self." It cannot do this because there is no such thing as the material entity "sight and so forth, the objects of the self."

[When Dignāga refers to] the "quality of the subject" here, the subject in question is "sight and so forth." The "quality" is [them being] "objects of the noncomposite one." Both sides agree that "sight and so forth" constitutes the basis [of their discussion]. They also agree that what is at issue is whether these have the quality of being "objects of the noncomposite one." It is in this context that [the Sāṃkhya], under the impression that sight and so forth indeed possess such a quality, fuses the two together in the subject of his proof. Taking this as his subject, he then tries to establish that because such things are composites, they are "there to serve the purposes of the self." It is at this point that the master delivers his refutation of the proof in the form of the words "This is contrary in that it establishes that the quality of the subject is the exact opposite [of the one ascribed to it]." This informs us that "[being] composite" establishes the opposite of the quality [that the Sāṃkhya wants to attribute to] the subject "sight and so forth"—that is, the quality of them being "objects of the noncomposite one." Thus the reason is contrary to what [the Sāṃkhya] wants to establish.

In line with this explanation, the proof that the Sāṃkhya uses is "Sight and so forth, the objects of the noncomposite one [A], are there to serve the purposes of some other [B], because they are noncomposite [C]." The proof with the contrary reason is the one derived from or conveyed through [Dignāga's] refutation of that Sāṃkhya proof. It is, "Sight and so forth [A] are there to be used by the noncomposite one [B], because they are composites [C]." This is the proof described as the one in which the reason is "contrary to the quality of the subject." [284] It gains this name from the fact that while the Sāṃkhya uses "sight and so forth" as the *subject* of his proof and assumes that these things have the *quality* of being "the objects of the noncomposite one," the reason [he uses] is contrary to "sight and so forth" being the basis for the attribution of such a quality.

The [treatises may seem to] represent the reason as one that differs from other contrary reasons, but this [only] derives from the way the proof in which it features is formulated in terms of refuting the Sāṃkhya. What the reason *itself* is contrary to is the nature of the *predicate* in the proof. So it is perfectly in keeping with what the treatises say on the matter.

When the Sāṃkhya uses the proof "Sight and so forth [A] are there to serve the purposes of the other, the noncomposite [cognitive] subject [B], because they are composites [C]," what he has in mind for the "other," whose purposes are served, is the "self." To refute this, the master Dignāga remarks, "This is contrary in that it establishes that the quality of the predicate is the exact opposite [of the one ascribed to it]."[763] It is in this proof that the basis of the quality and the quality ascribed to it are fused together in the predicate. "Serving the purposes" is the basis [of the attribution]. As to whose purposes are being served—just as a [specific] purpose, such as containing water, helps distinguish one thing [such as a pot] from others—the [specific] qualifier of the purposes here [identify] "the self" or "the self, the noncomposite [cognitive] subject"—since the two amount to the same thing here—as the one being served.

In saying that the reason in question "establishes that the quality of the predicate is the exact opposite [of the one ascribed to it]," what [Dignāga] means is that "[being] composites" would actually work as a correct reason if it were used to establish that sight and so forth are *not* there to serve the purposes of "the self, the noncomposite [cognitive] subject." And in saying that it is "contrary," he means that it is completely contrary to establishing that sight and so forth *are* there to serve the purposes of "the self, the noncomposite [cognitive] subject." To sum up, the contrary reason identified [by Dignāga] here is *derived* from the refutation of what the Sāṃkhya states. [Dignāga] asserts that this reason counts as an authentic contrary one, because it would serve as a correct one if it were used to establish the exact opposite of what the [Sāṃkhya] proposes.

Refuting incorrect positions

Others have given accounts of the contrary reason, in which they discuss such things as why [the treatises] talk about these reasons, how they are presented, and what counts as the example for each. But none of them have recognized the core issue. In setting out at some length what this core issue is, [most of their accounts] have been rebutted. As to other refutations that could be aimed at their assertions, there are simply too many to record here. [285]

However, we note that certain studious individuals claim that the "and so forth" in the phrase "sight and so forth" denotes the observed object and the immediate conditions. Hence they identify the subject of the Sāṃkhya proof as "all three conditions [that produce] a sense cognition."

[Response:] This is incorrect. According to the Sāṃkhya, the self, the conscious person, is able to experience the five objects by means of the senses, such as the eye—that is, sight. Aside from the eye and so forth, he does not believe in any sort of visual cognition—distinct from the self—that could allow it to view such things as physical forms. The analogy he uses to illustrate this situation is that of a person who dwells alone in a tower and is able to gaze out in every direction through a series of holes in the walls. This shows that the Sāṃkhya does not accept that there are "sense cognitions" distinct from the self. So why on earth would he be talking about the three conditions that [produce] such cognitions?

Also, treatises such as the *Compendium of Abhidharma* inform us that it was to demolish the notion of a self exactly like that espoused [by the Sāṃkhya] that the Blessed One, when he taught, broke things down into eighteen constituent elements—the eye element, the visual cognition element, and so on.[764] So all that you, the "studious one," have succeeded in doing is unfurling your standard, proclaiming that you are no more than a skimmer of the treatises.

Someone else asserts that "and so forth" denotes the [remaining] twenty-three objects of the Sāṃkhya's [classification], all of which [the Sāṃkhya] holds to be physical matter. This individual therefore identifies the proof's subject, "sight and so forth," as all twenty-four [of the Sāṃkhya's] objects.

[Response:] He has obviously not even looked at [Dignāga's earlier] statement, according to which the Buddhist has *already established* that the "sight and so forth" of the subject serve the purposes of others.

Someone else suggests that the subject, as far as the Sāṃkhya is concerned, is all twenty-four objects, whereas for the Buddhist, it is just the five senses.

[Response:] If that was the case, while the Sāṃkhya set out to prove that his "twenty-four objects of knowledge" are there to serve the purposes of some other, the Buddhist's response would amount to him saying that the Sāṃkhya proof does not work for him, because he, the Buddhist, has already established that "the five senses" serve the purposes of some other. So the Buddhist would be [guilty of] responding in a manner that bears no relation to what the Sāṃkhya proposes. [To this individual, we say,] don't exhibit [your foolishness] with such relish!

Anyway, [this individual's] analysis [only seeks] to determine such things as whether [the element] betraying that the "other" [in the Sāṃkhya proof] actually refers to the "self" is the subject, the reason, or whatever. This is a pitiful way to while away the day. What is the point of such an exercise? However much one analyzes, there is nothing to be said beyond what the master [Dharmakīrti] himself pronounced on such matters: "Even if he does not [openly] state his intention, it is determinable from the context."[765] [286]

Others propose that for the proof [seeking to establish] that "sound is permanent," "produced" is the contrary reason in which the nature of the predicate is refuted. It would follow that "produced" is a contrary reason in the refutation of sound being permanent. And the notion that it is a *correct* reason establishing that sound is impermanent collapses.[766] This concludes the description of contrary reasons.

When the skill required is that of determining a cow's age, even the most
intelligent person can look like a prize fool.
When the skill required is that of determining the complexities of logic,
who else in the whole wide world is there [to call on]?[767]

Reasons that are inconclusive

1. Defining characteristics
2. Varieties

A reason that is inconclusive is defined as "a reason with respect to which the property of the subject in the proof has been established, but the other party has not ascertained the relationship [underpinning] the pervasion."[768]

It has two varieties: inconclusive reasons that are *not shared* and inconclusive reasons that are *shared*. The first of the two is defined as "a reason that the other party—for whom it constitutes the property of the subject—has found neither among the class of similar instances nor the class of dissimilar instances." In the proof "Sound [A] is impermanent [B] because it is a heard thing [C]," "heard thing" is an example of this kind of reason.

Why then is this called an "inconclusive reason that is not shared"? This sort of reason is only involved with the proof's subject. Consequently, there can be no correct similar example to serve as the basis for ascertaining the relationship [underpinning] the pervasion [of the proof]. But what does this line "not involved with anything other than the subject" mean? Is the "other" that the reason has no involvement with something distinguished from it only in a [nominal, conceptual] sense of a separate isolate or in the [actual] sense of being a separate entity from it? If it was the first, it would follow that [the reason] "thing heard" is not even involved with known objects.[769] As for the second alternative, let us consider the proof "That which is devoid of momentariness [A] is devoid of production [B], because it is devoid of any functional activity [C]." [Based on the second alternative, according to which "other" denotes entities that are separate from the reason,] it follows that this reason must count as one that has no involvement with anything other than the subject, because it has no involvement with any entities other than those that are devoid of momentariness. But if one accepted that, it would follow that this proof—which is the [*correct*] [preparative] countering one, demonstrating the reverse pervasion for the proof "Sound is impermanent because it is produced"—counts as [one with an inconclusive reason of] the not-shared variety!

Some might dismiss those two alternatives, suggesting instead that "not involved with anything other than the subject" should be understood as referring to the fact that [a reason such as] "thing heard" is involved only with [the subject] "sound," in the sense that it is impossible to have a thing heard that is not a sound. [287]

[Response:] Then the same must also [apply to the aforesaid preparative countering] proof, which has "that which is devoid of momentariness" as its subject and "[because it is] devoid of any functional activity" as its reason, since it is impossible to have something "momentary" that is "devoid of any functional activity."

Some may reject all three of the preceding alternatives, asserting [instead] that to say "a thing heard is involved only with sound" means that there can be no valid cognition that ascertains, with respect to some locus, that a "thing heard" is a certain phenomenon without also ascertaining that sound is that phenomenon.

[Response:] But that would mean that it is impossible to have a locus with respect to which [someone] could have ascertained that "thing heard" is a defining characteristic without also ascertaining that sound is a defining characteristic. But [if that were the case], it would follow that the "sound of a conch" could never serve as the locus of illustration for a valid cognition to ascertain that "thing heard" is the characteristic that defines sound.

Someone else may propose that what [the line] means is that it is impossible to have ascertained by valid cognition that some phenomenon is a "thing heard" without also ascertaining that [the phenomenon] is a sound.

[Response:] Let us consider the proof "Actual thing [A] is impermanent

[B], because it is an actual thing not derived from effort [C]." It follows that [the reason] has no involvement with anything other than the subject, because it is impossible to have ascertained that something is an actual thing not derived from effort without ascertaining that it is an actual thing. But one cannot accept [this argument's conclusion], because "actual thing not derived from effort" *is* involved with something other than "actual thing." How so? Because it is involved with "phenomena not derived from effort," and this is something separate from and unrelated to [the subject] "actual thing."[770] "Phenomena not derived from effort" cannot be related to [the subject], since if negating what is not derived from effort necessarily ruled out actual thing, then it would be impossible to have an actual thing that *is* derived from effort! And equally, if negating actual thing ruled out [everything] not derived from effort, it would follow that "non-actual thing" is derived from effort!

Someone else claims that "thing heard is involved only with the subject [sound]" refers to "thing heard" encapsulating what it means to be a sound.

[Response:] But that amounts to saying, "That which encapsulates what it means to be sound is not involved with anything other than sound." That does not take us beyond the earlier analysis, since [one would still need to pose the same] questions about whether the "other"—that the encapsulation of sound is not involved with—refers to those things distinguished from sound only in the [nominal, conceptual] sense of a separate isolate and so forth. And since [his explanation] does not take us beyond the ones set out above, it is indistinguishable from them.

Someone else proposes that what the [line] means is that the substance that makes up [the reason] "thing heard" is necessarily the same as that which makes up [the subject] "sound," and vice versa.

[Response:] But then this must also apply elsewhere. And since it is also true of the proof "Something produced [A] is from the very moment of its formation destined for destruction [B], because its destruction is built into it by its causes [C]," it follows that this, the [correct] proof establishing non-reliance [on external agencies], also counts as an inconclusive one of the not shared variety. [288]

Here, then, is how to understand what the line "thing heard is not involved with anything other than [the subject] sound" means. Being heard is a quality specific to sound, and by virtue of this fact, unless one rids oneself of the doubt that sound might be permanent, there is no way to rid oneself of the same doubt regarding "thing heard." Summed up [in terms of the proof], there is no way for someone to ascertain the relationship that underpins the pervasion [for the proof "Sound is impermanent because it is a heard thing"]. This is because there is no [practical] way that anyone could use a similar example to ascertain that a heard thing is necessarily impermanent without also ascertaining that sound is impermanent. The sound of a conch, for instance, might be used as the similar example—the basis for ascertaining that whatever is a heard thing is impermanent. But in ascertaining that, [the party involved] could not fail also to ascertain that whatever is sound is impermanent.

Someone might object, saying that this must mean that a person who has ascertained that the sound of a conch is impermanent must also have ascertained that sound is impermanent. But then, he might say, it would be impossible for there to be some other party who has ascertained that the sound of a conch is impermanent but still clings to the idea that the sound of the Vedas is eternal.

[Response:] There is no such fault. Passages [in the treatises] that talk about "[using] the sound of a conch as the basis for ascertaining that a heard thing is necessarily impermanent" are providing, in a general sense, an illustration for discussing the ascertainment of that pervasion. The fact that the sound of a conch is mentioned as an example should not be construed to mean that it is the example that [could actually be] used to ascertain the pervasion [of the proof]. This is how [the treatises] are to be understood when they speak of "heard thing" as a reason that is not shared.

On occasions when [the treatises refer to proofs that] "lack an example that [instantiates] both reason and predicate" they are *not* necessarily denying the existence of a common locus for the reason and the predicate. What they mean is that there is no example that can serve as the basis for ascertaining the relationship between the reason and the predicate. Again, there is a great deal more to be said regarding such issues, but as the discussion could become a protracted one, I will not elaborate further now.

In the context of inconclusive reasons of the not shared variety—which are found in neither class—the [treatises] also cite the proof "The animate body [A] has a self [B] because it has life [C]." But in what sense is the reason not found in the class of dissimilar instances—that is, the selfless?

[Response:] Life is not observed in anything other than bodies that are animate. But whether such a body has a self or not remains the basis of this dispute. So the second party has not yet established that it is selfless. Therefore the relevant second party has not yet found whether a phenomenon ascertained to be selfless has life. Thus it is an [inconclusive reason] of the not-shared variety. With that, my description of this variety of inconclusive reason is completed.

Inconclusive reasons that are shared

An inconclusive reason that is shared is defined as "an inconclusive reason that the other party has found either among the class of similar instances or the class of dissimilar instances for the proof in question." [289]

There are three varieties of these: the inconclusive reason that [the other party] has (1) noticed is present in both of the classes, (2) found among the class of similar instances but not among the class of dissimilar instances, and (3) found among the class of dissimilar instances but not among the class of similar instances.

An example of the first is the reason in the proof "Sound [A] is permanent [B] because it is something comprehended [C]."

An example of the second is the reason in the proof "That other party, the person who speaks [A], is not omniscient [B] because he speaks [C]."

An example of the third is the reason in the proof "That other party, the person who speaks [A], is omniscient [B] because he speaks [C]."

[The treatises] classify the last two as cases where the second party has not found the reason among the class of "omniscient." This is taken from the point of view of a proof presented to a second party who has not established omniscience by valid cognition but wishes to know whether the specific individual before him is omniscient. [Neither of the proofs] could be presented by the follower of a non-Buddhist school to a Buddhist. This is because a Buddhist has already established the validity of what the Buddha taught.

There is an alternative classification of inconclusive reasons into (1) those in which the reason is present in both the class of similar instances and the class of dissimilar instances in the sense of encompassing [everything within them], (2) those in which the reason is present in the two classes but split with regard to both, (3) those in which the reason is present in the class of similar instances in the split sense and present in the class of dissimilar instances in the encompassing sense, and (4) those in which the reason is present in the class of similar instances in the encompassing sense and present in the class of dissimilar instances in the split sense.

An example of the first is the reason in the proof "Sound [A] is permanent [B] because it is a comprehended thing [C]."

An example of the second is the reason in the proof "Sound [A] is permanent [B] because it is not a tactile object [C]," when that proof is presented to a Vaiśeṣika. But why is this reason classified as split when there are no examples of tactile objects that are present [among the class of those that are permanent]? Well, it is true that there is no such thing as a permanent, enduring tactile object. Despite this, the Vaiśeṣika believes that there are four basic, elemental particles and that these are permanent. While the Vaiśeṣika therefore finds some permanent things to be nontactile, he does not "find" this with respect to others [i.e., certain elemental particles]. Thus, when [the treatises] classify this as a reason that is split with regard to the class of similar instances, they are describing it in terms of how the Vaiśeṣika understands it.

An example of the third variety is the reason in the proof "Sound [A] is not derived from effort [B] because it is impermanent [C]."

An example of the fourth is the reason in the proof "Sound [A] is derived from effort [B] because it is impermanent [C]."

What then does it mean in this context to say that something is either "found" or "not found" in the class of similar instances? It refers to *seeing* it in that class by means of valid cognition. "Seeing" here is not something determined by what anyone might simply *choose* to see. [290] It should be understood in terms of whether or not the second party has seen the thing. And this is not whether [in a general sense] valid cognition has seen the thing. The way of seeing here [can be explained] with regard to the proof "Sound [A] is something derived from effort [B] because it is impermanent [C]." To see the reason among the class of similar instances means to ascertain with a valid cognition that there is something that is both "derived from effort" and "impermanent"—that is, a common locus of the two is possible. This is all that is required. It does not mean, for instance, that [the second party] must ascertain with valid cognition that anything that is impermanent is necessarily derived from effort. This point should be extended to other inconclusive reasons in terms of how they work.

To sum up, whenever [the treatises talk of] an inconclusive reason being seen among the class of similar instances, it is only meant to denote that the other party has ascertained through valid cognition that it is *possible* to have a common locus [of the predicate and the reason]. It cannot mean that the party in question has seen that whatever is a case of the reason is necessarily a case of the predicate. If it did, he would need to ascertain that the reason is present *only* in the class of similar instances. And if he ascertained that, he would have ascertained with valid cognition the relationship [between the reason and predicate] and the proof's pervasion. But if [he ascertained that], it would ridiculously follow that the [inconclusive] reasons in these proofs qualify as correct ones, because they are ones with respect to which the property of the subject has been established, in addition to which both the relationship and pervasion [of the proofs] have been ascertained by valid cognition. In a similar fashion, to say that the reason is "not seen" among the class of dissimilar instances refers simply to valid cognition not ascertaining that a common locus is possible. It does not refer to valid cognition *ruling out* the possibility of such a common locus.

Tibetan logicians have classified [what the treatises refer to as] "inconclusive reasons with remainder" as a division within the category of inconclusive reasons of the shared variety. But I see no evidence either in the way of textual sources or logical arguments to support this view. The individuals who follow it are again like those caught up in the clamor prompted by the alarmed reports of the proverbial hare.

In fact, the "remainder" here is a reference to the residual uncertainty that the other party has regarding the relationship and the pervasion. Thus what it denotes is a situation in which the individual does not know [for sure] whether the reason is present only in the class of similar instances or is totally absent from the class of dissimilar instances. In that sense, *reason with remainder* is essentially synonymous with *inconclusive reason*. In any case, a reason with remainder can be defined as "a reason that is able only to engender uncertainty about the proof's relationship and pervasion in a person for whom that reason constitutes the property of the subject." Using "having a physical body" to infer that an individual has desirous attachment counts as an example of this. It is this that is clearly described in the [*Commentary on Pramāṇa*] passage:

> It is where simply not having seen [the thing]
> is [supposed to] demonstrate that it has been ruled out.
> That [reason] brings about only uncertainty
> because of which it is known as "[that] with remainder."[771]

This is clearly confirmed by Śākyabuddhi, whose comment on the stanza says:

> [Next] there is the question "What is the [reason] with remainder?"
>
> [Dharmakīrti responds] by describing the characteristics that define

> [such a reason] in the passage "It is where . . . ." The term *with remainder* is synonymous with *inconclusive.*[772] [291]

A great deal more could be said about inconclusive reasons, but again, since dealing with them all would take up too much space, I curtail the discussion here.

20. The Thesis of a Proof

What the [treatises' account] of inference involving a second party conveys by implication—that is, the probandum that the proof sets out to establish

1. Defining characteristics of a thesis
2. Varieties

Defining Characteristics

The probandum [i.e., the thesis] in a correct proof is defined as "that phenomenon that is understood in dependence on a reason fulfilling the three criteria and is [divided into] two nominally distinct [parts].[773]

There are two varieties: (1) a probandum in a proof that is for personal use and (2) a probandum in a proof that is for a second party.

The probandum in a correct proof that is for personal use

The first is defined as "that phenomenon, nominally divided into two [parts], that [an individual] comes to understand for himself by using a reason fulfilling the three criteria that has not been presented [to him] by another person."

This is divided into probanda in correct proofs for personal use that depend on (1) an effect reason, (2) a nature reason, or (3) a nonobservation reason.

Someone thinks that there is no distinction between a probandum in a proof that is for personal use and a probandum in a proof of the unprompted variety.

[Response:] This is obviously due to his ignorance regarding what distinguishes those two kinds of proof. With a proof of the unprompted variety, let alone it being something presented by a second party, it does not even involve any [process of] formal deliberation. It occurs, [for instance,] when a person is suddenly confronted by the sight of smoke on a mountain pass. He is able to call upon the knowledge he already has about the relationship between smoke and fire, which he gained *at an earlier point* [by observing what happens], for example, in the kitchen hearth, and can thus [immediately] infer the presence of fire. With a proof that is for personal use, while it is [equally] the case that there is no second party presenting it, the reasoning involves *sustained* personal deliberation, something that leads one to see how the reason establishes the probandum, allowing one to make the inference. [292]

Those who deny the existence of correct proofs of the personal variety, or if they accept them believe that they are the same as the unprompted kind, are intellectual juveniles. When it comes to issues of real import, rather than actually putting effort [into understanding them], they simply delight in the hearsay version.

It is a fact that those on the quest for the supreme states will never achieve their goals of liberation and enlightenment unless their practice is formed from the substance of the three types of knowledge—derived [respectively] from learning, deliberation, and meditation. So some consideration must be given to the natures of these types of knowledge. Their respective natures are as follows. Knowledge derived from meditation is not, in every instance, gained through relying [directly] on reasoning, since there is also yogic perception with the power to destroy the seeds of our distorted notions and which is induced by [meditative] experience. But that derived either from learning or deliberation necessarily relies on reasoning, although it may be in the form of either a valid cognition or the subsequent cognition induced by it. Learned understanding is necessarily generated through reliance on a reason. It occurs when, upon hearing what another person communicates to him, the individual is prompted to draw upon his recollection and become aware that [a certain thing] fulfills all three criteria of the reason [establishing the proof]. It is due to this that a correct reason that acts as the basis for this sort of learned understanding is referred to as a "correct reason that involves a second party."

Understanding derived from deliberation does not rely on being *taught* by another person. Instead, it is an inference that one arrives at oneself by means of a proper process of deliberation, through which one comes to recognize that a particular reason establishes [the probandum]. This understanding takes the form of either the inferential cognition realizing the thing one deduces [i.e., the probandum] or the subsequent cognition of that thing induced by such an inferential cognition. It is due to this that the correct reason that acts as the basis for this type of knowledge is known as the "correct reason in the personal domain."

There are those who hold that "learned knowledge" does not derive from relying on a correct reason and that it is just the realization of something that an individual gains through another person telling him that thing. They are under the impression that words alone are sufficient to inform us about what we should and should not embrace, and that there is no need to substantiate those things [for ourselves] with valid cognition.[774] As such, they are the most implacable enemies of true knowledge. I have an inexhaustible supply of wise words that I could convey to them, but I refrain from doing so, aware that,

Though their bows be heavily laden with the most excellent bounty,
the trees with abundant foliage are the ones disregarded
by the passing childish gang, in their ignorance.
Thus I keep the grove of fabulous trees I cultivate to modest proportions. [293]

The probandum in a proof that is for a second party

1. Defining characteristics
2. Varieties
3. Detailed explanation of the converse of what is not ruled out[775]

Defining characteristics

1. Refuting others' assertions
2. Setting out our own position

Refuting others' assertions

Someone defines the probandum of a proof involving a second party as "that in which the characteristics [of the thesis] are complete by virtue of being the thing denoted by the five terms, *entity* and so forth."

[Response:] It would follow that the probandum of *any* proof involving a second party is one denoted by the words [Dignāga used] to convey the definition of such a probandum, because the probandum of such a proof is the thing denoted by [Dignāga's] five terms, *entity* and so forth. But if [this individual] accepts that, it would follow [by extension] that any established basis [one might choose] must be the thing denoted by the words "that which can be an object known."[776]

Someone else defines this type of probandum as "that in which all five characteristics, entity and so forth, are complete."

[Response:] But what about the passage [in which Dignāga communicates the definition for this type of probandum] in the words "*entity, just, himself,* [*actual*] *assertion*, and *not ruled out*—[these] convey [the probandum]"?[777] It follows that this passage is a probandum in a proof involving a second party because it is something within which all five characteristics are complete.

Another individual defines the probandum of a proof involving a second party as "that thing in which all five of the characteristics denoted by *entity* and so forth are complete." He also claims that what the five terms, *entity* and so forth, denote is that "If *x* is the probandum [for a proof] involving a second party, it necessarily has the [five] characteristics of being something that the second party has not yet realized and so forth."

[Response:] It would follow that pot is that in which all five characteristics are complete. Why? Because it is the case that "If *x* is the probandum [for a proof] involving a second party, it necessarily has the [five] characteristics of being something that the second party has not yet realized and so forth."[778] If he agreed with that, it would follow that not only does pot count as a probandum in a proof involving a second party, the same line of reasoning could also be used for any established basis, meaning that every one of them would count as this type of probandum!

All [the definitions proposed by these individuals] also have another fault. Generally speaking, an authentic set of defining characteristics should be those that [allow] the meaning encapsulation of the thing being defined to appear to the mind. But [based on] the versions of the defining characteristics they propose, if the person in question is someone who already has the meaning encapsulating the probandum involving a second party clear in his mind, there would be no need to provide him with its defining characteristics. But if, [conversely,] the person was someone who needed the defining characteristics presented to him, the characteristics [as formulated by these individuals] would be incapable of conveying to his mind the meaning encapsulating what it is to be such a probandum. [This is because] unless someone already understands what each of the terms *entity* and so forth actually mean, he can have no idea of the thing to which they all refer. But none of the defining characteristics they propose convey to the mind of the person what any of those five terms really *mean*. [294] Without this information, there is no way that the encapsulation of a probandum in a proof involving a second person can appear to the mind of such a person.[779] It is therefore obvious that in the minds of those who propose the aforesaid definitions, there is no clue about the process occurring when a set of characteristics define a thing. So there is not the slightest whiff of the scholar about them.

Setting out our own position

The master Dignāga discussed the characteristics defining the probandum of a proof involving a second party in two separate passages. In his *Compendium of Pramāṇa* he says, "*Entity*, *just*, *himself*, *assertion*, and *not ruled out* convey [the probandum]." And in the *Entrance to Reasoning*, he remarked, "A probandum is also that which is to be established, it is what [someone] asserts, and it is not contradicted by the facts."[780]

As to how the characteristics are conveyed in the first passage, in response to the question about what the five terms, *entity* and so forth, mean, [Dignāga] states that to qualify as a probandum in the proof involving a second party, the thing in question must have the characteristics denoted by the five terms, *entity*, *just*, *himself*, *assertion*, and *not ruled out*. Hence it is (1) not [an entity] that the second party in question has already established and recalls, (2) [just the probandum and] not the probans presented to establish the probandum] in that context, (3) what the first party [himself] genuinely wishes to establish, (4) something that the first party actually accepts, and (5) not something ruled out by valid cognition. [Dignāga] indicates that if any of these five [characteristics] is absent, the thing in question does not qualify as a probandum in a proof involving a second party. The passage therefore communicates the set of characteristics defining a thesis in a proof involving a second party. Namely, it is "something that the first party himself asserts and actually wants [to establish], not something the second party has already established and recalls, and it is neither something presented as the reason in the present context nor something ruled out by valid cognition."

Thus the [first] term, *entity*, relates to the second party; the [subsequent] three—*assertion*, *himself*, and *just*—are [given] from the point of view of the first party; and *not ruled out* is from a more general perspective, meaning that the probandum is something that is not ruled out by *any* valid cognition. Consequently, when [Dignāga] explains what it is to be ruled out—the opposite of this [characteristic]—his discussion is necessarily a wide-ranging one, taking into account all the different types of valid cognition and what is to be ruled out by each.

Turning next to the defining characteristics of this type of probandum as presented in the *Entrance to Reasoning*, the passage tells us that the probandum in question is "something that can be established to the second party within the situation in question and that the first party actually asserts and wishes [to establish]." [295] This makes no explicit mention of the fact that the probandum should be something that is "not ruled out." This is, nevertheless, built into these characteristics, since nothing ruled out by valid cognition could have such characteristics.

What then distinguishes the two sets of characteristics that appear in the *Compendium of Pramāṇa* and the *Entrance to Reasoning*, and why was it deemed necessary to provide two versions? Essentially, these two do not differ, and either one can define [this type of probandum]. But [more specifically,] the version in the *Compendium of Pramāṇa* aims to address certain misconceptions surrounding this type of probandum. The version in the *Entrance to Reasoning*, on the other hand, simply delineates what is and is not [such a probandum]. How does the first passage counter misconceptions? It states that the probandum needs to be an "assertion." Without this, there could be the misconception that something advanced by a first party, not because he endorses it but just because it is stated in scripture, can qualify as a probandum. By stipulating that the probandum needs to be one that the first party proposing it actually asserts, the passage halts the misconception that this definition applies to such things [as the aforesaid scriptural assertion]. This is the way that the inclusion of *assertion* as part of the definition counters misconceptions [related to] that. One can extrapolate from this to understand how all the parts of the definition counter [their respective] misconceptions.

If that were not the case, and simply stating that the [probandum] is "asserted" was enough to divest someone of the conviction that any line of scripture can [genuinely] serve as a probandum, there would be no role left for valid cognition in countering misconceptions. Correct reasoning, inferential cognition, and all such things would similarly become pointless. In defining "substance," for example, it would follow that including mention of the fact that it is "produced" would alone [have the power] to divest anyone of the conviction that there are permanent substances or the notion that there can be impermanent substances that are not brought about by causes. Reasoning and inference would have no role to play in the process.[781]

Including "assertion" among the set of characteristics defining the probandum addresses cases like those of things that are stated in scripture but that [the first party may] not accept. If someone were to propose that the characteristics [of a probandum] also embraced such things, he would be forced to concede that there can be a probandum that the [first] party in the situation both asserts and does not assert. Thus, by including "asserted," the misconception that those characteristics also encompass statements of scripture that are not asserted [by the first party] is blocked. But, while [it can prevent the misunderstanding developing in the first place], it does nothing to dislodge the misconception from the mind of a person who is already convinced that a "second-party" probandum does not need to have such a characteristic. This is where logical reasoning—refuting the idea that absolutely anything stated in a scripture can serve as such a probandum—shows itself to be very far from lacking in purpose.

In a similar fashion, including "produced" among the characteristics that define what it is to be a substance helps prevent the misconception that the characteristics encompass such things as permanent substances that do not originate from causes. [296] This is why sets of defining characteristics of this kind are known as those that "counter misconceptions." But again, it will not block the notion in someone who is already convinced that a substance does not need to have the characteristic [of being produced]. This is where logical reasoning and inference [once more] come in.

Armed with this knowledge [about the countering of misconceptions], one will be able to explain how certain [sections within] well-known teachings, far from clashing, are perfectly compatible with each other. Without it, one will always feel like one who has become lost on his travels. The current crop of self-proclaimed scholars in this snowy mountain land have not even got as far as developing curiosity in this issue, so what chance is there that they actually understand it? I alone have explained it properly.

There are plenty of other matters related to the characteristics that define the second-party probandum that should be discussed. But these are covered at some length in the [*Commentary on Pramāṇa*] treatise itself, so I deal with them in the relevant work.[782]

Varieties

There are three: probanda in proofs involving a second party that use an effect, nature, or nonobservation as their reason.

Detailed explanation of the converse of what is not ruled out

What then does it mean to say that something is "ruled out by valid cognition"? And how many varieties of this are there? It should be understood that there are three ways that valid cognition might be said to counter a thing. Valid cognition counters the likes of self-grasping on a mental level. It counters a false proposition [or thesis] on the verbal level. And it counters the likes of "Sound is permanent" on the level of its purported object.

With the first, valid cognition counters the [self-grasping] mind by totally undermining the way it holds things to be. It is thereby able to arrest any further production of minds of that type. With regard to the second, to say that valid cognition counters a [false] thesis means that it undermines what the thesis or the words [expressing the thesis] propose, the way they portray things to be. In this way the valid cognition discredits the thesis or the words that communicate it. In the case of the third, valid cognition counters the thing in question by ruling out any possibility of [a permanent sound's] factuality.

When the [*Commentary on Pramāṇa*] says, "[Dignāga's *Compendium of Pramāṇa*] explains four ways of countering,"[783] it should be understood that [all four] work on this third level. Before valid cognition can counter a thing on the cognitive level (the way that someone's mind grasps it to be) or on the verbal level (the way that words depict that thing), it must already have negated it on the factual level—that is, it must have ruled out the possibility that there is such an object. This is exactly the point made in the passage "There is no way to rid oneself of that [notion] unless one counters its object."[784] [297]

In the present context, therefore, when the treatises talk of valid cognition "ruling out" a thing, they mean that valid cognition rules out the possibility, in broad terms, that the kind of thing in question exists. They are not referring to valid cognition halting [the continued] production of some misconception in the mind of those who adamantly maintain it. Nor do they mean the way that valid cognition negates things on the verbal or mental levels by undermining the correctness of certain statements or cognitions. The thing that the valid cognition rules out here is necessarily one that is not, in any real sense, established. Unless it were like this, it would follow that a common locus of something both established by valid cognition and ruled out by it is possible, because there is something that is ruled out by valid cognition but exists!

Some may dispute this, saying that although what valid cognition rules out is not established, the [object] of valid cognition's ruling out is.[785]

[Response:] But that is like saying that what valid cognition does not comprehend is not established, whereas the [object] of valid cognition's non-comprehension is. Now, it is true that there is a major distinction between, for example, a thing abandoned by a buddha and an abandonment of a buddha. But there is simply no parallel between that [and the present case]. An abandonment of a buddha [denotes something that] is necessarily a quality of a buddha, whereas the [object] of valid cognition's ruling out [could only refer to] something that valid cognition does not comprehend. What is negated by valid cognition and what is established by it categorically preclude each other. And if being the [object] of valid cognition's ruling out and valid cognition's comprehending do not preclude each other, neither can what valid cognition rules out and what it comprehends.

Someone else claims that what valid cognition rules out is established, because what valid cognition negates is established. This must be the case, he says, since valid cognition's negation of sound not being a thing heard is established.

[Response:] This is untenable. Based on this, it would follow that the totally nonexistent is established because the total nonexistence of the hare's horn is established. [What one should say is that] something negated by valid cognition is not an established basis. Sound not being a thing heard is not an established basis, but valid cognition's negation of sound not being a thing heard is. And that is because all known things are [confirmation] of that [negation].[786]

If something is "ruled out by valid cognition," it means that valid cognition negates any possibility that such a kind of thing [exists among] objects of knowledge.[787] Such things cannot be divided from their own side. References to "four divisions" [among them] here relate to the different ways that valid cognitions negate. Hence there are things ruled out by (1) valid perception, (2) valid inferential cognition dealing in demonstrable facts, (3) an assertion, and (4) common agreement [about names]. [298]

Someone defines something ruled out by valid cognition as "that which is negated by valid cognition." He also claims that *ruled out by valid cognition* is something that is not an established basis. But elsewhere, he has defined a definition as "that which has the three attributes of the encapsulated meaning." In his explanation of these three attributes, he says that for something [to qualify as a definition, its existence] must be "possible within its illustration."

[Response:] These positions contradict each other. Let us take as the subject "that which is negated by valid cognition." It must follow that it is possible for it [to exist] within [the illustration] "sound not being a thing heard."[788] Valid cognition negates sound not being a thing heard, since every phenomenon is a confirmation of the fact [that sound is a heard thing]. But it is not possible for "that which is negated by valid cognition" [to exist] within an illustration. If it was, then it would follow that [the subject] "total nonexistence" is something that valid cognition [could confirm the existence of, through] observing it in the hare's horn.

Anyone who accepts that the illustrator-illustrated model[789] works for things that do not exist is obliged to accept that the two things in question—the illustrator and the illustrated—are related to each other and also that the same [rules of] *coterminosity* apply equally to both.[790] As far as we are concerned, if you are someone who is prepared to posit a logical relationship between things that do not exist, we simply refuse to enter into discourse on the matter with you. We do not debate with madmen!

Quite aside from that, those who assert that the illustrator-illustrated model still works, even when the things in question are not established bases, must also accept that the cause and effect [order] of the establisher-established model can apply to them.[791] But if "ruled out" is a definiendum, one must accept that it therefore has a meaning encapsulating it. However, the only thing that "ruled out" could *be* is ruled out. So it would follow that [being ruled out] is something that defines itself and is its own individual isolate.[792] The [individuals in question here] should, at this point, give the matter some serious consideration. Since if they were to concede this, it would follow that "ruled out" is one with itself.[793] But would they not then end up having to decide whether all sorts of distinction, such as identicalness and difference, relatedness and preclusion, and so forth also apply to ["ruled out"] in spite of the fact that it is not an established basis? As far as I am concerned, if the thing in question is not an established basis, then no purpose could be served by having characteristics to define it; nor would that be feasible. Therefore I do not propose that "ruled out" has any defining characteristics.

Some may then ask, "Why is the same not the case for the *varieties* [of the ruled out]?" But it should be reiterated that the classification of four refers to what *is* ruled out, and it is in terms of these that one can speak of the four: what inferential cognition rules out, what perception rules out, and so forth. That is, what references to the fourfold division convey is that valid cognitions each have separate objects that they counter. We certainly do not assert that "the ruled out" itself forms the basis of a division, of which there are four distinct varieties. Indeed, the master [Dignāga] makes no reference either to "the ruled out" forming such a basis and has no description of any divisions [belonging to it].

Next, we examine the [treatises'] account of what is ruled out by valid perception.

What is ruled out by valid perception

1. Refuting others' assertions
2. Setting out our own position

Refuting others' assertions

First, someone defines that which is ruled out by valid perception as "the exact converse of the thing established by valid perception." [299] His example of this is "sound not being a thing heard."[794]

[Response:] We could point to the subject "that which is *not* established by valid perception." It would follow that it is something ruled out by valid perception, because it is the exact converse of what valid perception establishes. It is obviously the exact converse of that, since [what is not established by valid perception] *precludes* [that which is established by it] *in the sense of mutual opposition*. But if he accepts that [what is not established by valid perception is ruled out by it], it would follow that various objects of comprehension such as extremely hidden phenomena are ruled out by valid perception. Furthermore, it follows that [his example] "sound not being a thing heard" is the *direct preclusion* of that which is established by valid perception. In that manner, anyone who defines [what is ruled out by valid perception] in such a way is forced to accept that what a valid perception rules out is [limited to] that which is the direct preclusion [i.e., the exact converse] of the one it establishes.

Someone else defines what is ruled out by valid perception as "something proposed by an incorrect thesis, the direct opposite of which is established by valid perception." He adapts this same formula to define the other [three] things that are ruled out [by inferential cognition and so on].

[Response:] [Suppose that someone] advances the thesis "Sound is permanent." It would follow that in this case, "permanent" is something ruled out by valid cognition because it is "something proposed by an incorrect thesis, the direct opposite of which is established by valid cognition." He cannot deny the first part of this [i.e., that "permanent" is something proposed by an incorrect thesis]; otherwise it would follow that the statement "Sound is impermanent" does not communicate "impermanent." Hence he may accept [the argument]. But then what he needs to reflect upon is whether [it is actually the case] that if something communicates both "sound" and "impermanent," one is obliged to accept that it communicates "impermanent." [That notwithstanding,] once again, because a thing that is ruled out by valid perception is one that does not exist, we do not accept that there are characteristics to define it. Something like "sound not being a thing heard" is ruled out by valid perception. And in its case, "sound" is the basis for this ruling out—that about which something is ruled out. "Not [being] a thing heard" is what is ruled out with respect to it. What directly rules out this is [the fact of its being] "a thing heard." The grounds for ruling out—what allow it—are (1) [the fact that] valid perception establishes sound is a thing heard and (2) the inviolability of [the principles of] preclusion. The actual thing that rules out here is [the fact] of being a thing heard. But it is only by virtue of valid perception establishing [this fact] that the ruling out is made possible. That is why [the treatises] refer to "that which is ruled out by valid perception." This is the point made in the passage "The objects comprehended by perception and so forth also have [their names] assigned to them [according] to what [kind of cognition] comprehends them."[795]

Here, regarding what it means [when the treatises] say, "Sound being a thing heard is something comprehended by valid perception,"[796] the following question could be posed. [300] Does it refer to the fact that it is possible to have *a* valid perception comprehending that sound is a thing heard, or does it mean that the valid cognition comprehending that sound is a thing heard is necessarily a valid perception? It cannot be the first because it is [equally] possible to have a valid perception realizing that pot is impermanent. So it would follow that the object of the thesis "pot is permanent" [falls into the domain of] what should be ruled out by valid perception. There is good reason [to assert] that there are cases of such a perception, since it is possible to have a valid perception realizing all aspects of the truths. Thus the second alternative of the analysis is the one that must be accepted.

However, the valid cognition that comprehends [i.e., recognizes] that sound is a thing heard cannot be the consciousness that hears it. An auditory consciousness is certainly aware of sound, but it is not aware of sound *as* a thing heard. To recognize that sound is a thing heard, it would need to recognize it as the object of an auditory consciousness. And while the auditory consciousness is aware of sound by way of having that sound as its object, it does not comprehend [the fact that] it is aware of sound by way of having it as its object. "Produced," for instance, is a correct reason by way of being what establishes its thesis "Sound is impermanent," but it is not what establishes [itself to be] that correct reason.

Thus the valid perception that recognizes sound is the thing heard by an auditory consciousness is the *self-cognizing* perception experiencing that auditory consciousness. This self-cognition recognizes that the auditory consciousness has taken on the overt aspect of the sound. And implicit in this recognition is the awareness that sound is the object of the auditory consciousness.

It should be understood therefore that when [the treatises] state "Valid perception rules out sound not being a thing heard," the perception they are referring to is the self-cognizing one that experiences the auditory consciousness. If one were to assert that an auditory consciousness itself necessarily recognizes that sound is a thing heard, one would also have to [accept that] any such consciousness recognizes that sound is its object. That would mean that when a self-cognition is aware of the sense consciousness, the [same] self-cognition must also, necessarily, be aware that the sense consciousness is aware of itself. But that would make a situation in which one needed to prove to anyone with sense consciousness that he [also] had self-cognition in his continuum an impossibility!

Are all cases in which valid perception rules out something similar to this one? They are not. We might consider, for instance, the case where a valid perception rules out the absence of smoke in the kitchen. The valid perception in question observes the smoke in the kitchen. Therefore it is not a self-cognition.

How then are we to interpret the passage "It is [the word] *audible* that expresses the sense object"?[797] [301]

In that section, what [Dharmakīrti] unambiguously states is that recognizing [sound] to be a thing heard involves recognizing that it is the object perceived by a sense consciousness. And in that regard, the passage is entirely in keeping with my own position on the matter.

What is ruled out by inferential cognition dealing with demonstrable facts

Using what is proposed in the thesis "Pot is permanent" to illustrate, the basis—that about which something is ruled out—is "pot." What is ruled out about it is that it is "permanent." What actually rules this out is [the fact] that pot is impermanent. And valid inferential cognition's comprehension of this fact is what makes this ruling out feasible. The [remainder] can be understood through the illustration above.

WHAT IS RULED OUT IN THE CASE OF A [THESIS] ASSERTION

There are two varieties: that in which a thing is ruled out by the words of the statement asserting it, and that in which a thing is ruled out by [an inference dealing with a matter of] conviction. An example of the first is the thesis "Inferential cognition is not valid." This first [kind] also has two varieties: (1) that in which the thing is ruled out due to a clash within the thesis's own words and (2) that in which the thing is ruled out due to a clash between the thesis's overt and implied assertions. An example of the first is the thesis "[She is] a mother who is barren." An example of the second is the thesis "Valid cognitions with objects that they comprehend do not exist."

In cases like these, where a thing is ruled out by the words of the statement asserting it, [the questions are about] what the basis is, what it is that rules out, and so forth. Others have explained it in terms of the [aforesaid] thesis, "[She is] a mother who is barren," which they say makes two assertions: that the female in question is "a mother" and that she is "barren." They say that the latter assertion undermines the former, due to which this is described as "something that is ruled out due to a clash within the thesis's own words."

[Response:] This is incorrect. It would follow that [the way one should analyze this statement is to say that] the words "[She is] a mother who is barren" contains two *theses*—"The woman is a mother" and "The woman is barren"—and that it is because the object of one thesis rules out that of the other that they become "ruled out" and "ruler out," respectively, and are described as a case where something is ruled out due to a clash in the thesis's own words. This is completely untenable. It takes one female as the basis. But this female must, in fact, either be one who has given birth or not; there is no third alternative. Valid cognition must therefore have established either one or the other to be the case. The options for this are also limited; [the fact] must have been established by a valid perception or a valid inferential cognition dealing with demonstrable facts. Basically then, one of the two theses has been established by valid cognition, and it is this that rules out the one that is not established by valid cognition. [302] Hence, with this statement, the ruling out must be something done either by valid perception or by inferential cognition dealing with demonstrable facts. In either case, the idea that the ruling out occurs due to a clash on the level of the thesis's words is undermined.

As for the woman who serves as the basis with regard to whom something is ruled out here, assuming that she has given birth to a son and this has been established by valid cognition, [the question we pose to you is this]. Isn't what actually rules out her not having given birth the fact that she has? If not, then similarly, what actually rules out sound not being a thing heard cannot be the fact that it is heard. And if the thing that actually rules out here is that [fact], while it may be referred to as a case of something that is ruled out by the words of the statement asserting it, this must be nothing more than the words impeding each other.[798] And while the words in question may have been designated "ruler out" and "ruled out," [they are not really examples of such,] because the master and his followers have unequivocally declared in the treatises that these are not cases of one thing genuinely countering another. The [idea that they are genuine cases] also contradicts your own position [on this matter].

The same applies to what you have claimed about [other examples]. You have proposed that the statement "Inferential cognition is not valid" refers to a single cognition, with respect to which two theses—"The cognition is an inference" and "It is not valid [cognition]"—are asserted. And you have also proposed that the statement "Valid cognitions with objects that they comprehend do not exist" overtly asserts that valid cognitions do not exist but implicitly acknowledges that they do. And you say that in all of these cases, the clash is between the objects of the theses, and that this is what is meant by something being ruled out by the words of the statement that asserts it. Thus you have either failed to subject the matter to any analysis, or if you have analyzed them, have [produced] the shoddy [work] of an inferior intellect.

It is to be understood as follows. Using the example that the master himself has provided of something being ruled out by the words of the statement that asserts it, we should consider the way a thesis makes an assertion. So, with the statement "Inferential cognition is not valid," it is not that inferential cognition [in a general sense] is taken as a basis and the quality of "not being valid" is asserted about it. Instead, the basis [is a specific one], such as a cognition realizing that color is impermanent. In relation to this, two qualities, "inferential cognition" and "not valid," are asserted. And in the case of "[She is] a mother who is barren," the [thesis's] assertion is not that the mother is barren. Rather, a single female is taken as the basis, and the assertion is that she has the two [separate] qualities—that of being a mother and that of being barren. [303] In presenting the thesis "[She is] a mother who is barren" as an example, [the master chooses one] with two conflicting assertions—that a certain female is a mother and that the same female is barren. One should understand that this is similarly the case with [the choice] of the thesis "Inferential cognition is not valid" as an example. If it were otherwise, and the thesis "[She is] a mother who is barren" only made a single assertion, it could not [be an example] of two assertions clashing with each other. Instead, we would be dealing with a single assertion in which different parts of the wording conflicted with one another.

In the case of the thesis "Valid cognitions with objects that they comprehend do not exist," the overt assertion is that there is no such thing as a valid cognition. This statement is supposed to convince the person to whom it is addressed [what it says is the case], and it is [thus] delivered as though it were expressing an established fact. However, in suggesting that the listener can be sure of this [supposed] fact, the words assert by implication that [the person asserting it has certain knowledge of this fact] through having generated a nondeceptive cognition of it. So, while the overt assertion expressed in the thesis is that there is no such thing as a valid cognition that [knows a fact] nondeceptively, the assertion implied in the words is that there is a cognition that knows the fact [of that overt assertion] nondeceptively. These two assertions contradict each other, and that is why [the master] gave this as an example of a case where the overt and implied assertions clash with one another.

Even though the words of the statement betray [that the person who delivers it] accepts that what they express can be known by a nondeceptive cognition, this is not what "Valid cognitions with objects that they comprehend do not exist" is meant to convey. So [the master] did not present this thesis as an example of one in which the clash is between the overt and implied assertions of its object—what it [is intended] to convey. He gave it as an example of a thesis in which the overt [intended] assertion contradicts the implied [unintended] one. Correspondingly, we should describe it not as "a statement in which the overt and implied objects that it expresses clash" but as "a statement in which the overt and implied assertions clash [with each other]."

Let me now explain how something is ruled out by the words of the statement that assert it. In cases where the earlier and later [assertions of] the thesis contradict each other, the one ruled out is the object of the earlier assertion, whereas the one that rules it out is the object of the later assertion. As to how it rules that out, the later assertion impedes the establishment what the former assertion says. For instance, the earlier assertion may be that a particular female is a mother, with valid cognition having confirmed that she has given birth to a son. This assertion is one that [the person who makes it] could therefore substantiate by means of a correct reason. But once he makes the second assertion that the woman is barren, it will impede him from doing so. [304] Whatever reason he might present to establish the object of the first assertion, someone could point out that it is contradicted by the subsequent assertion, and the thesis is open to being discredited in this way. Unless he is prepared to drop the later assertion, therefore, the party [who proposes the thesis] will never have the opportunity to substantiate the earlier one. That said, it is not as though the later assertion can really *counter* the object of the earlier one. How could it? The first one is established by valid cognition.

In the case of the thesis "Valid cognitions with objects that they comprehend do not exist," the thing that is ruled out is the object it asserts. What rules it out is the implied assertion. As for the way it does this, the object of this implied assertion impedes the overt one being established. But since the object of that overt thesis is something not established, doesn't [the object of the implied one] counter it? It is only on the level of the thesis's words that the implied assertion contradicts the overt one. This does not [constitute] countering it. This is similar to the situation with the statement "Sound is impermanent," the words of which cannot [in any proper sense] counter the object of the thesis "Sound is permanent."

Thus, when [the treatises] talk of [a form of] ruling out that involves the thesis's own words, they only mean that one thing impedes another on the verbal level, not that one really counters [the other]. In this sense, these are not [genuine] cases of something being ruled out by valid cognition. To sum up then, when it is said that something is ruled out by the thesis's own words, what occurs is that one assertion made by the party in question impedes the establishment of the object of the other assertion he makes [within that thesis]. It could best be described, therefore, as a case of his later words undercutting his earlier ones. Those who characterize this as the words undermining their own potency are talking nonsense.

[As stated above,] in the case of something ruled out by valid inferential cognition dealing with demonstrable facts, the example given is the thesis "Pot is permanent." [That differs from the present variety] in that it involves a single basis—the pot—about which a single assertion—that it has the quality of being permanent—is made. And it is the object of that thesis that [the treatises] explain is ruled out by valid inferential cognition dealing with demonstrable facts.

A thing that is ruled out by [an inference dealing with a matter of] conviction

An example of something that is ruled out by [an inference dealing with a matter of] conviction is "Dharma [practices] such as generosity do not yield pleasure."[799] Dharmottara holds that to overtly assert that something is "Dharma" necessarily implies acceptance of its capacity to yield pleasure. [305] Thus, [in this example,] he identifies this earlier assertion [that the thing in question is Dharma] as the one that does the ruling out and the one following it—that [such practices] do not produce pleasure—as what it rules out. Dharmottara also claims that in the examples where the ruling out is done by other [kinds of] valid cognition, the two elements—the ruler out and the ruled out—need not be things that [the person in question] asserts. In the present case, however, he says that they do. He reasons that in those other cases, in which the ruling out is not that of an assertion—such as when, for instance, it is perception that rules out sound not being a thing heard—[the other party] need not be someone who asserts that sound is a thing heard. He says that conversely here, in cases where the ruling out is [in the domain of] assertions [relating to matters of conviction], both what counters and what is countered must be things that [the other party] has asserted.[800]

I will now explore the topic by subjecting it to analysis, in three sections: (1) what is ruled out, what rules out, and how it rules out, (2) whether an [authoritative] passage of scripture rules something out in the sense of countering it or impeding it, and (3) settling certain issues regarding the example [that the treatise supplies] of a false thesis.

Explaining what is ruled out, what rules out, and how it rules out

[In the example Dharmottara gives,] the basis—that with respect to which something is ruled out—is "Dharma [practices] such as generosity." That they "do not yield pleasure" is the thing ruled out about them, and "a passage from scripture that has been verified by means of the threefold analysis" alone is what rules this out. The way that such a passage rules out that [those practices do not yield pleasure] is not simply through impeding its establishment, but rather by actually countering it. The grounds for it being able to rule it out are that "[being] a passage from scripture that has been verified by means of the threefold analysis" serves as the correct reason establishing that the passage stating that Dharma [practices] such as generosity yield pleasure is nondeceptive [i.e., trustworthy] with regard to what it teaches. And in establishing this, it *counters* [the notion that such a passage] is deceptive. The logic behind this has been set out above.

Those who deny [the whole notion] of the correct logical proof of "conviction" cannot see how citing a passage that states a thing could be admissible as evidence of that thing's veracity. [While in this respect, they are right,] where they go astray is in making the generalization that a passage of scripture can never have a role in establishing or countering a thing, in the sense of correct logic. This is in every respect akin to someone who, seeing how "sound's production" is not admissible as the reason to establish [the thesis] that sound is impermanent, concludes that "[being] produced" can never serve as the reason to establish that thesis.[801] As such, it is a grave error.

Just citing a passage such as "From generosity, material resources; from discipline, pleasure" neither proves that what it states is correct nor disproves the converse of what it says. However, a passage that has been verified by the threefold analysis can serve as an authentic [logical] counter [to the converse], in that it disproves that there is anything deceptive about what [the passage] says. The [procedure for the analysis] is not [to begin from the point of] embracing the passage, accepting what it says, and then checking to see whether it can be verified using the threefold test. Instead, one first subjects the passage to the three forms of analysis, determining from the outset to accept it *only* if it can be verified by the process, and to *reject* it if it fails the test. [306] The passage one accepts and is convinced of will therefore have been verified by the threefold analysis, and that is why it is referred to as [an object of] "conviction." One uses such a reason [of conviction] to establish that the passage informing us that Dharma [practices] such as generosity yield pleasure is nondeceptive with regard to its content, and this is referred to as an "inference of conviction." The assertion that generosity does not yield pleasure runs counter to what this inferential cognition comprehends and is thus described as that which is "ruled out by an inference of conviction."

Explaining whether an [authoritative] passage of scripture rules out something in the sense of countering it or impeding it

[The *Commentary on Pramāṇa*] states, "If someone is not valid [with regard to a certain thing], the words [he speaks about that thing] cannot engage it."[802] A statement such as "Sound is impermanent" can be pronounced with confidence by someone who has realized its veracity for himself, and is one that he can assert is nondeceptive with regard to its content. Similarly, those who accept passages of scripture as the means of guiding their actions with respect to extremely hidden phenomena assert that those passages are nondeceptive with regard to their content.

[There are schools of thought that, while divided on] whether the passage of scripture rules a thing out by countering it or impeding [its establishment], agree that passages from scripture should be employed to investigate phenomena that are extremely hidden.[803] They also agree that to be convinced of the veracity of a passage is to accept that it is nondeceptive with regard to its content. Otherwise, they say, someone could deliver a statement like "Valid cognitions with objects that they comprehend do not exist" with conviction but without any evidence for accepting that its content is nondeceptive. Thus, [for both schools of thought,] to assert that a passage is valid is to acknowledge that it is nondeceptive [and correct] with regard to its content. Despite being divided on the [issue of how a passage rules something out], therefore, both groups agree that to investigate [a matter such as] whether or not practices like generosity yield maturing effects of the pleasurable variety, one must rely on passages from scripture. Thus they would both wholeheartedly accept the passage "From generosity, material resources; from discipline, pleasure"—which is to say that they agree that it is nondeceptive with regard to its content. They also agree that to assert that it is nondeceptive in this way is to assert that there is a correct reason that establishes this to be the case.

Still, they disagree on [the aforesaid issue] of whether the passage [rules something out by] actually countering it or just impeding it. [Let us look into what] separates them. [307] The master Dignāga did not espouse that authentic passages can be cited as correct reasons to establish the veracity of their own content. He was, however, [aware that there were] certain trainees who had yet to complete a thorough examination of the scriptural corpus. Such disciples were in no position to determine by means of valid cognition whether a particular statement passed the test of the threefold analysis. [Dignāga] wanted to provide this kind of disciple with a way to approach phenomena of the extremely hidden variety, so that they would be informed [about which actions] should be pursued and which rejected. With these disciples in mind, he proposed that scriptural statements such as "From generosity, material resources; from discipline, pleasure" could be regarded as an effect of the content it expresses, and taken from the perspective of these [individuals] purely as an *interim step*, he described such passages as effect reasons establishing their own content. This is what is referred to in *Commentary on Pramāṇa* where [Dharmakirti] states, "Acceptance [of the content is classified as an] effect reason."[804]

Despite the master Dignāga having explained it in this way, certain followers misinterpreted what the *Compendium of Pramāṇa* said here. They thought he meant that according to our [Buddhist] system, the existence of a passage of scripture was sufficient in every case to establish the [veracity of its] content and to counter [i.e., disprove] anything contrary to what that passage said. In support of this position, they argued that unless the scriptural passage "From generosity, material resources; from discipline, pleasure" itself established [the veracity of] its own content, since there was nothing else to prove [that veracity], then the things forming the basis of actions here—Dharma [practices] of generosity and so forth—would not be established by valid cognition. And if that were the case, there would not be two things in conflict with each other, since there would be no basis for conflict.[805]

According to those who advocate that [the most a scriptural passage can do] is impede [the converse of what it asserts], to hold that a scriptural passage itself can be cited as proof of what it says is to hold that it is able, from its own side, to prove its own content and counter the contrary. But since a scriptural passage is not like that, any claim such as "From generosity, material resources; from discipline, pleasure" can be no more than an assertion. And since that is the case, they say, a passage that states [the converse], that generosity and so forth do *not* yield material resources, would have an equal claim to be treated as "proof." Why? Because the only thing that could serve as the reason to establish the statement is that someone asserts it to be so, which can obviously be the case with such a statement. They therefore conclude that an authentic passage of scripture can neither constitute proof of what it asserts nor counter the contrary of what it asserts. [308]

In reality, however, [the treatises] do not teach that the two statements—one asserting that generosity gives rise to material resources, and the other asserting that it does not—carry equal weight or impede each other [in equal measure], because generosity giving rise to material resources is [a fact,] established by valid cognition! Thus the way that "impeding" should be understood here is this: if the passage stating that generosity gives rise to material resources was *itself* proof of the thing it asserted, then the one stating that generosity does not give rise to material resources would carry equal weight as proof of what it asserted. The passage stating that generosity does not give rise to material resources therefore impedes the one that says generosity gives rise to material resources serving as proof of what it asserts. [Correspondingly,] the passage stating that generosity gives rise to material resources impedes the one that says generosity does not give rise to material resources serving as proof of what it asserts. The reason that each is capable of impeding the other is that if one of them could count as proof of what it says, then the other one would, in equal measure, count as proof of what it says. Thus one *impedes* the other from serving as proof of what it says.

In summary, those who hold that one thing "impedes" the other do not mean by this that the two statements themselves impede each other. They mean that [the existence of] each passage impedes the other from counting as a probans that proves the thing it asserts. This is comparable, for instance, to the situation with the two theses "Sound is impermanent" and "Sound is permanent." Even though they do not carry equal weight [in terms of their veracity], their force is equal with respect to being cited as the probans establishing the things that they assert, in that the [existence of each] impedes the other from serving as the probans that can prove [the veracity of] its own content.

To conclude then, it was purely as an interim step for the type of trainees mentioned above, and from their perspective, that the master Dignāga proposed that a scriptural passage could serve as proof of what it asserted and counter the converse. However, he did *not* accept that in our own [Buddhist] system, a scriptural passage could in actuality counter anything. The description he would tend toward is that passages "impede [or prevent] each other" serving as proof of what they say. It was in reference to this that the master Dharmottara remarked, "[That they] impede is [Dignāga's actual] position. Nevertheless, as a provisional [measure], he maintained that they constituted 'counters.'"[806] And it is with this in mind that we understand statements like "That [scriptural] passages are *pramāṇa* has already been refuted."[807] [309]

If, however, one was to make the generalization that scriptural passages have no role to play in countering assertions that contradict what authentic scriptural passages say about extremely hidden objects, it would be a denial of the whole scriptural tradition and everything [determining] what should be either adopted or rejected. The claim of the current crop of self-proclaimed logicians is that both of the [competing] passages are equally capable of impeding each other. With regard to assertions about the existence or nonexistence of cause and effect, therefore, they claim that if one of them is established, they must both be, and if either is not established, then neither of them can be. Sensible persons would be well advised to block their ears against such misleading tales.

Settling certain issues regarding the example [that the treatise supplies] of a false thesis

As the example [of a false thesis], the master [Dharmakīrti] supplied, "Dharma [practices] such as generosity yield no pleasure [to an individual] after death."[808] He was not presenting this as the example of [a false thesis] within which "Dharma [practices] such as generosity" is the subject, "yield no pleasure" is the predicate, and the combination of these two formed the false thesis. [Neither did he propose that such a thesis is] the converse of the probandum "Dharma [practices] such as generosity yield pleasure" [and that the latter] could be established by using a correct reason. [This cannot have been his intention,] because a correct reason that would be capable of establishing that its subject "Dharma [practices] such as generosity" yield pleasure is an impossibility![809] In referring to "Dharma [practices] such as generosity," [Dharmakīrti] is not identifying the [actual] subject of a proof dealing with a matter of conviction. Rather, he is identifying something that an inference of conviction can establish.

Someone may claim that for the example, it would have been enough to have given "Generosity and so forth yield no pleasure," and that referring to them as "Dharma [practices]" was pointless.

[Response:] This is [intended as the example] for something that is ruled out by an assertion. [Dharmakīrti] included "Dharma" because he wanted to provide an illustration of a thesis with directly contradicting assertions—namely, one that accepts practices such as generosity are "Dharma" but proposes that they do not yield pleasure. [Again,] "Dharma [practices] such as generosity" is not presented as the subject in a correct proof dealing with a matter of conviction.

[When someone cites an authoritative scriptural passage,] how are we to distinguish between [that party's] own words and those of the scriptural passage? In a situation where the party accepts the passage in question, the words he utters can represent both those of the passage and his own. And as such, there is no distinction between the two in terms of them being nondeceptive with respect to what they say. [310] But it is only if the words he utters are *exactly* as they were [originally] formulated by the composer of the treatise that they are those of the passage. If he chooses to render them in his own way, they are his own. A [scriptural] treatise also represents the composer's own words, and [even if] these are verbalized by others, they can [still be] the words of the scripture.

This completes the account of things ruled out by a conviction.

A thing that is ruled out by common agreement [about names]

What this means in terms of [a statement] like "The sphere [marked] with the hare is not the moon" [is explained thus]: The sphere [marked] with the hare here forms the basis—that about which something is ruled out. That it is not legitimate for it to be denoted by the name "moon" is the thing ruled out about it. What rules this out is the legitimacy of the denotation. The grounds for this being ruled out are the fact of the legitimacy—something that is established by an inferential valid cognition using a correct reason [relating to the issue] of common agreement [about names].

One should be aware that when [the form of] ruling out relates to conviction or common agreement [about names], as on the previous occasions, what actually does the ruling out is a fact established by valid cognition. [The case regarding] reasons of common agreement has already been set out. [As we saw there, some] hold that the thing ruling out is not valid cognition. Some other issues relating to matters of common agreement and so forth will be explained in my commentarial exegesis on the [*Commentary on Pramāṇa*].

Apart from that, there are those who deny that inferential cognitions dealing with matters of common agreement are valid and, in the present context also, would say that while we may choose to talk about common agreement as though it involves something being countered, this is not in fact the case. To them, we can present the following argument. In terms of using the term "moon" to denote x, it follows that the legitimacy and illegitimacy [of the denotation] do not preclude each other in the sense of forming a mutual opposition. Why? Because valid cognition establishes neither that the denotation for x is legitimate nor that it is not legitimate. Not even the omniscient one could find a response to this attack. This concludes the account of a thing that is ruled out by common agreement [about names].

The way to explain what is ruled out by valid cognition has perplexed almost every erstwhile and current Tibetan "logician." In the present day, the people of this snowy mountain land have become as dumb as sheep when it comes to distinguishing between what is and is not correct. But for those viewing the world through jealous eyes, which flit like those of venomous snakes, what chance is there of correctly discriminating between beneficial and baneful? [311]

Comfortable accommodation for every fine account
has been provided in this vast mansion of an intellect.
It gloriously celebrates the illumination of all things
and is newly beautified with garlands of the freshest flowers of reasoning.

21. The Consequence

Explaining that which prepares the way for the proof statement

1. Account of the discrediting [statement]
2. Account of the way to respond to a consequence
3. Examination of subsidiary issues arising from these

The discrediting [statement]

Since *discrediting [statement]* and *consequence* are equivalent, my explanation proceeds from this standpoint. Accordingly, there are consequences that are correct and those that are false.

A correct consequence is defined as "an 'it follows' statement that cannot be countered by any appropriate response."

Correct consequences are of two varieties: those that project [i.e., convey] the probans [for the intended proof] and those that do not project the probans.[810]

The first is defined as "a correct consequence [containing] a predicate that, if reversed and [presented] to establish the reverse of the reason with respect to its subject, would [form a correct reason] fulfilling the three criteria."

There are two varieties: consequences that in their inversion project something of the same class as themselves, and those that in their inversion, project something of another class.[811] A consequence that in its inversion projects something of the same class as itself is defined as "an 'it follows' statement that, through an inversion, would give rise to a correct reason—one belonging to the same class of formulated proof as itself." An example is the consequence presented to a second party who holds that coldness continues to exist in a certain spot that has been engulfed by a raging fire—namely, "It follows that in that spot engulfed by raging fire [A] there is no engulfment by raging fire [B], because coldness continues to be present [there] [C]." This counts as an example of the first variety in that it is a consequence that employs the observation of a nature that precludes [what is being negated], and if this consequence is inverted, it elicits a reason [that similarly belongs to the class of reasons] that involve the observation of a nature that precludes [what is being negated]. [312]

[Second,] a consequence that in its reversal projects something of another class is defined as "an 'it follows' statement that, through an inversion, would give rise to a correct reason—one that does not belong to the same class of formulated proof as itself." An example of this is the consequence presented to a second party who holds that there is smoke on a nighttime ocean that has a wispy substance hanging over it—namely, "It follows that in the aforementioned spot [A] there is fire [B] because there is smoke [C]." If this consequence projected something that was the same class as itself, the reason [of the proof] that it projected should be one of the "effect" variety. But if inverted, what it actually projects is a reason of the "nonobservation of a cause" variety.

One should learn about the internal divisions of consequences that project [the proof's] reason from other writings [that have set these out in detail]. I have not written more about them here, as this would take up a good deal of space, and they are anyway quite straightforward.

A consequence that does not project the probans [for the intended proof] is defined as "a correct consequence [containing] a predicate that if reversed and [presented] to establish the reverse of the reason with respect to its subject, would not [form a correct reason] fulfilling the three criteria."

An example is the consequence presented to a second party who holds that [a cognition] that is free from conception is necessarily a perception—namely, "It follows that the sense cognition to which two moons appear [A] is a perception [B], because it is one that is free from conception [C]."

A false consequence is defined as "an 'it follows' statement that can be countered by any appropriate response." An example is the consequence "It follows that sound [A] is a substance [B] because it is permanent [C]" when presented to someone who holds that sound is permanent.

Next, we identify what it is that a consequence rules out. [Any second party who] responded to the consequence by accepting [its proposed] predicate would thereby basically have accepted something [i.e., a thesis] that is ruled out by valid cognition. And it is this that is referred to as "the thing ruled out by the consequence." So, for instance, by responding in the affirmative to the consequence "It follows that sound [A] is permanent [B]," the person in question would have accepted that sound is permanent—something that is ruled out by valid cognition. [But we see that] what the consequence proposes as the predicate and what it rules out are not [exactly] equivalent to each other. Someone who has asserted both that sound is permanent and that it is also produced might be presented with the consequence "It follows that sound [A] is derived from causes [B] because it is produced [C]." If he responded by saying that he agreed with this, he would in effect be accepting the consequence's predicate, but that [predicate] is not something ruled out by valid cognition, since valid cognition does not rule out sound being derived from causes.

Where it is said that "The reason of a consequence is established by valid cognition," it refers to the fact that the *presence* of the reason in the subject is something that the other party has established by means of valid cognition. So, while the reason may not be in keeping with his position, he cannot sensibly respond to it by stating that it is "not established." When it is said that "The pervasion is established by valid cognition," it should be understood in the same fashion. [313]

If the predicate [proposed in] the consequence is something that is not in line with what is asserted [by the other party] and is not ruled out by valid cognition, as long as that predicate is established by valid cognition, and a reason [appropriate to this] is presented, it can count as a proof that establishes [a position of] our own system. However, it *cannot* count as a consequence that discredits the position of another's system, since it is impossible to have a correct consequence [with the aforesaid features]. [That said,] as can easily be appreciated, it is perfectly feasible to have a correct consequence with both a reason and pervasion that have been established by valid cognition. While some have sought to use consequences as a means of "purging" the mouths and ears [of others], it appears that [the correct understanding of] what is ruled out by valid cognition has not yet penetrated [their own minds].

The way to respond to a consequence

If the presence of the consequence's predicate in the subject is established by valid cognition, as long as it does not leave one open to the charge of maintaining positions that contradict each other, one should respond to the consequence by saying "I accept." If the presence of the consequence's reason in the subject is not established by valid cognition, as long as it does not leave one open to the charge of maintaining contradictory positions, one should respond to the consequence by saying "The reason is not established." If the consequence's overt pervasion is neither established by valid cognition nor something one personally advocates, one should respond by saying "The pervasion is not established." And if one accepts none of the consequence's three spheres, one should respond by saying "I do not accept [any such position]." Not [being based on the target's] position is the gravest of faults in a consequence, and if [the consequence has] this flaw, it would be astounding if one did not expose it by means of this response.

In cases where whatever serves as the consequence's reason is necessarily a straight negation, the response "The subject is not established" will not work. [Conversely,] in cases where the thing that is the consequence's reason either itself is affirmative or is a negation that projects an affirmative phenomenon, if what is taken as the subject is not an established basis and is something one does not accept, one could respond by saying that "The subject is not established." But this will, [in such cases,] amount to the same as saying "The reason is not established."

Someone claims that if the single response "The pervasion is not established" were permissible both in those cases where the pervasion is contrary and in those where it is inconclusive, it would lead to the [unwanted] conclusion that being contrary and inconclusive belong to the same class [of fault].

[Response:] Then the same must apply when the individual in question himself responds that "The reason is not established," whereas it is in fact [more specifically] inconclusive.

This ends the brief account of the way to respond to a consequence. [314]

Examination of subsidiary issues arising from these

1. Account of the example [used in conjunction with] the reason
2. Account of [what counts as a] failing and a quality in the reason, example, and position.[812]

Explanation of the example [used in conjunction with] the reason

There are examples that are correct and those that are false. The first is defined as "that which serves as the basis for ascertaining the pervasion of the proof in question prior to ascertaining its probandum." There are two [kinds]. The first, the correct similar example, is defined as "that which serves as the basis for ascertaining the forward pervasion of the proof in question prior to ascertaining its probandum." This is divided into two: the correct similar example of the overt variety and the correct similar example of the corresponding-type variety. An illustration of the first is "pot" presented as the example for the proof "Sound is impermanent because it is produced." An illustration of the second is "[just as] the nonobservation of pot in a location devoid of any bulbous [vessels] necessarily means that there are none there" presented as the example for the proof "In the lump of clay [A] there is no pot [B], because no pot is observed [C]." The correct dissimilar example is defined as "that which serves as the basis for ascertaining the reverse pervasion of the proof in question prior to ascertaining its probandum." An illustration of this is "[noncomposite] space" presented as the dissimilar example for the proof "Sound is impermanent because it is produced."

The false example is defined as "that which is held to be the basis for ascertaining the pervasion of the proof in question prior to ascertaining its probandum but in dependence on which that proof's relationship-pervasion cannot be ascertained." This is also divided into the false similar example and the false dissimilar example. Their defining characteristics can be extrapolated from the preceding descriptions. Their illustrations are "space" and "pot" [presented] respectively as the similar example and the dissimilar example for the proof establishing that "Sound is impermanent." I proceed no further with these divisions, as the account will become too long.

Explanation of [what counts as] a failing and a quality in the reason, example, and position

1. Refuting others' assertions
2. Setting out our own position

Refuting others' assertions

With regard to the failings and qualities in the reason and in the position, someone identifies the failing as "that which the definitions of the reason and position respectively rule out" and the quality as the opposite of those [i.e., what each definition affirms].

[Response:] It would follow that the various misconceptions [about the reason and position] count as failings in them.

Someone else defines the failing in a reason as "something incongruent with the kind of characteristics that define a correct reason," and the failing in the position and so forth following the same pattern.

[Response:] To what does "incongruent with the kind of characteristics" refer? If it is simply supposed to mean anything that does not [fulfill] the three criteria, it would ridiculously follow that in the case of the proof

"Sound is impermanent because it is produced," the vast majority of known objects count as failings in a reason. [315]

Someone, of course, thinks that something that is "incongruent with the kind of characteristics" of, for instance, the property of the subject in a proof is just that which is *not* ascertained to be present, in accordance with the form of the proof, in the subject of interest.

[Response:] But if that was the case, it would follow that the similar example "pot" in the proof establishing "Sound is impermanent because it is produced" also counts as a failing in a reason.

Most of these [individuals] would agree that *x* being the correct reason of the proof in question when *x* [does not fulfill the definition of the property of the subject]—in that it is something not ascertained to be present, in accordance with the form of the proof, in the subject of interest—must count as a case of *x* being "incongruent with the kind of characteristics" defining the property of the subject and [is thus what] those characteristics [defining the property of the subject] rule out.

[Response:] According to that, it would follow that to be a failing in the reason, *x* must be something that is not an established basis. And by that reckoning, to be a reason with a failing is to be one that is flawless![813]

Someone else defines a failing in the reason as "something for which [the fulfillment of] any of the three criteria is unestablished."

[Response:] [Let us consider] the proof "Sound is impermanent because it is produced." It would follow that "produced," as a thing present—in accordance with the proof's form—within sound, counts as a failing in the reason, because it is something for which [the fulfillment of] any of the three criteria are [left] unestablished. He may deny that any of the three are [left] unestablished. But then it would follow that "'produced,' as a thing present—in accordance with the proof's form—within sound" is a correct reason [fulfilling all three criteria] in that proof.[814]

Someone else argues like this: "As far as a 'visual object' goes, the fact that it is *not* present—in accordance with the form of the proof in question—in sound, counts as a failing with regard to it being a correct reason in the proof that sound is impermanent. Why? Because it is the fact that 'visual object' [is not present in sound] that prevents it serving as a correct reason in that proof. [Conversely,] in terms of 'visual object' being a false reason, [the fact that it is not present in sound] counts as a *quality*, in that it is by virtue of that [nonpresence that visual object] is posited to be a false reason. [But among these two, he concludes,] a failing in a reason should [principally be understood in terms of] what makes something fail as a *correct* reason, not what makes it fail as a false one."

[Response:] He has simply not grasped how to undertake the analysis [to identify] the failing in a reason and which reason has such a failing. The analysis of the failing in a reason is to determine whether the basis with that failing—that is, the reason—is a correct or a false one. But he has interpreted the analysis as one that aims to determine whether the failing that a reason has is that by which it fails to be a correct reason or that which prevents it being a false one. To sum up, the analysis of the failing in a reason is the analysis of which reason has the failing. Given that fact, what reasons could be suitable [for such an analysis] other than those that are faulty?

Furthermore, in asserting what he does, he has basically claimed that because something is a property, it is a quality. But from this it would follow that it is *not* by virtue of having a failing that something is faulty and not by virtue of having a quality that [another] thing is [something] of quality.[815] [316] This is because, [for him, the thing] with a failing thereby has a property, and a property is a quality. But it is contradictory to say that a thing, by virtue of having a quality, is faulty.

Also, [based on his thinking,] the fact that someone is a sentient being must be the failing that prevents that individual being a buddha. So, with regard to being a buddha, being a sentient being must count as the failing. Thus it would follow that the self-grasping in the continuum of a sentient being [A] is the thing that needs to be eliminated with regard to the individual being a buddha [B], because it is a thing that [the individual] needs to eliminate and it prevents him being a buddha [C]. The reason and pervasion [of this argument] are the ones proposed [by the opponent]. But if he were to accept [its conclusion, we would say] that with regard to a sentient being being a buddha, the self-grasping in the sentient being's continuum cannot be what needs to be eliminated, because "a sentient being being a buddha" is not an established basis! What possible response could there be to this?

Someone claims that the failed reason and the failing in a reason are the same thing, as are the qualified and the quality.

[Response:] This defies direct experience, since the object universal [of each of the two, in both cases,] appear distinct from one another. What is more, it would follow that the bhikṣu and his vows are the same thing. It would also follow that the portion of production [that inheres in] sound is the same as that of production [in the general sense].

Others have claimed that [the two things in each of the two sets] are the same entity. Someone else has attacked [their position] by means of the consequence "If something that is a failing is necessarily faulty. . . ." But in doing this, he manages to expose the shortcomings [in his own reasoning abilities].

One can extrapolate from the way that others' assertions regarding a failing in a reason have been dealt with here to how those regarding [a failing in] the position and the example should be handled.

Setting out our own position

The failing in a reason is defined as "that by virtue of which the reason having it as a property is established to be a faulty reason for the proof in question, and a reason fulfilling the three criteria establishes it as such." An illustration of this, in the context of visual object being presented as the reason to establish that sound is impermanent, is the visual object's feature of not being present within sound.

The failing in an example is defined as "that by virtue of which the example having it as a property is established not to be a correct example for the proof in question, and a reason fulfilling the three criteria establishes it not to be such." The illustration of this, in the context of pot being presented as the example for the proof "Sound is permanent because it is an object of comprehension" is [the fact that] pot lacks permanence. [317]

The failing in the position is defined as "that by virtue of which the position having it as a property is established not to be a correct position for the proof in question, and a reason satisfying the three criteria establishes it not to be such." The illustration of this, in the context of the proof that sound is permanent, is [the feature] of permanence being present in sound, which is ruled out by valid cognition. The internal subdivisions of each of these are [obvious and] should be easy to understand. It should also be easy to understand that [the thing] within which the failing in a reason and the failing in the position are found can be the same, without [those failings] themselves needing to be the same. A common locus of the two is obviously possible, since in the context of the proof "Sound is permanent because it is permanent," not being present in sound is a failing in [both] permanents. But the way that the [*Commentary on Pramāṇa*] treatise describes this is something I will explain [in my commentarial exegesis] on that treatise.

Being a reason with a quality does not necessarily preclude being one with a failing. "Produced," presented as the reason to establish that sound is permanent, is both one with a quality and one with a failing. Production's presence in sound counts as a quality in that proof, whereas its being present solely in the class of dissimilar instances is a failing.[816] This illustrates how it also works in the case of the position and the example. As the example is an essential part of the reason, the failing in an example is subsumed within the failing in a reason. This completes the description of [what counts as] a failing and a quality with regard to the reason, example, and position.

That companion to the lotus [i.e., the sun] offers illumination,
that source of bounty [i.e., the ocean] supplies the wish-granting jewel,
and the garden of my intellect provides words of wisdom like a constant
 stream of honey:
such an abundance of virtuous riches befitting of a golden age!

This concludes the description of cognition, that which knows [the object], together with its subsidiary topics.

Part 3

How Cognition Engages Its Object

22. Varieties of Object and Ways of Cognizing

This has nine sections, with descriptions of (1) the negative and the affirmative, (2) preclusion and [logical] relationship, (3) the communicated and the communicating, (4) the universal and the particular, (5) the positive and the other-exclusion, (6) substantive and "reversed" [phenomena], (7) the single and the different, (8) the defining, the defined, and the illustration, and (9) the three times—the past and so forth. [318]

The negative and the affirmative

Regarding the first [section,] a negative[817] is defined as "that which the mind realizes through [taking on the] aspect of an overt exclusion of a negandum." The negation here [means] that when the universal of the thing in question appears to mind, the aspect through which it does this is that of an exclusion of the negandum. This is not a negation simply in the sense of an exclusion of what a thing is not [i.e., for *x*, the exclusion of non-*x*], since every object of knowledge remains in the state of excluding what it is not. Thus, even in cases when a negating particle [i.e., *non*] is not attached to the actual name of the thing in question, if *its cognition* [necessarily] involves an exclusion, and it is the aspect [of this exclusion] that appears in the mind, [that phenomenon] is referred to as "a negative." For this reason, all phenomena that are not actual things—object of knowledge, object of comprehension, and so forth—are regarded as negatives. The [reasoning] is as follows: "Object of knowledge [A] is a negative [B], because any cognition that realizes it overtly is necessarily one that [takes the] aspect of the exclusion of a negandum [C]. That in turn is because (1) a perception that has ["object of knowledge"] as an overt object is an impossibility, and (2) to any conceptual cognition that apprehends ["object of knowledge"], it appears as the opposite of non-object of knowledge.[818]

There are two kinds: those in which the negation is of the straight variety and those in which the negation is of the implicative variety. With the first of these, in the overt elimination of the negandum [through which] the object is cognized, no other phenomenon is conveyed or affirmed. For instance, a question as to whether it is acceptable for brahmans to drink alcohol [would be met with the response] "They should not drink alcohol." This simply excludes the notion of them drinking alcohol; it does not affirm anything about other substances they may or may not drink. As it says in the *Blaze of Reasoning*:

> The straight negation simply negates the entity of a thing. It does not affirm anything else that is other than the one in question but similar to it. For example, "Brahmans should not drink alcohol" negates just the [drinking of alcohol]; it does not say anything about other substances that they should or should not drink.[819] [319]

With the implicative negation [on the other hand], in the overt elimination of the negandum [through which] the object is cognized, some other phenomenon is conveyed or affirmed. When, for instance, someone wishes to indicate that a certain person belongs to the caste of "commoners" (*śūdra*),[820] he says, "This is not a brahman." It does not merely negate the person being a brahman but affirms that he belongs to another caste, that of the commoner. On this point, the *Blaze of Reasoning* says:

> The implicative negation, within negating the entity of the thing, affirms the entity of something that, while being similar to it, is other than it. For example, within negating [that the person is a brahman], "This is not a brahman" affirms that [he] is something similar but other than [a brahman: one] who is inferior to the brahman in terms of religious observances and learning and so forth—namely, one [who belongs to] the caste of commoners.[821]

Such a negation can convey the "other" phenomenon in four ways: (1) overtly, (2) by implication, (3) both overtly and by implication, or (4) through relying on the context. An example of the first is "The selfless exists," which in a single expression excludes a negandum and affirms another phenomenon. An example of the second is "Fat Devadatta doesn't eat anything during the day," which in effect indicates that he eats at night. An example of the third, "There's fat Devadatta, who doesn't eat anything during the day but isn't emaciated," is self-explanatory. An example of the fourth could occur in a situation where someone has determined that a specific individual belongs either to the ruler or brahman caste but is not sure which yet, and [a third person] says, "This is not a brahman." Rather than being something that the words of the statement expressly state, it is due to the context that he is shown to be of the ruler caste.

The way that other phenomena can be conveyed [by a negation] is limited to those three [i.e., overtly, by implication, through context], so any [negation] that conveys phenomena in one of these ways is an implicative negation. [A negation] that does not convey in any of those three ways is something else; it is a straight negation. As [the passage] cited by Avalokitavrata says:

> Negations [can either] indicate expressly,
> affirm in the same [set of] words, [or]
> by [the situation] though not by its own words.
> These are implicative negations: the others are [straight].[822]

Someone claims that whenever a thing is combined with a base that is affirmative, the [resultant combination] will be something affirmative.

[Response:] This is not tenable, because even though "brahman" itself is not just the exclusion of a negandum, "Brahmans should not drink alcohol" is such an exclusion. This is similar to the way that sound is an evident phenomenon, but sound [together with] impermanent [i.e., forming a thesis] is a hidden one.

Certain others assert that the basis [in the] combination should be identified as the "other phenomenon" conveyed [in the negation].

[Response:] This is also incorrect. In the case of "Brahmans should not drink alcohol," for example, "brahman" is the basis in terms of which one judges whether alcohol may be drunk; it is not the other phenomenon conveyed [through the negation]. [320]

An affirmative thing is defined as "a phenomenon that is able to appear to the cognition of which it is the object independently, without reliance on the elimination of a negandum." The examples of this are actual things.

This concludes the discussion on the negative and the affirmative.[823]

Preclusion and [logical] relationship

The second [section] has two [parts]: the characteristics defining [things as] preclusive and the varieties of preclusion. The first of these has:

1. Refuting others' assertions
2. Setting out our own position

Refuting others' assertions

Someone proposes that what defines things as preclusive is that they are "[in a state of being] at variance with each other."[824]

[A second individual, probes the first's position by] querying how he would refute the assertion that "the capacity [to engage in] activity" is the characteristic defining a pot.[825]

[The first responds by saying that it cannot be what defines a pot, since from this] "it would follow that a pillar is also a pot."

But [the second says that according to the first's definition] it would also follow that production and impermanent preclude each other.

[The first denies this,] claiming that production and impermanent are not "[in a state of being] at variance with each other."

The second retorts that equally, pillar is not that with "the capacity [to engage in] activity."

But the first says that it is, since it has "the capacity to support beams."

The second says that production and impermanent [must preclude each other, since] the characteristics that define them are at variance.

[Response:] There is no correspondence between the two cases. The fact that the characteristics defining two things vary does not mean that the things themselves are "at variance with each other," just as the fact that one definition precludes another does not necessarily mean that the things defined by those characteristics preclude each other.

According to someone else, the fact that two things have no common locus does not necessarily make them preclusive. He asserts that being preclusive must involve one thing [actively] countering the other. He argues that if the fact that [two] things lacked a common locus was enough to make them preclusive, one would be forced to say that cause and effect precluded one another. He refers to the passage in the [*Commentary on Pramāṇa*]:

> Because they [both] have self-grasping as their single cause
> and because they are cause and effect entities,
> desirous attachment and anger are mutually distinct,
> but they do not counter each other.[826]

He says that the commentaries on this explain the words to mean that *because* desirous attachment is the cause and anger its effect, the two cannot preclude each other. Similarly, he says blue, yellow, and so forth are not preclusive, since they do not actively counter one another.

[Response:] This is untenable. It would follow that permanent and impermanent do not qualify as preclusive, because they do not actively counter each other. That is the case, since neither one can negate [i.e., cancel out] the other.[827] [How could they?] Both of them are established by valid cognition. [321]

He may respond that even though, in a general sense, one does not counter the other, in terms of a phenomenon that is permanent, such as space, its permanence negates [its being] impermanent. And with a phenomenon that is impermanent, like sound, its impermanence negates [its being] permanent.

[Response:] Then the same must be the case for the likes of blue and yellow. What is more, unless produced and permanent precluded each other, produced could not be the correct reason establishing that sound is impermanent. So what is the reason that produced and permanent preclude each other?

He may respond that what makes them preclusive is the fact that (1) permanent and impermanent are directly preclusive [opposites] and (2) [the category of] produced things is totally pervaded [i.e., encompassed] by [the category of] impermanent ones.

[Response:] But again, it would follow [from this] that blue and yellow preclude each other. Why? Because (1) blue and non-blue constitute directly preclusive [opposites] and (2) [the category of] yellow is totally pervaded by [the category of] non-blue.[828] Furthermore, unless "[being] derived from effort" precluded the anti-predicate [i.e., permanent], it could not serve as a reason in the proof establishing that the sound of a conch is impermanent. So what is it that precludes something that is "derived from effort" from being permanent?

He might reply that it is the fact that it is impermanent.

[Response:] Again though, correspondingly, it would follow that something that is yellow is precluded from being blue, because it is [necessarily] non-blue. There is no other reason for [one precluding the other] than this, just as in the case [with "derived from effort" and "permanent"].

Some may [challenge our position with this argument] "In terms of the proof 'On the smoky pass there is fire, because there is smoke,' it follows that smoke is a *contrary* reason, because [while] it is the property of the subject, fire and smoke preclude each other."

[Response:] But [we could equally well argue this:] it follows that a proof using fire to establish the *absence* of coldness [in a certain location] is an affirmative one, because the fire that fulfills the three criteria is affirmative. They would have no response to this. Any number of attacks can be made against the position [espoused by the above individuals]. Only concerns about length have dissuaded me from relating any more of them here.

What the passage "Because they [both] have self-grasping as their single cause ..."[829] and commentaries on it actually tell us is that while it is true that if either desirous attachment or anger is manifest, the other cannot be manifest, this does not mean that either of them is an antidote to the other, able to eradicate it together with its seeds. Why? Because (1) there are cases where desirous attachment acts as the cause of anger, and vice versa, and (2) the original cause of both is self-grasping.

Those of you who claim that [what this passage] is saying is that because desirous attachment and anger are cause and effect, they *cannot* preclude each other in the sense of a mutual opposition, introduce something that is irrelevant and unrelated [to what the treatise discusses here]. And as your explanation does not get to the treatise's meaning, you have no justification for going through [the passage in the context of this discussion about preclusion]. So, by declaring that the treatise should be interpreted in this way, you "proponents of the [analytical] great works [approach]"[830] broadcast, in pitiful tones, the inadequacies [of your understanding].

Setting out our own position

The definition of [things being] preclusive is that "[they are] different and a common locus of them is impossible." [322] There are two varieties of preclusion: that which involves an antagonism and that which involves a mutual opposition. The former, an antagonistic preclusion, is defined as "that in which the actual things in question cannot coexist in equal strength for any sustained period." There are two varieties: that in which the antagonistic preclusion is between things that are physical material and that in which it is between things that are consciousness. An example of the first is heat and cold. An example of the second is self-grasping and the wisdom that perceives selflessness. Both these examples of antagonistic preclusion are *direct* preclusions. An example of an antagonistic preclusion where the things in question preclude each other *indirectly* is that between a vigorous body of smoke and intense cold. This is also known as a "preclusion involving countering by [another] valid cognition."[831] Why? Because the fact that where there is smoke there is fire is something we establish by means of valid cognition, and it is by virtue of fire and cold precluding each other in the antagonistic sense that we [understand] that smoke must also preclude cold in an [indirect] antagonistic sense.

Concerning the way in which these preclusions work, to learn about antagonistic preclusions between cognitions, one should consult what I have written elsewhere on the topic of the elements to be eradicated and their antidotes. As for the way it works in the case of [material things, like] heat and cold, others have explained it in the following manner. In the first instant, the two come into contact, then in the second, one weakens the strength of the other. Then, in the third instant, [the stronger one] breaks the sequence [of production for the weaker one]. They characterize the first one as "the powerful counter [force]" and the *cause* [in the process], and the other, "the weakened, the countered," as the *effect*.

[Response:] This position is untenable. [It suggests] that one thing can play the rôle of producing a phenomenon while also countering it, [whereas in fact] those two preclude each other. What actually happens with heat and cold is that in the first instant, they come into contact with each other. In the next, the second instant of coldness occurs, with the first moment of cold having acted as its substantial cause and the first instant of heat having acted as the contributory condition to its production. This [latter] makes the second instant of the cold into something whose capacity to produce its own effect is diminished. [Instants of] heat and cold such as these are cause and effect, and they do *not* preclude each other in the antagonistic sense. Then, the third instant of cold is produced. This third instant is created by the second instant of cold acting as its substantial cause, and the second instant of heat acting as its contributory condition. They make it into something that lacks the strength to create later instants of itself, in the form of its effects. These [instants of] heat and cold are also cause and effect, and it is not the case that one counters the other. That notwithstanding, we can talk of the heat as a *whole*, the entirety of which is composed of three temporal parts. We can also talk of the coldness as a *whole* comprising three temporal parts: the first of these parts has [full] productive capacity, the second is diminished in strength, and the third is totally incapacitated. So the heat and cold that preclude each other in this antagonistic sense are the heat and cold of those two *wholes*. [323] These are not cause and effect. And the reason that these—the heat and cold as wholes—preclude each other in the antagonistic sense is that their functions are incompatible with each other. Consequently, they are things that are unable to coexist for any sustained period of time with their respective productive capacities intact. That is because after they have come into contact in the first instant, the cold of the second instant will be of decreased capacity, and that of the third instant will have been rendered incapable of producing later instants of itself. Therefore the sequence of cold can no longer continue beyond the fourth instant. This process differs from the one involving light and dark. In that situation the light that is about to be produced and the darkness that is about to disappear occur simultaneously, and also the light that has been produced and darkness that has disappeared are simultaneous.

Someone affirms that heat and cold, as basic notions, are "counter and countered." But he also argues, "The coldness that is countered cannot be something that belongs to the present, since there is no way to counter a thing once it has already been produced." Added to this, he maintains that one of the most fundamental philosophical tenets is that all actual things belong to the present. We can only marvel at the carelessness [that leads] him to hold such blatantly contradictory positions.

Secondly, there is the preclusion of mutual opposition. *Preclusion* in this sense is defined as "that in which the phenomena in question are such that being either one excludes being the other." This also has two varieties, direct and indirect. The first is defined as "genuine opposites in the sense that the ruling out that something is either one of them will bring with it the understanding that it is the other." An example is "permanent and impermanent." The second [the indirect variety] is defined as "that in which one of the phenomena in question is precluded from being [the other] in the sense that it shares no common locus with it but is not the actual isolate reverse of that phenomenon." An example is "product and permanent." This indirect preclusion is also known as a "preclusion involving countering by [another] valid cognition." Why? Because by [establishing] that a certain thing was produced, one can negate it being permanent. But this is only on account of having already confirmed, with [another] valid cognition, that something that is produced is necessarily impermanent. To sum up then, things that preclude each other necessarily do so in the sense of a mutual opposition, whereas a preclusion involving countering by [another] valid cognition and an indirect preclusion are equivalent.

The passage [in the *Commentary on Pramāṇa*] that identifies direct preclusion in the antagonistic sense is "It is an entity that counters the [other] object; it is through its presence [that the other becomes] absent."[832] The passage that informs us about direct preclusion in the sense of a mutual opposition together with an example is "It is because the [two] are established to be mutually different, just as is the case with a thing that is constant and one that disintegrates."[833] [324] The passage "Because also it is countered by another valid cognition, just as, for instance, being necessarily true [is countered by] being contingent"[834] tells us that all indirect preclusions are cases of "preclusion involving countering by [another] valid cognition." This is an encapsulation of what it means to be an indirect preclusion, and having provided this, [Dharmakīrti] gives an example of [two things] that indirectly preclude each other in the sense of forming a mutual opposition. It encapsulates an indirect preclusion, since an indirect preclusion is defined as "a preclusion in which it is on account of a valid cognition establishing that *x* directly counters non-*x* that *y* is established to preclude non-*x*." That [encapsulation] also serves to illustrate what it is that defines a *direct* preclusion, in that [it also refers to] one phenomenon countering some other *without* having to rely on a further valid cognition informing it [about a separate] case where one thing has countered another.

[Logical] relationship

The definition of one thing [*x*] being related to phenomenon [*y*] is that "*x* and *y* are different from each other, and if *y* is ruled out, *x* is necessarily also ruled out."[835] There are two sorts of [logical relationship]: the nature variety and the causal variety. The definition of the first is "[the two things in question have] an unfailing concomitance with each other by virtue of them sharing the same nature identity." An example of two such things is "produced" and "impermanent." The definition of the second variety is "[the two things in question have] an unfailing concomitance with each other while having different nature identities. An example of this is smoke, as related to fire.

The valid cognition that ascertains a relationship of the nature variety is the same as the one responsible for ascertaining the relationship [underpinning] the pervasion within a proof of the nature variety. The valid cognition that ascertains the causal relationship is the same as the one responsible for ascertaining [that two things are] cause and effect. This is something one can understand by referring to what I have already explained [about the ascertainment of the pervasions].

A [logical] relationship is not established in any ultimate sense. If the relationship between produced and impermanence were true ultimately, then the difference between them would also have to be true in the ultimate sense—they would be truly different things. And if produced and impermanent were truly different things, they would need to be two distinct substances. While it is the case therefore that there is a [logical] relationship between "produced" and "impermanence," and that "produced" and "impermanence" are themselves truly established things, the relationship between them is not one that is established in any *true* sense. In a similar fashion, the relationship between fire and smoke is not established in any true sense. If it were, the conceptual cognitions that distinguish them and classify the fire as "that with which there is a relationship" and the smoke as "that which is related" would have to be unmistaken with respect to what appears to them. [325] That would need to be the case, because [those two identities of "related with" and "related"] would be established in a true sense, whereas for [such identities] to overtly appear to perception is in fact impossible. Using the same line of reasoning, one can demonstrate without difficulty that *preclusion* [itself] is also not established in any true sense. It is necessary therefore to skillfully distinguish between the isolate identity itself and things that have the identity, noting that while [logical] relationship and preclusion may not be established in the true sense, the [various] things that are either related to or preclude one another may be. The way that this works has been discussed at length above.[836] This completes the concise account of preclusion and [logical] relationship.

The communicated and the communicating

1. Defining characteristics
2. Varieties

With respect to the third [section,] the communicated thing [i.e., the object] is defined as "that which is conveyed by symbolic representation."[837] The communicating [medium] is defined as "that which conveys its object through symbolic representation." Every phenomenon is an object of communication, since there is no phenomenon that words cannot communicate.

Someone claims that the specifically characterized cannot be [adequately] captured in words.

[Response:] This is a massive error. It would follow that the name "moon" could not capture the sphere [marked] with the hare and that valid cognition verifies this [inability]. But if that were the case, the thesis "The name 'moon' can legitimately be used to denote the sphere [marked] with the hare," [far from being one verified] by valid cognition, would be something that it rules out.

Quite apart from that, if the claim were correct, it would follow that things that are ultimately true cannot be objects communicated by the teachings of the Buddha. It would also directly contradict [another of] the same individual's own positions—namely, that *both* kinds of comprehended object, those with specific and general characteristics, are "the communicated" [i.e., the subject matter] of the Pramāṇa treatises.

He might respond by saying that while the [scriptures and treatises deal with things that are ultimately true], they do so only from the excluding perspective.

[Response:] It would follow that the cognition realizing that things that are ultimately true are the object of the scriptures must also be an excluding engager. But if he accepts this, it would go against [another of his] claims—namely, that it is impossible for something that is true in an ultimate sense to serve as the object of a cognition that is an excluding engager.[838]

Another dolt, who assumes the outward appearance of a learned scholar, similarly maintains that words cannot capture what is specifically characterized.

[Response:] We notice that he also accepts that "[because] it exists" is a correct reason establishing that the name "moon" can communicate the sphere [marked] with the hare. No one beating him with a stick was needed to get him to accept these things; what an accommodating nature he has!

There are so many fearsome attacks that can be made against this notion that what is specifically characterized cannot be captured in words. Many of them have been made throughout the course of this work. But they are so numerous, how would it be possible to "capture" them all? [326] A specifically characterized thing is not, however, the overt object of the word that communicates it, since for that, it would need to be the object that appears to a conceptual cognition. One therefore needs to be aware [of this distinction]: something that is specifically characterized can necessarily be captured [and communicated] in words but is necessarily not the overt object [of the word] that communicates it. If something that is specifically characterized could not be overtly communicated in words, it would be impossible for conceptual cognition to realize it overtly. And if a conceptual cognition could not do that, it would follow either that "sound" and "impermanent" together [i.e., in the thesis "sound is impermanent"] cannot be realized directly by inferential valid cognition, or that those two together are permanent!

One should not [assert] that whatever a word overtly communicates is necessarily that word's overt object. The reason [for avoiding this assertion] is that it leads to the consequence that whatever a conceptual cognition overtly realizes is necessarily its explicit object. From this, it would in turn follow that whatever a conceptual cognition overtly realizes is necessarily its appearing object. And from this it would follow that [it is possible for] valid inferential cognition to comprehend a thing without overtly realizing it.

Someone with [inordinate] pride in his own scholarship accepts that the perception of a specifically characterized blue can induce a conceptual cognition, ascertaining that blue. But he also asserts that what is specifically characterized *cannot* be the object of conceptual cognition.

[Response:] This [may well] demonstrate that he "has an intellect that delights the gods," [but it] is nothing more than a straightforward case of holding directly contradictory theses. Illustrations of the object communicated have been provided above.

There are four separate ways to divide the communicating [medium]. The first, by way of entity [i.e., units of communication] is a threefold categorization into names, word formations, and letters. The first is defined as "a sound that communicates just the object's entity." This is divided into actual names and figurative names. An actual name is defined as "the name that is assigned in the initial symbolic labeling of the phenomenon and that can unfailingly communicate it." An example is "lion" as used for the king of the beasts. The figurative name is defined as "the name that is later assigned to the object of the actual name and that references a relationship or resemblance that the object in question has [to something else]." An example is "lion" when used for the child of a brahman. Figurative names are divided into those that make reference to relationships, such as calling sunlight "the sun," and those that make reference to a similarity, such as calling a medicinal ingredient "crow's feet." [327] As such things are easily understood, I will discuss them no further.

A *word formation* is defined as "a sound that communicates the object's entity conjoined with a property." An example is "Devadatta with blue clothes." A letter is defined as an intonation that, in isolation, does not communicate a meaning but is the stuff of which the type of sounds that do are composed. These can be divided into the letters that are vowels, [known as] *āli*, and the consonants *ka*, *kha*, and so on.[839] I have already refuted those who, through [an analysis] that splits them into individual instants, have tried to establish that names, word formations, and letters have no substantial existence.

Someone else argues that "A name or word formation can have no substantial existence, because they are what is described as 'nonassociated compounded things.'"[840]

[Response:] It follows that neither can impermanence have any substantial existence, because it is described as a nonassociated compounded thing. And if he concedes this, he [would essentially be] accepting that the only things that can be substantially existent are those that are permanent; a stance that would be truly astounding!

Why then are names and word formations described as nonassociated compounded things? This does not indicate that they, as entities, are not [real, substantive] things. Rather, it means that while names and word formations are the mediums of the objects they communicate, it is only due to thought having assigned them [this role] that they are such. And it is in reference to the lack of substantiveness [of the link between them and their objects that the masters] describe them as "nonassociated compounded things." What the section in the [*Commentary on Pramāṇa*] passage "Word formations and so forth are imputed, and not [substantive] things . . ."[841] does is pose the following question: "Since it is only due to being assigned as such by thought that a word formation or the like is the medium that communicates its object, that [word formation] is not the communicator of its object—the thing it communicates—in any real, substantive sense. So how can the relationship between a word formation or the like and the object it communicates be a real, substantive one?"

[To assert that] no name, word formation, or letter is substantially established contradicts the pronouncement that letters have their origin in the consciousness that is the impulse to articulate them. And as sounds that communicate meaning [would then effectively] become unfeasible, it would become impossible to convey meaning through symbolic representations. But that would make the whole exercise of [the Buddha] teaching by turning the wheels of Dharma a futile one! One would also have to accept that such things as telling lies have no [retributive] effect. It would also mean that what a speaker says cannot be used to deduce his motives. But if that were the case, how could one account for the passage "In that regard, [communicative] sounds are valid [i.e., reliable] . . ."?[842] The position [espoused by the aforesaid individual] invites a whole stream of serious attacks, but I have not related them at any length here.

Another way to divide the communicating [medium] is in terms of what it communicates: type-communicating terms and assemblage-communicating terms. [328] The first is defined as "a word, any literal content communicated by which is necessarily a universal." An example is the word *form*. A sound that conveys an assemblage is defined as "a word, any literal content communicated by which is necessarily a coarse entity." An example is the word *pot*.

From the perspective of a single basis, these two preclude each other. In the context of conveying "golden pot," [for instance], the word *pot* is a type-communicator, not an assemblage-communicator. But in the context of conveying the pot's form, it is an assemblage-communicator, not a type-communicator. However, if different [perspectival] bases are [taken into account], the two do not preclude each other. [Hence,] in reference to parts of the pot, such as its [visual] form, the word *pot* is an assemblage-communicator, whereas in reference to the instances of pot, it is a type-communicator.[843]

[The treatises distinguish between the two in terms of what they convey by describing] an assemblage-communicating word as being "devoid" of the thing with the assemblage and a type-communicating word as not being devoid of the thing with the type. As the [*Commentary on Pramāṇa*] says, "This, therefore, is the difference between [words] that communicate types and assemblages."[844] This is not saying that [the distinction between the two is that] a type-communicator conveys everything [belonging to] that type, whereas an assemblage-communicator does not convey everything [belonging to] the assemblage. Instead, it means that while the term *pot* can be used accurately for any individuation of pot, it can never be used accurately for such things as the [visual] form of pot.[845] I alone have the intellect that has been able to penetrate this point.

Another way to divide the communicating [medium] is in terms of how it represents its object: words that are *property communicators* and words that are *subject communicators*. The first is defined as "sound(s) that represent the thing that the speaker and listener have chosen to focus their attention on as a property." An example is "[the] cow's non-horseness." The second is defined as "sound(s) that represent the thing that the speaker and listener have chosen to focus their attention on as the basis of a property." An example is "[the] cow is [a] non-horse."[846]

Regarding what distinguishes property communicators and subject communicators, and what [the treatises mean when they say the distinction lies in] whether or not they are "devoid" of the communication of some other property, one individual claims that "devoid" and "not devoid" refer to whether the [respective sounds] "convey" or "do not convey" other properties.

[Response:] This is untenable. It would follow that "a cow's non-horseness" must convey every property of cow. [329] And if that were the case, it must even communicate the two types of selflessness [that are properties of cow]![847]

Someone else claims that the distinction [between property communicators and subject communicators] lies in whether they represent the phenomenon in question [i.e., the subject] as one that cannot or can serve as the basis for other properties.

[Response:] From this it would follow that a property communicator is necessarily inaccurate, because there is no such thing as a phenomenon that can serve as the basis for no property other than the one overtly referred to by the sound denoting that property. Thus we see that the assertions others have made about this are nothing more than the anguished expressions of those who find themselves unable to admit, "We haven't been able to fathom this!"

This is how it is: verbalizations are not produced by speakers independently. Their ability to convey meaning is determined by the speaker's wish to express something and the listener's wish to know it. When [the treatises] talk of "[being] devoid of other properties," they refer to how [certain verbalizations] represent the thing in question *as* a property, and in doing so, refrain from presenting it to the mind as an object that serves as a *basis*, supporting some other property. "Not [being] devoid of other properties" refers to how [other verbalizations] present a thing to the mind as an object that is the basis of a property. The way this works [in practice] is that a listener who hears just "non-horseness" will be aware of the numerous things, the buffalo and so on to which this "non-horseness" might [apply]. The wish to know which of them it is prompts him to inquire. The response that it is "the cow's non-horseness" informs him that the non-horseness is the basis of the property, and the cow, the property.[848] And it is this [representation] that allows him to distinguish this specific non-horseness from that of the buffalo and so forth. This is just as is the case, for instance, with "Rāhu's head." Rāhu is the property, since it is the phenomenon by means of which we understand that the head in question is to be distinguished from those of gods or humans. And the head is the basis of the property. Thus, [in the example above,] the verbalization represents the cow, in the isolated [abstract sense], as the property.

Alternatively, [a person] may be wondering about the cow and whether or not it is a non-horse. When he asks someone about it, that [second person] may choose to represent the cow as the basis and the non-horse as its property, and therefore formulate his response "The cow is a non-horse." This represents the cow as the basis that has the property of [being a] "non-horse."

While both verbalizations convey an isolated [abstraction] of "cow," one of them represents the cow as a property and is consequently classified as the *property communicator*. The latter represents the cow as the basis of a property and is thus the *subject communicator*. [330] Thus we come to fully comprehend that the point made [in the treatises] is that while both verbalizations may be indistinguishable in terms of the single phenomenon that they refer to [i.e., cow], they are distinguishable in terms of the way they represent it. While there may previously have been a few cursory mentions [of this distinction], until now no one has gained so much as a glimpse of this, the real point.

In a similar fashion, if someone is wondering whether the basis, a physical mass encompassing the distinctive neck hump, has the property of being a cow or a horse, a person who wants to inform him may state that it is "a cow, only." Using *only* as a distinguisher excludes horse and thereby represents cow[ness] as a property, and thus ["a cow, only"] counts as a verbalization that is a property communicator. [On the other hand,] when it is just the property-basis that a person wants to know about, someone else may choose to tell him that it is a "cow." This represents cow as the basis of the property, and thus ["cow"] counts as a verbalization that is a subject communicator. This completes the account of these two verbalizations.

A fourth way of dividing the communicating [medium] is in terms of the ways it excludes. There are three varieties: verbalizations that are (1) nonpossession excluders, (2) possession-by-others excluders, and (3) impossibility excluders. As to the nature of these, the word *indeed* is referred to as a *particle*. The grounds for this [description] are that it conveys meaning when it is conjoined with another word but is incapable of conveying anything when not so conjoined. When such a particle is attached to a property, and it excludes that the basis [in question] does not possess that property—thereby communicating that the basis possesses it—this particle is referred to as a verbalization that is a "nonpossession excluder." An example of this is "Caitra is an archer *indeed*."[849] If the articulation of the particle is one that connects it with a [certain] basis and excludes bases other than that one possessing the property, while [simultaneously] communicating that the basis in question has that property, this is referred to as a verbalization that is a "possession-by-others excluder." An example is "*Only* Pārtha is the archer." If an emphatic is attached [to the word] with the intention of excluding the impossibility of the basis having the property in question, it is an *impossibility excluder*. An example is "Blue is *certainly* possible for a lotus." This concludes the description of the communicated and the communicating. [331]

The universal and the particular

With respect to the fourth [section], a *universal* is defined as "a phenomenon that has concomitance with multiple phenomena [i.e., instances]." A *particular* is defined as "that which, in the sense of being encompassed by it, has its own type." As these have been covered at length in the preceding explanations, I will elaborate no further.[850]

The positive and the other-exclusion

In the fifth [section], *positive* [thing] and *appearance* [presenter][851] are equivalent and synonymous. An appearance [presenter] is defined as "an actual thing that plainly shows its own aspect to the perception that apprehends it."

One individual holds the view that if an appearance has objective existence, the same must be the case for an exclusion.

[Response:] [If that was correct, it would] equally apply [to the cognitions of those two]. Thus, if the "appearance engager"[852] [is a cognition that] engages an objectively existent thing, so too must the "excluding engager" be that. But that would contradict this individual's own stance on [cognitions] that engage through exclusion, according to which they *cannot* engage anything in an objective sense. Furthermore, if this individual was presented with the argument "because the appearance is ultimately real, it follows that the same must be the case for the other-exclusion," he would simply have no response.

[The same individual also argues against identifying visual form as an appearance,] because [he says,] "If visual form is by its nature an *appearance* [i.e., something that necessarily appears], it would mean that there can be no such thing as a blind person."

[Response:] Then equally, since visual form is by its nature an evident [phenomenon], it would also mean that there is no such thing as a blind person.

As to the nature of things [arrived at through] exclusion of other, all objects of knowledge are definitively divided into those that are negative and those that are affirmative. *Affirmative* [or positive phenomenon] and *appearance* [presenter] are equivalent, and every actual thing is both. Those that are *exclusions* and those that are *negative* are equivalent, and every non-actual thing is both.

Someone defines *exclusion* as "that which is the negation of what directly precludes [itself]." Based on this, he also argues, "Every phenomenon is the exclusion of another, since each of them is the exclusion of what does not accord with itself."

[Response:] This position is not sustainable. It would follow that every phenomenon is negative, because every one of them is the negation of what does not accord with itself, and also because every one of them is the negation of what directly precludes itself. This same line of reasoning also refutes the notion that something specifically characterized can be an exclusion. In any case, all such assertions are blatant rejections of the position frequently stated in the treatise system of the master [Dharmakīrti]—namely, that any exclusion of other is a construct. [332]

Someone else argues against specifically characterized things being exclusions, saying that if they were, it would follow that the perceptions [of them] must be excluding engagers.

[Response:] But then, correspondingly, because pot is an affirmative thing, it must follow that the conceptual cognition apprehending it is also an affirmative engager.

Another [individual] argues that only *factually correct* verbalizations and conceptual cognitions can be exclusions, since these are the ones that eliminate distorted notions.

[Response:] It would follow that all yogic perceptions are exclusions. He is also directly contradicting his own assertion that anything specifically characterized is precluded from being an exclusion. Anyway, he has already accepted that if something specifically characterized was an exclusion, it would follow that the perception of it would be an excluding engager. Hence we could argue, "It follows that the self-cognition perceiving a factually correct conceptual cognition is an excluding engager, because that factually correct conceptual cognition is an exclusion." The three spheres are [in place for this argument] and it is one to which he has no response. One can but marvel at [this individual's] intellect and its [prodigious] ability to bear the weight of such a massive load of contradictions!

As to the correct position, in his commentary on the passage "because a reversal has no [real] nature,"[853] the master Śākyabuddhi distinguishes between three exclusions.[854] These relate to the object [of the action], the action itself, and the instrument, respectively.[855] Regarding [the first, in the sense that it] can serve as the basis or the object for the action of exclusion, a specifically characterized pot is the "exclusion's object" [i.e., the exclusion's referent]. [Second,] the actual exclusion [in this case] is the simple exclusion of what is not pot. This is referred to as the "other-exclusion [as] straight negation." [Third,] that which appears to thought as the reverse of non-pot is the [instrument] by means of which the exclusion occurs. This is known as the "other-exclusion [as] implicative negation."

In line with this, the *Compendium of Suchness* says:

> Here there are two forms of exclusion:
> the implicative negation and the straight one.
> The implicative negation also has two forms,
> divided by way of the cognition and the object.[856]

The master Kamalaśīla has also given a detailed explanation of this in his commentary to the work.[857] Thus, in terms of exclusion, [we should talk of] "the exclusion's [referent] object(s)," "the exclusion [as] straight negation," and "the cognitive[-level] exclusion." The first are specifically characterized things, and "exclusion" is no more than a name attached to them in reference to the fact that they all [represent] the exclusion of what does not accord with themselves. The simple exclusion of non-pot is an exclusion [as] straight negation. That which appears to the conceptual cognition of pot as the reverse of non-pot is the cognitive[-level] exclusion. Since *exclusion* and *negation* are synonyms, these [last] two are genuine exclusions. [333] This *exclusion* denotes neither [the exclusion of] things that do not accord [with the one in question] nor [the elimination of] distorted notions. Instead, *other-exclusion* refers to the fact that the thing in question is one that can only become an object of mind through the [overt] exclusion or elimination of some negandum other [than itself]. Other-exclusion is therefore defined as "that which can only be realized through the explicit exclusion of a negandum." This has two varieties. The first, the straight negation-exclusion, is defined as "an other-exclusion that does not convey an affirmative phenomenon." The [second,] the implicative negation-exclusion, is defined as "an other-exclusion that conveys an affirmative phenomenon."

As to the cognitions that engage [these objects]: one that apprehends its object without relying on the explicit elimination of a negandum but does so by means of the independent aspect [of that object] is an *affirmative engager*. One that apprehends its object by means of eliminating a negandum is an *excluding engager*. That is what *excluding engager* denotes, and there are misleading and correct varieties of these. A cognition that, when taking a phenomenon as its overt object, does so by embracing all of its substantial qualities, not separating between that phenomenon and its substantial features, is known as an *appearance engager*. [Conversely,] a cognition that takes some of the phenomenon's substantial or isolated [qualities] as its object but not others, thereby distinguishing between them, is one that engages it selectively [i.e., through exclusion].

I have chosen not to approach this account of other-exclusion by setting out and refuting the various assertions of former scholars on the matter, as I feared this would become too lengthy. But [these have been dealt with] at some length above, in the course of the discussions about the manner that conceptual cognition apprehends its object—the generally characterized and so forth.

Substantive and "reverse" [phenomena]

With respect to the sixth [section, distinguishing between] substantive and "reverse" [phenomena], a *substantive [phenomenon]* is a real, specifically characterized one. A *reverse [phenomenon]* is one that is purely constructed by thought. As to the respective examples of these, "produced" and "impermanence" are the first, whereas the *difference* between "produced" and "impermanence" is the second. Here, "substance" and "phenomenon" are combined to form a single unit; there is no sixth-case, genitive [particle between] the two.[858] Hence [what is denoted is a "substantive phenomenon" rather than] a substance separate from its property, and [a "reverse phenomenon" rather] than a "reverse" [thing] separate from its property.

To state it succinctly, "substantive phenomenon" and "reverse phenomenon" refer to the same things as "substantial existent" and "imputed existent." [334] But that is [of course only taken] from the point of view that what distinguishes substantially existent phenomena from imputed existents is that the first has the capacity to function whereas the second does not. When earlier Tibetan scholars distinguished between substantial and imputed existents, they took the perspective that what separated the [two] phenomena was that [the first] was something able to stand independently, whereas [the second] was not. It was from this perspective that they went on to develop their various accounts of the substantial and the reverse, including the position that the definiendum—the thing defined—must have the "three properties of imputation," whereas the characteristics that defined it must have the "three properties of substance." Such was the way of those who followed the "[analytical] great texts' approach."[859] And while these days we find plenty of individuals espousing things about substantial and reversed [phenomena] that do not accord with any of the major works, I have not engaged in a detailed critique of these here.[860]

The single and the different

The seventh [section] concerns the single and the different. Something single is defined as "a phenomenon without separation." Those that are different are defined as "[things with] separation." There are two varieties of singularity. Things that are a single substance are defined as "[those that] arose as a nonseparate entity." An example is production and impermanence. A [conceptually] isolated single is defined as "a phenomenon that in terms of its individual isolate has no separation." An example is production and production.[861]

There are two varieties of difference. Things that are different substances are defined as "[those that] arose as separate entities." Things that are different in terms of [their conceptual] isolation are defined as "[those with] separate individual isolates." An example of the first is a pillar and a pot. An example of the second is production and impermanence. Issues such as whether things that are a single substance are necessarily single have been dealt with at length above.[862]

The defining, the defined, and the illustration

The definition of a definiendum—that is, the thing defined—is "that which has the three properties of the establisher." The three properties are (1) it is, in general terms, a definiendum, (2) it is not the definiendum of anything other than the defining characteristics in question, and (3) an illustration [embodying it] is possible. The definition of a definition is "that with the three properties of what is established." The three properties are (1) it is, in general terms, what defines [a thing], (2) it is not the definition of anything other than the definiendum in question, and (3) an illustration [embodying it] is possible. There are two varieties of definition: that which eliminates what does not accord [with the thing in question] and that which eliminates misconceptions. The way that they eliminate misconceptions has been explained above. An illustration is defined as "that which serves as the basis illustrating the thing defined in relation to what defines it." [335]

There is certainly much that can be said on the scheme involving the definiendum and so forth, but as there are so many side issues arising from it, I have not written any more here. But it is something that I will explain separately.

The three times—the past and so forth

The ninth [section deals with] the three times.[863] Someone defines a past [thing] as "that which has been produced and has ceased." He defines a future [thing] as "that which has not [yet] been produced but for which the causes exist." And he defines a present [thing] as "that which has been produced but has not [yet] ceased."

[Response:] This is untenable. It would follow that a past [thing] is necessarily a produced one, because such a thing has necessarily been produced. It would also follow that a future [thing] is necessarily a result, because it is necessarily something that has existent causes. The reasons for both [these arguments derive] directly [from his definitions]. But if he were to accept [their conclusions], it would follow that [things of the past and future] are actual things.

Someone else defines a past [thing] as "that which formerly existed" and a future one as "that which will arise."

[Response:] From this, it would follow that a present [thing] is an impossibility.

Another [individual proposes that] yesterday is an illustration. He claims that from the perspective of today, [yesterday] is something that illustrates the past, and that from today's perspective it is [also] "something that has been produced and has ceased" and so on.

[Response:] Based on that, one would have to accept that *today* is something that has "not been produced," "has been produced," and "has ceased," because that is what today is, from the perspectives of yesterday, today, and tomorrow, respectively. In short, this just amasses contradictions.

In our own system, that in the past is defined as "perished," that in the present is defined as "something that has been produced," whereas that in the future is defined as "that which has not been produced." An example of the first of these is a perished clay pot.[864] Pot is an example of the second. And the abstracted feature of a seed that has not yet been produced is an example of the third. This concludes the account of how cognition engages its object. [336]

Final words

Nurtured by the nectar of past virtuous deeds, this sandalwood mass with
its broad limbs, offers fragrant shade.
Its wise words, like drops of camphor, spread across the ground, deaden the
scorch of pernicious traditions.
And as nubile youths frolic precociously around it, the shimmering earth
beneath it shudders and quivers.

This splendid (*gelek*) tree of insight rids the land's rulers of their torments
and will, until the end of time, provide for every wish.

On his promontory on the great jeweled mountain of the Sugata's teachings
sits [the garuḍa] in delighted repose, viewing all with wide-eyed alertness.
The faintest movement from his mighty wings of logic would raise a great tempest raging in every direction,
churning the waters of insidious traditions and filling the heavens with glorious sunlight [illuminating] all things.
At the mere recollection of this fearless lord of winged creatures, the serpent legions of self-proclaimed scholars are immediately brought low.

My intellect is an immense structure, a wonderous tower of precious crystal in which every phenomenon is reflected.
It is a delightful *vīṇā* of pure reasoning that sings sonorously, affirming and dismissing with each stroke.
Is it not in celebration, heralding the dawn of a new age of understanding of the celebrated treatises that, on these snowy lands, the glorious sun sprinkles its vermillion rays?

And as I took up my fine writing implement to compose this clear mirror of description, revealing the true nature of all things, did all phenomena not shrink and shudder with anticipation?

My mind is a joyous habitat for myriad textual systems,
and it supports thousands of compelling reasons.
That the earth can bear the weight of such a jeweled mountain
is indeed a matter of great fortune! [337]

Having dressed himself in the immaculate costume of the Able One's conduct
and applied the nectar [makeup] of fine words to his face,
he stands before the throng ready to deliver words to delight the learned.
And as they set eyes on his countenance, the eager, intelligent [audience] is gratified.

Have those performers who lack the vision to see the truth for themselves
or the intellect to discern the message of the treatises,

and whose only aim is to gain the respect of the foolish, through repeating their borrowed scripts,
not yet wearied of their charade?

Those who have neither labored on the path of logic
nor discerned the way forged by the great charioteers,[865]
and who with tiny intellects [hide behind] a profusion of words, seeking sanctuary in citation,
are the most prize of fools.

Unaware of the extent of what the Able One taught
and without having fathomed the tenets of our own or others' systems,
some cling resolutely to formulas of their own creation.
Excited by gain and respect, these "spiritual guides" lure disciples with materiality.
Were they only to rest for some time, it would at least decrease the harm they do to the Conqueror's tradition.

With this, my mind is replete like the full moon, like the face of one drunk on the nectar of erudite description.
Intercourse with the beauteous one, the panoply of all things, and the play of nails[866] is over.
From the virtue brought about by the brilliance of the blooming night lilies of reasoning that it has produced,
may the gathering of clear-minded crested [young scholars be inspired to] strut in delight [like peacocks], with the swelling of their tail plumage seeming to compete with the expanding waters of the Buddhist tradition.

[In composing] this *Banisher of Ignorance: An Ornament of the Seven Treatises on Pramāṇa*, I bow to those charioteers in this snowy mountain land who are unsurpassed champions of the Conqueror's tradition. I especially humble myself before the crown ornaments of glorious scholars. One, for the present purpose, I must [impertinently] address by name: the holy and venerable Kumāramati [Rendawa]. There is also the one who is the crowning jewel among those who raise the saffron victory banner, the one whose pure enlightened deeds reach to every corner of the land, and who, in terms of maintaining the holy Dharma in exactly the way that the Conqueror intended, has no equal: the all-knowing splendor that is Losang Drakpa. I place my head at the feet of these holy, venerable greatly compassionate beings.

Having crossed to the far shore of [understanding] of the vast, ocean-like expanse of the tenets of our own system and others, and having [gained] the virtuous, fearless self-assurance of one who can correctly discern the intent of every one of the Sugata's teachings, [338] I, the logician and Śākya bhikṣu Gelek Palsang, have composed [this work] in that portion of the "wellspring of learning" that is the Nyangtö area in the [province of] Tsang known as Palbar [Monastery], the Grove of Brilliant Exposition, in Changra. May this contribute to the flourishing of the Conqueror's precious tradition and to its long continuing, so that it can sustain living beings.

Oṃ svasti.[867]

In a single analytic stride he takes the full measure
of the whole array of things comprehended on the three great levels.
The all-knowing protector of the Conqueror's holy Dharma realm,
the sun of exposition Gelek Pal, is victorious!

This supreme ornament of exposition on the Seven Treatises is a fabulous
offering:
it has rained down a multitude of flaming thunderbolts of refutation
to block the misleading paths along which others have strayed
and to logically establish the validity of the Three Jewels.

To further promote exposition and composition
and to demolish the mistaken statements of opponents through debate
here at the great monastic center of Tashi Lhunpo,
this work has been produced with the purest motives.

May whatever merit deriving from this act
[contribute] to the way of correct reasoning being understood by all,
to them always gaining the fortunate human existence
and entering the inestimable abode of a buddha's three bodies.

Within the expansive golden container of knowable things
stands the firm splendor of the marvelous mountain.

May the Buddha's teaching, source of benefit for multitudes of beings
with its great virtue, spread throughout the ten directions!

Svasti.

In this great monastic center of Tashi Lhundrup, may the Dharma-giving
[of such text production] increase and flow endlessly in a steady stream,
so that the magnificent tree of the Buddhadharma, source of all benefit and happiness, may thrive
and all living beings may partake of the supreme liberation that is its wonderful fruit!

Sarva jagataṃ!

On Preclusion and Relationship

Gyaltsab Darma Rinchen
(1364–1432)

[339] I bow before the venerable lamas,
who, under the guiding care of the conquerors' sons,
have mastered the essentials of symbolic [language] and logical reasoning
and use their learning and practice in the service of others.

One may wish to launch oneself into the ocean of scriptures
and declare one's intention to engage in the very heart of religious practice,
but without the capacity to investigate preclusion and relationship,
one's efforts will be little more than those of the blind struggling to discern
a physical form.

As developing one's realizations on the path to a level
where one can claim to have rid oneself of specific deluded misconceptions
depends on understanding the nature of preclusion and relationship,
I will explain these in accordance with their description in the treatises of
the learned masters.

What is the point of engaging
in ill-tempered, raucous controversies
with those whose loathing for the opponent's position creates turmoil in
their own minds
and who are bent on elevating themselves at the expense of their rivals?

It is instead to those individuals of good sense,
who wish to use logical reasoning to correctly realize selflessness and
thereby sever the root of samsara and gain entrance into the city of
liberation,
that I address myself here.

One may make various assertions about how the paths of the three vehicles are to be entered, how meditation on *this* particular path will give rise to *that* specific result, and how it is through the application of *this* particular antidote that one can eradicate *these* specific misconceptions. However, certitude about these matters can only develop once one has gained unerring knowledge of the two forms of preclusion and the two kinds of relationship. It is these that I will now explain, with the help of examples that are accessible to valid cognition operating in the conventional domain.

1. Analysis of preclusion
2. Analysis of relationship

1. Preclusion

Analysis of preclusion

1. Defining characteristics
2. Varieties
3. Why it is necessary to understand preclusion

Defining characteristics

1. Setting out the assertion of another [scholar]
2. Subjecting that assertion to critical scrutiny
3. Our own position [340]

Setting out the assertion of another [scholar]

One learned figure, attempting to characterize the lord of reasoning's thought on the matter, says that one thing precludes another when it negates [i.e., cancels out][868] that other thing, whereas one thing is related to another when [through its presence] it is able to confirm that other thing. He thus holds that blue and yellow do not, properly speaking, preclude one another.[869] To back this up, he points to the section in the *Ascertainment of Valid Cognition* where it says, "Hence only something that counters what one is seeking to establish is preclusive."[870]

Subjecting that assertion to critical scrutiny

[Response:] If, [as he suggests,] this passage is to be interpreted very literally, we would offer this analysis: It follows that permanent negates impermanent and vice versa, because permanent and impermanent preclude each other. He must accept this argument, as the pervasion [that to preclude something is to negate it] is the one he himself has proposed, whereas the reason [that permanent and impermanent preclude one another] is something that he has acknowledged elsewhere. Now, since these two [permanent and impermanent] preclude each other but theirs cannot be a mutually oppositional preclusion of the indirect variety, it must be that of the direct variety, such that one of them counters the other. But if it were the case that, of the two, impermanent is weaker than permanent, then any notion that impermanent could directly negate permanent in the sense of being in mutual opposition with it would be undermined. If, on the other hand, impermanent were the stronger of the two, this would [equally] contradict any idea that permanent could directly negate impermanent. Yet if the two were of equal strength, it would destroy any idea that they could respectively have the roles of "counter" and "countered."[871] So what response does he have to this?

In reply he may argue that preclusion is something that cannot be ascertained divorced from a subject, that it must be considered in relation to specific bases. He might propose that impermanence directly negates sound [being] permanent and therefore directly precludes it. [Similarly, he might say] that permanence directly negates noncomposite space [being] impermanent and [therefore] directly precludes it. And, he might say, it is due to their [instantiation] in these two that permanent and impermanent are to be understood as directly preclusive.

[Response:] Based on that [reasoning,] it would follow that blue and yellow are also preclusive, since something being the color of sapphire negates it being yellow. He has, I believe, essentially endorsed the three [spheres of this argument].

[He may then] *deny* that permanent and impermanent are directly preclusive when considered divorced from specific subjects.

[Response:] From this it would follow that there is no directly preclusive mutual opposition between single and different, since there is nothing that can be identified as [the instantiation of such a preclusion]. This is because "pot"—as a single thing—and "pot plus woolen cloth"—as different things—cannot be identified as that [instantiation].[872] The question of whether blue and yellow, or produced and permanent, respectively, could be considered preclusive [according to his system] should be judged in the same manner.

Regarding the aforesaid passage of the *Ascertainment of Valid Cognition*, what it actually asserts is that only those *reasons* that are counter to the thesis that someone is attempting to establish can be regarded as *contrary reasons*. It is not saying that preclusion is to be understood in terms of negating [i.e., canceling out]. [341] This is clear if one is aware of the context within which the passage occurs.

Our own position

The definition of a preclusion [between two things] is that [they are] "different and a common locus of them is impossible." These are the characteristics intended by the expounder of reason, [Dharmakīrti, something we see in the way that] he fends off the [potential] fault that a correct reason might be inconclusive. He refers to how the reverse pervasion] is something that one learns from the "[preparative] countering valid cognition." As the *Ascertainment of Valid Cognition* explains at some length, [this valid cognition helps establish the reverse pervasion by] countering the possibility that there could—in accordance with the form of the particular proof—be any *common locus* of the reason and the anti-predicate.

Thus [we learn through this] what it would mean for the reason to be present among the class of dissimilar examples—namely, a common locus of that reason and the anti-predicate would need to be possible. Given that, [we can reject the claims of those who say that] because "true existence" is itself neither truly single nor different, and also because "[that with the] three properties of imputation" is itself a definition, these are cases where the reasons of the proofs in question are present among the class of dissimilar examples.[873] [Their claims] betray a total ignorance of [the principles of] logic, since [following their thinking,] there would need to be a common locus of something that is "truly existent" and neither truly single nor different, and also a common locus of something that "has the three properties of imputation" and is not a definiendum. But [in reality, of course,] absolutely no one could establish that such common loci exist.

Varieties

There are two varieties of preclusion: the antagonistic preclusion and the preclusion of mutual opposition.

Antagonistic preclusion

1. Rejecting what is incorrect
2. Establishing what is correct

Rejecting what is incorrect

1. Outlining the position of an earlier scholar
2. Refuting that position

Outlining the position of an earlier scholar

That eminent exponent of logical reasoning in former times, the great spiritual guide [Chapa] Chökyi Sengé, divided antagonistic preclusion into two varieties:[874] (1) that in which [the thing precluded] is countered by an entity [that exists simultaneous with it] and (2) that in which [the thing precluded] is countered by a cause. He further divided the latter into those in which the cause is a direct one and those in which it is an indirect one. His [example of] the first [where what counters is an entity,] is heat countering cold, and that of the second [where what counters is a direct cause] is the supreme dharma level of the path of preparation countering those seeds that are to be eradicated by the dharma forbearance level regarding suffering [on the path of seeing]. His [example of] the third [where what counters is an indirect cause] is the indirect cause of light countering dark. [342]

He believed that there is a fundamental difference between the way that the transcendent path eradicates those seeds and the way that light counters darkness. He evidently thought along the following lines:[875] If that portion of the seeds that are to be disposed of by the uninterrupted path of the dharma forbearance level were no longer present at the time of that path, [the portion in question] must already have been disposed of, [meaning that the individual concerned would] already have gained a true cessation. But that would damage [the position] that the first [true] cessation and [true] path are attained simultaneously. Hence those seeds must still exist [at the time of the uninterrupted path]. And for [Chapa], what it means for the path to directly counter those seeds is for it to be the one directly responsible for making them incapable of re-producing any kind of thing similar to themselves. He thought that [the path directly responsible for this] could not therefore be the dharma forbearance level, because that would entail cause and effect existing simultaneously, so it must be the supreme dharma level.

However, [he believed that] in the case of light, darkness must already be ceasing when the [light] appears. So the direct cause of light cannot be the one directly responsible for countering darkness, since that would [again] entail cause and effect existing simultaneously. He thus held that it must be the *indirect* cause of light that was responsible for bringing darkness to the verge of cessation and making it into something that is incapable of reproducing any kind of thing similar to itself. He also stated that the thing countered [i.e., the darkness] is dispatched extremely swiftly, whereas in the case of the antidote and the thing it is eradicating, the two may be conjoined in the process for eons.

Refuting that position

[Response:] It follows from this that what directly eradicates that portion of the seeds allotted to the dharma forbearance level regarding suffering is *not* that dharma forbearance level [itself] but the [preceding] supreme dharma level of the path of preparation. That must be the case, because what it means here for an antidote to directly counter those seeds is for it to be the one directly responsible for making them incapable of re-producing any kind of thing similar to themselves, and this is a task performed not by that dharma forbearance level but by the supreme dharma level of the path of preparation. Both parts of the reason here are those that [Chapa] himself endorsed. But if he agreed with this conclusion, it would follow that *none* of the uninterrupted paths found within the paths of meditation in any of the three vehicles directly counters any of the respective portions of the seeds that are allotted to them for eradication. If he accepted this conclusion, since the released paths induced by each of those uninterrupted paths certainly cannot directly counter those seeds, he would be forced to concede that it is impossible for any transcendent path to destroy the seeds that need to be eradicated.

It would also follow that those capable of directly eradicating the seeds of delusion obscurations and obscurations to omniscience are ordinary beings [rather than āryas], because what directly counters the seeds that are supposed to be eradicated by the uninterrupted path of the dharma forbearance is the supreme dharma level on the path of preparation. But if that were accepted, it would follow that there could be an individual who had gained a true cessation without having directly realized selflessness! Accepting that would threaten the whole scheme of grounds and paths—one that [is premised on the position] that it is from the path of seeing onward that an individual is counted as [an ārya and] a Sangha Jewel. [343]

What is more, [Chapa's] view about how [the individual] *has* an abandonment or an antidote [unwittingly] allows for the simultaneous existence of cause and effect. It proposes that during the uninterrupted path, there must be some form of "acquisition" [that maintains the individual's connection with] the element that is to be eradicated [by that path].[876] But the notion that one can gain some form of "pre-eradication" prior to the actual one is a Vaibhāṣika view. In the context of setting out the systems of the great Mahayana pioneers it has no place.

That his opinion about the timescales for the processes of light countering dark and of the transcendent path eradicating the seeds is that they are vastly different demonstrates that he has failed to grasp what so many scriptures and commentarial treatises were aiming to convey when using [the former as] an analogy to illustrate [the latter], and also that he has failed to grasp the *Compendium of Abhidharma*'s position on the matter, which I will discuss below. Darkness has already ceased at the time light appears, and its lack of production is due to the fact that the immediate conditions required [for its production] failed to come together in the previous moment. [Darkness's absence] is *not* something achieved [affirmatively] through the impact of the antidote [i.e., light] having directly countered it. I will also elaborate on this below.

Furthermore, his explanation of the cause and effect [sequences] within which the uninterrupted path of the dharma forbearance and light are involved, and which lead to the direct elimination of those things that each is set to counter, encourages the idea that it is *they*—the path and the light themselves—that can be described as the ones directly responsible for countering [the seeds and darkness, respectively]. This is like a woman with a disfigured face parading in borrowed jewelry and taking the credit for its attractiveness.

Furthermore, if it really was the case that the supreme dharma level of the path of preparation is directly responsible for making the seeds that should be eradicated by the [subsequent] dharma forbearance regarding sufferings into [entities] incapable of re-producing any kind of thing similar to themselves, [that supreme dharma level] would need to be something that directly contributed [to those seeds' production]. But agreeing to that would be tantamount to accepting that [this supreme dharma level] was a common locus of something that both directly contributed [to the seeds' production] and directly countered them. Such a position would essentially contravene the rules of logic. Thinking along these lines, one can also work out other attacks that can be made on his position.

Antagonistic preclusion: establishing what is correct

1. Defining characteristics
2. Varieties
3. The way that one thing counters the other [in an antagonistic preclusion]

Defining characteristics

Antagonistic preclusion is defined as "a state of incompatibility in which [one thing], the eliminator, brings an end to the continued presence of [another], the eliminated."

The assertion that antagonistic preclusion can be defined simply in terms of "[that which] counters" has numerous flaws. [By extension it would mean that] blue and the perception apprehending it should not be classified as "object" and "subject." It would also mean that with this variety of preclusion, the "countered" could not be regarded to preclusive with "[that which] counters."[877] [344]

Varieties

The initial moment of the flame from a lamp that is gradually introduced into a particular location and the darkness [there] are examples of two things that are indirectly preclusive in an antagonistic sense, whereas the flame that directly counters [the dark] and darkness are directly preclusive.

The way that one thing counters the other [in an antagonistic preclusion]

1. The analogy
2. Applying this to the real area of interest
3. Countering objections

The analogy

Let us assume there is darkness in a room, and the enclosed nature of the space, covered by a roof, means that all the conditions are in place to ensure that, apart from [the possible introduction] of lamplight, there is nothing obvious that can interrupt the continued presence of darkness.[878] It is at this point that light from a flame gradually creeps in from the doorway. In the first instant, the causes [supporting] the continued presence of the darkness inside the enclosed space are still in place. But in the next instant, the causes [supporting] darkness and the light of the lamp that exists concurrently with them come into close proximity. This presence [of light] immediately makes [the darkness] into something incapable of subsequently re-producing anything similar to itself. And it also makes the light of the lamp [in the next instant], which is its direct effect, into a vigorous light. By the third instant, that [vigorous] lamplight will have been produced, and at the same time, the darkness in that enclosed space will have ceased. The fact that the darkness has not been produced at that point is due to the conditions that could directly give rise to it having failed to come together. It cannot be that the lamplight is still working to counter the darkness, because it would contradict [the principles of logic] to have simultaneous cause and effect or an effect that existed prior to its cause.

Thus the thing directly countered is the darkness, whereas that which counters it is the light of the lamp. And what "directly counter" means here is to *create*, immediately, that setting in which, due to the gradual introduction of the lamplight, the continuum of the thing countered has finally ceased. There can be no case [of a single thing] that is produced through having [another thing] both contributing to and countering its production, so what contributes to [production] here is the early temporal portions of the lamplight, and these do not preclude the entity of darkness. [But the light itself] is still the one that precludes the entity of darkness.

What must be understood therefore is that to directly counter here means to directly *create* the setting in which darkness is absent—a situation that occurs in the instant immediately following that in which light was produced, simultaneous with the darkness ceasing. Thus, although the earlier instant of light is the one responsible for making the darkness that is about to cease into something that is incapable of re-producing anything similar to itself, this does *not* constitute it directly countering [darkness]. That is because it is untenable for one thing to be the direct effect of another if a separate period of time intervenes between the two. [345]

A possible criticism of this might be that it allows for instants in which the light and darkness coexist compatibly. But this does not represent a flaw. [It must be granted that] every minute physical particle prevents any other particle from entering the space it occupies, in which sense it can be said that they do not coexist compatibly. But if the criticism is that [our position allows for instants of light and dark] to remain in close proximity with each other, this is a kind of "compatible coexistence" that we wholeheartedly accept. This coexistence cannot be [explained by asserting that] the particles of light and dark fluctuate and are only present alternately. That is because the process must be a continuous one, in which it is the sequential presence of the lamplight that gradually prevails over the darkness.

This process of countering should also be understood to occur in the case of heat and cold. There is no justification for saying that the antagonistic preclusion [of heat and cold] involves [countering by an] actual entity, whereas with light and dark it does not. It is equally true [of heat and cold] that a single spot cannot be occupied by a particle of both substances, and also that [particles of each] can coexist in close proximity, as it is with light and dark.

On no occasion did the master Dharmottara indicate that he believed the process, whether for heat and cold or for light and dark, was one that involved an initial instant of the two things coming into contact, a second where one is weakened, a third where a continuum is halted, and then the whole process beginning over again. So, when one scholar derides him by saying that his antagonistic preclusion must take a particularly long time, it is simply that scholar's failure to discern the other party's position. In the context of an antagonistic preclusion, the way that one thing counters another is by gradually depleting the causes that support [the production of] that other thing. For this reason the master Dharmottara chooses to describe it as "a preclusion arising from [actual] entities."[879] This form of preclusion must be ascertained on the level of continua rather than the subtle instants [comprising them]. For otherwise, ordinary beings, by means of perception, would be in no position to realize [that two things can] preclude each other.

Applying this to the real area of interest

It is on the path of preparation's supreme dharma level that the portion of seeds that the path of seeing's uninterrupted stage of dharma forbearance regarding suffering is responsible for eradicating reach their final instant. That earlier path is the one that makes these seeds into things that are incapable of subsequently re-producing anything similar to themselves, but that path does *not* count as their direct antidote. The uninterrupted path is on the verge of production at the same time as the seeds are on the verge of coming to an end. And as soon as the uninterrupted path has been produced, the seeds will have ended. The absence of the seeds at that point is due to a failure of the conditions [supporting their production] coming together, and it therefore constitutes a cessation of the *nonanalytical* variety. [346] It does not mark the attainment of an *analytical* cessation, since any true [i.e., analytical] cessation can only occur if it has been preceded by an uninterrupted path, through the operation of which that cessation is attained. Similarly, by the time someone reaches the stage of the uninterrupted path of the final continuum on the tenth ground, he will have no [actual] trace of the taint [of factors] associated with the unfavorable states. But still, he will not have achieved a true cessation of that taint, in which it is totally erased, nor will he have generated a released path [related to it], and in that sense, the period [in which that taint] is being countered has not yet ended. Thus [the taint] is still in the process of being eradicated rather than having already been totally eradicated. Only when the first instant of an omniscient consciousness has been produced can one speak of [the taint's] "total eradication."

Someone claims that by the time the path of seeing's uninterrupted path is reached, the seeds to be eradicated by this path are no longer present, whereas when the final continuum's uninterrupted path is reached, the seeds [it should eradicate] still exist. This is a case of him [trying to create] a homogenized position from tenet systems that are in conflict. The way that the knowledges and forbearances [of the path of seeing] are divided into sixteen according to the things that each eradicate is something that one can learn about from the explanations I have given in my expositions on the root treatises of [Maitreya's] *Unexcelled Continuum of the Mahayana* and the *Ornament of Realizations* as well as their [principal] commentaries.

Countering objections

Someone argues that our account contradicts what is said in the *Compendium of Abhidharma*. This subjects the manifest [forms of the elements that need to be eradicated] to an analysis in terms of the three times. It says that those of the past have already ceased, and therefore do not require eradication, those of the future have yet to occur, so [also] do not require eradication, whereas those of the present are not [manifest] at the time a transcendent path operates, so cannot be its main object for eradication.[880] The implication of this, he suggests, is that the seeds [of the things that need to be eradicated] must be present at the same time that the path is operational.

[Response:] That is not what [the treatise] means. What the section discusses is the way that a transcendent path counters seeds. Thus it points out that the process by which the uninterrupted stage of a transcendent path eradicates seeds cannot be one where it is *dispatching* those seeds that existed prior to the time that the [path] itself did, because these must already have ceased by the time that it arises and would therefore not require eradication. Nor can it be the case that the seeds it is responsible for eradicating could be dispatched—in the manner of a hammer smashing a pot—if they were those that are certain to be produced at some time in the future, since the [process is one that renders any] future production impossible. [Lastly, that path] cannot be eradicating those [seeds] that exist at the same time that it does, such that both of them will cease simultaneously, since the [seeds] cannot be present once [the path] is. How then does the process work? As was stated above, the uninterrupted path is about to come into being at the very same point in time that what it must eradicate—the aspects [associated with] the unfavorable states—are about to cease. Simultaneous with the former having been produced, the latter will have ceased. [347] And just after that, due to the lasting impact left by the antidote, the state is reached in which [those aspects] are rendered incapable of re-production—this is what it means to say that they have been "eradicated." This situation the [*Compendium of Abhidharma* asserts] parallels that of light and dark. So in the *Clear Meaning Commentary* [on the *Ornament of Realizations*, Haribhadra] is not saying that the [*Compendium of Abhidharma*'s] analogy for explaining the way the antidote eradicates should be kept and regarded as correct but that an alternative understanding of its intention needs to be sought.[881]

Those who try to explain the countering that occurs in an antagonistic preclusion as one that involves a cause *making* what it counters into an incapacitated thing have strayed from the intent of the figures of supreme authority who used light and dark as an analogy for the way that a transcendent path eradicates seeds.[882] The valid cognitions responsible for ascertaining this form of preclusion and the way that the countering occurs should be understandable from what I have explained here, so I will not elaborate further on these.

Preclusion of Mutual Opposition

1. Defining characteristics
2. Varieties
3. Delineation of [this] preclusion

Defining characteristics

Preclusion in the sense of mutual opposition is defined as "a state of incompatibility [between two things] such that the exclusion of one brings with it the [affirmative] discerning of the other."[883]

Someone contends that the masters Chapa and Dharmottara defined the preclusion of mutual opposition in terms of a [dichotomy that] divides things into those that do and do not have the capacity [to produce] a given result. He went on to claim that this position is untenable, since such a definition would exclude non-actual things such as object universals and a double moon from preclusions of mutual opposition.

[Response:] He has failed to understand what these masters actually said. In the *Ascertainment of Valid Cognition*, Dharmakīrti states, "The nature of individuations is such that they are not concomitant with one another. This is because their [productive] capacities, their appearances, and so forth are discrete."[884] Dharmottara's commentary[885] explains that what the passage asserts is that individuations [of a single thing] that are distinct substances cannot be concomitant with one another. He explains that [Dharmakīrti] presents two reasons why this is the case. The first is that they must be counted as distinct entities, in that while some of them have the capacity [to produce] a given result, others lack such a capacity. The second is that they appear to perception with differing object-aspects. What Dharmottara explains therefore is that individuations that are distinct substances can preclude each other in the sense that there is a mutual opposition between them, and that this preclusion can be in terms of them [respectively] having or lacking [a particular productive] capacity. But nowhere did he indicate that in every case [for this form] of preclusion, one of the elements involved is *necessarily* an actual thing. [348]

Varieties

Things such as permanent and impermanent preclude one another directly, whereas things such as blue and yellow preclude each other indirectly. That is, to discern the [presence] of impermanence within sound is necessarily to exclude the [presence of] permanence. [However,] the fact that one has been able to rule out that some third [item] is both the two [things in question] does not [necessarily] mean that one can ascertain that the two preclude each other directly. For instance, in ascertaining that the color of a piece of turquoise is blue, one necessarily rules out that it is yellow, but this does not mean that [blue and yellow] directly preclude each other.

In certain cases of indirect preclusion, one can only ascertain that the things involved preclude each other with [additional information], provided by a [preparative] countering valid cognition. For instance, ascertaining that sound is produced does not necessarily involve ruling out that it is permanent; [for that] one may still require [the support of] an additional [preparative] countering valid cognition, which rules out that there is a common locus [of produced and permanent].

In excluding the presence of permanence in sound, one will [also] discern the presence of impermanence [within it]. [However,] the fact that one has been able to rule out that two things are present in some third [item] will not [necessarily] mean that one can ascertain that the two [in question] preclude each other in a mutual opposition that is direct. For instance, the presence of impermanence within sound could be established by means of a valid cognition that excludes the presence of some *other*. But that does not necessarily mean that the two [impermanent and this other thing] are directly preclusive. In conclusion, [two things] only preclude each other directly if *the very act of eliminating one* [of them] *presents the other to valid cognition.*[886]

Delineation of [this] preclusion

The master Dharmottara stated, "The nature of [the thing in question] has certain characteristics that preclude [other] characteristics."[887] As this states, [preclusion is] where [the presence of one or more specific] characteristics [in a thing] excludes the [presence of one or more other] characteristics [in that thing]. So, for example, when something has the characteristic of impermanence, it is necessarily the case that it cannot have the characteristic of permanence. And when something has the characteristic of blue, it cannot have the characteristic of yellow. Thus certain characteristics oppose each other. And in the [affirmative] discerning of one, the nature of the other is "neutralized"—[that is,] excluded. Blue's nature therefore represents the total neutralization of the nature of the [other]. And in the act of excluding those things neutralized by the nature of blue, yellow—as something neutralized by blue's nature—is also excluded. However, the exclusion [of yellow] does not bring with it the [affirmative] discernment that [the item in question] has the nature of blue, since someone can still wonder whether it might be a *third alternative* [i.e., some color] that is neither [blue nor yellow].

Ascertaining a preclusion depends on being able to rule out that there is a valid cognition observing what [that preclusion] negates. Unless one can rule out that valid cognition observes sound to be permanent, for instance, one cannot rule out that sound [really] is permanent, and would therefore not be able to realize that it is impermanent. [349] For both varieties of preclusion, this means that their ascertainment relies on the nonobservation of something that should be apparent. Some might object, arguing that it would follow from this that there is no way to ascertain, with respect to sound, that impermanent and permanent are preclusive. Also, [they might say] it would be impossible to ascertain that a visible pot and an [inaccessible] *piśāci* preclude each other. But there are no such faults [with our position]. Permanence is impermanence neutralized. So, if sound had the nature of neutralized impermanence, it would never undergo any change—something that should be apparent. [Such a character] is ruled out through its failure to appear. [Similarly,] in the case of a visible pot, what one negates is not [the presence of] some inaccessible *piśāci*, an entity separate from the pot. Instead, one is negating that the visible pot itself has the nature of a *piśāci*. Therefore neither of these represent cases where the preclusion does not involve the nonobservation of that which should be apparent.

Why it is necessary to understand preclusion

The fundamental principles [of Buddhist] philosophy are outlined in the four seals of the official view. The facts set forth within these need to be verified using logical reasoning. In this context, without a genuine knowledge of preclusion, one cannot understand matters such as how [in a correct proof] the reason precludes the anti-predicate, how inferential cognition counters distorted notions, and also how, on the path, the wisdom directly realizing emptiness counters the two types of obscuration. Hence it is necessary for one to gain mastery of the two varieties of preclusion.

2. Relationship

Analysis of relationship

1. Defining characteristics
2. Varieties
3. Why it is necessary to comprehend [logical] relationship and understand that it is an imputed existent

Defining characteristics

The definition [of *x* being related to *y*] is "[*x* and *y*] are different, and the withdrawal of *y*—from which *x* is different—is certain to bring with it the removal of *x*." Only by ascertaining that [two things] are "removed" and "remover" can one ascertain that they are "pervaded" and "pervader" and, thereby, that [the first is] the "related thing" and [the second is] "that to which there is a relationship."[888] On occasions one might, for instance, observe smoke in a location where there is a crow or the absence of any crows in a location where there is no smoke. But this alone would not guarantee that [smoke and crow] are related. [350]

Varieties

1. Nature relationship
2. Causal relationship

Nature relationship

1. Defining characteristics
2. Delineation

Defining characteristics

[When the relationship is of the nature variety,] one should expand the general definition of relationship given above to indicate that "[the two] are not separate substances."

Delineation [of the nature relationship]

[The notion of one thing's removal entailing that of another is explainable in terms of facts] such as that the same inexorable force that imprints[889] production into a thing it creates is also the one that imprints impermanence into that thing. This [specific fact about production and impermanence] does not apply to all things that have a nature relationship. However, it is absolutely always the case [with this kind of relationship] that the withdrawal of certain properties that are of the same nature as the thing in question necessarily entails its own withdrawal [i.e., disappearance]. If that were not the case, the relationship would not be an unfailing one.

Causal relationship

1. Defining characteristics
2. Description of cause and effect in terms of their *informational relationship*

Defining characteristics

The causal relationship is defined as one in which "[two things] are separate substances, and the withdrawal of one of them brings with it the certainty that the other is also withdrawn." One thing [*x*] being causally related to another thing [*y*] does not always mean that *x* actually derives from *y*. This is because in the *Ascertainment of Valid Cognition*, [Dharmakīrti] established that the proof involving the nonobservation *of a direct effect* is a case in which the negated property [a cause] is related to the converse of the reason [an effect].[890] [On the other hand, it can be said that] there is absolutely no "informational relationship"[891] between the taste and visual form of molasses. Others assert that there is. But this must mean that you [others][892] are of the opinion that the response given by the lord of reasoning [Dharmakīrti] to criticisms [of his position] that the threefold categorization of [correct] reasons is a definitive and exhaustive one was wide of the mark. If you were right, the response Dharmakīrti *should* have given [about the "molasses proof"][893] was that "It is [just a straightforward] effect reason, and so it does not represent some 'fourth category.'" But in fact the master [Dharmakīrti] did not answer in that way. Instead, his denial that [the proof] posed any challenge to the [threefold] classification involved him describing this as [a special variety of reason, known as] a correct effect reason for *deducing a feature of the cause*, and explaining how this single proof gives rise to two separate inferences: one realizing that the taste of molasses at the earlier point had the potential to produce the visual form of [the present] molasses, and another, realizing [the existence of the present] visual form of molasses.[894] According to your [explanation], one is left wondering about the reason behind [Dharmakīrti's] choice of response here. Asserting that the reason constitutes an effect reason [giving rise to] the inference of a property of a cause [while also believing that there is an informational relationship between the taste and form of molasses] is a clear demonstration [that you] have not understood the system of reasoning. [351]

Description of cause and effect in terms of their informational relationship

[The following objection has been raised:] "The fact that two things are producer and produced means that they are also information and information yielder—that is, information about one can be gleaned from the other. However, every one of the features belonging to the *same simultaneous substance* as smoke is produced by fire, and every one of the properties belonging to the *same simultaneous substance* as fire produces smoke. So this must mean that every feature of smoke yields information about every feature of fire. And since this is the case, the features [of smoke] such as its bluish hue and its [being an actual] thing must be information about fire. [Similarly,] that the fire in question is a sandalwood fire and that it illuminates, blazes, and so forth must all be information yielded about fire. This must be so because unless [one can say] that smoke is produced when a sandalwood fire produces smoke, sandalwood smoke could not be counted as smoke."[895]

[Response:] There is no flaw [in our position]. While these [features can all be classified as either] producer or produced, that alone is not sufficient to make them [either] information [yielded] or information yielder. For while there are numerous abstracted features that are the same simultaneous substance as fire and smoke respectively, the only ones that count as the information here are those which, in addition to being features of fire, are producers of smoke in its every instance. And while there are numerous [conceptually] isolable portions that belong to the same simultaneous substance as smoke, the only ones that count as information yielders here are those that are necessarily the effects of fire and have an infallible link with smoke in its *every* instance. The more general qualities of smoke, such as its [being an actual] thing and being something physical, are not information yielders with respect to fire, because they can occur even when fire is absent. Also, ascertaining that something is a sandalwood fire does not count as ascertaining the producer of just smoke, since we observe cases where smoke occurs even when that particular type of fire is absent.[896]

[In a further objection] someone could argue that [our position] forces us to distinguish between features within the substance of smoke that are and are not produced by fire, and also those within the substance of fire that do and do not produce smoke, because of the way that the features cut across the information and the information yielder [division].

[Response:] As we have already explained, what [belongs to the categories of] produced and producer does not necessarily [belong to those of] information and information yielder.

Upon spotting smoke in the distance, it is through force of habit that the individual will, in the process of ascertainment, first identify it as "something," then as "something physical," and finally as "something that is smoke." The object of the first two of these [cognitions] is *not* the information yielder [with regard to] fire. [Rather,] it is asserted to be the object of the final ascertainment that is the information yielder about fire—[and that object is] a universal of [the properties of being] "something," "physical," and so forth that characterize smoke. [Conversely,] this would not be the case if [the individual in question] were mistaken with regard to both elements in the reason. [352] If, for example, he were to think, "This is a sail because there is a bird's nest at the peak," he would be mistaken about both the peak and the bird's nest, individually.[897]

If one is able to identify [the smoke in question] as a type of sandalwood smoke, it could obviously inform one of a sandalwood fire's [presence]. It would, nonetheless, be difficult to classify it as an accurate information yielder [with regard to] that fire.

As to which valid cognitions are responsible for ascertaining [that two things are] cause and effect, if a location was one in which fire and smoke are both present, to a sense perception of that space, the two could appear as though they are virtually merged. [Hence there should be] a *pair of perceptions regarding absences* of the two [in given locations]. After this, there should be a *pair that apprehend the entities that are cause and effect*—that is, one observing fire and then one observing smoke. Next, there should again be a *pair of perceptions regarding absences*—one observing that there is no fire, and then one observing that there is no smoke. It is by means of these *three sets of valid cognition* that any doubts [that could be entertained] about production being causeless or dependent on incongruous causes are removed and the [two things in question] are identified as cause and effect.[898]

Why it is necessary to comprehend [logical] relationship and understand that it is an imputed existent

Proper understanding of relationship is a vital and irreplaceable component within comprehension [of the broader Buddhist scheme. Certain fundamental principles,] such as that to accept something about what is pervaded commits one to accept something about that which pervades it, that a specific cause can give rise to a specific effect, that for such a specific effect to have materialized, it must have been preceded by a specific cause, and so forth, serve as the basis for the path and result in this scheme. One should rule out [the notion that] relationship is something substantially existent and understand that it only has imputed existence. The purpose behind this is expressed by the great brahmin [Śaṃkarānanda] in his commentary on the *Analysis of Relation*;[899] namely, it is to make one aware that it is only through ruling out that the person has a self-supporting, substantially existing [self] that one will be able to realize the selflessness of persons.

From the perspective of the conceptual cognition responsible for ascertaining the relationship between fire and smoke, the two must appear [to exist] simultaneously, and the smoke, [despite being] something fully formed, must still appear to be [in the process of production] relying on the fire. If the way that the two appeared [to that cognition] was an accurate reflection of the way that they are, fire and smoke would need to be simultaneous existents. The relationship between them therefore cannot be asserted to have substantial existence. In a similar fashion, the innate sense of grasping at a self of persons clings to [a notion of] the person as something self-supporting and substantially existent. And those whose philosophical tenets hold that there is a self of persons clutch to the idea that the self and the aggregates [subsist] like a master and his subjects. But if the [self of persons subsisted] in that way, it would have [an existence] independent of the aggregates. Hence a self of persons is refuted. [353] One should gain a better understanding from my other [writings on this matter], where I have dealt with this more thoroughly.

The source [*Compendium*] and the *Commentary* are vajra speech, smashing
the mountain of absolutism and nihilism clung to by our adversaries.
Preclusion and relationship are the treasured essentials they impart.
Relying on the pure path of reason and the kindness of my own lamas,
I have faithfully described them following Gyalnga Dunpa's tradition.[900]

I [dedicate] whatever pure virtue derives from these efforts
to dispelling the gloom of extreme views in all beings
so that, haloed by the light of pure logic,
they may gain entry to the omniscient Conqueror's citadel.

This definitive description of the principles of preclusion and relationship has been composed at the Geden Nampar Gyalwai Ling [Monastery] on the mountain of Drok Riwoché by the proponent of reasoning Darma Rinchen—who, over a sustained period of time, has partaken of the nectar of instruction of the holy and venerable Kumaramati and the magnificent precious lord Losang Drakpa, the great omniscient one in this age of decline.

The scribe has been the upholder of the Tripiṭaka Rinchen Chögyal.

May this contribute to the enduring survival and flourishing, in every possible way, of the precious tradition of Śākyamuni![901]

Oṃ svasti.[902]

In this great monastic center of Tashi Lhundrup, may the Dharma-giving
[of such publications] increase and flow endlessly in a steady stream,
so that the magnificent tree of the Buddhadharma, source of all benefit and happiness, thrives
and all living beings may partake of the supreme liberation that is its wonderful fruit!

Sarva mangalaṃ.

Mighty Pramāṇa Sun, "Banisher of Gloom from the Hearts of the Fortunate," Totally Illuminating the Profound and the Expansive

An Exposition on Valid Cognition in the Thousand Measures of *Clear Words*

Jamyang Shepa Ngawang Tsöndrü
(1648–1721)

1. Introduction

[355] *Namo gurumañjughoṣāya eṣṭadevīsvarasvatībhyām.*[903]
[Homage to Guru Mañjughoṣa and the goddess Sarasvatī.]

The complete Buddha, the captain who with brilliant, munificent instinct steers the course for beings,
the holy Dharma, the vessel whose nature is knowledge and release, delivering from the ocean of samsara,
and the irreversible Sangha, the company who are stewards of the glittering treasury of scripture and realization:
it is these Three Refuges, who convey us to the jeweled island of the two [most worthy] aims, that I bear aloft at my crown.

It was Nāgārjuna, with the mantra of logical reasoning, who drove away the clouds of extreme views,
so that in deep, cloudless heavens, the sun of the four *pramāṇas*
might reveal the detail of every variety of phenomena
and shine spectacularly, up to the present day, releasing the warmth of its benevolent luminosity.

How wonderous that we have this protector's own [spiritual] sons, themselves bright suns of piercing analysis,
and in particular, the excellent system of the Prāsaṅgika,
so that the ultimate sphere that he intended
has not been abandoned to false, gloomy trails of misinterpretation!

Glorious Mañjughoṣa, famed in every direction
as the forefather of all the conquerors
and embodied in the illustrious Losang Drakpa, essence of all conquerors,
never leave this place of honor that I offer you at the center of my heart!

And may I [continue to] receive the compassionate guardianship
of the magnificent pioneers, those champions of the protector's system,
and particularly that of the singular protector of every being, Losang Gyatso,
for whom no equal exists, either in the worldly realm or the quiescence beyond.

One can but marvel at the dispositions of those from this snowy land
who vainly regard themselves as upholders of the Middle Way but fraternize with base [classes],[904]
and claim that to assert emptiness is incompatible with the validation of things
and that the validation of things requires that emptiness be disregarded.

Avoiding all extremes, I will explain the fine system of the ultimate Middle Way,
which understands how, through perception, inference, scripture, and analogy,
the intimate complexities of every one of the four kinds of comprehended object are distinguished
while recognizing that their existence is nothing more than nominal.

Those who declare themselves to be followers of the Conqueror:
intelligent individuals who wish to get beyond shallow understanding
to the core of the Able One's intent, in which every extreme is averted,
should with impartiality and earnestness pay heed to what is said here! [356]

To explain a little about valid cognition according to the Prāsaṅgika, I will set out:

1. A general refutation of the Tibetan misconception that the Prāsaṅgika holds that valid cognition has no currency either as an actuality or as a designation
2. An accurate account of valid cognition as represented in the Prāsaṅgika's own treatises

A general refutation of the Tibetan misconception that the Prāsaṅgika holds that valid cognition has no currency either as an actuality or as a designation

Generally speaking, all proponents of tenets, Buddhist and non-Buddhist alike, accept the notion of valid cognition. All of them, be they of the realist or Prāsaṅgika schools, also agree with [the principle] that if the information derived from one [purported] "valid cognition" is undermined by another valid cognition, the former cannot, in fact, be a valid cognition. Thus there are many passages [that make this point], such as that in the *Distinction between the Two Truths* where it says, "A cognition's identity as valid is untrustworthy if it is undermined by another valid cognition."[905]

Here in Tibet, [formerly] there was no shortage of individuals who, while priding themselves on being Prāsaṅgika, rejected the notion of valid cognition. But all true scholars rejoiced when the revered father [Tsongkhapa], his [spiritual] sons, and their chief disciples issued their definitive rebuttal of that position, until all that survived of it was its name. However, [it was revived by] Taktsang Lotsāwa, out of his lust for material gain and personal respect and his attempt to gain recognition for himself with benefactors. He claimed that while those of the Prāsaṅgika [school] make reference to perception and inferential cognition, and thus acknowledge the concept of valid cognition, they do not believe that the [two] are, in fact, forms of valid cognition; nor do they even use the designation *valid cognition*.[906]

This assertion is totally unfounded. Candrakīrti himself employs the term *valid cognition* with respect to both of those [varieties], since [for him] there are four different means of valid cognition—perceptual, inferential, [and those that rely, respectively, on] scripture and on analogy. And each of those exist in a state of mutually supportive dependence with the objects that they comprehend, comparable with how long and short depend upon each other, such that the valid cognition's existence demands acceptance of the object it comprehends and vice versa. This is something [embedded] in the concept of *valid cognition* [expressed by] the Sanskrit term *pramāṇa*, where *māṇa* refers to "comprehension," and for there to be a comprehender, there must also be something comprehended by it. Hence *Clear Words* states:

> Thus it is explained that it is through the four valid cognitions that the world realizes things. And theirs is a mutual dependence, such that if there are valid cognitions, there must [also] be the things that they comprehend, and if there are things

> comprehended, there must [also] be valid cognitions. Neither valid cognition nor the things it comprehends are established independently, in their own right.[907] [357]

Someone claims that whereas valid cognition comprehending what is ultimately true is feasible, the same is not the case for that comprehending what is conventionally true. This is also incorrect. Why? Because even in conventional terms, there is (1) a being who [personifies] what it is to be valid, (2) his teachings, which embody valid authority, and (3) his awareness, which is valid cognition. As the sutra formula puts it:

> The Buddha, the Transcendent Victor,
> who is wisdom,
> who is sight,
> who is witness,
> who is valid, whose experience is knowledge[908]

And the *Precious Garland* says:

> Who is the [valid] authority superior
> to the Conqueror on this matter?[909]

This tells us that the Conqueror is *the* valid authority with respect to the Mahayana. In his autocommentary to *Entering the Middle Way*, Candrakīrti also states, "One determines the intention of a scripture [through reliance on] a treatise composed by a person who is a valid [authority] and seeing that the way it explains the passage is correct."[910] *Sixty Stanzas of Reasoning* says:

> It has been pronounced that whatever within this world appears to
> the likes of Brahmā to be true is, for the ārya being, deceptive.
> What else remains [to be said]?[911]

In his explanation of this section in the *Commentary on Sixty Stanzas of Reasoning,* Candrakīrti says:

> Because no one within the worldly realm is superior to Brahmā, when it comes to discerning suprasensory entities, he is [regarded as] pramāṇa. But while he may be the authority in that [domain],

> all the things that [he] perceives appear to him to have their own true identity, something that for āryas immediately [counts as] deceptive.[912]

And the *Precious Garland* says:

> His [i.e., the Buddha's] actions are in exact accordance with what he has taught.
> Hence his conduct is constantly reliable and unfaltering.
> Thus he is glorious, and within this world it is he who has the authority of holiness.[913]

There is also a passage in *Four Hundred Stanzas* that states, "To say that one exists whereas the other does not [is valid] neither in the ultimate [sense], nor in the worldly [one]."[914] In explaining this, [Candrakīrti's] *Commentary to Four Hundred Stanzas* says:

> When seeking to describe the things of the world, one should accept the validity of worldly notions, according to which internal and external entities are divided into five aggregates. Whereas, when the perspective is that of the [way] transcendent awareness perceives suchness, the five aggregates should be described as being empty of intrinsic existence. Otherwise, if parties affirm one thing while denying the other, neither suchness nor the world can be accounted for.[915] [358]

And in *Clear Words* he also states:

> Due to this, the assertion of the wise that "Only the pronouncements of the Buddha, the Blessed One, can be described as valid and authoritative" is correct, in that they are nondeceptive [i.e., do not mislead].[916]

This passage tells us about the notion of valid scripture: that scripture can be valid, on the grounds that in terms of both the things it describes and the words it uses to convey them, it does not mislead. In a similar vein, the glorious protector Nāgārjuna in his *Compendium of Sutras* announces:

> What is it that demonstrates that the appearance of a buddha is such an extremely rare occurrence?
> That is something that we can know by the fact that [he delivers] so many valid [authoritative] sutras.[917]

The great Saraha also said, "There is something that can convert [individuals] to the Mahayana—its system [composed] of valid treatises."[918]

Numerous such passages [make this point]. And to put it succinctly, there is no tenet system that rejects [the notion of] valid cognition.

An accurate account [of valid cognition] as represented in the Prāsaṅgika's own treatises[919]

To give an accurate account [of valid cognition] as represented in the Prāsaṅgika's own treatises, we must address the question of whether the description of the varieties, divisions, objects, and etymology of pramāṇa supplied by the Svātantrika and those [Buddhist schools] below them are tenable in this [Prāsaṅgika] system. An understanding of these matters is hindered by the fact that they received only brief treatment in the works of the revered father [Tsongkhapa] and his [spiritual] sons, and that [other] scholars have not elaborated upon them. I therefore deem it necessary to provide an account of the way that the positions of other schools regarding valid cognition are refuted, what valid cognition is in our own [Prāsaṅgika] system, and to deal with various issues related to these. I base this account on [Āryadeva's] *Four Hundred Stanzas* and its commentary [by Candrakīrti], [Nāgārjuna's] *Sixty Stanzas of Reasoning* and its commentary [by Candrakīrti], [Nāgārjuna's] *Dispeller of Dispute* and its commentary [by Nāgārjuna], but above all, on [Candrakīrti's] *Clear Words*.

2. Defense of Nāgārjuna's *Fundamental Treatise on the Middle Way*

1. The arguments of the logicians pertaining to [their understanding of] the necessity for valid cognition
2. Refuting their system's version of valid cognition
3. Setting out the valid cognition of our own system

The arguments of the logicians pertaining to [their understanding of] the necessity for valid cognition

1. Their attack [on Nāgārjuna's *Fundamental Treatise on the Middle Way*] with their argument [concerning] the existence of ascertainment
2. Their attack [on Nāgārjuna's treatise] with their argument [concerning] the absence of ascertainment

Their attack [on Nāgārjuna's *Fundamental Treatise on the Middle Way*] with their argument [concerning] the existence of ascertainment

Clear Words contains the passage: [359]

> At this point, there are those who argue thus: "Does the ascertainment that things lack production derive from valid cognition, or does it come about without it? If you propose that it is derived from valid cognition, you must state how many valid cognitions there are. What are the characteristics that define them? What are their objects? And are they produced from themselves, from other, from both, or do they arise causelessly? Conversely, you cannot reasonably suggest that it could be derived from something other than valid cognition. This is because the realization of anything comprehended must rely on valid cognition, since a thing that has not yet been realized cannot be realized

> without valid cognition. And if, due to the lack of valid cognition, a thing cannot be realized, how could this correct ascertainment [of yours] come about? Thus [your] claim that things have no production is unsustainable. Or it must be the case that your ascertainment that things have no production derives from the very same [source] as the one according to which those things exist. So, if for you there is ascertainment that things have no production, then [equally] for me why can't there [be ascertainment] that they are produced?"[920]

This attack is launched against the *Fundamental Treatise on the Middle Way* by those belonging to the Buddhist realist [schools] and some who are well versed in the logical arguments of the Pramāṇa system. They question whether what *Fundamental Treatise on the Middle Way* refers to as the "ascertainment" that things are not produced according to any of the four alternatives is derived from a cognition that is valid or one that is not. If it is the first, [they say,] then [Nāgārjuna's] treatise would be at fault, because that cognition must be one of the four means of valid cognition, and must also be produced according to one of the four alternatives, but his treatise fails to provide any details of such things, something that it should have done. This [question] is covered in the first section of the *Clear Words* passage quoted above, "At this point . . . do they arise causelessly?"

The argument [they] use against the second option [that the ascertainment derives from something that is not valid cognition] is as follows: "That such an ['ascertainment'] could realize anything is untenable, because [it is not something derived from valid cognition], and without valid cognition there cannot be realization of anything."

If this argument is accepted, they say, "It is no longer reasonable for you to maintain that things are not produced according to any of the four alternatives, because you have no correct ascertainment of that fact." This is conveyed in the second section of the *Clear Words* passage cited above: "Conversely, you cannot . . . is unsustainable." Jñānagarbha also declares, "Without valid cognition there can be no assertion that such and such a thing exists or is [one way or another]."[921]

Furthermore, they argue, "Just as it is the case that in making your statement that things are not produced, you 'ascertain' their nonproduction, the same applies to my statement of the reverse, because just as you declare, with such certainty, that '[Things] are not produced in any such way,' I, a realist, affirm with [equal] certainty, 'They are produced in just such a way.'" [360] [They continue,] "This must follow because our [respective] certainties are not [according to you] founded in valid cognition." This is contained in the third section of the *Clear Words* passage "Or it must be . . . they are produced?" Jñānagarbha also says, "A statement cannot make it so, otherwise it would mean that anything could exist."[922]

Their attack [on Nāgārjuna's treatise] with their argument [concerning] the absence of ascertainment

[*Clear Words* continues]:

> He then says, "If you yourself have no ascertainment that all things lack production, since it is a situation that you have not ascertained for yourself, there is no way you can induce realization [of that] in someone else, so your composition of the treatise must have been a futile exercise. Thus there has been no negation of all phenomena, and [consequently] they must exist."[923]

What this means is the following: "If you, a proponent of the Middle Way, have no ascertainment [of that lack of production], then it must follow that neither could I, in the course of our debate, gain ascertainment of such a lack of production, because you yourself do not have that ascertainment."

If this argument's conclusion were granted, it would mean that "It is not possible to induce the knowledge or realization of nonproduction in any other learner." But if that were accepted, then the conclusion would be "It follows that the composition of Nāgārjuna's treatise was a futile exercise." Thus nothing would have been achieved by the treatise's negation of production, and the production of all things must still be intrinsic to them. This is what is expressed in the passage from *Clear Words* cited immediately above.

By responding to these arguments, refuting the logicians' version of valid cognition

1. Addressing the issue of why the treatise does not refer to the valid cognition of demonstrable fact [as espoused by] the logicians
2. Refuting the valid cognition asserted by the logicians

Addressing the issue of why the treatise does not refer to the valid cognition of demonstrable fact [as espoused by] the Logicians

1. [Justification of] the treatise not providing an account of the varieties of valid cognition and other salient matters on the grounds that from the ultimate perspective, [there is no such thing] as either ascertainment or nonascertainment
2. [Justification of] the treatise not providing an account of the varieties of valid cognition and other salient matters on the grounds that contextually, such details do not belong here, since while such things may exist conventionally, the same is not the case from the perspective unique to our own [Madhyamaka] system, which [the treatise] is in the process of setting forth

[Justification of] the treatise not providing an account of the varieties of valid cognition and other salient matters on the grounds that from the ultimate perspective, [there is no such thing] as either ascertainment or nonascertainment

Clear Words says: [361]

> This is what we say [in response]: If, for us, there were any "ascertainment," it would need to be derived from something that either was or was not valid cognition. [But] there isn't such a thing. This is because, here, if there were nonascertainment, there would also be ascertainment, something that depended on it and countered it. But when for us there is no nonascertainment to start with, how could there be an ascertainment that is its opposite? It would need to be something that did not depend on other, related things, just as the longness and shortness of the donkey's horn [are not mutually dependent]. And when, in this way, there is no such nonascertainment, what [object] is it that one seeks to confirm by scrutinizing the valid cognition? And where does that leave [your questions] about the variety, characteristics, and object of the valid cognition, and whether it is produced from self, other, both, or arises causelessly? We will assert none of these are things.[924]

"Here" refers to the standpoint: the way that things actually exist from the perspective of the consciousness that investigates whether anything exists ultimately. From such a point of view, if there were any such thing as *nonascertainment*, there would also need to be its accompanying opposite, ascertainment, which opposed it. And if there were such a thing, it would [as you say] need to be one of the two [varieties] of ascertainment, [either] a correct one, such as that of the Middle Way view, or an erroneous one, such as that of those with nihilistic or eternalist views. It may well also be the case that these two would need to be derived from cognitions that were respectively valid and nonvalid. But there is no need to refer to either of them here since from the ultimate perspective, there is no ascertainment.

Alternatively, [this can be read as meaning that] views such as eternalism and nihilism may well be erroneous forms of *ascertainment*, but [in terms of classification] when distinguishing between cognitions that do or do not realize their objects, these fall into the latter category. Hence they cannot be counted as a form of ascertainment. Ascertainment—the thing that counters them—[on the other hand] must derive from a correct, or valid cognition, or from something that, if not a valid cognition, is a correct probans. And although this is a matter that really requires some explanation, here, [talking] from the ultimate perspective, it is something that has no existence. This is what is dealt with in the first portion of the passage, "This is what we say . . . there isn't such a thing."

The reasoning behind this is that if, in the ultimate sense, nonascertainment were to exist, in accordance [with the notion of] counter and countered, there would also need to be ascertainment to work against it. However, ultimately, neither [nonascertainment or ascertainment] exist. This is because while the two of them are, in a general sense, related and dependent on each other in terms of their [roles] as counter and countered, ultimately ascertainment is not connected with nonascertainment—the *other* on which it depends—because ultimately dependence is not tenable. Thus, for instance, while long and short are, in general, relative, the longness and shortness of the horn of a donkey are *not*. [362] This is what is revealed in the second portion of the passage "This is because, here, if there were nonascertainment . . . just as the longness and shortness of the donkey's horn [are not mutually dependent]." [Nāgārjuna is saying,] "In composing this *Treatise on the Middle Way*, we are under no obligation to set out things such as classifications of valid cognition because, in the context of investigating the ultimate, such things have as much existence as does the donkey's horn. And for the same reason, neither is it necessary to discuss according to which of the four alternatives [ascertainment] is produced." This is the point made in the last portion of the above passage, "And when, in this way . . . we will assert none of these are things."

[Justification of] the treatise not providing an account of the varieties of valid cognition and other salient matters on the grounds that contextually, such details do not belong here, since while such things may exist conventionally, the same is not the case from the perspective unique to our own [Madhyamaka] system, which [the treatise] is in the process of setting forth

1. The opponent's argument
2. Our response

The opponent's argument

He argues that our statement that things are not produced from any of the four alternatives is unsustainable, because we have no ascertainment that certifies such nonproduction. As *Clear Words* expresses it, "If it is something that you have no ascertainment of, how is it that you have this categorical assertion that 'Those things of yours are not [produced] from self, from other, from both, nor are they causeless'?"[925]

Our response

The response is delivered in the passage [of *Clear Words*] that follows it, "This is what we say [in response]. The categorical assertion . . . it is to reveal."[926] It says that while the categorical assertion or statement denying production from any of the four alternatives can, in general terms, be validated, this is not necessary when the perspective is that of the ultimate, nor when it is that of the Prāsaṅgika's own unique [understanding] of what is correct or that of which [the Prāsaṅgika] is cognizant. This is because this assertion, by virtue of its being confirmed by a valid cognition dealing in worldly conventions, is one that exists in worldly terms, whereas from the unique [perceptual] perspective of someone who maintains the Middle Way—that is, an ārya—it does not register. As *Clear Words* puts it, "This is what we say [in response]. The categorical assertion may exist according to the standards of correctness that the world sets for itself, but it does not [exist] for āryas."[927]

When the Prāsaṅgika says that the distinction between correct and false conventional things is not one of his own system, it comes down to the same point. Hence, from that perspective, [the Prāsaṅgika] rejects not only the basic notion of something that is conventional but even that what is ultimately true *exists*. A greater appreciation of this point can be gained from what follows below, with the discussion about the wish to reject all distinctions, how in emptiness all elaborations are negated, and how [the Prāsaṅgika] agrees with negation in terms of what is commonly [accepted]. [363] It is the failure to understand exactly this point that leads to so many false notions, [including] the beliefs that in the Prāsaṅgika system one cannot differentiate between correct and false conventional things and that there is no distinction between an [actual] horse and a dream one. Taktsang Lotsāwa's inability to provide an account of the *results of valid cognition* [acceptable to the Prāsaṅgika] stems from his failure to distinguish between the Prāsaṅgika's two positions—the public one and the [other] reflecting their own unique perspective.[928] One should not, therefore, approach such matters in a facile manner but instead investigate them thoroughly. If one's understanding of the matter is at variance with the way I have explained it here, one should be aware that it has certainly erred. This is because unless the point about the [Prāsaṅgika's two positions] is appreciated, one will fail to differentiate between the perspective of the ultimate, which is free from elaborations and transcends the world[ly], and that of worldly [conventions], the domain in which ordinary beings and āryas alike operate. So this slight digression has been a justified one.

At this juncture, the realist raises the question of whether, according to the unique purview of āryas, there is such a thing as reason. [The response is,] "From the unique perspective of an ārya, there can be no elaborations such as [what is logically] correct or incorrect, because from the perspective of the meditative equipoise of such a being, let alone notions of correctness, being or not being, verbalization, and so forth, even the ultimate truth that is the object of that equipoise does not exist, since [the meditative equipoise] is of one taste with its object—the straight absence of what has been negated." As *Clear Words* puts it: "For āryas, is there reason? Who can speak of [reason] existing or not existing? In terms of the ultimate, āryas say nothing. Hence, for those who have no [sense of] what is correct or incorrect, how can there be any elaborations about such things?"[929]

In response to this, the realist says, "If, according to the unique way that āryas perceive things, there is no [sense of what is] correct or logical, then there is no point in your making reasoned arguments. But if you refrain from doing that, there is no way that you can engender a realization of ultimate truth in worldly beings." [Nāgārjuna's] answer to this is, "Even though there are no such things as correctness or verbalization according to the āryas' unique perception, it is not as if there are no means of bringing worldly beings to realization of the ultimate. Āryas formulate numerous lines of reasoning for the sake of those worldly beings. But it is not that they, with the unique understanding of their own system, use worldly conventions to convey something that could be considered *correct* in terms of analysis of the ultimate. [364] Instead, they employ a notion of correctness that is agreed in the world, and it is by means of this that they induce realization of their own unique understanding [in worldly beings]." [Nāgārjuna] makes the first of these points when he says, "Expression is brought to an end because the activity of the mind has been brought to an end."[930] He makes the second point in the passage "We do not [seek to] explain these things without adopting [your] conventions."[931] In *Clear Words*, these points are expressed thus:

> "If āryas do not provide correct reasoning, how is it that they can engender realization of the ultimate in ordinary beings?" Āryas do not use the conventions of worldly expression to [convey] correct reasoning [of their own]. But to induce realization in others, they adopt only [the notions of] correct reasoning commonly accepted in the world. By this alone they bring realization to the world.[932]

Here, "only [the notions of] correct reasoning commonly accepted in the world" rules out that the [standards] in question are those of our own unique system. "Adopt" indicates that it is something they agree to, but only [in terms of] the "public" stance of one who follows the Middle Way.

As they do not accept any of the four alternatives [of production], these do not warrant mention here. The treatise endeavors to teach that [the view of] dependent origination is the antidote to all forms of superimposition regarding the object. And as valid cognition and its object are dealt with elsewhere, they are not explained here. *Clear Words* says:

> It is just as is the case with the body. Despite being impure, it is not perceived as such by those who are misled by their desirous attachment. In spite of its imperfections, they are entirely deluded by their superimposition of purity. To free such individ-

> uals from desirous attachment, the Tathāgata introduces them to the body's faults, which have been masked by the notion of the body as pure. [The Tathāgata] may do this by means of an emanation or by describing [the beauty of] such things as the hair of the celestial form.... In the present context [also], since āryas seek to induce ascertainment in those who cling to such things as the pot's existence, they will reason, "Just as [you] have accepted that there can be no production from self, something that existed prior to its production also cannot be produced, since [such a thing would already] exist."[933]

Thus, in the refutation of the type of self-production asserted by the Sāṃkhya, they reference the Sāṃkhya's own understanding of correct reasoning. [365] [Following this] *Clear Words* says:

> And, in those who assert that a sprout is not produced from things that are [completely] other than it, such as fire and charcoal, [āryas] will seek to induce ascertainment [by reasoning] that similarly, [a sprout] cannot [arise from] those things that they want to assert, such as a seed ... it is not reasonable.[934]

This describes how, by using reasoning [referencing the standards] of the other party, they refute production from [an]other. It also, by implication, refutes production from both [self and other] and causeless production. *Clear Words* then states:

> It is through [reference] only to the [standards] asserted by those [others] that [āryas] bring about realization [within those others].
>
> Things are, accordingly, not produced.[935]

What this indicates is that while for the follower of the Middle Way—the one who challenges the position of the other party in the debate—there are no autonomous reasons, it is by means of the [standards] asserted by that other party that he establishes, in line with the *Fundamental Treatise on the Middle Way*, that things are not produced. This is what is conveyed by "only to the [standards] asserted by those [others]"—words that, in the exclusion of one thing, bring the [affirmative] discerning of another.

The second point—that the treatise concentrates on teaching about dependent origination rather than valid cognition—is addressed by *Clear Words* in the passage:

> Thus it was initially to provide an antidote to the erroneous superimposition that [assigns to things] a nature that the first chapter was composed. Then the subsequent chapters were composed to counter the superimposition of certain qualities to [those things]. This is because its aim[936] is to show that within dependent origination, absolutely none of the qualities—whether it be that of the one who goes, that toward which one has gone, or the act of going—exist.[937]

This informs us that what the *Fundamental Treatise on the Middle Way* is expressly concerned with overtly conveying is ultimate truth. Since its object does not exist in conventional terms, why would an account of such things as valid cognition and autonomous reasons be given here? The [ultimate] is the primary point of the work. To approach it otherwise would be to lose sight of this fact. This is something that should be considered carefully.

3. General Refutation of Others' Assertions about Valid Cognition

REFUTING THE VALID COGNITION ASSERTED BY THE LOGICIANS

1. General refutation of their valid cognition
2. Specific refutation of their notion of perception

GENERAL REFUTATION OF THEIR VALID COGNITION

1. Refutation of the treatises of the logician and the Svātantrika
2. Refutation of the system according to which the bifurcation of valid cognition is the definitive way to divide it

REFUTATION OF THE TREATISES OF THE LOGICIAN AND THE SVĀTANTRIKA

1. The fault that their efforts have been futile
2. The fault that they have not [successfully] dealt with [the criticism related to] nonascertainment [366]

THE FAULT THAT THEIR EFFORTS HAVE BEEN FUTILE

Here, the opponent argues, "Just as we proponents of [intrinsic] nature refer in our treatises to this worldly notion of valid cognition and the object it comprehends as conventional, you must at least acknowledge the [kind of] valid cognition that is accepted in the world, because the realization of an object depends on valid cognition, and the ultimate also depends on realization of that." As *Clear Words* puts it, "He argues, 'It is this very notion of valid cognition and the object it comprehends—the one held in the world—that our treatises set out.'"[938] This would appear to be an argument [advanced by the] Svātantrika.

The Prāsaṅgika responds to it by questioning, "What purpose is there in talking about these in your treatises?"

The proponent of [intrinsic] nature [i.e., the Svātantrika] answers, "The purpose is this. Various logicians and realists, non-Buddhist and Buddhist alike, set forth their own specious ideas about what defines valid cognition in their respective treatises. But in doing so, they only succeed in undermining what they seek to define—namely, valid cognition. We proponents of [intrinsic] nature therefore provide the *correct* version of the defining characteristics of valid cognition in [our] commentaries on the *Fundamental Treatise on the Middle Way*—those that give a line-by-line explanation and those that concentrate on its import." As *Clear Words* says, "Well then, it is necessary to describe the purpose of talking about that. They may say, 'The logicians set forth their own specious ideas about the characteristic that defines valid cognition and, in doing so, undermine it. We therefore provide the correct version of its defining characteristics.'"[939]

The Prāsaṅgika rejoinder to this is to say, "Your efforts in this direction have been futile and irrational. In terms of the world or the realm of conventions, if it were the case that, by presenting erroneous versions of the characteristics that define valid cognition, these harmful logicians had done something [genuinely] detrimental to what was being defined—namely, perception and inferential cognition—then your efforts in this direction would have been worthy and served a purpose. However, it is not like that, because if [they have] set forth what defines and what is defined in an erroneous way, then both [just amount to] fictions." *Clear Words* says:

> This is also not fitting. If the harmful logicians' erroneous presentation of the defining characteristics were detrimental to the thing characterized in the worldly domain, then putting effort [to counter this] would prove a fruitful exercise. But since this is not the case, such efforts serve no purpose.[940]

The fault that they have not [successfully] dealt with [the criticism related to] nonascertainment

It is anyway the case that although you, the Svātantrika, [set out] to elucidate the correct or nonerroneous defining characteristics of valid cognition, you do not succeed. [367] This is because you fail to satisfactorily address the criticism made in [Nāgārjuna's] *Dispeller of Dispute*. There, the question posed is, "If objects are ascertained by valid cognition, is that valid cognition [established by] ascertaining itself, or by means of another? If it ascertained itself, the distinction between object and subject would be unfeasible, whereas if it was ascertained by means of another, it would lead to an infinite regress." As *Clear Words* says:

> Furthermore, you have also not succeeded in elucidating the correct defining characteristics, since you have failed to deal with the criticisms in *Dispeller of Dispute*, such as where it asks, "If realization of the object relies on valid cognition, what is it that discerns those valid cognitions?"[941]

This passage also refutes those among the Svātantrika who assert self-cognition.

Refutation of the system according to which the bifurcation of valid cognition is the definitive way to divide it

1. Outlining their position
2. Refutation of that

Outlining their position

The realist advocates that there is a definitive bifurcation of valid cognition into perception and inference, which derives from the [differing] manner that the two engage their [respective] objects. This is because there is a fundamental distinction between valid perception, which takes a specifically characterized actual thing as its held object, and valid inference, which takes a non-actual, generally characterized *śabdārtha* as its conceived object. He says that this in turn corresponds to the definitive bipartition among objects—the things that valid cognition comprehends—as these are necessarily either actual, specifically characterized things or non-actual, generally characterized ones. As the *Commentary on Pramāṇa* says, "As there are two objects of comprehension, there are two valid cognitions."[942] *Clear Words* thus states, "While [you propose] that there are two valid cognitions corresponding to the two [types of phenomena], the specifically and generally characterized . . . ."[943]

Refutation of their position

1. Refutation of the definitive bifurcation, which relies on the special gloss given to the term *lakṣaṇa*
2. Countering their attempts to rebut that [refutation]
3. Conclusion

Refutation of the definitive bifurcation, which relies on the special gloss given to the term *lakṣaṇa*

1. Refutation of the position that the term *lakṣaṇa* should be glossed as "that which acts [on the object]"
2. Refutation of the position that the term *lakṣaṇa* should be glossed as "the object [that is acted upon]"
3. Rebuttal of the defense against our attack on the first gloss [368]

Refutation of the position that the term *lakṣaṇa* should be glossed as "that which acts [on the object]"[944]

Regarding the realist position that the bifurcation of valid cognition is definitive and reflects a corresponding dichotomy among the things that it comprehends, we pose the following question. Should the *lakṣaṇa* [i.e., characteristics] of the "specific" and the "general" [objects] be understood to denote that which acts upon the object or the object that is acted upon—in other words, that which characterizes or that which is characterized? If [you assert that] it is the first, do the two things that act [as the specific and general characterizers] have a locus or thing [toward which their action] of characterization [is directed]? If they do, then the [twofold] division of valid cognition cannot be a definitive one, since quite apart from the two *lakṣaṇa* [i.e., the specific and the general characteristics] there would be another [class of] objects to be comprehended—the things that they characterize. *Clear Words* says, "So is there or is there not an object (*lakṣya*) to which the two characteristics (*lakṣaṇa*) belong? If there is, there must be a comprehended object other than the [two characteristics]. How then can there be [only] two valid cognitions?"[945]

[The logician's] response may be to deny that there is any such locus or object [for the action of] characterization. But then it would again follow that there could not be two valid cognitions, because there would be no locus or basis to which the two [characteristics] belonged, and without this, they would not be characteristics of anything. This is what is conveyed in *Clear Words*: "But if there is no locus for the characteristic, then there is no basis for it. And hence there can be no characteristic [depending on such a basis] either. How then can there be [only] two valid cognitions? . . . If the basis, the thing characterized, is not tenable, then neither can there be any characteristics [depending upon it]."[946]

Refutation of the position that the term lakṣaṇa should be glossed as "the object [that is acted upon]"

The [logician] says that the term *lakṣaṇa* could refer to any one of three components [within the action of characterization]: the thing characterizing, the actor, or the object. Thus *lakṣaṇa* might denote (1) the characterizer—in the [first] sense, of the thing through which there is an action of characterization, (2) the characterizer—in the [second] sense, of the agent who, through another, [performs] an action of characterization, or (3) the characterized, in the sense of that within which there is characterization—the locus of the characterization—its object.[947] Among these, [the logician proposes] that here *lakṣaṇa* refers to the object, meaning that in terms of distinguishing between the one acting and the one acted upon, it denotes the latter. [369] [He argues that] this understanding of the term *lakṣaṇa* as referring to the object is one that anyone can legitimately derive from it, because the secondary affix in the term *lakṣaṇa* [i.e., *ana*] need not be confined to meaning the one that performs the action. This is because, [according to the Sanskrit grammatical rule,] the situation for a *lyuṭ* affix is like that of a *kṛtya* [secondary] affix. As the [authoritative treatise on] Sanskrit grammar says, "Secondary affixes and *lyuṭ* affixes create various senses."[948] *Clear Words* says:

> He proposes that this is not to be [understood as] *lakṣaṇa* in the sense of being that which characterizes [something]. Instead, citing the [grammatical rule *kṛtyalyuṭo bahulam*], "secondary affixes and *lyuṭ* affixes create various senses [other than those specified]," he says that the *lyuṭ* affix [of the word *lakṣaṇa*] denotes the object, so that this is *lakṣaṇa* in the sense of what is characterized.[949]

There are two parts [to our response]:

1. A fault that parallels the earlier one
2. Refutation of the position that cognition can be the one performing the action [of characterizing]

A fault that parallels the earlier one

Well then, [if *lakṣaṇa* refers to the object characterized,] it would follow that nothing is being characterized, because there is nothing that is *doing* the characterization. If he rejects this, [insisting that the characterized and characterizer are distinct,] then it would follow, just as before, that the [basic division of] objects of comprehension must be threefold and [accordingly, the basic division of] valid cognition must also be threefold, because the object and that which acts on it—the characterized and the characterizer—are distinct. *Clear Words* states, "But even so, that *lakṣaṇa* cannot possibly characterize itself. And since that which does the characterizing must be distinct from the object [characterized], the same fault remains."[950]

Refutation of the position that cognition can be the one performing the action [of characterizing]

He might try to deny that there is any problem with asserting that the [twofold] distinction between the thing comprehended and the comprehender [that is, the object and valid cognition] is a definitive one by proposing that cognition is the *lakṣaṇa* [both in the sense of] being the thing characterized—the one that comprehends—and in the sense of the object that is comprehended, in addition to being counted among those things that are specifically characterized. *Clear Words* says, "He may believe that there is no problem [with his position], claiming that cognition performs the action, and also because it is included among specifically characterized [things]."[951]

This position has four faults:

1. The unwanted consequence that this once again leads to three objects [of cognition]
2. The unwanted consequence that the qualification [introduced by the logician means] that some *lakṣaṇa* cannot be objects of comprehension
3. The untenability of the locus of characterization being either identical to or distinct from the *lakṣaṇa*
4. The fault of [the logician's position] leaving no place for the agent responsible for the action

The unwanted consequence that this once again leads to three objects [of cognition]

Well then, since according to [you, the logician], it is the specific characteristics of the object of cognition alone that can serve as the object of the action, it follows that you must logically posit something other than the object of cognition as the entity that acts upon it. That is because you have chosen to cast aside the commonly accepted gloss of *lakṣaṇa,* according to which it denotes the thing that acts on the object, in favor of one that denotes the object acted upon, and you also [propose that] consciousness is that entity. [370] That [pervasion], in turn holds, because you posit that the specific characteristic(s) of a thing—such as "solidity" for earth, "experiencing" [i.e., sensing] for feeling, and "differentiating its own object" for [main] awareness—are what constitute the identities of those things and distinguish them from other phenomena. If you accept this, it must mean that, separate from the one acting [i.e., the cognition], there must be an object that is acted on, because the cognition, a thing with its own specific characteristics, is separate from the object that it cognizes. And if you acknowledge this, it would again follow that there are three objects [of cognition], meaning that the same problem remains regarding your assertion that the bifurcation of objects is the definitive way to divide them. *Clear Words* states:

> Here, what characterizes a thing's entity—[such as] solidity for earth, experiencing for feeling, and differentiating its own object for consciousness—is what marks it as individual and distinguishes it from others, and this is its specific characteristic. But this account of the particulars [of things], which follows common understanding, is what [you] cast aside [in your gloss of *lakṣaṇa*], as you assert it denotes the object of the action and consider consciousness as the one that does the action. Thus [you] must assert that only [one] specific characteristic of a thing is the object of the action whereas another specific characteristic is the one performing the action. Therefore, if it is the specific characteristic of consciousness that does the action, it must be the specific characteristic of something else that is the object of that action. So the original fault remains.[952]

The unwanted consequence that the qualification [introduced by the logician means] that some *lakṣaṇa* cannot be objects of comprehension

1. The actual fault
2. Rebuttal of his defense against our attack

The actual fault

He denies that needing to posit something else other than the object and performer of the action undermines his dichotomous division of objects of comprehension. This is because, he says, it is solidity and so forth that characterize things such as earth, and it is these [characteristics] alone that consciousness realizes, and which are [therefore] the objects of its action, and consciousness is not separate from its own specific characteristic(s). *Clear Words* states, "He might claim that it is only those things such as solidity and so forth that are realized by that consciousness, and it is these that are the object of its action, and that [consciousness] is not something separate from its own specific characteristic(s)."[953]

Based on that logic, it would follow that the characteristic specific to consciousness is not an object of comprehension, because it does not [serve as] the object that consciousness acts upon. [371] The reason is the one that he has asserted. The pervasion also holds, because he claims that the only thing that can be the object of comprehension is a specifically characterized one, an object that is acted upon. But if he were to accept [the argument's conclusion], it would follow that what he is advocating is that within the specifically-generally characterized bipartition of objects of comprehension, inside the category of specifically characterized things, it is necessary to differentiate between (1) those things that *are* objects of comprehension, in that they are the things characterized and [therefore] the objects acted upon [by consciousness], and (2) those that are *not* objects of comprehension, in that they are the specifically characterized things that do the characterizing. That is because this is [effectively] what he has just admitted. As *Clear Words* puts it:

> If that is so, well then, as the specific characteristic of the consciousness is not the object [of the action], it cannot be the thing that is comprehended, because only a specific characteristic that has the quality of being the object acted upon can be the thing comprehended. Therefore, with regard to [his] assertion "Objects of comprehension are of two [varieties], those specifically and those generally characterized," it becomes necessary for him to add the qualification "A portion of the specifically characterized ones *are* objects of comprehension, and they are classified as such [on the grounds that] they are the ones that are *characterized*. And [another] portion are not objects of comprehension, and those are classified as such due to being the ones that *characterize*."[954]

Rebuttal of his defense against our attack regarding the aforesaid qualification

1. Refutation of the position that what acts on the object is an other-knowing consciousness
2. Refutation of the position that what acts on the object is a self-cognizing consciousness

Refutation of the position that what acts on the object is an other-knowing consciousness

He claims, "There is no fault that the one performing the action is [thereby] excluded from being an object of comprehension, because that [performer, in its turn,] is also the object of comprehension for another consciousness, which apprehends it as something other than itself. This is because that [second] consciousness, which apprehends [the first] as other than itself, is the one performing the act of comprehending, whereas that [first] consciousness is the object of that action."

In response to this, we say that it would follow that there is an infinite regress, because the consciousness apprehending it as "other" in turn requires a further one, which is the agent of the action of comprehending, and that also requires a further consciousness [and so forth]. Also, there is the fault that the original object of comprehension is never actually cognized. *Clear Words* says, "If [he contends that] this also is an object acted on, that would also require something other [than it] doing the action. And even if one could establish that another consciousness had the identity of the one doing such an action [with respect to it], there would be the fault of an infinite regress."[955]

Refutation of the position that what acts on the object is a self-cognizing consciousness

He says there is no fault that the consciousness that is the agent is [itself] not an object of an action, since it is apprehended by self-cognition. [372] He proposes that there is such a thing as self-cognition, because an awareness has two portions: (1) one that cognizes "other" and illuminates [an outer] object, and (2) one that illuminates only its own nature—that is, a self-illuminating self-cognition. The [situation] is comparable with that of the flame of a lamp, within which is the [quality of] illuminating both an object and itself. *Clear Words* says:

> He may think, "Self-cognition exists. And because of cognizing itself, [the consciousness] is apprehended, and it is thereby the object of an action and belongs to the domain of things that are comprehended."[956]

The refutation of this position is dealt with in three sections:

1. Refuting self-cognition by means of logic
2. Refuting self-cognition by means of scripture
3. Conclusion

Refuting self-cognition by means of logic

Having identified the cognitive object, a specifically characterized thing, as the object of the action and consciousness itself as the agent of that action, he proposes that, with regard to that agent, a *further* internal distinction can be made, between the object and agent of an action. This is wrong, because [the idea that] consciousness has self-cognition is untenable. [Candrakīrti] issues a lengthy rebuttal to the notion of self-cognition in passages such as:

> It is not established that it experiences itself.
> They may [say that] subsequent recall proves that [an earlier self-cognition existed],
> but such a form of [ultimate recall], which is itself unproven,
> cannot be asserted to prove something that itself needs to be proved.[957]

And as *Clear Words* says:

> I state that self-cognition has been comprehensively refuted in *Entering the Middle Way*. It therefore makes no logical sense [to claim that] one thing with specific characteristics characterizes another thing with specific characteristics, and that the one [doing the] characterizing is "self-cognition."[958]

Furthermore, it follows that a self-cognizing consciousness cannot possibly be what comprehends the specific characteristic of the other consciousness, because that consciousness is not something that stands apart from its own characteristics. The pervasion holds, because [the logician's view] would require that the one acted upon and the one acting, [which are necessarily] separate, are encompassed within a locus that is single. As *Clear Words* states:

> Moreover, such a consciousness is not feasible. It cannot be separate from its own specific characteristics. And if there is no locus of characterization, there can be no foundation [for the action], and hence no characterizing operation. As [these things] cannot, in any sense, exist, how could there be self-cognition?[959]

Refuting self-cognition by means of scripture

Also, if there is such a thing as self-cognition, it would follow that the mind is able to comprehend itself. But if one agreed to that, it must follow that the blade of a sword could cut itself, and that the tip of a finger could touch itself. Such things are, however, contradicted by direct experience. *Clear Words* says:

> It is as stated in the *Questions of Ratnacūḍa Sutra*: "As he cannot truly observe the mind, he wonders where the mind came from. [He] searches the mind's continuum exhaustively, asking himself whether it is from the thing it observes that it arises. [373] [During this process of investigation,] he wonders whether what is observed is one thing while the mind is another, or whether the thing that is observed is [itself] the mind. But if, in this [situation], the thing observed was one thing while the mind was another, there would have to be two minds. However, if it were the case that the thing being observed was the mind, it would mean the mind would be seeing itself, but how could that be? The mind is unable to see itself. This is like, for instance, [the way] that the blade of a sword cannot cut itself, and the tip of a finger cannot touch itself..."[960] [This is] the way to engage in the pure activity of closely observing the mind . . . .

Conclusion

Self-cognition cannot tenably be the agent of the action, because of the welter of scriptural passages and lines of logical reasoning that establish that it does not exist. *Clear Words* says, "Thus self-cognition does not exist, and in its absence, what is [supposed to be] characterizing what?"[961]

The untenability of the locus of characterization being either identical to or distinct from the *lakṣaṇa*

Is the specific characteristic of the consciousness that [supposedly] comprehends a dependent [phenomenon] intrinsically distinct from the locus of characterization—the [cognitive] object—or indistinguishable from it? If that characteristic [of consciousness] were intrinsically distinct from the locus, it could not be the one that characterizes it, because it would be intrinsically distinct from it. This is just as something with the characteristic of having a stubby tail cannot characterize a cow. It would also follow that the locus could not serve as what is characterized in the process of characterization, because it would be intrinsically distinct from the characteristic(s) that characterize it. This is just as "the bulbous thing" [i.e., a pot] cannot characterize a pillar. *Clear Words* says:

> Also, one can question whether the characteristic is distinct from the locus of characterization or indistinguishable from it. If it were distinct from that, since the characteristic would be distinct from the locus of characterization, then just as something that is [patently] not the characteristic cannot [qualify as] that characteristic, then neither could it. [374] And as the locus of characterization would [correspondingly] be distinct from the characteristic, then just as something that is [patently] not the locus of characterization cannot [qualify as] the locus, then neither could it.[962]

Mastery of the [analytical] model of action, which distinguishes among the three components—the action, the agent, and the object—[is therefore essential] if one is to posit a scheme within which [the existence of] things is verified by valid cognition. Without this, one will not understand how, in spite of undertaking the deepest form of negation, one can [still credibly] maintain conventional reality. One should appreciate that it is for this reason that *Clear Words* deals with [this matter] at such length.[963]

It would also follow [from the logician's position] that the characterizer (*lakṣaṇa*) and the characterized (*lakṣya*) do not depend on each other in any way, because they are intrinsically different. He himself has asserted the reason, and the predicate also holds, because [Nāgārjuna declares], "A nature [must be something] inborn and independent of anything else."[964] Thus, for anything that is established intrinsically by means of its own nature, there can be no mutual dependency, such as that between the actor and the object of the action. But if [the logician] accepts this, then it again follows that the [thing in question] cannot be the locus of characterization for the other, because it would have a nature that is intrinsically distinct and entirely independent of it. Hence it would be [totally independent], like a flower [growing in] midair. *Clear Words* says:

> Likewise, because the characteristic (*lakṣaṇa*) would be distinct from the locus of characterization (*lakṣya*), it would mean that the locus was independent of the characteristic. It could not, therefore, be the locus of characterization, because it would be independent of that characteristic, comparable to a flower in midair.[965]

The same [Sanskrit] term [*lakṣya*] can be used for both the "locus of characterization" [in the sense of the illustration] and the "thing characterized" [in the sense of the definiendum]. In the present context, it should be understood to refer to [the latter, i.e.,] the definiendum—the thing being characterized.[966]

The converse of this would be that the two [characterizer and characterized] are intrinsically nondistinct—that is, indistinguishable from each other. But from this it would follow that in the case of "fit to be [regarded as] form," [the characteristic defining form,] the locus of the characterization—that is, the definiendum *form*—could not be characterized by it, because that [defining characteristic] would be indistinguishable from the [form] it defined. This is akin to the way that "fit to be [regarded as] form" is unable to [define or] characterize itself. As *Clear Words* puts it:

> If the characteristic and the locus of the characteristic were indistinguishable, since the [locus] would not be distinct from the characteristic, just as a characteristic cannot characterize its identity, [any idea that] the locus of characterization [can serve as] its own locus is discredited.[967]

In this passage, "its identity" denotes "its own identity" or "itself."

In a similar manner, it follows that with respect to form, the thing that [defines or] characterizes it—namely, its fitness to be [regarded as] form—could not be its defining characteristic, because [form] would be identical with that characteristic. This is akin to the way that "form"—the thing [defined or] characterized—is unable to characterize itself. As it says in *Clear Words*: [375]

> If the characteristic is other than the locus of characterization,
> that locus would be [rendered] characterless,
> [because as] you have clearly stated,
> a thing that is neither distinct nor the same as another thing, is one
> that does not exist.[968]

Also, "Because the *lakṣaṇa* [characteristic] would also not be distinct from the locus of characterization, it could not have the nature of the characteristic. Just as with the locus [in relation to] its [own] identity . . . ."[969] This merely serves as an illustration. What it should principally be applied to is the [twofold distinction between] *definer* and *defined*, in which [the characteristic referred to is the one that] defines a thing. That [was the case] for what preceded, and it is also the way that this [current discussion] should be understood. The pervasion in the above [argument] also holds, because there is no way to establish that two things [are related as] defining characteristic and thing defined, outside [understanding them to be either] identical or distinct. With regard to this, [*Fundamental Treatise on the Middle Way*] says:

> If it is the case that one thing
> can neither be established as identical with
> or different from another thing,
> in what sense is their existence established?[970]

[Concerning this,] *Clear Words* comments, "There are no means of establishing that [they are, respectively,] characteristic and locus of characterization apart from [referring to notions of] identicalness and otherness."[971]

[The logician] responds by saying, "If I held that the characteristic and locus of characterization were either identical to or discrete from each other, [my position] would have such a fault, but I make no such claim, because [the relationship between] them is incommunicable." *Clear Words* says, "If he responds that the [relationship between them is one that] exists in a manner that is incommunicable . . . ."[972]

But asserting that [the relationship they share] is incommunicable is also not a tenable position. One might be able to claim that the relationship is incommunicable for those who are entirely insensible to any distinction between characteristics and the things they define. But in lands and tenet systems where there is ignorance of those distinctions, there can be no analytical division between bases and their properties [allowing] realization that one is the characteristic and the other is the thing defined. And in such a situation, the two are not, therefore, the object and performer of an action, because within the domain of the incommunicable,[973] object and performer have no establishment [i.e., existence] at all. As *Clear Words* says:

> It is not like that. Incommunicability is for those who are ignorant of the distinctions between mutually dependent [elements]. But wherever there is no knowledge of this distinction, there can be no distinguishing [between] things as characteristic(s) or things defined by them. Hence neither of them [could be said to] exist. Therefore, within incommunicability, there is no establishment of them [at all].[974] [376]

THE FAULT OF [THE LOGICIAN'S POSITION] LEAVING NO PLACE FOR THE AGENT RESPONSIBLE FOR THE ACTION

What is more, it is untenable for a proponent of intrinsic identity, like you, to identify consciousness as the one that performs the action while saying nothing about the agent and the object [of an action], because [even] if consciousness *were* the one that did the action of comprehending the [cognitive] object, all three [components]—namely, (1) the comprehender or agent responsible for comprehending the object, (2) the instrument that performs the action, and (3) the object that is acted upon—are still required. It is just as is the case, for instance, [with the action] of chopping wood, where Devadatta is the agent responsible, the axe is the instrument, and the wood having been split into pieces is the object of the action. Thus there are three [components]: *agent, instrument, and object*. Without there being an agent responsible for the action, one cannot permissibly identify the consciousness as the instrument, and its having discerned its [cognitive] object as the object of the action—these [two] being what are indicated by the phrase "instrument and so forth" [in the *Clear Words* passage below]. [The situation] is just like that of chopping [wood], where unless there is an agent responsible for the action, those three components would become untenable. *Clear Words* states, "Furthermore, if consciousness is the instrument of the action, what would be the agent [of the action of] discerning the object? Without the agent responsible for the action, there can be no instrument and so forth, just as with the act of chopping."[975]

In response, [the logician] may contend that [by identifying] consciousness as the instrument, he does not incur the fault of there being no agent responsible for the action, because even though describing consciousness as the instrument may not [overtly] state that it is the agent, [it is nevertheless implicitly understood that] the basic awareness is the agent at work. As *Clear Words* says, "He might suggest that it is understood here that mind is the agent . . . ."[976]

This prompts the question of whether consciousness and basic awareness are identical or distinct. In the present context, consciousness should be understood as *a cognitive function*, whereas basic awareness is the main mind. This line also indicates that this basic awareness is the one being identified with the individual.[977] Nevertheless, since even in the [Buddhist] realist schools, there is no agent aside from a designation assigned to a basis, "agent" must be understood here in a sense of something that is just imputed. For [further discussion on these issues, one should consult Tsongkhapa's writings,] such as his *Stages of the Path* and commentaries on *Fundamental Treatise on the Middle Way* and *Entering the Middle Way*.[978]

[Our] response to the realist is that his identification of consciousness as the instrument and the basic awareness as the agent cannot be counted as legitimate even in his own system, because the functions that consciousness and basic awareness perform with regard to the object are distinct from each other. This is the case, since treatises of his own system state that the operation of basic awareness is just to regard the object, whereas what consciousness—that is, the *functions* of the mind—do is engage with the features that distinguish it. Thus *Distinguishing the Middle Way from the Extremes* says, "Of those, the basic awareness sees the object, [whereas] faculties within mind [deal with] distinguishing features of that"[979]—a point that is addressed in the treatise itself, its commentaries, and other works.[980] *Clear Words* says:

> This is also incorrect. It is like this. Observation of the basic object is the task [performed by] the mind, whereas engaging with the distinguishing features of the object is the task of the functions of mind. [It is you, after all, who] have asserted, "Of those, the basic awareness sees the object, [whereas] faculties within mind [deal with] distinguishing features of that."[981] [377]

He may deny that [his system] is at fault by claiming that while consciousness and basic awareness have distinct tasks, they also have a shared one, just as the human agent who cuts and the axe that is his implement have distinct roles but also share in the task of cutting the wood.

We would reject the appropriateness of this analogy. From the worldly perspective, one can differentiate between the two on the level of minor distinctions of role, in the sense that Devadatta, as the agent of the woodcutting, is the one who deals the blow, whereas the axe, as the implement, is the one that [immediately] inflicts the damage. But in terms of the *primary* task in which they are both engaged—namely, that of ensuring the wood is split into pieces—there is no distinction between them. He [the logician], however, has failed to identify a single principal task [in the situation in question,] in which both consciousness and basic awareness are [jointly] engaged. *Clear Words* states:

> It is by performing their minor roles in the action of whatever nature that the instrument and so forth [contribute] to the achievement of the principal action and thereby become [indispensable] components of that action—its object, instrument, and so forth. *Here,* [however,] the consciousness and basic awareness have no single, principal act in which they are [both involved].[982]

He might question what problem there would be with asserting that consciousness and basic awareness are indeed involved in a single, principal action.

To this, our response would be that maintaining that consciousness and basic awareness have a single, principal action in which they are both involved is not a viable position for him, because he asserts that the principal task of basic awareness is confined to grasping just the object in question, whereas the principal task of the cognitive functions is determining that object's features. This must be the case, because once the basic awareness just sees the object, its primary task is completed, whereas the same would not be true for the cognitive functions. With regard to specific distinctions [related to] the object, [he] accepts, for instance, that experiencing is the task of *feeling*, while the fine separation of the object's details is the task of *discrimination*, and that it is with the performance of these tasks that their principal actions are completed. Also, in the case of certain distracted states of mind, while concentration is [one of the functions] that accompany [awareness], it is due to its inability to perform its task to any significant degree that the mind is a distracted one. Such is the point made in [Maitreya's] *Distinguishing the Middle Way from the Extremes* and its commentaries. [378]

In terms of your [i.e., his] own system, therefore, it is untenable to identify, respectively, (1) consciousness as the instrument, (2) basic awareness as the agent, and (3) discerning the object as the action, since there is no single, primary action in which the instrument and the agent are [jointly] involved. This is because in terms of [recognizing] the basic object, consciousness is not the instrument, whereas with regard to [distinguishing] the object's features, basic awareness is not the agent. This means that he has still not escaped the earlier fault. *Clear Words* says, "So how is it? The basic awareness's primary task is discerning the basic object, whereas the primary task of consciousness is discerning the features of the object. Consciousness, therefore, is not the instrument, nor is mind the agent. Hence the original fault remains."[983]

This understanding of the magnificent Candrakīrti's commentary on the passage in *Distinguishing the Middle Way from the Extremes* is the one intended by the great lord [Tsongkhapa], Gyaltsab Jé, and the omniscient Gendun Drup. Some of our own scholars, rather than explaining "distinguishing features of that" as referring to distinctions of the object, take it to mean those of the mind. [Accordingly] they also identify the functions [associated with] mind as features of mind. But there are problems with this interpretation. One of these is that the aforesaid passage [in *Distinguishing the Middle Way from the Extremes*] represents the standpoint of a system that advocates a single awareness, because as Asaṅga himself states, "Since five are not tenable."[984] There are many issues related to this that cannot be pursued further here but that I intend to deal with in a separate work.[985]

Rejecting [the logician's] attempted rebuttal of our criticism about there being no place for the agent

1. His response to our criticism
2. Our refutation of that response

His response to our criticism

The [Buddhist] realist responds to our criticism by saying, "We assert that *agent* is a designation that has been attached to some basis and that, as such, it has no substantial existence. In spite of this, the object of the action and so forth—with 'and so forth' referring to what does the action—are, in conventional terms, substances. The agent can have no substantial existence, because various scriptures declare that 'All phenomena are without self.' The pervasion holds, because *self*, *agent*, and *adopter* are equivalent to one another." *Clear Words* says:

> He proposes that, because scripture declares that "All phenomena are without self," an agent is entirely absent. Hence, [he says,] the conventions of *action* and so forth can still exist despite there being no agent.[986]

As the three [Buddhist] realist schools completely deny the existence of an agent separate from the aggregates, it is necessary to add the predicate "substantially established" here [to the self in question]. [379] Furthermore, they agree that the action-executor-object [the three components of an action] exist in a conventional sense, and they do not distinguish among the three with regard to whether they have substantial reality.

Our refutation of that response

1. Rejecting the [realist's] interpretation of the scriptural passage
2. Refuting the analogy that the [realist] uses to illustrate the situation and countering his objections [to this refutation]
3. [Explaining the sense in which] analysis is inappropriate and how one must leave things in an unanalyzed [state]
4. How to posit phenomena conventionally
5. Why it is necessary to accept [the way that phenomena are posited conventionally]
6. Differentiating between skill and ignorance with regard to positing the two forms of "truth"

Rejecting the [realist's] interpretation of the scriptural passage

His interpretation of the scriptural pronouncement "All phenomena are without self" as one that while negating the substantial reality of the agent, still allows it for the object and instrument of the action is an incorrect one, because whether it be taken from the perspective of the coarse or subtle levels of selflessness, it cannot explain the meaning of that pronouncement in any credible way. As far as coarse selflessness goes, the object, instrument, and agent all equally lack a substantially existent "self." And as far as subtle selflessness is concerned, those three are equally lacking in intrinsic existence. *Clear Words* states, "This also is not the case, since [you] have not correctly grasped the pronouncement's meaning."[987] The object, instrument, and agent must be understood to share the same status, wherein they are equally selfless and equally conventionally existent. This is the manner in which they are set out in [Candrakīrti's] *Entering the Middle Way*, and there are numerous scriptural passages and logical arguments that discredit any departure from this position. These are as outlined in that work, in sections such as "If one is under the impression that there may be no agent but there is an object [for the action] . . . ."[988] [Candrakīrti] also states in *Clear Words*, "This is an issue that I have already dealt with in *Entering the Middle Way*."[989]

Refuting the analogy that the [realist] uses to illustrate the situation and countering his objections [to this refutation]

The realist argues, "Even if we identify the two *lakṣaṇa*s with the agent, this still does not mean that there must be three types of comprehended objects, since [we do not accept that] these characteristics are objects of comprehension separate from the locus in which they are characterized. This does not mean, however, that our position can be accused of leaving no place for the agent, because even though a property is not [in reality] something other than the basis to which it is attributed, thought nevertheless [distinguishes] the property from the basis.[990] This is comparable, for instance, to the way that, in worldly parlance, one can speak of "the pestle's body" and "Rāhu's head" despite the fact that there is no actual property of a pestle apart from the "body"-basis, and no property or attribute Rāhu apart from the head.[991] [380] Nonetheless, as far as thought is concerned, there *is* something that is the basis in each case. Thus, with respect to *solidity*, the characteristic that defines earth, even though there is [in actuality] no earth aside from that solidity, it is still permissible to speak of solidity being the characteristic that defines earth." As *Clear Words* says:

> He [proposes] that it is similar, for instance, to [the relationship between the elements in] "the pestle's body" and "Rāhu's head." There is no property distinct from the body and the head, but still there is [a reality to the separateness of] the property and property-basis. Similarly, [he suggests], there is no characteristic that is separate from the earth and so forth that such [characteris-

> tics] define, but [we] still speak of "the characteristic that defines earth."[992]

The explanation that I give here principally follows the treatment of the subject in the *Essence of Fine Elucidation*.[993]

To this, the one who espouses the absence of intrinsic existence responds that the proposed analogy does not work. Within the analogue itself, one can draw distinctions between bases and properties, counting the head and the body as one, and the pestle and Rāhu as the other. But even if these same distinctions of basis and property were applied to the target—that is, [the relationship between] solidity and earth—there is no question or doubt that requires settling. This means that there is no correspondence between the analogue and the target. Such is the case because mention of the words "body" and "head" will turn someone's thoughts toward those things, bringing with it the assumption that the two are bases of properties. Thus it will trigger in the individual the wish to know to which type of being among the six kinds and so forth, the body and head belong. With the intention of dispelling the idea that the body and head in question belong to such other beings, the one responsible for introducing the terms will attach them to the properties "pestle" and "Rāhu," thereby effectively settling the question. However, there is no earth that does not [embody] "solidity," so there is no corresponding question to be addressed. Hence the comparison fails. *Clear Words* states:

> That is not how it is, as there is no parallel [between the two]. The terms "body" and "head" function like those of "mind" and "hand," in that they are [understood to be] dependent [for their identity] on another accompanying thing. So, quite aside from the attention that the terms "body" and "head" [themselves] generate, mention of them will also engender [in the person] an expectation regarding the other thing that accompanies [each of them], as he wonders "Whose body is this?" and "Whose head is this?" The other [party], keen to dispel the notion that they are associated with other [unrelated] things, will inform [the person of that fact], in line with the conventions of the world, by means of the names of the properties, "pestle" and "Rāhu," and [thereby] resolve that question. But here there is no solidity and so forth apart from those of earth and so forth [themselves].

> Hence distinguishing between them in terms of the property and property-basis is not rational.[994] [381]

"Accompanying thing"[995] here is a generic term that [can encompass the] likes of a property and its basis, a predicate and the predicated, or the object and instrument [of an action]. But here the context determines that it should be understood as referring to a distinguishing feature and the thing to which it belongs. The "other [party]" is the individual distinct from the one in whose mind the question arises—that is, the one who settles the question. "Keen to dispel the notion that they are associated with other [unrelated] things" refers to the wish to rid the [first person of] any notion that the [body and head here] are those associated with the continua of things other than the pestle and Rāhu. "The conventions of the world" indicates that this does not constitute an analysis on the level of the ultimate but that it is something that remains within the realm of conventionality. The remainder of the passage is straightforward.

The realist responds by claiming, "While solidity and the like may not, as in the case with a pestle and a body, be different from each other in a preclusive sense, in the current context of describing *lakṣaṇa* as that which does the action, there is a practical reason for portraying them in such a way, meaning that this portrayal cannot be faulted. The reason relates to the way that non-Buddhist, *tīrthika* philosophers define any entity, asserting that the characteristic and locus of the characteristic are necessarily distinct things. The pervasion holds, since these non-Buddhist philosophers would see no problem with referring to solidity and so forth as the distinguishing features of earth and so forth—effectively [portraying] them as property and basis. As *Clear Words* says, "He might propose that since the non-Buddhist philosophers believe that [the characteristic] is distinct from the thing it characterizes, there would be nothing wrong here in [our choosing to depict] it as a distinguishing feature in accordance with that [belief]."[996]

The one who propounds the absence of intrinsic existence judges this attempt to defend the position to have failed, saying that the entirely fictional realities that the non-Buddhist philosophers create around such things as the property and basis, and the action and agent breach the [rules] of logic, and that our system is not prepared to indulge them. Were we to do so, we would also be obligated to accept such things as an unchanging and self-arisen cognition, that the words of the Vedas are eternal and the sole source of authority, and that there are six types of valid cognition or the like.

Clear Words says, "This is not the case. It would be improper to welcome into our system the creations of the *tīrthikas*, which breach [the rules of] logic. This would [further] demand the acceptance of additional types of valid cognition and so forth."[997] "So forth" includes other features that it would be necessary to accept, in accordance with these non-Buddhist philosophers' notions regarding such things as the object of valid cognition and the distinction between the object and the agent. [382]

[Explaining the sense in which] analysis is inappropriate and how one must leave things in an unanalyzed [state]

What is more, [the realist logician] argues that there is a correspondence between the analogue and target in that [just as is with the former, with the latter also,] when one engages in an analysis into the reality behind the designation,[998] the distinguishing feature is [found] not to be separate from the thing of which it is [said to be] a feature. But this is not tenable. That the body and the head are the bases or supports for the features, and that the pestle and Rāhu are the [respective] features or [properties] supported by them, is established convention. And things can only be established in such terms if they are not subjected to [the sort of] analysis or examination that delves into the reality behind the designation. Therefore his contention that the two have no conventional existence, and that they [can] be subjected to a search for some reality behind the designations, is not credible. *Clear Words* states:

> Moreover the pestle is dependent and is a feature of the body on which it relies, inasmuch as this is part of worldly convention, something that is not subjected to analysis. And Rāhu [also] is dependent on the head that is its basis. These exist as designations in the manner of things such as the person. Thus the analogy he proposes is not correct.[999]

Here [with regard to these analogies], if one delves into the [reality of such] conventional designations and tries to find some [real] foundation upon which they rest, one will fail to locate it. This is because it is Rāhu's head to which the name Rāhu is attached, and a search for the objects [respectively] designated "pestle" and "pestle head" will fail to find that they have any separate [reality].

The proponent of intrinsic existence may continue to deny that there is a problem with the analogy. He may argue that the [pestle and the head] appear discrete *as long as* they are not subjected to analysis beyond the designations, and that it is *only* when they are subjected to such an analysis that they are [discovered] not to be discrete. In this sense, he may claim, his analogy still works. He may say that the situation is comparable with that of determining the reality of a snake: when there is a coiled snake, a search for the designated entity will reveal [an actual] snake, whereas if there is only a coiled striped rope, a search will discover no hint of a snake. *Clear Words* says, "He may claim that because observing just that [informs us] that there is no entity separate from the body and head [in these cases], the analogy does work . . . ."[1000] This is the way that the Svātantrika and those in the schools below him posit phenomena. As the *Essence of Fine Elucidation* states, "Contained within this argument is the way that those aforesaid others posit phenomena to exist."[1001] Another question related to this will be explored below.

The position of the proponent of intrinsic existence is not sustainable, because [firstly] existence is [itself] a convention, and [secondly,] there can be no analysis for the reality behind the designation within the conventional [realm]. [383] That is the case, because existence is something that can be posited [only as long as one confines oneself to] the realm of worldly convention. If one subjects a convention to analysis, searching for a reality behind the designation, that [existence] can no longer be posited. Our own experience tells us that conventionalities must simply be left unanalyzed. As *Clear Words* states, "That is not the way it is, because worldly conventions are not subjected to such analysis, and because it is [only] without analysis that the things of the world exist."[1002]

What is more, it is not only [his] analogies that fail to stand up to a search for the reality behind the designation. The same can be said for the person and Devadatta. If one examines the way that Devadatta—the entity to which we assign the conventions "Devadatta's form" and "Devadatta's mind"—exists, and his [relation to that] form and mind, [one will discover that] neither his form nor his mind can be identified as Devadatta, but nor can Devadatta be found to exist outside them. That is the case, because if one searches for some reality behind the designation "Devadatta," there is none, and his unfindability within the context of such a search encapsulates what it means for him not to be existent from his own side, which is not to say that he does not exist. The first point [that there is no reality behind the designation] is established, because *Clear Words* says, "That is just how it is with the self, which upon investigation is definitely not something separate from form and so forth."[1003] Ārya [Nāgārjuna] also declares:

> The person is not earth and is not water,
> is not fire, not wind, and not space,
> is not consciousness, and is not all of them,
> and what person, other than those, is there?[1004]

The second point is also established to be the case, because the two [things cited in the] analogies exist as conventions in a manner that parallels the way that [Devadatta] exists in a deceptive [conventional] sense, as something [imputed] upon a set of aggregates. *Clear Words* states, "However, the analogy [still] does not work, because Rāhu and the pestle do exist, [albeit] in the deceptive fashion of the world, as does [the person], in dependence upon the aggregates."[1005]

How to posit phenomena conventionally

The way that things such as earth and solidity, which are classified as *characterized* and *characterizer*, should be posited is without analyzing [the reality behind] the designations. This is because if [as the realist proposed] they were to be subjected to an analysis into the reality behind the designations, they would not be found to [have any existence] separate from each other. But in spite of this unfindability, they exist in the deceptive, unanalyzed sense. The first point is established, because in terms of the aforesaid analysis, [if such separate existence were] found, it would be established that they existed from their own side, which would amount to them being truly existent. [384] As *Clear Words* says, "Likewise, upon examination, apart from solidity and so forth, there is no locus of characterization for earth and so forth. [And] there is also no characteristic apart from the locus of characterization."[1006]

The second point [that, despite their unfindability, they exist] is also established, because the only way that the existence of any phenomenon can be posited is in the deceptive, conventional sense. Thus the father Nāgārjuna and his [spiritual] son [Āryadeva] state that it is only in the relative terms of their mutual dependence that the existence of things can be posited. Here "only" rules out [the possibility that] they are entities [findable upon] examination. *Clear Words* says, "Despite that, they exist in the deceptive, conventional sense, and hence the masters have declared that it is only in their dependence on each other that things are established."[1007]

Why it is necessary to accept this as the only way that things can be posited conventionally

You, the realist and the Svātantrika, are obliged to accept that deceptive things are there [only] if we refrain from analyzing them in [the manner of] searching for the reality behind the designation. This is because not accepting that [would be tantamount to saying that the criterion] for a thing existing conventionally is that such a search must [result in that reality] being found, meaning that something deceptive would be established according to the standards [set for] an analysis into the ultimate. The pervasion holds, because in that situation, the subject analyzed would necessarily [have been revealed] to be suchness or something established in an ultimate sense, and *not* something that is established in a deceptive sense or is a deceptive object, whereas [in fact] logical analysis into the ultimate is *unable* to find not only something such as the pestle, but any phenomena at all—be they aggregates, elements, or sources—even in a conventional sense. The first point [that such an analysis should reveal suchness] is established, because *Clear Words* states, "You must certainly accept that it is just this way. If it were not so, would it not mean that deceptive [things] are correct? And if that were so, they could only be ultimate, not deceptive."[1008] The second point is established, because there is no true existence even in the conventional sense. As *Clear Words* says:

> If required to be correct according to such analysis, it is not just the likes of the pestle that become impossible. Even forms, feelings, and so forth do not exist according to such a [standard of] correctness, as will be outlined. And if one [also] had to concede that, like the pestle, these [form and feelings] did not exist in the deceptive sense, then since they did not, it would mean that they could not exist [at all].[1009]

Vasubandhu explains that being [logically] "correct," "permissible," and "acceptable"[1010] share similar meanings, and this can also be taken to apply here.[1011] What needs to be appreciated is that conventional and ultimate varieties of analyses apply separate standards. [385] The evidence supporting this is abundant, as I would now like to explain.

For the Svātantrika and those in the schools below him, any phenomenon that can be posited [should be findable, if one] looks into the reality behind the designation. But that alone would not mean that [a thing] is truly established. It must also, [for them,] be a *shared subject*, in that it is something that appears to both parties [in the discourse] to be something that has specific characteristics, a fact that they agree is confirmed by valid perception. On this level, they are all in accord, and due to this, there is also agreement among them regarding what characteristics define things like valid cognition and so forth. In this [Prāsaṅgika] system, however, things being that way would mean that they were truly established. And so far as the [process of] proving that things lack true existence goes, there can be no shared subject [for both parties]. [Accordingly, the Prāsaṅgika's] account of how something acts as a valid cognition with regard to that phenomenon and his explanation of perception, inference, and so forth also diverges [from those of the other schools]. Details of these will follow.

One should learn about the way things are posited to exist conventionally from what *Entering the Middle Way* has to say on the matter. [It informs us that] "This is established in dependence on the aggregates."[1012] It also says:

> Pots, woven materials, lattice fences, armies, forests, garlands, trees,
> households, chariot parts, boarding houses, and so forth—
> all such things likewise produced are explainable in this manner; it is realizable . . .
>
> Subjected to the "chariot" analysis, they are [found] not to exist in any of the seven ways.
> They exist in another manner, according to [the standards] agreed in the world.[1013]

Whichever form of examination is undertaken, be it [that which probes into] singularity and difference, or that of the sevenfold analysis, it [will reveal that what the other schools assert has] no reality in convention. Hence *Clear Words* says, "The way that things can [only be] posited in dependence [on others] has been covered extensively in *Entering the Middle Way*. So it should be consulted thoroughly."[1014]

Differentiating between skill and ignorance with regard to positing the two forms of "truth"

The Svātantrika may argue, "This form of ultimate analysis, which seeks to determine whether the locus characterized is distinct from the two types of characteristics, is not something [we] need [to get into], because I, a Svātantrika, deny true establishment for any phenomenon, including those involved in the process of characterization, such as valid cognition and its object of comprehension." But while he certainly rejects true existence, he still accepts the wisdom of the view widely held in the world, that the definitive bifurcation of valid cognition corresponds with the bipartition of the objects it comprehends. [386] *Clear Words* states:

> [He argues,] "What need is there for this form of detailed analysis? We do not claim that all of the conventions [relating to] valid cognition and [its] objects of comprehension are true. However, we accept this [scheme], as one that is established in the world."[1015]

The alternative way of explaining this [passage] is that it [reflects, more generally,] the thought of numerous Svātantrika treatises. *Distinction between the Two Truths*, [for instance,] says:

> Because [one accepts] the identity of things as they appear,
> one [should] not subject them to investigation.
> Through investigation, that [identity] will be altered,
> and [those things] will be undermined.[1016]

The Prāsaṅgika and the Svātantrika agree that objects are unfindable when they are subjected to analysis into the ultimate. But where they diverge is on what constitutes such an analysis—a difference that derives from their contrasting understandings of what is to be negated.

The Prāsaṅgika responds to [the Svātantrika's argument] by stating, "Whatever [might be said regarding] the logician's valid cognition and purpose, when it comes [simply] to positing things in terms of deceptive [truth], we agree with you in questioning the need to subject their manner of existence to rigorous investigation. What finds a deceptive thing is an erroneous cognition, and [such a thing] exists in as much as it exists for that cognition. With regard to their *purpose*, these deceptive [things] may not [represent] reality, but to discard them would be to deprive oneself of the opportunity of completing the two collections. *Clear Words* makes the first of these points when it says, "We also question why it is necessary to subject the conventions of the world to such rigorous scrutiny. They are found only in as much as their identities exist for a deceptive, erroneous [cognition]."[1017] There is a further question regarding this, but I will address it below.

Clear Words makes the second point in the passage "[This is] the cause [producing] the basic virtue that leads those who strive for liberation to it."[1018] The *Fundamental Treatise on the Middle Way* also states, "Without reliance on convention, there is no way to realize the sacred [ultimate]."[1019]

The [one responsible for] the erroneous appearance is deceptive ignorance, together with the imprints [it leaves]. These have yet to be curbed and cannot be, until one realizes suchness in the manner of never again arising from [meditative equipoise on] it. Once achieved, this will occasion an unimaginable transformation in one's state. *Clear Words* says, "This is the way it will remain until one realizes suchness."[1020] [387] With regard to this, certain rational individuals have presented [the following analysis]:

> It has been argued that in terms of the Prāsaṅgika's understanding of deceptive [truth], the things that are "found" by mistaken and unmistaken cognitions respectively must preclude one another, because there must be a difference between what is erroneous and not erroneous. But if one were to accept [this reasoning], it would follow that the thing found by the *inferential awareness [of the final state]*[1021] could not be the ultimate, since that [cognition] is a mistaken one. Similarly, something that was deceptively [i.e., conventionally] true could not be found by the omniscient mind, because such a thing is found by and is exclusively the object of a mistaken or erroneous cognition. The reason is established, because as already noted, *Clear Words* says, "They are found only in as much as their identities exist for a deceptive, erroneous [cognition]." The pervasion also holds, because "only" here excludes [them being] objects found by unmistaken cognition.

This [analysis is] outlined in the *Essence of Fine Elucidation*, "It may be proposed that [being] a thing found by a mistaken cognition and [being] a nonerroneous object of knowledge preclude each other . . . because the word *only* excludes its being found by an unmistaken cognition."[1022]

The first of the faults [identified by these individuals] does not apply [to the position], for in spite of the fact that being a thing found by a mistaken cognition and being an ultimate truth preclude each other, it does not mean that something found by the inferential awareness [of the final state]—in the sense of being the object that it apprehends—is precluded from being an ultimate truth. That is the case because while such an inferential cognition is a mistaken one, the object found by it—that is, the one it apprehends—does not count as a "thing found by mistaken cognition." For even though the cognition in question is a mistaken one, error in no way affects what it apprehends [of its object]. This is because that object exists in exactly the manner that the cognition apprehends it to, and deceptive appearance does not impact on what it apprehends in any way. The latter is the case, because the [only] object found by such an [inferential cognition]—the one that it apprehends—is necessarily an ultimate truth. As the *Essence of Fine Elucidation* puts it, "The first fault does not apply. The inferential awareness [of the final state] is mistaken with regard to its appearing object, but there is no contradiction in saying that the thing it finds is not the object found by mistaken cognition."[1023]

Someone might object to this, remarking that the way in which the inferential awareness in question conceives its object is [also] mistaken, because it is a cognition that is mistaken with regard to its conceptual object. *Thousand Measures* deals with this by rejecting the pervasion, and points out that the inferential cognition realizing sound to be impermanent is mistaken with regard to its conceived object.[1024] The [same work, which has the alternative title] *Providing the Fortunate with Sight*, says, "The Svātantrika and [those in other Buddhist] schools below him assert that inferential valid cognition is mistaken with regard to its appearing object but not its conceived object. [388] But here [in this system], such a position cannot be accepted."[1025]

Also, in the *Greater Stages of the Path* we find:

> So, even though the conceptual cognitions that apprehend such things as the aggregates being impermanent are mistaken with regard to their appearing object, valid cognition does nothing to undermine what they apprehend. Those [cognitions] can therefore be described as "nonerroneous," or "unmistaken." [Conversely,] sense consciousnesses are [not only] mistaken with regard to their appearing object, but there is also no portion of any of them that is not mistaken, and they cannot [therefore] be described as "unmistaken."[1026]

What this conveys is that valid sense consciousnesses [realizing form and so on] and inferential cognitions, such as those realizing impermanence, are similar in that they are both nondeceptive with respect to the main thing that they apprehend—that is, they are nondeceptive with respect to their *principal object*. There is, nevertheless, a distinction between them regarding whether they are mistaken in terms of their manner of apprehension; something determined by whether or not a [source of] error taints the apprehension of their principal object. This is because, despite the fact that they are similarly mistaken with respect to their appearing object, inferential cognition has an apprehended object that is not exactly equivalent to its appearing object, and this object is what it apprehends just as it actually is. Hence it is [said to be] unmistaken with respect to its apprehended object. Sense consciousness, on the other hand, has no apprehended object beyond the one that appears to it. And it does not grasp [that object] just as it actually is. This means that there is no [part] of its apprehended object with regard to which it is not mistaken, and hence [sense consciousness] cannot be described as "unmistaken in terms of its principal object." The question, however, that needs to be looked into here is whether the remarks of the father and [spiritual] son are in agreement.[1027]

The Prāsaṅgika declares, "In refuting you, the realist and the Svātantrika, [whose account] is at odds with the way that deceptive phenomena are posited, I am not wrecking conventionality. That is because, while you are not skilled in how to account for the two levels of truth, I, a Prāsaṅgika, have mastered it. Through your lack of skill, you subject certain things—that are, in the deceptive sense, phenomena, such as characterizer and characterized and the like—to an investigation into their [final] state, and having failed to find them, conclude that they do not exist." As *Clear Words* says, "As you are not skilled with regard to what is true ultimately and conventionally, you impose on certain [things] a standard, [then conclude that they] are not correct [according to it], and it is you who thereby wreck them, not [I]."[1028]

Conversely, "I, [Candrakīrti], who have gained mastery in these matters, can account for conventional phenomena within not subjecting them to analysis, and like a knowledgeable elder, I rely on the conventions of the world. [It is not these conventions] but just you, someone who seeks to destroy those such as 'pestle,' thereby forsaking a portion of conventionality, that I thwart." [389] As *Clear Words* says:

> As I have mastered how to account for deceptive truth, I can ally myself with the world, and with reasoning other than that which

> you employ to destroy a portion of convention, thwart you. And in the manner of an elder [dealing] with one who forsakes worldly tradition, it is you that I thwart, not deceptive [truth].[1029]

Thus, whether considered from the conventional or ultimate perspective, [the logician's] notion—that it is through an analysis into a reality behind the designation that the two forms of valid cognition are to be posited—is still subject to the same fault. This is because if it is from the conventional perspective, the earlier problem remains, since if there is a characteristic, there must also be something that it characterizes, whereas if it is from the ultimate perspective, there are no such things as characteristics, the characterized, or valid cognition. This is the point conveyed in *Clear Words*: "Therefore, if... how could there possibly be two valid cognitions?"[1030]

Countering their attempts to rebut our refutation of the definitive bifurcation of valid cognition, which relies on them giving a special gloss to the term *lakṣaṇa*

The logician and the Svātantrika may claim that there is a way for them to avoid these criticisms. This is by them denying that a "special gloss" for *lakṣaṇa*—whether it be in terms of specific and general characteristics or in the general sense [encompassing both]—need presuppose a connection between the object and agent of the action as set out [by the Prāsaṅgika] during the earlier discussion. *Clear Words* says, "Should he deny that the 'special gloss' presupposes a connection between the object and agent of the action . . . ."[1031]

The Prāsaṅgika responds, "Maintaining the position you now propose will be extremely problematic for you. This is because, by invoking an example such as the process of characterization, you are saying that the model for the linguistic analysis of action can be applied to the threefold distinction among the characteristic, the thing characterized, and the locus of characterization. What is more, while an action like Devadatta's chopping wood with an axe is steeped in the relations between the components of that model for linguistic analysis, and though you are [content] to use the designations for those, what you [now] try to do is deny that they reflect any reality. How dismal this is! It turns out that in your approach to conventional language, you the logician and the Svātantrika are guided not by any form of logical reasoning but simply by arbitrary choice." *Clear Words* states, "This is extraordinary! You use only the language that embraces the connection between object and agent, in spite [of the fact that you] do not accept the reality of object, agent, and so forth that the words [convey]. Oh, this is incredible! [390] You are guided simply by whimsy."[1032]

Conclusion

You dismiss the conventions of scripturally based valid cognition and comprehension through analogy as further forms of valid cognition on the grounds that they do not apprehend objects other than the two that you advocate [for perception and inference]—namely, those with specific or general characteristics. But this is a position that you cannot sustain, since there is no reason to support your assertion that objects of comprehension are divided into those with specific and general characteristics in the way that you contend. *Clear Words* says, "As it is not the case that such a dichotomous division of objects of comprehension exists, the [fact that] the scriptural [valid cognitions] and so forth do not have things with specific and general characteristics as their objects cannot be grounds for [rejecting] them as further means of valid cognition."[1033]

4. Specific Refutation of Others' Notions about Perception

Specific refutation of their version of perception (pratyakṣa)

1. [Explaining how] the characteristic of perception proposed by them fails to encompass [all that it should]
2. Their account not being tenable in terms of either of the two types of truth
3. Refutation of their derivation for the term *pratyakṣa*
4. [Rejecting] "free from conception" as a characteristic that defines perception

[Explaining how] the characteristic of perception proposed by them fails to encompass [all that it should]

1. Setting out the actual fault [in their account]
2. Countering the attempted rebuttal of our criticism

Setting out the actual fault that the characteristic of perception proposed by them does not encompass [all that it should][1034]

You [the logician] have also proposed that the characteristic defining perception (*pratyakṣa*) is that its [object], upon examination, is [found to be] one that is discerned by valid perception, such as in the case of the pot, examination [of which reveals that it is] composed of the eight [constituent] substances, and about which it is [permissible] to say, "The pot is *pratyakṣa* [i.e., it is perceivable]." But the characteristic [of perceivability] fails to encompass [what it is supposed to, in the manner you propose]. How so? Because in regard to the conventional application of the term [*pratyakṣa*], (1) if one were to subject the pot to examination, as will be explained below, [what this would reveal] is that it is *not* perceivable, in that not all of [its constituent substances] can be perceived, whereas (2) when, in the unexamined, uncritical manner of the world, a person says about something, "It is *pratyakṣa*," this does *not* represent a figurative description of the object [but rather, a literally correct one]. *Clear Words* says, "Also, because it does not embrace the ordinary language of the world, such as when it is said, 'The pot is *pratyakṣa*' and . . . the characteristic is not one that encompasses."[1035] [391]

They may try to deny that there is any fault [that pot and the like are not fully perceived], citing the fact that the perception of an ārya distinguishes [all] eight [constituent] substances, those of visual form, smell, and so forth. But this [argument] is not admissible, because they have accepted that the conventions in terms of which diverse deceptive objects are established are those of worldly beings not those of āryas. *Clear Words* states, "Because you have accepted the conventions are not those of āryas, the characteristic does not encompass [what it should]. Hence this is not tenable."[1036]

Countering the attempted rebuttal of our criticism

1. Their attempt to escape the criticism
2. Our rejection of that

Their attempt to escape the criticism

He says, "The criticism regarding the statement 'The pot is *pratyakṣa*' is not warranted.[1037] Although the pot—the 'appropriator'—may not itself be *pratyakṣa* [in the sense of something that is directly perceivable], the [constituent elements] appropriated [within it], such as the color blue, are [perceivable] on account of them being things discerned by valid sense perception. Thus, by way of the [constituents] that it appropriates, the pot is [figuratively] designated *pratyakṣa* [i.e., "perceivable"]. This is comparable to the situation with the Buddha's appearance in the world. Although this event is actually the *cause* of happiness, the event itself is described as a happy one, as when it is said, 'The Buddha's appearance in the world is a happy [occurrence].' In a similar way, it is the pot, the effect, to which the description *pratyakṣa* is assigned, whereas what is actually *perceivable* is the blue and so forth that are its causes." *Clear Words* says:

> He may claim that because the blue and so forth—those [constituents] that are "appropriated" in the case of the pot—are discerned by valid perception, the [pot] is [said to be] *pratyakṣa*. Thus it is just as [a description that relates to] an effect may be

> given to the cause, such as when it is said that "The appearance of a Buddha is a happy [event]." In a similar fashion, it is the causes, such as blue, that are perceivable, but the pot itself that is referred to as *pratyakṣa*, a case of the effect [being described in terms] of the cause.[1038]

Our rejection of that

1. Rejecting the rebuttal by showing that the analogy does not work
2. Rejecting the rebuttal by pointing out its absurd consequence
3. Conclusion

Rejecting the rebuttal by showing that the analogy does not work

There is no [parallel within the analogy that justifies] referring to the pot [figuratively] as *pratyakṣa* [i.e., perceivable]. The Buddha's appearance in the world is seen to be distinct from the [associated] happiness, and [this appearance] is something with a composite identity, within the nature of which are the characteristics of being transitory and dissatisfactory. And in addition, much hardship is involved [in its achievement], meaning that it can hardly be happy. Hence what the description refers to is the happiness that other migrating beings will gain from that appearance [not that of the appearance itself]. In the case of the pot, conversely, there is no perceivable entity apart from the eight substances [that constitute it]. As *Clear Words* states: [392]

> The designation of the object cannot tenably be [explained] in such a fashion. The appearance [of the Buddha] is something that the world sees as distinct from the happiness. Moreover, because that [appearance's] nature has the characteristic of being a composite, and because it is also the result of a multitude of hardships, it is definitely not happiness. When that [appearance in the world] is said to be "happy," that [happiness] is something extraneous to it, meaning that it would be reasonable to use [the description for] the object [i.e., the appearance] in a figurative sense. But here, in terms of the statement "Pot is *pratyakṣa*," there is no imperceptible [i.e., non-*pratyakṣa*] thing separate from that referred to as "pot," by virtue of which that [pot could] gain the figurative designation "perceivable" [i.e., *pratyakṣa*].[1039]

He may then suggest that the very fact that there is no pot separate from the features of blue and so forth justifies its being [figuratively] designated "perceivable." *Clear Words* says, "It might be proposed that because there is no pot distinct from the blue and so forth, the [pot] is figuratively *pratyakṣa*."[1040] But [based on that logic,] the designation would have to be [judged] as an entirely inappropriate one, since there is no basis for the designation "pot." It would be comparable to the way that it is improper to ascribe sharpness to the horn on the head of a donkey. *Clear Words* says, "From that point of view, the figurative designation would be even more inappropriate, because there would be nothing [acting as] the basis for the designation. There can be no figurative ascription of sharpness to the horn of a donkey."[1041]

Rejecting the rebuttal by pointing out its absurd consequence

The Prāsaṅgika furthermore argues, "It would also follow that blue and so forth are themselves *pratyakṣa* (perceivable) only in a figurative sense, because there is no blue and so forth aside from the [pot's constituent] earth element and so on. The pervasion [of this consequence] holds, because your reason for classifying pot as a figurative *pratyakṣa* was the fact that there is no pot aside from its eight [constituent] substances. You have already agreed to this. But you cannot accept the [argument's conclusion], as it would force you into accepting others that would further undermine your position, such as that all established bases must be figurative *pratyakṣa* and that blue and so forth would *not* be figurative *pratyakṣa*—conclusions that blatantly contradict each other." *Clear Words* says:

> Furthermore, he may propose that because a pot, an [indispensable] part of worldly convention, is not distinct from the blue and so forth [that constitute it, pot] is understood to be a figurative "perceivable" [i.e., *pratyakṣa*]. But according to that, since blue and so forth are also not separate from earth and so on, blue and so forth must also be understood to be figurative "perceivables."[1042] [393]

The logic employed when investigating whether something is *pratyakṣa* in an actual or figurative sense should be exactly the same, whether the subject is blue or the pot. This is the intention of the ārya father and spiritual son [Nāgārjuna and Āryadeva]. In *Four Hundred Stanzas* it states:

Just as there is no pot
aside from the [constituent] form and so forth,
similarly, there is no form
aside from the [constituent] wind [element].[1043]

Conclusion

Their view that [perceivability] is a defining characteristic of *pratyakṣa*, in the sense that upon examination [the object in question will be revealed] to be a thing that is discerned by valid perception is untenable, because [on the one hand] it fails to include the unexamined linguistic conventions [relied on] in the world, such as when someone says, "The pot is *pratyakṣa* [i.e., obvious] to me," and [on the other,] if [that characteristic] must be [arrived at] through examination, the criticism that has already been made remains. *Clear Words* says, "Thus, because such conventional forms of expression are not encompassed by that characteristic, it does not cover [all that it should]."[1044]

Their account not being tenable in terms of either of the two types of truth

The Prāsaṅgika asks the proponent of intrinsic existence whether his contention that pot [itself] is *not pratyakṣa* (perceivable), whereas its color blue and so forth *are*, is [to be understood] from the ultimate or conventional standpoint. If it were the first, [the Prāsaṅgika says,] It would follow that just as examination of [an entity such as a] pot or a pillar cannot be asserted to [reveal] something perceivable, separate from its eight [constituent] substances, then neither can it be asserted that blue and so forth are perceivable, since (1) if blue and so forth are themselves subjected to examination, [they are revealed] not to be separate from their four constituent elements, and (2) those [four] are not objects of sight and so forth. That follows, because in seeing the pot's visual form,[1045] one does not behold the entire pot. *Clear Words* says, "From the perspective of the insight awareness of suchness, the pot and so forth and blue and so forth are not held to be *pratyakṣa* [perceivable]."[1046] And [Āryadeva] states, "When one sees [its] form, one does not see all of the pot."[1047] In [Candrakīrti's] *Commentary to Four Hundred Stanzas*, his explanation of these lines is contained in the passage "Analyzing this ... [one who] investigates things and is expert with regard to their nature [knows that] in seeing just a facet of one of them, it is not possible to see the whole, and that to make claims such as that 'The pot is perceptible' is inappropriate."[1048] [394] The pervasion holds, because this is not simply the case for visual forms but for every sound, smell, taste, and tactility, which when similarly subjected to individual examination cannot be found. *Four Hundred Stanzas* says:

> By means of this analysis,
> fragrant aromas, sweet tastes, and soft [surfaces],
> all of these, are to be negated
> by one with superior intellect.[1049]

And in his commentary, [Candrakīrti] explains:

> Each of those [things] is also an appropriator [gathering together] the eight substances. Hence, [while] each object is apprehended by whichever of the respective six senses corresponds to its nature, none of them is apprehended in every one of its aspects. What individual who understood suchness would claim, therefore, that the likes of nutmeg flowers, molasses, or blossom of the cotton tree are perceivable [*pratyakṣa*] to him?[1050]

[Secondly, if the matter is] from the conventional standpoint, it would be illogical to claim that analysis leads one to differentiate between the two [the pot and its constituents], because just as the blue color [of the pot] is counted as *pratyakṣa* [perceivable] in deceptive, conventional terms, on the grounds that it is judged to be so by the world, the pot must also, correspondingly, be counted as *pratyakṣa*. This follows, because it is only when subjected to analysis that the [pot] is revealed not to be *pratyakṣa*, whereas conventionally, a trouble-free sense cognition that apprehends its color is regarded as the valid one that perceives [pot]. *Clear Words* says, "In terms of the conventional judgments of the world, one must accept that pot and so forth are perceivable [*pratyakṣa*]."[1051] And [Candrakīrti's] *Commentary to Four Hundred Stanzas* states, "As [the world does not] subject a thing's nature to dissection, one should accept whatever works in the world. And treating its notions as the standard, one can definitely say, 'The pot is *pratyakṣa* [perceivable, i.e., obvious] to me.'"[1052] This totally demolishes the view of Drapa Sherab Rinchen [i.e., Taktsang Lotsāwa] that in the deceptive domain of conventionality, it is not possible for a cognition to be a valid one.[1053]

[Refutation of the logician's] derivation of the term pratyakṣa

1. The Prāsaṅgika's own understanding of the term's derivation
2. Refutation of how earlier commentators and Pramāṇa logicians have accounted for the derivation

The Prāsaṅgika's own understanding of the term's derivation

Not only does [the Prāsaṅgika] regard the aforesaid explanations of what *pratyakṣa* means as untenable, he also has a different explanation of the term's derivation. [395] [For him,] the term *pratyakṣa* is used in reference to the likes of pot and blue in the sense of its meaning "[that toward which] the senses are directed." That [gloss is supported] by the fact that the derivation of *pratyakṣa* is [essentially] the same as that of *aparokṣa* [i.e., nonhidden], because *manifest* (*abhimukī*), *perceivable* (*pratyakṣa*), and *sensory object* are all [interchangeable] synonyms, whereas [conversely] *hidden*, *imperceptible*, and *nonsensory* are also synonymous. As [Amarasiṃha's catalogue of] *Synonyms* states:

> *Perceivable* and *sensory object*,
> *hidden* and *imperceptible*[1054]

This [also] reflects the view that is broadly accepted in the world. *Clear Words* says, "Furthermore, with regard to [the derivation of] the term, because *pratyakṣa* conveys 'a thing that is nonhidden,' something is *pratyakṣa* [perceivable] in that it is 'that toward which the senses are directed.'"[1055] This is the case, because in stating that "*pratyakṣa* conveys 'a thing that is nonhidden,'" [Candrakīrti] affirms that the two have the same derivation.

Separating the elements comprising the [compound] term *pratyakṣa* yields *prati* and *akṣa*. Generally speaking, *prati* can [act as] a distributive or an emphatic, or it can indicate "repetition" or [something that is] "initial," whereas *akṣa* relates to the senses. Consequently, no tenet school can explain the derivation for "manifest" and "hidden" [phenomena] without making reference to the senses. The derivation for the term *pratyakṣa* [relating to "manifest"] is as has been explained. [Whereas regarding "hidden,"] separating the elements comprising *aintriyakam*,[1056] the term for "*object* of the senses," gives *intri*[1057] for "senses," and *iyaka*, which can be explained as referring to their object. And if one separates the elements in the term for "hidden," *pratyadhyakṣa*, *prati* is as explained above, whereas *adhyakṣa* is separated into *ati-akṣa*, conveying the notion of something that is totally beyond [the sphere of] the senses [i.e., extrasensory]. Hence it essentially corresponds with the [other] term for "hidden" [*parokṣa*]. And while a very literal reading of *atīntriyam*[1058]—a term equivalent to *non-pratyakṣa*—yields only *ati-intriyam*, which [literally] translates as "emphatically a sense object," if one translates what the term actually conveys, it yields "directed to the dimension completely beyond the object of the senses." Thus the premier logician Dharmottara, in his [commentary on the *Ascertainment of Pramāṇa* known as] *The "Shorter" Correct*, states, "*Prati* is an abbreviation [indicating that 'each] depends on its own [respective one]' and refers to that which depends on a sense—that is, 'perception,'"[1059] and "[within this,] 'dependence on the sense powers' is the rationale for the derivation."[1060]

There are many other such statements [presenting] the grounds for [rooting] explanation of "hidden" and "manifest" in terms of dependency on the senses. One should therefore refrain from repeating the sloppy descriptions about "hidden" and "manifest" of those who have failed to grasp those grounds. [396]

Thus [for the Prāsaṅgika,] the nonhidden—those things such as pot and blue, which are the overt objects of sense perception—are *pratyakṣa*, in that they are the objects toward which the senses are directed. *Clear Words* says, "In being known as 'that toward which the senses are directed,' nonhidden things, such as pot and blue, are established to be *pratyakṣa*."[1061] [Also,] it is the thought of [Candrakīrti] that if one does not understand *pratyakṣa* [in the sense of manifest] and hidden in terms of the object, but interprets *pratyakṣa* [instead] in terms of the cognition that depends on the senses, it would follow that every sense cognition is a perception and that mental perception is an impossibility.

Once [one treats] the object and the subject that directly perceives it as [existing in a state of] mutual dependence, it is the object [that is understood to be] the actual *pratyakṣa*, whereas the subject is *pratyakṣa* in only a nominative sense.[1062] This is because [firstly,] from such a perspective, it is the object that is *manifest* [*pratyakṣa*] to the subject. [Secondly,] the subject is [obviously] not *manifest* [*pratyakṣa*] to the [object]; rather it is designated *pratyakṣa* ["perception"] by virtue of the fact that it comprehends a manifest [perceivable] object. Also [thirdly, Candrakīrti stresses,] "In the context of worldly conventions, neither of us can afford to reject the world's way of seeing things. Hence we must posit actual and nominative *pratyakṣa* in these terms." The first of these points is established, as the *Commentary to Four Hundred Stanzas* states, "According to that, while it is not correct to understand consciousness as *pratyakṣa*, it is correct for the object. With regard to such things as the waxing moon, it is from the sense object that there is a perception arising simultaneously from the continua of many."[1063]

The second point is established, because as *Clear Words* says, "The cognition that discerns the [object] is referred to as *pratyakṣa* due to having a *pratyakṣa* [object] as its cause—similar to the manner that a hay fire and a straw fire [gain their names]."[1064] The pervasion holds, because just like a fire is designated "hay fire" or "straw fire" with reference to its cause, a cognition is referred to as "perception" [*pratyakṣa*] on the basis of its object being a manifest one [*pratyakṣa*].

The third point is established, because the *Commentary to Four Hundred Stanzas* says:

> [Regarding] the meaning of some worldly [convention], it would also not be right to reject what the world sees in favor of some other understanding. Thus, according to the world, it is only to objects that [the name] *pratyakṣa* applies in the actual sense, whereas for cognition it is a [figurative] designation.[1065] [397]

"*Pratyakṣa* applies in the actual sense" means that the term *pratyakṣa* properly denotes the object.

Therefore, while the Svātantrika and those in the schools below him hold that the real *pratyakṣa* is the cognition, whereas for its object the designation is only a figurative one, this [position] is not tenable, because it accords neither with the language conventions of the world nor with the unique insight of āryas. The *Commentary to Four Hundred Stanzas* states, "According to others, the actual [denotation of] the term *pratyakṣa* is a cognition, and with regard to the object, it is a figurative [designation]. But this is not the worldly [understanding], because there is absolutely no such convention in the world."[1066] Some misinterpret such [statements, taking them to mean] that only objects such as form are *pratyakṣa*, whereas subjects such as visual [cognition], the person, and so forth are not. But this is incorrect, because in the understanding of the world, they are all equally *pratyakṣa*.

The *Commentary to Four Hundred Stanzas* also says, "In the understanding of the world, pot is *pratyakṣa*, as are the eye and so forth. And as the appropriator of those is also *pratyakṣa*, there is no fault [in our position]."[1067]

The pervasion holds, because the "appropriator of those" refers to the one who appropriates the visual [cognition] and so forth—namely, the person—since there is both a connection[1068] between the *appropriated* and the *appropriator* and a convention of referring to them in these terms. And even though the passage does not overtly mention "cognition," other sections support the view that what ["eye and so forth"] refer to is perception and the perceivable—that is, *pratyakṣa*. It should be noted, however, that this does not clash [with the general position]; the sense powers are [counted as] hidden, even if their five base supports are perceivable.

Refutation of how earlier commentators and Pramāṇa logicians have accounted for the derivation

1. Outlining their position
2. Refutation of that

Outlining the position of the earlier commentators and Pramāṇa logicians on the derivation of pratyakṣa

Some earlier [proponents of the] Svātantrika and Pramāṇa [systems] claimed that the denotation *prati-akṣa* or "perception" derives from the fact that it refers to (1) [a set of] cognitions, (2) each of which have their own respective sense powers. [398] Thus they explain it in terms of a particular [kind of perception], and engagement with a sense power. The thinking behind this explanation is that the [sense perception] apprehends [its object] through engagement with a sense power. This is evidently a misinterpretation of statements such as that by Dignāga, who said, "Their names are determined by the sense powers."[1069] *Clear Words* says, "Since it is stated that '[These] engage with their respective sense powers,' they explain the etymology of *pratyakṣa* in terms of a particular [i.e., a sense perception]."[1070]

Refutation of that explanation

1. How the [derivation] should be explained in terms of the object
2. [Describing how the proposed] repetition is not sufficiently inclusive

How the derivation of pratyakṣa should be explained in terms of the object

1. Refutation of the [position that the derivation of *pratyakṣa* is explainable in terms of it linking the cognitive] subject with the sense power(s)
2. Refutation of the [position that the derivation] is explainable in terms of a unique cause [for sense perception]

3. Explanation of how the number and nature of valid cognitions are determined by their objects
4. The unwanted consequence [that in their explanation of the derivation, they] dismiss commonly accepted verbal schemes

Refutation of the [position that the derivation of pratyakṣa is explainable in terms of it linking the cognitive] subject with the sense power(s)

The Prāsaṅgika [responds to the proponents of the Svātantrika and Pramāṇa systems] by saying, "Identifying cognition as *pratyakṣa* and then explaining [the derivation] in terms of those particular [cognitions] that engage with their respective sense powers is incorrect, because firstly, the five sense cognitions that are perceptions are *not* [correctly speaking] the 'sense powers' subjects,' and secondly, they are [correctly speaking] subjects of their objects, form and so forth.[1071] The first is the case, since they [are unable to cognize] these sense powers, which, as stated in Abhidharma [literature], are constituted by that variety of form that is indemonstrable but has physical resistance."[1072] *Clear Words* says, "Because cognition is not the subject with regard to the sense powers."[1073] The second is the case, because if one identifies *pratyakṣa* as cognition and then interprets [*prati* as denoting a distributive] repetition with regard to its engaged object,[1074] one should explain the derivation as referring to the fact that they "engage their respective objects or respective entities." Reading it [instead] as that they engage with their sense powers, and [trying to explain the derivation] in terms of a particular [kind of perception], is untenable. *Clear Words* states, "Since [it is] the object [that actually determines] the subject, the explanation in terms of the particular is incorrect. It should be [read as] 'respective objects' or 'respective entities.'"[1075]

Refutation of the [position that the derivation] is explainable in terms of a unique cause [for sense perception]

The proponents of the Pramāṇa and Svātantrika [systems] answer, "We admit the point that you, the Prāsaṅgika, makes is true. Just as you have explained, it is not that perceptions engage by taking sense powers as their objects. [399] Their engagement is with the entities that are their respective [objects]. But there is a very important purpose behind our describing them in the way we do. And that is because this makes it easier to realize that the cognitions that depend on their respective sense powers are perceptions, free from any conception. This purpose justifies the way we use the terminology, which [denotes perception through reference to] the unique cause that distinguishes it. This is comparable to [other situations, like that of] sense cognition. It requires *both* the object and the sense power be present for its production, but [between the two], it is its unique, distinguishing cause [i.e., the sense power] that ordains it should be known as a *visual* [literally, *eye*] *perception* as opposed to a *form perception*. We also observe many other comparable examples where the name something is known by [references the cause] unique to it, such as a *drumbeat* or a *barley sprout*. [It was due to this that] Dignāga declared, 'Because they are their unique causes, their names are determined by the sense powers.'"[1076] *Clear Words* says:

> He may acknowledge that the incidence of a [sense] cognition is something that depends on both the [object and sense power]. Despite this, [he might say,] it is their bases [the sense powers] that govern [whether] these perceptions are clear or weak, and that also [regulate them,] such that change in one brings about [commensurate] alteration in the other. Thus, [he might say,] it is its base that determines that it be called the visual ["eye"] cognition. And in a similar way, even though [sense perceptions] engage with the respective entities [that are their objects], they are cognitions that engage by depending on their respective sense powers, [and] it is these bases that determine that they are called *pratyakṣa* [perception]. This is like [the cases] we see with the drumbeat and barley sprout, where [the things] are designated by the causes that distinguish them.[1077]

In addition to this [purpose], within the derivation [of the term *pratyakṣa*]—that is, "dependence on the senses"—the Pramāṇa adherent also finds the rationale behind its usage, understanding it to refer to the instrument, that by means of which the entity is made evident, rather than to the object [of the action], that which is made apparent. *The Correct* states:

> [Within this] "dependence on the sense powers" is the rationale for the derivation. Regarding what the term applies to, it is that which makes the nature [of some object] evident—the cognition [to which] the entity is evident, that which is known as *pratyakṣa*.[1078]

In spite of this, these logicians do not feel that their derivation of *pratyakṣa* has the problem of being too restrictive. They argue that the rationale for applying the term [*pratyakṣa*] is found in this dependence on the sense power, which is *embodied* in one individual instance or particular of cognition [i.e., sense perception], and with this, serving as a representative, its application is [extended] to all four kinds of perception, including the three that do not depend on sense powers—mental perception, self-cognition, and yogic perception. [400] They claim that this is similar, for instance,[1079] with [what is found in] the treatises on Sanskrit [derivations] that inform us, "By virtue of the fact that it goes, it is [designated] 'cow'"[1080]—that is, the rationale for using the name *gauḥ* ("cow") is [found in] the act of going in which the cow engages.[1081] And despite the fact that [some cows], such as the calf in the womb, may not be engaged in that action, it is also used for them. *The Correct* says:

> One should understand that the dependence on sense powers is embodied in a single instance of cognition and that it is in this representative that the rationale [for the term's] usage [is found]. It is by virtue of this that *pratyakṣa* is used for all four [kinds of] perception. One should understand, for example, [when it is said that] "It is by virtue of the fact that it goes that it is [designated] *cow*," the act of going is embodied in one thing that [serves as the] representative of cowness and [provides the] rationale for usage [of the term *cow*]. The rationale for the same term *cow* being used for a fetus, devoid of propulsion, is [found in this representativeness].[1082]

Unless one appreciates these [points, there is a risk that] "the sunrise of one's refutation and assertion appears prior to it dawning on the opponent,"[1083] so one should investigate them with refined reasoning and not just accept matters hastily.

In response to this, the Prāsaṅgika says, "The case of the term *pratyakṣa* has no parallel with the earlier one [you cited] of the six cognitions being denoted by their governing conditions—that is, their respective bases, the sense powers that are individual to each. This is because (1) in that earlier case, if the six cognitions were denoted by their respective objects [with terms like] *form cognition* and so forth, it would not separate them from each other [sufficiently clearly], whereas if they are denoted by their bases, the sense powers, it makes distinguishing among them easy, and (2) in your explanation of the derivation of *pratyakṣa*, [you indicated] that you want the term to not merely convey sense perception but one of its particulars, a nondeceptive cognition. But if that is the case, denoting [perceptions] by referring to their sense powers proves to be of no help whatsoever. The first of these points is established, since the term *form cognition* does not allow one to determine whether the cognition in question is a visual or mental cognition [of form]—something that can also be said about terms such as *sound cognition*—because a mental cognition can engage exactly the same object as a visual or [other sense] perception, simultaneously with that [visual or other sense perception]. The reason is established, since this is the point made in passages such as the one in the Abhidharma where it states, 'Those things [known by] the two cognitions [sense and mental] are the five external [objects].'[1084] The pervasion also holds, since if their objects were used to denote them, there would be uncertainty [about which of the two cognitions was being referred to], whereas by using their bases, [any such uncertainty] is eliminated." *Clear Words* says:

> This case is not comparable to the earlier one. [401] There, if the objects of the cognitions were [used to] denote them [with names] such as "form cognition," it would not distinguish the six cognitions from one another, because mental cognition engages the same objects as visual cognition and so forth [i.e., the remaining sense cognitions], simultaneously with the [visual cognition and so forth]. Thus, if one referred to "cognition" in reference to one of the six cognitions [described by an] object like blue, it would prompt someone to wonder whether this cognition is one derived from a physical sense power or from the mental [sense power]. Denoting them through reference to their bases [on the other hand, allows one to] distinguish between them, even though the mental cognition engages the object of the visual and other [sense] cognitions.[1085]

It is necessary to add a qualification regarding the two cognitions having a single object, but this will be dealt with below.

[The Prāsaṅgika continues,] "The second part of our reason [criticizing the idea that *pratyakṣa* can specifically denote a nondeceptive cognition] is established, since you assert that the majority of sense perceptions are not valid. So, if what you really seek to demonstrate is that valid perception is necessarily free from conception, and [as such,] is a valid source of knowledge, there is no point in denoting it by referring to its base [a sense power]." *Clear Words* states:

> In the present context of wanting to communicate the characteristic that defines valid cognition, because [you] assert that only [a cognition] that is free from conception can be *pratyakṣa*, what you [actually] wish to show is that [perception] is distinguished from conception [by this feature]. But we see no point then in denoting [perception] by way of its unique cause.[1086]

Explanation of how the number and nature of valid cognitions are determined by their objects

The Prāsaṅgika impresses on the logician and certain Svātantrikas that they should explain the derivation of valid *pratyakṣa* [perception] purely in terms of the object, since referencing unique sense powers is of absolutely no use [in explaining it]. This is because the number of valid cognition's [varieties] and the nature of each depends on the objects. *Clear Words* says, "As denoting it by the sense powers is of no use here, it is entirely correct to describe it in terms of the object."[1087]

Not only is the nature of a valid cognition determined by its object of comprehension, so are the number [of varieties], since it is by virtue of manifest objects that there is valid perception and by virtue of hidden objects that there is valid inferential cognition. The first of these has been established, since it has already been demonstrated, in conjunction with an example, that the subject is identified as perception due to comprehending an object that is a manifest one. [402]

Someone asserts that what is *pratyakṣa* [manifest] for an ārya buddha is necessarily *pratyakṣa*. But [if that were accepted,] one would end up with an outright contradiction, as one would be forced to accept that [equally] what is not a hidden [phenomenon] for an ārya buddha is not a hidden [phenomenon]. In the present situation of describing [ordinary] worldly conventions, to analyze things from the perspective of the transcendent awareness of an ārya buddha would be to conflate [the Prāsaṅgika's] public and unique standpoints, and to confuse [differing] contexts. It would also clash with [what is stated in] works such as [Tsongkhapa's] *Golden Garland of Fine Elucidation* and *Illuminating the Intent*.

The second point [that it is by virtue of hidden objects that there is valid inferential cognition] is established, since there are three types of hidden phenomena—namely, the slightly hidden, the extremely hidden, and those hidden phenomena that can permissibly be comprehended through reference to an analogous manifest [i.e., *pratyakṣa*] phenomenon.[1088] And it is owing to these [three objects] that there are three varieties of inferential cognition. It is by virtue of the first that there is inferential cognition [regarding a] matter of established convention,[1089] by virtue of the second that there is valid cognition [associated with] scripture or inferential cognition [related to] conviction, and by virtue of the third that there is valid cognition that comprehends through analogy. As *Clear Words* says, "[The number of] valid cognitions . . . ."[1090]

Alternatively, the objects that valid cognition comprehends can also be said to determine the *number* [of its varieties], because there are four [varieties] of such object—the manifest [*pratyakṣa*], the slightly hidden, the extremely hidden, and the hidden [phenomena] that are ascertained through an analogy that is manifest [*pratyakṣa*]. Thus, [correspondingly,] there are [four kinds] of valid cognition—valid perception, valid inferential cognition, valid cognition [associated with] scripture or valid cognition [related to] conviction, and valid cognition that comprehends through analogy. As *Clear Words* says, "The number of valid cognitions is dictated by the objects comprehended and . . . ."[1091] "And" indicates that this [dependence on the object] is something that applies not just to the number [of varieties] but also to the establishment [of valid cognition] itself. [Hence] the fact that valid cognitions are able to verify their own existence without self-cognition is also something that relies on the objects they comprehend. This is because even without self-cognition, the fact that the aspect of the object comprehended by the valid cognition appears to it, the comprehender, is by itself enough for it to establish or "gain" its existence. The situation is comparable with that of something such as a sense perception apprehending blue, in that it is in the [act of] comprehending blue that the sense perception's existence is "gained"—that is, realized. And when it says here, "Simply by conforming with the aspect of the object [that each one] comprehends . . . ," [the treatise informs us of] the manner of comprehension, and by using the term "simply," it refutes the notion that self-cognition [is required] to substantiate [the existence of valid cognition]. The first of these points is confirmed, as [the full passage describing the manner of comprehension] says, "Simply by conforming with the aspect of the object [that each one] comprehends, the valid cognitions gain their own existence and establish themselves."[1092] [403] The second point is also confirmed, as *Illuminating the Intent* says [about this]:

> It is in the aspect of the objects they comprehend appearing to them that the valid cognitions establish their own existence. The term "simply" is included [in *Clear Words* to address] the views of the Cittamātra and the Sautrāntika, according to which . . . [this] refutes the notion that it is self-cognition that substantiates [valid cognition's existence]. It [effectively] means that simply in its establishing the object it comprehends, [the valid cognition] establishes [itself].[1093]

What this teaches is that such is the case not only for valid cognition but also for nonvalid, false cognitions—nonconceptual ones, such as a cognition of a double moon and conceptual ones, such as the conceptual grasping at the self. That is, they are all valid perceptions with respect to what *appears* to them. And since they comprehend [what appears to them], they are capable of inducing ascertainment of their own existence without needing to refer to any other valid cognition.

Several earlier Tibetans who composed *Thousand Measures* [commentaries] on *Clear Words*, and those who subsequently wrote *annotations*, proposed that the number of [types of] valid cognition depends on the definitive bipartition of objects of comprehension into those with specific and general characteristics. But this explanation is one that Candrakīrti already rejected. And whether one [divides things up into those that are] definitions and definienda or those with specific and general characteristics, as explained below, what they all share is that they can be objects for validly *perceiving* cognitions. Rational individuals should therefore dismiss [what these earlier Tibetans proposed]. And unless one accounts for the [aforesaid] passage in terms of manifest and hidden things being the respective objects of perception and inferential cognition in the manner outlined, one will be unable to explain its meaning. There will be more on this point below.

The unwanted consequence [that in their explanation of the derivation, they] dismiss commonly accepted verbal schemes

Those who advocate [that things have] an intrinsic nature claim, "It is correct to explain the derivation of *pratyakṣa* or "perception" not in terms of the object but, as already stated, purely in terms of [a set of] bases—the sense powers—of a particular [kind of perception], since it is a matter of wide acceptance in the world that when one refers to *pratyakṣa*, it is with the intention of conveying cognitions that engage [their objects] by means of depending on their own respective sense powers. [Conversely,] Candrakīrti, your explanation of the derivation in terms of the cognitions' respective objects (*pratyartha*) has no such currency."[1094] In support of the first point, they cite Pramāṇa literature, where it declares that "*Pratyakṣa* is free from conception and unmistaken."[1095] They also quote Dharmottara, who remarks, "*Pratyakṣa* communicates the thing being characterized. What *pratyakṣa* denotes is commonly accepted to be a cognition that makes [something] manifest. It is free from conception and is unmistaken."[1096] [404] *Clear Words* also says, "If [he] says that this is because in the world, it is commonly accepted that the term *pratyakṣa* expresses [a certain] intended meaning . . . ."[1097]

The second point [questioning Candrakīrti's gloss] is also presented in *Clear Words*, in the passage [setting out the objection] "'[Their] respective objects' (*pratyartha*) is not the term that is commonly accepted. The explanation [we] rely on therefore is solely in terms of the bases for a particular [kind of perception]."[1098]

The Prāsaṅgika responds, "Your explanation is not correct. We both agree that the term *pratyakṣa* is one commonly used in the worldly setting. However, [we assert that] its actual sense is not [to be gained from] splitting [its components in the way you suggest] but by using it in accordance with its accepted [meaning] in the world as referring [to something] manifest and nonhidden. Your [approach] of splitting the word and understanding it [in terms of a distributive] repetition that [references] the sense powers is inappropriate. Whereas the way that I, the [Prāsaṅgika,] takes it, understanding it to mean an object that is manifest, is in perfect agreement with the worldly convention on the matter." *Clear Words* states, "[We] say: this term *pratyakṣa* is certainly one that is commonly accepted in the world. But we use it in exactly the way it is used in the world."[1099]

The [Pramāṇa logician] may deny this [Prāsaṅgika approach]. But that would mean that, within the context of accounting for worldly conventions, he is rejecting the commonly accepted understanding of the term, because as outlined above, while [supposedly] explaining worldly conventions, he dismisses the worldly practice of using *pratyakṣa* to denote the object in favor of an account that seeks to explain it as referring, through [a set of] bases—the sense powers—to a particular [kind of perception]. As *Clear Words* states, "In rejecting the sense that it has in the world and [instead] explaining it in terms of a particular [perception, you] are also rejecting the commonly accepted term."[1100]

[The Prāsaṅgika continues,] "Your interpretation of *pratyakṣa*—according to which it means '[Each] engaging with its respective sense powers' or '[Each] engaging in dependence on their respective sense powers,' such that you understand it in terms of a [distributive] repetition [combined with] reference to the sense power bases—does not work, because the evidence against both of these has been set out, and there is more to follow to counter the tenability of this understanding of the repetition. *Clear Words* states, "Thus *pratyakṣa* does not work like that."[1101] [405]

[Describing how the proposed] repetition is not sufficiently inclusive

Not only is his explanation of [*pratyakṣa*] in terms of a particular [sense cognition] through [reference to that cognition's sense power] basis untenable, his reading of *prati* as a [distributive] repetition denoting "respective" is also untenable, because there are numerous temporal portions of sense perceptions that this repetition does not cover. Although he might try to deny that there are any such sense perceptions, the [Prāsaṅgika says,] "Take a single instant of a visual cognition, relying on a single instant of a sense power. It follows that it is not *pratyakṣa* [perception], because neither sense of the [distributive] repetition can be said to refer to it, in that it is neither 'what engages with [their] respective sense powers' nor 'what engages through depending on [their] respective sense powers.' And that is because it is a *single* cognition, relying on a *single* sense power." *Clear Words* states, "Because the [distributive] repetition makes no sense [here, it means that] a single instant of visual cognition relying on a single instant of sense power cannot be a perception."[1102]

His response may be, "Although these glosses do not apply to such a single instant, the [distributive] repetition nevertheless still encompasses perception [*pratyakṣa*], since I do not accept that each individual instant constitutes a perception but rather that only a sequence [of such instants] is capable of making its object manifest." But this argument is not a credible one, because if the perception is absent in each instant, there is no way that it can be present in the assemblage. *Clear Words* says, "What is not *pratyakṣa* in every [instant] cannot be it in the many."[1103]

[The Prāsaṅgika further argues,] "That [single instant] cannot be a perception, because of not being '[what] engage through depending on [their] respective sense powers.' The pervasion is the one advanced [by you, the

Pramāṇa logician]. And you cannot challenge the reason, since that [instant of cognition] is one that relies on just a *single* instant of its own unique, distinguishing governing condition, the visual sense power—a point that is easy to establish. The pervasion also holds, because the instant of the sense power and the instant of the cognition associated with it [are things that] perish immediately upon arising. On this point, [Candrakīrti's] *Commentary to Four Hundred Stanzas* states:

> Well then, how could a single instant of cognition be perception [*pratyakṣa*]? It is not [something that can] engage through depending on respective sense powers, because it [relies on] a unique, distinguishing [cause], and [also] because an instant of a sense power and an instant of cognition perish as soon as they arise.[1104]

Extending this [principle] to [other] objects and sense powers, it becomes feasible to maintain that a single instant of visual cognition can realize a single instant of form. [406] As this is the same in the context of mental perception, which will be discussed below, it means that [according to this system] there can be ordinary beings who perceptually realize subtle impermanence.

[The Pramāṇa logician] may argue, "If one divides a sense power and a form-source into each of their respective minute [constituent] particles, then the basis and observed [object] that they [originally were] no longer remain, since the first five consciousnesses [i.e., sense cognitions] have, as their bases, sense powers that are *assemblages* composed of minute particles and, [as their objects,] observable [things] that are *assemblages* or *composites* constituted of minute particles. This situation is like that of someone with a certain eye complaint, who despite seeing hairs floating before his eyes, cannot distinguish individual strands." The *Commentary to Four Hundred Stanzas* states:

> He may say that, as the group of five [sense] consciousnesses have bases and observed objects that are composites, it is not that one can discern each individual minute particle of the sense power or each individual minute particle of the object, which are [respectively] the basis and [thing] observed by it, [just] as one with a certain eye complaint does not see individual strands of hair."[1105]

Hence, [they argue,] the [visual] form and other sources that serve as objects observed [by perception] are collections of tiny particles, each of which, [as a part] within the cause, [contributes] to the production of that cognition. Similarly, when the particles [that form] the visual or other sense powers are amassed together, each of them serves as the basis [of the cognition], since what the group of the first five [sense] consciousnesses observe are composites. Thus [the Pramāṇa logician] denies that [his position] can be criticized on the grounds that the [distributive] repetition does not cover all [forms of] perception, because even though a single instant is not [in isolation] asserted to be perception, it is still legitimate to describe it as something that depends on each of the particles [that go to form] its basis, the sense powers. The *Commentary to Four Hundred Stanzas* says, "He may propose that each individual [constituent] within the composite is [part of] the causal entity and that similarly each individual particle [within] the composite of the eye [sense power] and so forth are a cause."[1106] This [argument] is consistent with [the general thinking] of the Sautrāntika and Bhāviveka but is actually one created [by Candrakīrti] and inserted into the discussion about the [distributive] repetition.

The Prāsaṅgika responds by saying, "This position is untenable, both because the analogy does not match [the target] and because the target is also flawed. The first is the case, because someone with the eye complaint [associated with] blurred vision *is* able to distinguish between individual strands of hair; it is only when there is some [additional] problem related to his sight that he does not.[1107] But with regard to the particles of the sense power, there is no [additional] basis for the cognition outside the composite formed by these particles. The *Commentary to Four Hundred Stanzas* states: [407]

> The analogue does not match [the target], since someone who has the [complaint associated with] blurred vision can distinguish each individual strand of hair. [Only] if there is [also another] problem with [his] sight will he not see [such]. As for the particles of the sense power, outside the context of them being massed together [to form the composite sense power], none of the particles, individually, is seen to be the basis for the [associated] cognition. Thus it is not logical to ascribe [the identity] of a basis to each one of them contained within the composite individually.[1108]

Second, [the target is flawed,] because [even when considered together,] it is impossible for the minute particles of the sense power to have gained anything through the repetition or addition of "[each of them] depending on their respective [bases]." If none of the individual particles of the sense power, in isolation, have any [causal] capacity to act as the basis for consciousness, then neither could any of them have such a capacity individually during the time that they are collected together in the composite, since prior [to being part of the collection], none of them would [even] have the capacity to form the physical dimensions of the sense power. If, for instance, [individual grains of] sand have a capacity of some small sort, then something of the same order but of much greater magnitude must be observed in a large mass [of sand]. If, on the other hand, the capacity is absent in them individually, the same will be observed to be true of them massed together. Correspondingly, it is by dint of a single blade of vegetation having the capability to entrap a bee that, when massed together, [many such blades] will have the power to restrain an elephant. And the fact that each individual sesame seed has a small amount of oil means that a whole load of them is capable of yielding enough oil to fill a whole jar. [This point is made in the] *Commentary to Four Hundred Stanzas,* in the section "[Grains of] sand are seen to have a modest [amount of] some capability; what they [have when part of] a composite is consistent with that . . . as it is possible for a load of them to yield a whole jar full of grain oil, [but] since none of the individual particles of sense power, independent of their inclusion within the composite, are a basis of cognition, it is impossible for anything to be added to them when considered as particles [together]."[1109]

The [distributive] repetition of the wording [proposed by the logician] fails to be sufficiently inclusive with regard to the sense powers not only from the point of view of their particles but also from the point of view of [their] temporal instants, since the sense powers are also momentary. This is easy to establish. And because of this [momentariness, each of these instants] will cease simultaneously with its [associated] consciousnesses.

[In conclusion, the Prāsaṅgika says,] "Your [derivation of *pratyakṣa*], which you say refers to 'cognitions situated in their own respective sense powers,' is incorrect, because the [distributive] repetition you explain does not cover [all instances of perception] and because, among other faults, it confuses what constitute the actual and figurative forms of *pratyakṣa*." Thus the *Commentary to Four Hundred Stanzas* states:

> And because the [sense power] is also momentary, and approaches its end together with its cognition, how could [any] addition to it be possible? Therefore, [to assert that] they are called *pratyakṣa*

> because they are cognitions and they depend on their respective sense powers is incorrect.[1110] [408]

Thus, whether [understood in terms of] "engaging with a sense power," "engaging [an object] in dependence on a sense power," or "situated within a sense power," the [notion of the distributive] repetition is refuted.

The proponent of intrinsic nature answers this by saying, "There is no problem [with my position], since I do not advocate that a cognition, in its individual [temporal] instants, is perception. Instead, I maintain that only a cognition that is a composite formed from a series of many instants can be a perception [*pratyakṣa*]. And simultaneous with that cognition, there are the series of instants forming the composite of the sense power [acting as that cognition's] basis. Because one can justifiably speak [of the perception] in terms of its 'dependence on the various moments of a sense power,' criticisms of the repetition [with its reference to plurality] are avoided. The point in the previous reason [i.e., that individual temporal instants of cognition are not perception] is established, because an ordinary being is incapable of performing any action within the duration of time [known as] a 'shortest instant,' since the [minimum that is required is an] 'action-completion instant,' which is necessarily composed of a series of moments." As the *Commentary to Four Hundred Stanzas* expresses this, "He may say that because the composite cognitions are situated in whichever of the sense powers corresponds to their nature, the particular explanation [of the derivation for *pratyakṣa* can be understood in terms of the perception's] instants."[1111]

The Prāsaṅgika responds, "This [stance] is not tenable because, as I have already explained, one cannot talk of single instants of a visual cognition in that way. And the sense power and the perception—which are composites—have no substantial existence aside from that of those instants. So there is no [sensible way of explaining how] a composite cognition depends on a sense power that is also a composite [but does not depend on the instants in that composite]. That would be like saying, for instance, that the roof of a four-pillared structure is supported by the *group* of four pillars while denying that any of the four support it." Concerning this, the *Commentary to Four Hundred Stanzas* says, "This is also not how it is. Why not? Because [his] particular explanation is impossible in terms of a single instant of visual cognition, and because there is also no way that a composite without substantial existence could depend on the sense powers."[1112] A case could be made for interpreting "without substantial existence" to mean "lacking true existence," but since the opponents here include among their ranks those of the Svātantrika school, who while denying true existence affirm substantial existence [for some things], it is better to read it as it stands.

When the repetition is [examined] with such an abundance of sophisticated reasoning
and the positions of the various tenet systems on the manifest and hidden are delineated with such clarity, [409]
could we not be forgiven for wondering whether Candrakīrti himself has returned?

The true intention of the ārya father and [spiritual] son remained unfathomed
by masters of logic from India and Tibet in their masses
but is revealed by you, [Candrakīrti,] like a splendid waxing moon amid the sparkling constellations,
and the conquerors beam with satisfaction.

And you, Tsongkhapa, who are Mañjuśrī in human guise,
illuminate the whole of samsara and nirvana to the devoted.
And it is as though with loving hands bearing a vessel brimming with profound knowledge you extend it toward my crown
to anoint me, announcing, "Now this is yours."

[Rejecting] "free from conception" as a characteristic that defines perception

1. Outlining the [logician's] position
2. Refutation of that position

Outlining the [logician's] position

Four Hundred Stanzas says:

> When one sees [its] form,
> one does not see all of the pot.
> So who with an understanding of suchness
> would claim that pot is *pratyakṣa* [perceivable]?[1113]

This indicates that when subjected to examination, [even] an object such as a pot is [revealed] not to be *pratyakṣa*. The logician who propounds intrinsic existence says, "You, the Prāsaṅgika, refute [the notion that] pot is *pratyakṣa*, but this refutation is illogical, because it serves not the slightest purpose. It is like refuting that sound is the thing apprehended by visual cognition. That is because we *also* assert that the pot is not *pratyakṣa*." Regarding the reasoning [behind this], according to the Vaibhāṣika and the Sautrāntika following scripture, form and the like are not specifically characterized.[1114] For the Cittamātra, they are not things included among the kind of [autonomous,] specifically characterized phenomena that make up the observed object of meditative equipoise.[1115] [Form and the like] are, however, the objects of the type of cognition denoted by the term *pratyakṣa* [perception]. As such, while cognition is actual *pratyakṣa*, its object is *pratyakṣa* in a figurative sense. This is the point made in the *Commentary to Four Hundred Stanzas* in the passage:

> In regard to this, the logicians say it is not that *pratyakṣa* is for pot [and so forth] exclusively. [The term] does not [actually] denote the [autonomous] specific characteristics of things such as form. But since [form and so forth] are the objects of visual and [other] cognitions—those that [the term] *pratyakṣa* [properly] conveys—[that term] is assigned to them in a figurative sense . . . because of this, they say, there is no point in refuting that they are *pratyakṣa*. [410] Just as with refuting that sound is the thing apprehended by visual cognition, it is not logical to refute [*pratyakṣa*] with respect to this pot.[1116]

The Prāsaṅgika then questions the logician as to what he holds *pratyakṣa* to be. He responds by saying that he holds it to be a type of consciousness. And since conceptual objects lack distinctness, he believes that such a cognition must be free from conception. As Dignāga declares, "*Pratyakṣa* [is a cognition] that is free from conception [the latter being what deals with] conjoining names, types, and so forth."[1117] Referring to this, the *Commentary to Four Hundred Stanzas* says, "This logician has totally divested it of its worldly sense. . . . He declares that *pratyakṣa* is consciousness. And what sort of consciousness? That which is free from conception."[1118]

What kind of conception is this? He asserts that it is a conceptual cognition that merges the name and the object. And in the case of a pot, it [merges] all those [instances] that have the same type, while in the case of things with different varieties, such as trees, it [merges by subsuming them] within an assemblage universal. As the *Commentary on Pramāṇa* states,

"Any consciousness that holds the *śabdārtha* [relating to a certain thing] is a conceptual cognition [of that thing]."[1119]

And the *Commentary to Four Hundred Stanzas* says, "What is [this] conception? It is a creative discrimination that is involved in superimposing name(s) and type(s) on an entity."[1120] "Creative discrimination" does not denote that a conceptual cognition is [actually] a form of discrimination; rather it describes the way that it assigns various [identities and features] to an object—a conceptual cognition being equivalent to an excluding engager. "Creative" refers to its mastery, indicating that conceptual cognition is skilled in differentiating and detailing the object.

[In summary, for the logicians,] the five sense consciousnesses are *pratyakṣa*, because they are free from such kinds of conception, and also because they are nondeceptive cognitions, which engage only with the object's individual characteristics as they really are, in a way that language and thought cannot capture. And the derivation of *pratyakṣa* is justified by the fact that those [sense perceptions] "are situated in their respective sense powers." On this point, the *Commentary to Four Hundred Stanzas* says:

> Due to being free from that [conception], the five sense consciousnesses engage solely with the [autonomous,] specific characteristics of their objects, which cannot be captured [by others]. Hence they can [rightfully] be referred to as *pratyakṣa*, in that they are [cognitions] that are situated in their respective sense powers.[1121] [411]

Refutation of that position

1. [Candrakīrti's] refutation of that position in the *Commentary to Four Hundred Stanzas*
2. [Candrakīrti's] refutation of that position in *Clear Words*

[Candrakīrti's] refutation of that position in the *Commentary to Four Hundred Stanzas*

The *Commentary to Four Hundred Stanzas* does not [specifically] refute the notion that [*pratyakṣa* is a cognition] "free from conception." But it attacks the attempt to explain the derivation of *pratyakṣa* in terms of the [distributive] repetition and rebuts [efforts to] defend that position. It thereby establishes that the actual *pratyakṣa* is the object, whereas the subject [the perception] is only figuratively designated such. In addition, it sets out another refutation, arguing against the view that sense cognitions can be valid perceptions [*pratyakṣa*] that validate the [autonomous] specific characteristics or nature of the object. The first of these [refutations] has already been detailed, and is dealt with in the section [of the treatise] that says, "Well then, how could a single instant of cognition be perception [*pratyakṣa*]? . . . And as the appropriator of those is also *pratyakṣa*, there is no fault [in our position]."[1122] Most of the knotty issues relating to this have already been laid out and discussed.

The second refutation is presented in the section of the commentary that says, "His assigning [the identity of] *pratyakṣa* to sense cognition, and furthermore examining it [in terms of its being] a valid cognition, is totally wide of the mark . . . Because it would follow that it is a valid cognition."[1123] The refutation ends with the conclusion, "Thus this logician . . . ."[1124] This second refutation is complicated, as Jé Rinpoché [Tsongkhapa] has remarked, so I will briefly outline how it proceeds.

The approach of this logician—who, between the object and the subject, chooses to identify *pratyakṣa* exclusively with the subject and also asserts that it is valid cognition—is entirely wide of the mark or irrelevant [to the issue at hand]. This is because, having made that choice between the object and subject, this logician goes on to attribute the identity of *pratyakṣa* to a sense consciousness that is free from conception and is unmistaken, when it has no such identity. He then further proceeds to treat the [autonomous] specific characteristics of the five objects, such as form, as the overt object [of these consciousnesses] and view them as valid cognitions that are nondeceptive and unmistaken with respect to such [objects]. The *Commentary to Four Hundred Stanzas* says, "His assigning [the identity of] *pratyakṣa* to sense cognition, and furthermore examining it [in terms of its being] a valid cognition, is totally wide of the mark . . . ."[1125] [412]

"Assigning [the identity of] *pratyakṣa*" refers to how, of the two, he chooses to assign the identity of the actual *pratyakṣa* to something that does not have it [i.e., the subject]. "Furthermore" is a reference to how he also treats the consciousness that he regards as *pratyakṣa* as one that is a valid cognition. And it is not enough that the valid cognition in question be one that is nondeceptive, he requires that it also be fresh and unmistaken. It is these [stipulations that Candrakīrti] judges to be wide of the mark with regard to the passage at hand.

The view of the logician or the propounder of intrinsic nature is that the five sense consciousnesses are valid cognitions with respect to the [autonomous] specific characteristics of form and so forth that are their objects. But this is not tenable, because these [consciousnesses] are not nondeceptive with regard to whether those objects are established by way of their own [autonomous] specific characteristics. The pervasion holds, because we see that as far as the world is concerned, being nondeceptive is the characteristic that defines a valid cognition. The reason is also established, as the Blessed One pronounced on many occasions, within [the context of] both the Hinayana and Mahayana, that consciousness is false and is comparable to an illusion. In [various] Mahayana sutras, he proclaimed, "All discrimination and worldly habitats are characterized by falsehood and deception,"[1126] "Alas, what is composed is transitory,"[1127] and "A phenomenon that is deceptive is [itself] false."[1128] He also stated:

> That composite thing is a deceptive phenomenon
> and a phenomenon that irrevocably perishes.[1129]

Elsewhere he declared:

> Form is like flecks of foam,
> feelings resemble bubbles,
> discrimination is like a mirage,
> compositional factors are similar to the [insubstantial] banana tree,
> and consciousness is akin to an illusion.
> This is what Arkabandhu ("Friend of the Sun") has pronounced.[1130]

And the *King of Samādhis Sutra* says:

> These phenomena are like foam and a banana tree,
> similar to an illusion, like a flash of lightning,
> like the moon [reflected] in the water, and resembling a mirage.[1131]

The *Commentary to Four Hundred Stanzas* states:

> [That] is totally wide of the mark. It is nondeceptive cognition that is regarded, in the world, as valid. And on the subject of consciousness, the Blessed One has pronounced that, due to being something that is composite, it is characterized by falseness and deception and is comparable to an illusion.[1132]

Those of the [Buddhist realist] śrāvaka grouping do not gloss this "falseness" and "deception" in terms of the lack of true or intrinsic existence. Instead, they see them as the antipodes of the [qualities of] "truth" and "holiness" attributed [to nirvana] in the line that immediately follows that first passage, which informs us, "This nirvana is the one sole truth and holy [object]." [413] The Sanskrit equivalents of these two terms, *vatya*[1133] and *pata*,[1134] can be read as "truth," "holy," or "eternal." So [what the two terms convey, according to these groupings, is that the phenomena in question are] "nonpermanent" or "impermanent." Hence they would deny that there is any pervasion [between the Buddha's statements and the Prāsaṅgika's conclusion]. They also [understand] the other passages in a similar fashion, interpreting the five analogies as respectively communicating the impurity and compositeness of form, the fleetingness of feelings, and so forth. And even though the *King of Samādhis Sutra* teaches the lack of true existence, one presumes that they do not accept that it does. Those who deny that śrāvakas and pratyekabuddhas can realize the selflessness of phenomena or that this form of selflessness is revealed in the Hinayana scriptures either have to follow [that Hinayana] interpretation of these passages or account for them by saying that they refer to the selflessness of persons.

The Prāsaṅgika supports the aforesaid pervasion by arguing that a cognition cannot reasonably be credited with [the veracity of] nondeceptiveness with respect to an object when that cognition and the way that it holds its object is false and comparable to an illusion. And even though the Prāsaṅgika says that [the opponent here] has already admitted that the reason is correct, if [that opponent] still challenges this, [the Prāsaṅgika] can respond with the argument "The five sense consciousnesses that you believe to be valid cognitions with respect to the [autonomous] specific characteristics of form and so forth cannot be nondeceptive with respect to such characteristics, because while the form and so forth exist in one manner, they appear to these cognitions or are held by them to exist in another. The situation is comparable to that of a sense cognition to which the moon appears as double." The *Commentary to Four Hundred Stanzas* says, "That which has the trait of being false and deceptive and is similar to an illusion cannot be nondeceptive, because things appear to it other than the way that they exist."[1135]

[As already noted,] in their own remarks on this issue, the *Stages of the Path* and *Thousand Measures* state that such consciousnesses are mistaken with regard to that [appearing] object, but that this does not preclude them from being valid cognitions. It is important to be aware of the qualification [that is necessary here] and the reason why being one [i.e., mistaken with regard to the appearing object] does not preclude being the other [i.e., being valid cognition]. On this matter, the *Stages of the Path* says:

> Put succinctly, those sense consciousnesses are not valid cognitions with respect to the [autonomous] specific characteristics of the five objects, in that they are deceived in terms of the appearance of the [autonomous] specific characteristics of the five objects. This is because while the five objects are empty of [self-defining, autonomous] specific characteristics, they appear [to these consciousnesses] to have such characteristics. [Candrakīrti] considers them to be comparable to a consciousness to which the moon appears as double.[1136]

While that is the case, it cannot plausibly be asserted that [the sense consciousnesses] are valid cognitions of such [characteristics], as this would lead to the absurd consequence that all consciousnesses are valid ones. As the *Commentary to Four Hundred Stanzas* says, "And while that is the case, it cannot plausibly be asserted that they are valid cognitions, for this would lead to the consequence that all consciousnesses are valid cognitions."[1137] This effectively counters Chöje Gyensang's claim that nonconceptual false cognitions can also be valid ones.[1138] [414]

We note a number of spurious remarks by Taktsang Lotsāwa relating to this section of the *Stages of the Path*. These include his claim "It is incorrect to say that the realists assert that a cognition's validity with regard to the five objects necessarily also entails it validating [autonomous] specific characteristics, because the [realists also] accept [that there are] phenomena that are without specific characteristics."[1139] Our response to this is to reject [his assertion] that the five objects have any characteristics that are not specific [and autonomous] according to the realists. Furthermore, we say, [it follows that the realists] *do* assert that [a cognition's being valid with regard to the five objects necessarily also] involves its validating [autonomous] individual characteristics, because this is the view attributed to them by Candrakīrti when he outlines the position of the opponent. His *Commentary to Four Hundred Stanzas* says:

> Due to being free from that [conception, they say,] the five sense consciousnesses engage solely with the [autonomous] specific

> characteristics of their objects, which cannot be captured [by others]. Hence they can [rightfully] be referred to as *pratyakṣa* in that they are [cognitions] that are situated in their respective sense powers.[1140]

Thus the three spheres are in place, [and Taktsang's position is thereby exposed as being irredeemably flawed].

In addition to this, it also follows [from Taktsang's interpretation] that in the [Buddhist realist] system there is no such thing as valid cognitions that comprehend the five objects with [autonomous] specific characteristics, because [according to him] the five sense cognitions that comprehend the five objects do not comprehend objects with [autonomous] specific characteristics. He cannot challenge the pervasion [of this argument], as that would leave him open to a number of other charges. It would mean, for instance, that there is no real distinction between the way that an excluding engager and an [affirmative] comprehensive engager engage [their respective objects]. And it would follow that the [Buddhist] realists would not be in a position to agree with the majority of statements in the *Commentary on Pramāṇa* and *Ascertainment of Valid Cognition*, which take the standpoint that [when] perception experiences [an object], it sees at the same time all of those features that belong to the same simultaneous substantial entity [i.e., those that are within that object]. And that would mean that [the Buddhist realists] would be unable to lay claim to any of the passages that [express this position].

All [these faults] arise from the fact that according to the position that [Taktsang Lotsāwa] attributes [to the Buddhist realists], the sense perception of form apprehends form itself alone, and none of its features, meaning, therefore, that [perception] would operate in the same way that the word *form* or the concept of form do—that is, by holding form alone.

Even if [Taktsang Lotsāwa] were to concede the root [point of the argument above],[1141] it would follow that passages such as "As there are two objects of comprehension, there are two valid cognitions,"[1142] must be unacceptable [to those schools]. It would also render the notion of a shared subject [for both parties] unsustainable.

Thus it is the pronouncements of Jé Rinpoché [Tsongkhapa] alone, which are the products of a systematic investigation through multitudinous lines of reasoning, that can be deemed valid. In light of this, [we note what] the *Stages of the Path* says about this topic:

> In this regard, the realists maintain that if form, sound, and so forth did not have intrinsic natures that are established by way of [autonomous] specific characteristics, they would be nonthings, without the capacity to perform any sort of function. It is on account of this that as far as they are concerned, if valid perception failed to [validate] the [autonomous] specific characteristics of the five objects, there would be no sense in which it could be counted as a valid cognition of those five objects [at all], and to be a valid cognition with respect to the five objects [necessarily involves] validating their [autonomous] characteristics.[1143] [415]

This is [of course] given from the point of view of valid perception. It is categorically not referring to inferential cognition.

[Candrakīrti's] refutation of the position that perception has the characteristic of being "free from conception" as set out in *Clear Words*

The assertion of the logician and the Svātantrika that *pratyakṣa* is a cognition that is free from conception is not an acceptable one, since there is no sound evidence to substantiate it, either in the form of authoritative scriptural sources or logical arguments, whereas the scriptural and logical evidence against it is plentiful. Considering [first] the logical argument: With regard to *pratyakṣa*, the analysis or identification of it as valid cognition is rendered valueless, because it insists that only *cognition that is free from conception* can be regarded as *pratyakṣa*. The reason [is what members of those schools themselves] accept. The pervasion also holds, in that according to worldly understanding it is form and so forth that are actually *pratyakṣa* [in the sense of being manifest or visible], whereas valid perception is only figuratively designated such, by virtue of having such things as its objects. And insisting that only cognition free from conception is [*pratyakṣa*] also defies the linguistic conventions of the world. This matters, since the [two parties engaged in the discourse] also aim to describe valid cognition and the object it comprehends in terms of worldly conventions. *Clear Words* says:

> Because [they] assert that only cognition that is free from conception can be regarded as *pratyakṣa*, because there is no such worldly convention, and because they also aim to describe valid cognition and what it comprehends in terms of worldly conven-

> tions, their analysis of *pratyakṣa* [identifying it as] valid perception has no value.[1144]

The chief opponent this targets is the Svātantrika, and it is delivered in the wake of him stating, "What need have we for the form of detailed analysis to which the other party [subjects such things]? We account [for this] in terms of the conventions of the world."[1145] For him to say that *pratyakṣa* refers not only to cognition free from conception but also to valid perception is to defy the linguistic conventions of the world. As far as the world is concerned, to realize an object through one's own direct experience is to perceive it. There is no requirement that this be free from conception. As explained below, there are plentiful cases of direct experience within conceptual cognition, such as the sensation of pleasure [that accompanies a thought]. And it is in reference to such pleasurable sensations that in common parlance one might say, "It's something I've directly experienced myself." [416] This is what *Clear Words* refers to when it states, "because there is no such worldly convention...."[1146]

Considering [second] the scriptural evidence regarding the assertion, while we find no source to support it, there is evidence against it. Someone argues that it is correct to [identify] *pratyakṣa* as [cognition that is] free from conception, citing the scripture that states, "With a basic visual awareness, one cognizes blue, but does not think 'blue.'"[1147] According to him, this passage supports the assertion, because it teaches that "free from conception and unmistaken" are the characteristics that define *pratyakṣa*. He also proposes that the Svātantrika and those in the schools below him hold this to be the case, citing the passage in [Kamalaśīla's] *Commentary on the Difficult Points [of the Compendium of Suchness]*, where it says:

> The characteristics that define *pratyakṣa* are that it is free from mistake and conception. The Blessed One declared "With a basic visual awareness [one cognizes blue but does not think 'blue.'"] Since this [indicates] that it "cognizes blue," it conveys that it is a subject that is nonerroneous and thus that it is unmistaken. And since it states that [the cognition] "does not think 'blue,'" it rules out [the notion that it] grasps an entity by conjoining it with a name and [hence] conveys that it is "free from conception."[1148]

[In response we say that] the scriptural passage does not support his assertion, nor do we accept that his reading of the passage is correct, since it fails to take account of the context [of its delivery]. This is because the passage "With a basic visual awareness . . ." was not spoken in the context of communicating a characteristic that defines *pratyakṣa*. So, let alone saying anything about mental perception, this does not even reveal anything about mental cognition, as what it refers to is the five sense awarenesses, since it teaches that they lack [the cognitive functions of] reflective analysis and deliberative evaluation,[1149] due to which they are regarded as witless. *Clear Words* states, "Also, because the passage 'With a basic visual awareness one cognizes blue but does not think *blue*' is not [spoken] in the context of communicating the characteristics that define *pratyakṣa*, and because it is one that teaches that the five basic sense awarenesses are witless . . . ."[1150] Hence the assertion that only cognition that is free from conception can be *pratyakṣa* is not substantiated, since this is not what is taught in the scripture. *Clear Words* says, "Neither is it [stated] in scripture that only cognition that is free from conception is *pratyakṣa*. So this [assertion of yours] is not correct."[1151]

As will be explained, the *Commentary to Four Hundred Stanzas* informs us that mental perception has reflective analysis. So, while the mental perceptions in the continua of sentient beings are not free from conception in the way that sense cognitions are, they can still be valid perceptions and have a vivid appearance [of their object], because conception does not preclude some degree of vividness.[1152] And it is also widely accepted that an entity can be "vividly" represented in language and thought. [417] the *Commentary on Pramāṇa* says:

> The cognition with a vivid appearance [of its object]
> is held to be free from conception and unmistaken.[1153]

While the appearance [for mental perceptions] may not be as vivid [as that for sense perception], even the *Commentary on Pramāṇa* system does not contest that they possess a degree of vividness, since [the *Commentary*] contains numerous passages such as:

> Unhinged by desire, fear, or grief,
> one can be plagued by visions of thieves and so forth.[1154]

Thus, in this [Prāsaṅgika] system, a cognition's being conceptual is not necessarily incompatible with its comprehending its object in a direct manner. This point and the criticisms of others regarding yogic perception, and so forth, are considered below.

5. Valid Cognition according to the Prāsaṅgika System

Setting out the valid cognition of our own [Prāsaṅgika] system

1. Demonstrating the correctness of our system on valid cognition
2. Resolving certain knotty issues [related to it]

Demonstrating the correctness of our own system on valid cognition

1. The characteristics that define valid cognition
2. Its varieties
3. Its object
4. The way that valid cognition and objects of comprehension are established

There are various reasons for organizing the topic in this [fourfold] fashion, including the fact that it makes it much easier to understand the whole system relating to valid cognition. As *Clear Words* puts it, "You must state how many valid cognitions there are. What are the characteristics that define them? What are their objects?"[1155]

The characteristics that define valid cognition

[First,] the definition of a valid cognition is "[being] a nondeceptive cognition." The *Commentary to Four Hundred Stanzas* states, "It is nondeceptive cognition that, in the world, is regarded as valid."[1156] [The passage's] reference to "in the world" establishes [that the characteristics defining valid cognition] should be understood not in terms of things that are truly established or that [can be found] through an analysis into a reality behind the designation, but according to the standards of worldly convention. Thus one cannot explain the translation of the Sanskrit term for valid cognition, *pramāṇa*, in terms of *pra* meaning "initial" or "fresh," and *māṇa* meaning "comprehension," as that would make the majority of correct or nondeceptive cognitions invalid ones—something that is contrary to common understanding. It would also present one with various difficulties, such as being unable to locate the "initial" portion of valid cognition. In *Dispeller of Dispute*, for instance, [Nāgārjuna] argues:

> Neither in the initial [stage]
> nor in the middle or at the end is it established.[1157] [418]

The *Commentary to Four Hundred Stanzas* says:

> Neither is it correct [to say] that [something] seen by worldly beings is really seen vividly, just as it is, because that validity is simply what accords with the world, and because it is established that the thing it observes is characterized by falseness and deceptiveness.[1158]

Here then [in the Prāsaṅgika system], *pramāṇa* should be understood as "proper comprehension," as it is in reference to comprehending a thing properly or accurately that it is "valid cognition." Or [it can be said that] it is valid cognition in the sense that it comprehends its primary or main object. The first [gloss] is a legitimate one, as [scripture] gives "a wisdom that properly distinguishes phenomena" as the illustration of valid cognition. This is stated in the *Teaching of Akṣayamati Sutra*:

> That which properly knows virtuous and nonvirtuous phenomena is wisdom. That which analyzes the phenomena that have been distinguished is wisdom. Because it makes manifest the dharmas of the āryas, wisdom is valid. Wisdom . . . is what properly and accurately realizes all forms of obscuration and impediment.[1159]

Despite things being false and deceptive, it is possible, as this sutra describes, to comprehend them accurately, because we accept the existence of correct theses and correct reasoning. The second gloss is a legitimate one, in that *pra*, as a superlative, can denote "main." Thus it can be "valid cognition" in the sense that it comprehends its main [object], since "best," "foremost," and "main" are all notions with common currency in the world. The emphatic [*pra*] must refer to the thing comprehended, since *māṇa* represents what comprehends it.

One should be aware that the phrase "in the world" has a number of different possible connotations. In terms of the worldly-transcendent bipartition, something that is "in the world" necessarily has to be deceptively [i.e., conventionally] true. And in terms of whether a thing exists among worldly conventions or ultimately, all phenomena are of "the world," in that they exist [among conventions]. The conventional distinction between the comprehended and the comprehender, [for instance,] is one that has no place within the ārya's meditative equipoise. There is consequently no alternative to understanding it as belonging to the domain of worldly conventions. Hence it is categorically not the case that the Prāsaṅgika rejects whatever the world accepts. Nor is it the case that, [since things like the comprehended-comprehender distinction belong to the world,] they are unacceptable in the Prāsaṅgika's own scheme of things. As is frequently declared [in sutra], "I accept whatever is in the worldly domain."[1160] And this delivers a decisive refutation to the position espoused by Taktsang Lotsāwa. [419]

The varieties of valid cognition

There are four varieties of valid cognition, which can also be subsumed into two. What comprehends objects that are manifest is perception. Objects that are hidden are [divided into] those that are slightly hidden and those that are extremely hidden. What comprehends the former is inferential cognition. What comprehends the latter is valid cognition [associated with] scripture. There is also valid cognition through analogy, which comprehends a hidden object through reference to an analogue that is manifest. These are the four. By subsuming the latter three varieties into inferential cognition, these [four] may be reduced to two. *Clear Words* says, "It is thus established that the world realizes objects by means of four valid cognitions."[1161]

The number of valid cognitions is therefore determined by [the things valid cognition] comprehends. This is because the objects of the three forms of analyses—namely, the manifest, the slightly hidden, and the extremely hidden—constitute three domains of comprehension, whereas, it also proves necessary [to add to these] an *object of analogy*, which involves the blending or amalgamation of the manifest and the hidden, thus making four [in total]. What is more, other classifications of valid cognition, such as the one determined by a twofold division of objects of comprehension into those with specific and general characteristics, have already been ruled out. As *Clear Words* says, "The number of valid cognitions is dictated by the objects comprehended and . . . ."[1162] "Dictated by the objects comprehended" indicates that there are different divisions of objects of comprehension and that the divisions of valid cognition correspond with these. Unless [the words] are interpreted in this way, one would be forced to say that valid cognition is *controlled* by objects of comprehension, something that would be inconsistent with the pronouncement cited below that their dependence on each other is of equal measure. The way to understand this is [by looking at how the principle of] being "dictated by another" works in the case of a mutual exclusion-affirmation.[1163] Again, *Clear Words* says:

> Once the bifurcation of comprehended things is no longer in place, [valid cognition associated with] scripture and so forth can no longer be [dismissed] as other forms [of valid cognition] on the grounds that [their] objects are neither those with specific nor those with general characteristics.[1164] [420]

While those of the Svātantrika school and below give no prominence to the notion of the four valid cognitions, they are certainly what was intended by the ārya father and [spiritual] son—a fact confirmed by the way that both Nāgārjuna's *Dispeller of Dispute* and his commentary to it feature the nomenclature and number of this fourfold classification of valid cognitions, the manner that they comprehend their objects, and the means by which they are verified. *Dispeller of Dispute* says:

> If you deny things that have been observed by perception,
> then the perception that observed them also does not exist.
>
> Inference, scripture, analogy,
> [and] everything established by inference, scripture,
> and by means of analogy
> [would also be negated] in response to [this absence of]
> perception.[1165]

This passage uses the nomenclature and number of the fourfold classification of valid cognition in its negation of true existence. *Dispeller of Dispute* also says:

If valid cognition established itself,
then this valid cognition of yours would be wholly established
and would not depend on the objects it comprehends . . .

Valid cognitions do not establish themselves,
they are not [established] through mutual dependence
by other valid cognitions, nor by what they comprehend,
[but] neither are they causeless.[1166]

This indicates the way that objects comprehended by [these] valid cognitions are established. *Dispeller of Dispute* says:

If it is valid cognition that conclusively establishes those objects of yours,
then state what it is that conclusively establishes those valid cognitions of yours.
If you think that another valid cognition [establishes it],
there would be an infinite regress . . .
[it would] dispel the gloom in all worlds.[1167]

This considers and then rejects the notion that self-cognition and so forth could be what substantiates valid cognition. *Dispeller of Dispute* furthermore includes the passage:

An emanation created by an emanation . . . .[1168]

And [the section]:

[Those who have] mastered the state of things,
[and hold that] some phenomena are virtuous due to their virtuous nature
[should be able to provide] a detailed account [of that and] also for every other phenomenon in similar fashion . . .
For whom there is emptiness, all things remain possible.[1169]

What these explain is that in our system, the four valid cognitions, four domains of knowledge, and everything, including virtue, remain viable. And within this refutation of self-cognition, the way that things can still exist is represented. Thus, *Illuminating the Intent* states, "For the account of four valid cognitions, one should rely on the root *Dispeller of Dispute* and its commentary."[1170]

Hence a considerable number of Tibetan scholars belonging to the erstwhile [generation] attributed "more" valid cognitions to the Prāsaṅgika and the "fewer" of the definitive twofold division to the Svātantrika and those in the schools below him. Later Tibetans such as Taktsang Lotsāwa have said that the Prāsaṅgika system denies the fourfold division of valid cognition. These are claims that are not founded in thorough investigation. [421] The feasibility of four valid cognitions was not refuted even [by Dharmakīrti] in the *Commentary on Pramāṇa*, which is not to say that the bipartition between perception and inference is regarded as any less definitive, since those [four] are explained as being subsumed within the twofold division of perception and inference. The assertions [of those Tibetans are therefore] works of pure speculation [by those] who have not even seen Śāntarakṣita's explanation to the above effect in his *Compendium of Suchness*.

[Although a slight departure from the main discussion,] elaboration of this point is entirely warranted. This nomenclature and typological classification of valid cognition is not the invention of later monk-scholars and masters but is something that has simply always been there. The Conqueror frequently refers to it throughout the higher and lower scriptural collections. *Elucidating the Intention Sutra*, which is a commentary on the import of sutras relating to both Hinayana and Mahayana, says, "Thus the reasoning *establishing correctness* fully verifies [a thing] by means of the five characteristics associated with valid perception, valid inferential cognition, and valid cognition relating to an [authoritative] scripture in which there is confidence."[1171] This passage reveals how something is verified by means of the three forms of analyses. The [sutra] also uses the term "conjoined [with a homogenous] analogy," as it elaborates:

> What then are the five types of characteristics of full verification? They are the characteristic [relating to] that which is manifestly observed, the characteristic [relating to] what is manifestly observed in dependence on that [first one], the characteristic [relating to something] conjoining with a homogenous analogy, the characteristic [relating to] rigorous confirmation, and the characteristic [relating to] something that is stated in a completely pure scripture.[1172]

This passage reveals both the way a thing is verified by means of the three analyses and the objects of the four valid cognitions. "Manifestly observed" refers to the objects of the three types of valid perception. "In dependence on that" denotes [what becomes] the object of inference [through being cognized] by means of that perception. The third refers to the object of the [valid cognition] that comprehends through analogy. The fourth indicates the way that those three valid cognitions confirm [their respective objects]. And the fifth clearly identifies the object of valid cognition [associated with] scripture. The same sutra [covers these further] in the section, "With respect to that, all composite things are impermanent . . . one should know this to be the characteristic [relating to] something that is stated in a completely pure scripture."[1173]

Valid perception is defined as "a cognition that does not overtly rely on a correct reason as its basis but is nondeceptive with respect to its apprehended object, that manifest thing (*pratyakṣa*) that it comprehends." The explanation given above establishes that these characteristics fully encompass [all instances of] what they define. In the present [Prāsaṅgika] context, the fact that a cognition is a valid perception *with respect to something* does not necessarily mean that it is a valid perception. [422] Whether the thing in question is one [classified as] characterizer or characterized, and whether it is, according to the realist schools, a specific or general characteristic, if it is "in the world"—in the sense that it exists for a worldly cognition, through such a cognition having its aspect—then it is an object that is manifest (*pratyakṣa*) and nonhidden for the [cognitive] subject in question. And it is by token of this that the subject is also affirmed to be a valid perception (*pratyakṣa*) with reference to that object. *Clear Words* states:

> Whether it be [the thing] characterized, a specific or general characteristic, what exists for the world is everything that it manifestly observes, and which is, because of that, not hidden [with respect] to it. Due to that, [the object,] together with the subject that has its aspect, is *pratyakṣa*.[1174]

This tells us that any cognition to which things appear dualistically is necessarily a valid perception of its own [manifestly] appearing object. "For the world" indicates that the perspective referred to is that of worldly cognition. "Exists for" refers to the presence that the object or its aspect has for such a cognition. The remainder of the passage describes how the object and subject, in dependence on each other, are respectively classified as actual and figurative *pratyakṣa*. This is how things are explained in [Tsongkhapa's] *Illuminating the Intent*.

This system maintains therefore that in cases such as when the moon appears double, or when strands of hair appear to fall in the space [before the viewer's eyes], such appearances are also manifestly perceived. This does not, however, contradict the way that those belonging to the world understand such matters, since they share the view that what determines whether sense cognitions are perceptions or not is whether they are affected [by defects] such as the [affliction associated with] blurredness. For [a cognition without a defect,] such a thing [as the falling hairs] does not manifestly appear, and [that cognition] is consequently not a perception of it. Neither can that [cognition] induce ascertainment [of that thing], so it cannot have been a valid cognition of it. [Conversely,] to [a cognition with the defect, such a thing] manifestly appears, and hence there is a perception [of the appearance]. And since that [cognition] is capable, without reference to any other valid cognition, of inducing ascertainment of the presence of that [appearance], it is also a valid cognition [of it]. *Clear Words* states, "From the point of view of cognitions without [the defect] of the blurredness, a double moon and so forth are not manifest (*pratyakṣa*), whereas from the point of view of those with the blurredness, they are absolutely manifest."[1175] [423]

Sense perception

There are three varieties of valid perception—sense perception, mental perception, and yogic perception—each of which is discussed on numerous occasions in Prāsaṅgika accounts. These three can be subsumed into two, those that directly rely on a physical sense power as their governing condition and those that rely solely on a mental sense power as that condition. The first of these is divided into the five sense perceptions, whereas the second is composed of mental perception and yogic perception. *Illuminating the Intent* states, "They are limited to valid cognitions that rely directly on a physical sense power and those that rely solely on a mental sense power."[1176]

Valid sense perception is defined as "a cognition that relies directly on its governing condition, a physical sense power, and is nondeceptive with respect to its apprehended object, a manifest thing." The characteristics defining [all five sense perceptions follow this pattern]: from perception apprehending [visual] form, which is defined as "a cognition that relies directly on its governing condition, a visual [sense power], and is nondeceptive with respect to its apprehended object, a visual form,"[1177] through to perception apprehending tactility, which is defined as "a cognition that relies directly on its governing condition, the corporeal sense power, and is nondeceptive with respect to its apprehended object, a tactile object."

Upon examination the five sense powers are [found to] arise from the [physical] elements and to be material, and so they cannot [themselves] apprehend objects. But from the unstudied perspective of valid cognitions involved with worldly conventions, we should accept that the six, the eye and so forth, are the senses, that the six sources, [visual] form and so forth, are their six objects, and also that it is due to the coming together of sense and object that the six cognitions come about. One must also acknowledge that [such matters] are the ripening effects of karma [and thus] are beyond our ken. The first point is established, since the *Commentary to Four Hundred Stanzas* states, "Here, the six, the eye and so forth, are the six senses, and visual form and so forth are, corresponding to the nature of each, their six objects. And it is due to the senses and the consciousnesses that the group of six consciousnesses come about."[1178] [424] The same work also says, "The eye sees only [visual] forms, not smells or so forth, since the objects [of the respective senses] are distinct."[1179] If subjected to examination, [the senses] are unfindable, but when not so subjected, they are valid [knowers of these objects], because the *King of Samādhis Sutra* states:

> [With regard to that], the eye, the ear, and the nose are not valid.
> The tongue, the body, and the mind are not valid.
> If these senses were valid [with regard to thatness],
> what would an ārya path do for anyone?
> Because these senses are not valid,
> being by nature neutral, physical matter . . . .[1180]

This establishes the above, since in singling out *thatness* and negating that [the senses] are valid [knowers of it, the passage] implicitly conveys that they are valid [knowers] of deceptive [conventional] objects. This is confirmed by [Candrakīrti's] *Commentary on Sixty Stanzas of Reasoning* where it says, "In viewing [things] as existing, they do not see thatness."[1181] And it is why the Blessed One's pronouncement "[With regard to that], the eye, the ear, and the nose are not valid . . ."[1182] is cited. The *Commentary to Four Hundred Stanzas* says, "At this point it indicates that the five, the eye and so on, arise from the [physical] elements. Each is distinct, as their actions [are directed at] different objects. Thus it is [the case] that the eye sees only forms and does not hear sounds. And also that the ear hears sounds and does not see only forms."[1183]

The second part of the reason is established, since in the context of worldly understanding, it is inappropriate to contradict direct experience, and to deny that the eye sees form would be to do just that. And even if one treats each sense as the governing factor, the reason why the eye serves as governing condition for seeing forms and not that for hearing sounds must be accounted for by saying that [finally] it is one of those unfathomable matters relating to the ripening of karma, since in the sutra collections it talks of how, for the snake and [also] the people of the Godānīya continent, it is their eyes that sense sounds. The *Compendium of Suchness* also states, "That the snake listens with its eyes is [something] commonly accepted."[1184] And the *Commentary to Four Hundred Stanzas* remarks:

> Thus, regarding such matters of the world, the wise do not only see them and concur with the sort of analysis described, but they accept them as unfathomable [issues relating to] the ripening effects of karma. [They] accept that the whole of the world [exists] in the manner of a conjuration, created by an illusory conjurer. What is experienced cannot be challenged. And that experience [says], "Even though the eye is derived from the [physical] elements, it sees only form and does not hear sound."[1185] [425]

That [commentary] also cites a number of sources in support of this. It explains, therefore, that despite them being false, in the manner of one emanation yielding another or one illusion yielding another, worldly matters such as the [eye and so forth] comprehending [form and so forth] must still be accepted. Taktsang Lotsāwa's contention that what exists in a false manner cannot serve as an object for valid cognition is [therefore] tantamount to finding fault with the Conqueror and the ārya father and [spiritual] son, because it contradicts so many such [authoritative] pronouncements and logical reasons. "Shape" is explained as being something that is included in both the first and the fifth sources [i.e., form source and tactile source].

Mental perception

Valid mental perception is defined as "a cognition that directly relies only on its unique governing condition, a mental sense power, does not rely on calm abiding, special insight, and so forth, and is nondeceptive with respect to its apprehended object, a manifest thing." While all tenet schools agree on these [characteristics], what distinguishes the Prāsaṅgika from the Svātantrika and those in the schools below him is that they hold the majority of these [cognitions] to be conceptual. As far as the [Prāsaṅgika is concerned], there are many examples of mental perceptions that think in terms of predication and so forth. This makes it necessary to remove "free from conception" from the characteristics that define valid perception, which is the [Prāsaṅgika's] reason for refuting [this characteristic]. The evidence for this has already been presented.

There are many varieties of mental perception. Among these are those mental perceptions that have been induced by the five sense perceptions and that have the aspect of the five objects. There are also mental perceptions with the aspect of internal sensations such as pleasure. There are mental perceptions with a phenomenon-source as their object. And there are also mental perceptions such as those that recall the events of the distant past. There are five of the first [variety, induced by sense perception]. These arise once the sense perception apprehending [one of] the five objects has ceased, and they have the aspect of what the sense apprehended but are mental, conceptual cognitions. The *Commentary to Four Hundred Stanzas* states:

> A consciousness that derives from a physical sense is produced to discern the aspect of a present object. The object and the cognition, being [subject to the process of] momentary disintegration, [advance] to their cessation, but a mental cognition arises thereafter. [426] That [mental cognition], which is produced in accordance with the causal force of the visual consciousness and so forth, will arise conceiving of the aspect of the consciousness that originated in the senses and will be generated with its aspect.[1186]

This [passage] establishes that [these mental perceptions have such a character], since "conceiving of the aspect of the consciousness that originated in the senses" specifies that the identity of this cognition is conceptual.

Such a mental perception is necessarily one that (1) has something belonging to the past as its object, (2) is a conceptual cognition, and (3) is only produced subsequent to the sense cognition that induced it. That it is a conceptual cognition is easy to understand. That it has an object belonging to the past is a point that will be discussed below. [The third feature]—that it is not until a sense perception has ceased to operate that such a mental perception can be produced—is the one that is misunderstood and gives rise to [the error] of those in the Mahayana system who assert that there can only be a single consciousness. [Nāgārjuna's] *Precious Garland* [also] states:

> When the mental [cognition] observes and realizes,
> the aspect of a past object that has been observed by the senses . . . .[1187]

And [Gyaltsab] Darma Rinchen's commentary to these lines says, "Because when the mind observes and realizes the aspect of the object that has already been observed by the sense and is an object of the past at the [mind's] own time, it thinks of [that object] as [such and such], and a single continuum cannot contain numerous thoughts simultaneously."[1188] The *Commentary to Four Hundred Stanzas* also states, "Here, when the visual cognition that has been produced in dependence on the eye and form ceases, it does so simultaneously with the sense and the object. Once it ceases, the very same thing that has already been seen will next be apprehended by the mind."[1189] "Already been seen . . ." indicates that this [mental cognition] has an object belonging to the past.

Is it the case, then, that the [Prāsaṅgika] understands the Abhidharma passage "Those things [known by] the two cognitions [sense and mental] are the five external [objects]"[1190] in the same way as the [follower of the] Pramāṇa [tradition]? He does not. According to this [Prāsaṅgika school], the context of stating that the visual cognition and the mental perception that it induces have the "same" object is that of them not being subjected to analysis. But when they are subjected to analysis, their objects [are revealed] not to be the same. The first point is established, as it is one dealt with in the *Commentary to Four Hundred Stanzas* section that says, "So how then are [the words] taken from the Abhidharma to be interpreted? . . . It is in terms of worldly conventions that something is said to be known by two consciousnesses."[1191] The second point is established, since [Āryadeva's] *Four Hundred Stanzas* remarks, "Likewise, two consciousnesses do not know the same object."[1192] [427] And in [his] commentary to that, [Candrakīrti] says, "The two consciousnesses do not, therefore, know a single object."[1193] Each of the aforementioned five mental perceptions has [two varieties]—those induced by sense cognitions that were valid and those induced by sense cognitions that were false—since [even] the sense cognition to which the moon appears as double induces a valid mental perception with regard to what appears to it.

Second, there are three varieties of mental perception with the aspect of an [internal] sensation, [those with the aspect] of pleasure and so forth. *Entering the Middle Way* states, "Feeling has the character of a sensation."[1194] And the section on the analysis of time in the *Commentary to Four Hundred Stanzas* says, "[Unlike] feelings and so forth, it does not [have] the aspect of experiencing a sensation."[1195] "And so forth" in this [passage] indicates [that there are also] mental perceptions that comprehend objects and have the aspect of sensation but are not induced by the senses.

Third, there are mental perceptions with a phenomenon-source as their object, such as minds that, without making any sort of differentiation between reality and fiction, grasp to a notion of "I," and those that grasp to the notion of "mine." There are also recollective cognitions that are induced by [the minds] that grasp at the two forms of self and that ascertain what appears [to those minds]. There are also those mental perceptions that grasp to such things as permanence, or to a dream, and have the aspect of sensations—that is, experiencing. This is [supported by] the *Commentary to Four Hundred Stanzas* in passages such as the one cited immediately above, and also where it says, "[It is] like the recollection, during the waking state, of an object experienced within a dream."[1196] There are also numerous passages in Jé [Tsongkhapa's] works identifying the notion that holds "I"—without making any sort of differentiation between reality and fiction—as the conventional valid cognition responsible for the establishment of "I."

Fourth, there are also many mental perceptions that recall [what belongs to] the past. There are those that recollect external [things] and those that recollect internal ones. For each of these, there are mental perceptions that recall [things] of the immediate past and those that recall [things] of the distant past. The first of these include the five mental perceptions induced by the five sense cognitions. It also includes the five mental perceptions that, immediately after one of the five sense cognitions have apprehended an object, recall, "I have experienced this object." Both the root [*Four Hundred Stanzas*] and [Candrakīrti's] commentary specify that these do not know their objects directly as the sense cognitions do but [instead] recall them. [428] Also, *Illuminating the Intent* says, "It is stated that first sense cognition knows the objects of form and so forth directly and that it is due to sense cognition that mental perception knows them, though not in the direct manner that sense cognition does. It is also stated that this is a [form of] recollection."[1197]

[Khedrup Jé's] *Providing the Fortunate with Sight* similarly affirms that it is due to a sense cognition that a mental cognition recalls the object.[1198] This tells us that a mental perception produced due to a sense cognition is not vivid and that it is [a form of] recollection. However, it does not mean that all mental perceptions lack vividness, nor that they are necessarily recollections, since many of them, such as the three feelings, [experience] objects that are present at their own time. Also, works such as [Tsongkhapa's] *Stages of the Path* and *Dispelling the Gloom of Erroneous Views*[1199] explicitly state that the three coarser feelings, and among these, pleasure and suffering especially, have a vivid aspect.

The root [*Four Hundred Stanzas*] and its commentary convey the point about this [mental perception] being a form of recollection in the following manner. *Four Hundred Stanzas* states:

> The thing that has already been seen does not reappear,
> and the cognition [of it] is not reproduced.
> Thus "recollection" arises in a false fashion
> and [relates to] its object totally falsely.[1200]

On this, [Candrakīrti's] commentary says, "The identity of a thing—as it is at the present time, one that is seen directly by the present cognition—will never appear again. [And] that the same object can be discerned by two consciousnesses has already been rejected . . . Thus what recollection observes is a thing of the past."[1201]

There are also the second kind [i.e., those that relate to the distant past] because there are things that, due to the imprint they left on the mind, can be recalled with a vivid image, but at the point of their recollection have long since ceased and retreated into the past, and [as such] no longer exist, having no more reality than illusions. It is, for instance, possible to have recollection of perishing from a mortal wound as if it happened yesterday, even though eons may have passed. And due to the imponderable power of dependent connections, it is possible for the footprint of a pigeon on a straw roof to be seen in the yogurt [inside the home] below it.[1202] *Four Hundred Stanzas* states:

> If [you hold that] the self [must be] permanent
> because it recollects past existences,
> then why not [hold that] the body is permanent
> because we see on it the scars of former [lives]?[1203]

[Candrakīrti's] comments on this [are contained in the section] "Here, the body of the present life will bear a scar resulting from the wound received from a weapon or something in a former existence. . . . In that the composite continuum, which so clearly [displays] its causal attributes, is purely impermanent, the appropriator of that, the self that is imputed to it, can [logically] be said to remember former existences."[1204] [429] This kind of cognition recollecting [previous existences] is also developed by many bodhisattvas, not by means of concentration but through the power of prayer—something that [further] establishes this [form of] mental perception. However, not all recollection is mental perception, as there are a whole range of recollections induced by inferential cognitions realizing hidden objects such as selflessness and impermanence. What is more, not every valid cognition falls into one of the four [categories]. The division of valid cognitions into four is made from the standpoint of the objects that such cognitions comprehend and is not intended to be a division of the exhaustive variety. Thus, while valid cognitions are subsumed within the fourfold categorization of perception and inferences, an individual cognition may not be any one of them. And in the case of a conceptual mental perception, if none among the objects that it apprehends are manifest (*pratyakṣa*), it does not count as valid perception. This is because only those cognitions with objects that are manifest are classified as perception.

Yogic perception

Yogic perception is defined as "a cognition that arises directly from its unique governing condition, the concentration that unites calm abiding and special insight, and that due to perceiving its apprehended object—one of the features of the four truths or either the coarse or subtle forms of selflessness—directly, is nondeceptive with respect to that."

It is *yogic* in the sense that the union of calm abiding and special insight has been attained and it depends on this. And while [things such as] the two forms of selflessness and so forth are, in general, hidden [phenomena], for the transcendent awareness that realizes them directly, they are *pratyakṣa* and manifest. So, in terms of its (*pratyakṣa*) object, this awareness can be identified as "valid *pratyakṣa*"—[an identification] that is justified because the Blessed One himself affirmed it. [This identification] is also justified because the object the awareness apprehends is manifest *to it*. [And also,] even though the object of such an awareness is a hidden [phenomenon] in general, that awareness engages the object's aspect in a manner that is entirely accurate, meaning that by the *standards* of worldly convention, it can be regarded as a valid *pratyakṣa* of that [object].

The first point, [that the Blessed One affirmed that this is "valid *pratyakṣa*" in terms of its object,] is established since the *Commentary on Sixty Stanzas of Reasoning* states, "Thus there is no inconsistency in a cognition being a *pratyakṣa*, even though it is one that the deceptive world does not [itself] observe,"[1205] and, "Thus [the Buddha] affirmed that cognition of the nonproduction of suffering is also *pratyakṣa*."[1206] [430] *Illuminating the Intent* also states, "*Commentary on Sixty Stanzas of Reasoning* relates how the Teacher, the Buddha, affirmed that true cessations are cognized manifestly."[1207]

The second point, [that the object is manifest to that awareness,] is established since the *Commentary on Sixty Stanzas of Reasoning* states, "A cognition, the operation of which accurately discerns a thing just as it is, is a perception of that. Therefore this system is correct."[1208] Thus that is what is required in order to [count as a cognition that] validly perceives something that is a hidden [phenomenon].

The third point, [that the awareness satisfies the standards of worldly convention for being regarded as a valid *pratyakṣa* of that object,] is established, since the *Commentary on Sixty Stanzas of Reasoning* says:

> As the nature of the cognition involved, like the thing it observes, is that of something that is not produced, it is [able] to engage the object accurately, observing it exactly the way it is. And in the world also, it is due to [observing a thing] in this fashion that something is said to perceive [that thing] . . . [A local] informs the traveler, "There is no water in the location, [and if you go to check for yourself] my words will be made manifest (*pratyakṣa*)." Thus it is also definitely the case in the world that not observing what is not there can be "manifest" (*pratyakṣa*).[1209]

It should be noted that this also demonstrates that the notion the Svātantrika and those in the schools below him have of perception (*pratyakṣa*) does not conform with that of the world, whereas our school's understanding is entirely compatible with it.

The Cittamātra school and above[1210] advocate that a yogic perceiver must have [some form of] selflessness as its overt object and that dualistic appearances with respect to that must have ceased. Those in the realist camp, such as the Vaibhāṣika and Sautrāntika schools, hold that the object overtly apprehended by any perception is necessarily something with specific characteristics.[1211] They maintain that initially, during [the paths of] accumulation and preparation, the selflessness of persons is realized by means of an object universal. It is through [continuous] meditation that complete familiarity with [selflessness] is gained. And this leads to the object—something impermanent and without portions, having only specific characteristics, unalloyed with general characteristics but *devoid* of a self—becoming "manifest." The *Compendium of Pramāṇa* says, "Yogis behold only what is taught by the gurus, an entity that is unalloyed."[1212] This is covered in the *Commentary on Sixty Stanzas of Reasoning* in the section "What the yogis behold is only that which derives directly from what the gurus have taught, an object that is unalloyed with conceptuality and is without superimpositions . . . [What they] realize is purely a thing, devoid of any earlier and later portions."[1213] [431]

The Prāsaṅgika responds, "This is not tenable, because things with specific and general characteristics are objects of knowledge that are meant to preclude each other, but here, meditation on a selflessness with general characteristics [supposedly] culminates in the manifestation of a thing with specific characteristics on which [the individual] has not been meditating. The reason is established, because you have asserted that it is meditation on a conceptually constructed selflessness with general characteristics that creates familiarity with an entity that has specific characteristics, a thing unalloyed with any general characteristics, which [thereby] becomes the overt object [of the yogic perception]. You have also insisted that the object overtly apprehended by any perception is necessarily something with specific characteristics." If [the realist] were to challenge the pervasion, [the Prāsaṅgika would respond,] "It follows that all phenomena that the individual has not meditated on become perceivable [to him], because while he meditated on something with general characteristics, what this [manifests] is something with purely specific characteristics, on which he has not meditated." If [the realist] accepted this argument, it would place him in a ridiculous position. Thus, as the *Commentary on Sixty Stanzas of Reasoning* phrases this:

> Since [he has] asserted that things with specific and general characteristics are discrete, it is not tenable for the application of meditation that has a general aspect to culminate in [perception] of an object with specific characteristics. If one subjects [his] statements on this matter to decisive examination, [they are seen to] entirely lack coherence [and force him into] a ridiculous extreme.[1214]

That [passage] sets out the ridiculous position [he is forced into]. The rest is straightforward. There are various other attacks [that could be made on the realist stance], but these are not related [in the commentary].

Yogic perceivers can be divided in various ways. These include the threefold categorization of yogic perceptions in the continua of the three [kinds of] āryas. There are also the various yogic perceptions in the continua of ordinary beings, realizing [objects such as] impermanence and so forth—the sixteen attributes of the four truths—on the coarse level, or the lack of a substantially existent self. That there are yogic perceivers in the continua of ordinary beings is something stated unequivocally [by Khedrup Gelek Palsang] in the [*Thousand Measures:*] *Providing the Fortunate with Sight*. It is also the intention of the second conqueror [Tsongkhapa], as it makes up part of his notes on the unique features of the Prāsaṅgika system.[1215] It is also the thought behind many passages in the *Commentary to Entering the Middle Way*, such as "Despite not having gained the view of thatness, one can determine such things as impermanence by valid cognition ... That [they] are capable of realizing that selflessness, through perception, is established by lines of reasoning that prove [the existence of] yogic perceivers."[1216] Moreover, this is also the intention [of Śāntideva] in *Entering the Bodhisattva Way*, where we find lines such as, "Even though they have no delusions, they are seen to have karmic propensities."[1217] Furthermore, it reflects the Blessed One's own intention. [432] The *Closely Guarded Concentration Sutra* contains words such as, "The truths for āryas ... And [such an individual] thinks, 'I have become an arhat.'"[1218] These [refer to the cases of individuals who] manifest [qualities of] knowledge and abandonment with regard to the four truths and, through meditating on the path [associated with them], achieve a state that they believe is arhatship. That sutra relates that despite being Buddhists, such individuals can develop doubts in the Buddha at the time of their deaths and be reborn in hell. The [conclusion] that such individuals are ordinary beings is, therefore, inescapable. This sutra is also cited in both *Clear Words* and the *Compendium of Sutras*, indicating that the ārya father and [spiritual] son are among the many who understand it this way. Hence the attempts of those Tibetans who contest Jé [Tsongkhapa's] explanation are thoroughly refuted.

Inferential valid cognition

Valid inferential cognition is defined as "a cognition that relies on a reason as its basis and is nondeceptive with respect to its apprehended object, the hidden [phenomenon] that it comprehends." As it would be illogical to employ a reason [to establish] what is already manifest, the apprehended object of an inferential cognition must be something that is hidden. Hence the object of an inferential cognition is a hidden [phenomenon]. A hidden [phenomenon] is something that must be realized by means of a reason. That reason cannot be mistaken with respect to the thesis that it is set to prove, so it must not be (1) contrary [to it], (2) inconclusive, (3) unestablished, or (4) associated with lingering doubts. The inference should thus be a cognition derived from a reason that is unmistaken with regard to the thesis. As to how [such a cognition] is generated, the reason in question is taken and [its] relationship [to the predicate] recalled, following which the thesis is inferred—that is, a valid cognition comprehending that [thesis] is produced. As *Elucidating the Intention Sutra* says:

> All composite things are momentary . . . It is by means of what is observed manifestly that what is not manifest can be inferred. And whatever is in accord with that is situated in it and has the characteristic of being observed in a manifest fashion . . . .[1219]

And *Clear Words* says, "The cognition with an object that is a hidden [phenomenon], one generated from a reason that is unmistaken with respect to the thesis, is an inference."[1220] It is also [communicated] in *The Correct* in the passage "This [indicates] that the valid cognitive awareness that has established the property of the subject and what pervades it [is the one that] ascertains it to be the reason. Through this, a cognitive inference is produced . . . Inference is what derives from the thing that is to be established through the mediation of the cognition of the reason."[1221] [433]

I have made a point of properly explaining this section of *Clear Words* relating to inference, having noted that other scholars have neglected it. While this [section] can be seen to supply the characteristics defining [inference], the evidence substantiating it, and the derivation of its name, for the sake of those with feeble intellect, I here spell out that derivation in simple terms. There is a rationale for using "valid subsequent inference" to denote the valid inferential cognition realizing selflessness in that [such a cognition] can be referred to as (1) a "subsequent inference," in the sense that it [involves] the comprehension of a thesis that has been inferred following the taking of a reason and the recollection of its relationship [to the predicate], and (2) a "valid cognition," in the sense that it is totally nondeceptive about or has the measure of its primary object or the thing it comprehends. The first part of this derivation is established by the fact that, while *anu* and *māna*—the [two portions of] *anumāna*, the [Sanskrit] equivalent of *inferential cognition*—respectively denote "subsequent" and "comprehension," the import of *māna* [in the present context] determines that it should be translated as "inferential [comprehension]." As the passage from *Clear Words* above says, "The cognition with an object that is a hidden [phenomenon], one generated from a reason that is unmistaken with respect to the thesis, is an inference."[1222] And *The "Shorter" Correct* states, "That which infers [the thesis] after it has taken a reason and recollected its relationship [to the predicate] is subsequent inference."[1223]

[Valid inferential cognition] can be divided into those turned toward and realizing things in terms of their reality and those realizing things in terms of their diversity.[1224] Each of these has three varieties: (1) inferential cognition,[1225] (2) valid cognition [associated] with scripture or inference [relating to] conviction, and (3) [inferential cognition] of analogy.

Regarding those realizing things in terms of their reality, an example of the first of the three varieties is an inference that relies on the reason "[because it is] dependently related" to realize that the sprout is without true existence. [Regarding the second variety,] generally speaking, all those in the Cittamātra and Madhyamaka [schools] agree that the principal object comprehended by a valid cognition [associated] with scripture is something that is extremely hidden. Dharmakīrti states, "When moving into the third domain [of knowledge], citing a passage of scripture is the procedure of the wise."[1226] But as will be explained, it is possible, at least theoretically, to have a valid cognition [associated with] scripture that realizes selflessness. So [an example of the second variety of] inferential cognition could be one that uses the reason "[because it is] a scripture that has been verified by means of the threefold analysis" to realize that the extensive Mother [*Prajñāpāramitā Sutra*][1227] is nondeceptive with respect to the thing it teaches, the true cessation (that is) *dharmakāya*. [An example of the] third is an inferential cognition that uses the analogy of the reflection of a face in the mirror not existing the way it appears to realize that the sprout, likewise, lacks the true existence it appears to have. [434] Among the three [types] of reason—effect, nature, and nonobservation—this is pervaded by the latter, since the reason upon which [such an inferential cognition] depends is necessarily a negative one.

This first category also contains both those that depend on the operation of a consequence and those that depend on the presentation of a proof. The latter is straightforward and has already been covered. Regarding those that depend on the operation of a consequence, the section on special insight in the *Greater Stages of the Path* states, "When this is done by means of a consequence, it is in dependence on the operation [of that consequence] that the inference is produced, and there will be no overt [presentation] of a proof statement to establish the thesis."[1228] Logical reasoning can also be used to establish this [point], because for an opponent of sharp faculties, a consequence alerting [him] to a contradiction [in his own position] can, by means of [confronting him with] valid counter evidence, convey to him the irreconcilability in his own thesis and thereby give rise to an inferential cognition realizing that the object of his thesis does not exist. A consequence can also be deployed [simply] to communicate the inconsistency within an incorrect position, as is the case, for example, when a proof statement connecting dissimilar phenomena is presented to the right opponent. With respect to this, *Clear Words* says, "If one uses this alone in the debate, will the opposing party not yield?"[1229] And, when someone of sharp faculties is made aware of evidence that counters his thesis, he will disclaim his original tenet and generate a valid cognition realizing that the object of his thesis does not exist. The special insight section of the *Greater Stages of the Path* contains passages such as "Once one who asserts [intrinsic] nature sees that the evidence presented to him is counter to this, he will reject the tenet holding to the existence of a nature established by way of its own identity,"[1230] and also "Once [he] realizes, through valid cognition, that a thing is not established by way of its own identity, [he will] relinquish the realist tenet."[1231] The Prāsaṅgika and the Svātantrika [it should be remembered] each have their own respective [literal] meanings.[1232]

Hence those of you who, on occasions, either unknowingly cast doubt on the Great Lord Jé [Tsongkhapa's] excellent explanations or who, in the manner of someone crazed, just oppose them with no reason other than because they are what he said, should desist. Only once you have composed yourselves and have engaged in a dispassionate examination of the matters in question should you pronounce judgment. [435]

Valid cognition [associated with] scripture

Valid cognition [associated with] scripture is defined as "a cognition that relies, as a reason, on a [section of] scripture that has been verified by means of the threefold analysis, and is nondeceptive with respect to what it comprehends—the hidden [phenomenon] that is the object of that scriptural passage." For something that is manifest, one does not even require logical reasoning to establish it, so it goes without saying that there is no need for scripture. As for hidden [phenomena], the lord of reasoning [Dharmakīrti] says "Who would suggest that for every examination one must turn to scripture?"[1233] As this indicates, things such as the impermanence of sound can easily be established by means of logical reasoning, and if a scripture was required in order to do that, the ridiculous conclusion would be that nothing could be [proved] without the citation of some passage of scripture. Thus scripture is not necessary [with regard to such things]. The object comprehended by a valid cognition [associated with] scripture is one that is extremely hidden and lies beyond the ken of the senses. It is explained that the [section of] scripture in question must be one whose contents have been verified by means of the threefold analysis. This must determine (1) whether what [the section] asserts is something known by perception and whether it contradicts perceptual experience, (2) whether [what it asserts] contradicts logic, reasoning, and what the world accepts to be the case, and (3) whether the scripture has internal inconsistencies regarding either its overt and implicative meanings or what different sections of it assert.[1234]

The scripture's content must also be something regarding which a valid cognition [relating to] conviction can gain ascertainment. *Clear Words* says, "Those words of which one becomes convinced and whose object is something outside [the scope of] the senses and is known directly is *scripture*."[1235] "Something outside [the scope of] the senses" refers to the object of such a valid cognition. "Of which one becomes convinced" refers to its having been verified by means of the threefold analysis. It also conveys valid cognition [associated with] scripture or inference of conviction. "Those words" conveys scripture or authoritative scripture, because here [in the Prāsaṅgika system, as in other Buddhist schools] it is also held to be the case that certain scriptures are valid.

[The Prāsaṅgika] also holds that certain persons and that which comprehends an object [i.e., a cognition] are valid. The first is established, since there are numerous passages [referring to these authoritative scriptures], such as, for instance, [Candrakīrti's *Clear Words*,] which states, "*Compendium of Sutras* says, 'This is something that can be known from many authoritative scriptures,'"[1236] and *Entering the Middle Way Autocommentary*, which says, "Scriptural passages that are nonerroneous [are] valid."[1237] The second [that certain persons are valid] is also established, since *Precious Garland* states, "Who is the valid [authority] superior to the Conqueror on this matter?"[1238] and [*Entering the Middle Way*] refers to "a treatise composed by a person who is a valid [authority]."[1239] The third point [that there are valid cognitions] is established, since [comprehension can] refer to (1) the comprehender, in the sense of the individual who does the comprehending, (2) the instrument, that by means of which there is comprehension, or (3) the object, that which is comprehended.[1240] [436] The first of these is the agent. The second is the instrument and [cognitive] subject, which is valid cognition. The third is the object of the action and the thing comprehended. This is in line with the analysis [of action] set out earlier, distinguishing between what is acted on and what acts, since it is in relation to an agent, instrument, and object that the terms *valid* [*cognition*] and *comprehension* communicate [their meaning]. In this, they are like the word *feeling* and the phrase *cutting of wood*. As *Illuminating the Intent* expresses this:

> Since *feeling* (*vedanā*) is a word with agent, instrument, and object dimensions, it can be translated [to denote] the person who *feels*, that by means of which [the person] *feels*, or what is *felt*. The second of these is valid cognition, that faculty in mind [classified as] "feeling." The third is that of which one is aware—namely, pleasure, suffering, or [a sensation that is] neutral.[1241]

Clear Words also states:

> Furthermore, if consciousness is the instrument of the action, what would be the agent [of the action of] discerning the object? Without the agent responsible for the action, there can be no instrument and so forth. Just as with the act of cutting . . . This is extraordinary! You use only the language that embraces the connection between object and agent, in spite [of the fact that you] do not accept the reality of object, agent, and so forth that the words [convey]. Oh, this is incredible! You are guided simply by whimsy.[1242]

It should be understood that [what this expresses] is applicable to many situations.

Regarding the derivation of the word *āgama-pramāṇa* ["scriptural pramāṇa"], *āgama* may refer to such things as scriptural passages, sudden appearances, and so forth, whereas *pramāṇa* denotes what is valid [and authoritative]. Based on this understanding, the rationale for using "valid scripture" to describe the three Mother Prajñāpāramitā Sutras is that they are [firstly] "scripture" in three senses—(1) having being transmitted through a line [of those who] have rid themselves of imperfections, (2) being that which informs fully, and (3) being that which progresses. [Secondly,] they are "valid" in the sense of being correct and nondeceptive with regard to their meaning.

The three glosses in the first [part of the] derivation are established [as correct], since that is the meaning of *āgama*, the Sanskrit equivalent of "scripture," explained in the [Sanskrit treatises on] definitive etymologies. In its commentary to the fifteenth chapter of the *Fundamental Treatise on the Middle Way*, *Clear Words* says:

> Therefore, (1) because it has been handed down [through a succession of] those who have rid themselves of imperfections [and in whom there can be] confidence, (2) because it fully informs, in that it fully informs about the reality of thatness, and (3) because it progresses, in that through dependence on it one can advance to the freedom beyond the sorrows of the world, the teachings of the Fully Enlightened One, the Buddha, alone, are recognized as "scripture." [437] And due to their lack of correctness, the canonical works of other systems are definitely not recognized as valid [authority] and [holy] "scripture."[1243]

Also, at this point in *Ocean of Reasoning*, [Tsongkhapa] says, "Explained in terms of the derivation of the [Sanskrit] equivalent of 'scripture,' it is scripture in the sense of being handed down by those who have rid themselves of all imperfections and in whom there can be confidence . . . [for which reason they are] recognized."[1244]

The second [part of the derivation] is established [as correct], since *Clear Words* states, "Only the pronouncements of the Blessed One are described as valid, in that they are correct and therefore nondeceptive."[1245] And [Tsongkhapa's] commentary to that says, "It is the pronouncements of the Conqueror alone that are regarded as valid [authority], since they are correct, and thereby nondeceptive."[1246]

[Similarly,] there is a rationale for using "valid cognition [associated with] scripture" to describe the inferences of conviction that, through reliance on the *King Dhāraṇīśvara Sutra* and *Teaching of Akṣayamati Sutra*, realize the three secrets of the buddhas and bodhisattvas. [This rationale] is that those two sutras (1) satisfy all three meanings of "scripture" according to the glosses outlined above, and (2) it is by depending on [the two scriptures] that the inferences [they give rise to] are nondeceptive with respect to their object, and are [thus] describable as "valid."[1247] This is similar to the way that the sixth [i.e., genitive] case in [the phrase] "fire of sandalwood" communicates that the fire in question is one that arises in dependence on sandalwood [i.e., is a sandalwood fire]. *Providing the Fortunate with Sight* says, "*Scriptural valid cognition* [that is, 'valid cognition associated with scripture'] is an inference of conviction, which comprehends something that is extremely hidden."[1248] This is a point that can also be gleaned from such works as [Dharmakīrti's] *Commentary* [*on Pramāṇa*] and [Śāntarakṣita's] *Compendium of Suchness*.

Regarding the "scripture" of other systems, *Heart of the Middle Way* says:

> Being a text handed down in an unbroken tradition,
> it is claimed, is what makes it a "scripture."
> But since the same applies to everyone's texts,
> what is it that gives [what they say any] certainty?[1249]

That is, if, as the other schools claim, being passed down as part of a tradition makes something a scripture, it would follow that even the Cārvāka treatises are "scriptures." Hence the claim is unsustainable. This also serves to refute those elder Tibetans who are under the impression that merely having something with [a tradition of] continuous transmission is sufficient to make it Dharma. It also indicates that one should not hold onto generic sayings unquestioningly, as though they contain some essential truth. All Buddhists are in agreement that words [embodying] direct (*pratyakṣa*) knowledge of something extremely hidden are "scripture." As detailed in *Commentary on Pramāṇa*, to gain such knowledge, it is necessary to have rid oneself of imperfections or obscurations. All those in the Cittamātra and the Madhyamaka schools concur that the [scripture in question] must have been verified by the threefold analysis. [438] This is what *Clear Words* refers to in the passage [cited above] with the words "and is known directly,"[1250] the remainder of which has already been explained. Kamalaśīla has also pronounced that:

> Some [individuals] learn [from scripture] about the effects [of actions] that are not yet manifest and [also] the extent to which

> the huge advantages [of the higher aims] or [the abjectness of the] lower states [respectively result from] the engagement in or rejection of certain practices. Since [this learning] could not come about without [these individuals] relying on authoritative scripture, [we] see some who are brought to engage [in practice] by means of the words. But that fact alone does not [represent] a weakening of [the need] to have realization, since it is by employing a special method [that such individuals] engage. This is because there is no method of engaging with an object that is an extremely hidden entity except through scriptures. Hence it is very definitely through scripture that one must become engaged.[1251]

This passage describes how one relies on scripture to engage with things that are extremely hidden and how words bring about engagement. In a similar vein, *Heart of the Middle Way* asserts:

> If it is knowledge [conveyed in] words able to withstand critical
> examination,
> it is *scripture*.
> Initially, they should be objects for examination,
> and later, [there can be conviction] in what they convey.[1252]

The first two lines of this stanza encapsulate what scripture is, and the latter two reveal the sequence of its acceptance. And although here [in *Clear Words*, as cited above,] it refers only to "something outside [the scope of] the senses," the object of this valid cognition is primarily something that is extremely hidden. Again, as the *Thousand Measures* says, "Scriptural valid cognition is an inference of conviction, which comprehends something that is extremely hidden."[1253]

Valid cognition through analogy

Valid cognition through analogy is defined as "an inferential cognition that relies on the resemblance or analogousness of something that has already been realized as a correct reason to realize that an entity hidden to the individual [involved] resembles that analogous thing." It would not be enough for this simply to involve the realization of some object based on an illustrative example, as this would render [this cognition] indistinguishable from the inference that is the second of the fourfold categories of valid cognition—something that could be the source of various criticisms, such as that this category would be superfluous and redundant. It is therefore necessary that what this cognition apprehends is that the target resembles the analogue, such as in the inference where an individual thinks, "The sprout, for instance, lacks reality, just like the reflection of the face in the mirror," or "A *gayal* resembles a cow." [439] *Clear Words* states, "To realize the object experienced from something resembling it is to comprehend it through analogy, as, for instance, when one thinks, 'A *gayal* resembles a cow.'"[1254] The pervasion holds, as the example [cited for the analogy] indicates that it [should involve] the sense that "*x* resembles *y*," which means that what is apprehended is not just the [target] entity but the thing to which it bears a resemblance.

Furthermore, [what the term in question] literally means is "comprehension [of what is] close," which translates to something like "comprehending an analogy." The rationale here is that the Sanskrit equivalent is *upamānam*, which, when split into its constituents, yields *upa* and *māna*—[words] that translate as "close" and "comprehension," respectively.[1255] Hence "comprehension [of what is] close" means comprehending the thing that closely resembles the [target] entity. Such is the case, because what "close" refers to is the resemblance—that is, the closeness—of the analogue to the entity, and "close comprehension" derives from the fact that it is this analogue that is comprehended. The rationale is [also found in] the frequency with which *upamānam* is rendered "analogy." To say, then, that "the [target] entity is realized *from* something resembling it" means that there is "realization of the entity's resemblance *to* that [analogue]" or "realization of the entity*'s* resemblance," since there are numerous situations where another grammatical case has been assigned to [convey] meaning [that actually belongs to the territory of] the second and sixth grammatical cases and so forth.[1256]

According to some, for this [kind of valid cognition to occur], the presentation of a separate formal proof is necessary. But this is simply a case of their failure to understand the point made by the Prāsaṅgika, who states that a consequence alone can be enough to arrest the erroneous views of an opponent, without the need to present a proof. One should be aware that while it [may sometimes] depend on the formulation of a [separate] proof, what is [absolutely] necessary is that the thing to which [the entity bears] resemblance is apprehended.

Divided by way of its objects, there are two kinds of valid cognition from analogy, that directed toward the deceptive [conventional] and that directed toward the ultimate. Each can further be divided into (1) those that rely on a consequence, (2) those that rely on a formulated proof, and (3) those that rely on a proof statement. Stated succinctly, what one needs to understand is that this valid cognition [involving] the "comprehension [of what is] close" is an inference that apprehends the resemblance between the analogue and the [target] entity, [and it occurs] at the point that the reason is presented. It is *not* [the kind of] inferential cognition that realizes the probandum *nor* one that ascertains the forward and reverse pervasions and so on. Candrakīrti declares that although the realist wants to establish that phenomena are truly existent, he cannot identify any example-analogy for this and therefore does not succeed, whereas the Mādhyamika does.[1257] Also, the lord [Tsongkhapa] distinguishes between a property-basis and the example-analogue, in terms of how easy each is to realize. All the lower tenet schools also assert that there is no way to establish [a proof's thesis] if the example-analogue and the [target] entity do not match. [440] [Having taken all these into account,] to convey how important it is that the example-analogue and [target] entity fit with each other, I have devoted a separate section to describing the "valid cognition [of what is] close" [i.e., valid cognition through analogy], an expansion that has been entirely warranted.

All of this has been to provide a comprehensive response to the opponent's question regarding the varieties of valid cognition and the characteristics defining them. Hence, in addition to the fourfold division and the characteristics that define [these four], the derivations of the terms denoting each of them have also been clearly set out. [Candrakīrti's] *Commentary to Four Hundred Stanzas* and *Commentary on Sixty Stanzas of Reasoning* are evidently earlier compositions. These were followed by [his] *Entering the Middle Way* and its [auto]commentary, and then finally this work *Clear Words*. The *Commentary to Four Hundred Stanzas* briefly outlines the characteristics defining valid cognition in general, and having deemed that sufficient to facilitate an understanding of those characteristics, [Candrakīrti] did not overtly explain them in this last work.

6. The Objects of Valid Cognition

The objects of valid cognition

The point of explaining valid cognition through a fourfold division is as has just been set out—namely, that it is by means of the four valid cognitions that objects are realized. And since this [division] cannot logically be something that [exists] ultimately, it must belong to the domain of worldly conventions. Or [it can be said that], since the realization of objects is something that does not meet the standards of ultimate analysis, it must be explained in terms of worldly conventions. And that is why the [preceding] account explained how manifest and hidden objects, respectively, are comprehended. [That is what] *Clear Words* [refers to when it] says, "Because of that, it is through the four valid cognitions that the realization of things in the world is explained."[1258]

The question "What are their objects?" is one mainly addressed by this [statement, albeit] implicitly. The reason why the author does not deal with it explicitly here has already been explained in the refutation of other systems' understanding of *pratyakṣa*. [Candrakīrti] also judged it unnecessary to [respond to it explicitly], having already clearly identified the things that each valid cognition comprehends when he explained the defining characteristics and varieties.

So is the [Prāsaṅgika's understanding] of manifest [i.e., evident] and hidden [phenomena] compatible with that of the lower tenet schools? They are totally irreconcilable, because [the Prāsaṅgika maintains] that to hold, as the lower schools do, that manifest and hidden [phenomena] are coextensive[1259] approaches an analysis into the reality behind the designations "manifest" and "hidden," a level on which neither is established and nothing could be [classified as] either of them. [441] This point can be understood by reflecting on the manner that a search into the reality behind the designation is conducted. This system, therefore, rejects the lower schools' twofold division of objects of comprehension into those with specific and general characteristics. While it acknowledges a nominal distinction between specific and general characteristics, it does not hold that these delineate two separate objects of valid cognition. This is because there are many cases of conceptual mental perceptions that overtly comprehend general characteristics and numerous inferential cognitions that overtly comprehend specific characteristics. What is more, in the present context, impermanence, the two kinds of selflessness, and so forth are described in terms of general characteristics, whereas things such as "fit to be [regarded as] form" is a specific characteristic.[1260] Thus, while there are things that valid cognitions comprehend—including the two truths, the four truths, and so on—if one needed to identify separate objects for the two valid cognitions according to this system, one should distinguish, respectively, between the manifest and hidden [phenomena rather than between specifically and generally characterized], a point that has regularly cropped up in the discussion on what defines [the various valid cognitions].

But would this not mean that everything that exists is [classified as] an object realized by valid perception? That is categorically not the case, since in this system, it is unacceptable to hold that every known thing is valid perception's object of comprehension. This is because there are plenty of hidden phenomena that are objects overtly comprehended by inferential cognition. This point is made in the *Commentary to Four Hundred Stanzas* in the line "Not all things are understood by cognitions that are perception, since there are also things realized by inferential cognition."[1261] This is commenting on the passage in *Four Hundred Stanzas* that says:

> Someone who develops doubt in the Buddha's pronouncements
> with respect to that which is hidden
> should rely on [what he taught on] emptiness
> and just gain conviction in that.[1262]

And this is a point [at which the treatise] distinguishes between the manifest and the hidden. There is also obviously a reason why it is in the context of discussing the objects of the two valid cognitions that the precious Jé [Tsongkhapa] cites this very passage. A manifest phenomenon, therefore, is defined as "something overtly comprehended by any of the valid perceptions of worldly beings that depend on one of the six senses." Any of the six sources, such as external [visual] form, are illustrations of this. "Object of any of the six senses," "manifest [phenomenon]," and "[thing] overtly comprehended by valid perception" are all equivalent. [Listing synonyms,] the *Treasury of Amara* says, "*Perceivable* and *sensory object*."[1263] Also, *Clear Words* states, "With regard to [the derivation of] the term, because *pratyakṣa* conveys 'a thing that is nonhidden . . . .'"[1264] [442] The supporting sources, the derivation, and so forth were provided above. A hidden phenomenon is defined as "an entity that is beyond [the scope of], or is other than, what is overtly comprehended by any of the six valid perceptions of worldly beings that depend on one of the six senses." This, "object beyond the ken of the senses," and "that overtly comprehended by inferential cognition" are equivalent. The *Treasury of Amara* says, "*Hidden* and *imperceptible*,"[1265] and *Clear Words* states, "Something outside [the scope of] the senses."[1266] Illustrations of this are the impermanence of sound, the two kinds of selflessness, and karmic causal connections. The varieties, derivation, and so on and the supporting sources have been provided above.

Resolving certain knotty issues

One individual with a particular passion for Pramāṇa claims, "An established basis is necessarily something overtly comprehended by valid perception, because it is necessarily something overtly comprehended by the individual valid perception that realizes it." To this, [we respond that] there is categorically no pervasion! In retort, he might argue, "Well then, because [according to you] there is no pervasion to this, it must follow that for a thing to be comprehended by valid perception, it must be comprehended by *each and every* valid perception." In response we would say that this is an even more blatant example of there being no pervasion. And we would further respond, "It follows that an established basis is necessarily something apprehended by a visual cognition, because it is necessarily something apprehended by the individual visual cognition that realizes it. The pervasion is the one that you asserted, and the reason is established, since everything is apprehended by the visual cognition of an ārya buddha." He might deny the pervasion, but to this, we would say, "Well then, because [you say] there is no pervasion to this, it must follow that for something to be apprehended by visual cognition, [that thing] must be apprehended by *each and every* visual cognition. Again, the pervasion is the one you have proposed, and from this what beckons is a whole series [of consequences, each of which has in place] the three spheres [that show your position is irredeemably flawed]." He may then yield the earlier point. But from this it would follow that tactile objects and sounds are also [things apprehended by visual cognition], because they are [each apprehended by the individual visual cognition of an ārya buddha that realizes them]. Although the pervasion is one that he has agreed to, the [conclusion] cannot be accepted, since it is the position of all four [Buddhist] tenet schools that objects of the tactile source and sound source do not impinge on the domain of objects comprehended by visual cognition. It is [strictly] maintained in both the higher and lower Abhidharma systems that the six sources are the objects of their respective [six] senses. The *Commentary on Pramāṇa* also states, "Because the sense consciousnesses are fixed,"[1267] referring to the five senses cognitions being fixed with regard to their respective objects. Also, *Four Hundred Stanzas* says:

> If it were like that [and the two were inseparable],
> how would it not be that the eye itself
> was apprehending both?[1268]

Which is to say, it would absurdly follow [that the cognition in question] could apprehend both visual-source and tactile-source [objects]. And there are a vast number of such [passages where the same point is made]. [443] Furthermore, we would say [to this person], "You, who hold that to be an established basis is necessarily to be a hidden [phenomenon], go ahead and proclaim that the pot you see standing before you and the [food] that you are eating are hidden [phenomena]!"

The individual may be concerned that, if being manifest for an ārya buddha is not sufficient grounds for [classifying] something as manifest, it would mean that when it comes to establishing objects, between buddhas and sentient beings, we are giving primacy to the latter. To this we would say, "Well then, it follows that anything that is an established basis is necessarily a nonhidden phenomenon, because it is necessarily not hidden for an ārya buddha. The pervasion is the one you yourself asserted. And to confirm the reason, we can simply make use of the arguments and quotations you yourself deployed, such as the passage, '[A buddha] who has the eye to which no phenomena are hidden.' If you try to deny the pervasion, then the very charge that you make—that when it comes to establishing objects, [our position] gives primacy [to the perspective] of sentient beings over that of buddhas—is one that you are guilty of in a very "manifest" fashion! But if you accept that basic [argument], then it would follow that there are *no* hidden phenomena, because to be an established basis is necessarily to be nonhidden. And what response can you have to this [consequence], since the three spheres [are all in place]? The pervasion [to this last consequence] holds, since you proposed that anything that is an established basis is necessarily manifest, and the reason is also the one you endorsed. And as regards that pervasion, [as has already been noted,] *Clear Words* states, "*Pratyakṣa* conveys 'a thing that is nonhidden.'"[1269]

Regarding the establishment of objects, it is therefore not the case that in this [Prāsaṅgika system, the perspective of] sentient beings is given primacy over that of enlightened beings. However, what is presently under discussion is the world's [distinction between] manifest and hidden. So who, save a crazed person, would introduce into this the perspective of bodhisattvas and āryas who have transcended the world, and especially the perspective of ārya buddhas? It is as inappropriate as if, for instance, during a discussion about ultimate truth—something beyond [the scope of the] world—someone were to start talking about worldly beings, saying "I think they see things this way but not that way." However, in the context of discussing worldly conventions, there is no way to explain things unless one grants validity to what worldly beings see. For instance, one cannot engage with a barbarian in another tongue but must use his own language. This point is made in *Four Hundred Stanzas* and [Candrakīrti's] commentary to it. *Four Hundred Stanzas* states:

> Just as a barbarian cannot grasp [things]
> in a language other than his own,
> worldly beings cannot grasp [things],
> unless it is in [the language of] the world.[1270]

And also:

> To state that one [thing] exists [but] the other does not
> [is correct] neither on the ultimate [level] nor on the worldly one.[1271]

In [Candrakīrti's] commentary to this, he says: [444]

> When accepting the things of the world, one should acknowledge the validity of notions of the world, according to which internal and external entities are divided into five aggregates. Whereas, when [the perspective] is that of the [way that the] transcendent awareness perceives suchness, the five aggregates should be treated as being empty of intrinsic existence.[1272]

There are also numerous passages in [Candrakīrti's] *Entering the Middle Way* and his *Clear Words* stating that what is deceptive [i.e., conventional] is not something that is established from the perspective of āryas. It is also necessary, when [interpreting] the treatise, to follow the example set by Jé [Tsongkhapa] regarding the personal instruction he received from Mañjuśrī—taking into account every [dimension, including] the text's principal and subsidiary subjects, the purpose and individuals to whom it was directed, its overt and implied import, the context of its delivery, and the internal relation between its various sections.

The way that valid cognition and objects of comprehension are established

Regarding the way that valid cognition and the object it comprehends are established, the two are in a state of mutual dependence, such that for the thing comprehended to exist there must be the valid cognition and for the valid cognition to exist there must be the thing that it comprehends. If the converse were the case, the establishment of the object comprehended would not, by itself, mean the existence of the valid cognition comprehending it. But that would mean that the valid cognition is not established, since no amount of searching [relating to] the comprehender [alone]—that is, to valid cognition—can determine whether what ascertains [and establishes it] is itself or some other. Also, when subjected to analysis, it becomes impossible [to explain] how a comprehended thing and the comprehender, which occur sequentially, can depend on each other. It must, therefore, be accepted that their dependence is mutual, and one of simultaneity: they are simultaneously established. The first of these points has already been addressed, [and relates to a position that Nāgārjuna] rules out in his *Dispeller of Dispute*, in passages such as, "If valid cognition established itself..."[1273] and "If you think that another valid cognition [establishes it], there would be an infinite regress."[1274] The second point is correct, since there are various flaws arising from [the notion of sequential dependence]. For instance, if the object comprehended was established prior to valid cognition, it would be something that did not depend on the valid cognition [that comprehended it] and would not be the object of comprehension. And if the valid cognition was established prior to the object of comprehension, it would not depend on the object it comprehended and would not be a valid cognition. *Dispeller of Dispute* says:

If the establishment [of the valid cognition] always
depends on the thing it comprehends,
then the establishment of the thing comprehended
does not depend on the valid cognition.

And if those objects of comprehension can be established
without depending on valid cognitions,
what [need would there be] for [valid cognitions to] establish them?
And what would valid cognition be establishing?

And if for you it is the valid cognitions
that depend on the objects they comprehend for their establishment,
then according to you, valid cognitions and the objects they
comprehend
would definitely be reversed.[1275] [445]

The third point [regarding the simultaneity of their relationship] is correct, because mutual dependency is not limited to something between an object comprehended and a valid cognition, but it is what makes everything possible, including cause and effect, long and short, the mountain over there [as opposed to] the one over here, and [with regards to the path,] what is to be eradicated and the antidote [used against it]. In addition to which, the holy beings have identified the mutual dependency of things as the grounds for them lacking intrinsic existence—something that it is necessary to accept. This is a matter that should be explained in conjunction with their pronouncements. *Dispeller of Dispute* says:

If for you it is by means of the valid cognition
that the thing comprehended is established,
and by means of the comprehended thing that the valid cognition is
established,
then for you, neither of these things are established.[1276]

This conveys that both valid cognition and what it comprehends are not established intrinsically. And [Candrakīrti's] *Entering the Middle Way* states, "The holy beings have declared that what is established through mutual dependence is not established."[1277] And the autocommentary says:

> He may grant that the cognition exists due to a capacity in that [object, since] it is from the [object] that cognition arises, and it is in this sense that they depend on one another. But [we say] this necessarily means that the cognition does not exist intrinsically. The analysis of the [object and cognition] should be like that, for instance, [of length]: because there is "long," there is "short," and because there is "short," there is "long." And because there is "far," there is "near," and because there is "near," there is "far." Thus, in the establishment of such things, there is nothing intrinsic.[1278]

This analysis, in which things are understood to exist in a state of mutual dependency, is one that contrasts with and is distinguished from that of the [realist] śrāvaka schools, which explain length, for instance, in terms of a self-determining dimension, with *long* being formed of a chain of three or more minute particles, and *short* being what is unable to form [adherence] beyond that of two minute particles. As it states in *Clear Words*:

> They are established in mutual dependence on one another. Because there are valid cognitions, there are objects comprehended, and because there are objects comprehended, there are valid cognitions. A valid cognition and a thing comprehended do not exist by way of their own natures.[1279]

Thus, whether the valid cognition in question comprehends something that is true in the ultimate or conventional sense, in the context of its comprehending that object, that valid cognition's *existence* can be accounted for without needing to assert that what realizes it is itself or some other valid cognition. [The valid cognition exists] by virtue of the fact that at that time its object is what it comprehends. The pervasion holds, since the comprehension of the object within that [particular] context establishes its [identity] as the valid cognition comprehending that object—[an identity] that it need not rely on any further valid cognition to verify. [446] Such is the case, because immediately following that valid cognition, an ascertainment with the sense of having comprehended [that object] is induced. This is comparable to the way that someone can have a recollection of having been poisoned when he recalls being [bitten] by a certain rodent. *Clear Words* says, "Simply by conforming with the aspect of the objects they comprehend, the valid cognitions gain their own existence and establish themselves."[1280] And *Illuminating the Intent* includes passages such as:

> If its establishment of the thing it comprehends was insufficient by itself to establish a valid cognition, and it was necessary, as others contend, for that valid cognition to establish itself, it would mean that it did so independent of the thing it comprehends.[1281]

And:

> At that point, the subject does not have the sense of experiencing itself. This is comparable to the way that one does not have the sense of being poisoned at the point that one is being bitten . . .[1282] It is simply in recalling the object that the subject is recalled. There is no need, therefore, for a separate recollection of the subject.[1283]

Hence, in the present context too, the view that every cognition must realize itself should be recognized as one that contradicts all logical and scriptural evidence, including the pronouncement that to experience a thing is to experience its traits and also the statement that mind does not cognize itself. Furthermore, [it should be recognized] that to hunt for some reality beyond the level of imputation—instead of [accepting that] a valid cognition and the object it comprehends are nominally existent—is to be duped by the chimera of the realist schools. It is, therefore, by way of the profound relationship of interdependent establishment that it becomes feasible to explain [the scheme of things] in a manner that does not contradict the perceptions of the world and that accords with its conventions. *Clear Words* states, "Thus it is feasible to explain things exactly as they are perceived and known to be in the world."[1284]

Regarding the second, one should consult the section on resolving difficult points in my text *Decisive Analysis on the Middle Way*,[1285] where it will be addressed.

Through the force of your ardent prayers and the power of your compassion,
it is you, with the profound secrets of your body, speech, and mind, who
stand out among the conquerors and their [spiritual] sons,
like the waxing moon set among the constellations.
O second conqueror, source of wisdom, reside in my heart!

The splendid system of the pioneer Nāgārjuna, that sun of the Buddhist
teachings in the land of āryas,
as illuminated in the works of the sole companion of the night lotus, the
moon [Candrakīrti], master of the ten grounds,[1286]
is what glows here, as nectar light, unadulterated by any realist assertion.

My three doors [of action] are thoroughly disciplined by the three trainings,
my heart is constantly devoted to the gurus and deities. [447]
And [now], as though Sarasvatī has emanated ten million tongues,
this immaculate account breaks forth [from me] like an ocean wave.

At the start I learned with the help of many masters,
in the middle I meditated and divested myself of conceptual elaborations,
and having gained certainty, I finally [trod] the path of the fortunate.
How then could this [work] be like the stale writings of others?

The ultimate may be indescribable like the vastness of the heavens,
within which the conventional, while false, bristles with illusory detail.
But amid the union of appearance and emptiness, what part of illusory play
could lie beyond the experience of this illusory yogi-conjuror?

Though there are no phenomena other than a pattern of names,
on the level of appearances, may the illusory, noble five-faced [lion][1287]
still vanquish the illusory elephant of ignorance
so that the illusion-like city of omniscience can be gained!

May this [work] emerge from the mountain of my training
as the supreme orb, master of the twelve [divisions of] excellent speech,[1288]
to grace the mental skies of all the fortunate ones,
beneath which a hundred thousand confusion-dispelling lotuses of
profundity and vastness can bloom!

Having received his share of the Dharma in the form of the three kinds of vows and so forth at the feet of the great conqueror [the Fifth Dalai Lama], then having trained with total surrender and devotion at the feet of numerous spiritual guides, such as the father Jamyang Lama Tri Rinpoché[1289] and his [spiritual] sons, the Śākya bhikṣu Jamyang Shepai Dorjé set off on the ocean of our own and others' tenet systems before finally arriving at the far shore of mastery. And having gained, in particular, an unerring discrimination that provides insights into the mysteries of myriad sutras and tantras, he composed this work, *Mighty Pramāṇa Sun, "Banisher of Gloom from the Hearts of the Fortunate," Totally Illuminating the Profound and the Expansive: An Exposition on Valid Cognition in the Thousand Measures of Clear Words*, in his place of residence on the glorious mountain of Riwo Gephel where ḍākinīs congregate, in the [quarters known as] Gurkhang Deden Nyiö Khyilwa within Thekchok Terdzö Khachö.

Oṃ svasti.[1290]

From this monastic center of the auspicious [right-]coiled [conch],
may the Dharma-giving [of such text production] gently rain as nectar
on the ground of the Able One's teachings
so that the fortunate gathering of cultivators can enjoy the fruits of benefit and happiness!

Śubhamastu sarva jagataṃ.

Appendix 1. Table of Tibetan Transliteration

Amdo	A mdo
Bodong Choklé Namgyal	Bo dong Phyogs las rnam rgyal
Changkya Losang Chöden	Lcang skya Blo bzang chos ldan
Changra	Lcang ra
Chapa Chökyi Sengé	Phywa pa Chos kyi seng ge
Chödrak Gyatso	Chos grags rgya mtsho
Chöjé Gyensang	Chos rje Rgyan bzang
Chomden Rikpai Raldri	Bcom ldan Rig(s) pa'i ral gri
Chöwang Drakpa	Chos dbang grags pa
Dakpo Kagyü	Dwags po bka' brgyud
Darma Rinchen	Dar ma rin chen
Darṭik	Dar ṭik
Desi Sangyé Gyatso	Sde srid Sangs rgyas rgya mtsho
Doklung	Gdog lung
Döndrup Gyatso	Don grub rgya mtsho
Drapa Sherab Rinchen	Sgra pa Shes rab rin chen
Drepung	'Bras spungs
Drikung	'Bri gung
Drok Riwoché	'Brog ri bo che
Duldzin Drakpa Gyaltsen	'Dul 'dzin Grags pa rgyal mtshan
Düsum Khyenpa (Chökyi Drakpa)	Dus gsum mkhyen pa (Chos kyi grags pa)
Dzungar	Jun gar
Gampopa (Sönam Rinchen)	Sgam po pa (Bsod nams rin chen)
Geden Nampar Gyalwai Ling	Dge ldan rnam par rgyal ba'i gling
Gelek Palsang	Dge legs dpal bzang
Geluk	Dge lugs
Gendun Drup	Dge 'dun grub
Gö Lotsāwa	'Gos Lo tsā ba
Gomang	Sgo mang
Gungru Chöjung (Chökyi Jungné)	Gung ru Chos 'byung (Chos kyi 'byung gnas)

Gungru Gyaltsen Sangpo	Gung ru Rgyal mtshan bzang po
Gurkhang Deden Nyiö Khyilwa	Gur khang Bde ldan nyi 'od 'khyil ba
Gyalnga Dunpa	Rgyal rnga bdun pa
Gyaltsab Jé (Darma Rinchen)	Rgyal tshab rje (Dar ma rin chen)
Gyantsé	Rgyal rtse
Gyümé	Rgyud smad
Hortön	Hor ston
Jamyang Shepa	'Jam dbyangs bzhad pa
Jikten Gönpo	'Jig rten mgon po
Jowo	Jo bo
Kachupa	Bka' bcu pa
Kadam	Bka' gdams
Kagyü	Bka' brgyud
Kalsang Gyatso	Bskal bzang rgya mtsho
Kawa Paltsek	Ska ba dpal brtsegs
Khedrup Jé (Gelek Palsang)	Mkhas grub rje (Dge legs dpal bzang)
Khyungpo Draksé	Khyung po grags se
Labrang Tashikhyil	Bla brang bkra shis 'khyil
Lama Tri Rinpoché	Bla ma Khri rin po che
Latö Jang	La stod byang
Layakpa Jangchup Ngödrup	La yag pa Byang chub dngos grub
Lhasang Khan	Lha bzang han
Lhetra Ting	Lhas khra ting
Loden Sangpo	Blo ldan bzang po
Ma Lotsāwa (Gewai Lodrö)	Rma Lo tsā ba (Dge ba'i blo gros)
Muzing	Smu rdzing
Narthang	Snar thang
Nenying	Gnas rnying
Ngamring	Ngam ring
Ngawang Losang Gyatso	Ngag dbang blo bzang rgya mtsho
Ngawang Tsöndrü	Ngag dbang brtson 'grus
Ngok Lekpai Sherab	Rngog Legs pa'i shes rab
Ngok Loden Sherab	Rngog Blo ldan shes rab
Ngorchen Kunga Sangpo	Ngor chen Kun dga' bzang po
Nyangtö	Nyang stod
Nyingma	Rnying ma
Palbar	Dpal 'bar
Palkhor Chödé	Dpal 'khor chos sde
Panam	Pa snam
Patsab Nyima Drak	Pa tshab Nyi ma grags

Phabongkha Jamyang Drakpa	Pha bong kha 'Jam dbyangs grags pa
Phakmo Drupa (Dorjé Gyalpo)	Phag mo gru pa (Rdo rje rgyal po)
Pharchin	Phar phyin
Rabten Kunsang Phak	Rab brtan kun bzang 'phags
Rendawa (Shönü Lodrö)	Red mda' ba (Gzhon nu blo gros)
Rinchen Chögyal	Rin chen chos rgyal
Riwo Dangchen	Ri bo mdangs can
Riwo Gephel	Ri bo dge 'phel
Rongtön Sheja Kunrik	Rong ston Shes bya kun rig
Sakya	Sa skya
Sakya Paṇḍita (Kunga Gyaltsen)	Sa skya Paṇḍita (Kun dga' rgyal mtshan)
Sangphu	Gsang phu
Sangyé Gyatso	Sangs rgyas rgya mtsho
Shākya Chokden	Shākya Mchog ldan
Shang Tsalpa (Tsöndrü Drakpa)	Zhang Tshal pa (Brtson 'grus grags pa)
Shangshung Chöwang Drakpa	Zhang zhung Chos dbang grags pa
Sönam Gyaltsen	Bsod nams Rgyal mtshan
Taktsang Lotsāwa (Sherab Rinchen)	Stag tshang Lo tsā ba (Shes rab rin chen)
Tashi Lhundrup	Bkra shis lhun grub
Tashi Lhunpo	Bkra shis lhun po
Thangsakpa (Shönu Gyaltsen)	Thang sag pa (Gzhon nu rgyal mtshan)
Thekchok Terdzö Khachö	Theg mchog mter mdzod mkha' spyod
Tsang	Gtsang
Tsangyang Gyatso	Tshangs dbyangs rgya mtsho
Tso Ngön	Mtsho sngon
Tsongkhapa (Losang Drakpa)	Tsong kha pa (Blo bzang grags pa)
Tsunpa Tönshön	Btsun pa Ston gzhon
Ü	Dbu
Yaktön Sangyé Pal	G.yag ston Sangs rgyas dpal

Appendix 2. Text Outlines

The "outlines" (*sa bcad*) are an important Tibetan organizational feature of complex texts, especially those in the tradition of scholasticism. This appendix presents the outlines as they appear in the three works, with some very minor modifications. Hence the chapter titles listed in the table of contents, which are not original features, are not reproduced here. As with the three main sections of the first text (highlighted in bold) the main heading for each section is introduced, followed by any internal divisions within it, listed as numbered subsections. The Tibetan system uses only basic ordinal numbers (equivalent to "first," "second," etc., in English) both for major sections and their subdivisions. This system of the "first of the first," "second of the first," etc., is essentially retained in the appendix, although digits are used in place of ordinal numerals. As in the translation, italics are used to mark subdivisions that are reïntroduced as main headings, to have further subdivisions made within them. Note that subdivisions that are later reintroduced as main headings are screened back in gray type when they are first introduced as subdivisions, whereas those not further subdivided are not screened back. The page numbers from the Tibetan edition of the text have also been added in parentheses for main headings and for subdivisions that are remote from where they are first introduced. Notes in this appendix comment on parts of the outlines that seem unclear or inconsistent, and all page numbers in the notes refer to the Tibetan edition.

Banisher of Ignorance
Khedrup Jé

The intention of the Pramāṇa treatises (4)
1. The aim of the Pramāṇa treatises
2. How [the achievement of] that aim depends on these treatises 12
3. A call to value treatises that have such an aim 12
4. The core subject matter of these treatises

The aim of the Pramāṇa treatises (5)
1. Countering certain misconceptions associated with the aim
2. The actual aim 9

Countering certain misconceptions associated with the aim (5)
1. Countering the misconception that the Pramāṇa treatises are not relevant to those engaged in the quest for liberation 4
2. Countering the misconception that Pramāṇa treatises are not relevant to the location in question 8
3. Countering the view of those who, while conceding that the Pramāṇa treatises have an aim, believe it to be an inferior one 9

The core subject matter of these treatises (13)
1. Identifying the core subject matter of the treatises 13
2. Detailed exposition

Detailed exposition (15)
1. **Description of the object: the thing known**
2. **Description of cognition: that which knows it** (84)
3. **How cognition engages its object** (317)

Description of the object: the thing known (15)
1. Enumeration [of equivalents for "object"]
2. Defining characteristics
3. Varieties

Enumeration [of equivalents] (15)

1. Refutation of others' assertions 15
2. Setting out our own position 18
3. Dealing with objections [to that position] 19

Defining characteristics [of object] (20)

1. Refutation of others' assertions 20
2. Setting out our own position 20
3. Dealing with objections [to that position] 20

Varieties [of object] (21)

1. Refutation of others' assertions 21
2. Setting out our own position

Setting out our own position [Four ways of dividing the object] (22)

1. The object in terms how it is comprehended or appears to the valid cognition that is its subject
2. (?)*
3. Division of objects by way of their identities (65)
4. Categorizing objects in terms of how their subjects apprehend them, [conceive them,] and so forth (78)

The object in terms of how it is comprehended or appears to the valid cognition that is its subject

1. Evident and hidden [things]
2. The specifically and generally characterized

* The Tibetan text (p. 21) says that there are four "ways of dividing" (*dbye sgo*) object, the first of which is in terms of "how the object is comprehended or appears to the valid cognition that is its subject." Khedrup Jé then introduces two pairs of divisions: (1) evident and hidden things, (2) the specifically and generally characterized. He seems to suggest that these represent two alternative forms of categorization within this first "way." The next way of dividing objects encountered in the text—in terms of "identity" (p. 65)—has no number assigned to it, whereas the one following it—in terms of "how their subjects apprehend them, etc." (p. 78)—is clearly stated to be the fourth. It would appear, therefore, that one of the ways of dividing objects is missing. It seems likely to me that the two pairs initially introduced as belonging to the same category, or way of dividing objects, were later treated as if they formed separate ones—i.e., instead of just constituting the first in the fourfold sets of division, they were treated as the first and second.

Evident and hidden [things] (22)
1. Defining characteristics
2. Varieties
3. Analysis of whether evident and hidden things preclude each other 24

The defining characteristics (22)
1. Refutation of others' assertions 22
2. Setting out our own position 23

Varieties (23)
1. Refutation of others' assertions 23
2. Setting out our own position 24

The specifically and the generally characterized (31)
1. How the perceptual and inferential dichotomy of valid cognition is determined by the specifically and generally characterized dichotomy of comprehended things Etymological derivation of the terms "specifically characterized" and "generally characterized" 31
2. Etymological derivation of the terms "specifically characterized" and "generally characterized"
3. Description of specifically and generally characterized entities

Description of specifically and generally characterized entities (32)
1. Delineating specific characterization
2. Delineating general characterization

Delineating specific characterization (32)
1. Defining characteristics 32
2. Identification of the illustration

Identification of the illustration (33)

1. (?) Countering the view that an actual thing need not be specifically characterized* 36
2. (?) Countering the position that the likes of actual thing do not constitute substances† 37
3. (?) Our own system‡ 49

Delineating general characterization (52)

1. What defines general characterization 52
2. Identification of the illustration 52

Several ancillary topics that have special significance with regard to the discussion on specific and general characterization§ (62)

Division of objects by way of their identities (65)

1. Etymological description of the two truths 65
2. Defining characteristics 66
3. Identification of their respective illustrations

Identification of their respective illustrations (67)

1. Refuting others' assertions 67
2. Setting out our own position 73

---

* This subdivision (pp. 36–49) was not mentioned at the start of "Delineating specific characterization," and so it was not assigned a number. It seems likely (although not entirely certain) that it was intended to be seen as part of "Identification of the illustration" rather than an independent section.

† See note above.

‡ At the end of "Delineating specific characterization," another unnamed, unnumbered section (pp. 49–52) appears, where Khedrup Jé sets out his own position. Again, it seems likely (but not certain) that it was supposed to be part of "Identification of the illustration."

§ This last section (pp. 62–65) contains information relevant to both specific and general characterization and seems like a subdivision of "The specifically and the generally characterized," but it was not mentioned in the text when that heading was introduced (p. 31).

Categorizing objects in terms of how their subjects apprehend them, [conceive them,] and so forth (78)

1. Refutation of others' assertions 78
2. Setting out our own position 82

Description of cognition: that which knows [the object] (84)

*Awareness** (84)

1. Awareness that is not valid
2. Awareness that is valid

Awareness that is not valid (84)

1. Conceptual cognition
2. Nonconceptual false cognition 88

Conceptual cognition (85)

1. Defining characteristics 85
2. Varieties

Varieties (86)

1. Valid inferential cognition 87
2. Subsequent cognition

Subsequent cognition (87)

1. Refutation of others' assertions 87
2. Setting forth our own position 88

Awareness that is valid (89)

1. Defining characteristics
2. Varieties

* At the start of this second major section, Khedrup Jé says that there are two ways of dividing awareness. He then discusses the distinction between awareness that is not valid and awareness that is valid. He describes this as a division by way of its "function" (*byed las*). The second way of dividing it does not seem to feature in the later text. So it is unclear what it is and whether Khedrup Jé ever intended to include it or had simply wanted to make the point that the tradition recognizes two main ways of dividing awareness.

Defining characteristics (89)

1. Refutation of others' assertions 89
2. Setting forth our own position

Setting forth our own position (97)

1. The actual defining characteristics [of valid cognition] 97
2. The valid cognition that ascertains those defining characteristics

The valid cognition that ascertains those defining characteristics (100)

1. Setting forth our own position 100
2. Refutation of others' assertions 100

Varieties of valid cognition (102)

1. Valid perception
2. Valid inferential cognition (202)

Valid perception (103)

1. Defining characteristics 103
2. Varieties
3. Valid perception and its results

Varieties (107)

1. Valid sense perception
2. Valid mental perception (147)
3. Valid self-cognition (157)
4. Yogic perception (166)

Valid sense perception (107)

1. Literal meaning of the term *sense perception* 107
2. Defining characteristics 108
3. Varieties 108
4. Explanation of the three conditions

Explanation of the three conditions (108)

1. An analysis of whether the group of causes for a sense consciousness is limited to the three conditions
2. Setting out the nature of each of the three conditions

An analysis of whether the group of causes for a sense consciousness is limited to the three conditions (108)

1. Refutation of others' assertions
2. Setting forth our own position

Setting forth our own position (111)

Setting out the nature of each of the three conditions [that produce a] sense consciousness 111

1. In the Sautrāntika system
2. In the Cittamātra system

The three conditions according to the Sautrāntika system (111)

1. The governing condition 111
2. The observed [object] condition 112
3. The immediate condition 119

The three conditions according to the Cittamātra system (127)

1. Identification of the observed [object] condition of sense perception
2. Identification of the governing condition of sense perception 146
3. Identification of the immediate condition of sense perception 146

Identification of the object condition of sense perception according to the Cittamātra system (127)

1. An account of the object condition 127
2. Subsidiary topic: a discussion about the reasoning [establishing] the "simultaneity of object and perception"

[Subsidiary Topic:] A discussion about the reasoning [establishing] the "simultaneity of object and subject" (133)

1. Discussion on the aim of this [logical] proof 133
2. Formulating the proof and identifying its three components 134
3. Establishing [the reason's fulfillment of] each of the [three] criteria 144

[Varieties of valid perception:] Valid mental perception (147)

1. Refutation of others' assertions 147
2. Setting forth our own position
3. Dealing with objections [to our position] 156

Setting forth our own position (153)

1. Defining characteristics 153
2. Varieties 153
3. Manner of production 154
4. Subsidiary topic: identifying the mental sense power 154

[Varieties of valid perception:] Self-cognizing valid perception (157)

1. Refutation of others' assertions
2. Setting forth our own position 163
3. Dealing with objections [to our position] 165

Refutation of other's assertions (158)

1. Refuting the idea that every awareness is essentially a self-cognition 158
2. Refuting the view that a self-cognizing perception has no object 160

[Varieties of valid perception:] Yogic perception (166)

1. Defining characteristics 166
2. Varieties 166
3. Description of the four truths

Description of the four truths (166)

1. General discussion on the four truths
1. Specific discussion about the aspect of selflessness

General discussion of the four truths (166)

1. The identity of each of the four truths
2. The definitiveness of the [fourfold] enumeration 170
3. The definitiveness of the order 170

The identity of each of the four truths (166)

1. True sufferings 166
2. True origins 168
3. True cessations 168
4. True paths 169

Specific discussion about the aspect of selflessness (172)

1. Identifying the two selves that are to be negated 172
2. Explaining the logical proofs that refute the two selves
3. How one meditates on selflessness 176
4. How one eradicates self-grasping by means of that meditation 182

Explaining the logical proofs that refute the two selves (175)

1. Formulating the [proof's] reason 175
2. Establishing the reason's [fulfillment of the] three criteria

Establishing the reason's [fulfillment of the] three criteria (175)

1. Establishing the pervasion 175
2. Establishing the property of the subject 175

Valid perception and its results (184)

1. Refutation of others' assertions 186
2. Setting forth our own position

Setting forth our own position (194)

1. The first conceptual analysis of valid cognition and its result: that involving other- cognition 194
2. The second conceptual analysis of valid cognition and its result: that involving self-cognition 195
3. The establishment of those models 195

Valid inferential cognition (202)

1. Literal meaning 202
2. Varieties

Varieties of inferential valid cognition (202)

1. Inferential cognition in the personal domain 203
2. Inferential valid cognition involving another party

Inferential cognition involving another party (205)

1. The actual account of inferential cognition involving another party
2. What this account conveys overtly: the description of logical reasons
3. What this account conveys implicitly: the description of the probandum that is to be logically established (291)
4. The description of that which prepares the way for the proof statement (311)

The actual account of inferential cognition involving another party (205)

1. List of synonymous terms 205
2. Literal meaning of the term 205
3. Defining characteristics 206
4. Identifying the illustrations [of proof statements]

Identifying the illustrations [used in] an inference involving another party (208)

1. Description of the varieties 208
2. Examination of whether there can be a proof statement comprising only a single element

Examination of whether there can be a proof statement comprising only a single element (211)

1. Refutation of others' assertions 211
2. Setting forth our own position 214

What the account of inference involving another party conveys overtly: the description of logical reasons (218)

1. Description of the correct logical reason
2. Description of its opposite, the fallacious logical reason (272)

Description of the correct logical reason (218)

1. Defining characteristics
2. Examination of the scheme
3. Varieties (234)

Defining characteristics of a correct logical reason (218)

1. Refutation of others' assertions 218
2. Setting forth our own position 219

Varieties of correct logical reason (234)
1. Logical reasons divided in terms of the type of evidence that they use
2. Logical reasons divided in terms of what type of thing they set out to prove (253)
3. Logical reasons divided in terms of the domain with which they deal (266)

Logical reasons divided in terms of the type of evidence that they use (234)
1. *Effect* as a correct reason
2. *Nature* as a correct reason
3. *Nonobservation* as a correct reason

Effect as a correct reason (234)
1. Literal meaning 234
2. Defining characteristics 234
3. Varieties
4. Analysis of the scheme

Varieties (234)
1. Correct effect-reason of the variety that "overtly proves a cause" 235
2. Correct effect-reason of the variety that "proves there was a preceding cause" 235
3. Correct effect-reason of the variety that "establishes the detail of a specific cause" 235
4. Correct effect-reason of the variety that "establishes a cause in terms of an individual isolated identity" 235
5. Correct effect-reason for "deducing a feature of a cause" 235

Analysis of the scheme (235)
1. Identifying the reason, the subject, and the predicate
2. Explaining which valid cognitions are responsible for ascertaining that each of the three criteria [are fulfilled] 236
3. Addressing the qualm that this type of reasoning is flawed 238

Identifying the reason, subject, and predicate (235)
1. Refutation of others' assertions 235
2. Setting forth our own position 236

Nature as a correct reason (238)

1. Defining characteristics 238
2. Varieties
3. Explaining which valid cognitions are responsible for ascertaining that each of the three criteria [are fulfilled] 239

Varieties (239)

1. Correct reason of nature of the "plain" variety 235
2. Correct reason of nature of the "specified dependence" variety 235

Nonobservation as a correct reason (241)

1. Defining characteristics 241
2. Varieties

Varieties (243)

1. Correct reason involving the nonobservation of something that is not accessible
2. Correct reason involving the nonobservation of something that should be apparent

[Proofs that use] the nonobservation of a thing that is not accessible as their reason:

Whether "nonobservation of a thing that is not accessible" should be regarded as a literal or figurative [designation] (243)

1. Refutation of others' assertions 243
2. Setting forth our own position 246

[Proofs that use] the nonobservation of a thing that should be apparent as their reason (246)

1. Defining characteristics 246
2. Varieties

Varieties (246)

1. Those that involve the *nonobservation* of something related to [the element negated] being used as the correct reason
2. Those that involve the *observation* of something that precludes [the

element negated] being used as the correct reason (251)

Those that involve the nonobservation of something related to [the element negated] being used as the correct reason (246)

1. Those involving the nonobservation of a cause [of the element negated] 246
2. Those involving the nonobservation of something that encompasses it 247
3. Those involving the nonobservation of something that is the same nature as it
4. Those involving the nonobservation of something that is a direct effect of it 251

A proof involving the nonobservation of something that is the same nature as [the element negated] (248)

1. Defining characteristics 248
2. Identifying the illustration

Identifying the illustration (248)

1. Refutation of others' assertions 248
2. Setting forth our own position 250

Those that involve the observation of something that precludes [the element being negated] that is being used as the correct reason (251)

1. Reasons that depend on an antagonistic preclusion
2. Reasons that depend on a preclusion of mutual opposition 252

Reasons that depend on an antagonistic preclusion (252)

1. The four that involve the observation of a *nature* that precludes [the element that is being negated]
2. The four that involve the observation of an *effect* that precludes [the element that is being negated]
3. The four that involve the observation of something *encompassed* that precludes [the element that is being negated]

The four that involve the observation of a nature that precludes [the element that is being negated] (252)

1. The observation of a nature that precludes a nature
2. The observation of a nature that precludes a cause

3. The observation of a nature that precludes an effect
4. The observation of a nature that precludes an encompasser

The four that involve the observation of an effect that precludes [the element that is being negated] (252)

1. The observation of an effect that precludes a nature
2. The observation of an effect that precludes a cause
3. The observation of an effect that precludes an effect
4. The observation of an effect that precludes an encompasser

The four that involve the observation of something encompassed that precludes [the element that is being negated] (252)

1. The observation of something encompassed that precludes a nature
2. The observation of something encompassed that precludes a cause
3. The observation of something encompassed that precludes an effect
4. The observation of something encompassed that precludes an encompasser

Logical reasons divided in terms of what type of thing they set out to prove (253)

1. Correct reasons [dealing with] demonstrable facts and realities 253
2. Correct reasons [relating to matters of] conviction
3. Correct reasons [dealing with] the issue of common agreement [about names]

Correct reasons [relating to matters of] conviction (253)

1. Refutation of others' assertions
2. Setting out our own position 258
3. Dealing with objections [to our position] 262

Refutation of others' assertions (253)

1. Refuting those who reject the feasibility of [using] correct logical proofs in matters relating to conviction 253
2. Refuting those who accept their feasibility, but propose a different model for them 255

Correct reasons [dealing with] the issue of common agreement [about names] (262)

1. Refutation of others' assertions 262
2. Setting out our own position 264

Logical reasons divided in terms of the domain with which they deal (266)

1. Correct logical reasons that establish the thing [meant]
2. Correct logical reasons that establish names and expressions

The cognition that grasps the reason (268)

1. Refutation of others' assertions 268
2. Setting out our own position 271
3. Dealing with objections [to our position] 271

The inverse [of the correct reason], the false logical reason (272)

1. Defining characteristics 272
2. Varieties

Varieties (272)

1. Reasons that are not confirmed
2. Reasons that are contrary [to the thesis proposed] (276)
3. Reasons that are inconclusive (286)

Reasons that are not confirmed (272)

1. Reasons that are unconfirmed on factual grounds
2. Reasons that are unconfirmed due to [inadequate] knowledge
3. Reasons that are unconfirmed due to the protagonists [in the debate]

Reasons that are unconfirmed on factual grounds (272)

1. Reasons not confirmed because the thing [cited as the] reason is an impossible one
2. Reasons not confirmed because the thing [cited as the] subject is an impossible one
3. Reasons not confirmed because there is no [logical] relationship between the basis [i.e., the subject] and the reason
4. Reasons not confirmed because a portion of the reason cannot be found in the subject
5. Reasons not confirmed because a portion of the subject cannot be found in the reason

Reasons that are unconfirmed due to [inadequate] knowledge (273)
1. Those that fail due to doubts
2. Those that fail because of the subject of interest 273

Those that fail due to doubts (273)
1. Those that fail due to doubts regarding the subject
2. Those that fail due to doubts regarding the reason
3. Those that fail because of doubts surrounding the [logical] relationship between the subject and the reason

Reasons that are unconfirmed because of [inadequate knowledge] regarding the subject of interest (274)
1. Those that fail because the basis of discussion [i.e., the subject] and the reason are identical
2. Those that fail because the basis and the predicate are identical
3. Those that fail because the predicate and the reason are identical

Reasons that are unconfirmed due to the protagonists [in the debate] (274)
1. Those that fail because of the first party
2. Those that fail because of the second party
3. Those that fail because of both parties

Reasons that are contrary [to the thesis proposed] (276)
1. Defining characteristics 276
2. Varieties

Varieties (276)
1. Those that derive from the refutation of the nature of the predicate
2. Those that derive from the refutation of the nature of the subject
3. Those that derive from the refutation of a quality of the predicate
4. Those that derive from the refutation of a quality of the subject

The way that the proof should be formulated [for 2] (276)
1. Refuting others' assertions 276
2. Setting out our own position 278

The examples of the contrary reasons [for 3 and 4] that derive from refutations of a quality of the predicate and a quality of the subject (280)

1. Setting out the correct position 280
2. Refuting incorrect positions 284

Reasons that are inconclusive (286)

1. Defining characteristics 286
2. Varieties

Varieties (286)

1. Inconclusive reasons that are not shared 286
2. Inconclusive reasons that are shared

Inconclusive reasons that are shared (289)

1. An inconclusive reason that [the other party] has noticed is present in both of the classes
2. An inconclusive reason that [the other party] has found among the class of similar instances but not among the class of dissimilar instances
3. An inconclusive reason that [the other party] has found among the class of dissimilar instances but not among the class of similar instances

An alternative, [fourfold] classification of inconclusive reasons (289)

1. Those in which the reason is present in both the class of similar instances and the class of dissimilar instances in the sense of encompassing [everything within them]
2. Those in which the reason is present in the two classes but split with regard to both
3. Those in which the reason is present in the class of similar instances in the split sense and present in the class of dissimilar instances in the encompassing sense
4. Those in which the reason is present in the class of similar instances in the encompassing sense and present in the class of dissimilar instances in the split sense

What the [treatises' account] of inference involving a second party conveys by implication—that is, the probandum that the proof sets out to establish (291)

1. Defining characteristics of a probandum [i.e., thesis] 291
2. Varieties

Varieties (291)

1. The probandum in a correct proof that is for personal use
2. The probandum in a correct proof that is for a second party

The thesis in a correct proof that is for personal use (291)

1. Probanda in correct proofs for personal use that depend on an effect-reason 291
2. Probanda in correct proofs for personal use that depend on a same nature-reason 291
3. Probanda in correct proofs for personal use that depend on a non-observation reason 291

Theses in proofs for a second party (293)

1. Defining characteristics
2. Varieties
3. Detailed explanation of the converse of what is not ruled out

Defining characteristics (293)

1. Refuting others' assertions 293
2. Setting out our own position 294

Varieties (296)

1. Probanda in proofs involving a second party that use an effect as their reason
2. Probanda in proofs involving a second party that use nature as their reason
3. Probanda in proofs involving a second party that use nonobservation as their reason

Detailed explanation of the converse of what is not ruled out (297)

1. Things ruled out by valid perception
2. Things ruled out by valid inferential cognition dealing in demonstrable facts 301
3. Things ruled out through an assertion
4. Things ruled out by common agreement [about names] 310

What is ruled out by valid perception (298)

1. Refuting others' assertions 298
2. Setting out our own position[1291]

What is ruled out in the case of a [thesis] assertion (301)

1. A thing that is ruled out by the statement asserting it 301
2. A thing that is ruled out by [an inference dealing with a matter of] conviction

A thing that is ruled out by [an inference dealing with a matter of] conviction (304)

1. What is ruled out, what rules out, and how it rules out 305
2. Whether an [authoritative] passage of scripture rules something out in the sense of countering it or impeding it 306
3. Settling certain issues regarding the example [that the treatise supplies] of a false thesis 309

Explaining that which prepares the way for the proof statement [from 205] (311)

1. Account of the discrediting [statement; i.e., the consequence] 311
2. Account of the way to respond to a consequence 313
3. Examination of subsidiary issues arising from these

Examination of subsidiary issues arising from these (314)

1. Account of the example [used in conjunction with] the reason 314
2. Explanation of [what counts as a] failing and a quality in the reason, example, and position

Explanation of [what counts as] a failing and a quality in the reason, example, and position (314)

1. Refuting others' assertions 314
2. Setting out our own position 316

How cognition engages its object (317)

1. The negative and the affirmative 318
2. Preclusion and [logical] relationship
3. The communicated and the communicating
4. The universal and the particular 331
5. The positive and the other-exclusion 331
6. Substantive and "reverse" [phenomena] 333
7. The single and the different 334
8. The defining, the defined, and the illustration 334
9. The three times—the past and so forth 335

Preclusion and [logical] relationship (320)
1. The characteristics that define [things as] preclusive
2. Varieties

The characteristics that define [things as] preclusive (320)
1. Refuting others' assertions 320
2. Setting out of our own position 321

The communicated and the communicating (325)
1. Defining characteristics 325
2. Varieties 326

On Preclusion and Relationship
Gyaltsab Jé

Analysis of preclusion (339)
1. Defining characteristics [of preclusion]
2. Varieties
3. Why it is necessary to understand preclusion 349

Defining characteristics (339)
1. Outlining the assertion of another [scholar] 340
2. Subjecting that assertion to critical scrutiny 340
3. Our own position 341

Varieties (341)
1. Antagonistic preclusion
2. Preclusion of mutual opposition

Antagonistic preclusion (341)
1. Rejecting what is incorrect
2. Establishing what is correct

Rejecting what is incorrect (341)
1. Outlining the position of an earlier scholar 341
2. Refuting that position 342

Establishing what is correct (343)
1. Defining characteristics 343
2. Varieties 344
3. The way that one thing counters the other [with this kind of preclusion]

The way that one thing counters the other [with this kind of preclusion] (344)
1. The analogy 344
2. Applying this to the real area of interest 345
3. Countering objections 346

Preclusion of Mutual Opposition (347)
1. Defining characteristics 347
2. Varieties 347
3. Delineation of [this] preclusion 348

Analysis of relationship (349)
1. Defining characteristics 349
2. Varieties
3. Why it is necessary to comprehend [logical] relationship and understand it is an imputed existent 352

Varieties (350)
1. Nature relationship
2. Causal relationship

Relationship of the same nature
1. Defining characteristics 350
2. Delineation 350

Causal relationship (350)
1. Defining characteristics 350
2. Description of cause and effect in terms of their informational relationship 351

Mighty Pramāṇa Sun
Jamyang Shepa

1. A general refutation of the Tibetan misconception that the Prāsaṅgika holds that valid cognition, both as an actuality and a designation, has no currency 356
2. An accurate account [of valid cognition] as represented in the Prāsaṅgika's own treatises

An accurate account [of valid cognition] as represented in the Prāsaṅgika's own treatises (356)
1. The arguments of the logicians pertaining to [their understanding of] the necessity for valid cognition (*pramāṇa*)
2. Refuting their system's version of valid cognition
3. Setting out the valid cognition of our own system (417)

The arguments of the logicians pertaining to [their understanding of] the necessity for valid cognition (pramāṇa) (358)
1. Their attack [on Nāgārjuna's *Fundamental Treatise on the Middle Way*] with their argument [concerning] the existence of ascertainment 358
2. Their attack [on Nāgārjuna's treatise] with their argument [concerning] the absence of ascertainment 360

[By responding to these arguments] refuting the logicians' version of valid cognition (360)
1. Addressing the issue of why the treatise does not refer to the valid cognition of demonstrable fact [as espoused by] the logicians
2. Refuting the valid cognition asserted by the logicians

Addressing the issue of why the treatise does not refer to the valid cognition of demonstrable fact [as espoused by] the logicians (361)
1. [Justification of] the treatise not providing an account of the varieties of valid cognition and other salient matters on the grounds that from the ultimate perspective, [there is no such thing] as either ascertainment or nonascertainment 362
2. [Justification of] the treatise not providing an account of the varieties of valid cognition and other salient matters on the grounds that contextually, such details do not belong here, since while such things

may exist conventionally, the same is not the case from the perspective unique to our own [Madhyamaka] system, which [the treatise] is in the process of setting forth

[Justification of] the treatise not providing an account of the varieties of valid cognition and other salient matters on the grounds that contextually, such details do not belong here, since while such things may exist conventionally, the same is not the case from the perspective unique to our own [Madhyamaka] system, which [the treatise] is in the process of setting forth (362)

1. The opponent's argument 362
2. Our response 362

Refuting the valid cognition asserted by the logicians (365)

1. General refutation of their valid cognition
2. Specific refutation of their notion of perception [*pratyakṣa*] (390)

General refutation of their valid cognition (365)

1. Refutation of the treatises of the logician and the Svātantrika
2. Refutation of the system according to which the bifurcation of valid cognition is the definitive way to divide it

Refutation of the treatises of the logician and the Svātantrika (365)

1. The fault that their efforts have been futile 365
2. The fault that they have not [successfully] dealt with [the criticism related to] nonascertainment 366

Refutation of the system according to which the bifurcation of valid cognition is the definitive way to divide it (367)

1. Outlining their position 367
2. Refutation of that

Refutation of their position (367)

1. Refutation of the definitive bifurcation, which relies on the special gloss given to the term *lakṣaṇa* [characteristic]
2. Countering their attempts to rebut that 389
3. Conclusion 390

Refutation of the definitive bifurcation, which relies on the special gloss given to the term lakṣaṇa *[characteristic]* (367)

1. Refutation of the position that the term *lakṣaṇa* should be glossed as *that which acts [on the object]* 368
2. Refutation of the position that the term *lakṣaṇa* should be glossed as *the object [that is acted on]*
3. Rebuttal of the defense against our attack on the first gloss

Refutation of the position that glosses the term lakṣaṇa *as the object [that is acted on]* (368)

1. A fault that parallels the earlier one 368
2. Refutation of the position that cognition can be the one performing the action [of characterizing]

Refutation of the position that cognition can be the one performing the action [of characterizing] (369)

1. The unwanted consequence that this once more leads to three objects [of cognition] 369
2. The unwanted consequence that the qualification [introduced by the logician means] that some *lakṣaṇa* cannot be objects of comprehension
3. The untenability of the locus of the characterization being either identical to or distinct from the *lakṣaṇa* 370
4. The fault of it leaving no place for the agent, responsible for the action (376)

The unwanted consequence that the qualification [the logician introduces means] that some lakṣaṇa *cannot be objects of comprehension* (370)

1. The actual fault
2. Rebuttal of his defense against our attack

Rebuttal of his defense against our attack regarding the aforesaid qualification (371)

1. Refutation of the position that what acts on the object is an other-knowing consciousness 371
2. Refutation of the position that what acts on the object is a self-cognizing consciousness

Refutation of the position that what acts on the object is a consciousness of the self-cognizing variety (371)

1. Refuting self-cognition by means of logic 372
2. Refuting self-cognition by means of scripture 372
3. Conclusion

The fault of [the logician's position] leaving no place for the agent, responsible for the action (376)

Rejecting [the logician's] attempted rebuttal of our criticism about there being no place for the agent (378)

1. His response to our criticism 378
2. Our refutation of that response

Our refutation of that response (379)

1. Rejecting the [realist's] interpretation of the scriptural passage 379
2. Refuting the analogy that the [realist] uses to illustrate the situation and countering his objections [to this refutation] 379
3. [Explaining the sense in which] analysis is inappropriate and how one must leave things in an unanalyzed [state] 382
4. How to posit phenomena conventionally 383
5. Why it is necessary to accept [the way that they are posited conventionally] 384
6. Differentiating between skill and ignorance with regard to positing the two forms of "truth" 385

*Specific refutation of their version of perception [*pratyakṣa*]* (390)

1. [Explaining how] the characteristic of perception proposed by them fails to encompass [all that it should]
2. Their account not being tenable in terms of either one of the two types of truth 393
3. Refutation of their derivation for the term *pratyakṣa* (394)
4. [Rejecting] "free from conception" as a characteristic that defines perception (409)

[Explaining how] the characteristic of perception proposed by them fails to encompass [all that it should] (390)

1. Setting out the actual fault [in their account] 390
2. Countering the attempted rebuttal of our criticism

Countering the attempted rebuttal of our criticism (391)
1. Their attempt to escape the criticism 391
2. Our rejection of that

Our rejection of that (391)
1. Rejecting the rebuttal by showing that the analogy does not work 391
2. Rejecting the rebuttal by pointing out its absurd consequence 392
3. Conclusion 393

[Refutation of the logician's] derivation of the term pratyakṣa (394)
1. The Prāsaṅgikas' own understanding of the term's derivation 394
2. Refutation of how earlier commentators and Pramāṇa logicians have accounted for the derivation

Refutation of how earlier commentators and Pramāṇa logicians have accounted for the derivation (397)
1. Outlining their position 397
2. Refutation of that

Refutation of that explanation (398)
1. How the [derivation] should be explained in terms of the object
2. [Describing how the proposed] repetition is not sufficiently inclusive 405

How the derivation of pratyakṣa should be explained in terms of the object (398)
1. Refutation of the [position that the derivation of *pratyakṣa* is explainable in terms of its linking the cognitive] subject with the sense power(s) 398
2. Refutation of the [position that the derivation] is explainable in terms of a unique cause [for sense perception] 398
3. Explanation of how the number and nature of valid cognitions are determined by their objects 401
4. The unwanted consequence [that their explanation of the derivation is one that] dismisses commonly accepted verbal schemes 403

[Rejecting] "free from conception" as a characteristic that defines perception (409)

1. Outlining the [logician's] position 409
2. Refutation of that

Refutation of that [position] (411)

1. [Candrakīrti's] refutation of that position in the *Commentary to Four Hundred Stanzas* 411
2. [Candrakīrti's] refutation of that position in *Clear Words* 415

Setting out the valid cognition of our own [Prāsaṅgika] system (417)

1. Demonstrating the correctness of our system on valid cognition
2. Resolving certain knotty issues [related to it] 442

Demonstrating the correctness of our own system on valid cognition (417)

1. The characteristics that define valid cognition 417
2. Its varieties
3. Its object 440
4. The way that valid cognition and objects of comprehension are established 444

Varieties (419)

1. Perception: what comprehends objects that are manifest
2. Inferential cognition: what comprehends the slightly hidden 432
3. Valid cognition [associated with] scripture: what comprehends the extremely hidden 435
4. Valid cognition through analogy, which comprehends a hidden object through reference to a manifest model 438

Perception (423)

1. Sense perception 423
2. Mental perception 425
3. Yogic perception 429

Notes

1. Volumes within *The Library of Tibetan Classics* series are intended to make selected classics of Tibetan writing accessible to an audience beyond the specialist. As such, in the hope of producing a smoother reading experience, they generally do not include features that are standard in academic translations—such as the frequent insertion of lengthy, technical notes and parenthetical remarks, the citation of multiple secondary sources, and the excavation of issues dealt with in the text. This has posed special challenges with regard to the current volume, both because of the sophisticated nature of its material and the concise manner in which our Tibetan authors often present their thinking and arguments. As with the other volumes in the series, the sources cited by them have been identified where possible and reference details included in notes. But additional notes have been provided to bring clarity at points where the text is particularly dense or the reader is likely to need some essential piece of information to fully understand the discussion.
2. *Heart of the Middle Way* (*Madhyamakahṛdaya*) 9.18, Toh 3855 Tengyur, dbu ma, *dza*, 32a3.
3. For further reading on the Pramāṇa tradition, see John Dunne's *Foundations of Dharmakīrti's Philosophy* and Tom J. F. Tillemans's *Scripture, Logic, Language*. For those wanting to delve deeper into the intricacies of the Tibetan Pramāṇa tradition, Georges Dreyfus's *Recognizing Reality* remains unmatched.
4. The only serious Buddhist alternative to this twofold model, a fourfold one associated with Madhyamaka, is discussed below.
5. Frauwallner, "Vasubandhu's Vādaviddhih."
6. Gö Lotsāwa, *Blue Annals*, 421.
7. Tib. *Tshad ma sde bdun*.
8. For more on the Tibetan translations of the *Pramāṇavārttika*, see note 242.
9. Gö Lotsāwa, *Blue Annals*, 97.
10. *Tshad ma rnying pa*.
11. Gö Lotsāwa, *Blue Annals*, 418.
12. In the text, "pot" is a translation of the Tibetan term *bum pa*. It simply denotes a vessel used for carrying and storing water, typically one that is bulbous with a small opening. When our authors refer to it, no special religious or other significance is implied.
13. There are two ways that x could pervade y. Pictured as two concentric circles, x could be the larger, covering the whole of y with room to spare. Alternatively, the two circles could be the same size, such that their circumferences are exactly equal. While in this second case x still pervades y, it would be just as true to say that y pervades x. For more on this see note 652.

14. *Madhyamakāvatārabhāṣya*, Toh 3862 Tengyur, dbu ma, *'a*, 222a3.
15. *Madhyamakopadeśa*, Toh 3929 Tengyur, dbu ma, *ki*, 96a5.
16. For details of these see Tillemans, "Sur le *parārthānumāna* en logique bouddhique," 74–75.
17. Several separate terms in Tibetan have commonly been used for component C (these include *rtags*, *gtan tshigs*, or *rgyu mtshan*). Some in the later Geluk tradition make slight distinctions among these. But more generally, they are treated as equivalent, and our authors do not distinguish among them. In Geluk writings, there is a preference for the term *rtags*, which is based on the Sanskrit *liṅga* and translates as "sign" or "inferential mark." But throughout I have chosen to use the more relatable "reason," the usual translation of *gtan tshigs* or *rgyu mtshan*, based on the Sanskrit *hetu*.
18. Mainly reflecting Khedrup Jé's understanding of the three, the translation "criteria" is used in this volume.
19. As Khedrup Jé explains in the first text (pp. 373–74), while the vocabulary may be the same, the pervasions of the proof and the consequence are different from each other.
20. For more information, see Samuels, "The Tibetan Institutionalisation of Disputation."
21. Hugon, "Arguments by Parallels in the Epistemological Works of Phya pa Chos kyi seng ge."
22. Roy W. Perrett's *An Introduction to Indian Philosophy* and Jonardon Ganeri's *Indian Logic* are good examples of such works.
23. There are questions about the relation between different strands of materialist thinking and philosophy in ancient and classical India, and to whom exactly the names Cārvāka and Lokāyata referred. However, Tibetan authors made no distinctions and used a single designation for them (*Rgyang 'phen pa*). For the sake of convenience, Cārvāka is used to translate this designation throughout the volume.
24. Dunne, *Foundations of Dharmakīrti's Philosophy*, 3n6.
25. Dreyfus, *Recognizing Reality*, 410.
26. *Weapon of Reasoning*, 13b–14b.
27. However, they do engage in minor discussions about certain points, such as the idea that particular passages can be described as "common" to the two systems or even to the two vehicles. See, for instance, pages 241–42.
28. See Jackson, "The Status of Pramāṇa Doctrine According to Sa skya Paṇḍita and Other Tibetan Masters."
29. *Ornament of the Mahayana Sutras* (*Mahāyānasūtrālaṃkāra*) 2.6, Toh 4020 Tengyur, sems tsam, *phi*, 2b2.
30. Layakpa Jangchup Ngödrup, *Ornament Clarifying the Essence [of Gampopa's Four Dharmas]*, 265.
31. *Ocean of Pramāṇa [Canonical] Writings.*
32. More accurately, in this Tibetan context, these individuals talked of *tsema* (*tshad ma*), the term used to translate *pramāṇa*.
33. Khedrup Jé, *Record of [Dharmas] Received*, 3a–b.
34. This dispute has been covered more than the others, with contributions from Heimbel in "The Dispute Between mKhas grub rJe and Ngor chen" and Dachille in *Searching for the Body*.

35. Some of the studies by Yael Bentor, including "Did Mkhas grub rje Challenge the Authenticity of the Sa skya *lam 'bras* Tradition?" throw light on specific areas in which Khedrup Jé found himself at odds with Sakya scholars on issues of authenticity and interpretation.
36. See Samuels, "Challenging the Curriculum: The Course of Studies in Buddhist Monasteries of Medieval Tibet and Beyond."
37. He is also referred to as Jamyang Shepai Dorjé.
38. The other two are the *Guide Through the Path of Pramāṇa* and the *Extensive Presentation on the Results of Valid Cognition*. Leonard van der Kuijp has written a summary for each of the four works in the first of a series of articles, *Studies in the Life and Thought of Mkhas-grub-rje 1*.
39. Khedrup Jé mainly speaks of the scholars he refutes in the third person. But he addresses some more directly, in the second person. It might seem likely that Khedrup Jé would reserve "you" for living figures, and since some of the individuals are identifiable, a more precise dating of this work may still be possible. However, there are some questions about whether Khedrup Jé is consistent in his use of addresses.
40. Van der Kuijp, *Studies in the Life and Thought of Mkhas-grub-rje 1*, 78.
41. I plan to go into more detail about this encounter in a separate work.
42. The other ten, mainly following the order they appear in the Zhol par khang edition of his Collected Works, are (1) *Explanation of Pramāṇasamuccaya*, (2) *Extensive Pramāṇa Memorandum*, (3) *Condensation of the Illuminator of the Path to Liberation: Commentary to Pramāṇavārttika*, (4) *Essence of the Sun: Explanation of Sambandhaparīkṣā*, (5) *Guide Through the Path of Pramāṇa*, (6) *Memorandum of the Perception Chapter of Pramāṇavārttika*, (7) *Illuminator of the Path to Liberation: Commentary to Pramāṇavārttika*, (8) *Illumination of the Intent: Extensive Commentary on the Pramāṇaviniścaya*, (9) *Essence Treasure of Fine Elucidation: Commentary to Nyāyabindu*, and (10) *Commentary on Treasure of Pramāṇa Reasoning*.
43. Shākya Chokden, *History of the Pramāṇa Tradition*, 22a.
44. See note 1289.
45. The present text by Jamyang Shepa has been partially translated into German by Chizuko Yoshimizu in *Die Erkenntnislehre des Prāsaṅgika-Madhyamaka nach dem Tshig gsal stoṅ thun gyi tshad ma'i rnam bshad des 'Jam dbyaṅs bshad pa'i rdo rje*, whereas Khedrup Jé's text has been translated into English as *A Dose of Emptiness* by José Cabezón.
46. The last word of the Sanskrit title (an equivalent for "banisher") is missing and was presumably omitted during the text's production.
47. This non-Buddhist Indian figure remains unidentified. The spelling of his name here is based on the Tibetan *Gling skyes*.
48. Maitreya, *Mahāyānasūtrālaṃkāra*, 2.6, Toh 4020 Tengyur, sems tsam, *phi*, 2b2. The original context for these words is a section describing the various ways in which the Mahayana is superior to the Hinayana. The passage emphasizes the relative shortcomings of logical reasoning, which is here treated as emblematic of conceptual understanding. Nevertheless, Khedrup Jé regards it as affirming a place for such understanding on the spiritual path, albeit one that is intended to lead to perception.

49. The topic of how a conceptual consciousness is able to know a thing is widely discussed in this work. The object universal (Tib. *don spyi*, Skt. *arthasāmānya*)—sometimes translated as "meaning generality" or even "concept"—is key to the explanation of this topic. A conceptual consciousness engages with its main object not directly but in a mediated fashion. As such, it relies on an object universal, which appears to a conceptual consciousness and is thus described as its appearing object. This is distinguished from its engaged object, which is the object that is the focus of its attention and that it may be realizing.
50. Each of the three Buddhist spiritual vehicles—those of the bodhisattva, pratyekabuddha, and śrāvaka—is described in terms of five sequential paths—the paths of accumulation, preparation, seeing, meditation, and no-more learning. The supreme dharma level is the last stage of the path of preparation. It immediately precedes the path of seeing, where reality is first experienced directly.
51. Maitreya, *Mahāyānasūtrālaṃkāra*, 12.60, Toh 4020 Tengyur, sems tsam, *phi*, 15b4.
52. Tib. *gtan tshigs kyi rig pa*, Skt. *hetuvidyā*.
53. The author refers to a common analytical tool of Tibetan scholasticism. This is employed to sum up how two things, or more precisely, categories of existent thing, relate to each other and where the boundaries between them lie. According to this, there are only four possible ways that any two things, *x* and *y*, might stand in relation to one another. Therefore, *x* and *y* may be such that (1) they are preclusive—that is, mutually exclusive (*'gal ba*), (2) they are coterminous (*don gcig*), (3) *x*, being more extensive, entirely encompasses *y*, or (4) *x* only partially encompasses *y*. In technical language, the third is referred to as a three-point (*mu gsum*) relationship, and the fourth a four-point (*mu bzhi*) relationship.
54. Although the author identifies this passage as coming from the *Abhidharma Sutra*, the sutra in question remains unidentified. The same words are cited in numerous Indian works, including Dignāga's autocommentary to his *Compendium of Pramāṇa* (*Pramāṇasamuccayavṛtti*), chap. 1, Toh 4204 Tengyur, tshad ma, *ce*, 15b2.
55. This line or a similar version is found in various sutras, including the *Bodhisattva's Scriptural Collection* (*Bodhisattvapiṭaka*), Toh 56 Kangyur, dkon brtsegs, *kha*, 85b4, the *Play in Full* (*Lalitavistara*), Toh 95 Kangyur, mdo sde, *kha*, 89b3, and the *Precious Discourse on the Blessed One's Extensive Wisdom That Leads to Infinite Certainty* (*Niṣṭhāgatabhagavajjñānavaipulyasūtraratnānanta*), Toh 99 Kangyur, mdo sde, *ga*, 22b5.
56. *Daśadharmasūtra*, Toh 53 Kangyur, dkon brtsegs, *kha*, 167b7.
57. A very similar line appears in the *History of Kanakavarṇa* (*Kanakavarṇapūrvayoga*), Toh 350 Kangyur, mdo sde, *a*, 53a5.
58. *Sutra Teaching How All Phenomena Are Without Any Origin* (*Sarvadharmāpravṛttinirdeśasūtra*), Toh 180 Kangyur, mdo sde, *ma*, 275a5.
59. *Sutra Teaching How All Phenomena Are Without Any Origin* (*Sarvadharmāpravṛttinirdeśasūtra*), Toh 180 Kangyur, mdo sde, *ma*, 275a4.
60. This section refers to the most important typology of reasons. They are divided into (1) effect reasons, (2) nature reasons, and (3) nonobservation reasons. The last refers to the major subdivision within the second category. Later in this text there are separate sections dealing with each of the above individually.
61. *Hundred Accounts of Noble Deeds Beginning with That of Pūrṇa* (*Pūrṇapra-*

mukhāvadānaśataka), Toh 343 Kangyur, mdo sde, *am*, 278b6. This account derives from the conversion of the wandering mendicant brahman Dīrghanakha ("Long Nailed One"), whose name alludes to one of his past ascetic practices. The work cited here should not be confused with the one preceding it in the Kangyur—*Questions of Dīrghanakha the Wandering Mendicant* (*Dīrghanakhaparivrājakaparipṛcchā*), Toh 342—which focuses on the same individual. Various sources appear to agree on the structure of the exchange during the initial encounter between the Buddha and the mendicant, where Dīrghanakha expresses his philosophically skeptical position and then the Buddha undermines Dīrghanakha's assertion by inverting it. However, these sources offer differing versions of how the original view is expressed. The current author's rendition, centering on Dīrghanakha's claim about his ability to "tolerate" (*bzod pa*), is unusual, although Sakya Paṇḍita also used it. The Dergé version instead has "assert" (*'dod pa*), whereas the version in the Pāli canon (*Dhiganaka Sutta*, MN 74) is generally translated as "believe."

62. This formula is found in various sutras, including *Hundred Deeds* (*Karmaśataka*), Toh 340, Kangyur, mdo sde, *a*, 109a5.
63. This passage does not appear in the Kangyur collection of sutras, but the latter half is located in *Tantra of Great Power* (*Mahābalatantra*), Toh 391 Kangyur, rgyud, *ga*, 1, 216b6.
64. *Ornament of the Mahayana Sutras* (*Mahāyānasūtrālaṃkāra*), 9.9, Toh 4020 Tengyur, sems tsam, *phi*, 7b7. The full stanza, which identifies features displayed by one whose progress on the Mahayana path has become irreversible, says:

    [Having] a mind that logically analyzes the good Dharma,
    never [being subject to] obstructions from evil spirits,
    gaining the special [attainments] and [being able to] discredit the position of others—
    these are the characteristics of unassailability's full maturation.

65. Candrakīrti, *Madhyamakāvatāra*, 6.116, Toh 3861 Tengyur, dbu ma, *'a*, 210a1.
66. At least four different Sanskrit terms featured in the names of Pramāṇa works could justifiably be translated as "commentary"—*ṭīkā* (sometimes *ṭika* or *ṭika*), *vārttika*, *vṛtti*, and *pañjikā*. Aside from the first, which was used as a loanword, Tibetans created their own range of terms (*rnam 'grel*, *'grel p/ba*, *'grel bshad*, and *dka' 'grel*) to translate these and also appear to have expanded the vocabulary through addition of the concept of "autocommentary" (*rang 'grel*). Translating every title that incorporates one of these terms as "commentary" would be confusing, and so it seems fitting to reserve *vārttika* for the most important text, *Commentary on Pramāṇa* (*Pramāṇavārttika*). To help distinguish among the others, several *rough* descriptive terms have been added—"direct commentary" (*ṭīkā*), "running commentary" (*'grel b/pa*), "explanatory commentary" (*'grel bshad*), and "commentary on difficult points" (*dka' 'grel*). These reflect variations present in both the Tibetan and Sanskrit names but are used mainly as a matter of convenience. There may be less variation in the structure of these works than their names imply. In the last case, while the Tibetan term chosen for *pañjikā* (*dka' 'grel*) may literally translate as "commentary on difficult points," the works do not always display dedication to the suggested purpose.
67. *Pramāṇavārttika* 1.214, 102b6. The numbering of stanzas for the *Pramāṇavārttika* here follows that in *The Writings of Dharmakīrti*, the second volume within the series of Tibetan critical editions (*Rgya gzhung sne che bdam sgrig pod phreng*)

edited by Thupten Jinpa. Depending on whether the introductory lines of the original are included in the count, enumerations of these stanzas can vary slightly. In their original Sanskrit, the *Pramāṇavārttika* and numerous other Buddhist works were composed in *kārikās*, a metrical form with two lines. In Tibetan, the two lines were invariably translated into a stanza with four lines of equal length. To reflect the Tibetan conception and description of the materials our authors worked with, the term *stanza*, rather than *kārikā*, is used throughout this volume. The number of lines in the English translation of a Tibetan stanza generally correspond to the number in the original. Although in the interests of clarity, four lines have occasionally been translated as two.

68. *Pramāṇavārttika* 4.108, 143b3.
69. *Pramāṇavārttika* 1.217, 102b7.
70. Tib. *mchod sbyin*, Skt. *yajña*.
71. "Myopic persons" (Tib. *tshur mthong*) is another way of describing ordinary beings, particularly those who concern themselves with the immediate experience and short-term goals of worldly existence rather than with long-term spiritual aims. Later in the text this expression is used in a more specific way, with "myopic" denoting "non-āryas"—that is, ordinary beings who have yet to achieve the state of an ārya.
72. These are the three criteria that a correct reason must fulfill, which were first described clearly by Dignāga. Their technical names are *property of the subject*, *forward pervasion*, and *reverse pervasion*. These are expanded upon below.
73. Here I have translated the Tibetan term *lus* as "core," rather than the more literal "body." "Body" would sound like it referred to the main section of a work, whereas what is meant here is a core group of topics that are not limited to a single text. As seen below, this core or "body" is distinguished from various "offshoots" or, literally, "limbs" (*yan lag*).
74. Dignāga's *Entrance to Reasoning* (*Nyāyamukha*) appears not to have been translated into Tibetan. But these lines are found in Śaṅkarasvāmin's *Entranceway to Reasoning* (*Nyāyapraveśaka*), Toh 4208 Tengyur, tshad ma, *ce*, 88b6. Due to confusion apparently arising from the similarity in their names (*Rigs pa'i sgo* versus *Rigs pa la 'jug pa'i sgo*), the Tibetan tradition has generally attributed the latter work to Dignāga. Furthermore, although the stanza cited by the author here is the version most commonly used by Tibetan scholars, the order of the lines differs in the Dergé Tengyur, where the first two lines are switched with the last two, so that the stanza begins with "Proof [statements]..."
75. Although Dharmakīrti's *Commentary on Pramāṇa* (*Pramāṇavārttika*) is presented as an explanation of Dignāga's *Compendium of Pramāṇa* (*Pramāṇasamuccaya*), there is disparity in the number and order of their chapters. The *Commentary* has four chapters: (1) Personal Inference, (2) Establishing Pramāṇa, (3) Perception, and (4) Inference for Others. The six chapters of the *Compendium* are (1) Inference and Perception, (2) Personal Inference, (3) Inference for Others, (4) Examples, (5) Other-Exclusion, (6) False Rejoinders. The second chapter of the *Commentary on Pramāṇa* is ostensibly devoted to establishing that the Buddha is a valid authority. Khedrup Jé claims that this is the main point of Pramāṇa treatises as a whole. The *Compendium of Pramāṇa* has no separate chapter on the topic, although the topic is the theme of its opening stanza praising the Buddha. The three chapters identified here by Khedrup Jé are therefore those that are essentially

common to both works. He goes on to explain how the three additional chapters of the *Compendium of Pramāṇa* are subsumed into those of the *Commentary on Pramāṇa.*

76. Our text contains only a short discussion of one variety of (self-defeating) rejoinder. "Rejoinders" is the usual translation for this kind of response (Skt. *jāti*). While the sixth chapter of Dignāga's *Compendium* gives its own presentation of the subject, the notion and systematic classification of these rejoinders goes back to non-Buddhist writings, especially the *Nyāyasūtras*. These are emphasized as responses that are ineffective, rather than ones that inflict further damage on the positions of those who issue them. But my translation includes "self-defeating" in reference to the term (*ltag chod*) chosen by Tibetan translators to denote these rejoinders. The popular etymology for this conjures the image of someone who, while attempting to strike at a target with an axe, inadvertently delivers a blow to himself with the back of the axe head.

77. In this first section, the author defines what it means to be an object. He first seeks to refute the reason that some use to deny that *object* (*yul*), *known thing* (*shes bya*), and *comprehended thing* (*gzhal bya*) can be counted as equivalent. As we now enter the main body of the text, we see this shift in approach, with refutation of the views of rival scholars preceding the author's articulation of his own position.

78. In line with custom, the author withholds the names of most of the Tibetan scholars whose positions he rejects. Since the majority of these individuals remain unidentified and some of the relevant works do not seem to have survived, it is often not possible to verify the accuracy of Khedrup Jé's representation of these other scholars' positions. However, according to his depiction, the first opponent's reluctance to count known thing and comprehended thing as equivalent seems to derive from his understanding of what "knowing" and "comprehension" imply. To say that a thing is known seems to imply nothing more to him than that there is some, perhaps vague, awareness of it. But to say that a thing is comprehended must mean that it is correctly realized. This seems to be why he argues that if cognitions were not just aware of their objects but comprehended them, those cognitions would all need to be entirely correct and valid.

79. A term such as *pot*, like a cognition, is classified as a subject, in that it has its object, pot. No special significance is attached to a pot (Tib. *bum pa*). As mentioned in the introduction, it is simply a favorite example for those in the Pramāṇa tradition.

80. To "go against" (*'bud pa*) is an expression used frequently in this text by Khedrup Jé. It is not common even in literature associated with scholasticism, although the works in which it appears are usually from the fourteenth or fifteenth century. The literal meaning of the word is "push," but here it is obviously a technical term, used to indicate the impact of the assertion that an opponent is now making upon one that he has previously made. It therefore carries the sense that one position dislodges or ousts the other. The concept does not appear to originate in Indian writings and may well derive from Tibetan disputation practice.

81. This phrase (*phud mtshams kyang khas blangs so*) appears a few times in the first text. It is obviously intended to reinforce the preceding phrase, in which the author denies the opponent the opportunity of making a certain response, since it would "go against" one of his other assertions. It most likely means that the opponent accepts the criteria for judging that one position has gone against another.

82. *Pramāṇavārttika* 3.53, 120b3.

83. *Pramāṇavārttika* 3.64, 121a2.
84. What follows are Khedrup Jé's arguments supporting a position now commonly associated with the Geluk—namely, that the existence of generally characterized things, like that of specifically characterized ones, is verified by valid cognition. This position was discussed in the introduction.
85. This is an example of a type of hypothetical argument mentioned in the introduction. The way Khedrup Jé phrases the argument suggests that a third individual proposes it.
86. Even in the course of attacking what he characterizes as a single position, Khedrup Jé's references to the opponents sometimes shift between singular and plural, or second and third persons. In such cases, he appears to group certain scholars together as equally guilty of a particular erroneous way of thinking. The shift to a second person and/or singular reference often signals that he is now choosing to pick on a very specific claim made by one member of this group. Since the scholars in question remain largely unidentified, it is not possible to say whether there was as much homogeneity among them as Khedrup Jé's attacks imply.
87. *Pramāṇavārttika* 3.65, 121a2.
88. *Pramāṇavārttika* 4.265, 150a1.
89. This is the first occurrence in the text of a technical expression, the "three spheres" (*'khor gsum*), which as mentioned in the introduction, is related to the consequence. Here we are dealing not with the consequence in theory (in terms of what role it might have in either inducing realization) or in classification (in the sense of determining to which category of consequence a particular example belongs) but with the consequence in practice, as a tool of argumentation. In the context of its use in these texts, although the consequence cannot be equated exactly with a *reductio ad absurdum* argument, in common with that, the consequence can be used affirmatively to argue for one position by pointing out how some given alternative leads to contradiction or incoherence. This usage is apparent in the present case, in which Khedrup Jé seeks to establish that to be a conventional object is to be a genuine existent and not merely something imagined. But we also see numerous examples within the text where consequences do not have this affirmative dimension but are simply employed to undermine the credibility of a position or an opponent. Apart from a criticism, such consequences tell us nothing about the author's own views on the matter. However, according to the way that Khedrup Jé and other Geluk scholars define the correct (or successful) consequence, its *overt* goal is a very immediate one—namely, to deprive the opponent of any reasonable answer. And when Khedrup Jé declares that the *three spheres* are in place, he is asserting that his argument has achieved the textbook goal of the consequence, in that it has left the opponent without any logical response. More generally, including in the context of monastic debate as currently practiced, "three spheres" is the expression one party uses to accuse the other of voicing positions that contradict each other. Scholarly consensus holds that the three are separate elements. The Tibetan word (*'khor*) that conveys circularity is translated here as "spheres," giving the sense that these are elements with their own domains. A reference to the three spheres implies that these domains conflict with each other. How each of the three spheres are to be identified is not a matter of universal agreement, although one explanation says that they refer to the reason, the pervasion, and the conclusion that should logically arise from those two. Later in the text Khedrup Jé gives his own understanding of the three. But the variations in the way they are

identified are minor; they do not alter how the consequence is employed or what it is intended to achieve. When, as in the present situation, the three spheres are said to be in place, it means that positions the opponent accepts or has signaled keenness to uphold are now served up to him as the reason and pervasion of a new argument (i.e., the consequence). These elements lead logically to the argument's conclusion. And while the opponent might try to avoid acceptance of that conclusion, since it is supposed to be derived solely from his own assertions, acceptance is inescapable. He therefore has no response, save that of abandoning at least one of the positions he would otherwise wish to keep.

Khedrup Jé clearly advocated reference to the "three spheres" in argumentation but he was not the first, since the expression was being used well over a century before his birth. A more literal translation of the expression would be "three rotations." And in monastic debate, the gesture that accompanies its articulation is that of circling one's prayer beads around the head of the opponent. It seems likely that both the term and gesture allude to the Tibetan word for being in a state of confusion (*mgo 'khor ba*), which literally means that one's "head is spinning."

90. The perspective that the opponent refers to here is that of conception. The "excluding perspective" (*sel ngo*) is one of the many ways that the distinction between conceptual cognition and perception is reinforced. This references the theory of *other-exclusion* (*apoha*), according to which a conceptual cognition engages an object not affirmatively but through elimination—blocking out what is not that object. This excluding perspective is presented as the counterpart to the "appearance perspective" or "perspective of appearance" (*snang ngo*). There is more discussion on both perspectives below.
91. The first two texts in this volume both have sections on the topic of preclusion. The distinctions between direct and indirect preclusions are explained in these sections.
92. "Actual thing" is used to translate the term *dngos po*. In many contexts it can be rendered "thing," in the sense of an entity. "Actual" has been added to indicate the Geluk gloss on the term in their writings on the Pramāṇa tradition. The actual thing is on the affirmative side of the basic dichotomies of phenomena explained in the introduction to this volume. Hence it is equivalent with phenomena that are impermanent, functioning, and specifically characterized.
93. As discussed later in the text, there is a twofold division of negations: a negation of the *straight* or nonimplicative variety (Tib. *med dgag*, Skt. *prasajyapratiṣedha*) does nothing but negate. A negation of the implicative variety (Tib. *ma yin dgag*, Skt. *paryudāsapratiṣedha*), through negating one thing, also suggests or affirms another.
94. *Pramāṇavārttika* 1.1, 94b4.
95. As mentioned in the introduction, this is another major position that is now associated with the Geluk. In refuting that actual things are limited to these smallest units of consciousness and matter, Khedrup Jé is affirming that all things that function and are subject to change—large or small, part or part-possessor—are equally real and not conceptual constructs.
96. The *piśāca* (Tib. *sha za*) is supposed to be a form of flesh-devouring spirit that is invisible to ordinary humans. In the Pramāṇa literature, there is little interest in the *piśāca* itself, but it is cited as the standard example of a *remote entity* (*bskal don*), a class of things that—for various reasons, including distance, time, nature,

or the limitations of the perceptual apparatus of a potential viewer—might lie beyond that viewer's immediate ken. The idea here is that even if such a spirit were right in front of us, we would not be aware of it. The *piśāca* features prominently later, in one of the main divisions of negative reasoning—nonobservation reasons—with important implications for the limits of our knowledge. To claim that we can be certain of the presence or absence of this type of spirit in a place before us challenges a basic tenet of the tradition.

97. Sakya Paṇḍita, *Treasure of Pramāṇa Reasoning*, 1.11, 3a1. This is the only time in the work that Khedrup Jé presents his sources in this fashion, citing a Tibetan author before citing Dharmakīrti.
98. *Pramāṇavārttika* 3.53, 120b3.
99. *Pramāṇavārttika* 1.186, 101b5.
100. *Pramāṇavārttika* 4.263, 149b7.
101. Here Khedrup Jé appears to equate affirmative phenomena with actual or impermanent things and negative phenomena with permanent ones. This does not represent a standard Geluk view.
102. Despite the slight difference in wording, this appears to be citing Dharmakīrti. See *Commentary on Pramāṇa Autocommentary* (*Pramāṇavārttikavṛtti*), Toh 4216 Tengyur, tshad ma, *ce*, 316a2.
103. As mentioned above, the most important classification of correct reasons divides them into three types. One of these is the nature reason. A proof that uses this reason uses the relation shared by two things—i.e., that they have the same nature—to derive an inference. This type of reason and the relation upon which it depends are recurrent topics throughout the text. In the later section on correct reasons, the author goes into the subcategory of nature reason in more depth, but some elaboration is necessary here in order for the reader to make sense of this debate. There are two subcategories of nature reason. The first is the *plain* or unqualified variety. The second is the reason of the *specified dependence* variety. Most of the discussion about what exactly separates the two varieties centers on production, with the idea that the first variety of reason is unadorned in that it conveys a property of the subject in question but reveals nothing about the specifics of that subject's production. Conversely, the second variety conveys something about its origin. The main reason under discussion here is referred to in the passage from *Commentary on Pramāṇa*. The standard formulation of this reason and the proof in which it is used, as understood by many Tibetan scholars, is "Sound is impermanent because it exists." Since "exists" conveys nothing about the specifics of the sound's production, this is generally considered to be an example of a plain nature reason. In the text, Khedrup Jé criticizes the opponent's formulation of the reason. The opponent has ditched the simple "exists" in favor of his alternative. But Khedrup Jé argues that the basic notion of the plain nature reason is lost in the opponent's more complicated formulation. This, Khedrup Jé says, has effectively removed the basis for distinguishing between the two subcategories.
104. The two Tibetan terms, *shes pa* and *rig pa*, function both as nouns and verbs, a fact that is often exploited in debates. The annotations in brackets are intended to convey this double dimension.
105. Again, the author uses the phrase *phud mtshams kyang khas blangs so* mentioned above (note 81).

106. The moon is obviously single rather than double. Nevertheless, there are clearly cases of individuals who see double. Such perceptions are faulty, but a double moon may appear to them. And as such, it could be said that there is an awareness of double moon. Khedrup Jé argues that by stipulating that an object must be a phenomenon, the opponent is obliged to accept that even something like a double moon must be a phenomenon and thereby an existent, since it is something of which there is an awareness.
107. According to these opponents, only correct cognitions have objects, because to be an object is to exist and be verified by valid cognition. Hence, if dysfunctional cognitions such as those that see a double moon had objects, they could not be false.
108. The nuance conveyed here is typical not only of this author but of the tradition as a whole. He says that anything cognized by awareness necessarily exists. Similarly, anything that is an object of awareness exists. But this does not mean that what is cognized by *any* awareness exists or that the object of *any* consciousness is an object. For instance, the sense cognition of the double moon is false, but the double moon is nevertheless its object and that of which it is aware.
109. Tib. *spyi khyab sgos khyab*.
110. This unidentified opponent posits a novel third category outside the usual dichotomy of actual and non-actual things. These mutual or shared phenomena (*thun mong gi chos*) seem to be intended to bridge the gap between particular instances and universals. The understandings of how particulars relate to universals and of the exact nature of universals themselves are central areas that distinguish between what Dreyfus characterizes as antirealist and moderate realist positions. Such positions separate Sakya Paṇḍita from Geluk thinkers. For more on this, see Dreyfus, *Recognizing Reality*, 154–70.
111. This is the first significant use of the important term *aspect* (*ākāra*, *rnam pa*). For more on *ākāra* and variations of its usage in Buddhist Abhidharma and Pramāṇa writings, see Birgit Kellner, "Changing Frames in Buddhist Thought." What should be appreciated here is that "aspect" encompasses many meanings. For instance, in literature relating to Maitreya's *Ornament of Realizations* (*Abhisamayālaṃkāra*), references to "aspect of the object" can refer to the object itself, whereas in the context of the sixteen aspects of the four truths, the aspect is a feature or quality. Perhaps its most familiar usage is in Buddhist theories of cognition and especially perception, where the aspect of the object refers to a representation of that object. But even within discussions on perception, Khedrup Jé occasionally focuses on different dimensions of aspect; sometimes he describes it more like an image and on others as an appearance. In addition to these various slants on aspect, there are also different *types*, such as the "object-aspect" and "subject-aspect."

    Returning to the aspect in perception, Tibetan scholars rank the Indian Buddhist tenet systems within the doxographic model based, at least partly, on the role they assign to the aspect. Thus, among these schools, the Vaibhāṣika's stance is usually said to be the crudest, because it has no place for the aspect. It might therefore be described, in Western philosophical terms, as a form of direct or naive realism. A position usually ascribed to the Sautrāntika and some of the schools above is far more familiar. For them, perception of a thing is only possible because the perception in question *has* the aspect of its object. This is usually explained to mean that the perception has some likeness to the object. In Western philosophical terms, this theory might be described as a form of representational realism. In Buddhism, this notion of correspondence between subject and object is invoked both when it comes to judgments about the veracity and accurateness of individual cognitions (i.e., whether they truly reflect what is there) and indeed the whole theory of what constitutes reality, since a truth only exists to the extent that it can be verified by cognition, which in some sense must accord with it. This aspect, understood as a likeness or representation of the object, is usually described as playing a mediating role between the object and subject, although as we see shortly, Khedrup Jé, like other Geluk scholars, has his own view on this. At the heart of the matter is how the aspect should be identified, how it is aligned with the subject and object, and how exactly it facilitates the process of perception.

112. The honorific language (*gsung pa* and *bzhad pa*) used by the author to report this view is at variance with his usual tone and indicates that he has respect for the individual who espoused it. Although the individual in question remains unidentified, the definition is clearly based upon on words in the first chapter of Dharmakīrti's *Ascertainment of Pramāṇa* (*Pramāṇaviniścaya*). The opponent's use of the term *experiential* probably stems from a wish to identify the evident with the empirical.

113. In the Sautrāntika system, "experiencer" is generally understood to refer to self-cognition, and the "experienced" is the awareness that is its overt object.

114. The stance of the opponents here seems to favor a Cittamātra view, according to which there are no externally established entities. These opponents presumably feel that if the perceptions in question here (*don rig mngon sum*) were realizing these entities by virtue of their own identities, it would clash with the idea that such entities lack external reality.

115. This is first major shift in the use of *aspect* referred to above (note 111). As mentioned there, the key role often assigned to the aspect in the Buddhist theory of perception is that of mediating between the subject and the object. For the realist in particular, this rests on the aspect's ability to accurately reflect an objective reality. But here we see Khedrup Jé introduce a facet of the aspect that is more akin to a *subjective* image or impression. He returns several times to the same scenario—of two people gazing at another individual—always as one that is problematic for the realist stance. The crux of this problem is that the differing perspectives that the people have on the individual are supposed to derive from sense cognitions rather than conceptual ones. These are not their thoughts or views about the individual, which might be triggered upon seeing him. Instead, they are divergent perspectives of the individual *within* perception itself. For the realist, this intrusion of the subjective into the realm of perception is unwelcome and has definite implications for the external reality that the perception is supposed to reflect. The scenario Khedrup Jé refers to and the argument he uses are derived from the third chapter of Dharmakīrti's *Commentary on Pramāṇa*. The lines in which they appear are cited on page 339.

116. Khedrup Jé will go on to develop what he says here about the aspect *presenting* (*shar ba*) itself. The same term can be understood to describe the aspect as *arising*. The important point is that, unlike the opponent, he is not speaking about the aspect as something that presents itself *to* the perception.

117. In Pramāṇa writings, sound and impermanence are regularly grouped together (*sgra dang mi rtag pa'i tshogs don*), since the combination of the two form the pro-

bandum in the proof "Sound is impermanent because it is produced." Here, however, reference to their combination is intended in a simpler sense. These are just two things that one might, in speech or thought, group together.

118. This division has been attributed to Dharmottara. According to it, an intentional utterance should lie outside the five situations (*gnas skabs lnga*)—namely, those of mental disturbance, sleep, an unthinking habit, unconscious copying or repeating, and a verbal slip.

119. The wording here (*kun mkhyen ye shes mi srid par thal lo*) could alternatively be read as "That would preposterously make omniscient wisdom an impossibility!"

120. The divine eye (Tib. *lha'i mig*, Skt. *divyacakṣus*) is one of the five superknowledges (Tib. *mngon shes lnga*, Skt. *pañcābhijña*). As such, it is held to be a power that can only be achieved by developing a particular state of concentration but which ordinary beings including non-Buddhists can attain. The special feature of the divine eye is that it sees all forms without hindrance. Hence, Khedrup Jé reasons, it must also be able to see physical sense powers.

121. This distinction between self-cognition (*rang rig*) and other-cognition (*gzhan rig* or *gzhan don rig pa*) is cited frequently. When, for instance, someone sees the color blue, there is a visual perception directed outward, toward the object blue that seems separate from the perceiver: this is other-cognition. But within the same experience, there is simultaneously a part of the cognition turned inward, which takes the visual perception itself as its overt object: this is self-cognition. Belief in self-cognition is found among the Sautrāntika and Cittamātra schools but also among some Madhyamaka thinkers. In Buddhist epistemological theory, self-cognition holds a key position. A thing can only be said to exist if it is verified by valid cognition. But what verifies the valid cognition itself? This is the most important role assigned to self-cognition, which perceives other-cognitions in an unmistaken manner irrespective of whether those cognitions are correct. If valid cognition is the foundation of knowledge, self-cognition, for those who assert its existence, is the epistemological backstop.

122. Tib. *gsal ba zhe 'dod la khas len pas*. Khedrup Jé acknowledges that the opponent has made no overt assertion about cause and effect. He also acknowledges that the reason and pervasion of the argument that he uses against the opponent are not ones that the latter has openly stated. Nevertheless Khedrup Jé proposes that this reason and pervasion can be elicited from what the opponent has said regarding evident and hidden things.

123. As mentioned above, these are the three criteria of a correct reason, the first clear formulation of which is generally attributed to Dignāga. Here the three are contrasted with the three varieties of incorrect reason. The link between the two sets of three is an accepted one, since Dharmakīrti connects each of the three varieties of incorrect reason with a seperate flaw, explaining how in the fulfillment of the three criteria each of the respective flaws is countered. Or, in a more literal rendering of what appears below, the fulfillment of each of the three criteria of the correct reason represents the *elimination* of a flaw found within each of the three categories of incorrect reason. The content of the current exchange between Khedrup Jé and this opponent is involved, but it boils down to a straightforward question: If division x is said to stem from or be directly linked to division y, to what extent must x mirror y?

124. The wording used in this exchange is terse, but Khedrup Jé's general point is clear. The fact that one division derives from another does not mean that there must be a direct correspondence between the two in every respect. The crucial issue that this is leading to, as the author is about to elaborate, is how the twofold division of objects of comprehension relates to the twofold division of the means of valid cognition.
125. *Pramāṇavārttika* 3.63, 121a1.
126. *Pramāṇavārttika* 1.15, 95a6.
127. *Commentary on the Difficult Points in the Pramāṇavārttika* (*Pramāṇavārttika-pañjikā*), chap. 3, Toh 4217, Tengyur, tshad ma, *che*, 146b2. The organization of the various Sanskrit commentaries on Dharmakīrti's treatise mirrors its four chapters. However, in some cases, not all of their four chapters exist in Tibetan translation. Devendrabuddhi's work, for instance, only has the commentary on the second, third, and fourth of Dharmakīrti's chapters. Hence, Devendrabuddhi's work starts with his commentary on the second chapter of *Commentary on Pramāṇa.*
128. *Direct Commentary on the Commentary on Pramāṇa* (*Pramāṇavārttikaṭikā*), chap. 3, Toh 4220 Tengyur, tshad ma, *nye*, 168b4.
129. As mentioned in the introduction to this volume, the author uses discussion about the relation between evident and hidden phenomena to make a broader point—namely, that notwithstanding the prominence of many rigid dichotomies, Buddhist epistemology also takes perspectives into account.
130. As in many other cases, here we have a single Tibetan word with a variety of applications or connotations, which cannot be captured by a single English word. In the context of the present twofold division of phenomena, the term *mngon 'gyur* is translated as "evident." But the author also here hints at another dimension, indicated by the use of "manifest" in the translation, which describes the *way* that they are realized. This second gloss is favored by the Prāsaṅgika. Hence the term is translated as "manifest" rather than "evident" throughout the third text in this volume.
131. The distinctions between these various objects are clarified later. As will become apparent, one should not assume that the *held object* (*gzung yul*) of a cognition means the same as an object that is held by a cognition. The "held object" is a technical term with a particular set of parameters. But there may be certain things that do not fit those parameters but could still quite correctly be described as objects that a particular cognition holds. The tradition revels in making such finesses.
132. The term *śabdārtha* (Tib. *sgra don*) is left in the original Sanskrit. Discussion about it follows shortly in Khedrup Jé's text and the accompanying note (141).
133. Throughout this volume, the first of the three criteria for a correct reason has been translated as "property of the subject." This rendering reflects how the source term (Tib. *phyogs chos*, Skt. *pakṣadharma*) is meant to be understood. A more literal translation would be "property of the position" or "property of the thesis." The question of how best to express the concept has a long history of discourse attached to it, going back to Dignāga's time. Especially in the Tibetan tradition, Dharmakīrti's major treatise is presented not just as a commentary on Dignāga's *Compendium of Pramāṇa* but as a defense of Dignāga's system. The very first concrete issue that Dharmakīrti's commentary addresses after the introductory stanzas is Dignāga's idiosyncratic use of the aforementioned term. Dharmakīrti's explana-

tion was aimed at Dignāga's critics, who said that given what Dignāga intended to convey about the first criterion of the correct reason, the term he chose was wrong, because it referred to the property of the proof's *thesis* (i.e., the subject plus the predicate), whereas the property in question was that of the *subject*. Dharmakīrti argued that while the term refers to the "position/thesis," it should primarily be understood to denote the subject, and that Dignāga chose it as a way of simultaneously embracing the different elements of the proof. Therefore the name for the first criterion should be translated more literally as "property of the position." Dharmakīrti's defense, expressed at some length in the autocommentary, turns from a justification of Dignāga's term into a hermeneutical exegesis on the employment of nonliteral terms in Buddhist scriptures and treatises. This discussion, which is so firmly rooted in the opening lines of the *Commentary on Pramāṇa*, is addressed by Khedrup Jé in his own commentary on that work. Since the literal translation of the term would introduce a further level of complication that none of the works in this volume ever directly address, I have chosen a rendering that is closest to its intended meaning.

134. *Pramāṇavārttika* 3.1, 118b3.
135. *Pramāṇasamuccaya* 2.1, 4a1.
136. A point made earlier was that certain Tibetan technical terms have a single form but that this may be interpreted as a noun or a verb. Depending on their position in the statement, others can be understood as a noun or an adjective. For example, *mi rtag pa* may be interpreted as "impermanence" or "impermanent." Here, likewise, the term *spyi mtshan* could denote "general characterization" or "generally characterized thing."
137. *Pramāṇavārttika* 3.1, 118b3.
138. In line with a common practice of Tibetan scholasticism, Khedrup Jé sets out to explore a topic by framing it as a discussion intended to resolve what might appear to be conflicting statements made by authoritative figures or works. The issues that he proposes might be seen to be in conflict here are that (1) the probandum (i.e., the thesis) of the proof is normally understood to comprise two elements, a subject and a predicate, (2) a probandum is usually also equated with a thing that is overtly realized by inferential valid cognition, and (3) generally characterized thing is an example of something that is overtly comprehended by valid cognition, but being single, it does not conform to the usual notion of probandum consisting of the aforementioned two elements.
139. *Pramāṇasamuccaya* 2.1, 4a1.
140. Despite the slightly ambiguous way that Khedrup Jé phrases this point, his question is quite basic: Can valid inferential cognition realize general characterization in isolation or not? He states that it cannot realize it in isolation, since an inferential cognition necessarily relies on a proof. By way of illustration, he refers to a proof that has "The *śabdārtha* of pot is generally characterized" as its probandum. He says that in this, general characterization is conjoined with the *śabdārtha* of pot. So it forms part but not the whole of the probandum.
141. The *śabdārtha* of any given term relates to its meaning. In certain contexts, such as when dealing with etymologies, *śabdārtha* can simply convey the sense of a word. But in Pramāṇa writings, the usage and analysis of the term engages with meaning on a deeper level. Generally speaking, the *śabdārtha* of pot can be understood as

what the term *pot* "means" or "indicates," but there is a difference of opinions on how exactly it is to be read, which is why it has been left untranslated here. Both the Sanskrit term and the Tibetan *sgra don* are composed of two elements. These respectively mean "sound" or "word" and "object" or "meaning." Some Tibetan scholars say that the two elements should be read separately, as "word *and* meaning/object," whereas others say that they should be conjoined, as "meaning/object *of* the word," i.e., the word's meaning/object. These differing interpretations, *śabdārtha*'s exact role, and how it is distinguished from the universal are discussed below in the text and accompanying notes.

142. *Pramāṇavārttika* 3.1, 118b3.
143. *Pramāṇavārttika* 3.54, 120b3.
144. Tib. *song ba'i gzhal bya.*
145. *Pramāṇavārttika* 3.1, 118b3.
146. *Pramāṇavārttika* 3.54, 120b3.
147. *Pramāṇavārttika* 3.1, 118b3.
148. Those of the Prāsaṅgika school say that the term translated here as "specifically characterized" carries the connotation of something with its own independent nature. As set out in the third text in this volume, Candrakīrti attacks the notion of phenomena being able to exist in such a way. Generally speaking, in expositions of Pramāṇa thinking according to Dignāga and Dharmakīrti, the Prāsaṅgika viewpoint is not taken into consideration. But Khedrup Jé serves a brief reminder that the discussion here fits into a grander doxographic scheme. He says that the Pramāṇa tradition's gloss on specific characterization must be compatible with Prāsaṅgika criticisms of that understanding.
149. Literally, the "isolated encapsulation of specific characterization" (*rang mtshan gyi don ldog*).
150. The illustration and definition of a thing are clearly different from each other, since what the author cites as the illustration of specific characterization is something he has just denied is its definition. Geluk thinkers rely upon a threefold model, which distinguishes between the *definition* (*mtshan nyid*), *definiendum* (*mtshon bya*), and *illustration* (*mtshan gzhi*). They make continuous reference to this model when explaining how, from the perspective of a single individual, *x* comes to be known or understood, named, and classified. Generally speaking, unless a definition is understood, there can be no knowledge of its definiendum. The illustration of *x* is usually held to be something that helps in the process of linking its definition and its definiendum. As its name suggests, it is meant in some way to embody *x*. But unlike the definition, it need not be watertight—that is, *x*'s illustration need not be entirely coterminous with *x*'s definition. Many more such minor distinctions between these three become apparent later in this text. In the third text, aspects of this model reappear, but this time in the hands of the Prāsaṅgika, who question the lower school's understanding of *characteristic* (*lakṣaṇa* or *lakṣya*).
151. Tibetan does not generally distinguish between singular and plural in nouns. Nor does it require the use of definite or indefinite articles. Whether a particular noun refers to one or many is mainly understood through context. It is important to keep this in mind for the following discussion. Pot, a pot, pots, the pot, etc., are all translations of the same Tibetan term, *bum pa*. The fact that the same term might be understood in different ways is an asset for Tibetan authors in their discussions on the relation between universals and particulars. In the translation, when articles

or plural markers are added—"the pot," "pots," etc.—the pots in question are particulars. When "pot" alone is used, it is more *likely* to denote a universal.

152. Tib. *rang gi gsal ba la rjes su 'gro ba.*
153. This whole section and especially what are represented as the mistakes of the present opponent are crucial for understanding the author's (and by extension the Geluk's) positions on the relation between universals and particulars. There are obviously difficulties in explaining how a single universal relates to its many particulars. This might seem to be less problematic when all the particulars are generally characterized, meaning that both universal and particular are conceptual constructs. But such is not the case when the particulars have their own identities that are not constructed by thought and exist in different locations and times. How can the universal maintain a relationship with these diverse particulars, and what is the nature of that universal? According to the "moderate realist" position of the Geluk, universals such as pot and actual thing—the particulars of which are all, without exception, real, functioning entities—are not generic or generally characterized. Such universals must be concomitant with their particulars. The particulars must also instantiate these universals—which would be impossible if the universal were generally characterized. Hence, the universal of pot cannot be anything other than a pot. It must also be present in each of its instances. This idea is reflected in the language used in Geluk writings, which does not speak of "universal pot" and "particular pots" or recognize such a distinction. Instead, there is only "pot" and its particulars.
154. In epistemological terms, another key distinction is made between *comprehensive engagers* and *excluding engagers*. A perception is said to engage its object comprehensively, which is generally explained to mean that the multiple features of its objects present themselves to it and it engages them accordingly. Conversely, a conceptual cognition engages its object in a selective manner. Put another way, in line with the *apoha* theory, thought and language engage their objects not affirmatively but through exclusion. The author makes references to the distinction between these two forms of object engagement throughout the text and devotes a separate section to them.
155. The notion of a *purely abstracted thing*, or literally, "thing alone" (Tib. *dngos po tsam*), is relied upon by many of those who, unlike Geluk thinkers, take an "antirealist" stance on the relation between the universal and its particulars. For them, there must be a purely abstracted version (not unlike a Platonic universal) of pot, to which any particular pot, in some sense, corresponds or refers. This purely abstracted object is the subject of regular attacks by Khedrup Jé.
156. *Pramāṇavārttika* 3.1, 118b3.
157. Tib. *ba lang dkar zal ma yin pa las log pa'i ldog pa*. In line with the *apoha* theory, a category is not an affirmative reality that comes from the side of the object. It only becomes an object of mind through a negation of what does not belong to the category. More literally, the category of *x* is the exclusion of non-*x*.
158. The two are separately related to impermanence in the sense that each individually is encompassed by the category of impermanence. More details about the distinction between things that are and are not derived from effort or exertion—and specifically sounds that are either of those two—will come in the discussion on inconclusive reasons.
159. The argument's reason is that "actual thing derived from effort" and "[actual thing]

not derived from effort" are each related to impermanence, in the sense that they each share the same nature as it.

160. By rejecting the reason outlined in the note immediately above, the opponent is obviously denying that "actual thing derived from effort" shares the same nature as impermanence. Khedrup Jé's consequence is based on this denial.

161. Tib. *tha dad yin pa'i cha.*

162. Depending on its position in a statement, a single Tibetan term (*bdag med*) translates either as "selfless" (i.e., lacking a self) or "selflessness." Debaters sometimes exploit this potential double meaning by using the term together with "if." Thus a single assertion can mean either "If *x* is selfless" or "If *x* is selflessness." It is also very difficult to respond in the negative to these assertions without seeming to imply that there could be something that is not selfless. Khedrup Jé's argument partly relies on this ambiguity, but in other respects it is clear. He proposes that, based on the opponent's own line of reasoning, one is lead to the conclusion that selflessness is a substance. This is, however, unacceptable, because selflessness is permanent whereas a substance is necessarily impermanent.

163. *Pramāṇavārttika* 1.45, 96b1.

164. Tib. *thogs bcas kyi gzugs*. "Forms with physical resistance" are coarser material substances that impede movement in other like things and can themselves also be impeded. These are contrasted with material substances that are not gross material and do not impede movement, which are known as "forms without physical resistance" (*thogs med kyi gzugs*). The main discussion about the distinction between these two kinds of forms occurs in the Abhidharma literature.

165. Khedrup Jé, like other Geluk authors, regards the Vijñaptika system as equivalent to Cittamātra. As already stated, both the realist view of the Sautrāntika and the idealist perspective of the Cittamātra are represented in *Commentary on Pramāṇa*. For the Sautrāntika, blue causes the perception of blue, in the sense of there being a real external object preceding the perception; according to the realist, the two must be sequential, and hence there is a time-lapse between the blue *out there* and the one experienced. For the Cittamātra, blue and its perception are simultaneous.

166. Here Khedrup Jé introduces the term *subject-aspect*. This relates to a distinction described in note 121—that between self-cognition and other-cognition. The subject-aspect is associated with the self-cognition, whereas the object-aspect is associated with the other-cognition. These designations distinguish the two cognitions on the basis of whether they are primarily directed inward at the subject, the perception of blue, or directed outward at the object blue.

167. Khedrup Jé returns to the identification of the object-aspect and subject-aspect repeatedly throughout the text. The issues behind this are discussed in note 342.

168. *Pramāṇavārttika* 1.43, 96a7.

169. *Pramāṇavārttika* 1.45, 96b1.

170. Tib. *grub bde dbyer med kyi rdzas gcig.*

171. *Pramāṇavārttika* 1.58, 97a1.

172. Dharmakīrti, (*Pramāṇavārttikavṛtti*), Toh 4216 Tengyur, tshad ma, *ce*, 275b5.

173. The reasoning here is that the *śabdārtha* of pot—that is, the thing indicated by the term "pot" —is counted as a conceptual construct, as remarked earlier. As such, it cannot directly appear to the sense consciousness of an ordinary being.

174. The term *asaṃkhyeya* (Tib. *grangs med*) literally suggests a period that is incalculable, but it actually refers to a specific number, which according to some accounts is 10^{140}.
175. Three conditions are necessary to produce a sense perception such as a visual consciousness. These are the observed [object] condition (*dmigs rkyen*), the governing condition (*bdag rkyen*), and the immediately preceding condition (*de ma thag rkyen*). As suggested here, the first is the object of such a visual consciousness. The three are discussed at length below.
176. Maitreya, *Ornament of Realizations* (*Abhisamayālaṃkāra*), 4.60, Toh 3786 Tengyur, shes phyin, *ka*, 9a4.
177. Tib. *rnam pa gtad pa.*
178. Tib. *skye mched*, Skt. *āyatana.*
179. Khedrup Jé's exact criticism is not immediately apparent. But he probably means that although the opponent denies that continua constitute substances, external objects could not appear to the sense consciousnesses of myopic beings unless they were continua.
180. Tib. *rang 'dra'i rnam pa*. The language used here relies on the realists' notion that there is an object *out there*. This reaches the consciousness through an aspect that is supposed to resemble the object—that is, through some "representation" of the object. A consciousness's ability to take on the aspect of the thing that is presented to it is what allows it to cognize that thing.
181. *Pramāṇavārttika* 3.321, 130b6.
182. Sound is often regarded as being different from the other four objects of the sense consciousnesses, in that the only sound that an entity such as a pot can be said to have is the one it elicits when struck by another physical entity.
183. Tib. *rigs 'dra'i rgyun.*
184. Tib. *gzugs kyi chung ngu'i mthar thug pa.*
185. Khedrup Jé addresses the opponent's apparent denial that continua can form distinct or separate substances. He briefly shifts the focus from continua formed by moments of time to continua formed by physical particles. He points out that if two sets of indivisible particles do not share the same location, it does not mean that they cannot form distinct substances.
186. Tib. *'dres pa.*
187. Cows are stock examples used in discussions about universals and particulars in Pramāṇa literature.
188. Universal itself is generally characterized, but something can *be* a universal—it may instantiate a universal—without being generally characterized. The Geluk rule of thumb on the matter is as follows. If all or some of the particulars of a universal are generally characterized, then the universal too is generally characterized. Universal itself is a universal, since it has various particulars. Some of its particulars—such as permanent and existent—are generally characterized. So universal too is generally characterized. Some of universal's other particulars—such as pot and actual thing—are universals, but since all their particulars are specifically characterized, they too are specifically characterized. In Geluk thinking, the suggestion that any kind of pot—whether it is asserted to be a universal or a particular—would be incapable of performing the function of a pot is deemed not to hold water.
189. *Pramāṇavārttika* 1.78, 97b5.

190. This is one of the clearest statements on how Khedrup Jé—and by extension, other members of the Geluk tradition—explain the role of *śabdārtha*. The *śabdārtha* is a purely conceptual object, which is to say that it is *necessarily* a construct. This is a feature that distinguishes it from a universal. But in spite of this artificial nature, the *śabdārtha* of *x* is the mentally constructed basis we refer to when determining that this or that thing is an *x*. In that sense, it is what the name for *x* "means." And it is also what allows us to gather various things and say that because they have the required attribute(s), they all belong to the same group.
191. As we see here, in Geluk thinking, the "universal" (Skt. *sāmānya*, Tib. *spyi*) is anything but an abstract notion. As already mentioned, the Geluk view can be described as a form of moderate realism. It does not deny the existence of universals, as is the case with "nominalism," but equally, in line with general Buddhist philosophical thinking, it resolutely rejects the extreme realism of Indian non-Buddhist schools such as the Nyāya and Vaiśeṣika, which proposes that certain universals must be eternal. Geluk thinking also contrasts with the stance of Sakya scholars, which is more antirealist. For Sakya scholars, only particulars or individuations can be specifically characterized. Universals are necessarily generally characterized and thus constructed by thought. Here, Khedrup Jé clearly articulates his moderate realist position. He says that the universal is to be understood as the commonality that certain things have: their homogeneity. Specifically characterized things are entirely independent of the mind. Their homogeneity exists in the properties inhering within them rather than being imposed upon them by thought. Therefore, as far as specifically characterized phenomena are concerned, universals do not belong to the realm of conceptuality. Instead, they are to be found among impermanent, functioning particulars and individuations.
192. *Pramāṇavārttika* 1.172, 101a4.
193. *Pramāṇavārttika* 2.14, 108a3.
194. The source of this is unclear.
195. *Pramāṇavārttika* 3.1, 118b3.
196. *Pramāṇavārttika* 3.3, 118b4.
197. Tib. *gtso bo* or, sometimes, *spyi gtso bo*.
198. *Pramāṇavārttika* 1.167, 101a2.
199. *Pramāṇavārttika* 1.152, 100b1.
200. *Pramāṇavārttika* 1.166, 101a1.
201. Tib. *snang ba*.
202. Tib. *btags pa*.
203. Two things appear to the conceptual consciousness that judges golden pot to be a pot. One is the golden pot itself, and the other is the *śabdārtha* of pot. But only the latter overtly appears and is the held object of that conceptual consciousness. At this point in the text, Khedrup Jé clearly distinguishes between these two, describing the former as an "appearance" and the latter as a "construct." But the conceptual consciousness itself does not distinguish between these two, and both of them appear to it to be a pot. Hence, in what follows, when Khedrup Jé uses phrases such as "that which appears to be pot" or "that which presents itself to conceptual cognition as if it is a pot," he is taking into account *both* things that appear to be pot.
204. Tib. *zhen pa*.
205. Tib. *gzugs brnyan*.

206. Here "objectified" (*dngos po ba*) means something that actually exists within the object, whereas "nonobjectified" refers to something that is superimposed on the object.
207. *Pramāṇavārttika* 1.72, 97b2.
208. *Pramāṇavārttika* 1.46, 96b2.
209. *Pramāṇavārttika* 4.230, 148b2.
210. *Pramāṇavārttika* 2.6, 107b6.
211. *Pramāṇavārttika* 4.222, 148a5.
212. What Khedrup Jé intends by "it is a false cognition with respect to that" is not entirely clear, since neither he nor the opponent regard the valid inferential cognition that sound is impermanent as a false one. The *śabdārtha* of sound being impermanent is the cognition's held object, not the one it comprehends. So one plausible meaning is that *if* that inferential cognition held the *śabdārtha* to be impermanent, it *would be* a false cognition.
213. *Pramāṇavārttika* 1.46, 96b2. Again, the complete line reads, "If inferential cognition also apprehended an actual thing, then when it ascertained one [of that thing's] features, it would have to apprehend every one of them."
214. *Pramāṇavārttika* 4.230, 148b2.
215. *Pramāṇavārttika* 1.85–86, 98a1.
216. *Pramāṇavārttika* 1.86, 98a2.
217. *Pramāṇavārttika* 1.70–71, 97b1.
218. *Pramāṇavārttika* 1.70, 97a7.
219. *Pramāṇavārttika* 1.131–32, 99b4.
220. Tib. *brda'i yul.*
221. *Pramāṇavārttika* 1.92, 98a5.
222. The process of naming with which the Pramāṇa literature concerns itself most is not that of the origins of words—when and by whom the object *x* was christened with the name *y*—but that in which an individual comes to learn that the name *y* is the correct one assigned to the object *x*. This is conceived of as a two-stage process: the initial point when the label or designation is applied (*brda' dus*), such as when someone first introduces the individual to the designation's usage, and then the point where the individual, having made the link between the designation and the object (and thereby the extent and range of the designation's usage), is able to primarily rely on that designation as the *signifier* of the object (*tha snyad dus*).
223. *Pramāṇavārttika* 1.138, 99b7.
224. Tib. *brda' sbyor ba'i yul.*
225. Tib. *brda' sbyar ba'i gzhi.*
226. Khedrup Jé counters the idea that the process of understanding what a cow is—i.e., being able to recognize the animal and apply its name correctly—is purely internal and simply involves the formation and manipulation of conceptual and linguistic elements, by saying that it must instead be rooted in experience, with a real cow as its basis. Despite asserting that the basis must be a sentient and specifically characterized cow, he is equally keen to counter any suggestion that the process could be an affirmative one. The understanding is gained when the individual in question has been able to use the real creature to isolate those features that define a cow and sees them as extendable to other like creatures. It is only the individual's ability to block out "non-cow"—i.e., what does not belong among those characteristics—that makes such an isolation achievable.

227. *Pramāṇavārttika* 1.92, 98a5.
228. In this section, Khedrup Jé refers to different varieties of *conceptual isolation* (Tib. *ldog pa*). The common thread is that they all involve some form of abstraction. The term, which literally means "reversed," is a reference to the process through which an object is engaged by thought according to the *apoha* theory—that one conceives of cow, for example, through eliminating non-cow. In Tibetan scholasticism, these conceptual isolations were developed into analytical tools. The reference to "isolation" in the names of some varieties, such as the "isolated type-identity" (*ldog pa rigs*), seems mainly intended as a reminder that the thing in question (i.e., a "type") is a phenomenon constructed by thought rather than one with an independent existence. But other varieties of conceptual isolation are intended to bring analytical preciseness by separating elements that might otherwise be conflated. The three most prominent conceptual isolations have some parallels with the definition–illustration–definiendum scheme. They are (1) the *isolate of encapsulation* (*don ldog*), (2) the *isolate of instantiation* (*gzhi ldog*), and (3) the *individual isolate* (*rang ldog*). As the names of the first two suggest, they respectively refer *only* to things that are *x* and the features that encapsulate what it is to be *x*. The individual isolate has a number of functions but is generally regarded as the most important of the three, and when "conceptual isolation" (*ldog pa*) appears alone, it should usually be understood to denote this individual isolate. The individual isolate highlights thought's ability to select and focus on just a single thing. Thus the individual isolate of *x* refers to *nothing* but *x*. In referring to *x* alone, it excludes not only such things as *x*'s name, but even the various instantiations of *x*, *x*'s defining features, and so forth. Khedrup Jé refers to all three isolations in this text, but their technical names are not always included in the translation. To indicate more clearly what the isolate refers to in each case, I have translated, for example, "encapsulates what it means to be *x*," rather than "encapsulation isolate for *x*." At this point in the text, Khedrup Jé distinguishes between the individual isolate and the instantiation isolate. He thereby separates identities such as *subject* from the things that instantiate those identities, such as a pot.
229. *Pramāṇavārttika* 1.40, 96a5.
230. In Tibetan, these three are *rigs 'dra ba dang mi 'dra ba*, *rigs mthun pa dang mi mthun pa*, and *rigs gcig dang mi gcig pa*.
231. Tib. *nyer len*, Skt. *upādāna*. In other contexts—such as when rebirth is described as a process that involves the individual *taking on* a new set of aggregates—the same term can be translated as "appropriating."
232. Khedrup Jé explains that there are two different ways of looking at type. As the example of the barley seeds illustrates, the first is an explanation based on origins. He also says that with respect to types, there is no real distinction between "likeness," "sameness," and "similarity"—they are different ways of describing correspondence. Despite this, here and elsewhere in the text he shows a preference for using the designation "similar substantial type" (*rdzas rigs mthun pa*) when referring to the type based on origins
233. Śākyabuddhi, *Direct Commentary on the Pramāṇavārttika* (*Pramāṇavārttikaṭīkā*), chap. 2, Toh 4220 Tengyur, tshad ma, *nye*, 125a7.
234. Śākyabuddhi, *Direct Commentary on the Pramāṇavārttika* (*Pramāṇavārttikaṭīkā*),

chap. 2, Toh 4220 Tengyur, tshad ma, *nye*, 125b6. The wording in the Dergé edition differs very slightly.

235. *Pramāṇavārttika* 3.184, 125b2.
236. Tib. *ldog pa rigs mthun pa.*
237. The Tibetan name (*shing sha pa*) is sometimes identified as the *Aquilaria agallocha* tree, the source of agarwood (Tib. *a ka ru* or *a ga ru*). But its use here is derived from the Pramāṇa literature, where it appears to denote *śiṃśapā*, the Indian rosewood tree (*Dalbergia sissoo*).
238. *Pramāṇavārttika* 1.162, 100b6.
239. Tib. *mngon par brjod pa'i bag chags.*
240. The phrase contains an internal self-reference, since what is translated here as "glory" (*dpal*) is a syllable of the author's name Palsang.
241. *Pramāṇavārttika* 1.68–69, 97a7.
242. Work on the first Tibetan translation of the *Pramāṇavārttika* began during the "earlier diffusion," but it is uncertain whether it was ever completed. The colophon of the current version of Dharmakīrti's work in the Dergé and other Tengyur editions tells us about the subsequent history. The treatise was translated by Ma Lotsāwa (Gewai Lodrö, 1044–89/90) and Subhūtiśrīśānti (d.u.). The colophon says that following this there was another translation by Loden Sangpo—an alias of Ngok Lotsāwa Loden Sherab—undertaken with the Kashmiri scholar Bhavyarāja. It seems likely that this translation was a revised version of the initial one. Finally, the colophon suggests there was a major revision of the translation by Sakya Paṇḍita in conjunction with Śākyaśrībhadra; later tradition came to regard this one as definitive. However, as discussed by Eli Franco in "The Tibetan Translations of the Pramāṇavārttika," the translations of three direct commentaries on the *Pramāṇavārttika* by Devendrabuddhi, Prajñākaragupta, and Ravigupta have alternative versions of many lines of the original embedded within them, which were translated independently. By Khedrup Jé's time, scholars almost always cited the words from the Sakya Paṇḍita version. But the alternative translation of the line provided here continued to attract attention for the useful extra dimension it provided and crops up occasionally in discussions about the etymology of the Sanskrit terms for the two truths in Tibetan commentarial writings on both Pramāṇa and Madhyamaka. This version of the line appears in Dharmakīrti's *Commentary on Pramāṇa Autocommentary* (Toh 4216 Tengyur, tshad ma, *ce*, 282b6), which was apparently translated by Ma Lotsāwa and Subhūtiśrīśānti and hence also undoubtedly featured in their version of the *Commentary on Pramāṇa* itself.
243. The Sanskrit term under discussion here, which translates as "conventional" in "conventional truth," is *saṃvṛti*. Khedrup Jé explains Dharmakīrti's description of this term's derivation. The later Tibetan translation of the passage uses the term *sgrib byed*, suggesting that the notion *saṃvṛti* is based on is concealment or obscuration. But Khedrup Jé points out that the earlier translators chose instead *kun rdzob*. This has a more disruptive connotation, suggesting that *saṃvṛti* is based on the idea of misleading or deceiving.
244. *Pramāṇavārttika* 3.3, 118b4.
245. *Pramāṇavārttika* 3.1, 118b3.
246. *Pramāṇavārttika* 3.3, 118b4. The full stanza runs:

    Whatever is capable of performing a function ultimately:

that here is what ultimately exists.
The other [kind of object] is conventionally existent.
These two are called the specifically and the generally characterized.

247. Tib. *don dam cha med.*
248. Tib. *yang dag kun rdzob.*
249. Vasubandhu, *Abhidharmakośa*, 6.4, Toh 4089 Tengyur, mngon pa, *ku*, 18b6.
250. In line with the notion of "isolates," these "conceptually isolable portions" (*ldog pa'i cha shas*) can be the real features or attributes of some specifically characterized substratum or basis, such as the various qualities of a pot, including its impermanence. In reality, as reflected in the way that they are perceived, these qualities do not exist separately from that basis but inhere within it. Nevertheless, on the conceptual and linguistic levels, we are able to distinguish or isolate these qualities from the basis to which they belong.
251. Khedrup Jé argues that from the perspective of the number of conceptually isolable portions that can be attributed to them, there is no fundamental difference between permanent phenomena and indivisible physical particles. There may seem to be an almost infinite number of things that can be negated about each. For instance, a permanent phenomenon is not a physical particle, a pot, a pillar, etc., just as an indivisible physical particle is not permanent, a pot, a pillar, etc. But in line with the thinking of the *apoha* theory, for each of these negations, the reverse must be correct of the thing in question. Hence, permanent phenomenon is the reverse of non-physical particle, etc., and physical particle is the reverse of impermanent, etc.
252. Tib. *kha dog gi rdzas.*
253. Vasubandhu, *Abhidharmakośa*, 4.3, Toh 4089 Tengyur, mngon pa, *ku*, 11a1.
254. *Pramāṇavārttika* 2.11, 108a1.
255. In the Geluk system, Asaṅga and Vasubandhu are seen as belonging to a different branch of the Cittamātra school from that of Dignāga and Dharmakīrti.
256. Tib. *kun tu tha snyed pa'i tshad ma.*
257. Tib. *log pa'i kun rdzob.*
258. The "object" and "actor" (referred to here as *bya byed*) represents another of the tradition's major binaries. The "object" here should be understood to denote that toward which an action is directed, and the "actor" the one which acts upon that object. This distinction forms the basis of an analysis of actions, predominantly those indicated by transitive verbs. This model of analysis comes under greater scrutiny in the third text of this volume.
259. Tib. *rnam par bcad tsam.*
260. In the Cittamātra system as famously represented in the works of Vasubandhu and Asaṅga, within the theory of the three natures, understanding the ultimate involves realizing that the sense of separation between subject and object—in which physical objects appear to exist as external substantial realities—is illusory. The absence of this distinction is the *perfect, immutable nature* (Skt. *pariniṣpann-asvabhāva*, Tib. *'gyur med yongs grub*).
261. The opponent here proposes that only the indivisible particles and temporal portions of a pot are realities, whereas the pot itself is a construct. These indivisible constituents are for him "true things" (*bden dngos*). Here Khedrup Jé targets the relationship that these "true things," as particulars, have to their universal. Explain-

ing this relationship is seen as problematic for those who, like this opponent, assert that the universal is a pure abstraction and thus an entirely different order of thing to its "true" particulars. In the earlier discussion on universals and particulars, in which the purely abstracted thing featured, Khedrup Jé indicated that he has in mind a group of scholars rather than a single individual. The present opponent seems willing to concede that the purely abstracted thing is subject to disintegration, but like the earlier opponents, he still views it as a universal and as such, something fundamentally different from its particulars.

262. Khedrup Jé directs his criticism against the idea that the "indivisibles" or "true things" form a separate class among impermanent objects. According to him, the opponent holds that these indivisibles are the constituents of reality, and that in this role, they maintain their state in a way that coarser entities are not able to do. But for Khedrup Jé, this implies that they have always existed and are therefore permanent. Finally, he says, the opponent's position means that he has no way to respond to another proposition. The proposition put forward by this hypothetical third party is open to interpretation. But Khedrup Jé uses it to play with the "produced but not ceased" definition of the opponent, pointing to the fact that while the negation of a nonthing may be possible, the ceasing of a nonthing (i.e., something that has never existed) is not. But this final line also seems to allude to what immediately follows in the text, where reference is made to the Madhyamaka negation of production.
263. According to Abhidharma philosophy, gender distinctions are based on distinct essences or powers. Just as the respective sense powers determine whether the consciousness derived from it is visual, auditory, etc., these essences determine an individual's gender.
264. This refers back to the section "Countering the position that the likes of actual thing do not constitute substances," where an opponent proposed that for those in the realist schools to maintain that blue is a coarse entity and something that overtly appears to the visual perception while denying that a "whole" in possession of different parts can overtly appear to an unmistaken awareness should be regarded as a contradiction in their system.
265. It is clear from other sources that the opponent Khedrup Jé refers to here is Bodong Choklé Namgyal.
266. In more technical language, one must distinguish between "individual isolate" (*rang ldog*) and "isolated instantiation" (*gzhi ldog*).
267. The original Sanskrit term for "whole" here is *anavayin*. It specifically denotes the concept of a whole according to the Vaiśeṣika and Nyāya systems. Tibetans translated this in a very transparent fashion as *yan lag can*, which can literally be rendered "[that which] has parts."
268. Tib. *shar cha* and *nub cha*.
269. As mentioned elsewhere in the text, the Sautrāntika holds that a material object such as a building is made up of particles that each have imprinted directions (east, west, etc.). But these are not to be confused with directions relating to these objects' position in space. Even though an indivisible particle itself lacks these directional, component parts on the subtler material level, it is still situated in space and surrounded by other such particles with directions relative to it.
270. Tib. *sna tshogs gnyis med*.

271. Tib. *sgo nga phyed tshal ba.*
272. Tib. *rnam shes grangs mnyam pa.*
273. Tib. *rnam bden pa* and *rnam brdzun pa.*
274. Tib. *rnam brdzun dri med pa* and *dri bcas.*
275. Prajñākaragupta composed the *Ornament Commentary to Pramāṇavārttika* (*Pramāṇavārttikālaṃkāra*). But as was the custom among Tibetan scholars of the time, Khedrup Jé refers to Prajñākaragupta not by his name but as the "author of the *Ornament.*"
276. *Pramāṇavārttika* 3.214–16, 126b4.
277. Tib. *gnyis chos.*
278. Tib. *btags yod.*
279. Maitreya, *Abhisamayālaṃkāra*, 8.16, Toh 3786 Tengyur, shes phyin, *ka*, 12a3.
280. This fourfold division is generally thought to have its origin in the Sangphu tradition. The Tibetan for these four terms are *snang yul, gzung yul, zhen yul,* and *'jug yul.*
281. The opponent wishes to avoid any suggestion that a conceptual cognition engages its object in a manner similar to perception—that is, through an actual thing, such as a material object, presenting itself to the cognition. But Khedrup Jé attacks his assertion that the conceptual cognition can have an overt object that is not an appearing object. The terms for "actual thing" and "overt object" employ the same syllable (*dngos*) in Tibetan, a fact that Khedrup Jé exploits in his argument.
282. *Pramāṇaviniścaya* chap. 3, 208b6. The word for "object" (*yul*) does not appear in the Dergé version.
283. "Adversary" and "friend" here assumes people who respectively are negatively and positively disposed to the individual in question.
284. *Pramāṇavārttika* 1.152, 100b1.
285. *Pramāṇaviniścaya* chap. 2, 168a6. The Dergé version differs very slightly.
286. Here, and more widely in the Tibetan Pramāṇa tradition, there is much discussion about the exact function of the "ascertaining awareness" (Tib. *nges shes*, Skt. *Niścayajñāna*).
287. Dharmakīrti, *Commentary on Pramāṇa Autocommentary* (*Pramāṇavārttikavṛtti*), Toh 4216 Tengyur, tshad ma, *ce*, 278a6.
288. The opponent proposes that the only object a conceptual cognition has is a conceptual object. For him, something cannot be the object of such a cognition unless that cognition *conceives* of it. He also tries to exclude the cognition itself from the equation, since he wants to avoid any suggestion that what such a cognition conceives of is itself rather than its actual object, such as a pot. Khedrup Jé responds that a conceptual cognition is not limited to its conceptual object. It also has an appearing object, but this is not something of which it conceives.
289. Tib. *zhen pa'i brjod bya.*
290. *Pramāṇavārttika* 3.224, 127a2.
291. Devendrabuddhi. *Commentary on the Difficult Points of the Pramāṇavārttika* (*Pramāṇavārttikapañjikā*), chap. 2, Toh 4217, tshad ma *che* 197a6.
292. The Tibetan term *skra shad 'dzags snang*—which literally means (that in which) "strands of hair appear to descend" (before the eyes)—almost certainly refers to the condition of *myodesopsia*. Tibetan scholastic authors regularly rely on it either as an example of a false visual consciousness or as an analogy for ignorance.

293. The "entity held" (Tib. *gzung don*) sounds similar to the "held object" (*gzung yul*) but carries a stronger sense of a thing that exists in a domain separate from the subject and could occasion a perception.
294. *Pramāṇavārttika* 3.9, 118b7.
295. *Pramāṇavārttika* 3.406, 134a2.
296. *Pramāṇavārttika* 3.66, 121a2.
297. The division between awareness that is valid and awareness that is not valid gives rise to a sevenfold categorization, which has its origins in Sangphu scholarship. This divides awareness into (1) perception, (2) inferential cognition, (3) subsequent cognition, (4) correct assumption, (5) [awareness to which something] appears but is not ascertained, (6) doubt, and (7) false cognition. This categorization has been standard in the Geluk tradition for centuries and forms the core of the basic study materials called *blo rig*, "Awareness and Cognition" (or, in some versions, *blo rigs*, "Types of Awareness"). The sevenfold categorization presents types of awareness on a descending scale of cognition, beginning with perception, the clearest form, which represents the ideal for realization, down to false cognition, which is furthest away from that goal. Khedrup Jé makes no direct reference to the sevenfold categorization in this work, although he covers most of its territory. This lack of reference is not an unconscious omission. Khedrup Jé is signaling his effective rejection of the sevenfold categorization associated with Sangphu. In this regard he is in line with Sakya Paṇḍita's tradition as represented in the *Treasure of Pramāṇa Reasoning* and its autocommentary. These works challenge previous understandings of categories 3 to 5 within the sevenfold division. Hence Khedrup Jé makes no reference to correct assumption (*yid dpyod*). There is more on this below (note 307). He also calls into question [awareness to which something] appears but is not ascertained and disagrees with earlier understandings of subsequent cognition. In all three respects he differs from mainstream Geluk scholarship.
298. Here we return to the debate on how the term *śabdārtha* is to be understood.
299. Tib. *'dre rung ba*. The earlier section on specifically and generally characterized phenomena described how thought can be said to "merge" things. There, merging related to thought's capacity for abstraction—how its ability to focus on certain common features, while disregarding specifics of space, time, etc., allows it to group things together into types or kinds. The current section of the text turns to another facet of thought's capacity for merging: the way it melds a thing and its name. Generally, thought does not overtly *mistake* the name for the thing to which it is attached, but it allows for the two to become sufficiently merged on a mental level so that words can stand for or signify those things. Here, the reference to "mergeability" is important. It does not suggest that individuals go around thinking, "These two can be merged," but instead it means that we have a linguistic propensity, such that even prior to the acquisition of language, thought predisposes us to start melding words and objects.
300. Tib. *sgra spyi*. For Khedrup Jé and other Geluk thinkers, the sound universal is akin to a sound image.
301. These scholars wanted to make the point that for those who have acquired language, names and things already appear to be merged, and so it makes no sense to describe them as seeming to have the *potential* for merging. But Khedrup Jé argues that to accept that this feature of mergeability does not encompass—and

is therefore not applicable to—individuals with language is to negate it for them. Hence, for such individuals, names and things must seem to *lack* any potential for merging.

302. *Pramāṇavārttika* 3.287, 129b1.
303. *Pramāṇavārttika* 3.287, 129b1.
304. *Pramāṇavārttika* 1.206, 102b1.
305. *Pramāṇaviniścaya*, chap. 1, 154b1.
306. The distinction is based on two scenarios. The first envisions an individual who, at some earlier point in time, was introduced to a name or label such as "cow" but either did not encounter an actual cow at that time or did not yet understand that the label could be applied through extension to particulars other than the one immediately present. The situation referred to in the first definition therefore refers to a later time, when the individual makes the link between the label and the object, grasping how the two fit together and thereby conjoins the stage of "labeling" (i.e., introduction) with that of "usage" (i.e., correct application). In the scenario for the second variety of conceptual cognition, there is no predetermined name or label, although the individual is obviously someone who can clearly identify a stick (or staff) and a person. Upon encountering some other person, the individual also observes that he is carrying a stick. This is foremost in his mind for some reason, and he conjoins the two, leading him to a conceptual or verbal characterization such as "the person with the stick" or the "stick-possessing person." These two forms of conceptual cognition might appear to work in different domains—with the first primarily concerned with the linguistic dimension and correct classification, and the second based on observation and creative description. However, Khedrup Jé says that both aspects of thought are at play in certain cases, such as the inferential realization that sound is impermanent. That is to say, just as the realization cannot simply be a process of labeling, it also cannot merely be an experience outside the realm of words and categorization.
307. As mentioned above (note 297), Khedrup Jé finds no place for "correct assumption." Other Geluk scholars regard this as an important bridge between those types of awareness that can realize their object (the first three within the sevenfold division) and those that cannot (the last three in that division). This is because correct assumption is usually explained as a cognition that is correct but has not yet realized its object, in which sense it represents knowledge that is not entirely stable. So it usually has a central place in descriptions of how to progress toward realization of an object, being regarded as the step before inference. Gendun Drup, for instance, defines it "an awareness that, without depending on a correct reason, apprehends a hidden object that [the individual] has not previously realized." See *Ornament of Reasoning*, 379. Interestingly, the example that Khedrup Jé refers to here in relation to doubt—the thought that there must be water in the well—is the same one that Gendun Drup uses for a correct assumption. However, in this case, Khedrup Jé is not countering Gendun Drup, since Gendun Drup's work was composed later.
308. Tib. *dmigs rnam mi 'dzin.*
309. Khedrup Jé questions whether the expression "latent doubt" (*bag la nyal gyi the tshom*) has any place in the textual tradition, although he admits that the similar "latency for doubt" (*the tshom gyi bag la nyal*) has currency. But the more

important point he makes here is that in neither case could the things that these expressions describe count as doubt. Doubt is necessarily a manifest form of awareness, not something existing as a latency.

310. The view of subsequent cognition that Khedrup Jé sets out in this section differs considerably from the Geluk mainstream, which holds that such cognition can be either perception or inference.
311. *Pramāṇavārttika* 2.3, 107b4.
312. Sakya Paṇḍita, *Treasure of Pramāṇa Reasoning* 2.12, 4b1.
313. This definition also differs significantly from that given by other Geluk scholars. This is closely linked with Khedrup Jé's understanding of valid cognition, detailed below.
314. The scholar has not stipulated that the consciousness in question must be an other-cognition. Thus a self-cognition of the sense consciousness, which is necessarily concomitant with it, would fulfill the definition and count as a nonconceptual false consciousness.
315. *Pramāṇavārttika* 2.1, 107b3.
316. *Pramāṇavārttika* 2.5, 107b5.
317. In the original Sanskrit of the second line, Dharmakīrti uses a syllable (*vā*) that is often translated as "or." However, the same syllable can denote "also." The Tibetan translation of the syllable (*kyang*) and the majority of Tibetan interpretations of the line clearly lean toward the "also" reading.
318. *Commentary on the Difficult Points in the Pramāṇavārttika* (*Pramāṇavārttikapañjikā*), chap. 2, Toh 4217 Tengyur, tshad ma, *che*, 5b5.
319. *Direct Commentary on the Pramāṇavārttika* (*Pramāṇavārttikaṭīkā*), chap. 2, Toh 4220 Tengyur, tshad ma, *nye*, 79a6.
320. This is the definition of valid cognition that has proved the most popular among Geluk scholars. Historically, it has been the most widely accepted version of the definition in Tibetan scholasticism. But Khedrup Jé defines valid cognition in another way, as we see later in the text. Hence this is one of those points on which his view differs from that of the Geluk mainstream.
321. Sakya Paṇḍita, *Treasure of Pramāṇa Reasoning*, 8.34, 15a3.
322. This may be a reference to Yaktön Sangyé Pal, *Commentary to the Treasure of Pramāṇa Reasoning*, chap. 8, 89b3.
323. Here again, we encounter the "individual isolate" (*rang ldog*), which this time is distinguished from the "isolated encapsulation" (*don ldog*). The latter is similar, though not exactly equivalent, to the definition of a thing, whereas the former is basically used here as an alternative way of referring to the definiendum. The point Khedrup Jé makes is that there are two circumstances in which it might be permissible to have two different passages defining valid cognition. The first would be when at least one of the passages has a specific purpose, such as addressing a certain misconception, and in such cases, the passages might not be expressed in the same way, since their aims may differ. The second circumstance would be when either of the two passages is only providing *part* of the definition, such as when the author wants to devote separate passages to individual features, since a single definition may encompass a number of features. But Khedrup Jé rejects that either of these two circumstances could apply in the present situation. He evokes the *isolated encapsulation*, something which must capture the *whole* of the thing being defined

rather than a partial definition. He says that this was Sakya Paṇḍita's argument. If the two definitions involved were both comprehensive and completely different from each other, they would require two distinct definienda.

324. *Pramāṇavārttikālaṃkāra*, Toh 4221 Tengyur, tshad ma.

325. The tradition of offering a short synopsis of the different positions on the definition of valid cognition among Dharmakīrti's Indian commentators goes back some way in the Tibetan tradition of scholasticism. Chapa Chökyi Sengé includes such a section, which later scholars clearly referenced. See *Banisher of Ignorance [Relating to] Pramāṇa*, 32a4. According to his explanation, of the two features of "nondeceptiveness" and "illumination" that Dharmakīrti set out, the author of the *Ornament* held that the combination of the two was the definition, Devendrabuddhi said that either would suffice, Dharmottara said that the former alone was the definition, and the great brahmin identified something akin to the latter ("realization of the object") as the definition. Chapa Chökyi Sengé then goes on to elaborate on the position of the author of the *Ornament* (Prajñākaragupta) at some length.

326. Here, "accurately discern" (*yongs su bcad pa*) and the related term "discern" (*yongs gcod*) both generally cover the same territory as realizing or establishing something by valid cognition. But most frequently in Geluk writings and in Tibetan scholasticism more widely they connotate an *affirmative* cognition (i.e., one that realizes a thing in an affirmative manner). This connotation becomes obvious when the second term is used in conjunction with its partner, "exclusion" (*rnam bcad*), which refers to the realization of a thing by means of an overt negation. The affirming-excluding combination features most prominently in discussions on preclusion. However, Khedrup Jé's understanding of what it means to "discern" a thing differs from that of others in the tradition. As we see in the way that he defines valid cognition (p. 205), he believes that *every* such cognition, whether affirmative or negative, accurately discerns an object. Thus it appears that discerning and realizing are essentially the same for him.

327. *Pramāṇaviniścayaṭīkā* chap. 1, 9a4.

328. *Pramāṇaviniścayaṭīkā* chap. 1, 9b1.

329. The wording differs in Chapa Chökyi Sengé's definition of valid cognition, but the description is close enough for us to suspect that he may have been targeted here, although perhaps indirectly. See Chapa, *Banisher of Ignorance*, 33a and 33b.

330. *Pramāṇavārttika* 2.1, 107b3.

331. *Pramāṇavārttika* 2.5, 107b5.

332. As stated in note 317, the syllable in the second line can be translated as "also" or as "or." This opponent seems to be closer to the second reading and arrives at "neither" through a negation of "or/either."

333. Tib. *sgra byung gi shes pa*.

334. *Pramāṇavārttika* 2.3, 107b4.

335. *Pramāṇavārttika* 2.1, 107b3.

336. *Pramāṇavārttika* 2.1, 107b3.

337. *Pramāṇavārttika* 2.1, 107b3.

338. *Pramāṇavārttika* 2.5, 107b5.

339. *Pramāṇavārttika* 2.1, 107b3.

340. This is Khedrup Jé's abbreviated version of the longer formula provided by the unnamed scholar.

341. As discussed elsewhere, every correct proof has a thesis, which the proof is intended to establish. Equally, every proof has a negandum, which can generally be understood as the opposite of that thesis. For instance, through establishing that sound is impermanent—that is, impermanence is a quality of sound—one negates that sound is permanent—that is, permanence is a quality of sound. Here, the proof is "permanent [A] is devoid of production [B], because it is devoid of functional activity [C]." But in trying to find a place for the specifically characterized in the process, the opponent says that what the inferential cognition arising from this proof realizes is "specifically characterized product, which is the reverse of something permanent." According to Khedrup Jé, this results in the nonsensical situation in which what one wants to establish about the subject (i.e., permanent) is something negative and generally characterized (i.e., that it is devoid of production), one is instead establishing something affirmative and specifically characterized—namely, a "specifically characterized product, which is the reverse of something permanent."

342. Khedrup Jé's returns to this point about the correct identification of the object-aspect often and with great insistence. Two essential pieces of background information will help the reader understand why he finds this necessary. These relate to (1) Geluk scholarship's rejection of the standard idea of representationalism in perception and (2) the need to account for the role of the aspect in perception in the wake of that rejection. The distinction between the object-aspect and the subject-aspect can be traced to Indian Pramāṇa writings, but the identity of the object-aspect was a particular issue in Tibetan scholasticism, because of its key place in the model of perception. According to later scholars such as Shākya Chokden, Chapa Chökyi Sengé had left unanswered questions about the object-aspect. See *History of the Pramāṇa Tradition*, 20a. But there is more to Khedrup Jé's constant revisiting of the object-aspect than merely rectifying a lacuna. The fact that an object acts as a cause for perception means that it must precede it. But a perception must therefore cognize something that no longer exists. For Sakya writers, part of the solution to this problem lay in describing an episode of perception in terms of three separate elements: the object, the subject-aspect, and the object-aspect. For them, the subject-aspect was the cognition itself, the perception. The object-aspect was a representation of the object. This notion of the aspect as a representation or likeness of the object was introduced in note 111. It is generally described as a medium by means of which the object is conveyed to cognition. An advantage is that it could be explained to exist simultaneously with the subject, thereby overcoming the problem of the time lapse between object and subject. In this representational model of perception, the aspect is clearly not the object itself. Geluk writers approached perception from a more philosophically realist perspective. Accordingly, they reduced the elements involved in the episode to just two, the object and the perception. They still used the terms *subject-aspect* and *object-aspect*, but behind this was their insistence that the object-aspect is not a separate, third element. Khedrup Jé usually reduces this to an insistence on the "correct" identification of the object-aspect, but implicit in this is his assertion that object-aspect must be equated with one of the two remaining elements involved

in the episode of perception, given that a place for any third element is denied. In broader terms, he is rejecting one model of perception—what could be referred to as a standard model of "representationalism"—in favor of the more realistic one, advocated by himself, Gyaltsab Jé, and later generations of Geluk thinkers. Georges Dreyfus provides a very useful summary of the issues at stake in *Recognizing Reality*, 406–19. Given this divergence of opinion regarding models of perception, it is worth bearing in mind that terms such as *appearance* (*snang ba*) can have different meaning for various scholars. As mentioned earlier (note 116), Khedrup Jé starts to describe the aspect as something that "presents" or "arises." The term in question is not new, but he uses it in an unusual way, as part of his alternative way of explaining the role of the aspect in perception. Since he wishes to get away from the idea of the time-lapse between the object and subject, and also that the aspect can serve as the medium because it can "travel" from the earlier object to the subject, he explains the process of perception as one in which the aspect presents or arises *within*, rather than *to*, the subject. This is meant to indicate that the aspect's existence is simultaneous with that of the subject, not that of the object. Another area of debate that Geluk scholars' denial of a third element involved in perception—and their related identification of the object-aspect—touches upon is that of self-cognition. For these scholars, the subject-aspect and object-aspect are two parts of the same perceptual experience. The object-aspect is that portion of the perception cognizing the external object, whereas the subject-object is the self-cognition—that portion of the perception that is aware of its awareness of that object—and the two form a single substance. This identification of the two facets of the perception—one directed outward to the external object and the other facing inward, to that cognition—contrasts with that made by their Sakya counterparts, and it is one that Khedrup Jé restates several times. Another divide between Geluk and Sakya thinkers on the nature of self-cognition is also referenced here. In making the aforesaid distinction between the outward-facing and inward-facing portions of perception, there is also a rejection of the idea that every cognition is a self-cognition of its own nature. Again, this is a point that Khedrup Jé reiterates throughout the text.

343. *Pramāṇavārttika* 2.7, 107b6.

344. That is to say, the individual first realizes selflessness by means of inferential valid cognition, then gains familiarity with this selflessness on the path of preparation. This process leads to direct cognition or perception of selflessness on the path of seeing. If the stages did not proceed in this manner, Khedrup Jé argues, it would follow that those who reach the path of seeing and thereby achieve the state of an ārya still have not perceived selflessness, the agreed measure of attaining that state.

345. On this and other occasions in texts within this volume, Devadatta represents an everyman, not the miscreant cousin of the Buddha. The tradition of using the name in this fashion seems to have its origins in Sanskrit works on grammar.

346. As we see, Khedrup Jé rejects the idea that a valid cognition can only realize an object if it does so newly or freshly, and he does not include this feature in his definition below. In this respect, he differs from most other Geluk scholars. There is also a related difference in their understandings of subsequent cognition. For other Geluk scholars, only the initial instant of a cognition has sufficient freshness to qualify as valid, but since later portions of the same continuum of cognition

(i.e., the second moment onward) still realize their object, they must be classified as subsequent cognitions. Most of the discussion about them centers on their immediate relationship with valid cognition. For Khedrup Jé, valid cognition is not limited to that initial instant. So his explanation of subsequent cognition takes him elsewhere, as he identifies it with *recollection.*

347. Khedrup Jé has a separate section on mental perception below. What he suggests here is that if mental perception is extremely hidden, with the implication that it is simply too fleeting for the individual to notice its presence, then it would be incapable of performing the cognitive functions assigned to it.

348. The view that perception is capable of eliminating distortions, and that this is not just a function of conceptual ascertainment, is one that later scholars correctly associate with Chapa Chökyi Sengé. Here Khedrup Jé appears to reject this view, and thereby deny that the elimination of distortion(s) is a basic function of valid cognition. If this is indeed what he asserts, this would be another case of him differing from the Geluk mainstream.

349. *Pramāṇaviniścaya* chap. 1, 152b4.

350. *Pramāṇavārttika* 2.1, 107b3.

351. *Pramāṇavārttika* 2.3, 107b4.

352. *Pramāṇavārttika* 2.5, 107b5.

353. *Pramāṇavārttika* 3.53–54, 120b3.

354. *Pramāṇavārttika* 1.179, 101b1.

355. *Pramāṇavārttika* 1.211, 102b4.

356. *Pramāṇavārttika* 2.1, 107b3.

357. *Pramāṇavārttika* 2.6, 107b6.

358. *Pramāṇaviniścayaṭīkā* chap. 1, 9a1.

359. *Pramāṇaviniścayaṭīkā* chap. 1, 9b1.

360. The scholars referred to by Khedrup Jé understand Dharmottara as asserting that when an ordinary being has a sense perception of blue, it is only the first temporal portion of that perception that is a valid cognition. The subsequent temporal portions of that perception cannot be valid cognitions, since they simply follow on from that first portion without engaging a new object through their own power. However, Khedrup Jé contends that elsewhere Dharmottara asserts that a valid mental perception of blue is induced by a valid sense perception of blue. This would mean that in such a case, even though the mental perception is only discerning what the sense perception has already discerned, it is *not* disqualified from being a valid cognition. Khedrup Jé says that these assertions are not consistent.

361. *Pramāṇavārttika* 2.4, 107b5.

362. *Pramāṇavārttika* 2.5, 107b5.

363. *Pramāṇavārttika* 2.5, 107b5.

364. Khedrup Jé employs a slight play on words, since the "personal insight" (*rang rig*) that he refers to could alternatively be read as "self-cognition."

365. Tib. *gzhan las nges kyi tshad ma.*

366. This is another of the standard examples cited in the literature. The poetic truth it rests on is that the light or sparkle of a jewel can be seen even when the jewel itself is concealed.

367. Sakya Paṇḍita, *Treasure of Pramāṇa Reasoning*, 8.56, 16a4. There is general agreement that "inattentive" (*yid ma gtad*) refers to a perception that occurs at a time

that the person is distracted by something else. Regarding the perception of a "beginner" (*dang po ba*), there is less agreement, with some scholars identifying it as the perception of a newborn baby and others as a perception generated during the stage of language acquisition. However, in rejecting these two as examples of valid cognition that ascertain dependently, Khedrup Jé seems to be rebutting a large portion of Sakya scholarship.

368. Phrases like this one, *nam mkha' la bsdad pa*, are used a couple of times in this volume. They connote views and discourse that are detached and fail to get to grips with the real issues.
369. Prajñākaragupta, *Ornament Commentary to Pramāṇavārttika* (*Pramāṇavārttikālaṃkāra*), Toh 4221 Tengyur, tshad ma, *te*, 206a1. The second line in the Dergé version differs slightly.
370. That is to say, since the two elements of the division are jointly exhaustive, any third possibility not encompassed by them is ruled out.
371. Khedrup Jé identifies the twofold division of valid cognition as an example of the *misconception-countering* variety of definitive categorizations. With his last remark he implies that it does not fulfill the requirements of the *excluded third* variety.
372. *Pramāṇasamuccaya* 1.3, 1b4.
373. By this, Khedrup Jé means that a self-cognition forms the same substance as the consciousness that it experiences. So, even though the self-cognition in question itself is a perception, it would be problematic to assert that it is free from conceptual cognition, since the conceptual cognition is the thing it experiences and with which it forms a single substance.
374. Individual isolates are necessarily restrictive. The only thing that can *be* the individual isolate of pot, for example, is pot. Clay pot, golden pot, and so forth do not count as individual isolates of pot because they are not identical with it. Similarly, the only thing that can be the individual isolate of conception (*rtog pa'i ldog pa*) is conception itself. Various types of conception, such as inferential cognitions, do not therefore count. More generally, individual isolates play little part in the explanation of definitions since the characteristics within a definition almost necessarily have many instantiations.
375. *Pramāṇaviniścaya* chap. 1, 154b1.
376. *Pramāṇavārttika* 2.112, 111b6.
377. Here Khedrup Jé rejects the category of cognition known as *(awareness to which something) appears but is not ascertained* (*snang la ma nges*). This type of cognition is the fifth category in sevenfold division of awareness (see note 297 above). Khedrup Jé's rejection of this type of awareness is a major distinguishing feature of his epistemological system.
378. A large section of scholarship is reluctant to accept that a single moon appears to such an awareness, because of the logical implication that a portion of the awareness must be unmistaken. Khedrup Jé appeals to experience to counter this thinking.
379. Sakya Paṇḍita, *Treasure of Pramāṇa Reasoning*, 9.1, 16b1. The second line (*nyid kyis tshad ma grub pa yin*) does not appear in the Sakya Kabum version.
380. *Pramāṇaviniścaya*, chap. 2, 167a6.
381. This form of reasoning is discussed in detail below.
382. Sakya Paṇḍita, *Treasure of Pramāṇa Reasoning*, 9.2, 16b2.

383. Sakya Paṇḍita, *Treasure of Pramāṇa Reasoning Autocommentary*, chap. 9, 107b2 (132b2).
384. Sakya Paṇḍita, *Treasure of Pramāṇa Reasoning*, 1.28, 3b5.
385. Khedrup Jé returns to the issue of the *Treasure of Pramāṇa Reasoning*'s autocommentary below.
386. *Pramāṇasamuccaya* 1.4, 1b4.
387. *Pramāṇavārttika* 1.223, 103a3.
388. *Pramāṇavārttika* 3.264–65, 128b2.
389. *Pramāṇavārttika* 3.526, 138b5. My translation of this line incorporates an amendment to the last syllable from *mod* to *med*. It now matches the corresponding line Khedrup Jé gives below, when he repeats the position of this individual. Without the change, the line would mean the exact opposite of what the opponent is arguing. That the amended version is now also consistent with the line that appears in the Dergé version is coincidental. Khedrup Jé goes into detail about this second passage below. His discussion centers on the meaning of one word in this line, which is here translated as "light/appearance." The word also features in the first passage the opponent cites, where it was simply translated as "light" (Tib. *snang ba*, Skt. *pratibhā*). But in that first passage, there is no question that it denotes "light," meaning natural illumination. In the second passage, I have translated the same word as "light/appearance," to reflect the two ways in which it can be interpreted. That is, it could be read as "light," in the sense of external illumination. But it could also be understood as what "appears," denoting that of which the cognition is immediately aware.
390. *Commentary on the Difficult Points in the Pramāṇavārttika* (*Pramāṇavārttikapañjikā*), chap. 2, Toh 4217 Tengyur, tshad ma, *che*, 206b5.
391. These are the first three lines of 3.526 from Dharmakīrti's *Commentary on Pramāṇa*. The third line is the one in question, but it does not match the version cited just above. Nor does it conform with the Dergé edition. The reason is explained fully in the next note.
392. What Khedrup Jé is doing at this point requires clarification. On a previous occasion (see page 161), he demonstrated his willingness to look beyond a single translation of the *Commentary on Pramāṇa* to see what another translation might contribute to understanding. But in the present highly unusual case, he appears to be consulting *three* different translations of the same passage. Based on this comparison, he observes that there are two quite different readings of the text. These come about not because translators had diverging opinions about the best way to render certain words in Tibetan, as on the previous occasion, but because translators and commentators alike disagreed about *whose* position the words reflect. That is to say, Dharmakīrti's treatise includes not only his own views but also those of scholars from other systems to whom he is responding. This is what distinguishes the two versions to which Khedrup Jé refers. As he explains, based on the first version of the line he presents, it is voicing an opponent's position, but based on the second version, it reflects Dharmakīrti's own system. Both versions of the passage Khedrup Jé cites differ from the one in the Dergé edition. But he also had access to that third version, as confirmed by the fact that he cites it elsewhere, in an extended discussion of the passage in question. See *Ocean of Reasoning*, vol. *da*, 202b–203b. Of the two versions that he comments on here, the first is also cited by Lama Dampa Sönam Gyaltsen

(1312–75) in his *Commentary on the Pramāṇavārttika: Essence of Fine Elucidation*, 552. The source of the second version has yet to be located, although it has some correspondences with yet another version of the line cited by Tsunpa Tönshön (1224–?). See *Explanation of the Pramāṇavārttika*, 373. As stated above (note 243), there were a number of full Tibetan translations of the *Commentary on Pramāṇa* and also separate translations of individual passages contained within various commentaries. Nevertheless, to have so many competing versions of a single line was extremely unusual. Further investigation is needed to determine exactly how many versions of the passage existed and the exact provenance of the two cited by Khedrup Jé. But the focus here must be on the meaning of the two versions that he refers to in the present work.

As to the context of the line's appearance in Dharmakīrti's treatise, it is in a section establishing the existence of self-cognition, which describes its intimate relationship with memory. In the course of the discussion, Dharmakīrti refutes various Buddhists and non-Buddhists who deny self-cognition. This he does by serially rejecting their alternative explanations of how it is possible for the individual to be aware that a cognition has occurred and develop a memory of such an awareness even without self-cognition. The discussion is lengthy and spans various topics. In the current section, the opponent, who seems to be identified as a Vaiśeṣika, has effectively rejected the distinction between other-cognition and self-cognition. He therefore has to explain how a single cognition/perception is capable of inducing a recollection of an object, such as an external form, and also of the awareness of that object. The opponent seeks to do this by saying that rather than cognizing both object and subject simultaneously, perception shifts between awareness of those two. But Dharmakīrti questions how this is possible. His analysis of the opponent's position is that it refers to three separate elements—namely, the form that is the "apprehended object" of the perception and two versions of the perception, one that perceives the form and another that takes that perception of form as its object. Following the way they are designated in some commentaries, these two are referred to in the translation as the "earlier" and "later" consciousnesses. This last element sounds similar in function to self-cognition, but as the designation "later" indicates, unlike the self-cognition—which, according to Dharmakīrti, is an inherent part of perception and occurs simultaneous with its object—the one that the opponent proposes must be produced by the preceding perception of form that serves as its object. The similarity between the Buddhist self-cognition and the "later consciousness" attributed to the opponent may have been one of the factors leading to different readings of whose position Dharmakīrti was represented in the line in question. Regardless of the interpretation of the line, however, the issue under discussion in the stanza is exactly what characterizes the "producer" and "apprehended (object)" of a perception.

393. Although the discussion about the meaning of the passage is complex, Khedrup Jé's analysis of how to read the second passage is straightforward. In the second version of the passage, the word in question must be interpreted as "appearance" and cannot mean "light." And while the word *might* be interpreted as such in the first version, the position being expressed there is not Dharmakīrti's own. Whatever the case, neither version supports the opponent's case. Khedrup Jé's explanation of the original passage supports the idea that it expresses Dharmakīrti's own

position. For some reason, he does not address the fact that the first version of the passage seems to be saying the opposite of what the Tibetan who cites it appears to be arguing (i.e., it says that the appearance/light is *not* apprehended). In fact, looking at Khedrup Jé's explanation, one might even wonder about the relevance of mentioning light here. Interestingly, in the Dergé version, the line preceding the one in question contains two syllables that might be read as "day [and] night" (*nyin mtshan*). However, most Tibetan commentators apparently interpret this as a mistake and amend the first syllable to *nyid*. Based on this, their explanations of the stanza make no mention of "day and night," or indeed of *light*.

394. *Pramāṇavārttika* 3.460–61, 136a2.
395. Valid cognitions and their results are dealt with at length in a section below (pp. 321–44).
396. Tib. *shes pa la yul gyi rnam pa 'char ba*.
397. Tib. *bum pa'i spyi rnam*.
398. Khedrup Jé's here equates *clear* with *not unclear*. To understand his thinking in such cases, it is important to recall the two principles of Geluk argumentation mentioned in the introduction to this volume. These are that (1) a double negation equates to an affirmation, and (2) the rejection of an assertion is viewed as tantamount to the assertion of its converse. Khedrup Jé is also making the point that the foremost means of verifying a thing's existence is valid perception rather valid inferential cognition.
399. Tib. *phyi rol gzugs kyi rnam pa shar ba'i cha*.
400. The phrase *mig shes la rnam pa shar ba* would invariably be understood to mean that an aspect is presenting itself *to* the visual awareness. But in keeping with the way that Khedrup Jé identifies and object-aspect, he gives it an idiosyncratic slant. It must therefore be read as "an aspect arises within the awareness" or even "the awareness arises in the aspect (of the object)." For background on this, see note 342.
401. *Pramāṇavārttika* 3.224, 127a2.
402. *Pramāṇavārttika* 3.341, 131b2.
403. *Pramāṇavārttika* 3.341, 131b2.
404. Khedrup Jé gives "corresponding immediate condition" (*mtshungs pa de ma thag rkyen*) as the full version of the name for variety of condition.
405. Tib. *'gog pa'i snyoms 'jug*, Skt. *nirodhasamāpatti*. This form of concentrative absorption belongs to the highest, ninth level, beyond the four form and formless concentrations. The concentrations are regarded as common to Buddhist and non-Buddhist traditions, but certain of them are employed as bases for meditative states on the Buddhist path. As the name of this one suggests, it is a state in which cognitive functions are highly attenuated. As Khedrup Jé's discussion of it illustrates, the higher concentrations are commonly referred to in debates about which is suitable to be used for the path and about the foundational consciousness. In the latter case, the question is how different Buddhist schools can account for the continuity of the person when an individual's consciousness is in such an attenuated state.
406. Tib. *kun gzhi'i rnam shes*, Skt. *ālayavijñāna*.
407. More about this "deluded awareness" (*nyon yid*) and its relation to the foundational consciousness will follow shortly.

408. Tib. *sgo lnga'i rnam shes.*
409. The source of this paraphrased passage has yet to be identified.
410. Geluk scholars usually contrast *imputed existents* (*btags yod*) with *substantial existents* (*rdzas yod*). This division is not generally equated with the basic dichotomies discussed in the introduction (permanent-impermanent, generally and specifically characterized, etc.), in that certain actual things, such as the person, are regarded as imputed existents. But here Khedrup Jé says that the Sautrāntika do not believe that actual things can be imputed existents. And in the section below on "Substantive and 'reversed' [properties]," he states even more clearly that he equates imputed existents with permanent things.
411. Tib. *'du shes med pa'i snyoms 'jug.*
412. *Pramāṇavārttika* 3.178, 125a6. The translation in the Dergé edition differs slightly. See the note below.
413. *Pramāṇavārttika* 3.178, 125a6. The passage is the same as the one cited above, but this time it includes "seen" (*mthong ba*), whereas on the previous occasion the verb it used was "operate" or "engage" (*'jug pa*). The "seen" version matches what appears in Dergé and other Tengyur editions. But scholars during Khedrup Jé's time preferred the "operate" version, which presumably featured in an earlier translation of the line.
414. Tib. *'jig lta*, Skt. *satkāyadṛṣṭi.*
415. Tib. *nyon mongs can gyi ma rig pa.*
416. *Pramāṇavārttika* 3.264, 128b2.
417. *Pramāṇavārttika* 2.165, 113b7.
418. This section on the three conditions that produce a sense consciousness sets out the standpoints of the Sautrāntika and Cittamātra systems because both are represented in the *Commentary on Pramāṇa*. The position of the individual that Khedrup Jé reports here should be understood in the context of the related commentarial discussion about which of the two perspectives Dharmakīrti is taking in certain passages of his treatise. The individual here cites the second chapter of the treatise as the source of the two passages in question, even though the first belongs more correctly to the third chapter.
419. *Pramāṇavārttika* 2.40, 109a3.
420. Prajñākaragupta, *Ornament Commentary to Pramāṇavārttika* (*Pramāṇavārttikālaṃkāra*), Toh 4221, Tengyur, tshad ma, *te*, 96a7.
421. *Commentary on the Pramāṇavārttika* (*Pramāṇavārttikavṛtti*) chap. 2, Toh 4224, Tengyur tshad ma *pe*, 347a2. Ravigupta's work, spanning two volumes in the Dergé collection, is a commentary on the second and third chapters of Dharmakīrti's treatise.
422. Tib. *rnam smin gyi 'bras bu.*
423. *Pramāṇavārttika* 2.149, 113a5.
424. Khedrup Jé appears to suggest that it is difficult to reconcile the Cittamātra rejection of externally established entities with their acceptance of the classification of three conditions of perception. That rejection means that the object condition cannot be a condition in the straightforward sequential sense of the realist. And yet, he says, the classification of the three conditions demands some correspondence among the three. He proposes that there are certain things that, if accepted for one condition, must be accepted for all three.

425. In a more literal rendering of the technical phraseology, this reads "different [conceptual] isolates within [things of] a single nature" (*ngo bo gcig la ldog pa tha dad*).
426. *Pramāṇavārttika* 3.388, 133a6.
427. Here "simultaneity" (Tib. *lhan cig dmigs nges*) refers specifically to the relation between the object and perception according to the Cittamātra position. This reverses the Buddhist realist view that the object exists outside the perceiver and causes the perception, and contends that object and perception arise from a single substance and as such have a simultaneous existence.
428. *Ālambanaparīkṣā*, stanza 6, Toh 4205 Tengyur, tshad ma, *ce*, 86a3.
429. Dignāga, *Analysis of Objects of Cognition* (*Ālambanaparīkṣā*), stanza 7, Toh 4205 Tengyur, tshad ma, *ce*, 86a4. "Alternatively" does not appear in the root text but is in the autocommentary, *Ālambanaparīkṣāvṛtti*, Toh 4206 Tengyur, tshad ma, *ce*, 87a4.
430. Dignāga, *Analysis of Objects of Cognition* (*Ālambanaparīkṣā*), stanza 7, Toh 4205 Tengyur, tshad ma, *ce*, 86a4.
431. Dignāga, *Analysis of Objects of Cognition* (*Ālambanaparīkṣā*), stanza 6, Toh 4205 Tengyur, tshad ma, *ce*, 86a3.
432. Dignāga, *Analysis of Objects of Cognition* (*Ālambanaparīkṣā*), stanza 6, Toh 4205 Tengyur, tshad ma, *ce*, 86a3.
433. Khedrup Jé suggests that those responsible for such readings are accustomed to listening to teachings but lack the intellectual training to understand their import. Two of the three reasons he gives for rejecting the interpretation are that it would make Dignāga guilty of two grave errors of treatise composition: namely, introducing an unwarranted repetition and making an irrelevant or untimely statement.
434. According to Khedrup Jé, it is in the second passage that Dignāga presents his own thought. Khedrup Jé also identifies the proof that he says the passage conveys. He will then go on to argue that others have misidentified the elements of this proof. To sum up, he says that it is wrong to formulate the proof "*X* is the object condition, because it supplies the capacity." Instead, he says, the correct formulation is, "Capacity *x* is the object condition, because it supplies (later consciousnesses) in successive stages."
435. Khedrup Jé argues that the proof presented by Dignāga concerns a capacity and in what sense it counts as the object condition. He sees a problem with identifying the capacity as part of the reason, as that would inevitably require the identification of another element as the proof's subject, thus making the whole proof into one that is "about" something else. He then considers two versions of what this other proof might be trying to establish and why each is unacceptable. His turn of phrase for the first one, saying that it would be "unconnected," is a little opaque. But the pervasion would essentially be "because something provides the later consciousness with the capacity, it is the object condition of that later consciousness." Khedrup Jé judges that this would be problematic, in that the capacity would cease to be a cause of later consciousness, since it would be a capacity within that consciousness itself, existing together with it. This would preclude it from being the object condition, which is necessarily a cause. The thinking on the second hypothetical proof is clear. The proof would be to establish that the unidentified subject *x* was the object condition because it provided a capacity to a consciousness *y* that preceded the sense consciousness *z*. But this involves a three-stage process, in which *x* directly causes *y*, which in turn directly causes *z*. However, that would

mean that *x* would only cause *z* indirectly. This would go against the idea of the object condition, which should be an immediate cause.

436. Tib. *rigs mthun gyi bag chags*.
437. *Ālambanaparīkṣāvṛtti*, Toh 4206 Tengyur, tshad ma, *ce*, 87b1.
438. Khedrup Jé asserts that the statement about the two characteristics can accommodate both standpoints on the observed condition, by which he means that this was Dignāga's intention.
439. Dignāga, *Ālambanaparīkṣāvṛtti*, Toh 4206 Tengyur, tshad ma, *ce*, 87a7. The last two syllables of the passage cited by Khedrup Jé are *'thad do*, whereas the Dergé version reads *mthong ngo*. A translation of the line based in the second version would read, "Thus it is the internal object with the two features that is seen to be the object condition."
440. As outlined in his criticisms of other commentators, Khedrup Jé feels that it is a mistake to assert that the *object condition* should be understood literally, as something that is both the object and the cause of a perception of an object, such as blue. At the same time, he believes the way that the object condition is explained must not totally lose sight of those two elements. Khedrup Jé's solution is to say that Dignāga's own position is communicated in the second passage. This affirms that the object condition must be the cause of the perception. But Khedrup Jé says that the passage also identifies the object condition as a capacity present in the earlier consciousness that produced the perception. A capacity clearly could not qualify as the object of the perception. However, the link with the object is not lost, since, of the various productive capacities present in that earlier consciousness, the one referred to as the "object condition" is identified as being responsible for generating the perception in the aspect of the object.
441. The "proof of simultaneity," or more literally "proof of the necessary co-observation (of object and subject)" (Skt. *sahopalambhaniyama*) seeks to establish that certain objects and the perception of those objects can never be observed or apprehended separately and leads to the conclusion that they arise from a single substance.
442. The reference here is to one of the six "superknowledges" (Tib. *mngon shes*, Skt. *abhijñā*), specifically the "superknowledge of knowing others' minds" (Tib. *gzhan sems shes pa'i mngon shes*, Skt. *paracittajñāna*). As the name suggests, such a consciousness is said to have another's mind as its object. The superknowledge to which Khedrup Jé's refers belongs to the continuum of some person other than Devadatta and takes Devadatta's mind as its object. Hence the subject, the superknowledge, and the object, Devadatta's mind, are in the continua of separate individuals and, as such, have no relevance to what the proof of simultaneity sets out to establish.
443. As we see below, Khedrup Jé asserts that what the proof sets out to establish relates to what might be termed "common sense objects." Its subject, therefore, is simply blue. As becomes clear in this section, he is also making several points about how to craft a proof that is intended to establish something to one or more second parties. It should be phrased in a manner that potential second parties find acceptable and not contain elements that they find objectionable. In the present case, the proof is for the benefit of those belonging to the Buddhist realist schools, the Vaibhāṣika and Sautrāntika. As such, elements within the formulation, such as the subject, should be capable of accommodating the views of both. Neither of the

two schools would raise philosophical or methodological objections to the subject "blue." But proofs with more technical formulations, including those that identify the "aspect of blue" as the subject would fail, since at least one of the parties would object to it on the grounds that it did not exist.

444. This refers back to the author's identification of the object-aspect.
445. This last clause (*mig shes la sngon por snang ba yod pa'i phyir*) is open to interpretation.
446. Vasubandhu, *Abhidharmakośa*, 1.42, Toh 4089 Tengyur, mngon pa, *ku*, 3b4.
447. *Pramāṇavārttika* 3.388, 133a6.
448. Tib. *yang dag par*.
449. *Twenty Stanzas* (*Viṃśatikā*), stanza 12, Toh 4056 Tengyur, sems tsam, *shi*, 3b3.
450. This refers a class of "false ripostes" or "self-defeating rejoinders" (Tib. *ltag chod*, Skt. *jāti*). Prior to Dignāga, Indian logicians, most notably those in the non-Buddhist Nyāya school, had enumerated the various flawed ways in which someone, attempting to thwart an attack on his position, might seek to respond with an argument of his own. Dignāga—and following him, Dharmakīrti—rejected the need to create comprehensive classifications, but they did define the specific variety to which Khedrup Jé refers here. This variety (Tib. *'bras mtshungs kyi ltag chod*; Skt. *kāryasama*) can be rendered more fully as "self-defeating rejoinder whose reason is similar to the one it attempts to refute with respect to being an effect." Based on Sanskrit sources, Watanabe Toshikazu ("Dharmakīrti on False Rejoinders (*jāti*).") discusses Dharmakīrti's interest in this particular form of rejoinder. In Indian philosophical literature, distinctions between the various *jāti* are explained with reference to the standard proofs such as "Sound is impermanent because it is produced." The "effect" in the name derives from this understanding and an analysis of how the production is to be understood. Khedrup Jé cites this proof, immediately below, as the example of such a rejoinder. How exactly he considers it to be an example of the "effect" variety is less clear, although his criticism of it is that it introduces a spurious stipulation, intended to befuddle the other party.
451. This is another of the rare occasions that Khedrup Jé uses an honorific verb when relating the view in question. This language is often used as a sign of respect for the other party, but Khedrup Jé does not hold back on his criticisms of the unidentified interlocutor.
452. Khedrup Jé again affirms his position that both the object-aspect and subject-aspect must be identified as cognitions. In the case of a perception of blue, he says that the perception of blue is the object-aspect and the self-cognition of that perception the subject-aspect. He argues that by misidentifying the subject-aspect as the perception of blue, his opponent is effectively denying the existence of self-cognition.
453. The presentation of the "valid cognition, its result, and what it comprehends"—which is regularly shortened to "valid cognition and its results"—was derived from Dignāga and developed by Dharmakīrti. It was further extended in the Tibetan tradition. Khedrup Jé deals with it more systematically below but also devotes one of his other four works on Pramāṇa to the topic. Broadly speaking, it represents an analysis of the cognitive process, but more specifically, in the Tibetan tradition, a way of examining Dharmakīrti's epistemological positions through a series of models, each of which has three constituents: a subject—that is, a valid

cognition—its object, and the result. On the most basic level, the *result(s)* are various productive outcomes of generating different valid cognitions. But as the later section reveals, *result* in this context has different layers of meaning. The models vary according to the type of valid cognition and the tenet system involved. Khedrup Jé here refers to a model described from the Cittamātra perspective. As we see later, he regards this model as the most prevalent. A major point being made through this model is that in a standard cognitive event, there is not simply a subject and object; rather, there are two facets to the subject—in that the individual is both aware of the object and of being aware. This is also important with respect to understanding selflessness, since Khedrup Jé identifies the distinctions among these three as the self of phenomena.

Returning to Khedrup Jé's argument at the present point in the text, he says that the distinctions among the three elements in the valid cognition and its results model must apply to the conventional level, not the ultimate one, on which all such distinctions disappear. The charge against the opponent here is that based on his misidentification of the elements involved, the three remain separate both from the conventional and from ultimate perspectives.

454. Valid cognitions are nondeceptive and are also rooted in perception. Another fundamental tenet of this system is that valid cognitions cannot contradict each other. Hence a basic test for the correctness of a thesis is whether there are any valid cognitions that challenge and thereby "invalidate" it. Valid cognitions, therefore, serve as the basis for determining what exists conventionally. Conceptual cognitions are by definition mistaken or erroneous, which means there is necessarily a discrepancy between the way things *appear* to them and the way that they are in reality. As reiterated numerous times in the text, this discrepancy need not prevent them from being nondeceptive, but it means that perception is regarded as superior to conceptual cognition. Due to this, conceptual cognitions cannot serve as the foundation for determining what and how things exist.

455. Khedrup Jé asserts that the proof of simultaneity is based on personal experience. To establish to someone that a thing cannot be separated from the cognition of that thing, it is necessary to rely on an everyday object and subject, such as blue and the perception of it, since these both lie in the realm of experience for the individual to whom the proof is presented. Omniscient wisdom, however, is a type of cognition that lies outside the personal experience of such a person, and if it was presented as the proof's subject or part of that subject, the individual would be in no position to establish any of its characteristics or properties. There would be no practical way, therefore, that such a proof could work.

456. Although he does not use the designation, Khedrup Jé is essentially referring to the category of "nonassociated compounded things" (Tib. *ldan min 'du byed*, Skt. *viprayuktasaṃskāra*), which are impermanent phenomena that are neither matter nor consciousness.

457. Tib. *snang gzugs*. Here this refers to what appears to be form but is not.

458. *Pramāṇaviniścaya* chap. 1, 166a2.

459. The similar example is, generally speaking, supposed to aid realization of the proof's forward pervasion—and thereby the proof itself—by offering some parallel that is already within the experience of the person to whom the proof is presented. The cognition of a double moon seems to offer this: while two moons

might appear to a faulty sense consciousness to be outside the subject, this is obviously an error. And it is not difficult for an individual to understand that, contrary to appearances, the two moons have no existence separate from that consciousness. In a similar fashion, an object such as blue appears to be an external reality, but according to the Cittamātra, it is not; it is of a substance that is not separate from the perception of blue. Khedrup Jé's objection to this similar example is that while the actual perception of the blue in question is a valid cognition, the cognition of two moons can only be a false one. Although this seems to suggest that for him, in the Cittamātra or Pramāṇa system, a cognition that is erroneous can never serve as the basis for the realization of one that is nondeceptive, the matter requires further examination.

460. *Pramāṇavārttika* 3.388, 133a6.
461. *Pramāṇavārttika* 3.387, 133a5.
462. *Pramāṇavārttika* 3.388, 133a6.
463. Tib. *bdag gcig tu 'brel.*
464. *Pramāṇavārttika* 3.388, 133a6.
465. Based on a clear distinction in the original texts, the term *rnam shes* (Skt. *vijñāna*) has been translated in two ways in this volume. It is sometimes rendered simply as "consciousness" or "mind," reflecting the nontechnical usage. On other occasions, it is translated as "main awareness," and our authors use the Tibetan term to denote the basic entity of mind, viewed as something that is simply capable of knowing its object. This is distinguished from the various functions and faculties of mind, the so-called mental factors. In the second usage, the main awareness—which is used interchangeably with terms like *sems*, *yid*, and *gtso sems*—together with the mental functions, form a binary division (Tib. *sems sems 'byung*, Skt. *cittacaitta*) within the sphere of consciousness.
466. *Foundation for Yoga Practitioners: Compendium of Ascertainment* (*Yogācārabhūmiviniścayasaṃgrahaṇī*) section 3 (*phung po'i dngos po la mkhas*), Toh 4038, Tengyur, sems tsam, *zhi*, 77b7.
467. This appears to be a paraphrased version of an argument attributed to Asaṅga.
468. In Tibetan writings, this issue is generally reduced to the question of whether a main awareness and the functions associated with it are the same *substance* or separate ones. But the discourse from which this arises was a much broader one, among different schools of Abhidharma philosophy in India, which partly explains why Asaṅga and Vasubandhu are cited here. Questions about the relationship between a main awareness and the various processes of cognition occurring together with it are reported to have preoccupied Vaibhāṣika thinkers in particular.
469. *Analysis of Objects of Cognition* (*Ālambanaparīkṣā*), stanzas 7–8, Toh 4205 Tengyur, tshad ma, *ce*, 86a4.
470. Dharmakīrti, *Commentary on Pramāṇa Autocommentary* (*Pramāṇavārttikavṛtti*), Toh 4216 Tengyur, tshad ma, *ce*, 278a6.
471. This is presumably an imperfect rendering of *akṣa*. The position attributed to Prajñākaragupta here relates to the etymology of the Sanskrit terms for "perception" (*pratyakṣa*). The third text within this volume discusses this word at length (see pp. 605–38).
472. Tib. *spel nas skyes pa*.
473. See *Pramāṇaviniścayaṭīkā* chap. 1, 87a3.

474. The author rectifies what he says are certain misrepresentations of Dharmottara's view by Tibetan scholars. However, he still concludes that he does not side with Dharmottara's account of mental perception.
475. As remarked above in note 121, self-cognition represents an epistemological backstop. Unless one can rely on self-cognizing perception to verify a mental event, there is no way of establishing that it ever occurred. Related to this, an oft-stated principle of the tradition is that individuals cannot be unaware of their own minds.
476. Tib. *'gal rkyen*.
477. In his attempt to establish that the second instant onward of a sense perception is a mental perception, the opponent essentially gave the reason "(because) it is a perception that can only arise once the earlier awareness that is its substantial cause has come to an end." Khedrup Jé points out that this fails logically, since this reason is true not just of the second instant but also the first, which the opponent clearly does not intend, as he is trying to draw a fundamental distinction between the two in saying the first is a sense perception whereas the second is a mental perception.
478. Khedrup Jé here refers to "certain commentators" on Sakya Paṇḍita's work. He then attacks those who identify a sense consciousness that has just ceased as "the governing condition of the mental consciousness." However, this is exactly the phrase found in the *Treasure of Pramāṇa Reasoning Autocommentary*. See chap. 9, 109a. While some, including Bodong Choklé Namgyal, had questioned whether the work identified as the autocommentary had truly been authored by Sakya Paṇḍita, Khedrup Jé is known to have argued against that. Khedrup Jé never openly challenges that authorship in his references to the work in this volume. But the possibility remains that when he composed the current work, he was less sure about the provenance of the "autocommentary" and that he may be expressing his doubt here, in an uncharacteristically veiled fashion.
479. Sakya Paṇḍita, *Treasure of Pramāṇa Reasoning*, 9.7, 16b4.
480. Sakya Paṇḍita, *Treasure of Pramāṇa Reasoning*, 9.9, 16b6.
481. Tib. *'gros*.
482. Vasubandhu, *Abhidharmakośa*, 1.17, Toh 4089 Tengyur, mngon pa, *ku*, 2b3.
483. Khedrup Jé presents this as an alternative to "Any of the immediately preceding six...," the first part of the *Abhidharmakośa* passage just cited. The first version is from the first Tibetan translation of the *Abhidharmakośa* done by Jinamitra and Kawa Paltsek in the early ninth century. Although there was a later revision of this, and at least one more full translation of the treatise, undertaken by Smṛtijñānakīrti (ca. 960–1040), the first version remained dominant in Tibet. But regarding this line, Khedrup Jé suggests that a later translation, probably the one by Smṛtijñānakīrti, was clearer.
484. Khedrup Jé is saying that in the Abhidharma system of the Vaibhāṣika, the mental sense power of the mental consciousness is to be found in the *set* of consciousnesses that preceded that consciousness. He says that "any" should not be construed to mean that just one of the six coming to an end would be enough to present the opportunity for the mental perception to arise.
485. According to the Pramāṇa system, only objects of the present can be substances. Those belonging to the past and future have no such concrete, functional existence.
486. Tib. *de ma thag pa'i gnas su gyur pa'i yid shes*.

487. Tib. *rdzas rigs mthun pa.*
488. Tib. *ldog pa rigs mthun.*
489. Tib. *ldog pa rigs mi 'dra ba.*
490. As mentioned in the introduction, a distinctive feature of Geluk epistemology is its view on self-cognition. It is in this section that Khedrup Jé sets out most clearly his opposition to a view on self-cognition that was especially prevalent among Sakya scholars.
491. *Pramāṇavārttika* 3.443, 135a7.
492. In the later section on Valid Cognition and Its Result, Khedrup Jé describes this as the "predominant view." We can surmise that it is a model that the unidentified opponent here either espoused or was assumed to agree with. When Khedrup Jé references it here, he is saying that the analysis that yields this agreed model is basically the same as that for the proposed model. So, if the opponent accepts one, he must also accept the other.
493. Khedrup Jé refers to his now familiar identification of the object-aspect and subject-aspect. But his basic argument is that if, as the opponent proposes, an awareness necessarily cognizes its own nature, the distinction between other-cognition and self-cognition essentially disappears. Hence the object-aspect and subject-aspect become almost interchangeable.
494. *Pramāṇavārttika* 1.57, 97a1.
495. *Pramāṇavārttika* 3.257, 128a6.
496. That is, in the Buddhist view, the feeling of pleasure can accompany one's experience of an external object, but the pleasure itself is not the object of the sense consciousness.
497. *Pramāṇavārttika* 3.444, 135a7.
498. This argument resembles the one made by Sönam Gyaltsen (*Essence of Fine Elucidation*, 776), and Khedrup Jé may partly have had him in mind. But as noted below, it is also possible to identify another likely opponent.
499. Sakya Paṇḍita, *Treasure of Pramāṇa Reasoning*, 9.10, 16b6.
500. *Pramāṇavārttika* 3.329, 131a2.
501. Sakya Paṇḍita, *Treasure of Pramāṇa Reasoning*, 8.32, 15a4.
502. As has been noted, one feature of this work is the way Khedrup Jé sometimes switches personal pronouns. On this occasion he begins by talking about the opponent in the third person but suddenly changes to a direct address. The quotation Khedrup Jé uses also allows us to identify the individual addressed in the second person as Yaktön Sangyé Pal. Whether in this case Khedrup Jé switches his criticisms from Sönam Gyaltsen to Yaktön Sangyé Pal requires more investigation.
503. Yaktön Sangyé Pal, *Commentary to the Treasure of Pramāṇa Reasoning*, 8. 150–52.
504. *Pramāṇavārttika* 3.353, 132a1.
505. As discussed in a note 393 above, Dharmakīrti uses memory to establish the existence of self-cognition. Khedrup Jé refers to another proof Dharmakīrti uses below.
506. Sakya Paṇḍita, *Treasure of Pramāṇa Reasoning*, 9.10, 16b6.
507. *Pramāṇavārttika* 3.370, 132b3. The wording differs slightly in the Dergé edition. The proof establishes that the awareness of an object such as blue is accompanied by the experience of being aware, and that these are part of the same consciousness.

Once one has established that a consciousness has these two facets or sides it is said to be relatively easy to understand that one of them is self-cognition.

508. This is the nub of Khedrup Jé's thinking on the object-aspect. The passage by Bhāviveka that he cites immediately below appears to be the main Indian treatise source for his interpretation.
509. Bhāviveka, *Tarkajvālā*, chap. 5, Toh 3856 Tengyur, dbu ma, *dza*, 211a1. In the Dergé edition, there is no "or."
510. *Pramāṇavārttika* 3.287, 129b1.
511. The words immediately preceding the two lines just cited are "Any consciousness that holds the śabdārtha [relating to a certain thing] is a conceptual cognition [of that thing]." In the Geluk tradition, this is treated as Dharmakīrti's key statement on what distinguishes conceptual cognition from others, and it is featured a number of times in this volume. It is in fact Dharmakīrti's response to an opponent who argues that because delusions are counted as conceptual, the same must be true of the self-cognitions that experience them. In the lines cited by Khedrup Jé here, Dharmakīrti is explaining why such a self-cognition is not a conceptual awareness but a perception.
512. Tib. *bden pa'i rnam pa.*
513. The author might be referring to his *Exposition on [Haribhadra's] Clear Meaning Commentary on the Ornament of Realizations, ka*, 42b1. This, however, is uncertain since it has not yet been ascertained whether that was composed before the present work.
514. *Pramāṇavārttika* 2.146, 113a3.
515. Tib. *sred pa.*
516. *Pramāṇavārttika* 2.189–90, 114b6.
517. *Pramāṇavārttika* 2.220, 116a1.
518. *Pramāṇavārttika* 2.257, 117a7.
519. According to a philosophy now particularly associated with the non-Buddhist figure Bhartṛhari (fifth century CE), everything evolves out of a single principle known as *śabdabrahman*. This is a "word essence," which is identified with ultimate reality. Hence language and the universe are said to be an indivisible whole.
520. Tib. *so sor brtags 'gog*, Skt. *pratisaṃkhyānirodha.*
521. Tib. *so sor brtags min 'gog pa*, Skt. *apratisaṃkhyānirodha.*
522. Apart from a slight variation in the translation, a passage like this appears in a work by Jitāri: *Analysis of the Sugata's System* (*Sugatamatavibhaṅga*), Toh 3899 Tengyur, dbu ma, *a*, 7b7. This in turn is similar to a passage in Āryadeva's *Compendium of the Essence of Knowledge-Insight* (*Jñānasārasamuccaya*), Toh 3851 Tengyur, dbu ma, *tsha*, 27b1.
523. Again, Khedrup Jé switches to a direct address.
524. Tib. *kun nas nyon mongs kyi phyogs.*
525. Tib. *rnam byang kyi phyogs.*
526. *Pramāṇavārttika* 2.134, 112b3.
527. *Pramāṇavārttika* 2.218, 115b7.
528. Tib. *'jig tshogs la lta ba.* This is what some translations render the *identity view.*
529. Tib. *nga tsam.*
530. *Phung po dang mtshan nyid mi mthun pa'i rang rkya thub pa'i rdzas yod.* Khedrup Jé's second use of this description looks like a quotation, but it seems to be

intended more as a formula. It appears in the works of Tsongkhapa but goes back several centuries before him.

531. Tib. *rtag gcig rang dbang can gyi gang zag.*
532. *Pramāṇavārttika* 2.218, 115b7.
533. Tib. *'gal zla dmigs pa*. Despite the fact that this uses the *observation* of something to disprove the presence of another, it is still classed as a "reason of nonobservation." There is more explanation of this below.
534. In more technical language, this is an "isolated encapsulation" (*don ldog*).
535. *Pramāṇavārttika* 2.254, 117a6.
536. The path that releases (*grol byed kyi lam*) is similar in name and meaning to the *released path* (*rnam grol lam*) discussed in the section on true paths. But the path that matures (*smin byed kyi lam*) is clearly a much broader category than the uninterrupted path (*bar chad med lam*) of that earlier division.
537. Tib. *sdug bsngal gyi sdug bsngal.*
538. *Pramāṇavārttika* 2.253, 117a5.
539. The sensation of cold in the analogy is counted as the cause of the goosebumps mentioned in the previous analogy.
540. Tib. *bsod nams cha mthun (gyi dge ba).*
541. Tib. *thar pa cha mthun gyi dge ba.*
542. *Pramāṇavārttika* 2.251, 117a5.
543. *Pramāṇavārttika* 2.136–37, 112b5.
544. Tib. *nyon grib.*
545. Khedrup Jé discusses this in his work entitled *Exposition on [Haribhadra's] Clear Meaning Commentary on the Ornament of Realizations*, 63a–b. But it is uncertain whether that is the section to which he is referring here.
546. In Tibetan, the two are respectively *tshad ma'i chod pa'i 'bras bu* and *tshad ma'i ma chod pa'i 'bras bu.*
547. *Pramāṇavārttika* 2.3, 107b4.
548. Tib. *tshad ma'i bskyed 'bras.*
549. Khedrup Jé refers to another binary scheme, the two elements of which are the *establisher* (*rnam par 'jog byed*) and the *established* (*rnam par gzhag bya*). Here, *establishment* does not denote the way that things actually exist or come into existence but the way that they become established or settled for the individual. Certain closely associated things, such as a definition its definiendum, can only be understood in a particular order. The one understood first is the "establisher" and is designated as such because of the role it has in helping the individual understand the second, the "established." The order in which they are understood or cognized also determines the sequence in which they should be presented to the individual, so reference to this scheme is common in descriptions of how information is to be imparted. Khedrup Jé draws attention to the practice of calling the *establisher* the "cause" and the *established* the "result" and how this is intended to convey the order in which they are understood or introduced. But in reality, a definition and its definiendum, or a basis and its quality, necessarily exist simultaneously so cannot be genuine cause and effect. Hence, Khedrup Jé says, in situations such as this one, "result" should be understood as a figurative designation.
550. *Pramāṇavārttika* 2.4, 107b5.
551. This identifies the names of three elements under discussion. But the first, as

explained here, is not so much the valid cognition itself as the facet or quality that makes the valid cognition what it is.

552. While the other two elements, a subject and an object, are identifiable entities, the "result" here can best be thought of as a functional outcome that the individual gains through the cognitive event.
553. Tib. *phrugs gsum.*
554. Tib. *tshad ma'i 'bras rtog dang po* etc.
555. Tib. *don lkog na mo.*
556. Tib. *yang dag par.*
557. The terms attributed to this individual differ slightly from those of others. He refers to the "aspect of the object" (*gzung ba'i rnam pa*), as an "imagined" (*btags ba pa*) cognition of "the (external) entity" (*don rig*), "(that which has the) subject-aspect" (*'dzin pa'i rnam pa*), and "the designation *self-cognition*" (*rang rig pa'i tha snyad*).
558. According to the opposing commentator, rather than being a passive acceptance, the "uncritical" understanding is a "mistaken" way of viewing things. The error it makes, he says, is to misidentify a particular aspect by seeing it as an external entity. It would seem the aspect in question can only be the object-aspect, since the subject-aspect plays no part in the first model. Khedrup Jé's tersely stated argument appears to be that the opponent's version of the model could not be correct, because it would mean that the mistake being made by this "uncritical" understanding is to identify the object-aspect (i.e., the valid cognition) as an external entity. That would indeed be a mistake, but it is simply not the one that this outwardly directed awareness, viewing some apparently external entity such as blue, is making.
559. A point that Khedrup Jé makes a number of times in this section, with varying degrees of clarity, is that the subject-aspect derives its identity from observation of the object-aspect. The latter, in turn, derives its identity as valid cognition through its observation of an object that is in reality the same nature as it. These identities cannot depend on or refer in any way to an imagined external entity. And since what the valid cognition observes is an object that is in its own nature, then if it observed an external entity, it would follow that such an entity was in its own nature.
560. *Pramāṇavārttika* 3.341–52, 131b2.
561. *Pramāṇaviniścaya* chap. 1, 165a2. The verb in the Dergé edition is *rnam par 'jog pa.*
562. *Pramāṇasamuccaya* 1.8, 2a2.
563. *Pramāṇavārttika* 3.301–19, 130a2.
564. *Pramāṇasamuccaya* 1.8, 2a3.
565. *Pramāṇavārttika* 3.320–40, 130b5.
566. *Pramāṇasamuccaya* 1.10, 2a4. In the Dergé version, this is "valid cognition" rather than "self-cognition."
567. *Pramāṇavārttika* 3.341–52, 131b2.
568. *Pramāṇavārttika* 3.320, 130b5.
569. *Pramāṇavārttika* 3.353, 132a1.
570. Tib. *kun rdzob rnam par 'jog pa'i ngor.*
571. *Pramāṇavārttika* 3.306, 130a5.
572. *Pramāṇavārttika* 3.310, 130a7.

573. The reference to "conceptual analysis" is clearly out of place here and probably derives from a scribal error. Most likely, "conceptual analysis" (*'bras rtog*) has mistakenly been added to what originally read simply "the third" (*gsum pa*), since this is very obviously a reference to the third misconception that the author identified immediately above.
574. *Pramāṇavārttika* 3.305, 130a4. The version in the Dergé edition has *'gas* instead of *'gags*.
575. *Pramāṇavārttika* 3.341–52, 131b2.
576. Khedrup Jé devotes two separate subsections to the first two conceptual analyses, in which he identifies his position on the three elements in each of the two models. In place of where we might expect to find a similar exposition of the third conceptual analysis, we instead find the discussion "The establishment of those models." This is because in contrast to the commentators he refutes above, Khedrup Jé does not accept a third model distinguishable from the first two. He makes his position clearer in *Ocean of Reasoning*, his commentary to Dharmakīrti's *Pramāṇavārttika* (chapter 3, 128b). He says that the models of the first two analyses for respectively understanding other-cognitions and self-cognitions cover the essential territory. The third analysis is intended as a further elaboration on the first two and serves as the basis for further exploring misconceptions that might arise with regard to them.
577. *Pramāṇavārttika* 3.342–44, 131b2.
578. *Pramāṇavārttika* 3.345, 131b4.
579. Khedrup Jé explains that Dharmakīrti's emphasis on self-cognition as the result allows him to separate the *experience* of the object from the question of its existence.
580. *Pramāṇavārttika* 3.341–45, 131b2.
581. *Pramāṇavārttika* 3.346, 131b4.
582. *Pramāṇavārttika* 3.346–49, 131b4.
583. *Pramāṇavārttika* 3.346, 131b4.
584. *Pramāṇavārttika* 3.347–49, 131b5.
585. *Pramāṇavārttika* 3.349–50, 131b6.
586. That is, the ascertainment (i.e., the thought recognizing) that the person is aware of blue is something that only comes about *after* the sense consciousness and owing to it.
587. Dignāga, *Analysis of Objects of Cognition* (*Ālambanaparīkṣā*), chap. 6, Toh 4205 Tengyur, tshad ma, *ce*, 86a3.
588. *Pramāṇavārttika* 3.350, 131b6.
589. *Pramāṇavārttika* 3.350, 131b6.
590. *Pramāṇavārttika* 3.349, 131b6.
591. *Analysis of Objects of Cognition* (*Ālambanaparīkṣā*), chap. 7, Toh 4205, Tengyur, tshad ma, *ce*, 86a4. The Dergé version says *ngo bo gang yin dbang po'ang yin*, rather than *rang gi ngo bo rig pa yin*, which might seem to significantly alter the meaning.
592. *Pramāṇavārttika* 3.387, 133a5.
593. Khedrup Jé refers to the section "Establishing each of the [three] criteria [of the proof's reason]" in relation to the logic establishing the simultaneity of object and subject (pp. 264–67).
594. *Pramāṇavārttika* 3.351–52, 131b6.

595. *Pramāṇasamuccaya* 2.1, 4a1.

596. *Pramāṇaviniścayaṭīkā* chap. 2, 168a6. The wording in the Dergé edition differs considerably.

597. The tradition distinguishes between an "actual name" (*dngos ming*) and a "figurative name" (*btags ming*). This division forms part of its hermeneutic analysis and interpretation of scriptures and treatises. The analysis seeks to explain why the Buddha and his chief commentators should choose to refer to certain things by names that are not their actual ones. The theory behind the analysis is that such variant uses of language always have some discoverable intended purpose and that this relates to the audience toward whom the words were originally directed. The analytical tool it uses is encapsulated in a threefold formula that is to be applied to any nonliteral use of terminology within canonical works. This is obviously not to determine whether the original nonstandard usage of the designation was acceptable. But commentators' accounts of why a nonstandard designation was used sometimes differ, so the analysis is used to examine the credibility of their interpretations. According to the threefold formula, any nonliteral designation must have (1) a rationale or justification, a demonstrable link with reality rather than being something that was assigned randomly, (2) a purpose, what the unconventional usage is intended to show, and (3) evidence countering the literalness of the designation, a reason why the thing to which the name *x* is applied cannot actually be an *x*.

598. One of the most important discourses shaping the Indian tradition of logic was about the correct formulation of the proof statement. This discourse stretched over many centuries and involved scholars from various philosophical schools, although Buddhist and Nyāya thinkers were especially active in it. They sought to determine the ideal formulation by means of which a proof could be conveyed to another party to induce an inference. This meant identifying the essential components of a correct proof statement. For reasons that will now be explained in the text, Buddhist logicians following Dignāga argued that the main aim of the proof statement was to convey the reason's fulfillment of the three criteria. They denied that it needed to include a formal presentation (i.e., a "verbal formulation") of the proof's probandum or thesis. They saw such a formulation as a recapitulation of what a correct proof statement should already have conveyed to the other party, and they therefore dismissed it as superfluous.

599. Tib. *gsal byed*.

600. The very precise discipline of textual analysis of scriptures and authoritative treatises is premised on the idea that their speakers or composers make no mistakes. Neither the Buddha nor his most reliable commentators would make an unwarranted repetition, since this would constitute an error. If something is repeated, just as in cases where canonical works use language unconventionally (see note 598), there must be some didactic purpose. The words in question must actually denote different things or be intended to achieve different ends. Deciphering these meaning and identifying their purposes is the task of later scholars.

601. Khedrup Jé argues that the wording of Dignāga's definition conveys the essential elements of a correct proof statement, so there would be no point in him repeating the point figuratively through the designation. This appears to suggest an order in which the two sets of words are understood, probably evoking the principle

that realizing the definition of a thing must precede correct understanding of any names and designations applied to it.

602. Although Khedrup Jé's response is oblique, he appears to deny any direct parallel between what the words of the correct proof statement and the words of the treatise, communicating the definition, should convey. What is essential for the proof statement is that it contains only those elements that can immediately engender an inference (i.e., the reason's fulfillment of the three criteria). Hence, even though the thesis is as much a component of the proof as the reason, this does not mean that it has an equal capacity for engendering the inference.
603. Adding a negation here, *yin* is emended to *ma yin*.
604. Khedrup Jé and the other interlocutor agree that the verbalization of the thesis is not an essential component of the correct proof statement and that reasoning can be employed to refute that it is such. But when this other interlocutor proposes a reason that could be used for this purpose, Khedrup Jé objects to it on technical grounds. He views the pattern of the reason as flawed, and points to another situation in which a reason based on the same pattern would create problems for the individual who used it.
605. *Pramāṇasamuccaya* 3.1, 6a5.
606. Tib. *yan lag lnga ldan gyi sgrub pa'i ngag.*
607. *Pramāṇaviniścaya* chap. 3, 198b1. The wording in the Dergé version differs considerably.
608. Prajñākaragupta, *Ornament Commentary to the Pramāṇavārttika* (*Pramāṇavārttikālaṃkāra*), chap. 4, Toh 4221, Tengyur, tshad ma, *the*, 123a5.
609. According to the Dergé catalogue, this is Dignāga, *Nyāyamukha*, Toh 4208 Tengyur, tshad ma, *ce*, 89a4, but it is actually the *Entranceway to Reasoning* (*Nyāyapraveśaka*) by Śaṅkarasvāmin.
610. As above, this is catalogued as Dignāga's *Nyāyamukha*, Toh 4208 Tengyur, tshad ma, *ce*, 89a5, but it is actually Śaṅkarasvāmin's *Nyāyapraveśaka*.
611. *Pramāṇavārttika* 1.28, 95b6.
612. *Pramāṇavārttika* 4.22, 140a4.
613. *Pramāṇavārttika* 1.27, 95b6. The wording in second line of the Dergé version differs very slightly.
614. *Pramāṇavārttika* 4.23, 140a5.
615. *Pramāṇavārttika* 4.35, 140b5. The Dergé version has a different verb (*bslad pa*), according to which the translation would read "This is something infected by ignorance."
616. The phrase "in accordance with the form of the proof" (*'god tshul dang mthun par*) is frequently included in definitions of the three criteria and is explained below; see note 675.
617. Khedrup Jé sees inconsistencies in the way that this group explains the property of the subject. Their definition of it is tight, but when it comes to the statement conveying that property, their standards appear surprisingly lax, seeming to require little more than someone saying "Sound is produced" to the relevant party.
618. The logical step that Khedrup Jé takes as his argument progresses from the previous line to this one is not entirely clear.
619. Khedrup Jé seems to argue that there are at least three different statements that

could serve as correct proof statement in the situation in question, apparently depending on the individual.

620. According to Khedrup Jé, these opponents make the mistake of proposing that the main requirement of a correct proof statement is just that it articulates the fulfillment of the three criteria. As he clarifies below in his own explanation of the function of correct proof statement, it should not *introduce* the three criteria to the second party so much as allow him to consolidate the ascertainment of them that has already been gained.
621. *Commentary on Pramāṇa Autocommentary* (*Pramāṇavārttikavṛtti*), Toh 4216 Tengyur, tshad ma, *ce*, 268a3. Only the second part of this passage appears in the existing version of the autocommentary. But the passage that Khedrup Jé cites appears so regularly in Tibetan writings that we can be sure that it was regarded by authors as an accurate (although perhaps paraphrased) representation of Dharmakīrti's position.
622. Ruling out a "third alternative" or "third possibility" (Tib. *phung po gsum pa*) is key to establishing that certain elements form jointly exhaustive dichotomies, but is also important more generally to the system of logic in which binaries feature so heavily.
623. The explanation of this "[preparative] countering proof" is on pages 397–99 and note 682.
624. *Pramāṇavārttika* 4.20, 140a3.
625. *Pramāṇavārttika* 1.27, 95b6.
626. *Pramāṇavārttika* 1. 27–28, 95b6. I have supplied some of the lines that Khedrup Jé gave in abbreviated form.
627. Yamāri's *Total Purity: An Explanation of the Ornament Commentary on the Pramāṇavārttika* (*Pramāṇavārttikālaṃkāraṭīkāsupariśuddha*), chap. 4, Toh 4226 Tengyur, tshad ma, *tse* 5a7.
628. *Pramāṇavārttika* 1.27, 95b6.
629. Khedrup Jé's criticism of Yamāri's commentary on these words seems to be that they suggest an exchange during a debate, in which the first party still needs to convince the second party that the reason is correct, rather than that they describe the first party helping the "knowledgeable" second party to realization of the proof.
630. *Pramāṇavārttika* 1.15, 95a6.
631. There are different ways to encapsulate what *pervasion* means. In one, it is about two categories and simply means that one encompasses the other. In another, it is about the things contained within those categories, that if something belongs to category *x*, it also belongs to category *y*. In this section Khedrup Jé scrutinizes how different scholars define the forward and reverse pervasions. They all agree that the forward pervasion is the predicate's encompassing the reason and that the reverse pervasion is the inverse of the same fact. The question is how to formulate these precisely. In English there are numerous ways to express one thing's pervasion of another. Reflecting the two encapsulations referred to above, to convey that the predicate *impermanent* pervades the reason *produced*, one can either say "whatever is produced is impermanent" or "if something is produced, it is necessarily impermanent." These sound like slightly different assertions, perhaps with the second being logically derived from the first. However, both would be perfectly

valid translations of the *same* Tibetan statement, although since the second uses the conditional *if*, it is slightly closer to the Tibetan in a literal sense. The ability of the Tibetan to accommodate what might sound like different assertions in English is useful to bear in mind when reading the translation.

632. I have translated the reason (*gzhi grub yin na / de gnyis ka yin pas khyab pa'i phyir*) as "because if something is an established basis, these two facts are always that." This is a formula of a kind not uncommon in Tibetan literature associated with debate, but it is open to different interpretations. A more literal rendering would be "because if *x* is an established basis, *it* must be both of those two." There are basically two different ways in which such a statement may be intended. The first is that it makes a genuine assertion with some philosophical import. In the present case, the individual could be using it to make the point that the pervasions embody two noncontingent *facts*—that something produced is necessarily impermanent and that something permanent is necessarily not produced—and there is nothing in existence (i.e., no established basis) that can be shown to contradict these. Hence they must be accepted as true. Later in the text (note 786) Khedrup Jé uses a reason that contains a similar assertion. However, the second way it might be intended is very different. The reason is formulated in a manner that is regarded as technically problematic. In particular, the incorporation of "if" (see note 778) within the reason means that it contains its own internal pervasion. And anyone presented with such a reason in debate is unsure how this internal pervasion relates to the consequence's main pervasion. In short, the debate format makes it virtually impossible to respond to such reasons in a satisfactory manner, and they tend to be introduced mischievously. Khedrup Jé interprets the other scholar's use of the formula in this second manner and responds accordingly in his criticism of the argument.
633. Tib. *sgrub byed kyi yan lag*.
634. Khedrup Jé does not tell us why these individuals assert that the components of the probans for this proof are permanent, so we are unclear about their thinking. But there are also some aspects of Khedrup Jé's attack that are unclear. However, the tension that Khedrup Jé identifies is between a reason such as "produced" needing to embody or instantiate the pervasions and those pervasions being defined as conceptually constructed facts. He seems to be keen to reject those positions that he feels stray toward the latter.
635. As we saw in the previous paragraph, these individuals assert that the components of the proof's probans are permanent, which means that they must be non-actual things.
636. Highlighting the vague and ineffectual nature of the reason introduced by one of the individuals, Khedrup Jé simply throws it back at him.
637. To be totally absent from that class would mean that it is not permanent.
638. This is another occurrence of the oblique phrase mentioned above (note 81), although the spelling of the first syllable (*phung* instead of *phud*) is different and almost certainly incorrect.
639. Khedrup Jé now switches personal pronouns and addresses the whole group directly.
640. Khedrup Jé argues that based on the opponents' position, the reverse pervasion of this proof must be "a thing that is not comprehended is necessarily impermanent."

Such a pervasion would clearly be incorrect. Nonexistents are not comprehended, which obviously does not mean that they are impermanent.

641. As featured on page 461, this is commonly agreed to be an incorrect reason of the "inconclusive" variety. A correct reason should only be present in the class of similar instances. But this one fails because the reason is present in *both* the class of similar instances and the class of dissimilar instances. In other words, some comprehended things are permanent, whereas others are impermanent.
642. *Pramāṇaviniścaya* chap. 2, 168b7.
643. *Pramāṇaviniścaya* chap. 2, 169b1.
644. Dharmakīrti, *Nyāyabindu*, chap. 2, Toh 4212 Tengyur, tshad ma, *ce*, 231a7.
645. Dharmakīrti, *Hetubindu*, Toh 4213 Tengyur, tshad ma, *ce*, 238b.
646. Tib. *rjes khyab*, *ldog khyab*, *dngos khyab*, and *bzlog pa'i khyab pa* or *go bzlog pa'i khyab pa*.
647. See note 654 for why this proof is classified as incorrect.
648. Tib. *sgrub byed 'phen pa'i thal 'gyur*.
649. As pointed out in the introduction, the consequence is regarded as a *verbal* formulation. The pervasions and assertions contained within it, and the elements it refers to, must hold together in a logical sense, but this does not mean that valid cognition can establish their reality.
650. For Khedrup Jé, the problem with the other scholars' formulations of the pervasions is that they do not focus on concomitance and nonconcomitance. For him, these two mean ascertaining the presence and absence of things within the two classes.
651. Each of the three criteria of the correct reason has its own foundation. For the property of the subject, this foundation is that subject of interest. For the forward and reverse pervasions, the foundations are, respectively, the class of similar instances and class of dissimilar instances. Khedrup Jé deals with the latter two foundations first. Up to this point in the text, the second element in the proof has generally been referred to as the *predicate*, and has seemed like a single quality of a thing, such as the *impermanence* of sound. But within a pervasion, this same element must represent a whole category, such as things that are *impermanent*. Viewed in this way, the second element is referred to as the "class of similar instances" and its opposite is the "class of dissimilar instances." Much of the analysis in this section is about how it is possible to realize a class of things.
652. In any correct proof—A is B because of C—B must totally encompass C, such that there is no instance of C that is not also one of B. This might manifest in two ways. B and C may be entirely coterminous, and encompass exactly the same range of things, as is the case with impermanent and produced. Or B can represent the larger category and thus encompass more than C. In this second situation, since some cases of B match those of C but others do not, B's encompassing of C is said to be divided into two (*cha gnyis su 'jug pa*). The proof "The sound of a conch [A] is impermanent [B] because it is something derived from effort [C]" is an example of this, since there are obviously many things that are impermanent but are not derived from (conscious) effort, such as any number of phenomena that occur naturally. But Khedrup Jé argues that based on the opponent's reasoning, this could no longer count as an example of a proof in which the B category is divided. This is because, he asserts, congruity between the reason and the predicate would demand that the two are coterminous.

653. These two are held to be examples of incorrect proofs. But even for these, it is generally held that the classes of similar and dissimilar instances should be identifiable.
654. Although "Sound is impermanent because it is a heard thing" might appear to be a correct proof, it is identified in the Pramāṇa treatises as faulty or, more specifically, as inconclusive. The problem is basically that no one could qualify as a correct second party for such a proof. "Heard thing" is the definition of sound, and while it is definitely not the case that generally, by realizing the definition of a thing, one realizes its definiendum, scholars say that anyone realizing that a thing heard is impermanent would also necessarily realize that sound is impermanent. What distinguishes the "not shared" subcategory is explained in Khedrup Jé's section on inconclusive reasons; see pages 457–61 and note 768.
655. As on other occasions, Khedrup Jé argues against simplistically transferring from one domain to another.
656. The translations "class of similar instances" and "similar instance(s)" derive from a single Tibetan term (*mthun phyogs*); the Tibetan concept accommodates both. Similarly, "class of dissimilar instances" and "dissimilar instance(s)" are translations of just one term (*mi mthun phyogs*).
657. *Known thing* (also referred to as *object of knowledge*) is coterminous with *existent*. Known thing and existent themselves are counted as permanent (see note 188). They also encompass everything (i.e., all permanent and impermanent things). But the fact that they encompass impermanent does not mean that impermanent itself or anything that is impermanent has to be permanent.
658. Tib. *khegs pa*.
659. Tib. *bsal ba*.
660. Tib. *rang ldog nas*.
661. This position is expressed by Gyaltsab Jé in his *Commentary to Nyāyabindu* (47a2). The wording matches almost exactly that used by Khedrup Jé here: *des na rtags yin na shes 'dod chos can grub pas khyab kyang rtags yang dag gi shes 'dod chos can yin na grub mi dgos te*. The colophon of that text says that it was composed at Ganden, meaning that the dates would appear to fit.
662. The *śabdārtha* is relied on by a conceptual cognition, not a perception. Since the Seven Treatises appear to suggest that someone confirms the property of the subject in this case by seeing the location, it would exclude the involvement of conceptual consciousness.
663. This formulation (*shes bya thams cad de yin pa'i phyir*) has some similarity with one used by an opponent above (see note 632), although here it is intended in a serious manner.
664. This is a reference to Kamalaśīla's *Illumination of the Middle Way*, which argues that while the reason and predicate may be simple negations and the subject something that does not exist, the proof can still be a correct one. See, for example, *Madhyamakāloka*, Toh 3887 Tengyur, dbu ma, *sa*, 173b–174a.
665. *Pramāṇasamuccaya* 3.2, 6a6.
666. *Pramāṇavārttika* 4.91, 143a1.
667. *Pramāṇasamuccaya* 4.5, 8b7. The wording in the Dergé version differs slightly.
668. The Tibetan term for *probandum* (*bsgrub bya*) is built upon the future form of a verb and literally denotes "that which is to be established." The designation for *correct reason* (*rtags yang dag*) makes no reference to an action and carries no future connotations.

669. Here "reason," "subject," and "predicate" render *rtags*, *chos*, and *don*.
670. Tib. *rlom tshod.*
671. Tib. *song tshod.*
672. Permanent is designated the *anti-predicate* (*dgag bya'i chos*) of this proof in that it is the element that one necessarily negates about sound (the subject) in the process of establishing impermanent (the predicate) about sound. By extension, the predicate in every proof must have an identifiable anti-predicate.
673. Reasoning dealing with demonstrable facts cannot establish what specific causes gave rise to the form of the aggregates that a particular person has adopted and nature of the manifest sufferings that the person experiences. But it can be used to establish that causes for the aggregates must have existed. Khedrup Jé refers to the individual isolate (*rang ldog*) here as a means of separating causes, in the general sense, from their specifics, and to convey that it is only the former that the proof is establishing.
674. This impossibility is explained in the next note.
675. There is no single copula verb "to be" in Tibetan. Instead, two sets of verbs, those of identity and existence—the most prominent examples of which are respectively the verbs *yin* (*pa*) and *yod* (*pa*)—broadly cover a similar range of functions between them as the English verb. The statements "*X* is fire" and "*X* is on the hill" use a single verb in English, but their Tibetan equivalents use the verbs of identity and existence, respectively. When expressing more fixed notions of being, such as the category to which a thing belongs, a verb of identity is generally used. When expressing something about a thing that is not part of its character but is a potentially changeable fact about it, such as its location at any one time, a verb of existence is used. Importantly, however, this second kind of verb is not just used to express transitory states but also the existence in more general sense—i.e., that a certain thing is an "existent." Verbs of existence also denote "having," such as when one says "*X* has quality *y*." The distinction between the two also impacts on the formulation of proofs, and whenever the phrase "in accordance with the form of the proof" is included in a definition, it indicates that the element(s) in question should match each other in terms of either an identity or existence formulation. Tibetan scholars agree on the need for the elements in the proof to correspond with each other in this way. But there are differences of opinion on whether, for instance, the predicate of the proof is "fire" or "fire exists." That is, some scholars view the verbs as part of the "grammar" of the proof and regard them as separate from the elements to which they are added. Other scholars say that they constitute part of the elements themselves and are inseparable. Khedrup Jé belongs more in the second camp. But his arguments here tell us that he regards *being*—in the sense of identity—as the default. That is, unless someone specifically *adds* a copula verb of existence to it, "fire" alone, unaccompanied by any verb, must be understood to carry an implicit assertion about "being fire." We also see in the current discussion that Khedrup Jé feels that "congruity" between two things entails identity. So, if *x* is congruous with *y*, it means that *x* is *y*.
676. The sense power and mental consciousness (i.e., the governing condition and immediate condition) cannot alone produce the visual consciousness. A visual form (i.e., the object condition) is also required. This is the "other" cause to which the predicate alludes. But the proof is intended only to establish that the visual

consciousness must *have* such a cause (i.e., that such a cause exists) rather than to identify it. Khedrup Jé's complicated argument is that since the opponent denies that "having" is built into the subject and predicate, it means that the default must apply, so they must be understood to contain assertions of being. To put it simply, an assertion that "*x* has *y*" is thereby transformed into an assertion that "*x* is *y*." The last step of Khedrup Jé's argument seems to rely on his reading "other than" (*las gzhan*) as a negation. Other scholars might question this.

677. According to the Pramāṇa tradition, an individual can come to realize that certain things are cause and effect based on personal observation. The analysis and discussion centers on the minimum number of valid cognitions required to elicit the knowledge. It is generally held that more than one valid cognition is needed, and since the valid cognitions are seen to work together to provide the necessary information, they are referred to as "sets" (*phrugs*).
678. Tib. *khyab 'brel.*
679. *Pramāṇavārttika*, 1.34, 96a2.
680. Tib. *tha snyad sgrub pa.*
681. Tib. *bltos med kyi rtags.* See next note and glossary.
682. Tib. *gnod pa can gyi rtags*. For an individual to realize the forward and reverse pervasions of a reason in a proof, it may be necessary to rely on other proofs to establish each of those two pervasions individually. Khedrup Jé's explanation of these proofs is firmly rooted in the Indian Pramāṇa treatises, where they are described as being precursors to establishing the main proof "Sound is impermanent because it is produced." While the proofs of *nonreliance* and *countering* are preparatory, they are also correct proofs in their own right, and later Khedrup Jé refers to the inferential valid cognitions that they engender. The name of the second proof does not indicate that its main purpose is to counter an assertion during argumentation. Instead it refers to its very specific task in the process of generating an inferential cognition. To bring about certainty with regard to the reverse pervasion—i.e., that the reason is totally absent from the class of dissimilar instances—it must rule out, or "counter," the possibility that something can be a common locus of the reason and the anti-predicate. That means, in this case, it must rule out the possibility that something could be both produced and permanent. It is in establishing the main proof, rather than the countering proof, that the individual realizes impermanence. Hence the tradition holds that an individual can realize that a produced thing is not permanent without yet having realized that it is impermanent. There is a good deal of discussion about this point among Tibetan scholars.
683. *Commentary on Pramāṇa Autocommentary* (*Pramāṇavārttikavṛtti*), Toh 4216 Tengyur, tshad ma, *ce*, 266b7.
684. Tib. *'brel ba'i don ldog.*
685. Tib. *gsal ba'i dbye ba.*
686. Tib. *'gal zla dmigs pa'i rtags.*
687. Tib. *rang ldog gzhi ldog gi rnam dbye.*
688. *Pramāṇavārttika* 4.262, 149b6.
689. *Pramāṇavārttika* 1.198, 102a4.
690. As hinted above (note 96), in proofs that use as their reason the nonobservation of something that is "not accessible," the point can be to establish the limitations of our ability to cognize a certain thing in a given set of circumstances. For instance,

the presence of a *piśāci* spirit may feature in such a proof. The proof is *not* intended to establish that such a *piśāci* is definitely not present but rather that an individual may not be in a position to judge whether it is present or not in a particular place, since the *piśāci* may lie outside the perceptual range of that individual. A proof that relies on such a reason must have a negandum—i.e., something that it rules out—but the *piśāci* cannot be that, because the proof is not designed to negate it. Nevertheless, since the *piśāci* is central to the proof and is also linked with that negandum, it is known as the "referent for the anti-predicate" (*dgag bya'i chos kyi don*) in the proof.

691. Tib. *blo'i tha snyad.*
692. Tib. *tha snyad sgrub pa.*
693. *Pramāṇavārttika* 1.200, 102a5.
694. The example of the termite mound crops up a number of times in Indian Pramāṇa literature. Such mounds may have central "chimneys" that function to regulate temperature. But in exactly what circumstances something emerging from the mound might be mistaken for smoke is uncertain.
695. This follows because according to this individual, the smoke would not be apparent even if it were present.
696. This passage, which Khedrup Jé says is from the autocommentary, remains unidentified, although if his remark about Śākyabuddhi's commentary on it below is correct, it should appear in the first few folios of the autocommentary. Hence this may be an established paraphrasing of Dharmakīrti's position.
697. Khedrup Jé reads the "nature" referred to in this passage not as the nature of what is being negated, smoke, but that of its cause, fire.
698. Śākyabuddhi, *Direct Commentary on the Pramāṇavārttika* (*Pramāṇavārttikaṭīkā*), chap. 1, Toh 4220 Tengyur, tshad ma, *je*, 17b4. The wording in the Dergé version differs.
699. This is the standard example of a correct proof in this category. "That which is observed by valid cognition" is asserted by most scholars to be the definition of existent. So many see this proof's reason, that pot is not observed by valid cognition, as a definition of its predicate (literally that "pot does not exist"). This gives rise to questions about what exactly such proofs are establishing and whether what they are primarily concerned with is correct designations.
700. *Pramāṇavārttika* 1.29, 95b7.
701. Śākyabuddhi, *Direct Commentary on the Pramāṇavārttika* (*Pramāṇavārttikaṭīkā*), chap. 1, Toh 4220 Tengyur, tshad ma, *je*, 44a5. The wording in the Dergé version is slightly different (*yang zhes bya ba ni dgag pa'i tha snyad bsgrub pa'i yang ngo / gtan tshigs ni rtags so*).
702. *Tha snyad byar rung.*
703. Tib. *bum pa med pa'i tha snyad.*
704. Khedrup Jé argues that the issue of whether an expression can legitimately be used is separate from whether the content of that expression is correct. So to establish to someone that it is legitimate to use the expression "there are no pots" may not bring that individual any closer to realizing that there are no pots in a particular location. Questions about the legitimacy of using particular designations are covered in the section "Correct reasons [dealing with] the issue of common agreement [about names]" (pp. 426–30).

705. *Pramāṇavārttika* 3.99, 122a5.
706. *Pramāṇavārttika* 4.265, 150a1.
707. *Pramāṇavārttika* 4.269, 150a3.
708. As remarked above (note 550), when the *establisher* and *established* are referred to as "cause" and "effect," it should not be viewed as a literal description in the sense of the former producing the latter. Instead, it indicates the sequence of their comprehension, since an individual first understands the establisher then the established.
709. The apparent disparity between the fact that these reasons are in the "non-observation" category while they actually involve the observation of a thing is indirectly addressed by Khedrup Jé below (p. 424). The point he makes is that even if the observation of something is cited as the reason, the probandum in such a proof is a negation.
710. "Antagonistic" and "mutual opposition" are the two forms of preclusion accepted in the tradition. They are discussed at some length by Gyaltsab Jé in the second text of this volume.
711. Vasubandhu, *Treasury of the Abhidharma* (*Abhidharmakośa*), 4.38, Toh 4089 Tengyur, mngon pa, *ku*, 12a6.
712. The most important point made in this discussion is that the existence of the category of reasons dealing with matters of conviction should *not* be interpreted to mean that one can simply use a reference in scripture as evidence in the sense that its status as scripture alone is enough to establish that what it says is true. Instead, using a reason belonging to this category obliges one to undertake some form of *analysis* of the scriptural passage's content.
713. This oft-cited passage is an Indian commentarial formulation of content attributed to the Buddha. It appears in Nāgārjuna, *Precious Garland* (*Ratnāvalī*), 5.38, Toh 4158 Tengyur, spring yig, *ge*, 123b1.
714. See note 675.
715. *Pramāṇavārttika* 1.214, 102b6.
716. *Pramāṇavārttika* 1.215, 102b6.
717. *Pramāṇavārttika* 1.215, 102b6.
718. *Pramāṇavārttika* 1.214, 102b5.
719. *Pramāṇavārttika* 1.214, 102b5.
720. *Pramāṇavārttika* 1.214, 102b6.
721. *Pramāṇavārttika* 1.215, 102b6.
722. *Pramāṇavārttika* 1.215, 102b6.
723. *Pramāṇavārttika* 1.215, 102b6.
724. That is, the content is not carved up into separate portions, each of which is then paired with a corresponding tool of analysis. Instead, the content is treated as a single domain, and the tools of the three analyses work on it collectively.
725. Scriptures are regarded as sound and are therefore heard by auditory cognition.
726. Tib. *gnod byed kyi tshad ma bzhi.* These four are perception and the three kinds of inferential valid cognition. What they each rule out is discussed below in the "Detailed explanation of the converse of what is not ruled out" (pp. 741–83).
727. *Pramāṇavārttika* 4.102, 143a7.
728. The main purpose of setting out this division of reason is to reaffirm the Buddhist philosophical principle that there is no logical or inherent relationship between an

object and its name. When authors like Khedrup Jé discuss how language relates to the things it denotes, one of their main aims from the Pramāṇa perspective is to counter the tendency exemplified by certain non-Buddhist Indian schools to essentialize and concretize the relationship. Even when Khedrup Jé is directly attacking a Tibetan scholar, he will often accuse him of falling into a similar trap. The theme running through much of the discussion is therefore the denial that the name and the thing share any sort of "special relationship" that has been ordained by some godhead, determined by a principle, or suggested by an essence inhering in that thing. But the refutation of a special relationship still leaves open many questions about how a name is attached to a thing and what the basis is for distinguishing between the correct and incorrect usage of names and, more generally, language. The additional slant to this for someone like Khedrup Jé, in the Pramāṇa context, is whether any of the answers to such questions can be established by means of logic. This is what leads the tradition to reject the route of etymology. The argument of those who say that the correct usage of a term is to be discovered in its derivation is very familiar to us. But while Geluk scholasticism encourages knowledge and analysis of etymologies, it sees a limited role for them in terms of logic. Etymologies are informative, but they cannot serve as the basis for the formulation of pervasions, watertight assertions, or negations. Nor is conventional usage identified as the arbiter of correctness in the linguistic sphere in the Geluk interpretation of Pramāṇa, although this is an issue explored in the third text in this volume, where we see differences emerging between Pramāṇa and Madhyamaka thinking on this issue. However, the points that Geluk scholars strongly emphasize when discussing the "common agreement" division is that what determines naming is choice and that choices are arbitrary. The simple fact of a thing's existence or its imaginability is enough to qualify it as one to which some name can be assigned: *x* can justifiably be referred to by the name *y* just because *x* exists. This does not mean that one could simply choose to assign names randomly hereafter. These things have become established by common agreement, or more properly by acceptance. The observations made here are about usage, and the insight is that things *could*, just as well, have been given different names.

729. Tib. *sgras brjod rung*. Following the Indian Pramāṇa treatises, this discussion about the legitimacy of using certain names for things uses the example of "moon" (Tib. *zla ba*). The analysis involves distinguishing between the thing and its name. To avoid the repetition and confusion that would ensue from using "moon" to denote both, it describes the thing as "(that which) has the hare." This is based on *śaśin*, a Sanskrit name for the moon. The Buddhist spin on this is that the hare or rabbit in question is the Buddha, who in an earlier existence (as a bodhisattva), gave his life for others by jumping into a fire, so impressing Brahmā that he imprinted the hare's image on the moon. But this actually reaches back into pre-Buddhist folklore. The idea of the so-called moon rabbit—i.e., the rabbit or hare whose image can be seen in the moon—is found in a number of cultures, in Asia and beyond. However, neither the figure nor its background has any special relevance to the discussion here. What is translated here as "sphere [marked] with the hare" is simply the standard subject used in the discussion of this category of proof.

730. Tib. *brda'*.

731. Nāgārjuna, *Fundamental Treatise on the Middle Way* (*Mūlamadhyamakakārikā*), 24.10, Toh 3824 Tengyur, dbu ma, *tsa*, 15a2.
732. Here the text incorrectly reads "class of similar instances" and has been corrected to fit with what appears below.
733. *Pramāṇavārttika* 1.97, 98a7.
734. The more literal (though uninformative) translation of *sgrub tshul gyi sgo nas* is "by way of the manner that they establish." Based on the context and historical debates about what separates the two divisions discussed here, *don* is translated as "thing [meant]," and *tha snyad* is rendered "names and expressions."
735. The designations for these two may appear to suggest a straightforward division between an object and the name attached to it. As also becomes clear, the distinction hinges on the separation between a definiendum and a definition. *However*, for Khedrup Jé and those in the Geluk tradition, neither the definiendum nor the definition are regarded as words. For instance, the definition—or more correctly, the characteristics defining—something such as a pot are that it is "a bulbous, flat-based (thing) able to perform the function of containing water," whereas the definiendum is the pot itself. In reality these are not, of course, distinguishable; only in the realm of words and thought is any separation between them possible. But there is still an *order* in which they can be known. That is, one first needs to recognize and isolate a certain set of characteristics—being bulbous, etc.—before one can understand that what these encapsulate is a "pot." What divides the two forms of reason under discussion here, therefore, is not that the first relates exclusively to objects whereas the second works with names and labels. It is true, however, that words and language are a stronger feature in the second.
736. While the inferential cognition is sometimes described as "that which has the reason" (*rtags can*), it must itself be preceded by the "cognition that grasps the reason" (*rtags 'dzin sems*). The information required to establish the property of the subject and the pervasions is drawn from different sources (i.e., separate perceptions and inferences). The individual must finally gather this information together to realize that the reason fulfills all three criteria, at which point the reason is said to be *grasped*. However, as Khedrup Jé explains in this section, scholars did not agree on the identity of this cognition.
737. This is a paraphrased version of Prajñākaragupta, *Ornament Commentary to Pramāṇavārttika* (*Pramāṇavārttikālaṃkāra*), Toh 4221 Tengyur, tshad ma, *te*, 214a.
738. This seems to be a highly paraphrased version of *Pramāṇaviniścayaṭīkā* chap. 2, 174b.
739. Śākyabuddhi, *Direct Commentary on Pramāṇavārttika* (*Pramāṇavārttikaṭīkā*), chap. 3, Toh 4220 Tengyur, tshad ma, *nye*, 173a6. This is a slightly abbreviated version of what appears in the Dergé edition.
740. *Pramāṇasamuccaya* 1.7, 2a2.
741. More literally, Khedrup Jé describes *fulfilling the three criteria* as the "isolated encapsulation" of a correct reason. Since he has already given this as the definition of a correct reason (p. 368), in this case he appears to treat the definition and isolated encapsulation as equivalent, although he does not always do this.
742. Here "recollection" (Tib. *dran pa*) is more about *bringing to mind* certain facts than remembering something from the past. The individual is literally required to

re-collect or gather together different facts that were cognized at earlier points in time.

743. The actual source for this is Dignāga, *Compendium of Pramāṇa Autocommentary* (*Pramāṇasamuccayavṛtti*), chap. 2, Toh 4204 Tengyur, tshad ma, *ce*, 35b2.
744. This "hare" is different from the ones in the two previous references (i.e., the "hare's horn" and the alternative name for the moon). The "proverbial hare" is the central character in a tale that has similarities with those in story cycles from other lands. In the Tibetan version, a stick falls into a well, and upon hearing the echoing sound, a hare believes that it issues from a beast. As the hare rapidly moves away from the well, the beast grows ever more dreadful in his imagination. Eventually, the hare races through the forest or jungle in a state of great agitation, shouting to the other animals to warn them of the horror. To conjure up the image of the proverbial hare in response to what someone says is to pour scorn on it and portray it as a confused, agitated, or baseless report.
745. The further objection seems to be that since it can equally be argued that something interposes between the reason and cognition of the reason, if the treatise was being consistent, it would not say that the first causes the second.
746. *Pramāṇavārttika* 3.81, 121b3.
747. As remarked above (note 240) Khedrup Jé sometimes buries self-references within his poetic lines. Here "true excellence" is his first name, Gelek (*dge legs*).
748. This is a clear articulation of the point made in the introduction.
749. Tib. *nges dka' sla*.
750. Tib. *dngos gyur gyi nam mkha'*.
751. This designation (*phyogs chos can*) notably features in the **Wheel of Reasoning: The Two-Headed Drum*, a short work attributed to Dignāga. The history of this work and its title (which in Sanskrit is now usually identified as *Hetucakraḍamaru*) are a little complicated but are picked apart by He and van der Kuijp 2016. This work focuses on the "nine reasons with the property of the subject in the thesis" (*phyogs chos can gyi gtan tshigs dgu*). The individual who Khedrup Jé refers to does not appear to be referencing these nine directly. But he asserts that a proof of the thesis-subject type requires a subject that *exists*. Since the Buddhist position is that space is not a real entity, he finds fault with the proof as it is originally formulated. As we have seen earlier in Khedrup Jé's text (pp. 381–84), the issue of whether it is necessary for the various elements of the proof to be existents has been a popular topic of discourse among Indian and Tibetan scholars.
752. The individual makes the distinction between *smras chos* and *zhe 'dod*.
753. *Pramāṇavārttika* 4.142, 145a1.
754. This is very similar to an unflattering remark made earlier (see note 369), but the reference to space here is also probably a pun on the space that is the topic of the discussion.
755. That is, all contrary proofs are defined by the *same* characteristic that Khedrup Jé identifies here. Whatever distinctions the Pramāṇa treatises seem to make should be understood as arising from Buddhist analyses of individual flaws in the reasons/proofs that non-Buddhist schools put forth. It does not mean that there are actually different categories of contrary reason with separate definitions.
756. *Pramāṇavārttika* 4.31, 140b2.
757. *Pramāṇaviniścaya* chap. 3, 190b6.
758. According to the Dergé catalogue, this is Dignāga, *Entrance to Reasoning*

(*Nyāyamukha*), Toh 4208 Tengyur, tshad ma, *ce*, 91a4. The work is actually *Entranceway to Reasoning* (*Nyāyapraveśaka*) by Śaṅkarasvāmin. The wording is also slightly different in the Dergé version.

759. See note above.

760. On two previous occasions, in the context of correct reasons, Khedrup Jé rejected this sort of distinction between the "actual" and "intended" proofs/reasons. Here, his analysis is of incorrect reasons, and he is considering a case where two proofs are derived from the same situation.

761. Here in the Tibetan, the terms for "noncomposite" (*'dus pa ma yin pa*) and "[cognitive] subject" (*yul can*) are conjoined by a particle that is classified as indicating the sixth case in the grammatical system, the genitive. Like the genitive in English, this set of particles can conjoin two elements to express that they are separate entities, and that the first possesses the second—e.g., if one wanted to communicate the Tibetan equivalent of "the farmer's cow." But there is another function of these particles that has no direct correspondence to the English genitive, where the two conjoined elements are not separate entities and the first describes the second. It is this second function that Khedrup Jé refers to here. Essentially what he says is that the word combination in question should be read as "noncomposite subject" and not "noncomposite's subject."

762. Catalogued as Dignāga, *Entrance to Reasoning* (*Nyāyamukha*), Toh 4208 Tengyur, tshad ma, *ce*, 91a5, but this is actually Śaṅkarasvāmin, *Entranceway to Reasoning* (*Nyāyapraveśaka*). The wording is also slightly different in the Dergé version.

763. Catalogued as Dignāga, *Nyāyamukha*, Toh 4208 Tengyur, tshad ma, *ce*, 91a2, but this is actually the *Entranceway to Reasoning* (*Nyāyapraveśaka*) by Śaṅkarasvāmin. The wording is slightly different in the Dergé version.

764. Asaṅga, *Abhidharmasamuccaya*, chap. 1, Toh 4049 Tengyur, sems tsam, *ri*.

765. *Pramāṇavārttika* 4.31, 140b2.

766. The last part of this section is slightly puzzling. Khedrup Jé began the section by identifying "Sound is permanent because it is produced" as the example of the first of the four contrary reasons, that in which the nature of the predicate of the proof is refuted. This is also the example of the reason given in Dignāga's **Wheel of Reasoning*. However, here the text appears to reject this. The corresponding passages in other versions of the text appear to match this one. The only solution I can see, apart from suggesting that the text might be corrupt at this point, is to propose that Khedrup Jé faults these individuals for failing to explain the standard examples of contrary reasons in the way that he does—i.e., that they are formulations "derived" from specific refutations.

767. Khedrup Jé says that the best qualification for performing a specific task is possession of the requisite skill. Someone such as a cattle farmer, for instance, can be an expert in judging a cow's age by the state of its teeth, whereas a better educated or more intelligent person without the necessary experience and skill may be hopeless at the task. Khedrup Jé implies that his expertise in logic uniquely qualifies him to perform the task of discerning its intricacies.

768. As the definition of this class of incorrect reason shows, inconclusive reasons are those for which another party has established the property of the subject but not the relationship necessary for the pervasion. The two subcategories of inconclusive reason both reference the notion of being "shared" (Tib. *thun mong ba*). The literal meaning of this term remains vague. But what those in the "shared"

subcategory have in common is that at least part of the reason is found in either the similar or dissimilar class. Those in the other subcategory are conversely *not* found among either class. Their name appears to derive from the fact that they are inconclusive reasons that are *not* of the "shared" variety (hence they are translated as "not shared" rather than "unshared"). Nevertheless, Khedrup Jé deals with this second subcategory first, seemingly because it has sparked more debate. The issue is about two statements cited in many scholarly Tibetan writings—namely, "the thing heard is not involved with anything other than [the subject] sound" (*mnyan bya sgra gzhan las mi 'jug*) and "the reason is not involved with anything other than the subject" (*rtags chos can las gzhan la mi 'jug*). These are both attributed to Dignāga and are said to convey a defining characteristic of the "not shared" variety. The exact source of these statements is unclear, and it seems likely that they are paraphrased. But the **Hetucakraḍamaru*, attributed to Dignāga, explicitly identifies the reason in the proof "Sound is impermanent because it is a heard thing" as the example of an inconclusive one of the not-shared variety. Why this proof is regarded as flawed is discussed above (note 654). But in this section of the text, the question is what Dignāga meant when he said that heard thing is *not involved with anything other* than sound. Tibetan scholars seem to have extrapolated from this to come up with the second statement, saying that an inconclusive reason of the not-shared variety must be one that is not involved with anything but the subject. Most of the discussion that follows in this section is about the meaning of "other" and "involved." Khedrup Jé criticizes various scholars' interpretations of these, saying that the features that they identify are *also* found among certain correct reasons, so they cannot be exclusive to this category of inconclusive reason. He argues that they could not therefore be what Dignāga meant.

769. Here the assertion is that heard thing is not involved with what is "other" than itself. But in what sense is this *otherness* intended? According to one of Tibetan scholasticism's favorite forms of analysis, things can be distinct from each other in one of two ways. The distinctions between them may be purely nominal, existing only on the conceptual level, or they may be substantive and real, inhering in the things themselves. Khedrup Jé first dismisses the possibility that the otherness here could be purely conceptual. On that level, even known thing is other than heard thing, simply by virtue of the fact that it is not identical with heard thing. Khedrup Jé argues that this is far too restrictive and cannot be what Dignāga meant by his statement.

770. "Phenomena not derived from effort" is a wider category than "actual thing not derived from effort," since, unlike the latter, it includes all permanent things. It is also a category that the latter belongs to and is, hence, involved with.

771. *Pramāṇavārttika* 1.14, 95a6.

772. Śākyabuddhi, *Direct Commentary on Pramāṇavārttika* (*Pramāṇavārttikaṭīkā*), chap. 1, Toh 4220 Tengyur, tshad ma, *je*, 27b5.

773. There are three separate terms that might be translated as "thesis." They all refer to different facets of what is essentially the same thing—the combined subject and predicate portions of the proof—what someone sets out to establish by means of reason. The term *dam bca'* is used primarily in the context of disputation, and refers to a thesis in the sense of being something that one party advances and might want to defend but others might seek to attack. The term used in the present section

of the text is *bsgrub bya*, which translates literally as "probandum." This technical language reflects that the concern lies more with the structure and mechanics of the proof. Accordingly, with this as their pivot, the various elements of the proof are assigned different designations. Here, the "probandum" is literally "that which is to be established." The "probans" (*sgrub byed*) is "that which establishes"—the reason that constitutes the evidence substantiating or confirming the thesis. And the "property of the probandum" or the predicate is "the quality being established (of the subject)." The third term (Tib. *phyogs*, Skt. *pakṣa*) that could be translated as thesis is often rendered more literally as "position." It does not feature much in this volume.

774. This is another succinct summary of the tradition's thinking.

775. The discussion here all springs from the way that Dignāga defined the correct thesis or probandum in *Pramāṇasamuccaya*. He did this through reference to five terms, and the following section explores what each of the five mean. This explains the curious phrasing of the subheading, which is a reference to the last of the five features—namely, that the content of a correct thesis must be something that is not ruled out by valid cognition. In the act of realizing its object, a valid cognition also always rules out something else (i.e., it negates some fact that is incorrect about that object). This section explores the fifth feature of the probandum, together with its converse—that is, what valid cognition and others are capable of ruling out.

776. "That which can be an object known" or "that which is fit to be known" (*blo yul du bya rung*) is held by some scholars to be the definition of *established basis* and by others to be the definition of *object of knowledge*. To say that something is "fit" to be known here does not indicate that understanding has any sort of limitation—it does not mean that while certain things are known, others await discovery, or are even unknowable. *What is known* is regarded as equivalent to *what exists*.

777. *Pramāṇasamuccaya* 3.2, 6a6. The wording of the translation in the Dergé version differs slightly.

778. In the explanation of the definition he proposes, the opponent introduces a conditional statement that essentially takes the form "If it is *x*, then it is *y*." Khedrup Jé's criticism is based on this. The problem he sees was encountered in an earlier section, when someone used a reason containing an internal pervasion (see note 632). Generally, there are no restrictions on the content and length of elements such as the predicate or reason. But they should not be logical statements in their own right, since this opens up complications in their relationship with the other elements of the proof or consequence.

779. Khedrup Jé refers here to a number of important principles relating to the Geluk theory of definitions, either mentioned or alluded to in the introduction. One part of the theory views the definition and the definiendum as categories. It concerns itself with establishing that the categories are coterminous, meaning that every instantiation of one is an instantiation of the other. The definition must therefore be entirely watertight, meaning that it can only be regarded as correct if it encompasses everything it needs to and excludes everything that does not belong. But what Khedrup Jé refers to in the text at this point is another important aspect, that of the definition's role in generating knowledge and bringing about cognition. If *x* is the definition and *y* is the definiendum, then *x* must be simpler to understand

than *y*. An understanding of *x* must also generally precede that of *y*. It should be possible to "spell out" *x* and explain the characteristics comprising it separately. But *x* should not be self-referential in this—it must be possible to understand *x* without needing to refer to *y* or refer back to any portion of *x*. As was remarked in the introduction, in a general sense, the tradition's theory of definitions shares affinities with principles of dictionary compilation. But the Geluk tradition goes much further in developing the epistemological dimension of this. Thus the disallowing of any portion of *x* being used to explain *x* is partly to avert the fallacy of circular logic. But as seen here in the text, this also has an interesting practical dimension. It should, at least in theory, be possible to identify an individual who comes to know *y* through knowing *x* and also explain how the process of understanding or cognition unfolds. As Khedrup Jé suggests here, some things must be ruled out as definitions on the grounds that there is no conceivable situation or set of circumstances in which they could feasibly function as definitions.

780. According to the Dergé catalogue, this is Dignāga, *Nyāyamukha*, Toh 4208 Tengyur, tshad ma, *ce*. But this work is actually Śaṅkarasvāmin, *Entranceway to Reasoning* (*Nyāyapraveśaka*). The passage cited here does not correspond directly to any in the Dergé version of the work, although one line on 89b2 has some similarities with its wording.

781. This is another succinct summary of the tradition's thinking.

782. On this and similar occasions, Khedrup Jé is referring the reader to his other major work on Pramāṇa, *Ocean of Reasoning: Extensive Explanation of the Commentary on Pramāṇa.*

783. *Pramāṇavārttika* 4.92, 143a1.

784. *Pramāṇavārttika* 2.222, 116a3.

785. Differences between the grammar of Tibetan and English make this point a little difficult to get across. But this individual uses a particle that, despite having certain similarities with one indicating the genitive case, belongs to the instrumental case—that is, he replaces the more normal *tshad mas bsal ba* with *tshad ma'i bsal ba*—and implies that this allows for a finer distinction to be made. Khedrup Jé dismisses this, arguing that this supposed finesse achieves nothing.

786. "Thing heard" is the definition of sound, so the two are technically equivalent. Khedrup Jé's argument can be summed up: when two things, *x* and *y*, are equivalent, *x* not being *y* is not true, but the negation of *x* not being *y* is true. His final line literally means "All known things are [confirmation] of that" (*shes bya thams cad de yin pa'i phyir*), and like the example above (see notes 632 and 663), is used earnestly and not as a piece of trickery. But here it is simply offered in support of this argument. It can be understood to mean that nothing in existence counters the aforementioned fact, and by implication, there is nothing that does not confirm it. In other words, whatever object we might choose to speak of, that negation remains a fact.

787. Here, and more generally, when a thing is said to be "possible" or a "possibility" (*srid pa*), this simply means that it exists or can exist (within a category, and so forth), even if a given individual may not yet have cognized this fact. It should not be confused with logical possibility, in the sense of a proposition that cannot be disproved according to the rules of some logical system. Nor does it mean something that may be true in some *possible* world, distinguished from the actual one.

788. That is, according to the opponent's description, anything defined must have an illustration through which it is instantiated. "A thing heard" is the definition of sound, and in establishing that to be the case, valid cognition must rule out that sound is *not* a thing heard. Thus "Sound is not a thing heard" should be able to serve as an illustration of something that is negated by valid cognition. But since it does not exist, how can it be the illustration of that? And if nothing can serve as such an illustration of *ruled out by valid cognition*, how can the latter be said to qualify as a thing defined?

789. Tib. *mtshan mtshon gyi rnam gzhag*. The illustration helps one to forge the link between definition and definiendum. Thus the "model" formed by these three mutually supporting elements is one way of referring to the tradition's theory of definitions. Aspects of this are discussed throughout the text and are summarized in note 779. At the theory's heart is the idea that a thing is embodied by a characteristic or set of characteristics that define it. "Personal" characteristics, such as aspects of someone's individuality, or those confined to single, unique objects, are not of interest here. The tradition concerns itself with those that define classes or groups of things, and that might have value in terms of the extension of knowledge.

790. Tib. *khyab mnyam*. This terse formulation is one of the text's few explicit mentions of a principle that is vital to Geluk thinking, especially in its theory of definitions. As already discussed, a definition must be easier to understand than a definiendum, and in this sense, the two are not equal. However, in another, logical sense, they must be entirely equal, in that to serve as definition and definiendum, the two must share the exact same boundaries. This is expressed in terms of the "rules of coterminosity," which apply both to being (or identity) and existence (or presence) of the things in question. Using x and y to represent these, the rules of "coterminosity" are that (1) anything that is x is necessarily y, and vice versa, (2) anything that is not x is not y, and vice versa, (3) wherever there is x there is y, and vice versa, and (4) wherever there is no x there is no y, and vice versa.

791. See notes 549 and 789.

792. As mentioned in note 779, definitions generally apply to many things. The idea that something has no instantiations is seen as logically problematic.

793. That a thing is one with itself is regarded as fundamental to its existence. Being one with itself is therefore denied for things that do not exist.

794. This appears to be Rongtön Sheja Kunrik, *Solar Essence*, 308b–309a.

795. *Pramāṇavārttika* 4.110, 143b4.

796. Being comprehended by valid cognition is introduced into the discussion at this point as the converse of being ruled out by valid cognition. Furthermore, the things that valid cognition is said to comprehend or rule out are distinguished from those that valid inference comprehends or rule out. In this regard the two cognitions have separate domains.

797. *Pramāṇavārttika* 4.135, 144b4.

798. There is more on what it means for one statement to "impede" another in the next section.

799. In this section, Khedrup Jé refers to the assertion "Dharma [practices] such as generosity yield pleasure" as the thesis. However, as he explains below, this thesis could not serve as the probandum of a proof dealing with a matter of conviction. It should more accurately be described as the *content* of the passage of scripture

that serves as the subject in such a proof. Nevertheless, at the point that the proof is established, the content of the passage is realized to be nondeceptive. And the realization that the thesis is nondeceptive must in some way rule out its converse (or antithesis), "Dharma [practices] such as generosity do not yield pleasure." In this section Khedrup Jé considers how this is the case.

800. *Pramāṇaviniścayaṭīkā* chap. 3, 43a6.
801. A proof that aims to establish that sound is impermanent can use "(because it is) produced" as its reason, but not "(because it is) sound's production." This is explained by the fact that realization of a proof's pervasion must precede realization of its thesis. If "(because it is) sound's production" was the proof's reason, anyone who realized the pervasion would ascertain that "sound's production" is present only in the class of impermanent things, and thus, in realizing the pervasion, would essentially have established the thesis "Sound is impermanent."
802. *Pramāṇavārttika* 4.94, 143a3.
803. Khedrup Jé identifies two main views on how the thesis rules out its converse or antithesis. According to some, the thesis genuinely "counters" the antithesis, which here means to totally invalidate it. Others deny that the thesis has the power to do this, saying instead that all it can do is "impede" the antithesis, meaning that it can prevent it from being established. Both Geluk and Sakya scholars engaged in the debate over which view was correct, but they were not split neatly across this divide. Khedrup Jé is measured in his comments. His description steers a careful course, as he tries to show how the existence of the category of proofs/inferences of conviction must be understood not to challenge certain important principles. There is a section similar to this one in Gendun Drup's *Ornament of Pramāṇa Reasoning* (346–50). But the conclusions Gendrun Drup reaches are slightly different.
804. *Pramāṇavārttika* 4.92, 143a2.
805. Thus these individuals assert that there must be some basis, established by valid cognition, with respect to which the factual thesis and its converse—namely, the antithesis, that the practices do and not yield the results in question—are in direct conflict.
806. *Pramāṇaviniścayaṭīkā* chap. 3, 43b4.
807. *Pramāṇavārttika* 4.101, 143a6.
808. *Pramāṇaviniścaya* chap. 3, 196b7.
809. The main point that Khedrup Jé and others want to communicate through their examination of proofs dealing with matters of conviction is that "because the Buddha said so" cannot directly be used as a reason to logically establish things that are extremely hidden. Thus the way to structure a correct proof involving a matter of conviction is *not* to use something like "Dharma [practices] such as generosity" as a subject and "yield pleasure" as the predicate. Instead, the subject for this type of proof must be a passage of scripture, and the remainder of the proof must present evidence that the content of that passage has been subjected to the required analysis.
810. Tib. *sgrub byed 'phen pa'i thal 'gyur* and *sgrub byed mi 'phen pa'i thal 'gyur.*
811. Tib. *bzlog pa rang rigs 'phen pa'i thal 'gyur* and *gzhan rigs 'phen pa'i thal 'gyur.*
812. Tib. *phyogs*. As mentioned in the earlier note 113, "position" is an alternative name for the thesis.
813. Khedrup Jé says that to explain the phrase in question, these opponents find it necessary to evoke the hypothetical example of something (x) that manages to be

the correct reason despite not meeting the criteria. But he argues that this hypothetical thing is one that does not exist. Any failing attributed to it must therefore be only an imagined one. The Tibetan for "without failing" (*skyon med*), like the English "flawless," suggests more than just the absence of some flaw; it connotes something that is immaculate and unblemished.

814. Although Khedrup Jé's argument is not entirely clear, he is perhaps playing on the Tibetan term translated here as "any" (*gang rung*), which is problematic when combined with a negation in the argumentation format.

815. The Tibetan word here (*yon tan*) has similar positive connotations to the English "quality." A person "with qualities" (*yon tan can*) can also be interpreted as someone who is "qualified," in the sense of being educated or learned. But unlike the English word, the Tibetan one is almost never used in a neutral sense.

816. Khedrup Jé revisits the distinction he seemed to reject above. But we note that in keeping with what he wrote earlier, he only distinguishes between a quality and a failing in terms of a single, *incorrect* reason and proof.

817. The Tibetan term here (*dgag pa*) encompasses "negation" and "negative (thing)," and both senses are covered in the discussion, without switches between the two being signposted. The first should be understood as an exclusion that occurs in the domains of thought and language, whereas the second is a thing arrived at through that exclusion. Discourses on "negation" center on how such exclusions appear in the mind and are articulated in words. But in those on the "negative," the focus is on the things to which these negations refer. For instance, non-pot can be treated as akin to a quality—not an affirmative trait but a mentally constructed fact about things that are not pots (i.e., their non-potness). "Pillar," for instance, is a non-pot or can be said to have the quality of being a non-pot. Non-pot can also be regarded as something that itself has properties, such as when it is said that "non-pot exists" or "non-pot is present in location *x*." And since not being a pot is true of many things, "non-pot" can also be viewed as a category to which everything (both actual and non-actual) other than pots belongs.

818. This does not represent standard Geluk thinking. There is universal agreement that object of knowledge is a construct and therefore permanent—which is true of any universal that numbers constructs among its particulars. But in mainstream Geluk, the corollary of this is *not* that such things are necessarily negative. Khedrup Jé restates his position at the end of the current section. But he neither elaborates much on his reasoning nor refers to any opponents of his view. It seems unlikely, therefore, that he saw himself as challenging any orthodox line on this matter.

819. Bhāviveka, *Tarkajvālā*, Toh 3856 Tengyur, dbu ma, *dza*, 59b5.

820. This is generally represented as the lowest of the four "castes" (*varṇas*) and stands at the opposite end of the scale to the brahman. Not being a brahman, however, does not necessarily mean that one is a *śūdra*. So the statement here might be intended as one that is understood through context, as described in one of the examples below.

821. Bhāviveka, *Tarkajvālā*, Toh 3856 Tengyur, dbu ma, *dza*, 59b4.

822. Avalokitavrata, *Prajñāpradīpaṭīkā*, Toh 3859, Tengyur, dbu ma, *wa*, 63b6.

823. Khedrup Jé makes a tidy equation between affirmative phenomena and actual things on the one hand, and between negative phenomena and permanent (or conceptually constructed) phenomena on the other. What he says here suggests

that his thinking stems from a more expansive notion of dependence (or a more restricted notion of independence) than most other Geluk scholars. So, for him, anything that can only be understood through a negation *depends* on a negandum, and as such, is not entirely independent. Hence he aligns this form of reliance with lacking individual characteristics, causes, and so forth.

824. Tib. *mi mthun par gnas pa.*
825. This is an unusual passage, since Khedrup Jé appears to present himself as a witness to an exchange between two other parties. When he finally intervenes, he does not, as we might expect, dismiss the positions of both parties. Instead, he says that the argument one of them used against the definition proposed by the other was not a sound one. This, despite the fact that he rejects the definition himself.
826. *Pramāṇavārttika* 2.212, 115b4.
827. According to the particular slant that Khedrup Jé puts on the Tibetan word translated as "negate" (*'gog pa*), here it means to actively cancel out or nullify.
828. That is to say, just as it is the case that produced is pervaded (i.e., encompassed) by impermanent, meaning that whatever is produced is necessarily impermanent, yellow is pervaded by non-blue, meaning that whatever is yellow is necessarily non-blue.
829. *Pramāṇavārttika* 2.212, 115b4.
830. This designation (*gzhung lugs pa*) was used to refer to scholars of the Sangphu tradition.
831. Tib. *tshad mas gnod 'gal.*
832. *Pramāṇavārttika* 4.278, 150b2.
833. *Pramāṇavārttika* 4.279, 150b2.
834. *Pramāṇavārttika* 4.279, 150b2. A single word difference in the Dergé version (*des gyur* instead of *nges gyur*) alters the reading significantly.
835. The term Khedrup Jé uses here stresses that the "ruling out" (*khegs pa*) of *x* or *y* is an act of comprehension. The terms Gyaltsab Jé chooses when defining logical relationship (p. 547) bring out another dimension, highlighting that this ruling out is conceptual.
836. Khedrup Jé says that in the foregoing text he has detailed the various cases in which it is necessary to separate between the scheme or classification itself and the things to which it applies.
837. Tib. *brda'i dbang gis rang yul go byed.*
838. The "excluding perspective" (*sel ngo*) and the related "excluding engager" (*sel 'jug*) were introduced earlier (see note 90 and the glossary).
839. Tibetan and Sanskrit make similar formal distinctions between vowels and consonants but, when identifying the consonants, represent them as having an inherent *a* sound.
840. Khedrup Jé alluded to this category (*ldan min 'du byed*) above (see note 456), but this is the only point in the text where it is directly named.
841. *Pramāṇavārttika* 1.238, 103b4.
842. *Pramāṇavārttika* 2.2, 107b4.
843. Khedrup Jé makes the point that the single term *pot* can be used in different situations, so there is nothing wrong with saying that it is a type-communicator in one situation and an assemblage-communicator in another. However, when viewed as embedded within certain word combinations, such as "golden pot" or "pot's form,"

it can only be one or the other, depending on what the word combinations in question are intended to convey.

844. *Pramāṇavārttika* 2.101, 111b1.

845. As with other topics covered within the nine summaries in the third section of this work, Khedrup Jé deals with this very concisely. He explores it at much greater length in the *Ocean of Reasoning*, his commentary to Dharmakīrti's *Commentary on Pramāṇa*, chap. 2, 61b–62b. The present work does not discuss the overt objects of these type-communicating and assemblage-communicating words. These are known as *type universals* (*rigs spyi*) and *assemblage universals* (*tshogs spyi*). The term usually translated as "universal" (Tib. *spyi*, Skt. *sāmānya*) features heavily in Geluk Pramāṇa writings. It functions as an independent term but is also used in the names of more specific varieties of "universal," like the aforementioned type universal and assemblage universal, as well as those encountered earlier in the text like the object universal and sound universal. A common interpretation of Dharmakīrti on the distinction between type universals and assemblage universals is that the things covered by or conceptually gathered together within the type universal are homogenous ones, whereas those gathered together within the assemblage universal (or perhaps the "collection universal") are heterogeneous ones. This is indeed one of the views that Jamyang Shepa puts forth in the third text in this volume prior to rejecting it. But to reiterate a point made in the introduction, Geluk understanding of the concept does not always accord with expectations and perhaps stretches the idea of a "universal." For Geluk scholars, the overt theme running through the various iterations is not necessarily universality or generality per se, but the idea of something within which many parts or elements are gathered or contained. In the strict sense, these elements are the particulars or individuations of a thing. The type universal obviously conforms with this, since it covers many things that are of the same type, which are necessarily homogenous. This is not literally the case for the assemblage universal, which as Khedrup Jé's explanation of pot hints, refers to a material assemblage. Here, the things in question are its diverse parts, and these are neither homogenous nor individuations of the pot (in that they are not themselves pots). For this reason, Geluk scholars generally do not count the assemblage universal as a genuine form of universal. Still, it is enumerated together with the others in that those parts are *gathered within* or encompassed by the pot.

846. The distinction between property communicators and subject communicators—which Dharmakīrti covers in the same section of chapter 2 in his treatise as the one dealing with assemblage communicators and type communicators—is explained through referring to "examples." The main question is how the words *within* these examples (i.e., combinations of words) relate to each other. The issues are complicated not only by differences between English and Tibetan but also by those between Tibetan and Sanskrit. But the terms *horseness* and *horse* derive from a single Tibetan term (*rta*), and likewise *non-horseness* and *non-horse* are essentially the same in Tibetan (*rta ma yin* {*pa*}). The crucial distinction between the examples for the property communicators and subject communicators is that the first includes a genitive particle. When non-horseness is conjoined with cow by means of this particle, it is regarded as making what it denotes very specific—this is the *cow's* non-horseness.

847. When it is asserted that the difference between property communicators and

subject communicators lies in whether the two convey other properties, it is usually understood to mean that the property communicator, by virtue of its specificity (e.g., that the non-horseness it conveys is that of cow) is the one that *excludes* other properties. Khedrup Jé's accusation against the individual in question here is that either through misunderstanding or clumsiness, instead of correctly aligning exclusion with non-conveying and nonexclusion with conveying, he identifies the negative notion of exclusion with the positive one of conveying. Hence he ends up with the property communicator conveying other properties. The consequence that Khedrup Jé draws from this is that "non-horseness of cow" conveys *all* the "non-horse" properties of cow, including that of its selflessness.

848. At first glance, these examples appear to be in the wrong order. But this is neither a mistake of a translator or scribe nor Khedrup Jé's own unusual take on the matter. Generally speaking, the vocabulary used to convey the distinction between a *subject, base*, etc., and the *quality, attribute*, etc., that belongs to it is close enough in Tibetan to what exists in English as to present no major challenges to translation. *However*, here there is a difference associated with the sixth (i.e., genitive) grammatical case arising out of the Sanskrit and reproduced in the Tibetan. It manifests in what appears to be a counterintuitive reversal of what constitutes the "basis" (*khyad gzhi*) and the "property" (*khyad chos*). If asked to distinguish between the property and subject (i.e., the basis) in "cow's non-horseness," one would be likely to identify "cow" as the subject, and "non-horseness" as the property it possesses. But here, the opposite is the case. Non-horseness is the subject/basis, and only when something else is appended to it can it become particularized. When "cow" is added, this non-horseness gains specificity, being distinguished, for instance, from the buffalo's non-horseness. As the one that makes the distinction, "cow" is therefore regarded as the distinguishing feature or property.

849. The word to which the particle is attached and qualifies is "archer." In Tibetan, which has no true indefinite particle, this is attached immediately after the name here, akin to "archer indeed."

850. Khedrup Jé appears to refer readers back to the long section on specifically and generally characterized things, although discussions about the distinctions between the universal and the particular could be said to pervade the whole text.

851. The term translated as "positive" here (*sgrub pa*) is the same the one used for "affirmative" in the first of the nine sections ("The negative and the affirmative"). Khedrup Jé starts here by declaring that the *positive* should be regarded as equivalent to what literally translates as "appearance" (*snang ba*). In the present context, the term *appearance* does not refer to an image or representation of another—something that may appear to be *x* but in reality is not. Instead, it denotes the *actual* thing—that is, a specifically characterized phenomenon, capable of presenting *itself* (i.e., its *own* appearance) to perception.

852. Tib. *snang 'jug*. The more common term for this is "comprehensive engager" (*sgrub 'jug*).

853. *Pramāṇavārttika* 1.169, 101a3.

854. Śākyabuddhi, *Direct Commentary on the Pramāṇavārttika* (*Pramāṇavārttikaṭīkā*), chap. 1, Toh 4220 Tengyur, tshad ma, *je*, 200b3.

855. What follows are two alternative, but very similar, threefold divisions of exclusion. The threefold division of other-exclusion—usually based on the second ver-

sion here—recurs throughout later Geluk scholastic literature, and is a staple of the Collected Topics works. Khedrup Jé's explanation of the three follows Śākyabuddhi and brings a good deal of clarity to the area. The three are neither different varieties of exclusion nor indeed all actually exclusions. Rather, they are the three elements involved within the action of exclusion. There is a longer parallel discussion of the divisions in chapter 1 of Khedrup Jé's *Ocean of Reasoning* (129b–133a).

856. Śāntarakṣita, *Tattvasaṃgraha*, chap. 20, Toh 4266 Tengyur, tshad ma, *ze*, 37b4.

857. *Commentary on the Difficult Points of the Compendium of Suchness* (*Tattvasaṃgrahapañjikā*), chap. 20, Toh 4267 Tengyur, tshad ma, *ze*, 338a6.

858. The two different functions of the sixth-case grammatical particles are explained above (see note 761). Khedrup Jé states here that the two words in the combination should be understood to refer to a single entity. Generally, the second word (*chos*) can denote either "phenomenon" or "property." Reading the two as separate is more likely to give rise to the second reading, which Khedrup Jé says is incorrect.

859. As noted above (see note 830), Khedrup Jé uses this designation to denote scholars of the Sangphu tradition. The criticism he makes at this point in the text certainly also applies to Chapa Chökyi Sengé, whose *Banisher of Ignorance [Relating to] Pramāṇa* explains the way that *definiendum* and *definition* are themselves defined in a manner referred to by Khedrup Jé.

860. Tradition ascribes the creation of the distinction between substantive and reversed properties to Chapa Chökyi Sengé, and there is some historical evidence to support this. Khedrup Jé's criticism here is clearly directed at Chapa Chökyi Sengé and those who followed the approach developed at Sangphu Monastery. Later, composers of works in the Collected Topics genre, which was first developed at Sangphu but was later adopted in the Geluk tradition, apparently based themselves on Chapa Chökyi Sengé's original division, and assigned an independent chapter to the topic of substantive and reversed properties. As the name suggests, the "substantive" property is tied to the notion of a substance—something that is generally understood to be affirmative and concrete. A "reverse" property refers not to the reverse *of* a property (i.e., a non-property), but one that is reached through a process of exclusion. Khedrup Jé's explanation is a much simpler conception of what distinguishes the two than that found in the Collected Topics works, and his comments here are a somewhat restrained criticism of the latter.

861. Tibetan generally distinguishes between "single" (*gcig*, a word that also means "one") and "same" (*gcig pa*). That is, the first denotes an individual thing that is not part of a pair or larger group, whereas the second refers to two or more things that, due to either being identical or sharing some variety of close correspondence, are judged to match one another. However, within the binary under discussion here, which is one of the most ubiquitous in Mahayana analytical thinking, the two terms and concepts converge, with one word (*gcig*) encompassing *both*. This convergence explains what might seem to the outsider to be a failure to respect the borders separating two different concepts. That said, it is usually clear from the context *which* of the two understandings is being referenced. In Madhyamaka analysis, it is more common to encounter the *single* meaning, whereas in Pramāṇa thinking, more attention is given to the notion of *sameness* (i.e., different ways in which two or more things might count as being the same). In his extremely brief treatment of this binary, however, Khedrup Jé here identifies what binds

these two concepts of singularity and sameness together, namely, the *absence of separation*.

862. Khedrup Jé dealt with the topic at some length in his analysis of specifically characterized phenomena.
863. This section deals with a topic that has featured in Buddhist scholarly discourse for many centuries. In spite of the title, it is less about time itself than objects within time, and what it means for something to belong to any of the three times. Outside discussions on Madhyamaka, Tibetan scholars have generally aligned "actual" existence with belonging to the present.
864. "Clay pot" (*rdza bum*) seems more likely than the "substantial pot" (*rdzas bum*) that appears in the text.
865. The notion of a "charioteer" (Tib. *shing rta srol 'byed*) denotes someone who plays a trailblazing or groundbreaking role and typically refers to Nāgārjuna and Asaṅga, in recognition of their establishment of the Madhyamaka and Cittamātra systems.
866. The text literally says, "the play of falling nails" (*sen mo lhung ba'i rtse dga'*), but I am unsure about the role of "falling" here. "Play of nails" is also opaque.
867. The final verses of dedication and the Sanskrit phrases are not part of the Khedrup Jé's original composition. They were appended to the version of the text that was produced at Tashi Lhunpo Monastery.
868. For Khedrup Jé on this, see page 507 and note 827.
869. There are similarities between this individual's position and the one refuted in Khedrup Jé's section on preclusion. In both cases, the individual asserts that blue and yellow do not preclude one another and also seems to hold that "countering" is central to preclusion (although this last point is clearer in Khedrup Jé's text). One of the responses of the opponent in both cases is also the same, and it does not seem unlikely that it is in fact the same person, although we cannot be certain of this. But by comparing the two sections, we see not only correspondences in the ways that Gyaltsab Jé and Khedrup Jé argue but also the slightly different avenues of reasoning that each explore.
870. *Pramāṇaviniścaya* chap. 3, 194a5.
871. According to the opponent, countering necessarily involves two things with separate roles, the "counter" (*gnod byed*) and the "countered" (*gnod bya*). Gyaltsab Jé raises the question of whether this suggests a disparity in the strength of the two elements. But he is not rejecting the relevance of countering to preclusion. Rather, as we see below, he is saying that it characterizes only one variety of preclusion.
872. Gyaltsab Jé introduces a conundrum. The opponent now insists that two things, such as permanent and impermanent, can only be posited as directly preclusive if there is a specific base in which this can be demonstrated—that is, something that instantiates that preclusion. But how is an instantiation possible for two things that preclude each other? The pot and the woolen cloth exist, as an ad hoc couple of individual things. But there is nothing that can be both, since a common locus of them is not possible. So to say that they instantiate anything becomes problematic.
873. The two proofs that Gyaltsab Jé refers to are:
    1. *X* [A] does not truly exist [B], because it is neither truly single nor truly different [C].

2. *X* [A] is a definiendum [B], because it has the three properties of imputation [C].

He alludes to the fact that other scholars identified these as examples that posed challenges to the system of logic or broke its rules. They argued that even though these were widely accepted to be correct proofs, they did not fulfill one of its basic criteria. A correct proof demands that the reason be totally absent from the class of dissimilar instances—a principle encapsulated in the third of the correct reason's three criteria. But these scholars claimed that in the two proofs in question, the reason was in fact present in that class. It is perhaps not necessary to go into the thinking behind this claim here since it involves intricacies of the theory of definitions. More important is the point made by Gyaltsab Jé that the way that one goes about establishing the presence or absence of a thing in a certain class is in terms of common loci. That is, to establish that object *x* is present in class *y*, one must determine that a common locus of *x* and *y* exists, and to establish that *x* is absent from *y* one must determine that no common locus of them exists. The even more specific point he makes here is that a common locus must be something that instantiates *x* and *y*—i.e., it must be a genuine case of something that *is* both *x* and *y*. Gyaltsab Jé says that the misguided arguments and examples introduced by these other scholars show that they have failed to recognize that this is the correct approach.

874. The section Gyaltsab Jé refers to is in Chapa Chökyi Sengé's *Banisher of Ignorance [Relating to] Pramāṇa*, 68a–b.

875. Preclusion is considered here in terms of how it relates to the progression from the path of preparation to the path of seeing (i.e., advancing from the second of the five paths to the third). More specifically, it refers to the last stage of the path of preparation, the *supreme dharma level*, and the first stage of the path of seeing, *the dharma forbearance level*, regarding sufferings (also see note 50). It is upon progression to the latter that the individual first realizes emptiness or selflessness directly, i.e., through perception, and thereby becomes an ārya. This initial perception of the truth begins the process of actually countering elements (starting with certain "seeds") that ārya paths alone can eradicate. This ability to eradicate is what makes these ārya paths "true paths." The paths that actually engage in eradication are called "transcendent" or "supramundane" paths. Within these, there are two serial stages, the uninterrupted path and the released path (see note 537). The former is the one that actually counters the undesired element. With the latter, the individual gains freedom from what was being countered and thereby achieves a "true cessation."

876. "Acquisition" (Tib. *thob pa*, Skt. *prāpti*), sometimes translated as "obtainment," belongs to the category of nonassociated compounded things. Some details about it are found in Chim Jampaiyang, *Ornament of Abhidharma*, 245–57. Buddhist thinkers in India sought to explain how the individual's association with certain nonmaterial phenomena was maintained over time. The Vaibhāṣika school posited that aquisition was an entity or quality, due to the presence of which individual's mindstream could be said to *possess* or *have* certain nonphyscial things, even when, as in the case of previous actions, their performance was confined to the past, or in the case of some states of abandonment attainable through the path, they had yet to be fully achieved. Even though there was no Vaibhāṣika school in Tibet, Chapa

Chökyi Sengé was perhaps the most prominent figure to be criticized for adopting aspects of Vaibhāṣika philosophy.

877. Gyaltsab Jé asserts that preclusion cannot be defined through reference to a single element. Whether antagonistic preclusion is described in terms of elimination or countering, there are necessarily two elements involved, and the definition should reflect this. Arguing against the opponent's thinking, Gyaltsab Jé first draws a parallel. In Tibetan, the term for "[cognitive] subject" (*yul can*) literally means "that which has an *object*." He suggests therefore that unless object and subject are viewed in relational terms and as mutually dependent, their concepts make no sense. His second argument is that by seeking to define antagonistic preclusion purely in terms of something that *counters*, the opponent has excluded the thing that is countered from the equation, meaning that the definition does not apply to it.

878. It is essential to understand that darkness is not being regarded here as the *absence* of light. Light, dark, heat, and cold are all affirmative phenomena. They are viewed as physical matter, composed of particles. This is one of the features that distinguishes the analogy from the target.

879. *Pramāṇaviniścayaṭīkā* chap. 2, 206a1. The wording does not match the Dergé version exactly.

880. Asaṅga, *Abhidharmasamuccaya*, chap. 2, Toh 4049 Tengyur, sems tsam, *ri*, 85a3. The Dergé version translates as "How is it dispatched? It is not from something of the past, since that has already ceased. It is not from something of the future, since that has not occurred. It is not that which is now arisen, since that does not operate concurrent with the path" (*gang zhig gang las spong zhe na / 'das pa ni 'gags pa'i phyir ma yin no / ma 'ongs pa ni ma byung ba'i phyir ma yin no / da ltar byung ba ni lam dang mnyam du mi 'jug pa'i phyir ma yin no*).

881. As discussed by Paṇchen Sönam Drakpa, in his *Lamp Illuminating the Meaning*, 191–93, for those in the Hinayana system, as described in Vasubandhu's *Treasury of the Abhidharma*, for the uninterrupted path to work, the element it eradicates must be manifest together with it. Those in the Mahayana system reject this and explain the process as Gyaltsab Jé has. The section in *Compendium of Abhidharma* is raised as an objection, with the opponent suggesting that Asaṅga implied that the seeds are present, meaning that he held the view that something needed to be manifest for the path to work against it. Gyaltsab Jé rebuts this and again explains that the process is one that involves simultaneity, in that the path is on the verge of production at the same time that the elements to be eradicated, including the seeds, are on the verge of destruction, but once the uninterrupted path is actually generated, the eradication is complete, so the two are never present together. Gyaltsab Jé also refers to an analogy used by Haribhadra to explain the process. He likens the element being eradicated to a thief and says that the point that the thief has been expelled from one's home and the door having been closed behind him occur simultaneously. Thus, Gyaltsab Jé asserts, Haribhadra was not calling for Asaṅga's analogy to be replaced or to be explained in another manner, since he regarded it as correct as it stood.

882. To summarize Gyaltsab Jé's position with respect to this first type of preclusion, it is not that *x* counters *y* by attacking and weakening it. If it did, one would need to assert that *y* (in its now weakened state) was the *effect* of *x*. But this would go against the whole notion of Buddhist causality, which is based on the idea that a

cause is something that "aids" or "helps" an effect come into existence, as expressed in the definition of a cause, which is "that which helps produce." So the notion of *x* simultaneously helping and incapacitating *y* would be regarded as paradoxical. Gyaltsab Jé proposes instead that it is through the arising of *x* that *y* is *deprived* of the conditions it requires to reproduce.

883. With this form of preclusion, in the negation of *x*, there is necessarily the affirmation of *y*. This process is not explained to be a methodical one. It is simply that when one correctly negates a certain thing, such as *x*, *y* is automatically or naturally affirmed. Furthermore, the "exclusion" (*rnam bcad*) and "[affirmative] discerning" (*yongs gcod*) of this definition indicate that these are forms of *realization* (one with a negative aspect, the other with a positive aspect). That is to say, the discussion is not concerned with exclusion and affirmation in an abstract sphere of logic but on the level of cognition.

884. *Pramāṇaviniścaya* chap. 1, 157b4.

885. *Pramāṇaviniścayaṭīkā* chap. 1. This seems to be a highly paraphrased version of the position Dharmottara sets out, beginning on the line identified.

886. Summing up the main point made by Gyaltsab Jé in this section, for two things to be preclusive in the sense of a mutual opposition that is direct, it must be the case that the affirmation of one necessarily brings with it the exclusion of the other, and also that the exclusion of one necessarily brings with it the affirmation of the other. That is, the result is the same whether taken from the affirming or negating perspective. Gyaltsab Jé is saying that the two things in question must be mutually exclusive in the sense that they have no common locus, and he also alludes to the fact that this kind of direct preclusion requires that the two things be *jointly exhaustive* in that they form a division that encompasses everything. The mention of valid cognition in the final line reiterates the point that exclusion and affirmation are actions of *realization*.

887. *Pramāṇaviniścayaṭīkā* chap. 1, 206a5.

888. Gyaltsab Jé's definition of relationship has the same two characteristics as Khedrup Jé's (p. 511)—namely, that the two elements are different and that if one is ruled out so is the other. But he elaborates by saying that there are three binary characterizations of the two elements that apply here. These characterizations reflect the fact that what is being established here is that *x* is related to *y*. Accordingly *x* is described as the "related thing" (*'brel pa*), and *y* is "that to which there is a relationship" (*'brel yul*). *Y* is therefore the basis for asserting the relationship. So, even though *y* does not literally "remove" *x*, *y*'s withdrawal from the picture entails *x* also being "removed." Similarly, Gyaltsab Jé characterizes *x* as the one pervaded by *y*, since without the pervader, there can be no thing "pervaded."

889. This locution is unusual, since imprinting is usually used to describe a process that happens *to* the mind. But here it denotes a trait that is literally "stamped" (*lag rjes 'jog pa*) into the nature of a thing.

890. The "causal relationship" is that of an effect being related to a cause. An effect must always have been preceded by a cause, and all deductions about that cause are premised on that fact. However, there is no logical relationship between a cause and an effect—or more strictly speaking, a cause is not related *to* its effect. Gyaltsab Jé here refers to what might appear to be the one exception to this—the category of correct reasons that involve the nonobservation of a direct cause. As the examples

cited by Khedrup Jé also show (pp. 412–13), this relies on the notion of an "inexorable productive power." This refers to a state that a cause can reach on the very threshold of yielding its effect, when the force or momentum toward production is unstoppable.

891. The "informational relationship" is not a third variety in addition to the causal and nature ones. It is instead an alternative perspective, focusing on the roles the elements in the relationship play in the yielding of information or knowledge. Again, it involves a bipartition, dividing things into *information providers* (*go byed*) and *provided information* (*go bya*). Specifically, in the context of inference, the distinction is between things *from* which one can deduce, and what it is that one can deduce or learn from them. To be "informed" in this context is, once more, to gain certain knowledge through valid cognition.

892. Gyaltsab Jé engages in some pronoun-switching here. He refers to "others" who make the claim (i.e., third-person plural) but then switches to "you" (second-person singular) as he elaborates on the problem with the position.

893. This is the proof that Khedrup Jé referred to on pages 221 and 390 (also see next note).

894. *Pramāṇavārttika* 1.10, 95a4. The line alluded to here is "That arose from an effect reason." (*de ni 'bras bu'i rtags las skyes*). When Dharmakīrti set out the threefold division of correct reasons—causal, nature, and nonobservation—he also explored several potential objections. One of these was the proof regarding the taste and form of a piece of molasses. Khedrup Jé set out the proof in the first text (p. 390) and referred to it a number of times but never elaborated on this particular debate. The objection raised against the proof was that it appeared to involve using the visual form of the molasses to make a deduction about its taste, despite the fact that the two have no causal relationship. And unless the proof relied on a causal relationship (it was argued), it could not be counted as an authentic one with an effect reason. Gyaltsab Jé now refers back to Dharmakīrti's response. If there were a causal relationship between the taste and the form of the molasses, Gyaltsab Jé says, then Dharmakīrti's answer to the objection would simply have been to affirm that relationship, and thereby establish that the proof belonged to the category of those that use correct effect reasons. But instead, Dharmakīrti acknowledged that there was no such relationship, and set out on a different route to explain how the proof yields information.

895. Gyaltsab Jé is again referring to a hypothetical objection that Dharmakīrti himself raised. Once more, the first chapter of *Commentary on Pramāṇa* is the original source, but the question was further developed in the autocommentary (*Pramāṇavārttikavṛtti*), Toh 4216 Tengyur, tshad ma, *ce*, 262b4.

896. With regard to using smoke to make inferences about fire, not all the features of those two things count as either information or yielders of information. Gyaltsab Jé distinguishes three groups. Features of the two that are either conceptual constructs or are shared with various things other than fire or smoke are too generalized for the informational relationship. Conversely, features that are true only of certain instances of fire or smoke are too specific. Only those features that are exclusive to all instances of fire or smoke are encompassed by the informational relationship.

897. *Compendium of Abhidharma* mentions using a bird's nest to make a deduction, although it does not specify what can be deduced from it. But the apparent reference to a "sail" (*g.yor mo*) is unfamiliar. It seems more likely to be of Indian rather

than Tibetan origin. Gyaltsab Jé also suggests that the individual is mistaken about the bird's nest. Although some Indian ships in ancient and medieval times appear to have featured a structure comparable to the "crow's nest" of Western ships, I am unsure whether avian imagery was ever used.

898. Compare Gyaltsab Jé's account of this with Khedrup Jé's in the first text (notes 393–94).
899. *Following [Dharmakīrti's] Analysis of Relation* (*Sambandhaparīkṣānusāra*), chap. 1, Toh 4237 Tengyur, tshad ma, *zhe*, 22a4.
900. The Indian commentator (Tib. Rgyal rnga bdun pa) to whom Gyaltsab Jé refers here is almost certainly Dharmottara. The present work deals with material covered in Dharmakīrti's *Analysis of Relation* and briefly mentions the "great brahmin" (Śaṃkarānanda), who is one of its Indian commentators. But Gyaltsab Jé does not cite Dharmakīrti's treatise here and does not project this work as one within its direct commentarial tradition. But he does, notably, defend Dharmottara's interpretations. The name cited in the closing stanzas is neither the usual Tibetan rendering for Dharmottara (Chos mchog) nor the one Gyaltsab Jé uses for Dharmottara in the text. But other Tibetan scholars during this era—such as Gewa Gyaltsen in his *Commentarial Ornament on Compendium of Pramāṇa* (folio 72b)—do use it for Dharmottara.
901. This line appears to have been added by the scribe, Rinchen Chögyal.
902. The final verse of dedication and the two Sanskrit phrases are not part of the Gyaltsab Jé's original composition. They were appended to the version of the text that was produced at Tashi Lhunpo Monastery.
903. In the final portion, *eṣṭa* should read *iṣṭa*. I also assume that *svarasvatī* should be *sarasvatī*.
904. This insult is a little obscure, but the first word here denotes "weavers," meaning that whole phrase (*thag mkhan rkang pa'i mched zla*) almost certainly refers to those who consort with or partner members of artisan classes, many of whom have been held in low regard in traditional Tibetan culture.
905. Jñānagarbha, *Satyadvayavibhaṅga*, stanza 27, Toh 3881 Tengyur, dbu ma, *sa*, 2b7.
906. The figure Jamyang Shepa refers to a number of times as Taktsang Lotsāwa is the scholar Sherab Rinchen (1405–77). Unlike the earlier tradition, exemplified by Khedrup Jé's work, Geluk authors such as Jamyang Shepa were more inclined to identify some of those they were refuting. But the named targets were a relatively small group, most commonly those who had been the strongest critics of Tsongkhapa's interpretations during the early days of the Geluk school's formation. The work of Taktsang Lotsāwa that Jamyang Shepa particularly has in mind here is his *Comprehensive Knowledge of Philosophical Tenets*. In this (93b), Taktsang Lotsāwa opposes the idea that the Prāsaṅgika system has a presentation of four kinds of valid cognition. Jamyang Shepa also devotes a good portion of his own *Great Exposition of Philosophical Tenets* to refuting Taktsang Lotsāwa's position.
907. *Prasannapadā*, 25b5.
908. *Ascertaining the Discipline: Upāli's Questions* (*Vinayaviniścayopālipariprcchā*), Toh 68 Kangyur, dkon brtsegs, *ca*, 121a1.
909. Nāgārjuna, *Ratnāvalī*, 4.91, Toh 4158 Tengyur, spring yig, *ge*, 121b4.
910. *Madhyamakāvatārabhāṣya*, chap. 6, Toh 3862, Tengyur, dbu ma, *'a*, 245a1.
911. Nāgārjuna, *Yuktiṣaṣṭika*, stanza 28, Toh 3825 Tengyur, dbu ma, *tsa*, 21b1.
912. *Yuktiṣaṣṭikāvṛtti*, Toh 3864 Tengyur, dbu ma, *ya*, 19b1.

913. Nāgārjuna, *Ratnāvalī*, 3.75, Toh 4158 Tengyur, spring yig, *ge*, 117a6.
914. Āryadeva, *Catuḥśataka*, 16.24, Toh 3846 Tengyur, dbu ma, *tsha*, 18a4.
915. *Catuḥśatakaṭīkā* chap. 16, 238a7.
916. *Prasannapadā* chap. 15, 90b6.
917. *Sūtrasamuccaya*, Toh 3934 Tengyur, dbu ma, *ki*, 148b1.
918. *Treasury of Doha* (*Dohakośa*) Toh 2224, Tengyur, rgyud 'grel, *wi*, 71a5.
919. On several occasions, the version of a subheading when first introduced differs from the one appearing when the section is actually covered in the text. But the discrepancies tend to be minor and have a minimal or no effect on the translation.
920. *Prasannapadā*, 18b6.
921. *Commentary on Distinction between the Two Truths* (*Satyadvayavibhaṅgavṛtti*), Toh 3882 Tengyur, dbu ma, *sa*, 8b6.
922. *Commentary on Distinction between the Two Truths* (*Satyadvayavibhaṅgavṛtti*), Toh 3882 Tengyur, dbu ma, *sa*, 9a1.
923. *Prasannapadā*, 19a2.
924. *Prasannapadā*, 19a3.
925. *Prasannapadā*, 19a6.
926. *Prasannapadā*, 19b7–20a4.
927. *Prasannapadā*, 19b1.
928. The "Prāsaṅgika's public position" (*thal 'gyur ba'i lugs tsam*) relates to conventional reality and involves accepting the standards of correctness and so on observed in the world. This contrasts with the Prāsaṅgika's "unique system" (*thun mong ma yin pa'i lugs*), which is based on an ārya's experience of emptiness. From this perspective, conventional phenomena, including correctness, simply do not appear.
929. *Prasannapadā*, 19b1.
930. *Fundamental Treatise on the Middle Way* (*Mūlamadhyamakakārikā*), 18.7, Toh 3824 Tengyur, dbu ma, *tsa*, 11a2.
931. *Dispeller of Dispute* (*Vigrahavyāvartanī*), stanza 28, Toh 3828 Tengyur, dbu ma, *tsa*, 27b7.
932. *Prasannapadā*, 19b2.
933. *Prasannapadā*, 19b3–7.
934. *Prasannapadā*, 19b7–20a2.
935. *Prasannapadā*, 20a2.
936. It is possible that a common scribal or printing error has occurred here, and that "it aims to..." (*de'i don*) was supposed to read "it is from the perspective of...." (*de'i ngo na*).
937. *Prasannapadā*, 20a3.
938. *Prasannapadā*, 20a4.
939. *Prasannapadā*, 20a5.
940. *Prasannapadā*, 20a5.
941. *Prasannapadā*, 20a6.
942. *Pramāṇavārttika* 3.1, 118b3.
943. *Prasannapadā*, 20a7.
944. Closely following *Prasannapadā*, Jamyang Shepa now begins a lengthy discussion on the exact meaning of the Sanskrit term *lakṣaṇa*, which is usually translated as "characteristic(s)." This is intended to bring scrutiny to the identification of the characteristic, and what occurs in the *act* of characterization. The term *lakṣaṇa* has

a companion term, *lakṣya*, which in this context can be translated as "the characterized." Candrakīrti initially appears simply to be criticizing the way that some have glossed the term *lakṣaṇa*, but this develops into what is widely understood to be an attack on the worldview of the Pramāṇa system. The term in question is the basis for the distinction between things that are specifically characterized (*svalakṣaṇa*) and those that are generally characterized (*sāmānyalakṣaṇa*). It therefore represents the foundation of the ontological dichotomy that underpins the epistemological model. Candrakīrti's basic argument is that followers of the Pramāṇa system cannot give a convincing account of what the term is supposed to convey, and that their model, premised on the idea of the fundamental distinction between the two objects, is therefore undermined. But there is a further dimension to this. The same term *lakṣaṇa* is the one used to translate *definition* or *defining characteristics* (Tib. *mtshan nyid*). So the attack also potentially undercuts one of the most important concepts of the Tibetan epistemological tradition—namely, that it is possible to define a thing and that valid cognition can gain certain knowledge of that thing through its defining characteristics.

945. *Prasannapadā*, 20b1.

946. *Prasannapadā*, 20b1.

947. The discussion has so far referred to the binary divide between the Sanskrit terms *lakṣaṇa* and *lakṣya* and concentrated on the relationship between the characterizer and the characterized. But here Jamyang Shepa introduces a threefold division, behind which lie two different analytical frameworks relied on within Tibetan scholasticism. The first has already been encountered in Khedrup Jé's text. It relates to a *theory of definitions* that goes back to the Sangphu tradition but was later embraced by Geluk scholars. As we saw in Khedrup Jé's text, in addition to the definition and definiendum, there is a third component—the "illustration." These three comprise a model that is used when explaining the elements and process involved in a person coming to understand the correct application of a specific definition. Here the illustration is a particular example that embodies the characteristic(s) in question and allows a person to make the link between the definition and definiendum. The second framework relates to a linguistic analysis of action and is named "action-executor-object" (*bya byed las gsum*) after its three component parts. But the better description of this is the one Jamyang Shepa uses later in the text, following Candrakīrti, when he refers to the "agent-instrument-object" model. The classic example used for explaining this is the action of chopping wood (which appears later in the text). In this, the axe is the "instrument" by means of which the action is performed, the person wielding the axe is the "agent," and the wood—as the thing toward which the action is directed—is the "object." Jamyang Shepa sometimes interrupts the binary symmetry by referencing one of these threefold divisions and, occasionally, as at the present point in the text, combines elements from both.

948. Pāṇini, *Sutras on Grammar* (*Vyākaraṇasūtra*), chap. 3, Toh 4420, Tengyur, sna tshogs, *to*, 23a5, etc. Here the logician cites classical Sanskrit grammar to justify his glossing of the term. The information relating to the specific point or "rule" that he refers to is dispersed in the Tibetan translations of works on Sanskrit grammar, but their main source is the *Aṣṭādhyāyī* composed by Pāṇini. The rule known as *kṛtyalyuṭo bahulam* appears in book 3, chap. 3, *sūtra* 113, where it says, "The affixes

called *kritya* [3.1.95] and the affix *lyuṭ* are diversely applicable and have other senses than those taught before."

949. *Prasannapadā*, 20b2.
950. *Prasannapadā*, 20b3.
951. *Prasannapadā*, 20b3.
952. *Prasannapadā*, 20b4.
953. *Prasannapadā*, 20b6.
954. *Prasannapadā*, 20b7.
955. *Prasannapadā*, 21a2.
956. *Prasannapadā*, 21a3.
957. *Entering the Middle Way* (*Madhyamakāvatāra*), 6.72, Toh 3861 Tengyur, dbu ma, *'a*, 207b4.
958. *Prasannapadā*, 21a3.
959. *Prasannapadā*, 21a4.
960. *Questions of Ratnacūḍa Sutra* (*Ratnacūḍaparipṛcchāsūtra*), Toh 91 Kangyur, dkon brtsegs, *cha*, 227a1–227a6.
961. *Prasannapadā*, 21b4.
962. *Prasannapadā*, 21b4.
963. This is an example of the subtle slants that Jamyang Shepa puts on the treatise. Candrakīrti's analysis may appear to be aimed at undermining the logician's position. But Candrakīrti's real design, Jamyang Shepa says, is to encourage us to think more about the model of action. Dissecting the action—identifying its components and their roles—is the only way for us to understand how conventional reality remains viable in the face of all the negation involved with the realization of emptiness. What Candrakīrti says, therefore, is to be understood more as a heuristic device than a refutation.
964. *Fundamental Treatise on the Middle Way* (*Mūlamadhyamakakārikā*), 15.2, Toh 3824 Tengyur, dbu ma, *tsa*, 8b5.
965. *Prasannapadā*, 21b5.
966. Jamyang Shepa says that the single Sanskrit term (*lakṣya*) can be understood in either of two ways but that here it refers to the second. This clarification is necessary because, as mentioned in a note above (944), the discussion in Sanskrit involves only two terms or concepts, *lakṣaṇa* and *lakṣya*—characterizer and characterized. However, in the Tibetan tradition this is extended to three, because "the characterized" (*lakṣya*) could be understood to refer either to the "definiendum" (*mtshon bya*) or the "illustration" (*mtshan gzhi*).
967. *Prasannapadā*, 21b6.
968. *Prasannapadā*, 22a1.
969. *Prasannapadā*, 21b7.
970. Nāgārjuna, *Mūlamadhyamakakārikā*, 2.21, Toh 3824 Tengyur, dbu ma, *tsa*, 3a4.
971. *Prasannapadā*, 22a1.
972. *Prasannapadā*, 22a2.
973. According to many interpretations of Pramāṇa, Dharmakīrti talked about the limits of language and proposed that certain entities and relations are incommunicable, inexpressible, or indescribable (Skt. *anupākhyeya*). Such an interpretation is not favored by Geluk thinkers, who are cautious about employing the idea of inexpressibility. To expand on a point touched upon in the introduction, in Geluk philosophical writings, inexpressibility is largely reserved for describing the limits

of language in conveying *experiences*, especially that of the ultimate. But since a central tenet is that the ultimate is to be approached through language and reasoning, conventional realities (entities, categories, etc.), and even ultimate truth itself, must be capturable and communicable. Although Jamyang Shepa makes no direct reference to the Pramāṇa system here, Candrakīrti's rebuttal of incommunicability is one that he, along with other Geluk thinkers, would wholeheartedly endorse. For them, the implication of this rebuttal is that things *can* be captured in language, although particular factors, relating to culture, society, or education may prevent this in certain situations.

974. *Prasannapadā*, 22a2.
975. *Prasannapadā*, 22a4.
976. *Prasannapadā*, 22a5.
977. Here Jamyang Shepa refers to a distinction that was discussed above (note 466) in Khedrup Jé's text. Thus the "basic awareness" or "main mind" refers to a basic cognizance of the object. This is distinguished from the more specific cognitive functions attached to a main mind. Depending on the context, the term *consciousness* (Tib. *shes pa*) can denote different things. But as Jamyang Shepa states, it is used in the discussion here to designate the cognitive functions rather than the basic awareness.
978. The first is a reference to the special insight sections of the *Greater* and *Middle-Length Stages of the Path*. The other two are Tsongkhapa's *Ocean of Reasoning* and *Illuminating the Intent.*
979. Maitreya, *Madhyāntavibhāga*, chap. 1, Toh 4021 Tengyur, sems tsam, *phi*, 9, 40b6.
980. The Tibetan of the second line (*de yi khyad par sems las byung*) contains an ambiguous expression, which I have translated as "of that" here. Based on this ambiguity, Tibetan scholars derived two distinct interpretations. Some read "that" as referring to the *object* of the preceding line. The reading for them is "While the basic awareness sees the object, the functions of mind deal with that object's distinctions." Others have interpreted "that" as a reference to the *mind* in the preceding line, yielding "the distinctions within consciousness are the functions arising within it." Toward the end of this section, Jamyang Shepa acknowledges this difference—he sides with the first interpretation, which he portrays as more widespread.
981. *Prasannapadā*, 22a5.
982. *Prasannapadā*, 22a6.
983. *Prasannapadā*, 22a7.
984. *Foundation for Yoga Practitioners: Compendium of Ascertainment* (*Yogācārabhūmiviniścayasaṃgrahaṇī*), section 3, Toh 4038 Tengyur, sems tsam, *zhi*, 77b7.
985. This relates back to the previous point about the two interpretations of the line in question. Jamyang Shepa seems to feel that talking about distinctions within consciousness goes against the idea of the individual having a single consciousness.
986. *Prasannapadā*, 22b1.
987. *Prasannapadā*, 22b1.
988. *Madhyamakāvatāra*, 6.136, Toh 3861, Tengyur, dbu ma, *'a*, 211a2.
989. *Prasannapadā*, 22b2.
990. This is the same distinction between the property and property-basis that was encountered in Khedrup Jé's text (see note 848). Accordingly, contrary to what might be expected, in the case of "head of the pestle," it is the pestle, not the head, that is the property.

991. Among contemporary academics, there are differences of opinion about whether the Sanskrit term used by Candrakīrti actually refers to a "pestle." However, following the standard Tibetan scholastic understanding, Candrakīrti cites the pestle and Rāhu as "well-known" examples of things that in ordinary discourse may be referred to as having a "body" and "head" respectively, when everyone knows that they do not and that this is just a manner of speaking. In the case of the pestle, its clubbed shape means that it is essentially all *body*. Rāhu is a figure in Indian astrology and myth. In the former, he is identified as a dark celestial identity and is paired with Ketu. According to mythology, Rāhuketu was originally a deity whose head was later severed from his body. Hence, while Ketu is all "body," Rāhu is all "head."
992. *Prasannapadā*, 22b2.
993. *Legs bshad snying po*. This refers to Tsongkhapa's *Differentiating the Interpretive and the Definitive*.
994. *Prasannapadā*, 22b3.
995. Tib. *lhan cig 'byung ba'i dngos po*.
996. *Prasannapadā*, 22b5.
997. *Prasannapadā*, 22b6.
998. Tib. *btags don btsal ba*.
999. *Prasannapadā*, 22b7.
1000. *Prasannapadā*, 23a1.
1001. Tsongkhapa, *Essence of Fine Elucidation*, 66b2.
1002. *Prasannapadā*, 23a1.
1003. *Prasannapadā*, 23a2.
1004. *Precious Garland* (*Ratnāvalī*) 1.79, Toh 4158 Tengyur, spring yig, *ge*, 109b7.
1005. *Prasannapadā*, 23a2.
1006. *Prasannapadā*, 23a3.
1007. *Prasannapadā*, 23a3.
1008. *Prasannapadā*, 23a4.
1009. *Prasannapadā*, 23a4.
1010. "Correct," "permissible," and "acceptable" are used here to translate *'thad pa*, *rigs pa*, and *rung ba*.
1011. *Principles of Exegesis* (*Vyākhyāyukti*), chap. 1, Toh 4061 Tengyur, sems tsam, *shi*, 32b7. This identification is tentative. The section does not present the issue in the clearcut manner that Jamyang Shepa suggests.
1012. Candrakīrti, *Madhyamakāvatāra*, 6.149, Toh 3861 Tengyur, dbu ma, *'a*, 211b4.
1013. Candrakīrti, *Madhyamakāvatāra*, 6.165–66, Toh 3861, Tengyur, dbu ma, *'a*, 212a7.
1014. *Prasannapadā*, 23a6.
1015. *Prasannapadā*, 23a6.
1016. Jñānagarbha, *Satyadvayavibhaṅga*, stanza 21, Toh 3881 Tengyur, dbu ma, *sa*, 2b4. The Dergé version has "nature" (*rang bzhin*) instead of "as they appear" (*snang bzhin*).
1017. *Prasannapadā*, 23a7.
1018. *Prasannapadā*, 23b1.
1019. The text says *dbus mtha' las*, but this is clearly a mistake. It should read *dbu ma las*. Nāgārjuna, *Mūlamadhyamakakārikā*, 24.10, Toh 3824 Tengyur, dbu ma, *tsa*, 15a2.
1020. *Prasannapadā*, 23b1.

1021. Tib. *rig shes rjes dpag.* The term *rig shes* is generally reserved for cognitions of ultimate truth.

1022. Tsongkhapa, *Differentiating the Interpretive and the Definitive*, 88a6–b2.

1023. Tsongkhapa, *Differentiating the Interpretive and the Definitive*, 88b2.

1024. In his *Thousand Measures*, Khedrup Jé chooses to cite the inferential cognition realizing sound to be impermanent since it is such a clear example of an awareness that is mistaken but is still able to comprehend its object. Thus he accepts that such an inferential awareness is mistaken with regard to its conceptual object, but denies that this entails it being mistaken about the *way* it conceives that object. Again, the thinking seems to be that although an inferential awareness, like other conceptual cognitions, is classified as a mistaken one, error does not affect the way that it apprehends its object.

1025. Khedrup Jé, *Providing the Fortunate with Sight*, 227a6.

1026. Tsongkhapa, *Greater Stages of the Path*, 407a2.

1027. The unreliability of sense consciousnesses is discussed below (pp. 630–36) and comes down to the issue of how they see specific characteristics. But to sum up the potential difference that Jamyang Shepa draws attention to here, Khedrup Jé, in his *Thousand Measures*, suggests that while for the lower schools, it is permissible to say that inferential cognition is mistaken with regard to its appearing object but not with regard to its conceived object, the same distinction does not work in the Prāsaṅgika system. This implies that in the Prāsaṅgika system, inferential cognition should be described as mistaken with respect to both objects. However, Jamyang Shepa wonders whether Tsongkhapa's remarks in his *Greater Stages of the Path*, where he distinguishes between the appearing and apprehended object of an inferential cognition in the Prāsaṅgika system, suggest that an inferential cognition should be described as unmistaken with regard to its conceptual object.

1028. *Prasannapadā*, 23b1.

1029. *Prasannapadā*, 23b2.

1030. *Prasannapadā*, 23b3–4.

1031. *Prasannapadā*, 23b4.

1032. *Prasannapadā*, 23b5.

1033. *Prasannapadā*, 23b6.

1034. The logician's system is built on an ontological dichotomy according to which any object of knowledge is either specifically characterized or generally characterized. This came under attack in the previous section. Candrakīrti next shifts attention to its companion, the epistemological dichotomy, according to which there are only two epistemic means or *pramāṇa* that can provide us with certain knowledge—that is, perception and inference. Candrakīrti focuses first on perception by calling upon the logician to explain the etymological route through which he arrives at the term he uses for perception. As with the discussion about *lakṣaṇa*, this might initially appear to be a pedantic issue about the correct usage of the Sanskrit term *pratyakṣa.* But Candrakīrti is using it to question the coherency of the logician's system and what he sees as its failure to reflect conventional understanding—in short, its conflict with the world of conventions. The matters dealt with, therefore, have real philosophical implications, but the vehicle for the discussion is the etymology or derivation of Sanskrit words. It relies on the dimensions of meaning to a term for which there is no direct parallel in English *or* Tibetan. But essentially, Candrakīrti criticizes the etymological understanding of the term *pratyakṣa*, which the logician explains as having been derived from the object. That is, the logician claims that *pratyakṣa* (perception) gains its name from *pratyakṣa* (the object of that perception)—those things that are "perceivable"—and that what is perceivable is manifest things: the sights, sounds, and so forth that surround us in the world.

1035. *Prasannapadā*, 23b6.

1036. *Prasannapadā*, 23b6

1037. Here the text refers to the pot and its constituent parts respectively as the "appropriator" and the "appropriated." The pot is the "appropriator" in the sense of being that within which the various parts are *gathered*. But it should again be stressed that in Geluk thinking, the Pramāṇa logician's analysis does *not* conclude that the pot has less reality than those constituents. The pot is regarded as the part-possessor, but this does not make it into an abstract notion or conventional designation assigned to those parts. So, although Jamyang Shepa recounts Candrakīrti's characterization of the logician's assertion, which says that the pot is only perceivable in a figurative sense, this position is not in line with mainstream Geluk understanding of the Pramāṇa tradition's stance.

1038. *Prasannapadā*, 23b7.

1039. *Prasannapadā*, 24a1.

1040. *Prasannapadā*, 24a3.

1041. *Prasannapadā*, 24a4.

1042. *Prasannapadā*, 24a4.

1043. Āryadeva, *Catuḥśataka*, 14.15, Toh 3846 Tengyur, dbu ma, *tsha*, 15b6.

1044. *Prasannapadā*, 24a6.

1045. "Visual form" here is more literally translated "form source" (Tib. *gzugs kyi skye mched*).

1046. *Prasannapadā*, 24a7.

1047. *Four Hundred Stanzas* (*Catuḥśataka*), 13.1, Toh 3846 Tengyur, dbu ma, *tsha*, 14a5.

1048. *Catuḥśatakaṭīkā* chap. 13, 196a4–6.

1049. Āryadeva, *Catuḥśataka*, 13.2, Toh 3846 Tengyur, dbu ma, *tsha*, 14a6.

1050. *Catuḥśatakaṭīkā* chap. 13, 198a7.

1051. *Prasannapadā*, 24a7.

1052. *Catuḥśatakaṭīkā* chap. 13, 196a5.

1053. This may be referring to the claim made by Taktsang Lotsāwa that it would be contradictory for the Prāsaṅgika to hold that conventional objects are misleading but their subjects (i.e., valid cognitions) are nondeceptive. *Comprehensive Knowledge of Philosophical Tenets*, 94a3.

1054. *Treasury of Amara* (*Amarakośa*), chap. 3, Toh 4299 Tengyur, sgra mdo, *se*, 211b6.

1055. *Prasannapadā*, 24b1.

1056. There are issues with some of the Sanskrit in this section. On a few occasions, letters from the dental and retroflex groups in the Sanskrit alphabet appear to have been mixed up with each other. In Tibetan, the same letters (in normal and reversed form) are used to represent the two sets respectively. But it is difficult to determine at which stage of the journey from composition to print reproduction these apparent mistakes might have crept in. Here *ainṭriyaka* should probably be *aindriyaka*.

1057. This should probably be *indri*.

1058. This should probably be *atīndriya*.

1059. *Extensive Commentary on Drop of Logic* (*Nyāyabinduṭīkā*) chap. 1, Toh 4231 Tengyur, tshad ma, *we*, 42b5. The start of this passage does not match what appears in the Dergé version. The second part is close, but the exact wording appears in *Direct Commentary on the Ascertainment of Pramāṇa* (*Pramāṇaviniścayaṭīkā*) chap. 1, 7b5. Dharmottara was the author of these two commentaries. Tibetan scholars used the name the *Correct* for both but distinguished between them by referring to the two as "Shorter" and "More Extensive," respectively. However, as here, on a later occasion also (p. 658), no exact match for words that Jamyang Shepa says are from *The "Shorter" Correct* appear in that work, although wording *closer* to them is found in the "More Extensive" (i.e., *Pramāṇaviniścayaṭīkā*). In the Tengyur, this commentary is split into two parts, one with the first and second chapters and the other with the third chapter alone. But even this division does not help clarify Jamyang Shepa's reference to the "Shorter."

1060. *Pramāṇaviniścayaṭīkā* chap. 1, 7b5.

1061. *Prasannapadā*, 24b2.

1062. This is the opposite of the logician's position. Candrakīrti has already pointed out problems with the logician's view that *pratyakṣa* is used for the sense object in a figurative sense. He now criticizes the logician's understanding of the term's derivation, arguing that the correct way to understand it should accord with the way it is used in everyday language.

1063. *Catuḥśatakaṭīkā* chap. 13, 197b1.

1064. *Prasannapadā*, 24b3.

1065. *Catuḥśatakaṭīkā* chap. 13, 197b1.

1066. *Catuḥśatakaṭīkā* chap. 13, 197b2.

1067. *Catuḥśatakaṭīkā* chap. 13, 197b4.

1068. Reading *'brel ba* for *'grel ba*.

1069. *Pramāṇasamuccaya* 1.4, 1b4.

1070. *Prasannapadā*, 24b3.

1071. As we have seen, the Pramāṇa tradition supports its view that *pratyakṣa* denotes perception by citing Dignāga's explanation of the term's etymology. Thus it breaks the term down into *prati-akṣa*, and says that the two components refer to a set of "cognitions" (*akṣa*) that respectively rely on "their own" (*prati*) sense powers. The fact that the perceptions have distinct sense powers is seen to explain why they cognize five different kinds of objects—sights, sounds, etc. Since the two are understood to be linked by a genitive case marker, according to the derivation, the term literally means "their sense power's cognition," i.e., the cognition of the sense power. Candrakīrti now attacks this idea, arguing that although it could be said that the cognitions are subjects of the objects they perceive, the Pramāṇa tradition's reversal of this, effectively describing them as the subjects of their sense powers, makes no sense. The discussion partly comes back to the idea of subject and object being mutually dependent designations or realities.

1072. As remarked in note 164, in Abhidharma writings, a distinction is made between forms that do and do not have physical resistance. Much of the discourse relating to the latter category focuses on the issue of what has been translated as "unperceived physicality" or "invisible physicality" (Skt. *avijñaptirūpa*, Tib. *rnam par rig byed ma yin pa'i gzugs*), a type of form that some Buddhist schools deny exists. But as the present discussion about sense powers shows, these are not the only type of forms that are asserted to have an unusual kind of existence that challenges common notions of materiality.

1073. *Prasannapadā*, 24b3.

1074. The term translated here as "repetition" (Tib. *zlos pa*) is one that Candrakīrti uses in reference to the derivation of *pratyakṣa* that he criticizes here. This is a repetition not in the sense of a single recurring word, concept, or the like but rather, as Jamyang Shepa describes it, in the sense of an equal distribution among a plurality of things, such as is conveyed in English by the combination of "each" and "respective," as in "each *x* has its respective *y*."

1075. *Prasannapadā*, 24b4.

1076. *Pramāṇasamuccaya* 1.4, 1b4.

1077. *Prasannapadā*, 24b4.

1078. *Pramāṇaviniścayaṭīkā* chap. 1, 7b5.

1079. The cow was introduced in Khedrup Jé's discussions about specifically and generally characterized things, the *apoha* theory, and definitions. We now find the etymology of the Sanskrit word for "cow" (*gauḥ*) entering the debate, as those in the Pramāṇa tradition look for a parallel that justifies their derivation of *pratyakṣa*. This exchange also involves an unusual reversal, since those in the Pramāṇa tradition must answer the charge that their derivation is too restrictive. Expressed in logical terms, this means that there is a fault with their pervasion, in that it does not encompass all that it should—i.e., there are many examples of perception that are not covered by their etymology of *pratyakṣa*. This is one of several points in this work that Jamyang Shepa takes the role of an observer and reporter of the debate. Were he to interject here and give the Geluk perspective on this matter, he would surely side with those in the Pramāṇa tradition, since in Geluk thinking, while pervasions must be watertight in correct proofs, etymologies do not work on the same principles and are not accountable to logical rules.

1080. Durgāsiṃha, *Rules for [Suffixes Forming Verbal Derivatives Beginning with] Uṇ etc. [in the Kātantra System of Sanskrit Grammar]* (*Kalāpoṇādisūtra*), Toh 4425 Tengyur, sna tshogs, *no*, 33b3. In relation to rule 86.2.28, the text says, "From *gami* comes *ḍo*" (*ga mi las ḍo'o*). Also, Durgāsiṃha, *Autocommentary to [Rules for Suffixes Forming Verbal Derivatives Beginning with] Uṇ etc. [in the Kātantra System of Sanskrit Grammar]* (*Uṇādivṛtti*), Toh 4426 Tengyur, sna tshogs, *no*, 48a5. Regarding rule 86.2.28, it says, *der gau: sa la sogs pa'o*. In the original Sanskrit this is *gam lrī ga taugacchatī ti*, which translates as *der 'gro bas na ba lang go*, "By virtue of the fact that it goes, it is [designated] *cow*."

1081. Here it is perhaps better to think of the characteristic action associated with cows as that of "roaming" or "wandering" rather than simply "going."

1082. *Pramāṇaviniścayaṭīkā* chap. 1, 7b6.

1083. This is a variation of a Tibetan saying (*phyogs snga'i nam ma langs bar dgag pa'i nyi ma 'char ba*) that is frequently encountered in the Geluk dialectical tradition. Its provenance is unclear, but it was probably adapted from a preexisting popular saying that evokes the natural order of things being reversed—i.e., sunrise occurring prior to dawn. It is generally understood to refer to a precipitous action. In this context, it is used to denote someone who presumptuously ascribes a position to an opponent without having checked that it is one that the opponent actually holds and then sets about refuting that position. And while the imagery may seem to suggest that the individual is ahead of his opponent in that the position could be one that has not yet "dawned" upon the latter but may do so later, this is ultimately a criticism that the individual is not properly engaging with the opponent and embarks on a perhaps lengthy refutation of a position that no one holds. Why exactly Jamyang Shepa chooses to use it to end this section is unclear.

1084. Vasubandhu, *Treasury of the Abhidharma* (*Abhidharmakośa*), 1.48, Toh 4089 Tengyur, mngon pa, *ku*, 3b7.

1085. *Prasannapadā*, 24b6.

1086. *Prasannapadā*, 25a2.

1087. *Prasannapadā*, 25a3.

1088. This marks the first real point at which Jamyang Shepa ventures into the territory of how the Prāsaṅgika explanation of valid cognition departs from that of the lower schools. Geluk scholars say that the Pramāṇa tradition recognizes two possible objects of inferential valid cognition: slightly and extremely hidden phenomena. Jamyang Shepa now posits a third, which he says can serve as the object for the valid cognition of analogy. He introduces this third category without any fanfare and does not elaborate on it here. But his classifying the object of the analogy as a hidden one, within the sphere of inferential cognition, is an important first step in his argument that the fourfold division of valid cognitions can be subsumed within the twofold model, without challenging it.

1089. This volume contains two different translations for a single Tibetan designation (*grags pa'i rjes dpag*). In Khedrup Jé's text, this is the name of the second variety of inferential cognition within the Pramāṇa system's threefold division. These three are the inferential cognition dealing with (1) demonstrable facts, (2) the issue of common agreement [about names], and (3) matters of conviction. The objects of the first type of inferential cognition are said to be slightly hidden phenomena and those of the third, extremely hidden. There are differing views among Geluk scholars about the objects of the second, but these do not generally take us beyond the division of the two types of hidden object. Here in Jamyang Shepa's work, reflecting the Prāsaṅgika understanding, the objects of those first two inferential cognitions of the Pramāṇa system—dealing with "demonstrable facts" and "matters of agreement [about names]"—are collapsed into the much broader category. The designation for this is the same one used for the second inferential cognition of the Pramāṇa system (i.e., *grags pa'i rjes dpag*). But to indicate that it no longer refers to the narrow issue of the legitimacy but denotes an expansive notion of conventional reality, it is translated as "an inferential cognition [regarding a] matter of established convention."

1090. *Prasannapadā*, 25a3.

1091. *Prasannapadā*, 25a3.

1092. *Prasannapadā*, 25a3.

1093. Tsongkhapa, *Illuminating the Intent*, 161b4–6. For the full version of these lines see the *Library of Tibetan Classics* translation of Tsongkhapa's work by Thupten Jinpa, 350–51.

1094. Candrakīrti argues that *pratyakṣa* be understood in terms of cognitions that rely on their respective objects. It is this gloss that the logician refers to when he says that Candrakīrti's explanation of the derivation ends up with him using another Sanskrit term, *pratyartha*, which can be read as "[their] respective objects." The logician also claims that this word does not form part of worldly vocabulary.

1095. *Pramāṇaviniścaya* chap. 1, 154a7.

1096. *Pramāṇaviniścayaṭīkā* chap. 1, 37a7.
1097. *Prasannapadā*, 25a4.
1098. *Prasannapadā*, 25a4.
1099. *Prasannapadā*, 25a4.
1100. *Prasannapadā*, 25a5.
1101. *Prasannapadā*, 25a5.
1102. *Prasannapadā*, 25a6.
1103. *Prasannapadā*, 25a6.
1104. *Catuḥśatakaṭīkā* chap. 13, 196b4.
1105. *Catuḥśatakaṭīkā* chap. 13, 196b5.
1106. *Catuḥśatakaṭīkā* chap. 13, 196b6.
1107. As mentioned above (note 292), this analogy—of eye conditions and what the sufferer mistakenly sees due to them—has been a popular one in Buddhist writings. That earlier note identified *myodesopsia* as the condition that scholars are likely referring to when they talk of an individual seeing "descending" hairs. The phrase used here is different and sounds more like the person simply has "blurred vision" (*rab rib can*), but in other respects it seems to be a specific complaint that also results in seeing "strands of hair." Candrakīrti's response makes one wonder whether there was complete agreement among Buddhist scholars about which condition and set of symptoms they were discussing.
1108. *Catuḥśatakaṭīkā* chap. 13, 196b7.
1109. *Catuḥśatakaṭīkā* chap. 13, 197a1–4.
1110. *Catuḥśatakaṭīkā* chap. 13, 197a5.
1111. *Catuḥśatakaṭīkā* chap. 13, 197a5.
1112. *Catuḥśatakaṭīkā* chap. 13, 197a6.
1113. *Catuḥśataka*, 13.1, Toh 3846 Tengyur, dbu ma, *tsha*, 14a5.
1114. The beginning of the Tibetan sentence is extremely terse, and some syllables may be missing. This could have some bearing on the fact that the assertion attributed to the two groups here does not seem consistent with something that Jamyang Shepa says later in the text (p. 654 and note 1211).
1115. Jamyang Shepa now gradually turns to Candrakīrti's criticisms of the logician's view that valid cognition is nondeceptive with regard to the specific or individual characteristics of its object. It is very apparent that the idea of specifically characterized things (*svalakṣaṇa*) is crucial to the logician. But the Prāsaṅgika—in the form of Candrakīrti—proposes that the very concept of such a characteristic implies autonomy and independence. He attacks the idea that such a thing could exist. Here "autonomous" has been added in brackets to indicate the aspect of *svalakṣaṇa* that Candrakīrti now chooses to target.
1116. *Catuḥśatakaṭīkā* chap. 13, 196a6–b2.
1117. *Pramāṇasamuccaya* 1.3, 1b4.
1118. *Catuḥśatakaṭīkā* chap. 13, 196b2–3.
1119. *Pramāṇavārttika* 3.287, 129b1.
1120. *Catuḥśatakaṭīkā* chap. 13, 196b3.
1121. *Catuḥśatakaṭīkā* chap. 13, 196b4.
1122. *Catuḥśatakaṭīkā* chap. 13, 196b4–197b5.
1123. *Catuḥśatakaṭīkā* chap. 13, 196b5–7.
1124. *Catuḥśatakaṭīkā* chap. 13, 196b7.
1125. *Catuḥśatakaṭīkā* chap. 13, 196b5.

1126. *Deliberation on the Dharma Sutra* (*Dharmasaṃgītisūtra*), Toh 238 Kangyur, mdo sde, *zha*, 6b1, and *Prasannapadā*, 13b3. Jamyang Shepa gives what appears to be a paraphrased version of the passages from these sources.

1127. *Impermanence Sutra* (*Anityatāsūtra*), Toh 310 Kangyur, mdo sde, *sa*, 157a4, and *Chapters of Utterances on Specific Topics* (*Udānavarga*), Toh 326 Kangyur, mdo sde, *sa*, 209a2.

1128. *Lion's Roar of Śrīmālādevī Sutra* (*Śrīmālādevīsiṃhanādasūtra*) Toh 92 Kangyur, dkon brtsegs, *cha*, 272b4 and *Prasannapadā*, 13b3. The citation appears to be a paraphrase.

1129. Buddhapālita, *Buddhapālita's Commentary on Fundamental Treatise on the Middle Way* (*Buddhapālitamūlamadhyamakavṛtti*), chap. 13, Toh 3842 Tengyur, dbu ma, *tsa*, 217b5. The sutra cited here has not been identified.

1130. *Miraculous Play of Mañjuśrī* (*Mañjuśrīvikrīḍita*), Toh 96 Kangyur, mdo sde, *kha*, 239b7, and the *Sutra Teaching the Unfathomable Sphere of a Buddha* (*Acintyabuddhaviṣayanirdeśasūtra*) Toh 79 Kangyur, dkon brtsegs, *ca*, 272a6. In both cases, the final line differs from that cited by the author. However, the passage with the matching last line appears in *Saṃyutta Nikāya* 22.95, the *Lump of Foam Sutta* (*Phena Sutta*), taught in Ayojjhā. See translation in Bodhi, *Connected Discourses*, 952. But Jamyang Shepa surely takes the lines in question from Candrakīrti, who cites them in his *Madhyamakāvatārabhāṣya*, 227b2.

1131. *Samādhirājasūtra* chap. 20, Toh 127 Kangyur, mdo sde, *da*, 70b7. The wording differs from that in the Dergé version.

1132. *Catuḥśatakaṭīkā* 13, 197b5.

1133. This should probably be *satya*.

1134. This should perhaps read *pāvana*.

1135. *Catuḥśatakaṭīkā* chap. 13, 197b6.

1136. Tsongkhapa, *Greater Stages of the Path*, 398a2.

1137. *Catuḥśatakaṭīkā* chap. 13, 197b7.

1138. Chöjé Gyensang (Gungru Gyaltsen Sangpo, 1383–1450) was another of Tsongkhapa's direct disciples. Jamyang Shepa refutes a position that Chöjé Gyensang expressed in his work known as *A Thousand Measures [of Madhyamaka]* (pp. 144–45). This is not a commentary on *Clear Words*. Structured like a work on tenets, it is mostly devoted to the Madhymaka schools. Chöjé Gyensang should not be confused with Gungru Chöjung (Gungru Chökyi Jungné, sixteenth–seventeenth centuries), who, as the seventeenth abbot of Gomang, was a predecessor of Jamyang Shepa, and whose writings were used as the textbooks at Gomang prior to being replaced by those of Jamyang Shepa.

1139. Taktsang Lotsāwa, *Comprehensive Knowledge of Philosophical Tenets*, 96a–b.

1140. *Catuḥśatakaṭīkā* chap. 13, 196b4.

1141. That is, if Taktsang Lotsāwa were to accept that since for the Buddhist realist schools, the five sense cognitions do not comprehend objects with autonomous specific characteristics, for them, there are no such things as valid cognitions that comprehend the five objects with such characteristics.

1142. *Pramāṇavārttika* 3.1, 118b3.

1143. Tsongkhapa, *Greater Stages of the Path*, 398a4.

1144. *Prasannapadā*, 25a7.

1145. These appears to be a paraphrase of *Prasannapadā*, 23a6.

1146. *Prasannapadā*, 25a7.

1147. This passage is cited in *Prasannapadā*, 25a7. It was also used by Khedrup Jé (pages 79–80).
1148. *Tattvasaṃgrahapañjikā*, Toh 4267 Tengyur, tshad ma, *ze*, 143b3.
1149. Tib. *rtog pa* and *dpyod pa*.
1150. *Prasannapadā*, 25a7.
1151. *Prasannapadā*, 25b1.
1152. The Prāsaṅgika (or Candrakīrti's) position on mental perception is also considered to be a major departure from that of the logician and has been identified by various Geluk authors as a key distinguishing feature of Prāsaṅgika epistemology.
1153. *Pramāṇavārttika* 3.299, 130a1. The second line of the Dergé version differs slightly, reading *de ni rtog med gnyis gar yang* instead of *de ni rtog bral ma 'khrul 'dod*.
1154. *Pramāṇavārttika* 3.282, 129a5.
1155. *Prasannapadā*, 18b6. This is a perfect example of Jamyang Shepa's affirmative reading of Candrakīrti's position. In a more usual reading of these lines, Candrakīrti is challenging followers of the Pramāṇa system to set out what they believe, so that he may refute them in their own terms. But Jamyang Shepa takes it instead as an endorsement of the procedure in scholasticism, with Candrakīrti stating that it is necessary to clearly delineate the foundations of the system to ensure a stable structure.
1156. *Catuḥśatakaṭīkā* chap. 13, 197b5.
1157. *Vigrahavyāvartanī*, stanza 32, Toh 3828 Tengyur, dbu ma, *tsa*, 28a2. Here Jamyang Shepa uses Nāgārjuna's argument about the unfindability of things in an unusual fashion, suggesting that it creates problems for followers of the Pramāṇa system who assert that the initial moment of valid cognition needs to be "fresh." As we saw in the first text, the majority of scholars in the Tibetan Pramāṇa tradition define valid cognition as "a fresh and nondeceptive consciousness," or something very similar.
1158. *Catuḥśatakaṭīkā* chap. 13, 202b3.
1159. *Akṣayamatinirdeśa*, Toh 175 Kangyur, mdo sde, *ma*, 129a6–129a7.
1160. The verbatim version of this pithy line has not been located in current editions of the Kangyur, and it may well have been paraphrased. However, in Indian and Tibetan commentarial writings, this line is frequently coupled with a related formula, "I do not dispute with the world" (*nga ni 'jig rten dang mi rtsod do*). This latter one appears in a number of sutras, including the *Chapter Explaining the Three Vows* (*Trisaṃvaranirdeśaparivartasūtra*), Toh 45 Kangyur, dkon brtsegs, *ka*, 9b5, and the *Great Parinirvāṇa Sutra* (*Mahāparinirvāṇasūtra*), Toh 119 Kangyur, mdo sde, *ta*, 247a5.
1161. *Prasannapadā*, 25b5.
1162. *Prasannapadā*, 25a3.
1163. Jamyang Shepa refers back to the principle explained by Gyaltsab Jé (p. 543 and note 883) in relation to a preclusion of mutual opposition, according to which the exclusion of one thing necessarily brings with it the discerning of another, and vice versa.
1164. *Prasannapadā*, 23b6.
1165. Nāgārjuna, *Vigrahavyāvartanī*, stanzas 5–6, Toh 3828 Tengyur, dbu ma, *tsa*, 27a4.
1166. Nāgārjuna, *Vigrahavyāvartanī*, stanzas 40–51, Toh 3828 Tengyur, dbu ma, *tsa*, 28a6–b4.
1167. Nāgārjuna, *Vigrahavyāvartanī*, stanzas 31–39, Toh 3828 Tengyur, dbu ma, *tsa*, 28a2–6.

1168. Nāgārjuna, *Vigrahavyāvartanī*, stanza 23, Toh 3828 Tengyur, dbu ma, *tsa*, 27b5.
1169. Nāgārjuna, *Vigrahavyāvartanī*, stanzas 52–70, Toh 3828, Tengyur, dbu ma, *tsa*, 28b4–29a5.
1170. Tsongkhapa, *Illuminating the Intent*, 162b3. See also translation by Thupten Jinpa in Tsongkhapa, *Illuminating the Intent*, 352.
1171. *Saṃdhinirmocanasūtra*, chap. 10, Toh 106 Kangyur, mdo sde, *ca*, 52a4.
1172. *Elucidating the Intention Sutra* (*Saṃdhinirmocana*), chap. 10, Toh 106 Kangyur, mdo sde, *ca*, 51a7.
1173. *Elucidating the Intention Sutra* (*Saṃdhinirmocana*), chap. 10, Toh 106, Kangyur, mdo sde, *ca*, 51b1–7.
1174. *Prasannapadā*, 25b2.
1175. *Prasannapadā*, 25b3.
1176. Tsongkhapa, *Illuminating the Intent*, 162b2. See also translation by Thupten Jinpa in Tsongkhapa, *Illuminating the Intent*, 352.
1177. "Visual form" here is more literally translated "form source" (Tib. *gzugs kyi skye mched*).
1178. *Catuḥśatakaṭīkā* chap. 11, 180a1.
1179. *Catuḥśatakaṭīkā* chap. 13, 196a4.
1180. *Samādhirājasūtra*, chap. 9, Toh 127 Kangyur, mdo sde, *da*, 26b5.
1181. *Yuktiṣaṣṭikāvṛtti*, Toh 3864 Tengyur, dbu ma, *ya*, 5a7. The Dergé version differs slightly.
1182. *King of Samādhis Sutra* (*Samādhirājasūtra*), chap. 9, Toh 127 Kangyur, mdo sde, *da*, 26b5.
1183. *Catuḥśatakaṭīkā* chap. 13, 201a5.
1184. Śāntarakṣita, *Tattvasaṃgraha*, chap. 30, Toh 4266 Tengyur, tshad ma, *ze*, 123b5.
1185. *Catuḥśatakaṭīkā* chap. 13, 201b6.
1186. *Catuḥśatakaṭīkā* chap. 11, 180b2.
1187. *Ratnāvalī* 4.53, Toh 4158 Tengyur, spring yig, *ge*, 120a5.
1188. Gyaltsab Darma Rinchen, *Commentary to the Precious Garland*, 55a3.
1189. *Catuḥśatakaṭīkā* chap. 13, 205b5.
1190. Vasubandhu, *Treasury of the Abhidharma* (*Abhidharmakośa*), 1.48, Toh 4089, Tengyur, mngon pa, *ku*, 3b7.
1191. *Catuḥśatakaṭīkā* chap. 11, 180b1–4.
1192. *Catuḥśataka* 11.18, Toh 3846, Tengyur, dbu ma, *tsha*, 12b7.
1193. *Catuḥśatakaṭīkā* chap. 11, 180b4.
1194. Candrakīrti, *Madhyamakāvatāra*, 6.201, Toh 3861 Tengyur, dbu ma, *'a*, 214a4.
1195. *Catuḥśatakaṭīkā* chap. 11, 171b3.
1196. *Catuḥśatakaṭīkā* chap. 11, 183a5.
1197. Tsongkhapa, *Illuminating the Intent*, 163a1. See also translation by Thupten Jinpa in Tsongkhapa, *Illuminating the Intent*, 353.
1198. Khedrup Jé, *Thousand Measures*, 224b6.
1199. The second work to which Jamyang Shepa refers here would appear most likely to be Khedrup Jé's *Lamp Dispelling the Gloom*, but a passage matching the one he cites has not been located.
1200. *Four Hundred Stanzas* (*Catuḥśataka*), 11.25, Toh 3846 Tengyur, dbu ma, *tsha*, 13a4.
1201. *Catuḥśatakaṭīkā* chap. 11, 182b4–183a1.
1202. Reference to this belief is found in Candrakīrti's commentary, *Catuḥśatakaṭīkā*,

chap. 10, 162a6. Despite a slight question about whether the term appearing in the Tibetan (*zho*) actually refers to yogurt or mud used for plastering, the belief itself is clear. Candrakīrti talks of how, despite the fact that it is impossible that there could have been any direct physical contact between a pigeon on the well-thatched roof of a house and the yogurt in a container within that house, what seems to be the footprints of the pigeon can still appear on the surface of that yogurt.

1203. Āryadeva, *Four Hundred Stanzas* (*Catuḥśataka*), 10.7, Toh 3846 Tengyur, dbu ma, *tsha*, 11b1.

1204. *Catuḥśatakaṭīkā* chap. 10, 162a2–5.

1205. *Yuktiṣaṣṭikāvṛtti*, Toh 3864 Tengyur, dbu ma, *ya*, 10a1.

1206. Candrakīrti, *Commentary to the Sixty Stanzas of Reasoning* (*Yuktiṣaṣṭikāvṛtti*), Toh 3864, Tengyur, dbu ma, *ya*, 9b4. Differing slightly, the wording in the Dergé version reads "passage" rather than "system."

1207. Tsongkhapa, *Illuminating the Intent*, 62a5. See also translation by Thupten Jinpa in Tsongkhapa, *Illuminating the Intent*, 152–53.

1208. *Yuktiṣaṣṭikāvṛtti*, Toh 3864 Tengyur, dbu ma, *ya*, 10a2. The wording in the Dergé version differs slightly.

1209. Candrakīrti, *Commentary to the Sixty Stanzas of Reasoning* (*Yuktiṣaṣṭikāvṛtti*), Toh 3864 Tengyur, dbu ma, *ya*, 9b5–10a1.

1210. "And above" seems intended to include the Svātantrika but not the Prāsaṅgika.

1211. What this sentence says seems entirely correct, but it appears to clash with an assertion mentioned above (p. 629 and note 1114), regarding which there may be some doubts.

1212. *Pramāṇasamuccaya* 1.6, 2a1.

1213. *Yuktiṣaṣṭikāvṛtti*, Toh 3864 Tengyur, dbu ma, *ya*, 9a7–9b2. The wording in the Dergé version differs slightly.

1214. *Yuktiṣaṣṭikāvṛtti*, Toh 3864 Tengyur, dbu ma, *ya*, 9b3. The wording in the Dergé version differs slightly.

1215. Tsongkhapa, *Notes on the Eight Difficult Points*, 11b6–12a1. Jamyang Shepa is probably referring to this section. While not stating the point as directly as Jamyang Shepa proposes, Tsongkhapa suggests that it is possible for non-āryas to develop "clear appearance" (*gsal snang*) with regard to the selflessness of persons.

1216. Tsongkhapa, *Illuminating the Intent*, 27b1 and 27a4. Confusingly, Jamyang Shepa reverses the order of the lines that appear in Tsongkhapa's work. Nevertheless he is undoubtedly referring to the section that contains both of them. For a full translation of this section by Thupten Jinpa in Tsongkhapa, *Illuminating the Intent*, 80–83.

1217. *Bodhisattvacaryāvatāra* 9.45, Toh 3871 Tengyur, dbu ma, *la*, 32b3.

1218. The author is paraphrasing a passage cited by Candrakīrti, *Prasannapadā*, chap. 24, 171b4–173a6. The *Closely Guarded Concentration Sutra* (*Dhyāyitamuṣṭisūtra*) remains unidentified. But a section with some similarities to the present one appears in the *Sutra Teaching How All Phenomena Are Without Any Origin* (*Sarvadharmāpravṛttinirdeśasūtra*) Toh 180 Kanygur, mdo sde, *ma*, 275b–278a.

1219. *Saṃdhinirmocana*, Toh 106 Kangyur, mdo sde, *ca*, 51b2–4.

1220. *Prasannapadā*, 25b4.

1221. *Pramāṇaviniścayaṭīkā* chap. 1, 36b6–37a1.

1222. *Prasannapadā*, 25b4.

1223. Dharmottara, *Extensive Commentary on Drop of Logic* (*Nyāyabinduṭīkā*), chap. 1, Toh 4231 Tengyur, tshad ma, *we*, 40a4. This resembles what appears in the Dergé version. But the actual passage is in *Pramāṇaviniścayaṭīkā* chap. 1, 8a1 (see note 1059).
1224. Tib. *ji lta ba* and *ji snyed pa*.
1225. The uninformative name of the first category makes it seem indistinguishable from the thing of which it is supposed to be a subdivision, but Jamyang Shepa's description shows that he is using it as a catchall for inferential cognitions other than those of scripture or analogy.
1226. *Pramāṇavārttika* 4.51, 141a7. The second clause of this passage in the version of the text in the Dergé edition differs: *bstan bcos len pa rigs ldan yin*.
1227. The three Prajñāpāramitā sutras usually designated Mother, to which Jamyang Shepa refers here and later, are *Śatasāhasrikā-prajñāpāramitāsūtra*, *Pañcaviṃśatisāhasrikāprajñāpāramitāsūtra*, and *Aṣṭasāhasrikā-prajñāpāramitāsūtra*—the Prajñāpāramitā sutras in 100,000, 25,000, and 8,000 lines respectively.
1228. Tsongkhapa, *Greater Stages of the Path*, 486a2.
1229. *Prasannapadā*, 5b7. The wording in the Dergé version differs very slightly.
1230. Tsongkhapa, *Greater Stages of the Path*, 460b5.
1231. Tsongkhapa, *Greater Stages of the Path*, 461b1.
1232. Jamyang Shepa reminds the reader that the names of the two Madhyamaka subschools are said to derive from their respective dependence on consequences and autonomous proofs.
1233. *Pramāṇavārttika* 4.53, 141a7.
1234. For Khedrup Jé's remarks on the same matter, see p. 420.
1235. *Prasannapadā*, 25b4.
1236. *Sūtrasamuccaya*, Toh 3934 Tengyur, dbu ma, *ki*, 1148b2.
1237. *Madhyamakāvatārabhāṣya*, chap. 6, Toh 3862 Tengyur, dbu ma, *'a*, 245a1. While this seems to be the passage that Jamyang Shepa has in mind, the Dergé version does not include "valid." The formulation cited by the author here is closer to what is found in Jayānanda, *Commentary to Entering the Middle Way* (*Madhyamakāvatāraṭīkā*), Toh 3870 Tengyur, dbu ma, *ra*, 113a. At this point in his commentary to Candrakīrti's work, Jayānanda goes into some depth about how scriptural passages are asserted to be valid. However, Candrakīrti argues for the same case in *Clear Words* chap. 15, 90b.
1238. Nāgārjuna, *Ratnāvalī*, 4.91, Toh 4158 Tengyur, spring yig, *ge*, 121b4.
1239. *Madhyamakāvatārabhāṣya* chap. 6, Toh 3862, Tengyur, dbu ma, *'a*, 245a1.
1240. Jamyang Shepa reprises the analytical model he relied on above (p. 585 and note 947).
1241. Tsongkhapa, *Illuminating the Intent*, 163a5. See also translation by Thupten Jinpa in Tsongkhapa, *Illuminating the Intent*, 353.
1242. *Prasannapadā*, 22a4–23b5.
1243. *Prasannapadā* chap. 15, 90b7.
1244. Tsongkhapa, *Ocean of Reasoning*, 160b6–161a2.
1245. Candrakīrti, *Prasannapadā*, chap. 15, Toh 3860 Tengyur, dbu ma, *'a*, 90b7.
1246. Tsongkhapa, *Ocean of Reasoning*, 160b5.
1247. Jamyang Shepa reaches back to the derivation of the Sanskrit name for the class of valid cognition under discussion here to help explain the class itself and also why

it is permissible to describe a scripture as "valid." For the latter, he makes a link between scripture and valid cognition in terms of their nondeceptiveness. With respect to the Sanskrit name (*āgama-pramāṇa*), he gives the Buddhist derivation for each of the two elements, "scripture" and "valid cognition." In the Tibetan designation for this (*lung gi tshad ma*)—which I have translated as "valid cognition [associated with] scripture"—the two elements are connected together by the grammatical particle, identified with the sixth (genitive) case. Since sixth case grammatical particles have more than one function, authors often specify which function the particle in individual instances is performing, to clarify the relationship between the two conjoined elements. These functions are described in a note (761) attached to Khedrup Jé's discussion on the relation between "noncomposite" and "[cognitive] subject." Jamyang Shepa is essentially saying that the combination of elements in the name here should be understood to produce a meaning akin to "scriptural valid cognition."

1248. Khedrup Gelek Palsang, *Thousand Measures*, 224b1.
1249. *Madhyamakahṛdaya*, 9.18, Toh 3855 Tengyur, dbu ma, *dza*, 32a3.
1250. *Prasannapadā*, 25b4.
1251. *Commentary on the Difficult Points of the Compendium of Suchness, Tattvasaṃgrahapañjikā*, Toh 4267 Tengyur, tshad ma, *ze*, 135b1.
1252. *Madhyamakahṛdaya* 9.19, Toh 3855 Tengyur, dbu ma, *dza*, 32a4.
1253. Khedrup Jé, *Thousand Measures*, 224b1.
1254. *Prasannapadā*, 25b4.
1255. The Sanskrit term for "analogy" here is *upamānam*. Based on the Sanskrit etymology of this term, the Tibetan translation for this—(*dpe*) *nyer 'jal*—incorporates a word for "close" and is rendered literally as "comprehension of a close example." This explains Jamyang Shepa's many references to something that is "close."
1256. The different grammatical particles used to express these in Tibetan roughly equate with the English prepositions (indicated in italics). In brief, Jamyang Shepa says that explanations of this variety of inference commonly express the relation between the elements involved using the fifth case (e.g. "from"), whereas the second case (e.g. "to") and the sixth case (e.g. "'s") are more correct here and give a better sense of that relation.
1257. Here, to indicate that a shift has occurred, the term that was previously translated as "analogy" has been rendered "example-analogy." The Sanskrit word for "analogy" cited above (*upamānam*) is different from the one for "example" (*dṛṣṭana*), as in the "similar example" and the "dissimilar example" used to establish the forward and reverse pervasions within a proof. But a single Tibetan term (*dpe*) is used for both those Sanskrit terms. As employed in relation to the proof, the example of a thing is generally held to be something that should instantiate it. Obviously, however, an analogy for something is necessarily *not* that thing. The fact that a single term is used for those two concepts does not usually create problems in discussions on classical Buddhist Pramāṇa, simply because the analogy is generally held to have no real epistemological value. But Jamyang Shepa's description of valid cognition through analogy places it squarely in the domain of logical proofs and inferential cognitions, and his use of the Tibetan term in this section is clearly intended to encompass both example and analogy. This could be seen to place it at odds with the Pramāṇa tradition's general understanding of the "example" (*dṛṣṭana*),

and we have seen various points in this volume where criticisms have been made against examples that fail on account of the fact that they do not actually instantiate what they are supposed to be illustrating (see, for instance, pp. 451 and 457). It should be said, however, that there has been a widespread acknowledgment among Tibetan scholars that, in terms of proofs establishing emptiness, certain things presented as "examples" actually function more like analogies. This is the implicit conclusion of many debates on how the reflection of a face in a mirror can serve as a so-called example when establishing that something lacks true existence. Jamyang Shepa's explanation of this form of valid cognition certainly references these debates and their conclusions. But his bringing together of analogy and example here is not a widely accepted Prāsaṅgika slant on Pramāṇa. It seems more to reflect a Geluk scholar's wish to circumscribe the epistemological scope of analogy.

1258. *Prasannapadā*, 25b5.

1259. The section of Khedrup Jé's text that explores whether these two preclude each other (pp. 106–14) is very relevant to this point.

1260. Revisiting an earlier point, the Sanskrit term *svalakṣaṇa* yields a number of Tibetan terms and concepts, which are all linked by the fact that they refer to characteristics that are *individualized* in some way. Jamyang Shepa says that when a Prāsaṅgika uses *svalakṣaṇa*, it does not convey a "specifically characterized (phenomena)" but rather is simply to be understood as a "definition," in the sense of a set of characteristics that distinguish a certain phenomenon, such as form, from others. Similarly, he says that the Prāsaṅgika may speak of "*general* characteristics" (*sāmānyalakṣaṇa*) but that this does not refer to "generally characterized phenomena." Although he does not expand on what he means when he says that "impermanence, the two kinds of selflessness, and so forth" are to be understood in terms of general characteristics, it seems very likely that he just means that each of these is true of *many* phenomena. This corresponds with the way Prajñāmokṣa's *Commentary to [Atiśa's] Middle Way Instruction* explains Atiśa's reference to the twofold division, and how "general characteristics" is essentially to be understood in the manner of the four seals—that all composite things are impermanent, all contaminated things are (in the nature of) suffering, all phenomena are empty and selfless, and nirvana is peace.

1261. *Catuḥśatakaṭīkā* chap. 11, 186b4.

1262. Āryadeva, *Catuḥśataka*, 12.5, Toh 3846 Tengyur, dbu ma, *tsha*, 13a7.

1263. Amarasiṃha, *Amarakośa*, chap. 13, Toh 4299 Tengyur, sgra mdo, *se*, 211b6.

1264. *Prasannapadā*, 24b2.

1265. Amarasiṃha, *Amarakośa*, chap. 13, Toh 4299 Tengyur, sgra mdo, *se*, 211b6.

1266. *Prasannapadā*, 25b4.

1267. *Pramāṇavārttika* 3.257, 128a6.

1268. Āryadeva, *Catuḥśataka*, 13.8, Toh 3846 Tengyur, dbu ma, *tsha*, 14b2.

1269. *Prasannapadā*, 24b1.

1270. Āryadeva, *Catuḥśataka*, 8.19, Toh 3846 Tengyur, dbu ma, *tsha*, 9b7.

1271. Āryadeva, *Catuḥśataka*, 16.24, Toh 3846 Tengyur, dbu ma, *tsha*, 18a4.

1272. *Catuḥśatakaṭīkā* chap. 16, 238a7.

1273. *Vigrahavyāvartanī*, stanza 40, Toh 3828 Tengyur, dbu ma, *tsa*, 28a6.

1274. *Vigrahavyāvartanī*, stanza 31, Toh 3828 Tengyur, dbu ma, *tsa*, 28a2.

1275. *Vigrahavyāvartanī*, stanzas 44–46, Toh 3828 Tengyur, dbu ma, *tsa*, 28a7. The first two lines in the Dergé edition differ slightly.

1276. *Vigrahavyāvartanī*, stanza 47, Toh 3828 Tengyur, dbu ma, *tsa*, 28b2. The first line differs slightly from the Dergé version.
1277. *Madhyamakāvatāra* 6.58, Toh 3861 Tengyur, dbu ma, *'a*, 207a2.
1278. *Madhyamakāvatārabhāṣya* chap. 6, Toh 3862, Tengyur, dbu ma, *'a*, 267a4.
1279. *Prasannapadā*, 25b5.
1280. *Prasannapadā*, 25a3.
1281. Tsongkhapa, *Illuminating the Intent*, 162a1. See also translation by Thupten Jinpa in Tsongkhapa, *Illuminating the Intent*, 351.
1282. This figure is used in the context of the Prāsaṅgika refutation of self-cognition. Self-cognition is criticized on the grounds that positing it leads to an infinite regress, since if the other-cognition requires a self-cognition to verify it, the self-cognition would in turn require another valid cognition to perform a similar role, and so forth. The rodent is used to evoke an alternative model of explanation. Certain rodents are said to infect or "poison" one through their bite. At the time of being bitten, the person can be fully cognizant of what has occurred, but awareness of having been infected may only come later. It is when certain conditions subsequently bring the ailment arising from the infection to the fore that retrospective awareness is gained and the person establishes the "poisoning."
1283. Tsongkhapa, *Illuminating the Intent*, 160b5–161a5. See also translation by Thupten Jinpa in Tsongkhapa, *Illuminating the Intent*, 349.
1284. *Prasannapadā*, 25b6.
1285. Jamyang Shepa, *Decisive Analysis of the Madhyamakāvatāra*.
1286. The second line calls upon a Sanskrit poetic synonym for the moon, *kumudabandhu*, which translates literally as "companion of (or friend to) the night lotus." But the words actually refer to Candrakīrti, since *candra* means "moon."
1287. Tib. *gdong lnga pa*. Skt. *pañcānana*. Explanations of this name vary. Some take it literally to denote five faces and describe what each symbolizes. Others take it to refer to the large size of the lion's head or open mouth.
1288. In likening his work to the sun, Jamyang Shepa brings together two counts of twelve. "Master of the twelve" references a Sanskrit poetic synonym for the sun that depicts it as chief of the *ādityas*, a class of twelve solar deities. The second count of twelve seems to reference the twelve classes of Buddhist scripture (Tib. *gsung rab yan lag bcu gnyis*, Skt. *dvādaśāṅgapravacana*).
1289. As mentioned in the volume's introduction, it seems likely that this is Döndrup Gyatso (also known as Hortön Döndrup Gyatso), who became the forty-eighth Ganden throneholder in 1702. But prior to this, he had been the abbot of Gomang and then, later, the abbot of Gyümé. He was also one of Jamyang Shepa's main teachers, although there are some questions about when and where their encounters occurred and which of the tenures is referred to here in the colophon.
1290. The final verse of dedication and the two Sanskrit phrases are not part of Jamyang Shepa's original composition. They were appended to the version of the text that was produced at Labrang Tashikhyil Monastery.
1291. This subheading is introduced at the beginning but does not appear explicitly in the text.

Glossary

Note: Where a clearly identified Sanskrit source term exists, this has been included. But it should be noted that this glossary primarily reflects Geluk scholarship's understanding of the terms, which occasionally differs from that of others.

actual thing (Tib. *dngos po*, Skt. *vastu*, *bhāva*, etc.). An impermanent entity that functions, has its own characteristics, and the existence of which is independent of the conceptual mind.

antagonistic preclusion (*lhan cig mi gnas 'gal*). That state of incompatibility between two actual (i.e., impermanent) things, meaning that they cannot coexist in the same locus for any sustained period.

anti-predicate (*dgag bya'i chos*). The element that is negated when establishing that a subject has a particular predicate. Thus, in establishing that sound is impermanent, one negates that it is the anti-predicate, permanent.

appearing object (*snang yul*, *pratibhāsaviṣaya*). That which is most immediately present to the cognitive subject. For a conceptual cognition, this is the medium through which the main object is reached. For a perception, which gets at its object directly, without relying on a medium, this is the main object itself.

ascertainment. See entry below.

ascertaining awareness (*nges shes*, *niścayajñāna*). A correct cognition that brings with it knowledge about its object that is certain. Ascertainment is usually explained as a conceptual function.

aspect (*rnam pa*, *ākāra*). Various meanings, see note 111.

basis of negation (*dgag gzhi*). The subject in a proof or consequence, about which something is being ruled out.

circular [definition, etc.] (*rtogs pa phan tshun brten pa*). A flaw in an argument or in an account of how knowledge of a thing is to be gained, in which *x* is introduced to explain or justify *y*, but *x* cannot be explained or justified without reference back to *y*. The Tibetan literally means "each realization depending on the other."

cognition that grasps the reason (*rtags 'dzin sems*). The cognition generated when someone is first able to gather together different pieces of knowledge about a thing to realize that it fulfills all three criteria required of a correct reason.

common locus (Tib. *gzhi mthun*, Skt. *samānādhikaraṇa* or *samānādhibaraṇa*). An instantiation of two different qualities or things. Pot, for instance, is a common locus of physical matter and an existent thing.

comprehended object or **comprehended thing** (*gzhal bya, prameya*). An entity that exists and is therefore known.

comprehensive engager (*sgrub 'jug, vidhipravṛtti*). A cognition that engages its object not in a selective manner but affirmatively, such that the various features of that object (rather than just the object itself) appear to it. Perception is a comprehensive engager, in contrast to conceptual cognition.

conceived object (*zhen yul*). The main object that a conceptual cognition gets at or engages in, as opposed to the medium by means of which it is able to reach that object.

conceptual construct (*sgro btags, samāropa*). Something superimposed by thought but nevertheless useful or necessary for making sense of the world, using language, and gaining knowledge.

conceptual isolation (*ldog pa*). Based on the principle of the *apoha* theory, this is a mental abstraction that arrives at a specific object through a process of double negation. For more on the individual varieties, see note 228.

consequence (*thal 'gyur, prāsaṅga*). An argument that largely mirrors the proof in structure but is used to criticize the position of an opponent and is built upon the opponent's own assertions, as signaled by the necessary inclusion of the expression "it follows."

correct reason (*rtags yang dag, samyakliṅga*). Something that fulfills the three prescribed criteria (see entry for *three criteria*) and is thereby qualified to establish a thesis in a proof. More literally, this is a correct *sign* or *mark* (see note 17).

(preparative) countering valid cognition (*gnod byed kyi tshad ma, bādhakapramāṇa*). An inferential valid cognition that allows an individual to establish the reverse pervasion of another, main proof. As set out in the text (see pp. 397–99 and note 682), the proof that is the basis of such an inferential cognition is designed to rule out that the reason and anti-predicate of the main proof have a common locus.

(accurately) discern (*yongs gcod, pariccheda*). To realize an object, and for many scholars (see note 326), to do so in an affirmative fashion.

definiendum (*mtshon bya, lakṣya*). The thing defined or embodied by a definition (rather than just the name or label applied to a thing). One member of the definition-illustration-definiendum triad.

definition (*mtshan nyid, lakṣaṇa*). The characteristic or set of characteristics (rather than a set of words or verbal formula) that delineate a thing. One member of the definition-illustration-definiendum triad.

discrediting statement (*sun 'byin, dūṣaṇa*). A refutation conforming to a prescribed pattern that in Tibetan scholasticism is largely equated with the consequence.

dissimilar example (*mi mthun dpe, vidṛṣṭānta*). A thing that is used to help establish the reverse pervasion by means of a negative contrast. Thus for the proof "Sound is impermanent because it is produced," noncomposite space (which is permanent) is presented as a dissimilar example.

dissimilar instance. A thing that belongs to the class of dissimilar instances (see next entry).

(class of) dissimilar instances (*mi mthun phyogs, vipakṣa*). The thing or class of things that constitute the opposite of the similar instances in a proof.

(mental) distortion (*sgro 'dogs, adhyāropa*). An incorrect imposition—usually the specific false attribution of a quality—or the consciousness responsible for that attribution, which a valid cognition is able to rectify or counter.

effect reason (*'bras bu'i rtags, kāryahetu*). One of the three principal divisions of correct reason. This forms part of a proof that uses an effect to make affirmative deductions about a cause.

engaged object. See entry for *object of engagement.*

equivalent (*don gcig, ekārtha*). Two or more things that are completely coterminous.

established basis (*gzhi grub*). A thing that is established by valid cognition and is therefore an existent. The basis about (literally, "upon") which various qualities can be established.

evident (*mngon gyur, abhimukī*). A class of phenomena that can, generally speaking, be cognized by perception without needing to rely on inference. Evident things are contrasted with the class of the hidden.

excluding engager (*sel 'jug, apohapravṛtti*). A designation used for both conceptual cognitions and communicative sounds, both of which engage their objects by means of overt elimination.

excluding perspective (*sel ngo*). Conceptual cognition's viewpoint of its object, in that such a cognition is only capable of engaging that object in an eliminative fashion, not an affirmative one.

exclusion (*sel ba, apoha*). The act of elimination through which conceptual cognitions and communicative sounds are able to engage their objects. Or more generally, the name of the theory describing that. Also see entry for *other-exclusion*.

extremely hidden thing (*shin tu lkog gyur, atyantaparokṣa*). A hidden thing that an ordinary being must rely on the contents of scripture and an inference dealing with a matter of conviction to realize.

false cognition (*log shes, mithyājñāna*). A cognition that is completely spurious and provides incorrect information.

first party (*snga rgol, pūrvavādin*). In a debate between two persons, the one who conveys a proof to the other, seeking to induce in him an inference. In most cases this is identified as the Buddhist, presenting a correct proof.

forward pervasion (*rjes khyab, anvayavyāpti*). The second of the three criteria for a correct reason, that it should be fully present in the class of similar instances. Thus, in terms of the proof "Sound is impermanent because it is produced," every case of a thing that is produced belongs to the category of things that are impermanent.

generally characterized (entity) (*spyi mtshan, sāmānyalakṣaṇa*). Something that depends on the conceptual mind for its existence.

governing condition (*bdag rkyen, adhipatipratyaya*). One of the three main conditions or causes—the other two being the object and immediate conditions—with a role in producing a sense perception. This condition determines that each of the six kinds of sense perception—from the visual through to the mental—experiences only its own kind of object and not others.

held object (*gzung yul*). This object of cognition is identified in the same way as the appearing object.

hidden (thing) (*lkog gyur, parokṣa*). A phenomenon that must initially be realized by means of an inferential cognition. There are two varieties, slightly hidden and extremely hidden.

illustration (*mtshan gzhi, lakṣya*). Something that embodies the defining characteristics and helps an individual make the link between those characteristics and the definiendum.

immediate condition or **immediately preceding condition** (*de ma thag rkyen, samanatarapratyaya*). One of the three main conditions or causes—the other two being the governing and object conditions—with a role in producing a sense perception. The immediate condition is a consciousness from which the perception directly arises, without necessarily sharing the same object as it.

implicative negation (*ma yin dgag, paryudāsa*). One of the two varieties of negation, the other being *straight negation*. With this variety, within the negation of one thing there is the suggestion or affirmation of another.

inference or **inferential cognition** (*rjes dpag, anumāṇa*). A correct conceptual cognition that realizes its object and is generated by relying on a logical proof, embodied by a reason.

inference of conviction (*yid ches kyi rjes dpag, āptānumāṇa*). This—more properly to be understood as *an inference that deals with a matter of conviction*—is an inferential cognition derived from an associated proof that uses the fact that a particular passage of scripture has withstood a prescribed form of analysis to establish that the content of that passage is nondeceptive.

inference (dealing with) demonstrable facts and realities (*dngos stobs kyi rjes dpag, vastubalapravṛttānumāna*). An inference about a phenomenon or phenomena that are slightly hidden—i.e., hidden entities that do not fall within the domain of scriptural inference. A correct inferential cognition of this variety relies on a proof that uses knowledge from the domains of the slightly hidden and the evident to realize another slightly hidden entity.

inference (dealing with) the issue of common agreement (about names) (*grags pa'i rjes dpag*). An inferential cognition derived from a proof that is concerned with establishing a particular principle that governs the usage of names.

infinite regress (*thug med du thal*). The logical flaw of trying to account for a process by attributing a particular function to a certain entity, but that entity in turn requiring another similar entity to perform a corresponding function with respect to it, and so on. Accusations that such a fault has been incurred are most frequently made in relation to explanations of processes and elements involved in cognition.

manifest (phenomenon). See entry for "evident."

(preclusion of) mutual opposition (*phan tshun phan 'gal*). A state of incompatibility between two things, such that something being one of them necessarily rules out its being the other.

nature reason (*rang bzhin gyi rtags, svabhāvahetu*). One of the three principal divisions of correct reason. This forms part of a proof that uses the fact that two things share the same nature to make affirmative deductions about one of them based on the other.

negandum (*dgag bya*). An element that is ruled out or negated through a verbal or mental process. In the context of the proof, the negandum is the opposite of the probandum. As such, it represents an *anti-thesis*—a combination of the subject and the anti-predicate—that of which the probandum represents a negation. For instance, if the probandum is "Sound is impermanent," the negandum is "Sound is permanent."

non-actual thing (*dngos med, abhāva*). The converse of an actual thing, a category that includes both permanent phenomena and nonexistent entities.

nondeceptive (*mi slu ba, avisaṃvādi*). Rather than the mere absence of deceptiveness, the quality of being totally reliable and trustworthy, in the sense of being the source of certain and incontestable information and knowledge.

(reason involving the) nonobservation of a thing that is not accessible (*mi snang ba ma dmigs pa'i rtags*). One of the two main subdivisions of nonobservation reasons. This one uses the fact of nonaccessibility—meaning that even if the thing in question were to be present within the specified object or location, the individual or type of individual concerned would be in no position to observe it—to make a logical deduction.

(reason involving the) nonobservation of a thing that should be apparent (*snang rung ma dmigs pa'i rtags*). One of the two main subdivisions of nonobservation reasons. This relies on the fact that if the thing in question were present within the specified object or location, the individual in question should be able to observe it to make a logical deduction. This kind of reason is typically used to establish that the thing in question is not present in a particular location or that it does not exist at all.

nonobservation reason (*ma dmigs pa'i rtags, anupalabdhihetu*). One of the three principal divisions of correct reason. This forms part of a proof that uses facts—such as that a certain thing is not observed in a specific time and place, or by a particular individual—to make deductions of a negative aspect.

(preparative) nonreliance valid cognition (*bltos med kyi tshad ma*). An inferential valid cognition that allows an individual to establish the forward pervasion of another, main proof.

object (*yul, viṣaya*). A thing that is known or conveyed by a *subject* (i.e., a cognition or a communicative sound).

(observed) object condition (*dmigs rkyen, ālambanapratyaya*). One of the three main conditions or causes—the other two being the governing and immediate conditions—with a role in producing a sense perception. This is generally identified as the object of the perception—i.e., in the case of a perception of pot, the pot—and is explained as the thing chiefly responsible for making the perception take on the aspect that it does.

object of engagement (*'jug yul, pravṛttiviṣaya*). The object that a cognition or consciousness is directed toward or focused upon. Pot, for instance, is the object of engagement both for the perception of pot and the conceptual cognition of pot.

object-aspect (*gzung rnam, grāhyākāra*). The outward-looking cognition that is directed, for instance, toward an external object, as opposed to that which is inward-looking (the latter being known as the *subject-aspect*).

object universal (*don spyi, arthasāmānya*). The appearing object of a conceptual cognition. That by means of which such a cognition is able to engage the object upon which it focuses.

other-cognition (*gzhan rig*). That portion of the consciousness other than self-cognition; it is directed toward the object rather than the subject.

other-exclusion (*gzhan sel, anyāpoha*). Essentially the same as *exclusion*, but this designation is used more when the discussions are about the divisions of exclusion and the things arrived at through exclusion.

other party. Same as *second party*.

particular (*bye brag, vaśeṣa*). Something that belongs to a type or kind and is an instance or individuation of a universal.

perception (*mngon sum, pratyakṣa*). A cognition that realizes its object directly and in a nonconceptual fashion.

pervasion (*khyab pa, vyāpti*). The notion of encompassment that serves as the basis for a theory of logical entailment. In the classic sense, *x* "pervades" *y* when *x*, as a category, covers and includes every case of *y*. Once a *pervasion* between the two is established, it allows for deductions, since where there is *y* there must be *x*, and so forth. In the non-classic sense of Tibetan argumentation, the pervasion is simply logical necessity, meaning that if *y* is true, then so must *x* be.

preclusion (*'gal ba, virodha*). A principle underpinning Buddhist logic. Two things preclude each other if they are different and a common locus of them is impossible.

predicate (*bsgrub bya'i chos, don*, etc.). The element that occupies the second position in a proof or consequence—i.e., in the thesis "Sound is impermanent," *impermanent* is the predicate.

probandum (*sgrub bya, sādhya*). The technical name for "that which is to be established"—that is, the thesis of the proof.

probans (*sgrub byed*). The technical name for the reason, the part of the proof that establishes the thesis.

proof (Tib. *sbyor ba*, Skt. *prayoga*, etc.). That which is presented to establish a thesis, and if correct, can induce an inferential cognition realizing that thesis. In the Tibetan tradition, direct designations for the proof are used rarely. The preference is to refer to the proof through its constituent parts, *especially* the reason. A reason can only be correct within the context of a specific proof. Tibetan authors therefore see the correct reason, with its three criteria fulfilled, as the embodiment of the correct proof, and they regularly refer to the reason (usually by the name *rtags*) to communicate the proof.

proof statement (*sgrub ngag*). The verbal formulation of the proof, which the Tibetan tradition distinguishes from the proof itself.

property of the probandum (*bsgrub bya'i chos, sādhyadharma*). The second component within the probandum or thesis—i.e., the one occupying the predicate position. This could more accurately be described as the "property *within* the probandum."

property of the subject (*phyogs chos, pakṣadharmatā*). The first of the three criteria of the correct reason. It is the ascertainment that the reason is present in the subject as its property.

referent for the anti-predicate (*dgag bya'i chos kyi don*). In a nonobservation proof of the "not accessible" variety, an element such as the *piśāca* spirit may be described as a thing that is not observed. But since the proof is not designed to rule out the presence of the *piśāca*, it does not form part of the negandum. The classification of the *piśāca* as the referent for the anti-predicate is, however, a recognition that the anti-predicate is constructed around it.

relationship (*'brel ba, saṃbhandha*). Another underpinning of the logical system. Two things are logically related only if the withdrawal or negation of one of them also necessarily brings with it the withdrawal or negation of the other.

remote entity (*bskal don*). A class of things that—for various reasons, including distance, time, nature, or the limitations of the perceptual apparatus of a potential viewer—might lie beyond that viewer's immediate ken.

reverse pervasion (*ldog khyab, vyatirekavyāpti*). The third of the three criteria for a correct reason, that it should be totally absent from the class of dissimilar instances. Thus, in terms of the proof "Sound is impermanent because it is produced," it means that no case of a thing that is produced is present in the category of things that are permanent.

same simultaneous substantial entity or **same simultaneous substance** (*grub bde dbyer med kyi rdzas gcig*). Two or more impermanent features, qualities, etc., that belong to a single substantial entity but do not necessarily belong to the same sense domain, such as the shape and smell of a pot.

scriptural inference (*lung gi rjes dpag*). Same as *inference of conviction.*

scriptural valid cognition (*lung gi tshad ma, āgamapramāṇa*). Same as *valid cognition of conviction.*

second party (*phyi rgol, uttaravādin*). In a debate between two persons, the one to whom a proof is presented, so that it may induce in him an inference. In most cases in the Pramāṇa writings, this is identified as the non-Buddhist.

self-cognition (Tib. *rang rig*, Skt. *svasaṃvedana* or *svasaṃvitti*). That portion of every conscious experience that is directed inward toward the subject (i.e., consciousness) and is therefore aware of being aware.

similar example (*mthun dpe, sadṛṣṭānta*). A thing that is used to help establish the forward pervasion in that it draws attention to a quality shared with the reason, affirming that the reason belongs among the class of similar instances.

similar instance. A thing that belongs to the class of similar instances (see next entry).

(class of) similar instances (*mthun phyogs*). That class of things that a proof seeks to establish the subject belongs to exclusively. In the proof "Sound is impermanent because it is produced," this is impermanent (things).

slightly hidden thing (*cung zad lkog gyur*). A hidden thing that falls within the domain of demonstrable facts and realities, and which can be realized by relying on proofs that deal with these, as opposed to relying on scripture.

specifically characterized [phenomenon] (*rang mtshan, svalakṣaṇa*). Something impermanent, occupying a place in time and space, and existing independently of mind.

straight (or nonimplicative) negation (*med dgag, prasajyapratiṣedha*). One of the two basic varieties of negation (the other being the *implicative negation*). With this negation, no other thing is suggested or affirmed through the negation—it is simply an absence.

subject (*yul can*). Literally, "that which has an object"—i.e., either a cognition, a communicative sound, or a person.

subject (*chos can, dharmin*). The first element in the proof and also the consequence.

subject of interest (*shes 'dod chos can*). The same as the proof's subject—i.e., what the second party wishes to know something about.

subject-aspect (*'dzin rnam, grāhakākāra*). The same as the *self-cognition*.

substance (*rdzas, dravya*). An impermanent thing, typically presented as a substratum, and as such, distinguished from the features inhering in it. Since substances are also seen as phenomena that exist independently, they are also frequently contrasted with those that are conceptually constructed.

three criteria (*tshul gsum, trairūpya*). The three conditions or standards that something must meet to qualify as a correct reason. These are the property of the subject, the forward pervasion, and the reverse pervasion.

three spheres (*'khor gsum*). An expression used in argumentation by someone attacking an opponent's position by means of consequences. It amounts to an accusation that elements within the opponent's position are in such a direct state of conflict with each other that the position is no longer logically viable (see note 89).

universal (*spyi, sāmānya*). Something that has particular instances or individuations.

valid cognition (*tshad ma, pramāṇa*). A cognition that brings with it correct and certain knowledge of a thing. It has two varieties, perception and inference.

Bibliography

Works Cited or Mentioned by the Authors

Kangyur

Ascertaining the Discipline: Upāli's Questions. Vinayaviniścayopālipariprcchā. 'Dul ba rnam par gtan la dbab pa nye bar 'khor gyis zhus pa. Toh 68, dkon brtsegs *ca.*

Bodhisattva's Scriptural Collection. Bodhisattvapiṭaka. Byang chub sems dpa'i sde snod. Toh 56, dkon brtsegs *kha.*

Chapter Explaining the Three Vows. Trisaṃvaranirdeśaparivarta. Sdom pa gsum bstan pa'i le'u. Toh 45, dkon brtsegs *ka.*

Chapters of Utterances on Specific Topics. Udānavarga. Ched du brjod pa'i tshoms. Toh 326, mdo sde *sa.*

Closely Guarded Concentration Sutra. Bsam gtan dpe mkhyud kyi mdo. Possibly an alternative title for the *Sutra Teaching How All Phenomena Are Without Any Origin. Sarvadharmāpravṛttinirdeśasūtra. Chos thams cad 'byung ba med par bstan pa'i mdo.* Toh 180, mdo sde *ma.*

Deliberation on the Dharma Sutra. Dharmasaṃgītisūtra. Chos yang dag par sdud pa'i mdo. Toh 238, mdo sde *zha.*

Elucidating the Intention Sutra. Saṃdhinirmocana. Mdo sde dgongs 'grel. Toh 106, mdo sde *ca.*

Great Parinirvāṇa Sutra. Mahāparinirvāṇasūtra. Yongs su mya ngan las 'das pa chen po'i mdo. Toh 119, mdo sde *ta.*

History of Kanakavarṇa. Kanakavarṇapūrvayoga. Gser mdog gi sngon gyi sbyor ba. Toh 350, mdo sde *a.*

Hundred Accounts of Noble Deeds Beginning with That of Pūrṇa. Pūrṇapramukhāvadānaśataka. Gang po la sogs pa'i rtogs pa brjod pa brgya pa. Toh 343, mdo sde *am.*

Hundred Deeds. Karmaśataka. Las brgya pa. Toh 340, mdo sde *a.*

Impermanence Sutra. Anityatāsūtra. Mi rtag pa nyid kyi mdo. Toh 310, mdo sde *sa.*

King Dhāraṇīśvara Sutra. Dhāraṇīśvararājesūtra. Gzungs rgyal kyi mdo. It is unclear whether this is Toh 62, 95, 147, or 522.

King of Samādhis Sutra. Samādhirājasūtra. Ting nge 'dzin gyi rgyal po'i mdo. Toh 127, mdo sde *da.*

Lion's Roar of Śrīmālādevī Sutra. Śrīmālādevīsiṃhanādasūtra. Lha mo dpal phreng gi seng ge'i sgra'i mdo. Toh 92, dkon brtsegs *ma.*

Lump of Foam Sutta. Pāli: *Phena Sutta. Yang dag ldan pa'i mdo. Saṃyutta Nikāya* 22.95 (Bodhi, *Connected Discourses,* 951–53).

Miraculous Play of Mañjuśrī. Mañjuśrīvikrīḍita. 'Jam dpal rnam par rol pa. Toh 96, mdo sde *kha.*

Play in Full Sutra. Lalitavistarasūtra. Rgya cher rol pa'i mdo. Toh 95, mdo sde *kha.*

Precious Discourse on the Blessed One's Extensive Wisdom That Leads to Infinite Certainty. Niṣṭhāgatabhagavajjñānavaipulyasūtraratnānanta. Bcom ldan 'das kyi ye shes rgyas pa'i mdo sde rin po che mtha' yas pa mthar phyin pa. Toh 99, mdo sde *ga.*

Questions of Dīrghanakha the Wandering Mendicant. Dīrghanakhaparivrājakaparipṛcchāsūtra. Kun tu rgyus pa sen rings kyis zhus pa'i mdo. Toh 342, mdo sde *a.*

Questions of Ratnacūḍa Sutra. Ratnacūḍaparipṛcchāsūtra. Gtsug na rin po ches zhus pa'i mdo. Toh 91, dkon brtsegs *cha.*

Sutra Teaching How All Phenomena Are Without Any Origin. Sarvadharmāpravṛttinirdeśasūtra. Chos thams cad 'byung ba med par bstan pa'i mdo. Toh 180, mdo sde *ma.*

Sutra Teaching the Unfathomable Sphere of a Buddha. Acintyabuddhaviṣayanirdeśasūtra. Sangs rgyas kyi yul bsam gyis mi khyab pa bstan pa'i mdo. Toh 79, dkon brtsegs *ca.*

Tantra of Great Power. Mahābalatantra. Dpal stobs po che'i rgyud kyi rgyal po. Toh 391, rgyud *ga.*

Teaching of Akṣayamati Sutra. Akṣayamatinirdeśasūtra. Blo gros mi zad pas bstan pa. Toh 175, mdo sde *ma.*

Ten Grounds Sutra. Daśadharmasūtra. Chos bcu pa'i mdo. Toh 53, dkon brtsegs *kha.*

Tengyur

Amarasiṃha. *Treasury of Amara. Amarakośa. 'Chi ba med pa'i mdzod.* Toh 4299, sgra mdo *se.*

Āryadeva. *Compendium of the Essence of Knowledge-Insight. Jñānasārasamuccaya. Ye shes snying po kun las btus pa.* Toh 3851, dbu ma *tsha.*

———. *Four Hundred Stanzas. Catuḥśataka. (Dbu ma) Bzhi brgya pa.* Toh 3846, dbu ma *tsha.*

Asaṅga. *Compendium of Abhidharma. Abhidharmasamuccaya. Mngon pa kun btus.* Toh 4049, sems tsam *ri.*

———. *Foundation for Yoga Practitioners: Compendium of Ascertainment. Yogācārabhūmiviniścayasaṃgrahaṇī. Rnal 'byor spyod pa'i sa rnam par gtan la dbab pa bsdu ba.* Toh 4038, sems tsam *zhi* and *zi.*

Avalokitavrata. *Extensive Commentary on (Bhāviveka's) "Lamp of Wisdom." Prajñāpradīpaṭīkā, Shes rab sgron ma rgya cher 'grel pa.* Toh 3859, dbu ma *wa, zha,* and *za.*

Bhāviveka. *Blaze of Reasoning: Commentary on the Heart of the Middle Way. Tarkajvālā. Dbu ma snying po'i 'grel pa rtog ge'i 'bar ba.* Toh 3856, dbu ma *dza.*

———. *Heart of the Middle Way. Madhyamakahṛdaya. Dbu ma'i snying po.* Toh 3855, dbu ma *dza.*

Buddhapālita. *Buddhapālita's Commentary on Fundamental Treatise on the Middle Way. Buddhapālitamūlamadhyamakavṛtti. Dbu ma rtsa ba'i 'grel pa buddha pā li ta.* Toh 3842, dbu ma *tsa.*

Candrakīrti. *Clear Words. Prasannapadā. Dbu ma tshig gsal.* Toh 3860, dbu ma *'a.*

———. *Commentary to Four Hundred Stanzas. Catuḥśatakaṭīkā. Dbu ma bzhi rgya pa'i 'grel ba.* Toh 3865, dbu ma *ya.*

———. *Commentary on Sixty Stanzas of Reasoning. Yuktiṣaṣṭikāvṛtti. Rigs pa drug cu pa'i 'grel pa.* Toh 3864, dbu ma *ya.*

———. *Entering the Middle Way. Madhyamakāvatāra. Dbu ma la 'jug pa.* Toh 3861, dbu ma *'a.*

———. *Entering the Middle Way Autocommentary. Madhyamakāvatārabhāṣya. Dbu ma la 'jug pa'i bshad pa.* Toh 3862, dbu ma *'a.*

Devendrabuddhi. *Commentary on the Difficult Points in the Pramāṇavārttika. Pramāṇavārttikapañjikā. Tshad ma rnam 'grel gyi dka' 'grel.* Toh 4217, tshad ma *che.*

Dharmakīrti. *Ascertainment of Pramāṇa. Pramāṇaviniścaya. Tshad ma rnam nges.* Toh 4211, tshad ma *ce.*

———. *Commentary on Pramāṇa. Pramāṇavārttika. Tshad ma rnam 'grel.* Toh 4210, tshad ma *ce.*

———. *Commentary on Pramāṇa Autocommentary. Pramāṇavārttikavṛtti* [or *Svavṛtti*]. *Tshad ma rnam 'grel gyi 'grel ba* (*rang 'grel*). Toh 4216, tshad ma *ce.*

———. *Drop of Logic. Nyāyabindu. Tshad ma rigs pa'i thigs pa.* Toh 4212, tshad ma *ce.*

———. *Drop of Reasoning. Hetubindu. Gtan tshigs kyi thigs pa.* Toh 4213, tshad ma *ce.*

Dharmottara. *Direct Commentary on Ascertainment of Pramāṇa (Chapters 1 and 2). Pramāṇaviniścayaṭīkā. Tshad ma rnam nges pa'i 'grel bshad. Tshad ma rnam par nges pa'i ṭīka 'thad ldan zhes bya ba (le'u dang po dang gnyis pa).* Toh 4229, tshad ma *dze.*

———. *Direct Commentary on Ascertainment of Pramāṇa (Chapter 3). Pramāṇaviniścayaṭīkā. Tshad ma rnam nges pa'i 'grel bshad. Tshad ma rnam par nges pa'i ṭīka 'thad ldan zhes bya ba (le'u gsum pa).* Toh 4227, tshad ma *tshe.*

———. *Extensive Commentary on Drop of Logic. Nyāyabinduṭīkā. Rigs pa'i thigs pa'i rgya cher 'grel pa.* Toh 4231, tshad ma *we.*

Dignāga. *Analysis of Objects of Cognition. Ālambanaparīkṣā. Dmigs pa brtag pa.* Toh 4205, tshad ma *ce.*

———. *Analysis of Objects of Cognition Autocommentary. Ālambanaparīkṣāvṛtti. Dmigs pa brtag pa'i 'grel pa.* Toh 4206, tshad ma *ce.*

———. *Compendium of Pramāṇa. Pramāṇasamuccaya. Tshad ma kun las btus pa.* Toh 4203, tshad ma *ce.*

———. *Compendium of Pramāṇa Autocommentary. Pramāṇasamuccayavṛtti. Tshad ma kun btus pa'i 'grel ba* (*rang 'grel*). Toh 4204, tshad ma *ce.*

———. *Entrance to Reasoning. Nyāyamukha. Rigs pa la 'jug pa.* (see entry for Śaṅkarasvāmin).

Durgāsiṃha. *Autocommentary to (Rules for Suffixes forming Verbal Derivatives beginning with) Uṇ etc. (in the Kātantra System of Sanskrit Grammar). Uṇādivṛtti. Uṇa la sogs pa'i 'grel pa.* Toh 4426, sna tshogs *no.*

———. *Rules for (Suffixes forming Verbal Derivatives beginning with) Uṇ etc. (in the Kātantra System of Sanskrit Grammar). Kalāpoṇādisūtra. Ka lā pa'i uṇa la sogs pa'i mdo.* Toh 4425, sna tshogs *no.*

Guṇaprabha. *Vinaya Sutra. Vinayasūtra. 'Dul ba'i mdo.* Toh 4117, 'dul ba *wu.*

Haribhadra. *Clear Meaning: Commentary* (*on the Ornament of Realizations*). (*Sphuṭārtha*) *Abhisamayālaṃkāranāmaprajñāpāramitopadeśaśāstravṛtti.* (*'Grel ba don gsal*) *Shes rab kyi pha rol tu phyin pa'i man ngag gi bstan bcos mngon par rtogs pa'i rgyan zhes bya ba'i 'grel pa.* Toh 3793, shes phyin *ja.*

Jayānanda. *Commentary to Entering the Middle Way. Madhyamakāvatāraṭīkā. Dbu ma la 'jug pa'i 'grel bshad.* Toh 3870, dbu ma *ra.*

Jitāri. *Analysis of the Sugata's System. Sugatamatavibhaṅga. Bde bar gshegs pa gzhung rnam par 'byed pa.* Toh 3899, dbu ma *a.*

Jñānagarbha. *Commentary on Distinction between the Two Truths. Satyadvayavibhaṅgavṛtti. Bden gnyis rnam par 'byed pa'i 'grel pa.* Toh 3882, dbu ma *sa.*

———. *Distinction between the Two Truths. Satyadvayavibhaṅga. Dden pa gnyis rnam par 'byed pa'i tshig le'u byas pa.* Toh 3881, dbu ma *sa.*

Kamalaśīla. *Commentary on the Difficult Points of the Compendium of Suchness. Tattvasaṃgrahapañjikā. De kho na nyid bsdus pa'i dka' 'grel.* Toh 4267, tshad ma *ze* and *'e.*

———. *Illumination of the Middle Way. Madhyamakāloka. Dbu ma snang ba.* Toh 3887, dbu ma *sa.*

Maitreya. *Distinguishing the Middle Way from the Extremes. Madhyāntavibhāga* or *Madhyāntavibhaṅga. Dbus dang mtha' rnam par 'byed pa.* Toh 4021, sems tsam *phi.*

———. *Ornament of Realizations. Abhisamayālaṃkāra. Mngon rtogs rgyan.* Toh 3786, shes phyin *ka.*

———. *Ornament of the Mahayana Sutras. Mahāyānasūtrālaṃkāra. Mdo sde rgyan.* Toh 4020, sems tsam *phi.*

———. *Unexcelled Continuum of the Mahayana. Mahāyānottaratantra. Theg pa chen po rgyud bla ma.* Toh 4024, sems tsam *phi.*

Nāgārjuna. *Commentary on Dispeller of Dispute. Vigrahavyāvartanīvṛtti. Rtsod pa bzlog pa'i 'grel pa.* Toh 3832, dbu ma *tsa.*

———. *Compendium of Sutras. Sūtrasamuccaya. Mdo kun las btus pa.* Toh 3934, dbu ma *ki.*

———. *Dispeller of Dispute. Vigrahavyāvartanī. Rtsod pa bzlog pa.* Toh 3828, dbu ma *tsa.*

———. *Fundamental Treatise on the Middle Way. Mūlamadhyamakakārikā. Dbu ma rtsa ba'i tshig le'ur byas pa.* Toh 3824, dbu ma *tsa.*

———. *Precious Garland. Ratnāvalī. Rin po che'i phreng ba.* Toh 4158, spring yig *ge.*

———. *Sixty Stanzas of Reasoning. Yuktiṣaṣṭikā. Rigs pa drug cu pa.* Toh 3825, dbu ma *tsa.*

Pāṇini. *Sutras on (Sanskrit) Grammar. Vyākaraṇasūtra. Brda sprod pa pā ṇi ni'i mdo.* Toh 4420, sna tshogs *to.*

Prajñākaragupta. *Ornament Commentary to the Pramāṇavārttika. Pramāṇavārttikālaṃkāra. Tshad ma rnam 'grel gyi rgyan.* Toh 4221, tshad ma *te* and *the*.

Ravigupta. *Commentary on the Pramāṇavārttika. Pramāṇavārttikavṛtti. Tshad ma rnam 'grel gyi 'grel pa.* Toh 4224, tshad ma *pe*.

Sahara. *Treasury of Doha. Dohakoṣa. Do ha mdzod kyi glu.* Toh 2224, rgyud 'grel *wi*.

Śākyabuddhi. *Direct Commentary on the Pramāṇavārttika. Pramāṇavārttika-ṭīkā. Tshad ma rnam 'grel gyi 'grel bshad.* Toh 4220, tshad ma *je* and *nye*.

Śaṅkaranandana. *Following (Dharmakīrti's) Analysis of Relation. Sambandhaparīkṣānusāra. 'Brel ba brtag pa'i rjes su 'brang ba.* Toh 4237, tshad ma *zhe*.

Śaṅkarasvāmin (although attributed to Dignāga in the Tibetan catalogue). *Entranceway to Reasoning: A Treatise on Pramāṇa. Nyāyapraveśaka. Tshad ma'i bstan bcos rigs pa la 'jug pa.* Toh 4208, tshad ma *ce*.

Śāntarakṣita. *Compendium of Suchness. Tattvasaṃgraha. De kho na nyid bsdus pa.* Toh 4266, tshad ma *ze*.

———. *Ornament to the Middle Way. Madhyamakālaṃkāra. Dbu ma rgyan.* Toh 3884, dbu ma *sa*.

Śāntideva. *Entering the Bodhisattva Way. Bodhisattvacaryāvatāra. Byang chub sems dpa'i spyod pa la 'jug pa.* Toh 3871, dbu ma *la*.

Vasubandhu. *Principles of Exegesis. Vyākhyāyukti. Rnam par bshad pa'i rigs pa.* Toh 4061, sems tsam *shi*.

———. *Treasury of the Abhidharma. Abhidharmakośa. Chos mngon pa'i mdzod.* Toh 4089, mngon pa *ku*.

———. *Twenty Stanzas. Viṃśatikā. Nyi shu pa.* Toh 4056, sems tsam *shi*.

Yamāri. *Total Purity: Explanation of Ornament of the Commentary on Pramāṇa. Pramāṇavārttikālaṃkāraṭīkāsupariśuddhānāma. Tshad ma rnam 'grel rgyan gyi 'grel bshad shin tu yongs su dag pa zhes bya ba.* Toh 4226, tshad ma *phe*, *be*, *me*, and *tse*.

Tibetan Works

Chapa Chökyi Sengé (Phywa pa Chos kyi Seng ge). *Banisher of Ignorance (Relating to) Pramāṇa. Tshad ma yid kyi mun sel.* Manuscript in Bka' gdams gsung 'bum phyogs bsgrigs—first release, 8:439–634. Si khron: Si khron mi rigs dpe skrun khang, 2006.

Chöjé Gyensang / Gungru Gyaltsen Sangpo (Chos rje rgyan bzang / Gung ru Rgyal mtshan bzang po). *A Thousand Measures (of Madhyamaka). Dbu ma stong thun.* In *Gung ru rgyal mtshan bzang po'i stong thun dang rnam thar.* Lha sa: Ser gtsug nang bstan dpe rnying 'tshol bsdu phyogs sgrig khang, 2011.

Gyaltsab Jé Darma Rinchen (Rgyal tshab Dar ma rin chen). *Commentary to Nāgārjuna's Precious Garland. Rin chen phreng ba'i 'grel ba.* Zhol par khang Collected Works, vol. *ka*. New Delhi: Mongolian Lama Guru Deva, 1982.

———. *Commentary to Nyāyabindu. Tshad ma rigs thigs kyi 'grel pa legs bshad snying po'i gter.* Zhol par khang Collected Works, vol. *nya*. New Delhi: Mongolian Lama Guru Deva, 1982 (possible reference).

———. *On Preclusion and Relationship. 'Gal ba 'gal 'brel gyi rnam gzhag.* Delhi: Institute of Tibetan Classics, 2006.

Jamyang Shepa ('Jam dbyangs bzhad pa'i rdo rje). *Decisive Analysis of the Madhyamakāvatāra. Dbu ma 'jug pa'i mtha' dpyod.* In *Collected Works of 'Jam-dbyaṅs-bźad-pa'i-rdo-rje*, vol. 9. New Delhi: Ngawang Gelek Demo, 1973.

———. *Mighty Pramāṇa Sun, "Banisher of Gloom from the Hearts of the Fortunate," Totally Illuminating the Profound and the Expansive: An Exposition on the Valid Cognition in the Thousand Measures of Clear Words. Tshig gsal stong thun gyi tshad ma'i rnam bshad zab rgyas kun gsal tshad ma'i 'od brgya 'bar ba skal bzang snying gi mun sel.* Delhi: Institute of Tibetan Classics, 2006.

Khedrup Jé Gelek Palsang (Mkhas grub Dge legs dpal bzang). *Banisher of Ignorance: An Ornament of the Seven Treatises on Pramāṇa. Tshad ma sde bdun gyi rgyan yid kyi mun sel.* Delhi: Institute of Tibetan Classics, 2006.

———. *Exposition on (Haribhadra's) Clear Meaning Commentary on the Ornament of Realizations. 'Grel pa don gsal gyi rnam bshad rtogs dka'i snang ba.* Zhol par khang Collected Works, vol. *ka*. New Delhi: Mongolian Lama Guru Deva, 1982.

———. *Lamp Dispelling the Gloom: Guide to the View. Lta khrid mun sel sgron me.* Zhol par khang Collected Works, vol. *ta*. New Delhi: Mongolian Lama Guru Deva, 1982 (possible reference).

———. *Ocean of Reasoning: Extensive Explanation of Commentary on Pramāṇa. (Ṭīk chen) Tshad ma rnam 'grel gyi rgya cher bshad pa rigs pa'i rgya mtsho.* Zhol par khang Collected Works, vols. *tha* and *da*. New Delhi: Mongolian Lama Guru Deva, 1982.

———. *Thousand Measures: Providing the Fortunate with Sight. Zab mo stong pa nyid kyi de kho na nyid rab tu gsal bar byed pa'i bstan bcos skal bzang mig 'byed.* Zhol par khang Collected Works, vol. *ka*. New Delhi: Mongolian Lama Guru Deva, 1982.

Sakya Paṇḍita Kunga Gyaltsen (Sa skya Paṇḍita Kun dga' rgyal mtshan) *Treasure of Pramāṇa Reasoning. Tshad ma rigs pa'i gter.* Sa skya bka' 'bum (Collected works of the five great masters of the Sakya tradition—reproduced from the 1736 Sde dge edition), vol. *da*. Dehra Dun: Sakya Centre, 1992–93.

———. *Treasure of Pramāṇa Reasoning Autocommentary. Tshad ma rigs gter rang 'grel.* Sa skya bka' 'bum (Collected works of the five great masters of the Sakya tradition—reproduced from the 1736 Sde dge edition), vol. *da*. Dehra Dun: Sakya Centre, 1992–93.

Taktsang Lotsāwa Sherab Rinchen (Stag tshang lo tsā ba Shes rab rin chen). *Comprehensive Knowledge of Philosophical Tenets. Grub mtha' kun shes.* Stag tshang lo tsā ba Shes rab rin chen kyi gsung skor (Collected Writings), vol. *ka*. Kathmandu: Sa skya rgyal yongs gsung rab slob gnyer khang, 2007.

Tsongkhapa Losang Drakpa (Tsong kha pa Blo bzang grags pa). *Differentiating the Interpretive and the Definitive: Essence of Fine Elucidation. Drang ba dang nges pa'i don rnam par phye ba'i bstan bcos legs bshad snying po.* Zhol par khang Collected Works, vol. *pha*. New Delhi: Mongolian Lama Guru Deva, 1978–79.

———. *Golden Garland of Fine Elucidation. Phar phyin ṭikka legs bshad gser gyi phreng ba.* Zhol par khang Collected Works, vol. *tsa* and *tsha*. New Delhi: Mongolian Lama Guru Deva, 1978–79.

———. *Greater Stages of the Path. Byang chub lam rim chen mo.* Zhol par khang Collected Works, vol. *pa*. (Special insight section: *Lhag mthong chen mo.*) New Delhi: Mongolian Lama Guru Deva, 1978–79.

———. *Illuminating the Intent of (Candrakīrti's) Entering the Middle Way. Dbu ma la 'jug pa'i rnam bshad dgongs pa rab gsal.* Zhol par khang Collected Works, vol. *ma*. New Delhi: Mongolian Lama Guru Deva, 1978–79.

———. *Notes on the Eight Difficult Points. Dka' gnad brgyad kyi zin bris rje'i gsung bzhin brjed byang du bkod pa.* Zhol par khang Collected Works, vol. *ba*. New Delhi: Mongolian Lama Guru Deva, 1978–79.

———. *Ocean of Reasoning: Commentary to Nāgārjuna's Mūlamadhyamakakārikā. Dbu ma rtsa ba'i tshig le'ur byas pa shes rab ces bya ba'i rnam bshad rigs pa'i rgya mtsho* (*Rtsa she ṭik chen*). Zhol par khang Collected Works, vol. *ba*. New Delhi: Mongolian Lama Guru, 1978–79.

Yaktön Sangyé Pal (G.yag ston Sangs rgyas dpal). *Commentary to the Treasure of Pramāṇa Reasoning. Sde bdun gyi dgongs 'grel tshad ma rigs pa'i gter gyi de kho na nyid gsal bar byed pa rigs pa'i 'od 'phro ba*. Tshad ma'i 'grel pa phyogs bsgrigs, vol. 8. Rdzong sar khams bye'i slob gling thub bstan dar rgyas gling, 2009.

Works Referred to by the Translator

Asaṅga. *Foundation for Yoga Practitioners: The Levels of Spiritual Practice. Yogācārabhūmi-bhūmivastu. Rnal 'byor spyod pa'i sa las dngos gzhi sa mang po*. Toh 4035 Tengyur, sems tsam *tshi*.

Atiśa (Dīpaṃkaraśrījñāna). *Instruction on the Middle Way. Madhyamakopadeśa. Dbu ma'i man ngag*. Toh 3929 Tengyur, dbu ma *ki*.

Bentor, Yael. "Did Mkhas grub rje Challenge the Authenticity of the Sa skya *lam 'bras* Tradition?" In *Fifteenth Century Tibet: Cultural Blossoming and Political Unrest*, edited by Volker Caumanns and Marta Sernesi, 227–48. LIRI Seminar Proceedings Series 8. Lumbini: Lumbini International Research Institute, 2017.

Bodhi, Bhikkhu, trans. *The Connected Discourses of the Buddha: A Translation of the Saṃyutta Nikāya*. Boston: Wisdom Publications, 2000.

Cabezón, José Ignacio. *A Dose of Emptiness: An Annotated Translation of the sTong thun chen mo of mKhas grub dGe legs dpal bzang*. New York: State University of New York Press, 1992.

Chim Jampaiyang. *Ornament of Abhidharma: A Commentary on Vasubandhu's Abhidharmakośa*. Translated by Ian James Coghlan. The Library of Tibetan Classics 23. Somerville, MA: Wisdom Publications, 2018.

Chödrak Gyatso (Chos grags rgya mtsho). *Tshad ma rigs gzhung rgya mtsho. Ocean of Pramāṇa [Canonical] Writings*. Thimbu: Topga Tulku, 1973.

Chomden Rikpai Raldri (Bcom ldan Rigs pa'i ral gri). *Analysis of Relation: Floral Ornament. 'Brel ba brtag pa rgyan gyi me tog*, Collected Works, vol. *tha*, Lhasa: Khams sprul bsod nams don grub, 2006.

———. *Weapon of Reasoning: Summary of Pramāṇa. Tshad ma bsdus pa rigs pa'i mtshon cha*. Sa skya'i dpe rnying bsdus sgrig khang, (n.d.).

Dachille, Rae Erin. *Searching for the Body: A Contemporary Perspective on Tibetan Buddhist Tantra*. New York: Columbia University Press, 2022.

Dignāga. **Wheel of Reasoning: The Two-Headed Drum. *Hetucakraḍamaru. Gtan tshigs kyi 'khor lo gtan la dbab pa.* Toh 4209 Tengyur, tshad ma *ce*.

Dreyfus, Georges, B. J. *Recognizing Reality: Dharmakīrti's Philosophy and Its Tibetan Interpretations.* Delhi: Sri Satguru Publications, 1997.

Dunne, John, D. *Foundations of Dharmakīrti's Philosophy.* Boston: Wisdom Publications, 2004.

Franco, Eli. "The Tibetan Translations of the Pramāṇavārttika and the Development of Translation Methods from Sanskrit to Tibetan." In *Proceedings of the 7th Seminar of the International Association for Tibetan Studies, Graz 1995*, edited by H. Krasser, T. Much, E. Steinkellner, and H. Tauscher, 277–88. Vienna: Verlag der Österreichischen Akademie der Wissenschaften, 1997.

Frauwallner, Erich. "Vasubandhu's Vādaviddhih." *Wiener Zeitschrift für die Kunde Süd-und Ost-Asiens* 1 (1957): 2–43.

Ganeri, Jonardon, ed. *Indian Logic: A Reader.* New York: Routledge, 2001.

Gendun Drup (Dge 'dun grub). *Ornament of Reasoning: [For the] Great Pramāṇa Treatises. Tshad ma'i bstan bcos chen mo rigs pa'i rgyan.* Lhasa: Ser gtsug nang bstan dpe rnying 'tshol bsdu phyogs sgrig khang, 2010.

Gewa Gyaltsen (Rigs pa'i dbang phyug Dge ba rgyal mtshan). *Commentarial Ornament on (Dignāga's) Compendium of Pramāṇa. Tshad ma kun las btus pa zhes bya ba'i rab tu byed pa'i rgyan.* Dehra Dun: Sakya College, 1999.

Gö Lotsāwa Shönu Pal ('Gos lo tsā wa, Gzhon nu dpal). *Blue Annals. Deb ther sngon po.* Chengdu: Si khron mi rigs dpe skrun khang, 1984.

Gyaltsab Jé Darma Rinchen (Rgyal tshab Dar ma rin chen). *Commentary on (Sakya Paṇḍita's) Treasure of Pramāṇa Reasoning. Rgyal tshab rje'i tshad ma rigs gter 'grel pa.* Kathmandu: Sa skya rgyal yongs gsung rab slob gnyer khang, 2007.

———. *Condensation of the Illuminator of the Path to Liberation: (Commentary to Dharmakīrti's) Pramāṇavārttika. Rnam 'grel thar lam gsal byed bsdus don.* Zhol par khang Collected Works, vol. *ca*. New Delhi: Mongolian Lama Guru Deva, 1982.

———. *Essence of the Sun: Explanation of (Dharmakīrti's) Sambandhaparīkṣā. 'Brel ba brtag pa'i rnam bshad nyi ma'i snying po.* Zhol par khang Collected Works, vol. *ca*. New Delhi: Mongolian Lama Guru Deva, 1982.

———. *Explanation of (Dignāga's) Pramāṇasamuccaya. Tshad ma mdo'i rnam bshad.* Zhol par khang Collected Works, vol. *nga*. New Delhi: Mongolian Lama Guru Deva, 1982.

———. *Extensive Pramāṇa Memorandum. Tshad ma'i brjed byang chen mo.* Zhol par khang Collected Works, vol. *nga*. New Delhi: Mongolian Lama Guru Deva, 1982.

———. *Guide Through the Path of Pramāṇa Tshad ma'i lam khrid.* Zhol par khang Collected Works, vol. *ca*. New Delhi: Mongolian Lama Guru Deva, 1982.

———. *Illumination of the Intent: Extensive Commentary on [Dharmakīrti's] Pramāṇaviniścaya. Tshad ma rnam nges kyi ṭīk chen dgongs pa rab gsal.* Zhol par khang Collected Works, vols. *ja* and *nya*. New Delhi: Mongolian Lama Guru Deva, 1982.

———. *Illuminator of the Path to Liberation: [Commentary to Dharmakīrti's] Pramāṇavārttika. Rnam 'grel thar lam gsal byed.* Zhol par khang Collected Works, vol. *cha*. New Delhi: Mongolian Lama Guru Deva, 1982.

———. *Memorandum of the Perception Chapter of the Pramāṇavārttika. Mngon sum le'u'i brjed byang.* Zhol par khang Collected Works, vol. *ca*. New Delhi: Mongolian Lama Guru Deva, 1982.

He, Huanhuan, and Leonard W. J. van der Kuijp, "Once Again on the *Hetucakraḍamaru: Rotating the Wheels." *Journal of Indian Philosophy* 44 (2016): 267–302.

Heimbel, Jörg. "The Dispute Between mKhas grub rJe and Ngor chen: Its Representation and Role in Tibetan Life-Writing." In *Fifteenth Century Tibet: Cultural Blossoming and Political Unrest*, edited by Volker Caumanns and Marta Sernesi, 249–89. LIRI Seminar Proceedings Series 8. Lumbini: Lumbini International Research Institute, 2017.

Hugon, Pascale. "Arguments by Parallels in the Epistemological Works of Phya pa Chos kyi seng ge." *Argumentation* 22.1 (2008): 93–114.

Jackson, David. "The Status of Pramāṇa Doctrine According to Sa skya Paṇḍita and Other Tibetan Masters: Theoretical Discipline or Doctrine of Liberation?" In *The Buddhist Forum (1991–1993): Papers in Honor and Appreciation of Professor David Seyfort Ruegg's Contribution to Indological, Buddhist and Tibetan Studies*, edited by Tadeusz Skorupski and Ulrich Pagel, 3:85–129. New Delhi: Heritage, 1995.

Jamyang Shepa ('Jam dbyangs bzhad pa'i rdo rje). *Autobiographical Verses. 'Jam dbyangs bzhad pa'i rdo rje'i rnam thar bka' rtsom tshigs bcad ma.* Collected Works, vol. 1. New Delhi: Ngawang Gelek Demo, 1974.

———. *Decisive Analysis of Pramāṇavārttika. Tshad ma rnam 'grel gyi mtha' dpyod.* Collected Works, vol. 13. New Delhi: Ngawang Gelek Demo, 1974.

———. *Great Exposition of Philosophical Tenets. Grub mtha' chen mo*, comprising the root text (*Grub mtha' rnam bzhag 'khrul spong gdong lnga'i sgra dbyangs*) and the autocommentary (*Grub mtha'i rnam bshad lung rigs rgya mtsho skye dgu'i re ba kun skong*). Collected Works, vol.14. New Delhi: Ngawang Gelek Demo, 1973.

Kellner, Birgit. "Changing Frames in Buddhist Thought: The Concept of *Ākāra* in Abhidharma and in Buddhist Epistemological Analysis." *Journal of Indian Philosophy* 42 (2014): 275–95.

Khedrup Jé Gelek Palsang (Mkhas grub Dge legs dpal bzang). *Entrance Point for the Faithful: The Marvelous Biography of the Great Lama Tsongkhapa. Rje btsun bla ma Tsong kha pa chen po'i ngo mtshar rmad du byung ba'i rnam thar dad pa'i 'jug ngogs*. Zhol par khang Collection, vol. *ka*. New Delhi: Mongolian Lama Guru Deva, 1978–79.

———. *Extensive Presentation on the Results of Valid Cognition. Tshad 'bras kyi rnam gzhag chen mo*. Zhol par khang Collection, vol. *na*. New Delhi: Mongolian Lama Guru Deva, 1982.

———. *Guide Through the Path of Pramāṇa. Tshad ma'i lam khrid*. Based on old Bkra shis lhun po redaction, vol. 12. New Delhi: Ngawang Gelek Demo, 1985.

———. *Record of (Dharma) Received. Mkhas grub thams cad mkhyen pa dge legs dpal bzang po'i gsan yig*. Based on old Bkra shis lhun po redaction, vol. *ka*. New Delhi: Ngawang Gelek Demo, 1985.

Layakpa Jangchup Ngödrup (La yag pa Byang chub dngos grub). *Ornament Clarifying the Essence (of Gampopa's Four Dharmas). Mnyam med dwags po'i chos bzhir grags pa'i rtsa gzhung gi 'grel pa snying po gsal ba'i rgyan*. In *Blo gros mtha' yas pa'i mdzod*, 3:51–392. Nepal: Rigpe Dorje Publications, Pullahari Monastery, 2008.

Losang Gyatso, Phukhang Geshé (Phu khang dge bshes Blo bzang rgya mtsho). *The Advanced Path of Reasoning: Compendium of Essentials for the Field of Study of Awareness. Rigs lam che ba blo rigs kyi rnam gzhag nyer mkho kun btus*. New Delhi: Lochen Rinpoche, 1985.

MacDonald, Anne. *In Clear Words: The Prasannapadā, Chapter One*. Vienna: Österreichische Akademie der Wissenschaften, 2015.

Nāgārjuna. *Treatise on Pulverization. Vaidalyaprakaraṇa. Zhib mo rnam par 'thag pa'i rab tu byed pa*. Toh 3830 Tengyur, dbu ma *tsa*.

Paṇchen Sönam Drakpa (Paṇchen Bsod nams grags pa). *Lamp Illuminating the Meaning of the Mother (Prajñāpāramitā). Yum don gsal ba'i sgron me: Phar phyin spyi don*. Collected Works of Paṇchen Sönam Drakpa, vol. 3. Mundgod: Drepung Loseling Library Society, 2015.

Perrett, Roy. W. *An Introduction to Indian Philosophy.* Cambridge: Cambridge University Press, 2016.

Prajñāmokṣa. *Commentary to [Atiśa's] Instruction on the Middle Way. Madhyamakopadeśavṛtti. Dbu ma'i man ngag gi 'grel pa.* Toh 3931 Tengyur, dbu ma *ki.*

Rongtön Sheja Kunrik (Rong ston Shes bya kun rig). *Solar Essence: Explanation of Treasure of Pramāṇa Reasoning. Tshad ma rigs pa'i gter gyi rnam bshad nyi ma'i snying po.* Skye dgu mdo: Gangs ljongs rig rgyan gsung rab par khang, 2004.

Samuels, Jonathan. "Challenging the Curriculum: The Course of Studies in Buddhist Monasteries of Medieval Tibet and Beyond." *The Eastern Buddhist* 1:1, Third Series (2021): 89–129.

———. "The Tibetan Institutionalisation of Disputation: Understanding a Medieval Monastic Practice." *Medieval Worlds* 12, (2020): 96–120.

Shākya Chokden (Shākya mchog ldan). *History of the Pramāṇa Tradition. (Tshad ma'i 'byung tshul) Tshad ma'i mdo dang bstan bcos kyi shing rta'i srol rnams ji ltar 'byung ba'i tshul gtam du bya ba nyin mor byed pa'i snang bas dpyod ldan mtha' dag dga' bar byed pa* Collected Works, vol. *dza.* Kathmandu: Sachen International, Guru Lama, 2006.

Smith, E. Gene. "Introduction" to the Collected Works of 'Jam dbyangs bzhad pa'i rdo rje, vol. 13. New Delhi: Ngawang Gelek Demo, 1974.

Sönam Gyaltsen, Lama Dampa (Bla ma dam pa Bsod nams rgyal mtshan). *Commentary on the Pramāṇavārttika: Essence of Fine Elucidation. Tshad ma rnam 'grel gyi 'grel pa legs par bshad pa'i snying po.* In *Tshad ma kun btus dang rnam 'grel gyi rtsa 'grel gces btus.* Chengdu: Si khron bod yig dpe rnying bsdu sgrig khang, n.d.

Tillemans, Tom, J. F. *Dharmakīrti's Pramāṇavārttika: An Annotated Translation of the Fourth Chapter (Parārthānumāna).* Vienna: Österreichische Akademie der Wissenschaften, 2000.

———. *Scripture, Logic, Language: Essays on Dharmakīrti and His Tibetan Successors.* Boston: Wisdom Publications, 1999.

———. "Sur le *parārthānumāna* en logique bouddhique." *Etudes Asiatiques* 38.2 (1984), 73-99.

Toshikazu, Watanabe. "Dharmakīrti on False Rejoinders (*jāti*)." *Journal of Indian and Buddhist Studies* 58.3 (2010): 1235–40.

Tsongkhapa. *Illuminating the Intent: An Exposition of Candrakīrti's Entering the Middle Way.* Translated by Thupten Jinpa. The Library of Tibetan Classics 19. Somerville, MA: Wisdom Publications, 2021.

Tsunpa Tönshön (Btsun pa ston gzhon). *Explanation of the Pramāṇa-vārttika: Ornament of the Snowy Realm. Rnam 'grel gyi rnam bshad gangs can gyi rgyan.* Beijing: Krung go'i bod kyi shes rig dpe skrun khang, 1993.

van der Kuijp, Leonard W. J. "Studies in the Life and Thought of Mkhas grub rje I: Mkhas grub rje's Epistemological Oeuvre and His Philosophical Remarks on Dignaga's Pramanasamuccaya." *Berliner Indologische Studien* 1 (1985): 75–105.

Yoshimizu, Chizuko. "Die Erkenntnislehre des Prāsaṅgika-Madhyamaka nach dem *Tshig gsal stoṅ thun gyi tshad ma'i rnam bshad* des 'Jam dbyaṅs bshad pa'i rdo rje": Einleitung, Textanalyse, Übersetzung. Vienna: Arbeitskreis für Tibetische und Buddhistische Studien, Universität Wien, 1996.

Index

Abhidharma, 77, 222, 670
forms with physical resistance in, 730n164
gender in, 737n263
on main awareness and mental factors, 755n468
object condition in, 250
sense powers in, 226, 615, 799n1072
two truths in, 14
Abhidharma Sutra, 79–80
absorption of nondiscrimination, 236
abstraction, 24, 280, 739n299. *See also* purely abstracted things
accurate discernment, 197–98, 205, 206–7, 216, 347, 654, 742n326
acquisition, 537, 787n876
action-executor-object, 575, 582, 589–90, 793n947
actual things, 101, 169, 294, 505, 519, 738n281, 781n823
effort and, 124, 729nn158–59
and existent things, equivalency refuted, 96–97, 721n92
identity of, 156–58
illustration, 137–38
in inconclusive reasons, 458–59
mistaken views on, 97, 121, 260, 721n95
as specifically characterized, 174
as ultimate truth, 174
as universals, 152
valid cognition of, 181, 208
affirmation, 152
in consequences, responding to, 494
in mutual opposition preclusion, 543, 789n883, 789n886
specifically characterized entities and, 147–49, 150–51
affirmative cognition, 742n326
affirmative phenomena, 18, 505, 519, 520, 781n823, 788n878
agent-instrument-object, 585–88, 589, 602–3, 661, 793n947, 807n1240
aggregates, 236
in Cittamātra, 255
definitive enumeration of, 265–66
self and, 303, 304–5, 308–9, 551, 597
suffering of, 298, 309, 311
See also view associated with transitory composite
Akṣapāda Gautama, 39, 79
Amdo, 60, 61, 63
analogies and examples, 428
adversary and friend, 180, 231–32, 256, 338, 339, 738n283
barley seeds, 157, 734n232
barren mother, 478–80, 481
barren woman's son, 301, 302
bird's nest, 550, 790n897
blue lotus, 134, 152, 153–54
Buddha's appearance in world, 606, 607
chariot analysis, 597
chopping wood, 585–86, 587, 602–3, 661, 793n947
cow, name of, 617, 800n1079
cows of different colors, 124, 139, 140, 142, 157, 729n157, 731n187
donkey's horns, 564, 565, 608
elephant examined by sightless beings, 239, 294–95, 381

escaping sun by leaping into flames, 85
fire on mountain, 102, 103
five-faced lion, 676, 810n1287
floating hairs, 184–85, 624, 625, 738n292, 802n1107
flower in midair, 583
footing on a bubble, 87
generosity (conviction proofs), 415, 417–18, 421, 423–24, 482, 779n799
gold, assaying, 3, 81
goosebumps, 312, 413, 759n539
hare, proverbial, 438, 463, 774n744
hare's horns, 17, 43, 95, 277, 307, 329, 383, 417, 472
illusionist, 289–90
jewel's sparkle, 210–11, 745n366
lamp and flame, 215, 539
light expelling darkness, 206, 536, 537–38, 539–41, 543, 788n878
mirages, 214, 359, 632
mirror's reflection, 658, 665, 808–9n1257
molasses, 221, 390, 548, 790n894
moon (common agreement), 426–27, 428–30, 488, 513, 772n729
pestle's body, 590–92, 593, 595, 596, 795n990, 796n991
pigeon's footprint, 652, 805n1202
piśāca spirit, 97, 401–5, 721n96, 769–70n690
Rāhu's head, 590–92, 593, 595, 796n991
rodent bite, recollection of, 674, 675, 810n1282
rope imagined as snake, 428, 594
salt flavoring food, 82
seed and sprout, 569
single day, 143
sword's blade cutting itself/finger's tip touching itself, 581
termite mounds, 406, 770n694
veiled face, 314
See also double moon; fire and smoke; pots; sound as impermanent
analytical cessation, 301, 541
antagonistic preclusion, 412–13
definition, 538–39, 788n877, 788n882
of material things, 509–10
mistaken views, 536–38, 787n876
anti-predicate, 386–87, 768n672
in countering reasons, 769n682
in effect reasoning, 391
in nonobservation reasons, 402, 403–4
preclusion and, 507, 535
antirealism, 723n110
antithesis, 780n803, 780n805
apoha theory, 729n154, 729n157, 734n228, 736n251, 800n1079. *See also* exclusion; other-exclusion (*anyāpoha*)
appearance perspective, 290, 721n90
appearance presenters, 519, 520, 784n851
appearing objects, 110
and conceptual cognition, relationship of, 144–47, 179–80, 183, 738n281, 738n288
and held object, equivalency of, 184–85
inferential cognition and, 601
in Sautrāntika, 230–31
of sense consciousness, mistaken understandings, 230
apprehended object, 166, 747–48n392
defining, 223
of doubt, 191–92
inferential cognition of, 601, 657
of mental perception, 649
of sense perception, 646–47
valid perception of, 645
of yogic perception, 653
appropriator and appropriated, 606, 610, 614, 798n1037
argumentation, 34–36, 37, 47
arhatship, 238, 316, 317, 656
ārya buddhas, 619, 669–70, 671
Āryadeva, 68, 245, 595. See also *Four Hundred Stanzas*
āryas, 300, 537, 558–59, 566, 606, 792n928
ārya's meditative equipoise, 175, 193, 567, 641
Asaṅga, 8, 786n865
Cittamātra system of, 165, 736n255, 736n260
Compendium of Abhidharma, 7, 456, 538, 542, 543, 788nn880–81, 790n897

Foundation for Yoga Practitioners, 7, 265–66, 588
on mental sense power, 280
ascertaining awareness, 181, 182, 270, 287
ascertaining cognition, 191, 192, 205, 286–87, 561–63, 565
ascertaining consciousness, 321
Ascertainment of Valid Cognition (Dharmakīrti), 8, 88, 411, 724n112
on appearing objects, 179
on conceptual cognition, merging and, 190
on consciousness, accurate aspects presented to, 333
on contrary reasons, 448–50
on dissimilar examples, 255
on individuations as nonconcomitant, 543
on inference involving another party, 352
on nonobservation of direct effect, 548, 789n890
on objects of valid cognition, 181
on perception, 213–14, 635
on preclusion, 533, 534
Sakya Paṇḍita and, 11
on three criteria, 373
Tibetan commentaries, 10
on valid cognition, 205, 217, 535
aspect, 229
in Cittamātra, 232, 251
experiential, 102
four ways of appearing, 227
image, 104, 724n115
meanings, range of, 723n111
observed object condition and, 226–27, 250
perception and, 109
as presenting itself, 104, 233–34, 724n116
sense consciousness and, 247–48
universal, 228
See also object-aspect; subject-aspect
assemblage universal, 629–30, 783n845
assemblage-communicating terms, 515–16, 782n843, 788n845
Atiśa, 10
Instruction on the Middle Way, 25
"three combined rivers of bodhicitta," 55
ātman. *See* self
Avalokitavrata; *Prajñāpradīpaṭīkā*, 505
awareness
equivalent terms, 189
main (*see* basic awareness)
objects of, 100, 723n108
pramāṇa rooted in, 3
sevenfold categorization, 739n297, 740n307
single, 106, 305–6, 588, 650, 795n985
unmistaken, 125, 132, 737n264
to which something appears but is not ascertained, 215, 739n297, 746n377
See also ascertaining awareness; deluded awareness
Awareness and Cognition (*blo rig*), 739n297

Banisher of Ignorance (Chapa Chökyi Sengé), 11, 66, 742n325
on antagonistic preclusion, 536–37
on conceptual ascertainment, 745n348
on consequences, 30
on mutual opposition preclusion, 543–44
parallel argument used by, 35–36
on valid cognition, 742n329
Banisher of Ignorance (Khedrup Jé), 18
on Cittamātra and Madhyamaka, relationship of, 45
colophon, 526–27
composition, 64–65
content outline, 77
defense of Pramāṇa in, 50
final words, 524–26
homage, 75–77
honorific language in, 724n112, 753n451
opponents in, 719n78, 720n86
on personalized instructions, 51
pronouns in, 757n502
sources, citation of, 722n97

structure, 65–66
Tashi Lhunpo appendage, 527–28, 786n867
time period, 43–44
translator's relationship with, 66–67
bases, valid and nonvalid, 209
basic awareness, 275
and cognitive functions, relationship of, 265–66, 280, 755n465, 755n468
and consciousness, relationship of, 586–88, 795n977, 795n980
neither starting nor ending point of, 313–15
basis. *See* subjects (logical reasons)
basis of negation, 200–201
Bhartṛhari, 758n519
Bhāviveka, 30, 625
Blaze of Reasoning, 293–94, 504
Heart of the Middle Way, 2, 663, 664
Bhavyarāja, 735n242
binary divisions, 13–18
bodhicitta. *See* mind generation (*bodhicitta*)
Bodong Choklé Namgyal, 56, 66, 737n265, 756n478
body
and consciousness, non-Buddhist views, 240–41
substantial cause for, 242, 244
suspension absorption and, 235–36, 239–40
Brahmā, 85, 266, 311, 558, 772n729
Buddha Śākyamuni
authority of, 15, 82–83, 84–85, 558–60
in conviction proof, 419–20
doubt in, 656
faultlessness of, 86, 89
homage, 75, 555
and logic, commitment to, 33–34, 80
as pramāṇa, 3
as ultimate source of knowledge, 1
buddhas
in conviction proofs, 416–17
knowledge of non-actual things, 175–77
three secrets of, 663
valid cognition of, 203, 205
See also ārya buddhas

calm abiding, 318
calm abiding and special insight, uniting, 653
Candrakīrti, 18, 676
Bhāviveka and, 30
Commentary on Sixty Stanzas of Reasoning, 558–59, 560, 647, 654, 655, 666
Entering the Middle Way Autocommentary, 25, 558, 660, 666, 673–74
See also *Clear Words*; *Commentary to Four Hundred Stanzas*; *Entering the Middle Way*
Cārvāka/Lokāyata schools, 38, 85, 94, 168–69, 255, 273, 291, 394, 663, 714n23, 719nn80–81
categorical assertions, 566
causal condition, 271
causal relationship, 548–49, 789n890, 790n894
cause and effect/causality, 15, 788n882
analyzing, 246–47
basis for, 305
denying, 415
informational relationship of, 549–50, 790n896
mutual dependency of, 673
personal observation of, 393, 769n677
preclusion of, 106
relationship between, 112, 231, 303, 487
simultaneous, 93–94, 245–46, 250, 536, 537
as substances, 136–37
Changkya Losang Chöden, 61
Changra Monastery, 56, 64
Chapa Chökyi Sengé, 10, 11, 51, 743n342, 785n860, 787n876. See also *Banisher of Ignorance*
characteristics (Skt. *lakṣana*), 15–16, 40, 173–74
Chödrak Gyatso, Seventh Karmapa, 51
Chöjé Gyensang (Gungru Gyaltsen Sangpo), 634, 803n1138

Chomden Rikpai Raldri, 44, 67
circular definitions, 224–25, 777–78n779
Cittamātra tradition (Yogācāra), 127, 134, 260, 621, 730n165
  aspects in, 233, 234
  conceptual cognition in, 128
  external entities in, 232, 249, 252, 724n114, 750n424
  and Madhyamaka, relationship of, 4–5, 45
  perception in, 128, 218, 290, 730n165
  proof of simultaneity in, 266
  scripture in, 663
  self-cognition in, 292, 293, 725n121
  selflessness in, 307
  sense perception in, 214, 220, 230
  in Seven Treatises, 174
  specifically characterized things in, 629
  subschools, 165, 172
  substance in, 127
  three natures in, 736n260
  two truths in, 163
  ultimate in, 162
  valid cognition and result models in, 323, 326, 327
  valid cognition associated with scripture in, 658
  valid perception in, 217
  yogic perceivers in, 654
  See also False Aspectarian Cittamātra; True Aspectarian Cittamātra
Clear Words (Candrakīrti), 12–13, 68–69, 560, 639, 656, 659, 672, 794n963, 804n1155
  on agent, instrument, action, 585–86, 588, 589, 590, 661
  on analogy, 665
  on analysis of worldly convention, 593, 594, 596, 598
  on ascertainment, 561–62, 563
  on basic awareness, 586, 587
  on body, 568–69
  on Buddha's authority, 559–60
  on characteristic and locus of characterization, 582, 583, 584, 595
  on dependent existence, 595–96, 597
  on incommunicability, 585, 794n973
  on *lakṣana*, refuting mistaken views, 574, 575, 576, 592
  on mutual dependence, 674–75
  on nonascertainment, 572–73
  on nonproduction, 566, 569
  on object of comprehension, 603
  on objects of other-knowing consciousness, 579
  on perception as free from conception, 636–38
  on *pratyakṣa*, conventional language and, 606–7, 608, 609, 610, 645
  on *pratyakṣa*, derivation, 611, 612, 613, 669
  on *pratyakṣa*, distributive repetition, 623
  on *pratyakṣa*, intended meaning, 622–23
  on *pratyakṣa*, object of, 671
  on *pratyakṣa*, unique cause, 616
  on *pratyakṣa* and sense powers, 614, 615
  on *pratyakṣa* as cognition, 618, 619
  on property and property-basis, 590–92
  on reasons, ārya's perspective, 567, 568
  on scripture, 660, 662, 664
  on self, investigating, 594–95
  on self-cognition, 580, 581
  on specifically characterized things, 577, 578
  on suchness, 599
  on superimposition, 570
  on two truths, 601–2
  on valid cognition, four types, 557–58, 620, 641, 667
  on valid cognition, objects of, 642
  on valid cognition, two forms, 602
  on valid subsequent inference, 657–58
  on worldly conventions, 675
  on worldly valid cognition, 571, 572
Closely Guarded Concentration Sutra, 656
coarse entities, 143
  and continua, differences between, 135
  in realist schools, 132–34
  as specifically characterized, 141

as substances, refuting, 120, 130–31
two truths and, 169–70
cognition grasping the reason
correct reasons and, 437–38
mistaken views, refuting, 433–37
cognitions, 403
equivalent terms, 189
exclusion and affirmation in, 544, 789n883, 789n886
factually correct and factually incorrect, distinguishing, 181
in Indian pramāṇa tradition, 3
lakṣana as, refuting, 576–77, 578
pratyakṣa as, refuting, 612, 613–14, 615
valid and nonvalid, preclusion of, 106
See also individual cognitions
Collected Topics genre, 65, 784–85n855, 785n860
commentarial tradition, 11, 717n66
Commentary on Pramāṇa (Dharmakīrti), 8, 20, 83, 122, 293–94, 717n66, 724n115
on antagonistic preclusion, 510–11
on apprehended object of sense consciousness, 223, 747n392, 748n393
on ascertaining cognition, objects of, 287
chapters, number, and order of, 88–89, 718n75
on characterless phenomena, 173
on classification, 151–52
on conceptual cognition, 153, 629–30
on contrary reasons, 448, 457
on conviction proofs, 421–22, 423
on dissimilar examples, 255
on effect reasons, 394, 485
on engagement preceded cognition, 402, 403
on four truths, sequence of, 302
Gyaltsab Jé's commentary, 48
on held objects, 183
on identity, 156
on ignorance, 221
on implicative meaning, 357
on inconclusive reasons with remainder, 463
on inference, two forms, 19
Jamyang Shepa and, 62
on karmas as governing conditions, 244
Khedrup Jé's commentaries, 64
on mind and sense powers, relationship of, 242
on names, 154, 430
on nonobservation reasons, 400, 409, 411
on objects, naming, 476
on perception, 635
on pervasions, 397
on preclusions, 506, 508
on proof statements, 356
on reason and predicate, 97
on reasons, capacity to understand, 364
on same type, 158
on scripture, 425, 486, 658, 660, 663
on self, four mental notions, 238
on self-cognition, 285, 286, 288, 292, 294, 339, 342, 757n507
on selflessness, 309
on selflessness of phenomena, 318
on sense consciousness, 224, 670
on sense powers, 222
on suffering of aggregates, 298
on suffering of compositionality, 311
tenets represented in, 241–42, 317–18, 324, 750n418
on three criteria, 364, 368
Tibetan translations and revisions, 8, 10, 11, 735n242, 747n392
Tibetan view of, 726n133
on true origins, 299
on type- and assemblage-communication, 516
on valid cognition, defining characteristics, 195, 203
on valid cognition, need for, 321
on valid cognition, objects of, 337, 341–42
on valid cognition, specifically characterized things and, 206–7
on valid cognition, two types, 17, 573, 644
on validity and language, 483–84

on vivid appearance, 638
on word formations, 515
Commentary on the Difficult Points in the Pramāṇavārttika (Devendrabuddhi)
on Dharmakīrti's tenet system, 172
on evident and hidden phenomena, 107–8
on objects and aspect, 183
on sense powers and light, 222–23
on subsequent cognition, 193
on valid cognition, defining characteristics, 195, 196, 742n325
on valid inferential cognition, 210–11
Commentary on the Difficult Points of the Compendium of Suchness (Kamalaśīla), 637, 663–64
Commentary to Four Hundred Stanzas (Candrakīrti), 559, 560, 666
on consciousness, 632, 634–35
on creative discrimination, 630
on illusion, 633
on inferential cognition, 668
on mental perception, 638, 649
on mental perception and sense perception, relationship of, 650
on perceptibility, 609, 610, 624
on *pratyakṣa*, derivation, 630, 631
on *pratyakṣa* as figurative, 613, 629
on recollection, 651, 652, 653
on sensation, 651
on sense perception, 647, 648
on sense power, 624, 625, 626–27
on valid cognition, 639, 640
on worldly and transcendent awarenesses, 671
on yogic perception, 654
common agreement about names
reasoning, 429, 771n728
defining, 428
mistaken views, refuting, 426–27
ruling out by, 473
valid cognitions in, 428–30
common locus, 152, 153–54, 535, 538, 786–87n873, 789n886
communication
cognition from, 198–99
communicated and communicating in, 512–14
four divisions of, 514–18
Compendium of Pramāṇa (Dignāga), 7–8, 15, 77, 384
chapters, number, and order of, 88, 718n75
on correct reasoning, ascertaining, 384
on false rejoinders, 20
on inference, two kinds, 345, 346
on inference involving another, 350, 351, 762n601
intent of, 82–85
on mental perception, 270–71
on perception, 213
on *pratyakṣa*, 629
on proof statements, 352, 762n598
on scripture, mistaken understandings, 485–86, 780n805
on sense powers, 219, 614, 616, 799n1071
on thesis, five terms, 467–68, 469, 470, 777n775
on valid cognition, 472
on yogic perception, 655
comprehended and comprehender, 167, 576, 641, 672
comprehended objects, 100, 200
as communicated, 513
divisions of, 641–42
as evident or hidden, 107
inferential valid cognition of, 285, 347
misconceptions about, 336, 340–42
synonyms, 98
threefold division, 575–76, 590
twofold division, 115–16, 122, 621, 726n124
twofold division, Prāsaṅgika rejection, 667–68
in valid cognition and result models (correct), 333–34
in valid cognition and result models (mistaken), 323–24, 325–29
valid cognition of, 198, 199, 200, 205, 206, 209, 557–58
valid perception of, 115–16

comprehensive engagers. *See under* engagers
conceived objects, 110, 179, 185
  conceptual cognition of, 144–47, 180–81, 183, 191, 228, 738n288
  valid inference and, 573, 600, 797n1027
conceptual ascertainment, 745n348
conceptual cognition, 551, 758n511
  as affirmative engager, 520
  of appearing and conceived objects, 144–47, 228
  and appearing objects, relationship of, 179–80, 738n281
  cognition grasping the reason as, 435
  communication and, 513–14
  conceived objects and, 180–81, 183, 738n288
  definition, 190–91
  direct experience within, 637, 638
  of generally characterized entities, 143–46, 732n203
  held objects of, 185
  logical relationship and, 512
  mental perception and, 269–70, 649
  as mistaken, distinctions in, 144–45, 600
  as mistaken by definition, 754n454
  mistaken views on, 189–90, 216, 739n299
  name and object merged in, 629–30
  and perception, distinctions between, 213, 721n90
  and self-cognition as single substance, refuting, 128, 730n173
  shared nature of entities in, 227–28
  and specifically characterized entities, 94, 146–47
  two varieties, 191–92, 740n306
  of universals, 152–53
conceptual consciousness
  conventional truth and, 161–62
  inference as, 18
  object universals and, 716n49
  and perception, relationship of, 210
  as perception, refuting, 256
  simultaneous, refuting, 237, 238
  and valid cognition, relationship of, 207–8
conceptual constructs, 41, 112, 154, 166, 169
  in Cittamātra, 172
  coarse continua as, refuting, 181–82
  generally characterized entities as, 43, 46
  insubstantially existent and totally imagined, distinguishing between, 43
  noncomposed things and, 44
  in reasons, 151, 156, 387, 394
  śabdhārtha as, 145
  selflessness as, 175
  universals and, 140, 141, 142, 729n153
conceptual false cognition, 191
conceptual isolations, 24, 523, 734n228
conceptual objects, 140, 181, 183, 600, 629, 732n190, 738n288, 797n1024, 797n1027
consciousness, 104–5, 332, 755n465
  and appearing objects, relationship of, 180
  communication and, 515
  equivalent terms, 189
  as illusory, 632
  impermanence of, 15
  nature of, 294
  nondualistic, 172
  objects of, 214–15
  and physical body, non-Buddhist views, 240–41
  Sautrāntika view, 102, 724n113
  sense perception and, 259
  six kinds, 279, 280
  smallest/indivisible units of, 97, 118, 122, 164–65, 721n95, 736n261
consequences, 20, 21, 30–31, 88, 720n89
  analysis and classification of, 35
  Buddha's use of, 80
  correct, definition and varieties, 491–92
  false, defining, 492
  in Geluk school, importance of, 25, 26
  in live debate and textual, distinction between, 34
  overt pervasion in, 374

responding to, 493–95
ruling out by, 492–93
textual and live, distinctions in, 34
that project probans of a proof, 375
valid cognition in establishing, 493
valid cognition through analogy in, 665, 666
as verbal formulation, 766n649
contaminants, 235
continua
coarse, 181–82
consciousnesses in individual, number of, 279, 280
distortions in, eliminating, 205, 745n347
example of, 143
maturing, 310
as mental perception, 273
preclusion in, 541
sense consciousnesses as, 276
sound as, 134–35, 731n182
as specifically characterized, 141
as substances, 120, 133–35, 136–38, 731n179, 731n185
units of time and, 135–36
contrary reasons, 168
authentic, 450
definition and varieties, 446, 448, 774n755
incorrect positions, refuting, 455–57
preclusion and, 534
quality of predicate in, 450–54, 455, 457
quality of subject in, 454–55
subject's nature, correct view, 448–50
subject's nature, mistaken views, 444–48, 775n766
conventional existence
in Cittamātra, 326
correct and false, 566, 567
denying, 291
establishing, 95–96
language and, 794–95n973
negation and, 582, 794n963
Prāsaṅgika view, 595–97
purpose of teaching, 152
conventional truth
defining characteristics, 162–63
denying, 154, 427
erroneous consciousness of, 173
etymological description, 161–62, 735n243
Prāsaṅgika view, 566–67, 598–99, 601–2
two levels, 43
and valid cognition, relationship of, 198
conventional valid cognitions, 95, 196–97, 259, 651, 754n454
conviction proofs, 420, 780n809
denying, 483
formulating, 421–25
models of, refuting, 417–20
as unfeasible, refuting, 414–17, 771n712
correct assumption, 739n297, 740n307
correct reasons, 726n133, 767n668
ascertainment by both parties, examining, 384–85
defining characteristics, 367–68
demonstrable fact type, 414–16, 420, 427
divisions of, 389, 414, 431
establishing thing meant, 431, 432, 773n735
failing in, 498
forward and reverse pervasions in, 374
inferential cognition and, 4
involving second party, 466
with nonexistent subject, 381–83
Prāsaṅgika views on, 657
presenting and becoming, distinction between, 363
three types, 722n103
See also three criteria for correct reasons; individual types of reasons
coterminosity, 474, 779n790
counter and countered, 509, 510–11, 534, 536, 538, 539, 540–41, 565, 786n869, 786n871, 788n877
countering reasons, preparative, 396–99, 458, 769n682
craving attachment, 298, 299, 303, 311
cyclic existence. *See* samsara

Dakpo Kagyü, 50–51
debate
  assertiveness of, 35
  consequence in, 30–31
  Khedrup Jé and Bodongpa, 56, 66
  paradigm, 20–21
  Pramāṇa system and, 53
  proofs embedded in, 27
deceptive truth, 598–99, 601–2. *See also* conventional truth
definiendum, 728n150, 793n947
  and definition, relationship of, 18, 36–37, 431–33, 474, 773n735, 779n789
  definitions of, 196, 522, 523
  Geluk understanding of, 46, 777n779, 792–93n944
definitions/defining characteristics, 535, 786–87n873, 793n947
  circular, 224–25, 777–78n779
  definition, 522, 523
  Geluk understanding of, 46, 53, 777n779, 779n790, 792–93n944
  and illustrations, difference between, 728n150
  purpose, 468
  three flaws, 199
  See also under definiendum
definitive categorizations, 211–12, 220, 746n371
deluded awareness, 235, 237–38
delusions, 14, 18, 68, 221, 303
  antidote to, 301
  eradicating, 21, 22
  root of, 304
  seeds of, separation from, 300
  self of persons and, 308–9
  suffering from, 298
  as true origins, 299, 303
dependent connection, 652
dependent origination, 568, 570
Desi Sangyé Gyatso, 62, 64
designated existence, 175
designations, reality behind, 593–94, 595, 596, 597, 602, 639–40, 667–68
desire realm, 238–39, 240, 241, 242, 303
determinate location, 117, 139, 143–44, 729n153
determinate time, 117, 139–40, 143–44, 729n153
Devadatta, 204, 594, 744n345
Devendrabuddhi, 8, 163, 174, 735n242. See also *Commentary on the Difficult Points in the Pramāṇavārttika*
Dharmakīrti, 34, 86, 753n453
  Analysis of Relation, 67
  Commentary of Pramāṇa Autocommentary, 98, 269, 361, 407, 770n696
  Dignāga and, 37, 40
  Drop of Logic, 373
  Drop of Reasoning, 373
  Geluk understanding of, 42–43, 44
  homage, 76
  influence of, 3–4, 13
  on mental perception, 271
  philosophical tradition of, 6, 45, 172
  proof statements of, 30
  Science of Disputation, 39
  Tibetan views of, 7–9, 27
  See also *Ascertainment of Valid Cognition*; *Commentary on Pramāṇa*
Dharmottara, 8, 62, 172, 197–98, 742n325, 791n900. See also *Direct Commentary on Ascertainment of Pramāṇa*; *Extensive Commentary on Drop of Logic*
dichotomies, 13–18, 173, 362, 371
Dignāga, 34, 37, 40, 86, 726n133, 753n453
  Analysis of the Objects of Cognition, 217, 248–50, 267, 342, 751n433
  Analysis of the Objects of Cognition Autocommentary, 251, 752n438
  Compendium of Pramāṇa Autocommentary, 438, 774n743
  on contrary reasons, 449, 453–55
  on conviction through inference, 25
  Entrance to Reasoning, 87, 354–55, 469, 470, 718n74, 763n609, 778n780
  homage, 76
  influence of, 3–4, 13
  philosophical tradition, 6
  proof statements of, 30

Tibetan views of, 7–9, 27
**Wheel of Reasoning*, 774n751, 775n766
See also *Compendium of Pramāṇa*
Direct Commentary on Ascertainment of Pramāṇa (Dharmottara), 799n1059
on cognitions grasping the reason, 434
on engagement, 198
on inference, 346, 657
on mental perception, clarifying and refuting, 270–74, 756n474
on mutual opposition preclusion, 543–44, 545
on *pratyakṣa*, 612, 616, 617, 622
on preclusion arising from actual entities, 540–41
on scripture, 486
on valid cognition, 208, 209, 745n360
on valid cognition, ruling out by, 482
Direct Commentary on the Commentary on Pramāṇa (Śākyabuddhi)
on cognition grasping the reason, 434
on Dharmakīrti's tenet system, 172
on hidden and evident phenomena, 108
on inconclusive reasons with remainder, 463–64
on negation, expression of, 409
on nonobservation of cause, 407
on subsequent cognition, 193
on types, classifying, 157
on valid cognition, 195
Dīrghanakha, 80, 716n61
discrediting statements, 20, 21, 79, 88. *See also* consequences
Dispeller of Dispute (Nāgārjuna), 68, 560, 639
on valid cognition, establishment of, 672–73
on valid cognition, fourfold, 642–43, 644
on valid cognition and ascertainment, 572, 573
dissimilar examples, 28, 255, 354, 355, 378, 495, 535, 808n1257
dissimilar instances, class of, 354, 355, 356, 357, 766n641
in common agreement about names, 427
in correct reasons, 370–71, 372, 373, 766n651, 767n653
in countering reasons, 769n682
definition, correct, 379
definitions, incorrect, 376–77
failing in, 499
in inconclusive reasons, 460, 461, 463
in nature reasons, 398
in pervasion, 308, 375
preclusion and, 535, 786n873
varieties, 379–81
distortions, mental, 146, 175, 191, 198, 214
divine eye, 105, 725n120
Doklung Valley, 54
Döndrup Gyatso, 61, 68, 677, 810n1287
double moon
manifest appearance of, 646
mutual opposition preclusion, 543
as object, 99, 100, 325, 723n106–8
sense cognition of, 184, 185, 215–16, 217, 218, 633, 634, 746n378
as similar example, 263–64
valid mental perception of, 650
doubt, 191–92, 740n309
dreaming consciousness, 194
Drepung Monastery, 62–63
Dreyfus, Georges, 43, 46
Drikung Kagyü, 49
Drok Riwoché, 552
Duldzin Drakpa Gyaltsen, 59, 60
Düsum Khyenpa, First Karmapa, 51
Dzungar Mongols, 63–64

effect reasons, 80
ascertainment in, 393–94
cognition grasping the reason in, 433
consequences in, 492
conviction proofs and, 419
deducting feature of cause, 548–49, 790n894
literal meaning and defining characteristics, 389
probandum for personal use, 465
probandum for second party, 471
qualms about, 394–95
reason, subject, predicate in, 391–92

varieties, 390–91, 768n673
effort, actual things and, 124, 729nn158–59
eight constituent substances, 119, 128, 605, 606, 607, 608, 609, 610
Elucidating the Intention Sutra, 644, 645, 657
emptiness, 17, 298
direct perception of, 19
Geluk view, 43, 45
inference of, 22
Prāsaṅgika view, 567, 792n928
encapsulation isolate, 734n228
engaged objects, 110, 181–82, 197–98
and object universals, distinguishing, 716n49
valid cognition of, mistaken views, 200–201
valid cognition of, two senses, 185–86, 206–8
engagers
affirmative, 520, 521
comprehensive and excluding, distinction between, 118, 729n154
comprehensive/appearance, 124, 126, 127, 150, 151, 270, 519, 522, 635, 784n852
excluding, 179, 430, 513, 519, 520, 521–22, 635
entailment, 24
Entering the Middle Way (Candrakīrti), 13, 68, 666, 672
on conceptual analysis, 81
on conventional existence, 597
in Geluk school, 12
on mutual dependence, 673
on object, instrument, agent, 590
on self-cognition, 580
on sensation, 651
entities
actual and non-actual, 15
same, being part of, 264, 265
two natures of, 227
in Hindu philosophical schools, 38–39
See also external entities
eons, three countless, 130, 731n174
established basis, 254–56, 468, 496
equivalent terms, 98, 200
known objects and, 467, 777n776
mental perception as, 277
mere self of phenomena as, 305–6
mistaken understandings, 111, 120–21, 126, 208
in nonobservation reasons, 404
pervasion and, 374
reverse pervasion and, 378
subject as, 381–83
valid cognition's negation and, 473
valid perception and, 669–70
establisher-established, 322, 412, 474, 759n549, 771n708
eternalism, 460, 565, 592–93, 633
evident phenomena, 102–4, 106–8, 423
example-analogy, 666, 808n1257
examples (proof statements), 808n1257
correct, defining, 494–95
failing in, 498
false, defining, 495
similar, 28, 263, 264, 754n459
See also dissimilar examples; similar examples
excluded third definitive categorization, 212, 362, 397, 545, 746n371, 764n622
excluders, three types, 518
excluding perspective, 96, 289–90, 291, 513, 721n90
exclusion, 124, 519–20, 729n157, 742n326. See also *apoha* theory; other-exclusion (*anyāpoha*)
existents, two types, 98–99, 722n101
experienced and experiencer, 102, 293, 724n113
Extensive Commentary on Drop of Logic (Dharmottara), 10, 658, 799n1059
external entities, 45
Cittamātra view of, 232, 249, 252, 724n114, 750n424
conventional and ultimate, 257–58
Sautrāntika views, misunderstanding, 227
sense consciousness and, 229, 230
in three turnings, 171–72

in valid cognition and result models (correct), 337–40
in valid cognition and result models (mistaken), 323, 324–29, 760n558
extremely hidden phenomenon
in conviction proofs, 415–17, 419, 420, 423
inference and, 26, 347
mental perception as, refuting, 271, 272
scripture and, 484–85, 486, 660, 663
extremes of exaggeration and denial, 81–82

faculties of parties
in correct reasons, 432
for effect reasons, 393
for nature reasons, 396
for proof statements, 356–57, 358, 361–62, 364–65
False Aspectarian Cittamātra, 172, 260, 290–91, 323–24, 325–26
false cognitions, 100, 145, 210, 286, 621, 723n107
faults, identifying, 261–62
fire and smoke, 23, 24, 326
as cause and effect, 136–37
cognition grasping the reason and, 433–34
as effect reason, 390–92, 768n673
inference and, 22, 211
informational relationship and, 549–50, 790n896
nighttime ocean and, 405–7, 492
unprompted proof, 466
five fields of learning, 79
five omnipresent mental functions, 236
five paths, 716n50. *See also individual paths*
five portal sense consciousnesses/perceptions, 235, 237, 244, 256
five situations (*gnas skabs lnga*), 105, 725n118
form realms, 238–39, 240
formless realms, 240, 241, 242, 244
forms with physical resistance, 126–27, 730n164
forward pervasion, 264–65, 718n72
ascertainment of, 380
concomitance and nonconcomitance in, 375, 766n650
definitions, 373, 376
foundation, 766n651
preparative nonreliance reason in, 396–97, 769n682
and proof statement, relationship of, 350–51
foundational consciousness, 235, 236, 237–39
Four Hundred Stanzas (Āryadeva), 559, 560, 608–9, 610
on hidden phenomena, 668
on recollection, 652
on sense and mental consciousnesses, 650, 651
on sense consciousness and their objects, 670
on worldly beings, 671
four seals, 546
four truths
enumeration, 302
order, 302–4
Pramāṇa treatises and, 82
in realizing selflessness, 310, 312
yogic perception of, 653, 656
function
in defining valid cognition, 207
in dividing awareness, 189, 739n297
generally characterized entities and, 141
perception and, 216
specifically characterized entities and, 118, 121–23, 141
two truths and, 166–67, 174
twofold division of objects and, 163, 735n246
Fundamental Treatise on the Middle Way (Nāgārjuna), 12
on ascertainment, 561–63
on convention, need for, 599
on *nature*, 582
on nonproduction, 566, 569
Svātantrika commentaries on, 572
on ultimate, realizing, 427
ultimate perspective of, 564–66, 570

Gampopa Sönam Rinchen, 50
Ganden Monastery, 47, 54, 57, 59, 60, 67
Ganden tradition, 12
Geden Nampar Gyalwai Ling, 552
Geluk Pramāṇa
critiques of, 48–49, 792–93n944
definition and definiendum, order of, 773n735
distinctions in, 42–46
etymology in, 771–72n728
importance of, 53
objects of sense and mental cognitions in, 650
opponents, identity of, 50–51
origins, 42
other traditions and, 1–3
self-cognition in, 757n490
tantra and, 53
See also logicians
Geluk tradition, 12
on antithesis, 780n803
on characteristics, two types, 16–17
consequence in, importance of, 30, 31
debate paradigm in, 21–22
dichotomy in, 17
etymologies in, 800n1079
Gyaltsab Jé's influence, 59–60
inexpressibility in, 794n973
intellectual consistency in, 47–48
Khedrup Jé's influence, 57
moderate realism of, 46, 723n110, 729n153, 732n191
origins, 47
perception approach of, 743n342
Pramāṇa and Madhyamaka as distinct in, 12
scholasticism of, 48–49, 51–52, 63
scripture and reasoning in, 25
two truths in, 14–15
gender, 169, 737n263
Gendun Drup, First Dalai Lama, 588. See also *Ornament of Reasoning*
generally characterized entities, 16–18
as communicated, 513
as conceptual constructs, 141
definition, 143
etymological derivation, 116
Geluk view, 43, 94, 95–96, 720n85
as held objects, 211
illustration, 143–46
inferential valid cognition of, 112–13, 727n138, 727n140
Prāsaṅgika view, 642, 655, 668
and specifically characterized, as mutually exclusive, 46
universals as, 731n188
"go against," 94, 719nn80–81
Gö Lotsāwa, *Blue Annals*, 7, 10, 12
Gomang College, 48, 61, 62, 63, 68
governing cause, 222–23
governing condition, 731n175
of maturing effects, 244
of mental and sense perception, differentiating, 278
of mental perception, 648–49
as mental sense power, 274, 275
mistaken sense consciousness and, 184–85
of sense consciousnesses, 219, 220, 222, 747n389, 276
of sense consciousnesses (Cittamātra), 247, 248, 267
of sense consciousnesses (Sautrāntika), 224–25
of sense perception, 219, 220, 648
valid perception and, 646
great charioteers, 526, 786n865
Guṇaprabha; *Vinaya Sutra*, 79
Gyalnga Dunpa, 551, 791n900
Gyaltsab Darma Rinchen, 54, 588
Commentary to Nyāyabindu, 767n657
Commentary to the Precious Garland, 650
on Dharmakīrti, 8
Extensive Pramāṇa Memorandum, 50
as Ganden throneholder, 57, 58, 59
in Geluk school, role of, 47
Illuminator of the Path to Liberation, 48, 59–60
life events, key, 58–59
Pramāṇa works of, 67, 715n42
Rendawa and, 55

written works, 59–60
See also *On Preclusion and Relationship*
Gyantsé, 56
Gyümé Tantric College, 61

Haribhadra; *Clear Meaning*, 132, 543, 788n881
held entity, 185, 226–27, 739n293
held objects, 110, 181, 185, 211, 726n131, 733n212
conceptual cognition of, 183
as generally characterized, 146
as generally characterized, refuting, 121–23
of mistaken sense consciousness, 184–85
in Sautrāntika, 230–31
as specifically characterized, 573
unmistaken cognition of, 162
of valid inferential cognition, 286
Heshang, 152
hidden phenomena, 83, 285–86
buddhas' awareness of, 177
conviction proofs and, 423, 424
defining, 104, 108
established basis as, 670
and evident, preclusion of, 106–8
inference of, 25–26, 347, 348, 619, 620, 621, 657, 658, 668
and manifest, distinctions in, 671
mistaken views, 95, 102–4, 323, 325
occasional, 102
Prāsaṅgika views, 620, 667–69
three varieties, 105, 620, 801n1088
valid cognition associated with scripture of, 659–60
yogic perception of, 653–54
Hinayana tradition, 5, 633, 644, 788n881
Hugon, Pascale, 35–36

identity itself and thing having identity, distinguishing, 152, 169, 400, 512, 737n266
ignorance
as cause of existence, 299
as cause of faults, 221
deceptive, 599
deluded, 238
nonafflicted, 317
as substantial cause of consciousness, 241
illustrations, 793n947
of actual things, 137–38
definition, 523
Geluk understanding, 46, 728n150
of proof statements, similar and dissimilar phenomena in, 354
of specifically and generally characterized entities, distinction in, 141
of two truths, 174
illustrator-illustrated model, 474, 779n789
imagined cognition, 327, 760n557
immediate condition/immediately preceding condition, 209, 731n175, 749n404
of consciousness, post-absorption, 239
of mental perception, 280, 281
mistaken sense consciousness and, 184–85
of samsara, 299
of sense consciousnesses (Cittamātra), 246, 247, 267
of sense consciousnesses (Sautrāntika), 225, 234–43
of sense consciousnesses, mental perception as, 271, 274, 275, 278
impermanence, 15
of actual things, 124, 729nn158–59
of aggregates, 298, 309
clear recollection of, 113–14
direct perception of, 19
inference of, 22
and permanence, preclusion examples, 506–7, 510, 533–34, 544, 545
as pervasion, 24
suffering of compositionality and, 310–11
See also sound as impermanent
implicative negation, 400, 504–5, 521, 721n93
imprints/seeds, 227, 260

in Cittamātra, 232, 251
for continuity of kind, 251
eradicating, 311, 317, 542, 788n881
mistaken views of, 243–44
of obscurations of knowledge, 175
paths countering, 536, 537–38, 787n875
recollection and, 652
stability of, 217, 218
as substantial cause of body, 242
imputation, Geluk understanding, 45
imputed existents, 40, 236, 522, 551, 750n410
inappropriate analysis, 593–95
inclusive reasons, 377, 378, 767n654, 775n768
inconclusive reasons
definition, 457, 775n768
not shared and shared, 457–61
with remainder, 463–64
in similar and dissimilar classes, 461–63
incorrect reasons, threefold division, 107, 725n123
India, 20, 21, 37–38, 753n450
Indian Buddhism, 25
binaries in, 14
demise of, 11
epistemological tradition in, 2
four philosophical schools of, 5
influences, 44
pramāṇa tradition in, 3–4
Indian Pramāṇa tradition, 11, 51, 743n342
conciseness in, 28
development, 6–7
fourfold division of pramāṇa in, 13
in Geluk tradition, 7–9
historical impact of, 42
on logical proofs, 26–27
scripture in, 25–26
sources, 8
indirect causes, 220–22
individual isolates, 196, 734n228, 737n266, 741n323
of conception, 213, 746n374
effect reasons and, 390, 768n673
as generally characterized, 156
of self, 381
individual nature, 117–18, 139, 143–44
inference [dealing with] common agreement about names, 488. *See also* common agreement about names reasoning
inference [dealing with] demonstrable facts and realities, 312, 473, 477–78, 481–82, 564
inference for oneself and another, 19
inference of conviction, 26, 482–83, 663, 779n799. *See also* conviction proofs; valid cognition [associated with] scripture
inference/inferential cognition, 87, 88, 200, 216
apprehending actual things, refuting, 150, 733n213
ascertainment induced by, 202
and cognition grasping reason, relationship of, 433–34, 435–37, 438, 773n736
conceptual cognition and, 191, 740n306
correct, 25, 31
divisions of, 212
effect reason and, 80
in engendering proof statements, 350, 763n602
of evident and hidden things, analysis, 106–8
extremely hidden phenomena and, 26
held objects and, 181
hidden things and, 102–3
knowledge from, 466–67
necessity of, 52
objects of, 207, 601, 797n1027
and other thoughts, distinction between, 24
overt and implicit realization by, 108–9, 110–11
as pramāṇa, 3, 4
Prāsaṅgika view, 557
proof statements and, 21
in realization, Geluk emphasis on, 19, 22–23
recollection's role in, 364

of selflessness of person, 308
specifically characterized entities and, 147
and subsequent cognition, relationship of, 192–93
as valid cognition, 17–18
and valid inference, distinguishing, 216
varieties, 801n1089
inferential awareness of final state, 599, 600
inferential cognition in personal domain, 345, 347
inferential cognition involving another party
defining characteristics, 351, 353
literal meaning and purpose, 349–50
similar and dissimilar phenomena varieties, 353–57
synonyms, 349
inferential valid cognition, 201, 211
in conviction proofs, 415, 416–17
definition (Prāsaṅgika), 620, 656–58
Dignāga's presentation, 345–47
held objects and, 185
of hidden phenomena, 104, 108
hypothetical argument on, 94–95, 720n85
literal meaning, 345
as mistaken, distinctions in, 215, 216–17
mistaken views, refuting, 112
in nature reasons, 396–99
objects of, 208, 285, 573
probandum and, 112–13
as relying on logic, 86
self-cognition and, 286–87
of selflessness, 203, 318, 744n344
specifically characterized entities and, 121–23, 149–50
valid cognition and its result model for, 347–48
varieties, 658–59, 807n1225
informational relationship, 548, 789n891
instantiation isolates, 156, 734n228, 737n266
intermediate existence, 240, 241, 242
interpretative teachings, 171, 172
isolable portions, 164–65, 736nn250–51
isolated encapsulations, 196, 309, 741n323, 759n534, 773n741
isolated type, 157–58, 281–82, 457–58

Jackson, David, 49
Jamyang Lama Tri Rinpoché, 677, 810n1289
Jamyang Shepa, 18, 715n37
Autobiographical Verses, 60–61
Decisive Analysis on the Middle Way, 675
life events, key, 60–63
textbooks and written works, 48, 63
See also *Mighty Pramāṇa Sun*
Jikten Gönpo, 49
Jinamitra, 756n483
Jñānagarbha
Commentary on Distinction between the Two Truths, 562, 563
Distinction between the Two Truths, 557, 598

kachupa title, 56, 58, 61
Kadam tradition, 10, 44, 51
Kagyü traditions, 49, 50–51. *See also* Dakpo Kagyü; Drikung Kagyü
Kalsang Gyatso, Seventh Dalai Lama, 63
Kamalaśīla, 8, 12, 383, 521, 767n664. See also *Commentary on the Difficult Points of the Compendium of Suchness*
karma
Buddha's comprehension of, 15
denying, 415
in non-Buddhist schools, 39
physical body and, 242, 244
in realist schools, 132
ripening, 647, 648
root of, 304
self of persons and, 305, 308–9
as true origins, 299, 303
Kawa Paltsek, 756n483
Khedrup Gelek Palsang
on Dharmakīrti, 8
as Ganden throneholder, 60
Geluk Pramāṇa and, 42

Guide Through the Path of Pramāṇa, 18
individuality of, 47–48
life events, key, 54–57
name, 159, 439, 735n240, 774n744
Ocean of Reasoning, 64, 65
Pramāṇa works of, 64, 715n38
on pramāṇa's role in Buddhism, 7, 32–33
refutations by, identity in, 715n39
Thousand Measures, 68, 69, 600, 621, 633, 651–52, 663, 664, 797n1027
written works, 57–58
See also *Banisher of Ignorance*
Khyungpo Draksé, 10
King Dhāraṇīśvara Sutra, 662–63
King of Samādhis Sutra, 632, 633, 647
knowledge
definition's role in, 468–69, 777n779
Geluk view of, 1, 2, 23
three types, 19, 85, 87, 466–67
known things, 99
and comprehended things, equivalency, 93–94, 719n78
in correct reasons, 377, 380, 383
synonyms, 98
Kokonor Lake, 63

Labrang Tashikhyil Monastery, 63, 810n1290
lakṣana, 792n944
Jamyang Shepa's threefold division, 575, 583, 602, 793n947, 794n966
and *lakṣya*, relationship of, 574, 575–76, 582–85, 592–93, 595
objects of comprehension and, 577–78
language
acquisition of, 189–90, 739n299, 739n301
conventional, 771–72n728
limits of, 585, 794n973
oppositional approach in, 14
realist theory, criticism of, 42
Layakpa Jangchup Ngödrup; *Ornament Clarifying the Essence of Gampopa's Four Dharmas*, 50
learning, internal, 78–81
letters, substance of, 120, 129–30
Lhasang Khan, 62
Lhetra Ting, 60
liberation
in communicated instructions, 84–85
in non-Buddhist schools, 39
Pramāṇa treatises and, 78–81
resolve for, 315–16
Lingkyé, 78
logical reasoning, 3–4, 43, 78
in attaining Mahayana goal, 318
binaries in, 14
in Buddhist path, variant views, 50–51
Geluk view, 47
inference rooted in, 22–23
necessity of, 52
of Pramāṇa system, 53, 79
Prāsaṅgika view, 659
for realization, necessity of, 19
relation and pervasion in, 23–24, 713n13
and scripture, relationship between, 25–26, 34
Tibetan verbs in, 768n675
logical relationships, 67–68, 511–12, 547, 551, 782n835, 789n888. *See also* causal relationship; nature relationship
logicians
on *lakṣana*, 574–75, 585–89, 590, 591, 602–3, 793n948
on *pratyakṣa*, 605–9, 614, 615–16, 628–30, 797n1034, 799n1071
on sense consciousness, 631–32
on specifically characterized things, 576–77
on valid cognition, 571–72
Losang Gyatso, 556

Ma Lotsāwa, 10, 735n242
Madhyamaka tradition, 5, 68, 131–32, 242, 785n861
and Cittamātra, relationship of, 4–5, 45
non-Buddhist parallels in, 41
Pramāṇa tradition and, 8, 52–53
production in, 168, 737n262
scripture in, 663
self-cognition in, 725n121
in Tibet, development of, 12

on valid cognition associated with scripture, 658
See also Prāsaṅgika Madhyamaka; Svātantrika Madhyamaka
Mahayana tradition, 4–5, 84, 171, 307, 318, 560, 644, 788n881
Maitreya, 50
Distinguishing the Middle Way from the Extremes, 586, 588
Ornament of Realizations, 176, 542, 723n111
Ornament of the Mahayana Sutras, 78, 79, 81, 715n48, 717n64
Unexcelled Continuum of the Mahayana, 542
manifest (*abhimukī*), 611, 613
manifest objects, 619, 620
for buddhas and sentient beings, establishing, 670–72
of mental perception, 653
Prāsaṅgika view, 667–69
of valid perception, 645, 646
of yogic perception, 653–54, 655
Mañjughoṣa/Mañjuśrī, 75, 76, 555, 672
materialism, 38, 714n23
meditation
direct perception during, 19
Geluk views of, 29
personalized instructions in, 51–52
primacy of, 50
on selflessness, 309, 310–18
specific and general characteristics in, 655
meditative equipoise, 234–35, 238, 629. *See also* ārya's meditative equipoise
memory. *See* recollection
mental consciousnesses, 239
in effect reasons, 392, 768n676
imprints in, 242, 243
mental sense power and, 279–80
observed object condition and, 225
physical body and, 241
sense consciousnesses and, 219
suspension absorption and, 235, 236–37
mental factors/faculties, 40, 265–66, 269, 755n465
mental perception, 209, 262
definitions, 277, 648–49
as extremely hidden, refuting, 205, 745n347
mental sense power and, 280
mistaken views, 269–77, 279
pratyakṣa and, 617
production, 278, 281, 282
varieties, 278, 649–53
vivid appearance of, 638
See also under sense perceptions
mental sense powers, 219, 274–75, 279–80, 646
mergeability, 189–91, 739n299, 739n301
Mighty Pramāṇa Sun (Jamyang Shepa), 53
Clear Words and, 13
colophon and Tashikhyil appendage, 677, 810n1290
concluding verses, 676
homage and intent, 555–56
overview, 68–69
pramāṇa divisions in, 13, 39
sources, 560
Mīmāṃsā school, 38, 331–32
mind, 755n465
Buddhist and non-Buddhist views of, 41–42
equivalent terms, 189
mind generation (*bodhicitta*), 84, 316–17
Miraculous Play of Mañjuśrī, 632
misconception-countering definitive categorization, 212, 746n371
mistaken cognitions, 96, 112, 162, 184, 232, 599–601
momentariness, 143, 458, 649, 657
āryas' perception of, 175
impermanence and, 432–33
sense powers and, 626–27
Mother. *See* Prajñāpāramitā Sutras
mutual dependency, 672–75
mutual exclusion affirmation, 642, 804n1163
mutual opposition preclusion, 412, 413, 508, 533–34, 804n1163
definition, 510–11, 543–44, 789n833, 789n886

delineation, 545
valid perception and, 475
varieties, 544
Muzing temple, 55

Nāgārjuna, 8, 30, 68, 245, 595, 676, 786n865
Compendium of Sutras, 559–60, 656, 660
homage, 555
Precious Garland, 558, 559, 595, 650, 660–61
Sixty Stanzas of Reasoning, 558, 560
Treatise on Pulverization, 39
See also *Dispeller of Dispute*; *Fundamental Treatise on the Middle Way*
name of effect/result assigned to cause, 349, 437
names, 154
actual and figurative, distinguishing, 514, 762n597
conceptual cognition and, 191
experience and, 733n226
naming merging with named thing, 189–90, 739n299, 739n301
as nonassociated compounded things, 515
two stages of, 155–56, 733n222
names and expressions
correct reasons establishing, 431–33, 773n735
ending, 568
in nonobservation nature reasons, 408–10, 770n704
Narthang Monastery, 44
nature reasons, 80, 408–10, 770n704
ascertainment in, 396–99
conviction proofs and, 419
defining characteristics, 395
probandum for personal use, 465
probandum for second party, 471
varieties, 99, 395–96, 722n103
nature relationship, 547–48, 789n889
negandum, 503–5, 743n341
existent things and, 98
in nonobservation reasons, 399, 769–70n690
other-exclusion and, 521
specifically characterized things and, 116, 117
negation, 17, 18, 152, 781n817
double, as affirmation, 47, 729n398
Prāsaṅgika view, 567
preclusion and, 505, 519–20, 534
specifically characterized entities and, 147–49, 150–51
Svātantrika and Prāsaṅgika differences in, 598
twofold division, 721n93
See also basis of negation
negative phenomena, 18, 159, 503, 781n817, 781n823
negative reasons, 200–201, 207, 400, 431–32, 721–22n96
Nenying Monastery, 57, 58
Ngamring Monastery, 54, 56
Ngawang Losang Gyatso, Fifth Dalai Lama, 61, 62, 677
Ngok Lekpai Sherab, 10
Ngok Loden Sherab (Ngok Lotsāwa), 10–11, 735n242
Ngorchen Kunga Sangpo, 56
nihilism, 154, 290, 291, 565
Nirgrantha (Jain) tradition, 38, 40, 256, 444, 445
nirvana, 4, 312, 315, 633
non-actual things, 101, 129, 150, 159, 168, 174, 386, 519, 737n262
nonanalytical cessations, 301, 541
nonascertainment, 564–66, 572–73
nonassociated compounded things, 514–15, 754n456, 787n876
nonconceptual cognition, 184, 185, 234–37
nonconceptual false cognition, 194, 213, 226, 237, 634, 741n314
nondeceptive consciousness
in defining valid cognition, 195–98, 199, 205, 207
pratyakṣa as, refuting, 618–19, 630
nonobservation reasons, 44, 80
of cause, 402–5, 406, 409

consequences in, 492
conviction proofs and, 419
defining characteristics, 399–400
of direct cause, 412–13, 789n890
inferential cognition and, 658
of nature, 308, 309, 313, 403–4, 405, 406, 411–12
observation in, 392, 412, 771n709
observation of something that is preclusive, 309, 399, 759n533
probandum for personal use, 465
probandum for second party, 471
of same nature, 407, 408–10, 411–13, 770n699
of things not accessible, 401–5, 769n690
valid perception and, 111
of what should be apparent, 167, 265, 403, 404, 405–7, 545
nonproduction, 562–63, 566–67, 569, 654
nonreliance reasons, preparative, 396–97, 769n682
Nyāya school, 13, 27, 38, 753n450
Buddhist critiques of, 41–42, 287, 732n191
Pramāṇa tradition and, 39–40
proof statements in, 762n598
"whole" in, 737n266
Nyāyasūtras, 39, 79, 719n76
Nyingma tradition, 64

object and actor, 166, 173–74, 580, 583, 736n258
object and subject, 18
clinging excessively to, 328, 330
correspondence between, 723–24n111
as mistaken thought, 173
as mutually dependent, 612, 788n877
perception's role between, 724n115
simultaneity of (*see* proof of simultaneity)
object condition. *See* observed object condition
object universals, 78, 189, 655, 716n49
as conceived objects, refuting, 181
in correct proofs, 386, 387
failing reasons and, 496
inferential cognition of, 110–11
mutual opposition preclusion and, 543
valid inferential cognition of, 348
object-aspect, 232–33, 261
in Cittamātra True Aspectarians, 172
as cognition, 258–59, 753n452
of conceptual cognition, 145
as engaged objects, refuting, 201, 743n342
Geluk understanding of, 46
mutual opposition preclusion and, 544
pratyakṣa and, 620–21, 645–46
self-cognition and, 286, 289–90, 292, 293–94, 757n493, 758n508
of sense consciousness, presenting, 228–31, 729n400
in valid cognition and result models (correct), 334, 335, 340, 341
in valid cognition and result models (mistaken), 323–24, 325–29, 760n558
object-meanings, 191
objects
ascertaining nature, 201–2
categorizing, 101–2, 179, 738n280
defining characteristics, 99–100
known things and, 93–97, 719nn77–78
objectified and nonobjectified, 146, 733n206
synonyms, 98
and their names, relationship of, 42, 414, 415–16, 426, 771–72n728, 772n729
valid cognition determined by, 641–42
valid cognition ruling out, 472–73, 474–75
See also individual types
objects of engagement. *See* engaged objects
objects of knowledge
in Cittamātra, 257
divisions of, 212, 519
mistaken cognition and, 599–601
negation and, 503, 781n818
in Sāṃkhya, 450, 452, 456
valid cognition and, 473

objects of thought, two categories, 428
obscurations to knowledge, 175, 537
observed object condition, 130, 222, 731n175
  correct stance, 248–51, 751nn434–35, 752n438, 752n440
  in effect reasons, 768n676
  of mental perception, 278, 280
  of sense consciousnesses (Cittamātra), 245–51
  of sense consciousnesses (Sautrāntika), 225, 226–34
omniscient awareness/consciousness, 111, 203, 227, 255, 312, 318, 401, 541, 542
On Preclusion and Relationship (Gyaltsab Jé)
  colophon and Tashi Lhumpo appendage, 552, 791n902
  homage and intent, 531–32
  overview, 67–68
  time period, 43–44
opponents, fictional and actual, 65–66
Opponents of Parity, 172, 234
Ornament Commentary to the Pramāṇavārttika (Prajñākaragupta)
  on cognition grasping the reason, 433–34, 435
  on Dharmakīrti's tenet, 172
  on inferential valid cognition, 353
  on jewel's sparkle, 210, 211
  on mental perceptions, misunderstandings about, 269–70
  on physical body, 242
  on subsequent cognition, 193
  on valid cognition, defining characteristics, 196
Ornament of Reasoning (Gendun Drup), 64, 66, 740n307
other-cognition, 183, 290
  mental perception and, 277, 278
  nonconceptual, 184
  object-aspect, 127, 730n166
  in Sautrāntika valid cognition models, 324–25
  and self-cognition, distinctions in, 105, 285, 288, 293, 725n121
  sense perception and, 229
other-exclusion (*anyāpoha*), 24, 179, 519, 520–22
  conceptual cognition, 721n90
  labeling and, 155, 733n226
  threefold division, 520–21, 784n855
other-knowing consciousnesses, 219–20, 579
otherness, 457–59, 776n769
overt pervasion, 374–75, 494

Palbar Monastery, 527
Palkhor Chödé Monastery, 56, 64
Pāṇini; *Sutras on Grammar*, 575, 793n948
particles, 135, 257
  actual things and, 97, 721n95
  basic awareness and, 314
  objects of perception as, 624–26
  as part-possessing whole, 170
  as specifically characterized entities, 118
  specifically characterized things and, 122
  substance and, 131, 136, 731n185
  two truths and, 169
  as ultimate truth, 164–65, 736n251, 736n261
particulars, 18
  definition, 519
  Geluk understanding of, 46
  inference and, 23
  mutual phenomena and, 723n110
  and *śabdārtha*, relationship of, 146
  universals and, 46, 168, 729n153, 736n261
part-possessing whole, 132, 133, 170, 314, 737n267
path of accumulation, 301, 655
path of meditation, 19, 297, 301, 318, 537
path of no-more learning, 297, 301
path of preparation, 297, 301
  objects on, 655
  path of seeing and, 235
  selflessness and, 203, 744n344
  supreme dharma level, 78, 536, 537, 538, 541, 716n50, 787n875

path of seeing, 19, 537, 716n50
arising, 235, 318
dharma forbearance level, 536, 538, 541–43, 787n875
misconceptions about, 82
selflessness on, 744n344
as true path, 301
yogic perceivers on, 297
path that matures, 310, 759n536
Patsab Nyima Drak, 12, 68
perception, 19, 45, 87, 88, 620, 754n454
as actual thing, 123
aspect in, 102, 723n111, 743n342
cognition grasping the reason and, 435
as comprehensive engager, 126
conceptual, 121–23
conceptual cognition and, 738n281
of evident and hidden things, analysis of, 106–8
first and later portions of, 208–9, 745n360
foundational consciousness as, refuting, 237
as free from conception, refuting, 636–38
Geluk understanding of, 46
inattentive, 210, 745n367
inferential cognition and, 348
models, variant views on, 743n342
as pramāṇa, in Indian tradition, 3
Prāsaṅgika view, 557
role of, 724n115
self-cognizing and other-cognizing, 105, 725n121
as valid cognition, 17, 208, 209–10
and valid perception, distinguishing, 214–15, 216–17
perfect, immutable nature (third nature), 166, 736n260
permanence, 15, 138, 167–68, 736n251, 736n261, 781n823
personalized instructions, 51, 714n32
pervasion, 31, 714n10
ascertaining, 361
in connecting similar and dissimilar phenomena, 355, 356–57
of consequence, 33
contrary, 386
definitions, 369–72, 764n631, 765n632, 765n640
divided, 376, 766n652
in effect reasons, 393, 394
establishing, 308
expression of, 358
four types, 373–74
general and specific, 100
internal, 765n632, 777n778
in nonobservation reasons, 412
preclusion and, 533
preclusion and relationship in, 67
ruling out, 387
and thesis, relationship of, 359, 780n801
valid cognition in establishing, 493
See also forward pervasion; reverse pervasion
Phabongkha Jamyang Drakpa, 61
Phakmo Drupa Dorjé Gyalpo, 51
phenomena
as "characterless," 173–74
conceptually constructed, 156, 781n823
correct conventional, 164
deceptive, 632–33
as dream-like, 131–32
as evident or hidden, 22, 105
functioning and not functioning, distinction between, 116
in Hindu philosophical schools, 41
noncomposed/unconditioned, 44
nonexistence and nonobservation, as identical, 411
not derived from effort, 459, 776n770
single and different, 523, 785n861
substantive and reverse, 522, 785n860
See also affirmative phenomena; negative phenomena; positive phenomena
phenomenon-source, 649, 651
physical sense powers
mental perception and, 278
sense perception and, 217, 219, 275, 276, 756n478
valid cognition and its result model and, 336–37
valid perception and, 646

as wholly hidden phenomena, refuting, 104, 105, 725n120
position. *See* thesis
positive phenomena, 519, 520, 784n851
pots, 143, 713n12
for activity and efficacy, 15
for cause and effect, 94, 719n79
golden pot, 119–20, 129, 143–44, 146, 732n203
for mutual phenomena, 101
negation and, 17, 46
nonobservation reasons on, 403–4, 408, 409–10, 411, 770n704
perceivability of, 605–9, 628–29, 798n1037
proof statements and, 21
self-production and, 245
simultaneity and, 262
for specifically characterized entities, 16
substance and, 118, 119, 124, 128–29, 138
for universals, 46
practitioners, faith-based, 81, 87
Prajñākaragupta, 8, 735n242. See also *Ornament Commentary to the Pramāṇavārttika*
Prajñāmokṣa; *Commentary to Atiśa's Middle Way Instruction*, 809n1260
Prajñāpāramitā Sutras, 658, 662, 807n1227
pramāṇa
in Indian, variant views, 2–3
in non-Buddhist schools, 39
Prāsaṅgika view, 639–40, 804n1157
See also Geluk Pramāṇa; Tibetan Pramāṇa tradition
Pramāṇa Summary, 66
Pramāṇa treatises
aim of, 82–85
core subject matter, 87–89
misconceptions about, 77–82
value of, 86–87
Prāsaṅgika Madhyamaka, 6, 13
on cognition and objects as illusory, 633
conventional truth in, 566–67
in Geluk school, dominance of, 12
inferential cognition in, 797n1027, 801n1089
misconceptions about, 557–60, 641, 644, 650
name, significance of, 659, 807m1232
nonproduction in, 566–67
public and unique systems in, 567, 568, 619, 792n928
specific [self] characterization in, 117, 728n148
substance in, 40
svalakṣana in, 809n1260
Svātantrika and, 30, 571–72, 649
two truths in, 601
valid cognition in, four varieties, 557–58, 620, 641–46, 666, 667, 801n1088 (*see also individual type*)
valid cognition in, four varieties as non-definitive, 653
valid cognition in, sources for, 560
pratyakṣa
distributive repetition and, 623–28
as figurative or actual, 608–9, 626–27, 629, 630–31, 636, 646
as free from conception, 628–30
logicians' view, 605–9, 612–16, 797n1034, 799n1062, 799n1071
Prāsaṅgika views, 611–14, 617–19, 622–23, 645, 797n1034, 801n1094
Svātantrika views, 609–10, 613, 614, 615–16, 621–23, 637, 654
two truths and, 609–10
yogic perception and, 653–54
pratyekabuddhas, 297, 316, 317, 318, 633
preclusion, 67–68, 546
affirming-excluding in, 742n326
arising from actual entities, 540–41
Buddha's teaching about, 80
definitions, correct, 508–9, 535
definitions, mistaken, 506–8, 533–34, 786n869
direct, 475
direct and indirect, 508–9
involving countering by another valid cognition, 508–9, 510, 511

as not established, 512
varieties, 412–13, 508–9
See also antagonistic preclusion; mutual opposition preclusion
predicates, 28, 40, 385–87, 400, 409, 493, 766n651
predisposition for linguistic formulation, 159
probandum. *See* thesis
probans. *See* reasons
production, 270, 398–99, 562, 568
proof of simultaneity, 266, 752nn442–43
aim of, 252–53
formulating and identifying components, 253–54, 752n443
fulfillment of three criteria, 264–66
incorrect views in establishing, 254–63
personal experience in, 754n455
simultaneity, meaning in, 260–63
proof statements, 20, 21, 79, 80, 88
cognition grasping the reason and, 438
correct formulation of, 350–51, 362–63, 762n598, 763n602, 763n604
as correct verbalization of sign, 351
flaws of, 351–53, 354–55, 364
opponents, two kinds, 361–62
Prāsaṅgika view, 659
purpose, 363–64
single element in, refuting, 358–61
three criteria in, role of, 361, 363–64, 764n620
valid cognition through analogy in, 666
proofs, 25, 752n443, 786–87n873, 808n1257
affirmative, 431–32
affirmative and negative, distinction between, 424
analysis and classification of, 35
and consequences, distinctions between, 31, 32, 714n19
establishing expression, 409–10
example, 28
existence variety, 354, 369, 377, 418, 768n675
formulating, 307–8
in Geluk school, importance of, 25, 26, 27–29
identity variety, 354, 369, 376–77, 386, 418, 768n675
intended and unintended results, 480
models, 26–30, 40
Prāsaṅgika view, 665–66
precision in, 27–29
and thesis, relationship of, 743n341
of thesis-subject, 446–47, 774n751
threefold model, 728n150
unprompted, 465–66
property and property basis, 40, 590–92, 795n990
property communicators, 516–18, 783nn846–47, 784n848
property of the probandum, 151, 776–77n773
property of the subject, 111, 264, 360, 718n72, 726n133, 763n617
ascertaining, 361, 367–68
confirming, 381
definitions, 372–73
establishing, 308–9
foundation, 766n651
purely abstracted things, 119, 729n155, 736–37n261

Qoshot Mongols, 62–63, 64
Questions of Ratnacūḍa Sutra, 581

Rabten Kunsang Phak, 56
Ravigupta, 242, 735n242
realism
Buddhist schools, 117, 131–32, 169
moderate, 46, 723n110
naive, 723n111
pejorative stance toward, 40–41
representational, 723–24n111
reasons, 33, 152, 776–77n773
actual and intended proof in, 453, 457, 775n760
ārya's perspective on, 567–68, 569
autonomous, 569, 570
failing, 495–98

identifying, 385–87
naming, 390
and predicate, relationship between, 97, 365, 412, 460
in proofs, 28, 714n17
quality in, 497–99, 781n815
typology, 80, 716n60
unconfirmed, 386
See also individual types
rebirth, 22, 240, 241, 242, 303, 652–53
recollection, 744–45n346
in cognition grasping the reason, 434–35, 436, 437–38, 773n742
conceptual consciousness and, 208
mental perception and, 651–53
range of, 653
self-cognition and, 291, 747–48n392, 757n505
valid cognition and, 203
reductio ad absurdum, 30
referent for anti-predicate, 402, 769–70n690
referents for labeling, 154–56
refuge, 85
rejoinders, 88, 718n76
false, 20
self-defeating (similar effect), 258, 753n450
relationships. *See* logical relationships
released path/path that releases, 300, 310, 537, 541, 759n536, 787n875
remote entity, 97, 401, 404–5, 406, 721n96
Rendawa Shönü Lodrö, 55, 58, 526
representationalism, 743n342
resultant sense consciousness, 224, 225
reverse pervasion, 264–65, 374, 718n72
concomitance and nonconcomitance in, 375, 766n650
definition, 373
established basis and, 378
foundation, 766n651
preparative countering reasons/valid cognition in, 396–99, 535, 769n682
Rinchen Chögyal, 552, 791n901
Riwo Dangchen Monastery, 56, 64
Riwo Gephel retreat, 61–62, 68, 677
Rongtön Sheja Kunrik, 56, 59

śabdabrahman ("word essence"), 300, 758n519
śabdārtha, 185, 727n141
as appearing object of conceptual cognition, 190–91
deluded awareness and, 238
as exclusion of other, 179
as generally characterized, 113, 727n140
as held object, 121–23
illustration, 144, 732n203
mistaken views, 145–46, 190
naming as pointless, 154–56
of nonexistents, 381–83, 767n662
objects and, 110
perception and, 128, 730n173
presenting to conceptual cognition, 146
role of, 140, 732n190
Sakya Monastery, 11, 12, 55, 58
Sakya Paṇḍita, 723n110
antirealist view, 46
on consequences, 30
Khedrup Jé and, 58
Pramāṇavārttika revision by, 735n242
Treasure of Pramāṇa Reasoning Autocommentary, 218, 756n478
See also *Treasure of Pramāṇa Reasoning*
Sakya tradition
on antithesis, 780n803
and Geluk tradition, contrasts between, 732n191, 757n490
Khedrup Jé and, 55, 58
on perception, three elements, 743n342
scholasticism in, 49
Śākyabuddhi, 8, 163, 174, 210–11, 365. See also *Direct Commentary on the Commentary on Pramāṇa*
Śākyaśrībhadra, 735n242
same simultaneous substantial entity, 127–28, 549, 635
Śaṃkarānanda (great brahmin), 197, 278, 365, 551, 742n325, 791n900
Sāṃkhya school, 27, 38, 351
Buddhist critiques of, 41–42

contrary reasoning of, 450–55, 456–57
self-production in, 245, 569
substance in, 157–58
unconfirmed reasonings of, 444–45
universals in, 141–42
samsara, 39, 86, 298, 303, 310–11, 315
Sangphu Monastery, 10, 51, 793n947
awareness categorization from, 739n297
decline of, 12
definition theory from, 46
Gyaltsab Jé at, 59
Jamyang Shepa at, 61
object categorization from, 738n280
proponents of the analytical great works approach of, 508, 522, 782n830, 785nn859–60
scholasticism at, 66, 68
"summaries" genre at, 11
Śāntarakṣita, 8, 12
Compendium of Suchness, 521, 644, 648, 663
Ornament to the Middle Way, 172
Śāntideva; *Entering the Bodhisattva Way*, 656
Saraha; *Treasury of Doha*, 560
Sarasvatī, 555, 676
Sautrāntika school, 5, 328, 329, 332, 621, 625
actual things in, 260
aspect in, 102, 253, 723n111
conceptual cognition in, 128
Dharmakīrti and, 6, 45
indivisibility in, 170–71, 737n269
perception in, 217, 654–55, 730n165
as realists, 40
self-cognition in, 292, 293, 725n121
selflessness in, 307
sense consciousness in, 224–44
sense perception in, 214, 218, 220
in Seven Treatises, 174
specifically characterized things in, 629
substance in, 127
three systems (Śāntarakṣita), 172
true cessations in, 301
two systems in, 165
two truths in, 163, 164
ultimate in, 162
valid cognition and result models in, 323, 324–25, 331, 333, 335, 338–39
scripture
authority of, 558–60
citing, accuracy in, 487–88
conviction proofs and, 414–15, 416, 417–18, 428, 771n712
countering and impeding by, 483–84
on illusory nature of phenomena, 632
of other systems, 663
on *pratyakṣa*, 637–38
as probandum, variant views, 470
reasoning establishing correctness in, 644
as reliable source of truth, 3
repetition in, 350, 762n600
ruling out by, 482–83
shared by two vehicles, 241–42
threefold analysis of, 420–21, 422, 483, 644–45, 659, 660, 663, 771n724
See also conviction proofs; valid cognition [associated with] scripture
sectarianism, 49, 63
self
attachment to, 303
equivalent terms, 589
investigating, 311–12
logical reasoning on, 304, 381–82
permanent, unitary, independent, 305, 308
reasonings on, 372
straight negation of, 175
in Hindu philosophical schools, 39
self of persons
identifying, 304–5
and person, distinction between, 305, 306
refuting, 307–9, 551
self of phenomenon, 753–54n453
identifying, 304, 305–7
and phenomenon, differentiating, 306
reasoning on, 312
refuting, 307
self-cognition, 184, 283, 747–48n392, 756n475

acting on object, refuting, 180, 579–81
appearing objects of, 180
in Cittamātra, 259
in common agreement about names, 430
every awareness as, refuting, 285–88
in Geluk and Sakya traditions, divergence in, 743n342, 757n490
Khedrup Je's view, 292–94
mental perception and, 272, 278, 282
and object-aspect, refuting mistakes, 231–33
and other-cognition, distinction between, 105, 285, 288, 293, 725n121
as perception, 294, 758n511
Prāsaṅgika view, 643–44, 675, 810n1282
pratyakṣa and, 617
sense consciousness and, 233–34
subject-aspect, 127, 730n166
in Svātantrika, refuting, 573
valid cognition and, 209, 620–21
in valid cognition and result models (correct), 334
in valid cognition and result models (mistaken), 323–24, 325–33
self-cognizing perception, 105, 229, 477
mistaken understandings, 128, 194, 213, 260–61, 262, 741n314
in proof of simultaneity, 264
subject-aspect as, 127
as without objects, refuting, 288–91
self-grasping, 253
cause of, eradicating, 304
investigating, 311–12
referent object of, 305
as root of samsara, 299, 315
selflessness and, 261, 306, 309, 316–18
suffering from, 298
valid cognition countering, 472, 778n785
selflessness, 17, 193, 307
of aggregates, 298, 299
as conceptual consciousness, refuting, 174–75
direct perception of, 19, 203, 744n344, 787n875
Geluk understanding of, 43
as impaired conventional phenomena, refuting, 166
inference of, 22, 657–58
meditation on, 309, 310–18
as nonexistent, refuting, 97
object, instrument, agent of, 589–90
perception of, 125
as permanent, refuting, 126, 730n162
Pramāṇa treatises and, 78–79, 82
yogic perception of, 653, 654
selflessness of persons, 317
clear appearance in, 806n1215
in first turning, 171
realizing, 309–10, 551, 655
selflessness of phenomena, 171
self-production, 245, 569
self-supporting person, 308–9
self-supporting substance, 304, 305, 306, 307–8, 381, 758n530
self-supporting substantial existence, 307–8, 551
sense bases, 133, 242
sense consciousnesses/cognitions, 194, 219, 797n1027
cognitive functions, lacking, 638
as deceptive and nondeceptive, 217–18
logicians' view, 630
mistaken, 99, 184, 185
objects of, 180, 287, 601, 635, 669–70, 757n496, 803n1141
objects presenting to, 133, 731n180
in Sautrāntika and Cittamātra, differences, 233
self-cognition and, 477
three conditions of, 220–23
three qualities, separate, 225
valid cognition and, 341–42
as valid perception, 631
sense objects, 252–53, 267, 274, 278, 453, 477, 612, 613, 752n443
sense perceptions, 209, 217, 259–60
of absences, 109
definition (Khedrup Jé), 219–20
definition (Prāsaṅgika), 646–48
definition, mistaken, 274–75

meaning, literal, 219
and mental perception, differentiating, 269–71
and mental perception, mistaken views, 273–74, 275, 276, 280, 756n477
and mental perception, relationship of, 278, 281–83, 650–52
non-Buddhist views, 213
in nonobservation reasons, 408
three conditions for, 80, 130–31, 731n175
varieties, 220
sense powers
arising of, 647
cognition associated with, 624–27
in effect reasons, 392, 768n676
as governing condition, 219, 220
as hidden, 614
and mind, relationship of, 242
pratyakṣa and, 614, 615–18, 622, 799n1071
in Sautrāntika and Cittamātra, differences in, 267
and sense consciousness, relationship of, 225–26
See also mental sense powers; physical sense powers
sentience, 256
sentient beings, 1, 316
set of causes, 274
Seven Treatises on Pramāṇa
Banisher of Ignorance and, 77
Cittamātra perspective in, 45
as False Aspectarian, refuting, 290–91, 326
foundational consciousness as incompatible with, 239
Khedrup Jé's categorization of, 79–80
nonexistence in, 95
purposes of studying, 82–83, 86
subject matter, 88–89
three criteria in, 368
in Tibetan tradition, 7–8
as True Aspectarian who are Opponents of Parity Cittamātra, 172–77
two approaches in, 171–72
Shākya Chokden, 67, 743n342
Shang Tsalpa Tsöndrü Drakpa, 51
Shangshung Chöwang Drakpa, 69
"Shorter" Correct. See *Extensive Commentary on Drop of Logic* (Dharmottara)
signifiers, 733n222
similar examples, 28, 141, 263–64, 354–55, 383, 391, 460, 494–96, 754n459
similar instances, class of, 377, 766n641, 766n651, 767n653
in correct proof statement, 354, 355, 356, 357, 361, 372, 373
definition, correct, 379
definitions, incorrect, 376–78
inconclusive reasons in, 461–63
in pervasion, 308, 369–70, 375
varieties, 379–80
similar substance type, 157, 158, 549, 734n232
simultaneous observation, 218, 262–63
singularity and difference, 523, 534, 785n861, 786n872
Śiva, 75, 85
six superknowledges, 752n442
slightly hidden phenomena, 422, 620, 641, 801n1089
Smith, Gene, 62
Smṛtijñānakīrti, 756n483
Sönam Gyaltsen, 757n498, 757n502
sound as impermanent, 201
consequence of accepting, 31–32
correct proof, 373, 743n341
as evident or hidden, 104–5, 724n117
expositional model, example, 29–30
flawed proof statement, 352
held objects and, 185
individual and shared natures and, 228
inferential cognition of, 110–11, 112, 113–14, 138, 150, 286–87, 733n212
mental perception and, 272
mistaken cognition and, 96, 600, 797n1024
nature reasons on, 395–96
perception of, 125, 148–50, 215
pervasion and thesis in, 483, 780n801

preclusion and, 544
production reason, 358, 359–61, 377, 378, 385–87
proof establishing an expression, 410
scripture and, 660
substance and, 118–19
"thing heard" reason, 377, 378, 767n654
valid perception and, 148
sound universal, 189–91, 739n300, 783n845
space
in contrary reasoning, 446–50
mistaken views on, 97, 121, 721n95
as non-actual thing, 207
noncomposite, 200, 202, 301, 354, 355, 363, 369, 371, 379, 397, 495, 534, 765n640
specifically characterized entities, 16–18, 809n1260
as actual things, refuting, 147–51
communication and, 512–14
comprehension of, 98
as conceived objects of conceptual cognition, refuting, 180–81, 573
in correct proofs, 386, 387
defining, 117
in defining valid cognition, 206–7, 208
determinate identity of, 156–58
determinate location, time, and individual nature, 139–40
engaged objects and, 202
etymological derivation, 116
exclusion and, 520, 521
Geluk understanding of, 43, 45–46, 720n85
and generally characterized, as mutually exclusive, 46
as held objects, 211, 286
illustrations, 117, 118–21
mistaken views, 121–23, 162–63
as objects of cognition alone, refuting, 576–77
Prāsaṅgika view, 642, 654–55, 667–68, 802n1115
as referent for labeling, 154–56
self-cognition and, 580–81
three times and, 129
and ultimate existence, relationship of, 164, 174
universals and, 140–41, 729n153
valid cognition and, 200–201, 207–8, 630–34
valid perception and, 111
Śrāvaka tradition, 5, 171, 674
attainment in, 316
goal of, 318
selflessness in, 307, 317, 633
tenets, 162
yogic perceivers in, 297
straight (nonimplicative) negation, 97, 503–4, 505, 521, 721n93
analytical cessation as, 301
in consequences, responding to, 494
contrary reasons and, 448–49
in nonobservation reasons, 400
of self, 175
unconfirmed reasons and, 442
Subhūtiśrīśānti, 735n242
subject communicators, 516–18, 783nn846–47, 784n848
subject-aspect, 127, 730n166, 743n342
as cognition, 258–59, 753n452
identity of, 760n559
and object-aspect, relationship of, 233
self-cognition and, 234, 260–61, 286, 288, 289–90, 292, 757n493
of sense consciousness, 229
in valid cognition and result models (correct), 340, 341
in valid cognition and result models (mistaken), 323–24, 325–29
subjects (logical reasons), 40
as conventional truth, 152
identifying, 385–87
and predicate, relationship of, 376–78, 766n652
proof statement and, 21
role of, 383–84
shared by realists and idealists, 254
subsequent cognition, 114, 739n297, 744n346
conventional, 198

definition, 193–94, 741n313
knowledge from, 466–67
mistaken views, 148
mistaken views, refuting, 192–93, 196, 204, 741n310
self-cognition and, 291
of sense consciousness, 342, 761n586
and valid cognition, relationship of, 205, 208, 271
subsequent inference, 657–58
substance, 138, 246
basic awareness as, refuting, 314
conceptual cognition as, 213, 746n373
imprints and, 243
Indic roots of concept, 40
logical relationship and, 512
in nature relationships, 547, 548
in non-Buddhist philosophy, 142–43
object and subject as separate, 252–53
Pramāṇa system view of, 280, 756n485
self of phenomena and, 306
self-cognition as, refuting, 290–91
of sense and mental perception, separate, 281–82, 283
shape and, 165
simultaneity of separate, refuting, 265–66
single, 123–29
single and different, 523
specifically characterized entities and, 118–21
universals and, 140
of valid cognition and its result, misunderstanding, 336–37, 340
in Hindu philosophical schools, 41
See also similar substance type
substantial causes, 234–37, 240
basic awareness and, 314
in classifying types, 157
of consciousness, post-absorption, 239
contributory conditions and, 247
of physical body, 242
and substantial types, 281–82
substantial existence, 522
and imputed existence, distinctions between, 40, 551
lack of, 514–15, 588–89, 627, 628
mental sense power and, 276
Svātantrika view, 628
substantial existents, 175, 522, 750n410
substantive phenomena, 522, 785n860
suchness, 172, 301, 559, 596, 599, 609, 610, 628, 671
suffering
of aggregates, 298, 309, 311
eradicating, 312
of others, wish for freedom from, 316–17
Pramāṇa study and, 49–50
three forms, 310–11
See also true sufferings
superimposition, 568, 570, 630
supramundane paths. *See* transcendent/supramundane paths
suspension absorption, 260, 749n405
arising from, 235–37, 239–40
engaging, 238
mental consciousness in, 239–41
sense consciousness in, refuting, 256
Svātantrika Madhyamaka, 6, 12, 30, 560, 649
conventional existence in, 596, 597
inferential valid cognition in, 600
lakṣana's special gloss in, 602–3
misconceptions about, 644
name, significance of, 659, 807m1232
nonascertainment in, 572–73
phenomena in, 594
Prāsaṅgika and, 30, 571–72, 649
pratyakṣa in, 609–10, 613, 614, 615–16, 621–23, 637, 654
sense consciousnesses in, 631–32, 633–34
substantial existence in, 628
valid cognition in, 571–72, 642

Taktsang Lotsāwa Sherab Rinchen, 557, 567, 610, 634–35, 641, 644, 648, 791n906, 798n1053, 803n1141
tantra, 51–52, 53, 57
Tashi Lhunpo Monastery, 527, 528, 552, 786n867, 791n902

Teaching of Akṣayamati Sutra, 640, 662–63
ten grounds, 238, 541, 542
Ten Grounds Sutra, 80
tenet systems, 5, 14–15, 723n111
textbooks (*yig cha*), 48
Thangsakpa, 12
thatness, 647, 656, 662
thesis, 28, 30, 727n138, 767n668
  assertions ruled out by statement's words, 478–81, 487
  as conventional truth, 152
  in conviction proofs, 423
  correct proofs and, 743n341
  curiosity regarding, 384, 385, 445
  defining characteristics and, 196
  disproved, 381
  failing, mistaken understandings, 495–98
  false, 472, 487–88
  flawed, 352
  for personal use, 465–67
  and pervasion, relationship of, 359, 780n801
  and probans, relationship of, 350
  and proof statement, relationship of, 359, 418
  translations of, 776n773
  valid inferential cognition and, 112–13
thesis for second party
  definitions, correct, 470–71
  definitions, mistaken, 466–69, 777n778
  Dignāga's five terms on, 467–68, 469, 777n775
  varieties, 471
three criteria for correct reasons, 714n18
  correct understanding, 373–75
  Dignāga's definition, 29–30, 718n72
  direct perception of, 86, 89
  encapsulating correct reason, 437, 773n741
  faulty, 357, 359–60
  incorrect reasons and, 107, 725n123
  mistaken understandings, 368–72
three kinds of individuals, 316–17
three natures, 736n260
Three Refuges, 555
three spheres, 34, 720n89
three spiritual types, 84
three times, 119–21, 523–24, 542, 786n863
three vehicles, 82, 84–85
threefold investigation, 83
Tibet, 8
  Central, political turmoil in, 62–64
  Indian pramāṇa tradition in, 3–4, 42
Tibetan Buddhism
  earlier and later diffusions, 8
  Indian philosophical schools in, 5–6
  pramāṇa's place in, 4–5
  schools, distinguishing, 47, 49
Tibetan Pramāṇa tradition
  in Buddhism, role of, 32–33
  formal logic in, 25
  in Geluk school, 12, 13, 18–21, 53
  non-Buddhist traditions and, 37–40
  three waves, 9–13
  two truths in, 14–15
Tibetan scholasticism, 35, 79, 716n53, 742n325
  binaries in, 14
  conceptual isolates in, 734n228
  debate paradigm in, 20
  definitions in, importance of, 18
  Indian influences in, 11
  object-aspect in, 743n342
  origins, 49
  on valid cognition, 741n320
time
  minutest units of, 131, 171, 272–73
  mistaken views on, 97, 121, 721n95
  See also three times
transcendent/supramundane paths, 537–38, 542–43, 787n875
Treasure of Pramāṇa Reasoning (Sakya Paṇḍita), 11, 59, 275, 290–91, 739n297, 756n478
  composition, 64
  Khedrup Jé and, 65, 66
  on mental sense power, 280
  on perception, 217, 218, 278
  on relation and preclusion, 67

on self-cognition, 288, 292
on sense powers, physical and mental, 276–77
on subsequent cognition, 193
on valid cognition, 196, 289
Treasury of Amara, 611, 669
Treasury of the Abhidharma (Vasubandhu)
on five objects, cognition of, 618
on mental sense power, 279
on objects of sense and mental cognitions, 650
on paths and seeds, 788n881
on *prātimokṣa*, 415
on sense power, 254
Tibetan translations, 756n483
on two truths, 164, 165
treatises
author's intent and work, distinguishing, 45
grave errors in composing, 751n433
interpreting, 672
True Aspectarian Cittamātra, 172, 233, 260, 323, 326
true cessations, 537, 658
attaining, 541
four aspects, 300
as manifest object, 654
and true path, relationship of, 302, 536, 787n875
variant views on, 301–2
true existence
Madhyamaka view, 132
Prāsaṅgika view, 596, 597
preclusion and, 535
realist view, 633
Svātantrika view, 598, 627–28
of universals, 152–53
true origins, 299, 300
true paths, 300–301, 302, 536, 787n875
true sufferings
four aspects, 298–99
illustrations, 297–98
Tsang, 54, 55–56, 57, 58
Tsangyang Gyatso, Sixth Dalai Lama, 62
Tsongkhapa, 44, 527, 557, 560, 586, 588, 619, 633, 652, 672
disciples, 54, 59, 69
Entrance Point for the Faithful, 54, 57
Essence of Fine Elucidation, 591, 594, 599, 600, 796n993
and Geluk school, role in, 47
Greater Stages of the Path, 600, 634, 636, 659, 797n1027
Gyaltsab Jé and, 58, 59, 60
Gyaltsab Jé's views and, 48
homage, 555
Illuminating the Intent, 619, 621, 644, 646, 651, 654, 656, 661, 675
Khedrup Jé and, 55–56, 57, 58
Notes on the Eight Difficult Points, 656
Ocean of Reasoning, 662
Pramāṇa interpretations of, 42
Record of Teachings Received, 54
two collections, 227, 599
two obscurations, 318–19, 537
two truths, 152
function in distinguishing, 166–67
Svātantrika and Prāsaṅgika views, compared, 598–602
in tenet systems, variations, 14–15
valid cognition and, 558
See also conventional truth; ultimate truth
type-communicating terms, 515–16, 782n843, 783n845
types, two ways of understanding, 156–57, 158–59, 734n232

Ü, 55, 57, 59, 61
ultimate (*paramārtha*), 132
analysis of, 596, 598, 667
language in approaching, 794–95n973
realization by worldly beings, 568
ultimate existence, 95–96, 151–52
ultimate indivisibles, 164, 166
ultimate truth, 329, 564–66, 671
communicating, 513
defining characteristics, 162–63
etymological description, 162
function, mistaken views regarding, 163–67

Geluk understanding of, 17, 43, 46
unconfirmed reasons
definition, 441
due to protagonists, 444–46
on factual grounds, 441–42
failure due to doubt, 442
failure due to subject, 443–44
uncontaminated transcendent awareness, 310
uncontaminated transcendent path, 234–35
uninterrupted paths, 300, 301, 536, 537, 538, 541–42, 759n536, 787n875, 788n881
universals, 18, 146
actual things and, 140, 141–43, 731n188
commonality of, 140–41
definition, 519
Geluk view of, 141, 732n191, 783n845
held objects as, 146
inference and, 23
mistaken views, 179, 180
mutual phenomena and, 723n110
names and, 430
in nature reasons, 399
negandum and, 503
and particulars, mistaken views, 729n153
and particulars, nonexclusivity, 46
and particulars, relationship of, 168, 736n261
perception of, 119, 124
specifically characterized entities and, 129
true establishment of, refuting, 152–53
type and assemblage, 788n845
Upāli's Questions, 558

Vaibhāṣika school, 5, 242, 328, 330–31, 332, 337–38
acquisition in, 787n876
actual things in, 260
main awareness and mental factors in, 755n468
mental sense power in, 279–80, 756n483
perception in, 218, 654–55
as realists, 40, 723n111
and Sautrāntika, differences in, 232
self-cognition and, 292
sense powers in, 226, 253–54
specifically characterized things in, 629
true cessations in, 301
Vaiśeṣika school, 38, 40, 432
Buddhist critiques of, 41–42, 732n191, 747–48n392
consciousness in, 272
contrary reasoning of, 446–47, 448–50
inconclusive reasoning of, 462
substance and, 120
universals in, 142
on whole and parts, 170, 737n266
valid cognition, 3, 81, 181, 283, 294, 476–77, 779n796
of absences, 109–10, 111
and ascertainment, role of, 561–62, 565, 572–73
in authenticating Dharma, 83, 84, 89
buddhas' awareness and, 177
of cause and effect, 550
in Cittamātra, 259, 323, 326, 327
cognition grasping the reason and, 434, 435–36, 438
in inconclusive reasons, 462–63
constructs and, 43
conventional and ultimate, 196–97
countering, 397–99, 425, 769n682, 771n726
definition (Geluk standard), 195–96, 741n320
definition (Khedrup Jé), 205–9
definition (Prāsaṅgika), 639–41
definitions, mistaken, 195–205
informational relationships and, 790n891
knowledge from, 466–67
logical relationships and, 511
and mental perception, relationship of, 270–71, 272, 273
nature and varieties, objects in determining, 619

in object classification, 102
operation of, 149–50
Prāsaṅgika view, 557–58, 598, 602–3, 620, 641–46, 666, 667, 672–75, 801n1088
pratyakṣa as, refuting, 631
preclusion and, 545
preparative countering, 535, 544, 789n886
realist views, 633–35
for realization, necessity of, 19
ruling out by, 467, 468, 471–75, 492–93, 777n775, 778n786, 779n788
and self-cognition, relationship of, 209, 289, 725n121
simultaneous observation and, 263
of specifically characterized things, 147–48
Svātantrika and Prāsaṅgika views, compared, 597
that ascertains dependently, 210, 745–46n367
of three criteria, 437–38
in Tibetan scholasticism, 13
two definitions as permissible, 196, 741n323
of two truths, 166–67
twofold division, 109–10, 115–16, 162–63, 573, 574, 726n124, 746n371
of ultimate, 46, 95–96, 342–43
as unable to comprehend anything, refuting, 94–95, 96
and valid perception, relationship of, 476
See also inferential valid cognition; valid cognition and its results; valid perception
valid cognition and its results, 286, 343, 753n453, 760n552
in Cittamātra, 259
mediated and unmediated results, 321–22
other-cognition analysis, 333–34, 336–37, 761n576
overt comprehension in, 348
predominant view, 757n492
self-cognition analysis, 334–36, 761n579
standard model, refuting, 289–90
three-set models, refuting, 323–33
valid cognition [associated with] scripture, 641, 658, 662–63, 807n1247
āgama-pramāṇa derivation, 661–62, 807–8n1247
definition, 659–60
See also conviction proofs
valid cognition through analogy, 641, 645
analogy, meaning in, 665, 808n1255
definition, 664–65
two kinds, 665–66
valid perception, 122, 211, 283, 668–69
ascertaining awareness and, 182
in conviction proofs, 424
definition (Pramāṇa), 213–15
definition (Prāsaṅgika), 645–46
in effect reasons, 393–94
of evident phenomena, 104
as foremost, 729n398
four categories, 217
of generally characterized things as held objects, refuting, 121–23
and inference, relationship of, 103
of manifest objects, 619, 621
mistaken views, refuting, 111–12, 148, 149, 215–16
in nature reasons, 396
overt and implicit realization by, 109
ruling out by, 473, 475–77
sense powers and, 226
Svātantrika view, 597, 637
as valid cognition (Prāsaṅgika), 620
varieties, 646
van der Kuijp, Leonard, 65
Vasubandhu, 7, 8, 250
Cittamātra system of, 165, 736n255, 736n260
Principles of Exegesis, 596
Twenty Stanzas, 257
See also *Treasury of the Abhidharma*
Vedas, 25, 38–39

view associated with transitory composite, 238, 305
view of self, 238
Vijñāptika. *See* Cittamātra tradition (Yogācāra)

wheel of Dharma, 171
wisdom realizing selflessness, 306, 312–15
word formation, 514–15
worldly conventions, 650
- agreement with, 13, 568, 622, 641, 671, 675
- analysis and, 593, 594
- perceivability and, 608, 612–13, 619
- sense perception and, 647, 648
- valid cognition and, 566, 636–37, 639–40, 667
- valid perception and, 645

wrong views, 415

Yaktön Sangyé Pal, 59, 757n502
Yamāri, 163, 365, 764n629
Yoga school (Hindu), 38
yogic perception, 466
- Khedrup Je's views, 297
- Prāsaṅgika views, 653–55
- *pratyakṣa* and, 617

About the Translator

JONATHAN SAMUELS (Sherab Gyatso) received his Geluk education as a monk at monasteries in India, beginning at the Institute of Buddhist Dialectics in Dharamsala, and gained the title of *geshe* at Drepung Loseling Monastery. He also holds a DPhil in Oriental studies from Oxford University. He was the principal teacher for the Lotsawa Rinchen Zangpo Translator Program in Dharamsala, served as interpreter for his teacher Gen Lobsang Gyatso, translated several of his books, including *Bodhicitta: Cultivating the Compassionate Mind of Enlightenment*, and wrote the Tibetan language guide *Colloquial Tibetan: The Complete Course for Beginners*. He has held posts at Oxford University and Heidelberg University. He currently works for the Austrian Academy of Sciences in Vienna.

Institute of Tibetan Classics

The Institute of Tibetan Classics is a nonprofit, charitable educational organization based in Montreal, Canada. It is dedicated to two primary objectives: (1) to preserve and promote the study and deep appreciation of Tibet's rich intellectual, spiritual, and artistic heritage, especially among the Tibetan-speaking communities worldwide; and (2) to make the classical Tibetan knowledge and literature a truly global heritage, its spiritual and intellectual resources open to all.

To learn more about the Institute of Tibetan Classics and its various projects, please visit www.tibetanclassics.org or write to this address:

Institute of Tibetan Classics
304 Aberdare Road
Montreal (Quebec) H3P 3K3
Canada

The Library of Tibetan Classics

"This new series edited by Thupten Jinpa and published by Wisdom Publications is a landmark in the study of Tibetan culture in general and Tibetan Buddhism in particular. Each volume contains a lucid introduction and outstanding translations that, while aimed at the general public, will benefit those in the field of Tibetan Studies immensely as well."

—Leonard van der Kuijp, Harvard University

"This is an invaluable set of translations by highly competent scholar-practitioners. The series spans the breadth of the history of Tibetan religion, providing entry to a vast culture of spiritual cultivation."

—Jeffrey Hopkins, University of Virginia

"Erudite in all respects, this series is at the same time accessible and engagingly translated. As such, it belongs in all college and university libraries as well as in good public libraries. *The Library of Tibetan Classics* is on its way to becoming a truly extraordinary spiritual and literary accomplishment."

—Janice D. Willis, Wesleyan University

Following is a list of the thirty-two proposed volumes in *The Library of Tibetan Classics*. Some volumes are translations of single texts, while others are compilations of multiple texts, and each volume will be roughly the same length. Except for those volumes already published, the renderings of titles below are tentative and liable to change. The Institute of Tibetan Classics has contracted numerous established translators in its efforts, and work is progressing on all the volumes concurrently.

1. *Mind Training: The Great Collection*, compiled by Shönu Gyalchok and Könchok Gyaltsen (fifteenth century). NOW AVAILABLE
2. *The Book of Kadam: The Core Texts*, attributed to Atiśa and Dromtönpa (eleventh century). NOW AVAILABLE
3. *The Great Chariot: A Treatise on the Great Perfection*, Longchen Rapjampa (1308–63)
4. *Taking the Result As the Path: Core Teachings of the Sakya Lamdré Tradition*, Jamyang Khyentsé Wangchuk (1524–68) et al. NOW AVAILABLE
5. *Mahāmudrā and Related Instructions: Core Teachings of the Kagyü Schools*. NOW AVAILABLE
6. *Stages of the Path and the Oral Transmission: Selected Teachings of the Geluk School*. NOW AVAILABLE
7. *Mountain Dharma: An Ocean of Definitive Meaning*, Dölpopa Sherab Gyaltsen (1292–1361). NOW AVAILABLE
8. *Four Tibetan Lineages: Core Teachings of Pacification, Severance, Shangpa Kagyü, and Bodong*, Jamgön Kongtrül (1813–99). NOW AVAILABLE
9. *The Tradition of Everlasting Bön: Five Key Texts on Scripture, Tantra, and the Great Perfection*. NOW AVAILABLE
10. *Stages of the Buddha's Teachings: Three Key Texts*. NOW AVAILABLE
11. *The Bodhisattva Ideal: Selected Key Texts*
12. *The Ethics of the Three Codes*
13. *Sādhanas: Vajrayana Buddhist Meditation Manuals*
14. *Ornament of Stainless Light: An Exposition of the Kālacakra Tantra*, Khedrup Norsang Gyatso (1423–1513). NOW AVAILABLE
15. *A Lamp to Illuminate the Five Stages: Teachings on the Guhyasamāja Tantra*, Tsongkhapa (1357–1419). NOW AVAILABLE
16. *The Perfection of Wisdom Tradition: Three Essential Works*
17. *Treatises on Buddha Nature*
18. *Differentiations of the Profound View: Interpretations of Emptiness in Tibet*
19. *Illuminating the Intent: An Exposition of Candrakīrti's Entering the Middle Way*, Tsongkhapa (1357–1419). NOW AVAILABLE
20. *Buddhist Epistemology in the Sakya School: Three Key Texts*
21. *Buddhist Epistemology in the Geluk School: Three Key Texts*. NOW AVAILABLE
22. *Tibetan Buddhist Psychology and Phenomenology: Selected Texts*

23. *Ornament of Abhidharma: A Commentary on the Abhidharmakośa*, Chim Jampaiyang (thirteenth century). NOW AVAILABLE
24. *Beautiful Adornment of Mount Meru: A Presentation of Classical Indian Philosophies*, Changkya Rölpai Dorjé (1717–86). NOW AVAILABLE
25. *The Crystal Mirror of Philosophical Systems: A Tibetan Study of Asian Religious Thought*, Thuken Losang Chökyi Nyima (1737–1802). NOW AVAILABLE
26. *Gateway for Being Learned and Realized: Selected Texts*
27. *The Tibetan Book of Everyday Wisdom: A Thousand Years of Sage Advice*. NOW AVAILABLE
28. *Mirror of Beryl: A Historical Introduction to Tibetan Medicine*, Desi Sangyé Gyatso (1653–1705). NOW AVAILABLE
29. *Selected Texts on Tibetan Astronomy and Astrology*
30. *Art and Literature: An Anthology*
31. *Tales from the Tibetan Operas*. NOW AVAILABLE
32. *A History of Buddhism in India and Tibet*, Khepa Deu (thirteenth century). NOW AVAILABLE

To receive a brochure describing all the volumes or to stay informed about *The Library of Tibetan Classics*, please write to:

support@wisdompubs.org

or send a request by post to:

Wisdom Publications
Attn: Library of Tibetan Classics
132 Perry Street
New York, NY 10014 USA

The complete catalog containing descriptions of each volume can also be found online at wisdom.org.

Become a Benefactor of the Library of Tibetan Classics

The Library of Tibetan Classics' scope, importance, and commitment to the finest quality make it a tremendous financial undertaking. We invite you to become a benefactor, joining us in creating this profoundly important human resource. Contributors of two thousand dollars or more will receive a copy of each future volume as it becomes available, and will have their names listed in all subsequent volumes. Larger donations will go even further in supporting *The Library of Tibetan Classics*, preserving the creativity, wisdom, and scholarship of centuries past, so that it may help illuminate the world for future generations.

To contribute, please either visit our website at wisdom.org, call us at (617) 776-7416, or send a check made out to Wisdom Publications or credit card information to the address below.

Library of Tibetan Classics Fund
Wisdom Publications
132 Perry Street
New York, NY 10014
USA

Please note that contributions of lesser amounts are also welcome and are invaluable to the development of the series. Wisdom is a 501(c)(3) nonprofit corporation, and all contributions are tax-deductible to the extent allowed by law.

If you have any questions, please do not hesitate to call us or email us at support@wisdompubs.org.

To keep up to date on the status of *The Library of Tibetan Classics*, visit the series page on our website, and subscribe to our newsletter while you are there.

About Wisdom Publications

Wisdom Publications is the leading publisher of classic and contemporary Buddhist books and practical works on mindfulness. To learn more about us or to explore our other books, please visit our website at wisdom.org or contact us at the address below.

Wisdom Publications
132 Perry Street
New York, NY 10014 USA

We are a 501(c)(3) organization, and donations in support of our mission are tax deductible.

Wisdom Publications is affiliated with the Foundation for the Preservation of the Mahayana Tradition (FPMT).